S0-BDP-227

# Literature of Travel and Exploration

*VOLUME ONE*

*A TO F*

# LITERATURE OF TRAVEL AND EXPLORATION

## AN ENCYCLOPEDIA

*VOLUME ONE*
*A TO F*

JENNIFER SPEAKE, EDITOR

Fitzroy Dearborn
An Imprint of the Taylor & Francis Group
New York London

Published in 2003 by
Fitzroy Dearborn
An imprint of the Taylor & Francis Group
29 West 35th Street
New York, NY 10001

Published in Great Britain by
Fitzroy Dearborn
An imprint of the Taylor & Francis Group
11 New Fetter Lane
London EC4P 4EE



Fitzroy Dearborn is an imprint of the Taylor & Francis Group



10 9 8 7 6 5 4 3 2 1

**Library of Congress Cataloging-in-Publication Data**

Literature of travel and exploration : an encyclopedia / Jennifer
Speake, editor.
p. cm.
ISBN 1-57958-247-8 (hb : set : alk. paper)-ISBN 1-57958-425-X (hb:
vol. 1: alk. paper)-ISBN 1-57958-424-1 (hb : vol. 2: alk. paper)-ISBN
1-57958-440-3 (hb : vol. 3: alk. paper)
1. Voyages and travels. 2. Travelers' writings. 3. Travel writing.
I. Speake, Jennifer.
II. Title.
G465.L565 2003
910.4′03—dc21
2003005352

ISBN 1-57958-247-8 (3-volume set)
ISBN 1-57958-425-X (Volume 1)
ISBN 1-57958-424-1 (Volume 2)
ISBN 1-57958-440-3 (Volume 3)

# Contents

# Preface

*Perceiving that the Great Khan took a pleasure in hearing accounts of whatever was new to him respecting the customs and manners of people and the peculiar circumstances of distant countries, he endeavoured wherever he went to obtain correct information on these subjects and made notes of all he saw and heard, in order to gratify the curiosity of his master.*

—*Marco Polo*

Curiosity, information, pleasure—not much has changed in the underlying compact between travel writers and their audience since Marco Polo's visit to the court of the Mongul Great Khan, Kublai, in the thirteenth century. Viewed over time, however, the literature of travel and exploration has taken on a bewildering multiplicity of forms and functions, and it is the purpose of this encyclopedia to provide some basic waymarks in an extraordinarily rich and varied landscape. The book is intended in the first place to provide a reference tool for teachers, researchers, and students looking for a starting point in what has become a rapidly evolving academic discipline. It is also hoped that it will afford information and pleasure to the individual aficionado of travel writing. Intending travelers are a third group of readers who may find valuable pointers and insights in accounts of the experiences of earlier travelers in the regions that they plan to visit. The ambitious scope of the project, from the classical world to the present, from Herodotus to space exploration, precludes any claim to comprehensiveness, but what it does aim to do for all those who use it is to open up the immense, intriguing possibilities of the ever expanding horizons of travel writing.

The entries number more than six hundred and are arranged in alphabetical order. They fall into a number of subject categories, of which by far the largest two are those on geographical entities and on individuals. The former are surveys, often extensive, on countries, regions, cities, routes, and other features, and they offer an overview of how a particular place has been experienced and presented at various times by different travelers with a range of personal agendas. Such agendas may be the gratification of simple wanderlust or a more deliberate quest for scientific knowledge, religious enlightenment, military glory, or mercantile advancement, to name just some of the motives that drew, and still draw, people to distant lands—or they may be a combination of two or more such factors. To take a simple example, a text on India and Indians as experienced by an eighteenth-century servant of the British East India Company and one by a modern seeker after spiritual wisdom illuminate, in their very different ways, the story of Westerners' ongoing engagement with this vast land and its complex culture. The geographical survey articles are designed to set such very disparate texts in their physical and historical contexts, but the way in which countries and regions are broken down for these entries is governed not so much by strict geographical or temporal criteria but according to how, or whether, the different components were or are significant in the history of exploration or travel. Thus Sakhalin warrants a separate entry on account of the long-running debate about its status as island or peninsula. The larger country entries may be divided arbitrarily into centuries (as with England and France), broken at a date that is historically significant (Greece, Japan), or subdivided geographically (United States) as seemed most convenient given the nature and volume of the literature that they have generated.

The second major category, that of articles on individual writers, focuses on authors who have been significant practitioners of travel writing, mainly, but by no means exclusively, in English. In this latter category the net has been cast widely to take in not only the authors of the great travel classics (Marco Polo, Charles Doughty, Apsley Cherry-Garrard) and the oeuvres of the dedicated world travelers (Nicolas Bouvier, Ida Pfeiffer, Paul Theroux) but also more obscure figures whose accounts of their journeys may be lacking in high literary polish but that nonetheless unfold a fascinating human story: Kate Marsden and her heroic endeavors on behalf of the lepers of Siberia, tough Samuel Hearne, dourly coping with starvation and frostbite in northern Canada, and John Rae, revealing the (literally) unpalatable truth about the ill-fated Franklin expedition.

To complement the two principal categories of entry, the book offers a number of other angles of approach to the field by including, for example, articles on various methods of transportation, on individuals and organizations that have promoted exploration and travel, on different subgenres in travel writing, and on issues and topics relevant to the theorization of subject. A list of the entries broken down under geographic and thematic headings can be viewed at a glance on pages xxv–xxxi.

Entries are structured into two sections: an essay, ranging in length from about 1,000 to 5,000 words, and a bibliography. Further details of many of the texts listed in the bibliographies can be found on the encyclopedia's website, www.routledge-ny.com/travellit. In addition, articles on individuals include a short biography. Readers who find that a person or place in which they are interested is not featured as a separate entry are encouraged to pursue their inquiries by consulting the analytical listings in the index.

The illustrations, in a range of media (manuscript drawings, woodcuts, photographs, and so on), have been carefully researched and selected to complement more than 230 of the entries. In addition to the factual information they convey, illustrations are a barometer of the significance attached by authors, publishers, and contemporary readers to the visual aspect of travel books; from woodcuts in early Renaissance texts, where one fantasy cityscape can do duty for half a dozen towns, to the specificity of the Victorian topographical drawing and the modern photograph, the pictures in the works are an integral element in the story of the literature of travel and exploration. In addition, illustrations—or the absence of them—are, like other physical aspects of a book (typography, paper, binding), highly revealing to the modern reader of the way in which the original publishers intended the works to be received by their target readership. As Dickens put it in *Martin Chuzzlewit*, "the dainty frontispiece and trim vignette [point] like handposts on the outskirts of great cities, to the rich stock of incident beyond" (ch. 5).

# Acknowledgments

Around 300 people have been involved with this project over the protracted period of the book's preparation, and it would be impracticable to attempt to thank each of them individually by name. First and biggest thanks should go to the members of the advisory panel; their knowledge and support have been invaluable, and they have often worn a second hat as contributors, thus being doubly generous with their time and expertise. The enthusiasm of the contributors for the project has been a huge encouragement, with many articles written not only out of an academic engagement with their subject but also with affection and brio.

On the publishing side, special thanks go to Lesley Henderson, who conceived the idea for the book; to Daniel Kirkpatrick, Stuart Midgeley, Robert Balchin, Cathy Johns, Chris Murray, Caroline Howlett, and others at FDP who worked in various capacities on the avalanche of incoming text; and to Alison Worthington, who had the daunting task of copyediting the whole. Mark O'Malley at Routledge landed the tricky job of taking over the practicalities of the project at a late stage in its development. Others who have offered advice and assistance—or simply the opportunity for discussion—include: Dr. George Bishop; Deborah Manley and other members of ASTENE; and Carl Thompson and Sarah Moss, whose seminars at Oxford helped expand my horizons at an early stage of the project.

For the illustrations, the marvelous resources of the library at the Travellers Club in London were generously made available by the library committee; particular thanks to Thomas A. Sutherland and Sheila Markham for access to this treasure trove, and thanks, too, to Philip de Bay for taking the photographs. Thanks also to Cefn Newsham of Oxford for the photographs of books in my own collection. Olivia Fraser and William Dalrymple kindly granted permission to reproduce the endpaper map in *From the Holy Mountain*.

# Introduction

The theme of travel runs through all the great literatures of the world—predictably so, since the metaphor of life as a journey is a powerful one that resonates across time and across cultures. In the European tradition, there is the archetypal myth of Ulysses sailing out beyond the known world, beyond the pillars of Hercules, or there is Dante journeying through Hell and up Mount Purgatory into the extraterrestrial realms of Paradise. Great epic poems in many languages recount crusading journeys, knightly quests, fantastical voyages, journeys by sea and on land, journeys that conclude with a homecoming or that go on without end.

It is hardly surprising, therefore, that travelers who write about actual journeys they have undertaken are often in some way influenced by that fictitious writing, and indeed the boundaries between fact and fiction in what we shall call the genre of travel writing are often hard to discern. Travelers write about what they see, and their perceptions are shaped by the cultural context from which they come and by all that they have read and experienced in that culture. So the early travelers to the Americas wrote about curiously formed creatures and amazing human beings in terms that often bore stronger resemblances to images familiar to readers of popular romances of the day than to any description that we might recognize as scientific. When trying to describe what was foreign to them, travel writers had to fall back either on the familiar and banal or on the fictitious and fantastical. Hence the difficulties some travelers had in describing creatures that appeared to belong to no clearly definable species, such as penguins or armadillos, and the charming variations on terms for those creatures of the New World known in English as guinea pigs and in Spanish as little rabbits of the Indies.

Equally, travel writers write for a designated audience, whose expectations are similarly shaped by their own context. Travel writing is therefore a particular form of writing, closely akin to translation. Like the translator, the travel writer shapes material in such a way that readers may have access to whatever situations and places, known or unknown, are being described. Sometimes travel-writing conventions lead writers to favor an ethnographical or anthropological stance, at other times travel writers are indistinguishable from novelists or writers of memoirs, but always the object of their gaze is a culture different from their own. Travel writing has built into its very existence a notion of otherness. It is premised on a binary opposition between home and elsewhere, and however fuzzy ideas of "home" might be, ideas of otherness are invariably present regardless of the ideological stance of the writer. Writing about other places, other contexts, involves writing (albeit implicitly) about one's own context, about oneself. Hence all travel writing exists in a dialectical relationship between two distinct places—that designated by the writer and perhaps also by readers as "home," and that designated as the cultural other. This is a tradition that goes back as far as Tacitus, who, in his *Germania*, writes about the matriarchal tribe of the Sitones and as a good Roman male was so appalled by the fact that "woman is the ruling sex" that he remarks tersely that this is a measure of their decline "I will not say below freedom, but even below slavery."

The essays in this volume trace the complex history of travel writing from its earliest manifestations in the ancient world to the present day. Interestingly, travel writing today is hugely successful, perhaps more so than at any other time, and it is particularly popular in the Anglo-American world. Writers like Bruce Chatwin, William Dalrymple, Patrick Leigh Fermor, Norman Lewis, Jan Morris, Eric Newby, Paul Theroux, and Colin Thubron have become bestselling authors on the basis of their travel books, and most bookstores have whole sections devoted to travel writing. It is tempting to speculate that this may have come about as a result of the increase in travel generally, as millions more people fly to distant holiday destinations every year, but it may also be because of the residual colonial history that still remains powerfully present in Britain. The British empire, after all, was built on an export policy of world proportions, whereby British products were manufactured and sold overseas and British culture was exported as part of a civilizing mission. The U.S. melting-pot policy of the nineteenth century and beyond was likewise constructed upon the idea of one preferred cultural model over all others. Both the British and the American models posited their own culture as the most desirable, yet at the same time there was widespread interest in those cultures perceived as less developed, less civilized, and more "primitive." The explosion of adventure literature for boys in the nineteenth century by writers such as R.M. Ballantyne, Robert Louis Stevenson, Rider Haggard, and G.A. Henty shows how far the popular interest in places beyond the safe bounds of known countries had developed. Joseph Bristow, in his study of that literature, defines the books as stories of "fearless endeavour in a world populated by savage races, dangerous pirates, and related manifestations of the 'other' to be encountered on voyages towards dark and unexplored continents" (Bristow, 1991).

Through the pages of adventure stories, boys could explore strange new worlds and experience from the safety of their own homes the thrill of exploring unknown territories. At the same time, their parents avidly read the stream of publications by travelers eager to make their mark on the scientific community and reach the pinnacle of being admitted to the Royal Geographical Society. The latter half of the nineteenth and the early years of the twentieth century saw a great number of such publications by travelers and explorers like Richard Burton, Charles Doughty, John Speke, and Henry Yule, and also by an increasing number of women, such as Isabella Bird, Mary Kingsley, and Lucie Duff Gordon. Public interest in exploration narratives and in travel writing generally was so great that dozens of missionaries, military officers, journalists, diplomats, and many of the wives who accompanied their husbands produced accounts of their journeys.

Interest in travel writing grew steadily throughout the nineteenth century, fueled by the rapid expansion of tourism as an increasingly profitable industry. The idea of the "tourist" as distinct from the "traveler" is still current in travel literature, though when the term *tourist* was first coined in the late eighteenth century it did not have the derogatory connotations it quickly came to acquire. Paul Fussell, one of the leading experts on travel writing, defines the difference as follows: "Tourism as not self-directed but externally directed. You go not where you want to go but where the industry has decreed that you shall go. Tourism soothes you by comfort and familiarity and shields you from the shocks of novelty and oddity. It confirms your prior view of the world instead of shaking it up" (Fussell, 1987).

Travel writing trades on this idea of difference, and there is a whole subgenre of travel writing that describes the hardships and traumas of travel, as if to reinforce the gap that divides the "true" traveler from the armchair traveler, who can only ever aspire to become a tourist. There is an elitism here that at times can be disturbing for the reader, though the best travel writing avoids this pitfall either through self-deprecatory humor, as is the case with Eric Newby, Redmond O'Hanlon, and Dervla Murphy, or through sheer energy and exuberance, as in the writings of Isabella Bird. Guidebooks of the 1990s have gone a long way toward eradicating the artificial traveler-tourist divide, and series such as the Rough Guides and the Lonely Planet Guides serve both as sources of information and as travel books in their own right.

The earliest travel accounts were produced to provide essential information on other cultures for political or diplomatic purposes. Marco Polo's account of his travels across Asia is one of the classic texts of early travel writing, but equally interesting is the account of a similar journey undertaken as part of a diplomatic mission by Friar Odoric of Pordenone in the early fourteenth century. In the same period, Ibn Battuta wrote an account of his travels in Asia and Africa, an extraordinary journey that took him some seven years, covered 75,000 miles, and led him to become the only known person of his time to have visited the lands of every Muslim ruler.

The age of exploration resulted in large numbers of travel accounts being produced. Antonio Pigafetta wrote a firsthand account of Magellan's epic voyage around the world, while Bernal Díaz de Castillo and Fray Bartolomé de Las Casas left detailed records of the Spanish conquest of Latin America. At the same time, another strand of travel writing was emerging, exemplified by Fynes Moryson's chatty, highly personal, eccentric book, full of minute details about food, inns, and local customs, *An Itinerary Containing His Ten Yeeres Travels thorow Twelve Dominions*, published in 1617. What we might loosely term political and personal travel writing developed along parallel tracks, and by the latter half of the eighteenth century, with the growing popularity of the Grand Tour, dozens of young men, mostly English, were writing their own accounts of their educational journeys. One such account, not published until 1930, is *An Englishman at Home and Abroad 1792–1828 with Some Recollections of Napoleon: Being Extracts from the Diaries of J.B. Scott of Bungay, Suffolk*, an entertaining book that tells us a great deal about what the Grand Tour meant to a fairly typical young Englishman who obviously saw the journey as the highlight of his life.

The age of the Grand Tour was also an age of changing sensibility, and with the advent of Romantic ideas came new perspectives on landscape and travel. Byron's Childe Harold epitomizes the new sensibility, seeing beauty verging on the sublime in scenery that a previous generation would have found unpleasant or even threatening. The Alps, the Scottish Highlands, and the fells of the Lake District all acquired a dignity and splendor for the Romantic mind that find their way into travel writing. The two best-known European volcanoes, Etna and Vesuvius, which had traditionally been described in terms of hellishness and perceived as symbols of nature's most ugly, threatening aspect, were transformed into symbols of nature's power and grandeur. Throughout the nineteenth century, travelers were to seek out such landscapes, with Iceland proving particularly popular. The description of the Serbian forest in Alexander Kinglake's *Eothen; or, Traces of Travel Brought Home from the East* (1844) is a good example of the way in which the Romantic imagination could be utilized to create an impression of brooding uneasiness:

> Endless and endless now on either side the tall oaks closed in their ranks, and stood gloomily lowering over us, as grim as an army of giants with a thousand years' pay in arrears. One strived, with listening ear, to catch some tidings of that Forest World within—some stirring of beasts, some night bird's scream; but all was quite hushed, except the voice of the cicalas that peopled every bough, and filled the depths of the forest through and through with one same hum everlasting—more stilling than very silence. (Kinglake, 1982)

Voyages outside Europe proved a rich source of travel literature, as the expansion of education to the middle classes resulted in widespread interest in new scientific discoveries. Captain Cook's journals, Alexander von Humboldt's personal narrative of his travels in the Americas between 1799 and 1804, Charles Waterton's detailed descriptions of the flora and fauna of the Americas in the early nineteenth century, and Charles Darwin's epic *Voyage of the Beagle* (1839) are but a few of the dozens of books that fueled popular interest in science and exploration, while a series of publications on archaeological finds in the Near and Middle East had an impact on the burgeoning tourist trade. Thomas Cook organized his first excursion in 1841, shepherding 570 people from Leicester to nearby Loughborough to attend a temperance rally on a specially chartered train. The advent of the railways gave Cook the opportunity to develop his schemes for organized travel, and in 1855 the first Cook's tour to Europe took place. Much of the expansion of travel in the nineteenth century followed technological developments, and the advent of mass railways led to much greater freedom of movement for ever larger numbers people.

Beside the scientific interest in travel, another strand of travel writing continued to be highly personal. This form of travel writing was focused on the exploits of one individual, and the establishment of that individual's credentials of authenticity was of great importance. Claims that travelers and explorers might make had to be verified; the bitter clash between Burton and Speke over the source of the Nile following their troubled expedition of the 1850s shows all too clearly what could happen even to distinguished men who failed to produce concrete evidence to validate their claims. Fraudulent travel accounts abound, and Burton's *Personal Narrative of a Pilgrimage to El-Medinah and Meccah* (1855–1856), in which he insists that he managed to travel to the holy city of Mecca in disguise, is still the subject of debate today.

In the twentieth century, travel writing came to be an object of study in its own right, and the last two decades have seen a steady stream of publications that have sought to map out the history of travel writing, to theorize it, and to investigate key questions of ethics and issues of identity. Mary Louise Pratt's important study of colonial landscape, the work of James Clifford, James Buzard, Paul Fussell, the growing number of studies deriving from work in cultural geography, representation theory, and postcolonial studies have resulted in a rich fund of secondary materials that complement the primary texts produced by travel writers. Of particular significance is research into issues of gender and travel writing.

In her controversial book *Feminism and Geography: The Limits of Geographical Knowledge*, Gillian Rose argues that the academic discipline of geography has always been dominated by men. In this respect, it mirrors the history of travel, for this too has been predominantly a man's activity. The voyages of discovery, the mapmaking and surveying that were the objectives of so many journeys, were almost all undertaken by men alone. Almost no women were elected to the prestigious Royal Geographical Society in London until 1913, and only a small percentage were elected thereafter. Yet the contribution of women travel writers has been considerable, from Lady Mary Wortley Montagu, whose commonsense account of life in the Turkish harem of the Sultan of Istanbul in the eighteenth century should be set against the erotic fantasizing of male writers denied entry to all-female spaces, to Sara Wheeler, writing in the 1990s about being a lone woman traveling in the male-dominated world of Antarctica. What is particularly interesting about the writing of women like Isabella Bird or Margaret Fountaine is the disparity between their lives in bourgeois British society and the freedom of movement, both physical and psychological, that they were able to enjoy when traveling. Many of these writers bring their own particular subjectivity into their writing, allowing us insights not only into the places they visited but also into their personal responses to events and to people. That subjectivity is increasingly present in men's writing also, as exploration literature becomes less prominent and a more self-reflective writing appeals more strongly to readers. Such writers as Jan Morris and Colin Thubron move at times close to lyrical writing, elsewhere close to metaphysics. Here is Jan (formerly James) Morris creating an evocative portrait of Venice in a single beautifully crafted sentence: "It is a gnarled but gorgeous city: and as the boat approaches through the last church-crowned islands, and a jet fighter screams splendidly out of the sun, so the whole scene seems to shimmer—with pinkness, with age, with self-satisfaction, with sadness, with delight" (Morris, 1960).

Venice has been the subject of travel writing for centuries, but other places have featured more or less prominently at different times. In the seventeenth century, accounts of travels in the Americas or the Indies were popular, while Australasia became fashionable after the voyages of James Cook. The nineteenth century is, to a large extent, dominated by accounts of explorations to Africa, though expeditions to lesser-known parts of the globe, such as the Amazon jungle or the polar regions, were also popular subjects. Three regions have perhaps been more consistently romanticized than any others—the North and South Poles, the deserts of Arabia and Persia, and the expanse of plains and great mountain ranges of central Asia, the Hindu Kush, and Tibet. All are places where human endurance is tested to its limits; all are also places where boundaries are hard to define and where past and present are fused in the nomadic lifestyles of the inhabitants. In the 1990s there was a sharp increase in books about Antarctica, the Northwest Passage, and central Asia, with one traveler after another writing about their experiences in these, the least urbanized areas of the planet. Perhaps the popular desire to read more about such places reflects a nostalgia for a world before globalization, or perhaps the travel writers are tapping into an atavistic desire for Xanadu, for caverns measureless to man or for spaces of total whiteness on which no human imprint can be seen.

The contributors to this volume in their essays trace many different patterns in travel writing across the ages. No single volume could ever hope to cover the vast range of texts that have been and continue to be written about travel, but this book does at the very least succeed in drawing a map for all those armchair travelers who seek to enlarge their own horizons by reading about someone else's journeys.

Susan Bassnett

## Bibliography

Bristow, Joseph, *Empire Boys: Adventures in a Man's World*, London: Unwin Hyman, 1991.

Fussell, Paul (editor), *The Norton Book of Travel*, New York and London: Norton, 1987.

Kinglake, Alexander William, *Eothen; or, Traces of Travel Brought Home from the East*, London: Ollivier, 1844, New York: Wiley and Putnam, 1845; with an introduction by Jan Morris, Oxford: Oxford University Press, 1982.

Mann, Ethel (editor), *An Englishman at Home and Abroad, 1792–1828, with Some Recollections of Napoleon: Being Extracts from the Diaries of J.B. Scott of Bungay, Suffolk*, London: Heath Cranton, 1930.

Morris, James, *Venice*, London: Faber, 1960; 3rd revised edition, 1993.

Rose, Gillian, *Feminism and Geography: The Limits of Geographical Knowledge*, Cambridge: Polity Press, and Minneapolis: University of Minnesota Press, 1993.

Tacitus, Cornelius, *Tacitus on Britain and Germany*, translated by H. Mattingly, London: Penguin, 1948.

# Board of Advisors

# Alphabetical List of Entries

## D



## E

# Thematic List of Entries

## AMERICA: NORTH



## AMERICA: SOUTH



## ARCTIC AND ANTARCTIC



## ART AND TRAVEL

## ASIA: CENTRAL

Central Asia, Russian Exploration
Central Asia, Western Travelers
Fa-hsien
Fleming, Peter
Gobi Desert
Great Game
Hedin, Sven
Maillart, Ella
Mannerheim, Carl Gustav Emil
Odoric of Pordenone
Polo, Marco
Rubruck, Guillaume de
Samarkand
Semenov, Petr Petrovich
Stein, Aurel
Tibet
Tsybikov, Gombozhab
Turkestan
Younghusband, Francis

## ASIA: EAST

Beijing (Peking)
China
David, Armand
David-Néel, Alexandra
Fa-hsien
Hearn, Lafcadio
Japan, Pre-1853
Japan, Modern
Kaempfer, Engelbert
Korea
Malraux, André
Przheval'skii, Nicolai M.
Ricci, Matteo

## ASIA: SOUTH AND INDIAN OCEAN

Afghanistan
Albuquerque, Afonso de
Bernier, François
Bontekoe, Willem
Buckingham, James Silk
Burma / Myanmar
Burnes, Alexander
Byron, Robert
Camões, Luís Vaz de
Conti, Niccolò dei
Coryate, Thomas
Curzon, George
Dalrymple, Alexander
Dalrymple, William
Della Valle, Pietro
Eden, Emily
French Indochina
Garnier, Marie-Joseph-François
Graaff, Nicolaus de
Haafner, Jacob
Hawkins, William
Heber, Reginald
India, Modern
India, Moghul
India, South
Indian Ocean Islands
Indian Subcontinent, Up to 1500
Kashmir
Knox, Robert
Linschoten, Jan Huyghen
Lodewycksz, Willem
Madagascar
Malaya / Malaysia
Mekong River
Methwold, William
Moorcroft, William
Nikitin, Afanasii
Pakistan
Pinto, Fernao Mendes
Rennell, James
Roberts, Emma
Roe, Sir Thomas
Sassetti, Filippo
Singapore
Sri Lanka
Tavernier, Jean-Baptiste
Texeira, Pedro
Thailand / Siam
Varthema, Ludovico
Yule, Henry

## AUSTRALASIA AND PACIFIC

Australia
Bali
Borneo
Eyre, Edward
Fiji
Flinders, Matthew
Forrest, John
Java
King, Philip Parker
New Zealand
Pacific Ocean, Exploration Across
Pacific Ocean, Exploration along American West Coast
Pacific Ocean, Post-Exploration
Pacific Ocean Islands
Papua New Guinea
Philippines
Samoa
Stuart, John McDouall
Sturt, Charles
Tahiti

## CLASSICAL ANTIQUITY

Alexander the Great
Apollonius of Tyana
Greece, Ancient Hellenic World
Herodotus
Megasthenes
Odyssey
Pausanias

## EURASIA: NORTHERN



## EUROPE: MEDITERRANEAN



## EUROPE: NORTHERN

## GENRES AND PUBLICATIONS



## JOURNEY TYPES AND ROUTES



## MARITIME AND CIRCUMNAVIGATION



## MIDDLE EAST

## MISCELLANEOUS AND LITERARY



## NEAR EAST



## ORGANIZATIONS AND SOCIETIES



## PUBLISHERS AND PUBLISHING

## SCIENCE AND TRAVEL



## THEMES AND ISSUES



## TRANSPORTATION



## WORLD TRAVELERS

## ACOSTA, JOSÉ DE (1540–1600) *Spanish Jesuit Priest and Historian*

José de Acosta's most significant writing resulted directly from his work as a missionary in Spain's American colonies. He spent 14 years in Peru and almost another year in Mexico, and during that time he traveled widely and wrote incessantly, not merely recording his experiences, observations, and the stories he heard from explorers and other travelers, but analyzing the numerous questions that confronted him about the natural world and the life and customs of the Indians. The works that resulted—published following his return to Spain in 1587—demonstrate his remarkable knowledge of the sciences, mathematics, geography, history, and social issues, in addition to the matters of Christian doctrine that were of paramount concern to him throughout his life.

In the 1570s, Acosta visited many different towns in the interior of the viceroyalty of Peru, such as Arequipa, Cuzco, and La Paz. He reviewed the missionary work that was being carried out in such places, and also accompanied the viceroy, Francisco de Toledo, on some of his visits to different areas of the vast territory. Acosta learned Quechua, the dominant indigenous language, and studied the history and culture of the Inca empire. Many of the sermons, Bible teachings, and reflections upon Christian faith that resulted from his missionary work were published in Spain many years later, and comprised a substantial body of religious writing. However, it was Acosta's ability to reflect critically upon all aspects of colonial life, including the missionary enterprise, that produced his most original work. He was at pains to establish clear moral principles for the diffusion of Christianity, and to ensure fair treatment for the Indians. When another missionary, Alonso Sánchez, argued that to spread the gospel effectively in China force had to precede religious teaching, as had happened in some parts of Spanish America, Acosta vigorously combated such ideas. He wrote two letters in 1587 arguing that war was not a moral means for disseminating the Christian doctrine.

Acosta's *De Procuranda Indorum Salute*, believed to be the first book written by a Jesuit in America, examined such moral issues in greater depth. Based on the observations he had made of Indian culture during his travels, Acosta argued that Christian teaching in the Americas needed to be more flexible, with the methods varied in accordance with the variations in the patterns of life of the different Indian communities. He was outspoken in his criticism of colonial administrators and churchmen, whom he saw as too often concerned more with their own prosperity than with efficient and just government and effective religious teaching. The Indians were not to be enslaved, he argued, but treated with compassion. The difficulties frequently encountered in preaching the faith were the result not so much of the Indians' deficiencies as of the inadequacies of the missionaries themselves. It was an audacious work, proposing a new approach to Christian missions, based on a clearer sense of vocation and self-sacrifice and involving a greater understanding of Indian culture.

Acosta's best-known work is his *Historia natural y moral de las Indias* (*A Natural and Moral History of the Indies*), a lengthy and wide-ranging study of the natural environment of the American continent, its great pre-Hispanic civilizations, and the consequences of Spanish conquest and colonization. Published in its complete form in 1590, it was one of the most important contributions to Spanish scientific thought of the period. It made an immediate impact in Spain, where the educated elite was eager for information about the American colonies, and six editions were published within three years of its appearance. It was then translated into several other major European languages. Its detailed description, philosophical discussion, and elegant style made it a highly influential work, and it served as a model for many writers who followed.

The work is divided into seven parts, or books, the first four of which focus on the natural environment of the Americas. A keen observer, Acosta describes flora, fauna, and such features as land formations, currents, and climatic conditions. Wherever possible, he seeks explanations. Although influenced by classical thought, which he had studied in depth, Acosta used his own experiences and studies to challenge some of the assumptions made by such classical scholars as Aristotle. His inquiring mind frequently led him to make detours during his travels to examine something of special interest to him. Centuries later, Alexander von Humboldt would acknowledge the importance of Acosta's work and his skill as a natural scientist. Of particular interest are Acosta's detailed observations on the relationship between humans and the natural world, describing such activities as silver mining and whale hunting, the effects of altitude sickness in the Andes, and the uses made of the coca leaf by the Indian communities.

In parts 5 and 6 of *Historia natural*, Acosta discusses such "moral matters" as the government, religious practices, and culture of the Indians of Peru and Mexico, combining his own observations of their life with his readings of other writers on the subject, such as Polo de Ondegardo and Juan de Tovar. This dedication to the study of Indian civilization has led some critics to identify Acosta as an important precursor of anthropology and ethnography in the Americas. In the seventh and final book of *Historia natural*, Acosta concludes that divine providence had led Spain to the new continent in order to implant the Catholic faith. As is to be expected, theological doctrine at times imposed constraints on Acosta's scientific thinking, but it is his continual questioning and insistence upon analysis that sets *Historia natural* apart from most other scholarly works on Spanish America produced during the first century of colonialism.

MARK DINNEEN

### Biography

Born in Medina del Campo, Castile, Spain, September 1540. Joined the Jesuit order as a boy. Studied theology and philosophy in Alcalá de Henares, 1559–1567. Ordained as a priest in 1566, age 26. Set off for the Americas, 1571, to serve as a missionary. Spent ten months on the island of Hispaniola, in the Caribbean, and then worked in Peru, 1572–1586, and in Mexico for ten months, 1586–1587. Returned to Spain that year, partly because of disillusion he felt on account of internal conflicts within the Jesuit order. His major works were published in Spain after his return, written from the unfinished manuscripts and substantial notes he brought back with him. Died in Salamanca, 15 February 1600.

### References and Further Reading

Acosta, José de, *De Procuranda Indorum Salute*, 1588; as *De Procuranda Indorum Salute*, translated and edited by G. Stewart McIntosh, 2 vols., 1996.

Acosta, José de, *Historia natural y moral de las Indias*, 1590; as *A Natural and Moral History of the Indies*, translated by Edward Grimston, 1604; edited by Clements R. Markham, 2 vols., 1880; reprinted, 1970.

Acosta, José de, "Escritos menores" (letters, essays, and other short documents), in *Obras del Padre José de Acosta*, edited by Francisco Mateos, 1954.

*See also* **New World Chronicles**

## AFGHANISTAN

Among the features of the area now lying within the borders of Afghanistan that have determined its ethnic, political, and cultural history is its distance from the sea, which has kept the country separate from the seaborne mercantile empires that grew up in the Indian Ocean. The mountains in the center, east, and northeast, fringed by stretches of desert and semidesert, have allowed independence to be maintained from most of the great land empires that have ravaged but rarely held the land. Even though long-term control has been difficult to establish, the area has always been a crossroads of ethnic and military movement and camel caravans carrying trade across the Eurasian landmass. In the place names, in the landscape, and in the ethnic groups inhabiting it can be seen the traces of the Achaemenid Persians of the sixth century BCE; Alexander the Great's Greeks of the fourth century BCE and their successors, who eventually merged into the Buddhist culture of northern India; the Muslim Arabs of the seventh century CE; the Mongols of the thirteenth century CE; and others. The region's major river systems, the Oxus/Amu-Darya/Jayhun, the Kunar and

Kabul rivers flowing east to join the Indus, the Helmand draining the Hazarajat, and the Haray Rud flowing west via Jam and Herat have allowed trade between Iran and India, and between China and central Asia, throughout history.

Beginning in the seventh century, Afghanistan was incorporated, with difficulty, into the "Dar al-Islam" Islamic commonwealth; the last pockets of pagan resistance were mopped up in Laghman only in the seventeenth century and Nuristan in the late nineteenth century. Traces of Arab bedouin garrison tribes survive in the north near Balkh. From the late seventh century, Afghanistan's foreign relations and increasingly its internal social and political relations were molded by the precepts of Islam. The eleventh-century Nasiri Khusro and fourteenth-century Ibn Battuta traveled in the area using the networks typical of Muslim society: religious colleges, hospices, caravanserais and trade caravans, as well as the progresses of influential emirs and vizers. Ibn Battuta is one of the early travelers who mentions bandits, called Afghans, in the Sulaiman mountains—their name had not yet been given to the area, which was still reckoned part of Khorasan, or Turkestan, or the farthest reaches of northwestern India. The seventeenth-century Safavids in Iran and Moghuls in India fought over the area of Afghanistan, with the frontier of control fluctuating around Balkh and Kandahar: this accounts for sectarian (Shi'i versus Sunni) and linguistic (Farsi versus Pushtu) features of the area today.

Afghanistan has been the center of Turkish Muslim empires, in the eleventh century under the Ghaznavids at Ghazni and in the fifteenth century under the Teimurids at Herat. Pushtun/Afghan tribes and Turk/Uzbek clans expanded not only in Afghanistan but also raided widely into Iran and India, sometimes for no more than slaves and booty, sometimes to build ephemeral empires—the fifteenth-century Lodins and sixteenth-century Suris in India, the eighteenth-century Hotakis in Iran, and the eighteenth-century Abdalis in Kashmir, the Rohillas in northern India, and so on. Obviously, the Muslim invasions of India—the Ghurids, the Ghaznavids, the Moghuls—passed largely through Afghanistan, as can be read in the memoirs of the sixteenth-century emperor Babur, who always retained a special affection for the clear dry air of Kabul, where he chose to be buried.

The growth of the British Indian and Russian central Asian empires in the nineteenth century led to the squeezing of Afghanistan as a buffer state to be preserved within narrower borders (defined in the St. Petersburg Convention of 1907) that cut right across ethnic boundaries. This led to the still current situation of the large Pushtun populations shared between Afghanistan and Pakistan; the Baluch people shared between Afghanistan, Pakistan, and Iran; and the Uzbeks and Turkmens shared between Afghanistan and central Asia. This has, naturally, blurred the edges of political control, taxes, trade, and smuggling, and of course also of travel writing. Much of this travel writing developed out of nineteenth-century intelligence-gathering operations, often by British officers concerned with the security of the northwest frontier of India. Afghanistan was justifiably suspicious of Westerners before and after the three wars with British India and operated an almost closed-border policy, which accounts for the almost total absence of the missionary writing that elsewhere (for example, in Iran and India) is useful as a supplement to the writings of other travelers. Since trade has never been a major motive of Western penetration of this area, Western travel writing has been primarily military, political, and ethnographic in focus, especially in the period of Anglo-Russian rivalry in the nineteenth century and, more recently, during the period of U.S.-Soviet rivalry.

Images of wild-eyed, bearded, and turbaned tribesmen have had a long history in shaping Western perceptions of the country (frontispiece to vol. 2 of Arthur Conolly's *Journey to the North of India*, second edition, 1838). *Courtesy of the Travellers Club, London; Bridgeman Art Library, agent.*

Travel writing about Afghanistan can be roughly divided into the following stages: Alexander the Great and his historians, from the third century BC to the second century AD; the Buddhist pilgrims, from the fourth to the seventh century AD; the Muslims, especially Nasiri Khusro, Ibn Battuta, and the emperor Babur; early Europeans such as Marco Polo in the 1270s and Benedict de Goes in 1603; colonial penetration from India, beginning with Mountstuart Elphinstone in 1809 and continuing up until the 1842 disaster memorably recounted by Lady Sale; the closed period before the modernization of the country, with the brief incursion by Sir George Robertson in 1890 to the still unenlightened pagans of Nuristan and the visit of Lord Curzon to the "Iron Emir" in 1894; the wartime escapades of Oskar von Niedermayer in 1915 and Fitzroy Maclean in 1938; the twentieth-century Grand Tourists such as Robert Byron in 1933, Nicolas Bouvier in 1953, Eric Newby in 1956, and Peter Levi in 1969; archaeologists and anthropologists, scholars and residents like the great French Dominican Serge de Beaurecueil, and war journalists who traveled in Afghanistan after the 1979 Soviet invasion—Radek Sikorski (traveled 1987), Peregrine Hodson (traveled 1984), and Sandy Gall (traveled 1982)—and during the ensuing jihad and more recent chaotic civil war.

BRUCE WANNELL

### References and Further Reading

Arrian, *The Life of Alexander the Great*, translated by Aubrey de Sélincourt, 1958; also as *History of Alexander and Indica*, translated by P.A. Brunt, 2 vols., 1976–1983 (Loeb edition).
Babur, Zahiruddin, *The Babur-nama in English: Memoirs of Babur*, translated by Annette Susannah Beveridge, 2 vols., 1921.
Balsan, François, *Inquisitions de Kaboul au Golfe persique*, 1949.
Beaurecueil, Serge de, *Mes Enfants de Kaboul*, 1983.
Bellew, H.W., *Journal of a Political Mission to Afghanistan, in 1857*, 1862; reprinted, 1978.
Bellew, H.W., *From the Indus to the Tigris: A Narrative of a Journey through the Countries of Balochistan, Afghanistan, Khorassan and Iran, in 1872*, 1874; reprinted, 1977.
Bonvalot, Gabriel, *En Asie Centrale, de Moscou en Bactriane*, 1884.
Bouvier, Nicolas, *L'Usage du monde*, drawings by Thierry Vernet, 1963; as *The Way of the World*, translated by Robyn Marsack, 1992.
Burnes, Alexander, *Travels into Bokhara, Being the Account of a Journey from India to Cabool, Tartary and Persia*, 3 vols., 1834.
Burnes, Alexander, *Cabool, Being a Personal Narrative*, 1842; reprinted, 1973.
Byron, Robert, *The Road to Oxiana*, 1937.
Chaffetz, David, *A Journey through Afghanistan: A Memorial*, 1981.
Cobbold, Ralph P., *Innermost Asia: Travel and Sport in the Pamirs*, 1900.
Conolly, Arthur, *Journey to the North of India: Overland from England, through Russia, Persia, and Affghaunistaun*, 2 vols., 1834; second edition, 1838.
Curzon, George Nathaniel (Marquess Curzon of Kedleston), *Tales of Travel*, 1923; reprinted, 1988.
Danziger, Nick, *Danziger's Travels: Beyond Forbidden Frontiers*, 1987.
Darmesteter, James, *Lettres sur l'Inde, à la frontière afghane*, 1888.
Elliot, Jason, *An Unexpected Light: Travels in Afghanistan*, 1999.
Elphinstone, Mountstuart, *An Account of the Kingdom of Caubul*, 1815; 3rd edition, 2 vols., 1839; reprinted, 1972.
Eyre, Vincent, *The Military Operations at Cabul Which Ended in the Retreat and Destruction of the British Army, January 1842*, 1843; as *Journal of an Afghanistan Prisoner*, 1976.
Fa-hsien, *A Record of Buddhistic Kingdoms*, translated by James Legge, 1886; reprinted, 1991.
Ferrier, J.P., *Caravan Journeys and Wanderings in Persia, Afghanistan, Turkistan, and Beloochistan*, translated by William Jesse, 1856; 2nd edition, 1857; reprinted, 1971.
Forbes, Rosita, *Forbidden Road: Kabul to Samarkand*, 1937.
Forster, George, *A Journey from Bengal to England, through the Northern Part of India, Kashmire, Afghanistan, and Persia, and into Russia, by the Caspian Sea*, 2 vols., 1798.
Fox, Ernest F., *Travels in Afghanistan, 1937–1938*, 1943.
Gall, Sandy, *Behind Russian Lines: An Afghan Journal*, 1983.
Goes, Benedict de, *Purchas His Pilgrimes*, 4 vols., 1625; reprinted as *Hakluytus Posthumus; or, Purchas His Pilgrimes*, 20 vols., 1905–1907.
Gray, John Alfred, *At the Court of the Amir: A Narrative*, 1895.
Harlan, Josiah, *Central Asia: Personal Narrative . . . 1823–1841*, edited by Frank E. Ross, 1939.
Hodson, Peregrine, *Under a Sickle Moon: Journey through Afghanistan*, 1986.
Hsuan Tsang, *Si-Yu-Ki: Buddhist Records of the Western World*, translated by Samuel Beal, 2 vols., 1884.
Ibn Battuta, *Travels of Ibn Battuta, AD 1325–1354*, translated by H.A.R. Gibb, 5 vols., 1958–2000 (vol. 4 with C.F. Beckingham).
'Izzatullah, Mir, *Travels in Central Asia by Meer Izzut-Oollah in the Years 1812–13*, translated by Captain Henderson, 1872.
Kessel, Joseph, *Afghanistan*, translated by Bernadette Folliot, 1959.
Khalili, Khalilullah, *'Ayyari az Khorasan*, 1980.
Khusro, Nasiri, *Sefer nameh: Relation du voyage de Nassiri Khosrau*, edited and translated by Charles Schefer, 1881; reprinted, 1970; as *The Book of Travels (Safarnama)*, translated by W.M. Thackston Jr., 1986.
Klass, Rosanne, *Land of the High Flags: A Travel-Memoir of Afghanistan*, 1964; as *Afghanistan: Land of the High Flags*, 1966.
Levi, Peter, *The Light Garden of the Angel King: Journeys in Afghanistan*, 1972.
Maclean, Fitzroy, *Eastern Approaches*, 1949.
Masson, Charles, *Narrative of Various Journeys in Balochistan, Afghanistan, and the Panjab*, 4 vols., 1842–1844; reprinted, 1974–1977.
Mohana Lala, Munshi, *Journal of a Tour through the Panjab, Afghanistan, Turkistan, Khorasan, and Part of Persia*, 1834.
Mohana Lala, Munshi, *Travels in the Panjab, Afghanistan, and Turkistan*, 1846; reprinted, 1971.
Moorcroft, William, and George Trebeck, *Travels in the Himalayan Provinces of Hindustan and the Panjab*, 2 vols., 1841; reprinted, 1979.
Morgenstierne, Georg, *Report on a Linguistic Mission to Afghanistan*, 1926.
Myrdal, Jan, *Kreuzweg der Kulturen: Ein Buch über Afghanistan* [Crossroads of Cultures: A Book about Afghanistan], 1964.
Newby, Eric, *A Short Walk in the Hindu Kush*, 1958.
Niedermayer, Oskar von, and Ernst Diez, *Afganistan*, 1924.
Outram, Sir James, *Rough Notes of the Campaign in Sinde and Affghanistan in 1838–1839*, 1840.
Palmer, Louis, *Adventures in Afghanistan*, 1990.
Polo, Marco, *The Book of Ser Marco Polo*, edited and translated by Henry Yule, 2 vols., 1871; 3rd edition, revised by Henri Cordier, 1903; as *Marco Polo: The Description of the World*, edited and translated by A.C. Moule and Paul Pelliot, 2 vols., 1938, reprinted, 1976.
Robertson, George Scott, *The Kafirs of the Hindu-Kush*, 1896, reprinted, 1974.
Sale, Lady Florentia, *A Journal of the Disasters in Affghanistan 1841–42*, 1843; as *The First Afghan War*, edited by Patrick Macrory, 1969.

Sikorski, Radek, *Dust of the Saints: A Journey to Herat in Time of War*, 1989.
Stark, Freya, *The Minaret of Djam*, 1970.
Stirling, Edward, *The Journals of Edward Stirling—in Persia and Afghanistan 1828–1829*, edited by Jonathan L. Lee, 1991.
Stocqueler, J.H., *Memorials of Affghanistan . . . between the Years 1838 and 1842*, 1843.
Tate, G.P., *Seistan: A Memoir on the History, Topography, Ruins, and People of the Country*, 2 vols., 1910–1912; reprinted, 1977.
Thesiger, Wilfrid, *Among the Mountains: Travels through Asia*, 1998.
Thornton, Ernest, and Annie Thornton, *Leaves from an Afghan Scrapbook*, 1910.
Toynbee, Arnold, *Between Oxus and Jumna*, 1961.
Vigne, G.T., *A Personal Narrative of a Visit to Ghuzni, Kabul, and Afghanistan*, 1840; reprinted, 1982.
Wood, John, *A Personal Narrative of a Journey to the Source of the River Oxus*, 1841; as *A Journey to the Source of the River Oxus*, edited by Alexander Wood, 1872, reprinted, 1976.
Yate, C.E., *Northern Afghanistan; or, Letters from the Afghan Boundary Commission*, 1888.
Yate, C.E., *Khurasan and Sistan*, 1900.

*See also* **Great Game**

## AIRPLANES

Given how drastically the advent of the airplane changed travel on a global scale throughout the twentieth century, it has engendered very little in the way of travel literature. What does exist seems to fall chronologically on either side of World War II. In the early twentieth century, the airplane was not chiefly used for the benefit of passenger travel; it was used for mail transport (as in the United States, which in 1924 instituted the first scheduled night flights courtesy of the Air Mail Service), for air battles, for setting records (usually in exchange for a substantial monetary award or financial backing), and for entertainment. Before World War II, commercial plane travel was a kind of luxurious adventure; passengers might be given first-class treatment and amenities while being sprayed with icy runway mud through draughty air vents. Pressurized commercial aircraft came into operation in 1940, but World War II disrupted existing passenger services. After the war, the great passenger airlines began to pare down their amenities and focus on economy and efficiency, and suddenly air travel became a common occurrence; at the same time, it became unmemorable.

The timescale involved is really rather breathtaking. Graham Coster (1960–) argues that perhaps aviation has not inspired the century's writers because it happened so fast (1997). Wilbur Wright (1867–1912) and Orville Wright (1871–1948) made their historic first powered flight at Kitty Hawk, North Carolina, in 1903; the world's first scheduled passenger service operated in Florida in 1914. In 1917, Deutsche Luft Reederei was formed, the forerunner of the modern airline Lufthansa, though they did not run a scheduled service until 1919. By 1921, the British government was subsidizing the "glamorous" London–Paris route, frequented mostly by American film stars and businessmen. In 1927, Charles Lindbergh (1902–1974) made the first solo flight across the Atlantic; in the early 1930s, Lindbergh plotted possible passenger routes across both the Atlantic and the Pacific, with his wife, Anne Morrow Lindbergh (1906–2001), as traveling companion and radio operator. By the latter half of the 1930s, transatlantic passenger travel was common.

Both of the Lindberghs wrote about their pioneering flying experiences. So did the American Amelia Earhart (1897–1937), the Frenchmen Antoine de St.-Exupéry (1900–1944), and the Briton Beryl Markham (1902–1986). Markham was raised in Kenya and learned to fly there, and St.-Exupéry's regular employment as a pilot occurred in North Africa and South America, so these writers do represent a wide spectrum of flying experience around the world. Many of their books are still available today, though it may be difficult for the modern traveler to understand the nostalgic attitude that seems to pervade the writing of these early fliers. St.-Exupéry's *Wind, Sand and Stars* (1939), based on the author's early flights and training and the characters he encountered, was published while the author was still in his thirties; but his perspective is that of one looking back as though from a great distance on events and techniques, now obsolete, which happened scarcely 15 years earlier. Charles Lindbergh takes a similar tone in his foreword to Anne Morrow Lindbergh's *Listen! The Wind* (1938), when he explains that the description of a survey flight made only five years earlier "is about a period in aviation which is now gone, but which was probably more interesting than any the future will bring . . . The 'stratosphere' planes of the future will cross the ocean without any sense of the water below."

The novels and travelogues produced by this group of writers almost universally describe experiences that occurred between 1920 and 1940, for in terms of age the authors are very close contemporaries of one another. Earhart was the first woman to cross the Atlantic by air (as a passenger), and set a women's altitude record in 1922; she published books in 1928 and 1932, and even the existing notes of her failed trip around the world were published in 1937, as *Last Flight*, after her disappearance in the Pacific earlier that year. St.-Exupéry, who took his first flight at the age of 12 a mere nine years after Kitty Hawk, was a commercial airline pilot and a novelist by the time he was 30; his novels *Southern Mail* (1929) and *Night Flight* (1931) were based firmly in his own experiences working air mail services in Morocco and South America. Charles Lindbergh's first book, *We, Pilot and Plane*, appeared in 1927, the same year as his historic flight across the Atlantic; in it he describes all the excitement and daredevilry associated with being a pioneering pilot, from wing-walking to parachuting. Markham, who in 1936 became the first woman to fly the Atlantic solo from east to west, published a memoir titled *West with the Night* in 1983, in which she describes learning to fly in Kenya in the 1930s and her various paid jobs there as a pilot. The book also describes her flight to England from Kenya with Bror Blixen, and her subsequent record-setting flight from England to Newfoundland.

By far the most eloquent of these writers are St.-Exupéry and Anne Morrow Lindbergh. St.-Exupéry is enamored of people and landscapes and the interrelationships between the two, culminating in his memorable plane crash in the desert (recounted in a single chapter of *Wind, Sand and Stars*, but also alluded to in his classic children's book *The Little Prince*, of 1943). Lindbergh's reminiscences (1935 and 1938), are true travelogue, and are as much about her experiences on the ground as in the sky; she talks of the magic of the clash between new and old (1935), of what a "fairy tale" it was to be flying in the early days when the pilot had to rock the plane to attract the passenger's attention over the noise of the wind and the engines, of the peculiar problems one encountered in the roles of radio operator, explorer, and ambassador, and of one's luggage bounded by weight restrictions: "'I want a pair of shoes,' I would say, entering a shop, 'that I can wear at balls and dinners, and also at teas and receptions, and also for semi-sport dresses, and also for bedroom slippers.'"

Less obvious references to the airplane and its role in twentieth-century travel are hidden within longer works that do not actually focus on the airplane itself. In *The Last Tycoon* (1941), the unfinished final novel of F. Scott Fitzgerald (1896–1940), there is a brilliant cameo of passenger travel along the Atlantic–Pacific route across the United States in the 1930s: "There has been nothing like the airports since the days of the stage-stops . . . airports lead you way back in history like oases, like the stops on the great trade routes." Karen Blixen (1885–1962), writing as Isak Dinesen, provides similar cameos in her memoir *Out of Africa* (1937), describing her experiences of passenger flight over the Great Rift Valley in Kenya in the 1920s. Occasionally, a telling travel experience is captured briefly in a poem, as in Paulette Jiles's "Night Flight to Attiwapiskat" (in Fraser, 1991).

Another untapped source to be considered is that of the fighter pilot. Wartime flying in both world wars inspired a great deal of pulp fiction about air aces and dogfights, and individual memoirs of fighter pilots became (and still are) a popular form of literature. But it is not exactly travel literature, and in general the writing is mediocre or ghostwritten, the focus being not on travel but on the events of war. Nevertheless, a few names stand out in this genre of adventure writing, whose skill as writers turns their wartime flying experiences into a kind of travelogue: Cecil Lewis (1898–1997), Don Charlwood (1915–), Roald Dahl (1916–1990), and St.-Exupéry are notable among these. Lewis's memoir *Sagittarius Rising* (1936) contains stunning descriptions of the very early days of flying, of the hazards of being a flier in World War I, and of flight in China in the 1920s.

Of recent interest is Graham Coster's 1997 collection of flying vignettes in *The Wild Blue Yonder: The Picador Book of Aviation*. A more individual memoir is *A Pirate Looks at Fifty* (1998), by Jimmy Buffett (1946–), chronicling the author's travels around the Caribbean in a seaplane or "flying boat." William Langewiesche, known for his travel writing on the Sahara desert, has recently published *Inside the Sky* (1998), in which travel, people, events, and experiences are unfailingly interconnected with the airplane with an eloquence and spirit not known since perhaps the days of Anne Morrow Lindbergh and St.-Exupéry; the great difference is that Langewiesche writes as both commercial passenger and pilot, as one experienced with modern air travel and not as a pioneer. Indeed, he describes a conversation with a fellow passenger who mistakes the Pacific Ocean for the Napa Valley, proving true Charles Lindbergh's prophecy that the modern air traveler will not be aware of the water below. The notable, noteworthy airplane journeys seem to remain with the individual; they occur aboard small aircraft rather than aboard the packed commercial airliners. Whether as pilot or passenger, one's experience of flying seems to be as a solitary activity, whose fascination is caught early on in the 1919 poem "An Irish Airman Foresees His Death," by W.B. Yeats (1865–1939): "A lonely impulse of delight / drove to this tumult in the clouds."

ELIZABETH E. WEIN

### References and Further Reading


Buffett, Jimmy, *A Pirate Looks at Fifty*, 1998.

Charlwood, D.E., *No Moon Tonight*, 1956.

Coster, Graham, *The Wild Blue Yonder: The Picador Book of Aviation*, 1997.

Coster, Graham, *Corsairville: The Last Domain of the Flying Boat*, 2000.

Dahl, Roald, *Going Solo*, 1986.

Earhart, Amelia, *20 Hrs. 40 Min.: Our Flight in the Friendship: The American Girl, First across the Atlantic by Air, Tells Her Story*, 1928; reprinted, 1980.

Earhart, Amelia, *The Fun of It: Random Records of My Own Flying and of Women in Aviation*, 1932.
Earhart, Amelia, *Last Flight*, arranged by George Palmer Putnam, 1937.
Fawcett, Edward Douglas, *From Heston to the High Alps: A Chat about Joy-Flying*, 1936.
Fraser, Keath (editor), *Bad Trips*, 1991; as *Worst Journeys: The Picador Book of Travel*, 1992.
Hemingway, Ernest, "A Paris-to-Strasbourg Flight," 1922.
Hemingway, Ernest, "A Christmas Gift," 1954.
Langewiesche, William, *Inside the Sky: A Meditation on Flight*, 1998.
Lewis, Cecil, *Sagittarius Rising*, 1936.
Lindbergh, Anne Morrow, *North to the Orient*, with maps by Charles A. Lindbergh, 1935.
Lindbergh, Anne Morrow, *Listen! The Wind*, with a foreword and maps by Charles A. Lindbergh, 1938.
Lindbergh, Charles A., *We, Pilot and Plane*, 1927; expanded as *The Spirit of St. Louis*, 1953.
Lindbergh, Charles A., *Of Flight and Life*, 1948.
Markham, Beryl, *West with the Night*, 1983; as *The Illustrated West with the Night*, abridged by Elizabeth Claridge, 1989.
St.-Exupéry, Antoine de, *Terre des hommes*, 1939; as *Wind, Sand and Stars*, translated by Lewis Galantière, 1939; translated and with an introduction by William Rees, 1995.
St.-Exupéry, Antoine de, *Pilote de guerre*, 1942; as *Flight to Arras*, translated by Lewis Galantière, illustrated by Bernard Lamotte, 1942; translated by William Rees, 1995.

*See also* **Balloons and Airships**

## ALASKA

On 30 March 1867, William Henry Seward (1801–1872), U.S. Secretary of State, signed the cession treaty that secured Russian America for the United States. Derided by the *New York Herald* as "Walrussia" and "Icebergia," the 586,400-square-mile territory cost a mere $7.2 million and was quickly renamed Alaska from the native Aleutian peoples' word *Alak' shak* or *Al-ay' ek-sa*, meaning "the great country."

For the previous two centuries, the coast of Russian America had witnessed Russian, British, and Spanish territorial rivalries, and a period of intense exploration. Spurred on by colonialism, an urgency to determine whether Siberia and North America were connected by land, and the search for a Northeast Passage (a sea route to China via the north coast of Siberia), the earliest European exploration of the area was Russian.

In 1725, Vitus Jonassen Bering (1681–1741), a Dane in the service of Peter the Great (1672–1725), began an expedition to determine whether the Asian and North American continents were contiguous. In 1728, he sailed from the Kamchatka River through what would be named the Bering Strait and into the Arctic Ocean, reaching 67° N. Bering charted the area, but poor weather prevented any sighting of the North American coastline. To resolve the question of continental separation, Bering led the Great Northern Expedition (1733–1743). He reached the Alaskan coast on St. Elias Day, 16 July 1741, and named the highest mountain St. Elias.

Sitka, founded by the Russians on this site in 1804 under the name of Novoarkhangelsk (New Archangel), only passed into United States control in 1867; its Russian character is plainly visible in some of the buildings in this waterfront view (from Frederick Whymper's *Travel and Adventure in the Territory of Alaska*, 1868). *Courtesy of British Library, London.*

Although knowledge of continental separation is generally attributed to Bering, both his 1728 voyage and his discovery had been preempted by almost 80 years. In 1648, fur hunters led by an illiterate Cossack, Semen Dezhnev (1605–1673), had already confirmed that Asia and North America were divided by sailing from the Kolyma River to the Anadyr River through the Bering Strait. The log of Dezhnev's voyage lay forgotten in the Russian archives at Yakutsk until the German historian Gerhard Friedrich Müller (1705–1783) discovered it in 1736. It was to become source material for Bering's second voyage and for Captain James Cook (1728–1779).

On his third and final voyage (1776–1779), Cook attempted to discover a Northeast Passage between the Pacific and the North Sea and a northwest passage around Canada and Alaska. He sighted America at 45° N and began a survey that took him as far as the Bering Strait (70° N). He sailed into Prince William Sound on 12 May 1778 and on 26 May discovered Cook Inlet. On 25 August, ice forced him to sail south, and he surveyed the opposite coast of Siberia.

Throughout this period, territorial rivalries smoldered. In July 1774, Captain Juan Perez had reached the southern coast of Alaska to substantiate Spanish claims to the territory and to oust Russian fur traders. The following year, Juan Francisco de la Bodega y Quadra (1743–1794) and Don Francisco Antonio Mourelle (1755–1820), also in the service of the king of Spain, discovered Bucareli Bay and reached 58° N before returning to Mexico. However, by 1784 Grigorii Ivanovich Shelikhov (1747–1795) had founded a permanent settlement on Kodiak Island and claimed the adjoining coast for Russia.

By the nineteenth century, the focus of exploration had moved from Alaska's islands and coastline to its interior. During his second overland expedition (1825–1827), Sir John Franklin (1786–1847) explored from the mouth of the Mackenzie River in northwest Canada to Beechey Point in Alaska. A second party, led by the surgeon and naturalist Sir John Richardson (1787–1865), followed the coast eastward from the Mackenzie to the Copper River.

From 1859 to 1861, Robert Kennicott (1835–1866) explored Russian America collecting mammal and bird specimens. In 1865, the Western Union Telegraph Company appointed him head naturalist on their expedition to survey a 700-mile telegraph route from the Seward Peninsula to Fort Yukon. However, when the expedition's steamer failed the party had to winter at the native village of Nulato, where Kennicott died. William Healey Dall (1845–1927), a natural historian, malacologist, paleontologist, and an authority on the flora, fauna, geography, and indigenous peoples of Alaska, replaced Kennicott.

Although only 21, Dall had already spent the latter half of 1865 in the Aleutian Islands devoting himself to the first systematic examination of marine fauna. Dall now made the first detailed investigation of the Alaskan interior, also mapping much of the Yukon River. His *Alaska and Its Resources* (1870) is a detailed appraisal of the natural resources of Alaska. Between 1871 and 1879, he made coastal surveys of the Aleutian Islands and Alaska that resulted in his *Pacific Coast Pilot: Coasts and Islands of Alaska* (1879). In 1899, Dall again traveled to Alaska as part of the Harriman Alaska Expedition, funded by the railroad giant Edward H. Harriman (1848–1909).

In 1883, Alaska's first pleasure steamer entered Glacier Bay, and Alaska became a tourist destination. Ella Higginson (1862–1940), traveler and author of *Alaska: The Great Country* (1917), noted that "from June to September, thousands of people 'go to Alaska' . . . they take passage at Seattle on the most luxurious steamers that run up the famed 'inside passage' to Juneau, Sitka, Wrangell, and Skaguay." However, pondering the vastness of the country, she remarked wryly, "The person who contents himself with this will know as little about Alaska as a foreigner who landed in New York, went straight to Niagara Falls and returned at once to his own country, would know about America."

Alongside tourism, scientific, cartographical, and paleontological expeditions spanned the late nineteenth and early twentieth centuries. In 1891, Lieutenant Frederick Schwatka (1849–1892), a member of the Alaska Exploring Expedition of 1883, returned to Alaska, and Israel C. Russell (1852–1906) journeyed to Mount St. Elias. In 1904 and 1907, the Smithsonian dispatched expeditions in search of mammoth and Pleistocene fossil vertebrates. However, it was between 1897 and 1900 that Alaska was to witness a greater influx of travelers and writers than it had ever seen or is likely to see again. Gold "stampeders," including Jack London (1876–1916) and Joaquin Miller (1839–1913), trekked, sledded, and sailed to the Klondike goldfields to seek their fortunes.

IAN N. HIGGINSON

## References and Further Reading

Bodega y Quadra, Juan Francisco de la, *Carta de los descrubrimientos hechos en la costa N.O. de la America Septentrional*, 1792.

Campbell, Robert, *The Discovery and Exploration of the Youcon (Pelly) River by the Discoverer, Robert Campbell*, 1885.

Carmack, George Washington, *My Experiences in the Yukon*, 1933.

Cook, Frederick A., *To the Top of the Continent: Discovery, Exploration and Adventure in Sub-Arctic Alaska: The First Ascent of Mt. McKinley, 1903–1906*, 1908.

Dall, William H., *Alaska and Its Resources*, 1870.

Dall, William H., *Scientific Results of the Exploration of Alaska, during the Years 1865–1874 by the Parties under the Charge of W.H. Dall*, 1876.

Dall, William H., *Pacific Coast Pilot: Coasts and Islands of Alaska*, 1879.

Dall, William H., *Report of the International Polar Expedition to Point Barrow, Alaska, in Response to the Resolution of the* [US] *House of Representatives of December 11, 1884*, 1885.

Dall, William H., *The Yukon Territory; The Narrative of W.H. Dall, Leader of the Expedition to Alaska in 1866–1868; The Narrative of an Exploration Made in 1887 in the Yukon District*, 1898.

DeGraf, Anna, *Pioneering on the Yukon, 1892–1917*, edited by Roger S. Brown, 1992.

Franklin, John, *Narrative of a Second Expedition to the Shores of the Polar Seas, in the Years 1825, 1826, and 1827*, 1828.

Franklin, John, *Sir John Franklin's Journals and Correspondence: The Second Arctic Land Expedition, 1825–1827*, edited by Richard C. Davis, 1998.

Haskell, William B., *Two Years in the Klondike and Alaskan Gold-fields, 1896–1898: A Thrilling Narrative of Life in the Gold Mines and Camps*, 1898; reprinted, 1998.

Higginson, Ella, *Alaska: The Great Country*, 1908; revised and augmented edition, 1917.

La Pérouse, Jean François de Galaup, Comte de, *Voyage autour du monde*, 4 vols., 1797; as *A Voyage around the World, in the Years 1785, 1786, 1787, and 1788*, 2 vols., 1798.

Lugrin, Charles H., *Yukon Gold Fields Map Showing Routes from Victoria, B.C., to the Various Mining Camps on the Yukon River and Its Branches, Mining Regulations of the Dominion Government and Forms of Application: Together with a Table of Distances, Extracts from Mr. Ogilvie's Reports, and Other Information*, 1897.

McGuire, Thomas, *99 Days on the Yukon: An Account of What Was Seen and Heard in the Company of Charles A. Wolf, Gentleman Canoeist*, 1977.

Merriam, C. Hart, *Results of a Biological Reconnaissance of the Yukon River Region*, 1900.

Mourelle, Francisco Antonio, *Journal of a Voyage in 1775 to Explore the Coast of America*, 1781.

Ogilvie, William, *Report of Wm. Ogilvie Exploration Survey of the Yukon River District*, 1887.
Ogilvie, William, *Early Days on the Yukon and the Story of Its Gold Finds*, 1913.
Pike, Warburton, *Through the Subarctic Forest: A Record of a Canoe Journey from Fort Wrangel to the Pelley Lakes and down to the Yukon River to the Behring Sea*, 1896.
Raymond, Charles W., *Report of a Reconnaissance of the Yukon River, Alaska Territory, July to September, 1869*, 1871.
Russell, Israel C., *A Journey up the Yukon River*, 1889.
Russell, Israel C., *An Expedition to Mount St. Elias*, 1891.
Schwatka, Frederick, *Along Alaska's Great River: A Popular Account of the Travels of the Alaska Exploring Expedition of 1883, along the Great Yukon River, from Its Source to Its Mouth, in the British North-West Territory, and in the Territory of Alaska*, 1885.
Schwatka, Frederick, *Report of a Military Reconnaissance Made in Alaska in 1883*, 1885.
Schwatka, Frederick, *A Summer in Alaska: A Popular Account of the Travels of an Alaska Exploring Expedition along the Great Yukon River, from Its Source to Its Mouth, in the British Northwest Territory, and in the Territory of Alaska*, 1891.
Schwatka, Frederick, *Schwatka's Last Search: The New York Ledger Expedition through Unknown Alaska and British America, Including the Journal of Charles Willard Hayes, 1891*, edited by Arland S. Harris, 1996.
Scidmore, Eliza Ruhamah, *Appletons' Guide-Book to Alaska and the Northwest Coast, Including the Shores of Washington, British Columbia, Southeastern Alaska, the Aleutian and the Seal Islands, the Bering and the Arctic Coasts, the Yukon River and Klondike District*, 1899.
Stuck, Hudson, *Ten Thousand Miles with a Dog Sled: A Narrative of Winter Travel in Interior Alaska*, 1914.
Whymper, Frederick, *Travel and Adventure in the Territory of Alaska, Formerly Russian America, Now Ceded to the United States, and in Various Other Parts of the North Pacific*, 1868.

*See also* **Russian-American Company; Yukon River**

## ALBANIA

From the time of Byron to the late twentieth century, Albania has drawn travelers attracted to its cultural and geographical remoteness: the country is by far the poorest and least developed in Europe. At the same time, much English-language travel writing about Albania has taken the excitement of isolation as a sufficient subject in itself. Only a handful of writers have been able to approach the country on its own terms, with the benefit of knowledge and a sense of context.

This is unsurprising, given that Albanian culture remains, in many respects, difficult to access. The language has no close relationship to any other now spoken. The territory is historically divided, by the Shkumbini River, into two very different sectors, northern high and southern low Albania. During the period of Communist rule, Albania declared itself the world's first atheist state, yet it continues to share in the inheritance of three major religions, Catholicism, Eastern Orthodoxy, and Islam.

The town of Berat in the early nineteenth century, drawn by British architect Charles Robert Cockerell, who accompanied Thomas Smart Hughes on a visit to Ali Pasha (from Hughes's *Travels in Sicily, Greece and Albania*, 1820). *Courtesy of the Travellers Club, London; Bridgeman Art Library, agent.*

Albania was part of the Ottoman empire from the late fifteenth century until the achievement of national independence in 1912. The name of the country, and the exact origin of the Albanian people, are both obscure. The word *Albania* first surfaces in medieval Latin and Greek. Modern Albanians, on the other hand, call their homeland Shqipëri, and have increasingly done so since the early nineteenth century. Folk belief has related this term, not very plausibly, to an Albanian word for "eagle," which accounts for the plethora of travel books featuring eagles in their title.

From the early nineteenth century on, the word *Albania* was used by writers in two senses. It was applied to the Albanian homeland, an area that coincided in many ways with the outline of the modern state. It was also applied to the area of southern Epirus under the control of the semiautonomous chieftain Ali Pasha (1744–1822). This included Ioannina, which Ali made his chief city in 1809. The sector was predominantly Greek-speaking and now lies firmly within the borders of modern Greece.

The best informed of the early writers on Albania was William Leake, who arrived in Ioannina in 1809 as British representative at the court of Ali Pasha. Anglo-French rivalry for Ali's support in the unstable political environment of the eastern Mediterranean was mirrored in a personal hostility between Leake and the French representative at Ioannina, François Pouqueville. The latter also wrote at length about the area, though much less reliably.

It was Lord Byron who consolidated a growing fashion for Albanian travel. Attracted by the possibility of meeting Ali Pasha, he went to Ioannina with John Cam Hobhouse in October 1809. They finally encountered Ali farther north, in Tepelene, and Byron wrote proudly, "With the exception of Major Leake . . . no other Englishmen have ever advanced beyond [Ioannina] into the interior." Byron's fantasy of Albania, as one of the world's wild places, has been the mainstay of most English travel writing about the country ever since:

> Land of Albania! let me bend mine eyes
> On thee, thou rugged nurse of savage men!
>
> (*Childe Harold's Pilgrimage*, canto 2, lines 338–339)

The publication of the first two cantos of *Childe Harold* in 1812, and their instant success, placed Albania firmly on the imaginative map of Europe.

The young Benjamin Disraeli visited Albania (by which he meant southern Epirus) in 1830. In an energetic letter to his father, dated 25 October 1830, he recorded his impressions of "this savage land of anarchy" and his vast enjoyment of "the now obsolete magnificence of Oriental Life." Much of the letter subsequently passed into his novel *Contarini Fleming* (1832).

Following Ali Pasha's death in 1822, there are very few English accounts of Albania in the rest of the century. One exception, however, is also one of the most memorable: Edward Lear's *Journals of a Landscape Painter in Albania*. Lear made two journeys through Albania, in September–November 1848 and April–June 1849. He traveled widely, saw the great inland cities of Berate and Gjirokast, and felt the "deadly cold loneliness" of Ali's now ruined city of Tepelene.

In the mid-nineteenth century, the center of gravity for writing on Albania shifted to Austria and, a little later, to Italy, a reflection of political developments and the strategic importance of the Albanian coastline to those two countries. The writing becomes much more informed, less driven by a fantasy of the remote. The work of Johann von Hahn (1854) is of particular importance. Significant too are the books by Theodor Ippen (1907), Karl Steinmetz (1904), Eugenio Barbarich (1905), and Vico Mantegazza (1912).

In the English-speaking world, there was a resurgence of interest at the turn of the twentieth century. Most famous among English writers of that period was Edith Durham (1863–1944). She began traveling in the Balkans in her late thirties and became deeply involved in the politics of the area. Many towns in Albania still have a street named after her, and she was one of the few foreigners whose memory survived the cultural cleansing of the Communist period. Durham was a close associate of Aubrey Herbert (1880–1923), who was a leading advocate of the Albanian cause in England and the writer of a posthumously published memoir on Albania at the time of the Second Balkan War of 1912, *Ben Kendim* (1924).

The period from 1900 to about 1935 was the golden age of Albanian travel writing. Among a large number of works there is the distinguished journalism of J.D. Bourchier (1850–1920); Gabriel Louis Jaray's elegantly detailed accounts of his travels, *L'Albanie inconnue* (1913) and *Au Jeune Royaume d'Albanie* (1914); René Puaux's *La Malheureuse Épire* (1914); Rose Wilder Lane's *The Peaks of Shala* (1922); and the work of the English Albanologist Joseph Swire, *Albania* (1929) and *King Zog's Albania* (1937).

The dearth of travel writing on Albania after World War II is entirely due to political circumstances. Following the accession to power of the Communists under Enver Hoxha in 1944, the country gradually turned its back on the outside world. Hoxha's rule also brought severe internal repression and, until his death in 1985, very little leisure travel was possible in the country. Thereafter, with gradually improving political conditions, there has been a resumption of interest in and publications on Albania.

STEPHEN MINTA

### References and Further Reading


Anagosti, Vasil, *The Terraces of Lukova*, 1985.

Baldacci, Antonio, *Itinerari Albanesi, 1892–1902*, 1917.

Barbarich, Eugenio, *Albania*, 1905.

Benson, Theodora, *The Unambitious Journey*, 1935.

Bourcart, Jacques, *L'Albanie et les Albanais*, 1921.

Brown, H.A., *A Winter in Albania*, 1888.

Cabanes, Pierre, *Albanie: Le pays des aigles*, 1994.

Carver, Robert, *The Accursed Mountains: Journeys in Albania*, 1998.

Ceretti, Giampietro, *L'Albania in grigio verde: Appunti di un viaggio da Valona a Salonicco*, 1918.

Cora, Guido, *Cenni generali intorno ad un viaggio nella Bassa Albania . . . compiuto dal settembre 1874 al gennaio 1875*, 1875.

Degrand, A., *Souvenirs de la Haute-Albanie*, 1901.

Disraeli, Benjamin, *Contarini Fleming: A Psychological Auto-Biography*, 1832.

Disraeli, Benjamin, *Letters*, edited by J.A.W. Gunn et al., vol. 1: *1815–1834*, 1982.

Durham, M. Edith, *The Burden of the Balkans*, 1905.

Durham, M. Edith, *High Albania*, 1909.

Durham, M. Edith, *The Struggle for Scutari*, 1914.

Durham, M. Edith, *Twenty Years of Balkan Tangle*, 1920.

Durham, M. Edith, *Some Tribal Origins, Laws and Customs of the Balkans*, 1928.

Edmonds, Paul, *To the Land of the Eagle: Travels in Montenegro and Albania*, 1927.

Emerson, June, *Albania: The Search for the Eagle's Song*, 1990.

Ghiglione, Piero, *Montagne d'Albania*, 1941.

Gordon, George [Lord Byron], *Childe Harold's Pilgrimage*, cantos 1 and 2, 1812.

Gordon, Jan, and Cora J. Gordon, *Two Vagabonds in Albania*, 1927.

Gordon, Thomas, *History of the Greek Revolution*, 2 vols., 1832.

Grogan, Ellinor, *The Life of J.D. Bourchier*, 1926.

Hahn, Johann Georg von, *Albanesische Studien*, 3 vols., 1854.

Hahn, Johann Georg von, *Reise durch die Gebiete des Drin und Wardar*, 1867.
Hecquard, Hyacinthe, *Histoire et description de la Haute-Albanie ou Guégarie*, 1858.
Herbert, Aubrey, *Ben Kendim: A Record of Eastern Travel*, edited by Desmond MacCarthy, 1924.
Heseltine, Nigel, *Scarred Background: A Journey through Albania*, 1938.
Hobhouse, J.C., *A Journey through Albania, and Other Provinces of Turkey in Europe and Asia, to Constantinople, during the Years 1809–1810*, 2 vols., 1813.
Holland, Henry, *Travels in the Ionian Isles, Albania, Thessaly, Macedonia, etc. during the Years 1812 and 1813*, 2 vols., 1815.
Hughes, Thomas Smart, *Travels in Sicily, Greece and Albania*, 2 vols., 1820.
Ippen, Theodor A., *Skutari und die nordalbanische Küstenebene*, 1907.
Jaray, Gabriel Louis, *L'Albanie inconnue*, 1913.
Jaray, Gabriel Louis, *Au Jeune Royaume d'Albanie . . .*, 1914.
Jaray, Gabriel Louis, *Les Albanais*, 1920.
Joliffe, Thomas R., *Narrative of an Excursion from Corfu to Smyrna, Comprising a Progress through Albania and the North of Greece*, 1827.
Kadaré, Ismaïl, *Gjirokastër, la ville de pierre*, translated from Albanian, c. 1997.
Knight, E.F., *Albania: A Narrative of Recent Travel*, 1880.
Lane, Rose Wilder, *The Peaks of Shala: Being a Record of Certain Wanderings among the Hill-Tribes of Albania*, 1922.
Leake, William Martin, *Researches in Greece*, part 1, 1814.
Leake, William Martin, *Travels in Northern Greece*, 4 vols., 1835.
Lear, Edward, *Journals of a Landscape Painter in Albania*, 1851.
Mantegazza, Vico, *L'Albania*, 1912.
Matthews, Ronald, *Sons of the Eagle: Wanderings in Albania*, 1937.
Newby, Eric, *On the Shores of the Mediterranean*, 1984.
Newman, Bernard, *Albanian Back-Door*, 1936.
Nopcsa, Ferencz [Baron], *Aus Sala und Klementi: Albanische Wanderungen*, 1910.
Peacock, Wadham, *Albania, the Foundling State of Europe*, 1914.
Pouqueville, F.C.H.L., *Voyage en Morée, à Constantinople, en Albanie, et dans plusieurs autres parties de l'Empire Othoman, pendant les années 1798, 1799, 1800 et 1801*, 3 vols., 1805; translated anonymously as *Travels through the Morea, Albania and Other Parts of the Ottoman Empire to Constantinople during the Years 1798, 1799, 1800*, 1806.
Pouqueville, F.C.H.L., *Mémoire sur la vie et la puissanced'Ali-Pacha, visir de Janina*, 1820.
Pouqueville, F.C.H.L., *Voyage dans la Grèce*, 5 vols., 1820–1821; 2nd edition, as *Voyage de la Grèce*, 6 vols., 1826–1827.
Puaux, René, *La Malheureuse Épire*, 1914; as *The Sorrows of Epirus*, 1918.
Sherer, Stan, *Long Life to Your Children! A Portrait of High Albania*, 1997.
Siebertz, Paul, *Albanien und die Albanesen*, 1910.
Steinmetz, Karl, *Eine Reise durch die Hochländergaue Oberalbaniens*, 1904.
Steinmetz, Karl, *Ein Vorstosz in die nordalbanischen Alpen*, 1905.
Swire, J., *Albania: The Rise of a Kingdom*, 1929.
Swire, J., *King Zog's Albania*, 1937.
Thornton, Philip, *Dead Puppets Dance*, 1937.
Tilman, H.W., *When Men and Mountains Meet: Himalayas*, 1946.
Walker, Mary Adelaide, *Through Macedonia to the Albanian Lakes*, 1864.
Zaimi, Nexhmie, *Daughter of the Eagle: The Autobiography of an Albanian Girl*, 1937.

*See also* **Balkans, pre-1914**

## ALBUQUERQUE, AFONSO DE (c. 1460–1515) *Portuguese Admiral and Viceroy of India*

Afonso de Albuquerque was a soldier, statesman, navigator, admiral, administrator, diplomat, strategist, ideologist, and, above all, patriot. His work carried the stamp of the Portuguese empire. Albuquerque believed in a colonization that would benefit both conquerors and conquered. He dreamed of a mixed Indian-Portuguese race, educated, participating in their region's politics, fairer than before, respecting customs and religion, subject not to an oppressing king but to a bigger kingdom to which they belonged. Governing with a strong hand, unsupported in his concepts, he was not given the due credit and had no special rewards in a career totally dedicated to the glory of a small nation and its king.

Son of Gonçalo de Albuquerque, of noble ancestry, Albuquerque frequented the court of Afonso V (1432–1481), having received the usual education of a nobleman. The first 40 years of his life were spent at the service of three kings, participating in several inland and maritime military deeds. Some years in Morocco taught him the customs and beliefs of the Muslims. His presence at the court gave him the opportunity to establish important friendships and to meet the adventurous navigators who went ever further in their explorations. He was knowledgeable in the classics and mastered Latin, but exercised his literary talent only in epistolary writing, fluent and personal. His letters to Manuel I, compiled by his son Brás de Albuquerque and first published in 1557, are an important source for those interested in Portuguese oriental expansion.

Albuquerque made his first trip to India in 1503, commanding three vessels in the same expedition as his cousin Francisco de Albuquerque and António de Saldanha. An important account of this trip is given by the Tuscan Giovanni da Empoli in one of the few surviving documents of that time, the others having been destroyed in the Lisbon earthquake of 1755. Albuquerque had received orders from Manuel I to build a fort in Cochin, make war on Calicut (whose Muslim samorim had killed the Portuguese left at a trading station and had stolen all its merchandise), and establish further commercial relations in the area. Albuquerque left India in January 1504, carrying precious gifts to Manuel I, and reported directly to the king his observations on the possible expansion of the Portuguese empire. His ideas included the control of trade routes through the conquest of strategic positions in the Indian Ocean, from Bab-el-Mandeb to the Strait of Malacca, and obstructing the Muslim trade in spices and other merchandise through the Red Sea.

In order to proceed with these plans, Albuquerque was again sent to the East in the armada of Tristão da Cunha (who baptized newfound islands in the Atlantic Ocean with his name). A terrible plague was devastating Lisbon, and this led to the necessity of recruiting prisoners for the crew; Albuquerque was quoted as saying he had more fights on his ship than there were fights in the whole city of Salamanca. Without a pilot, he took charge and managed to catch up the main part of the fleet, which had departed earlier. While da Cunha's role was essentially commercial, Albuquerque was charged of a wider mission, being secretly appointed the second viceroy, succeeding Francisco de Almeida, whose authority expired in 1508. After the construction of a fort on the strategic island of Socotra, Albuquerque, nominated *capitão-mor* (admiral) of Arabia, was to patrol the coast and conquer that which he thought convenient, such as the main ports of Oman and the rich city of Hormuz, which he made tributary to the kingdom of Portugal.

Albuquerque had to leave the fort of Hormuz while it was still under construction and travel to India in 1508, in order to deal with the disobedience of his captains and to fulfill his responsibilities as viceroy. Soon after, on 2 February 1509, Almeida destroyed the Muslim fleet at the Battle of Diu, helping to establish Portuguese control over the spice trade. Returning to Cochin, Almeida refused to accept Albuquerque's authority and ordered his imprisonment in September. Albuquerque was freed later in 1509, upon the arrival of Fernando Coutinho from Lisbon, who confirmed his appointment as viceroy; Coutinho was also under orders to conduct an armed expedition against Calicut. Albuquerque, although seriously wounded in the disastrous battle, managed to save some men, but Coutinho lost his life. Albuquerque went on to a series of victories, always accomplished with inadequate supplies. In 1510, Albuquerque was invited to help the people in Goa fight against the oppression of the Ottoman troops, but he soon had to abandon the effort because of the superior strength of the Muslim forces. The Portuguese eventually regained Goa on 25 November, after a strenuous fight.

In 1511, Albuquerque went with his armada to Malacca, center of the East Indian spice trade, to try to free Portuguese captives. After fruitless attempts to negotiate with the sultan, Albuquerque attacked and conquered the city, which was guarded by 20,000 men and war elephants. He constructed a fort and left for India, his ships filled with rich prizes. Unfortunately, his boat sank, and he and his crew escaped with only their lives. He returned to Goa, again under Ottoman attack, but once more defeated the Turks in sea and land fighting, and also conquered the fort of Benastarim.

In 1513, Albuquerque became the first European admiral to sail in the Red Sea. His attempts to conquer Aden failed because of faulty siege equipment, but he entered Bab-el-Mandeb, thus completing the Portuguese control of the Far Eastern spice trade. In the following year, he was occupied with administrative and diplomatic work in India, having succeeded in making peace with Calicut. In 1515, he tried to complete construction of the fort at Hormuz, this time with no resistance and with the approval of the local ruler, who accepted protection from the Portuguese against his ambitious ministers. Albuquerque's plans were thus complete: the Portuguese, strong in nautical science and in artillery, controlled all the main ports of the Indian Ocean.

Albuquerque's most famous remark—"bad relations with the King for the sake of his men, and bad relations with his men for the sake of the King"—was made on his way back to India in November 1515. When his brilliant conquests became known, envy arose among many ambitious people in Portugal, accompanied by the anger of his enemies. They combined to demote him, and Lopo Soares de Albergaria was appointed the new viceroy without Albuquerque's being consulted. Exhausted and ill after nine years of campaigns in a pestilent climate, Albuquerque, upon hearing this news, had time only to dictate his last letter to Manuel I, reminding him of his services and asking protection for his natural son, Brás. He died on a boat off the coast, at the site of Goa, deeply mourned by the population. He acquired no personal fortune during his long service. However, his wide-ranging knowledge and extraordinary charisma arouse fascination to this day.

Manuel I, later regretting his ingratitude, took care of Brás de Albuquerque (1501–1587), who changed his name for his father's, Afonso. Brás was well educated by the monks of Saint Eloy, and went on to hold important positions in the kingdom. He was responsible for the publication of his father's letters, a work of historical veracity and power: *Comentários do grande Afonso de Albuquerque*.

PATRICIA LOPES BASTOS

## Biography

Born probably near Lisbon, c. 1460. Fought in the Battle of Toro, 1476. Participated in the naval expedition to help the King of Naples in his fight against the

Turks, 1480. Departed to Morocco after Afonso's death, 1481. Returned to Portugal as a member of the royal guard commanded by Mascarenhas and soon after nominated *estribeiromor* of João II (1455–1495). Returned to Morocco after João II's death, 1495. Went back to Portugal as a member of the royal guard of Manuel I (1469–1521). Sailed to India with Portuguese fleet, 1503. Returned to Lisbon, 1504. Set out again for the Orient with Tristão da Cunha, traveled through Mozambique and Madagascar, 1506. Departed to the Oman coast and started construction on fort of Hormuz, 1507. Secured control of the Persian Gulf and went to India, 1508. Imprisoned and released, appointed second viceroy of India, 1509. Conquered Goa and other ports on Malabar coast, 1510. Established naval control of commerce from the Red Sea to Malacca and access to the Moluccas (Spice Islands), Japan, and China, 1510–1515. Recaptured Hormuz, 1515. Learned by mistake of his removal as viceroy and died, weakened by a lasting case of dysentery, on a boat at the site of Goa, 16 December 1515.

### References and Further Reading

Albuquerque, Afonso de, *Comentários do grande Afonso de Albuquerque, capitão geral que foi das Indias Orientais*, 1557, edited by António Baião, 2 vols., 1922–1923; as *The Commentaries of the Great Afonso Dalboquerque, Second Viceroy of India*, translated by Walter de Grey Birch, 4 vols., 1875–1884; reprinted, 1970.

Albuquerque, Afonso de, *Cartas*, edited by Raymundo Antonio de Bulhão Pato, 7 vols., 1884–.

Albuquerque, Afonso de, *Albuquerque, Caesar of the East: Selected Texts by Afonso de Albuquerque and His Son*, edited and translated by John Villiers and T.F. Earle, 1990.

## ALEXANDER THE GREAT (356–323 BCE)

***Macedonian King and Soldier***

His military genius, great courage, and the lasting cultural impact of his empire earned Alexander his nickname "the Great." His enormous conquests and ceaseless search for the ends of the earth stirred the imagination of his contemporaries and of all generations after him. The history of his life was from the beginning intertwined with legend, so it has always been hard to define what Alexander was actually aiming at. When he died in Babylon in 323 BCE, his empire reached from Greece to Egypt, and from the Mediterranean to northern India.

Alexander was born the son of Olympias, of the royal house of Epirus and Philip II, king of Macedon. Philip had converted Macedon into a strong, strictly organized state, and had achieved supremacy in Greece thanks to clever diplomacy, cunning bribery, and ruthless military action. The Macedonian army became a formidable force, consisting of a phalanx of multiple ranks of infantry soldiers armed with six-meter pikes. When Philip was murdered in 336, Alexander promptly eliminated all challengers to his right to succeed. A swift military expedition in southern Greece made him in effect head of the League of Corinth. Thebes revolted, but it paid a heavy toll; after its devastation, the inhabitants were enslaved. Soon after, in 334, Alexander embarked on a war against the Persian empire. It was meant as an act of revenge for Persian aggression in the past. With his army of about 50,000 soldiers, Alexander took Asia Minor, and liberated the Greek cities along the coast. He met with heavy resistance at Tyre and other places in the eastern Mediterranean, but the Egyptians welcomed him as their great liberator. In 331, Alexander started his campaign against Darius III, king of Persia. Darius had already been defeated at Issus in 333, but had been able to escape. He now suffered a second, crushing defeat at Gaugamela (near Arbela, in Mesopotamia), but again fled. Setting off in pursuit, Alexander took possession of the rich Persian cities of Babylon, Susa, and Persepolis. Finally, in the late spring of 330, east of Ecbatana (present-day Hamadan), Darius was found, murdered by Bessus. In 327, the great war against Persia ended with the conquest of remote areas such as Hyrcania, Bactria, and Sogdiana; Bessus, the usurper of Darius's power, was executed.

As soon as Alexander attempted to strengthen the eastern frontiers of his empire, he was drawn into new wars. India, where his mythical forebears Heracles and Dionysus had once set foot, attracted him. After a successful invasion of the Indian Punjab, Alexander moved toward an uncertain destination, until his disaffected soldiers forced him to abandon his ill-defined plan. The army returned over the River Hyphasis (Beas) to Patala at the head of the Indus delta. A long journey full of hardship through the deserts of Gedrosia (Baluchistan) ended with Alexander's return to Susa in the winter of 325–324. While he was planning new conquests in Arabia and in the west, Alexander, after a short illness, died unexpectedly in Babylon in June 323; his death may have been a poisoning. After a period of turmoil, the western part of the empire was divided among Alexander's Macedonian generals, who founded the great dynasties of the now Hellenized world: the Ptolemies (mainly Egypt, Cyrene, Cyprus, and parts of Syria), the Seleucids (northern Syria and the southern half of Asia Minor), and the Antigonids (Macedonia and Thessaly, and to a certain extent the Greek homeland).

Colossal, often ruthless, military feats seem to dominate Alexander's biography, but his conduct shows how he had learned to reckon with the political support needed for his actions. He had many other talents, some natural, some the result of his childhood training at the hands of fine teachers, one of whom was probably Aristotle. Alexander's boundless desire to explore remote areas is testimony to his curiosity; the legend of the cutting of the Gordian knot is an illustration of his inventiveness. Another feature of his personality is his profound admiration for Greek culture, culminating in his love of Homer's *Iliad.* That he saw the protection of Greek culture as a political legitimation for his devastating war against the Persian empire is symbolized by his visit to Homer's Troy (Ilium), where he made sacrifices to Athene and to Priam, whom he regarded as one of the Greeks. On the administrative level, Alexander promoted Greek colonization and the foundation of new cities (such as Alexandria in Egypt), so as to create political stability and unity in his new empire. His marriage to Roxane, daughter of a Bactrian leader, was meant to be a stimulus to marriages between Greeks and Asians. He respected local customs and hierarchies, favored Persian ceremonies, and left many satraps and local rulers in office. This pro-Persian policy, and his absolute style of government in imitation of the Persian kings, was destined to become unpopular with the Greeks. At an earlier stage they had already complained about his visit to the temple of Ammon in the oasis at Siwah in Egypt in 331, where the oracle had addressed him as the son of Ammon Zeus, confirming the claim that he was of divine origin. In this way the overconfident conqueror gradually drifted away from his old Greek friends and from his own soldiers. Some plotted against him in 327, but they were mercilessly executed.

Little has been preserved of the many contemporary writings on Alexander. The authors of these writings were either among those participating in Alexander's campaigns, or else had access to firsthand information. But the material they left inspired later generations of Greek and Latin authors. The main works that survived are Arrian's restrained historical description of Alexander's military campaigns; Plutarch's anecdotal character sketch; Diodorus Siculus's history, which contains many fragments of authors now lost; Quintus Curtius Rufus's biography, concentrating on the psychological changes in Alexander's life; and Justin's extract from Pompeius Trogus. A large number of unhistorical and legendary stories about Alexander are found in the late Hellenistic (probably third-century CE) so-called Alexander Romance, which was erroneously attributed to Alexander's own historian, Callisthenes. The Alexander Romance was transmitted in many different forms in both European and Asian languages. These fantastic stories, such as Alexander's aerial and submarine adventures, aroused much interest in the Middle Ages. They helped to make Alexander the most revered historical figure of antiquity in that period. In the Renaissance, a more factual picture of Alexander emerged after the rediscovery of the ancient authors previously mentioned.

ZWEDER VON MARTELS

## Biography

Born in Pella, Macedon, 356 BCE, son of King Philip II of Macedon and Olympias, princess of Epirus. Taught by Aristotle. Defended Macedon against the Maedi, 340. Fought at the battle of Chaeronea, 338. Fled with his mother to Epirus after her divorce from Philip; later went to Illyria. Returned to Macedon and was reconciled with Philip. Inherited his father's title after his assassination, 336. Crossed the Hellespont and traveled through Asia Minor to Egypt, leading the Macedonian military campaign against the Persian empire, 334–327. Married Roxane, daughter of the Bactrian leader Oxyartes, c. 328. Killed his friend, Clitus, provoking unrest in the Macedonian army, c. 328. Successfully invaded the Punjab, India, 326. Returned to Susa, 325–324. Became ill in Babylon, either with malaria or from poisoning, 323. Died in Babylon, 10 or 13 June 323 BCE.

### References and Further Reading


Arrian, *Arrian*, translated by P.A. Brunt, 2 vols., 1976–1983 (Loeb edition).

Diodorus Siculus, *Library of History*, book 17 (in vol. 8), edited and translated by C. Bradford Welles, vol. 422, 1963 (Loeb edition).

Justin, *Epitome of the Philippic History of Pompeius Trogus, Books 11–12*, translated by J.C. Yardley, with commentary by Waldemar Heckel, 1997.

Plutarch, *Plutarch's Lives*, vol. 7, edited and translated by Bernadotte Perrin, vol. 99, 1919; reprinted, 1967 (Loeb edition).

Quintus Curtius Rufus, *History of Alexander*, edited and translated by J.C. Rolfe, vols. 368–369, 1946 (Loeb edition).

Stoneman, Richard (editor and translator), *The Greek Alexander Romance*, 1991.


*See also* **Greece, Ancient Hellenic World**

## ALPS

Generations of travelers have looked upon the Alps as a region of passage, a boundary between what the Romans thought of as the cold, "barbarous" north and the warm, "civilized" south. The principal routes led from north to south, rather than along the valleys running from east to west, and were determined primarily by accessibility and the time of year. The most famous of early journeys remains that made by Hannibal and his elephants across the western Alps. The Romans left behind an extensive road system that remained the basis of travel through the region for many centuries.

In the Middle Ages, traffic was commercial, religious, diplomatic, or military. Travelers from the Rhône and Rhine valleys usually crossed by the Mont Cenis Pass to Susa or by the Great St. Bernard to Turin and Milan. The opening of the St. Gotthard Pass created a shorter, more direct route across the central Alps, linking the Rhine valley to Milan. By the fourteenth century, the most popular route led from Augsburg in southern Germany to Innsbruck and over the Brenner Pass to Verona. A less dangerous route passed through Salzburg, Vienna, and Styria and Carinthia in the eastern Alps. The lot of Alpine travelers was eased by hospices, many dating from around the time of the First Crusade: the most famous were those on the Great St. Bernard and the St. Gotthard.

Travelers did not linger in the high mountain passes and valleys of the Alps, fearing storms, avalanches, and bandits. The narrow paths of the decaying road system were accessible only by mules and horses. Apart from occasional visitors like Petrarch, few travelers were interested in mountains, and it was not until the middle of the sixteenth century that Hans Fries was recorded as making a journey in the mountains for pleasure (De Beer, 1930) and the naturalist Conrad Gesner (1516–1565) took a scientific interest in the study of mountain environments. The British traveler Fynes Moryson wrote of his solitary journey in 1595 across the western Alps without even a footman, "I think very few have done [it] but myself."

Reminder of the superstitious awe with which the Alps were for centuries regarded: the strange light effect seen after the fatal accident on the first ascent of the Matterhorn in 1865 (engraved frontispiece to Edward Whymper's *Scrambles amongst the Alps*, 1871). *Courtesy of British Library, London.*

In the seventeenth century, British travelers like Gilbert Burnet (1643–1715) were interested in the history and religious life of the western Alps but not in the mountains themselves. By the beginning of the next century, scientifically minded travelers, including Johann Jakob Scheuchzer (1672–1733), from Zurich, began to make tours through the mountains. Scheuchzer's account of his complicated itineraries included descriptions of dragons. Burnet's son William reported to the Royal Society on his 1708 visit to the Grindelwald glaciers. German literary and philosophical interest in mountains was reinforced by Albrecht von Haller (1708–1777), whose poem "Die Alpen" (1732) was inspired by his travels. Most Grand Tourists continued to dislike mountains, though William Windham's description of his attempt to climb Mont Blanc in 1741 helped to make Chamonix into a mountaineering center.

After the end of the Seven Years' War (1756–1763), Alpine travel became more popular and the scientific exploration of the mountains began in earnest. Horace-Bénedict de Saussure's accounts of his travels and observations came to be regarded as the most influential. Like his rival Marc-Théodore Bourrit (1739–1818), Saussure (1740–1799) was determined to climb Mont Blanc and, though he was not the first to do so, he finally succeeded in 1786. Viewing glaciers became fashionable, but William Coxe (1747–1828), who made four visits to Switzerland in the 1770s and 1780s, expressed disappointment in those at Grindelwald. His admiration for other aspects of the scenery was evidence of the changes in taste that made the Alps increasingly attractive to tourists as they began to seek experiences of the sublime in ways that anticipated romantic attitudes to nature.

Improvements to the roads made the mountains more accessible. Rousseau's *La Nouvelle Héloïse* (1760) generated many literary and artistic pilgrimages to the Valais, where French travelers in particular took an idealized view of Alpine life. A passion for untamed nature encouraged the antiquarian Karl von Bonstetten (1716–1792) to "bathe his soul in pure nature," declaring that geology was "the true poetry of the Alps." Other visitors included Goethe (1749–1832), the Baron de Frenilly (1768–1828), and Wordsworth (1770–1850), whose walking tour helped to set a fashion. The new aesthetic of the sublime based on feeling encouraged female appreciation of the mountains. Subjective impressions of the beauty of the mountains became commonplace.

After the end of the revolutionary wars in 1814, the influence of romanticism brought many more visitors to the mountains. Schiller's *William Tell* (1803–1804) reinforced the association of the Swiss Grisons with the values of liberty, independence, and democracy. By contrast, visitors crossing into Alpine Austria complained of the bureaucratic and autocratic nature of the Hapsburg regime. In the 1840s, the new railways created simpler routes, determined primarily by topography, which encouraged the development of new resorts. Travel over the high passes continued to be on horseback or by sleigh until the construction of railway tunnels in the last quarter of the century. Of the many visitors to the Swiss Alps, few had much new to say, but, as in the case of John Ruskin (1819–1900), love of the Alps often generated enthusiastic accounts of their beauties. Most of the major peaks in the High Alps had already been climbed by Swiss, Austrian, or French mountaineers by 1854, when the so-called golden age of British mountaineering began. This culminated in the ascent of the Matterhorn in 1865, the only large peak still unconquered. Edward Whymper's account of the dramatic and controversial event, in which four lives were lost, remains one of the classics of the mountaineering genre.

The numerous memoirs published by members of the British Alpine Club (founded in 1857) were mostly concerned with topography rather than the history and peoples of the region. Long-established visitors to the region like Leslie Stephen (1832–1904) resented the tourists flooding what he dubbed the "playground of the world." A different kind of tourist—for example, Amelia Edwards (1831–1892)—looked for "untrodden peaks and unfrequented valleys" in unknown areas like the Dolomites, now made more accessible by the railway over the Brenner.

Despite new methods of travel, including guideless climbing, skiing, bicycling, and the motorcar, valleys in the more remote areas of the southeastern Alps remained secluded well into the twentieth century, when the customs and traditions of their inhabitants, threatened by or re-created for tourists, became the subject of anthropological interest.

JILL STEWARD

## References and Further Reading


Ball, John (editor), *Peaks, Passes and Glaciers: A Series of Excursions by Members of the Alpine Club*, 1859.

Beaumont, Albanis, *Travels through the Rhaetian Alps, in the Year 1786, from Italy to Gemany, through the Tyrol*, 1792.

Belloc, Hilaire, *The Path to Rome*, 1902.

Bourrit, Marc-Théodore, *Description des glaciéres, glaciers et amas de glace du duché de Savoie*, 1773; as *A Relation of a Journey to the Glaciers in the Duchy of Savoy*, translated by Charles and Fred Davy, 1775.

Burnaby, Elizabeth, *The High Alps in Winter; or, Mountaineering in Search of Health*, 1883.

Burnet, Gilbert, *Some Letters Containing What Seem'd Most Remarkable in Switzerland, Italy, &c.*, 1686; as *Bishop Burnet's Travels through Switzerland, Italy, Some Parts of Germany, &c. . . . To Which Is Added an Appendix, Containing Some Remarks on Switzerland and Italy, Writ by a Person of Quality*, 1725; reissued, 1737.

Churchill, George, and Josiah Gilbert, *The Dolomite Mountains: Excursions through Tyrol, Carinthia, Carniola, and Friuli in 1861, 1862, and 1863*, 1864.

Coryate, Thomas, *Coryats Crudities*, 1611; revised edition, 1776; reprinted, 2 vols., 1905; with an introduction by William M. Schutte, 1978.

Coxe, William, *Travels in Switzerland, and in the Country of the Grisons, In a Series of Letters to William Melmoth*, 3 vols., 1789.

D'Angeville, Henriette, *Mon Excursion au Mont Blanc*, 1838; as *My Ascent of Mont Blanc*, translated by Jennifer Barnes, with an introduction by Dervla Murphy, 1992.

De Beer, Gavin, *Early Travellers in the Alps*, London: Sidgwick and Jackson, 1930; New York: October House, 1967.

Edwards, Amelia B., *Untrodden Peaks and Unfrequented Valleys: A Midsummer Ramble in the Dolomites*, 1873; reprinted with a new introduction by Philippa Levine, 1986.

Forbes, James D., *Travels through the Alps of Savoy and Other Parts of the Pennine Chain: With Observations on the Phenomena of Glaciers*, 1843; as *A Tour of Mont Blanc and of Monte Rosa*, 1855.

Frenilly, August François Fauveau, Marquis de, *Souvenirs du Baron de Frenilly, pair de France (1768–1828)*, 1890–1901; as *Recollections of Baron de Frenilly, Peer of France (1768–1828)*, translated by Frederic Lees, with an introduction and notes by Arthur Chuquet, 1905.

Gesner, Conrad, "On the Admiration of Mountains, the Prefatory Letter Addressed to Jacob Avienus, Physician," in his pamphlet "*On Milk and Substances Prepared from Milk,*" *A Description of the Riven Mountain, Commonly Called Mount Pilatus . . . First Printed at Zurich in 1543*; translated by H.B.D. Soulé, edited by W. Dock, with bibliographical notes by W. Dock and J.M. Thorington, 1937.

Goethe, Johann Wolfgang von, *Reise-Tagebuch von Karlsbad nach Rom*, 1786; edited by Eberhard Haufe, 1971.

Grohmann, Paul, *Wanderungen in den Dolomiten* [Wanderings in the Dolomites], 1877.

Montaigne, Michel de, *Journal de Voyage de Michel de Montaigne en Italie: Par la Suisse & l'Allemagne en 1580 & 1581*, 2 vols., 1774; as *The Journal of Montaigne's Travels in Italy by Way of Switzerland and Germany in 1580 and 1581*, translated and edited by W.G. Waters, 3 vols., 1903; as *The Diary of Montaigne's Journey to Italy in 1580 and 1581*, translated by E.J. Trechmann, 1929; as *Montaigne's Travel Journal*, translated by Donald M. Frame, 1983.

Morrell, Jemima, *The Proceedings of the Junior United Alpine Club*, 1863; as *Miss Jemima's Swiss Journal: The First Conducted Tour of Switzerland*, 1963; reprinted, 1998.

Moryson, Fynes, *An Itinerary Written by Fynes Moryson, Gent, First in the Latin Tongue and Then Translated by Him into English: Containing His Ten Years Travel through the Twelve Dominions of Germany, Behmerland, Switzerland, Netherland, Denmarke, Poland, Italy, Turkey, France, England, Scotland and Ireland*, 1617; reprinted, 1907.

Pennell, Elizabeth Robins, *Over the Alps on a Bicycle*, illustrated by Joseph Pennell, 1898.
Philipon, Marie Jean (afterward Madame Roland de la Platière), *Voyage en Suisse* [Swiss Journey], 1787; edited by Gavin De Beer, 1937.
Ray, John, *Observations Topographical, Moral and Physiological, Made in a Journey through Part of the Low-Countries, Germany, Italy and France*, 1673; as *Travels through the Low-Countries, Germany, Italy and France: With Curious Observations Natural, Topographical, Moral, Physiological, &c.: Also, a Catalogue of Plants, Found Spontaneously Growing in Those Parts and Their Virtues, To Which Is Added an Account of the Travels of Francis Willoughby, Esq., through Great Part of Spain*, 2 vols., 1693; corrected edition, 1738.
Ruskin, John, "Of Mountain Beauty," in his *Modern Painters*, vol. 4, part 5, 1856.
Saussure, Horace-Bénedict de, *Voyages dans les Alpes*, 4 vols., 1779–1796.
Scheuchzer, Johann Jakob, and Isaac Newton, *Ouresiphoites Helveticus; sive Itinera Alpina tria: In quibus incolae, animalia, plantae, montium altitudines barometricae, coeli & soli temperies, aquae medicatae, mineralia, metalla, lapides figurati*, 1708; as *Beschreibung der Natur-Geschichten des Sweitzerlandes* [A Swiss Mountain Haunt; or, Three Alpine Journeys: In Which the Inhabitants, Living Creatures, Plants, Barometric Heights of the Mountains, Temperatures of the Sky and Sun, Medicinal Waters, Minerals, Metals, Decorative Stones and Other Fossils: And Anything Else in the Nature, the Arts and Antiquities of the Swiss and Rhaetian Alps Which Is Rare and Worthy of Note, Is Explained and Illustrated with Pictures], 3 vols., 1706–1708; as *Geschichte des Schweizerlandes, samt seinen Reisen über die Schweizerische Gebirge* [History of Switzerland Together with His Travels over the Swiss Mountains], 2 vols., revised and edited by Johann Georg Sulzer, 1746.
Stephen, Leslie, *The Playground of Europe*, 1871.
Sulzer, Johann Georg, *Unterredungen über die Schönheit der Natur* [Conversations on the Beauty of Nature], 1750; as *Unterredungen über die Schönheit der Natur: Moralische Betrachtungen über besondere Gegenstände der Naturlehre* [Conversations on the Beauty of Nature: Moral Observations on Particular Objects of Nature Study], 1770; reprinted, 1971.
Töpffer, Rodolphe, *Voyages en Zigzag; ou, Excursions d'un pensionnat en vacances dans les cantons Suisses et sur le revers Italien des Alpes* [Zigzag Travels; or, Boarding School Rambles in the Swiss Cantons and on the Italian Side of the Alps], 1844.
Tyndall, John, *The Glaciers of the Alps: Being a Narrative of Excursions and Ascents, an Account of the Origin and Phenomena of Glaciers and an Exposition of the Physical Principles to Which They Are Related*, 1860; reprinted, 1856.
Whymper, Edward, *Scrambles amongst the Alps in the Years 1860–1869*, 1871; reissued with additional material from the author's unpublished diaries and an introduction by Ronald W. Clark, revised and edited by H.E.G. Tyndale, 1936; unabridged, reorganized version of 1871 edition, 1996.
Williams, Helen Maria, "Rapturous Subliminity, the Solitariness of Nature. . .," in her *A Tour in Switzerland; or, a View of the Present State of the Governments and Manners of These Cantons . . . with Comparative Sketches of the Present State of Paris*, 2 vols., 1798.
Wills, Alfred, *Wanderings among the High Alps*, 1858.
Windham, William, *An Account of the Glaciers or Ice Alps in Savoy*, 1744.
Wordsworth, William, *Descriptive Sketches Taken during a Pedestrian Tour in the Italian Grisons, Swiss and Savoyard Alps*, 1793; edited by Eric Birdsall, 1984.

*See also* **Central Europe**

## AMAZON RIVER

The basin of the Amazon River stretches from the Atlantic to the eastern slopes of the Andes. It has more than 1,000 tributaries that drain a territory of more than 6 million square miles. The enormous outflow of water and sediment through its vast estuary noticeably discolors and dilutes the Atlantic Ocean as far as 150 miles offshore. The Spaniard Vicente Yáñez Pinzón noted this phenomenon when he was navigating up the Brazil coastline in 1499. As the first European to discover the river, he named it Santa Maria de la Mar Dulce, or "the Freshwater Sea."

It was not until after the conquest of Peru that Spanish adventurers turned their attention to the Amazon, driven by rumors that the fabulous riches of the empire of "El Dorado" and the "land of cinnamon" lay somewhere in the jungles of the eastern slopes of the Andes. Gonzalo Pizarro's expedition struggled down the Coca to the Napo in 1541. Short of supplies and recognizing that the rivers ran east, Pizarro ordered Francisco de Orellana to take a brigantine and forage ahead. Swept inexorably downstream by the force of the current, Orellana's party entered the Amazon and followed it to the sea. He returned to Spain with accounts of the riches of the Omagua tribes settled on the main river between the Putumayo and Japurá, and of women warriors encountered downstream of the Madeira. His attempt in 1545 to return with a small fleet to what had rapidly become known as the Rio del las Amazonas met with disaster in the delta. It would be 15 years before another Peruvian, Pedro de Ursúa, set off with a disorderly expedition down the tributary Huallaga toward the El Dorado of the Omaguas. Ursúa and the party's leaders were rapidly disposed of by their men. The mutinous rabble built two large boats and retraced Orellana's journey to the Atlantic, led by their psychopathic campmaster Lope de Aguirre. The Dominican friar Gaspar de Carvajal produced a fascinating eyewitness report of Orellana's epic descent of the Amazon, as did the soldier Francisco Vasquez, who managed to survive Lope de Aguirre's crazed wanderings. These accounts were extracted by contemporary Spanish chroniclers, but neither was actually published until some 350 years later.

Seventeenth-century accounts of travel on the Amazon stemmed from international skirmishes for control of the river, and from accompanying missionary activities. The Portuguese founded Belém in Pará in 1616 as a defense against Dutch, English, and Irish intruders who had already established settlements along the North Channel of the delta and the lower reaches of the Xingu. The Englishman William Davies reconnoitered the North Channel in 1608, recording his impressions of the native peoples and strange animals and fish he had encountered, as well as tales of the island of Morria, inhabited only by warrior women. By the early 1630s, Portuguese slave raids, missions, and military expeditions had pacified the tribes in the river mouth and driven other European colonists out. The movement to reestablish an independent Portuguese crown in the later 1630s made the authorities in Brazil anxious to make a claim to the inner reaches of the Amazon, to counter incursions from Spanish Peru. In 1637, when two Spanish Franciscans who had been working among the tribes of the Napo journeyed by canoe down to Belém, the viceroy of Brazil quickly countered by sending Pedro Teixeira upriver to Quito, with sealed orders to fix a boundary between Peru and Brazil in the upper reaches of the Amazon. The Jesuit Christoval de Acuña, who accompanied Teixeira on the return trip downriver, published a superb account of the journey in 1641. The record of a similar voyage by two Spanish Franciscans in 1651 was not published until 1879 (see Cruz). *The Journal of the Travels and Labours of Father Samuel Fritz*, a Jesuit operating out of Peru who ministered to a huge parish on the upper Amazon between 1685 and 1711, was not printed until 1922. Fritz was the first to draw a reasonably accurate map of the course of the main river to Pará.

Amazon travel literature produced in the Age of Reason was a by-product of scientific inquiry. In 1735, the Spanish Crown allowed a team of savants, backed by the French Académie des Sciences, to travel to Quito to make astronomical observations that would settle the length of a degree of longitude at the equator and definitively resolve the heated international debate as to the shape of the Earth. After seven arduous years in the Andes, the expedition broke up. Its geographer, Charles-Marie de la Condamine, determined to return to France from Cayenne and rafted down the Amazon to Belém. La Condamine's popularized account of his adventure among "new plants, new animals and new men," of his experiments with arrow poison, and his musings as to whether there remained any vestige of the "feminine republic" of the Amazons, provoked instant and continuing interest after its publication in 1745. Its value to armchair travelers was enhanced, after 1773, by the addition of an appendix written by Jean Godin des Odonais. A mathematician on the original expedition, Godin had followed La Condamine down to Cayenne in 1750. Nineteen years later, his long-suffering wife set out from Peru to join him, enduring the loss of all her companions and surviving horrific privations en route. Godin's record of his wife's sufferings excited enormous interest, the stories circulating in textual and oral form for more than half a century. The publication of the manuscript of "Diario da viagem filosófica" (see Ferreira), illustrated with exquisitely detailed watercolors of Amazonian Indians and fauna, produced by a Portuguese scholarly expedition that explored the Negro, Branco, Madeira, Guaporé, and Mamoré tributaries in 1783 to 1792, was interrupted by the Napoleonic wars. The text and illustrations became separated and were not recompiled for publication until the late 1800s.

In the nineteenth century, the Amazon became a magnet for natural scientists. The publication of the results of Alexander von Humboldt's extended travels across the watershed of the Orinoco into Amazonia, during which he verified the linkage between the two great waterways through the Negro and the Cassiquiare canal, met with great acclaim. Charles Waterton, the first naturalist to emulate Humboldt's feats (between 1812 and 1824), spent relatively little time on the Amazon. However, after 1840, when the upheavals associated with the struggle for Brazilian independence had subsided, numerous American and European naturalists explored upstream from Belém past the Negro, collecting thousands of specimens of insects, reptiles, fish, and plants. Strong public interest in their endeavors encouraged Henry Bates, Alfred Russel Wallace, W.L. Herndon, Louis Agassiz, and others to publish excellent narratives that combined scientific observation with hair-raising tales of brushes with piranhas, electric eels, anacondas and boa constrictors, poisonous snakes, and crocodiles.

The close of the first decade of the twentieth century also saw the end of the 60-year rubber boom, which had brought a second tide of fortune-seeking adventurers into the Amazon valley and at the same time raised international concerns about the treatment of its native inhabitants by the rubber companies. These two themes of adventure and conservation have dominated Amazon travel literature in the past century. The Amazon valley has continued to send out the siren call of the "unknown of the present" to adventurers and scientists, but the airstrips and roads that have made its inner reaches steadily more accessible are connected to development initiatives that threaten to destroy both its surviving native peoples and its delicate ecological balance. On the adventure side of the ledger, those who wish to read about the Amazon have been able to choose from classic tales of vagabondage, searches for lost Inca cities, arduous journeys along unmapped southern tributaries, and encounters with headhunters. Colonel Fawcett's disappearance while seeking Atlantis in the jungles of the Mato Grosso combined all these elements and spawned several accounts by those who set out to retrace his last journey into the wilderness (see books by Cowell, Dyott, and Fleming).

Since the later 1950s, however, journalists, anthropologists, and natural scientists have used the medium of the travel account to bring the consequences of development in Amazonia before a global audience. Eyewitness records of the efforts of the Villas Boas brothers to mediate contact with rainforest tribes within the Xingu National Park, of the work of Jacques Lizot among the Yanomami, and of the violent conflict between cattle ranchers and rubber tappers and between tribes and miners have jostled with those of searches for medicinal plants and pink dolphins. A mixture of travelogue, scientific observation, and political polemic on environmental stewardship and human justice, the more recent works have a wide appeal to a more traveled and globally conscious readership, but leave disturbing questions about the right of the inhabitants of Amazonia to map out their own future, free from the interventions of well-meaning or exploitative outsiders.

JOYCE LORIMER

## References and Further Reading


Acuña, Christoval de, *Nuevo Descubrimiento del Gran Rio de las Amazonas*, 1641.

Adalbert, Prince of Prussia, *Travels of His Royal Highness Prince Adalbert of Prussia, in the South of Europe and in Brazil, with a Voyage up the Amazon and Its Tributary the Xingú, Now First Explored*, 2 vols., translated by R.H. Schomburgk and J.E. Taylor, 1849.

Agassiz, Louis, and Elizabeth Agassiz, *A Journey in Brazil*, 1868.

Allen, Benedict, *Mad White Giant: A Journey to the Heart of the Amazon Jungle*, 1985.

Allen, Benedict, *Through Jaguar Eyes: Crossing the Amazon Basin*, 1994.

Almagro, Manuel de, *Breve descripción de los viajes hechos en América por la Comisión Científica enviada por el Gobierno de SMC durante los años de 1862 a 1866*, 1866.

Almeida, F.L.J., *Diáro da viagem pelas Capitanios do Pará, Río Negra, Mato-Grosso, Cuyabá e S. Paulo, nos annos de 1780 a 1790*, 1841.

Bates, Henry Walter, *The Naturalist on the River Amazons*, 2 vols., 1863.

Bidou, Henry, *900 Lieues sur l'Amazone*, 1938.

Biocca, Ettore, *Yanoáma*, translated by Dennis Rhodes, 1970.

Branston, Brian, *The Last Great Journey on Earth*, 1970.

Browne, C. Barrington, and William Lidstone, *Fifteen Thousand Miles on the Amazon and Its Tributaries*, 1878.

Carvajal, Gaspar de, *Descubrimiento del río de las Amazonas*, edited by José Toribio Medina, 1894; as *The Discovery of the Amazon*, translated by Bertram T. Lee, 1934.

Castelnau, Francis de, et al., *Expédition dans les parties centrales de l'Amérique du Sud*, 7 parts, 1850–1859.

Cherrie, George K., *Dark Trails: Adventures of a Naturalist*, 1930.

Clough, R. Stewart, *"The Amazons": Diary of a Twelvemonth's Journey . . . on a Mission of Inquiry up the River Amazon, for the South American Missionary Society*, 1873.

Coudreau, Henri Anatole, *Voyage au Rio Branco, aux Montagnes de la Lune, au Haut Trombetta*, 1886.

Coudreau, Henri Anatole, *La France équinoxiale*, 2 vols., 1886–1887.

Coudreau, Henri Anatole, *Voyage au Tapajoz*, 1897.

Coudreau, Henri Anatole, *Voyage au Tocantins-Araguaya*, 1897.

Cousteau, Jacques-Yves, and Mose Richards, *Jacques Cousteau's Amazon Journey*, 1984.

Cowell, Adrian, *The Heart of the Forest*, 1960.

Cowell, Adrian, *The Tribe That Hides from Man*, 1973.

Craig, Neville B., *Recollections of an Ill-Fated Expedition to the Head-waters of the Madeira River in Brazil*, 1907.

Cruz, Laureano de la, *Nuevo descubrimiento del Río de Marañón llamado de las Amazonas*, written 1653; in *Saggio da bibliografia geografica, storica, etnografica Sanfrancescana*, by Marcellino da Civezza, 1879: 269–300.

Davies, William, *A True Relation of the Travailes and Most Miserable Captivitie of William Davies, Barber-Surgion of London, under the Duke of Florence*, 1614.

Domville-Fife, Charles William, *Among Wild Tribes of the Amazons: An Account of Exploration and Adventure on the Mighty Amazon and Its Confluents, with Descriptions of the Savage Head-Hunting and Anthropophagous Tribes Inhabiting Their Banks*, 1924.

Duguid, Julian, *Green Hell: Adventures in the Mysterious Jungles of Eastern Bolivia*, 1931.

Duguid, Julian, *Tiger Man: An Odyssey of Freedom*, 1932.

Dwyer, Augusta, *Into the Amazon: Chico Mendes and the Struggle for the Rain Forest*, 1990.

Dyott, G.M., *On the Trail of the Unknown: In the Wilds of Ecuador and the Amazon*, 1926.

Dyott, G.M., *Man-Hunting in the Jungle*, 1930.

Edwards, William Henry, *A Voyage up the River Amazon, Including a Residence at Pará*, 1847.

Fawcett, Percy Harrison, *Exploration Fawcett: Arranged from His Manuscripts, Letters, Log-books, and Records, by Brian Fawcett*, 1953.

Ferreira, Alexandre Rodrigues, "Diario de viagem filosófica pelas capitanias do Grão Pará, Rio Negro, Mato Grosso e Cuiabá," in *Revista Trimensal do Instituto Histórico Geográphico e Ethnográphico do Brasil* 48 (1885): 1–234; 51 (1888): 5–166.

Fleming, Peter, *Brazilian Adventure*, 1933.

Flornoy, Bertrand, *Haut-Amazone*, 1939; as *Jivaro: Among the Headshrinkers of the Amazon*, translated by Jean Pace, 1953.

Flornoy, Bertrand, *Découverte des sources: Des Andes à la forêt Amazonienne*, 1946.

Forest, Jesse de, "Journal du voyage faict par les pères des familles envoyés par Messieurs les Directeurs de la Compagnée des Indes occidentales pour visiter la coste de Gujane," translated in *A Walloon Family in America: Lockwood de Forest and his Forbears, 1500–1848: Together with A Voyage to Guiana, Being the Journal of Jesse de Forest and His Colonists, 1623–1625*, edited by Emily Johnston de Forest, 2 vols., 1914: vol. 2, pp. 191–235.

Foster, Harry L., *A Tropical Tramp with the Tourists*, 1925.

Fritz, Samuel, *The Journal of the Travels and Labours of Father Samuel Fritz in the River of the Amazons between 1686 and 1723*, translated and edited by George Edmundson, 1922.

Fritz, W., Up de Graff, *Headhunters of the Amazon: Seven Years of Exploration and Adventure*, 1923.

Gardner, George, *Travels in the Interior of Brazil . . . during the Years 1836–1841*, 1846; reprinted, 1973.

Gates, Reginald Ruggles, *A Botanist in the Amazon Valley*, 1927.

Gheerbrandt, Alain, *Journey to the Far Amazon: An Expedition into Unknown Territory*, translated by Edward Fitzgerald, 1954.
Grieve, Peter, *The Wilderness Voyage*, 1952.
Hanbury-Tenison, Marika, *For Better, for Worse*, 1972.
Hanbury-Tenison, Robin, *A Question of Survival for the Indians of Brazil*, 1973.
Hanson, Earl Parker, *Journey to Manaos*, 1938.
Harrison, John, *Up the Creek: An Amazon Adventure*, 1986.
Herndon, William Lewis, and Lardner Gibbon, *Exploration of the Valley of the Amazon, Made under the Direction of the Navy Department*, 2 vols., 1853–1854.
Hessel, Lizzie, *Lizzie: A Victorian Lady's Adventure*, edited by Tony Morrison, Ann Brown, and Anne Rose, 1985.
Holman, Alan, *White River, Brown Water: A Record-Making Kayak Journey down the Amazon*, 1985.
Humboldt, Alexander von, *Personal Narrative of Travels to the Equinoctial Regions of the New Continent, during the Years 1799–1804*, translated by Helen Maria Williams, 7 vols., 1814–1829.
Jiménez de la Espada, Marcos, *Diario de la expedición al Pacífico, llevada a cabo por una comisión de naturalistas españoles durante los años 1862–1865*, edited by Agustín Jesús Barreiro, 1928.
Kane, Joe, *Running the Amazon*, 1989.
La Condamine, Charles-Marie de, *Relation Abrégée d'un voyage fait dans l'intérieur de l'Amérique Méridionale, depuis la côte de la mer du sud, jusqu'aux côtes du Brésil et de la Guyane en descendant la rivière des Amazones*, 1745; as *A Succinct Abridgment of a Voyage Made within the Inland Parts of South-America*, 1747.
Lange, Algot, *In the Amazon Jungle: Adventures in Remote Parts of the Upper Amazon River, Including a Sojourn among Cannibal Indians*, edited in part by J. Odell Hauser, with an introduction by Frederick S. Dellenbaugh, 1912.
Lange, Algot, *The Lower Amazon: A Narrative of Exploration in the Little Known Regions of the State of Pará*, 1914.
Lutz, Dick, *Hidden Amazon*, 1999.
MacCreagh, Gordon, *White Waters and Black*, 1926.
McGovern, William Montgomery, *Jungle Paths and Inca Ruins*, 1927.
Marcoy, Paul, *Voyage à travers l'Amérique du sud*, 2 vols., 1869; as *A Journey across South America*, translated by Elihu Rich, 1873.
Maw, Henry Lister, *Journal of a Passage from the Pacific to the Atlantic, Crossing the Andes in the Northern Provinces of Peru and Descending the River Marañon, or Amazon*, 1829.
Maxwell, Nicole, *Witch-Doctor's Apprentice*, 1961.
Meunier, Jacques, and A.M. Savarin, *Le Chant du Silbaco: Chronique amazonienne*, 1991; as *The Amazonian Chronicles*, translated by Carol Christensen, 1994.
Miller, Leo E., *In the Wilds of South America: Six Years of Exploration in Colombia, Venezuela, British Guiana, Peru, Bolivia, Argentina, Paraguay, and Brazil*, 1919.
Montgomery, Sy, *Journey of the Pink Dolphins: An Amazon Quest*, 2000.
Nugent, Stephen, *Big Mouth: The Amazon Speaks*, 1990.
O'Hanlon, Redmond, *In Trouble Again: A Journey between the Orinoco and the Amazon*, 1988.
Orbigny, Alcide Dessalines d', *Voyage dans l'Amérique méridionale*, 9 vols., 1835–1847.
Orton, James, *The Andes and the Amazon; or, Across the Continent of South America*, 1870.
Ridgway, John, *Amazon Journey: From the Source to the Sea*, 1972.
Roosevelt, Theodore, *Through the Brazilian Wilderness*, 1914.
Savoy, Gene, *Antisuyo: The Search for the Lost Cities of the Amazon*, 1970.
Schulz-Kampfhenkel, Otto, *Riddle of Hell's Jungle: Expedition to Unexplored Primeval Forests of the River Amazon . . . with Extracts from the Diaries of His Friend Gerd Kahle*, translated by Violet M. MacDonald, 1940.
Shoumatoff, Alex, *The Rivers Amazon*, 1978; revised edition, 1986.
Smith, Anthony, *Mato Grosso: Last Virgin Land*, 1971.
Smyth, William, and Frederick Lowe, *Narrative of a Journey from Lima to Para, across the Andes and down the Amazon*, 1836.
Snow, Sebastian, *My Amazon Adventure*, 1953.
Spix, Johann Baptist von, and Carl Friedrich Philipp von Martius, *Travels in Brazil in the Years 1817–1820, Undertaken by Command of His Majesty the King of Bavaria*, translated by H.E. Lloyd, 2 vols., 1824.
Spruce, Richard, *Notes of a Botanist on the Amazon and the Andes*, edited by Alfred Russel Wallace, 1908.
Starkell, Don, *Paddle to the Amazon*, edited by Charles Wilkins, 1987.
Sting and Jean-Pierre Dutilleux, *Jungle Stories: The Fight for the Amazon*, 1989.
Tomlinson, H.M., *The Sea and the Jungle*, 1912; reprinted, 1989.
Vázquez, Francisco, "Relación verdadera de todo lo que sucedió en la jornada de Omagua y Dorado," in *Historiadores de Indias*, vol. 2, edited by Manuel Serrano y Sanz, 1909 (Nueva Biblioteca de Autores Españoles, vol. 15).
Von Hagen, Victor Wolfgang, *Off with Their Heads*, 1937.
Wallace, Alfred Russel, *A Narrative of Travels on the Amazon and Rio Negro*, 1853.
Waterton, Charles, *Wanderings in South America, the North-West of the United States, and the Antilles*, 1825.
Wickham, Henry Alexander, *Rough Notes of a Journey through the Wilderness, from Trinidad to Pará, Brazil, by Way of the Great Cataracts of the Orinoco, Atabapo, and Rio Negro*, 1872.
Zahm, J.A. (as H.J. Mozans), *Along the Andes and down the Amazon*, with an introduction by Theodore Roosevelt, 1911.
Zahm, J.A., *Through South America's Southland*, 1916.
Zahm, J.A., *The Quest of El Dorado: The Most Romantic Episode in the History of South American Conquest*, 1917.

*See also* **Brazil**

## AMUNDSEN, ROALD (1872–1928)

### *Norwegian Polar Explorer*

Roald Amundsen may legitimately be considered the greatest polar explorer of all time. Even as a young boy in Norway he had decided that he wanted to be a polar explorer. His chance came in 1897 when his application to sign on as second mate of *Belgica*, the expedition vessel of Lieutenant Adrien de Gerlache de Gomery's Belgian Antarctic expedition, was successful. The expedition made significant contributions to the exploration and mapping of the Antarctic peninsula and its off-lying islands. But then, in an almost suicidal move, since the expedition was not provisioned or equipped for a wintering, de Gerlache deliberately allowed his ship to be beset in the Bellingshausen Sea for a winter adrift in the pack ice. Scurvy broke out and ultimately killed one expedition member. Amundsen survived better than most and took careful notes on equipment, provisions, and his companions, with a view to planning his own future expeditions. *Belgica* survived this wintering, the first in the Antarctic, and escaped from her imprisonment in the pack in mid-March 1899.

On his return to Norway, after gaining some more sea time toward his master's certificate, Amundsen began preparing for his own polar expedition. He had set his sights on the Northwest Passage, planning to conduct studies of magnetism to give his project scientific respectability. He bought a small 47-ton fishing vessel, *Gjøa*, and sailed for the Northwest Passage on 16 June 1903 with a total complement of six men. Having traversed approximately half of the passage, Amundsen found an excellent wintering harbor at Gjøa Haven on King William Island; here *Gjøa* remained for two winters while Amundsen and his men carried out magnetic observations and made extensive sledge trips. A group of Netsilik Inuit settled near the ship during both winters, and Amundsen and his men learned a great deal from them about native clothing, hunting, sledge travel, igloo building, and so on. *Gjøa* got under way again in August 1905, westward bound, but having passed the Mackenzie Delta she was blocked by ice and forced to winter again. She finally emerged from the Bering Strait in early September 1906 and reached San Francisco on 19 October, the first vessel to make the transit of the Northwest Passage.

The polar explorer as national hero (jacket by Rees for Charles Turley's *Roald Amundsen: Explorer*, 1935). *Courtesy of the Stapleton Collection, London.*

Amundsen next set his sights on the North Pole. His plan involved a modified version of Nansen's trans-Arctic drift in *Fram*, but by starting farther east than Nansen he hoped that the drift would take his vessel right over the Pole. Nansen agreed to let him have *Fram* for this attempt. Forestalled when the news broke in the autumn of 1909 that first Dr. Frederick Cook and then Robert Peary had reached the North Pole, Amundsen publicly continued his preparations for his trans-Arctic drift, but privately he switched his aim to the South Pole, to which a British expedition under Captain Robert Scott was also bound. *Fram* sailed from Norway on 9 August 1910.

Amundsen established his base camp, Framheim, at the Bay of Whales in the southeast corner of the Ross Sea; Scott established his base at Cape Evans in McMurdo Sound in the southwest corner of the Ross Sea. Polar parties set out from both camps in the southern spring of 1911. Amundsen's party used skis and dog sledges; Scott's party initially used pony sledges, but later resorted to the brutal expedient of man hauling. Amundsen and his party reached the South Pole on 14 December 1911 then started back north along a trail of well-stocked and conspicuously marked depots, reaching Framheim in excellent health on 26 January 1912. By contrast, although Scott and his party reached the Pole, they all died, stormbound in their tent on the return journey.

Amundsen next set his sights northward again. This time he wanted to combine a transit of the Northeast Passage with a trans-Arctic drift, but with scientific observations rather than reaching the Pole as the main objective. He had a specially designed ship, *Maud*, built for the purpose. The expedition sailed from Oslo on 25 June 1918 and passed Cape Chelyuskin, the northernmost point of Eurasia, on 8 September, but was blocked by ice and forced to winter a short distance farther east. Getting under way again on 12 September 1919, *Maud* reached Chaun Inlet but here was again blocked by ice and was forced to winter a second time. Released from the ice in the summer of 1920, she ran south through the Bering Strait. At this point, Amundsen left the expedition; Dr. Harald Sverdrup now took command, and over the next five years completed a modified version of the planned ice drift.

All of Amundsen's further polar endeavors were in the air. Sharing the leadership of the expedition with Lincoln Ellsworth, Amundsen next attempted to fly to the North Pole from Kongsfjorden in Svalbard in two Dornier-Wal seaplanes, the *N24* and *N25*, taking off on 21 May 1925. They landed on a polynia at 87°43′ N (136 nautical miles from the Pole), but the *N24* was damaged by ice. Fuel and supplies were transferred from the crippled aircraft to the *N25*; when a runway had been laboriously leveled on the ice, the *N25* managed to take off and flew back south to Svalbard. But this near-success (or near-disaster) only whetted the appetites of Ellsworth and Amundsen. The next attempt was by airship. Amundsen bought a dirigible from Italy and rechristened it *Norge*. With Umberto Nobile at the controls, *Norge* took off from Kongsfjorden on 11 May 1926 and flew over the Pole at 1:25 AM on 12 May. Amundsen had now reached both poles. The dirigible landed at Teller, Alaska, in the early hours of 14 May, having completed the first crossing of the Arctic Ocean.

Two years later, when Nobile's dirigible *Italia* crashed on the sea ice north of Svalbard, a multinational search for the survivors began. Amundsen was invited by the French government to take charge of the French effort, in a large Latham seaplane piloted by Captain René Guilbaud. On 18 June 1928, with Amundsen on board, the Latham took off from Tromsø bound for Svalbard—and disappeared. On 31 August, a Norwegian fishing boat recovered one of the plane's floats from the water not far from Tromsø. No bodies were ever recovered.

Amundsen wrote (or coauthored) accounts of five of his expeditions and an autobiography. We are particularly indebted to Amundsen's biographer, Roland Huntford, fluent in Norwegian, who has read all of Amundsen's books (and a great deal of his correspondence and diaries) in the original Norwegian. Writing of Amundsen's *The Northwest Passage*, Huntford (1979) notes that it is a straightforward, almost bald account, with little embroidery, simple and direct, but with flashes of humor. The same remarks would apply to Amundsen's *The South Pole*; here the contrast with Robert Scott's elegant narrative of his fatal attempt at the South Pole (Scott, 1914) is particularly striking. But whatever his shortcomings as a writer (if indeed these are considered shortcomings), as a polar explorer Amundsen had no equal.

WILLIAM BARR

## Biography

Born Roald Engebreth Gravning Amudsen in Borge, near Christiania (Oslo), Norway, 16 July 1872, youngest of four sons of a ship's captain and shipowner. Moved with his family to Oslo, late 1872. Skied extensively as a youth; made two extended ski trips across the Hardangervidda wilderness between Oslo and Bergen, 1893 and 1896. Studied medicine briefly at Oslo University, c. 1892–1894. Made first sea expedition with the sealing vessel *Magdalena*, 1894. Obtained his mate's certificate, 1895. Leader or coleader of six of seven expeditions between 1894 and 1901; experienced seven polar winters. Served as first mate on board *Belgica*, expedition ship of the Belgian Antarctic Expedition (1897–1899), the first expedition to winter in the Antarctic. Received his skipper's licence, 1900. Made the first transit of the Northwest Passage in *Gjøa*, 1903–1906. Led the first expedition to reach the South Pole, arriving on 14 December 1911. Took *Maud* through the Northeast Passage, wintering twice en route, 1918–1920, completing his circumnavigation of the Arctic Ocean. Flew with Lincoln Ellsworth to within 136 nautical miles of the North Pole in two Dornier seaplanes, 1925. Made first trans-Arctic flight with Ellsworth and Umberto Nobile in the dirigible *Norge*, from Svalbard via the North Pole to Teller, Alaska, 1926. Disappeared in the Arctic while flying from Tromsø to rescue Nobile and the survivors of the crash of the dirigible *Italia*, June 1928.

## References and Further Reading


Amundsen, Roald, *Nordvest-passagen*, 2 vols., 1907; as *The North-West Passage: Being the Record of a Voyage of Exploration of the Ship "Gjøa" 1903–1907*, 1908.

Amundsen, Roald, *Sydpolen*, 2 vols., 1912; as *The South Pole: An Account of the Norwegian Antarctic Expedition in the "Fram," 1910–1912*, translated by A.G. Chater, 1912.

Amundsen, Roald, *Nordostpassagen: Maudfaerden langs Asiens Kyst 1918–1920*, 1921.

Amundsen, Roald, *Gjennem luften till 88° Nord*, with Lincoln Ellsworth and other members of the expedition, 1925; as *Our Polar Flight: The Amundsen-Ellsworth Polar Flight*, 1925; as *My Polar Flight*, 1925.

Amundsen, Roald, *Den Første flukt over Polhavet*, with Lincoln Ellsworth and others, 1926; as *The First Flight across the Polar Sea*, 1927; also as *First Crossing of the Polar Sea*, 1927.

Amundsen, Roald, *Mitt liv som polarforsker*, 1927; as *My Life as an Explorer*, 1927.


# ANDES

This South American mountain range, one of the longest in the world, presents a continuous landscape of towering heights, with few and very difficult passes (Quindio in Colombia and Uspallata in Argentina are among the best known). In Patagonia, the mountains are smaller, and the sea makes its way between them, forming fjords. Lakes with glaciers are also common. Archaeological investigations have uncovered the design of a huge road network constructed and used by the Incas, the *camino del Inca*, which kept the whole empire united. It runs from north of the equator to the center of Argentina and Chile.

Accounts of the Andes have existed since America was first explored by Europeans. The *cronistas de In-*

*dias* were the first to describe the landscape of the mountains. Alonso de Ovalle (1601–1651) and Reginaldo de Lizárraga (c. 1545–1615), as well as Concolorcorvo (b. c. 1706), wrote travel reports of the Andean views.

During the Enlightenment, the precise determination of geographic features was the aim of famous travelers, among them Charles-Marie de La Condamine (1701–1774), who published the report about his scientific investigations in 1745 and 1751, and Alexander von Humboldt, who wrote an outstanding work about his trip with Aimé Bonpland from 1799 to 1804, *Voyage aux régions équinoxiales du Nouveau Continent*, which included vast territories in the Andes of Colombia, Ecuador, and Peru. In the same scientific perspective are the expeditions of Malaspina from 1789 to 1794, with Tadeo Haenke, and of Fitzroy from 1826 to 1836, with Charles Darwin. These travelers describe the Andes in detail, and often famous artists such as Pallière and Brambila contribute illustrations to the reports. Scientific journeys continued throughout the nineteenth century, representative examples being those of Alcide D. d'Orbigny from 1826 to 1833, Johann Jakob von Tschudi from 1838 to 1842, Hermann Burmeister from 1857 to 1860, and Charles Wiener in 1877.

During the nineteenth century, interest in the economic potential of the Andes attracted many travelers, especially English ones, in search of investments for their countrymen. Good examples are Samuel Haigh, John Miers, Peter Schmidtmeyer, Robert Proctor, Alexander Caldcleugh, Francis Bond Head, Joseph Andrews, Edmond Temple, Campbell Scarlett, and Ignacio Rickard. The plan for Andean railways—real engineering wonders as a result of building difficulties and the altitude (2,000 to 4,000 meters or more)—was the theme of some reports of the second half of the century. The English engineer Robert Crawford started a survey for the building of a trans-Andean railway in 1871. The Argentine diplomat Santiago Estrada commented on the monumental railway from Lima to La Oroya in the Peruvian Andes in 1872. The German scientist Max von Thielmann remarked on the pros and cons of a railway between Chile and Argentina during his trip of 1879. The Chilean politician Benjamín Vicuña Mackenna made an exploratory trip—an account of which was published in 1885—to study the area and to help determine the best route for the building of a railway from Buenos Aires to Valparaiso, which eventually materialized as the BAP (Buenos Aires al Pacífico).

More recently, other interests have replaced economic potential: sightseeing, archaeological treasures, and the exoticism of remote places. In the south, the attraction of the Andes is identified with the appeal of Patagonia as a distant world. A good example is Bruce Chatwin's book (1977).

A mule falls from the icy trail through the Uspallata Pass (frontispiece to Alexander Caldcleugh's *Travels in South America*, 1825). *Courtesy of the Travellers Club, London; Bridgeman Art Library, agent.*

The situation of the Andes between Argentina and Chile has produced interesting texts by travelers of both nations. Wars of independence impelled the movement across the Andes of armies, producing military reports such as General Espejo's *El paso de los Andes* (1876) and General Miller's memoirs (1828). Civil wars on both sides of the border produced exile texts. Some examples are the memoirs of Sarmiento (1961) and Aráoz de la Madrid (1947) in the time of Juan Manuel de Rosas's government, and Pablo Neruda's anecdotes of his life as a runaway, also in the twentieth century.

The means of transport used by travelers across the dangerous mountains is a way of distinguishing between different reports. Historically, travelers would rent a train of mules with one or more *arrieros* to guide them or even to carry the traveler on their back; others, such as Lieutenant Charles Brand in the winter of 1827, would cross the mountains on foot. The French adventurer Auguste Guinnard was forced to cross the Andes on foot in 1861 when he managed to escape from the Indians in Patagonia who had kept him captive for three years. The Argentine Eduardo Bradley wrote about his pioneering crossing by balloon in 1916. The first attempt to cross the Andes by plane ended Benjamín Matienzo's life in 1919. It was the beginning of a tradition of air crossing that included the flights of Antoine de St.-Exupéry and his fellows, and the establishment of the air mail in southern South America, as well as the recent unfortunate expedition and tragic accident of the Uruguayan plane with a party of sportsmen and their families. The grim story of the survival of the group is told in the book *Alive* (Read, 1974), which was later made into a movie.

Travel texts abound with details of the vicissitudes of traversing the Andes. Often mentioned are the dangers of lonely and winding roads and the need to trust incomprehensible local guides, as well as the obligation to carry as much food as was needed for the long journey through uninhabited passes. More menacing was the threat of snowstorms, which could make the roads impassable. Typical refuges known as *casuchas* were to be found in six different places between Mendoza and Santa Rosa de los Andes. They date back to Spanish rule during the eighteenth century, when the viceroy of Peru ordered the building of these small constructions with vaulted roofs to protect postmen and other travelers during stormy weather. They are usually mentioned in travelers' narratives.

Frontier disputes occurred often between Argentina and Chile, which is unsurprising given the difficulties of determining with fairness the exact place where their borders should run. There are various experts' reports on the subject, such as that of Francisco Perito Moreno (1876), a connoisseur of the Patagonian Andes. In this context, many travelers' texts, inspired by the greatness of nature to be experienced while crossing the Andes, plead soberly for peace.

ELENA DUPLANCIC DE ELGUETA

## References and Further Reading


Andrews, Joseph, *Journey from Buenos Ayres through the Provinces of Cordova, Tucuman, and Salta to Potosí: Thence by the Deserts of Caranja to Arica, and Subsequently to Santiago de Chile and Coquimbo*, 12 vols., 1827; reprinted, 1971.

Aráoz de la Madrid, *Memorias*, vol. 4, 1947.

Bradley, Eduardo, *La travesía de los Andes en globo*, 1917.

Brand, Charles, *Journal of a Voyage to Peru: A Passage across the Cordillera of the Andes, in the Winter of 1827, Performed on Foot in the Snow, and a Journey across the Pampas*, 1828.

Burmeister, Hermann, *Reise durch die La Plata-Staaten, mit besonderer Rücksicht auf die physische Beschaffenheit und den kulturzustand der Argentinischen Republik: Ausgeführt in den Jahren 1857, 1858–1859 und 1860*, 2 vols., 1861.

Caldcleugh, Alexander, *Travels in South America, during the Years 1819–20–21: Containing an Account of the Present State of Brazil, Buenos Ayres, and Chile*, 1825.

Chatwin, Bruce, *In Patagonia*, 1977.

Concolorcorvo (Calixto Bustamante Carlos Inca), *El Lazarillo de ciegos caminantes desde Buenos Aires hasta Lima*, 1773; facsimile, 1997; as *El Lazarillo: A Guide for Inexperienced Travelers between Buenos Aires and Lima*, translated by Walter D. Kline, 1965.

Crawford, Robert, *Across the Pampas and the Andes*, 1884.

Darwin, Charles, *Journal of Researches into the Geology and Natural History of Various Countries Visited by HMS* Beagle, *under the Command of Captain Fitzroy, R.N., from 1832 to 1836* (vol. 3 of *Narrative of the Surveying Voyages of His Majesty's Ships Adventure and Beagle*, edited by Robert Fitzroy), 1839; revised edition, 1845; as *The Voyage of the Beagle*, 1909.

Espejo, Gerónimo, *El paso de los Andes: Crónica histórica de las operaciones del ejército de los Andes para la restauración de Chile en 1817, por el General Gerónimo Espejo (Antiguo Ayudante del Estado Mayor del mismo Ejército)*, 1876; reprinted, 1953.

Estrada, Santiago, *Viajes*, 2 vols., 1889; as *Viajes y otras paginas literarias*, 1938.

Guinnard, Auguste, *Trois Ans d'esclavage chez les Patagons*, 2nd edition, 1864; edited by Jean-Paul Duvoils, 1979; as *Three Years' Slavery among the Patagonians: An Account of His Captivity*, translated by Charles S. Cheltnam, 1871.

Haigh, Samuel, *Sketches of Buenos Ayres and Chile*, 1829.

Head, Francis Bond, *Rough Notes Taken during Some Rapid Journeys across the Pampas and among the Andes*, 1826.

Hibbert, Captain Edward, *Narrative of a Journey from Santiago de Chile to Buenos Aires in July and August, 1821*, 1824.

Humboldt, Alexander von, and Aimé Bonpland, *Voyage aux régions équinoxiales du Nouveau Continent, fait en 1799, 1800, 1801, 1802, 1803 et 1804 par Al. de Humboldt et A. Bonpland: Rédigé par Alexandre de Humboldt*, part 1: *Relation historique*, 3 vols., 1814–1825; as *Personal Narrative of Travels to the Equinoctial Regions of the New Continent, during the Years 1799–1804*, translated by Helen Maria Williams, 7 vols., 1814–1829.

La Condamine, Charles-Marie de, *Journal du voyage fait par ordre du roi, à l'equateur, servant d'introduction historique à la Mesure des trois premiers degrés du méridien*, 1751.

Lizárraga, Reginaldo de, *Descripción y población de las Indias*, 1609; as *Descripción breve de toda la tierra del Perú, Tucumán, Río de la Plata y Chile*, 1908; reprinted, 1999.

Miers, John, *Travels in Chile and La Plata, Including Accounts Respecting the Geography, Geology, Statistics, Government, Finances, Agriculture, Manners and Customs, and the Mining Operations in Chile, Collected during a Residence of Several Years in These Countries*, 1826.

Miller, John, *Memoirs of General Miller*, 1828.

Moreno, Francisco P., *Viaje a la Patagonia austral*, 1876–1877, 18 2nd edition, 1879; reprinted, 1997.

Orbigny, Alcide Dessalines d', *Voyage dans l'Amérique Méridionale . . . exécuté pendant les années 1826–1833*, 9 vols., 1835–1847.

Ovalle, Alonso de, *Histórica relación del reino de Chile y de las Misiones y ministerios que ejercita en él la Compañía de Jesús*, 1646; reprinted, 1969; as *An Historical Relation of the Kingdom of Chile*, 1649.

Proctor, Robert, *Narrative of a Journey across the Cordillera of the Andes and of a Residence in Lima and Other Parts of Peru, in the Years 1823 and 1824*, 1825.

Read, Piers Paul, *Alive: The Story of the Andes Survivors*, 1974.

Rickard, Francis Ignacio, *The Mineral and Other Resources in the Argentine Republic (La Plata) in 1869: Report upon the Mining Districts, Mines and Establishments in the Argentine Republic in 1868–69*, 1870.

Sarmiento, Domingo Faustino, "Las Cordilleras," in his *Memorias*, vol. 5, 1961.

Scarlett, Peter Campbell, *South America and the Pacific; Comprising a Journey across the Pampas and the Andes, from Buenos Ayres to Valparaiso, Lima, and Panama: With Remarks upon the Isthmus*, 1838.

Schmidtmeyer, Peter, *Travels into Chile over the Andes, in the Years 1820 and 1821*, 1824.

Temple, Edmond, *Travels in Various Parts of Peru, Including a Year's Residence in Potosi*, 1830.

Thielmann, Max von, *Vier Wege durch Amerika* [Four Routes through America], 1879.

Tschudi, Johann Jakob von, *Reisen durch die Andes von Süd Amerika, von Cordova nach Cobija im Jahre 1858*, 1860.

Tschudi, Johann Jakob von, *Reisen durch Südamerika* [Travels through South America], 5 vols., 1866–1869; reprinted, 1971.

Vicuña Mackenna, Benjamín, *A través de los Andes: Estudio sobre la mejor ubicación del futuro ferrocarril interoceánico entre el Atlántico y el Pacífico en la América del Sur*, 1885.

*See also* **Chile; Peru**

## ANJOU, PETER (1796–1869) *Russian Navy Officer and Explorer*

Peter Anjou (in Russian, Petr Fedorovich Anzhu) was born into a Lutheran family who in the eighteenth century had moved from France to Russia. His father, Fedor Anjou, was a civil servant in the Russian empire and wanted his son to become a naval officer. In the Naval Corps of Cadets in St. Petersburg, Anjou became friends with the Baltic German Ferdinand von Wrangell (in Russian, Ferdinand Petrovich Vrangel) (1797–1870), whose close contacts with the leading naval officers of Russia helped Anjou to become the leader of the Ust'ianskoi group of the Russian northeast Siberian expedition (1820–1824). Wrangell was appointed the leader of the Kolymskoi group.

The most important geographical discoveries made by Russian Cossacks and travelers in the seventeenth and eighteenth centuries concerned the numerous islands located in the coastal waters off Siberia. In spite of the very important discoveries made, the picture of the Siberian coastline still remained incomplete, and the northern extent of the Alaska peninsula remained unknown. The Russian Cossacks Stepan Andreev and Iakov Sannikov were convinced that they had seen extensive landmasses, the first one north of the Medvezh'i Ostrova (Bear Islands), and the second north of Kotel'nyi and Novaia Sibir' islands, respectively. Ornithological signs had led the British seafarer James Cook to suppose that there existed a vast land in the Arctic Ocean. His crew member James Burney believed that a peninsula between Mys Shelagskii and Cape North connected the American and Asian continents. The task of the two expedition groups was to find and map these lands, together with the known Siberian islands and the coastline from the mouth of the Olenek, if possible, up to the Bering Strait. The group guided by Anjou, which consisted of the steersmen Il'ia Avtonomovich Berezhnykh, Petr Ivanovich Il'in, the medical doctor Aleksei Ivanovich Figurin, the sailor Ignatev, and the fitter Voronkov, had to map the coastline of the Arctic Ocean from the Olenek up to the Indigirka and the New Siberian Islands located in the Arctic Ocean.

The expeditions of Anjou were carried out mainly with the help of dog teams and reindeer, but also with horses and boats. In the spring and summer of 1821, the islands Stolbovoi, Kotel'nyi, Faddeev, and the Novaia Sibir', and the coast from the mouth of the Iana up to the mouth of the Indigirka were mapped and described. As a result of the expedition, the existence of lands that Sannikov, a traveling companion of Mathias von Hedenström (in Russian, Matvei Gedenshtröm), claimed to have seen north of the above-mentioned islands in 1810 was not confirmed. Instead, the existence of a thin ice-cover northeast of the island Novaia Sibir' was established, implying the presence of the open sea in the vicinity.

During the 1822 expedition, Anjou had to finish the mapping of the New Siberian Islands and to draw on the map the Malyi and Bolshoi Liakhovskii islands and the coastal area from the mouth of the Yana up to the mouth of the Olenek that had remained unmapped the year before. The existence of the so-called Sannikov Land had to be established. Both Liakhovskii islands, the coastal area, and the Lena River were mapped in the inland direction. But the search for Sannikov Land failed; instead of discovering land, Anjou and his team found an extensive polynia north of the New Siberian Islands. Claiming that an extensive voyage on the open sea was the only way to find the supposed land, Anjou recommended to the governor of Siberia, Mikhail Mikhailovich Speranskii, that he organize the trip. The governor rejected the proposal, considering the trip risky and likely to prove negative, and insisted on the study of the sea area west of the New Siberian Islands. In 1823, Anjou fulfilled this task. He mapped the Vasil'evskii and Semenovskii islands and established that the polynia extended to the west of the New Siberian Islands. As a result of Anjou's expedition, the whole coastal area between the Olenek and the Indigirka, and the New Siberian Islands, was precisely mapped, data were collected on the geology (by A.I. Figurin), climate, vegetation cover, and fauna of this region, and the existence of Sannikov Land was disproved. (The myth of Sannikov Land continued to spread until the beginning of the twentieth century.)

The results of the Anjou expedition, from the point of view of further exploration of the Arctic Ocean, were as important as those of the simultaneous Wrangell expedition, an account of which was published in German, Russian, English, and French (while the diaries of the Anjou expedition were destroyed by a fire in January 1837 in Anjou's house). Wrangell's expedition mapped the coast of the Arctic Ocean from the mouth of the Kolyma up to Cape North and showed that Burney's supposition that the peninsula between Cape Shelagskii and Cape North connected the American and Asian continents was a mistake and that the so-called Andreev Land north of the Medvezh'i Ostrova was a fiction. However, on the basis of Chukchi statements he supposed that there was an undiscovered land north of Cape Iakan, but he could not prove it. He did prove the existence of a polynia opposite the coastal area he had studied. It was one of the most significant discoveries for further exploration of the Arctic Ocean in the second half of the nineteenth century, because it established the existence of the open sea and thus served as a basis for several important theories concerning the physical geography of the Arctic Ocean.

Anjou was involved in exploration again in 1825 to 1826, when he was a member of a military topographic mission to the coasts of the Caspian and Aral Seas, led by the Baltic German Friedrich Rembert von Berg, a Russian military officer and statesman. The aim of the mission was to determine the feasibility of joining these two inland seas by a channel and taking control of the Aral Sea region. During the expedition, Anjou was in charge of the barometric measuring of the route and he established that the surface of the Aral Sea was 117.6 feet above that of the Caspian Sea.

ERKI TAMMIKSAAR

## Biography

Born Petr Fedorovich Anzhu in Vyshnii Volok, Government Tver', Russia, 26 February 1796 (Gregorian calendar). Attended St. Petersburg Naval Military Academy, 1808–1811. Sailed the Baltic Sea on several Russian ships. One of the leaders of the Russian northeast Siberian expedition, 1820–1824. Member of a military topographic mission in Central Asia, 1825. Married the widow of the English traveler John Dundas Cochrane (née Kseniia Ivanovna Loginova), 1828. Made further excursions on Russian ships in the Black and the Baltic Seas, 1830s. Head of the port of Kronstadt, 1844–1849. Member of the Learned Marine Committee, 1850–1855. Director of the Department of Ship Forests, 1855–1868. Vice admiral from 1854. Died in St. Petersburg, 24 December 1869.

# ANTARCTICA

Ancient and medieval philosophers speculated about the existence of a huge southern continent (Terra Australis Incognita), but it was not until the early-nineteenth century that the Antarctic continent was actually seen. During that century, explorers traveled ever farther south, mapping the coastline and making short sorties inland, many of them publishing expedition accounts that thrilled a public hungry for knowledge of unknown places. The heroic age of Antarctic exploration began at the end of the nineteenth century and continued through World War I, and men like Robert Falcon Scott, Roald Amundsen, and Ernest Shackleton added accounts of their adventures to the ever growing literature about the Great White South. The frigid, mysterious wilderness inspired other authors, too, and through the years renowned fiction writers such as James Fenimore Cooper (*The Sea Lions; or, the Lost Sealers*, 1849), Jules Verne (*The Sphinx of the Ice Fields*, 1898), and Agatha Christie (*Ordeal by Innocence*, 1958) drew inspiration from it.

The golden age of exploration in the fifteenth and sixteenth centuries saw intrepid adventurers like Ferdinand Magellan, Francis Drake, and John Davis dipping southward and discovering Tierra del Fuego, the Drake Passage, and the Falkland Islands. Drake's chaplain, Francis Fletcher, wrote an engaging description of penguins in *The World Encompassed* (1628). Perhaps inspired by popular conceptions of the far south, the first Antarctic novel, *Mundus Alter et Idem* (1605), by "Mercurius Brittanicus" (Joseph Hall, Bishop of Norwich), used a theoretical southern continent as a setting for an anti-utopian society.

However, it was not until the late eighteenth century that books on Antarctica began to appear in large numbers. By this time, many of the sub-Antarctic islands had been discovered, and Captain James Cook had crossed the Antarctic Circle in 1773. Cook's account (*Voyage toward the South Pole, and round the World*) was published in 1777. However, it was clear from public interest in the adventure that money might be made from writing about it, and several expedition members scrambled to make arrangements with publishers. Gunner's mate John Marra had extracts published from his account as early as December 1775, and George Forster's full book came out a few weeks before Cook's, despite attempts by the Admiralty to suppress it.

All these accounts were in circulation before the southern continent had even been sighted. However, Cook's description of abundant marine populations enticed sealers to abandon the failing stocks in the north and turn south; it is possible that members of these expeditions were the first to sight the continent. The first official sightings, however, were on expeditions under the command of Nathaniel Palmer, Thaddeus von Bellingshausen, and Edward Bransfield in 1820. The following decades saw Antarctic waters dominated by the sealers, who were highly competitive and kept maps and charts to themselves. The owners of the sealing and whaling company Enderby Brothers were exceptions. Samuel Enderby and his sons—Charles, Henry, and George—actively encouraged their captains to explore and to make their findings public. They passed John Biscoe's account of the expedition on *Tula* to the Royal Geographical Society for publication, while Charles Enderby wrote an account of the Auckland Islands in 1849, urging the government to establish a settlement there.

Although little was being written about the Antarctic during the sealing years, the continent still fasci-

The gramophone was taken along as a morale-raiser on Shackleton's 1907 to 1909 expedition—and the penguins seemed to enjoy it too (from Shackleton's *The Heart of the Antarctic*, 1909). *Courtesy of the Travellers Club, London; Bridgeman Art Library, agent.*

nated the public. Several fiction writers capitalized on this interest, including Edgar Allan Poe. In 1830, he published a short novel entitled *The Narrative of Arthur Gordon Pym of Nantucket*, a grisly tale full of cannibalism and other horrors. To counterbalance the whiteness of the North Pole, Poe's south polar inhabitants were black, clothed in the fur of black animals and with a deep-rooted terror of anything white. Another Antarctic story by Poe was *Ms Found in a Bottle* (1831), which described the plight of a man on a ship being drawn into a great vortex at the South Pole. On a similar theme, James de Mille's *A Strange Message Found in a Copper Cylinder* (1888) is a tale of people in a warm south polar land with a vast inland sea.

With sealers' accounts mostly unavailable, it was left to governments to chart the Antarctic. The intellectual Frenchman Jules-Sébastian-César Dumont d'Urville led an expedition from 1837 to 1840, and published his account in 1841. At the same time, the irascible American Charles Wilkes led his ill-prepared and unseaworthy flotilla to the Antarctic, sighting what he named Wilkes Land and producing the monograph *Narrative of the United States Exploring Expedition during the Years 1838, 1839, 1840, 1841 and 1842*, which was published in 1845. Wilkes was an unpopular captain, whose crew clamored for his court-martial upon return. The antithesis of Wilkes was James Clark Ross, an experienced and efficient navigator who discovered the Ross Sea, Victoria Land, and the towering white cliffs of the Ross Ice Shelf. His detailed study *A Voyage of Discovery and Research in the Southern and Antarctic Regions during the Years 1839–1843*, was published in 1847.

After Ross's triumphant return to England, Antarctic exploration went through a period of decline. The seal colonies had been decimated by unscrupulous sealers, and the vast, cold Antarctic waters were considered too distant and dangerous to attract the interest of whalers—at least as long as the northern stocks were plentiful. Governments perceived the south as unprofitable, a huge white wilderness of no economic value. Consequently, attention turned to Africa and the Arctic, where the searches for the sources of the Nile and the fabled Northwest Passage were under way.

By the 1890s, however, the overexploitation of whales in the north meant that whalers began seeking new hunting grounds. Whaling companies sent ships south for the rich stocks around the Antarctic peninsula. Technological advances made as a result of exploring the Arctic meant that ships were faster, stronger, and steam-powered. They were now in a position to penetrate the pack ice that hugs the Antarctic coast and to begin exploring the mysterious interior.

In 1895, the Sixth International Geographical Congress helped launch a new era of Antarctic exploration. Among the first expeditions was one led by Baron Adrien de Gerlache, whose ship *Belgica* became trapped in the ice off the Antarctic peninsula in 1898. Unable to escape, the crew, which included a young Roald Amundsen, spent a miserable winter enduring insanity, scurvy, and starvation. The ship's surgeon, Frederick Cook (later to achieve notoriety with his fraudulent claims to have attained the North Pole), wrote a vivid account of the ordeal in *Through the First Antarctic Night*, published in 1900. De Gerlache's own account was published in French in 1902, but was not translated into English until 1998.

In 1899, Norwegian-born Carsten Borchgrevink and the crew of *Southern Cross* became the first to winter on the continent itself (see *First on the Antarctic Continent*, 1901). In the ensuing several years, a number of major national expeditions went south, including a German one (1901–1903) commanded by Erich von Drygalski (1865–1949), a Scottish one (1902–1904) under the scientist William Speirs Bruce (1867–1921), and a Swedish one led by Otto Nordenskjöld (1869–1928), whose riveting book *Antarctic; or, Two Years amongst the Ice of the South Pole* was published in 1905. Meanwhile, Scott led the British National Antarctic Expedition, and in 1902 made the first serious attempt on the South Pole with Edward Wilson and Ernest Shackleton. This heroic period gave rise to some of the most enduring and popular expedition accounts ever written, including Scott's *The Voyage of the "Discovery"* (1905).

Jean-Baptiste Charcot represented France by leading two expeditions to the Antarctic, in 1903 to 1905 and 1908 to 1910. He married a granddaughter of the novelist Victor Hugo, but the marriage was not a success (she divorced him on grounds of desertion during his second winter in the Antarctic). The scientific success of his first wintering in the south led to funding for a second expedition, which resulted in the charting of 1,250 miles of coastline. The official expedition account ran to a staggering 28 volumes, though most readers might prefer to tackle the shorter account in *The Voyage of the "Why Not?" in the Antarctic* (1911).

Upon his return from Scott's first expedition, Shackleton organized his own attempt on the South Pole. In early 1908, he reached Ross Island, where he built a compact little hut at Cape Royds. The next spring, he set off toward the Pole. Exhausted and with inadequate supplies and deteriorating weather, Shackleton's party had to turn back only 97 nautical miles short of their goal. Nevertheless, Shackleton returned to London to a hero's welcome, and his book *The Heart of the Antarctic* (1909) tells the story of his journey. The expedition is also notable for its production of the first book published in Antarctica. Entitled *Aurora Australis*, it was 120 pages long and illustrated with aluminum printing plates, and the literary contributions from expedition members were painstakingly typeset by Frank Wild and Ernest Joyce.

The geographic South Pole was not the only goal of Shackleton's expedition. In 1909, Douglas Mawson was one of a party of three to reach the magnetic South Pole, which they claimed for the British empire. Afterwards, Mawson was invited to join the venture organized by Scott in 1910, but he declined the offer in order to lead his own expedition. His intention was to chart the coast later to be claimed as Australian Antarctic Territory. However, Mawson had unwittingly selected the windiest place on earth for his quarters, and his account, aptly named *The Home of the Blizzard* (1915), tells of winds that blew for days at speeds of between 60 and 80 miles per hour. In 1912, Mawson and his companions Xavier Merz and B.E.S. Ninnis pushed southeastward with a dog team to explore George V Land. Ninnis disappeared down a crevasse, and Merz died shortly after, leaving Mawson alone, exhausted, and with dwindling supplies. His return to base camp is one of the most remarkable of all Antarctic tales.

However, it is the story of Scott and Amundsen and the "race to the Pole" that captured the imagination of a generation. On 17 January 1912, after an agonizing journey in poor weather, Scott and four companions reached the South Pole, only to find that Amundsen's party of five had reached it more than a month before. Scott and his companions died on the homeward journey, while Amundsen returned to an enthusiastic welcome in Norway. Scott was an outstanding writer, and his intensely moving diaries, recovered from his frozen body the following summer, were published posthumously as the two-volume *Scott's Last Expedition* (1913). Meanwhile, Amundsen published an account of his success, *The South Pole* (1912).

Scott's was not the only book by a member of his expedition. The photographer Herbert Ponting wrote *The Great White South* (1921), detailing his artist's impressions of life in the hut at Cape Evans and the wildlife he watched for hours at a time for the perfect photograph. Similarly, Apsley Cherry-Garrard's description of the nightmarish winter journey undertaken to Cape Crozier with Edward Wilson and "Birdie" Bowers (both of whom died with Scott the following summer) is a classic account of polar exploration. Hampered by violent Antarctic storms, the trio traveled 65 miles in temperatures that plummeted to −77°F. Cherry-Garrard left his readers in no doubt of his views on the matter by naming his book *The Worst Journey in the World* (1922).

Undeterred by the deaths of his former companions, Shackleton began to plan the "greatest polar journey ever attempted"—the crossing of Antarctica. He did not succeed in his objective, but the journey he did undertake is one of the most remarkable in the history of exploration. In 1914, his ship, *Endurance*, was crushed in the ice, forcing the crew to abandon her and travel across the ice carrying all their supplies. They reached Elephant Island, and Shackleton undertook an 800-mile voyage in an open boat to fetch help. Landing on the wrong side of South Georgia, he was then obliged to struggle over 17 miles of glaciers and mountains to reach a whaling station. Shackleton's account (*South: The Story of Shackleton's Last Expedition, 1914–1917*) was published on his return in 1919.

Shackleton's journey was the last in the heroic age. By the time he returned, England was in the grip of World War I, and governments had lost interest in the Antarctic. It was not until the late 1920s that a resurgence of interest led to the use of airplanes to chart the still largely unexplored interior. Richard Evelyn Byrd struggled to keep the lure of the south alive with flights across the Pole and spells of self-imposed solitude (see his books *Little America* and *Alone*, published in 1930 and 1938, respectively), while Lincoln Ellsworth flew from one side of the continent to the other in 1935.

After World War II, major government expeditions concentrating on science, such as Operation Highjump (1946–1947) and the International Geophysical Year (1958–1959), became the norm. Many explorers wrote accounts of the still primitive conditions on the continent of adventure: Thomas Charles (*Ice Is Where You Find It*, 1951), William Menster (*Strong Men South*, 1949), and George J. Dufek (*Operation Deepfreeze*, 1957). Vivian Fuchs and Edmund Hillary joined forces to cross the Antarctic using motor sledges, though the press quickly latched on to the fact that the two men did not much like each other—an aspect of the trans-

Antarctic expedition that was addressed in the published accounts of both explorers.

Today the Antarctic is protected from exploitation and military occupation by the Antarctic Treaty, and human activity there is limited to that of scientists, a growing number of tourists, and a few adventurers who seek to raise funds for future jaunts by writing about their experiences. Readers are faced with an ever growing number of books written by men and women who have walked, driven, or skied to the Pole, but few of them offer much that is original or different. In 1996, Lonely Planet produced the first mass-market travel guide to the continent, though access for most visitors is restricted to acquiring a berth on a tourist ship, as there are no youth hostels or cheap restaurants in the Antarctic. In 2000, Bernard Stonehouse went one better, writing *The Last Continent: Discovering Antarctica*, so far the best Antarctica travel guide on the market.

Finally, fiction writers continue to use the Antarctic as a backdrop for their stories (see Clive Cussler's *Iceberg*, 1975, and *Shock Wave*, 1997), and William Dietrich's *Ice Reich*, 1998); the National Science Foundation established its Artists' Programme specifically to provide artists and writers with an opportunity to travel south. Science-fiction guru Kim Stanley Robinson was a guest; his novel *Antarctica* (1997) reads almost like a diary of his personal experiences, reminiscent of the expedition accounts of the first travelers to the far south.

ELIZABETH CRUWYS

### References and Further Reading


Amundsen, Roald, *The South Pole: An Account of the Norwegian Antarctic Expedition in the "Fram," 1910–1912*, translated by A.G. Chater, 1912.

Borchgrevink, C.E., *First on the Antarctic Continent: Being an Account of the British Antarctic Expedition, 1898–1900*, 1901.

Brown, Robert Neal Rudmose, R.C. Mossmann, and J.H. Harvey Pirie, *The Voyage of the "Scotia": Being the Second of a Voyage of Exploration in Antarctic Seas by Three of the Staff*, 1906; reprinted, 1978.

Bruce, William Speirs, *The Log of the "Scotia" Expedition, 1902–4*, edited by Peter Speake, 1992.

Byrd, Richard Evelyn, *Little America: Aerial Exploration in the Antarctic, the Flight to the South Pole*, 1930.

Charcot, Jean-Baptiste, *The Voyage of the "Why Not?" in the Antarctic*, 1911; as *The Voyage of the "Pourquois Pas?": The Journal of the Second French South Polar Expedition, 1908–1910*, 1978.

Charles, Thomas, *Ice Is Where You Find It*, 1951.

Cherry-Garrard, Apsley, *The Worst Journey in the World: Antarctic, 1910–1913*, 1922.

Cook, Frederick A., *Through the First Antarctic Night, 1898–1899*, 1900.

Cook, James, *Voyage toward the South Pole, and round the World: Performed in His Majesty's Ships the Resolution and Adventure, in the Years 1772, 1773, 1774, and 1775*, 1777.

Dufet, George J., *Operation Deepfreeze*, 1957.

Dumont d'Urville, Jules-Sébastian-César, *Voyage au Pole Sud et dans l'oceanie sur les corvettes l'Astrolabe et la Zélée: Executé par ordre du Roi pendant les annees 1837–1840* [Voyage to the South Pole and Oceania in the Corvettes *Astrolabe* and *Zélée*: Executed by Order of the King during the Years 1837–1840], 1841.

Enderby, Charles, *The Auckland Islands: A Short Account of Their Climate, Soul, and Productions, and the Advantages of Establishing a Settlement at Port Ross for the Carrying Out the Southern Whale Fisheries*, London: Pelham Richardson, 1849.

Fletcher, Francis, *The World Encompassed, by Sir Francis Drake*, 1628.

Fuchs, Vivian, *The Crossing of Antarctica: The Commonwealth Trans-Antarctic Expedition, 1955–1958*, 1958.

Fuchs, Vivian, *Of Ice and Men: The Story of the British Antarctic Survey, 1943–1973*, 1982.

Fuchs, Vivian, *A Time to Speak: An Autobiography*, 1990.

Gerlache, Adrien de, *Voyage de la "Belgica": Quinze mois dous l'Antarctique*, 1902; as *Fifteen Months in the Antarctic*, translated by Maurice Raraty, 1998.

Hillary, Edmund, *No Latitude for Error*, 1961.

Hillary, Edmund, *Nothing Venture, Nothing Win*, 1975.

Hurley, Frank, *Shackleton's Argonauts: A Saga of the Antarctic Ice-Packs*, 1948.

Marra, John, *Journal of the Resolution's Voyage in 1772, 1773, 1774 and 1775*, 1775.

Mawson, Douglas, *The Home of the Blizzard: Being the Story of the Australasian Antarctic Expedition, 1911–1914*, 1915.

Menster, William, *Strong Men South*, 1949.

Nordenskjöld, Otto, *Antarctic; or, Two Years Amongst the Ice of the South Pole*, 1905.

Ponting, Herbert G., *The Great White South*, 1921.

Ross, James Clark, *A Voyage of Discovery and Research in the Southern and Antarctic Regions, during the Years 1839–1843*, 1847.

Scott, Robert Falcon, *The Voyage of the "Discovery,"* 1905.

Scott, Robert Falcon, *Scott's Last Expedition: The Journals of Captain R.F. Scott*, 1913.

Shackleton, E.H., *The Heart of the Antarctic: Being the Story of the British Antarctic Expedition, 1907–1909*, 1909.

Shackleton, E.H., *South: The Story of Shackleton's Last Expedition, 1914–1917*, 1919.

Wheeler, Sara, *Terra Incognita: Travels in Antarctica*, 1996.

Wild, Frank, *Shackleton's Last Voyage: The Story of the "Quest,"* 1923.

Wilkes, Charles, *Narrative of the United States Exploring Expedition during the Years 1838, 1839, 1840, 1841 and 1842*, 1845.

Wilson, Edward, *Diary of the Terra Nova Expedition to the Antarctic, 1910–1912*, edited by H.G.R. King, 1972.


## APOLLONIUS OF TYANA *Greek*

### *Philosopher and Traveler*

Almost nothing is known of the historical Apollonius. He was probably born early in the first century CE, in Tyana in Cappadocia, and died before 100 CE. What we know of this pre-Christian holy man—including the narrative of his extensive travels—comes from a biography (it is more of a hagiography) written by the great third-century Sophistic writer Philostratus between about 222 and 235. There is no doubt that Philostratus embroidered what was already a semilegendary tradition—possibly not, until then, a coherent narrative account—of a famous magician and wonder-worker whose career in the Roman East has been rightly compared with that of his slightly earlier contemporaries, Jesus and Paul. Much of what now comprises the eight books of Philostratus's *Life of Apollonius* (an exceptionally long biography by Greco-Roman standards) must be the author's invention. Certainly Philostratus's work (a more precise translation of the title would be *In Honor of Apollonius of Tyana*) had an enormous impact—we know of a cult of Apollonius (through amulets, temples, and various religious activities) that continued at least into the fifth century in pagan circles in Rome and the Greek-speaking East. And the Christian bishop Eusebius felt the need in the fourth century to write a refutation of Philostratus (in his *Contra Hieroclem*), arguing that Apollonius was not a true holy man but a charlatan magician.

Philostratus's Apollonius is a divine sage—a paragon of wisdom, a worker of miracles, and a restorer of the polytheistic Hellenic religious culture of the Greco-Roman tradition. In all of this he is distinctly comparable to Christ, except that the Gospel writers present Jesus as restoring his own Jewish religious tradition as opposed to that of the Hellenic world. As a significant part of the rhetorical argument of the *Life*, Philostratus presents Apollonius as a traveler extraordinaire—to Arabia, Babylon, India, Asia Minor, Greece, Rome, Gades, Libya, and Egypt. In the theme of his travels, Apollonius resembles less the literary representation of Christ than that of St. Paul, both in the *Acts of the Apostles* and in the apocryphal and novelistic *Acts of Paul and Thecla*, which circulated at about the same time as Philostratus's *Life of Apollonius*. In exploiting a narrative frame of travels, Philostratus borrows from the important tropes of travel in the ancient romantic fiction contemporary with him (in which the conceit of travel to faraway lands usually dominates the adventures that separate hero and heroine, as in Chariton's novel *Chaereas and Callirhoe* and Achilles Tatius's *Leucippe and Clitophon*). The travel theme became de rigueur also in philosophical or religious biography, in which the hero is often shown visiting foreign lands as part of his education (thus, Jesus went to Egypt in Matthew 3:13–3:15, while Pythagoras went to Egypt in Porphyry's *Life*, 6–8, and in Iamblichus's *Life*, 12–19). While such fictional travel may have had little relation to the realities of the ancient journey or to the actual accounts of voyages that survive from antiquity (such as the *periploi* of various merchants or the *Periegesis* of Pausanias), not only does it reflect popular views of what travel was like for the privileged elite, but it must also have helped to formulate ideals of travel that themselves informed the desires, actual voyages, and written texts of Greco-Roman travelers (most of them now lost to us).

Apollonius is represented as acquiring his philosophical education through his travels to the East—especially his journey to the Brahmans in India, among whom he learns self-knowledge. In penetrating the enclaves of the Indian philosophers, he is presented as surpassing the greatest of all pseudohistorical travelers in the Greco-Roman tradition, namely Heracles, Dionysus, and Alexander the Great. Education into spiritual perfection in India (still a vivid trope of travel writing in the West) enables Apollonius to demonstrate mastery both at home in Greece and Asia Minor and on his confrontation with the naked sages (*gymnosophistae*) of Ethiopia, whom he meets and with whom he debates during his trip to Egypt to discover the sources of the Nile. This spiritual mastery not only gives Apollonius authority with philosophers and priests, but also enables him to outwit the emperor Domitian—represented as an enemy of philosophy—whom he confronts in the course of his second (and last) trip to Rome. While the travels are used as a metaphor of the progress toward and attainment of divine perfection in the sage, they also serve to demonstrate Apollonius's spiritual control over the empire (whose religious system Philostratus portrays Apollonius as revitalizing). The sage travels to the empire's peripheries on all sides except the north, and to the center, where he meets the emperor. Many of his more local journeys are pilgrimages, during which Apollonius visits sacred sites, oracles, and graves of heroes, but surpasses the normal pilgrim by giving advice, correcting the rites, and communing with the local deity. Toward the end of the *Life* (8:15), Apollonius arrives in Olympia—itself a major center of pan-Hellenic pilgrimage—not as a pilgrim but more as a destination of pilgrimage in his own right, attracting devotees from throughout the Greek-speaking world.

The importance of the topos of travel to Philostratus's *Life of Apollonius* should not, then, be read as a guide to actuality, nor dismissed as a "mere" rhetorical trope. Rather, it reflects a virtuoso literary use of a theme characteristic of fiction in order to create a sacred history of an obscure wonder-worker whom Philostratus constructed as the paradigmatic holy man for the Roman empire. For the purposes of this encyclopedia, devoted to travel and travel writing, it is worth reflecting on the power of the metaphorical implications of travel and how sophisticated their literary use in the third century was. Many recent uses of the travel theme—especially the journey east in search of spiritual education—are indebted directly or indirectly to

Philostratus's masterly treatment in the *Life of Apollonius of Tyana*.

JAŚ ELSNER

## Biography

Little is known of his life. The only full account, by Philostratus, states that he was born at Tyana, in Cappadocia, at the beginning of the first century CE and died during the reign of Nerva (96–98 CE). He was an ascetic wandering teacher and visited India. He became the posthumous object of a cult that attracted the patronage of Severan emperors.

### References and Further Reading

Philostratus, *Flavii Philostrati Opera*, edited by C.L. Kayser, vol. 1, 1870.

Philostratus, *The Life of Apollonius of Tyana*, translated by F.C. Conybeare, 2 vols., 1912–1950.

*See also* **Greece, Ancient Hellenic World**

# ARABIA

Geographical entities—real or imagined—with enticing names like Arabia, El Dorado, Samarkand, Shangri-La, Tibet, Timbuktu, and Xanadu have been exposed to or born of Western myth making. Arabia has been conjuring up images of mystery, romance, and adventure since antiquity. The classical authors divided Arabia into three zones: Arabia Petraea, including the Sinai peninsula; Arabia Deserta, comprising the Syrian desert, the northern extension of the peninsula; and Arabia Felix—Araby the Blest, as it was known in English—which originally comprised almost the entire peninsula, but over time came to signify only those southwestern areas blessed with myrrh and frankincense.

Knowledge of Arabia grew out of the ancient world's quest for rare fragrances. In time, other motives drew new entrepreneurs and intrepid travelers to the peninsula. The age of discovery, with the endeavor to establish new routes for the spice trade, brought Europeans to the Red Sea and the Persian Gulf. They were followed by those for whom the holy and, for non-Muslims, forbidden cities Mecca and Medina were coveted goals. The Enlightenment witnessed the first scientific expeditions, and the romantics arrived in search of the noble savage whom they thought was to be found in the bedouin. The Great Game in Central Asia had its appendage in Arabia with European Orientalists-cum-imperial agents "exploring" Arabia in the nineteenth century, continuing with the intrusion of scholars as agents from both the Central Powers and the Allies during World War I. Among the more tangible incentives have been coffee, pearls, horses, oil, and leaves of the *qat* tree. There were also, of course, those who wanted to map the unmapped and be the first to cross al-Rub'al-Khali, the formidable Empty Quarter, which is the largest continuous body of sand in the world, or to find the fabled city of ancient Arabia, the Atlantis of the Sands, with the help of photographs taken from the space shuttle *Challenger*.

Although Mecca and Medina seem to have been closed to all but believers right from the beginning, the Portuguese presence, especially after 1517, when the Ottomans took over as guardians of the holy cities, caused a much stricter adherence to this prohibition. Those known to have penetrated Arabia before the eighteenth century were mostly merchants, soldiers, renegades, captives, or shipwreck survivors whose writings, if any, have not survived. An exception are accounts of journeys made, or alleged to have been made, to Mecca. Unfortunately, many of them are spurious and related by men who, although widely traveled, never actually visited Mecca.

The lure of the exotic on the cover of Lady Anne Blunt's *A Pilgrimage to Nejd* (1881). *Courtesy of the Travellers Club, London; Bridgeman Art Library, agent.*

The first authentic narrative of Arabia to become known in Europe was by Ludovico di Varthema, who visited Mecca and Medina in 1504. His dictum that "the testimony of one eye-witness is worth more than ten heard-says" held true, as the book, first published in Italian and translated into Latin, German, French, Spanish, Dutch, and English, became immensely popular. It was not until 1704, when the Englishman Joseph Pitts (c. 1663–1730s) published an account of his involuntary pilgrimage to Mecca and Medina in 1685, that new and more accurate information reached Europe. Pitts's book remained for some reason rather unknown, even in England.

To expand the information given in the Bible and to extrapolate between the biblical patriarchs and contemporary bedouin was one of the main goals of the first scientific expedition sent to the Arabian peninsula. The two outstanding members were Carsten Niebuhr (1733–1815) and the Helsinki-born pupil of Linnaeus, Peter Forsskål (1732–1763). Niebuhr, as the sole survivor, took care of the publishing of Forsskål's descriptions of the flora and fauna encountered, but Forsskål's detailed diary in Swedish from 1761 to his death in 1763 was not published until 1950. In the same category, though defying all attempts at classification, belongs Charles Montagu Doughty (1843–1926). His *Travels in Arabia Deserta* (1888), full as it is of anthropological, archaeological, geographical, geological, historical, and linguistic observations, and being the record of a traveler's nightmare, is, after all, motivated by observing the Bedouin as living a replica of the nomadic, patriarchal life of the Old Testament. In 1971, two atavistic travelers, Arabist William R. Polk (b. 1929) and photographer William J. Mares, made a quixotic journey, a quest for the culture of the desert, crossing the Great Nafud from Riyadh to Amman, a month-long camel trip of about 1,240 miles. They had with them a ghostly comrade on their trip, thc sixth-century poet Labid, whose poem Polk was about to translate. The journey was undertaken to experience the feelings, sights, and the concerns of Labid, and the crossing of the desert resulted in two wonderful books, *Passing Brave* (1973) and *The Golden Ode* (1974), which, taken together, constitute one of the best twentieth-century travelogues of Arabia and, at the same time, an unsurpassed insight into pre-Islamic Arabia.

The French invasion of Egypt in 1798 was primarily motivated by a desire to strike a blow at England and its interests in India. This led to British involvement not only in Egypt but also in Arabia, as the thoroughfare to India. Picturing this political situation enables us to understand why each and every traveler to the peninsula was, or was suspected of being, a spy and agent of one or more of the European powers. The travelers were almost without exception fluent in Arabic and had, with full awareness, taken the character of a Muslim to crown their travels with the pilgrimage to Mecca. The Catalan Domingo Badía y Leblich (1766–1818) assumed the role of a scion to the once ruling Abbasid caliphs, calling himself Ali Bey al-Abbasi, and traveled in a princely fashion among the Arab potentates. He visited Mecca in 1807, and was the first to determine the city's position by astronomical observations and to give an eyewitness report of the rising power of the puritan Wahhabi movement, destined to determine the ideological climate in the twentieth century. Ali Bey died mysteriously in 1818 while traveling for a second time to Mecca, apparently of dysentery but, according to the French for whom he had been working, poisoned by the British. The next agent *in spe* to enter Mecca, in 1809, was the Russian subject Ulrich Jasper Seetzen (1767–1811). Together with Georg August Wallin (1811–1852), he was without doubt the best-qualified scholarly traveler to the peninsula. Seetzen had written to the czar affirming that after performing the pilgrimage to Mecca and obtaining the coveted title of hajji he would be at the czar's disposal for Russian intelligence in central Asia. After visiting the holy cities, Seetzen traveled widely in the southern parts of the peninsula until he was murdered in the vicinity of Mocha in September 1811. Seetzen's notes pertaining to the pilgrimage and to his last years were lost.

British involvement in inter-Arabian affairs began with Captain George Forster Sadleir's (1789–1859) sea-to-sea crossing of Arabia from east to west in 1819. He was sent as an emissary to Ibrahim, the son of Muhammed Ali, who in 1818 had conquered Dir'iyya, the Wahhabi stronghold, with an address of congratulations and a sword of honor. Sadleir's own instructions were to concert the necessary arrangements with Ibrahim with a view to the complete reduction of the Wahhabi power. It has been said of Sadleir that rarely have the laurels of geographic exploration dropped on the head of one more reluctant and less suited. His having no Arabic and no knowledge of the ways of the desert, his hatred of Arabia, and his loathing of the Bedouin made him quite immune to the fascination later exercised by the Bedouin over the romantics who would follow him. Another British officer, James Raymond Wellsted (1805–1842) with the Bombay Marine, the naval arm of the British East India Company, contributed greatly in the 1830s to the knowledge of southern Arabia and Socotra, considered as a coaling station en route to India. In the felicitous words of Robin Bidwell (1976), it is a pleasure to read Wellsted because he, quite frankly, enjoyed himself in Arabia and is not ashamed to let us know it. Wellsted had the greatest of all gifts in an explorer—an intuitive understanding of the people he met and a sympathy with them.

Four books paved the way for the romantic traveler of the nineteenth century and, of equal significance, created at home a reading public eagerly anticipating engagingly written publications of insights into the exotic but nevertheless familiar landscape. These ABCD books of romantic travel were the *Arabian Nights*, the Bible, *Childe Harold's Pilgrimage*, and the *Description de l'Égypte*, by the French savants accompanying Napoleon to Egypt from 1798 to 1801. With this already half-painted canvas in their camel saddlebags, some ill-adjusted misfits and escapists from the conventions of an industrialized Europe proceeded to create some of the best nineteenth-century travel literature. The romantic traveler, to quote Sir Isaiah Berlin (1999), "is indeed an individual, the outsider, the adventurer, the outlaw, he who defies society and accepted values, and follows his own—it may be to his doom, but this is better than conformity, enslavement to mediocrity." And the paragon for these ideals, the anarchist not ruined by civilization, was the Bedouin.

Johann Ludwig Burckhardt (1784–1817), a Swiss by birth but writing in English, has left us a sympathetic picture of the Bedouin, although his fame as an explorer of Arabia rests, deservedly so, upon the posthumously published description of his pilgrimage to Mecca. As a proof of the accuracy of Burckhardt's relation has been cited the fact that Sir Richard F. Burton (1821–1890), perhaps the most romantic figure of his time, found nothing to add and no way to improve on it and simply quotes his predecessor's account. Bearing in mind how Burton appropriated John Payne's translation of the *Arabian Nights* when preparing his own makes this assertion questionable.

The first sea-to-sea crossing from west to east was accomplished by William Gifford Palgrave (1826–1888), a British Jesuit of Jewish background, whose travels in Arabia (1862–1863) were undertaken with Napoleon III's political and financial support and the blessings of Pope Pius IX. Palgrave's travelogue (1865) achieved immediate success, but for almost a century his veracity was questioned and it was even suggested that he never set foot in Arabia (see Braude, 1999).

As M. Trautz (1932) remarked so appositely, each decade of the middle of the nineteenth century is marked by one traveler of capital importance in the history of Arabian exploration: Wallin in the 1840s, Burton in the 1850s, Palgrave in the 1860s, and Doughty in the 1870s. They were all poets, creating what they saw more in accordance with their expectations than with their experience. These poetic guides gave way in the twentieth century to still more adventurist guides from equally accomplished travelers. These were scholars and explorers who acted as advisers to their governments during and after World War I. Despite the efforts of two accomplished desert travelers, Captain William H.I. Shakespear (1879–1915), who was killed in action while fighting on the side of the troops of Ibn Saud, and Harry St. John Bridger Philby (1885–1960), another personal friend of Ibn Saud, the century-long British distrust of the Wahhabis led the British to support—with the guidance of Colonel Thomas Edward Lawrence (1888–1935)—the Hashemites of Mecca as *the* political and religious force in Arabia after the war. This decision was to have reverberations beyond Arabia and for a long time to come. Lawrence's vade mecum was Doughty's *Travels in Arabia Deserta*, the only book in English on Arabian travel that can compete in popularity with his own renowned memoir of the war years, *Seven Pillars of Wisdom* (1935). Lawrence had a second coming in the 1960s with David Lean's film *Lawrence of Arabia* (1962); the visual image of Lawrence's Arabia has, perchance, become confused with Peter O'Toole's Arabia.

No less remarkable scholars were attached to the Central Powers' war efforts: the German Max Freiherr von Oppenheim (1860–1946), author of the massive *Die Beduinen* (1939–1968), and Alois Musil (1868–1944), "Lawrence of Moravia" as he has been called, a Czech but a loyal subject of the Hapsburgs as long as the empire lasted and without doubt one of the greatest travelers to Arabia ever. It is strange that Musil is so little known, compared, for example, to his counterpart Lawrence, though his monumental contributions to our knowledge of north Arabia were published in the 1920s in English by the American Geographical Society.

"As I passed along the southern edge of the Great Southern desert of Arabia, the Empty Quarter, I knew that I was about to cross a line between legend and reality" (Buckley, 2000). A desert inside a desert must be the desert. In the 1920s and 1930s, it was the ultimate prize, the only remaining unknown quarter of the world. In 1930, two British travelers, Bertram Thomas (1892–1950) and Philby, each had his heart set on becoming the first European to cross the Empty Quarter. The race was won by Thomas, who between December 1930 and February 1931 made the crossing from south to north, bringing about suggestions that it was the end of the history of exploration (see Lawrence's foreword to Bertram Thomas, *Arabia Felix*).

The thwarted Philby, who had been captivated by the idea of crossing these sands since 1918, commenced his journey, from north to south, in January 1932, emerging 68 days later, in March 1932. "Greatest of Arabian explorers," reads the inscription on Philby's grave in Beirut. That may or may not be true, but he certainly saw more of Arabia during some 40 years than most, and he was a prolific documenter of his travels. To some, it was with his demise that the age of exploration ended (Bidwell, 1976). This is, in a way, true, at least concerning Arabia: by 1955, travelers had visited virtually all of the peninsula, which by then had been mapped with the aid of aerial photography. But the pronouncements of Lawrence and Bidwell have been proved not wholly accurate. Wilfred Thesiger (b. 1910), the opinionated neo-Victorian whose *Arabian Sands* (1959) stands second to nothing written about deserts in the last century, together with his and Lawrence of Arabia's biographer Michael Asher (b. 1953), have kept the tradition alive despite all ominous predictions.

For Europeans, the nineteenth century had created its own image of Arabia: a landscape of sand and romanticized desert values. But Yemen is different. Yemen is a place where one's received ideas on the nature of Arabia are entirely upset; as Tim Mackintosh-Smith (1997) put it, "Yemen was part of Arabia but the landscape looked like . . . well, nowhere else on Earth, and definitely not Arabia." Pace the Yemeni, who wondered why people spend thousands of dollars rushing round the world when they can chew *qat*, it was the *qat*-lovers who took modern readers to this lotusland in the 1990s. Eric Hansen began the genre in 1991, with his *Motoring with Mohammed*, a book much better than its title; it rose to its heights in 1997, with Tim Mackintosh-Smith's charming masterpiece *Yemen: Travels in Dictionary Land*, one of the best travel books ever, albeit of a different Arabia; the genre continued with Kevin Rushby's *Eating the Flowers of Paradise*, of 1998.

To the British, the Arabian desert and the Bedouin have been the subjects of a fascination quite out of proportion; as Lawrence writes in his foreword to Bertram Thomas's *Arabia Felix*, "the readable Arabian books are all in English, bar one; Jews, Swiss, Irishmen and Whatnots having conspired to help the Englishmen write them." In a more extensive treatment of this subject, some further German, French, Dutch, Italian, and even more British travelers might have been discussed here.

Common to most of those mentioned so far is that they turned the landscape of Arabia into a literary one, perhaps even an inner landscape. As William R. Polk (1973) found out,

> The desert, like a powerful magnet, changes those who come within its field. Many travelers have felt it to be an almost mystical experience; others, a challenge to their humanity, to their very survivability. Some have found peace, some despair. Others have created from inner resources monuments of literature, philosophy, and religion. Perhaps the desert is no more than a magnifying lens, something that enables man to write large whatever he truly is.

KAJ ÖHRNBERG

## References and Further Reading


Ali Bey [Domingo Badía y Leblich], *Voyages d'Ali-Bey el Abbassi en Afrique et en Asie, pendant les années 1803, 1804, 1805, 1806 et 1807*, 3 vols., 1814; as *Travels of Ali Bey in Morocco, Tripoli, Cyprus, Egypt, Arabia, Syria, and Turkey between the Years 1803 and 1807*, 2 vols., 1816.

Asher, Michael, *In Search of the Forty Days Road*, 1984.

Asher, Michael, *A Desert Dies*, 1986.

Asher, Michael, *Impossible Journey: Two Against the Sahara*, 1988.

Asher, Michael, *The Last of the Bedu: In Search of the Myth*, 1996.

Berlin, Isaiah, *The First and Last*, London: Granta, 1999.

Bidwell, Robin, *Travellers in Arabia*, London: Hamlyn, 1976.

Braude, Benjamin, " 'Jew' and Jesuit at the Origins of Arabism: William Gifford Palgrave," in *The Jewish Discovery of Islam: Studies in Honor of Bernard Lewis*, edited by Martin Kramer, Tel Aviv: Moshe Dàyàn Centre for Middle Eastern and African Studies, 1999.

Buckley, Martin, *Grains of Sand*, London: Hutchinson, 2000.

Burckhardt, Johann Ludwig, *Travels in Arabia, Comprehending an Account of Those Territories in Hedjaz Which the Mohammedans Regard as Sacred*, 2 vols., 1829.

Burckhardt, Johann Ludwig, *Notes on the Bedouins and Wahabys*, 2 vols., 1831.

Burton, Richard F., *Personal Narrative of a Pilgrimage to El-Medinah and Meccah*, 3 vols., 1855; memorial edition, 2 vols., 1893.

Burton, Richard F., *The Gold-Mines of Midian and the Ruined Midianite Cities: A Fortnight's Tour in North-western Arabia*, 1878.

Burton, Richard F., *The Land of Midian (Revisited)*, 2 vols., 1879.

Carruthers, Douglas, *Arabian Adventure: To the Great Nafud in Quest of the Oryx*, 1935.

Cheesman, R.E., *In Unknown Arabia*, 1926.

Cocker, Mark, *Loneliness and Time: British Travel Writing in the Twentieth Century*, 1992.

Cole, Donald Powell, *Nomads of the Nomads: The Al Murrah Bedouin of the Empty Quarter*, 1975.

Dickson, H.R.P., *The Arab of the Desert: A Glimpse into Badawin Life in Kuwait and Sau'di Arabia*, 1949.

Doughty, Charles M., *Travels in Arabia Deserta*, 2 vols., 1888.

Euting, Julius, *Tagbuch einer Reise in Inner-Arabien*, 2 vols., 1896–1914.

Fiennes, Ranulph, *Atlantis of the Sands: The Search for the Lost City of Ubar*, London: Bloomsbury, 1992.

Forsskål, Peter, *Resa till Lycklige Arabien: Dagbok 1761–1763* [Journey to Arabia Felix: Diary, 1761–1763], 1950.

Hansen, Eric, *Motoring with Mohammed: Journeys to Yemen and the Red Sea*, 1991.

Kinglake, Alexander W., *Eothen; or, Traces of Travel Brought Home from the East*, 1844.

Labid Ibn Rabiah, *The Golden Ode*, edited and translated by William R. Polk, with photographs by William J. Mares, 1974 [Arabic and English].

Lancaster, William, *The Rwala Bedouin Today*, 1981.

Lawrence, T.E., *Seven Pillars of Wisdom: A Triumph*, 1935.

Loti, Pierre, *Le Désert*, 1895; as *The Desert*, translated by Jay Paul Minn, 1993.

Mackintosh-Smith, Tim, *Yemen: Travels in Dictionary Land*, 1997; as *Yemen: The Unknown Arabia*, 2000.

Maltzan, Heinrich von, *Meine Wallfahrt nach Mekka*, 2 vols., 1865.

Musil, Alois, *Arabia Petraea*, 4 vols., 1907–1908.

Musil, Alois, *Arabia Deserta: A Topographical Itinerary*, 1927.
Musil, Alois, *The Manners and Customs of the Rwala Bedouins*, 1928.
Musil, Alois, *Northern Negd: A Topographical Itinerary*, 1928; reprinted, 1978.
Musil, Alois, *In The Arabian Desert*, 1930.
Niebuhr, Carsten, *Reisebeschreibung nach Arabien und andern umliegenden Ländern*, 3 vols., 1774–1837; as *Travels through Arabia and Other Countries in the East*, translated by Robert Heron, 2 vols., 1792.
Nölde, Eduard, *Reise nach Innerarabien, Kurdistan und Armenien, 1892*, 1895.
Oppenheim, Max Freiherr von, with Erich Bräunlich and Werner Caskel, *Die Beduinen*, 4 vols., 1939–1968.
Palgrave, William Gifford, *A Narrative of a Year's Journey through Central and Eastern Arabia, 1862–63*, 2 vols., 1865.
Philby, H. St. John B., *The Heart of Arabia*, 2 vols., 1922.
Philby, H. St. John B., *Arabia of the Wahhabis*, 1928.
Philby, H. St. John B., *The Empty Quarter*, 1933.
Philby, H. St. John B., *Sheba's Daughters*, 1939.
Philby, H. St. John B., "Palgrave in Arabia," *The Geographical Journal*, 109 (1947): 282–285.
Philby, H. St. John B., *Arabian Highlands*, 1952.
Philby, H. St. John B., *Forty Years in the Wilderness*, 1957.
Philby, H. St. John B., *The Land of Midian*, 1957.
Pitts, Joseph, *A True and Faithful Account of the Religion and Manners of the Mohammetans*, 1704; 4th edition, 1738; reprinted, 1971.
Polk, William R., and William J. Mares, *Passing Brave*, 1973.
Rushby, Kevin, *Eating the Flowers of Paradise: A Journey through the Drug Fields of Ethiopia and Yemen*, 1998.
Sadleir, George Forster, *Diary of a Journey across Arabia, from El Khatif in the Persian Gulf to Yambo on the Red Sea, during the Year 1819*, 1866; reprinted, 1977.
Seetzen, Ulrich Jasper, *Reisen durch Syrien, Palästina, Phönicien, die Transjordan-Länder, Arabia Petraea und Unter-Aegypten*, edited by Friedrich Kruse, 4 vols., 1854–1859.
Taylor, Andrew, *Travelling the Sands: Sagas of Exploration in the Arabian Peninsula*, Dubai: Motivate, 1995.
Thesiger, Wilfred, *Arabian Sands*, 1959.
Thesiger, Wilfred, *Desert, Marsh and Mountain: The World of a Nomad*, 1979.
Thesiger, Wilfred, *Visions of a Nomad*, 1987.
Thomas, Bertram, *Arabia Felix: Across the "Empty Quarter" of Arabia*, with a foreword by T.E. Lawrence, 1932.
Trautz, M., "G.A. Wallin and 'The Penetration of Arabia'," *Geographical Journal*, 76, 1930, pp. 248–252.
Varthema, Ludovico di, *Itinerario de Ludovico de Varthema Bolognese nello Egypto, nella Surria, nella Arabia deserta e felice, nella Persia, nella India e nella Ethiopia*, 1510; as *The Travels of Ludovico di Varthema in Egypt, Syria, Arabia Deserta and Arabia Felix, in Persia, India and Ethiopia, AD 1503 to 1508*, translated by John Winter Jones, edited by George Percy Badger, 1863.
Wallin, Georg August, "Notes Taken during a Journey through Part of Northern Arabia, in 1848," *Journal of the Royal Geographical Society*, 21 (1851): 293–344; reprinted in his *Travels in Arabia (1845 and 1848)*, 1979.
Wallin, Georg August, "Narrative of a Journey from Cairo to Medina and Mecca, by Suez, Arabá, Tawilá, al-Jauf, Jubbé, Háil, and Nejd, in 1845," *Journal of the Royal Geographical Society*, 24 (1854): 115–207; reprinted in his *Travels in Arabia (1845 and 1848)*, 1979.
Wallin, Georg August, "Narrative of a Journey from Cairo to Jerusalem, via Mount Sinai," translated by Norton Shaw, *Journal of the Royal Geographical Society*, 25 (1855): 260–290.
Wellsted, J.R., *Travels in Arabia*, 2 vols., 1838.

*See also* **Yemen**

## ARCTIC

The first Europeans to explore the far north were the Greeks in about 300 BCE, who may have gone as far as Iceland. Seven or eight centuries later, Celtic monks in search of remote and silent places for hermitages sailed north of the Scottish and Irish archipelago in fragile coracles, but they were not trying to see how far north they could go, and their wondering accounts reflect this. By about 1000 CE, Norse settlers in Iceland and Greenland were exploring the western Arctic in search of better fishing and hunting. The first person to write a theorized account of Arctic geography was Nicholas of Lynn, a young Franciscan who sailed north from Norway in the late fourteenth century until he found frozen seas and strange new lands inhabited by small people. His text does not survive, but it is quoted by some sixteenth-century writers and also by Chaucer in his treatise on the astrolabe. By the late fifteenth century, the sphericity of the earth was widely accepted, and rulers began to commission long-distance voyages of exploration for trade with the wondrous "Cathay" described by Marco Polo. Spain and Portugal looked south toward Cape Horn and the Cape of Good Hope, leaving the British, French, and Dutch to seek a route across the top of the earth to the fabled gold, silk, and spices of the Far East.

In 1551, the Company of Merchant Adventurers in London was established, and in 1553 Sir Hugh Willoughby and Richard Chancellor sailed from Deptford on the first official expedition in search of a Northeast Passage. Their fates presage those of many other Arctic explorers: Willoughby's ship was swept off course, and the crew, marooned near modern Murmansk, died slowly of exposure and starvation. Chancellor landed where Archangel now stands, and then traveled overland to Moscow. This resulted in the establishment of the Muscovy Company and the redirection of other exploration westward. In 1576, Martin Frobisher set off with two small ships to seek a passage to Cathay via the northwest. After reaching Greenland, which he did not recognize because contemporary maps showed it far to the east, Frobisher came upon Baffin Island and its apparently Asian inhabitants, one of whom caused nearly as much excitement in London as the black rocks thought to contain gold. Queen Elizabeth commissioned two further expeditions on the strength of the rocks, but when the rocks were eventually recognized as iron pyrites, doubt was thrown on all of Frobisher's discoveries. Nevertheless, hope (or greed) sprang eternal, and in 1585 John Davis set off to conduct a survey of Greenland and points west. Having reached the entrances of Baffin Bay and Hudson Strait, he returned convinced of the existence of a Northwest Passage, but in 1588 the appearance of the Spanish armada temporarily halted English Arctic exploration.

Meanwhile, the Dutchman Willem Barents, exploring northeastward, had passed the Kara Strait and found the Kara Sea to be ice-free. Barents went home triumphant, and returned the following year to find abundant whaling grounds and to attempt the first European overwintering in the Arctic. Scurvy and cold took their toll, but many of the crew eventually got home, only to find that the Dutch had set up their own East India Company using the southern route; there was thus no need for further Dutch Arctic exploration, although whaling there continued.

The Spanish sea-power threat having been dealt with, the British began to look north again, and in 1607 Henry Hudson, commissioned by the Muscovy Company, mapped Spitzbergen and Jan Mayen Island and identified rich fishing grounds. Hudson returned in 1608, when mutiny forced him home early, and sailed for America in 1609 and finally for the Northwest Passage in 1610. On this voyage, Hudson entered Hudson Bay and was convinced he had found the Northwest Passage, but he died after being marooned on Charlton Island by his mutinous crew. Hudson's crew had the foresight to bring his charts back, so Sir Thomas Button in 1612 and 1615 and Jens Munck in 1619 continued the exploration of Hudson Bay, followed in 1631 by James and Foxe. Meanwhile, in 1616 William Baffin, sailing north and west of the island that bears his name, mapped much of northern Greenland and the Canadian Arctic archipelago. All of this facilitated the founding of the Hudson's Bay Company in 1670, which became principally responsible for such exploration until the mid-eighteenth century.

As western European countries were scrambling to find trade routes to the Far East, Peter the Great saw that Russia had obvious advantages in this competition, and in 1725 he commissioned Vitus Bering to lead a crew from the Imperial Russian navy overland from Europe and across Asia and then across what is now the Bering Strait to what became Alaska. Bering achieved this on his second voyage, in 1740, but died when his ship was wrecked on Bering Island. There were a few western European Arctic voyages in the eighteenth century, almost all under the auspices of the Hudson's Bay Company, but in general most of the available resources were channeled toward the great South Sea and Antarctic voyages in this period. It was not until the end of the Napoleonic wars, in 1811, when employment for the vast British navy was needed, that further systematic British exploration of the Arctic took place, and by this time expeditions were sent in the name of science and cartography more often than trade and wealth. It should be said, however, that whalers and fishermen sailing out of Bristol, Whitby, and the Scottish ports continued to build up Arctic knowledge and expertise that were largely ignored by the naval officers and university graduates in charge of official exploration. The only exception was the Whitby whaler William Scoresby, whose *Account of the Arctic Regions* (1820) was more widely consulted.

Man-handling the boats through ice hummocks (from William Parry's *Narrative of an Attempt to Reach the North Pole*, 1828). *Courtesy of the Travellers Club, London; Bridgeman Art Library, agent.*

John Barrow became secretary to the admiralty in 1804, and spent the next 40 years contriving and directing polar exploration. The growing Russian presence in Alaska and down the west coast of America helped to justify the devotion of national resources to Arctic exploration. The Royal Geographical Society persuaded the British government to offer prizes for expeditions reaching points along the Northwest Passage, culminating at £20,000 for the first group to reach the Pacific from the Atlantic across the top of North America. In 1818, Barrow dispatched his first two polar expeditions. One, led by Captain Buchan with John Franklin as second in command, got no farther north than Spitzbergen before storms forced a return home. The second, led by John Ross with William Parry, was far more successful. Following an extraordinary encounter with the Inuit on Smith Sound, the expedition reached the end of Baffin Bay, where Ross was convinced he had seen a chain of mountains through the fog (the Croker mountains), blocking the way west, and insisted on returning to London immediately. Controversy raged when the expedition reached home, concluding with Ross's compulsory retirement on half-pay and Parry's promotion to lead Barrow's next Arctic expedition, in 1819.

Parry was unusual in his attention to the welfare of his crew. He carried freshly prepared lemon juice as well as various pickles to prevent scurvy, and was the first explorer to use canned food, which had to be specially prepared for him. He also participated in the new Anglican evangelical movement, conducting compulsory prayers on board. On 1 August 1819, Parry's ship *Hecla* entered Lancaster Sound, and a few days later he sailed over the place where Ross claimed to have seen the mountains. Eventually he found the channel blocked by ice, and turned west until he reached 110° W and earned a £5,000 bounty. By the end of September, *Hecla* and *Griper* were trapped in pack ice, and Parry prepared to overwinter as he had planned. He devised a timetable intended to ensure that the crew were always clean, well fed, well exercised, and without spare time or energy to contemplate the relentless cold, darkness, and confinement of a winter in the High Arctic, but the ice did not clear when spring came, and many of his men became seriously ill with scurvy. In August, concerned for his crew, Parry chiseled his way out of the ice; he returned to London and a hero's welcome. In 1821, equipped with refurbished ships, Parry set off again, and ruled out Repulse Bay before settling for the winter. Partly because of the refurbishments and partly because Parry grew huge quantities of mustard and cress, this winter went well, and there were cheerful visits to and from the local Inuit. But in June, once again, Parry had to saw his ships out of the ice and, though he thought he saw the Northwest Passage in August, the ice did not clear, and the crews prepared for another Arctic winter, cooperating with the Inuit to ensure the survival of both groups. By August 1823, most of the crew were seriously ill again, and the ice showed no signs of clearing. Parry turned for home.

Meanwhile, John Franklin had returned from a disastrous overland expedition, and the two men dined together before Parry departed for the Arctic again in May 1824. The ships reached Prince Regent Inlet in September and were immediately iced in, so the cold and hungry men passed another Arctic winter. But when summer came, *Fury* was driven onto a rocky beach and wrecked, so Parry returned with all his men in one ship. Meanwhile, Franklin mapped most of the American Arctic coast.

In 1826, Parry realized that his reputation could be redeemed by making the first attempt on the North Pole. Leaving his young and pregnant wife and ignoring Scoresby's advice to leave early and take dogs, Parry took James Clark Ross (John Ross's nephew) as second in command and began to drag sledges across the ice toward the Pole in July 1827. He had underestimated the amount of food required and had not prepared for jagged and slushy ice, and he gave up in August when his crew were dangerously ill with scurvy, frostbite, and exhaustion. Parry and Franklin were both knighted, however, and Parry did not go north again.

John Ross had been brooding at home since seeing the Croker mountains, and in 1829 he found private funding to try again. He and his nephew took a small steamship, the first in the Arctic, and found the warmest and clearest Arctic season of the century. However, after an easy passage that left him 300 miles beyond Parry's farthest point, winter closed in and Ross was trapped there for four years, until George Back came to his rescue.

In 1844, the navy began to appoint leaders of another Northwest Passage expedition, intending to use data and theories gathered by Hudson's Bay Company surveyors. James Clark Ross refused a leadership post, having just married on the condition that he would not go to the Arctic again. However, Franklin, anxious to restore his reputation after governing Tasmania unsuccessfully, accepted eagerly, despite his age and sedentary habits; he disappeared. It was in the course of the many attempts to find Franklin that the Americans first became involved in official polar exploration, notably Elisha Kent Kane and Robert McClure, who sailed through much of the Northwest Passage from the west and sledged along the coast of the rest of the passage while seeking Franklin. In March 1854, the navy announced that it considered Franklin and his men dead. Many of the search expeditions, including John Rae's and Elisha Kane's, were still in the Arctic. Kane returned to great celebrations in New York in 1855, but Franklin's wife, Jane, would not give up hope. In 1857, she sent a final expedition, led by Leopold M'Clintock, who completed the mapping of America's Arctic coast and found cairns and a group of Inuit who told him much about the Franklin expedition's last weeks. He returned in 1859 to general acclaim.

A printer from Cincinnati, Charles Francis Hall, remained unsatisfied with this end to the Franklin search and determined to set out for the Arctic himself. He raised the funds, and was extremely lucky to meet an Inuit couple, Ebierbing and Tookolito (known as Joe and Hannah), who spoke fluent English and were happy to accompany him. Also in the summer of 1860, a doctor called Isaac Hayes set out to investigate continuing rumors of an open polar sea surrounding the North Pole. He too had Inuit companions, a couple called Hans and Merkut and their baby, and succeeded in convincing himself—but no one else—that he had found an open sea at the north coast of Greenland. Hall mapped southern Baffin Island in 1862 and returned to the States to exhibit his Inuit guides until their baby died and he had enough money to go back to the Arctic.

He traveled for three years with various Inuit groups and with whalers (one of whom he shot during an argument) and found some more skeletons and relics of expeditions. Hall transferred his attention to the North Pole and set off with a crew composed of friends, whalers, and naval officers in 1871, picking up the long-suffering Hans and Merkut on the way. There were tensions among the crew, and that winter, after two weeks of sickness and apparent paranoia, Hall died of what was subsequently diagnosed as arsenic poisoning. The crew began to drink, and amid confusion in bad weather 19 people, including two Inuit families, were marooned on a drifting ice floe. They drifted for six months, subsisting on seals caught by the Inuit men, until a whaling ship rescued them off the Labrador coast.

The idea of using yet more public money for Arctic exploration was unpopular in Britain by this time, but growing American investment made the idea of planting the Union Jack on the top of the world appealing to the Victorian public. George Nares led a naval expedition that left in 1875 to find the North Pole. Nares traveled overland using sledges, pulled by men rather than dogs, and heavy tents. His men subsisted almost entirely on salt meat, and suffered appallingly from scurvy. They reached the northern coast of Greenland before turning back. There were no more Royal Navy Arctic expeditions until 1935.

In 1882 to 1883, as part of the first International Polar Year, an American expedition led by Adolphus Greely was sent to carry out scientific observation and also to get as far north as possible. The crew argued bitterly and threatened each other as they struggled through an Arctic winter in unbearably cramped conditions. When summer came, they made a dash for the North Pole, reaching 83°24′ N, the highest latitude reached by Europeans. This triumph was short-lived. Greely left the High Arctic precipitately, to find conditions worse and game scarcer farther south, and support vessels sent from home were unable to reach him. The party ended up stranded on an islet off Ellis Island, dying by inches of scurvy, frostbite, and starvation, and hating each other in their overcrowded hut. By June 1884, when a rescue party arrived, there were just seven survivors and the bodies of the others showed evidence of cannibalism.

The next expedition to set a new point farthest north was very different. Fridtjof Nansen had skied across the Greenland ice-cap in 1888 and, living with the Greenlandic Inuit, had observed that the pattern of driftwood suggested an Arctic current flowing from Siberia to Greenland. He tested this, and surveyed the High Arctic by designing a boat that would withstand months of being trapped in drifting ice and by choosing a crew who would be content to live on it and make scientific observations on their progress. He furnished the boat, *Fram*, as comfortably as possible, with a varied library and a piano as well as plenty of good food and fuel, but when it became clear that they were drifting around rather than toward the Pole, he and Hjalmar Johansen set off on snowshoes for the Pole. He reached a new farthest north latitude (86°13′ N) before fleeing the onset of winter. They were too late, however, and spent the winter in an ice cave, eating plenty of game and playing fantasy games until they encountered an English ship, which took them back to Norway, where *Fram* arrived a week later. Two years later, a Swede, Salomon Andrée, attempted to reach the North Pole by balloon, with predictably disastrous consequences, but by the end of the century the young Norwegian Roald Amundsen was sailing through the Northwest Passage.

The American Robert Peary was convinced that the Norwegians, especially Otto Sverdrup, were trying to reach the Pole rather than merely surveying the area, and was determined that the Americans would get there first. Peary was obsessive and ruthless, and had no qualms about selling the friends and relatives of his Inuit companions to the American Museum of National History, where they were housed in the basement until they died of pneumonia; their bodies were cut up and displayed. Peary's expedition marks the split between science and sport in Arctic travel, for he was not interested in the Arctic or its inhabitants except inasmuch as they would bring him fame. Peary made several improbable and undocumented claims about his achievements, including that he had discovered land that subsequently turned out not to exist. Peary took only five people on his final polar dash in 1909: his African American valet Matthew Henson and four Inuit guides, none of whom could calculate observations. He claimed, unbelievably, to have traveled much faster once the fully trained members of his party had turned back, and he kept no records of the day he later claimed to have reached the Pole. Meanwhile, Frederick Cook, also American, who had certainly survived two years in extremely harsh conditions in the High Arctic, claimed to have reached the Pole alone and said that he had left the papers proving it at Etah, in northern Greenland. Such papers were never recovered, and the controversy is still running.

Since World War I, the North Pole has been reached many times by ski, dog sledge, snowmobile, and airplane, by men and women traveling alone or in groups. Nearly all have been airlifted out after reaching the Pole and nearly all have had supplies air-dropped along the way. Arctic travel writing has proliferated; there are histories of exploration, breathless accounts of adventurous suffering, and, more recently, meditations on the extraordinary appeal of this difficult and beautiful landscape.

Sarah Moss

**References and Further Reading**

Back, George, *Arctic Artist: The Journal and Paintings of George Back, Midshipman with Franklin, 1819–1822*, edited by C.S. Houston, 1994.

Barrow, John, *Voyages of Discovery and Research in the Arctic Regions*, 1846.

Lopez, Barry, *Arctic Dreams: Imagination and Desire in a Northern Landscape*, 1986.

Lyon, George, *The Private Journal of Capt. G.F. Lyon*, 1824.

Nansen, Fridtjof, *Farthest North: Being the Record of a Voyage of Exploration of the Ship "Fram" 1893–96 . . .*, 2 vols., 1897.

Parry, William, *Journal of a Voyage for the Discovery of a North-West Passage from the Atlantic to the Pacific . . .*, 1821.

Scoresby, William, *An Account of the Arctic Regions*, 1820; reprinted, 1969.

*See also* **Greenland; Northeast Passage; Northwest Passage**

## ARGENTINA

Argentina and the River Plate (Rio de la Plata) bear names that reflect Spanish adventurers' dreams of silver wealth more than the poor reality. Early colonization was prevented by the hostility of the native peoples. The first settler, Juan Díaz de Solís, was murdered by the Querandí in 1516. Although Magellan (1519) and Sebastian Cabot (1527) had already made voyages of exploration, Pedro de Mendoza is regarded as the founder of (Santa María de los) Buenos Aires (1538). Sir Francis Drake, who went to South America in 1566, visited the Plate region several times before the second and definitive foundation of Buenos Aires by Juan de Garay in 1580. Although British sailors had traveled with the early Portuguese and Spanish discoverers, and other British citizens (missionaries, businessmen, smugglers, and pirates) displayed more than a passing interest in the Plate region during the sixteenth and seventeenth centuries, there was no attempt at a permanent settlement because of the lack of mineral wealth and the hostility of the indigenous population.

The establishment of the South Sea Company (1711) was a clear manifestation of Britain's political and commercial aims in the eighteenth century. The Treaty of Utrecht (1713), which ended the War of Spanish Succession, helped to establish trade links with the Plate region, including an infamous slave trade agreement. When the bubble burst in 1730, many of the traders stayed on. The best known of the ship doctors was Thomas Falkner (1702–1784), who converted to Catholicism, became a Jesuit, and on his return to Britain wrote an important record of his travels and experiences in *A Description of Patagonia* (1774). When Britain, after the loss of its North American colonies, sought a foothold on the southern continent, Falkner's book became a manual for the later travelers. Although Argentina would not officially gain its independence from Spain until 1816, many eager Britons could not await the inevitable emancipation process. In 1806 and 1807, several British citizens, with the unofficial connivance of the British government, took the law into their own hands. The failed *invasiones inglesas* of Sir Home Popham and the eventual disgrace of generals Whitelock and Beresford sparked the Argentine people in their quest for identity. One of the imprisoned officers was Major Alexander Gillespie, whose *Gleanings and Remarks* (1818) covers many aspects of local customs and religion, much superior to the other military memoirs of the time, such as those of Thomas Fernyhough, Lancelot Holland, and Alexander Crauford. Emeric Essex Vidal's 24 watercolors in his *Picturesque Illustrations of Buenos Ayres and Monte Video, Consisting of Twenty-Four Views* (1820) represent the first and main source of pictorial information about early Argentina.

The Buenos Aires skyline crowned with the "spacious and very elegant" cathedral (from John Pinkerton's *A General Collection of the Best and Most Interesting Voyages and Travels in all Parts of the World*, vol. 14, 1813). *Courtesy of the Travellers Club, London; Bridgeman Art Library, agent.*

Within a decade, British interest was mainly commercial, with a procession of mining consultants, engineers, metallurgists, and mineralogists making their way from Britain to Montevideo, to Buenos Aires, and across the Pampas, recording their experiences as they went; for example, in Peter Schmidtmeyer's *Travels into Chile, over the Andes* (1824) and J.A.B. Beaumont's *Travels in Buenos Ayres and the Adjacent Provinces of the Río de la Plata* (1828). Useful too is the merchant Samuel Haigh's *Sketches of Buenos Ayres, Chile, and Peru* (1831), but one of the best literary works of the decade is Joseph Andrews's *Journey from Buenos Ayres, through the Provinces of Cordova, Tucuman and Salta to Potosi* (1827). The rarest (for the bibliophile) and the most popular (from the literary point of view) is that published by the soldier-cum-mining engineer Sir Francis Bond Head ("Galloping Head"), *Rough Notes Taken during Some Rapid Journeys across the Pampas and among the Andes* (1826), whose graphic and impressionistic vision of the Pampa and its inhabitants, the gauchos, received a warm welcome in Britain and Argentina, where Head is revered. Thus it is no coincidence that Head's key work was quoted by later (often inferior) writers, like Charles Brand (1828), John MacDowall (1833), W.H.B. Webster (1834), P. Campbell Scarlett (1838), and many others.

The person who stimulated and oversaw this commercial and political activity was the British consul, Woodbine Parish. He returned home in 1838, and published the first edition of his *Buenos Ayres and the Provinces of the Río de la Plata* the following year. The more polished and expanded version of 1852 reveals not only his valuable information for settlers and investors, but also his personal interest in the geographical and archaeological riches of the country. The Robertson brothers, John Parish and William Parish, who had helped found the ill-fated Scottish colony in Monte Grande (1825), later published their *Letters on Paraguay* (1838–1839) and *Letters on South America* (1843), which were well written, full of interesting details, and fairer to the Catholic Argentines than were most of the works by other British travel writers. By midcentury, travel literature was flourishing: L. Hugh de Bonelli (1854), Robert Elwes (1854), William Hadfield (1854), W. Parker Snow (1857), and others produced volumes of interest and value. Industrial investigators like William MacCann (*Two Thousand Miles' Ride through the Argentine Provinces*, 1853) and Wilfrid Latham (*The States of the River Plate: Their Industries and Commerce*, 1866) published informative, literary works. The views of the scientists are reflected in the narrative of Robert Fitzroy (1839) and in Charles Darwin's journal of research (1839), both of *Beagle* renown. By the last third of the century, the narratives were becoming a little more literary and less commercially oriented: for example, Thomas Woodbine Hinchcliff's *South American Sketches* (1863), the British consul Thomas Hutchinson's *Buenos Aires and Argentine Gleanings* (1865), and, probably one of the most widely read, the exciting adventures recounted in George Chaworth Musters's *At Home with the Patagonians* (1871).

It was in about this period that Robert Bontine Cunninghame Graham (1852–1936) arrived as a youth in Argentina. Neither scientist nor industrial investigator, his intentions were vaguely commercial (to earn a living) and personal (to seek adventure). He found the life of the Pampa gaucho to his liking, and their activities were to form an important part of his literary output over the last 40 years of his career, when he produced hundreds of impressionistic sketches, mostly devoted to the Pampa way of life: "El Rodeo," "Los Indios," "The Captive," and many more in this vein (see Walker, 1978). Fittingly, he died in Buenos Aires in 1936, but not before making an emotional pilgrimage to the birthplace of his good friend and kindred spirit, W.H. Hudson. Although regarded, with Graham, as the best of *los viajeros ingleses*, in fact Hudson was born in Argentina and moved to Britain as an adult, where he achieved a great reputation as an outdoors essayist and naturalist. Lesser known are his South American romances, like *El Ombú* (1902), his essays, like *Idle Days in Patagonia* (1893), and his autobiography, *Far Away and Long Ago* (1918). It is a felicitous coincidence that Graham's protégé and biographer, the Swiss-Argentine Aimé F. Tschiffely, himself the author of many fine travel books and adventure stories—such as *The Tale of Two Horses* (1934), *Bridle Paths* (1936), and *This Way Southward* (1945)—should write a little biography of a not so well-known Englishman, *The Man from Woodpecker Creek* (1953), based on the life of E. Lucas Bridges (1874–1949), who had told his own story in detail in *The Uttermost Part of the Earth* (1948), about his life as the son of missionary parents in Patagonia. This magical region in the south of Argentina has intrigued writers right up to the present: Herbert Childs's *El Jimmy: Outlaw of Patagonia* (1936) is a colorful book of pioneer adventure; in our own time, Bruce Chatwin's splendid modern-day quest of wonder voyage *In Patagonia* (1977) and Paul Theroux's *The Old Patagonian Express* (1979) capture something of the spirit of this eternally attractive and mysterious land.

Of the many other travel writers who toured Argentina in the twentieth century, none is more famous than Graham Greene, whose *Travels with My Aunt* (1969) describes the fierce Chaco territory of northern Argentina. Less well known but no less effective is the important travel writing of sometime Argentinian resident Gordon Meyer, such as *The River and the People* (1965), the British naturalist Gerald Durrell's less serious accounts in *The Drunken Forest* (1956) and *The Whispering Land* (1961), and Christopher Isherwood's *The Condor and the Cows* (1949).

From its earliest days, Argentina has been a magnet for travelers. Not all of the travel writers had the literary skills of a Graham Greene or a W.H. Hudson, but soldiers, pioneers, missionaries, and diplomats all put pen to paper in their attempts to capture the essence of this fascinating land, as have countless amateurs, whose memoirs, chronicles, reports, journals, and letters have become the stuff of Argentine travel literature, and, incidentally, have been plowed back (through translation) into the field of national culture and social history.

JOHN WALKER

### References and Further Reading

Andrews, Joseph, *Journey from Buenos Ayres, through the Provinces of Cordova, Tucuman and Salta, to Potosi*, 2 vols., 1827; reprinted, 1971.

Beaumont, J.A.B., *Travels in Buenos Ayres and the Adjacent Provinces of the Río de la Plata, with Observations Intended for the Use of Persons Who Contemplate Emigrating to That Country, or Embarking Capital in Its Affairs*, 1828.

Bonelli, L. Hugh de, *Travels in Bolivia, with a Tour across the Pampas to Buenos Ayres*, 1854.

Brand, Charles, *Journal of a Voyage to Peru, a Passage across the Cordillera of the Andes . . . and a Journey across the Pampas*, 1828.

Bridges, E. Lucas, *The Uttermost Part of the Earth*, 1948.

Chatwin, Bruce, *In Patagonia*, 1977.

Childs, Herbert, *El Jimmy: Outlaw of Patagonia*, 1936.

Crawford, Robert, *Across the Pampas and the Andes*, 1884.

Darwin, Charles, *Journal of Researches into the Natural History and Geology of the Countries Visited during the Voyage of "H.M.S. Beagle" round the World*, 1839; revised edition, 1845.

Davie, John Constanse, *Letters from Paraguay: Describing the Settlements of Monte Video and Buenos Ayres*, 1805.

Durrell, Gerald, *The Drunken Forest*, 1956.

Durrell, Gerald, *The Whispering Land*, 1961.

Elwes, Robert, *A Sketcher's Tour round the World*, 1854.

Falkner, Thomas, *A Description of Patagonia and the Adjoining Parts of South America*, 1774; reprinted, 1935.

Fernyhough, Thomas, *Military Memoirs of Four Brothers*, 1829.

Fitzroy, Robert, *Narrative of the Surveying Voyages of His Majesty's Ships "Adventure" and "Beagle," between the Years 1826 and 1836*, vols. 1–2, 1839.

Gillespie, Alexander, *Gleanings and Remarks: Collected during Many Months of Residence at Buenos Ayres, and within the Upper Country*, 1818.

Greene, Graham, *Travels with My Aunt*, 1969.

Hadfield, William, *Brazil, the River Plate, and the Falkland Islands*, 1854.

Haigh, Samuel, *Sketches of Buenos Ayres, Chile, and Peru*, 1831.

Head, Francis Bond, *Rough Notes Taken during Some Rapid Journeys across the Pampas and among the Andes*, 1826.

Hinchcliff, Thomas Woodbine, *South American Sketches*, 1863.

Hutchinson, Thomas J., *Buenos Ayres and Argentine Gleanings*, 1865.

Isherwood, Christopher, *The Condor and the Cows*, 1949.

King, J. Anthony, *Twenty-Four Years in the Argentine Republic*, 1846.

Latham, Wilfrid, *The States of the River Plate: Their Industries and Commerce*, 1866.

Love, George Thomas, *A Five Years' Residence in Buenos Ayres, during the Years 1820 to 1825*, 1825.

MacCann, William, *Two Thousand Miles' Ride through the Argentine Provinces*, 2 vols., 1853.

Meyer, Gordon, *The River and the People*, 1965.

Miers, John, *Travels in Chile and La Plata*, 2 vols., 1826.

Mulhall, Michael G., *The English in South America*, 1878.

Mulhall, Mrs. M.G. (Marion McMurrough Mulhall), *Between the Amazon and the Andes; or, Ten Years of a Lady's Travels in the Pampas, Gran Chaco, Paraguay and Matto Grosso*, 1881.

Musters, George Chaworth, *At Home with the Patagonians: A Year's Wandering over Untrodden Ground from the Straits of Magellan to the Rio Negro*, 1871.

Parish, Woodbine, *Buenos Ayres and the Provinces of the Río de la Plata: From Their Discovery and Conquest by the Spaniards to the Establishment of Their Political Independence*, 1839; 2nd edition, 1852.

Robertson, J.P., and W.P. Robertson, *Letters on Paraguay, Comprising an Account of a Four Years' Residence in That Republic*, 3 vols., 1838–1839.

Robertson, J.P., and W.P. Robertson, *Letters on South America*, 3 vols., 1843.

Scarlett, P. Campbell, *South America and the Pacific: Comprising a Journey across the Pampas and the Andes, from Buenos Ayres to Valparaíso, Lima and Panamá*, 2 vols., 1838.

Schmidtmeyer, Peter, *Travels into Chile, over the Andes, in the Years 1820 and 1821*, 1824.

Snow, W. Parker, *Two Years' Cruise off Tierra del Fuego, the Falkland Islands, Patagonia, and in the River Plate: A Narrative of Life in the Southern Seas*, 1857.

Theroux, Paul, *The Old Patagonian Express: By Train through the Americas*, 1979.

Vidal, E.E., *Picturesque Illustrations of Buenos Ayres and Monte Video, Consisting of Twenty-Four Views: Accompanied with Descriptions of the Scenery, and of the Costumes, Manners, &c. of the Inhabitants of Those Cities and Their Environs*, 1820.

Walker, John (editor), *The South American Sketches of R.B. Cunninghame Graham*, 1978.

## ATHOS, MOUNT

The rugged and beautiful Athos peninsula in northern Greece has attracted travelers since at least the fifteenth century because of its unique Orthodox monastic community.

The peninsula was the site of five ancient cities. The Persian king Xerxes dug a canal through its neck in 481 BCE for the great fleet that he brought from Asia to subdue the troublesome Greeks. The mountain itself, which rises 2,033 meters from the sea in a pyramid of white limestone, was the subject of the fantasies of the architect Deinocrates, who proposed carving it in the image of Alexander the Great. Anchorites first settled on Athos around 800 CE. Organized monastic foundations spread later, under the protection of the Byzantine emperors, eventually developing into the self-governing community that still exists today: twenty monasteries under the spiritual authority of the Ecumenical Patriarch.

The opening of Mount Athos—the Holy Mountain—to the imagination of the West through travelers' records began with the Florentine priest Cristoforo Buondelmonti (d. 1430) in the early fifteenth century.

A detailed early account was that of the French naturalist Pierre Belon (1517–1555). Published in 1553 as part of a longer book describing his travels in the Levant, it became a point of reference for later writers. Belon pioneered the description of the natural history of the Levant. His interest extended to the customs of the regions he visited. Another who also set out to satisfy the growing Western interest in natural history was John Sibthorp (1758–1796), who visited Mount Athos twice during the expeditions that provided material for his classic publication *Flora Graeca.*

A more common motive for early visitors was an interest in the eastern Orthodox Church, whether its doctrines or its old manuscripts. Anglican and Jesuit priests and pilgrims from Orthodox lands, especially Russia, were all attracted. John Covel (1638–1722), chaplain for the Levant Company at Constantinople, who visited Athos in 1677, was the first English traveler to leave an account of the Holy Mountain. He visited most of the monasteries and wrote detailed notes on their architecture, relics, numbers of monks and dependents, taxes, the election of abbots, and the working life of the monasteries. The writings of travelers such as Covel are an essential source for information about the society and institutions—less so for the spiritual life—of the Holy Mountain, supplementing copious primary material in the Acts of the Monasteries and Lives of the Saints. They helped to satisfy the curiosity of patrons, bishops, and royalty about the Orthodox Church.

Growing interest in Greek lands and antiquities brought more travelers to Athos in the eighteenth and nineteenth centuries. Manuscripts were a strong attraction. The most famous of the manuscript-hunters was Robert Curzon (1810–1873), whose lively *Visits to Monasteries in the Levant*, published in 1849, has rarely been out of print. Curzon had little time for the churches, and less for the inner life of the monks. He helped to consolidate the image—already cultivated by travelers such as John Morritt of Rokeby (1772–1843)—of the ignorant monk, neglecting the priceless treasures under his nose.

More balanced observers include the great topographer William Martin Leake (1777–1860) in his *Travels in Northern Greece* (1835) and the Oxford geographer Henry Fanshawe Tozer (1829–1916) in his *Researches in the Highlands of Turkey* (1869). Tozer found in the mid-nineteenth century that the monks linked the future of the mountain with the future of Turkey: when, as they were convinced would happen, Greece regained Constantinople, the Holy Mountain would once again become the place of learning that they believed it to have been in former times. At about the same time, the German scholar J.P. Fallmerayer (1790–1861), notorious for trying to prove that the Greeks of

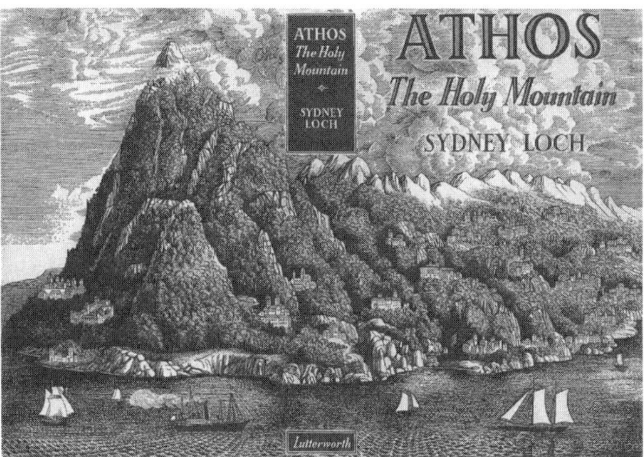


Jacket by W. McLaren, based on a nineteenth-century print, for Sydney Loch's *Athos: The Holy Mountain* (1957); a map and mini-guide are printed on the reverse.

his day had no true Greek blood in their veins, was so struck by the beauty and calm of the Holy Mountain that he fantasized about retiring there; the fantasy lasted only a few days. Another nineteenth-century visitor was Edward Lear (1812–1888), who visited Athos in 1856 and returned with a portfolio of 50 fine watercolor paintings. Lear found the atmosphere of Orthodox monasticism oppressive, objecting particularly to the exclusion of women from the mountain.

Among the many accounts by twentieth-century pilgrims and sightseers, those that bring new insights to bear include the books of Robert Byron (1905–1941), R.M. Dawkins (1871–1955), Sydney Loch, and Philip Sherrard, with the scandalous memoir by Ralph Brewster for light relief. Robert Byron's book *The Station* (1928) opened up for the general reader the glories of Byzantine art on Athos. Dawkins, in *The Monks of Athos* (1936), left a sympathetic account of the legends of the Holy Mountain, with much insight into monastic life and ways of thought. Loch, who came to Greece to work on the relief and settlement of refugees after the Asia Minor disaster of 1922, stayed on at Ouranopolis, on the neck of the Athos peninsula. His book *Athos: The Holy Mountain* was edited by his wife and published posthumously in 1957. Sherrard, who lived in Greece, was the only one of these authors to become a member of the Orthodox Church. His books enter into the imaginative world of the monks, conveying both the concrete, oppressive detail and the spiritual content of their lives, and defining the dilemmas that modernity and materialism pose for the Holy Mountain.

The thousands of pilgrims and curious visitors—all male—who visit Athos each year can now see evidence of a strong recent revival of monastic life: another in the cycle of changes in the history of the Holy Mountain, always within the stable framework that has endured since the tenth century. Visitors from the outside world have helped to illuminate this life. A notable Russian example is the charmingly illustrated eighteenth-century account of the monasteries by V.G. Barsky (1887). Greek contributions include the autobiographical *Anaphora ston Gkreko* (1961), by the great Cretan novelist Nikos Kazantzakis (1883–1957). The tradition of travelers' tales from the mountain continues, providing a colorful addition to the mass of scholarly works on the history of Athos and on Orthodox monasticism.

MICHAEL LLEWELLYN SMITH

### References and Further Reading

Barsky, Vasily Grigorovich, *Stranstvovaniia Vasilia Grigorovicha Barskago po sviatym mestam Vostoka s 1723 po 1747* [Travels of Basil Grigorovich Barsky in the Holy Places of the East from 1723 to 1747], 4 vols., 1885–1887.

Barsky, Vasily Grigorovich, *Vtoroe poseshchenie sviatoi Afonskoi gory Vasilia Grigorovicha-Barskago im samim opisannoe* [Basil Grigorovich Barsky's Second Visit to the Holy Mountain of Athos as Described by Himself], 1887.

Belon, Pierre, *Les Observations de plusieurs singularitez et choses mémorables*, 1553; as *Plurimarum Singularium et Memorabilium Rerum in Graecia, Asia, Aegypto, Iudaea, Arabia, aliisque exteris Provinciis ab ipso conspectarum Observationes*, translated into Latin by Carolus Clusius, 1589.

Brewster, Ralph H., *The 6,000 Beards of Athos*, 1935.

Buondelmonti, Cristoforo, *Librum Insularum Archipelagi*, 1824; as *Description des îles de l'Archipel . . . Version grecque par un anonyme, publiée d'après le manuscrit du Sérail avec une traduction française et un commentaire, par Émile Legrand*, 1897.

Byron, Robert, *The Station; Athos: Treasures and Men*, 1928; with an introduction by Christopher Sykes, 1949.

Choukas, Michael, *Black Angels of Athos*, 1935.

Covel, John, *Some Account of the Present Greek Church, with Reflections on Their Present Doctrine and Discipline*, 1722.

Curzon, George Nathaniel, Marquess Curzon of Kedleston, "Monasteries of the Levant," in his *Leaves from a Viceroy's Note-book and other Papers*, 1926; as *A Viceroy's India*, edited by Peter King, 1984.

Curzon, Robert, *Visits to Monasteries in the Levant*, 1849; with an introduction by D.G. Hogarth, 1916; with an introduction by Seton Dearden and a preface by Basil Blackwell, 1955.

Dalrymple, William, "The Monastery of Iviron, Mount Athos, Greece, 29 June 1994: The Feast of SS Peter and Paul," in his *From the Holy Mountain: A Journey in the Shadow of Byzantium*, 1997; as *From the Holy Mountain: A Journey among the Christians of the Middle East*, 1998.

Dapontes, Konstantinos, *Kepos Chariton* [Garden of the Graces], 1880.

Dawkins, R.M., *The Monks of Athos*, 1936.

Fallmerayer, Jakob Philipp, *Hagion Oros, oder Der Heilige Berg Athos* [The Agion Oros, or the Holy Mountain Athos], edited by Franz Hieronymus Riedl, 1978.

Georgirenes, Joseph, *A Description of the Present State of Samos, Nicaria, Patmos, and Mount Athos*, translated by Henry Denton, 1678.

Hasluck, F.W. (editor), "The First English Traveller's Account of Athos (1677)," *Annual of the British School at Athens*, 17 (1910–1911): 103–131.

Hasluck, F.W., *Athos and Its Monasteries*, 1924.

Kästner, Erhart, *Die Stundentrommel vom Heiligen Berg Athos* [The Beating of the Hours on the Holy Mountain Athos], 1956; as *Mount Athos: The Call from Sleep*, translated by Barry Sullivan, 1961.

Kazantzakis, Nikos, *Anaphora ston Gkreko: Myth istorema*, 1961; as *Report to Greco*, translated by P.A. Bien, 1965.

Khitrovo, Sofiya, *Itinéraires russes en Orient*, 1889.

Leake, William Martin, *Travels in Northern Greece*, vol. 3, 1835.

Loch, Joice Nankivell, *A Fringe of Blue: An Autobiography*, 1968.

Loch, Sydney, *Athos: The Holy Mountain*, 1957.

Morritt, John B.S., *The Letters of John B.S. Morritt of Rokeby, Descriptive of Journeys in Europe and Asia Minor in the Years 1794–96*, edited by G.E. Marindin, 1914.

Norwich, John Julius, and Reresby Sitwell, *Mount Athos*, with photos by the authors and A. Costa, 1966.

Papantoniou, Zacharias, *Hagion Oros* [The Holy Mountain], 1934.

Riley, Athelstan, *Athos, or the Mountain of the Monks*, 1887.

Rycaut, Sir Paul, *The Present State of the Greek and Armenian Churches, Anno Christi 1678*, 1679; reprinted, 1970.

Sandys, George, *A Relation of a Journey begun An. Dom. 1610*, 1615.

Sherrard, Philip, *Athos, the Mountain of Silence*, with photos by Paul du Marchie van Voorthuysen, 1960.

Sherrard, Philip, *Athos: The Holy Mountain*, with photos by Takis Zervoulakos, 1982.

Sibthorp, John, J.E. Smith, and John Lindley, *Flora Graeca*, 10 vols., 1806–1840.

Spencer, Matthew, *Athos*, 2000.

Talbot Rice, David, "The Monasteries of Mount Athos," *Antiquity*, 2/4 (December 1928): 443–451.

Tozer, Henry Fanshawe, *Researches in the Highlands of Turkey*, vol. 1, 1869.

Walpole, Robert (editor), *Memoirs Relating to European and Asiatic Turkey, edited from Manuscript Journals*, 1817.

*See also* **Greece, 1600–1821; Greece, post-1821**

## ATLANTIC OCEAN, EXPLORATIONS ACROSS

Because Noah had only three sons, medieval theologians limited the world to the three continents of Europe, Asia, and Africa. Rejecting as heretical the reports of Plato, Aristotle, and Pliny that intimated a great continent to the west, medieval cartographers influenced by Ptolemaic geography envisioned the Western Ocean as a remnant of the Flood, a vast, morally encoded expanse of water dotted with Blessed Islands, among which might be found the Fortunate Isles of St. Brendan, King Arthur's Avalon, Hy Brasil, and the Seven Cities of Antilla founded by seven Portuguese priests. Adherence to the tripartite vision of the world and Paolo Toscanelli's Arabic measurements of longitude 15 miles per degree too small predisposed the pious Christopher Columbus, achieving landfall in

Hispaniola, to mistake his location by some 8,000 miles and to boast in the *Letter to Santangel* (1493) that the Lord had crowned His ambassador's voyage with success.

By following migrating birds, Columbus located the trade winds and solved the chief logistical problem of transatlantic travel. Maps of the next century indicate trade winds with ships sailing at particular latitudes. To cross the Atlantic to the Caribbean, a vessel had to coast down Spain and Africa to Cape Cantin, course toward the Canaries, and set out due west for Hispaniola. The return trip through the Gulf Stream brought the vessel through the Florida channel up to Virginia and east toward the Azores. To cross to Brazil, a vessel needed to take a southwest course from the Canaries. Because of prevailing currents and winds, however, to get from the Caribbean to Brazil required two transatlantic voyages, north from the Caribbean to Virginia, east to the Azores, south to Africa, and southwest from the Canaries. In 1496, John Cabot drifted lazily toward Newfoundland. The northern route to Virginia was not discovered until 1614.

A clause in the Papal Bull of Partition of 1493 sealed Columbus's religious enthusiasm as a part of the rationale for the *mare clausum*, a principle whereby Spain enjoyed exclusive rights to all territory 100 leagues west of the Cape Verde Islands while Portugal owned all non-Christian territory to the east. The Treaty of Tordesillas (1494) adjusted the boundary between Spanish and Portuguese territory to 370 leagues west (47°32′56″ W) but did nothing to correct the moral geography on which it was founded. Outraged at this theology, in 1526 King Francis I of France asked to see the clause in Adam's will that excluded him from the division of the world. The first century and a half of Atlantic exploration thus unfolds as the collision of two great agendas: conservative Spanish attempts to protect and pursue their papal-derived rights, and the efforts of non-Spanish captains, diplomats, scholars, theologians, and princes to circumvent the mare clausum.

The Treaty of Tordesillas was an imprecise legal document. Confusion about the measurements of longitude allowed Portugal to expand its holdings in Brazil. Convenient misunderstanding of Spanish rights under the Papal Bull allowed Henry VII of England to issue a letters patent to John Cabot and his sons in 1496 to explore the Western Ocean above the latitude of Spain. Precedent allowed several later Atlantic ventures centered around John Cabot's surviving son, Sebastian. Dynastic alliances encouraged the Hapsburg Holy Roman emperor, Charles V, to grant Germans exclusive rights to African slave trading (begun in 1517, altered in 1538) and inland exploration in Venezuela and Paraguay. As consort to Queen Mary of England, Philip II licensed the Englishman John Hawkins to operate as a slave trader. Confusion about mixed crews had permitted Henry VII to commission Anglo-Portuguese voyages, and Flemish, French, and English sailors crewing Spanish vessels to the Indies often found themselves in positions to use their knowledge to undermine Spanish rights in later years.

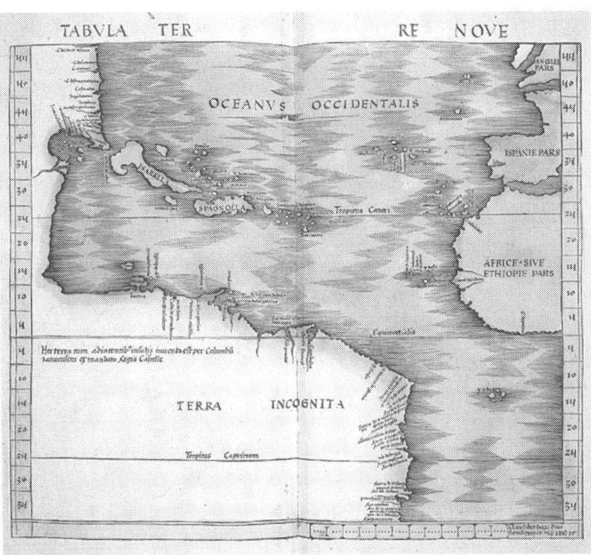


The state of knowledge in 1513 about what lay beyond the Atlantic: the *Tabula Terre Nove* ("Map of the New Land") was one of 20 new maps compiled by Martin Waldseemüller for the 1513 Strasbourg edition of Ptolemy's *Geographia*, published by Jacob Eszler and Georg Uberlin, a book that Nordenskiöld described as the "first modern atlas." *Courtesy of British Library, London.*

Violations of the mare clausum were frequently belligerent. From 1506 until the 1560s, French Huguenot privateers stationed in Florida and on the north coast of Hispaniola preyed on Spanish vessels. From 1577 to 1579, a privateering Francis Drake mapped out the Cape of Good Hope and, attempting to turn back through the Northwest Passage, charted the California coast. The year 1584 saw the Roanoke voyages to establish an English privateering colony that explored Chesapeake Bay. Dutch rebellion from 1568 to 1648 motivated the Dutch to win Brazil, Piet Hein to capture the Plate Fleet in 1628, and the Curteens firm to establish a network of trade routes throughout South America to root out the Iberian presence. In reprisal, the Spanish destroyed the Huguenot settlement in Florida in 1565, resisted the foundation of the Roanoke colony in 1585, attacked the English on Providence Island in 1635, and prepared to recapture Brazil from the Dutch in 1637 to 1638.

Competition for domain stimulated the widespread publication of discoveries, and these, in turn, invigorated the intellectual life of Europe. In 1499, Amerigo

Vespucci pronounced the West Indies a New World. As the eastern profile of the New World began to take shape on maps, scholars pored over classical and medieval materials to show that the ancients had known America as Odysseus's Island of Calypso, Plato's Lost City of Atlantis, a landmass discovered by Carthaginian merchants, Plutarch's Antipodes, Solomon's Ophir, Seneca's land beyond Thule, the Isle of Brasil, Portugal's Antillas, and Brendan's Fortunate Isles. This interest in the past had a political dimension. Winken de Worde's publication of the *Legend of Saint Brendan* (1520), Richard Willes's positioning of the legend of the windswept pilot early in the front matter to the *The Historie of Travayle in the East and West Indies* (1577), and George Peckham's *True Report of Sir Humphrey Gilbert's Voyage* (1584) manufactured a pre-Columbian Christian tradition of British travel to the Americas that the Spanish pope, Alexander VI (1492–1503), had not taken into consideration when bestowing the Western Ocean upon Spain.

Recovered legends propelled explorers onward. In 1512, the Fountain of Youth in the romance *Huon de Bordeaux* motivated Juan Ponce de Leon to sail to Florida and the Bahamas. From 1532 to 1615, the legend of El Dorado motivated four German forays into the interior of South America, four Spanish expeditions down the Amazon or the Orinoco, English reconnoitering around the mouth of the Amazon River in 1609, and Walter Raleigh's two ventures into Guiana in 1595 and 1614. The medieval idea of the West as a set of islands with a waterway to Japan moved Columbus to search out the Caribbean from 1492 to 1503, Balboa to cross the Isthmus of Panama on foot to the Pacific in 1513, and Magellan to chart the southern regions of Patagonia in 1520. To the north, persistently futile searches for a Northwest Passage by John and Sebastian Cabot (1496), Jacques Cartier (1534–1541), Martin Frobisher (1576–1578), Francis Drake (1577–1579), John Davies (1585–1589), George Waymouth (1602), Samuel de Champlain (1604–1615), John Knight (1606), Henry Hudson (1610), Thomas Button (1612), Gibbons (1614), William Baffin (1615), and Christopher Middleton (1742) succeeded in making known the extent of the great inland waterways of Hudson Bay, Baffin Bay, Button's Bay, the Saint Lawrence River, the Great Lakes region, the Hudson River, Chesapeake Bay, and the Atlantic and California coasts of North America.

Cartography made first landfall politically important. In the early eleventh century, the Icelander Lief Erickson landed in Canada; in 1311, the Malian emperor Abubakari may have successfully crossed the Atlantic, and decades before the anonymous windswept *Pilot* ever crossed paths with *Columbus*, Bristol fisherman may have been fishing the Grand Banks. However, no prior explorers had ever charted this territory. In the contentious milieu in which hagiography, old wives' tales, and oral tradition were refuted by maps, the notion of "Atlantic exploration" to mean "the mapping of particular coastlines" was born. The 1560s saw widespread vernacular publication of technical works about charting unfamiliar waters. Geography was in vogue in the universities and the courts of Europe. Spain set up a school for pilots, and Richard Hakluyt and Francis Drake sought to establish a similar school in England, but the Netherlands nurtured Europe's preeminent mapmakers.

As local knowledge, gained illicitly, gave the northern European states a practical advantage in the Americas, the Black Legend of the Spanish conquest helped Englishmen give their colonization the color of right at home. Drake organized the Cimarrones to attack the Spanish colonizers in 1572; Raleigh wooed Guiana in 1595; John Smith seduced Pocahontas, and Plimouth Plantation sat at table with the native Americans. Spain interpreted challenges to the moral authority of its empire as a challenge to papal authority, and the Inquisition was a powerful arm of Spanish imperial power. The first heretics subjected to an auto-da-fé in the New World were members of John Hawkins's crew captured in the ambush at San Juan de Ulúa in 1568, the incident that persuaded Elizabeth I to grant Francis Drake his letters of marque to attack Spanish vessels in his circumnavigation of the globe from 1577 to 1579.

The Inquisition had reason to be upset. To justify their violations of the mare clausum, northern European Protestants adopted Columbus's claims of divine assistance to articulate a doctrine of particular discovery. Particular discovery not only denied the exclusivity of the Spanish claim, it challenged fundamentally the pope's power to hold bound in heaven what he declared bound on earth, the foundational principle that entitled the papacy to preside over the division of the world.

As event interpretation on the ocean became an important subject in Protestant colonial discourse, Columbus became an international hero and Peter Martyr a theologian of stature. Before 1620, English advocates of New World colonization Richard Eden (1555), Richard Willes (1576), Richard Hakluyt (1587), and Michael Lok (1612) appended English accounts of travels across the ocean to newly focused editions of Peter Martyr de Angleria's *De orbe novo*. Published under slightly different titles, the volumes allowed their readers to imagine that God would assist English ambassadors to the New World as he had assisted Columbus.

As Protestant sailors navigating to the west employed event interpretation on the ocean to defy papal authority, Protestant preachers in England, France, Switzerland, and the Netherlands focused on scriptural texts that showed the ocean as a site of God's judgment. English sermons imagined Elizabethan and Jacobean Englishmen as new Israelites crossing the Red Sea. Anti-Catholic sermons on Jonah and Christ's miracles at sea abounded in England, France, Switzerland, and the Netherlands during the Reformation. In 1588, Protestant Europe was united in celebrating the defeat of the Spanish armada by storm at sea as the Divine Hand admonishing Philip II and the pope for persecuting Protestants.

By 1615, international theologizing of the ocean had culminated in the idea of the mare liberum, the principle of the liberty of the seas grounded in the contemplation of the Atlantic's essential nature. In 1609, the Dutch Hugo Grotius rationalized that just as the air and water were free and could not be possessed, so too the ocean was free. William Camden placed similar reasoning in the mouth of Elizabeth in his *Annales* (1615) of her reign. Samuel Purchas in *Hakluytus Posthumus* (1625) interpreted the motions of the winds as evidence that God wanted the oceans free. Giovanni Botero's *Observations on the Sea* (1635) declared that smaller waterways were useful for traffic while the Great Ocean was useful chiefly for the contemplation of God's nature.

J.P. CONLAN

## References and Further Reading


Andrews, Kenneth R. (editor), *English Privateering Voyages to the West Indies, 1588–1595*, 1959.

Asher, G.M. (editor), *Henry Hudson, the Navigator: The Original Documents in Which His Career Is Recorded*, 1860.

Barbour, Philip L. (editor), *The Jamestown Voyages under the First Charter, 1606–1609*, 2 vols., 1969.

Barr, William, and Glynawr Williams (editors), *Voyages to Hudson Bay in Search of a Northwest Passage, 1741–1747*, vol. 2: *The Voyage of William Moor and Francis Smith*, 1955.

Benzoni, Girolamo, *History of the New World, Shewing His Travels in America from AD 1541 to 1556*, translated and edited by W.H. Smyth, 1857; reprinted, 1970.

Burrage, Henry S. (editor), *Early English and French Voyages, Chiefly from Hakluyt, 1534–1608*, 1906.

Carvajal, Gaspar de, et al., *The Discovery of the Amazon According to the Account of Friar Gaspar de Carvajal and Other Documents*, edited by José Toribio Medina, translated by Bertram T. Lee, edited by H.C. Heaton, 1934.

Champlain, Samuel de, *Voyages of Samuel de Champlain, 1604–1618*, edited by W.L. Grant, 1907; reprinted, 1959.

Churchyard, Thomas, "A Matter Touching the Iourney of Sir Humphrey Gilbarte, Knight," in his *A Discourse of the Queenes Maiesties Entertainement in Suffolk and Norfolk*, 1578.

Cieza de León, Pedro, *The War of Las Salinas*, translated and edited by Clements Markham, 1923.

Coats, William, *The Geography of Hudson's Bay, Being the Remarks of Captain W. Coats in Many Voyages to That Locality, between the Years 1727 and 1751*, edited by John Barrow, 1852.

Columbus, Christopher, *The Four Voyages of Christopher Columbus*, edited and translated by J.M. Cohen, 1969.

*The Discovery and Conquest of Terra Florida by Don Ferdinando de Soto*, translated by Richard Hakluyt, 1611; edited by William B. Rye, 1851.

Dominguez, Luis L. (editor and translator), *The Conquest of the River Plate, 1535–1555*, 1891; reprinted, 1964.

Ellis, Thomas, *A True Report of the Third and Last Voyage into Meta Incognita: Achieved by the Worthie Capteine, M. Martine Frobisher, Esquire*, 1578.

Hakluyt, Richard, *Divers Voyages Touching the Discoverie of America, and the Ilands Adiacent unto the Same, Made First of All by Our Englishmen, and Afterward by the Frenchmen and Britons*, 1582; facsimile, 1967.

Hakluyt, Richard, *The Principall Navigations, Voiages and Discoveries of the English Nation*, 1589; facsimile, introduction by David B. Quinn and R.A. Skelton, 2 vols., 1965.

Jameson, J. Franklin (editor), *Narratives of New Netherland, 1609–1664*, 1909; reprinted, 1959.

Jane, Cecil (translator and editor), *Select Documents Illustrating the Four Voyages of Columbus*, 2 vols., 1930–1933; as *The Four Voyages of Columbus*, 1988.

Las Casas, Bartholomé de, *The Spanish Colonie*, translated by M.M.S., 1583; facsimile, 1977.

López de Gómara, Francisco, *Historia general de las Indias* [General History of the Indies, 1556], modernized by Pilar Guibelalde, 2 vols., 1965; part 2 as *The Pleasant Historie of the Conquest of the Weast India*, translated by Thomas Nicholas, 1578.

Lorimer, Joyce (editor), *English and Irish Settlement on the River Amazon, 1550–1646*, 1989.

Münster, Sebastian, *A Treatise of the Newe India*, translated by Richard Eden, 1553.

Nuttall, Zelia (translator and editor), *New Light on Drake: A Collection of Documents Relating to His Voyage of Circumnavigation, 1577–1580*, 1914.

Olson, Julius E, and Edward Gaylord Bourne (editors), *The Northmen, Columbus and Cabot, 985–1503*, 1906; reprinted, 1959.

Peckham, Sir George, *A True Reporte of the Late Discoveries and Possession Taken in the Right of the Crowne of Englande, of the Newfound Landes: By That Valiaunt and Worthye Gentleman Sir Humfrey Gilbert, Knight*, 1583.

Peter Martyr, *De orbe novo decades*, 1516, enlarged edition, edited by Antonio de Lebrija, 1530, facsimile, in his *Opera*, 1966; parts 1–3, with other material, as *The Decades of the Newe World or West India*, translated by Richard Eden, 1555, as *The History of Travayle in the East and West Indies*, revised by Richard Willes, 1577; complete, as *De orbe novo Petri Martyris Anglierii . . . decades octo*, translated by Richard Hakluyt, 1587; as *De Novo Orbe; or, The Historie of the West Indies*, translated by Richard Eden and Michael Lok, 1612.

Purchas, Samuel, *Purchas His Pilgrimes*, 4 vols., 1625; as *Hakluytus Posthumus; or, Purchas His Pilgrimes*, 20 vols., 1905–1907.

Quinn, David B. (editor), *The Voyages and Colonising Enterprises of Sir Humphrey Gilbert*, 2 vols., 1940.

Quinn, David B. (editor), *The Roanoke Voyages, 1584–1590*, 2 vols., 1952–1955.

Quinn, David B., and Alison M. Quinn (editors), *The English New England Voyages, 1602–1608*, 1983.

Rundall, Thomas (editor), *Narratives of Voyages towards the North-West, in Search of a Passage to Cathay and India*, 1849; reprinted, 1964.

Sarmiento de Gamboa, Pedro, *Narratives of the Voyages of Pedro Sarmiento Gamboa to the Straits of Magellan*, translated and edited by Clements R. Markham, 1895; reprinted, 1970.

Settle, Dionyse, *A True Reporte of the Laste Voyage into the West and Northwest Regions, &c., 1577, Worthily Atchieved by Capteine Frobisher*, 1577; facsimile, 1969.

Simón, Pedro, *The Expedition of Pedro de Ursua and Lope de Aguirre in Search of El Dorado and Omagua in 1560–61*, translated by William Bollaert, introduction by Clements R. Markham, 1861; reprinted, 1971.

Strachey, William, *The Historie of Travell into Virginia Britania (1612)*, edited by Louis B. Wright and Virginia Freund, 1953.

Williamson, James A. (editor), *The Voyages of the Cabots and the English Discovery of North America under Henry VII and Henry VIII*, 1929.

Zárate, Agustín de, *The Strange and Delectable History of the Discoverie and Conquest of the Provinces of Peru*, translated by Thomas Nicholas, 1581.

## ATLANTIC OCEAN, MIDDLE PASSAGE

Although trading in slaves dates back to ancient times and is chronicled in all known cultures, the slave trade that endured from the fifteenth to the nineteenth century under the auspices of the European maritime powers was marked by its expressly racial character and the particular nature of the westward transatlantic crossing, known as the Middle Passage. This was the second leg of a round-trip transatlantic voyage to and from the Americas that is popularly referred to as the triangular trade.

This trade was marked by an interchange of ships, goods, and human chattels that ostensibly began in a European port with ships transporting items of domestic European as well as imported Asian manufacture to be traded on the western coasts of Africa for slaves, who were then exchanged in the Caribbean and the Americas for local, colonial goods to fill the ships' hulls for the return voyage eastward across the Atlantic to the home port. According to this neat, geometric model of commercial activity, a single ship made all three legs of the voyage, thereby maximizing the profits of the European investors. Current research is revisionary, however, estimating that this model is oversimplified and economically untenable. The picture of the Atlantic slave trade emerging from recent scholarship is one of specialized ships and crews maintaining their respective legs of the trade route, with the "slavers," as the ships specializing in human cargo were called, becoming particularly noted for the crucial role they played in what has proved to be one of the greatest, though forced, migrations known to human history. Estimates of the number of slaves to make these 21- to 90-day transoceanic voyages vary, with figures ranging from the significant to those approaching holocaust proportions. Though the exact numbers may finally prove definitively incalculable, scholars currently approximate that 11 to 20 million Africans were forced to migrate to the Americas over a period of more than 400 years.

The slaves for this New World trade were purchased on the African Atlantic coast, with trading ports established on major waterways, from the Senegal River down to the Niger River on the Gulf of Guinea. The Portuguese exploration of the coast in the fifteenth century opened up a previously unexploited sea route for an exchange of goods and slaves with the African populations. Extensive land-based routes had existed on the continent and throughout the Mediterranean for centuries, but with their entry into extant African markets the Portuguese provided a speedy and sometimes more economical water route for goods desired in West Africa from the north of the continent and from Asia, Europe, and the Mediterranean. Most of the goods required by the coastal and interior African peoples were already being brought in by these overland routes before the arrival of the European. The European's influence did not have to do with the introduction to Africa of exotic or unusual goods from afar, as is frequently reported, but had more to do with the increased availability and volume of familiar merchandise. The coming of the European affected the expansion of the contemporary market for slaves by influencing the growth of western African markets overall and, ultimately, their direction.

One of the key issues that has set this particular slave trade apart in the annals of recent history is the appalling conditions of the voyages. On the heels of the initial Portuguese trade, sailing ships from Great Britain, France, and the Netherlands cruised the Guinea Coast of Africa for up to a year bartering, purchasing, gathering, and sometimes kidnapping Africans until they had reached a cargo ranging from 100 to 600 persons. Once under way, disease, mutiny, piracy, and violent weather conditions could hinder the progress of a ship and, therefore, any potential profits. In order to maximize profit, it was essential to embark with the maximum cargo and to minimize onboard rebellion.

So that the largest possible consignment of slaves might be stowed, the captives were wedged in horizontal rows of low-lying platforms that were stacked in tiers in the cargo holds. This arrangement allowed for a maximum of 6 feet by 16 inches of individual room per slave. They were unable to stand, stretch out, or even to roll themselves over. Oppressive heat, noxious fumes, and the general unventilated and unsanitary conditions caused diseases to spread rapidly, with the dead laying side by side with the living for days before being removed and unceremoniously dumped overboard. Sailors' lore has it that schools of sharks followed these slavers at sea as a result of the frequency and regularity of these expedient burials. For food the slaves were given rations twice a day, consisting most frequently of boiled rice, maize, or stewed yams. But if there were shortages on board, often occasioned by an unforeseen extension of the voyage, the already meager slave rations were cut before those of the sailors, further contributing to the spread of illness. The ship's company would resort to "dancing the slaves," forcing shackled African men to jump up and down in a macabre performance as a way to preserve their health. During this time, if a captain was particularly diligent about the safe arrival of the majority of his cargo, he would have the slave holds washed down by the crew. When these measures were not possible, the slaves were held in the hold in their oppressive conditions. It was this cold commodification of the enslaved, along with the ravaging conditions of the voyages and the high mortality rates during the crossing, that are the marked characteristics of this traffic across the Atlantic to the so-called new world.

STEPHANIE SMITH

### References and Further Reading


Barbot, Jean, "A Description of the Coasts of North and South Guinea," in *A Collection of Voyages and Travels*, edited by Awnsham Churchill and John Churchill, vol. 5, 1732; corrected edition as *The Writings of Jean Barbot on West Africa 1678–1712*, 2 vols., edited by P.E.H. Hair, 1992.

Equiano, Olaudah, *The Interesting Narrative of the Life of Olaudah Equiano; or, Gustavus Vassa, the African*, 2 vols., 1789; edited by Werner Sollors, 2001.

Falconbridge, Alexander, *An Account of the Slave Trade on the Coast of Africa*, 1788; reprinted, 1973.


*See also* **Slave Narratives**

## AUSTRALIA

In the seventeenth century, as European empires were extending beyond the previously known world, the concept of *terra australis* began to emerge as a reality. With the development of travel and exploration literature as a genre, speculation on the existence of such a landmass, fueled by occasional sightings, was replaced by the scientific and geographic obsession of its British occupiers and of other European maritime powers, accompanied by sociological interest in its occupants—both indigenous and newly arrived—and the workings of their societies. Innumerable books and articles based on individual travel experiences in Australia have been published in Europe, North America, and Australia, most of them in the nineteenth century.

Since classical times, there had been speculation on the existence of a great southern landmass. By the sixteenth century, Spain was already sending expeditions to seek this land, which Fernando Quiros in the early seventeenth century imagined abounded "with gold, silver, pearls, nutmegs, mace, ginger, and sugarcanes of an extraordinary size" (quoted in John Campbell's *Navigantium atque Itinerantium Bibliotheca*, 1744–1748). As a consequence of seventeenth-century Dutch maritime exploration, largely motivated by the desire to profit from such riches, much of Australia's northern, western, and southern coasts were charted, and the land was named New Holland to distinguish it from *terra australis incognita*, the elusive great southern continent. By the end of the 1670s, several accounts of Abel Janszoon Tasman's voyage to New Holland 40 years before had been published and translated into other languages. Early English descriptions of Australia include those of William Dampier, first in *A New Voyage round the World* (1697), and later in *A Voyage to New Holland* (1703, 1709), which described, though not always in flattering terms, the coastal appearance of western Australia, its Aboriginal inhabitants, and flora and fauna. (For more on the literature of these European voyages, see Williams and Frost, 1988.)

Watering party under attack at Goulburn Island, off the Arnhem Land coast (from Philip Parker King's *Narrative of a Survey of the Intertropical and Western Coasts of Australia*, 1827). *Courtesy of the Travellers Club, London; Bridgeman Art Library, agent.*

By the second half of the eighteenth century, with improved navigational techniques and new measuring instruments, both the French and the English separately set out to claim the South Pacific. The pursuit of science was a major aspect of late-eighteenth- and early-nineteenth-century voyages to Australia and the South Pacific. Bernard Smith has argued in *European Vision in the South Pacific* (1989) that by the late eighteenth century the around-the-world voyage was seen as especially suitable for young gentlemen serious about travel as a means of extending their scientific knowledge, and as an alternative to what some saw as the frivolous nature of the European Grand Tour. A young Joseph Banks accompanied James Cook, captain of *Endeavour*, on an expedition that observed the transit of Venus in Tahiti, and charted the east coast of Australia, stopping off to collect specimens and make acquaintance with the country and its inhabitants. Banks's detailed journal was published posthumously (though parts were included, along with excerpts from Cook's journals, in John Hawkesworth, 1773). It had been an important reference tool in his library, which developed as a center of scientific activity where he maintained a collection of specimens and illustrations from both his own and others' travels. Reports of *Endeavour*'s journey, Cook's accurate charting of Australia's east coast, the claiming (and naming) of New South Wales as a British colony, the anthropological interest in its native inhabitants, and the scientific interest aroused by the novelty of its fauna and flora—all helped contribute to an increasingly informed European view of Australia.

Banks was to become president of the Royal Society, and was instrumental in sending the expedition led by Arthur Phillip to begin the colonization of Australia at Sydney Cove in 1788. Although a primary purpose of this 1788 expedition was to establish a penal colony to relieve England's overcrowded jails, scientific interest continued, particularly now that England was extending and consolidating its empire. Travel and exploration were essential to this extension and consolidation. France's foothold in the South Pacific meant that there was some urgency to chart Australia's coastline—and find out what was there—not only to thwart French land claims, but also to establish British scientific superiority in a competitive, scientific Europe. Artists, naturalists, and scientifically inclined gentlemen accompanied voyages to record scientific detail. Weather patterns, seasonal changes, and life on board ship were noted, landscape features sketched and described, encounters with local Aborigines recorded, botanical and zoological specimens collected. So much detail was expected that some devised new means of recording it. Ferdinand Bauer, the artist on board Matthew Flinders's *Investigator*, did quick sketches of plants and animals, but marked each into segments in a number code corresponding to one of over 1,000 colors and their shades, so providing the means of later producing accurate color illustrations. Some of his exquisite colored plates were published in Matthew Flinders's *A Voyage to Terra Australis* (1814).

As well as challenging much conventional European knowledge, observations from colonial travels intrigued a public eager to find out more about the New World. On their return to Europe, artists might exhibit works produced on their Australian travels, or publish them as colored plates with brief descriptions of their subject matter, as did Joseph Lycett (1824), George French Angas (1847), and Eugen von Guerard (1867). Travel writing as a genre was well established in Europe by the late eighteenth century and was rich in Australian travel experiences; the same market that consumed works by Mary Shelley could also be interested in the books by Watkin Tench (1789 and 1793) and David Collins (1798).

Land exploration of New South Wales (named by the British) began almost as soon as the colonists arrived in 1788, and also aroused publishing interest. "Explorers' journals," as the writings became known, used a conventional day-by-day approach, but instead of descriptions of ancient monuments or lengthy discussions of local customs and manners to engage the reader's interest, these highlighted danger and a novel environment. Accounts covered such subjects as concern about dwindling water supplies, explorers surrounded by raging bush fires, as well as descriptions of (initially friendly) encounters with Aborigines, new species of flora and fauna, and the physical demands of making one's way through the bush. Explorers' journals continued to be a popular genre for much of the nineteenth century with the publication of those of John Oxley (1820), Ludwig Leichhardt (1847), and Ernest Giles (1875), among many others.

Although European women were generally not members of government-sponsored exploration parties, three "ladies" accompanied the explorer Charles Sturt on an expedition to survey land in South Australia. George Gawler, the governor of South Australia, hoped that favorable publicity surrounding the safe return of these ladies (one of whom was his own daughter) might persuade prospective European residents to settle in these districts. Charles Sturt's journals of the expedition were published in a South Australian newspaper (*The Register*, 4 January 1840), and some years later Eliza Davies, one of the "lady travelers," published an account in her autobiography (1881).

In a discussion of European literature on travel and exploration, it is easy to overlook Australian Aborigines except as objects of interest and fascination. There are no published travel accounts by Aborigines as we understand the genre. But Aborigines did on occasion interact with European explorers, and they are incorporated into some stories, assuming the status of dreaming figures. Many Aboriginal communities have stories of Captain Cook in which he "come from Big England" bringing the disastrous changes to Aboriginal life (Rose, 1989; Kolig, 1979).

As scenery was becoming a feature of much travel writing about Europe, so it was in accounts of Australia. In the early nineteenth century, Van Diemen's Land (later Tasmania) fit well into the new convention of the picturesque, its rivers winding through undulating hills, past occasional cottages with smoke curling out of chimneys (it was colder in the southernmost colony). Where scenery didn't fit the conventionally picturesque—there were no ivy-clad castle ruins and few shepherds—new conventions were established. The inlets of Sydney Harbour, with ancient rocks and gentle beaches surrounded by luxuriant growth, often with boats bobbing in a watery background, lasted long as an Australian idyll. Notions of the sublime provided another difference: snow-covered craggy mountain peaks came to represent the sublime in Europe, but the Australian version had craggy cliffs plunging into a vast sea of trees, which is how Charles Darwin described the Blue Mountains on his visit to New South Wales in 1836.

From the 1830s on, more and more books about Australian travel experiences were published, most in England, but some in Europe (especially France, perhaps because of the French outposts in the Pacific). Substantial accounts of Australia were included in larger world travel narratives. Books by George Bennett (1834) and James Holman (1834–1835), and the second volume of Marianne North's *Recollections* (1892), are good examples. There were also German, Italian, even Gaelic travel accounts. An official effort to encourage immigration meant that from this time Australian travel accounts might include appendices with practical information—the cost of living in different colonies, employment prospects—to help prospective immigrants. The gold rushes of the 1850s, with many prospectors from around the world trying their luck in the Australian goldfields, gave added impetus to the publication of books about Australia. Travel accounts of Australia continued to flourish throughout the nineteenth century and into the twentieth.

Travel to the colonies, either directly or as part of an around-the-world trip, provided useful professional experience for many men and some women. Artists, botanists, and those who were generally interested in natural history or social institutions had much to observe in the colonies. Perhaps the most famous of these is Charles Darwin, who visited Australia in 1836 as part of *Beagle*'s world voyage. Many travelers published accounts of their Australian experiences, including Anthony Trollope (1873) and Mark Twain (1897). Most of these accounts followed the general pattern of describing the nature of the culture and society of Australia's population (including Aborigines), natural history, and the political and economic dimensions of Antipodean society. Initially, there was much interest in the possibilities of a largely convict and military society. Later observers, including James Froude (1886), wrote with interest of the emerging democratic institutions of the colonies, as well as of local initiatives in, among other things, care of the underprivileged. The work of Rosamond and Florence Hill (1875) is another good example.

Travel in the colonies was not easy; rail networks did not extend across the colonies until the latter part of the nineteenth century. Before this time, the fastest travel was by steamboat along the coast or via the larger rivers. But much of the colonies was accessible only by coach and horse, usually along badly rutted roads. Frequent delays, inadequate transport, and unpredictable changes in travel plans, along with the possibility of danger to life and limb, delayed the development of mass tourism in most parts of the colonies until the 1890s. Prior to that, travel as a leisure activity was largely confined to the upper middle classes.

But travel wasn't the preserve only of gentlemen. As in other parts of the world, "lady travelers" frequented the colonies and wrote of their Australian travels, producing a significant number of published accounts. One of the first was a slim book by Mary Ann Parker published in 1795. As well as providing noteworthy accounts of Australian scenery, customs, manners, and social institutions, "feminine" interests provided another perspective, notably in botany with the pursuit of dainty flowers and ferns. Much of Louisa Atkinson's pioneering work on Australian ferns was published in local newspapers and journals as entertaining travel accounts intermixed with botanical details. (For a listing, see Clarke, 1990.) Other interesting examples of Australian travel literature in the nineteenth century by women include the works by Louisa Meredith (1861), Ellen Clacy (1853), and Mrs. Alan MacPherson (1860). Accounts of customs and manners, both of locals and of fellow travelers, almost always saw class and gender as important, particularly regarding the ways in which social status was maintained, and the local requirements for being a "lady." Some accounts discussed female employment and Aboriginal society; many included observations about the role of women. Substantial lists of nineteenth-century women's travel writing about Australia are provided by Debra Adelaide (1991) and Julia Horne (1995).

Most early-nineteenth-century travel accounts were published in England, and imported to Australia for a small, eager readership. Although they were not always written for locals, they did become a means of local self-definition. There emerged in Australia an increasing interest, even pride, in natural wonders and unusual phenomena, as well as in emerging social and political institutions. From the middle of the nineteenth-century, travel accounts about Australia were written not only for a market extending across the British empire, but also for a specifically local audience; some were published in colonial newspapers and periodicals. To celebrate Australia's centenary of British colonization, two substantial publications were produced presenting detailed travel description of the colonies—Garran (c. 1886–1887) and Morris (1889–

1890). Australian travel, then, was no longer primarily an imperial activity, one in which the outcomes of observations were determined elsewhere, but also had local uses, especially in helping to educate Australians about Australia and raising local scientific awareness.

Travel accounts published in Australia urged residents to undertake tours so that they might see for themselves the local natural and social phenomena, the geological curiosities of underground caves, the magnificence of tree-ferns, the bountiful colors of delicate wildflowers, prominent public institutions in major towns and cities, poor areas, rich areas, Aboriginal communities, town life, country life. In these accounts, Australia was a place where nature, the picturesque, and the sublime might be studied, as might the workings of a modern society, its democratic principles, the outcomes of public welfare, its cultural interests, and commercial enterprises. And the occasional unexpected adventure helped the story along.

In the first half of the twentieth century, this type of travel writing continued to be published for an Australian audience not only in newspapers and magazines but also as books by a growing local publishing industry. William Hatfield's *Australia through the Windscreen* (1936), Ernestine Hill's *The Great Australian Loneliness* (1937), and numerous titles by Frank Clune described the remote parts of Australia to readers in the coastal cities. Working within a genre that had been well established since the nineteenth century, they offered scientific explanations for unusual natural phenomena and social commentary as well as for the odd adventure. Travel magazines such as *Walkabout* were also bringing Australia to Australians in pictures as well as words.

In the 1950s, travel writing for a local audience began to decline, partly because tourism was by then well established and there was less reason for entrepreneurs to promote independent travel. Whereas travelers' tales were once an important way of conveying information about a place (and travel was the means to collect it), that role was now performed by historians, sociologists, political scientists, and other experts. The sense of wonder and adventure, elements central to travel writing, translated so well to the screen that Australian television travelers like Bill Peach, Robert Raymond, and the Leyland brothers had soon supplanted the traveler who relied on words alone. Internationally, however, travel writing about Australia has survived in works by Bruce Chatwin, Jan Morris, and others, though there is much less of it today than there was a century ago.

Julia Horne

## References and Further Reading


Ackermann, Jessie, *Australia from a Woman's Point of View*, 1913; facsimile, 1981.

Adelaide, Debra, *Biography of Australian Women's Literature, 1795–1990*, Port Melbourne: Thorpe–National Centre of Australian Studies, 1991.

Bennett, George, *Wanderings in New South Wales, Batavia, Pedir Coast, Singapore, and China, Being the Journal of a Naturalist in Those Countries, during 1832, 1833 and 1834*, 1834.

Chatwin, Bruce, *The Songlines*, 1987.

Clacy, Ellen, *A Lady's Visit to the Gold-Diggings of Australia in 1852–53*, 1853.

Clarke, Patricia, *Pioneer Writer: The Life of Louise Atkinson Novelist, Journalist, Naturalist*, Sydney and Boston: Allen and Unwin, 1990.

Clune, Frank, *Land of Australia: "Roaming in a Holden,"* 1953.

Collins, David, *An Account of the English Colony in New South Wales with Remarks on the Dispositions, Customs, Manners etc., of the Native Inhabitants of That Country*, 1798; foreword by Brian Fletcher, 1975.

Cook, Samuel, *The Jenolan Caves: An Excursion in Australian Wonderland*, 1889.

Cunningham, Peter, *Two Years in New South Wales*, 1827; edited by David S. MacMillan, 1966.

Dampier, William, *A New Voyage round the World*, 1697.

Dampier, William, *A Voyage to New Holland &c. in the Year 1699*, part 1, 1703, part 2, 1709; edited by James Spencer, 1981.

Darwin, Charles, *Journal of Researches into the Geology and Natural History of the Various Countries Visited by HMS Beagle under the Command of Captain Fitzroy, RN from 1832 to 1836*, 1839.

Darwin, Charles, *The Beagle Record: Selections from the Original Pictorial Records and Written Accounts of the Voyage of HMS Beagle*, edited by Richard Darwin Keynes, 1979.

Davies, Eliza, *The Story of an Earnest Life: A Woman's Adventures in Australia and in Two Voyages around the World*, 1881.

Dilke, Charles, *Greater Britain: Charles Dilke Visits Her New Lands, 1866 & 1867*, 1868; edited and abridged by Geoffrey Blainey, 1985.

Dixon, James, *Narrative of a Voyage to New South Wales and Van Diemen's Land in the Ship Skelton during the Year 1820 with Observations on the State of These Colonies, and a Variety of Information Calculated to Be Useful to Emigrants*, 1822.

Eisler, William, *The Furthest Shore: Images of Terra Australis from the Middle Ages to Captain Cook*, 1995.

Eisler, William, and Bernard Smith, *Terra Australis: The Furthest Shore*, 1988.

Field, Barron (editor), *Geographical Memoirs on New South Wales*, 1825.

Fitzpatrick, Kathleen (editor), *Australian Explorers: A Selection from Their Writings*, 1958.

Flinders, Mathew, *A Voyage to Terra Australis: Undertaken for the Purpose of Completing the Discovery of That Vast Country, and Prosecuted in the Years 1801, 1802, and 1803 . . .*, 2 vols. and atlas, 1814.

Froude, J.A., *Oceana: The Tempestuous Voyage of J.A. Froude, 1884 & 1885*, 1886; edited and abridged by Geoffrey Blainey, 1985.

Garran, Andrew (editor), *Picturesque Atlas of Australasia*, c. 1886–1887.

Gerstaecker, F., *Narrative of a Journey round the World Comprising a Winter Passage across the Andes to Chili, with a Visit to the Gold Regions of California and Australia, the South Sea Islands, Java, &c.*, 1853.

Giles, Ernest, *Geographic Travels in Central Australia from 1872 to 1874*, 1875.
Hall, Mary, *A Woman in the Antipodes and in the Far East*, 1914.
Hatfield, William, *Australia through the Windscreen*, 1936.
Hawkesworth, John, *An Account of the Voyages Undertaken by the Order of His Present Majesty for Making Discoveries in the South Hemisphere*, 1773.
Hill, Ernestine, *The Great Australian Loneliness*, 1937; as *Australian Frontier*, 1942.
Hill, Rosamond, and Florence Hill, *What We Saw in Australia*, 1875.
Hingston, J. (editor), *Guide for Excursionist from Melbourne*, 1868.
Holman, James, *A Voyage round the World, Including Travels in Africa, Asia, Australasia, America, etc. etc. from 1827 to 1832*, 1834–1835.
Horne, Julia, "Favourite Resorts: Aspects of Tourist Travel in Nineteenth-Century New South Wales" (dissertation), Sydney: University of New South Wales, 1995.
Inglis, James, *Our Australian Cousins*, 1880.
King, Philip Parker, *Narrative of a Survey of the Intertropical and Western Coasts of Australia Performed between the Years 1818 and 1822*, 1827.
Kolig, Erich, "Captain Cook in the Western Kimberley," in *Aborigines of the West: Their Past and Their Present*, edited by Ronald M. Berndt and Catherine H. Berndt, Nedlands: University of Western Australia Press, 1979.
Leichhardt, Ludwig, *Journal of an Overland Expedition in Australia . . . during the Years 1844–45*, 1847.
Lorck, Walter (editor), *New South Wales Picturesque Resorts Convenient to Railways: An Illustrated Guide to Some of the Principal Towns and Districts in New South Wales*, 1907.
Lycett, Joseph, *Views in Australia*, 1824.
Mackaness, George (editor), *Fourteen Journeys over the Blue Mountains of New South Wales, 1813–1841*, 1965.
Maclehose, James, *Picture of Sydney and Strangers' Guide in New South Wales for 1839*, 1839; facsimile, 1977.
MacPherson, Mrs. A., *My Experiences in Australia, Being Recollections of a Visit to the Australian Colonies in 1856–57*, 1860.
Macquarie, Lachlan, *Journals of His Tours in New South Wales and Van Diemen's Land, 1810–1822*, 1956.
Mann, D.D., *The Present Picture of New South Wales 1811*, 1811; reprinted, 1979.
Meredith, Louisa, *Notes and Sketches of New South Wales during a Residence in That Colony from 1839 to 1844*, 1846.
Meredith, Louisa, *Over the Straits: A Visit to Victoria*, 1861.
Millar, Ann (editor), *I See No End to Travelling: Journals of Australian Explorers, 1813–76*, 1986.
Morris, Edward Ellis, *Cassell's Picturesque Australasia*, 1889–1890.
Morris, Jan, *Sydney*, 1992.
North, Marianne, *Recollections of a Happy Life, Being the Autobiography of Marianne North*, 1892.
Oxley, John, *Journals of Two Expeditions into the Interior of New South Wales Undertaken by Order of the British Government, 1817–1818*, 1820.
Parker, Mary Ann, *A Voyage round the World*, 1795; facsimile, 1991.
Pesman, Roslyn Cooper, "Some Italian Views of Australia in the Nineteenth Century," *Journal of the Royal Australian Historical Society*, 70/3 (1984): 171–193.
Rose, Deborah Bird, "Remembrance," *Aboriginal History*, 13/1–13/2 (1989): 135–147.
Strzelecki, P.E. de, *Physical Description of New South Wales and Van Diemen's Land*, 1845; facsimile, 1967.
Tench, Watkin, *Narrative of the Expedition to Botany Bay*, 1789.
Tench, Watkin, *A Complete Account of the Settlement at Port Jackson*, 1793.
Trollope, Anthony, *Australia*, 1873; foreword by P.D. Edwards and R.B. Joyce, 1967.
Twain, Mark, *Following the Equator*, 1897; reprinted in part as *Mark Twain in Australia and New Zealand*, 1973.
Verschuur, G., *At the Antipodes: Travels in Australia, New Zealand, Fiji Islands, the New Hebrides, New Caledonia, and South America 1888–89*, translated by Mary Daniels, 1891.
von Guerard, Eugen, *Eugen von Guerard's Australian Landscapes*, 1867; facsimile, 1975.
Wilke, Charles, *Narrative of the United States Exploring Expedition during the Years 1838, 1839, 1840, 1841, 1842*, 1845.
Williams, Glyndwr, and Alan Frost (editors), *Terra Australis to Australia*, Melbourne: Oxford University Press, 1988.
Wood, G.A., "Explorations under Governor Phillip," *Journal of the Royal Australian Historical Society*, 12/1: 1–25.

## AL-AYYASHI (1628–1679) *Moroccan Sufi and Traveler*

An indefatigable traveler, a Sufi, a scholar, a biographer, and a poet, Abu Salim Abd Allah bin Mohammad al-Ayyashi left a detailed account of his journey between 1661 and 1663 from his native Tafilat in Morocco to Cairo, Mecca, and Medina, across the Sinai desert to Jerusalem, and then down the Palestinian coast to Cairo again, and back to Morocco through the Sahara route. The title that he gave to his account was *Ma' al-Mawaid*, but when it was published, in 1899, the title was expanded to *Rihlat al-Shaykh al-Imam Abi Salim al-Ayyashi* [The Journey of the Sheikh and Imam, Abu Salim al-Ayyashi].

Ayyashi's account is the finest example of the *rihla* (travel) genre of literature that appeared in Maghrebi writing. There were numerous types of *rihla* writing in early modern Arabic—the journey for learning, for travel, for discovery, and for pilgrimage—all of which were amalgamated in Ayyashi's account. He wrote not just a description of a pilgrimage to the holy sites in Hijaz and Palestine, but of peoples, ideas, landscapes, personal encounters and friendships, dangers, foods, and customs. Despite the numerous interpolations of poems of praise, prayers, lengthy invocations, and rhythmic prose, Ayyashi's account presents a detailed description of the Maghreb and the Mashriq in the second half of the seventeenth century and the difficult conditions with which travelers had to contend.

Maghrebi pilgrims and travelers predominantly used the sea route to Alexandria and from there to Cairo and the Hijaz, despite the danger of attack by Spanish, Sicilian, and Maltese pirates. Ayyashi, however, took the land route and provided one of the rare descriptions of the hinterlands of North Africa. He joined a caravan in Sijilmassa in central Morocco and traveled southeast toward Wadi Sawra in Algeria before turning north into Wadi Souf and then continuing via Tunis and Libya to Cairo. The journey was fraught with danger as travelers sometimes passed through arid terrain "with no [fire]wood, food, or drink, where the wind was so cold it came from hell"; at other times, they encountered robbers, though in all his *rihla*, Ayyashi was fortunate never to fall victim to them. Ayyashi described the foods and moneys he used, and the preachers and jurists he met; he also noted the water springs, the oases, the valleys, and the region's inhabitants, both urban and Bedouin. Indirectly, he showed how little the Ottoman rule extended into those southern regions of the North African regencies: while in Sakra, the Turks had defeated the Bedouin and built a fort; elsewhere, the Bedouin had kept the Turks away from them. Ayyashi also wrote down the curious and the coincidental: in Walin, a village of one man and a few of his women relatives, Ayyashi was stunned to find that manuscripts and written records had reached such a village; in Qulay'a, he stopped to visit the grave of his friend, Sidi Abu Hafs, who had died in 1660 and with whom Ayyashi had gone on a pilgrimage in 1649; in Wariqla, the inhabitants threw the clothes of their dead outside the city walls and celebrated the Fitr Eid with shooting, even inside their small mosque.

The same meticulous descriptions appear in Ayyashi's account of Cairo's mosques and jurists, libraries and Turkish officials. Throughout the journey, Ayyashi composed poems for the people who offered him hospitality, often mosque imams and sheikhs. He showed the extensive network of jurists and scholars who knew each other, read each other's works, and accommodated each other in the vast world of Ottoman Islam. In Mecca and Medina, Ayyashi was more interested in describing the scholars and holy men who resided there than in narrating the history of the sites. Holiness for him lay more in men than in monuments, and though he was always interested in the religious associations of the sites, he carefully recorded the discussions, debates, and judgments in which he was engaged, as well as the titles of books and other records of scholarship he encountered. Ayyashi showed how interconnected the world of Islam was where learned men knew about each other despite vast distances and national and jurisprudential differences. Wherever he went, he found jurists whose books he had read, and sheikhs (or their tombs) legendary for their wisdom and asceticism.

On his return from the Hijaz, Ayyashi decided to visit Palestine, *al-ard al-muqadassa al-mubaraka* (the blessed and holy land) and *thalith al-haramayn* (the third sanctuary). He had not planned the visit, because he knew how difficult it would be, but the holy land of Palestine seemed too close to miss, and so instead of cutting across the Sinai desert in the well-established pilgrimage route Ayyashi sent his books by ship to Cairo and turned north. He spent two months and traveled from Gaza to Ramla, and from Jerusalem to Hebron. Ayyashi described the majestic mosques and monuments of Palestine, but not at the price of human detail: he mentioned a Gazan sheikh who came to him and told him that he had once eaten a Moroccan meal that he had liked very much, couscous, and wondered whether the Moroccans were going to prepare it; later, Ayyashi felt offended after he saw Gazans walking through mosques with their shoes on, and even smoking in the *sahn*. In Ramla, he learned how the sheikh, Khair al-Deen Abu Ali, had planted with his own "blessed hand over a hundred thousand trees all of which bore fruit and of which he had eaten. And this was quite wonderful." Later, Ayyashi found out that the sheikh had started planting in the year 1017 AH (1608 CE) and that he had built over a thousand lintels and most of the khans in Ramla. "He told me that when he came to Ramla it had had little fruit, but he worked and planted . . . and now it is one of the most abundant of coastal cities."

As Lévi-Provençal (1922) has noted, Ayyashi's *rihla* is a veritable encyclopedia of Islamic lore about scholars and Sufis, mosques and shrines, from Morocco to Hijaz and from Fez to Jerusalem. No other Maghrebi writer compares with Ayyashi for detail and scope. His *rihla* is an engaging source of information about the travel routes and caravans, the cities and manners, the agriculture and the society, the devotions and debates of the early modern world of Islam.

NABIL MATAR

## Biography

Born near Tafilat, Morocco, 4 May 1628. Educated in jurisprudence by his father. Joined Sufi fraternity in Fez; received *ijaza* (certificate), July 1653. Spent most of his life traveling; lived in Mecca, Medina, Jerusalem, and Cairo. Died of the plague, 13 December 1679.

### References and Further Reading

Abu Salim Abd Allah bin Mohammad al-Ayyashi, *Rihlat al-Shaykh al-Imam Abi Salim al-Ayyashi*, 2 vols., 1899.

Lévi-Provençal, Évariste, *Les Historiens des Chorfa: Essai sur la littérature historique et biographique au Maroc du XVIe au XXe siècle*, Paris: Larose, 1922.

# B

## BACK, GEORGE (1796–1878) *British Naval Officer, Artist, and Arctic Explorer*

As an active player in the Royal Navy's initiatives in Arctic exploration in the first half of the nineteenth century, George Back participated in a total of five Arctic expeditions and commanded two of them. In terms of geographical distribution, his travels took him from northern Alaska to Svalbard, and he traveled by sailing ship, canoe, boat, and on foot and experienced practically every privation and hazard that Arctic exploration involved.

Back first went north at the age of 22 as midshipman on board HMS *Trent*, commanded by Lt. John Franklin, in 1818. Along with HMS *Dorothea*, commanded by Lt. David Buchan, Franklin was ordered to attempt to sail north past Svalbard, across the North Pole to the Bering Strait and the Pacific. The reality was that the two ships encountered impassable ice at 80°34′ N, and were severely damaged by the ice during a gale and were forced to retreat. This was the rough Arctic initiation experienced by Midshipman Back.

The following year (1819), Franklin selected Back as a member of his first overland expedition, as artist. Having established winter quarters at Fort Enterprise on Winter Lake, in the spring of 1820 the expedition descended the Coppermine River by canoe, then coasted eastward. The intricacies of Bathurst Inlet delayed their eastward progress, and at Point Turnagain on Kent Peninsula the expedition was forced to turn back. In view of the lateness of the season, the party started overland from the mouth of the Hood River, aiming for Fort Enterprise. With their supplies exhausted, and with little success at hunting, the expedition members were reduced to eating the lichen known as "tripe de roche" and began to die of starvation and exposure. Back went ahead, located a band of Yellowknife Native Americans, and brought help to his surviving companions at Fort Enterprise. Without Back's efforts, Franklin and Richardson would have died, and the course of Arctic history would have been very different.

In 1825, Back was selected by Franklin as a member of his second overland expedition (1825–1827). From a base at Fort Franklin on Great Bear Lake, Franklin and Back explored the coast by boat, westward from the Mackenzie Delta to Return Reef, just west of Prudhoe Bay on the Alaskan North Slope.

In 1829, Captain John Ross sailed for the Arctic on a private expedition aboard *Victory* to search for the Northwest Passage. When there was still no word from him in 1833, Lt. Back was dispatched by the Admiralty to mount a search for him via the Thle-wee-choh (Great Fish River), now the Back River. Having reconnoitered a route from Great Slave Lake to the head of the Back River, Back and party settled down for the winter at Fort Reliance, at the head of the east arm of Great Slave Lake. In April 1834, news reached Fort Reliance of Ross's safe return to Britain, but nonetheless Back was ordered to proceed to the Arctic coast and to explore as much of it as possible. Having built a boat on Artillery Lake, Back and his men descended the rapids of the Back River to its mouth and explored Chantrey Inlet as far north as Point Ogle. They returned safely upriver, wintered again at Fort Reliance, then returned to England.

The rigors of a portage, engraving after one of Back's own sketches (from *Narrative of the Arctic Land Expedition to the Mouth of the Great Fish River*, 1836). *Courtesy of the Travellers Club, London; Bridgeman Art Library, agent.*

The very next year (1836), the Admiralty again dispatched Back (now a captain) to the Arctic, this time on board the bomb vessel HMS *Terror*, with orders to proceed by sea to Repulse Bay or Wager Bay, then overland to the Arctic coast to explore the very substantial gap westward to Point Turnagain. In the event, Back did not even reach his suggested starting point. *Terror* became beset in the ice off the northeast coast of Southampton Island and drifted with the ice all winter, southward through Foxe Channel, then eastward through most of the length of Hudson Strait before being released, very severely damaged. Despite the sinking condition of his ship, Back nursed it back across the Atlantic, beaching it in Lough Swilly in Northern Ireland.

Back's accounts of three of his expeditions have been published, two during his lifetime and one posthumously and only recently. All three accounts are characterized by his ability to create vivid word pictures, whether they be of the view of the Clearwater Valley as seen from the north end of Methy Portage as he saw it during the two overland expeditions, of the terrifying rapids of the Back River, or of the equally terrifying experience of HMS *Terror* being lifted out of the water by rafting sea ice.

These prose pictures are matched or perhaps surpassed by his watercolors. The engraver did his best in reproducing them for the public account of his Back River expedition and of the voyage of HMS *Terror*. But we are extremely fortunate that his editors (Houston and MacLaren) have reproduced many of his water colors from Franklin's disastrous first overland expedition in color, in many cases in conjunction with the engraver's rendering of the same view. One has to be doubly impressed by the clarity and delicacy of these watercolors when one realizes that Back carried them and in some cases executed them under the grim conditions of the disastrous overland trek from Bathurst Inlet to Fort Enterprise, a trek that so few of his companions survived.

William Barr

### Biography

Born in Stockport, Lancashire, 6 November 1796. Joined HMS *Arethusa* as first-class volunteer, 15 September 1808. Captured by French in Spain, April 1809; prisoner of war at Verdun, 1809–1814. Returned to active duty in England, July 1814. Sailed to the Arctic as midshipman under Franklin in HMS *Trent*, 1818. Took part in Franklin's expedition to the Arctic coast east of the Coppermine River, 1819–1822. Promoted to rank of lieutenant, 1821. Served on Franklin's second overland expedition to the Mackenzie River and Arctic coastline, 1825–1827. Promoted to rank of commander, 1827. Volunteered to search for Sir John Ross in the Arctic; commanded an expedition by boat down Thle-wee-choh (Back River), mapping that river and Chantrey Inlet, 1833–1835. Commanded HMS *Terror* on unsuccessful Arctic voyage, 1836–1837. Received founder's medal and gold medal of the Royal Geographical Society, 1837. Knighted, 1839. Received gold medal of the Geographical Society of Paris, 1839. Promoted to rear admiral, 1857; vice admiral, 1863; admiral, 1876. Died in London, 23 June 1878.

### References and Further Reading

Back, George, *Canadian Airs, Collected by Captain George Back, R.N. during the Late Arctic Expedition under Captain Sir John Franklin, with Symphonies and Accompaniments by Edward Knight, Junior*, 1823.

Back, George, *Narrative of the Arctic Land Expedition to the Mouth of the Great Fish River, and along the Shores of the Arctic Ocean, in the Years 1833, 1834 and 1835*, 1836.

Back, George, *Narrative of an Expedition in HMS Terror, Undertaken with a View to Geographical Discovery on the Arctic Shores, in the Years 1836–37*, 1838.

Back, George, *Arctic Artist: The Journal and Paintings of George Back, Midshipman with Franklin, 1819–1822*, edited by C. Stuart Houston with commentary by I.S. MacLaren, 1994.

*See also* **Northwest Passage**

## BACKPACKING

The term *backpacking* does not immediately suggest a definite historical time frame, since people have been putting packs on their backs and walking to distant destinations for thousands of years. Given the vagueness of this term, one still might dare to state that contemporary readers and travelers are more likely to associate backpacking with the Appalachian Trail rather than the Oregon Trail, Thoreau's *The Maine Woods* rather than *Walden*, *An American Werewolf in London* rather than *Dances with Wolves*, John Muir rather than Emerson, Kathmandu rather than Canterbury. When trying to sketch a particular set of images for backpacking, I often recall this brief section from Sally Tisdale's infamous "Never Let the Locals See Your Map (Why Most Travel Writers Should Stay Home)" (1995): "The traveller becomes even more desperate for a pure experience, something authentic . . . The single traveller, the one with the small back-pack and the notebook, the one looking for the 'real' Java, the 'real' Sudan, wants something that the tour group does not."

Backpacking reveals more than a few crucial contradictions within the experience of travel. The traveler who might admit to being both hippie and Puritan, desperate and spontaneous, authentic and self-conscious, fiercely independent and socially privileged—this is the strange modern creature known as a backpacker. When one adds a notebook to the equipment list and an exotic destination to the itinerary, one begins to add further complicating factors about audiences, expectations, forms of expression, ways in which the single traveler speaks for and to a cultural group.

Having said that backpacking, as opposed to space travel or deep-sea exploration, has no clear time of origin, it could be argued that the impetus for a *literary* recognition of backpacking developed, at least in North America and Europe, during the nineteenth century. When one considers book 6 of Wordsworth's *The Prelude*, or Emerson's "Nature," or reads the declarations of Henry Thoreau, William Hazlitt, John Muir, or John Burroughs by candlelight in a tent during a snowstorm, it matters little whether they walked 15 miles or 50, whether they had a clear goal or not. In such readings, one can get a clear sense of how "rambling," to use Thomas Lyon's term, was far more than just taking a long walk in the country. Rambling was a personal declaration of independence that resonated with an increasingly large audience.

Public interest in backpacking dovetailed neatly with the development of American national parks or land preserves, which came with a very handy feature—hiking trails. Routes such as the Wonderland Trail in Mount Rainier National Park, the Long Trail in the Green Mountains of Vermont, the Muir Trail in the High Sierras, and perhaps the best-known trail, the Appalachian Trail, have one thing in common: they were all designed and completed during the early twentieth century. As Ronald Fisher explains (1972), such trails rely upon a vocabulary of optimism and challenge:

> I remembered the story of a backpacker who emerged from the trail into the parking lot at Newfound Gap in the Tennessee–North Carolina Smokies. A pudgy, sandaled tourist hailed him: "Hey, buddy, where's that path lead to?"
>
> The hiker silenced him with one word: "Maine."

Hiking trails also rely heavily on the myth of continuity; that is, the sense that one can relive the experience of previous explorers (especially those from the nineteenth century). In books and essays such as Colin Fletcher's *The Man Who Walked through Time* (1968), Sigurd Olson's "Ancient Trails" (1982), Galen Rowell's "The John Muir Trail: Along the High, Wild Sierra" (1989), Joe McGinniss's "The Brooks Range" (1980), Anne LaBastille's *Woodswoman* (1976), or *Backpacker* magazine's "Ten Best Trails of the World" (1988), backpacking is often praised for its elegant simplicity and its rigorous (but not violent) encounters with the natural world.

Tisdale's statement also reminds one that backpacking is not just a matter of long and lonely hikes in wilderness areas. Backpackers often mingle with other travelers and tourists, yet while sharing a similar space they often have drastically different plans. Backpackers seem more likely to tell tales of odd strangers, random misadventures, willful decisions to get lost, miserable sleeping arrangements, and questionable meals. (And, despite nasty rumors, backpackers also enjoy sex: Lonely Planet's *Brief Encounters: Stories of Love, Sex, and Travel* is just a more public forum for such welcome encounters.) The backpacker's sense of enlightened (or misguided) perception is, not surprisingly, associated with a strong sense of exclusion or contrast. Those pilgrims who share in the communal joy of an arduous or arbitrary trip often declare their opposition to the thick-waisted, middle-class vulgarity of stereotypical "tourists" or "consumers." In books such as Robert Kaplan's *The Ends of the Earth* (1996), Jack Kerouac's *The Dharma Bums* (1958), and just about any travelogue by Ernest Hemingway, Paul

Theroux, Mary Morris, or Edward Abbey, a clear line is drawn between the backpackers and the hordes.

Some writers go further than simply claiming to have an "authentic" experience of place. In books such as Peter Matthiessen's *The Snow Leopard* (1978) or Peter Jenkins's *A Walk across America* (1979), the act of backpacking is closely associated with the spiritual renewal of a person or perhaps even a large audience. At times these claims are made explicitly, as when Matthiessen states that his 250-mile trek to Crystal Mountain in Nepal would be a "true pilgrimage, a journey of the heart," or when Chris McCandless, the subject of Jon Krakauer's *Into the Wild* (1996), declares that his backpacking trek in Alaska will become "the climactic battle to kill the false being within and victoriously conclude the spiritual revolution." For those who wish to join the "revolution," guidebooks such as those from *Lonely Planet* provide refreshingly candid and practical tips for those who are literally living out of a backpack. It is also clear that such desires for simpler travel also match neatly with one other "revolution," namely the Internet revolution, which provides up-to-the-minute guidebooks and forums for many would-be trekkers.

Gene McQuillan

### References and Further Reading

Abbey, Edward, "A Walk in the Desert Hills," in his *Beyond the Wall: Essays from the Outside*, 1984.
Edwards, Mike W., and David Hiser, "Mexico to Canada on the Pacific Crest Trail," *National Geographic* (June 1971): 741–779.
Fisher, Ronald M., *The Appalachian Trail*, photographs by Dick Durrance II, foreword by Benton MacKaye, 1972.
Fletcher, Colin, *The Man Who Walked through Time*, 1968.
Harrison, Jim, "A Passacalgia on Getting Lost," in *On Nature: Nature, Landscape, and Natural History*, edited by Daniel Halpern, 1987.
Hemingway, Ernest, "Big Two-Hearted River," in his *In Our Time: Stories*, 1925.
Jenkins, Peter, *A Walk across America*, 1979.
Kaplan, Robert D., *The Ends of the Earth: A Journey to the Dawn of the 21st Century*, 1996.
Kerouac, Jack, *The Dharma Bums*, 1958.
Krakauer, Jon, *Into the Wild*, 1996.
LaBastille, Anne, *Woodswoman*, 1976.
Leopold, Aldo, "The Green Lagoons," in his *A Sand County Almanac*, illustrated by Charles W. Schwartz, 1949.
Matthiessen, Peter, *The Snow Leopard*, 1978.
McGinniss, Joe, "The Brooks Range," in his *Going to Extremes*, 1980.
Muir, John, "A Near View of the High Sierras," in *The Wilderness Reader*, edited by Frank Bergon, 1980.
Murdoch, Stephen, "Domesticity Never Looked So Exciting," *Newsweek* (3 July 2000): 11.
Olson, Sigurd F., "Ancient Trails," in his *Of Time and Place*, illustrations by Leslie Konba, 1982.
Rowell, Galen, "The John Muir Trail: Along the High, Wild Sierra," *National Geographic*, 175 (April 1989): 460–493.
Snyder, Gary, and Allen Ginsberg, "Glacier Peak Wilderness Area," in Snyder's *Earth House Hold: Technical Notes and Queries to Fellow Dharma Revolutionaries*, 1969.
Snyder, Gary, and Allen Ginsberg, "On the Path and off the Trail," *Antaeus*, 63 (Fall 1989): 227–238.
"Ten Best Hike-in Views" and "Ten Best Trails of the World," *Backpacker*, 16 (January 1988): 67–69.

*See also* **Tourism**

## BAEDEKER GUIDES

Born in Essen, Karl Baedeker (1801–1859) studied at Heidelberg and worked in Berlin before establishing his own publishing business in Koblenz in 1827. He had no initial plans for issuing travel guidebooks, but after he acquired a bankrupt publishing house in 1832 whose list included Johann August Klein's *Rheinreise von Mainz bis Köln*, Baedeker decided to revise the work personally and republish it. He added practical information on transportation and hotels and also described excursions to nearby places in Holland. Recognizing the frequent incompetence and unscrupulousness of many who served as personal guides, Baedeker sought to provide information that would allow travelers to visit different destinations without having to rely on anyone else. Several more titles were issued, and the guides became such a success that man, firm, and guide became synonymous.

Around the same time that Baedeker was establishing his line of guidebooks in Germany, the British publisher John Murray began issuing his own in London. With acknowledgment, Baedeker incorporated features that Murray had pioneered, including his most important innovation, the arrangement of descriptive and practical information along numbered routes extending between major destinations. Baedeker's guides were not without innovation, the most important being the star system. Starting in 1844, Baedeker began marking with an asterisk important sights that busy travelers should not miss. Later, he added a second asterisk to distinguish the very important from the important, and extended his star system to denote the quality of hotels and restaurants. Unquestionably, the star system greatly enhanced the usefulness of Baedeker's books, and most travel guides published since have adopted similar ways of denoting quality. As more astute travelers realized, asterisks could not indicate the finest travel experiences, which remained hidden from the average tourist's gaze. In *Italian Hours* (1909), Henry James observed, "It is behind the walls of the houses that old, old history is thick and that the multiplied stars of Baedeker might often best find their application."

After Karl Baedeker's death, his publishing empire passed to his sons, whose varying talents and ambitions allowed each to make unique contributions. The eldest, Ernst (1833–1861), added new titles to the firm's list. Most important, he began issuing Baedeker guides in English, thus making them useful for British and American travelers. After Ernst's death, Karl (1837–1911), the second son and an active mountain climber, used his personal experience and sense of adventure to enhance the guides he wrote. When Karl fell ill, Fritz (1844–1925), the third son, stepped in and greatly expanded the business. Fritz moved the firm to Leipzig in 1872 and issued many new titles, including what is considered the finest Baedeker of all, *Palestine and Syria* (1875). The business flourished, and the guides reached unprecedented sales levels. Fritz's strong leadership ensured that Baedekers would continue being published into the next century.

Baedekers gained an excellent reputation for their crisp, precise prose style, which influenced a variety of authors. Bertrand Russell, for example, claimed that his literary style had two models, Baedeker and Milton. One stylistic eccentricity common to Baedeker guidebooks is the use of parentheses, which were often inserted to provide practical information with little regard for the surrounding text. E.M. Forster brilliantly parodied the Baedeker parenthesis in *Where Angels Fear to Tread* (1905). Whereas one character is "not one to detect the hidden charms of Baedeker," another "could never read 'The view from the Rocca (small gratuity) is finest at sunset' without a catching at the heart." The guidebooks encouraged travelers who found errors to write to the firm so that mistakes could be remedied. In *A Tramp Abroad* (1880), Mark Twain, describing a hike to the summit of Rigi-Kulm, observed that because "Mr. Baedeker requests all tourists to call his attention to any errors which they may find in his guidebooks, I dropped him a line to inform him that when he said the foot journey from Wäggis to the summit was only three hours and a quarter, he missed it by just about three days." Mark Twain's complaint was an exception, however, for Baedekers had an excellent reputation for accuracy.

Like them or not, Baedekers became essential for travelers, and travel literature is rife with references to them. Henry James criticized what Baedekers symbolized—the crass, wide-eyed tourist—yet he could not help but confess that he, too, used them. Describing his arrival at the Hotel Byron in Switzerland, he explained that he had "Baedeker in hand, to 'do' the place." George Bernard Shaw wrote in *London Music* that he consulted one while traveling to the Bayreuth Festival in 1889: "Glancing though Baedeker as I bowl along Bayreuth-wards I perceive that the chief feature of the Wagner district is a great lunatic asylum." After T.S. Eliot's mother expressed her concern about her son's travel-readiness, he reassured her: "I have Baedekers." Eliot would later write a poem entitled "Burbank with a Baedeker: Bleistein with a Cigar." T.E. Lawrence took a copy of *Palestine and Syria* on his journeys through the Near East in 1909 and 1911. During World War I, the British War Office reprinted *Palestine and Syria* for distribution to servicemen stationed there.

The firm suffered greatly during World War I, but with Fritz Baedeker still in control it later recovered, and new editions of most of the guides to western Europe appeared in post-war editions. With Fritz's death, his son Hans succeeded his father and adapted the guidebooks to suit the times. World War II brought more hardship, and the company's records were obliterated when Leipzig was bombed. In terms of military history, Baedekers gained an infamous reputation during the war, for the Luftwaffe used starred items as a blueprint for bombing; German air raids on British places of cultural and historical importance in 1942 became known as Baedeker raids. The firm recovered after World War II, moving to Hamburg in 1948, and to

RUSSIA

WITH

TEHERAN, PORT ARTHUR, AND PEKING

HANDBOOK FOR TRAVELLERS

BY

KARL BAEDEKER

WITH 40 MAPS AND 78 PLANS

LEIPZIG: KARL BAEDEKER, PUBLISHER
LONDON: T. FISHER UNWIN, 1 ADELPHI TERRACE, W.C.
NEW YORK: CHARLES SCRIBNER'S SONS, 597 FIFTH AVE.
1914

*All rights reserved*

A Baedeker title page from the eve of World War I advertises destinations via Russia that would become impossible or problematic by that route for decades after the fall of the czarist empire. *Courtesy of the Travellers Club, London; Bridgeman Art Library, agent.*

Freiburg im Breisgau in 1956. To this day, Baedekers continue to be published and used by travelers worldwide.

KEVIN J. HAYES

*See also* **Guidebooks**

## BAFFIN, WILLIAM (c. 1584–1622) *English Navigator, Explorer, and Scientific Observer*

Described by Samuel Purchas as "that learned-unlearned Mariner and Mathematician" in *Purchas His Pilgrimes* (1625), William Baffin was an outstanding explorer and scientific observer. Through his skill, courage, and determination, he achieved success as a mariner, gaining successive and quick promotions. In exploration, he made a significant contribution to charting the coast of Greenland, and is most famous for his discovery and exploration of Baffin Bay. He was also a meticulous scientist who made detailed and accurate astronomical and hydrographical observations. His life can be seen as a series of attempts to solve some of the great navigational problems of his day. Yet, despite his significant achievements, Baffin remained remarkably modest. At the forefront of contemporary navigational knowledge, he nevertheless remained aware of the limits of that knowledge.

Baffin wrote about only four of the many voyages he undertook, and the accounts were all published by Purchas in *Purchas His Pilgrimes*. Though narratives of other voyages made by Baffin do exist, the combined writings cover only the last decade of his life. Almost nothing is known of his early life. It seems likely that he spent much of it aboard ship learning his profession, and that he was largely self-educated. Consequently, the scientific element of Baffin's writing is all the more remarkable.

Baffin's first narrative relates to his 1612 expedition to Greenland, during which he explored the coast around Holsteinsborg. It is his scientific records, however, that are truly impressive. With great ingenuity, he attempted to derive longitude by solar and lunar observations and a series of complex mathematical calculations. The methodology had problems, and Baffin noted that "this finding of the longitude . . . is somewhat difficult and troublesome, and there may be some small errour." However, his is one of the earliest records of a practical attempt to derive longitude, and Baffin did himself a disservice when he remarked, "[those that] are desirous to learne [the methodology], may in short space attaine to such knowledge."

The success of the 1612 voyage led to expeditions to Spitzbergen in 1613 and 1614. Sponsored by the Muscovy Company, these voyages combined further exploration of Greenland with whaling enterprises. Whaling was conducted in difficult, icy seas, amid intense international competition. In 1613, Baffin's fleet encountered 17 ships from France, Spain, and Holland, all engaged in whaling. Opportunities for exploration were limited, and Baffin concentrated on another scientific issue, that of the sun's refraction. His account details his methodology, and his conclusion is typically modest: "I suppose the Refraction is more or lesse according as the ayre is thicke or cleare, which I leave for better schollers to discusse." The 1614 voyage, in which further discoveries were made along the coast of Greenland despite the hazardous conditions, is not recorded by Baffin, although Fotherby's account is included in *Purchas His Pilgrimes*.

Baffin's experiences on the Spitzbergen voyages prepared him for his 1615 and 1616 voyages in search of a Northwest Passage. The 1615 voyage resulted in no new discoveries, but Baffin's journal is again interesting for its scientific entries. It includes a table detailing the daily latitude, longitude, and magnetic variation of the compass. It also shows Baffin trying another method of calculating longitude, this time by observing the altitude of the moon and another heavenly body, and then measuring the angular distance between them. Baffin's appears to be the first recorded attempt to put this method into practice at sea.

If the 1615 voyage was a disappointment in terms of discovery, the voyage of 1616 saw Baffin's greatest achievement. He discovered and explored a large part of Baffin Bay, considerably extending knowledge of the area to the north of the Davis Strait. As a result, Baffin became convinced that a Northwest Passage did not exist. Unfortunately, he failed to realize that the entrance to Lancaster Sound, which he discovered and named, was, indeed, the opening to the Northwest Passage. His failure is understandable given the dangers to navigation caused by an ice shelf that ran up the coast to the mouth of Lancaster Sound. However, it was not only the ice and storms, and "the difficultie of sayling so neere the Pole (upon a traverse)," which made exploration dangerous: "above all, the variation of the Compasse, whose wonderfull operation is . . . a thing almost incredible and matchlesse in all the world beside," meant that "without great care, and good observations, a true description could not have beene had."

The 1616 narrative was Baffin's last written account, though he participated in two further voyages. In 1617, he joined in the East India Company's seventh joint-stock voyage to the East, via the Red Sea. Baffin returned in 1619 and received a special payment for his "pains and good art in drawing out certain plots of the coast of Persia and the Red Sea, which are judged to have been very well . . . performed" (Markham, 1881).

Baffin's last voyage was another East India Company venture to the East. Difficult sailing conditions caused the voyage to become sidetracked by military considerations in the Persian Gulf. The Portuguese fleet was attacked, and the English joined the Persian army in attacking the Portuguese-held town of Kishm. It was during this raid on 23 January 1622, while measuring the height and distance of the town walls to facilitate more accurate shooting, that Baffin was killed. Thus, the skills of accurate observation and mathematical calculation, by which Baffin had achieved so much, ultimately cost him his life.

Baffin made his most significant geographical discoveries in the difficult and dangerous conditions of the Arctic Circle. His extensive experience, combined with his intellect and ambition, made him well suited to coping with the hardships of Arctic travel. Yet his writings also show his sharp mind giving practical application to the most advanced scientific theories of the day. His achievements as both "mariner and Mathematician" were remarkable. That he failed to discover the Northwest Passage, and did not find a practical method of taking longitude at sea, reflects less his own limitations than those of his age.

MATTHEW DAY

### Biography

Probably born in London, c. 1584. Pilot on voyage to Greenland for discovery, 1612; sailed to Spitzbergen for whaling and further exploration of Greenland, 1613 and 1614. Voyages in search of Northwest Passage, 1615 and 1616; to East Indies via Red Sea as master's mate, 1617–1619; to Persia as master, 1620–1622. Married, but name of wife and date of marriage unknown. Killed by gunshot outside Kishm, Persia, 23 January 1622.

### References and Further Reading

Baffin, William, "The Fourth Voyage of James Hall to Groeneland, wherein He was Set Forth by English Adventurers, Anno 1612, and Slaine by a Greenelander," "A Journal of the Voyage Made to Greenland with Five English Ships and a Pinasse, in the Yeere 1613," "A True Relation of Such Things as Happened in the Fourth Voyage for the Discoverie of the North-west Passage, Performed in the Yeere 1615," "A Briefe and True Relation or Journall, Contayning Such Accidents as Happened in the Fift Voyage, for the Discoverie of a Passage to the North-West, Set Forth at the Charges of the Right Worshipfull Sir Tho. Smith Knight, Sir Dudly Digges Knight, Master John Wostenholme Esquire, Master Alderman Jones, with Others, in the Good Ship Called the *Discoverie* of London; Robert Bileth Master, and My Selfe Pilot, Performed in the Yeere of our Lord 1616," and "Relation of the Fight of Foure English Ships with Foure Portugall Ships, Two Galliats, and Ten Frigats in the Gulfe of Persia, in the Monethes of December and January, 1620," in *Purchas His Pilgrimes*, edited by Samuel Purchas, 4 vols., 1625; as *Hakluytus Posthumus; or, Purchas His Pilgrimes*, 20 vols., 1905–1907.

Markham, Clements R. (editor), *The Voyages of William Baffin, 1612–1622*, 1881.

*See also* **Northwest Passage**

## BAINES, THOMAS (1820–1875) *British Artist, Traveler, and Explorer*

John Thomas Baines, better known as Thomas Baines, was born on 27 November 1820 in "the ancient borough and sea port of Kings Lynn" in Norfolk. On his paternal side he came from a seafaring family; his grandfather, Thomas Baines, was a master mariner who was captain of a whaling vessel. His father, John Baines, who was in the navy, spent some time at the Cape of Good Hope, in the Cape Squadron.

His mother appears to have been a strong-minded, determined woman who sent the young Thomas to the two local schools. At the age of 16, he had an accident that left him a cripple for the rest of his life. Because he was physically a small but sturdy man—only five feet four inches tall—his mother probably thought that a seafaring life would not be suitable, so she had him apprenticed to an "ornamental painter"—in other words, a signwriter. This is probably where he acquired his artistic skills and learned draftsmanship.

On his twenty-second birthday, he arrived in Cape Town, where he was to spend the next six years. We do not know why he went to Cape Town; possibly he was influenced by Captain Williams Roome, a Kings Lynn man, who was master of *Olivia*, the ship on which Baines arrived at the Cape. He could also have been motivated by his father's tales of the colony. In Cape Town, he started working as a coach painter. This was an important formative period of his life. Using the paints available in his daily work for making early canvasses of Cape life and scenery, he was persuaded by his friend Frederick Logier, organist of St. George's cathedral, to become a professional painter.

After being in Cape Town for six years, Baines was inspired by a fellow painter, George French Angus, to move to Grahamstown, and during the next few years he used it as a base to make three long and arduous trips into the interior. On the first, he spent three months traveling to the Orange River near Colesberg with the Liddle brothers. Subsequently, he made a solo trip on horseback and foot from Grahamstown to the mouth of the Kei River—a strenuous journey that gave him much experience. His next trip was with Joseph McCabe to Mooiriviersdorp (now Potchefstroom) on the Vaal River. They made an unsuccessful attempt to reach the great lake of the interior, Lake Ngami, but were prevented by the Boer republic of Transvaal from going through its territory. On his return to Grahamstown during the Eighth Frontier War, Baines joined Major General Henry Somerset's forces in the field, serving for six months as South Africa's first war artist.

Despite his slight build and the problem with his leg, he proved to be an intrepid and hardy traveler. After the Frontier War, he returned to England, where he joined A.C. Gregory's expedition to northern Australia. For over two years, from May 1855 to September 1857, he was with Gregory exploring northern Australia. One of his feats of endurance included a 700-mile journey in an open boat, which he navigated from Dutch Timor to the Albert River in northern Australia. After this expedition, he again returned to Britain and was pleased to get a position with the explorer and missionary David Livingstone, who was going to explore the Zambezi. This trip ended disastrously for Baines when Livingstone, who found it difficult to get along with white people, dismissed him on an unjust allegation of theft.

Artistically, too, this trip was a disaster: Livingstone retained most of the drawings Baines had made on the expedition. On his return to Cape Town, Baines joined James Chapman on a journey from Walvis Bay via Lake Ngami to the Victoria Falls, which he and Chapman were among the first seven white men to see.

Baines's accomplished drawing of the "Buffalo pear," made in the Cape in 1849 (from one of Baines's South African sketchbooks preserved in the Royal Geographical Society). *Courtesy of the Royal Geographical Society, London.*

When he returned from the Zambezi with Chapman, he spent 16 months with Charles John Andersson in Otjimbengu in what today is Namibia. During these 16 months, he sketched continually and made drawings for Andersson's book, *Notes on the Birds of Damaraland and the Adjacent Countries*. These drawings were not published until 1972, in *The Birds of South Africa*, by Thomas Baines, edited by R.F. Kennedy.

In 1868, while on a visit to England, Baines was asked by the South African Goldfields Company to lead an expedition to Matabeleland to obtain concessions from Chief Lobengula to exploit the newly found gold in what is now Zimbabwe. Between 1869 and 1872, he made two trips to obtain Lobengula's goodwill. He died in May 1875 while planning a third trip. The journeys he made in southern Africa made him one of the most widely traveled of South African explorers, and though he did not discover any new territory, he did reach areas that were previously little known to Europeans.

During the six years Baines had spent in Cape Town, he had sharpened his artistic skills considerably. Throughout his adventurous and active life, Baines continued to paint, sketch, and write. He kept voluminous diaries and journals, which were published several years after his death. Some 4,000 drawings and paintings have been found by the writer, making Baines one of the most prolific artists of South Africa of his time—and possibly of all time. To a large extent, he was a narrative painter. Like his writings, his drawings and paintings relate to incidents he witnessed and to the scenery and people he found interesting. In his journal, he wrote, "The better years of my life having been passed in Africa it is on the scenes there witnessed that my memory loves to dwell." Like Constable, he annotated his work in amazing detail, giving such information as time, date, place, and even, in the more studied oils, the length of time that elapsed between making the preliminary sketch and the finished painting. Through this narrative element in Baines's works, we learn much about his background and experiences, yet his paintings also show him to have been both imaginative and creative. On his death, the *Eastern Province Herald* wrote that "as an artist and traveller truth was his great characteristic."

Despite having no scientific education or training in the natural sciences, Baines's journals show that his interest in such things as geology and botanical science was reflected in his knowledge of scientific nomenclature. He sent sketches of his findings of new specimens to Sir William Hooker and his son Joseph Hooker, who sometimes named the specimens after him. Professor

J.P.R. Wallis, in *Thomas Baines of Kings Lynn*, lists 17 plants named after Baines, excluding the *Aloe bainesii*. Even insects interested him. A beetle found on the banks of the Mangwe River was named *Bolbotritus bainesii* by H.W. Bates.

His interest in geology enabled him to study rock formations, although he had very little knowledge of the subject. Tribute to him as a geologist has been paid to him by people like Sir Harry Johnson, who said that Baines's "gold discoveries in the Transvaal and Matabeleland are revolutionising the history of South Africa." He even made a contribution to South African cartography, and invented a method of measuring distances. His major feat in cartography was to produce a map of the Limpopo area from description, without having visited the area. His maps of Shepstone's visit to Zululand, and the sketches of the Zambezi that he made for Livingstone, show that he is second only to the latter as a cartographer in southern Africa.

Baines's modest discoveries as an explorer were, with the exception of the Australian ones, not well known, but there is no doubt that had he not been limited by lack of funds he would have made further explorations of much importance. When this multifaceted man died on 8 May 1875 in Durban, the *Natal Mercury* paid tribute to him as "a traveller, explorer, and as a brave, distinguished and single hearted man," but not as an artist. It was to be many years before his oeuvre was recognized as the work of an artist of considerable talent and not of a mere pictorial journalist and topographical recorder. Today, his works are recognized as being of enduring value. Through them, we are able to appreciate the world that provided the impetus to his imagination and his talent.

FRANK R. BRADLOW

### Biography

Born in Kings Lynn, Norfolk, 27 November 1822. Learned heraldic painting from a local coach-builder. Traveled to Cape Colony, 23 November 1847; moved to Grahamstown, 1848. Traveled with William and Joseph Liddle to the Orange River, 1848. Undertook the "solitary journey," traveling on his own, first on horseback and then on foot, to East London, 1849. Joined Joseph McCabe on an unsuccessful journey of exploration to reach Lake Ngami, 1850. Served as an artist in Lt. General Somerset's forces in the Eighth Frontier War, 1850–1853. Returned to England, 1853; joined A.C. Gregory's expedition to northern Australia, 1855. Joined David Livingstone as artist and storekeeper to his proposed expedition to the Zambezi, 1858. Dismissed by Livingstone. Joined James Chapman's expedition to the Zambezi, 1861. Took part in the war with the Damaras. His journals published as *Explorations in South-West Africa*, 1864. Published lithographic album *The Victoria Falls, Zambesi River*, 1865. Returned to Britain, 1865. Joined Robert Mann of Natal in an exploration of the goldfields of Matabeleland and an attempt to float the South African Goldfields Exploration Company, 1868. Met the Matabele chief, Lobengula, 1870. Remained in southern Africa, mapping routes and sketching, until his death. Elected a Fellow of the Royal Geographical Society, 1857. Died of dysentery in Durban, 8 May 1875.

### References and Further Reading


Baines, Thomas, *Journal of Residence in Africa, 1842–1853*, edited by R.F. Kennedy, vol. 2, 1861.

Baines, Thomas, *Explorations in South-West Africa*, 1864.

Baines, Thomas, *Various Articles, Nature and Art*, 1866.

Baines, Thomas, with William B. Lord, *Shifts and Expedients of Camp Life, Travel and Exploration*, 1871.

Baines, Thomas, *The Gold Regions of South Eastern Africa*, 1877.

Baines, Thomas, *The Northern Goldfields Diaries of Thomas Baines*, edited by J.P.R. Wallis, 3 vols., 1946.


### Illustrated Albums


Baines, Thomas, *Scenery and Events in South Africa: A Series of Views*, 1852.

Baines, Thomas, *The Victoria Falls, Zambesi River: Sketched on the Spot*, 1865.

Baines, Thomas, *The Birds of South Africa*, edited by R.F. Kennedy, 1972.


## BAKER, SAMUEL WHITE (1821–1893)

***British Traveler, Hunter, and Writer***

Samuel Baker believed that the hunting of large and dangerous animals was the best training a young man could have if he wanted to become an explorer or a soldier, as he wrote in *True Tales for My Grandsons* (1883). An energetic and accomplished traveler, Baker's books reflect his enthusiasm for the places he visited. The numerous editions and reprints of his works indicate that he was an inspired and entertaining writer, and that there was considerable public demand for them.

The son of a successful West India merchant, Baker received his early education in England before being sent to Germany, where he revealed an aptitude for languages. He married Henrietta Biddulph just after his twenty-first birthday, and fathered seven children, only three of whom survived him. He then visited Mauritius with his young family, helping to manage his father's estates, and this experience gave him a strong desire for further travel. In 1846, he went to Ceylon (Sri Lanka), drawn by the prospect of big game hunting, but then decided to found a British colony there.

He purchased land and then chartered a ship, which sailed from England in September 1848 to take him and 17 other adults to establish what would become a flourishing estate at Newera Eliya. During his nine years in Ceylon, Baker established a reputation as a hunter, and his book *The Rifle and the Hound in Ceylon* (1854) vividly described many of his exciting hunting experiences. His next book, *Eight Years' Wanderings in Ceylon* (1855), was a more general account of his travels.

After the death of his wife late in 1855, Baker spent some months traveling in eastern Europe and hunting wild boar. In 1859, while in the Turkish garrison town of Vidin, in what is today Bulgaria, he came across an Ottoman auction of slaves; on an impulse, he purchased a beautiful woman who was part of a group of Hungarian refugees who were being sold into bondage. This remarkable woman, Florence, soon became his second wife, and she accompanied Baker on most of his subsequent travels, often making the difference between failure and success.

After a year of managing the construction of a railway for the Danube and the Black Sea Railway Company, in 1861 Baker turned his eyes to Africa and the source of the Nile. Before heading south, however, the Bakers explored the Abyssinian tributaries of the Blue Nile, during which time they learned Arabic, endeared themselves to the local Arabs as a result of Baker's prowess as a hunter, and gained proof that sediments in the Nile originated in Abyssinian rivers. They marched into Khartoum in 1862, a year to the day from when they had set off east from Berber. *The Nile Tributaries of Abyssinia and the Sword Hunters of the Hamran Arabs* (1867) documents both their geographical discoveries and Baker's fascination with hunting.

In December 1862, the Bakers left Khartoum with a party of 96, heading up the Nile. At Gondokoro, they generously resupplied the expedition of John Hanning Speke and James Grant and were given a map by Grant, on which he had placed the lake that he had been told the Nile flowed into and then out of on its way north from Lake Victoria. The Bakers pressed toward the mysterious lake with a much-reduced party, all too reliant on a variety of hostile slave-traders. Progress was very slow, and while "enjoying" the enforced "hospitality" of a local king named Kamrasi, Baker was obliged to fend off enthusiastic offers for his wife. With the Bakers ill and desperate, in March 1864 the party reached the village of Mbakovia on the lake about which they had been told, a lake Baker named the Albert Nyanza. They explored the eastern edges of the lake and then followed the Nile to the magnificent Murchison Falls before heading north again. The story of this four-year expedition was told in Baker's vivid *The Albert Nyanza, Great Basin of the Nile*, which was published in 1866 and enjoyed numerous reprints and editions. On Baker's return to England, he was credited with helping to complete the work of Speke on the source of the Nile, and was honored with medals and a knighthood (1866). At this time, he produced his first attempt at a storybook, *Cast up by the Sea* (1868).

It was not long before the Bakers were on the move again, this time to Egypt, where in 1869 the Egyptian government appointed Baker governor general of the province of Equatoria. His remit was to bring the countries to the south of Gondokoro under Egyptian control, to suppress the slave trade, to initiate commerce with the south, and to encourage navigation in the equatorial lakes. He set out south from Khartoum in 1870, and annexed Gondokoro the next spring. He continued up the Nile, but the next two years consisted mainly of running battles with various African tribes and the Arab slaver Abu Su'ud, battles that Baker's forces usually won but that did not lead to any significant political reorganization of the area. Eventually, leaving behind a series of military stations, Baker returned to Khartoum, his four years in Equatoria having been a failure at almost every level. His experiences appeared in *Ismailïa* (1874), a two-volume work that was written in an astonishing 64 days.

Though Baker undertook no more significant expeditions, he and Florence did not stop traveling. They spent some time in Cyprus, where Baker penned *Cyprus as I Saw It in 1879* (1879). He also indulged his love of hunting in places as far away as India, Japan, and the west of the United States. Even when in his sixties, his skill and dedication to the hunt made him one of the most famous and successful animal killers of his day. *Wild Beasts and Their Ways* (1890) is a curious combination of natural history and how to destroy it.

Baker died just after Christmas in 1893 at his Devon estate, and his ashes were scattered near Worcester. In addition to his seven books about his travels, Baker wrote two storybooks and contributed numerous articles to such prestigious journals as *Nineteenth Century, Fortnightly*, and *National Review*. He was an intriguing man, with a raw enthusiasm and a sense of humor that often shines through in his books, which together rendered him a more appealing figure to his contemporaries than many other explorers. However, his mania for the wanton killing of masses of animals—he admitted that his greatest joy was "whole hecatombs of slaughter"—and his thorough contempt for black Africans and virtually every aspect of their cultures make him a less sympathetic figure today.

BEAU RIFFENBURGH

### Biography

Born in London, 8 June 1821, the son of a West India merchant. Brought up in Enfield; educated in Sussex, Gloucester, and Frankfurt. Married Henrietta Biddulph, 1842 (d. 1855): seven children. Managed family holdings in Mauritius, 1843–1845. Lived in Ceylon, establishing a plantation there, 1846–1855. Returned to England in poor health. Lived with Florence von Sass, from 1859. Worked on Danube–Black Sea railway, 1859. Went to Africa with Florence, 1861–1865. Discovered the Albert Nyanza (Lake Albert), 1864. Married Florence von Sass, 1865. Commanded by the viceroy of Egypt to set up military expedition to the Nile equatorial regions (Sudan), founded several garrisons there, and appointed governor general of these territories, 1869–1873. Continued to travel in Egypt, India, Japan, and Cyprus until his death. Awarded the Victoria Gold Medal of the Royal Geographical Society, 1865. Knighted, 1866. Died at his home at Sandford Orleigh, south Devon, 30 December 1893.

### References and Further Reading


Baker, Samuel White, *The Rifle and the Hound in Ceylon*, 1854.

Baker, Samuel White, *Eight Years' Wanderings in Ceylon*, 1855.

Baker, Samuel White, *The Albert Nyanza: Great Basin of the Nile, and Explorations of the Nile Sources*, 2 vols., 1866.

Baker, Samuel White, *The Nile Tributaries of Abyssinia and the Sword Hunters of the Hamran Arabs*, 1867.

Baker, Samuel White, *Cast up by the Sea*, 1868.

Baker, Samuel White, *Ismailïa: A Narrative of the Expedition to Central Africa, for the Suppression of the Slave Trade, Organized by Ismail, Khedive of Egypt*, 2 vols., 1874.

Baker, Samuel White, *Cyprus as I Saw It in 1879*, 1879.

Baker, Samuel White, *True Tales for My Grandsons*, 1883.

Baker, Samuel White, *Wild Beasts and Their Ways: Reminiscences of Europe, Asia, Africa, and America*, 1890.


## BALI, 1800–1970

Before 1800, the island of Bali had been regularly visited by European seafarers, traders, and travelers. It enjoyed a somewhat mixed reputation. Travelers reported that Hindu civilization seemed to have miraculously survived—witness the "Hindoo spectacles," temple ceremonies, and widow-burnings that could be attended. Others, such as Dirk van Hogendorp, a Dutch naval officer and administrator, described the inhabitants as "savage, wild, false, and warlike, lazy, unwilling to work and poor." Admiration and contempt alternated.

For most nineteenth-century travelers, Bali was part of a tour through the Indonesian archipelago. It was a small island (it measures some 2,100 square miles), adjacent to the more interesting Java, and usually visited for a few days only. In the first half of the century, it attracted mostly "official" visitors. British and Dutch colonial officials, naval and military officers, and an occasional missionary explored the island with an eye to conquest and exploitation. Many of them, however, took a lively interest in the inhabitants and their way of life and published sometimes fascinating reports of their experiences.

Initially, the existing ideas about a "Hinduistic" Bali were reinforced. Two British travelers have contributed to this image. Sir Thomas Stamford Raffles, governor of the Indonesian archipelago under British occupation (1811–1816) and John Crawfurd, a physician employed by the government, were the first to collect material on Bali's history and culture. They visited the island in 1814 and 1815 and were deeply impressed by what they believed to be the remnants of a Hindu civilization. They were followed by another "official" visitor, H.A. van den Broek, a Dutch military officer who visited Bali on a diplomatic mission in 1817 with the purpose of reinstating Dutch sovereignty. He provided an informative survey of administration, economy, social life, and customs of the Balinese kingdoms. Whereas both Raffles and Van den Broek had been interested in the mundane aspects of strategy and exploitation, another traveler was concerned with the prospects of spiritual conquest. Walter Medhurst, a British sinologist and missionary, visited the island in 1829 to see whether the population was in need of the Christian gospel. It was.

The upshot of these early reports was the creation of a number of fixed cultural stereotypes. Bali was ruled, it was thought, by strong trader-kings. The population was divided into castes. Widows and slaves followed their husbands and masters into cremation. Hindu ceremonies were carried out almost daily. Literature and language were based on Sanskrit heritage. In short, Bali was seen as an atavistic Hindu sanctuary in a Muslim world and a living reminiscence of pre-Muslim Java. Most of these assumptions, however, were wrong.

To the Dutch, Bali posed severe political problems. Its nine rajas stubbornly refused to acknowledge Dutch sovereignty and continued to practice such evils as the plunder of shipwrecks, slave trade, and internecine warfare. Moreover, foreign traders, including the Danish merchant Mads Lange, had settled on Bali's shores, W.A. van Hoëvell, a Protestant minister in Batavia, who traveled through Bali in 1847, warned against this intrusion of foreigners into (at least nominally) Dutch territory. Reports like Van Hoëvells's awakened the Dutch from their colonial slumber. In three subsequent expeditions (1846, 1848, and 1849), the colonial army invaded Bali and succeeded, albeit with great difficulty, in defeating the rajas. This opened up the island to an influx of travelers.

The new generation of travelers created a more varied and colorful image of Balinese society. They focused on village life and habits and customs, such as gambling and cockfighting. They were interested in, among other things, the relations between men and women and the sexual life of the inhabitants. R. van Eck, a Protestant missionary, published a lively description of Balinese peasant life (1878), giving drama and excitement a prominent place in his story. P.L. van Bloemen Waanders, an administrator, and many other observers, most of them Dutch, saw the Balinese village as a sort of small democratic republic and portrayed Balinese society as egalitarian rather than hierarchical. And none of them could refrain from singing the praises of Balinese women: "those wonderful lines, the soft brown skin, the robust and solid breasts, really, one must have lost every sense of aesthetics, if one doesn't find Balinese women attractive," wrote J. Jacobs, a Dutch physician who toured through Bali as a government vaccinator in 1883.

The dramatic events of 1906 and 1908 provided a decisive turning point in Balinese history and travel. In a short and nasty campaign, the colonial army broke Bali's last resistance against Dutch rule. The last two independent rajas of South Bali committed collective suicide (called *puputan*) with their courts by running unarmed and accompanied by all their womenfolk, children, and slaves right into the firing squads of the colonial military. This massacre embarrassed the Dutch considerably.

From that moment on, a new policy was pursued. The colonial authorities emphasized the uniqueness of Balinese culture, which they strove to preserve and protect. They started a campaign to attract the world's attention to the landscape, scenery, arts and architecture, religious ceremonies, and dances of Bali. In 1910, the first tourist information bureau for Bali was established, and Dutch- and English-language travel guides appeared. In 1924, a regular steamship service was opened to North Bali. In 1928, the Bali Hotel was built in Den Pasar. Within 20 years, an amazing tourist industry had developed, with over 1,000 visitors yearly.

A new era of luxurious and elitist travel had begun. Americans especially flooded the island, afterward publishing romantic reminiscences of their journey through the "garden of Eden" and "the last paradise," as Hickman Powell (an American journalist and adventurer) called it (1930). Powell's Bali was the creation of a successful colonial advertisement campaign, helped by the enthusiastic travelogues of Americans and other foreign visitors. The image presented was of an unspoiled country, inhabited by unspoiled, delicate, artistic, and spiritually rich people, from whom nervous people from the West could learn a lot.

In the early part of the twentieth century, Bali was also discovered by Western artists (not seldom homosexuals) and anthropologists. They have contributed enormously to the image of Bali as presented to the outer world. The first of them, W.O.J. Nieuwenkamp, who was also a talented author, explored Bali around the turn of the century. More influential, however, was Walter Spies, a German artist, who settled in Bali in 1925 and established a center of arts in Ubud. This center became a place of pilgrimage for all artistically minded Western visitors. Spies did more than anyone else to "design" Bali to the taste of the escapist Western traveler. Even Margaret Mead and her husband, Gregory Bateson, American anthropologists, went to Spies's place for deeper insight into the Balinese soul.

During World War II and the struggle for national independence (1945–1949), Bali was of course not a place most people would want to visit. There were few exceptions to this rule. One was K'tut Tantri, a British American woman-adventurer, who supported the Indonesian struggle for freedom enthusiastically. Few others stayed in Bali in the uneasy and violent 1950s and 1960s. Jef Last, a Dutch leftist author, wrote a sympathetic account (1955) of his stay in Bali, and a British couple, the Mathewses, lived in Den Pasar in the frightening early 1960s. The new Indonesian government soon understood the value of Bali as a living advertisement for modern Indonesia. Sukarno himself, the first president of the Indonesian republic, proclaimed Bali "the mother of Indonesian culture." It was, however, only under Suharto's new regime, in the 1970s, that Bali developed into one of the world's leading holiday resorts.

J.A. de Moor

## References and Further Reading

Baum, Vicki, *Liebe und Tod auf Bali*, 1937; as *Life and Death on Bali*, 1937; as *A Tale from Bali: The Powerful Account of a Holocaust in Paradise*, 1986.

Bloemen Waanders, P.L. van, "Aanteekeningen omtrent de zeden en gebruiken der Balinezen" [Notes on the Manners and Customs of the Balinese], *Tijdschrift voor Indische Taal-, Land- en Volkenkunde uitgegeven door het Bataviaasch Genootschap*, 8 (1859): 105–279.

Blom, Govert, *Lotgevallen op mijne reis naar Java, het verongelukken van het fregatschip Overyssel, nabij het eiland Baly, en terugreis naar Nederland met het fregatschip* Johanna Catharina [Adventures on My Journey to Java, the Shipwreck of the Frigate *Overyssel*, near the Island of Bali, and My Return Voyage to the Netherlands with the Frigate *Johanna Catharina*], 1841.

Broek, H.A. van den, "Verslag noopens het eiland Bali" [Report on the Island of Bali], *De Oosterling*, 1 (1835): 158–236.

Covarrubias, Miguel, *Island of Bali*, 1937.

Crawfurd, John, *History of the Indian Archipelago: Containing an Account of the Manners, Arts, Languages, Religions, Institutions, and Commerce of Its Inhabitants*, 3 vols., 1820.
Eck, R. van, "Schetsen van het eiland Bali" [Sketches of the Island of Bali], *Tijdschrift voor Nederlandsch-Indië*, 7 (1878): 85–130, 165–213, 325–356, 405–430; 8 (1879): 36–60, 104–134, 286–305, 365–387; 9 (1880): 1–39, 102–132, 195–221, 401–429.
Friederich, R., "A Preliminary Account of the Island of Bali," *Journal of the Indian Archipelago and Eastern Asia*, 3 (1849): 117–139 and 235–250.
Helms, Ludvig Verner, *Pioneering in the Far East and Journeys to California in 1849 and to the White Sea in 1878*, 1882.
Hoëvell, W.R. van, *Reis over Java, Madura en Bali in het midden van 1847* [Journey on Java, Madura, and Bali in mid-1847], 3 vols., 1849–1854.
Hogendorp, Dirk van, *Berigt van den tegenwoordigen toestand der Bataafsche bezittingen in Oost-Indiën en den handel op dezelve* [Report of the Current Situation of the Dutch Possessions in the East Indies and on the Trade with Them], 2nd edition, 1800.
Jacobs, J., *Eenigen tijd onder de Baliërs: Eene reisbeschrijving, met aan tekeningen betreffende hygiène, land- en volkenkunde van de eilanden Bali en Lombok* [Some Time among the Balinese: A Travelogue with Notes on Hygiene and Ethnography of the Islands of Bali and Lombok], 1883.
Kol, H.H. van, *Uit onze koloniën* [From Our Colonies], 1903.
Kol, H.H. van, *Driemaal dwars door Sumatra en zwerftochten door Bali* [Three Times Right across Sumatra and Rambles on Bali], 1914.
Last, Jef, *Bali in de kentering* [Bali in Transition], 1955.
Mathews, Anna, *The Night of Purnama*, 1965.
Mead, Margaret, and Gregory Bateson, *Balinese Character: A Photographic Analysis*, 1942.
Medhurst, W.H., and W. Tomlin, *Journal of a Tour along the Coast of Java and Bali*, 1830.
Nieuwenkamp, W.O.J., *Bali en Lombok: Zijnde een verzameling geïllustreerde reisherinneringen en studies omtrent land en volk, kunst en kunstnijverheid* [Bali and Lombok: Being a Collection of Illustrated Travel Reminiscences and Studies on Land and People, Art and Crafts], 3 vols., 1906–1910.
Powell, Hickman, *The Last Paradise*, 1930.
Raffles, Thomas Stamford, *The History of Java*, 2 vols., 1817; reprinted, 1965.
Tantri, K'tut, *Revolt in Paradise*, 1960.
Weede, H.M. van, *Indische reisherinneringen* [Netherlands Indies Travel Reminiscences], 1908.

## BALKANS, PRE-1914

The Balkans have been both a bridge and a barrier between Europe and Asia. Situated on a landmass that forms a natural connection between the two continents, this region has witnessed vast movements of peoples in the past. But because of their rugged terrain (*Balkan* in Turkish means "mountain") and generally turbulent history, travel in the Balkans, apart from the northern flatlands, has for centuries been synonymous with great physical effort, danger, and uncertainty. Technological advances in transport, even after the Middle Ages, were slow and uneven; four-wheeled carts, used in the rest of Europe for a long time previously, were a rarity: until the middle of the nineteenth century, the mountainous interior of the peninsula could be reached only on foot or on horseback. The main lines of communication were built on the routes of Roman roads, like the Via Militaris, which led from Belgrade through Sofia to Constantinople, using mostly river valleys. But the Roman routes in the western Balkans, which had to conform to the more difficult terrain, in later times often degenerated into narrow paths suitable only for foot travelers and horsemen.

Until the nineteenth century, most travel literature on the Balkans was written by Europeans crossing the peninsula on their way to the East. Thus, for most travelers the journey through the Balkans was incidental and secondary, a fact generally reflected in their travel accounts, where other regions and places were accorded much more space.

In the Middle Ages, travelers across the Balkans were mostly soldiers, pilgrims, merchants, and diplomats. The first two categories easily merged during the Crusades, as fighting for religion and pious travel became the same for many western European visitors to the Holy Land. Around the middle of the eleventh century, William Ingulf, the first Englishman known to have passed through the Balkan peninsula by land, traveled with a group of pilgrims to Jerusalem. An account of that journey can be found in *Ingulph's Chronicle of the Abbey of Croyland* (1854). In 1096, two prominent crusaders, Raymond IV (Count of Toulouse) and Ademar de Monteil, passed through Dalmatia ("Sclavonie") and Albania on their way to Constantinople. They were the first French travelers known to have visited the south Slavic lands. In 1192, the English king Richard I, returning from the Third Crusade, landed at Ragusa (Dubrovnik); this visit was recorded in several later chronicles. Another medieval traveler, the Frenchman Bertrandon de La Broquière, went on some sort of secret mission to the East and recorded his travel through the Balkans in 1433 in his *Le Voyage d'outremer* (1892).

By the early decades of the sixteenth century, as a result of the Reformation movement and the capture of the Holy Land by the Turks in 1517, the fashion for pilgrimages had almost come to an end in England. Arguably the last English pilgrim–travel writer to pass through the Balkans was Sir Richard Torkington, who in 1517 went to Jerusalem via Venice and recorded in his diary (published as *Ye Oldest Diarie of Englysshe Travell*, 1884) his enthusiasm both for relics and for good wine in the holy places he visited.

The expansion of trade in the age of discovery and an increase in diplomatic activity between Europe and Turkey encouraged new travelers and new travelogues. In 1530, the Slovene Benedikt Kuripečič (1490–) served as an interpreter for a diplomatic mission going from Ljubljana to Istanbul, where it was received by Suleiman the Magnificent. Kuripečič's *Itinerarium* (1531) reflects the European fear of Turkish power and contains valuable information on the conditions in the peninsula during the first century of Ottoman rule.

The sixteenth century witnessed the first permanent exchange of ambassadors between France and Turkey. But the first French envoy, sent to Istanbul in 1525, did not reach his destination: he and his 11 companions were massacred in Bosnia. In 1547, another French diplomat had better luck: ambassador Gabriel d'Aramon (1508–1553) passed through the Balkan interior on his way to Istanbul. This journey was described by one of his companions, Jean Chesneau, in his *Le Voyage de Monsieur d'Aramon* (1887).

In the second half of the sixteenth century, we find some precursors of latter-day tourists—people traveling for pleasure. Such were the Frenchmen Philippe Du Fresne-Canaye and Pierre Lescalopier, who in 1573 and 1574, respectively, traveled to Istanbul on the Dubrovnik road. Du Fresne-Canaye's travelogue *Le Voyage du Levant*, originally written in Italian, was later translated into French and published in Paris only in 1897. At the end of the sixteenth century, the same route was used by two English travelers—Captain Henry Austell and a man known to us only by his last name, Fox. Austell traveled in 1585 with a caravan of merchants, while Fox accompanied his master Henry Cavendish in 1589 on a trade trip to Istanbul. Their travel accounts provide scant yet valuable information on the Balkan hinterland at that time: Fox writes that carts are a rarity, that people are crude and poor, and that they yell from hilltop to hilltop to convey messages.

In the seventeenth century, the Balkans continued to be a transit region for western Europeans on their way to Turkey. The prevalent route was the one between Venice and Istanbul by sea down the Dalmatian coast, then inland from Split or Dubrovnik. That route seemed to be safer in the sixteenth and most of the seventeenth century than the northern one through the plains, probably because of frequent military engagements in the north. As before, the travelers remarked on the poverty of the countryside, the miserable condition of the caravanserais (travelers often called them "stables") and the roads, the depopulation of entire regions, and the oppressive conditions under which Christians ("Sclavonians" or "Illyrians") lived.

In 1611, a French ambassadorial party's voyage to Istanbul was described by Le Febvre in his text *Le Voyage de Monsieur de Sancy*. A notable description in this travelogue is that of a fair in Pirot, where the writer also notes the typical Serb folk musical instrument, the *gusle*. In 1620, the English traveler Peter Mundy (1600–1667) accompanied ambassador Paul Pindar on his return from Istanbul to England. Mundy's account (1907) is generally reliable and contains valuable information about the lands and the people he saw along the route (Istanbul–Sofia–Belgrade–Sarajevo–Split–Venice). The French consul in Syria, Louis Gédoyn, traveled to the Turkish capital in 1624, also via Split (the "Split road"), and discovered in Belgrade a widely based—or at least rumored—Christian plot to overthrow Turkish power in the Balkans (*Journal et correspondance de Gédoyn "le Turc,"* 1909). Ten years after Gédoyn, the Englishman Henry Blount (1602–1682) traveled on the same road and recorded his trip in *A Voyage into the Levant* (1636). This astute observer, whose views on other cultures are refreshingly objective for his time, experienced some dangerous encounters on the road, especially in Bosnia.

Dangers, including battles, were experienced also by the Turkish traveler Evliya Çelebi, who visited many lands in his decades-long journeys in Turkey, the Middle East, and Europe. His travels in the Balkans in the 1660s were recorded in the fifth and sixth volumes of his ten-volume *Seyahatnamesi* [Narrative of Travels], a work that survived only in later copies, so its authenticity (except perhaps for its pious verbosity) is questionable, at least in part.

In the second half of the seventeenth century, Western travelers started to make wider use of the northern route to Istanbul, via Vienna or Budapest. In 1665, the Scotsman John Burbury was part of a diplomatic mission going from Vienna to Istanbul. The group traveled in boats from Vienna to Belgrade, and from there by land, in wagons and on horseback, to the Turkish capital. Burbury's travelogue, entitled *A Relation of a Journey* (1671), possesses a great immediacy of observation and directness of writing rarely matched in other travel texts of the period.

From the last decades of the seventeenth century on, the British and the French grew interested in the Greco-Roman antiquities in the Balkans, and visitors began to observe—and note in their travel diaries—such monuments as the amphitheater in Pula and Diocletian's palace in Split. These "philosophical travelers" showed greater curiosity and expanded interests, including an awareness of the natural world, history, language, and economic life of the countries visited. One such traveler was the Englishman Edward Browne (1644–1708), who in 1669 went from Vienna to Greece and described in his *A Brief Account of Some Travels* (1673) such sights as dugouts in Srem, the different colors of the Danube and the Sava, and women's dresses in central Serbia. Later in the century, the British architect Robert Adam (1728–1792) went to examine some important Roman remains on the Adriatic coast and meticulously described them in *The Ruins of the Palace of the Emperor Diocletian at*

*Spalatro in Dalmatia* (1764). A decade later, the same region was visited by the Italian abbot Alberto Fortis (1741–1803), who portrayed it exhaustively in his *Viaggi in Dalmazia* (1774). Written in the form of letters to various people, this work deals ably with many aspects of Dalmatia—its natural phenomena, antiquities, folklore, language, and literature.

Toward the end of the eighteenth century, growing western European economic interests in the Balkans, especially commercial ones, led merchants, diplomats, and other travelers to the peninsula. Several countries (France, Austria, and Britain) established diplomatic offices in various parts of "Turkey-in-Europe," and some French consuls and other diplomatic officials left important testimonies of their Balkan experience, both ambulatory and sedentary. The French diplomat F.C.H.L. Poqueville traveled widely in Albania, Greece, and other parts of the Ottoman empire and wrote, among other works, *Voyage en Morée, à Constantinople, en Albanie* (1805). J.B.A. Chaumette des Fossés, a French consular official in Travnik, described his *Voyage en Bosnie dans les années 1807 et 1808* (1816). The French presence in Napoleon's Illyrian provinces from 1809 to 1813 generated much travel writing as many army officers, administrators, diplomats, and others set down impressions of France's new Balkan possessions.

The long-burning Eastern Question flared up as the nineteenth century progressed and Serbia and Greece started their independence movements, attracting much attention and some support from western European countries. Some Europeans were so attracted to the Balkans that they even wrote about fictional trips there, like Prosper Mérimée in his book *La Guzla* (1827). But many more wrote after having gone there on some mission, on business, or out of curiosity. Besides diplomats and merchants, travelers now included an even greater number of secret agents, historians, geographers, naturalists, archaeologists, painters, hunters, businessmen, and missionaries—and also journalists, who wanted to witness and report on current events, like wars and rebellions. In the last decades of the century, we also find the first modern tourists. They could now prepare for travel using guidebooks (like those published in England by John Murray) that were themselves interesting examples of travel writing, based as they were on their authors' actual visits to the Balkan lands—for Western travelers not only the most easterly but also the most oriental and exotic part of the Continent.

By midcentury, routes to and within the peninsula had become more varied, and destinations had multiplied. Many of these were explored by the French traveler Ami Boué (1794–1881), whose monumental four-volume work *La Turquie d'Europe* (1840) set the tone and subject matter for many subsequent travel writers. In 1844, the English Egyptologist John G. Wilkinson (1797–1875) made a tour of the southwestern Balkans and paid visits to the Montenegrin and Herzegovinian rulers (*Dalmatia and Montenegro*, 1848). A few years later, his countryman Edmund Spencer, who ventured (mainly on horseback) deeper into the Balkan interior, was struck by "vast forests" in Serbia and that country's "half-deserted" appearance (*Travels in European Turkey in 1850*, 1851). At about the same time, the Balkans were traversed by another Briton, James Henry Skene (1812?–1886), who published his travelogue anonymously in 1853 under the title *The Frontier Lands of the Christian and the Turk*. This work reads in some places like a novel or an adventure story, while in others it is a political commentary interspersed with descriptions of current and recent events in the Balkans.

More ideologically oriented than Skene's is the travel book of Aleksandar Giljferding (1831–1872), the Russian consul in Sarajevo in 1857, *Putovanje po Hercegovini, Bosni i Staroj Srbiji* [Travels in Herzegovina, Bosnia, and Old Serbia] (1859). While mainly interested in the status of Serbs and Orthodox Christianity in the Balkans and in the spread of pan-Slavism there, Giljferding as a travel writer offers interesting cultural insights and many captivating details. The German Otto Blau (1828–1879), another consul-travel writer in Bosnia (where he served from 1861 to 1872), was chiefly attracted to the natural world and wrote about plants and geography in his *Reisen in Bosnien und der Hertzegowina* (1877). Two British women, Adeline Paulina Irby (1831–1911) and Georgina Muir Mackenzie (1833–1874), traveled extensively in the Balkans during the 1860s, always accompanied by Turkish armed escorts and carrying a wooden bathtub, a carpet, and copies of the Bible for their missionary work. Their *Travels in the Slavonic Provinces of Turkey-in-Europe* (1866) covers most Balkan regions and describes journeys, people, and places from a female perspective.

In the mid- and late 1870s, several travelers visited the peninsula and witnessed, on purpose or by accident, the rapid crumbling of Turkish power in the Balkans, marked especially by upheavals and fighting in Bosnia and Herzegovina, Serbia, and Bulgaria. The young Briton Arthur J. Evans (1851–1941), the future archaeologist of Knossos fame, recorded much of what he saw of the natural world, physical and human geography, and historical evidence between the Sava and the Adriatic Sea in his book *Through Bosnia and the Herzegovina on Foot* (1876). At about the same time, the French author and skilled illustrator Charles Yriarte (1833–1898) wrote his account of the Bosnian/Herzegovinian rebellion in *Bosnie et Herzégovine: Souvenirs de voyage pendant l'insurrection* (1876) and of his other experiences in *Les Bords de l'Adriatique et le Monténégro* (1878).

In the late nineteenth century and at the beginning of the twentieth, as travel conditions in the Balkans improved, with better roads, railways, and European-style hotels, travelers and travel writers became more numerous and their interests, motivations, and perspectives still more varied. Yet one constant remained: for European (and some American) visitors, the main appeal of Balkan lands continued to be their perceived oriental and exotic quality, their fundamental differentness from the rest of the Continent. For many writers, the westernizing influence of Austria in parts of the peninsula, especially after 1878, only underscored the still vital cultural elements of centuries-long Turkish presence there. Some of this perspective is reflected in the titles of several travelogues, like those of the English authors Harry De Windt (1856–1933; *Through Savage Europe*, 1907) and William Miller (1864–1945), who made several journeys to the Balkans in the 1890s and wrote reliably about the region's past and present in his *Travels and Politics in the Near East* (1898).

In the early twentieth century, the renewed unrest in the peninsula attracted a number of interested travelers who wrote on many aspects of the region's intricate political situation. This was also a time when the number of women travelers to the Balkans started to increase; one of the most prominent writers, the English woman Mary Edith Durham (1863–1944), made six tours of the region (she, too, sometimes refers to the Balkans as the "Near East") and wrote several books, mainly on Albania. The people of the peninsula, she remarks in *The Burden of the Balkans* (1905), "live in their past to an extent which it is hard for us in the West to realize." The Greek Demetra Vaka also wrote about Albania and the eastern Balkans in her book *In the Shadow of Islam* (1911).

The car and the camera added a special flavor to both traveling and travel writing in the Balkans before World War I. The English traveler Maude M. Holbach made a tour of Dalmatia and Bosnia in the first decade of the century and wrote two travelogues: *Dalmatia* (1908) and *Bosnia and Herzegovina* (1910). In 1908, the American Frances Kinsley Hutchinson drove through the western part of the peninsula with her family and "kodaked" various scenes that she deemed "quaint and curious" (*Motoring in the Balkans*, 1909). The British major Percy E. Henderson wrote a richly photographed account of his tour of several Balkan lands in 1909 (*A British Officer in the Balkans*, 1909).

Until the nineteenth century, most travel writing about the Balkans was done by people who passed through the peninsula on their way to Turkey, the Middle East, or India, and much of it was not published until the nineteenth or twentieth century. Later, the Balkans often became the primary destination of travelers—mainly French, British, German, and Austrian—who in their travels and their accounts frequently focused on a particular region or theme. Unlike the early writers, the later ones provided more dependable and more varied information on the countries they visited; they also had an eye for the landscape and were generally more interested in the lifestyles of the people they described. The sum of their writings brought southeastern Europe closer to the rest of the Continent.

Omer Hadžiselimović

## References and Further Reading


Adam, Robert, *The Ruins of the Palace of the Emperor Diocletian at Spalatro in Dalmatia*, 1764.

Blau, Otto, *Reisen in Bosnien und der Hertzegowina: Topographische und pflanzengeographische Aufzeichnungen*, 1877.

Blount, Henry, *A Voyage into the Levant*, 1636.

Boué, Ami, *La Turquie d'Europe*, 4 vols., 1840.

Boué, Ami, *Recueil d'itinéraires dans la Turquie d'Europe*, 1854.

Browne, Edward, *A Brief Account of Some Travels in Hungaria, Servia, Bulgaria, Macedonia, Thessaly, Austria, Styria, Carinthia, Carniola and Friuli*, 1673; 2nd enlarged edition, 1685.

Burbury, John, *A Relation of a Journey of the Right Honourable My Lord Henry Howard, from London to Vienna, and thence to Constantinople*, 1671.

Chaumette des Fossés, J.B.A., *Voyage en Bosnie dans les années 1807 et 1808*, 1816.

Chesneau, Jean, *Voyage de Monsieur d'Aramon, ambassadeur pour le Roy en Levant*, 1887; reprinted, 1970.

De Windt, Harry, *Through Savage Europe, Being the Narrative of a Journey, throughout the Balkan States and European Russia*, 1907.

Du Fresne-Canaye, Philippe, *Le Voyage du Levant*, 1897; reprinted, 1980.

Durham, Mary Edith, *Through the Lands of the Serb*, 1904.

Durham, Mary Edith, *The Burden of the Balkans*, 1905.

Evans, Arthur, *Through Bosnia and the Herzegovina on Foot during the Insurrection, August and September 1875*, 1876.

Evans, Arthur, *Illyrian Letters*, 1878.

Evliya, Çelebi, *Narrative of Travels in Europe, Asia, and Africa*, 2 vols., translated from the Turkish by Joseph von Hammer, 1850.

Evliya, Çelebi, *Putopis: Odlomci o jugoslavenskim zemljama*, edited and translated by Hazim Šabanovic, 1967.

Fortis, Alberto, *Viaggi in Dalmazia*, 2 vols., 1774; as *Travels in Dalmatia*, 1778.

Gédoyn, Louis, *Journal et correspondance de Gédoyn "le Turc,"* 1909.

Giljferding, Aleksandar, *Putovanje po Hercegovini, Bosni i Staroj Srbiji*, [Travels in Herzegovina, Bosnia, and Old Serbia], 1972; 2nd Bosnian/Serbo-Croatian edition, 1996.

Henderson, Percy E., *A British Officer in the Balkans*, 1909.

Holbach, Maude M., *Dalmatia: The Land where East Meets West*, 1908.

Holbach, Maude M., *Bosnia and Herzegovina*, 1910.
Hutchinson, Frances Kinsley, *Motoring in the Balkans: Along the Highways of Dalmatia, Montenegro, the Herzogovina and Bosnia*, 1909.
Ingulf, Abbot of Crowland, *Ingulph's Chronicle of the Abbey of Croyland with the Continuations by Peter of Blois and Anonymous Writers*, translated from the Latin by Henry T. Riley, 1854.
Irby, Adeline Paulina, and Georgina Muir Mackenzie, *Travels in the Slavonic Provinces of Turkey-in-Europe*, 1866; 2nd, enlarged edition, 1877.
Kuripcčič, Bcncdikt, *Itinerarium oder die Botschaftsreise des Josef von Lamberg und Nicolas Jurischitz durch Bosnien, Serbien, Bulgarien nach Constantinopel 1530*, 1531.
Kuripečič, Benedikt, *Putopis kroz Bosnu, Srbiju, Bulgarsku i Rumeliju 1530.*
La Brocquière, Bertrandon de, *Le Voyage d'outremer*, edited by Ch. Schefer, 1892; as *The Voyage d'outremer*, translated and edited by Galen R. Kline, 1988.
Miller, William, *Travels and Politics in the Near East*, 1898.
Mundy, Peter, *The Travels of Peter Mundy, in Europe and Asia, 1608–1667*, 5 vols., edited by Richard Carnac Temple, 1907–1967.
Poqueville, F.C.H.L., *Voyage au Morée, à Constantinople, en Albanie et dans plusieurs autres parties de l'empire Ottoman pendant les années 1798, 1799, 1800 et 1801*, translated as *Travels through the Morea, Albania, and Other Parts of the Ottoman Empire . . .* , in Richard Phillips, *A Collection of Modern and Contemporary Voyages and Travels*, vol. 3, 1805–1810.
Skene, James Henry, *The Frontier Lands of the Christian and the Turk: Comprising Travels in the Regions of the Lower Danube, in 1850 and 1851*, 2 vols., 1853.
Spencer, Edmund, *Travels in European Turkey in 1850*, 2 vols., 1851.
Torkington, Richard, *Ye Oldest Diarie of Englysshe Travel*, edited by W.J. Loftie, 1884.
Vaka, Demetra, *In the Shadow of Islam*, 1911.
Wilkinson, J. Gardner, *Dalmatia and Montenegro: With a Journey to Mostar in Herzegovina*, 2 vols., 1848.
Yriarte, Charles, *Bosnie et Herzégovine: Souvenirs de voyage pendant l'insurrection*, 1876.
Yriarte, Charles, *Les Bords de l'Adriatique et le Monténégro*, 1878.

*See also* **Albania; Greece, 1600–1821; Greece, post-1821**

## BALLOONS AND AIRSHIPS

Balloons were used early in man's attempts to fly. Joseph and Étienne Montgolfier, on 4 June 1783, successfully launched an unmanned balloon in France. Later they launched a balloon with several animal passengers. The first manned balloon flight took place in November of that year when three Frenchmen sailed over Paris in a Montgolfier balloon. The flight lasted 23 minutes and covered about five and a half miles. Finally, in December, a flight was undertaken that lasted for two hours.

Perhaps because of their military and scientific applications, there has been extensive development of balloon technology (for instance, the introduction of pressurized cabins or capsules). Balloons were the first vehicles to approach the edge of space. Much of the advances in weather science have been possible thanks to intensive exploration by instrumented free balloons, which can travel up to heights of around 20 miles.

Balloons and airships have also been used in Arctic exploration; the pioneer was Salomon August Andrée (1854–1930), a Stockholm engineer who started planning for an attempt to reach the North Pole in a balloon. Backed by, among others, the king of Sweden, Oscar II, his balloon *Örnen* (The Eagle) started from Spitsbergen in July 1897. The flight lasted only 65 hours and ended just north of 82°N. After a crash landing on the ice, the three pilots (Andrée and fellow pilots Knut Fraenkel and Nils Strindberg) started walking south. They reached White Island, east of Spitsbergen, in October. There they perished. It was not until 1930 that the three frozen bodies were found and brought back to Sweden for burial.

The next attempt to reach the North Pole was made by the American journalist Walter Wellman in an airship in the first years of the new century.

In the 1920s, it was Roald Amundsen's ambition to fly over the North Pole. With the American Lincoln Ellsworth, he made an unsuccessful attempt in 1925 in the airship *Norge*. The flight resulted in the gathering of important new information about the Arctic. There was, however, a tragic follow-up. The Italian Umberto Nobile, who had designed *Norge*, two years later took its sister ship *Italia* on an Arctic flight. When nothing was heard from the expedition in six weeks, a search started. Amundsen flew in a search party, but his plane never came back. The second search expedition found *Italia*, which had crashed. Among the survivors was Nobile himself.

The airship era had begun when Count Ferdinand von Zeppelin flew his first airship, the zeppelin *LZ 1*, from the shores of Lake Constance in 1900 and ended when his company's great zeppelin *Hindenberg* caught fire and crashed at Lakehurst, New Jersey, on 6 May 1937. During this time, airships went from flimsy craft built largely of wood to the enormous but lightweight metal constructions of the 1920s and 1930s. What is left are the nonrigid blimps we see today.

It was not until 1978 that the Atlantic was crossed by a helium gas balloon, *Double Eagle II.* Launched from Maine in the United States, it covered 3,120 miles in 137 hours piloted by Maxie Anderson, Ben Abruzzo, and Larry Newman. Almost ten years later, the Atlantic was crossed for the first time in a hot air balloon, *Virgin Atlantic Flyer*, piloted by the British billionaire Richard Branson and the Swede Per Lindstrand. It was the fastest manned balloon, flying at an average speed of 97 miles per hour. It covered 3,075 miles in almost

32 hours. With the extremely high flying hot air balloons, the careful construction of the pressurized gondola for the aeronauts is essential.

In 1981, the Pacific was crossed for the first time by a manned balloon, *Double Eagle V*, piloted by Abruzzo, Rocky Aoki, Ron Clark, and Newman. It crossed from Japan to California (5,770 miles) in around 85 hours. The first hot air balloon to cross the Pacific, *Pacific Flyer*, was piloted by Branson and Lindstrand in 1991; they set off from Japan and landed in the Canadian Arctic after 46 hours and 6,761 miles. The Englishman John Ackroyd was responsible for constructing the gondolas in both Branson-Lindstrand flights. The great balloon exploration achievement was of course the attempt to fly around the world. There were a number of contestants in the 1990s, among them Branson-Lindstrand, but the eventual winner was the Swiss Bertrand Piccard and his companion Brian Jones, in the hot air balloon *Breitling Orbiter 3*. The balloon started in Switzerland on 1 March 1999 and landed in Egypt on March 21. Piccard and Jones were the first balloonists to circumnavigate the globe with a nonstop, nonrefueled flight, taking 19 days, 1 hour, and 49 minutes.

Ballooning has become a prominent sport all over the world, but it has not developed into an important means of travel. Balloons are used for shorter excursions but not for common travel.

BERTIL HÄGGMAN

### References and Further Reading

Ahlmann, H. W:son, editor, *Med Örnen mot Polen: Andrées polarexpedition år 1897 utgiven på grundval av S.A. Andrée, Nils Strindberg och Knut Fraenkel sommaren 1930 på Vitön funna anteckningar*, 1930.

Andrée, S.A., "Förslag till polarfärd med luftballong: Föredrag," 1895.

*See also* **Airplanes**

## BANKS, JOSEPH (1743–1820) *British Naturalist, Explorer, and Patron of Exploration*

Joseph Banks's father died in 1761, leaving his son, then in his first year at Oxford, a large fortune and the freedom to use it as he pleased. By then his taste for botany had already been encouraged by his mother, apparently with the help of Gerard's *Herball*. Instruction in botany at Oxford was less than adequate during the mid-eighteenth century, so Banks looked for a teacher in Cambridge and brought back Israel Lyons (1739–1775), botanist and astronomer, who was later recommended by his former pupil to be a member of the group that traveled with Constantine Phipps (1744–1792) on his voyage to the North Pole. After she was widowed, Banks's mother lived in a London house in Paradise Row, close to the Chelsea Physic Garden, where her son was able to pursue his botanical studies with the help of Philip Miller (1691–1771), the garden's curator, author of the *Gardeners Dictionary* (1731), and a central figure in the introduction of exotic plants.

Constantine Phipps was also Banks's companion on his own 1766 voyage in *Niger*, one of the naval ships patrolling the Newfoundland fisheries. With the advice of Daniel Solander (1736–1782), who had studied under the Swedish naturalist Carl Linnaeus (1707–1778), the two young men gathered equipment for collecting both plants and animals, as well as a handful of books to help in identifying their discoveries. The journey started from Plymouth, where Banks collected plants and made drawings and notes about fish and other animals before departing on 22 April. *Niger* arrived in St. John's, Newfoundland, on 11 May and stayed there for a month before going on to Croque on the Northern Peninsula, then to Château Bay in Labrador. There a blockhouse was built before the ship returned to St. John's, where it remained for two weeks. Just before *Niger* left for Lisbon in September, James Cook (1728–1779) arrived in *Grenville*. Though there is no proof that Cook and Banks first met in Newfoundland, it seems more than likely that they did. After a long pause (six weeks) in Lisbon, *Niger* returned to England. Back in London, Banks and his sister, Sarah Sophia (his only sibling), left their mother's house and took one of their own to provide more room for his rapidly growing library, herbarium, and other collections.

This journey might be regarded as preparation for a longer one that took Banks, Solander, and a team of naturalists and artists around the world on *Endeavour* with Captain Cook. The voyage was sponsored by the Royal Society with the particular object of observing the transit of Venus in June 1769 from Tahiti. Banks had been elected a fellow of the society in April 1766 and, as "a gentleman of large fortune, who is well versed in Natural History," was recommended (with seven colleagues) to join the travelers "for the advancement of useful knowledge" in this field. *Endeavour* left on 8 August 1768 and traveled via Madeira, Rio, Tierra del Fuego, Cape Horn, Tahiti, other Pacific islands, Australia and New Zealand, Batavia (where malaria and dysentery killed many of the crew, including the artist, Sydney Parkinson [1745?–1771]), and the Cape of Good Hope to return on 15 July 1771. "Immortal Banks, the glory of England and the whole world" (as Linnaeus described him in a letter of 6 August), received an enthusiastic welcome home. The young traveler, wearing a feather cloak from New Zealand, was painted by Benjamin West. The publication of drawings and descriptions of the 30,000 plants and 1,000 animals collected on the voyage was planned, and copperplates of the plants were engraved, but the whole set was not issued until the 1980s, when *Banks' Florilegium* was printed in color from the original plates.

The circumnavigation, followed by Banks's election as president of the Royal Society in 1778, established him as George III's "Minister of Philosophic Affairs." His influence on a great variety of projects can be traced in the annotated catalog of his correspondence—from the introduction of merino sheep to Australia and tea to India to the organization of the Royal Gardens at Kew as a center of botanical exploration, the establishment of the settlement at Botany Bay, and his patronage of Mungo Park (1771–1806), Matthew Flinders (1774–1814), and William Bligh (1754–1817), among many others. From 1777, his house and library in Soho Square served as the headquarters of scientific patronage, though his own plans for a second journey around the world with Cook, on *Resolution*, had been thwarted by the limitations of the space made available for his party. Instead, Banks and a group of friends made a shorter journey to Iceland from July to November 1772, pausing in the Hebrides on 13 August to look at the island of Staffa. His account of the place ("better than cathedrals"), the earliest description of its geology, was printed in the 1774 edition of Thomas Pennant's *Tour in Scotland* and in Uno von Troil's *Letters on Iceland*, in Swedish in 1777 and in English in 1780. The other outstanding feature of this journey was the ascent of Mount Hecla in Iceland, a brief diversion from the natural history of the place. Banks's collection of Icelandic plants was added to his herbarium; he also brought back 162 Icelandic manuscripts, which he presented to the British Museum Library. Eventually, his own library and other collections were bequeathed to the same institution, though a later series of sales scattered the letters and other manuscripts that had been left in the hands of his relatives.

SANDRA RAPHAEL

Banks as Royal Society grandee in his later years appears in a very different character from the resourceful young man who sailed with Captain Cook (mezzotint frontispiece to *The Journal of the Rt. Hon. Sir Joseph Banks*, 1896, from the 1815 portrait by Thomas Phillips). *Courtesy of British Library, London.*

## Biography

Born in London, 13 February 1743. Attended Harrow School briefly; later studied at Eton College, 1755–1760, and Christ Church, Oxford, 1760–1763. Inherited his father's estate, Revesby Abbey, near Boston, Lincolnshire, 1861. Elected a Fellow of the Royal Society, May 1766. Traveled to Newfoundland and Labrador, 1766; around the world on *Endeavour* with Captain Cook, 1768–1771; and to Iceland, 1772 (pausing at Staffa on the way). President of the Royal Society, 30 November 1778–1820. Helped to establish the African Association, sponsoring Mungo Park's expedition to Africa, 1788. Married Dorothea Weston-Hugessen, 1779. Knighted and created a baronet, 1781; invested with the Order of the Bath, 1795, and membership of the Privy Council, 1797. Awarded Honorary DCL of Oxford, 1771. Died at Spring Grove, Isleworth, Middlesex, 19 June 1820.

## References and Further Reading

Banks, Joseph, *The Banks Letters: A Calendar of the Manuscript Correspondence of Sir Joseph Banks*, edited by Warren R. Dawson, 1958; *Supplementary Letters*, 1962.

Banks, Joseph, *The Endeavour Journal of Joseph Banks, 1768–71*, edited by J.C. Beaglehole, 2 vols., 1962.

Banks, Joseph, *Joseph Banks in Newfoundland and Labrador, 1766: His Diary, Manuscripts and Collections*, edited by A.M. Lysaght, 1971.

Banks, Joseph, *The Letters of Sir Joseph Banks: A Selection 1768–1820*, edited by Neil Chambers, 2001.

Pennant, Thomas, *A Tour in Scotland, and Voyage to the Hebrides MDCCLXXII*, 1774 (pp. 261–269, plates 27–31, especially plate 28, "Fingal's Cave"); edited by Andrew Simmons, 1998.

*See also* **Scientific Traveling**

## BARROS, JOÃO DE (c. 1496–1570)

***Portuguese Historian and Writer***

Although João de Barros was not a great traveler, he is important in the field of travel literature as author of *Décadas da Ásia*, a work in which he celebrated the national glories resulting from overseas conquest and exploration by the Portuguese.

In spite of being an illegitimate child, Barros was descended from a noble family and was educated at court from an age when, according to him, he should have been "playing with his top." There he served Prince John (João), who became John III, as the prince's valet. Later in life, he would become one of the most prominent Renaissance scholars and one of the most elegant writers in Portugal.

Being a humanist, Barros had a vast range of interests, including history, geography, pedagogy, grammar, and architecture. He was even involved in religious debates, defending the expelled Jews and the so-called New Christians, who were being persecuted and ill-treated in Portugal at the time. He dealt with this critical issue in *Ropica Pnefma* (1532). From a literary point of view, he was also a man of his age and, always using vigorous language and a style worked to perfection, he cultivated different genres. These included a romance of chivalry (*Crónica do Imperador Clarimundo*, 1520), the reading of which may have influenced Manuel I to ask Barros to write an epic history of the Portuguese in Asia. The king's challenge was accepted, and, following the Roman model of Livy, Barros divided the related events into periods of ten years, hence the title "Decades." The *Décadas*, as we know them, are only a part of his original plan, which was divided into three parts: "Conquest" (including four sections: Europe, Africa, Asia, and Santa Cruz or Brazil), "Navigation," and "Commerce."

John III sent Barros to Africa, and on his return he started his public service. In 1525, he became treasurer of the House of India, later treasurer of the House of Mina and of the House of Ceuta, and finally steward of estate (*feitor*), thus administering the House of India between 1533 and 1567. During this period, because of his professional obligations, he had direct access to most of the information concerning the political, military, and maritime development of the empire. In his official position, Barros could ask questions of the returning soldiers, merchants, and administrators and read all the official correspondence, while he himself, as *feitor* of the House of India, was personally involved in the dispatch and return of the annual India fleets.

He compiled all this information and used it to write *Décadas da Ásia*, the epic historical account of Portuguese discoveries and conquests in the Orient to 1538. Barros published the first volume in 1552, and subsequent volumes in 1553 and 1563. The last volume, which appeared posthumously in 1615, covered the period from 1539 to the end of the century and was edited and partially written by Diogo do Couto. Barros's other works on geography, commerce, and navigation disappeared after his death.

His involvement in the confused history of the colonization of Maranhão, in Brazil, which eventually led to its occupation by the French in 1612, after Barros's death, was an unfortunate event in his life. His role in this affair was never clear, but as a result of his failure to colonize the territory he had been granted in 1535, he experienced great financial problems and lost most of his possessions. His failure also caused the death of many of the other participants in the adventure, compelling him to pay compensation to their bereaved families. As often happens, there are opposing views about this episode, and some historians, like Charles R. Boxer, even consider Barros to be one of the stimulating forces behind the colonization of Brazil itself.

Some scholars, like Hernâni Cidade, consider his writings more formative than informative. They also call our attention to the fact that, even in the *Décadas da Ásia*, despite the nationalist apology—whose origin is both the patriotic ideal of the Renaissance and the conscienceness of a historical mission to be fulfilled—there is a very strong pedagogical propensity in Barros's works. This marked tendency has earned him the reputation of being "a true pedagogue of good citizenship." Consequently, wanting to write an edifying history, he had to be selective and may, therefore, have compromised historical truth. He himself, in the prologue of the third "Decade," declares that historical truth should not predominate to the extent that it compels us to describe deeds that though "due to justicc could be seen as cruelty."

In spite of the justified accusations that his imperialist view of history and his expansionist euphoria interfered with Barros's impartiality as a reliable historical source, the literary brilliance of his oeuvre conferred on him his well-deserved fame as a distinguished humanist.

It is also worth mentioning that, even though he had not actually been there himself, he included in his work extremely vivid descriptions of the wonderful landscapes of Africa and of the Orient. These descriptions can be considered as his indirect contribution to the development of travel literature, and this facet of his literary career also helped turn him into an indisputable icon of Portuguese intellectual life in the sixteenth century.

MARIA LAURA PIRES

### Biography

Probably born at Vila Verde, Viseu, c. 1496. Illegitimate son of Lopo de Barros, the descendant of a northern Portuguese noble family. Began serving at court at an early age; sent by John III on a mission to San Jorge da Mina in Guinea, 1522. Returned, 1525. Appointed by John III to a post corresponding to crown administrator of the colonies in Africa and India, c. 1525. Devoted most of his life to the task of writing his historical chronicles celebrating the imperial deeds of the Portuguese in the East. Experienced financial problems after the loss of his estate in Brazil. Continued his literary work and retained his official position at court until 1567. Resigned his post at the House of India and retired to his property near Pombal. Died at Ribeira de Litém, near Pombal, 20 October 1570.

### References and Further Reading

Barros, João de, *Ásia de João de Barros dos Feitos que os Portugueses Fizeram no Descobrimento e Conquista dos Mares e Terras do Oriente: Primeira década*, 1552.

Barros, João de, *Segunda Década da Ásia de João de Barros*, 1553.

Barros, João de, *Terceira Década da Ásia*, 1563.

Barros, João de, *Quarta Década da Ásia de João de Barros . . . com notas e taboas geographicas de João Baptista Lavanha*, 1615.

Barros, João de, *Décadas da Ásia*, edited by A.A. Grillo and G.A. Grillo, 1886; edited by Hernâni Cidade and Manuel Múrias, 6th edition, 4 vols., 1945–1946; selection, edited by António Baião, 4 vols., 1945–1946.

Barros, João de, *The History of Ceylon, from the Earliest Times to 1600 AD*, translated and edited by Donald Ferguson, 1909 [extracted from *Ásia*].

Boxer, C.R., *João de Barros: Portuguese Humanist and Historian of Asia*, New Delhi: Concept Publishing Company, 1981.

Boxer, C.R., *Portuguese Seaborne Empire, 1415–1825*, London: Hutchinson, and New York: Knopf, 1969; reprinted, Manchester: Carcanet, 1991.

Buescu, Ana Isabel, "João de Barros: Humanismo, Mercancia e Celebração Imperial" [João de Barros: Humanism, Trade, and Imperial Celebration], *Oceanos*, 27 (July–September 1996): 10–27.

Buescu, Leonor, "João de Barros," *Verbo: Enciclopédia Luso-Brasileira de Cultura*, vol. 3, Lisbon: Verbo, 1965.

Cidade, Hernâni, *A Literatura Portuguesa e a Expansão Ultramarina* [Portuguese Literature and Overseas], vol. 1: *Os Séculos XV e XVI*, Lisbon: Agência Geral das Colónias, 1943; 2nd edition, Coimbra: Amado, 1963.

Cidade, Hernâni, "João de Barros: O que pensa da língua portuguesa, como a escreve" [João de Barros: What He Thinks about Portuguese Language, How He Writes It], *Boletim de Filologia* (Lisbon), 11 (1950): 281–303.

Cordeiro, Luciano, "Documentos sobre Viagens, Navegações e Conquistas dos Portugueses" [Documents about Travels, Navigations, and Conquests by the Portuguese], in his *Questões Histórico-Coloniais*, vol. 1, Lisbon: Agência Geral das Colónias, 1935.

Diffie, Bailey W., and George D. Winius, *The Foundations of the Portuguese Empire, 1415–1580*, Minneapolis: University of Minnesota Press, 1977.

Godinho, Vitorino Magalhães, *Documentos sobre a Expansão Portuguesa* [Documents about Portuguese Expansion], vols. 1–2, Lisbon: Gleba, 1943–1945; vol. 3, Lisbon: Cosmos, 1956.

Martins, Atílio A.R., *Subsídios para uma Edição Crítica da "Ásia" de João de Barros* [Contributions to a Critical Edition of Barros's *Ásia*], Braga: n.p., 1963.

Matos, Luís, "Acerca dos Inéditos de João de Barros" [About Barros's Unpublished Works], in *Actas do III Coloquio Internacional de Estudos Luso-Brasileiros (1957)*, 2 vols., Lisbon, 1959.

Moreira, Rafael, and William M. Thomas, "Desventuras de João de Barros: O Achado da Nau Aires da Cunha Naufragada em 1536," *Oceanos*, 27 (July–September 1996): 101.

Penrose, Boies, *Travel and Discovery in the Renaissance, 1420–1620*, Cambridge, Mass.: Harvard University Press, 1952; 2nd edition, 1955.

## BARROW, JOHN (1764–1848) *British Explorer, Writer, and Geographer*

John Barrow was born in humble circumstances near Ulverston, then in Lancashire, on 19 June 1764. As a young man, he went to sea and eventually obtained a position as secretary and attaché to Lord Macartney, ambassador to China and later governor of the Cape of Good Hope colony. Barrow accompanied the first British embassy to China in 1792, and after spending ten years in Southeast Asia and southern Africa he returned to England in 1802. In 1803, he was appointed second secretary to the Admiralty, a position he was to hold, with a brief interruption, for approximately 40 years.

Barrow recorded accounts of his travels with Macartney in three books: *Travels in China . . .* (1804), *A Voyage to Cochinchina, in the Years 1791 and 1793* (1806), and *An Account of Travels into the Interior of Southern Africa, in the years 1797 and 1798* (1801–1804). Barrow's writings proved to be not only popular, as subsequent English, French, German, and American editions indicate, but also useful to governments, merchants, and travelers alike. Barrow's text on southern Africa, for example, includes the first reliable map of the area.

During the period of Barrow's tenure at the Admiralty, agencies for the British government, and for the Admiralty in particular, took the lead in promoting and funding numerous voyages both to further the knowledge of geography and navigation and to expedite colonial initiatives. In 1815, Barrow replaced Sir Joseph Banks as the government's principal instigator of exploration. His first efforts were directed toward plotting the course of the Niger in Africa, but these soon proved unsuccessful. Perhaps because of a voyage to

Spitzbergen when he was 16, and perhaps because of the well-publicized and ongoing search for a Northwest Passage, Barrow then redirected his efforts to Arctic exploration. Barrow's influence was such that he was able to persuade the British government to fund several Arctic expeditions, including those of John Ross, David Buchan, William Parry, and the ill-fated John Franklin.

Barrow published the results of these expeditions in numerous articles in the *Quarterly Review* and in two books. The first book, *A Chronological History of Voyages into the Arctic Regions*, was published in 1818, and takes shape not as a factual history of Arctic exploration but rather as an extremely lively and entertaining account of both fictitious and actual travel narratives from the mid-ninth to the early eighteenth century. The second book, *Voyages of Discovery and Research within the Arctic Regions, from the Year 1818 to the Present Time*, appeared in 1846, and its style, while still very fluid, is much more detailed, factual, and, perhaps, scientific. Barrow's secondhand accounts of Arctic exploration raised questions about their authenticity, however, and John Ross's allegations of inconsistencies and inaccuracies in the works caused a rift between the two men that continued throughout the remainder of Barrow's life.

In his official capacity as second secretary to the Admiralty, Barrow was a prolific writer. Moreover, he somehow found time to write a number of other travel-related books: biographies of famous English admirals and explorers, including Francis Drake, Earl Howe, and Lord Anson; a manual of the description and function of mathematical drawing instruments used in navigation and cartography; and what has come to be regarded as the definitive account of the mutiny on HMS *Bounty*.

Barrow was a principal founder of the Royal Geographical Society, which originated as the Raleigh Traveller's Club in 1827, was reorganized as the Geographical Society of London in 1830, and was finally incorporated under its present name in 1859. The encouragement and assistance he gave to Arctic explorers resulted in several geographical features being named after him, including Barrow Strait (the entrance to the Northwest Passage), Cape Barrow (the northernmost cape on the North American continent), and Point Barrow, Alaska (the largest Inupiat Eskimo village in the world). Although Barrow did not live to see Amundsen's discovery of the Northwest Passage in 1904, his optimism and conviction that such a route existed continued to serve as a source of inspiration for Arctic explorers long after his death in 1848.

TERRY REILLY

### Biography

Born near Ulverston, Lancashire (now Cumbria), 19 June 1764, to a humble family. Educated at Town Bank Grammar School, Ulverston. Timekeeper at a foundry in Liverpool, 1778–1781. Went to sea on a Greenland whaler, c. 1781. Taught at a school in Greenwich, c. 1783–1785. Obtained a position as secretary and attaché to Lord Macartney, ambassador to China and later governor of the Cape of Good Hope colony. Accompanied the first British embassy to China, 1792; spent several years in Southeast Asia and southern Africa, 1790s. Married Anna Maria Trüter, c. 1798. Bought property in South Africa, 1800; forced to return to England after the Treaty of Amiens, 1802. Second secretary to the Admiralty, 1803–1806, 1807–1845. Initiated expeditions to survey the Arctic coast and discover the Northwest Passage, 1817–1818. A founder of the Royal Geographical Society, 1830, and one of its first presidents. Created baronet, 1835. Wrote prolifically, both travel narratives and travel-related biographies. Hon. LL D, Edinburgh University, 1821. Died in London, 23 November 1848.

### References and Further Reading

Barrow, John, *An Account of Travels into the Interior of Southern Africa, in the Years 1797 and 1798*, 2 vols., 1801–1804.
Barrow, John, *A Description of Pocket and Magazine Cases of Mathematical Drawing Instruments*, 1803.
Barrow, John, *Travels in China . . .*, 1804.
Barrow, John, *A Voyage to Cochinchina, in the Years 1792 and 1793*, 1806.
Barrow, John, *Some Account of the Public Life, and a Selection of the Unpublished Writings of the Earl of Macartney*, 1807.
Barrow, John, *A Chronological History of Voyages into the Arctic Regions; Undertaken Chiefly for the Purpose of Discovering a North-east, North-west, or Polar Passage between the Atlantic and Pacific*, 1818; reprinted, 1971.
Barrow, John, *The Life of George, Lord Anson, Admiral of the Fleet*, 1838.
Barrow, John, *The Life of Richard, Earl Howe, K.G. Admiral of the Fleet, and General of Marines*, 1838.
Barrow, John, *The Life, Voyages, and Exploits of Admiral Sir Francis Drake, Knt., with Numerous Original Letters from Him*, 1843; reprinted, 1900.
Barrow, John, *Voyages of Discovery and Research within the Arctic Regions, from the Year 1818 to the Present Time*, 1846.
Barrow, John, *The Eventful History of the Mutiny and Piratical Seizure of HMS Bounty: Its Causes and Consequences*, 1876.

*See also* **Northwest Passage**

## BARSKII, VASILII GRIGOROVICH (1702–1747) *Ukrainian Pilgrim, Monk, and Diarist*

Vasilii Grigorovich Barskii was born into a tradesman's family in Kiev. After studying at the Kiev Mogila Academy, the first institution of higher education in the Ukraine, he left without a degree in 1723 to travel by walking through Galicia, a province of the Austro-Hungarian empire, to L'vov (Lemberg, Poland) for medical treatment. He entered the local Jesuit academy for the spring term, but continued his travels on foot in July 1724. Because he walked everywhere overland, his travels lasted virtually all his life.

Barskii had, it seems, the mind of a perpetual pilgrim, drifting from one world to another: that of the traditional Russian, of the "enlightened" citizen of Europe, and of the rediscovered explorer of the Near East. His personality revealed both the dignity of a monk and the quality of a curious observer. He was obsessed with the idea of jotting down in detail everything he saw, frequently using the popular expression from old Russian pilgrims' tales "this I have seen with my own eyes" [Travels . . . in the East].

Barskii's meticulous accounts resemble an inventory rather than a tale. He was more of an artist and an observer, a systematic collector of data and architectural measurements, than a philosopher or spiritual seeker. Being a pilgrim and a monk, he paid much attention to the churches, monasteries, and the religious life in the countries he visited. His Mount Athos itinerary includes a concise description of the peninsula's geographical position, the condition of the monastic buildings and the church, a brief account of the monastic activities, the numbers and nationalities of the monks, the time spent in each monastery, and the distance in hours between them on his route.

Barskii differs from his Russian predecessors in that he did not record legends and miracles, but merely listed the famous icons and relics. However, he never allowed his religious commitment to hinder him from observing other aspects of life: "One ought to know that even though the people in the various Hungarian countries belong to different creeds they are nevertheless hospitable" [Travels . . . in the East].

Barskii's travel diary begins with a description of the journey from Kiev to L'vov. He visited some places only briefly, in others he stayed longer. With equal benevolence he describes the Magyars (Hungarians), the Slovaks, the Serbs, and the other people he met during his travels. He was particularly enthusiastic about the town Košice, where he noted that all the houses were of stone, that there was a complete sewerage system with clean streets, and that there were wells inside the houses. He also discovered that in Vienna "there are stone houses, which are tidy and beautiful, and outside each house a lantern is hanging on a handle" [Travels . . . in the East].

From L'vov, Barskii walked across Hungary with the intention of visiting the holy places of Christianity. He met the emperor Charles VI (1685–1740) in Vienna, visited the Santa Casa, or Holy House of the Virgin, at Loreto, and venerated the relics of St. Nicholas at Bari in southeastern Italy. Through Naples, Rome, and Florence, he reached Venice, where he embarked on a ship to Corfu and Cephalonia. From the Ionian islands, he sailed to Chios, where he met Patriarch Chrysanthos (1707–1731) of Jerusalem in 1725. From Thessaloniki, he sailed to Mount Athos. He visited Palestine, Jerusalem, and Cyprus, then sailed to Cairo, where he met Patriarch Cosmas II of Alexandria (d. 1736). Through Suez and Raithu, he continued to the monastery of St. Catherine on Mount Sinai, where he met expatriarch Jeremias III of Constantinople (1716–1726).

He set out again for Cairo, then Jerusalem, lived for a while in Tripoli, then in Dasmascus, where he met Patriarch Sylvester of Antiochia (1724–1766), who conferred the monastic habit on him in 1734. In honor of St. Basil the Great (330?–379), Barskii kept his first name as his monk's name at his baptism. From Damascus, Barskii sailed to Cyprus, then to Patmos, where he resided from 1737 to 1743. Invited by the Russian minister plenipotentiary, G. Všnjakov, he went to Constantinople and then revisited Mount Athos. He made his naturalistic drawings of each ruling monastery, which have been reproduced ever since in numerous pilgrims' books on Mount Athos. Then he went to Epirus, Crete, and returned from Constantinople to Ukraine by walking through Bulgaria, Wallachia, Moldavia, and Poland. Six weeks later, he died in Kiev, on 7 October 1747, at the age of 45.

Barskii's travel diaries, written en route in Church Slavonic with some Ukrainian traits, were kept by his mother and published three years after her death in 1778. The text was linguistically and stylistically revised by Prince Grigorii A. Potemkin. New editions appeared in 1785, 1795, 1800, and 1819. From 1885 to 1887, Nikolai Barsukov reedited Barskii's work from the original manuscript. Barskii's invaluable and well-known pen-and-ink drawings of all the ruling monasteries on Mount Athos are printed in this edition.

René Gothóni

## Biography

Born in Kiev, Russia, 1702. Attended Kiev Mogila Academy of Theology, c. 1720. Left the academy without a degree. Traveled to L'vov (now Lemberg), Poland, for medical treatment; attended the local Jesuit academy, 1723. Set out on a lifetime's journey through the Austro-Hungarian empire, July 1724: visited Italy, Greece, Palestine, Syria, Arabia, and Egypt. Returned to Kiev, 1747. Died in Kiev, 7 October 1747.

### References and Further Reading

Barskii, Vasilii Grigorovich, *Pěšechodca Vasiliia Grigoroviča Barskago-Plaki-Albova uroženca kievskago, monacha antiochiiskago, Putešestvie k'sviatym městam, v'Evropě, Azii i Afrikě nachodiaščiisia* [The Travels of the Pedestrian Vasilii Grigorovich Barskii of Kiev, Antiochian Monk, to Holy Places in Europe, Asia, and Africa], 1778.

Barskii, Vasilii Grigorovich, *Stranstvovaniia V.G. Barskogo po sviatym městam Vostoka s 1723 po 1747* [The Travels of Vasilii Grigorovich Barskii to Holy Places in the East from 1723 to 1747], edited by Nikolai Barsukov, 1885–1889.

## BARTH, HEINRICH (1821–1865) *German Explorer*

Heinrich Barth was born in Hamburg on 16 February 1821. In 1839, he entered the University of Berlin to study classics, then spent the following year in Italy. Upon his return, he entered the University of Berlin's law school and eventually completed his Ph.D. (1844) before going to London to study Arabic (he already spoke English, French, Italian, and Spanish). From 1845 to 1847, he traveled in Europe, North Africa, and the Levant; the results of his travels were published as *Wanderungen durch das punische und kyrenäische Küstenland* [Wanderings along the Punic and Cyrenaic Shores of the Mediterranean]. After returning to Europe, Barth became a faculty member at the University of Berlin, where he taught comparative geography and colonial commerce as an unsalaried lecturer. His academic career quickly ended and the university cancelled his classes because he was a poor teacher.

Fortunately for Barth, Christian Bunsen (1791–1860), the Prussian ambassador to Britain, arranged for him to accompany the British government's Mixed Scientific and Commercial Expedition to Central Africa under the command of James Richardson (1806–1851). Adolph Overweg (1822–1852), another German who was a geologist and astronomer, also joined the expedition.

On 30 November 1849, Richardson left London to meet Barth and Overweg in Tunis. Even before their travels began, it was evident that there was a disagreement about their mission. Richardson, a member of the Anti-Slavery Society, perceived the trip's purpose primarily in terms of ending the trans-Saharan slave trade by concluding commercial treaties with local rulers, while Barth and Overweg wanted to devote their efforts largely to scientific inquiry. Nevertheless, on 24 March 1850, the trio departed from Tunis for Tin Tellust in the Sahara via Murzuk, Ghat, Basakaf, and Selufiet.

At Tin Tellust, Barth left the expedition for a brief visit (10–30 October 1850) to Agadès. After he had rejoined Richardson and Overweg at Tagetel, it became evident that bickering between the three explorers about their goals and duties had probably doomed the expedition. In January 1851, the trio reached the southern Sahara in high spirits because of their good progress. However, financial problems prompted Barth and Overweg to part company from Richardson. They planned to reunite at Kukawa, the capital of the kingdom of Bornu. Sadly, Richardson died on 4 March 1851 at Ungouratona, near Kukawa.

Meanwhile, Barth and Overweg agreed to separate, the latter going east to Golan and Maridi while Barth went to Kano. After a one-month stay, during which Barth started a survey of the city that he believed would become an important commercial center for Europe, Barth journeyed east and, on 2 April 1851, arrived at Kukawa. Shortly thereafter, Overweg joined him. The two stayed in Kukawa for 18 months. During that time, Barth made trips to Yola, Kanem, Mousgou, and Masena, while Overweg explored Lake Chad. In July 1852, Barth received British government approval and some funding to continue the expedition.

At the urging of the Foreign Office, Barth abandoned plans for a transcontinental trip. Instead, on 25 November 1852, he started for Timbuktu alone, Overweg having died on 27 September. On 23 June 1853, Barth reached the town of Say on the Niger. He pushed on via Zinder, Kano, and Sokoto and arrived in Timbuktu on 23 September. Barth had hoped to remain in Timbuktu for only a short time, but the local authorities forced him to stay for six months. During that time, he completed a plan of the city.

Finally, on 18 March 1854, Barth departed with his protector, Sheik El Bakay. The two parted company at Gao. About 120 miles west of Kukuwa, Barth met Eduard Vogel (1829–1856), a German astronomer who had originally planned to join his expedition but was now embarked on his own explorations to Bauchi (on 8 February 1856, he was killed in Wadai). On 11 December 1854, Barth finally reached Kukuwa. He spent the next few months resting and preparing for the return journey. In May 1855, Barth left Kukuwa and arrived on 28 August in Tripoli, having passed through Bilma, Murzuk, and Socna. On 6 September 1855, he arrived in London.

Barth's expedition, which covered more than 10,000 miles, had taken more than five years. Ironically, he failed to make any significant original discoveries. However, his exploration of the upper part of the river Benue and his travels through the modern states of Cameroon, Chad, Niger, Nigeria, and Mali, all of which were recounted in detail in his journals, greatly advanced Europe's knowledge of the Sahara and west Africa. He also concluded commercial treaties with Bornu, Gwandu, and Sokoto, but Britain neglected to ensure their implementation.

In recognition of his achievements, the British government paid him £500 per annum from the time of Richardson's death, plus £1,000 after the publication of the first three volumes of his journals and another £1,000 upon completion of the project. In 1856, the Royal Geographical Society, which had no affiliation with the expedition, awarded Barth the Patron's Gold Medal and subsequently made him a foreign associate. He was also created Companion of the Bath. Regrettably, the publication of his journals, which scholars welcomed, elicited little public interest. As a result, Barth failed to gain the popular adulation he felt he deserved, and in 1859 he returned, embittered, to Germany. In 1863, he was appointed professor of geography at the University of Berlin. Barth also became president of the Berlin Geographical Society and founded the Carl Ritter Institute. Despite these achievements, he remained disillusioned, largely because his dream of obtaining a consulship in Siam (now Thailand) or Turkey never materialized, and also because the Royal Academy of Sciences refused to grant him full membership.

Despite these setbacks, Barth resumed his travels to several destinations in Europe and Asia Minor, including Trebizond to Scutari (1858), Spain (1861), Turkey (1862 and again in 1865), the Alps (1863), and Italy (1864). He also went to Dublin in 1857 and delivered a paper about the Niger to the British Association for the Advancement of Science, and found time in this hectic schedule to publish the three-volume *Collection of Vocabularies of Central African Languages* (1862, 1863). After a two-day illness, he died on 25 November 1865 and was buried in Berlin's Jerusalem Cemetery.

THOMAS OFCANSKY

### Biography

Born in Hamburg, Germany, 16 February 1821. Attended the University of Berlin, 1839–1844. Traveled in Europe, North Africa, and the Levant, 1845–1847. Taught for a short time at the University of Berlin, c. 1848. Part of the British government's Mixed Scientific and Commercial Expedition to Central Africa, 1849–1855. Lived in England, 1855–1859. Published his journals of the expedition, 1857–1858. Returned to Germany, 1859. Professor of geography at the University of Berlin, 1863. Traveled to Europe and Asia Minor, 1858–1865. Awarded the Royal Geographical Society's Patron's Gold Medal, 1856, and made a foreign associate. Founded Carl Ritter Institute. Died in Berlin, 25 November 1865.

### References and Further Reading

Barth, Heinrich, *Wanderungen durch die Küstenländer des Mittelmeeres*, vol. 1: *Wanderungen durch das punische und kyrenäische Küstenland* [Wanderings along the Punic and Cyrenaic Shores of the Mediterranean], 1849.

Barth, Heinrich, *Reisen und Entdeckungen in Nord- und Central-Africa in den Jahren 1849 bis 1855*, 5 vols., 1857–1858; as *Travels in North and Central Africa*, 5 vols., 1857–1858.

Barth, Heinrich, *Reise von Trapezunt durch die nördliche Hälfte Klein-Asiens nach Scutari im Herlost 1858*, 1860.

Barth, Heinrich, *Reise durch das Innere der europäischen Turkei*, 1864.

## BECKFORD, WILLIAM (1760–1844)

***British Novelist and Travel Writer***

Born into a wealthy Whig family with genealogical connections to the blood royal of both England and Scotland, William Beckford was intended to become a key figure in building and governing the empire. His notoriety, however, was independent of any political deeds. Instead, it centered on his literary and architectural projects; his art, antique, and book collections; and his bisexuality.

Beckford was ten when his father died, leaving him a colossal fortune. His mother, a Calvinist, directed his education. To her and Beckford's other guardians, mostly political associates of his father, grooming the boy for a public career meant having him privately tutored and keeping him isolated at Fonthill, the family estate in Wiltshire. To ease the solitude, Beckford indulged his penchant for fantasy. As a child, Beckford cultivated an active interest in oriental culture. This constituted a recurring pattern in his life and travel writings—using aesthetics and imagination to escape the present. Necessity also made his fascination with the Orient covert. His guardians were alarmed at his interests, and, at 13, he was made to burn all the oriental drawings he possessed.

Wealth facilitated Beckford's traveling. His first journey to the Continent came in 1777, when he was sent to relatives in Geneva to continue his education. His letters to friends in England convey an enthusiasm for scenery and ironic observations on manners, including his own. A self-absorbed Beckford returned to England in 1778. To draw him out, his guardians sent him on a tour of England in 1779, which resulted in Beckford's meeting William Courtenay, later the ninth duke of Devon, and acknowledging his homosexual feelings. Their relationship has been given varying interpretations, but all concur that it had a profound emotional effect. At this same time, Beckford was working on his first literary composition, "The Long Story," or "Centrical History." Later published as *The Vision* (1930), this work uses an imaginary voyage and travel literature as contexts in which to examine emotional intimacy, lost innocence, and the quest for knowledge.

Bored at home, Beckford conducted his Grand Tour through Holland, Germany, Austria, and Italy from 1780 to 1781 and again in 1782. He seemed relieved to be traveling again, but his upbringing, homosexual feelings, and aesthetic vision heightened his sense of isolation. His travel letters register what he saw, but their emphasis is on his subjective responses. The letters are confessional and remarkable for their display of his learning, especially in discussing Italian antiquities and painting, in their evocation of dreams and fantasies, and in how he seeks out and resolves disparities between the ideal and the real. Frequently, the letters evince an aesthetic of disdain: he desired a more refined form of art or music or physical demeanor to escape the offensive reality he was in. This attitude ensured his isolation as well as making the daydreams he recorded a congratulatory form of self-protection.

Beckford prepared these travel letters for publication as *Dreams, Waking Thoughts, and Incidents, in a Series of Letters, from Various Parts of Europe*. But in April 1783 he suppressed the edition of 500 even though it was already in press. Only six copies came into circulation. Various reasons have been advanced for his action: that the book's criticisms of the Dutch would compromise his political career; that the confessional and voluptuous tone did not reflect the sobriety expected in a politician; that the letters might be used as evidence in support of the rumors about Beckford's sexuality. That he was to be married the following month suggests that suppression formed part of his family's wishes. Nevertheless, the letters were revised and reprinted 51 years later as *Italy: With Sketches of Spain and Portugal, in a Series of Letters Written during a Residence in Those Countries* (2 vols., 1834).

The intended publication of *Dreams* in 1783 makes it among the first examples of romantic travel literature. *Dreams* begins on a note of self-consciousness directed to the reader: Beckford's fancies will supply the subject. These letters do not adhere to the eighteenth-century travel literary convention of *utile dulce*, instruct and please. Instead of the usual epistolary travel conventions of autobiography, topography, and facts, Beckford trebly subverted the genre. He satirized its expectations, gave it the sense of a personal dream vision rather than the notion of a shared common experience, and foregrounded his frustrations and aesthetic sensibilities. Even though the letters' revisions for their 1834 publication as *Sketches* toned down the effusions, Beckford still strove for effect. The prose is elegant; the stories rounded off with polish. Both *Dreams* and *Sketches* reflect the genre's transition from didacticism to entertainment. Travel literature gave Beckford a public framework within which to explore his individuality against a background of shifting geography.

Beckford's next journey to the Continent was not for pleasure. It came two years into his marriage and just after his election to Parliament. In 1784, he was accused of sexual misconduct with Courtenay. The charges were never substantiated, and evidence suggests that they were fabricated by Courtenay's uncle, a longtime political nemesis of the Beckfords. The ensuing vilification caused Beckford to leave for Switzerland. It was during this period that his wife died after bearing their second daughter and that *Vathek* (1786), the oriental tale that represents the culmination of his interest in the Middle East, was published.

During his first visit to Portugal in 1787, Beckford kept a journal, part of which he later edited for inclusion in *Sketches*. But the journey that formed the basis for his last travel book came while living there in 1794. He accompanied the prince regent of Portugal on an excursion to two wealthy ecclesiastical foundations. The literary account of this became *Recollections of an Excursion to the Monasteries of Alcobaça and Batalha* (1835). Unlike *Dreams* or its revised form *Sketches*, which had just been published the year before, *Recollections* is less confessional. Rather than the direct address to the reader used in his earlier travel works, *Recollections* has a stronger narrative quality. It offers anecdotes and impressionistic dialogs. It gives tableaux and rich descriptions of topics—people, chapels, tombs, monasteries, moonlight, nightingales, ceremonies—that aroused emotional responses, sometimes specified, sometimes hinted at, sometimes self-mocking. The episodes show mature descriptive and imaginative powers.

In 1796, Beckford returned to England, and three years later he began pulling down the old house at Fonthill and constructing a Gothic fantasy, Fonthill Abbey, that rendered in stone the luxurious, imaginative retreats described in his literary works. He remained there until forced to sell the estate in 1822, whereupon he moved to Bath.

Like Fonthill Abbey and *Vathek*, the travel books connect two periods. The concrete imagery and incorporation of facts and detail align them with the eighteenth century. Their introspection, energy, and emotional intensity make them harbingers of romanticism. As he did with architecture and orientalism, Beckford used travel literature to explore, define, protect, and display his personal aesthetic vision and imagination.

COLE WOODCOX

### Biography

Born either in Soho Square, London, or Fonthill, Wiltshire, 29 September 1760. Privately educated; received tuition in architecture and drawing from eminent tutors and piano lessons from Wolfgang Amadeus Mozart.

Inherited significant fortune on his father's death, 1770. Traveled to Geneva and Italy to complete his education, 1777–1778. Toured England; met Viscount William Courtenay, 1779. Returned to Italy, also visiting the Low Countries, Germany, and Austria, 1780–1782. Wrote the novel *Vathek* in French, 1782. Married Lady Margaret Gordon, daughter of the earl of Aboyne, May 1783: two daughters. Member of Parliament for Wells, Somerset, 1784–1790. Fled to Switzerland in exile after scandal over relationship with Courtenay, 1785. Margaret Beckford died in childbirth in Switzerland, 1786. Remained abroad, visiting Portugal, Spain, and France, 1787–1793. Member of Parliament for Hindon, Wiltshire, 1790–1794. Traveled in Portugal, 1794. Supervised the rebuilding of family home, Fonthill Abbey, 1799–1822. Returned to Portugal, 1798. Reelected as member of Parliament for Hindon, 1806–1820. Visited France, 1801, 1814, and 1819. Sold Fonthill estate and moved to Bath, 1822. Died in Bath, 2 May 1844.

### References and Further Reading

Beckford, William, *Dreams, Waking Thoughts and Incidents, in a Series of Letters, from Various Parts of Europe* (published anonymously), 1783; as *The Travel Diaries*, edited by Guy Chapman, 1928.

Beckford, William, *Italy, with Sketches of Spain and Portugal, in a Series of Letters Written during a Residence in Those Countries*, 2 vols., 1834.

Beckford, William, *Recollections of an Excursion to the Monasteries of Alcobaça and Batalha*, 1835; revised edition, 1840.

Beckford, William, *The Journal of William Beckford in Portugal and Spain, 1787–1788*, edited by Boyd Alexander, 1954.

*See also* **Orientalism**

## BEIJING (PEKING)

The site of present-day Beijing has been an important commercial and military center for over 2,000 years and a prime location for travelers since the Yüan (Mongol) dynasty (1206–1368) made the city, Ta-tu, their administrative capital in 1267. Marco Polo's (c. 1254–1324) *Description of the World* paints a picture of a wealthy and well-governed city; this image remained the dominant European one for centuries, though some recent scholarship raises doubt as to whether Marco Polo even made it to the capital.

The old Mongol capital was given its present name, Beijing (former common romanization: Peking, meaning "Northern Capital"), during the Ming dynasty (1368–1644). Matteo Ricci (1552–1610), an Italian Jesuit and father of Western sinology, as the first European to be educated in the Chinese traditions, portrayed Ming Beijing, with its orderly governance, peace, and prosperity, in a glowing light.

Travelers to Beijing were less content with the city, and China generally, by the beginning of the Manchu Qing dynasty (1644–1911). Francisco Pimentel, a Jesuit member of the Portuguese embassy of 1670, gave what was perhaps the first generally negative Western account of Beijing as cold, dusty, and insect-ridden, and cautioned against comparisons with European capitals: "One who hears of the grandeur of this capital will conceive of something like Lisbon, Rome, or Paris, but, so that he will not be deceived, I warn him that, if he entered it, he would think he was entering one of the poorest villages of Portugal."

Travel to Beijing figures prominently in Chinese travel accounts. The Chinese scholar Tai Ming-shih's *Diary of a Journey in the Year I-hai*, which documents his 1695 journey from Nanking to Beijing, reflects a growing sense of subjectivity and autobiographical awareness in Chinese travel literature. Tai's journey ended in frustration as customs officials harassed him, thus exposing his books to the rain.

John Bell's *A Journey from St. Petersburg to Pekin, 1719–1722*, offered an empirical portrait of court ceremony and the arts, Chinese women, and the nearby Great Wall. Perhaps Lord Macartney's mission of 1793 can be seen as a turning point as travelers from the increasingly democratically minded and industrial parts of the West began to turn against China, a country they perceived to be hopelessly stagnant. John Barrow's *Travels in China* (1804), a product of the mission, portrayed Manchu despotism in "terms of tyranny, oppression, and injustice."

Beijing began to look more like a dusty museum relic than the capital of a great empire to many Western travelers during the nineteenth and first decades of the twentieth century. The 1910 edition of *Cook's Handbook for Tourists to Peking* explained that the city was "little worthy of special attention." However, the end of the Qing dynasty began a new era of travel to Beijing. Travelers began to refract images of the capital through the prism of global revolutionary politics.

Derk Bodde's *Peking Diary: A Year of Revolution* (1950) is an eyewitness account of the collapse of the Kuomintang and spread of Communist control from August 1948 to October 1949, the author being excited at the atmosphere in Beijing, full of renewed hope and optimism. The creation of the People's Republic of China saw a substantial decrease in the number of foreign visitors to China, but many of those who continued to make the trip were to the left of the political spectrum in their own countries and found Communist Beijing to exemplify progress. The French feminist Simone de Beauvoir, in her *La Longue Marche* (1957), was not seduced by what remains she saw of the uniform *hu-t'ungs* (alleyways) of dynastic Beijing ("unity imposed by repetition") but did find the "classless society" of the Communist city to be extraordinary. Felix Greene, a resident of the United States and British passport holder, remarked in his *Awakened China: The Country Americans Don't Know* (1961), in sharp contrast to Qing travelers, "Peking is as clean or cleaner than many of the cities of England or America. No piles of garbage, no refuse, no smells, no cigarette stubs—and (it's true) almost no flies." In his *600 Million Chinese* (1957), Robert Guillain welcomed the repainting and renovation of the city that he had seen in decay during the 1930s: "I will leave it to others to lament this period, when the splendor of China was crumbling to dust."

Edgar Snow, who introduced Mao to the West in his *Red Star over China* (1937), noted in *The Other Side of the River: Red China Today* (1962) that Beijing was relatively silent and much cleaner than before, the public quarreling, rickshaws, brothels, bargaining, and drug dens having disappeared. Underlying most travel accounts from this period is a strong sense of doubt: one could not be sure that the "real" Beijing, or China, could be glimpsed from foreigner hotels and limited contact with the populace.

The Belgian scholar Pierre Ryckmans (pen name Simon Leys), a staunch critic of Chinese Communism, saw this newly found quiet to be emblematic of a China that had lost its essence. In his *Chinese Shadows* (1977), a harsh appraisal of the Cultural Revolution, Leys lamented the destruction of humanity that he perceived under the Communist regime: "For those who knew it in the past, Peking now appears to be a murdered town. The body is still there, the soul has gone. The *life* of Peking, which created never-ending theater in its streets and squares, the noisy and enjoyable life of the city has gone, leaving only the physical presence of a mute and monochromatic crowd." The Swiss journalist Lorenz Stucki, in his *Behind the Great Wall: An Appraisal of Mao's China* (1965), had been no less condemning:

> The dullness of Chinese cities, including Peking and Shanghai, is underlined by the lack of all those things that lend sparkle to the appearance of other cities: pretty girls; elegant women; an occasional whiff of the perfume of the mysterious world outside; elegant shop windows; antique shops in which one can make a great find; bookstores in which one likes to browse because they are not stocked solely with monotonous, stereotyped Party literature; a hidden small restaurant; somebody singing in a backyard instead of the blaring loudspeakers on the streets.

Travel accounts of Beijing during the Deng era generally tended to be more optimistic. Orville Schell's *Watch out for the Foreign Guests! China Encounters the West* (1980), *To Get Rich Is Glorious: China in the Eighties* (1984), and *Discos and Democracy: China in the Throes of Reform* (1988) portray the Chinese capital as a rapidly modernizing city with room for optimism. Nicholas Kristof and Sheryl WuDunn's *China Wakes: The Struggle for the Soul of a Rising Power* (1994) displayed confidence with regard to economic development in the People's Republic during the 1990s, but with an underlying concern about Beijing's growing social problems and the political future in the capital after the Tiananmen Square massacre, an event the authors were witness to.

JOSEPH EATON

## References and Further Reading


Barrow, John, *Travels in China: Containing Descriptions, Observations, and Comparisons, Made and Collected in the Course of a Short Residence at the Imperial Palace of Yuen-min-yuen, and on a Subsequent Journey through the Country from Pekin to Canton*, 1804.

Beauvoir, Simone de, *La Longue Marche: Essai sur la Chine*, 1957; as *The Long March*, translated by Austryn Wainhouse, 1958.

Bell, John, *A Journey from St. Petersburg to Pekin, 1719–1722*, edited by J.L. Stevenson, 1965.

Bodde, Derk, *Peking Diary: A Year of Revolution*, 1950.

Gordon-Cumming, Constance Frederica, *Wanderings in China*, 2 vols., 1886.

Greene, Felix, *Awakened China: The Country Americans Don't Know*, 1961; as *The Wall Has Two Sides: A Portrait of China Today*, 1962.

Greene, Felix, *A Curtain of Ignorance: How the American Public Has Been Misinformed about China*, 1964.

Guillain, Robert, *600 Millions de chinois sous le drapeau rouge*, 1956; as *600 Million Chinese*, translated Mervyn Savill, 1957; as *The Blue Ants: 600 Million Chinese under the Red Flag*, 1957.

Ides, Evert Ysbrants, *Three Years Travels from Moscow Overland to China: . . . To Which Is Annexd an Accurate Description of China by a Chinese Author* [D. Kdo], 1706.

Kristof, Nicholas D., and Sheryl WuDunn, *China Wakes: The Struggle for the Soul of a Rising Power*, 1994; revised edition, 1998.

Leys, Simon, *Chinese Shadows*, 1977.

Li, Chih-Ch'ang, *The Travels of an Alchemist: The Journey of the Taoist Ch'ang-Ch'un from China to the Hindukush at the Summons of Chingiz Khan, Recorded by His Disciple Li Chih-Ch'ang*, translated by Arthur Waley, 1931; reprinted, 1963.

Little, Archibald, *The Far East*, 1905.

Little, Archibald, *Gleanings from Fifty Years in China*, 1910.

Mirsky, Jeannette (editor), *The Great Chinese Travelers: An Anthology*, 1964.

Pimentel, Francisco, *Breve relação da jornada que fez à corte de Pekim o senhor Manoel de Saldanha, embaixador extraordinario del rey de Portugal ao emperador da China, e Tartaria (1667–1670)*, edited by C.R. Boxer and J.M. Braga, 1942.

Polo, Marco, *The Travels of Marco Polo*, translated by Ronald Latham, 1958.

Ricci, Matteo, *China in the Sixteenth Century: The Journals of Matthew Ricci, 1583–1610*, translated by Louis J. Gallagher, 1953.

Schell, Orville, *Watch out for the Foreign Guests! China Encounters the West*, 1980.
Schell, Orville, *To Get Rich Is Glorious: China in the Eighties*, 1984; revised edition, 1986.
Schell, Orville, *Discos and Democracy: China in the Throes of Reform*, 1988.
Snow, Edgar, *Red Star over China*, 1937; revised edition, 1968.
Snow, Edgar, *The Other Side of the River: Red China Today*, 1962.
Strassberg, Richard E. (translator and editor), *Inscribed Landscapes: Travel Writing from Imperial China*, 1994.
Stucki, Lorenz, *Behind the Great Wall: An Appraisal of Mao's China*, 1965.
Yule, Henry (translator and editor), *Cathay and the Way Thither, Being a Collection of Medieval Notices of China*, new edition, revised by Henri Cordier, 4 vols., 1913–1916.

*See also* **China**

## BELL, GERTRUDE (1868–1926) *British Traveler, Diplomat, and Amateur Archaeologist*

Born into a late-Victorian world of privilege with the British empire nearing its zenith, Gertrude Bell occupied a position at the forefront of a new, if small, wave of upper-middle-class women entering professions formerly accessible only to men and utilizing their intellectual talents in nondomestic endeavors. Like other British women throughout the nineteenth century and into the twentieth, Bell discovered that travel in the vast British empire provided a sense of personal liberation, as well as opportunities for professional training and advancement. Largely as a result of her travels and her writing about them, Bell became the most celebrated British woman of her generation in the Middle East.

Gertrude Bell was born into a family from the industrial north of England blessed with wealth, taste, education, and a strong work ethic. Her father was Thomas Hugh Bell, son of a Victorian captain of industry and heir to an ironworks and coal fortune. Her mother, Mary Shield Bell, the daughter of a prominent Newcastle food merchant, died when Gertrude's brother Maurice was born in 1871. At a time when most upper-middle-class girls were educated privately at home, Gertrude was allowed to attend Queen's College, London, and then became one of the first women students at Oxford, entering Lady Margaret Hall. A brilliant student, she left Oxford before the age of 20, with a first class in modern history. Bell was the first woman to achieve this distinction, and her educational attainments and later career exemplified the new opportunities for women that began to open up during her lifetime.

As a travel writer, Bell impresses the reader with her curiosity, intelligence, independence, and tireless energy. She produced works that reveal a fascinating combination of imperial hauteur with respect and admiration for people in the Middle East as individuals. In the preface to *The Desert and the Sown* (1907), Bell maintained that she would seek to impress Arab dignitaries by letting it be known that she came "of a great and honoured stock whose customs are inviolable." On the other hand, as a diplomat, she relished her involvement in Mesopotamian politics and welcomed delegations from all parts of the region, spending long hours talking to those who sought a meeting with her. In her letters, she remarks, "They are the people I love, I know every Tribal chief of any importance through the whole length and breadth of Iraq and I think them the backbone of the country."

Bell's lifelong interest in the Middle East began on a trip to the Ottoman empire during the summer and autumn after she left university. Later, traveling to Persia to visit maternal relatives in the diplomatic service in Teheran, Bell fell under the orientalist spell that had attracted so many British travelers before her, such as Hester Stanhope, Richard Burton, and Wilfrid and Anne Blunt. On her visit to Persia, barely 20, she began writing her first travel book, *Safar Nameh: Persian Pictures* (published anonymously in 1894). In Persia, Bell studied Farsi and began to translate the work of the thirteenth-century Persian poet Hafiz, as *Poems from the Divan of Hafiz* (1897), a translation still highly regarded. Bell's best-known travel book is *The Desert and the Sown* (1907), set in Lebanon, Palestine, and Syria, and published when Bell was 39. This travel book reveals Bell's trademark intelligence, wit, and ability to both tell and listen to stories. Sensitive to language and cultural nuance, Bell learned Arabic and often discussed classical Arabic poetry with her hosts along the road. She described a visit with one man in Syria who "knew the poets of the Ignorance [Pre-Islamic poets] by heart, and when he found that I had a scanty knowledge of them and a great love for them he quoted couplet after couplet." Fascinated by the architecture of the ancient Middle East, Bell also conducted archaeological excavations, writing about them in *The Thousand and One Churches* (1909), *Amurath to Amurath* (1911), and *The Palace and Mosque at Ukhaidir* (1914). Inspired by the travels of Anne and Wilfrid Scawen Blunt in Arabia on horseback, Bell set off in 1913 from Damascus on a very difficult journey into the central Arabian peninsula.

It was war that propelled Bell into political work and allowed her to put the knowledge she had gained on her many travels about the Middle East to profitable use. Through her travels in many remote areas, she developed long-standing personal contacts with many tribal leaders in Arabia, Syria, and Iraq, which proved valuable in her intelligence work for the British during World War I. Her talent for making maps also endeared her to her political superiors during and after the war.

Thus, it was Bell's forays into travel writing that laid the groundwork for her eventual eminence in the British foreign service.

As in the case of many travel writers, much of Bell's writing evolved from letters written to her family in England, mostly to her father, Hugh Bell, and her stepmother, Florence Olliffe Bell, who edited Gertrude's letters for publication in 1927. Also similar to a number of other travel writers, Gertrude Bell gradually became an expatriate, choosing to live out her life in the new state of Iraq, where she had found her most challenging and fulfilling work in helping to shape the post-war Middle East. World War I had a massive impact on Bell's decision to remain out of England. Bell was immensely excited about her role in helping to make history in Iraq after the war during the Mandate period, when various nationalist groups in several Arab territories were agitating for self-rule. However, she also remained in the Middle East because of a depressing sense of dislocation caused by the war. Despite her love of politics, Bell had very much wanted to be a wife and mother, but had never married. One early romance had ended with her parents' disapproval of the match and then the young man's death. Also before the war, Bell fell in love with a married man, Dick Doughty-Wylie, who was later killed at Gallipoli. Thus, Bell's decision to become a permanent traveler was one way of dealing with her personal grief, a grief shared by so many Europeans after the slaughter of the Great War finally ended.

Evolving from a traveler into a powerful British government official in Mesopotamia during and after the war, Bell came to believe that she was a part of the land that she had adopted. In 1918, she wrote from Baghdad, "I had a warm feeling of being part of it all. And so I am, you know; just as much as I'm part of English surroundings. It's a curious sense to have two native lands and to be wound into this one as with that by long links of associations" (*Letters*). In 1922, Bell wrote to her father of her conviction that "I'm more a citizen of Bagdad than many a Bagdadi born, and I'll wager that no Bagdadi cares more, or half so much, for the beauty of the river or the palm gardens or clings more closely to the rights of citizenship which I have acquired."

One result of Gertrude Bell's prominence first as a travel writer and later as a diplomat was that she became a cultural icon representing the British in the Middle East, just as Hester Stanhope had almost a century before. Both Stanhope and Bell acquired popular fame as "Queen of the Desert," and Gertrude Bell was referred to during the height of British power in Iraq as "the Khatun," or powerful lady of the court. As in the case of Stanhope, Bell's elegance, prestigious class background, and perceived political influence caused her to be regarded by Europeans, as well as many people of the Middle East, as a symbol of British imperialism itself.

Anne M. Lockwood

### Biography

Born at Washington Hall, County Durham, 14 July 1868. Brought up by her stepmother, Florence Olliffe. Attended Queen's College, London, at age 15. Attended Lady Margaret Hall, Oxford, 1886–1888. Traveled to Bucharest, Romania, and Ottoman Constantinople, 1888–1889. Visited Persia, 1892. Traveled widely in Europe, 1892–1899. Made her first around-the-world trip, 1897. Traveled to Jerusalem, 1899. Second around-the-world trip, 1902. Journeyed in Lebanon, Palestine, and Syria and through the Syrian desert to Mesopotamia, 1910–1911, conducting various archaeological investigations. Traveled from Damascus to Hail, Central Arabia, 1913–1914. Served briefly in the Red Cross at the beginning of World War I, then began British intelligence work at the Arab Bureau in Cairo, Egypt, 1915; worked with T.E. Lawrence. Served as political officer in Basra, beginning in 1916. After the armistice, was appointed Oriental Secretary to the British High Commissioner, Sir Percy Cox, in Baghdad, 1919–1923. Participated in Cairo conference to divide up the Middle East among the Allied Powers after World War I, 1921. Lived in Baghdad until her death. In Iraq, helped to direct British foreign policy and install Faisal I as king of Iraq, 1921. As director of antiquities, helped to establish the National Museum of Iraq in Baghdad, 1923. President of Salam Library; founding member of the antisuffrage league. Awarded CBE, 1917. Awarded Founder's Medal of the Royal Geographical Society, 1918. Died of a drug overdose in Baghdad, 12 July 1926.

### References and Further Reading


Bell, Gertrude, *Safar Nameh: Persian Pictures: A Book of Travel* (published anonymously), 1894; as *Persian Pictures*, 1928.

Bell, Gertrude, *The Desert and the Sown*, 1907; with an introduction by Sarah Graham-Brown, 1985; as *Syria: The Desert and the Sown*, 1907.

Bell, Gertrude, with W.M. Ramsay, *The Thousand and One Churches*, 1909.

Bell, Gertrude, "The Churches and Monasteries of Tur Abdin," in *Amida*, by Max van Berchem, 1910.

Bell, Gertrude, *Amurath to Amurath: Travels in Asia Minor and Persia*, 1911.

Bell, Gertrude, "Damascus," *Blackwood's Magazine*, 189 (April 1911).

Bell, Gertrude, "Asiatic Turkey under the Constitution," *Blackwood's Magazine*, 190 (October 1911).

Bell, Gertrude, "Post-Road through the Syrian Desert," *Living Age*, 280 (7 and 21 February 1914): 329–343 and 458–469.

Bell, Gertrude, *The Palace and Mosque at Ukhaidir: A Study in Early Mohammadan Architecture*, 1914.

## BELL, JOHN (1691–1780) *British Diplomat, Merchant, and Traveler*

John Bell was born in Antermony, Stirlingshire, Scotland, son of a nonjuring clergyman. After studying at Glasgow University, he graduated, apparently with medical qualifications, in 1713. Almost immediately, he set out for St. Petersburg, where he went with the intention of "seeking an opportunity of visiting some parts of Asia, at least those parts which border on Russia" (*Travels*). At St. Petersburg, he met a fellow Scot, Robert Areskine (1677–1718), Peter the Great's chief physician, who found him a paid position in the imminent Russian embassy to Persia led by A.P. Volynskii (1689–1740). During the course of this epic, three-year journey, which began in July 1715, Bell sailed down the Volga River as far as Astrakhan, crossed the Caspian Sea, and retraced the steps of Xenophon through the deserts of Kurdistan. The 140-man embassy arrived in Isfahan on 14 March 1717 but was not presented to Shah Sultan Husayn (r. 1694–1722), the last ruler of the Safavid dynasty, until seven weeks had passed. On its homeward journey, the party, laden with the shah's gifts for the Czar, passed six months in Shemakha in the Caucasus before finally returning to St. Petersburg in December 1718.

In July 1719, Bell left the city to accompany the Russian embassy to the Chinese emperor K'ang-hsi (1677–1722). The mission was led by L.V. Izmailov (1686–1738), the first Russian envoy to perform the kotow before the emperor (Pritchard, 1943). This journey took the Scotsman across the Urals and through Siberia, territory not previously described by a British writer. Although Russia was hardly well known to the English reading public in 1763 (the date of publication of Bell's work), Bell's interest was limited to its economic resources; for example, Baron Stroganov's salt pits at Solikamsk, which were responsible for about three-quarters of Russian production. Once he went beyond the Russian culture region, however, his descriptions thickened, reflecting an ethnological curiosity about non-Europeans. Bell was remarkably sensitive to the differences among the various peoples whose territory he traversed. The further he journeyed into Siberia and Mongolia, the more detailed and nuanced his descriptions became. Although he wrote favorably about their customs and manners, he dismissed the religious beliefs of the Eurasian peoples as "downright Paganism of the grossest kind." He took advantage of numerous opportunities to observe their shamans at close range. His initially open-minded attitude soon hardened into contempt. After watching a shaman of the Buratsky people perform "legerdemain tricks" such as "running himself through with a sword, and many others too trifling to mention," he concluded "that these shamans are a parcel of jugglers, who impose on the ignorant and credulous vulgar."

The embassy's impending arrival in China was announced by the sight of the Great Wall in the distance. "The appearance of it, running from one high rock to another, with square towers at certain intervals, is most magnificent," Bell recorded. It was in the mountainous regions just outside the wall, where he detected "a sensible alteration in the weather"—in the form of "a warm and pleasant air"—that he first registered his sense of having entered the Chinese empire. "Every thing now appeared to us as if we had arrived in another world," he recorded. At a "small Chinese monastery, situated on the declivity of a steep rock," he and his fellow travelers were regaled with green tea, "which was very agreeable." Also ensconced among the rocks were "little scattered cottages, with spots of cultivated ground, much resembling those romantick figures of landskips which are painted on the China-ware and other manufactures of this country." He was able to reassure his readers that such scenes were not "fanciful," but "really natural." After traversing a country full of villages and towns that had been devastated by a great earthquake the previous year, Bell arrived in Beijing on 18 November 1720. His account of his five months in the city is substantially devoted to the embassy's reception by the emperor, royalty, and leading officials. However, there are fascinating glimpses of Chinese urban culture, including markets, street theater, and factories.

Bell had scarcely arrived back from China when he was assigned a place in Peter the Great's entourage during his military expedition to Derbent. As Derbent was located close to the Persian border, the journey simply took him along a route he had already traversed twice before. He returned to St. Petersburg by December 1722. Soon afterward, he returned to Scotland. By 1734, though, he was back in St. Petersburg, where he obtained employment as private secretary to Claudius Rondeau, the British resident. The fourth and last phase of his major travels began in December 1737, when Rondeau sent him on a diplomatic mission to Constantinople. This time, he was obliged to travel virtually alone, with only a Turkish-speaking servant to share the rigors of the road. In Constantinople, where he arrived on 29 January 1738, he lodged with the British ambassador in the diplomatic enclave of Pera. He left the Ottoman capital on 8 April, returning to St. Petersburg on 17 May 1738.

After Rondeau died in 1739, Bell was the unofficial British representative in St. Petersburg until his successor, Edward Finch-Hatton (d. 1771), arrived in April

1740. Thereafter, Bell moved to Constantinople, where he worked as a merchant until 1746. He then returned to Scotland and resumed life as a country squire. (It is said that he often wore oriental costume while riding about his estate.) Around 1758, the earl of Grenville suggested that he produce a formal account of his extensive travels. By 1762, his manuscript was ready. Bell's *Travels from St. Petersburg in Russia to Diverse Parts of Asia* (1763), one of the most effortlessly readable of eighteenth-century travel books, was praised by the *Quarterly Review* in 1817 as "the best model perhaps for travel-writing in the English language." It also appeared in a Dublin pirate edition (1764), and in translations into French and Russian. It was last published as volume 7 of Pinkerton's *Voyages and Travels*. Despite the long interval that had elapsed between Bell's journeys and the writing of the *Travels*, the book is considered highly reliable. The view of Bell's modern editor, J.L. Stevenson, is that it must have been based on an extremely detailed journal that Bell had kept during the course of his travels.

James Paterson

### Biography

Born in Antermony, Stirlingshire, Scotland, 1691. Attended Glasgow University, c. 1709–1713. Traveled to Russia, departing on *Prosperity of Ramsgate*, July 1714. Engaged in the service of Czar Peter I (Peter the Great); took part in two Russian embassies: Volynskii's to Persia, 1715–1718, and Izmailov's to China, 1719–1721. Accompanied Peter the Great's military expedition to Derbent, 1722. Returned to Scotland, 1732–1733. Private secretary to Claudius Rondeau, the British resident in St. Petersburg, 1734–1739. Sent on diplomatic errand to Constantinople, 1737–1738. Unofficial British resident in St. Petersburg, 1739–1740. Worked as merchant in Constantinople, 1740–1746. Married Mary Peters, c. 1746. Returned to Scotland and lived as country squire from 1747, traveling again to Russia, 1751–1753. Published *Travels from St. Petersburg*, 1763. Died in Antermony, 1 July 1780.

### References and Further Reading

Bell, John, *Travels from St. Petersburg in Russia to Diverse Parts of Asia*, 2 vols., 1763.

Bell, John, *A Journey from St. Petersburg to Pekin, 1719–22*, edited by J.L. Stevenson, 1965.

Pritchard, Earl H., "The Kotow in the Macartney Embassy to China in 1793," *Far Eastern Quarterly*, 2/2, 1943: 163–203.

## BENJAMIN OF TUDELA *Jewish Traveler*

Though he is remembered as Rabbi Benjamin of Tudela, this twelfth-century author of a book of travels in Europe, Asia, and Africa may not have been a rabbi in the modern sense (the title was often honorific at that time, denoting simply a learned or respected individual), and the name of the town in his lifetime was Tuteila (only becoming Tudela more recently). Nevertheless, though his biography is limited to these simple details of name, locale, and authorship, and his writings are practically unknown to the world at large, Benjamin of Tudela has become something of a Jewish folk hero. Streets are named after him in Israeli cities, he is the subject of books and videos for children, and, perhaps most notably, his writings have spawned a long line of literary sequels and homages, from the 1885 satire *Travels and Adventures of Benjamin the Third*, by the "grandfather" of modern Yiddish literature, Mendele Mocher Seforim, to more contemporary works, such as Yehuda Amichai's poem *From Travels of a Latter-Day Benjamin of Tudela* (1975) and Jonathan Levi's novel *A Guide for the Perplexed* (1992). Despite these trappings of fame, however, Benjamin was no Jewish Marco Polo. His book was not intended to describe strange and distant places, but rather to catalog familiar if distant ones: Jewish communities around the world.

The twelfth century was a time of peril and opportunity in the Jewish world, and especially on the Iberian peninsula, where a Jewish "golden age" of learning and cultural achievement was under periodic siege from the twin attacks of the Christian reconquest and Muslim fundamentalist reaction. But in Christian Navarre, where Benjamin lived, the Jews were prospering, and it is not unlikely that his plan to survey far-flung Jewish communities was prompted by the mercantile success of Spanish Jewry, with trading partners throughout the Christian and Muslim worlds, combined with a sense of their precariousness, as those two cultures clashed in their midst.

All existing versions of Benjamin's works begin with a brief introduction identifying him and vouching for his perspicacity and the veracity of his account, before commencing Benjamin's first-person narrative. In this introduction, his patronymic and nationality are usually given ("Rabbi Benjamin, son of Jonah, of Navarre"), and the Jewish year 4933 (1173 CE) is cited as the date of his arrival in Castile at the end of his journey. In all extant versions of the works, the introduction also claims that Benjamin "made a record of all that he saw." Because this introduction is apparently written by someone other than Benjamin himself, and because the often terse descriptions provided in the existing narrative can hardly be "all that he saw," scholars disagree on whether, as seems likely, the book we have reproduces Benjamin's own account, with the introduction merely an early scribal addition, or whether it is all the work of a scribe who condensed and edited Benjamin's original notes.

Scholars do generally agree, however, on the dating of the journey, following Adler's suggestion that Benjamin probably left Navarre in late 1165 or 1166. According to his writings, Benjamin began by sailing southeast on the Ebro River, stopping first in present-day Saragossa, and then at the seaport of Tortosa. From there, Benjamin journeyed on land, following the Mediterranean coast, from Spain through France, with stops at Barcelona, Marseilles, and many smaller towns in between. From Marseilles, he embarked by ship for Genoa, and then traveled overland through Pisa to Rome—the first place where Benjamin devotes much space to describing historical buildings and other features, though even here the entry begins by discussing members of its small but renowned Jewish community, some of whom were employed by the pope. After Rome, Benjamin continued down the western seaboard of Italy, to Naples, Sorrento, and Salerno, before zigzagging through the Apennines to Bari, on the east coast, and finally arriving at Brindisi, where he took ship for Otranto, Corfu, and the Greek mainland. In Greece, Benjamin again kept mostly to the coast, traveling by land and sea; his stops included cities such as Corinth, Thebes, and Salonica (Thessaloniki), but not Athens, before his arrival in Constantinople, then the capital of the Byzantine empire.

Though there is only a slight alteration in the often pedestrian style of his narration, which tends to include more descriptive passages and more local legends in the accounts of the Middle East than it does in those of Italy or Greece, as Benjamin's narrative moves away from the major European population centers its historical importance grows considerably. In *The Decline and Fall of the Roman Empire*, the great eighteenth-century historian Edward Gibbon cites Benjamin's works several times in connection with Byzantium and the Holy Land, and almost every modern study of a remote or obscure Jewish community, from the Balkans and North Africa to the Middle East and central Asia, begins with Benjamin of Tudela's description, or uses his works as one of the first sources. As Benjamin heads south from Constantinople, first by sea through the islands of the eastern Mediterranean and then along the coasts of present-day Turkey, Syria, Lebanon, and Israel, he travels increasingly through areas familiar to him for their historical and biblical associations, and often identifies them by their ancient names. Travel in the land of Israel itself became difficult in the period of the Crusades, and that fact, combined with significant errors in Benjamin's account, suggests that here we have, possibly for the first time, descriptions of places Benjamin himself did not visit.

Fittingly, Benjamin probably arrived in Jerusalem about halfway through the six years of his journey. Though he gives Jerusalem no more space than he earlier devoted to Rome and Constantinople, Benjamin does include a long story about the accidental discovery of the tombs of the kings of Judah, including David and Solomon, and how these were subsequently closed up and hidden. Traveling south to Bethlehem and Hebron, Benjamin discovers a minor scam perpetrated on Christian pilgrims, then turns west to Jaffa and Ascalon, on the coast, north to the Sea of Galilee, and then on to Damascus.

Beginning in Damascus, another notable change in Benjamin's descriptions takes place: suddenly, the number of Jewish inhabitants begins to soar, from a few dozen or a few hundred, to thousands, in city after city, including Damascus, Palmyra, Aleppo, Mosul, and many others. In the Mesopotamian region, Benjamin claims that there are 10,000 or more Jewish residents in at least four different cities (Hadara, Okbara, Hillah, and Basra), and 40,000 in Baghdad alone. And in areas of the Arabian peninsula, Benjamin puts the Jewish population at 300,000 or more. The point here is not the preposterousness of these figures (after all, Yathrib—later Medina—had a prominent Jewish population when it invited Mohammed to move there from Mecca; at the same time, Yemen was part of the Abyssinian empire, and Ethiopian Jewry has been estimated in the millions during various centuries); rather, it is the lack of the usual details (the professions followed by the Jewish community and the names of its leaders), especially in proportion to the size of those populations, which make Benjamin's accounts of these areas seem secondhand, at best. As the narrative proceeds eastward, into the Persian empire as far as Samarkand, and from there to Tibet, India, and China, the details become increasingly unreliable; Benjamin uses phrases that suggest he did not personally make the trip, and identifies by name an informant for one of his stories, giving the impression that he himself may never have traveled farther east than the largely Jewish Persian city of Isfahan.

Benjamin's narrative returns from China, by way of Aden (and, mistakenly, Libya), to Abyssinia and Egypt. Benjamin himself probably visited Egypt in 1171, before embarking for Sicily; Cairo, Alexandria, and Messina are the last stops on his itinerary described at length. Though from Sicily Benjamin claims to have traveled through Italy to Germany, Bohemia, and France, all three areas are covered in a few paragraphs total, without the details that usually mark his firsthand accounts. On his return to Castile in 1173, however, and despite the episodes of unreliability in parts of his account, Benjamin became the first European travel writer to mention China, and his book—in addition to its importance as a historical and ethnographic document—marks a milestone in the development of the European image of Asia.

DAVID MESHER

### Biography

Born in Tuteila (present-day Tudela), Navarre, Spain, c. 1120s. Possibly became a rabbi. Probably left Navarre either late 1165 or 1166. Set out via Saragossa and traveled through Spain, France, Italy, and Greece, recording details of the Jewish communities there. Traveled to the Byzantine capital, Constantinople, and later visited Syria, Palestine, Mesopotamia, and Persia. Probably visited Egypt and Jerusalem, 1171. Probably returned from Persia via Sicily, reaching Castile in 1173, although his writings suggest he traveled on to China. Wrote an account of his travels in Hebrew, *Masa'ot shel Rabi Binyamin.*

### References and Further Reading

Benjamin of Tudela, *Masa'ot shel Rabi Binyamin/Itinerarium D. Beniaminis*, 1633.
Benjamin of Tudela, *The Itinerary of Rabbi Benjamin of Tudela*, edited and translated by A. Asher, 2 vols., 1840–1841.
Benjamin of Tudela, *The Itinerary of Benjamin of Tudela*, edited and translated by Marcus Nathan Adler, 1907.

## BENNETT, JAMES GORDON, JR. (1841–1918) *American Newspaper Owner and Expedition Financier*

Expeditions in the nineteenth century to regions hitherto unknown to Europeans, like the interior of Africa or the Arctic, needed not only intrepid and brave explorers, but money. James Gordon Bennett Jr. never set foot in the frigid wastes of the north or on the dusty African savannahs, but he paid others to do so. Henry Morton Stanley uttered the famous words "Doctor Livingstone, I presume" on a Bennett-funded expedition, and it was Bennett who both created and capitalized on a growing public thirst for firsthand details about journeys to unknown lands—especially if there were deaths, starvation, or other sensational aspects to the story.

Bennett was born on 10 May 1841, the son of James Gordon Bennett Sr., owner of the influential *New York Herald*, which had the largest circulation of any newspaper in the United States. He was educated in Paris until summoned to join the Union army in 1861, spending most of the American Civil War posted on the family yacht. In 1865, with the end of the war, Bennett joined the staff of the *Herald*, and was promoted to chief executive officer when his father retired two years later. He was an extraordinary judge of talent, and hired writers like Mark Twain, Walt Whitman, Charles Nordhoff, and Charles Edward Russell.

Bennett had an uncanny understanding of exactly what the American newspaper readership wanted, and he became the first newspaper proprietor to regularly create or manufacture the news accordingly. He had carefully taken note when his father had sent *Herald* correspondents around the United States to cover the Civil War. He believed that the descriptions of the areas from which the stories emanated were as important to the readers as anything that might be happening there. He therefore began to send reporters to cover not only events in strange places but the places themselves—these stories were some of the first travel writings to appear in the popular press. Bennett also quickly realized the value of *exclusive* news, so it was a logical progression for him to send correspondents as members of expeditions and then to organize and send the expeditions himself. In that way, he could first create the popular desire for information and then satisfy it with exclusive reports.

His first major attempt to create exclusive news was when he sent Stanley, one of his roving reporters, to find the Scottish medical missionary David Livingstone in central Africa. The introduction of Stanley's book *How I Found Livingstone* (1872) gives an account of the interview with Bennett in which he was given his commission. Bennett knew that whoever located the missing Livingstone would have a fabulous story to tell, and that the newspaper that printed it would benefit enormously. Stanley quotes Bennett as saying, "Draw a thousand pounds now, and when you have gone through that, draw another thousand, and when that is spent, draw another thousand, and when you have finished that, draw another thousand, and so on; but FIND LIVINGSTONE."

Stanley did find Livingstone, and the exclusive reports he sent to the *Herald* increased the newspaper's circulation and had the public clamoring for more. Several years later, after Livingstone had died, Bennett's *Herald* and the *Daily Telegraph* of London combined to fund Stanley's magnificent trans-Africa expedition (1874–1877), which answered the essential remaining questions about the major rivers and lakes of central Africa (see Stanley, 1878).

Bennett was also quick to grasp that the public was fascinated by the so-called Arctic questions—that is, whether there was a Northwest Passage and who would be the first to reach the North Pole. In 1873, his writers accompanied expeditions to search for *Polaris*, Charles Francis Hall's missing ship, and the thrilling accounts of hurricanes and storms at sea further increased the *Herald*'s readership. Two years later (1875), he sent Januarius Aloysius MacGahan on *Pan-*

*dora* to search for a Northwest Passage and to hunt for relics of the ill-fated Northwest Passage expedition under Sir John Franklin. MacGahan's vivid dispatches helped increase the circulation of the *Herald*, and his diaries were later published as a book, *Under the Northern Lights* (1876).

Because Bennett saw that the public still desired information regarding Franklin and his missing men, he proposed that *Herald* reporter William Henry Gilder accompany Lt. Frederick Schwatka on an expedition seeking them in the Canadian Arctic. A sledge journey of 3,251 miles followed, in which relics and skeletons were discovered. The journey was a considerable achievement, but was comparatively uneventful. Glitch-free expeditions do not sell newspapers, and Gilder's reports back to the *Herald*, on which his book *Schwatka's Search* (1881) was based, sensationalized the story.

Bennett's most sensational venture in the north was in his sponsorship of the North Pole expedition on *Jeannette*, under the command of George Washington De Long. Bennett's desire to create news and De Long's craving for fame combined to stage a disaster almost unparalleled in American exploration. In 1878, a year before *Jeannette* set sail, the Swedish explorer Adolf Erik Nordenskiöld had set out to navigate the Northeast Passage. Recalling his success with Stanley finding Livingstone, Bennett decided that De Long should find Nordenskiöld, even though there was nothing to suggest that Nordenskiöld needed assistance. With the possibility of two huge stories (the "rescue" of Nordenskiöld and the attainment of the North Pole) in the offing, Bennett assigned reporter Jerome Collins to the crew.

*Jeannette* never came close to finding Nordenskiöld. She steamed through the Bering Strait and then became stuck in the ice. She drifted helpless in the ice for two years until she was finally crushed, leaving the crew to take to the sea in three open boats. One was never seen again, and two reached the Lena delta. Collins and De Long died while awaiting rescue, leaving only members of the third boat, under George W. Melville, to struggle to safety. Meanwhile, Bennett had backed a rescue expedition, with Gilder as onboard reporter. This was no more successful than the *Jeannette* expedition had been, though it did prove that Gilder was an accomplished Arctic explorer and a valuable asset to the sales of the *Herald*. Bennett realized just how valuable Gilder was when Gilder intercepted Melville's report to the navy of his search for De Long and used it to write a story for the *Herald*, which thus had the scoop before any other newspaper knew that there was a story to be written. Gilder's book *Ice-Pack and Tundra* (1883) is a vivid account of his adventures.

Bennett promptly dispatched yet another reporter, John P. Jackson, to travel to the Lena delta to discover details of the death of De Long. Jackson traveled to De Long's icy grave and promptly exhumed him, sending lurid stories and sketches of the bodies to the *Herald*, which fascinated and delighted the reading public. Not everyone shared Bennett's pride in his reporters. Melville wrote a harsh condemnation in *In the Lena Delta* (1884): "I never dreamed that a person born in a Christian land would so far forget the respect due to our honored dead as to violate their sacred resting place for the purpose of concocting a sensational story."

The *Jeannette* fiasco was not the last Arctic controversy with Bennett at its heart. In 1909, Frederick Cook claimed to have reached the North Pole. Bennett promptly bought Cook's exclusive story and ran it in the *Herald*. Several days later, however, Robert E. Peary, who had previously sold his accounts to the *Herald* but was now supported by the *New York Times*, also claimed to have reached the North Pole. The two explorers and their respective newspapers were plunged into a controversy that provided them both with ample sensational reading matter for months.

Bennett remained a brilliant, but quixotic, proprietor for many years. His flamboyant lifestyle and quick, unpredictable temper made him many enemies, though the $30 million he is reputed to have spent as playboy, sportsman, traveler, and socialite doubtless bought him many friends, too. He was a major contributor to the development of American journalism, and his comment on the newspaper business perhaps summarizes his attitude to his work: "A great editor is one who knows where hell is going to break loose next and how to get a reporter first on the scene" (O'Connor, 1962). As one of America's most eligible bachelors, he staved off marriage until he was 73, and died four years later from a brain hemorrhage.

BEAU RIFFENBURGH

## Biography

Born in New York City, 10 May 1841. Son of the founder and editor of The *New York Herald*. Joined Union army, 1861, but saw no Civil War action. Joined The *New York Herald*, 1865: became managing editor, 1866; chief executive officer, 1867. Sponsored Henry Morton Stanley's expedition to look for David Livingstone in Africa, 1869; instigated and funded a number of significant Arctic ventures, including the sponsorship of George Washington De Long to discover the North Pole, 1879–1881. Moved to Europe, 1877; lived mainly in France. Married Maud Potter, Baroness de Reuter, widow of George de Reuter, September 1914. Died in Beaulieu, France, 14 May 1918.

### References and Further Reading

De Long, Emma (editor), *The Voyage of the Jeannette: The Ship and Ice Journals of George W. De Long*, 1883.
Gilder, William, *Schwatka's Search: Sledging in the Arctic in Quest of the Franklin Records*, 1881.
Gilder, William, *Ice-Pack and Tundra*, 1883.
MacGahan, J.A., *Under the Northern Lights*, 1876.
Melville, George W., *In the Lena Delta*, 1884.
O'Connor, Richard, *The Scandalous Mr. Bennett*, New York: Doubleday, 1962.
Stanley, Henry Morton, *How I Found Livingstone*, 1872.
Stanley, Henry Morton, *Through the Dark Continent*, 1878.

## BERING, VITUS (1681–1741) *Danish Explorer and Navigator*

Vitus Bering, a Danish seafarer who had a long career in the imperial Russian navy, is renowned for his command of two Russian voyages in the North Pacific, during the first of which (1728) he explored the strait now named for him and on the second (1741) "discovered" Alaska. A pragmatic and reserved man, Bering focused his energies on the challenges of navigation in uncharted, unforgiving seas. He showed little appreciation for travel writing or scholarship and, indeed, wrote remarkably little on his voyages. Bering's relevance to the field of travel literature lies in the fact that his voyages facilitated the beginnings of Russo-European exploration, scholarship, and colonialism in the North Pacific and northwest America.

Bering, known as a competent officer who had "been to India and kn[ew] his way around," received his first Pacific command in December 1724 by order of the westernizing Russian emperor Peter the Great (1672–1725). The emperor ordered Bering to find the "land that goes to the north [of Kamchatka]," which he believed to be part of America, to determine whether "European possession[s]" existed there, and to map its shores. Though the voyage spoke to important scientific questions of the day—the relation of Asia to America and the possibility of Arctic sea routes—it is likely that Peter was primarily motivated by the desire to expand the Russian fur trade to northwest America, thereby reviving the sagging state revenue from the trade.

Early in 1725, Bering departed from St. Petersburg for the Pacific with his officers, men, and supplies. Despite encountering several indigenous groups during the trek across Siberia, Bering's report to the admiralty makes only brief references to the "idolaters" and their lack of "good habits." Following an arduous journey, the party reached Avacha Bay on the Kamchatka Peninsula in spring 1728. From there, Bering's fragile vessel, *St. Gabriel*, which had been constructed on site, was put to sea on 13 July and proceeded north along the Asian coast to the Bering Strait. Standing at 67°18′ N on 16 August, having passed the Chukchi Peninsula without sighting America, Bering turned back, convinced that Asia and America were not connected. The following year, Bering sailed east, presumably attempting to locate America or islands near it, but found nothing. In 1730, he returned to St. Petersburg, satisfied that he had acted "according to the instructions of His Imperial Majesty," and delivered an uninspired account of the voyage.

The admiralty promoted Bering to the rank of captain commander on his return, but it considered the results of his voyage inconclusive. Bering had neither followed the north Siberian shore west to the Kolyma River (already familiar to the Russians) to establish with finality the lack of a land connection between Asia and America, nor had he reached the latter continent. Amid criticism of his leadership, Bering petitioned Empress Anna for command of a second voyage in the North Pacific. After considerable discussion, Bering received permission to form a second expedition in December 1732.

This project subsequently grew into one of the most ambitious undertakings in the annals of exploration and scientific inquiry. Not only was Bering to take two vessels to North America, subject the indigenous inhabitants to fur tribute, and ascertain other powers' designs in the region, but other sections of the expedition were to explore the entire Arctic coast of Siberia and reach Japan as well. Furthermore, a number of western European and Russian scholars, including G.F. Muller, J.G. Gmelin, S.P. Krasheninnikov, and G.W. Steller, were dispatched to study the "natural history" of lands and peoples all over Siberia, including distant Kamchatka. The works of Krasheninnikov and Steller remain fundamental texts of Siberian scholarship. As for Bering's contingent, he and second-in-command Aleksei Chirikov, accompanied by 500 men, again made the long, difficult passage across Siberia to Avacha Bay. When Kamchadal natives drafted to ferry supplies across the peninsula by dogsled resisted, Bering had the rebels flogged with the knout. Preparations for the sea voyage were not completed until summer 1741.

On 4 June 1741, *St. Peter*, commanded by Bering, and *St. Paul*, skippered by Chirikov, were put to sea. The vessels separated during a storm and proceeded to the American coast independently. Neither made lengthy landfalls or had extensive contact with Alaskan natives. *St. Peter* sighted Mount St. Elias along the Alaska coast in mid-July. Faced with unfamiliar waters and dwindling supplies, Bering reacted coolly, commenting on the necessity to "take into consideration . . . how far [they were] from home" (Steller, 1974). On 20 July, Bering allowed a brief reconnaissance of Kayak Island, where semisubterranean Chugach

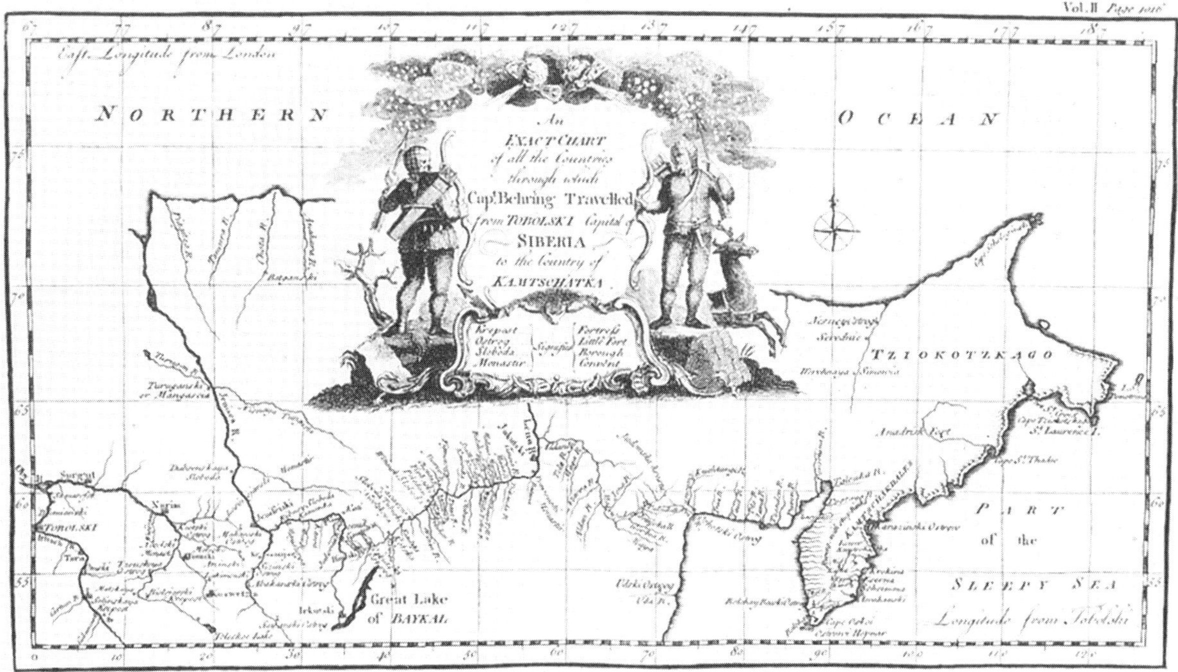


Bering's route across Siberia to Kamchatka (from Harris's *Navigantium atque Itinerantium Bibliotheca*, 1744); the cunningly positioned title partially conceals the contemporary ignorance about Siberia's northern coastline. *Courtesy of the Travellers Club, London; Bridgeman Art Library, agent.*

dwellings and human tracks in the sand were found. And in September, an encounter with "Americans" (Aleuts) occurred in the Shumagin Islands. These events were brief, however, and the accounts of Bering's officers reveal a marked lack of enthusiasm. It may be said that they saw but did not *observe*. Steller was outraged by the officers' lack of initiative. Their "stupidity" and "fear of a few unarmed and moreover timid savages [*wilden*]," he claimed, cut his scientific work short (Steller, 1974). Tragically, on the return voyage Bering and 19 others perished from scurvy. The survivors limped back to Avacha Bay in late August 1742, after many months stranded on the island of Bering's demise.

Bering's second voyage had fulfilled its objectives only partially (and that at enormous cost), and no account of it by his hand exists. Nevertheless, Bering made an important impact on the North Pacific and northwest America. The zoological and ethnographic tracts on coastal Alaska written by his adjunct, Steller, are the earliest scholarly field studies of the area. The sea route to Alaska established by Bering and Chirikov and the sea otter pelts their vessels brought back to Siberia facilitated and encouraged the encroachment of Russian fur companies into Alaska, to be followed by the Russian state and church. This irrevocably altered the ecology of the region and the culture of its inhabitants. Most important for present purposes, following Bering's "discovery" of northwest America, explorers, scholars, and merchant-adventurers from Russia, Britain, France, Spain, and the United States descended upon Alaska with increasing frequency, producing a significant volume of travel writing.

John C. Ehrhardt

### Biography

Born in Horsens, Denmark, 1681. Two voyages in service of the Dutch East India Company by 1703. Entered Russian navy as sublieutenant, 1704. Reached rank of captain, 1724. Served with Black Sea and Baltic fleets in wars with Ottoman empire and Sweden. Married Anna Matveevna: three sons. Commanded first Kamchatka expedition in eastern Siberia and the North Pacific, 1725–1730, exploring Bering Strait, 1728. Commanded second Russian expedition in eastern Siberia and the North Pacific, part of the Great Northern Expedition, beginning 1733. Reached Alaska coast in July 1741. Explored Kodiak Island; attempted to return to Siberia but shipwrecked on the shore of Bering Island, off the Kamchatka Peninsula coast, November 1741. Died of scurvy on Bering Island, 19 December 1741.

### References and Further Reading

Bering, Vitus, "Ekspeditsiia v Kamchatku Kapitana ot Flota Beringa" [Fleet Captain Bering's Expedition to Kamchatka], in *Ekspeditsiia Beringa: Sbornik dokumentov* [Bering's Expeditions: A Collection of Documents], edited by A.A. Pokrovskii, 1941.

Steller, Georg Wilheln, *Reise von Kamtschatka nach Amerika* [*Voyage from Kamchatka to America*], edited by Hanno Beck, Stuttgart: Brockhaus, 1974.

## BERLIN

A town since the thirteenth century, Berlin did not become prominent until after the Thirty Years' War when the kings of Prussia chose it as a place of residence and expanded the city limits. This aristocratic Berlin was the subject of a travel guidebook written by Friedrich Nicolai (1733–1811), who revised and enlarged his meticulously researched study, which left no stone unturned. He described Berlin and Potsdam's topography and demography, administrative and social institutions, trade and industry, schools and universities, libraries and museums, religion and courts, and even suggested a few tours through the parks and to the suburbs. The courtly city was also depicted in the travel accounts of renowned foreigners, among them the theologian John Toland (1670–1722), who visited Berlin in the early eighteenth century, and the midcentury visitors James Boswell (1740–1795) and Voltaire (1694–1778). The French philosopher lived from 1750 to 1753 at Sans-Souci, the country seat of Frederick the Great in Potsdam, and sketched his royal friend as well as the courtly intrigues in his correspondence and memoirs.

In the early nineteenth century, Heinrich Heine (1797–1856) visited Berlin and wrote three loosely organized letters about the city, using an anecdotal and journalistic style to express his displeasure with the aristocracy, the military, and the censor. He later incorporated the letters in his *Reisebilder*. For four months in 1821, Vicomte de Chateaubriand (1768–1848) stayed in Berlin as the French ambassador, and in his autobiography recounted his not-so-favorable impressions of the city. In 1840, the American editor and diplomat Theodore Sedgwick Fay (1807–1898) published a fictional tale about Berlin, which serves as the setting for a didactic romance about the terrible consequences of duelling.

The capital of the Second Reich after Germany's victory in the Franco-Prussian War, Berlin continued to grow rapidly and attracted an increasing number of artists and intellectuals. Foremost among Berlin's writers was Theodor Fontane (1819–1898), who established his fame with the publication of *Wanderungen durch die Mark Brandenburg*, which describes the author's excursions into the towns and countryside surrounding the capital. Fontane employed a mixture of factual description and narrative to tell provincial history and to portray the local people. Dealing in his novels with Berlin's upper-class milieu especially, he became Germany's leading realistic writer of the Wilhelmine era.

Social conditions were the focus of many other novels about Berlin. Max Kretzer (1854–1941), who was compared to Zola, depicted the lives of the city's workers and outcasts; Heinrich Seidel (1842–1906) wrote a popular series about a petty bourgeois protagonist; and the writer and philosopher Fritz Mauthner (1849–1923) published a trilogy about the city. Everyday life in Berlin was also the subject matter of the illustrated *Berlin under the New Empire*, written by the British foreign correspondent Henry Vizetelly (1820–1891). George Eliot visited the city twice (1854–1855 and 1870), used it in some of her fictional works, and compiled her *Recollections of Berlin*. The American historian George Bancroft served as a diplomat in the city from 1867 to 1874, and recorded in his letters and journals his meetings with many influential politicians, artists, and intellectuals.

In the first half of the twentieth century, the German capital became a protagonist in its own right in *Berlin Alexanderplatz* by Alfred Döblin (1878–1957). This high-modernist novel—turned into popular films in 1930 and 1980—tells the story of an ex-convict who tries to live a decent life but fails vis-à-vis the social and moral forces of the metropolis. The dark side of the city also fascinated the American expatriate Robert McAlmon (1896–1956), who composed a series of *Grim Fairy Tales* (his book's subtitle) about Berlin, and Christopher Isherwood (1904–1986), who wrote

Unter den Linden was redesigned by Frederick the Great as a neoclassical showpiece, with the eponymous lime trees flanking the central pedestrian boulevard (from A.B. Granville's *St. Petersburgh: A Journal of Travels to and from That Capital*, 1828). *Courtesy of the Travellers Club, London; Bridgeman Art Library, agent.*

three novels about Berlin under Nazi rule as well as a book of reflections on his years in Germany. His friend Stephen Spender (1909–1995), who was in the German capital from 1931 to 1932, recounted his Berlin experiences in his autobiography. A loving view of the city, though overshadowed by the rise of Adolf Hitler, was expressed by the novelist Thomas Wolfe (1900–1938), who visited Germany six times between 1926 and 1936; and a humorous perspective was offered by Sinclair Lewis (1885–1951) in his Grand Tour satire, *Dodsworth*, several chapters of which feature Berlin. The American novelist and historical writer Joseph Hergesheimer (1880–1954) visited several major European cities and devoted two chapters of a travel account to his impressions of the German capital. The Berlin of the 1920s and 1930s was also the setting of two Russian novels by Vladimir Nabokov (1899–1977), and the subject of a pictorial work by the French writer Jean Giraudoux (1882–1944).

From the end of World War II to the fall of the Iron Curtain, Berlin symbolized the twentieth century's struggle with the forces of totalitarianism. Herman Wouk (b. 1915), Danielle Steel (b. 1947), and Anthony Burgess (b. 1917) described Berlin as a war-torn battlefield or as the center of National Socialism; Thomas Berger (b. 1924), Leon Uris (b. 1924), and William Buckley (b. 1925) depicted the post-war situation of a city sandwiched between the free world and the Communist Bloc. This Berlin of the Cold War figured most prominently in the popular genre of the spy novel written by authors such as John Le Carré (b. 1931) and Len Deighton (b. 1929). A suspenseful Berlin drama of a nonpolitical sort was published by Patricia Highsmith (1921–1995), who, in *The Boy Who Followed Ripley*, offered her readers a tour through the entire city. As the capital of the German Democratic Republic, the divided Berlin was also the setting for the personal and political conflicts of East German citizens; among them, Stefan Heym (b. 1913) and Christa Wolf (b. 1929) described their embattled hometown in their stories and novels about Germany's recent history.

UDO NATTERMANN

### References and Further Reading

Bancroft, George, *The Life and Letters of George Bancroft*, 2 vols., edited by M.A. De Wolfe Howe, 1908.

Boswell, James, *Boswell on the Grand Tour: Germany and Switzerland, 1764*, edited by Frederick A. Pottle, 1953.

Chateaubriand, François René de, *Mémoires d'outre-tombe*, 1849–1850; as *The Memoirs of François René, Vicomte de Chateaubriand*, translated by Alexander Teixeira de Mattos, 1902.

Eliot, George, *George Eliot's Life: As Related in Her Letters and Journals*, 3 vols., edited by John W. Cross, 1885.

Fontane, Theodor, *Wanderungen durch die Mark Brandenburg* [Excursions through Mark Brandenburg], 4 vols., 1862–1882.

Giraudoux, Jean, *Rues et visages de Berlin*, 1930.

Heine, Heinrich, *Briefe aus Berlin*, 1827; in *Heine in Art and Letters*, translated by Elizabeth A. Sharp, 1895.

Hergesheimer, Joseph, *Berlin*, 1932.

Isherwood, Christopher, *Christopher and His Kind 1929–1939*, 1976.

Nicolai, Friedrich, *Beschreibung der königlichen Residenzstädte Berlin und Potsdam, aller daselbst befindlicher Merkwürdigkeiten, und der umliegenden Gegend* [Description of the Imperial Cities Berlin and Potsdam, Their Peculiarities, and Their Environs], 1769; revised, 1779.

Spender, Stephen, *World within World*, 1951.

Toland, John, *An Account of the Courts of Prussia and Hannover: Sent to a Minister of State in Holland*, 1705.

Vizetelly, Henry, *Berlin under the New Empire: Its Institutions, Inhabitants, Industry, Monuments, Museums, Social Life, Manners, and Amusements*, 2 vols., 1879.

Voltaire, *Les Oeuvres Complètes*, edited by Theodore Besterman et al., 1968.

*See also* **Germany**

## BERNIER, FRANÇOIS (1620–1688) *French Physician and Traveler*

François Bernier started his travels in order to see the world and spent twelve years (1656–1668) in the East. Of these, he worked for eight years as a physician at the Moghul court during the early rule of Aurangzeb. The beginning of his travels, however, was confined to Europe and was never properly described in writing. Leaving off his theological studies, he followed the French ambassador to Poland in 1646. From Poland, he went on to Italy and returned to France in 1650. Afterward, he completed an M.D. at the University of Montpellier, and in 1656 he started his great journey to the East.

The beginning of the journey is only partially known. Traveling through Palestine and Syria, he lived for about a year in Cairo. In 1658, he went by ship from Egypt to Jedda and Mocha. Learning there that Ethiopia was no longer safe for Roman Catholic travelers, he abandoned his original plan of going to Gondar and, embarking on an Indian ship, arrived in Surat at the end of 1658 or the beginning of 1659. From Surat, he continued on to the Moghul court in Agra. He soon attracted attention and became the court physician of Dara Shikoh, one of the princes competing for the crown. Parting from the prince, he took service in the retinue of the *Omrah* (minister) Danishmand Khan. With his patrons, he traveled in many parts of north India, visiting Delhi, Lahore (1664), and Kashmir (1665), then Varanasi and Bengal (in the company of Jean-Baptiste Tavernier) and Golconda in Deccan (1666). In 1667, he left the court and went to Surat, where he sent to France his *Mémoire sur l'établisse-*

*ment du commerce dans l'Inde* [Memoir about the Establishment of Trade in India], the manuscript of which was preserved in archives, but only published in the twentieth century. He left India in 1668, visited Shiraz, then the capital of Iran, and returned to France in 1669. For the rest of his life, he remained mainly at home, with the exception of a visit to England and the Netherlands in 1685.

There were many Europeans seeking a living in Iran and in Moghul India in the seventeenth century. The majority consisted of practical people, such as jewellers, painters, architects and other craftsmen, gun-makers, and soldiers of fortune. In this company, Bernier, as the pupil of the philosopher Pierre Gassendi, was the most prominent and the most learned and therefore also one of the best eyewitnesses of seventeenth-century India. He arrived in India during the war of succession and was thus able to see the rise of Aurangzeb. He was a keen observer and much interested in politics, and supplied important information on the recent history, politics, judicial system, and even religion of the Moghul empire. In his position as a physician, he was, unlike many other travelers, capable of moving in court circles and making important acquaintances. Writing in the period of the great expansion of European commercial interests in India, he had a wide and interested readership. His style is exact and lively, and anecdotes from many different sources testify to a good sense of humor.

Bernier did not write a coherent account of his travels. His work consists of two historical accounts, mainly founded on his firsthand observations, and of several letters. Details of his travels are partly culled from these, partly from the accounts of contemporary travelers such as Jean Chardin and Tavernier. The first of Bernier's own writings, the *History of the Late Revolution*, originally published in 1670 and dedicated to Louis XIV, briefly explains his coming to India and goes on to describe the war over the succession of Shah Jahan in 1655–1660. The author and his personal experiences are only occasionally brought into the picture. The second account, the *Particular Events*, relates events from the time of the victory of Aurangzeb up to the departure of the author from India, thus concluding the history. Much space is devoted to the description of various embassies arriving at Aurangzeb's court and to portraits of important Moghul nobles.

The *Letter to Monseigneur Colbert*, written soon after Bernier's return to France, contains a general account of the Moghul empire, its geography, society, administration, judicial system, economy, natural resources, and trade. At the end, he discusses the reasons for the apparent decline of Moghul India, explaining it mainly by the unstable system of land ownership and the defects of administration and jurisdiction. The *Letter to Monsieur de La Mothe Le Vayer*, written in Delhi in July 1663, is a separate description of Delhi and Agra, the two Moghul capitals. It also adds many details of Moghul court life and customs. He gives an account of the Jesuits who had been working in Agra since the days of Akbar, and expresses his skepticism about the missionaries' chances of success. The *Letter to Monsieur Chapelain*, written in Shiraz in October 1667, is an attempt at a description of the Hindus and their religion and society as separate from the ruling Muslims. It is mainly founded on information obtained from Father Roth, a German Jesuit working in Agra, but also from Kavindracharya Sarasvati, the famous Hindu scholar of Varanasi. Finally, the author's visit to Kashmir in 1665, together with Aurangzeb's army, is described in the series of nine *Letters to Monsieur de Merveilles*, written during the expedition itself. To the last letter are appended the answers to five queries presented to the author by Melchisédech Thévenot, the famous publisher of travels. The fourth of these contains a description of Bengal.

KLAUS KARTTUNEN

## Biography

Born in Joué-Etiau, Maine-et-Loire, France, 26 September 1620, son of Pierre Bernier, tenant farmer of the chapter of Angers. Orphaned at an early age; educated by an uncle. Studied in Paris for an ecclesiastical career and later at the Collège Royal under Pierre Gassendi. Traveled to the Netherlands and Poland with the Vicomte d'Arpajon, ambassador to Poland; involved with the election of the king of Poland, 1848. Made further travels to southern Germany and Italy. Joined Gassendi at Toulon, became involved in Gassendi's libel case against the astrologer J.-B. Morin, 1650. Studied medicine at the University of Montpellier; completed his doctorate in medicine in less than four months, 1652. Lived in Digne and Paris with Gassendi, 1652–1655. Traveled and practiced medicine in Palestine, Syria, Egypt, India, and Tibet, 1656–1669. Returned to France; settled in Paris and associated with a number of writers, including Racine and Molière. Lived with Madame de La Sablière for some years. Published a number of medical and philosophical books and articles. Traveled in France, Holland, and England in later life. Died of apoplexy in Paris, 22 September 1688.

## References and Further Reading

Bernier, François, *Histoire de la dernière Revolution des États du Grand Mogol*, 1670 (first part of his travel account); *Evenemens particuliers, où cequi s'est passé de plus considerable après la guerre pendant cinq ans, ou environ, dans*

*les États du grans Mogol*, 1670; *Suite des Mémoires sur l'empire du Grand Mogol*, 1671; together in 2 vols. as *Voyages de François Bernier, contenant la description des états du grand-mogol*, 1699; numerous reprints and editions, including *Voyage dans Les États du Grand Mogol*, with an introduction by F. Bhattacharya, 1981.
Bernier, François, *The History of the Late Revolution of the Empire of the Great Mogol*, 1671; *Particular Events; or, the Most Considerable Passages after the War of Five Years, or thereabout, in the Empire of the Great Mogol*, 1671; *A Continuation of the Memoires . . . Concerning the Empire of the Great Mogol*, 1672.
Bernier, François, *Bernier's Travels, Comprehending a Description of the Mogul Empire*, translated from the French by John Stewart, 1826.
Bernier, François, *Travels in the Mogul Empire*, translated from the French by Irving Brock, 2 vols., 1826.
Bernier, François, *Travels in the Mogul Empire, AD 1656–1668*, revised and improved edition based on Irving Brock's translation, and annotated by Archibald Constable, 1891; 2nd edition revised by Vincent A. Smith, 1916.

## BICYCLES

The first machine that is considered to be the precursor to the modern bicycle, the Draisienne, was invented in 1817 and enjoyed a brief period of fashionable acclaim in 1819, but it was not until the development of the front-driven velocipede in the 1860s that cycling began to be taken seriously as a form of long-distance touring transport. Even on these heavy and unwieldy machines with solid malleable-iron frames and carriage-style wooden wheels, travelers toured the length of Britain and France. Before this time, there is evidence that three- and four-wheeled manumotive and pedamotive machines were ridden considerable distances, but, with the exception of unpublished personal records (for example, H.H. Hodgson on a Sawyer machine in the 1850s; see Ritchie, 1975), reference to these is more the incredulity of reporters rather than the literature of travel. Perhaps the most famous is the article referring to "a gentleman from Dumfries" who had ridden from Cumnock to Glasgow (40 miles) in a day, published in three papers in 1842. Who the gentleman was and what his "velocipede" comprised is a vexing question in cycling history today.

The era of the front-driven velocipede (c. 1867–1870) established cycling as we would recognize it today, the favored machine being the bicycle, with riders' clubs, organized race meets, and a fledgling literature devoted to the activity. The publications of this period set the model for many that follow, in that most are guides to how to purchase, ride, and maintain the machines, but sometimes they include sections on touring, and there is an underlying assumption that this should be the aim of most riders.

However, it is the period of the high-wheeled machine, from about 1870 to 1890, that sees the flowering of a true literature of travel by cycle. These machines were elegant and increasingly light and quick. By 1880, they had become the fastest vehicles on the road, capable of sustained speeds of over 10 miles per hour over long distances, sprinting at nearer to 20 miles per hour, and scorching downhill at whatever the road and the rider's nerves would allow. The responsive performance, ease of riding, and lightness of the high machine, coupled with its unequaled riding position, tempted riders to take on challenging tours of epic proportions, which they often recorded in book form. These start appearing in the 1870s—for example, W. Saunders's account of Laumaille's *Paris to Vienna on a Bicycle* (1875) and W.S. Yorke Shuttleworth's *Eyatkuhnen to Langenweddingen by Bicycle* (1879)—but probably the most renowned, for the colorfulness of their journeys and the hardships they endured, are Karl Kron's *Ten Thousand Miles on a Bicycle* (1887) and Thomas Stevens's two-volume *Around the World on a Bicycle* (1887–1888). The epic ride with no shortage of hardship was to remain popular well after the high-wheeler had passed into history, an example being R.L. Jefferson's lively accounts of his experiences touring in Russia and Siberia.

A more homely, but equally interesting genre comes from tricyclists at this period. Tricycles were seen as the sedate mounts of the gentry and suitable for lady riders. A series of books by Joseph and Elizabeth Pennell describe their touring activities through Europe, including their honeymoon, which was taken as a tour on a tandem tricycle. Joseph was a skilled illustrator, and his work enhances these publications. S.R. Crockett's *Sweetheart Travellers* (1895) gives an account of the author's tours around rural Britain with his young daughters on a Humber equipped with child seats, again well illustrated, but not by the author.

The widescale acceptance of the rear-chain-driven safety bicycle, particularly after the introduction of pneumatic tires in the late 1880s, not only set the pattern of machine that is still familiar today, but allowed bicycling to reach a far wider constituency. At first, these machines remained the playthings of the wealthy, but after the high point of the mid–1890s "bicycle boom" the bicycle became progressively more demotic, and this is reflected in the nature of the writing associated with it. Many publications from the 1890s up to World War I are characterized by haute bourgeois interests. The Earl of Cavan's *With the Yacht, Camera, and Cycle in the Mediterranean* (1895) is a good example. The two well-known cyclo-novels based on actual rides, H.G. Wells's *The Wheels of Chance* (1896) and Jerome K. Jerome's *Three Men on the Bummel* (1900), are also interesting for their insights into social class and cycle touring. Bernard Newman's extensive output of books describing his tours, mainly around Europe in the 1930s, is typical of later writing.

An important class of literature of travel by cycle is that of the roadbook. These had been written for cyclists since the 1870s, but the two most notable series are those put out by the Cyclist's Touring Club in the 1890s (and revised in the 1910s) covering Britain and much of Europe, and the H.G. Inglis Contour series begun in 1896 and completed in 1908. The latter is particularly worthwhile, because Inglis seems to have personally ridden all the roads he describes, a total of some 40,000 miles. An associated genre is the detailed guide written from riding experiences, a type-form that continues to be put out by numerous authors.

It is reasonable to argue that by the early twentieth century, the key forms of cyclo-travel writing had been established. Most continue to be popular, but undoubtedly the long-distance tour, often through exotic (to their usually British or American writers) climes, remains the archetype. Examples are Nick Sanders's *The Great Bike Ride: Around the World in Eighty Days* (1988), and Ian Hibell and Clinton Trowbridge's *Into the Remote Places* (1984).

Cyclo-travel writing suggests that the cycle's primary use is sport and leisure or as "alternative" transport. Perhaps this is because the literature of cycling continues to be dominated by works in English written by authors from industrially developed Western nations, although cycling is often the only form of personal mechanized transport that is available to a significant portion of Third World populations. It is also notable that although the cycle is a form of transport that for much of its history has often experienced an impressive gender balance (more so-called ladies' bicycles were sold in the late 1890s than gentlemen's), this is not reflected in the authorship of cycling literature, which continues to be male-dominated. Exceptions to this include authors such as F.J. Erskine and Lillias Davidson, who wrote general guides with touring advice in the late nineteenth century; more recently, Dervla Murphy in the 1960s and contemporary writers Bettina Selby and Josie Dew have provided accounts of long-distance touring.

NICHOLAS ODDY

## References and Further Reading


Allen, Thomas Gaskell, and William Lewis Sachtleben, *Across Asia on a Bicycle: The Journey of Two American Students from Constantinople to Peking*, 1894.

Anderson, William C., *The Great Bicycle Expedition: Freewheeling through Europe with a Family, a Potted Plant—and Bicycle Seatus*, 1973.

Annis, William L., *Alaska Journal: A Cyclist's Adventure Tour in Southeast Alaska*, 1993.

Bailey, Glenn, *One Pedal at a Time: A Bicycle Journey around Australia*, 1995.

Baron, Stanley R., *Westward Ho! From Cambria to Cornwall*, 1934.

Bauer, Fred, *How Many Hills to Hillsboro?*, 1969.

Bell, David E.T., *The Highway Man*, edited by P. Blane, S.J. Hourston, and J.B. Gambles, 1970.

Berg, Ted, *Sweden and Back on a Bicycle: The Adventures of a Fourteen-Year-Old Traveling Alone*, 1956.

Biddulph, Eric, *A Gringo and a Bike in South America*, 1987.

Birchmore, Fred A., *Around the World on a Bicycle*, 1939.

Bolton, Alfred M., *Over the Pyrenees: A Bicyclist's Adventures among the Spaniards*, 1883.

Broad, Lucy, *A Woman's Wanderings the World Over*, 1909.

Brooks, Charles S., *A Thread of English Road*, 1924.

Bulfin, William (Che Buono), *Rambles in Eirinn*, 1907.

Burke, W.S., *Cycling in Bengal*, 1898.

Burston, G.W., and H.R. Stokes, *Round about the World on Bicycles*, 1890.

Callan, Hugh, *Wanderings on Wheel and on Foot through Europe*, 1887.

Callan, Hugh, *From the Clyde to the Jordan: Narrative of a Bicycle Journey*, 1895.

Cavan, Frederick Edward Gould Lambart, Earl of, *With the Yacht, Camera, and Cycle in the Mediterranean*, 1895.

Chandler, Alfred D., *A Bicycle Tour in England and Wales*, 1881.

Chilosà, *Waif and Stray: The Adventures of Two Tricycles*, 1896.

Coffey, Maria, *Three Moons in Vietnam: A Haphazard Journey by Boat and Bicycle*, 1996.

Cole, Grenville A.J., *The Gypsy Road: A Journey from Krakow to Coblentz*, 1894.

Cook, Dave, *Breaking Loose: An Account of an Overland Cycle Journey from London to Australia*, 1994.

Cowles, Frederick, *Vagabond Pilgrimage, Being the Record of a Journey from East Anglia to the West of England*, 1949.

Crane, Nicholas, and Richard Crane, *Bicycles up Kilimanjaro*, 1985.

Crane, Nick, *Atlas Biker: Mountainbiking in Morocco*, 1990.

Crane, Richard, and Nicholas Crane, *Journey to the Centre of the Earth*, 1987.

Crockett, S.R., *Sweetheart Travellers*, 1895.

Davar, Framji Jamshedji, *Cycling over the Roof of the World . . . The First Bicycle Journey over the Mighty Andes*, 1929.

Davar, Framji Jamshedji, *Across the Sahara*, 1937.

Davidson, Lillias, *Handbook for Lady Cyclists*, 1896.

Dew, Josie, *The Wind in My Wheels: Travel Tales from the Saddle*, 1992.

Dew, Josie, *Travels in a Strange State: Cycling across the U.S.A.*, 1994.

Downing, Rupert, *If I Laugh: The Chronicle of My Strange Adventures in the Great Paris Exodus—June 1940*, 1941.

Drorbaugh, Richard, *World Ride: Going the Extra Mile against Cancer*, 1995.

Duker, Peter, *Sting in the Tail: By Racing Bicycle around the World*, 1973.

Ellington, W.A., *Through the Ardennes and Luxembourg on Wheels*, 1891.

Elvin, Harold, *The Ride to Chandigarh*, 1957.

Elvin, Harold, *Avenue to the Door of the Dead*, 1961.

Elvin, Harold, *Elvin's Rides*, 1963.

Erskine, F.J., *Tricycling for Ladies*, 1885.

Faed [A.J. Wilson], *Two Trips to the Emerald Isle*, 1888.

Fraser, John Foster, *Round the World on a Wheel, Being the Narrative of a Bicycle Ride of Nineteen Thousand Two Hundred and Thirty-seven Miles through Seventeen Countries and across Three Continents by John Foster Fraser,*

*S. Edward Lunn and F.H. Lowe*, 1899; abridged edition, 1982.

Galen, Ralph W., *Two Wheels, Two Years and Three Continents: A Bicyclist's Dream Fulfilled*, 1997.

Garrison, Winfred Ernest, *Wheeling through Europe*, 1900.

Gidmark, David, *Journey across a Continent*, 1977.

Green, Anna, and Howard Green, *On a Bicycle Made for Two*, 1990.

Hakim, Adi B., et al., *With the Cyclists round the World*, 1928.

Hamsher, W. Papel, *The Balkans by Bicycle*, 1937.

Hanson, John, *Around the World in Cycle Clips: An Eye-Opening Journey through Calamities, Curries and Culture Shock*, 1990.

Hardinge, Rex, *South African Cinderella: A Trek through Ex-German South Africa*, 1937.

Harper, Charles G., *Cycle Rides round London*, 1902.

Hastings, Frederick, *The Spins of "The Cycling Parson,"* 1903.

Hibell, Ian, and Clinton Trowbridge, *Into the Remote Places*, 1984.

Howgate, Bernie, *Tales of a Travelling Man: Eight Years around the World on a Ten-Speed Bike*, 1990.

Inglis, Harry R.G., *The Contour Road Book of Scotland*, 1896.

Jackson, Keith, *Keith's Incredible Journey: Alaska–Tierra del Fuego*, 1984.

James, Charles, *Two on a Tandem, Being the . . . Account of the Tour of Two Men on a Bicycle*, 1896.

Jefferson, Robert L., *To Constantinople on a Bicycle: The Story of My Ride*, 1894.

Jefferson, Robert L., *Awheel to Moscow and Back: The Record of a Record Cycle Ride*, 1895.

Jefferson, Robert L., *Across Siberia on a Bicycle*, 1896.

Jefferson, Robert L., *A New Ride to Khiva*, 1899.

Jefferson, Robert L., *Through a Continent on Wheels*, illustrated by Harry Evans, 1899.

Jerome, Jerome K., *Three Men on the Bummel*, 1900.

Johnson, Barbara Mary, *Pilgrim on a Bicycle: Coast to Coast in Search of Community*, 1982.

Jose, A.W., *Two Awheel and Some Others Afoot in Australia*, 1903.

Kharas, K.J., R.D. Ghandhi, and R.D. Shroff, *Pedalling through the Afghan Wilds*, 1935.

Kron, Karl, *Ten Thousand Miles on a Bicycle*, 1887; reprinted, 1982.

Kshitisa, Chandra Vandyopadhyaya, *My Travels in the East*, 1936.

Kshitisa, Chandra Vandyopadhyaya, *Across the Near East*, 1938.

Le Gallienne, Richard, *Travels in England*, 1900.

Lovett, Richard A., *Freewheelin': A Solo Journey across America*, 1992.

Lynn, Ethel, *The Adventures of a Woman Hobo*, 1917.

Magnouloux, Bernard, *Travels with Rosinante: Five Years' Cycling round the World*, 1988.

McCulloch, Alan, *Trial by Tandem*, 1951.

Meakin, Budgett, *The Land of the Moors*, 1901; reprinted, 1986.

Melland, Frank H., and Edward H. Cholmeley, *Through the Heart of Africa*, 1912.

Murif, Jerome J., *From Ocean to Ocean: Across a Continent on a Bicycle: An Account of a Solitary Ride from Adelaide to Port Darwin*, 1897.

Murphy, Dervla, *Full Tilt: Ireland to India with a Bicycle*, 1965.

Murphy, Dervla, *The Waiting Land: A Spell in Nepal*, 1967.

Murphy, Dervla, *Transylvania and Beyond: A Travel Memoir*, 1992.

Murphy, Dervla, *The Ukimwi Road: From Kenya to Zimbabwe*, 1993.

Murphy, Dervla, *South from the Limpopo: Travels through South Africa*, 1997.

Mustoe, Anne, *Lone Traveller: One Woman, Two Wheels and the World*, 1998.

Nauticus, *Nauticus on His Hobby Horse; or, The Adventures of a Sailor during a Tricycle Cruise of 1,427 Miles*, 1880.

Nauticus, *Nauticus in Scotland: A Tricycle Tour of 2,462 Miles, Including Skye and the West Coast*, 1882.

Newby, Eric, *Round Ireland in Low Gear*, 1987.

Newman, Bernard, *In the Trail of the Three Musketeers*, 1934.

Newman, Bernard, *Pedalling Poland*, 1935.

Newman, Bernard, *The Blue Danube: Black Forest to Black Sea*, 1935.

Newman, Bernard, *Albanian Back-door*, 1936.

Newman, Bernard, *I Saw Spain*, 1937.

Newman, Bernard, *Ride to Russia*, 1938.

Newman, Bernard, *Baltic Roundabout*, 1939.

Newman, Bernard, *Savoy! Corsica! Tunis! Mussolini's Dream Lands*, 1940.

Newman, Bernard, *British Journey*, 1945.

Newman, Bernard, *Middle Eastern Journey*, 1947.

Newman, Bernard, *The Lazy Meuse*, 1949.

Newman, Bernard, *The Sisters Alsace Lorraine*, 1950.

Newman, Bernard, *Oberammergau Journey*, 1951.

Newman, Bernard, *Both Sides of the Pyrenees*, 1952.

Newman, Bernard, *Ride to Rome*, 1953.

Newman, Bernard, *Berlin and Back*, 1954.

Newman, Bernard, *Still Flows the Danube*, 1955.

Newman, Bernard, *Visa to Russia*, 1959.

Nicholl, Charles, *Borderlines: A Journey in Thailand and Burma*, 1988.

Nichols, Alan, *Journey: A Bicycle Odyssey through Central Asia*, 1991.

O'Connor, Frank, *Irish Miles*, 1947; reprinted with an introduction by Brendan Kennelly, 1988.

Pennell, Elizabeth Robins, *To Gipsyland*, illustrated by Joseph Pennell, 1893.

Pennell, Elizabeth Robins, *Over the Alps on a Bicycle*, illustrated by Joseph Pennell, 1898.

Pennell, Joseph, and Elizabeth Robins Pennell, *A Canterbury Pilgrimage*, 1885.

Pennell, Joseph, and Elizabeth Robins Pennell, *Two Pilgrims' Progress*, 1886; as *An Italian Pilgrimage*, 1887.

Pennell, Joseph, and Elizabeth Robins Pennell, *Our Sentimental Journey through France and Italy*, 1888.

Pham, Andrew X., *Catfish and Mandala: A Two-Wheeled Voyage through the Landscape and Memory of Vietnam*, 2000.

Pollock, Wilfred, *War and a Wheel: The Graeco-Turkish War as Seen from a Bicycle*, 1897.

Reynolds, Jim, *The Outer Path: Finding My Way in Tibet*, edited by Kathleen Hallam, introduction by the Dalai Lama, 1992.

Ritchie, Andrew, *King of the Road: An Illustrated History of Cycling*, London: Wildwood House, and Berkeley, California. Ten Speed Press, 1975.

Roberts, Stephen K., *Computing across America: The Bicycle Odyssey of a High-Tech Nomad*, 1988.

Rutter, Frank, *The Path to Paris: The Rambling Record of a Riverside Promenade*, illustrated by Hanslip Fletcher, 1908.

Sanders, Nick, *The Great Bike Ride: Around the World in Eighty Days*, 1988.

Sang Ye, with Nicholas Jose and Sue Trevaskes, *The Finish Line: A Long March by Bicycle through China and Australia*, 1994.

Savage, Barbara, *Miles from Nowhere: A Round-the-world Bicycle Adventure*, edited by Diane Hammond, 1983.

Selby, Bettina, *Riding the Mountains Down*, 1984.

Selby, Bettina, *Riding to Jerusalem*, 1985.
Selby, Bettina, *Riding the Desert Trail*, 1988.
Selby, Bettina, *The Fragile Islands: A Journey through the Outer Hebrides*, 1989.
Selby, Bettina, *Riding North One Summer*, 1990.
Selby, Bettina, *Frail Dream of Timbuktu*, 1991.
Selby, Bettina, *Beyond Ararat: A Journey through Eastern Turkey*, 1993.
Selby, Bettina, *Pilgrim's Road: A Journey to Santiago de Compostela*, 1994.
Selby, Bettina, *Like Water in a Dry Land: A Journey into Modern Israel*, 1996.
Sheldon-Williams, Inglis, *A Dawdle in France*, 1926.
Sheldon-Williams, Inglis, *A Dawdle in Lombardy and Venice*, 1928.
Shuttleworth, W.S. Yorke, *Eyatkuhnen to Langenweddingen by Bicycle*, 1879.
Stevens, Thomas, *Around the World on a Bicycle*, vol. 1: *From San Francisco to Teheran*, 1887.
Stevens, Thomas, *Around the World on a Bicycle*, vol. 2: *From Teheran to Yokohama*, 1888.
Sutherland, Louise, *I Follow the Wind*, 1960.
Thomson, Alex, and Nick Rossiter, *Ram Ram India: Notes from a Ride in the Subcontinent*, 1987.
Thwaites, Reuben Gold, *Our Cycling Tour in England*, 1892.
Urrutia, Virginia, *Two Wheels and a Taxi: A Slightly Daft Adventure in the Andes*, 1987.
Vantress, Sally, *Seeing Myself, Seeing the World: A Woman's Journey around the World on a Bicycle*, 1990.
Vernon, Tom, *Fat Man on a Bicycle*, 1981.
Vernon, Tom, *Fat Man on a Roman Road*, 1983.
Vernon, Tom, *Fat Man in Argentina*, 1990.
Vickers, Simon, *Between the Hammer and the Sickle: Across Russia by Bicycle*, 1992.
Wallington, Mark, *Destination Lapland: A Journey to the Far North*, 1987.
Wells, H.G., *The Wheels of Chance: A Holiday Adventure*, 1896.
Wilson, David A., *Ireland, a Bicycle and a Tin Whistle*, illustrated by Justin Palmer, 1995.
Winder, Tom, *Around the United States by Bicycle*, 1895.
Workman, Fanny Bullock, and William Hunter Workman, *Algerian Memories: A Bicycle Tour over the Atlas to the Sahara*, 1895.
Workman, Fanny Bullock, and William Hunter Workman, *Sketches Awheel in Fin de Siècle Iberia*, 1897.
Workman, Fanny Bullock, and William Hunter Workman, *Through Town and Jungle: 14,000 Miles Awheel among the Temples and Peoples of the Indian Plain*, 1904.
Wray, W. Fitzwater, *Across France in War Time*, 1916.
Young, Jim, and Elizabeth Young, *Bicycle Built for Two*, 1940.

## BIG GAME HUNTING

> *Hunting brings bodily health, improves sight and hearing, is an antidote to senility, and excellent training in the art of war . . . Our ancestors knew that hunting was the source of their success over their enemies and made the young men practice it . . . For they saw that the pleasure that young men take in hunting provides in itself many benefits. It makes them self-restrained and just, through education in true principles; and our ancestors recognized that to these they owed their success, especially in war.*
>
> —*Xenophon, Cynegeticus*

When the Greek soldier and hunter Xenophon (430?–355? BCE) wrote the *Cynegeticus*, he drew together ideals—of fitness, mastery, aggression, masculinity—that have tended to characterize big game hunting over the ensuing centuries. Though not strictly speaking a utilitarian practice (and so importantly distinct from other hunting forms), big game hunting nevertheless has its uses—perhaps none more distinctive, as the passage from Xenophon will suggest, than its instrumental role in the making of social power.

These characteristics emerge in some of the earliest accounts of what we recognize as big game hunting. Ashurbanipal (668–627 BCE) on his own hunting exploits in Assyria, Plutarch (47?–120?) on Alexander the Great (356–323 BCE) hunting in Persia, the biographer of the *Scriptores Historiae Augustae* on Hadrian (76–138) hunting in western Asia and northern Africa, Marco Polo (c. 1254–1323) on the grand hunts of Kublai Khan (1216–1294) in China—these accounts celebrate the hunter's regal supremacy and at the same time underscore the geographical stretch of his political power. They also tend to document hunting methods that, if brutal, are nevertheless held to be courageous. Thus such accounts exemplify the importance of courage and fair play to the meaning of sport and, in so doing, delineate big game hunting as an at once heroic and imperial practice.

This conception of big game hunting holds clear affinities with the rituals of "hunting at force" prevalent in Europe in the medieval and early modern periods and celebrated by such writers as William Twiti (*The Art of Hunting*, 1327), Gaston Phébus, comte de Foix (1331–1391; *Le Livre de la chasse*, 1387), Edward, second duke of York (1373?–1415; *The Master of Game*, 1406–1413), Juliana Berners (1388?–; *The Boke of Saint Albans*, 1486), George Turberville (1540?–1610?; *The Noble Arte of Venerie*, 1575), and Thomas Cokayne (1519?–1592; *A Short Treatise of Hunting*, 1591). But more germane still to the development of modern literatures of travel is the resonance of this model of big game hunting within the histories of Anglo-European imperial expansion. Often linked to the study of natural history, big game hunting was instrumental both to the manufacture of symbolic power and to the maintenance of practical control within the colonies. To the extent that the species of big game encountered by explorers, travelers, and settlers in the colonial contact zone were not just threatening competitors but also ready symbols of supposedly "exotic" difference, their slaughter could serve to affirm imperial mastery—an affirmation documented in the hunting trophies collected as a matter of course by imperial sportsmen. As John Mackenzie has argued, at the "high noon of empire hunting became a ritualised and occasionally spectacular display of white dominance. European world supremacy coincided with the peak of the hunting and shooting craze." By extension, the narrative accounts of sporting travel must have

*Courtesy of the Travellers Club, London; Bridgeman Art Library, agent.*

served not just to entertain their readers but to institute within them the values and beliefs—the imperial ideologies—that hunting as a practice had come to exemplify. These books were, in a sense, surrogate trophies.

In India, the seeds of the sporting craze seem to have been sown in the first decades of the nineteenth century. Though probably familiar with Indian hunting traditions from existing travel accounts (as for instance the chronicle of Moghul hunting practices found in the journals of Thomas Roe [1581–1644]), colonial agents tended before 1800 merely to observe Indian hunts; in the early decades of the new century, however, they came increasingly to hunt themselves. Narratives from this period, including most notably those by Thomas Williamson, Daniel Johnson (1767–1835), and Samuel Baker (1821–1893), outline in detail the abundant sporting opportunities in India—ones prompting what Baker calls "whole hecatombs of slaughter." According to these accounts, hunting enabled the emergence of a cross-cultural elite—a no doubt idealized picture sketched by Williamson and elaborated in subsequent narratives. In any event, the so-called Mutiny of 1857 provoked a significant rethinking of this vision and its attendant ideologies. After the uprising, the hunt became much more evidently a site for the demonstration of imperial mastery; in practice, Indians had now to serve or watch, not join, colonial agents in the rigors of sport. *The Wild Sports of India* (1860), by Henry Shakespear, gives insight into the logic underlying the transformation, arguing that the uprising would have been averted had the British practiced a more strenuous, less integrated hunting regimen. Thus, from the middle of the nineteenth century big game hunting in India occasioned the increasingly ostentatious display of imperial control. As narratives by G.P. Sanderson, Edward Braddon (1829–1904), A.I.R. Glasfurd, Sainthill Eardley-Wilmot (1852–1929), E.P. Stebbing (1870–1960), and W. Hogarth Todd make clear, well into the twentieth century the lesson was faithfully rehearsed by sportsmen and travelers for readers all across the empire.

Big game hunting played a similar role in the imperial conquest of Africa. Despite the fact that hunting contributed to subsistence, trade, and social life among Africa's indigenous peoples, white explorers and settlers tended to treat the rich diversity of game as an untapped resource. Hunting was a crucial component of imperial expansion, serving as a means to defend territory, to acquire resources for subsistence and trade (notably for the global market in ivory), and, as in India, to accumulate symbolic power. The nineteenth-century itinerary of big game hunters, beginning in southern Africa before shifting up into the central interior and the eastern regions, maps as well the increasing importance of such symbolic power in the rituals of the hunt. A number of sportsmen in the early nineteenth century, including William John Burchell (1782?–1863), Andrew Smith (1797–1872), and William Cornwallis Harris (1807–1848), helped to create a myth of African hunting intensely attractive to subsequent generations of hunters. Their narratives make big game hunting an extension of rational scientific endeavor; the brutal excesses of sport come to seem a natural part of science's taxonomic imperative. Harris's exploits in particular set the stage for two of the nineteenth century's most celebrated sporting travelers: Roualeyn Gordon Cumming (1820–1866), whose two-volume *Five Years of a Hunter's Life in the Far Interior of South Africa* (1850) documents the new standards in hunting profligacy that made its author a midcentury celebrity, and William Charles Baldwin, whose *African Hunting, from Natal to the Zambesi* (1863) graphically reveals the rapidity of extermination on the killing fields of southern Africa. Their narratives delineate a model of imperial sport that proved enabling for a number of subsequent hunters, including Frederick Selous (1851–1917), Arthur Neumann, Winston Churchill (1874–1965), Theodore Roosevelt (1858–1919), C.H. Stigand (1877–1919), and W.T. Shorthose, all of whom managed to extract from sporting adventure varying degrees of star power.

Much like their counterparts in India and Africa, imperial travelers to North America found what seemed to many of them a virtual paradise of game. Narratives by Rufus Sage (1817–1893), John Palliser (1807–1887), G.F. Berkeley (1800–1881), H.W. Herbert (1807–1858), G.O. Shields (1846–1925), Caspar Whitney (1862–1929), William Baillie-Grohman (1846–1925), William Temple Hornaday (1854–1937), and the Earl of Dunraven, Windham Thomas Wyndham-Quin (1841–1926), among others, document the diversity of big game found in North America and depict big game hunting as imperial adventure and the sportsman as imperial hero—a vision epitomized in the North American context by Roosevelt, whose account of sport in such narratives as *The Wilderness Hunter* (1893) and *Outdoor Pastimes of an American Hunter* (1905) served to disseminate to a wide readership his persona of strenuous livelihood—a persona regnant over American imperial politics in 1900.

Key within the nineteenth-century North American shooting cult was the buffalo. The hunting of bison by Native Americans had, since the earliest Spanish accounts, played a key role in the narrative invention of the newness, but also the translatability, of the "New World" (see, for example, de Benavides, 1630; Lewis and Clark, 1814; and Parkman, 1849). Of course, following white contact the buffalo hunt did not stay an exclusively aboriginal practice; it became a locus of cross-cultural contact, as narratives by Josiah Gregg

(1806–1850) and George Catlin (1796–1872) make plain. Yet in retrospect, the increasing participation of whites in the buffalo hunt underscores, more darkly, the institution's place within the repertoires of imperial domination. For many sporting travelers, the buffalo represented a special challenge, more ferocious, according to Alexander Ross (1783–1856), than either the polar bear or the Bengal tiger. If under the terms of the Louisiana Purchase of 1803 the U.S. government achieved possession of millions of buffalo in the abstract, the exploits of white sport hunters in the second half of the nineteenth century made such abstract ownership brutally material, serving to decimate the buffalo herds and devastate aboriginal ways of life all across the continent. Hunters such as Ross, Palliser, Frederick Graham (1820–1888), and Shields gloried in the thrills of this sport; by contrast, Hornaday's elegiac account "The Extermination of the American Bison" (1889) grimly depicts the scale of the slaughter—even as, ironically enough, it concludes by describing Hornaday's own hunt of bison for his taxidermic dioramas in the American Museum of Natural History in Washington, D.C.

Such ironies marked the growing investment by big game hunters, in the late nineteenth and early twentieth century, in the causes of preservation and subsequently conservation (see, for instance, Hornaday, 1913; Corbett, 1944). The appetite in the hunting cult for wholesale slaughter threatened the eventual obliteration of big game from the seeming Edens of empire. In response, many hunters began to reenvision their sporting habits in terms of cultural (and often explicitly racial) legacy, collecting specimens with which to stock the great natural history museums emergent in the late nineteenth century—or in some cases even becoming preeminent taxidermists in their own right (as, for example, did Hornaday and Rowland Ward ([1848?–1912]). Increasingly, such hunters also worked to preserve wildlife for future generations of sportsmen through game laws and parkland legislation. The commitment by such preservationists to the principle of a "commonwealth" of wildlife preserved for all seems in retrospect more than a little ironic, given that in many ways their efforts aimed less at curtailing sport than at reconstituting the terms of its pursuit, at managing animal resources for the continued benefit of an elite hunting class. With the growth of animal conservation in the twentieth century, however, big game hunting became an increasingly controversial, if persistently popular, practice. Though still undertaken by a sporting elite at present, rituals and narratives of big game hunting are no longer the means to social power they were at the height of the imperial shooting cult. Celebrity now attends new forms of environmental intervention and mastery.

MARK SIMPSON

## References and Further Reading


Akeley, Carl E., *In Brightest Africa*, 1923.

Akeley, Delia J., *Jungle Portraits*, 1930.

Baillie-Grohman, William A., *Camps in the Rockies*, 1882.

Baillie-Grohman, William A., *Sport in the Alps in the Past and Present*, 1896.

Baillie-Grohman, William A., *Fifteen Years' Sport and Life in the Hunting Grounds of Western America and British Columbia*, 1900.

Baker, Samuel W., *The Rifle and the Hound in Ceylon*, 1854.

Baker, Samuel W., *Eight Years' Wanderings in Ceylon*, 1855.

Baldwin, William Charles, *African Hunting, from Natal to the Zambesi*, 1863; 3rd edition, as *African Hunting and Adventure*, 1894.

Benavides, Alonso de, *Memorial*, 1630; as *Benavides' Memorial of 1630*, translated by Peter Forrestal, 1954.

Berkeley, Grantly F., *The English Sportsman in the Western Prairies*, 1861.

Berners, Juliana, *The Boke of Saint Albans*, 1486; facsimile, 1969.

Braddon, Edward, *Thirty Years of Shikar*, 1895.

Burchell, William John, *Travels in the Interior of Southern Africa*, 2 vols., 1822–1824; reprinted, 1953.

Burn-Murdoch, W.G., *Modern Whaling and Bear-Hunting*, 1917.

Catlin, George, *Illustrations of the Manners, Customs, and Condition of the North American Indians*, 1845.

Chapman, Abel, *Retrospect: Reminiscences and Impressions of a Hunter-Naturalist in Three Continents*, illustrations by Chapman, 1928.

Chapman, Abel, and Walter J. Buck, *Wild Spain*, 1893.

Churchill, Winston S., *My African Journey*, 1908.

Cokayne, Sir Thomas, *A Short Treatise of Hunting*, 1591; facsimile, 1932.

Corbett, Jim, *Man-Eaters of Kumaon*, 1944.

Cumming, Roualeyn Gordon, *Five Years of a Hunter's Life in the Far Interior of South Africa*, 2 vols., 1850.

Eardley-Wilmot, Sainthill, *Forest Life and Sport in India*, 1910.

Edward, second duke of York, *The Master of Game: The Oldest English Book on Hunting*, 1406–1413; edited by William A. and F. Baillie-Grohman, 1909.

Gaston Phébus, comte de Foix, *Le Livre de la chasse*, 1387; facsimile, 2 vols., 1976.

Gillmore, Parker, *Leaves from a Sportsman's Diary*, 1893.

Glasfurd, A.I.R, *Rifle and Romance in the Indian Jungle*, 1905.

Graham, Frederick Ulric, *Notes of a Sporting Expedition in the Far West of Canada, 1847*, edited by Jane Hermione Graham, 1898.

Gregg, Josiah, *Commerce of the Prairies*, 2 vols., 1844.

Grew, J.C., *Sport and Travel in the Far East*, 1910.

Grinnell, George Bird (editor), *Hunting at High Altitudes*, 1913.

Harris, William Cornwallis, *The Wild Sports of Southern Africa*, 1839.

Hemingway, Ernest, *Green Hills of Africa*, 1935.

Herbert, Henry William (as Frank Forester), *Field Sports in the United States and the British Provinces of America*, 2 vols., 1848; later editions as *Frank Forester's Field Sports*.

Herbert, Henry William, *American Game in Its Seasons*, 1853.

Herne, Peregrine, *Perils and Pleasures of a Hunter's Life; or, The Romance of Hunting*, 1854.

Hibben, Frank C., *Hunting American Lions*, illustrated by Paul Bransom, 1948.

Hornaday, William T., *Two Years in the Jungle: The Experiences of a Hunter and Naturalist in India, Ceylon, the Malay Peninsula and Borneo*, 1885.

Hornaday, William T., "The Extermination of the American Bison," *Smithsonian Institution Annual Report, 1886–87*, part 2 (1889).
Hornaday, William T., *Camp-Fires in the Canadian Rockies*, 1906.
Hornaday, William T., *Camp-Fires on Desert and Lava*, 1908.
Hornaday, William T., *Our Vanishing Wild Life: Its Extermination and Preservation*, 1913.
House, Edward J., *A Hunter's Camp-Fires*, 1909.
Johnson, Daniel, *Sketches of Field Sports as Followed by the Natives of India*, 1822.
Jones, C.J., *Buffalo Jones' Forty Years of Adventure*, 1899.
Leveson, Henry Astbury, *Sport in Many Lands*, 2 vols., 1877.
Lewis, Meriwether, William Clark, et al., *History of the Expedition under the Command of Captains Lewis and Clark to the Sources of the Missouri*, edited by Nicholas Biddle, 2 vols., 1814.
Markham, Gervase, *Countrey Contentments*, 1615; facsimile, 1973.
Martindale, Thomas, *Sport Indeed*, 1901.
Martindale, Thomas, *With Gun and Guide*, 1910.
Murphy, John Mortimer, *Sporting Adventures in the Far West*, 1879.
Neumann, Arthur H., *Elephant-Hunting in East Equatorial Africa*, 1898.
Palliser, John, *Solitary Rambles and Adventures of a Hunter in the Prairies*, 1853.
Parkman, Francis, *The California and Oregon Trail*, 1849.
Phillips, John C., *A Sportsman's Scrapbook*, 1928.
Phillips, John C., *A Sportsman's Second Scrapbook*, 1933.
Phillipps-Wolley, Clive, *Big Game Shooting*, 2 vols., 1894.
Polo, Marco, *The Description of the World*, edited and translated by A.C. Moule and Paul Pelliot, 2 vols., 1938.
Prichard, H.V.H., *Hunting Camps in Wood and Wilderness*, 1910.
Roe, Thomas, *The Embassy of Sir Thomas Roe to the Court of the Great Mogul, 1615–1619, as Narrated in His Journal and Correspondence*, edited by William Foster, 2 vols., 1899.
Roosevelt, Theodore, *Hunting Trips of a Ranchman*, 1885.
Roosevelt, Theodore, *The Wilderness Hunter: An Account of the Big Game of the United States and Its Chase with Horse, Hound, and Rifle*, 1893.
Roosevelt, Theodore, *Outdoor Pastimes of an American Hunter*, 1905.
Roosevelt, Theodore, *African Game Trails*, 1910.
Roosevelt, Theodore, and George Bird Grinnell (editors), *Hunting in Many Lands*, 1895.
Ross, Alexander, *The Fur Hunters of the Far West*, 2 vols., 1855.
Rudolf of Austria, *Notes on Sport and Ornithology*, translated by C.G. Danford, 1889.
Sabretache, *Monarchy and the Chase*, 1948.
Sage, Rufus B., *Rocky Mountain Life*, 1857.
Sanderson, G.P., *Thirteen Years among the Wild Beasts of India*, 1878.
Selous, Frederick Courteney, *A Hunter's Wanderings in Africa*, 1881; 5th edition, 1907.
Selous, Percy, *Travel and Big Game*, 1897.
Seton-Karr, H.W., *Ten Years' Wild Sports in Foreign Lands; or, Travels in the Eighties*, 1889.
Shakespear, Henry, *The Wild Sports of India*, 1860.
Shields, G.O., *Rustlings in the Rockies*, 1883.
Shields, G.O. (editor), *The Big Game of North America*, 1890.
Shorthose, W.T., *Sport and Adventure in Africa*, 1923.
Smith, Andrew, *Illustrations of the Zoology of South Africa*, 5 vols., 1838–1849.
Stebbing, E.P., *The Diary of a Sportsman Naturalist in India*, 1920.
Stigand, C.H., *Hunting the Elephant in Africa*, introduction by Theodore Roosevelt, 1913.
Todd, W. Hogarth, *Work, Sport and Play: An Englishman's Life in India before the War*, 1928.
Turbervile, George (attributed), *The Noble Arte of Venerie or Hunting*, 1575.
Turner-Turner, J., *Three Years' Hunting and Trapping in America and the Great North-West*, 1888.
Twiti, William, *The Art of Hunting*, 1327; edited by Bror Danielsson, 1977.
Ward, Rowland, *The Sportsman's Handbook to Practical Collecting, Preserving, and Artistic Setting-up of Trophies and Specimens*, 1880; 11th edition, 1923.
Webber, C.W., *The Hunter-Naturalist*, 1851.
Whitney, Caspar, *On Snow-shoes to the Barren Grounds*, 1896.
Whitney, Caspar, *Musk-ox, Bison, Sheep and Goat*, 1904.
Williamson, Thomas, *Oriental Field Sports*, 2 vols., 1808.
Wyndham-Quin, Windham Thomas, Earl of Dunraven, *Canadian Nights*, 1914.
Wyndham-Quin, Windham Thomas, *Hunting in the Yellowstone*, 1917.
Xenophon and Arrian, *Xenophon and Arrian on Hunting*, edited by A.A. Phillips and M.M. Willcock, 1999.

## BIRD, ISABELLA L. (1831–1904) *British Travel Writer*

By the time of her death, Isabella Lucy Bird (or Mrs. John Bishop) was not only famous, she was a moral exemplar: her life story, complete with many of the typical tropes of a hagiography (such as examples of infant piety or early heroism), joined the legends of Queen Victoria and Florence Nightingale in cheaply produced volumes presented as Sunday school prizes.

Her father spent his early years in Calcutta, but returned to England after the death of his first wife to enter the church. His second wife, Isabella's mother, was connected to the Wilberforce family, and shared their energetic moral enthusiasm. From her youth, Isabella Bird suffered from a succession of vague illnesses. When her doctors first prescribed a long sea voyage, she traveled to Nova Scotia, Canada, and to the western frontier of the United States, and on her return John Murray published her account, *The Englishwoman in America*, in 1856. What she records is scarcely remarkable, save for its zest. Unlike Mrs. Trollope (*The Domestic Manners of the Americans*, 1832) or Charles Dickens (*American Notes*, 1842) Miss Bird enjoyed herself thoroughly.

Although it was 20 years before she embarked on the series of journeys that made her famous, the characteristic rhythms of her career were shaped. With the profits from her first book, she provided equipment for families cleared from the western Highlands of Scotland, whose plight she had observed during family holidays. After her father's death, she and her mother and sister Henrietta moved to Edinburgh, and eventually to Tobermory, where Isabella pursued this work, traveling around Britain and America, fund-raising and lecturing until her health gave out and her physicians once again prescribed travel. New York, the Mediterranean, and New Zealand were ineffective. But in Hawaii and in Colorado on her way back home, she bloomed. The two books she produced (edited versions of her letters to stay-at-home Henrietta) are both primarily narratives of the journey as self-discovery. Indeed, *A Lady's Life in the Rocky Mountains* (1879) is a quintessential tale of a pious Victorian spinster's liberation. The published account of her relationship with "Rocky Mountain Jim" is more veiled than the original letters, but its emotional charge is still evident.

It was perhaps because she feared that *A Lady's Life* had revealed too much that her next work, *Unbeaten Tracks in Japan* (1880), is so much more consciously the work of a serious geographer and ethnographer. She had once again paid for her pleasures with a round of good works that eventually prostrated her, but the obliging physician who ordered her to travel again probably had something more relaxing in mind than her journey to Hokkaido, alone save for a Japanese servant. Miss Bird had been a precise and systematic observer of the natural world since childhood. Her botanical expertise and her descriptions of volcanic activity in Hawaii had won her scientific respect, and now she regarded the reception of her account of a region and people (the Ainu), then almost unknown to the West, as a vindication of "the right of a woman to do anything which she can do well" (Stoddart, 1906). The scholarship and statistics are a little too assiduous, but her evocation of atmosphere and pride in the achievement enliven the narrative.

The chronic ill health that permitted her travels never spoiled them. She could eat anything, endure any climate, and was little affected by high altitudes. Although she doubtless exaggerated her hardiness, the constant celebration of her presence in danger or discomfort, far from the amenities of genteel Edinburgh, is an implicit challenge to conventional femininity. Her account of a brief visit to the "Golden Chersonese" (Malaysia), on her way home from Japan, is at heart an unabashed account of her freedom to share the company, pleasures, and business of men.

However, the devoted suitor she eventually married at the age of 50 had little taste for travel. As Dr. John Bishop rather wanly observed, his one rival was "the high tableland of Central Asia" (Stoddart, 1906), and it was indeed there that she headed after his death in 1886. She had always been devout, but now she began to be more explicitly pious. In Hawaii, she had been contemptuous of the narrow-mindedness of the American missionaries; now she became an active supporter of mission work, although the same practical instincts that had inspired her help for Highland emigrants convinced her that evangelism needed to be bolstered by material aid. She established one of several hospitals or orphanages in her husband's name at Srinagar, and from there traveled through Tibet to the Karakoram Pass. Mighty scenery, physical hardship, and an exhilarating sense of being a long way from home combine to make *Among the Tibetans* (1894) the liveliest of her later works.

The homestead in Estes Park, Colorado, below Longs Peak, where Isabella Bird kept house for "Rocky Mountain Jim" (from *A Lady's Life in the Rocky Mountains*, 1879). *Courtesy of British Library, London.*

Before its publication, however, she had produced *Journeys in Persia and Kurdistan* (1891), and it is here that she becomes more strident in her advocacy of Christianity and correspondingly scathing in her opinions of Islam. Her agenda may have been partly determined by the nature of the expedition she accompanied, a hush-hush mission headed by Major Herbert Sawyer to establish a winter route from Baghdad to Teheran. As a bit player in the Great Game, she was not allowed to publish much detail about the landscape or even its flora, and her account of the misery of the local people is politically colored.

Moreover, the large expedition was not to her taste, and her subsequent journeys to Korea and the Yangtze Valley are at their most vivid when she is most isolated from her own kind. Her contemporaries admired her accounts of unfamiliar religious practices and of missionary endeavors in China, and her insight into local conditions was respected by politicians as well as geographers: she was one of the first women to become a Fellow of the Royal Geographical Society and its Scottish equivalent. Much of her expertise has long been superseded, and her forthright opinions and attitudes belong to her own era. What remains of value, however, is the quality of her descriptive writing, and her unashamed relish for adventure.

CICELY PALSER HAVELY

## Biography

Born Isabella Lucy Bird in Boroughbridge, Yorkshire, 15 October 1831, daughter of Edward Bird, a clergyman. Educated by her mother at home; lived in Tattenhall, Cheshire, Birmingham, and Huntingdonshire, taking holidays in Edinburgh and the Western Isles. Suffered from ill health from an early age: traveled to the United States and Canada for health reasons, 1854 and 1857–1858. Moved with her family to Edinburgh after her father's death, 1858. Undertook philanthropic and social work; corresponded with John Bright on social issues; cofounded the Harris cloth-manufacturing industry. Lived in London and Edinburgh after her mother's death, 1867. Traveled around the world, visiting Australia, New Zealand, the Sandwich islands (now Hawaii), and the United States, especially the Rocky Mountains, 1872–1874. Returned to Edinburgh; traveled to Japan and Hong Kong, 1878. Nursed her invalid sister, Hennie, in Edinburgh and in Tobermory, Mull, until Hennie's death, 1880. Married Dr. John Bishop (d. 1886), 1881. Trained as a nurse at St. Mary's Hospital, Paddington, London, 1887. Joined the Baptist church in order to become a medical missionary, 1888. Traveled as a missionary to India, Central Asia, and Persia, 1889–1890; Korea, Hong Kong, and Japan, 1894–1895; Yangtze Valley, China, 1896. Founded hospitals in India, Korea, and China and an orphanage in Tokyo, Japan. Returned to Tobermory briefly, 1897. Lived in London, Huntingdonshire, and Edinburgh, 1897–1904. Traveled to Morocco, 1901. Fellow of the Royal Scottish Geographical Society, 1891, and the Royal Geographical Society, 1892. Died in Edinburgh, 7 October 1904.

## References and Further Reading


Bird, Isabella L., *The Englishwoman in America* (published anonymously), 1856.

Bird, Isabella L., *The Hawaiian Archipelago: Six Months among the Palm Groves, Coral Reefs, and Volcanoes of the Sandwich Islands*, 1875.

Bird, Isabella L., *A Lady's Life in the Rocky Mountains*, 1879; reprinted with an introduction by Daniel J. Boorstin, 1960; with an introduction by Pat Barr, 1982.

Bird, Isabella L., *Unbeaten Tracks in Japan: An Account of Travels in the Interior Including Visits to the Aborigines of Yezo and the Shrines of Nikkô and Isé*, 1880; as *Unbeaten Tracks in Japan: An Account of Travels on Horseback in the Interior Including Visits to the Aborigines of Yezo and the Shrines of Nikkô and Isé*, 1881.

Bird, Isabella L., *The Golden Chersonese and the Way Thither*, 1883.

Bird, Isabella L., *Journeys in Persia and Kurdistan: Including a Summer in the Upper Karun Region and a Visit to the Nestorian Rayahs*, 1891.

Bird, Isabella L., *Among the Tibetans*, 1894.

Bird, Isabella L., *Korea and Her Neighbours: A Narrative of Travel, with an Account of the Recent Vicissitudes and Present Position of the Country*, 1897.

Bird, Isabella L., *The Yangtze Valley and Beyond: An Account of Journeys in China, Chiefly in the Province of Sze Chuan and among the Man-Tze of the Somo Territory*, 1899.

Bird, Isabella L., *Chinese Picture*, 1900 (illustrations).

Bird, Isabella L., *This Grand Beyond: The Travels of Isabella Bird Bishop*, edited by Cicely Palser Havely, 1984.

Stoddart, Anna M., *The Life of Isabella Bird (Mrs Bishop), Hon. Member of the Oriental Society of Pekin [Sic], FRGS, FRSGS*, London: John Murray, 1906.


# BLACK SEA

References to the Black Sea and its exploration before Greek colonization are very rare. The Hittite king Telipinu described the dimensions of the empire of one of his forerunners by referring to its borders reaching the coast of the sea in the north as well as in the south. A famous literary text dealing with the queen of Kanesh/Nesha (Kültepe) and her 30 children records the exposure of the babies. They were placed in a kind of box, which then was thrown into the river. The river brought them down to the land Zalpuwa and farther, to the (Black) Sea, where the gods picked up the children and raised them. The Greek name Pontos Euxeinos shows that the Greeks were not the first ones to explore this area. It is a euphemism for Pontos Axeinos, which is derived from Iranian *akhshaena*, which means "black."

Our knowledge gets more detailed with the beginning of Greek colonization of the Black Sea, documented in archaeological, mythical, and literary sources of later times. The Greek presence starts to get visible in the archaeological record at the end of the seventh century BCE when the western and the southern coasts became known by Greek sailors. The eastern shores around the River Phasis and the legendary lands of Colchis and Aia were explored a little later, beginning in the middle of the sixth century. The famous myth connected with Jason and the Argonauts seems to mirror the very early stage of Greek exploration in which the Black Sea, or at least parts of it, had a tremendous and fantastic connotation. It is also this myth, whose existence is already mentioned in some stanzas of the Odyssey (12, 70–72), that guaranteed the Black Sea an enduring place in the geographical and literary worldview throughout antiquity, thanks to its various literary treatments reaching from Pindar (Pythian 4) (462 BCE), Apollonius Rhodius (third century BCE), Dionysius Scythobrachion (c. 100 BCE), and Valerius Flaccus (first century CE) to Orpheus's *Argonautika* (c. 400 CE).

Only at the end of the third quarter of the sixth century BCE did Greek knowledge about the Black Sea become more precise. In a fragment of Hecataeus of Miletus (around 500 BCE) the Greek name *pontos* appears for the first time. This whole area was important to the Mediterranean economy for the next two centuries, because many raw materials and resources were exported. We do not know the names of the explorers and discoverers who made this vast area accessible, but their explorations and knowledge found their way into literary sources that have been preserved. Herodotus (IV: 85ff) is the first to give a fairly exact description of the whole Black Sea and its dimensions. It has been questioned whether Herodotus personally visited this area, but, in any case, his description shows that the Black Sea was no longer an unknown field in the Greek world. Also, the territories around the sea and their peoples, cultures, and features were described. The mythic view was pushed back, but it was never completely banished. The Amazons, originally located south of the Black Sea, were transferred farther to the northeast, and throughout antiquity strange peoples with odd cultural features lived at its eastern and southeastern fringes.

After the third century BCE, the Black Sea lost importance. This development too is documented in the literary sources of this time. Many of these sources are preserved only indirectly in the geographical work of Strabo (63 BCE–19 CE), where little new information appears. A bit earlier, at the end of the second century BCE, there existed an anonymous description of the southern coast of the Black Sea and its hinterland (Pseudo-Scymnus), but already in this treatise traditional views played an important role. Only a famous digression in the preserved parts of the historical work of Polybius (200–120 BCE) gives a different picture with many new insights and details (IV: 38–44). It looks like a reaction to the ignorance of his time. This standard of information was never surpassed during antiquity. Furthermore, a description of the coast of the Black Sea is part of the oldest preserved periplous of Pseudo-Scylax of Caryanda (mid-fourth century BCE), and the one of Menippus of Pergamon (end of the first century BCE) also focused on this area.

Descriptions of the coast and its hinterland were also published during the time of the Roman empire. Pomponius Mela and Pliny the Elder (both first century BCE) showed great interest in this area and presented well-organized and rich material. But the extant traditions remained valid and important and were often more dominant than new exploration. A periplous of the whole Black Sea area, which is outstanding for the high quality of its information, was written by Arrian of Nicomedia (second century BCE), who was the governor of the province of Cappadocia and knew this territory personally. But again, in late antiquity the preserved descriptions present little new information. This is true even of the works of Ammianus Marcellinus (4 CE), whose digression is strongly dependent on traditional literatures and views (22.3: 1–48), and also for an anonymous periplous of all coasts of the Black Sea (Pseudo-Arrianus, 6 CE).

Byzantine literature is not rich in travel writing, though there have been many diplomatic and official missions that the historians have recorded. Most information concerning the Black Sea area is to be found in Constantine VII Porphyrogennetos's tenth-century books. *De Thematibus* (*peri ton thematon*) refers to geographic writers of the sixth century and the Justinian age (Stephen of Byzantium, Hierocles) and gives detailed information concerning cities, local stories, the people, and the political structure of provinces in the Byzantine empire. Andreas Libadenos (c. 1308–after 1361), an ecclesiastical and imperial official, served as undersecretary of a legation to Mameluke Egypt. His *Periegetike Historia* relates events up to 1355 and describes his journey, especially the history and landscape of northern Anatolia around Trebizond, his hometown. Matthew of Khazaria was sent to the Crimea in 1395 as an exarch and wrote a poem of 15-syllable verses in the form of a dialog between the poet and the city of Theodore (most probably Dory), which complains about her prolonged sufferings under siege and attacks. The work may mirror the campaigns of Timur's Mongols.

Byzantium did not manage to maintain military and economic control of the Black Sea in the thirteenth century. It came into conflict with Georgia, the Seljuk

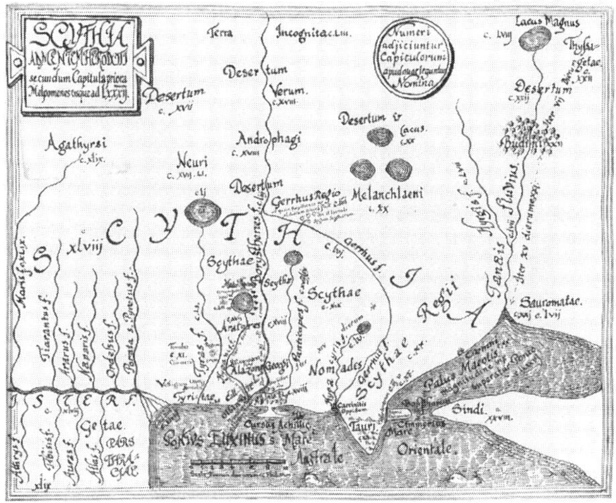


"Scythia," or the region north of the Black Sea, according to the information provided in Herodotus; the Black Sea is shown here under its classical name Pontus Euxinus (from E.H. Minns, *Scythians and Greeks*, 1913). *Courtesy of British Library, London.*

Turks, and the Mongols. From 1204 on, Italian naval powers—mainly Venice and Genoa—also dominated the region and established colonies there. Finally, the Byzantine emperor granted Genoa exclusive access and tax exemptions under the Treaty of Nymphaion in 1261. Giovanni di Piano Carpini, a cleric sent by the pope to the Mongol court of Batu Khan with a diplomatic mission, left from an Italian base, as did William of Rubruk (Guillaume de Rubrach; 1253) on a similar errand. The Polo brothers entered Mongol territory from Soldaïa on the Crimea in 1260 for their first journey. The Bavarian Johann Schiltberger (1380–1432), after being freed from Ottoman and then Mongol slavery, traveled along the coast of the Black Sea up to Georgia and gives detailed information concerning the areas he visited.

Skirmishes among the Italians weakened their position. After having recovered from the battle of Angora in 1402, the Ottomans obtained the supremacy in the Pontic area. In 1461, they conquered Trebizond, in 1475 Caffa, and in 1484 the markets at the mouth of the Danube were taken by Beyazit II. From then on, this region formed part of the Ottoman empire, and until the late eighteenth century travel to the Occident was obstructed and for this reason rare. Most travelogues were therefore written by escaped prisoners or envoys (see Gonzaléz de Clavijo, 1582; Membrè, 1542). Giovanni Antonio Menavino (1485–1534) fled in 1514 after having been a page of the Ottoman court for 13 years and describes at the end of his work the stages of his flight, specifically his travels with the Turkish army to Tabriz, passing along the southern coast of the Black Sea.

Travel reports from Russian ambassadors, who most often used the route from Azov to Constantinople, are rare, but there does exist one by Ivan Petrovich Novosiltsev (1519–1576) from 1570. The learned Turk Evliya Çelebi (1611–1684) refers to several long journeys he took as an individual or in an official capacity. His ten-volume *Seyahatname* [*Book of Travels*], a unique source, contains rich information on folklore, geography, and legends. He is, however, not always reliable, and some of the journeys are only fantasy. In book 2, he describes Trebizond, in books 7 and 8 the Crimea.

In 1774, after a lost war, Russia forced the Ottomans to open the Black Sea for trade, with the Treaty of Küçük Kainardschi. Moreover, it annexed the Crimean peninsula in 1783. Toward the end of the eighteenth century, the European powers started to compete for economic and military predominance in the area. This caused the Crimean War (1853–1856), during which Britain and France supported the Ottomans against Russia. As a result of this, the Black Sea was demilitarized and Britain kept close relations with Turkey. The officers Leopold G. Heath, Alexander Fisher Macintosh, and Adolphus Slade traveled the area during the Crimean War, as did the correspondent Laurence Oliphant. But theirs are only a few examples of a great many of the texts written by people involved in the war.

The accounts of Antoine-Ignace Anthoine de Saint-Joseph (1749–1826), Henry A.S. Dearborn (1751–1829), Nicolaus E. Kleemann (1736–1798), Claude Charles de Peyssonell (1727–1790), and Jean Baron de Reuilly (1780–1810) are the results of travel undertaken to collect facts of commercial conditions in the (after 1774) easily accessible region, but also contain descriptions of the voyages themselves and the traveled areas. Private, often aristocratic, travelers, like Lady Elizabeth Craven (1750–1828), Michael J. Quin (1796–1843), and William L.L.F. Baron De Ros (1797–1774), competed for importance with explorers interested in history, archaeology, geography, and geology, like Prince Démidov (1812–1870), the historian Jacob Philipp Fallmerayer (1790–1861), and Jean-Baptiste Lechevalier (1752–1836).

ROLAND STEINACHER AND ROBERT ROLLINGER

## References and Further Reading


Alexander, James Edward, *Travels to the Seat of War in the East, through Russia and the Crimea in 1829*, 2 vols., 1830.

Anthoine de Saint-Joseph, Antoine-Ignace, *Essai Historique sur le commerce et la navigation de la mer noire*, 1805.

Arnold, R. Arthur, *From the Levant, the Black Sea and the Danube*, 2 vols., 1868.

Arrian, *Périple du Pont-Euxin*, edited and translated by Alain Silberman, 1995.

Besse, Jean Charles de, *Voyage en Crimée au Caucase en Géorgie, 1829 et 1830, pour servir à l'histoire de Hongrie*, 1838.

Constantine VII Porphyrogennetos, *De Thematibus*, edited by Allesandro Pertusi, 1952.

Craven, Elisabeth (Countess), *A Journey through the Crimea to Constantinople, in a Series of Letters from the Right Honourable E. Lady C. to His Serene Highness the Margrave of Brandenbourg*, 1789.

Curtis, William Eleroy, *Around the Black Sea, Asia Minor, Armenia, Caucasus, Circassia, Daghestan, the Crimea and Roumania*, 1911.

Dearborn, Henry A.S., *A Memoir on the Commerce and Navigation of the Black Sea, and the Trade and Maritime Geography of Turkey and Egypt*, 2 vols., 1819.

Démidov, Anatole de, *Voyage dans la Russie méridionale et la Crimée, par la Hongrie, la Valachie et la Moldavie, exécuté en 1837*, 4 vols., 1840–1842; vol. 1 of the first edition translated as *Travels in Southern Russia and the Crimea, through Hungary, Wallachia and Moldavia during the Year 1837*, 1853.

De Ros, William Lennox Lascelles Fitzgerald, *Journal of a Tour in the Principalities, Crimea, and Countries adjacent to the Black Sea in the Years 1835–1836*, 1855.

Engelhardt, Moritz, and Friedrich Parrot, *Reise in die Krim und den Kaukasus*, 1815.

Eton, William, *A Concise Account of the Commerce and Navigation of the Black Sea: From Recent and Authentic Information*, 1805.

Evliya Çelebi, *Seyahatnamesi*, 10 vols., 1896–1938; as *Müntekhabat-i Ewliya Çelebi*, edited by Ahmed Djewdet and Nedjib Asim, vols. 1–6 in arabic letters, 7–10 in Latin script, 1896–1938; parts as *Narrative of Travels in Europe, Asia, and Africa in the Seventeenth Century*, translated by Joseph von Hammer, 1834–1850; *Evliya Çelebi's Book of Travels: Land and People of the Ottoman Empire in the Seventeenth Century: A Corpus of Partial Editions*, translated by Klaus Kreiser, 1988–2000.

Fallmerayer, Jacob Philipp, *Fragmente aus dem Orient*, 2 parts, 1845.

Gonzaléz de Clavijo, Ruy, *Historia del gran Tamorlan*, 1582; as *Narrative of the Embassy of Ruy Gonzalez de Clavijo to the Court of Timour, at Samarcand, AD 1403–6*, translated by Clement R. Markham, 1859.

Guthrie, Maria, *A Tour Performed in the Years 1795–96 through the Taurida or Crimea: The Ancient Kingdom of Bosphorus, the Once-Powerful Republic of Tauric Chersa, and All the Other Countries on the North Shore of the Euxine*, 1802.

Heath, Leopold George, *Letters from the Black Sea during the Crimean War, 1854–1855*, 1897.

Holderness, Mary, *New Russia: Journey from Riga to the Crimea by Way of Kiev; with Some Account of the Colonization and the Manners and Customs of the Colonists of New Russia*, 1823.

Ignatij, Smolensk, *Russian Travelers to Constantinople in the Fourteenth and Fifteenth Centuries*, translated and edited by George P. Majesta, 1984.

Kleemann, Nicolaus Ernst, *Reisen von Wien über Belgrad bis Kilianova durch die Butschiak-Tartarey über Kavschan, Bender in die Krimm, dann von Kaffa nach Konstantinopel, nach Smirna, und durch den Archipelagum nach Triest und Wien in den Jahren 1768, 1769 und 1770*, 1771.

Kohl, J.G., *Reisen in Südrussland*, 1843; as *Russia: St. Petersburg, Moscow, Kharkoff, Riga, Odessa, the German Provinces on the Baltic, the Steppes, the Crimea, and the Interior of the Empire*, 1842.

Lechevalier, Jean-Baptiste, *Voyage de la Propontide et du Pont-Euxin avec la carte générale de ces deux mers*, 2 vols., 1800.

Libadenos, Andrew, *Andreou Libadenou bios kai erga*, edited by Odysseus Lampsides, 1975.

Macintosh, Alexander Fisher, *A Military Tour in European Turkey, the Crimea, and on the Eastern Shores of the Black Sea*, 2 vols., 1854.

Membrè, Michele, *Relazione di Persia*, 1542; as *Mission to the Lord Sophy of Persia, 1539–1542*, translated with an introduction and notes by A.H. Morton, 1993.

Menavino, Giovanni Antonio, *I cinque libri della legge, religione et vita de 'Turchi: et della corte et d'alcune guerre del Gran Turco: Di Giovan Antonio Menavino Genovese de Vultri: Oltre cio, una Prophetia de' Mahomettani, et la miseria de' prigioni, et de' Christiani, che vivono sotto 'l Gran Turco et altre cose Turchese, non piu vedute: Tradotte da M. Lodovico Domenichi*, 1548.

Montadon, Charles H., *Guide du voyageur en Crimée: Orné des cartes et précédé d'une introduction sur les differentes manièrs de se rendre d'Odessa en Crimée*, 1834.

Müller, Karl (editor), *Geographi Graeci Minores*, 2 vols., 1855–1861; reprinted, 1965.

Novosiltsev, Ivan Petrovich, 1570; in *Puteshestviya Russkikh Poslov*, 16–17, (1954): 63–99.

Oliphant, Laurence, *The Russian Shores of the Black Sea in the Autumn of 1852: With a Voyage down the Volga, and a Tour through the Country of the Don Cossacks*, 1853.

Peyssonell, Claude Charles de, *Traité sur le commerce de la mer noire*, 1787.

Potocki, Jan, *Memoire sur un noveau Peryple du Pont-Euxin ainsi que sur la plus ancienne histoire de peuple du Taurus, du Caucase et de la Scythie*, 1795.

Quin, Michael Joseph., *A Steam Voyage down the Danube, with Sketches of Hungary, Wallachia, Servia and Turkey*, 2 vols., 1835.

Reuilly, Jean Baron de, *Voyage en Crimée et sur les bords de la mer Noire, pendant l'année 1803*, 1806; as *Travels in the Crimea, and along the Shores of the Black Sea*, 1807.

Schiltberger, Johann, *Hie vahet an d' schildberger der vil wunders erfaren hatt in der heydenschafft und in d'türcken*, 1473; as *The Bondage and Travels of Johann Schiltberger: A Native of Bavaria in Europe, Asia and Africa 1396–1427*, translated by Buchan Telfer and Philipp Bruun, 1879.

Seymour, H.D., *Russia on the Black Sea and Sea of Asoff: Being a Narrative of Travels in the Crimea and Bordering Provinces; with Notices of the Naval, Military and Commercial Resources of Those Countries*, 1855.

Slade, Adolphus, *Records of Travels in Turkey, Greece, &c. and of a Cruise in the Black Sea, with the Capitan Pasha, in the Years 1829, 1830, and 1831*, 2 vols., 1833.

Slade, Adolphus, *Travels in Germany and Russia: Including a Steam Voyage by the Danube and the Euxine from Vienna to Constantinople, in 1838–1839*, 1840.

Spencer, Edmund, *Travels in Circassia, Krim-Tartary, &c., Including a Steam Voyage down the Danube from Vienna to Constantinople, and round the Black Sea in 1836*, 2 vols., 1837; as *Turkey, Russia, the Black Sea, and Circassia*, 1854.

Steinbuechel von Rheinwall, Anton, *Neueste Dampfschiffahrt von Wien nach Trapezunt, oder die grosse Donaustrasse zu einem der reichsten Ansitze des asiatischen Welthandels*, 1838.

Struve, Johann Christian von, *Reise eines jungen Russen von Wien über Jassy in die Krim*, 1801; as *Travels in the Crimea: A History of the Embassy from Petersburg to Constantinople in 1793*, 1802.

Taitbout de Marigny, Jacques Victor Edouard, *Voyages en Circassie (en 1818) par le Chevalier Taitbout de Marigny: Avec vues, etc.*, 1836; as *Three Voyages in the Black Sea to the Coast of Circassia*, 1837.

Telfer, John Buchan, *The Crimea and Transcaucasia: Being the Narrative of a Journey in the Kouban, in Gouria, Georgia, Armenia, Ossety, Ineritia, Swannety, and Mingrelia and in the Tauric Range*, 2 vols., 1876.

Verne, Jules, *Kéraban-le-têtu*, 2 vols., 1883; as *Keraban the Inflexible*, 2 vols., 1884–1885.


*See also* **Caucasus, Russian Exploration; Caucasus, Western Visitors; Crimea**

## BLIXEN, KAREN (1885–1962) *Danish Short-Story Writer, Novelist, and Translator*

Born Karen Christentze Dinesen, Karen Blixen took the name Isak—which in Hebrew means "the one who laughs"—for her pen name, but her family called her Tanne, her friends Tania, and, after she married Baron Bror von Blixen-Finecke, she called herself the baroness. She moved from Denmark to the East African protectorate of Kenya in 1914, establishing herself on her 6,000-acre coffee plantation in the highlands bordering the Ngong hills. She lived in Kenya from 1914 to 1931, and her life there inspired her to write *Out of Africa* (1937) and *Shadows on the Grass* (1960). These two works—perhaps more than any others about colonial Kenya—served to mythologize and romanticize Africa and the colonial adventure.

*Out of Africa* is in part autobiography. Blixen describes her experiences as a coffee plantation owner, her relationship with the Africans who lived and worked on her farm, her friendships with aristocratic British expatriates like Berkeley Cole, her relationship with the dashing British adventurer Denys Finch Hatton, and the failure of her coffee enterprise, which resulted in the sale of the farm and her return to Denmark. Even though Blixen states at the beginning of *Out of Africa* that she will "write down as accurately as possible [her] experiences on the farm, with the country and with some of the inhabitants" as "it may have a sort of historical interest," she does not offer her readers a factual record of her life. In fact, Blixen rearranges and omits details of her Kenyan experiences in order to create a romantic vision of Africa and of her life there.

In *Out of Africa*, Blixen strips Africa of everything tedious and ordinary. The country becomes Blixen's metaphor for beauty, aristocracy, and honor as she understood these concepts, as well as her utopia and paradise. She creates a pristine landscape dominated by freedom, adventure, and power: "Everything that you saw made for greatness and freedom, and unequalled nobility." Aristocrats, exiles, and outcasts from the industrial world populate this romantic, feudal world. Both Cole and Finch Hatton, for example, are anachronisms, the former belonging in spirit to the Elizabethan world, the latter to the Restoration court. The Africans are also aristocrats because they live with a sense of pride, courage, and nobility. Even European visitors to the farm, such as Old Knudson and Emmanuelson, are aristocrats. For Blixen, Old Knudson is a romantic rebel who abhors and lives outside the law, while the vagabond wanderer Emmanuelson is a heroic figure of tragedy.

In this feudal world, Blixen, the only woman in the company of extraordinary men, finds freedom from conventional gender roles, a consequence of her privileged status as a white European in colonial Kenya. She farms, hunts big game, acts as doctor and judge to the Kikuyu tribespeople living on her farm, and leads a supplies caravan to the British forces encamped on the German East African border during World War I. In her narrative, Blixen places herself at the heart of the colonial adventure, making her life seem at times a whirlwind of exotic experiences and adventures.

Blixen wrote *Out of Africa* after she had returned permanently to Denmark and thus was separated by time, space, and experience from the mythic Africa she evokes in her memoir. Indeed, the mood of *Out of Africa* is elegiac and nostalgic; the reader senses Blixen's pain at being separated from this mythic, romantic world to which she could not return. The death of Finch Hatton in an air crash signals the end of Blixen's idyll in Africa. Shortly thereafter, she is forced to sell the farm, losing her home, her friends, and her independence in the process. "I had a farm in Africa," Blixen writes at the start of her narrative, and it is the tragedy of that loss that permeates the work.

Published 24 years after *Out of Africa*, *Shadows on the Grass* also focuses on Blixen's experiences in Africa. The work consists of four short essays. In the opening chapter, "Farah," Blixen describes her special bond with her beloved Somali servant Farah Aden, likening their relationship to a covenant and a creative unity. Farah was not a mere servant but Blixen's confidante and support during hard times. "I talked to him about my worries as about my successes, and he knew of all that I thought or did," Blixen writes. In "Barua a Soldani," Blixen tells of receiving a letter from the king of Denmark, thanking her for her gift of a lion's skin. On the day she receives the letter, an accident occurs on the farm. A falling tree strikes a young Kikuyu. Blixen, as the doctor of the farm, is called to alleviate the boy's pain. Having no morphine, she decides to use the letter as a talisman, telling the boy that as a "Barua a Soldani," it will relieve his pain. The boy's pain does subside, and the letter becomes for the natives a renowned charm with mysterious healing powers. For Blixen, however, the letter takes on greater significance as a covenant "signed between the Europeans and the Africans—no similar document of this same relationship is likely to be drawn up again." "The Great Gesture" refers to the Europeans' wiping away of African traditions, replacing them with aspects of Western civilization, a process that Blixen opposed. The final chapter, "Echoes on the Hills," offers an epilogue to Blixen's narrative. The reader learns of her various plans to return to Africa, none of which came to fruition, and of the actual fate of those servants and friends who so enriched her life.

Recent critics of *Out of Africa* have focused on deconstructing the narrative's process of mythopoesis in an attempt to demonstrate either that Blixen embraces racist views or that she challenges the racial ideologies of colonialism. While some of her references to the native Africans may make modern readers uncomfortable (such as her tendency to compare the Africans to wild animals or children), Blixen is usually highly perceptive, particularly about the differences between European and African culture, and appreciative of what she learns from "her" Africans. Moreover, Blixen's African works, despite being pastoral romances, do have some historical value, as they capture some of the social and political changes affecting British East Africa as well as the decline of the African wilderness in the face of colonial expansion.

HARICLEA ZENGOS

### Biography

Born Karen Christentze Dinesen at Rungstedlund, north of Copenhagen, Denmark, 17 April 1885. Educated privately in Denmark, England, Switzerland, Italy, and France. Married Baron Bror von Blixen-Finecke, 1914, and they went to Kenya to manage a coffee plantation. After her divorce in 1921, she stayed on until 1931, when, the coffee market having declined, she returned to her family home. Met the English hunter Denys Finch Hatton, 1918; became his companion and lover. Finch Hatton died in a plane crash, May 1931. Lived permanently at Rungstedlund, from 1931. Established the Rungstedlund Foundation, securing the family estate and the surrounding land as a bird reserve after her death. She had been contributing items to Danish periodicals since 1905 under the pseudonym Osceola, but her first two books, *Seven Gothic Tales* (1934) and *Out of Africa* (1937), were written first in English and appeared under the name Isak Dinesen. Cofounder of the literary journal *Heretica*. Founding member of the Danish Academy, 1960. Died from malnutrition at Rungstedlund, 7 September 1962.

### References and Further Reading

Blixen, Karen, *Out of Africa*, 1937; as *Den afrikanske farm*, 1937.

Blixen, Karen, *Shadows on the Grass*, 1960; as *Skygger paa graesset*, 1960.

Blixen, Karen, *Breve fra Afrika*, 2 vols., edited by Frans Lasson, 1978; as *Letters from Africa, 1914–1931*, translated by Anne Born, 1 vol., 1981.

## BLUE NILE

The Blue Nile, whose source lies in highland Ethiopia, is known as "Al-Bahr al-Azraq" in Arabic, and as "Abbay" in Amharic. Along with the Atbara, it contributes more than 80 percent of the Nile's total water supply, the remainder coming mainly from the White Nile, which stretches down to the Great Lakes plateau in Central Africa. That the Nile had two major tributaries (the Blue and the White Nile) was already an accepted idea in late medieval cartography, even though it was recurrently identified with the biblical Ghion (one of the four rivers flowing from Eden). Also, most maps of Africa up to the late seventeenth century extended the Nile's double hydrographical basin too far south in the continent (sometimes right down to the Cape region). Correspondingly, Ethiopia's dimensions were also too exaggerated until the late seventeenth century. For a long time, the Ethiopian plateau was conceived as a metaphorical Eden embedded in eastern Africa, from where flowed the Nile's waters.

Inspired by the British Royal Geographical Society, European geographers began distinguishing the Blue Nile from the "Nile proper" in the mid-nineteenth century. This fact is interesting, for it reflects the strong connection between cultural worldview, geographical exploration, and political imperialism. On the one hand, the colonization of Sudan, and, on the other, the maintenance of Ethiopia's formal independence in the height of the "scramble for Africa" by rival European imperial powers, boosted British interest in the exploration of the White Nile beyond Khartoum, where both tributaries meet. The view that the White, and not the Blue, was the "Nile proper," is intimately tied up with this exploratory and imperial impulse. Until then, however, the Blue Nile had been the main focus of European travelers' and geographers' attention.

From classical times, the persistent search for the sources of the Nile had always been related to the inquiries into the nature of its paradoxical floods—occurring in the summer and not in winter, contrary to

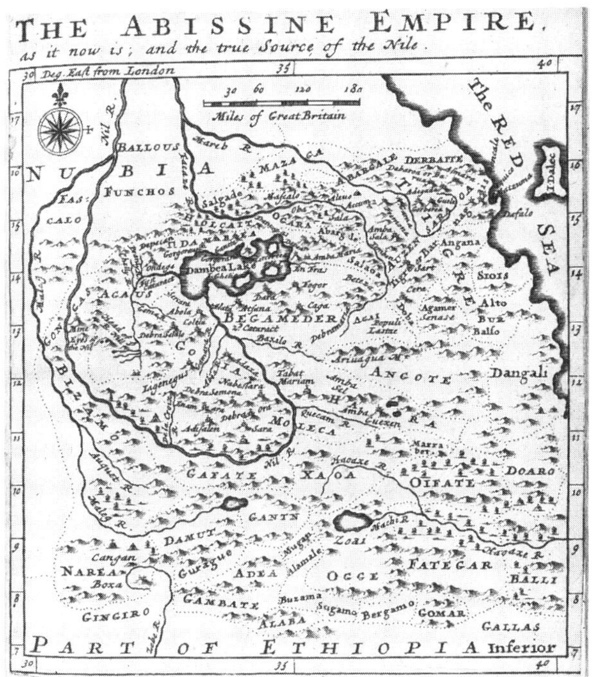


The Jesuits brought the cartography of Ethiopia out of the Middle Ages; Tellez's map is based on the work of Pero Paez, who describes seeing the source of the Blue Nile in 1613 (from Balthazar Tellez SJ's *Travels of the Jesuits in Ethiopia* reprinted in vol. 7 of *A New Collection of Voyages and Travels into All Parts of the World*, London, 1710). *Courtesy of British Library, London.*

other Mediterranean rivers. Herodotus (fifth century BCE), who reported Egyptian exploration of the Upper Nile in his *History* (book 2), questioned the credibility of different explanations of the mysterious floods. One, in particular, seemed to him most implausible: in summer, the waters of the ocean would be pushed through subterranean tunnels to emerge from deep abysses at the top of a high mountain. Curiously enough, this was the theory that was preferred by most Western writers for more than a millennium.

In late antiquity, the Nile was seen as the hydrographic axis of the African continent, its sources supposedly being located to the southwest. Pomponius Mela (first century CE), who in his *De Situ Orbis* mentions those sources in the antipodes of the known world, establishes a clear distinction between the eastern and the western parts of Africa. Pliny (23–79) relates that Emperor Nero sent parties in search of the source of the Nile, which was to be found south of the Atlas Mountains, in West Africa. He also notes that, after running to the east, the river's waters seemed to disappear under the desert sands, to reappear later in East Africa, whence they would then flow north toward Egypt.

Paulus Orosius (380?–after 417), Cosmas Indicopleustes (sixth century), and other ancient Christian cosmographers tried to correlate the classical thesis about the particularities of African hydrography with the idea that the Nile flowed from the Earthly Paradise. For this reason, they tended to favor an eastern origin of the river that, in their opinion, separated Asia from Africa, much as the Danube divided Europe from Asia. It must also be remembered that, in their views, the Far East, and particularly the Earthly Paradise—represented as a high mountain—lay nearer the celestial spheres than any other parts of the Earth. In his *Imago mundi*, Pierre d'Ailly (late fourteenth century) underlines "the fact that in reality the Earthly Paradise is at the East," and stresses that "there is a greater probability of the Nile originating in the East than in the West."

Frequent efforts were made to reconcile these theological views with travelers' information that suggested a less schematic hydrographic network in which the Nile had not one but two sources, one located in East Africa and the other to the west. References to rivers disappearing in the desert, to subterranean tunnels, and to lakes and confluences deep in the interior of the African continent multiplied in Vincent of Beauvais's *Speculum historiale* and in *The Book of Knowledge* (fourteenth century).

In the fifteenth and sixteenth centuries, Christian Ethiopia, the supposed kingdom of the legendary Prester John, was to be explored and described in close relation to such cosmographic conceptions. New information about Ethiopia further exaggerated its dimension in relation to the rest of the continent. Portuguese seamen exploring West African coasts and rivers in the fifteenth century recurrently referred to the sovereigns of the different kingdoms they encountered as vassals of the (Ethiopian) Prester John, and saw rivers such as the Senegal, Niger, and Congo as part of the mythical hydrographical network of the Nile. The existence of an oriental Christian kingdom of unknown and exaggerated dimensions in a mountainous territory geographically distinct from the rest of the African continent adjacent to the source of the (Blue) Nile was a geographic cliché that was still in full vigor in the late eighteenth century.

The information about the upper Nile basin contained in the *Ethiopian Itineraries* (lists of place names with an indication of distance in days, with complementary geographical information, which served as guides for European travelers to Ethiopia in the fifteenth and sixteenth centuries), well known to Italian cartographers, conditioned the image of Africa as an inhabited area, in the *Modern Tables*—the maps and charts included in the fifteenth-century versions of Ptolemy's *Geography*. In those *Tables*, as in Fra Mauro's *World Map*, the place names on the banks of the continent-wide River Nile were the same as the Ethiopian towns mentioned in the *Itineraries*. Arab geographers and travel writers such as Ibn Hawqal (943–977), al-Idrisi (c. 1099–1154), Abu al-Fida (1273–1331), and Ibn Battuta (1304–1368?) were also very informative sources about the Upper Nile region.

The publication in 1540 of Francisco Álvares's *True Information of the Lands of the Prester John of the Indies* increased this tendency, as can be observed in late-sixteenth-century maps. Such maps, which also showed an oversized Ethiopia, presented a rather less coherent image of the Nile than the *Modern Tables*, but a much more detailed (if more fantastical) representation of African political divisions, based on the topography brought from Ethiopia by Francisco Álvares. The sources of the Nile and the Mountains of the Moon occupied the center of the continent, and the Ethiopian territory was covered with important cities and sumptuous palaces and churches.

As detailed firsthand information about Ethiopia started to be published in Europe, the inadequacy between the reported Ethiopian reality and the medieval utopia of Prester John became manifest. Even so, the fantastical ideas about a subterranean connection between the ocean and the Ethiopian plateaus had not been abandoned. In his *Historia ecclesiastica* (1610), the Dominican Luis de Urreta informed his readers that the waters of Lake Tana, in Ethiopia, were supplied by the Indian Ocean. The Jesuit missionary Pero Paez (1564–1622), the first European to visit and describe the sources of the Blue Nile, explicitly refuted this thesis. In chapter 26 of the *History of Ethiopia*, Paez narrated his visit to the sources of the river and explained the cause of the floods (namely, the monsoon rains). To better clarify a thousand-year-old enigma, Paez tasted the water to confirm that it was not salty. He also "lowered a spear into one of the sources; after eleven spans [the spear] seemed to touch the roots of trees laying on the border of the cliff." Paez could thus finally prove that the sources of the Nile were not deep abysses, fed by the Indian Ocean.

In their explorations, their measurements, and their inquiries, Paez and other Jesuit missionaries were the first to accurately represent Ethiopia in land maps and to dismiss the age-old ideas about the peculiar nature of the River Nile. In one such map, annexed to the manuscript of Manuel Almeida's *Historia geral de Ethiopia* (published by Balthazar Tellez in 1660), the region's dimensions and proportions, and the emplacement of the Blue Nile's source and initial course, are already approximately equivalent to their modern cartographic representation.

The Jesuit missionaries were the first European writers to reach the source of the Blue Nile by Lake Tana, to demonstrate its accessibility, and to reject the exaggerated dimensions traditionally ascribed to Ethiopia. But most of their writings were left unpublished, and European cartographers of the seventeenth and eighteenth centuries disregarded their geographical findings. Instead, they propounded the old idea of a Central African lake that supplied a unified network of rivers and streams.

This vision would definitely change some time after the publication of James Bruce's *Travels to Discover the Source of the Nile*, in 1790. The description of his travels from Cairo to the Upper Nile basin and toward the Blue Nile source was extremely valuable, not only in geographic terms, but also in feeding European popular imagination about the mixture of African wilderness and the oriental decadence of Cairo, Massawa, Gondar, and Sennar. Charles-Jacques Poncet had traveled via Sennar and into Ethiopia in 1699, but he hadn't visited the Blue Nile source. But Bruce, who retraced Poncet's route, wrote an intensely personal report of his perilous travels disguised as a dervish, and of his romantic relations with the Ethiopian princess Ozoro Esther and with Sittina, the woman ruler of Shendi, in Sudan.

In the wake of the 1798 French military expedition in Upper Egypt, led by the Napoleonic general Desaix and described by Dominic Vivant, Baron de Denon, European travel and exploration of the Nile basin, beyond the cataracts of Aswan, followed the Turkish military push south, led by Mohammed Ali. The travelers Thomas Legh and Reverend Charles Smelt met a strange character in Ibrim, south of Philae. Johann Ludwig Burckhardt, a Swiss traveler who dressed after the Turkish fashion, had set out from England with the help of the Association for Promoting the Discovery of the Interior Parts of Africa. He went as far as Shendi and wrote very extensive and detailed notes of his expedition. The call of the Nile kept drawing "antiquarian visitors" eager to dress as Turks and to ride upstream toward Sennar and the Blue Nile's source. In 1821, at Meroë, George Waddington, a fellow of Trinity College, Cambridge, met an obscure American adventurer, George Bethune English. At Shendi, he also made the acquaintance of Frédéric Cailliaud, a French intellectual who had accompanied one of Mohammed Ali's sons, Ismail, in a slave-raiding tour to the Ethiopian border, past Roseires. In the 1850s, travels in the Upper Nile became somewhat fashionable among European travelers. These included George Melly, the writer Gustave Flaubert, Lady Duff Gordon, Bayard Taylor, and Doctor Theodor Bilharz. The big game hunter Samuel Baker, with his wife, in 1861–1862, as well as the Dutch travel writer Juan Maria Shuver, in 1880–1882, further explored the Atbara and the Blue Nile.

Another big game hunter, the American W.N. Macmillan, tried in vain, in 1902–1905, to make the journey to Lake Tana from Khartoum but gave up near the Ethiopian border, while his Norwegian companion, the explorer B.H. Jensen, failed to make the descent of the river between Lake Tana and the border. Likewise, the British explorer Arthur Hayes explored Lake Tana, the Blue Nile, and the Atbara valleys, but without managing the complete exploration of the mythical river's bed. It wasn't until 1930, thanks to the British colonel R.E. Cheesman, that the last 300 miles of unmapped territory toward the Blue Nile's source were systematically explored and measured.

MANUEL JOÃO RÃMOS

## References and Further Reading


Abu al-Fida, *Kitab Taqwim al-buldan*, edited by J.T. Reinaud and William MacGuckin de Slane, 1840.

Ailly, Pierre d', *Imago mundi*, translated into English by Edwin F. Keever, 1948.

al-Idrisi, *Geographie d'Édrisi*, translated by P. Amédée Jaubert, 2 vols., 1836–1840; reprinted, 1984.

Almeida, Manuel de, *Historia geral de Ethiopia a Alta ou Abassia*, in *Rerum aethiopicarum scriptores occidentales inediti a saeculo XVI ad XIX*, edited by Camillo Beccari, vols. 5–7, 1907–1908; parts translated as *Some Records of Ethiopia, 1593–1646*, translated and edited by C.F. Beckingham and G.W.B. Huntingford, 1954.

Álvares, Francisco, *Verdadeira informação das terras do preste João, segundo vio e escreueu ho Padre Francisco Aluares capellam del rey nosso senhor*, 1540; as *The Prester John of the Indies: A True Relation of the Lands of the Prester John, Being the Narrative of the Portuguese Embassy to Ethiopia in 1520*, translated by Lord Stanley of Alderley,

1881; revised and edited with additional material by C.F. Beckingham and G.W.B. Huntingford, 2 vols., 1961.
Baker, Samuel W., *The Nile Tributaries of Abyssinia, and the Sword Hunters of the Hamran Arabs*, 1867.
Bruce, James, *Travels to Discover the Source of the Nile, in the Years 1768, 1769, 1770, 1771, 1772 and 1773*, 5 vols., 1790.
Burckhardt, Johann Ludwig, *Reisen in Nubien*, 1820; as *Travels in Nubia*, 2nd edition, 1822; reprinted, 1978.
Cailliaud, Frédéric, *Voyage à Méroé, au Fleuve Blanc, au-delà de Fâzoql dans le midi du royaume de Sennâr*, 4 vols., 1826–1827; reprinted, 1972.
Cheesman, R.E., *Lake Tana and the Blue Nile: An Abyssinain Quest*, 1936; reprinted, 1968.
Cosmas Indicopleustes, *Ellas topografia*, in *Patrologiae Graeca*, vol. 88, 1860; as *The Christian Topography of Cosmas*, translated by J.W. McCrindle, 1897.
Denon, Vivant, *Voyage dans la Basse et la Haute Egypte pendant les campagnes du général Bonaparte*, 2 vols., 1802, edited by Hélène Guichard, Adrien Goetz, and Martine Reid, 1998; as *Travels in Upper and Lower Egypt*, translated by Francis Blagdon, 2 vols., 1802; translated by Arthur Aikin, 3 vols., 1803.
Duff Gordon, Lucie, Lady, *Letters from Egypt, 1863–65*, edited by Sarah Austin, 1865.
English, George Bethune, *A Narrative of the Expedition to Dongola and Sennaar: Under the Command of His Excellence Ismael Pasha, Undertaken by Order of His Highness Mehemmed Ali Pasha, Viceroy of Egypt*, 1822.
Hayes, Arthur J., *The Source of the Blue Nile: A Record of a Journey through the Soudan to Lake Tsana in Western Abyssinia, and of the Return to Egypt by the Valley of the Atbara, with a Note on the Religion, Customs, etc. of Abyssinia*, with an entomological appendix by E.B. Poulton, 1905.
Herodotus, *The History of Herodotus*, translated by George Rawlinson, 4 vols., 1858–1860, and many later editions: especially book 2.
Holland, Trevenen J., and Henry M. Hozier, *Record of the Expedition to Abyssinia*, 2 vols., 1870.
Ibn Battuta, *Travels of Ibn Battuta AD 1325–1354*, translated by H.A.R. Gibb, 5 vols. (vol. 4 with C.F. Beckingham), 1958–2000.
Ibn Hawqal, *Kitab Surat al-ard*, edited by J.H. Kramers, 2 vols., 1938–1939; as *Configuration de la terre*, translated by J.H. Kramers and G. Wiet, 1964.
Legh, Thomas, *Narrative of a Journey in Egypt, and the Country of the Cataracts*, 1816.
*Libro del conoscimiento de todos los reinos e tierras e señorios que son por el mundo e de las señales e armas que han cada tierra e señorio por si et de los reyes e señores que los proveen* [mid-fourteenth century], edited by Marcos Jimenez del Espada, 1877; as *The Book of Knowledge of All Kingdoms*, edited and translated by Nancy F. Marino, 1999.
Mela, Pomponius, *De situ orbis libri III*, edited by Abraham Gronovius, 1748; as *Pomponius Mela's Description of the World*, translated by F.E. Romer, 1998.
Melly, George, *Khartoum, and the Blue and White Niles*, 2 vols., 1851.
Paez, Pero, *Historia Aethiopiae*, in *Rerum aethiopicarum scriptores occidentales inediti a saeculo XVI ad XIX*, edited by Camillo Beccari, vols. 2–3, 1905–1906.
Pliny the Elder, *Natural History*, vol. 2, translated by H. Rackham, 1942: especially book 5.
Poncet, Charles-Jacques, "Relation Abrégée du voyage que M. Charles Poncet fit en Éthiopie en 1698, 1699 et 1700," in *Lettres Édifiantes et curieuses écrites des missions étrangères par quelques missionaries de la Compagnie de Jésus*, book 4, part 2, 1704: 251–443; as *A Voyage to Aethiopia, Made in the Years 1698, 1699, and 1700, Describing Particularly That Famous Empire*, 1709.
Schuver, Juan Maria, *Reisen in oberen Nilgebiet: Erlebnisse und Beobachtungen auf der Wasserscheide zwischen Blauem und Weissem Nil und in den ägyptisch-abessinischen Grenzländern 1881 und 1882*, 1883; as *Juan Maria Schuver's Travels in North East Africa, 1880–1883*, edited by Wendy James, Gerd Baumann, and Douglas H. Johnson, 1996.
Urreta, Luis de, *Historia ecclesiastica, politica, natural y moral de los grandes y remotos reynos de la Etiopia, monarchia del emperador llamado Preste Juan de las Indias*, 1610.
Vincent of Beauvais, *Speculum historiale*, 4 vols., 1473; as *Miroir Historial*, translated by Jehan du Vignay, 5 vols., 1495–1496.
Waddington, George, and Barnard Hanbury, *Journal of a Visit to Some Parts of Ethiopia*, 1822.

*See also* **Ethiopia/Abyssinia**

## BLUNT, WILFRID SCAWEN (1840–1922) AND LADY ANNE (1837–1917) *British Travelers*

English poet, horse-breeder, orientalist, and advocate of Muslim causes, Wilfrid came from a land-owning Sussex family. After his father's early death, Wilfrid's mother let their lands and reared her children in London, often taking them to Europe. Following his mother's conversion to Roman Catholicism, Wilfrid was sent to Catholic schools. Although he was to lose his faith, he remained attached to religious shrines, theological discussions, and Bible study, a spiritual hunger that later drew him to Islam. He entered Britain's diplomatic service when he was 18 and was posted to Athens, various European cities, and Buenos Aires. After marrying Annabella Noel, who had an independent income, Wilfrid resigned from the foreign service in 1869 and spent his life breeding horses, traveling in Arab lands, writing poetry, and backing Egyptian political causes.

Anne Isabella Noel, generally called Lady Anne, was the granddaughter of Lord Byron. She was reared by her mother, who died when Lady Anne was 15, and then by her grandmother. Educated by private tutors and at Swiss boarding schools, she was interested in mathematics, music, painting, and horses. Anne and Wilfrid shared their Near Eastern adventures, starting with a journey in 1873 to Constantinople, where they bought pack-horses and supplies and, accompanied by a semimilitary escort and a translator, they spent six weeks exploring rural Anatolia. By talking to local peasants through their interpreter, they came back believing in the "honest goodness" of the rural Turks despite their bad government. Although Wilfrid noted their hardships, he also felt that Muslims suffered little persecution and enjoyed freedom from a remote and weak regime. When Wilfrid and Anne visited Algeria the following year, however, they were shocked at France's oppression of its settled Muslim subjects and charmed by the culture of the camel-breeding nomadic tribes. Unable to go to Ethiopia in 1876 as they had hoped, they landed in Suez, hired camels and Arab guides, and set out to explore Egypt's Western Desert. When they first met Egyptian peasants, the Blunts noted their honesty, industry, and suffering at the hands of moneylenders and tax collectors.

Happier as a traveling couple than on their Sussex estate, Anne and Wilfrid hired horses, camels, and guides and journeyed to Mesopotamia and Persia in 1877–1878 and then to the Arabian desert in 1879, arduous travels that Anne describes in *Bedouin Tribes of the Euphrates* (1879) and *A Pilgrimage to Nejd* (1881). The latter journey was one of the first made by Europeans to northern Arabia, and her books corrected errors in earlier explorers' accounts. The Blunts mastered both written and spoken Arabic, became devoted to Bedouin tribes and their culture, and started buying the horses that later became known as the Crabbet Stud, which began the breeding of authentic Arabians in the West. Despite a secular upbringing, Anne became a Catholic after having a mystical vision while nursing Wilfrid during one of their Arabian journeys. For Wilfrid, the result of these travels was his attachment to Islam and the Arabs.

Their increasing disillusionment with British imperial rule, following a trip to India, led them to return to Egypt in 1880. Although they briefly visited Jedda, Wilfrid contracted malaria, and Anne decided they must return to Cairo. There Wilfrid began studying Islamic history and institutions with a former student of Jamal al-Din al-Afghani, the pan-Islamic leader who had lived in Cairo in the 1870s. His tutor introduced him to Jamal al-Din's disciple, Muhammad 'Abduh. Their friendship profoundly colored Wilfrid's thinking and bound him to Egypt. In 1881, he wrote *The Future of Islam* (1882), in which he argued that Britain could help the Muslims by setting up an Arab caliphate based in Mecca, led by Mohammed's descendants and severed from the Ottoman sultanate. His proposal later contributed to the rise of Arab nationalism.

In seeking this Arab caliph, Wilfrid pinned his hopes on Col. Ahmad 'Urabi, who led Egypt's first nationalist movement, in 1881–1882. Although British leaders regarded 'Urabi's movement as a mutiny by discontented officers against Egypt's established order, Blunt came to see it as a revolution of the Arabic-speaking peasants for constitutional government and against their Turkish and Circassian rulers. His *Secret History of the English Occupation of Egypt* (1907) relates his involvement, in Cairo and London, with this movement. He expended much of his political influence—and Lady Anne's fortune—trying to persuade Britain's consul in Cairo, Gladstone's cabinet, and the British public to support 'Urabi's nationalists against the old Turco-Circassian regime. He opposed Britain's military occupation of Egypt in September 1882. When 'Urabi and his friends were captured and charged with treason, Blunt demanded that the nationalists receive a public trial, hired British barristers to represent them, and managed to arrange that they should be exiled and not executed. In that same year, the Blunts purchased an orchard at Shaykh 'Ubayd, near Cairo. Banned from Egypt for several years, once they could assure the British government that they would refrain from local politics it allowed them to return there. They turned Shaykh 'Ubayd into an Elysian retreat, built a cottage, received their guests wearing Arab robes and burnooses, and served Egyptian foods. Viewing their land as a feudal domain, they harbored peasants who tended their trees and Bedouin who herded their flocks. They built up a collection of Arabian horses, some of which were shipped to England to form part of the Crabbet Stud. Because of failing health, Wilfrid never left England after 1905, but Lady Anne returned to Shaykh 'Ubayd to superintend the property and to manage their horses. Estranged from her husband, she wintered at Shaykh 'Ubayd until 1915, then lived in Egypt until her death, while Wilfrid stayed in Sussex.

The Blunts' strong attachment to Egypt is rare among English people. Their earlier exposure to Arab tribes had taught them a culture scarcely related to Egyptian conditions. Wilfrid's proposal in *The Future of Islam* for an Arab caliphate was assailed by Egypt's nationalists during the British occupation. However, because he backed 'Urabi, he is one of the few English

Lady Anne with an Arab horse; the Blunts used mares they brought back from Arabia to establish a stud farm at their English home, Crabbet, in Sussex (frontispiece to *A Pilgrimage to Nejd*, 1881). *Courtesy of the Travellers Club, London; Bridgeman Art Library, agent.*

political writers respected by modern Egyptians, and his *Secret History* has been translated into Arabic.

ARTHUR GOLDSCHMIDT JR.

## Biography

### *Wilfrid Scawen Blunt*

Born at Petworth House, Sussex, 17 August 1840. Educated at Stonyhurst and Oscott. Traveled in various European countries as a child. Entered diplomatic service, 1858; held a variety of posts in Europe and South America, 1858–1869; lived in Greece, 1860. Married Lady Anne Isabella Noel, 1869: one daughter. Retired from diplomatic service, 1869. Traveled to Anatolia, 1873; Algeria, 1874; Egypt, 1876; Spain, 1877; Syria and Mesopotamia, 1877–1878; northern Arabia and Persia, 1878–1879; India, 1879, 1883–1884. Wintered in Egypt, 1880–1881, 1887–1905; Siwa, 1897. Built a house in Cairo, 1881. Wrote *The Future of Islam*, 1881. Advised Col. Ahmad 'Urabi and other Egyptian nationalists, 1881–1882. Stood unsuccessfully for election as member of Parliament, 1885, 1886. Went to Ireland; imprisoned briefly for support of tenant farmers, 1887. Later published portions of his diaries in *The Secret History of the English Occupation of Egypt*, 1907; *India under Ripon*, 1909; *Gordon at Khartoum*, 1912, and *My Diaries*, 2 volumes, 1919–1920. Died in Southwater, Sussex, 10 September 1922.

### *Anne Blunt*

Born Anne Isabella Noel in London, 22 September 1837. Brought up by her mother and then by her grandmother (the widow of Lord Byron); educated by tutors and at Swiss boarding school. Traveled in various European countries as a child; met Wilfrid Scawen Blunt in Italy, 1866. Married Blunt, 1869: one daughter. Traveled to Anatolia, 1873; Algeria, 1874; Egypt, 1876; Syria and Mesopotamia, 1877–1878; northern Arabia and Persia, 1878–1879; India, 1879, 1883. Wintered in Egypt, 1880–1881, 1887–1915; remained in Egypt, 1915–1917. Succeeded as Baroness Wentworth, 1917. Died in Cairo, 15 December 1917.

## References and Further Reading


Blunt, Anne, *Bedouin Tribes of the Euphrates*, edited by W.S. Blunt, 2 vols., 1879; reprinted, 1968.

Blunt, Anne, *A Pilgrimage to Nejd: The Cradle of the Arab Race*, 1881; facsimile with an introduction by Dervla Murphy, 1985.

Blunt, Anne, *Journals and Correspondence 1878–1917*, edited by Rosemary Archer and James Fleming, 1986.

Blunt, Wilfrid, *The Future of Islam*, 1882.

Blunt, Wilfrid, *Secret History of the English Occupation of Egypt: Being a Personal Narrative of Events*, 1907.

Blunt, Wilfrid, *My Diaries: Being a Personal Narrative of Events 1888–1914*, 2 vols., 1919–1920.


# BONTEKOE, WILLEM (1587–1657) *Dutch Sailor and Explorer*

In 1646, the Hoorn bookseller Jan Jansz Deutel published the first edition of the book that was to become the most popular travel story of the Low Countries: *Iovrnael ofte gedenckwaerdige beschrijvinghe vande Oost-Indische reyse van Willem Ysbrantsz. Bontekoe van Hoorn* [Journal; or, The Memorable Description of the East Indian Voyage of Willem Ysbrantsz. Bontekoe of Hoorn]. The dramatic adventures of Captain Bontekoe and his crew on their journey to the Dutch East Indies had taken place more than 20 years earlier. On 28 December 1618, his brand-new ship, *Nieuw Hoorn*, sailed from Holland to the East Indies. The ship had almost reached its destination when disaster struck on 19 November 1619. A fire on board the ship spread to the well-stocked gunpowder store and caused a tremendous explosion. Some of the men were able to leave the burning ship in time, but Bontekoe was still on board at the time of the explosion. He miraculously survived, and after many wanderings returned to his birthplace, Hoorn. There he lived quietly, until the local publisher Deutel persuaded him in 1646 to tell the spectacular story of his travels. The Mennonite Deutel clearly wanted to use Bontekoe to show his readers the merits of good faith and devotion. The journal could therefore be read as a religious example in the wrapping of a sensational travel story.

Bontekoe's journal may nevertheless be classified as a "travel journal," a popular genre of travel accounts based on ships' logbooks that originated at the end of the sixteenth century with the return of the first Dutch explorers from East India. In the middle of the seventeenth century, a second variety of travel stories became popular, not because of the exploratory contents but because of the spectacular nature of the journeys. The journal of Bontekoe fits well into this tradition of shipwreck and disaster, but its popularity far exceeded that of other Dutch travel works.

From the very first edition, the book was an enormous success. The same year, Deutel had it reprinted, and the following year the first pirated editions were printed in Rotterdam and Utrecht. The original publisher reacted in 1648 by releasing a cheaper reprint. In his foreword, he complains about the "parrots" that pirated his successful book. This revised edition of the book marked the beginning of a true "Bontekoe craze" in the Netherlands in the second half of the seventeenth century. Many publishers profited from Bontekoe's popularity by producing one or more editions of his journal, making it a true best-seller.

Over the years, the book underwent a typographical metamorphosis, culminating in the 1663 edition published by the Amsterdam publisher Gillis Joosten Saeghman. He abridged the text and adapted the typographical form to please a broad public. By setting the text in two columns, using cheap woodcuts instead of the original copper engravings, and reducing the amount of paper used, he met the needs of less experienced readers with less money to spend. Thus the journal of Bontekoe was incorporated into the tradition of popular literature.

Its popularity continued in the eighteenth century, allowing the various editions to be printed even more cheaply. Though the typographical form of the book did not change essentially, the quality of the printing and the paper used deteriorated sharply. In order to keep the publishing costs as low as possible, the illustrations were made from woodblocks that originated from seventeenth-century editions. Newly made blocks were cut in a rough fashion. Characteristic of this development is the portrait of Bontekoe that was included in the preliminaries of the earliest editions and later became the standard illustration of the title page. Over the years, Bontekoe's picture moved farther and farther away from the original large copper engraving of 1646. From the coarse woodcuts used in the late eighteenth century, the proud sea hero can barely be recognized. Between 1810 and 1830, the last Dutch edition appeared in the old tradition, but this by no means signified the end of Bontekoe.

In the meantime, the adventures of Bontekoe had crossed the Dutch borders, finding a warm reception in German and French collections of travel stories. As early as 1648, Bontekoe's *Denckwürdige Reyse* appeared as the twenty-fourth part in the collection of Levinus Hulsius in Frankfurt. Several other German translations followed in the seventeenth and eighteenth centuries. In France, the journal was included in Melchisédech Thévenot's *Relation de divers voyages curieux* in 1663. Another French edition was printed in Amsterdam in 1681. In the eighteenth century, the distribution of Bontekoe in French travel collections continued. True international popularity came with its inclusion in Abbé Prévost's *Histoire Générale des voyages* (1750), followed by a renovated version by the prolific German pedagogue Joachim Campe in his *Sammlung . . . Reisebeschreibungen für die Jugend* (1788). Both Prévost and Campe were translated into various European languages.

So Bontekoe made his way into the European canon of stories of disaster and shipwrecks, thanks mainly to the spectacular explosion of his ship (though some foreign editors held serious doubts about the authenticity of the events described). In the Netherlands, the story of Bontekoe remained popular in the nineteenth and twentieth centuries. A number of edited versions of the journal were published there, specially adapted for new generations of readers. In the former Dutch colonies, the journal of Bontekoe was translated into Malay, Javanese, and Sundanese, also for educational purposes. The first complete English translation appeared in 1929, in both an English and an American edition, which was even translated into Chinese in 1982. In 1972, a new German edition was published, showing the continuing interest in Bontekoe. To commemorate the 350th anniversary of the first edition of Bontekoe's account in 1996, a new Dutch edition was published together with a descriptive bibliography of all recorded editions, adaptations, and translations of Bontekoe.

In 1924, the Dutch author Johan Fabricius based his children's book *De scheepsjongens van Bontekoe* on the original story of Bontekoe. More than 20 editions of this popular adaptation were published, it was translated into eight languages, adapted as a newspaper comic strip and a television broadcast, and even now the book continues to be reprinted. Thus Bontekoe lives on for new generations of readers in the Netherlands and abroad.

GARRELT VERHOEVEN

## Biography

Born in Hoorn, Holland, 1587. Followed his father as commander of the ship *Bontekoe*, to which his name refers. Captured by Barbary pirates, 1617; released after a ransom had been paid. Engaged by the East India Company to be captain of *Nieuw Hoorn*, 1618. Shipwrecked after explosion off the coast of Sumatra, 1619. Engaged in East India to serve on several ships. Made four voyages in the area; returned to the Netherlands, 1625. Resigned from the East India Company and returned to Hoorn, working as a merchant there. Travel journal published, 1646. Died in Hoorn, 1657.

## References and Further Reading


Bontekoe, Willem, *Iovrnael ofte gedenckwaerdige beschrijvinghe vande Oost-Indische reyse van Willem Ysbrantsz. Bontekoe van Hoorn*, 1646.

Bontekoe, Willem, *Memorable Description of the East Indian Voyage, 1618–25*, translated by Mrs. C.B. Bodde-Hodgkinson and Pieter Geyl, with an introduction and notes by Geyl, 1929; reprinted, 1992.

Bontekoe, Willem, *Journalen van de gedenckwaerdige reijsen, 1618–1625*, edited by G.J. Hoogewerff, 1952 (Werken uitgegeven door de Linschoten-Vereeniging, vol. 54).

Bontekoe, Willem, *Journael ofte gedenckwaerdige beschrijvinghe: De wonderlijke avonturen van een schipper in de Oost, 1618–1625*, edited by V.D. Roeper, 1996.

## BORNEO

Sindbad the Sailor made landfall on Borneo. Ibn Battuta, traveling in the neighborhood in the 1340s, remarked deadly seas and a possible site for the Sailor's roc. For other visitors of the period, the island's appeal owed more to its supplies of gold, camphor, gums, perfumed oils, spices, gems, and slaves. Reports of Borneo's "sweet riches" had already percolated through Asia into Europe; Marco Polo (1254–c. 1323) had noted a great and profitable junk traffic between China and the island. In 1521, Magellan's fleet visited the port-capital of Bruni. Antonio Pigafetta's (c. 1480/91–c. 1534) description of gorgeously caparisoned elephants, allusions to pearls as big as hens' eggs, and keen eye for glittering detail did nothing to dash European hopes.

Over the next two centuries, the Dutch and English East India companies set about supplying the demand for eastern spices. In 1718, Captain Daniel Beeckman, English East India Company official, diverted consumers with alarming tales of his adventures in the skin trade in Banjarmasin on the southern coast. The term *Oran Ootan*, or "wild man," entered the lexicon, adding extra piquancy and a certain ethnological implication to the English quest for pepper.

In the nineteenth century, James Brooke (1803–1866), English gentleman-adventurer, ensured that Borneo would figure in Western imaginations and encyclopedias as rather more, or less, than Pigafetta's luminous projection. Aided by British naval might and complacent locals, Brooke suppressed piracy in Sarawak, in return securing a pledge granting him sole rights to the district.

Protected by Brooke's arms and reputation, government officers and professional scientists opened up the forested interiors. Hugh Low (1824–1905), Brooke's private secretary, began identifying the country's flora, fauna, and peoples; his travels took him "more into the country, and amongst the tribes of aborigines, than any other Englishman." Spenser St. John (1825–?), Brooke's second secretary and British envoy, further publicized the region with his *Life in the Forests of the Far East* (1862). He made two audacious journeys—an ascent of the Limbang River to its source, and, with Low, a trek through Trusan into northeastern Borneo to the top of southeast Asia's highest mountain, Kinabalu. Unlike Low, he was less interested in advertising the island's actual productions than in discovering a marvelous lake that lay just over the next ridge.

Scientific inquiry, however, rather than Sindbaddian romance or commerce, remained the official motive for travel. In the 1850s, Alfred Russel Wallace was in Sarawak, examining orangutans with the aim of expanding Europe's knowledge of the "great Man-like ape." He also cataloged over 1,000 species of moths in the rains of Mount Mattang and spent two months trekking through Hill-Dyak country. But it was another orangutan hunter, Odoardo Beccari (1843–1920), Italian botanist and collector, who, in the 1860s, most thoroughly, and bad-temperedly, slogged through the wildernesses of Brooke's growing raj. He got as far as the Kapuas region of Dutch territory, where he had a run-in with famished dogs whose treatment of his hat was to survive 40 years in his memory untarnished by sentiment.

Tourism also put in its own more leisured appearance. The first of Sarawak's tourists was Frederick Boyle (b. 1841), Victorian gentleman and fellow of the Royal Geographical Society. His account of his tours of the newly pacified territories is laced with condescension and imperial drollery. "Most of the women," he observes of the Kennowit people, "were of astonishing age and amusing ugliness" (1865). Such observations contrast with the more generous representations given by Sarawak government officials and other more chastened visitors. Wallace's famous remark that "the better specimens of savages are much superior to the lower examples of civilised peoples" was inspired by his brush with Hill-Dyaks.

Sarawak now became a happy hunting ground for collectors. In 1878, William T. Hornaday (1854–1937), American hunter and taxidermist, waded through Wallace's swamps at Simunjon, picking off orangutans for North American museums. More generally, the country was explored by government officers who could combine official duties with less slaughterous science. Robert W. Shelford (1872–1912), naturalist, had seven years, as curator of the Sarawak museum, in which to become an expert on cockroaches. Charles

*Pax Britannica* arrives at a Borneo village (frontispiece to vol. 2 of Rodney Mundy's *Narrative of Events in Borneo and Celebes, Down to the Occupation of Labuan*, 1848, based on the journals of James Brooke, Rajah of Sarawak). *Courtesy of the Travellers Club, London; Bridgeman Art Library, agent.*

Hose (1863–1929), residential officer on the Baram, used his 23 years of service to produce scholarly accounts of "pagan tribes" and "natural man," as well as a popular narrative of field trips.

Dutch Borneo, too, was heavily trampled by government officials, explorers, romantics, and scientists; some of these marched through the central regions, leaving the names of mountain ranges in their wakes. In 1878, Carl Bock (1849–1932), Norwegian naturalist and explorer, protected by an army of bodyguards and porters, combed central Borneo for "tailed men," headhunters, and cannibals. His *The Head-Hunters of Borneo* (1881) inspired a compendious, sometimes lurid travel literature promoting Borneo's real or imagined decapitators. In the early 1920s, Bock's compatriot Carl Lumholtz (1851–1922), explorer and ethnographer, armed with a camera, anthropometric callipers, and a harder head, visited the tail-less tribes of the same area. Another of the region's more scrupulous visitors was Hendrik Tillema (1870–1952), Dutch hygienist and ethnographer, who spent the late 1920s and early 1930s exploring the Apo-Kayan district. Like Lumholtz, he left a photographic record of sobering historical value.

Less glamorous than its neighbors, North Borneo was the special province of missionaries and colonial officers. When it was noticed by a wider audience, it was principally through the efforts of visitors to Mount Kinabalu.

While many early European travelers to Borneo were attracted by its natural wealth, ethnological differences, missionary potential, or the chance to be "first" at something, others were drawn by the lure of the exotic—of those marvels that, like St. John's lake or Bock's tailed men, could only ever be realized in fantasy. Their successors have been no less avid for that which lies over the next ridge. They have gone to hunt heads, search for the "extinct" Bornean rhinoceros, interview "wild men" for *Time-Life*, experience "dragons" and isolation, find paradise, or photograph a rain forest that is always vanishing.

PIERS SMITH

### References and Further Reading


Alder, W.F., *Men of the Inner Jungle*, 1923.

Alliston, Cyril, *In the Shadow of Kinabalu*, 1961.

Alliston, Cyril, *Threatened Paradise: North Borneo and Its Peoples*, 1966.

Arnold, Guy, *Longhouse and Jungle: An Expedition to Sarawak*, 1959.

Banks, Edward, *A Naturalist in Sarawak*, 1949.

Barclay, James, *A Stroll through Borneo*, 1980.

Beccari, Odoardo, *Nelli foresti di Borneo: Viaggi e ricerche di un naturalista*, 1902; as *Wanderings in the Great Forests of Borneo: Travels and Researches of a Naturalist in Sarawak*, translated by Enrico H. Giglioli, 1904, with an introduction by the Earl of Cranbrook, 1986.

Beebe, William, *Pheasant Jungles*, 1927.

Beeckman, Daniel, *A Voyage to and from the Island of Borneo, in the East Indies*, 1718.

Belcher, Edward, *Narrative of the Voyage of H.M.S. Samarang, during the Years 1843–46*, 2 vols., 1848.

Bickmore, Albert S., *Travels in the East Indian Archipelago*, 1868.

Bisch, Jörgen, *Ulu-verdens ende: Rejse i Borneos jungle*, 1960; as *Ulu: The World's End*, translated by Reginald Spink, 1961.

Bock, Carl, *The Head-Hunters of Borneo: A Narrative of Travel up the Mahakkam and down the Barito*, 1881.

Boyle, Frederick, *Adventures among the Dyaks of Borneo*, 1865.

Brooke, Charles, *Ten Years in Sarawak*, 2 vols., 1866.

Brooke, James, *A Letter from Borneo, with Notices of the Country and Its Inhabitants: Addressed to James Gardner, Esq.*, edited by John C. Templer, 1842.

Brooke, Margaret, *My Life in Sarawak*, 1913.

Bruce, Charles, *Twenty Years in Borneo*, 1924.

Burbidge, F.W., *The Gardens of the Sun; or, A Naturalist's Journal on the Mountains and in the Forests and Swamps of Borneo and the Sulu Archipelago*, 1880.

Collingwood, Cuthbert, *Rambles of a Naturalist on the Shores and Waters of the China Sea, Being Observations in Natural History during a Voyage to China, Formosa, Borneo, Singapore, etc., Made in Her Majesty's Vessels in 1866 and 1867*, 1868.

Cook, Oscar, *Borneo: The Stealer of Hearts*, 1924.

Cotteau, E., *Quelques notes sur Sarawak*, 1886.

Crocker, W.M. (editor), *Waiting for the Tide; or, Scraps and Scrawls from Sarawak*, 1875.

Currey, L.E., *Borneo*, 1933.

De Leeuw, Hendrik, *Crossroads of the Java Sea*, 1931.

Denison, Noel, *Jottings Made during a Tour amongst the Land Dyaks of Upper Sarawak*, 1879.

Dickson, Mora, *A Season in Sarawak*, 1962.

Dickson, Mora, *Longhouse in Sarawak*, 1971.

Domalain, Jean-Yves, *Panjamon: Une Expérience de la vie sauvage*, 1971; as *Panjamon: I Was a Head-Hunter*, translated by Len Ortzen, 1972.

Earl, George Windsor, *The Eastern Seas; or, Voyages and Adventures in the Indian Archipelago, in 1832–33–34*, 1837; reprinted, with an introduction by C.M. Turnbull, 1971.

Emmerich-Högen, Ferdinand, *Kopfjäger auf Borneo* [Borneo Headhunters], 1935.

Enriquez, C.M., *Kinabalu: The Haunted Mountain of Borneo*, 1927.

Evans, Ivor H.N., *Among Primitive Peoples in Borneo: A Description of the Lives, Habits and Customs of the Piratical Headhunters of North Borneo*, 1922; reprinted, 1990.

Furness, William Henry, *The Home-Life of Borneo Head-Hunters: Its Festivals and Folklore*, 1902.

Geddes, W.R., *Nine Dayak Nights*, 1957.

Gersi, Douchan, *Bornéo, dans les ténèbres de la jungle-femelle: La Dramatique Aventure de trois hommes en plein inconnu*, 1976.

Gersi, Douchan, *Explorer*, 1987.

Gomes, Edwin H., *Seventeen Years among the Sea Dyaks of Borneo: A Record of Intimate Association with the Natives of the Bornean Jungles*, 1911.

Grant, Charles, *A Tour among the Dyaks of Sarawak in 1858*, 1864.

Green, Eda, *Borneo: The Land of River and Palm*, 1909.

Groeneveldt, W.P., *Notes on the Malay Archipelago and Malacca, Compiled from Chinese Sources*, 1876.

Haddon, Alfred C., *Head-Hunters: Black, White and Brown*, 1901.

Hanbury-Tenison, Marika, *A Slice of Spice: Travels to the Indonesian Islands*, 1974.

Hanbury-Tenison, Robin, *A Pattern of Peoples: A Journey among the Tribes of Indonesia's Outer Islands*, 1975.

Hanbury-Tenison, Robin, *Mulu: The Rain Forest*, 1980.

Harrisson, Tom (editor), *Borneo Jungle: An Account of the Oxford University Expedition to Sarawak 1932*, 1938.

Harrisson, Tom, *Innermost Borneo: Ten Years' Exploration and Research*, 1959.

Harrisson, Tom, *World Within: A Borneo Story*, 1959; reprinted, 1984.

Hatton, Frank, *North Borneo: Explorations and Adventures on the Equator, with Biographical Sketch and Notes by Joseph Hatton*, 1885.

Hatton, Joseph, *The New Ceylon, Being a Sketch of North Borneo or Sabah*, 1881.

Helbig, Karl, *Urwaldwildnis Borneo: 3,000 kilometer Zick-Zack-Marsch durch Asiens grosste Insel* [Borneo's Jungle Wilderness: A 3,000 Kilometer Zig zag March across Asia's Largest Island], 1940.

Helbig, Karl, *Eine Durchquerung der Insel Borneo (Kalimantan): Nach den Tagebüchern aus dem Jahre 1937* [A Crossing of the Island of Borneo: From Journals for the Year 1937], 1982.

Hornaday, William T., *Two Years in the Jungle: The Experiences of a Hunter and Naturalist in India, Ceylon, the Malay Peninsula and Borneo*, 1885; as *The Experiences of a Hunter and Naturalist in the Malay Peninsula and Borneo*, with an introduction by J.M. Gullick, 1993.

Hose, Charles, *Fifty Years of Romance and Research; or, A Jungle-Wallah at Large*, 1927; as *Fifty Years of Romance and Research in Borneo*, with an introduction by Brian Durrans, 1994.

Hose, Charles, *The Field-Book of a Jungle-Wallah, Being a Description of Shore, River and Forest Life in Sarawak*, 1929; reprinted, 1985.

Huxley, Aldous, *Jesting Pilate: The Diary of a Journey*, 1926; reprinted, 1985.

Ivanoff, Pierre, *Chez les coupeurs de tête de Bornéo*, 1955; as *Headhunters of Borneo*, translated by Edward Fitzgerald, 1958.

Iwata Keiji, *Kami no jiruigaku: Fushigi no basho o megutte* [Anthropology of Gods: A Tour of Mythical Places], 1985.

Johnston, Tracy, *Shooting the Boh: A Woman's Voyage down the Wildest River in Borneo*, 1992.

Jongejans, J., *Ons mooi Indië: Uit Dajakland; Kijkjes in het leven van den koppensneller en zijne omgeving* [Our Beautiful Indies: Out of the Land of the Dyaks; The Everyday Life and Surroundings of the Headhunter], 1922.

Keith, Agnes, *Land below the Wind*, 1939.

Keppel, Henry, *Expedition to Borneo of H.M.S. Dido for the Suppression of Piracy, with Extracts from the Journals of James Brooke Esq.*, 2 vols., 1846; reprinted, with an introduction by R.H.W. Reece, 1991.

Klum, Mattias, *Borneo Rain Forest*, 1998.

Krohn, William O., *In Borneo Jungles: Among the Dyak Headhunters*, 1927; reprinted, 1991.

Kükenthal, Willy Georg, *Forschungsreise in den Molukken und in Borneo*, 1896.

Lim Poh Chiang, *Among the Dayaks*, 1989.

Linklater, Andro, *Wild People: Fighting and Writing about Borneo's Head-Hunters*, 1990.

Low, Hugh, *Sarawak, Its Inhabitants and Productions: Being Notes during a Residency in That Country with H.H. the Rajah Brooke*, 1848; reprinted, 1988.

Lumholtz, Carl, *Through Central Borneo: An Account of Two Years' Travel in the Land of the Head-Hunters between the Years 1913 and 1917*, 2 vols., 1920; with an introduction by Victor T. King, 1991.

MacDonald, David W., *Expedition to Borneo: The Search for Proboscis Monkeys and Other Creatures*, 1982.

MacDonald, Malcolm, *Borneo People*, 1956.

McDougall, Harriette, *Sketches of Our Life at Sarawak*, 1882; with an introduction by R.H.W. Reece and A.J.M. Saint, 1992.

Marryat, Frank S., *Borneo and the Indian Archipelago, with Drawings of Costume and Scenery*, 1848.

Miller, Charles Constant, *Black Borneo*, 1942.

Mjöberg, Eric Georg, *I Tropikernas villande urskogar: Aventyr och upplevelser i Nederlandska Indien*, 1928; as *Forest Life and Adventures in the Malay Archipelago*, translated by Anna Barwell, 1930.

Mjöberg, Eric Georg, *Bornéo: L'Île des chasseurs de tétes*, 1934.

Moody, Geoffrey T., *Coral in the Sand*, 1962.

Moor, J.H., *Notices of the Indian Archipelago, and Adjacent Countries: Being a Collection of Papers Relating to Borneo, Celebes, Bali, Java, Sumatra, Nias, the Philippine Islands, Sulus, Siam, Cochin China, Malayan Peninsula, &c.*, 1837.

Muller, Kal, *Borneo: Journey into the Tropical Rainforest*, 1996.

Mundy, Rodney, *Narrative of Events in Borneo and Celebes, down to the Occupation of Labuan: From the Journals of James Brooke, Esq., together with a Narrative of the Operations of H.M.S. Iris*, 2 vols., 1848.

Nieuwenhuis, A.W., *In centraal Borneo: Reis van Pontianak naar Samarinda*, 1900.

Nieuwenhuis, A.W., *Quer durch Borneo: Ergebnisse seiner Reisen in den Jahren 1894, 1896–97 und 1898–1900*, 2 vols., 1907.

O'Hanlon, Redmond, *Into the Heart of Borneo: An Account of a Journey Made in 1983 to the Mountains of Batu Tiban with James Fenton*, 1984.

Oost, Jan, *Onder koppensnellers op Borneo*, 1916.

Pfeffer, Pierre, *Bivouacs à Bornéo*, 1963.

Pfeiffer, Ida, *A Lady's Second Journey round the World: From London to the Cape of Good Hope, Borneo, Java, Sumatra, Celebes, Ceram, the Moluccas, etc., California, Panama, Peru, Ecuador, and the United States*, 1856.

Piazzini, Guy, *Chez les rescapés du déluge*, 1959; as *The Children of Lilith: A French Exploration into the Up-River Country of Borneo*, translated by Peter Green, 1960.

Plessen, Viktor von, *Bei den Kopfjäegern von Borneo: Ein Reisetagebuch*, 1944.

Pryer, Ada, *A Decade in Borneo*, 1894.

Rawlins, Douglas (editor), *Borneo Venture*, 1969.

Ritchie, James, *Bruno Manser: The Inside Story*, 1994.

Ross, John Dill, *Sixty Years' Life and Adventure in the Far East*, 2 vols., 1911.

Rutter, Owen, *Triumphant Pilgrimage: An English Muslim's Journey from Sarawak to Mecca*, 1937.

St. John, Spenser, *Life in the Forests of the Far East; or, Travels in Sarawak and Northern Borneo*, 2 vols., 1862; reprinted, with an introduction by Tom Harrisson, 1974.

Sargent, Wyn, *My Life with the Headhunters*, 1974.

Schwaner, C.A.L.M., *Borneo: Beschrijving van het stroomgebied van den Barito, en reizen langs eenige voorname rivieren van het zuid-oostelük gedeelte van det eiland . . . op last*

*van het gouvernement van Nederl. Indie gedaan in de jaren 1843–184*, 2 vols., 1853–1854.
Sharp, Arthur Frederick, *The Wings of the Morning*, 1954.
Shelford, Robert W., *A Naturalist in Borneo*, edited and with an introduction by Edward B. Poulton, 1916; reprinted, 1985.
Spalding, Linda, *A Dark Place in the Jungle*, 1999.
Tehupeiorij, J.E., *Onder de Dajaks in Centraal-Borneo: Een reisverhaal*, 1906.
Teo, Albert C.K., *Journey through Borneo*, 1994.
Tillema, Hendrik F., *Apo-Kajan: Een filmreis naar en door Centraal-Borneo, 1938 afbeeldingen*, 1938; as *A Journey among the Peoples of Central Borneo in Word and Picture*, translated by Victor T. King, 1989.
Treacher, W.H., *British Borneo: Sketches of Brunai, Sarawak, Labuan, and North Borneo*, 1891.
Villard, Mady, *Bornéo: Chez les hommes aux longues oreilles*, 1975.
Wallace, Alfred Russel, *The Malay Archipelago: The Land of the Orang-Utan and the Bird of Paradise: A Narrative of Travel, with Studies of Man and Nature*, 2 vols., 1869; reprinted, with an introduction by John Bastin, 1986.
Walker, H. Wilfrid, *Wanderings among South Sea Savages and in Borneo and the Philippines*, 1910.
Whitehead, John, *The Exploration of Mount Kina Balu, North Borneo*, 1893.
Wilson, John Kennedy, *Budu; or, Twenty Years in Sarawak*, 1969.
Young, Gavin, *In Search of Conrad*, 1991.

## BORROW, GEORGE (1803–1881) *British Traveler, Writer, Translator, and Philologist*

George Borrow was born near East Dereham, Norfolk, the second child of a recruiting officer in the West Norfolk militia and his wife, said to be of Huguenot descent. As a military family during the Napoleonic wars, the Borrows led a peripatetic existence, and Borrow's education was interrupted in 1815–1816 when "Captain" Borrow—he possessed the title but never the pay of captain—was stationed in Ireland. There, Borrow came into contact with the excluded people who haunted his imagination all his life: gypsies, tinkers, and other dispossessed Irish. Borrow attended Norwich Grammar School for three years, where he showed a gift for languages, if little else. On leaving school, he became articled to a Norwich law firm for five years, during which time he met William Taylor, a writer and dilettante philosopher, and under Taylor's influence Borrow decided to abandon law for a writing career. In 1824, when his apprenticeship ended (and his father died), Borrow moved to London and began a miserable period of hack writing and translation, mostly for the publisher Sir Richard Phillips. Fascinated by northern European languages and folk cultures, Borrow published translations of Danish, Dutch, and German ballads and tales in Phillips's periodicals *The Monthly Magazine* and *Universal Review*, and in 1826 he published *Romantic Ballads* privately. However, Borrow probably learned his craft best by working on the six-volume *Celebrated Trials* (1825), an unoriginal but vivid collection of rogues' lives in the eighteenth-century *Newgate Calendar* style; no doubt it also strengthened his tendency to identify with social outsiders. Depressed and enervated by a life of indoor drudgery, Borrow intermittently disappeared, and from 1825 to 1832 he wandered across Britain and Europe, his means of living unknown. He later drew on this "veiled period" for his fictionalized memoirs, *Lavengro* (1851) and *The Romany Rye* (1857), but his account cannot be verified independently.

In 1833, Borrow applied successfully for the job of agent to the British and Foreign Bible Society, recognizing that this was the ideal vehicle for his talents: travel and languages. He spent 1833 to 1835 in St. Petersburg preparing an edition of the Bible in Manchu, having amazed his employers by mastering the language in only a few weeks. Characteristically, he found time to translate Russian and Turkish folk tales, including Pushkin's story *The Talisman* (St. Petersburg, 1835). By the winter of 1835, Borrow was in Spain on the first of three journeys to the Iberian Peninsula, distributing copies of the New Testament. It was a dangerous time for such work; there had been civil war in Spain since the 1820 revolution, and in 1835 Palmerston sent a British force to Spain, ostensibly in a peacekeeping role but actually in support of the royalists (Borrow was arrested three times, to his delight). His letters to the society form the basis of *The Bible in Spain* (1843), a picaresque travel account that was an instant success. Though he worked zealously to promote the society's work, Borrow was no missionary, and his violent anti-Catholic prejudice stemmed from his instinctive hatred of authority rather than from religious conviction. He loved languages, especially if lost or marginalized, such as Romany or Calo (Spanish gypsy), words, speech, argot, and robbers' cant; he recorded and analyzed what he heard, and can be regarded as an amateur philologist and ethnologist who inspired serious interest in gypsy and Celtic languages and cultures; his own studies, such as the linguistic charts in his study of European gypsies, *The Zincali* (1841), verge on the imaginary.

Borrow returned to England in 1840, married, and attempted to settle down to country life at his wife's Norfolk estate, but by 1844 he was once again traveling through Europe and, by his own account, reached Constantinople. He seems to have passed through Budapest, Bucharest, and perhaps part of Albania, returning home via Salonica (Thessaloniki), Venice, Rome, Marseilles, and Paris, as usual collecting conversations in several languages. Back in Norfolk, he worked on *Lavengro*, aware that the author of *The Bible in Spain* and *The Zincali* had much to live up to; however, *Lavengro* and its sequel *The Romany Rye* disappointed the reading public and the critics, many of whom were simply bewildered by the strange, dreaming figure of Lavengro, Borrow's fictional alter ego. From 1853 to 1860, Borrow explored Britain's Celtic fringe (Scotland and the Isles, Ireland, Wales, Cornwall, and the Isle of Man), sometimes accompanied by his wife and stepdaughter, more often alone; *Wild Wales* (1862) restored his critical reputation slightly. By now, Borrow was outdated as a travel writer as well as a philologist, and a late work on the Romany language, *Romano Lavo-Lil* (1874), revealed plainly that contemporary scholarship had rendered his work obsolete. His last years were spent in bitter obscurity, and although *Lavengro* remained in print in various cheap editions, Borrow played no part in English literary life after 1870.

The late Victorian and early-twentieth-century quest to uncover a lost, preindustrial natural world helped to renew interest in Borrow's writings, and the publication of his letters contributed to his emerging cult. W.I. Knapp's idealizing biography figured Borrow as an authentic scholar gypsy (Borrow appears not to have read Matthew Arnold, or indeed any contemporary English literature), and Edmund Gosse remarked on Borrow's "masculine intelligence." It is from this period that the word *Borrovian* enters the language, with its suggestions of long rural walks and a love of plain speech and rough company. *Lavengro* remains the text on which Borrow's reputation rests, though *The Bible in Spain* contains his most successful travel writing.

HILARY WEEKS

### Biography

Born near East Dereham, Norfolk, 5 July 1803. Educated at schools in Huddersfield and Clonmel, Ireland; later at Edinburgh High School and at Norwich Grammar School, 1816–1819. Articled as legal clerk to William Simpson, solicitor, Norwich, 1819–1824. Traveled between London, Norwich, France, Spain, and Portugal, studying the languages, 1825–1832. Agent and correspondent to the British and Foreign Bible Society, 1833–1840: in Russia, 1833–1835, and on three missions to the Iberian peninsula and North Africa (November 1835–September 1836; November 1836–September 1838; December 1838–April 1840). Married a widow, Mary Skepper Clarke, 1840 (d. 1869): one stepdaughter. Traveled extensively in Europe and Asia in 1844, possibly to Constantinople (Istanbul) and through Romania, Hungary, Albania, and Greece. Acquired estate in Oulton Broad, Norfolk; lived there from 1840, moving to Great Yarmouth in 1853. From 1849 until his death, he undertook walking tours through the British Isles, notably in Wales, 1854–1857. Moved to London, 1860. Returned to Oulton, 1874. Lived in Norwich, late 1870s. Died in Oulton, Norfolk, 26 July 1881.

### References and Further Reading

Borrow, George, *The Bible in Spain; or, The Journeys, Adventures, and Imprisonments of an Englishman in an Attempt to Circulate the Scriptures in the Peninsula*, 3 vols., 1843.
Borrow, George, *Lavengro*, 3 vols., 1851.
Borrow, George, *The Romany Rye*, 2 vols., 1857.
Borrow, George, *Wild Wales*, 3 vols., 1862.
Borrow, George, *Letters of George Borrow to the British and Foreign Bible Society*, edited by T.H. Darlow, 1911.
Borrow, George, *Letters to His Mother Ann Borrow*, 1913.
Borrow, George, *Letters to His Wife Mary Borrow*, 1913.
Borrow, George, *A Journey to Eastern Europe in 1844 (Thirteen Letters)*, edited by Angus M. Fraser, 1981.

## BOSWELL, JAMES (1740–1795) *Scottish Lawyer, Journalist, and Biographer*

James Boswell's ancient family was related to the royal houses of Bruce and Stuart. The son of a Scottish judge and classicist, he abandoned naive military ambitions for the law, but was best known in his own time as the author of several books, quarried from the journals (unpublished until the twentieth century) that he kept for most of his adult life.

The earliest journals deal with a Scottish "jaunt" in autumn 1762, and a brilliantly dramatized narrative of the young rake amid London's high and low life in 1762–1763, when he first met Samuel Johnson. Partly written for correspondents back home, these are explorations of his favorite subject—himself—in testing situations. The London journal displays his talent for acute description of people rather than places, and wonderfully lifelike rendering of dialog. He was sent for a year of legal study in Holland (for which his full journal is lost, but other documents survive), then made his Grand Tour: Germany and Switzerland in 1764; Italy, Corsica, and France in 1765–1766—all were carefully journalized, showing that, while he could respond appropriately to dramatic scenery or classical ruins, his real interest was in people. Touring the Hebrides a decade later, he wrote, "A landscape or view of any kind is defective, in my opinion, without some human figures to give it animation." On the Continent, these included scholars, artists, high-born ladies and "monsters" of the streets, British travelers such as the radical politician John Wilkes and the son of Lord Bute, and Jacobite survivors at the Roman court of the "Old Pretender." Boswell did battle at Ferney with Voltaire on religion, noting, "For a certain portion of time there was a fair opposition," and he had a personal triumph in challenging the reclusive Rousseau with his self-dramatization as "a man of singular merit, as a man with a feeling heart, a sensitive and melancholy spirit," and cajoling him into six interviews.

Encouraged by Rousseau, Boswell visited Corsica (1765), then the focus of political thinkers for its independence struggle against the "old" Europe of Genoa but not well known at firsthand. Impressed by the personal qualities of its leader, General Paoli, Boswell energetically campaigned to raise British funds and arms; an ironic consequence of his failure was that one of the first babies born under the conquering French jurisdiction was Napoleon Bonaparte, son of Paoli's adjutant. Influential in Boswell's campaign was his *Account of Corsica* (1768), partly an unoriginal synthesis of geography and history, partly the journal of his tour, drawing a narrative from his diaries to present the Rousseauist theme of Corsican primitive simplicity together with the classical heroism of Paoli. At a stroke, it gave him a European reputation, being widely serialized, and translated (partly even into Russian), and selling well in America. The poet Thomas Gray, no friend of Boswell, succumbed to its "artless technique": "any fool may write a most valuable book by chance if he will only tell us what he heard and saw with veracity." Johnson understood his achievement better: "There is between the History and the Journal that difference which will always be found between notions borrowed from without and notions generated within. Your History was copied from books; your Journal rose out of your own experience and observation." Although pilloried by reviewers for stylistic faults such as Scotticisms, from the age of 29 the author was made, as "Corsica Boswell," a public figure: "I had got upon a rock in Corsica and jumped into the middle of life."

In 1773, Boswell, using his social connections to procure invitations from clan chiefs and Edinburgh literati, finally persuaded the elderly Johnson to make a three-month tour up the east coast of Scotland, via Aberdeen and Inverness, thence to Skye, Mull, and other islands, to Boswell's ancestral home at Auchinleck, and back to Edinburgh, which tour he duly reported in contemporary newspapers. Boswell's original journal, rediscovered in 1930, is as usual concerned less with place—important towns such as Inverness and Aberdeen are hardly described—than with objects suggestive of antiquity or Gaelic feudal life, and stories of the Second Sight. The romantic Hebridean scenes that would enrapture nineteenth-century travelers provoke little real enthusiasm. Boswell focuses instead on the "gallant highlanders," especially those involved in the 1745 rebellion and the escape of Bonnie Prince Charlie: Flora MacDonald and her husband evoke all his old "Jacobite" feelings. The journal has valuable historical material on the rising, of which he never made his intended history. His other great subject, part of his long-term biographical project, is his controlled experiment in placing the allegedly Scottophobic Johnson in an alien environment, setting him topics of discussion: "it was I who always 'set him a-going.' The fountain was locked up till I interfered." The result is sharp observation of personality, recorded through dramatic detailing of conversation.

Encouraged by favorable responses to his private journal from select readers such as Sir Joshua Reynolds, Boswell staked out his position as Johnson's biographer after his death by publishing in 1785 *The Journal of a Tour to the Hebrides*, only now recognized as a significant reworking of the original account. He cut much of the topography and autobiography to focus on the potential conflict between the Scots and the "John Bull . . . true-born Englishman," playing down Johnson's rudeness to and about Scottish hosts: Boswell's relative, Lady Macdonald, "would sink a ninety-gun ship. She is so dull—so heavy." Lord Macaulay's clerical grand-uncle was "the most ignorant booby and the grossest bastard."

Despite this toning down and some stylistic formalizing, the *Tour* was a sensational and controversial book because of its frankness in importing the material and techniques of Boswell's private journals into the public arena: he survived the 20 Rowlandson-Collings caricatures based on its episodes, the threats of Lord Macdonald—the repeated butt of criticism in the journal—and a feud with Johnson's former patron, Mrs. Thrale. Further polished for the second edition, the *Tour* was a huge commercial success and established Boswell as an idiosyncratic classic, interested

Frontispiece to Thomas Rowlandson and Samuel Collings's *The Picturesque Beauties of Boswell*, 1786, which caricatured the tour to the Hebrides Boswell undertook with Johnson (shown helping to pull the cart). *Courtesy of British Library, London.*

in travel for what it revealed about himself and his fellows.

IAN MCGOWAN

### Biography

Born in Edinburgh, 29 October 1740, eldest son of a Scottish judge, later Lord Auchinleck. Educated privately and at Edinburgh High School. Attended the University of Edinburgh, 1753–1758; studied philosophy and literature under Adam Smith at the University of Glasgow, 1759–1760. Planned, then abandoned, a career in the army. Visited London frequently, from 1760 on. Met Samuel Johnson, 1763. Studied law at the University of Utrecht, Holland, 1763–1764; made Grand Tour of Europe, 1764–1766, visiting Corsica in 1765. Became Scots advocate (barrister), 1766; married his cousin Margaret Montgomerie, 1769: seven children (two died in infancy). Elected as a member of Johnson's literary club; toured Scotland with Johnson, 1773. Inherited his father's estate and became Laird of Auchinleck, 1782. Called to the English bar, at the Middle Temple, 1786. Recorder of Carlisle, 1788–1790. Settled in London after the death of his wife, 1789. Published *The Life of Samuel Johnson*, 1791. Died in London, 19 May 1795.

### References and Further Reading

Boswell, James, *An Account of Corsica: The Journal of a Tour to That Island; and Memoirs of Pascal Paoli*, 1768.
Boswell, James, *British Essays in Favour of the Brave Corsicans*, 1769.
Boswell, James, *The Journal of a Tour to the Hebrides, with Samuel Johnson LL.D.*, 1785; 2nd edition, 1785; 3rd edition, 1786; edited by Frederick A. Pottle and Charles H. Bennett, 1936; revised and enlarged edition, 1963.
Boswell, James, *Boswell's London Journal, 1762–1763*, with an introduction and notes by Frederick A. Pottle, 1950.
Boswell, James, *Boswell in Holland, 1763–1764, Including His Correspondence with Belle de Zuylen (Zelide)*, 1952.
Boswell, James, *Boswell on the Grand Tour: Germany and Switzerland, 1764*, edited by Frederick A. Pottle, 1953.
Boswell, James, *Boswell on the Grand Tour: Italy, Corsica, and France, 1765–1766*, edited by Frank Brady and Frederick A. Pottle, 1955.
McGowan, Ian (editor), *Journey to the Hebrides*, Edinburgh: Canongate, 1996.
Powell, L.F. (editor), *Boswell's Life of Johnson*, vol. 5: *The Tour to the Hebrides*, Oxford: Clarendon Press, 1950; revised edition, 1964.

*See also* **Johnson, Samuel**

## BOUGAINVILLE, LOUIS ANTOINE DE (1729–1811) *French Scientist and Explorer*

While the vast majority of contemporary readers are unlikely to recognize the name of Louis Antoine de Bougainville beyond the eponymous small shrublike vine with purplish flowers that he brought back from South America in 1765, Bougainville was the epitome of the world traveler in eighteenth-century France and responsible in great part for the consideration of the voyage of circumnavigation as, beyond its political, economic, and scientific aspirations, a major cultural enterprise.

Bougainville's extensive education in law and mathematics provided the intellectual foundation and impetus for his voyage around the world; his subsequent military career, which he embarked upon in 1750, provided valuable practical experience for the journey. Sent to Canada in 1756 as a captain, Bougainville fought in the Battle of Quebec (1759) during the Seven Years' War (1756–1763). Following the defeat of France and its loss of all remaining Canadian territories, Bougainville sought governmental support for a series of military expeditions to the Malouine Islands (the Falkland Islands) with the hope of establishing a permanent French settlement to accommodate Acadian emigrants who had been persecuted and deported since France had ceded Acadia to England under the Treaty of Utrecht (1713). Bougainville was ultimately forced to secure private financial support for the two trips he made to the Falklands beginning in 1763. While Bougainville's Falklands campaign ended in failure with French interests turned over to Spain and England, the political prominence of these trips to the Southern Hemisphere paved the way for governmental approval for the first French circumnavigation which, after several delays and false starts, departed from Saint-Malo, France, on 15 December 1766.

Accompanying Bougainville and his crew aboard the frigate *La Boudeuse* and the supply ship *L'Etoile* were a host of naturalists, draftsmen, and astronomers. Among the most significant of these specialists was the astronomer Pierre-Antoine Véron. In the absence of reliable instruments of longitudinal measurement such as the chronometer, then being perfected both in England and France, navigation in the mid-eighteenth century was, at best, a mathematically complicated, approximate procedure ridden with potential errors. Véron's presence aboard *La Boudeuse* was significant because he was able to make thousands of readings and measurements that, when compared to existing maps and charts, corrected the errors of many previous navigators and cartographers. The exact location of many Pacific islands was established during the trip and the expedition determined with precision the width of the Pacific Ocean.

On 5 April 1768, the French ships, sailing westward through the Pacific, arrived at the island of Tahiti, where European visitors had first arrived in 1767, led by Samuel Wallis. The friendly islanders received the weary French sailors with a hospitality the travelers did not expect. Meeting the ships were canoes filled with Tahitian women who had been stripped bare of their daily garments. The accompanying Tahitian men encouraged the French sailors to choose a woman and go to shore with her. The islanders' apparent sexual freedom and the lush tropical beauty of their home prompted the naming of the island "La Nouvelle Cythère" (New Cythera) after the Greek island where Aphrodite had a temple and which was an important symbol in eighteenth-century French painting and erotic fiction. Despite the fact that *La Boudeuse* and *L'Etoile* spent only two weeks at the island, the description of Tahiti and its inhabitants comprises two full chapters out of 18 in Bougainville's *Description d'un voyage autour du monde*.

Shortly before the ships' departure on 15 April 1768, the islanders' leader, Ereti, asked Bougainville that the French take with them a Tahitian man named Aotourou who desired to accompany them on their voyage. Bougainville and his officers agreed and Aotourou joined the expedition. As the circumnavigation continued through the eastern Pacific, to the Moluccas, Batavia, and on to the Indian Ocean where landfall was planned at the French colonies on the Ile de France (Mauritius) and the Ile de Bourbon (Réunion), those aboard learned a great deal about Tahitian society and its customs from the new companion, information that served to further valorize in the eyes of the Frenchmen Tahiti's stature as an island paradise. After the return to France of *La Boudeuse* on 6 March 1769 and *L'Etoile* on 24 April 1769, Aotourou circulated among Paris's fashionable and intellectual circles. He inspired, along with Bougainville's own complimentary description of Tahiti in the account of his circumnavigation that appeared in October 1769, Denis Diderot's *Supplément au voyage de Bougainville* (1772), a seminal text in the Enlightenment philosophical debate on the state of nature and the figure of the noble savage. Bougainville later entrusted Aotourou to a merchant captain bound for the Ile de France; precise directions were provided in order to chart a course to Tahiti, but it is unknown whether Aotourou ever returned to his native island.

Although Bougainville's circumnavigation was a political and economic failure that did not significantly expand France's colonial territories or extend French interests in the spice trade through the Indian Ocean, it did provide a wealth of scientific and geographical detail about the Pacific Ocean and secured for Bougainville a prominent place in French military and intellectual history.

LEONARD R. KOOS

## Biography

Born in Paris, 11 or 12 November 1729. Studied law and worked as a lawyer for the Parlement de Paris until 1752. Published the two-volume mathematical work *Traité de calcul intégral*, 1752–1756. Joined the *mousquetaires noirs* (black musketeers). Appointed secretary to the French embassy in London, 1755. Elected to the Royal Society of London, 1756. Served as aide-de-camp to General Montcalm, 1756. Served in Quebec with the French army, 1756–1758; took part in the capture of Fort Oswego, 1757. Promoted to rank of colonel, 1759. Served as aide-de-camp to General Choisel-Stainville and traveled to Germany where he was wounded. Appointed ship's captain; traveled to the Malouines (the Falkland Islands) in two expeditionary missions, 1764 and 1765. Traveled around the world on *La Boudeuse*, 1766–1769. Appointed secretary to Louis XV, 1772. Served as *chef d'escadre* (commodore) in North America in campaigns against the British, 1779–1782. Married Flore-Josèphe de Longchamps de Montendu, 1779. Court-martialed after the defeat of the French fleet near Martinique, 1782. Collaborated on the plans of La Pérouse's proposed voyage, 1785. Promoted to post of vice-admiral, 1791. Took his family to live on his estate near Coutances, Normandy, during the French revolution, and resigned from public life; was imprisoned and released after the fall of Robespierre. Elected a member of the French Institute. Lived in the Chateau de Suisnes, Brie, after 1799. Appointed by Napoleon as senator to the imperial senate, count of the First Empire, 1808, and grand-officier de la Legion d'Honneur. Died in Paris, 31 August 1811.

## References and Further Reading


Bougainville, Louis Antoine de, *Mémoire sur l'état de la Nouvelle France à l'époque de la guerre de Sept Ans*, 1756.

Bougainville, Louis Antoine de, *Mémoire sur les découvertes et établissements faits le long des côtes d'Afrique par Hannon, amiral de Carthage*, 1761.

Bougainville, Louis Antoine de, *Mémoires Divers sur le Canada*, 1762.

Bougainville, Louis Antoine de, *[Description d'un] Voyage autour du monde*, 2 vols., 1771; revised edition, 1772; edited by Jacques Proust, 1982; as *A Voyage round the World*, translated by John (Johann) Reinhold Forster, 1772.

Bougainville, Louis Antoine de, *Essai sur l'île de Tahiti, située dans la mer du Sud; et sur l'esprit et les moeurs de ses habitants*, 1779.

Bougainville, Louis Antoine de, *Essai Historique sur les navigations anciennes et modernes dans les plus hautes latitudes septentrionales*, 1801.

Bougainville, Louis Antoine de, *Adventure in the Wilderness: The American Journals of Louis Antoine de Bougainville, 1756–1760*, edited and translated by Edward P. Hamilton, 1964.

Bougainville, Louis Antoine de, *Écrits sur le Canada: mémoires-journal-lettres*, edited by Roland Lamontagne, 1993.

## BOUVIER, NICOLAS (1929–1998) *Swiss Travel Writer*

Nicolas Bouvier was born on 6 March 1929 in the village of Grand-Lancy near Geneva. His family was well known in academic circles in Geneva. His grandfather, Bernard Bouvier, had been rector of the University of Geneva and his father became university librarian. Bouvier's interest in traveling began early. At the age of 16 he went alone by train to Italy and stayed in Florence. This was not characteristic behavior for a teenager from his social background but he received the backing of his father who told him to travel to all the places he had never been to and tell him about it. This the young Bouvier did in his correspondence home. He was a prolific letter writer and the early missives were useful finger exercises for his later writings. He began to write short pieces for the prestigious Geneva newspaper *La Tribune* and in 1947, on the strength of his press card, traveled to Finland where he was particularly struck by the solitary beauty of Lapland. Bouvier decided to study Sanskrit and medieval history at the University of Geneva; though he finished his degree and had originally intended to do a Ph.D. in history on French and English responses to empire, his restlessness drew him away from the academic career that had been almost predestined by his family circumstances.

In June 1953, after finishing his final examinations he left Geneva in a Fiat Topolino intending to join his old schoolfriend, the artist Thierry Vernet, in Yugoslavia. The account of the journey, *L'Usage du monde* (1963), which ends with Bouvier alone in the Khyber Pass in December 1954, has become one of the classics of French travel writing in the twentieth century. The account is both a description of the peoples and cultures Bouvier meets en route to his ultimate destination in Afghanistan and also a reflection on the nature of the traveling itself. Travel is seen as a form of *enlightenment* but in a very particular sense of the word. The travel writer leaves behind the weight of the past, social background, cultural assumptions, and quotidian worries, and in a suitably purged state is then ready to absorb the polyphonic complexity of the world. As Bouvier observes in a typical passage in *L'Usage du monde*,

> Comme une eau, le monde vous traverse et pour un temps vous prête ses couleurs. Puis se retire, et vous replace devant ce vide qu'on porte en soi, devant cette espèce d'insuffisance centrale de l'âme qu'il faut bien apprendre à côtoyer, à combattre, et qui, paradoxalement, est peut-être notre moteur le plus sûr.

> Like water, the world passes through you and for a while you take on its colours. Then it ebbs away and you are faced again with the emptiness you carry inside, this kind of basic inadequacy of the soul that you have to learn to know and to fight against, and which, paradoxically, is perhaps our greatest driving force.

The lightness is a form of asceticism that involves both a concern with the physical labor of travel and an almost mystical attentiveness to the material presence of reality. Bouvier's writing from the beginning is haunted by a sense of physical and mental fragility that invests his experiences of moment and place with an almost visionary intensity. *L'Usage du monde* is not however a monument to meditative self-importance and the text is graced by a fine irony and an appreciation of laughter and humor as the coin of communication between people of very different linguistic and cultural backgrounds. Nine years elapsed after the trip before *L'Usage du monde* was published. Bouvier wrote slowly and was obsessed with establishing a perfect adequacy between words and things. Writerly scrupulousness was not the only reason for the tardy publication of the account. The early 1960s in the French-language publishing world were the heyday of the experimental novel, in particular, the *nouveau roman*. Travel writing as a genre seemed hopelessly antiquated in its commitment to a notion of the real and in its concern for narrative expressiveness. Publishers were not interested in new travel accounts and the book was finally published in 1963 at the author's expense. Even though the book was republished two years later, critical and public indifference to travel writing in the period led to many of the copies being pulped. Bouvier was bitterly disappointed by the initial reaction to his work. It was much later, in the late 1970s, with the reemergence of travel writing as an important literary genre in French, that Bouvier's work was hailed as a modern masterpiece and became a publishing success.

Bouvier traveled down through India in 1955 and eventually arrived in Ceylon (Sri Lanka). Exhausted by continuous travel and learning that his Swiss girlfriend wanted to leave him, Bouvier experienced nervous collapse. The account of this period in Ceylon is contained in *Le Poisson-scorpion* (1981), a text of remarkable, hallucinatory condensation. The descriptions of the turbulent insect life of his rented room are a mixture of lucid black humor and a tense, unnerving wretchedness. The darkness of his Ceylonese interlude was such that it was many years before Bouvier could bring himself to write about the traveler's island prison. Bouvier decided to head east and spent much of 1955–1956 in Japan. He eventually returned to Geneva but after the publication of his first travel account he decided to leave again for Japan in 1964. He traveled extensively in Japan in 1964 and 1965 and published an account in 1967 entitled simply *Japon*. He made further visits to Japan between 1966 and 1970 and *Japon* was republished with later Japanese travel pieces as *Chronique Japonaise* in 1975. The Japanese writings of Bouvier have a serenity that is absent from the earlier work and he was obviously fascinated by the coexistence of tradition and modernity in post war Japan. The Zen Buddhist celebration of frugality and paradox appealed to his own specific aesthetic sensibility but he was careful to avoid the kitsch Orientalism of Beat philosophy. Bouvier was continually attracted to extremities, to bare, windswept, forgotten places, which he preferred to visit in the empty winter months. In February 1985, he decided to stay on the largest of the three Aran islands, Inishmore, off the west coast of Ireland. *Journal d'Aran et d'autres lieux* (1990) contains the account of his period on Inishmore along with a number of other texts describing journeys to Japan, China, and Korea. On Inishmore, the elemental force of rain and wind coupled with the islanders' tales of the other world of fairy folk held his attention. It is the dramatic discontinuities rather than the nativist continuities in Irish history that perplex and fascinate the Swiss traveler.

In addition to his travel writing, Bouvier also published books on a variety of different subjects such as the history of Swiss French television, a biography of a family of Swiss photographers, and an account of folk art in Switzerland, and he was for years a professional photographer and collector of illustrations. The poetic sensibility evident in his travel accounts is also directly expressed in the anthology of his poems published in 1991 under the title *Le Dehors et le dedans* (revised edition 1997). Nicolas Bouvier died in his native Switzerland on 17 February 1998. He was intensely proud of the tradition of Swiss travel writing that included Platter, Paracelsus, Rousseau, Cingria, Eberhardt, and Cendrars. Nicolas Bouvier demonstrated magnificently in his own writing that Alpine claustrophobia was no obstacle but an invitation to an enthusiastic embrace of the worlds beyond the peaks.

MICHAEL CRONIN

### Biography

Born in Grand-Lancy, near Geneva, Switzerland, 6 March 1929. Traveled to Italy, 1945, and Finland, 1947. Studied law, literature, Sanskrit, and history at the University of Geneva, 1950–1954. Traveled from Switzerland to Afghanistan, 1953–1954. Traveled to India and Ceylon (Sri Lanka), 1955. Traveled in Eastern Europe and Asia with the painter Thierry Vernet, 1955–1956. Returned to Geneva, 1957. Married Eliane Petitpierre, 1958. Worked at various professions: photographer, broadcaster, collector of illustrations, tourist guide, lecturer. Returned to Japan, 1964–1965 and between 1966 and 1970. Travelled to the Aran Islands, Ireland, 1985. Died in Geneva, 17 February 1998.

### References and Further Reading

Bouvier, Nicolas, *L'Usage du monde*, 1963; as *The Way of the World*, translated by Robyn Marsack, with a foreword by Patrick Leigh Fermor, 1992.
Bouvier, Nicolas, *Japon*, 1967.
Bouvier, Nicolas, *Chronique Japonaise*, 1975; as *The Japanese Chronicles*, translated by Anne Dickerson, 1992.
Bouvier, Nicolas, *Le Poisson-scorpion*, 1981; as *The Scorpion-Fish*, translated by Robyn Marsack, 1987.
Bouvier, Nicolas, *Journal d'Aran et d'autres lieux*, 1990.

## BRAZIL

Travel writing on Brazil began with the accounts produced by European explorers and settlers at the beginning of the sixteenth century. The common objective was to document the flora, fauna, and inhabitants of the hitherto unknown land, exemplified by the descriptions given in the letters written by Amerigo Vespucci (1454–1512) and Pero Vaz de Caminha (c. 1449–1500). Full of wonder, they convey a vision of an earthly paradise. The later works of Pero de Magalhães Gândavo (dates unknown) and Gabriel Soares de Sousa (1540–1591) demonstrate how Portuguese accounts of their new colony became more detailed, scholarly, and systematic in the course of the sixteenth century, a process to which Jesuit missionaries such as José de Anchieta (1534–1597) and Manuel da Nóbrega (1517–1570) made an important contribution.

Travelers from other European countries also wrote informative accounts of sixteenth- and seventeenth-

How the wealthy got around in San Salvador: a hammock version of the sedan chair known as a *serpentin* (from A.F. Frézier, *Relation du voyage de la mer du sud aux côtes du Chily et du Perou fait pendant les années 1712, 1713 et 1714*, 1716). *Courtesy of the Travellers Club, London; Bridgeman Art Library, agent.*

century Brazil. The main interest of these works resides in their discussion of Indian life, about which there was great curiosity throughout Europe at the time. The account by Hans Staden, a German sailor, of his capture by Indians in 1552 caused a sensation in many European countries. Missionaries were the most important source of information about Indian culture, however. Colorful descriptions of the Indians of southern Brazil were written by the Franciscan friar Andrés Thevet (1502–1592), who spent only a few months in the country in 1555, and by the Protestant missionary Jean de Léry (1534–1613), whose account, published in 1578, is arguably the most detailed of the period. In addition to the substantial body of documentary writing left by these and other missionaries, such as Claude d'Abbeville (d. 1623) and Antony Sepp von Rechegg (1655–1733), there were chronicles of adventure produced by such travelers as Antony Knivet, who lived among Indians during part of an eight-year stay in Brazil, and William Davies, who briefly described his ten-week expedition to the Amazon as a slave on an Italian vessel in 1608.

European interest in the Brazilian Indian waned in the course of the seventeenth century, and travel writing focused increasingly on the economic and social life of different regions of the country. Richard Flecknoe's descriptions of Rio de Janeiro, where he spent six months in 1648, is a major example. The growing importance of the city as a port and political center is reflected in the large number of visitors it attracted in the eighteenth century, often as a stopover during a longer voyage. Among the most significant accounts of such visits were those by Louis de Bougainville (1729–1811), John White, and George Stauton, who all provided valuable details of the urban environment and its social activity. Descriptions of other parts of the country, albeit often brief, were written by other travelers, such as Major James Semple Lisle, who wrote about the far south, and the French scientist Charles-Marie de la Condamine (1701–1774), who described a journey along the Amazon River, with details of flora and fauna.

The nineteenth century was the most productive for travel writing on Brazil. Economic interest in the country was responsible for much of it, as the suppression of mercantilist controls and the growing awareness of commercial opportunities in Brazil encouraged overseas visitors. The largest number of resulting accounts were by British authors, one of whom, Thomas Ashe, used his description of life and customs to highlight commercial openings available to his fellow British merchants. Among those who produced more thorough documentation were John Mawe, whose stay in Brazil from 1808 to 1810 resulted in descriptions of such economic activities as mining, agriculture, and assorted handicrafts; Thomas Lindley, who was imprisoned in Salvador in the northeast for smuggling in 1802; and John Luccock (1770–1826), a Yorkshire merchant, whose ten-year residence in Brazil enabled him to give a detailed account of socioeconomic conditions. However, the most penetrating study in English of early-nineteenth-century Brazilian life was written by Henry Koster, who was born and brought up in Portugal and was fluent in Portuguese. Based on his travels in the northeast and his experience as a plantation owner there, Koster wrote a detailed record and carefully considered analysis of numerous aspects of life in the region.

Significant improvements to travel conditions and transport in the course of the century provided further incentive for visitors to Brazil. Some traveled widely in the country, such as the French botanist Auguste de Saint-Hilaire and the famous British explorer Richard Burton (1821–1890), who both produced extensive accounts that went beyond mere description to consider issues of society, culture, the economy, and the natural environment. Lengthy and detailed documents were produced on virtually every region. Robert Avé-Lallemant recounted his journeys through both the north and the south; George Gardner's writing, based on several years traveling, is particularly valuable for its descriptions of the interior; and the American pastor Daniel Kidder (1815–1891) described the many provinces he visited during his missionary work. As the century progressed, the contribution of women to this vast body of travel writing became increasingly important. The works by Maria Graham (1785–1842), Marion McMurrough Mulhall, and Marie Robinson are among the most notable examples. As might be expected, opinions of the country varied greatly. Some writers, like Charles Expilly, Carl Seidler, and John Codman were critical of Brazilian society, but others, such as Wolfgang Hoffmann-Harnisch, were impressed by the immense potential of the country.

Scientific expeditions provided the basis for many other nineteenth-century travel accounts. Two German scientists, Johann Baptist von Spix and Karl Friedrich Phillis von Martius, published one of the best known of such works between 1823 and 1831. Among the numerous naturalists who produced studies based on their travels were Louis and Elizabeth Agassiz, Henry Bates, Hermann Burmeister, William Edwards, Hercules Florence, Herbert Smith, and Alfred Russel Wallace (1823–1913). The works of many travel writers of the period concentrated on their own specialized interests, such as geography in the case of Elisée Reclus and Wilhelm Ludvig von Eschwege; ethnology in that of Prince Maximilian Wied-Neuwied and Karl von den Steinen; and social studies with Hastings Dent and Charles Ribeyrolles. Some texts were accompanied by valuable illustrations, the most notable example being the work of the artist Jean-Baptiste Debret (1768–1848), who, on his travels, painted or sketched landscapes, urban views, and scenes of daily life.

The production of travel writing on Brazil declined in the course of the twentieth century, particularly as documentary film became widely used to record events, patterns of life, and the natural environment. There were, however, some important accounts of adventurous expeditions undertaken in the early decades. The two best-known examples are Theodore Roosevelt's 1914 work *Through the Brazilian Wilderness*, recounting his participation in a hazardous journey along rivers in Mato Grosso and the Amazon, and Peter Fleming's *Brazilian Adventure* of 1933, a humorous account of his journey to solve the mystery of Colonel Percy Fawcett, who disappeared while exploring the interior of Brazil in 1925. At the same time, many well-known Brazilian writers recorded their travels to different regions of the country, inspired to explore its cultural diversity by the dynamism of the modernist movement that, from the 1920s to the 1940s, revolutionized all forms of national artistic expression. Among the writers involved were Ronald de Carvalho (1893–1935), Plínio Salgado (1895–1975), and, most notable of all, Mário de Andrade (1893–1945). Andrade's "ethnographic journeys" produced important studies of Brazilian folklore.

Travel narratives in the 1990s by such writers as Moritz Thomsen and Brian McPhee are an indication of the fascination that Brazil has continued to hold for foreign visitors. Much of the travel writing of this period has focused on specific issues, above all the threats facing the natural environment and the indigenous groups dependent upon it. One of the best examples is Stephen Nugent's *Big Mouth: The Amazon Speaks* (1990), which examines the stereotypical views of the Amazon that have become widely diffused, and discusses the environmental problems confronting the region.

MARK DINNEEN

### References and Further Reading


Agassiz, Louis and Elizabeth Agassiz, *A Journey in Brazil*, 1868; reprinted, 1969.

Anchieta, José de, *Cartas, informações, fragmentos históricose sermões*, edited by Afrânio Peixoto, 1933; reprinted, 1988.

Andrade, Mário de, *O turista aprendiz*, edited by Telê Porto Ancona Lopez, 1976.

Ashe, Thomas, *A Commercial View, and Geographical Sketch, of the Brasils in South America, and of the Island of Madeira*, 1812.

Avé-Lallemant, Robert, *Reise durch Sud-Brasilien im Jahre 1858*, 2 vols., 1859.

Avé-Lallemant, Robert, *Reise durch Nord-Brasilien im Jahre 1859*, 2 vols., 1860.

Bates, Henry Walter, *The Naturalist on the River Amazons*, 2 vols., 1863.

Bougainville, Louis de, *Voyage autour du monde*, 1771; as *A Voyage round the World*, translated by John Reinhold Forster, 1772; reprinted, 1967.

Burmeister, Hermann, *Reise nach Brasilien, durch die Provinzen von Rio de Janeiro und Minas Geraës*, 1853.

Burton, Richard F., *Explorations of the Highlands of the Brazil; with a Full Account of the Gold and Diamond Mines*, 2 vols., 1869.

Caminha, Pero Vaz de, *A carta de Pero Vaz de Caminha*, edited by Jaime Cortesão, 1943.

Claude, d'Abbeville, *Histoire de la mission des pères capucins en l'isle de Maragnan et terres circonvoisines ou et traicte des singularitez admirables et des meurs merueilleuses des indiens habitans de ce pays*, 1614.

Codman, John, *Ten Months in Brazil, with Incidents of Voyages and Travels, Descriptions of Scenery and Character, Notices of Commerce and Production*, 1867.

Davies, William, *A True Relation of the Travailes and Most Miserable Captivitie of William Davies, Barber-Surgion of London, under the Duke of Florence*, 1614.

Debret, Jean-Baptiste, *Voyage pittoresque et historique au Brésil*, 3 vols., 1834–1839.

Dent, Hastings Charles, *A Year in Brazil, with Notes on the Abolition of Slavery, the Finances of the Empire, Religion, Meteorology, Natural History, etc.*, 1886.

Durtain, Luc, *Imagens do Brasil e do Pampa*, translated by Ronald de Carvalho, 1933.

Edwards, William Henry, *A Voyage up the River Amazon, Including a Residence at Pará*, 1847.

Eschwege, Wilhelm Ludwig von, *Journal von Brasilien; oder, Vermischte Nachrichten aus Brasilien*, 2 vols., 1818.

Eschwege, Wilhelm Ludwig von, *Pluto Brasiliensis*, 1833.

Expilly, Charles, *Les Femmes et les moeurs du Brésil*, 1863.

Flecknoe, Richard, *A Relation of Ten Years Travels in Europe, Asia, Affrique and America*, 1654.

Fleming, Peter, *Brazilian Adventure*, 1933.

Florence, Hercules, *Voyage fluvial du Tieté à l'Amazone*, 1875.

Gândavo, Pero de Magalhães de, *Tratado da terra do Brasil*, written c. 1570.

Gândavo, Pero de Magalhães de, *História da Província de Santa Cruz a que vulgarmente chamamos Brasil*, 1576; as *The Histories of Brazil*, translated and edited by John B. Stetson, Jr., 2 vols., 1922.

Gardner, George, *Travels in the Interior of Brazil, Principally through the Northern Provinces, and the Gold and Diamond Districts, during the Years 1836–1841*, 1846; reprinted, 1973.

Graham, Maria, *Journal of a Voyage to Brazil, and Residence There, during Part of the Years 1821, 1822, 1823*, 1824; reprinted, 1969.

Hoffmann-Harnisch, Wolfgang, *Brasilien: Bildnis eines tropischen Grossreiches*, 1938.

Kidder, Daniel P., *Sketches of Residence and Travels in Brazil*, 2 vols., 1845.

Knivet, Anthony, *The Admirable Adventures and Strange Fortunes of Master Antonie Knivet, Which Went with Master Thomas Candish in His Second Voyage to the South Sea, 1591*, in *Purchas His Pilgrimes*, vol. 4, 1625.

Koster, Henry, *Travels in Brazil*, 1816.

La Condamine, Charles-Marie de, *Relation abrégée d'un voyage fait dans l'intérieur de l'Amérique Méridionale, depuis la côte de la Mer du Sud, jusqu'aux côtes du Brésil et de la Guyane, en descendant la rivière des Amazones*, 1745;

as *A Succinct Abridgment of a Voyage Made within the Inland Parts of South-America*, 1747.
Léry, Jean de, *Histoire d'un voyage fait en la terre du Brésil, autrement dite Amerique*, 1578; as *History of a Voyage to the Land of Brazil, Otherwise Called America*, translated by Janet Whatley, 1990.
Lindley, Thomas, *Narrative of a Voyage to Brasil: Terminating in the Seizure of a British Vessel, and the Imprisonment of the Author and the Ship's Crew by the Portuguese*, 1805.
Luccock, John, *Notes on Rio de Janeiro, and the Southern Parts of Brazil: Taken during a Residence of Ten Years in That Country, from 1808 to 1818*, 1820.
Mawe, John, *Travels in the Interior of Brazil, Particularly in the Gold and Diamond District of That Country*, 1812; 2nd edition, 1823.
McPhee, Brian, *Down the Nowhere River: A Brazilian Journey*, 1992.
Mulhall, Marion McMurrough, *Between the Amazon and Andes; or, Ten Years of a Lady's Travels in the Pampas, Gran Chaco, Paraguay and Matto Grosso*, 1881.
Nóbrega, Manuel da, *Cartas do Brasil (1549–1560)*, 1931; reprinted, 1988.
Nugent, Stephen, *Big Mouth: The Amazon Speaks*, 1990.
Reclus, Élisée, *Nouvelle Geógraphie universelle: La terre et les hommes*, vol. 19: *Amerique du Sud: l'Amazonie et la Plata*, 1894.
Ribeyrolles, Charles, *Brazil pittoresco*, 1859.
Roosevelt, Theodore, *Through the Brazilian Wilderness*, 1914.
Saint-Hilaire, Auguste de, *Voyages dans l'intérieur du Brésil*, 8 vols., 1830–1851.
Salgado, Plínio, *Geographía sentimental*, 1937.
Seidler, Carl, *Zehn Jahre in Brasilien während der Regierung Dom Pedro's und nach dessen Entthronung*, 2 vols., 1835.
Semple Lisle, James George, *The Life of Major J.G. Semple Lisle, Containing a Faithful Narrative of His Alternate Vicissitudes of Splendor and Misfortune*, 1799.
Sepp von Reinegg, Anton, *RR. PP. Antonii Sepp und Antonii Böhm . . . Reissbeschreibung, wie dieselbe aus Hispanien in Paraquariam kommen*, 1697; as *An Account of a Voyage from Spain to Paraquaria*, in *A Collection of Voyages and Travels*, edited by Awnsham Churchill, vol. 4, 1704.
Smith, Herbert H., *Brazil, the Amazons and the Coast*, 1879.
Sousa, Gabriel Soares de, *Tratado descritivo do Brasil em 1587*, edited by Francisco Adolfo de Varnhagen, 4th edition, 1971.
Spix, Johann Baptist von, and Carl Friedrich Philipp von Martius, *Reise in Brasilien in den Jahren 1817–1820*, 3 vols., 1823–1831; partial translation, as *Travels in Brazil in the Years 1817–1820*, translated by H.E. Lloyd, 2 vols., 1824.
Staden, Hans, *Warhaftige Historia und Beschreibung eyner Landtschafft der Wilden, Nacketen, Grimmigen Menschfresser Leuthen, in der Newenwelt America gelegen*, 1557; facsimile, 1925; as *Hans Staden: The True History of His Captivity, 1557*, translated and edited by Malcolm Letts, 1928.
Staunton, George, *An Authentic Account of an Embassy from the King of Great Britain to the Emperor of China*, 3 vols., 1797.
Steinen, Karl von den, *Durch Central-Brasilien*, 1886.
Steinen, Karl von den, *Unter den Naturvölkern Zentral-Brasiliens*, 1894.
Thevet, André, *Les Singularitez de la France antarctique, autrement nommée Amerique, et de plusieurs terres et isles découvertes de notre temps*, 1558; as *The New Found Worlde; or, Antarctike*, translated by Thomas Hacket, 1568, facsimile, 1971.
Thomsen, Moritz, *The Saddest Pleasure: A Journey on Two Rivers*, 1991.
Vespucci, Amerigo, letters to Lorenzo di Pier Francesco de' Medici, 1500 and 1502; in *The Letters of Amerigo Vespucci and Other Documents Illustrative of His Career*, translated by Clements R. Markham, 1894.
Wallace, Alfred Russel, *A Narrative of Travels on the Amazon and Rio Negro*, 1853; 2nd edition, 1889; reprinted, 1969.
White, John, *Journal of a Voyage to New South Wales*, 1790.
Wied-Neuwied, Prince Maximilian of, *Reise nach Brasilien in den Jahren 1815 bis 1817*, 2 vols., 1820–1821; as *Travels in Brazil, in the Years 1815, 1816, and 1817*, 1820.
Wright, Marie Robinson, *The New Brazil: Its Resources and Attractions*, 1901; 2nd edition, 1907.

*See also* **Amazon River**

## BRITO, BERNARDO GOMES DE (1688–c. 1759) *Portuguese Bibliophile*

A dedicated bibliophile gifted with a good memory and intelligence that compensated for his lack of scholarly education, Brito is mainly famous for his collection of reports of disasters that happened to Portuguese ships, the *História trágico-marítima, em que se escrevem cronologicamente os naufrágios que tiveram as naus de Portugal, depois que se pôs em exercício a navegação da Índia* [Tragic-Maritime History, wherein Are Written Chronologically the Shipwrecks That Happened to Portuguese Vessels, after the Navigation to India was Established]. Covering half a century of Portuguese nautical experiences (from 1552 to 1602), it is probably the first important work describing, in a direct and poignant way, the extremes of human tragedy on the seas. Although at times lacking in scientific precision, Brito's work is a compilation of realistic descriptions from survivors who had witnessed the most appalling conditions of suffering. These accounts, bare of any stylistic or literary apparatus, were obtained through oral transmission or copied from manuscript sources, which were abundant at the time. The *História trágico-marítima* is a document of precious historical value, particularly in connection with Portuguese maritime expansion. According to Diogo Barbosa de Machado, Bernardo Gomes de Brito prepared the *História* in five volumes, of which only two appeared (1735 and 1736). He also wrote two other works: *Virtudes pelas acções dos Portugueses obradas em todas as quatro partes do mundo autorizadas por vários Autores Portugueses* and *Sentenças, Máximas, e Apotegmas morais, e políticos escritos por Lugares-comuns*. Brito was apparently still alive when Machado published his *Biblioteca Lusitana*, in 1759.

PATRICIA LOPES BASTOS

### References and Further Reading

Brito, Bernardo Gomes de, *História trágico-marítima, em que se escrevem chronologicamente os naufrágios que tiveram as naus de Portugal, depois que se pôs em exercício a navegação da Índia*, 2 vols., 1735–1736; edited by António Sérgio, 3 vols., 1956–1957; as *The Tragic History of the Sea, 1589–1622: Narratives of the Shipwrecks of the Portuguese East Indiamen* São Thomé *(1589)*, Santo Alberto *(1593)*, São João Baptista *(1622) and the Journeys of the Survivors in South East Africa*, edited by C.R. Boxer, 1959; *Further Selections from the Tragic History of the Sea, 1559–1565: Narratives of the Shipwrecks of the Portuguese East Indiamen* Aguia *and* Garça *(1559)*, São Paulo *(1561) and the Misadventures of the Brazil-ship* Santo Antonio *(1565)*, edited and translated by C.R. Boxer, 1968.

*See also* **História Trágico-Marítima**

## BROOKE, ARTHUR DE CAPELL (1791–1858) *British Landowner and Traveler*

Sir Arthur de Capell Brooke is largely forgotten today, except, perhaps, among specialists in the history of travel, devotees of the British watercolor tradition, and historians of nineteenth-century Sweden, Norway, Finland, Spain, or Morocco. Yet the popularity and cultural influence of his books long outlasted his own lifetime. Indeed, for readers of English seeking information on the countries that Brooke visited, there were few accessible alternatives until after the expansion of mass travel following World War II had begun to generate writers, and readers, of new guidebooks and travel memoirs, describing lands that had once seemed physically and/or culturally remote from western Europe. Thus, as recently as 1952, nearly 100 years after Brooke's death, Frank Stagg cited Brooke as one among just five non-Norwegian sources on north Norway, preceded chronologically only by an Italian (Giuseppe or Joseph Acerbi) and a Prussian (Leopold von Buch).

However, now that the transition from travel as rare adventure to travel as mass experience has been completed, at least in western Europe and North America, Brooke and his writings have receded into a past that in many ways seems as remote from the early twenty-first century as northern Scandinavia, Spain, and Morocco must have seemed to his first readers. Brooke himself can appear to be almost a stereotype, if not an unconscious parody, of the nineteenth-century gentleman traveler. He was the eldest son and heir of a landowning baronet from the English Midlands; the proud possessor of detailed genealogies linking him to William the Conqueror, Henry III, and Richard II; the holder of an Oxford M.A. and of an army commission; a diligent recorder and sketcher of foreign lands, who left the Travellers Club because he thought, somewhat pompously, that too many of its members had not done enough traveling; the absentee landlord of an estate in Ireland; deputy lord lieutenant and sheriff of the county that contained the largest of his inherited estates; and an enthusiastic president of his tenants' cricket club.

Brooke deserves attention in particular for his three volumes on Scandinavia. His first two books, *Travels through Sweden, Norway, and Finmark* [sic] (1823) and *A Winter in Lapland and Sweden* (1827) form an account of his voyage by sea around the coast of Finnmark (northern Norway), and then overland into Sweden and Finland. (Finland was then a grand duchy ruled by the Russian emperor, hence Brooke's slightly startling references to "Russia.") The entry on Brooke in *The Dictionary of National Biography* attributes the books' success to their containing "much which at the time had the interest of novelty." Up to a point. Even in the 1820s, the many passages packed with evocations of the wonders of Nature and the primitiveness of the inhabitants, and, a fortiori, of Lapp (Sami) reindeer herders, must have seemed fairly familiar exercises to those living in the Romantic era. Nevertheless both books succeed in conveying some of the sense of wonder that Brooke felt at seeing the aurora borealis, experiencing the effects of the midnight sun, and gazing, uncomprehendingly but not wholly without sympathy, on the harsh lives and alien customs of Scandinavians. Nor is all the humor in them unintended. For example, it seems clear that Brooke himself was amused by the fact that, while he heard several accounts of sea serpents, both from people "of superior rank and education" and from "honest and artless" fisherfolk, he never saw for himself any evidence that they existed. Above all, perhaps, his own "honest and artless" watercolors of scenes in these northern climes, published in a third volume, *Winter Sketches in Lapland* (1827), are charming and, apparently, reliable records of ways of life that have largely vanished, as wooden shacks, reindeer-drawn sleds, and traditional costumes make way for manufactured products even beyond the Arctic Circle.

Similar strengths and weaknesses mark Brooke's last volume of travel writing (and painting), his *Sketches in Spain and Morocco* (1831). This appears to have had less commercial success than the earlier volumes, presumably because Spain and, to a lesser extent, Morocco were already better known to British readers than Lapland was. Here, even more than in his earlier books, Brooke concentrates his attention on landscapes and buildings, and deftly but somewhat routinely sketches his impressions of them in prose and in paint, while doing little to evoke the people of either country beyond repeating familiar stereotypes about hot blood, passionate natures, and the deadening effects (as he saw them) of Catholicism and Islam respectively. As a Protestant gentleman and an officer in His Majesty's army, Brooke clearly found it very difficult to take either of these "exotic" cultures on their own terms. Thus, if Brooke deserves a monument at all, it lies in the words and pictures with which he described Norway, Sweden, and Finland, and made these countries intriguing to generations of readers.

PATRICK HEENAN

### Biography

Born in Mayfair, London, 22 October 1791. Attended Magdalen College, Oxford: B.A., 1813; M.A., 1816. Entered army; reached rank of major by 1846. Traveled in Sweden, Norway, Spain, and Morocco from 1820 on; published four books of writings and watercolor sketches based on his travels, 1823–1831. Founding member of the Travellers Club, but resigned from it and became founding president of the Raleigh Club (later absorbed into the Royal Geographical Society), 1821; also a member of the Royal Society and the Royal Geographical Society. Succeeded to baronetcy, incumbency of the Great Oakley estate near Corby, Northamptonshire, and absentee ownership of the Ahadoe estate near Killeagh, County Cork, 1829. President of the Great Oakley Cricket Club; deputy lord lieutenant and sheriff of Northamptonshire. Married the widow of another landowner, J.J. Eyre, 1851. Died in 1858.

### References and Further Reading

Brooke, Arthur de Capell, *Travels through Sweden, Norway, and Finmark* [sic] *to the North Cape, in the Summer of 1820*, 1823.

Brooke, Arthur de Capell, *A Winter in Lapland and Sweden, with Various Observations Relating to Finmark* [sic] *and Its Inhabitants Made during a Residence at Hammerfest, near the North Cape*, 1826.

Brooke, Arthur de Capell, *Winter Sketches in Lapland, or Illustrations of a Journey from Alten, on the Shores of the Polar Sea, in 69 Degrees 55 Minutes North Latitude, through Norwegian, Russian* [sic], *and Swedish Lapland to Tornea, at the Entrance to the Gulf of Bothnia, Intended to Exhibit a Complete View of the Mode of Travelling with Reindeer, the Most Striking Incidents That Occurred during the Journey, and the General Character of the Scenery of Lapland and Sweden*, 1827.

Brooke, Arthur de Capell, *Sketches in Spain and Morocco*, 2 vols., 1831.

## BRUCE, JAMES (1730–1794) *British Traveler*

If Captain Cook was the first truly modern "scientific" maritime explorer, James Bruce has some claim to be the first scientific continental explorer. When he set out in 1768, his object was to establish the position of the source of the Nile for the sake of advancing knowledge. He did reach the source of the Blue Nile and provided a wealth of other geographical, botanical, and archaeological information on Ethiopia and the Nile Valley as well as gaining a unique knowledge of the Ethiopians as a result of his close involvement with them for two years.

Yet neither in his lifetime nor later did Bruce receive the respect and veneration accorded to Cook. This is partly because the quality of his astronomical observations and of his other scientific work has been overshadowed by controversies about his Ethiopian reports. Bruce was not an official explorer like Cook but a private traveler relying on the wealth created by coal mining on his Stirlingshire estate. Since Ethiopia has only intermittently been a principal object of British strategic interest, retrospective endorsement as a precursor of empire never followed for Bruce as it did with certain other travelers. Most important, perhaps, is the fact that his principal geographical discovery was really a rediscovery for the Western world of something that the Spanish Jesuit Pero Paez had established in 1613 and which, in any case, did not solve the problem of the ultimate source of the Nile. Bruce erred badly in trying to discredit what Paez and other priests had achieved in Ethiopia some 150 years before—Dr. Samuel Johnson exerted his great influence against him for this reason. Educated in England, Bruce was not really a product of the Scottish Enlightenment and so found few supporters even in his home country when he retreated to his estate in 1776.

All this said, it is nevertheless incorrect to assume, as does a recent biographer, that Bruce has remained unknown and unappreciated since his death. On the contrary, his standing has steadily become greater. Already well received and respected in France and in German-speaking Europe, Bruce was to have splendid second and third editions of his *Travels* produced in 1805 and 1813. Abridgments and summaries of his work have remained in print since 1790 and there have been a number of biographies, while historians of travel and of Africa have made regular reference to him.

Neither the existing biographies and studies of Bruce nor any of the shortened editions of his travel writing make any use of unpublished materials; a modern edition of his records is badly needed. Until that comes, it is on the basis of the published *Travels* that Bruce's importance must be assessed. His own 1790 effort is a delight to handle and read. The engravings are superb. His pomposity can be forgiven. Employed, as he said, "in the noblest of all occupations, that of exploring distant parts of the Globe" for its own sake and making it his principle "not that all men are equal, but that they are all brethren," Bruce was able to "set the example of mildness" in all his dealings with people as he proceeded from the Barbary Coast, in a series of adventurous journeys to the Abyssinian highlands via the Red Sea and Massawa. He was to return by an arduous route down the Nile Valley. The narrative of these journeys in the 1790 volumes has its faults: It is rather ill organized, being mixed up with a history of Ethiopia and disquisitions short and long on a variety of subjects. Bruce fails to acknowledge the contributions of his companion, Luigi Balugani, who ought at least to share the credit for the depictions of people, animals, and buildings. Above all, it is clear that what Bruce in retrospect wished he had said and done must often have been substituted for what actually did happen; his orotund speeches at moments of crisis, presumably in languages not his own, are simply not believable, however enjoyable to read. Having said this, one must immediately add that all the evidence, both internal, and, as far as that is possible, from independent sources, suggests that Bruce did not distort the truth in more fundamental ways. His real stature as a remarkable actor in the dramas he described, as well as an indispensable source of information on northern Africa, becomes clearer in the editions of his *Travels* in eight volumes of 1804–1805, which were edited by Alexander Murray on the basis of Bruce's own records and correspondence; they also incorporated a life by another considerable traveler in northeast Africa, Henry Salt. The publishing history of these volumes is complicated and they remain as difficult to acquire as the 1790 volumes. Although there are many later abridgments and summaries, the ordinary reader may well find the best way to sample Bruce is to use the 1964 selection from the 1804–1805 edition made by Beckingham, which concentrates on Ethiopia and also contains a useful short life.

What Bruce provides is a fundamentally accurate picture of the political and social situation in Ethiopia with its then intolerant church, its weak monarchy, and its powerful warlord regional rulers, especially Ras Michael of Tigre. The effects on the ancient empire of the surrounding Muslim peoples and of the Oromo ("Galla") people encroaching from the south are all apparent. Descriptions of how Ethiopians cut steaks from living cattle intrigue now as much as they were disbelieved in London in 1774. But it is Bruce himself who most attracts the reader. Large, brave, and apparently irrepressible whatever his difficulties, he could fire a tallow candle through a wooden table, break in a horse, or seduce a beautiful woman as the situation might require. His sexual conquests seem to have included Ras Michael's wife, the Queen Mother, and the beautiful princess Esther Ozoro. In this respect and others, he was fully integrated into the upper ranks of Ethiopian society and it is this that makes his account so compelling both for the historian and the general reader. The pleasure and profit obtained leads one to forgive Bruce his boasts about the Nile source and allow him his moment of glory "standing in that spot which had baffled the genius, industry and inquiry of both ancients and moderns, for the course of near three thousand years."

Bruce's India-ink drawing of the aqueduct at Cherchell in Algeria (reproduced in Playfair's *Travels in the Footsteps of Bruce*, 1877). *Courtesy of the Travellers Club, London; Bridgeman Art Library, agent.*

ROY BRIDGES

## Biography

Born at Kinnaird, Stirlingshire, Scotland, 14 December 1730. Attended Harrow School; later studied for the bar. Married Adriana Allan, daughter of a Scottish wine merchant, in 1754 and traveled to Spain and Portugal to inspect vintages. She died of tuberculosis in France, nine months after the marriage, 1754. Gave up wine business and devoted himself to travel in North Africa and Italy. Recruited Luigi Balugani as artistic assistant, studied Eastern history and languages, including Ge'ez and Arabic, and practiced architectural drawing. Consul in Algiers, 1763–1765; traveled widely in North Africa, Crete, and Syria, 1765–1768; reached Egypt, July 1768. Sailed along the Red Sea to Massawa, September 1769, and marched inland, reaching Gondar, February 1770. Associated with Ras Michael, ruler of Tigre. At the second attempt reached the source of the Blue Nile, south of Lake Tana, 14 November 1770. Traced the Blue Nile to the confluence with the White, crossed the Nubian desert, and reached Egypt in 1772. Traveled on to Marseilles, France, 1773; well-received there. Returned to London and to disbelief about his accounts of Ethiopia, 1774. Elected a fellow of the Royal Society. Retreated to his estate in Kinnaird; married Mary Dundas, May 1776 (died 1785). Prepared his travel writing for publication, 1785–1790. Died after a fall in Kinnaird, 27 April 1794.

### References and Further Reading

Bruce, James, *Travels to Discover the Source of the Nile in the Years 1768, 1769, 1770, 1771, 1772 and 1773*, 5 vols., 1790; 2nd edition, corrected and enlarged and edited by Alexander Murray with a life of Bruce by Henry Salt, 8 vols., 1804–1805; 3rd edition, 8 vols., 1813; abridged as *Travels to Discover the Source of the Nile*, selected and edited with an introduction by C.F. Beckingham, 1964.

## BRUIJN, CORNELIS DE (c. 1652–c. 1727)

### *Dutch Traveler and Painter*

Cornelis de Bruijn was born in The Hague. Of his early years not much is known, nor of his family background. The best sources for de Bruijn's life are his own two travel books.

In his youth he took painting and drawing lessons from Theodoor van der Schuer. If we may believe de Bruijn himself, he took these lessons because he wished to travel to foreign countries and there to paint and draw. In 1674, he embarked on his first long journey, traveling to Rome where he arrived at the end of the year. In Rome he became a member of the so-called Bentveughels, a society of Dutch and Flemish painters, who were notorious for their eating and drinking bouts. After 18 months in the Eternal City, he lived for some time in Livorno. There he apparently decided not to return to the Netherlands, but to prolong his journey in order to visit the Levant. In the summer of 1678, he arrived in Izmir (Smyrna) where he lived—interrupted by a stay of more than a year in Constantinople—until the beginning of 1681 when he sailed to Egypt, where he visited Cairo, Saqqara, and Alexandria. From Egypt he traveled on to Palestine. In the summer he went via Jaffa to Jerusalem and Bethlehem. He spent the winter months in Tripoli. In the spring of 1682 he traveled to Acre in order to visit Nazareth, Lake Tiberias, and Mount Tabor. In May of the same year he went to Aleppo, where he was to stay for almost a year. He intended to visit the ruins of Palmyra, but predatory Arab Bedouin prevented the realization of this plan. In April 1683, he embarked for Cyprus; from there he sailed to Antalya and traveled back by land—a highly unusual route—to Izmir. In October 1684, de Bruijn left Ottoman territory for Venice, where he lived for another eight years improving his painting skills as an apprentice of Carlo Loth. In March 1693, de Bruijn was back in The Hague.

The numerous drawings, watercolors, and paintings of ancient monuments, peoples, plants, animals, and cities that de Bruijn had made on the spot and brought back with him excited much admiration. Consequently, de Bruijn decided to publish, at his own financial risk, an itinerary of his travels illustrated with more than two hundred engravings. In 1698, *Reizen . . . door de vermaardste Deelen van Klein Asia* (*A Voyage to the Levant*) appeared. The book was a great success and was soon followed by translations into French (1700) and English (1702). In addition to his own notes, for the text of the itinerary de Bruijn used the work of other travelers, especially Jean de Thévenot, author of the *Voyage au Levant* (1664). De Bruijn carried with him on his journey Thévenot's itinerary as well as that of Pietro della Valle (1650). In the last months of 1700, de Bruijn traveled to England, possibly to discuss the publication of an English edition of his work.

In the summer of 1701, de Bruijn began his second great journey. By ship he traveled to Archangel and from there by sled to Moscow, where he arrived in February 1702. Letters of introduction from Nicolaas Witsen, merchant and mayor of Amsterdam, gave him access to Peter the Great, whom he met on several occasions. The czar admired de Bruijn's work and commissioned him to paint portraits of the royal nieces. In April 1703, de Bruijn left Moscow and, sailing down the Volga and across the Caspian Sea, arrived in November 1703 in Isfahan. After nearly a year there, he went on to Persepolis. He remained for nearly three months at this ancient Achaemenid palace complex in order to draw and describe the ruins most accurately; he inscribed his signature (still visible) on one of the monuments. From Persia he continued his travels by way of Bandar Abbas and Sri Lanka to Batavia (Jakarta), in the Dutch Indies, where he arrived in February 1706. In August of the same year, he returned home by the same route as that of his outward journey.

Back in the Netherlands in October 1708, de Bruijn immediately started preparations for his *Reizen over Moskovie* [*Travels into Moscovy*], which was published in 1711 and which was, like the earlier volume, beautifully illustrated with some 300 engravings. A French translation appeared in 1718 and an English one in 1720. The significance of de Bruijn's travel books lies in the fact that his descriptions and especially his drawings are very accurate compared to others of the same era. De Bruijn himself remarks that he had "made it an indispensable Law to my self, not to deviate in any respect from the Truth." His works greatly added to the European knowledge of foreign peoples, flora and fauna, and ancient monuments (especially Persepolis). A discussion with Gisbert Cuper, who had observed great differences between de Bruijn's description and drawings of Persepolis and those given in the recently published accounts by Jean Chardin and Engelbert Kaempfer, induced de Bruijn in 1714 to publish an apologetic work entitled *Aenmerkingen* [Remarks].

It is not known exactly how de Bruijn financed his travels. He was not a wealthy man and he does not

Among more usual exotica, Bernard Picart's frontispiece to de Bruijn's *Voyages* features one of the Achaemenid monuments at Persepolis, drawn by de Bruijn in 1704 (from [Corneille Le Brun], *Voyages . . . par le Muscovie, en Perse, et aux Indes Orientales*, first French edition, 1718). *Courtesy of the Travellers Club, London; Bridgeman Art Library, agent.*

seem to have had a Maecenas. He probably acquired the money from the sale of his paintings and drawings, as well as of antiquities and curiosities that he had assembled en route. The sale of his travel books must also have been a source of income. Nonetheless, de Bruijn's final years were fraught with hardship and he seems to have died a poor and lonely man at Zydebaelen, the estate near Utrecht of his protector David van Mollem.

During the eighteenth century de Bruijn's travel books were much appreciated and were reprinted several times. From the nineteenth century onwards interest in his work declined. Of the many drawings and paintings made by de Bruijn, only a very few have survived. The library of the University of Amsterdam possesses a unique edition of *Voyage au Levant* (1700), with engravings printed in color. The Rijksmuseum in Amsterdam has a portrait of de Bruijn painted by his friend Sir Godfrey Kneller.

JAN WILLEM DRIJVERS

### Biography

Born in The Hague, Netherlands, c. 1652. Learned painting and drawing from Theodoor van der Schuer. Traveled to Italy, settling in Rome, 1674–1676, and Livorno, 1677–1678. Traveled in Turkey, Rhodes, Egypt, Palestine, Syria, Cyprus, 1678–1684. Lived in Venice; apprenticed to the painter Carlo Loth, 1684–1692. Returned to The Hague, 1693; prepared and published first travel book, 1693–1698. Traveled to England, 1700–1701. Traveled to Moscow and through Russia, 1701–1703. Journeyed from Moscow to Persia; visited Isfahan and Persepolis, 1703–1705. Went to Batavia (Jakarta), 1706. Made return journey to the Netherlands, 1706–1708. Lived in the Netherlands in increasing poverty, from 1708 until his death. Published second travel book, 1711. Died at Zydebaelen, near Utrecht, c. 1727.

### References and Further Reading

Bruijn, Cornelis de, *Reizen van Cornelis de Bruyn, door de vermaardste Deelen van Klein Asia, de eylanden Scio, Rhodus, Cyprus, Metelino, Stanchio, etc. mitsgaders de voornaamste steden van Aegypten, Syrien en Palestina, verrijkt met meer als 200 kopere konstplaaten, vertoonende de beroemdste Landschappen, Steden, etc. alles door den auteur selfs na het leven afgetekend*, 1698; as *Voyage au Levant*, 1700; as *A Voyage to the Levant; or, Travels in the Principal Parts of Asia Minor . . .* , translated by J.W. London, 1702.

Bruijn, Cornelis de, *Reizen over Moskovie, door Persie en Indie: Verrykt met Driehondert konstplaten, Vertoonende De beroemdste lantschappen en steden, ook de byzondere dragten, beesten, gewassen en planten, die daer gevonden worden: Voor al derzelver oudheden En wel voornamentlyk heel uitvoerig, die van het heerlyke en van oudts de geheele werrelt door befaemde Hof van Persepolis, By de Persianen Tchilminar genaemt*, 1711.

Bruijn, Cornelis de, *Aenmerkingen Over de Printverbeeldingen van de Overblyfzelen van het Oude Persepolis. Onlangs uitgegeven door de Heeren Chardin en Kempfer, waer in derzelver mistekeningen en gebreken klaer worden aengewezen, door Cornelis de Bruin*, 1714.

Bruijn, Cornelis de, *Voyages de Corneille le Brun par la Moscovie, en Perse, et aux Indes Orientales . . . On y a ajouté la route qu'a suivie Mr. Isbrants, Ambassadeur de Moscovie, en traversant la Russie & la Tartarie, pour se rendre à la Chine. Et quelques remarques contre Mrs. Chardin & Kempfer. Avec une lettre écrite à l'Auteur, sur ce sujet*, 2 vols., 1718; translated as *Travels into Muscovy, Persia, and the East-Indies*, 2 vols., 1737.

## BRY, THEODORE DE (1528–1598) *Flemish Illustrator and Engraver*

Theodore de Bry was an engraver, printmaker, publisher, and goldsmith. Trained in Liège as a goldsmith and engraver, he was known (under the name Dietrich Brey) as a goldsmith in Strasbourg, where in 1560 he married Catherine Esslinger (d. 1570). He returned to Liège in 1561, where his eldest son, Johann Theodore de Bry, was born, but because of his Lutheran religious convictions de Bry left Liège again to establish citizenship in Strasbourg, where he lived from 1570 to c. 1586 and where his second son, Johann Israel de Bry (c. 1570–1611), was born. While there he came under the stylistic influence of the Parisian Huguenot Étienne Delaune, who had fled to Strasbourg in 1572. De Bry was married a second time, in 1570, to Catherine, daughter of the Frankfurt goldsmith Hans Rotlinger.

In 1588, the de Bry household moved permanently to Frankfurt while Theodore was in England (c. 1586–1589). He twice visited London, where he executed such works as 12 plates for *The Procession of the Knights of the Garter* and another 34 plates for *The Funeral of Sir Philip Sidney*. He also met the English geographer Richard Hakluyt, with whose assistance he collected materials for a finely illustrated collection of accounts of voyages and travels, *Collectiones peregrinationum in Indiam orientalem et Indiam occidentalem* (1590–1634), which was continued by his sons Johann Theodore and Johann Israel but not completed until 1634 by Matthäus Merian the Elder. Johann Theodore de Bry (1561–1623) was also trained as an engraver, etcher, printmaker, and publisher. He was a prolific printmaker and with his father and brother published two popular emblem books: *Emblemata nobilitate et vulgo scitu digna* (1593) and *Emblemata secularia* (1611).

Among the other works that the elder de Bry engraved is a set of plates illustrating Thomas Harriot's *A Briefe and True Report of the New Found Land of Virginia* (1590), making engraved copies after the watercolors of John White. These, with his copies after similar works by Jacques Le Moyne de Morgues, are among his best-known engravings and were used as illustrations in the ten volumes of American travel literature, the *Grands Voyages*, as well as the *Petits Voyages* (15 volumes) concerning Africa and Asia, that he and his sons published (Frankfurt am Main, 1590–1634). The *Grands Voyages* were a compilation of Girolamo Benzoni's *Historia del Nuevo Mundo* (1565), Thomas Harriot's *Briefe and True Report of the New Found Land of Virginia* and later accounts of the Virginia colony, the *Warhaftige Historia* (1557) of Hans Staden, Walter Ralegh's *Discoverie of Guiana* (1596), and Dutch accounts of voyages via the Straits of Magellan. These engravings and their accompanying texts were the medium through which many Europeans first came to view the peoples and landscapes of America.

De Bry also published a series of portraits, including Gerard Mercator (1512–1594) and Copernicus (1473–1543), engraved after drawings by Jean-Jacques Boissard (*Icones quinquaginta vivorum illustrium doctrine et eruditione praestantium ad vivum effectae*, Frankfurt-am-Main, 1597–1599). However, he is best known for his series of volumes chronicling many of the earliest expeditions to the Americas. De Bry, as a Lutheran, emphasized the cruelty of the Spanish conquerors toward the natives they encountered and likewise stressed the presence of other European nations in the New World through his presentation of their exploits in Virginia, Orinoco, Brazil, and the southern tip of the continent. Moreover, although his compilation was extensive and painstaking de Bry necessarily altered and distorted the visual materials he copied and for which the compilation is chiefly known. For example, there are significant differences between the illustrations that de Bry made to represent Brazilian cannibalism and the original woodcuts that appeared in Staden's account. It is arguable that he gave a much more negative and misogynist emphasis to Tupian ritual than was reported by Staden (Whitehead, 2000). Equally, in cases where there were no preexisting visual depictions, such as Raleigh's account of his voyage to Guiana, de Bry inferred or invented scenes to accompany the text. The epistemological status of the various illustrations to the volumes therefore varies considerably: some may be considered relatively faithful reworkings of eyewitness depictions, others represent reinterpretations of such depictions, while still others are attempts to render visually observations reported in text only. Therefore, despite the popularity and historical significance of the images, they must be treated carefully and their relation to original source materials critically assessed. One consequence of de Bry's personal ignorance of the scenes he portrays is that there is a marked tendency toward a generic representation of native peoples—the same feathered crowns and tasteful loin coverings may be viewed from North to South America without regard to the differences in materials, culture, and display that in fact existed. So too in lieu of knowledge of American landscape the backgrounds seem often redolent of European landscape, as is the case for the flora and fauna. Nevertheless the de Bry enterprise was not one of falsification, and it is clear that close attention was paid to the textual descriptions of manner, customs, and appearance. In this way de Bry certainly raised the level of depiction to a new standard and the copperplate engravings may be enjoyed in their own right, not just as reflections of vanished worlds.

De Bry's version of the meeting of Cortés and Montezuma highlights the dramatic contrast between the tight-packed ranks of the Spanish troops and the relaxed procession of near-naked Indians (engraving from de Bry's German edition of Las Casas's *Brevissima Relacion de la Destruycion de las Indias*, 1597). *Courtesy of British Library, London.*

NEIL L. WHITEHEAD

### Biography

Born in Liège (now in Belgium), 1528. Trained in Liège as a goldsmith and engraver. Worked as a goldsmith in Strasbourg, returning to Liège, 1561. Married Catherine Esslinger (d. 1570), 1560; two sons, Johann Theodore, born 1561, and Johann Israel, born before 1570, both of whom continued his travel publishing enterprises after his death. Escaped religious persecution by the Spanish and settled in Strasbourg, 1570. Worked as a goldsmith, under the name Dietrich de Brey, until 1578. While there came under the stylistic influence of the Parisian Huguenot Étienne Delaune, who had fled to Strasbourg in 1572. Married Catherine, daughter of the Frankfurt goldsmith Hans Rotlinger,

1570. Traveled to England, c. 1586–1589; met Richard Hakluyt and worked with him on collecting materials for his publications. Moved to Frankfurt-am-Main, 1588; established a printing and publishing business there. Died in Frankfurt, 27 March 1598.

### References and Further Reading

*Collectiones peregrinationum in Indiam orientalem et Indiam occidentalem*, 25 vols., 1590–1634; as *Americae, 1590–1634*, edited by Gereon Sievernich, 1990.

Whitehead, Neil L., "Hans Staden & the Cultural Politics of Cannibalism," *Hispanic American Historical Review*, 80/4, 2000: 721–751.

*See also* **Collections of Literature of Travel and Exploration, Anthologies; New World Chronicles**

## BUCCANEER NARRATIVES

The buccaneers were essentially pirates who preyed on Spanish ships and settlements in the Caribbean, and along the Pacific littoral of South America, during the latter half of the seventeenth century. At intervals they received tacit approval in England as instruments of unofficial foreign policy toward Spain. The buccaneers' antecedents were the English, French, and Dutch interlopers who infiltrated Spain's trade with her American colonies from the beginning of the sixteenth century. The traders gravitated to the sparsely inhabited island of Hispaniola (Haiti) for supplies of wood and water, and hunted wild oxen that they smoked or roasted on grills in the manner of Amerindians. By about 1650 this practice had inspired the English word *buckaneer* from the French *boucan*, "smoke," and *boucaner*, "to cure or smoke flesh."

After a Spanish fleet expelled the nascent French and English colonies on St. Kitts in 1629 a number of refugees made their way to Tortuga, an island adjacent to the *boucan* settlements on Hispaniola, which developed into a buccaneer stronghold. Swelled by a steady influx of renegades, runaway slaves, deserters, and logwood cutters from the forests of Central America, the buccaneer community sought to enrich itself by tapping Spain's silver lifeline. After years of disrupting trade at sea they switched their attacks to the mainland with the assault on New Segovia in Honduras in 1654. This marked the opening phase of a systematic campaign of terror against Spanish settlements. The buccaneers' most spectacular successes were achieved under the leadership of Henry Morgan whose feats are recorded in A.O. Exquemelin's *De Americaenesche Zee-Roovers* published in Amsterdam in 1678, and printed in English as *Bucaniers of America* in 1684.

Exquemelin's narrative describes how Morgan was commissioned by the governor of Jamaica, Thomas Modyford, to enhance the security of the island. Morgan interpreted his instructions liberally, effecting a series of preemptive strikes against Spanish towns throughout the region culminating in an assault on Panama. With the city in flames, Morgan barely managed to restrain his men from invading Peru. Exquemelin claims to give an eyewitness account of Morgan's "Unparalleled Exploits." Replete with sensational tales of daring and lush descriptions of exotic locales, Exquemelin's narrative is a festive historical romance with great appeal.

In April 1680, another party of buccaneers, under the leadership of Captain Peter Harris, crossed Darien to sack Panama for the second time. After failing to secure the town they hijacked some vessels anchored in the bay, and burst loose into the Pacific. For the next 18 months, mainly under the leadership of Captain Bartholomew Sharpe, the buccaneers scoured the coast in search of prizes. When Sharpe finally headed for home, he intended passing through the Straits of Magellan but a great storm blew him too far south so that he became, perforce, the first English captain to round the Horn in an easterly direction. Sharpe's exploits aroused intense interest at court when it became known that he had seized a secret book of charts and pilotage instructions from a prize off the coast of modern Ecuador. The charts represented hydrographic information covering the entire Pacific coastline from California to Cape Horn and their value, in English hands, was inestimable. King Charles II, prompted by Christopher Monck, duke of Albemarle, had the charts illicitly copied under the very nose of the Spanish ambassador to whom they had been returned.

Sharpe's narrative of the voyage, which survives in no fewer than eight manuscript versions, was first printed in Captain William Hacke's *A Collection of Original Voyages* in 1699. The provenance of the manuscripts reveals that senior members of the Royal Society, including its future president, Samuel Pepys, scrutinized the voyage closely. The drive by scientists to obtain disciplined, truthful voyage narratives had begun as early as 1666 when the society published "Directions for Seamen, Bound for Far Voyages" in *Philosophical Transactions*. The "Directions" guided mariners in the composition of their journals so that they might be rendered "pertinent and suitable for [the society's] purpose." Sharpe's narrative was crucial because in his passage round the Horn he had sailed farther south than anyone before. His descriptions of icebergs, and the flora and fauna he encountered in the Antarctic Ocean, were of unique interest to the society, as was his claim that the great southern continent, *Terra Australis Incognita*, was a fiction.

In addition to Sharpe, six members of his crew also left narratives of the voyage. Basil Ringrose, navigator and cartographer, seems to have left the most reliable account, which was published in an expanded edition of *Bucaniers of America* in 1685. William Dampier also recorded the expedition, his brief coverage being incorporated in *A New Voyage round the World*, published in 1697. The bias in Dampier's account is evidence of a meticulous editorial process designed to divorce the author from his buccaneering past. The editor, who may have been Hans Sloane, secretary and later president of the Royal Society, entirely refashioned Dampier's narrative to reflect information of scientific interest. A similar process is observable in Lionel Wafer's *A New Voyage and Description of the Isthmus of America* (1699). Wafer had abandoned the expedition in April 1681, with Dampier and about 40 others, intending to return across the isthmus to a rendezvous on the Atlantic coast. During the march overland a quantity of gunpowder was ignited accidentally, injuring Wafer's knee so badly that he had to be left behind at the mercy of "*wild* Indians." Wafer's spectacular narrative of his life among the Cuna tribe is superimposed on a natural history of Darien, edited to emphasize contemporary scientific preoccupations.

In March 1684, *Batchelor's Delight*, commanded by Captain John Cook, joined *Nicholas*, under Captain John Eaton, off Valdivia. Together they sailed to Juan Fernandez where they recovered a Moskito Indian whom Sharpe had marooned accidentally three years earlier. Dampier, who was on board *Batchelor's Delight*, describes how the castaway survived his island solitude in a passage, printed in *New Voyage*, which may have been a contributory source for Daniel Defoe's novel *Robinson Crusoe* (1719). After leaving Juan Fernandez, Cook and Eaton sailed for the Galapagos where Cook's pilot, William Ambrose Cowley, compiled the first English map of the archipelago. Cowley's map and a narrative he kept of his voyage were published in Hacke's *Collection*.

On 28 May 1685, in one of the last significant actions undertaken by the buccaneers, *Batchelor's Delight* and *Nicholas* assembled as part of a force of ten ships and almost a thousand men to blockade the Bay of Panama. Under the leadership of Captain Edward Davis, who had assumed command of *Batchelor's Delight*, the buccaneers prepared to intercept the Spanish treasure fleet from Lima. Dampier, Ringrose, and Wafer were among those present. Fourteen heavily armed Spanish vessels duly arrived but they were empty of treasure, having been forewarned of the buccaneers' presence. The Spaniards were resolved to fight, and although the ensuing battle proved to be inconclusive it was enough to fracture the buccaneers' alliance. Dampier's rueful observations on this occasion coincide with the start of a terminal decline in the buccaneers' fortunes: "Thus ended this days Work, and with it all that we had been projecting for 5 or 6 Months; when instead of making ourselves Masters of the Spanish Fleet and Treasure, we were glad to escape them" (*New Voyage*).

In 1685, hostilities broke out between France and Spain, and in 1689 England joined in on the Spanish side. Almost the last action of the buccaneers was the attack on Cartagena in 1697, led by the governor of the French possessions in Hispaniola. After Cartagena fell, the buccaneers, who made up about a third of the attacking force, were denied their due share of the booty. In retaliation they besieged the city until forced to disperse by a combined English and Dutch squadron. The buccaneers' heyday was finally eclipsed by the Treaty of Ryswick in 1697 that ended the Nine Years' War. The majority of the buccaneers were rehabilitated, entering the service of their respective countries, and others settled as planters, but the remainder reverted to outright pirates, infesting the coasts of North America until they were finally suppressed in the nineteenth century.

The rash of buccaneer narratives printed after 1697 reflects the fact that tales of voyages became the second most popular reading material, after religious works, in the early years of the eighteenth century. Buccaneers' journals were avidly sought by publishers as raw materials for a marketable product that was both instructive and pleasurable. Indeed, *utile dulce* became such a winning formula that the demand for authentic voyage stories outstripped supply. The scarcity of buccaneer journals was the result of two overriding factors. First, the survival of manuscripts at sea or in the tropics was often a matter of chance. Dampier's account of wading through jungle rivers with his journal preserved in a bamboo cane stopped with wax illustrates the problems he encountered. Second, literacy rates among seventeenth-century seamen were generally very low and few men were capable of keeping a journal. (The number of men who compiled narratives of Sharpe's voyage is exceptional, signifying that the buccaneers were able to recruit educated and intelligent men.) The shortage of genuine narratives encouraged enterprising authors to foist counterfeits upon a credulous public. Defoe's novels *Captain Singleton* (1720) and *A New Voyage round the World* (1725) are classic examples of this type.

The buccaneers' experience in remote areas of the world often meant that they were sought out for consultation by government officials and projectors of schemes. On 2 July 1697, Wafer was interviewed by John Locke and the other commissioners of the Council of Trade and Plantation concerning Darien and the projected Scots colony. Wafer's knowledge of Darien was also requested by the directors of the Company of Scotland Trading to Africa and the Indies (the Darien

Company), and the advice he gave them almost certainly influenced the siting of the disastrous Scots colony in 1698. The establishment of the South Sea Company in 1711 was partly inspired by intelligence gathered on buccaneering voyages concerning the viability of trade on America's Pacific rim. Narratives that incorporated speculative geography, particularly concerning the vast spaces of the Pacific, were highly prized by contemporary cartographers eager for the latest intelligence from abroad.

Speculative geography in at least one narrative carried an abiding legacy. According to Lionel Wafer, when *Batchelor's Delight*, under the command of Captain Davis, was in the latitude of 27°20′ S, some 500 leagues south of the Galapagos, the buccaneers observed "a range of high Land" which they took to be a group of islands. In his world map, which formed the frontispiece to Dampier's *New Voyage*, the cartographer Herman Moll faithfully represented "Davis Land" in the position stated by Wafer. In 1721, the Dutch West India Company fitted out three ships under Jacob Roggeveen to search for "Davis Land," and French and British ships were still looking for it at the end of the nineteenth century. The true identity of "Davis Land" still remains a puzzle. It may have been Easter Island, but it seems more likely that Davis and his men were deceived by a cloud bank.

JAMES WILLIAM KELLY

### References and Further Reading


#### *Manuscripts*

Bartholomew Sharpe's journal dated 1683, formerly Lot 245 in Christie's sale 13–14 June 1978. Now in private hands.

British Library, London, Sloane MS 46A. Copy of Sharpe's journal, c. 1685.

British Library, London, Sloane MS 46B. Copy of Sharpe's journal, 1683.

Cambridge, Pepys MSS 2610, 2874. Copies of Sharpe's journal both dated c. 1684.

Pierpont Morgan Library, New York, MS 3310. Copy of Sharpe's journal, 1695.

Naval History Library, Taunton, Somerset, MS 4. Copy of Sharpe's journal, 1698.

British Library, London, Sloane MS 3820. Basil Ringrose's journal (holograph), undated but before 1683.

British Library, London, Sloane MS 48. Copy of Basil Ringrose's journal by Phillip Dassigny with illustrations by William Hack.

British Library, London, Sloane MS 54. Cowley's journal.

British Library, London, Sloane MS 1050. Cowley's journal (another copy).

Lambeth Palace Library, London, MS 642. Cowley's journal (another copy).

British Library, London, Sloane MS 3236. Dampier's journal.

British Library, London, Addl. MS 33054. Wafer's journal.

#### *Books*

Dampier, William, *A New Voyage round the World . . .*, 1697; with an introduction by Percy G. Adams and a new introduction by Sir Albert Gray, 1968.

Defoe, Daniel, *The Life, Adventures, and Piracies, of the Famous Captain Singleton*, 1720; edited by Shiv K. Kumar, with an introduction by Penelope Wilson, 1990.

Defoe, Daniel, *A New Voyage round the World by a Course Never Sailed Before*, 1725; edited by G.A. Aitken, 1895.

Exquemelin, A.O., *De Americaenesche Zee Roovers*, 4 vols., 1678; as *The Bucaniers of America: The Second Volume Containing the Dangerous Voyage and Bold Attempts of Captain Bartholomew Sharp and Others . . . Written by Mr. Basil Ringrose, Gent. Who Was All along Present at Those Transactions*, 1684; as *The Buccaneers of America*, edited and with an introduction by Henry Powell, 1893; translated by Alexis Brown, 1969.

Hacke, William, *A Collection of Original Voyages*, 1699; facsimile, with an introduction by Glyndwr Williams, 1993.

Wafer, Lionel, *A New Voyage and Description of the Isthmus of America*, 1699; edited and with an introduction by L.E. Elliott Joyce, 1934.


*See also* **Pirates and Bandits**

## BUCKINGHAM, JAMES SILK (1786–1855) *British Traveler and Writer*

Born in Flushing, Cornwall, at the water's edge, in 1786, James Silk Buckingham took to the sea at the precocious age of ten. This first experience aboard a mail-packet to Lisbon only increased his taste for further voyages. As an adult, travel served the cause of reform for Buckingham, and the causes he championed included temperance, peace, and the plight of mariners.

Buckingham joined the navy in 1802 as a 16-year-old. The sailor's life was not as he expected. After seeing the fatal "round the fleet" flogging of a deserter, he deserted. The man-of-war had been "a perfect hell on earth." The next several years were challenging. He married, had a son, and took to the sea again. The financial misdeeds of a trustee of his father's estate had left Buckingham penniless. In 1807 he made his first voyage to the United States, a trip that left him disappointed at the sight of tobacco-chewing Americans, drunken Indians, and dreadful slavery. Soon after this voyage, Buckingham was promoted to captain. In his new position, Buckingham produced new rules of discipline for his men that included abstinence from all spirits and harsh language, mandatory weekly church attendance, enforced cleanliness, and suppression of dissatisfaction. His years of adventure as a captain included attack by pirates and continued failure at getting out of debt.

Buckingham was an extraordinarily perceptive traveler who took good notes that later resulted in numerous volumes of travel writing. He began his wanderings in Egypt and the Middle East in 1813, curious to learn more of the world and eager for mercantile success. The young "Frank," as all Europeans in the region were known at the time, was welcomed by the Nubians as a harbinger of good luck. On the way to Baghdad he posed, with mixed success, as a Muslim. Buckingham journeyed to Bombay in 1815 and again in 1816.

Buckingham's career in India was marked by his humanitarianism. After refusing to take the command of a slave ship to Zanzibar, Buckingham became the editor of a new periodical, the *Calcutta Journal*. The journal's wide-ranging discussions on colonial government and conditions in India led the governor-general to expel Buckingham from India and suppress the *Journal*. Back home in England, Buckingham furthered his literary career by founding the *Oriental Herald and Colonial Review* in 1824 and the important Victorian journal, the *Athenaeum*, in 1828. Through all his journalistic ventures, Buckingham thought it his duty to educate Britons as to the true condition of the empire and the world. His previous travels resulted in a series of travel books: *Travels in Palestine* (1821), *Travels among the Arab Tribes* (1825), *Travels in Mesopotamia* (1827), and *Travels in Assyria, Media, and Persia* (1829). A contemporary said of his work:

> He is one of those (a sadly-circumscribed number) few, who look with their own eyes on the things which lie before them, and who are gifted with the ability to supply mankind with vivid, original, and correct descriptions. (*London Literary Chronicle*, 10 March 1827)

Buckingham sustained his vocal criticism of the East India Company and ventured to Scotland and France to speak on reform. His adoption of the cause of temperance was at least partially influenced by his travels in the East. The sobriety of the heathen lands contrasted greatly with the drunkenness apparent throughout Christendom. In 1832, as a candidate for the parliamentary seat of Sheffield, Buckingham took a pledge to remain a teetotaller. His career in Parliament, though less than glorious, was devoted to social reform.

Buckingham proposed, in 1829, to sail around the world on a mission of "Temperance, Education, Benevolence, and Peace." Instead, the culmination of Buckingham's career was a second trip to the United States in 1837, a trip that lasted three years and brought him to all states but Arkansas and Florida. For Buckingham, America represented the best hope for reformers. His earlier travels had prepared him for such a journey; he could give a "more patient, more diligent, and more impartial examination of the country and its inhabitants" than previous, more chauvinistic British travelers. The product of Buckingham's travels was an encyclopedic eight volumes (three individual works) on America.

Buckingham generally saw a great future for the United States. He heaped much praise on the "steady and liberal patronage" by Americans of benevolent institutions: "Far beyond the immediate sphere of their own locality, they extend their benevolence to the remotest part of the world." He clearly believed that republicanism had led to prosperity and the rapid growth of the American population. The American women were "almost uniformly good-looking." He remarked of America's original inhabitants, "The complexion of the Indians, generally, resembles that of the nation of Hindoostan, more than that of any other people I had seen." Buckingham assured readers back home that the secret ballot was a success. Even the arts would soon flourish in America, despite the nation's relative infancy and the absence of leisure: "There are already indication that the arts are relished and enjoyed by many, and that they will, ere long, be successfully cultivated by more."

Not all, however, was perfect in the New Republic. Roads were horrible. The food was not much better: "The table however, was . . . more remarkable for superabundance of food than skill or delicacy in preparing it . . . [O]ne of the most valuable reforms that could be efforted in America would be a reform in the culinary and dietetic system of the country." On a more serious note, Buckingham was consistent in his condemnation of slavery even as he cautioned those who would speak against the institution while traveling through the United States.

Buckingham returned to Britain in 1840 and continued giving lectures. In 1849, he proposed a "model town" in his *National Evils and Practical Remedies*, based on the lessons learned during many years of travel. Buckingham died in 1855 and is buried in Kensal Green Cemetery, London.

JOSEPH EATON

## Biography

Born in Flushing, Cornwall, 25 August 1786. Joined the Royal Navy; deserted, 1802. Married Elizabeth Jennings, 1806. Merchant fleet captain, 1807–1810. Traveled in Egypt, India, and the Middle East, 1813–1817. Founded the *Calcutta Journal*, 1818. Expelled from India after criticism of the Indian government, 1823. Founded the *Athenaeum* journal, 1828. Member of Parliament for Sheffield, 1832. Toured the United States, 1837–1840. Helped to found the British and Foreign Institute, 1843. Toured Europe, 1847–1848. Proposed "model town" in 1849. President of the London Temperance League, 1851. Died in St. John's Wood, London, 30 June 1855.

## References and Further Reading

Buckingham, James Silk, *Travels in Palestine, through the Countries of Bashan and Gilead, East of the River Jordan, etc.*, 1821.

Buckingham, James Silk, *Travels among the Arab Tribes Inhabiting the Countries East of Syria and Palestine . . . etc.*, 1825.
Buckingham, James Silk, *Travels in Mesopotamia: Including a Journey from Aleppo to Bagdad, by the Route of Beer, Orfah, Diarbekr, Mardin and Mousul, etc.*, 2 vols., 1827.
Buckingham, James Silk, *Travels in Assyria, Media, and Persia etc.*, 2 vols., 1829.
Buckingham, James Silk, *Sketch of Mr. Buckingham's Life, Travels, Political and Literary Labours and Lectures on the Oriental World*, 1829; revised edition as *Improved Syllabus of Mr. Buckingham's Lectures on the Oriental World, Preceded by a Sketch of His Life, Travels and Writings, etc.*, 1830.
Buckingham, James Silk, *America, Historical, Statistic, and Descriptive*, 3 vols., 1841.
Buckingham, James Silk, *The Eastern and Western States of America*, 3 vols., 1842.
Buckingham, James Silk, *The Slave States of America*, 2 vols., 1842.
Buckingham, James Silk, *Canada, Nova Scotia, New Brunswick and the Other British Provinces in North America, with a Plan of National Colonization*, 1843.
Buckingham, James Silk, *Belgium, the Rhine, Switzerland, and Holland: An Autumnal Tour*, 2 vols., 1848.
Buckingham, James Silk, *France, Piedmont, Italy, Lombardy, the Tyrol, and Bavaria: An Autumnal Tour*, 1848.

## BUONDELMONTI, CRISTOFORO (c. 1385–1430) *Florentine Monk and Traveler*

Cristoforo Buondelmonti was born into a celebrated Florentine family. He learned Greek from Guarino da Verona and received a good education from Niccolò Niccoli, who gathered and supervised a humanist circle. In 1414, he was already a priest and rector of one of the churches in Florence—possibly Santa Maria sopr'Arno. At the end of the year, his passion for the Greek classics, especially history and poetry, together with his scholarly early Renaissance curiosity about man, took him to the island of Rhodes.

Buondelmonti's journey to the Mediterranean was facilitated through family connections: one branch of his family included the ruler of Ioánnina and another was connected with the duke of Athens, and with the ruler of Corinth. Cosimo de' Medici the Elder asked Buondelmonti to purchase Greek codices, and Niccolò Niccoli requested Greek books. There is still at least one codex that Buondelmonti brought back from Crete in the Biblioteca Laurenziana in Florence.

From Buondelmonti's itinerary it is fairly certain that the journey he describes lasted for about seven years, from 1414 to 1422. Using the island of Rhodes as a base, he crisscrossed the Aegean Sea from 1415, visiting Crete, the Hellespont, Constantinople, the peninsula of Mount Athos, and other islands. He used every kind of vessel available, and did not hesitate to embark on pirate ships. His ship was wrecked on a voyage from Rhodes to Chios and he and his companions found themselves on the deserted island of Foúrnoi near Samos. In 1415 he explored the island of Crete on horseback for 26 days and spent much time with the humanist Rinuccio d'Arezzo, who reminded him of a character in Aristophanes' comedy *Plutus*. He visited Crete again in 1417 and 1418, and explored Imbros and Andros in 1419. In 1420, he was back on Rhodes and two years later in Constantinople, then on Rhodes again in 1423. He continued to travel in the Greek archipelago, and he was still in Greece in 1430, but there are no details of his whereabouts up to his death later that year.

On Rhodes, writing in Latin and using the notes he made en route, he compiled his travel book on the Greek archipelago, now well known as *Librum insularum Archipelagi*, and sent it to Cardinal Giordano Orsini in 1422. The original manuscript was never printed, but the work survived in various fifteenth- and sixteenth-century copies. Not until four centuries later was a copy traced in Paris by the Swiss Gabriel Rudolf Ludwig von Sinner from Bern. He edited and published it in 1824.

Buondelmonti's account is written from the viewpoint of an observant outsider with an inquiring mind. Although the style is impressionist, the content is detailed and informative. Complementing the Old Russian diplomatic records of the abbots Paisios and Joachim, Buondelmonti provides the first empirical report of monastic conditions on Mount Athos. We can with good reason maintain that Mount Athos was discovered for the West principally by Cristoforo Buondelmonti and Pierre Belon. Buondelmonti came to Mount Athos from the island of Thasos for just a few days, visiting some monasteries, presumably those close to the sea. He does not mention them by name, and refers only to the fact that there were nearly 30 ruling monasteries in total.

Buondelmonti's reference to the number of monks living in the ruling monasteries—"I have counted myself in some monasteries one hundred monks, in others five hundred"—in conjunction with other records, enables us to be fairly sure that the monasteries he lodged in were Vatopedi and Great Lavra. This is supported by his assertion that the monks returned to their cells after morning service and took their meals alone there, a habit practiced only in the idiorrhythmic monasteries. At that time only Vatopedi and Great Lavra were idiorrhythmic. He also visited, at least briefly, one of the cenobitic monasteries, since he describes the monks there as following a more severe regime. Then he continued along the coast to Great Lavra and some of the separate *sketes* (cottages) in the monastic village of St. Anne. He visited some of the ruling monasteries along the western coast before finally heading to Thessaloniki.

Buondelmonti's description of the daily routine of the monks is more precise, but fragmentary. He took part in at least one morning service (*orthros*). Instead of providing a systematic description of the daily routines of the monks, he chose to build his account around his own impressions of the extraordinariness of Athos as a holy mountain inhabited by holy men. The monks are described as oriented totally toward Heaven and the Eternal Fatherland (Paradise), thereby atoning for the transgression of the First Father (Adam). They are also said to exercise in solitude, without any fear and unworried about "the gold money." They were content with little and did not fear those who held sovereign power, who could not harm them in any way. Neither did they fear ambushes or their fellow men.

Buondelmonti thus pictures the life of a monk in opposition, the antithesis of ordinary life at that time. His idealized picture is partly explained by the fact that he was himself a monk and that he visited Mount Athos only briefly. It could also be interpreted as a reflection of the fears, troubles, and worries ordinary men and he himself experienced in everyday life, especially during voyages in the pirate-ridden Mediterranean. In this respect, the account tells us as much about the medieval society in which Buondelmonti lived as it does about actual life on the Greek islands.

Buondelmonti's account is of great value, because he appears to have been one of the first Europeans to make a thorough survey of the Greek archipelago. He provided the basis for later cartographers and collected both ethnological and historical details about the Aegean islands at a time when little was known of Greece in the West.

René Gothóni

### Biography

Born in Florence, c. 1385. Learned Greek from Guarino da Verona. Received a good humanist education from Niccolò Niccoli. Became a priest and rector of a church in Florence, possibly Santa Maria sopr'Arno, by 1414. Settled on the island of Rhodes, late 1414. Traveled the islands and peninsulas of the Aegean Sea, 1414–1422. Sent his travel diary to Cardinal Giordano Orsini, 1422. Died 1430.

### References and Further Reading

Buondelmonti, Cristoforo, *Librum insularum Archipelagi* [Book of the Islands in the Archipelago], edited by Gabriel Rudolf Ludwig von Sinner, 1824 (written 1422).

## BURCHELL, WILLIAM JOHN (1781–1863) *British Naturalist and Traveler*

William John Burchell's fame rests upon the two-volume account of the first part of his travels in South Africa in the years 1811–1815. Comparatively little is known about his life before or after this South African episode despite the fact that he later traveled in Brazil on what seems to have been an equally remarkable series of scientific journeys.

Born into what was presumably a family of limited means, Burchell must nevertheless have received a good schooling. University education was substituted for by some sort of association with Kew Gardens, and practical experience as a naturalist on St. Helena. There, failure to secure a permanent post with the East India Company and some disagreement with the governor helped to persuade him to embark for Cape Town, but much more traumatic must have been the arrival on St. Helena of his fiancée. This lady announced she had married the captain of the ship on the way. Burchell never subsequently married. He commenced his travels, as he tells us, "in the purest spirit of independence" and free from "the mire of Sensuality and Selfishness" and anxious to enjoy "the genuine pleasure which Nature bestows only on those who view . . . the beauty and perfection of all her works."

Whether or not he was reacting as a jilted lover, Burchell certainly traveled as a child of the Enlightenment. Even if at first he expected to see examples of his fellow humans in a state of "primeval simplicity," he never believed in the "noble savage"; rather, he conceived people to be at different stages in the ascent from barbarism to civilization. The disillusioning examples of human behavior that Burchell saw in South Africa made him believe that regression was also possible. Only the natural world furnished the harmony desired by the Creator. Burchell resembles a deist as much as a conventional Christian and he certainly much disapproved of the work among Africans of missionaries. Although he was on friendly terms or traveled with some of them, his general verdict was that most were "self-deluded enthusiasts." Missionaries could reach the heights of "fanaticism and folly" when, for example, they condemned music and dancing by their converts (Burchell was a flautist of some accomplishment).

Burchell's greatest gifts were as a scientist. He was an explorer in the sense that he knew how to calculate latitudes and longitudes and entered some territory previously unseen by anyone capable of systematic description. Principally, however, he was a naturalist. The sheer number of specimens of animals and plants he collected (63,000) or noted and drew is astonishing. Burchell's skill in drawing was employed also to depict people and landscapes. Major delights for readers of his *Travels in the Interior of Southern Africa* are the colored plates and the vignettes.

Because he wanted to ensure accuracy and authenticity, Burchell prepared his pictures for publication himself. In the ten years between traveling and publication, he obviously prepared his text as well. Since his manuscript journals are lost, it is impossible to say how close the text is to what he originally noted. It does follow the sequence of his travels and he claimed that it provides "a faithful picture of occurrences and observations" and that he was "free of prejudice." Perhaps the prejudices of a late Enlightenment naturalist are less harmful than those of some travelers. Burchell was certainly capable of detaching himself to some extent from "normal" European assumptions as, for example, in his discussion of notions of territoriality among African peoples.

It is in showing his human sympathies rather more than in the demonstration of his scientific detachment that Burchell becomes an attractive writer. He condemned the still legal slavery and pleaded for justice for Africans at the hands of the colonists, and yet tried to be fair to the Boers. When, after language preparation, Burchell set out northward from Cape Town, he had an ox-wagon (later two) and about ten Khoi assistants. These were replaced as circumstances dictated over the next four years. Burchell's close association with his Khoi followers, especially Philip Willems and "Juli," makes a fascinating study. Most of the people Burchell encountered were also Khoi. Known then and subsequently by the derogatory term "Hottentots," these people had to a greater or lesser extent mixed with Europeans from the Cape. Burchell tells us that one of his objects was to discover whether they "had been rendered happier by their communication with . . . those enjoying the blessings of civilization." His melancholy conclusion was that they were neither happier nor wiser. This was even more true of the Khoisan ("Bushmen") whom Burchell describes in detail. At one point, he experimented with a group to discover whether they had any moral awareness and he later concluded that their low state of "social existence" must have to do with their lack of property. Property gradations might produce the relative advancement that he saw among the Bantu he began to encounter at the furthest reaches of his journey into what is now the very north of South Africa. The BaTlhaping (Bachapins) and some Xosa had not yet had much contact with Europeans and were "perfectly free from servile timidity." Even if the information that Burchell provides lacks some of the context that might be provided by a modern anthropologist, it is useful historical data as well as enlivened by warmth of attempted understanding.

*Equus burchelli*, the species of zebra most widespread in southern and eastern Africa, is named after the explorer (lithograph by Frank Howard from *Portraits of the Game and Wild Animals of Southern Africa drawn by W. Cornwallis Harris*, 1840). *Courtesy of the Travellers Club, London; Bridgeman Art Library, agent.*

It is his sympathy for diverse conditions of humanity together with his delight in the scenery and natural history of South Africa that make Burchell's work not only an important source for historians, but also a classic of African travel literature. Possibly a third volume on South Africa and another set on Brazil would have been even better, but we have to accept that the rest of Burchell's long life was an anticlimax, as perhaps he realized when he committed suicide. The best edition of Burchell's South African volumes is that edited by Schapera although even this is rare. Important studies by Helen Mackay were never, unfortunately, followed by a full-scale biography. It does not seem that studies of Burchell's Brazilian work have progressed far, although his notes and his botanical and zoological materials have survived.

Roy Bridges

## Biography

Born in Fulham, London, 23 July 1781. Attended Raleigh House Academy, Mitcham. Studied at the Royal Botanic Gardens, Kew. Schoolmaster on St. Helena island, 1805–1807; appointed naturalist to the East India Company on St. Helena, 1807–1810. Left St. Helena and sailed to Cape Town, South Africa, October 1810. Traveled north to Kuruman and beyond, returning via the Vaal–Orange confluence to the Great Kei River in the South East Cape, 1811–1815. Returned to England, 1815. Lived in Fulham, London, and developed his specimen collection, 1815–1818. Moved to Sevenoaks, Kent, 1819. Engaged in controversy with Barrow over information on South Africa in connection with emigration schemes, 1820–1822. Published two volumes on his travels in 1822–1824. Explored and collected in little-known parts of southern Brazil, 1825–1829. Returned to London, 1830, after the death of his father; lived in Fulham until his death. Hon. D.C.L., University of Oxford, 1834. Fellow of Linnean, Royal Geographical Societies. Committed suicide in London, 23 March 1863.

### References and Further Reading

Burchell, William, *Hints on Emigration to the Cape of Good Hope*, 1819.

Burchell, William, *Travels in the Interior of Southern Africa*, 2 vols., 1822–1824; reprinted with additional material and an introduction by I. Schapera, 1953; selections, edited by H. Clement Notcutt, 1935.

## BURCKHARDT, JOHANN LUDWIG (1784–1817) *Swiss Traveler*

Johann Ludwig Burckhardt (also known as John Lewis and Jean Louis Burckhardt) was born into a wealthy family of Basel silk manufacturers and forwarders. After university studies, he went to London in 1806, hoping to find an administrative position in the civil service. Unsuccessful, he took employment with the African Association in London with a view to resolving some of the geographical problems pertaining to the course of the Niger River. Under the Association's auspices Burckhardt made a number of journeys in greater Syria, Nubia, and western Arabia in preparation for an expedition from Cairo to Timbuktu. He died before he could set out on his planned western journey. His manuscript journals were subsequently edited and published by the African Association.

Burckhardt was accepted for employment by the African Association in 1808. After beginning the study of Arabic at Cambridge University, he traveled (March–July 1809) to Aleppo in disguise as the merchant Ibrahim bin Abdullah, a persona he continued to use until his death. He spent two and a half years in Aleppo learning to pass as a Muslim Arab, as well as studying Arabic and the Qur'an. He also collected a large number of Arabic manuscripts (subsequently sent to Cambridge University) and made several short expeditions. These included a round-trip to Baalbek, Mount Lebanon, and Damascus, and excursions to the Hauran and the Euphrates. A visit to Tadmor (ancient Palmyra) gave Burckhardt his first encounter with the Bedouin whose manners and way of life so impressed him that they formed the subject of his first treatise. In 1812, he traveled again in Lebanon, this time visiting Tripoli and Beirut. From Damascus he went south to the Hauran for a second time and as far as ancient Bosra and Jerash. Leaving Damascus again Burckhardt journeyed to the Sea of Galilee, met Lady Hester Stanhope in Nazareth, and traveled to Es Salt, Amman, and Kerak in Transjordan. Curiosity about some strange buildings and so-called monasteries near Ain Musa led to his becoming the first European to report a visit to Petra. Crossing the rift valley and the Sinai peninsula, he reached Cairo on 4 September 1812. There he resumed his scholarly activities.

Now able to pass as a Muslim Arab without arousing much suspicion, in January 1813 Burckhardt set out for Upper Egypt and Nubia, arguing to his employers that the information he would collect about African people would assist his planned western expedition. Unusually, he traveled by land and, pushing his permits to the limit, almost reached the Third Cataract on the Nile. On returning north, he discovered the sand-choked, rock-cut Great Temple of Ramesses II at Abu Simbel. After waiting at Esme for a caravan, Burckhardt made another expedition into Nubia. This took him south to Berber on the Nile, then through the territory of ancient Meroë and as far as Shendi, an important market for the eastern Sudan. From Shendi he traveled eastward to the Red Sea at Souakin. By now he had resolved to visit Mecca since the successful completion of the pilgrimage would strengthen his disguise as a returning pilgrim when eventually he set out for Timbuktu.

Burckhardt reached Jeddah on 18 July 1814. Here he fell seriously ill for the first time on his journeys. A visit to Muhammad Ali Pasha, ruler of Egypt, at his campaign headquarters in Taif led to a rigorous testing of his credentials as a Muslim that he passed successfully. He was thus allowed to visit Mecca and to perform the prescribed rituals in the Beitullah (Great Mosque). After another visit to Jeddah, Burchkardt lived for several months in Mecca and took part in the ceremonies associated with the great pilgrimage or Hajj. A subsequent visit to Jeddah revealed the brutal consequences of Muhammad Ali's recent defeat of the Wahhabi Islamic "fundamentalists." In January 1815, Burckhardt traveled to Medina where he became dangerously ill. Recovered three months later, he made his way to the Red Sea coast at Yambo only to find it afflicted with the plague. He escaped from the port, landed on Sinai, and traveled overland back to Cairo, where he arrived on 24 June 1815.

Apart from a month in Alexandria and two months exploring southern Sinai (including visits to St. Catherine's monastery), Burckhardt spent the remaining two and a half years of his life living modestly in Cairo, patiently waiting for a caravan that would take him to the Fezzan on his journey west. He spent his time completing the journals of his travels in Nubia and western Arabia, writing up his notes on the Wahhabis, studying Arabic literature, and editing a collection of Cairean Arabic proverbs made originally in the early eighteenth century. A recurrence of dysentery in October 1817 led to his death. Less than two months later, the Hajj caravan returned to Cairo, accompanied by pilgrims from West Africa.

Burckhardt traveled off the beaten track followed by many contemporary European travelers. More than them, he experienced considerable hardship and privation, as well as harassment from suspicious local people and travelers, especially in Nubia. His knowledge of written and spoken Arabic was remarkable for a European, as was his inside understanding of Islam. Although his disguise as a learned Muslim merchant secured access to sights and societies denied to contemporary European travelers (notably the Holy Cities and life among the Bedouin), it also hindered him in making notes in the field, which, for fear of discovery, had to be done surreptitiously. Nonetheless, he was meticulous in recording what he saw and heard. Where appropriate, as in the cases of Mecca and Medina, he supplemented this information from literary and documentary sources in Arabic. Accordingly, his detailed descriptions of early-nineteenth-century Jeddah, Mecca, and Medina are enormously valuable (and could not be bettered by Burton), as is his information on Shendi, while his studies of the Bedouin and the Wahhabis have provided the foundation for all subsequent anthropological and historical research on these topics. Finally, Burckhardt discovered "rose-red" Petra and the Great Temple at Abu Simbel.

MALCOLM WAGSTAFF

### Biography

Born in Lausanne, Switzerland, 15 November 1784. Educated at home and at school in Neuchâtel. Studied at the University of Leipzig, 1800–1804 and Göttingen, 1804–1806. Traveled to London, 1806. Introduced to Joseph Banks and the Association for Promoting the Discovery of the Interior Parts of Africa (the African Association), 1807–1808. Accepted as the Association's explorer, 1808. Studied Arabic in London and Cambridge; traveled to Syria, 1809. Explored in Syria, Lebanon, and Transjordan, 1809–1812. Discovered Petra, 1812. Made two journeys in Nubia, 1813–1814. Discovered the Great Temple at Abu Simbel, March 1813. Visited the Hejaz district of Arabia, including Jeddah, Mecca, Medina, and Yambo, 1814–1815. Traveled in southern Sinai, 1816. Died of dysentery in Cairo, 15 October 1817. Gravestone bears the name he assumed while traveling in Arabia, Ibrahim Ibn Abdullah.

### References and Further Reading

Burckhardt, Johann Ludwig, *Travels in Nubia*, edited by W.M. Leake, 1819.

Burckhardt, Johann Ludwig, *Travels in Syria and the Holy Land, etc.*, edited by W.M. Leake, 1822.

Burckhardt, Johann Ludwig, *Travels in Arabia, Comprehending an Account of Those Territories in Hedjaz Which the Mohammedans Regard as Sacred*, edited by William Ouseley, 2 vols., 1829.

Burckhardt, Johann Ludwig, *Notes on the Bedouins and Wahabys Collected during His Travels in the East*, edited by William Ouseley, 2 vols., 1830.

*Scheik Ibrahim* [Johann Ludwig Burckhardt], *Briefe an Eltern und Geschwister*, edited by Carl Burckhardt-Sarasin, 1956.

## BURMA / MYANMAR

The earliest recorded visit to Burma by a Westerner was probably that of the thirteenth-century traveler Marco Polo. The Portuguese explorer Fernão Mendes Pinto wrote of his adventures in Asia between 1537 and 1558 in his *Peregrinação*, and some of the book's most exciting and interesting episodes take place during his visit to Burma, including the Burmese invasion of Thailand and the siege of the old Thai capital of Ayutthaya. The First Englishman also visited in the sixteenth century: Ralph Fitch in 1586–1588. Fitch's enthusiastic description of the Shwe Dagon pagoda in Rangoon is often quoted: "of a wonderful bignesse, and all gilded from the foot to the toppe. It is the fairest place, as I suppose, that is in the world." A little later the Portuguese Augustinian missionary Friar Sebastião Manrique gave an account of his travels between Europe and Macau during the period 1629–1637 in *Itinerário de las missiones de l'India Oriental* (1649).

Burma's outside visitors were mainly missionaries during the sixteenth and seventeenth centuries. A history of missions by the Society of Jesus during the early 1600s is related by Father Fernão Guerreiro in *Jahangir and the Jesuits* (1930). It includes an account of the Portuguese adventurer, Philippe de Brito, who conquered and ruled part of Syriam from 1600 until his execution by the Burmese king in 1613.

Nearly 200 years later, the distinguished orientalist William Hunter, then an army surgeon, was stranded in Burma from August to September 1782, after the ship he was traveling in was dismasted in a storm. He produced a detailed and well-observed description of all aspects of life in the kingdom, *A Concise Account of the Kingdom of Pegu . . .* (1785), which was written with a view to stimulating the British East India Company's interest in trade in the region. With the advent of steamships, access to Burma from Europe became easier, and the early nineteenth century saw attempts by British, Dutch, and Portuguese traders to establish trading posts on the Bay of Bengal. A group of missionaries who arrived in 1813, led by the American Baptist Adoniram Judson (1788–1850), initiated serious study of the Burmese language. The Anglo-Burmese War (1824–1826) and two later wars resulted in the British East India Company's expansion into the whole of Burma by 1886.

This rapid opening up of the country inspired a number of travelogues and accounts, many written by members of British army expeditions looking to establish trade routes. John Anderson in *Mandalay to Momien* (1876) gives an account of Britain's attempts to find an overland route to China via Bhamo, one under Colonel Edward B. Sladen in 1868 and another in 1875 under Colonel Horace Browne. This chronicle includes route maps and descriptions of local peoples, such as the Kachins and Shans, encountered along the way. A more lively account of local people, trade, and customs was written by Holt S. Hallett during his travels in Thailand and the Shan States in 1876 as he was carrying out a survey of possible rail routes from Burma.

Another account that dates back to the late nineteenth century is a mainly geographical report written by Émile Roux. It chronicles an overland trip from Hanoi to Calcutta through an area that was identified as containing the sources of the Irrawaddy River. Led by Prince Henri d'Orléans, this French expedition covered several territories, including the upper Mekong valley, that were, at the time, unexplored by Westerners.

An altogether different genre of travel writing came from adventurers such as John Bradley. In his *Narrative of Sport and Travel in Burmah, Siam and the Malay Peninsula* (1876), Bradley writes of his visit in 1869 and his attempts to shoot every form of wildlife he came across. In a similar vein, the larger-than-life Victorian explorer, Sir George Scott (1851–1935) helped establish British colonial rule in the region and spent years mapping Burma's lawless frontiers. Author of *The Burman* (1882) and an accomplished photographer, Scott is also famed for having introduced soccer to Burma. His unpublished diaries are the inspiration for Andrew Marshall's *The Trouser People* (2002), in which the author recounts some of Scott's greatest adventures.

Hariot Georgina Blackwood gives some interesting impressions of Upper Burma in her journal from the time when she accompanied her husband, Frederick Temple Blackwood, Lord Dufferin, the Governor-General of India, on a visit to the country in February 1886. Lord Dufferin presided over the third Anglo-Burmese War and made the decision to annex the region on 1 January 1886. *Burma after the Conquest* (1886) by Grattan Geary also gives a detailed description of Upper Burma at the time of annexation.

Burma, by this time a province of British India, featured in a number of travelogues of the early twentieth century. Notable among these is W. Somerset Maugham's *The Gentleman in the Parlour* (1930), written after the author spent time during the 1920s traveling by canoe and riverboat, by rickshaw and pony from Rangoon to Mandalay and on to Haiphong in Vietnam. Maugham describes the Southeast Asian countryside and some of the people he meets along the way including British officials and other querulous Europeans stranded in the region. Insights into Burma during British rule can be gleaned from George Orwell's first novel, *Burmese Days* (1934). After serving six years in the Imperial Police in Burma, Orwell was well placed to observe life in the region, as well as the mood of the country during the 1920s. He conjures a picture of oppressive heat and humidity, of tropical downpours and racial tensions.

In 1937, Burma was established by the British as a colony separate from India; it became an important battleground during World War II. The Japanese invaded and by May 1942 had occupied most of the country. The Japanese were driven out in 1945, and Burma became fully independent in January 1948; in the decades since, Burma has suffered considerable political and economic instability. Revolts by the communists, Mons, and the hill peoples during the 1950s eventually culminated in Burma's becoming a military dictatorship under General Ne Win in 1962. An interesting travelogue by Austin Coates, *Invitation to an Eastern Feast* (1953), chronicles two visits to the country written at a time before the dictatorship imposed restrictions on such travel. It includes observations of a number of insurrections during the period 1948–1950. An account written by Norman Lewis, *Golden Earth* (1952), also captures this time in the nation's history. Writing about a visit in 1951, Lewis predicts that access will soon be restricted, and he attempts to capture the "old" Burma in his book.

One of the results of the political situation in the country was that from the 1960s until the late 1990s tourism was discouraged, and little emerged in the way of travel literature. One author who did travel through Burma during this time was Paul Theroux. In the early 1970s, Theroux set out to journey by train from London to Tokyo, and then back via the Trans-Siberian Express. His book *The Great Railway Bazaar* (1975) chronicles this journey and includes chapters on Theroux's train journeys from Rangoon to Mandalay and from Mandalay via Maymyo to Naung Peng in the Shan States of Upper Burma. A later, and considerably more perilous journey, was taken by Bertil Lintner and his Shan wife, Hseng Noung, mainly on foot across insurgent areas of northern Burma between 1985 and 1987. In his account, *Land of Jade* (1990), Lintner, a prolific writer on Southeast Asia, includes interviews with Naga, Kachin, communist, and Shan leaders and followers.

In 1987 and 1988, huge demonstrations demanded General Ne Win's resignation. A military coup led to General Saw Maung's taking control with the promise that elections would take place. At this time, the State Law and Order Restoration Council decreed that the country should be known as Myanmar, as part of an attempt to cast off colonial influences. Despite the military's best efforts, the National League for Democracy, led by Aung San Suu Kyi, won the elections in 1990. However, the ruling military junta ignored the election results and has continued its oppressive rule to this day. Much of the writing emerging from Burma during this period has chronicled the political turmoil and repression. Notable among these is Lintner's *Outrage: Burma's Struggle for Democracy* (1989) and *Freedom from Fear and Other Writings* (1991), a collection of pieces by and about Aung San Suu Kyi herself.

JANE LANIGAN

### References and Further Reading


Abbott, Gerry, *Inroads into Burma: A Travellers' Anthology*, 1997.

Adamson, C.H.E., *Narrative of an Official Visit to the King of Burmah, in March 1865, from Notes Made at That Time*, 1878.

Anderson, John, *Mandalay to Momien: A Narrative of the Two Expeditions to Western China of 1865 and 1875 under Colonel Edward B. Sladen and Colonel Horace Browne*, 1876.

Anonymous [Colesworthey Grant], *Rough Pencillings of a Rough Trip to Rangoon in 1846*, 1853.

Bowers, Alexander, *Bhamo Expedition: Report on the Practicability of Re-opening the Trade Route between Burmah and Western China*, 1869.

Bradley, John, *A Narrative of Sport and Travel in Burmah, Siam and the Malay Peninsula*, 1876.

Burn Murdoch, William G., *From Edinburgh to India and Burmah*, 1908.

Coates, Austin, *Invitation to an Eastern Feast*, 1953.

Colquhoun, A.R., and H.S. Hallett, *Report on the Railway Connexion of Burmah and China: With Account of Exploration-Survey*, 1888.

Curle, Richard, *Into the East: Notes on Burma and Malaya*, with a preface by Joseph Conrad, 1923.

Dufferin and Ava, Hariot Georgina Blackwood, Marchioness of, *Our Viceregal Life in India: Selections from My Journal, 1884–1888*, 2 vols., 1889; new edition, 1890.

Edmonds, Paul, *Peacocks and Pagodas*, 1924.

Enriquez, Colin Metcalf Dallas, *A Burmese Enchantment*, 1916.

Falla, Jonathan, *True Love and Bartholomew: Rebels on the Burmese Border*, 1991.

Gascoigne, Gwendolen Trench, *Among Pagodas and Fair Ladies: An Account of a Tour through Burma*, 1896.

Geary, Grattan, *Burma after the Conquest, Viewed in Its Political, Social and Commercial Aspects, from Mandalay*, 1886.

Gill, William John, *The River of Golden Sand: Being the Narrative of a Journey through China and Eastern Tibet to Burmah*, with an introduction by Henry Yule, 2 vols., 1880.

Gordon, Charles Alexander, *Our Trip to Burmah: With Notes on That Country*, 1876.

Guerreiro, Fernão, *Jahangir and the Jesuits: With an Account of the Travels of Benedict Goes and the Mission to Pegu from the Relations of Father Fernão Guerreiro, S.J.*, translated by C.H. Payne, 1930.

Hallett, Holt S., *A Thousand Miles on an Elephant in the Shan States*, 1890.

Hart, Mrs Ernest, *Picturesque Burma: Past and Present*, 1897.

Hunter, William, *A Concise Account of the Kingdom of Pegu, Its Climate, Produce, Trade and Government: The Manners and Customs of Its Inhabitants, Interspersed with Remarks Moral and Political*, 1785.

Kelly, R. Talbot, *Burma Painted and Described*, 1905.

Kessel, Joseph Elie, *La Vallée des rubis*, 1956; as *Mogok: The Valley of Rubies*, translated by Stella Rodway, 1960.

Kington, Miles, "The Burma Road," in *Great Journeys*, by Philip Jones Griffiths *et al.*, 1989.

Lach, Donald F., *Southeast Asia in the Eyes of Europe: The Sixteenth Century*, 1965.

Leicester, C.M., *A Holiday in Burma: With a Chapter on a Visit to Calcutta*, 1928.

Lewis, Norman, *Golden Earth: Travels in Burma*, 1952; reprinted, 1983.

Lintner, Bertil, *Land of Jade: A Journey through Insurgent Burma*, 1990; revised edition, 1996.

Malcom, Howard, *Travels in the Burman Empire*, 1840.

Manrique, Sebastião, *Itinerário de las Missiones de l'India Oriental*, 1649; edited by Luis Silviera, 1946; as *Travels of Fray Sebastien Manrique*, 1629–1643, 2 vols., 1927; reprinted, 1967.

Marshall, Andrew, *The Trouser People: Colonial Shadows in Modern-Day Burma*, 2002.

Maugham, W. Somerset, *The Gentleman in the Parlour: A Record of a Journey from Rangoon to Haiphong*, 1930.

Metford, Beatrix, *Where China Meets Burma: Life and Travels in the Burma-China Border Lands*, 1935.

Mitton, G.E., *A Bachelor Girl in Burma*, 1907.

O'Connor, V.C. Scott, *The Silken East: A Record of Life and Travel in Burma*, 2 vols., 1904; 2nd edition, 1928.

Orwell, George, *Burmese Days: A Novel*, 1934.

Pinto, Fernão Mendes, *Peregrinação*, 1614; as *The Travels of Mendes Pinto*, edited and translated by Rebecca D. Catz, 1989.

Polo, Marco, *The Book of Ser Marco Polo*, edited and translated by Henry Yule, 2 vols., 1871; 3rd edition, revised by Henri Cordier, 1903; as *Marco Polo: The Description of the World*, edited and translated by A.C. Moule and Paul Pelliot, 2 vols., 1938; reprinted, 1976; also as *The Travels of Marco Polo*, translated by Ronald Latham, 1958.

Raven-Hart, Rowland, *Canoe to Mandalay*, 1939.

Roux, Émile, *Aux Source de l'Irraouddi: D'Hanoi à Calcutta par terre*, 1897; as *Searching for the Sources of the Irrawaddy: With Prince Henri d'Orleans from Hanoi to Calcutta Overland*, translated and with an introduction by Walter E.J. Tips, 1999.

Scott, James George, *The Burman: His Life and Notions by Shway Yoe*, 2 vols., 1882.

Shaplen, Robert, *A Turning Wheel: Three Decades of the Asian Revolution as Witnessed by a Correspondent for The New Yorker*, 1979.

Smith, Nicol, *Burma Road: The Story of the World's Most Romantic Highway*, 1940.

Stanford, J.K., *Far Ridges: A Record of Travel in North-Eastern Burma 1938–39*, 1946.

Theroux, Paul, *The Great Railway Bazaar: By Train through Asia*, 1975.

Tucker, Shelby, *Among Insurgents: Walking through Burma*, 2000.

Vincent, Frank, *The Land of the White Elephant: Sights and Scenes in South-Eastern Asia: A Personal Narrative of Travel and Adventure in Farther India Embracing the Countries of Burma, Siam, Cambodia, and Cochin-China (1871–2)*, 1873; with an introduction by William L. Bradley, 1988.

Ward, Frank Kingdon, *In Farthest Burma: The Record of an Arduous Journey of Exploration and Research through the Unknown Frontier Territory of Burma and Tibet*, 1921.
Ward, Frank Kingdon, *Burma's Icy Mountains*, 1949.
Ward, Frank Kingdon, *Return to the Irrawaddy*, 1956.
Wheeler, J. Talboys, *Journal of a Voyage up the Irrawaddy to Mandalay and Bhamo*, 1871.
Williams, Clement, *Through Burma to Western China: Being Notes of a Journey in 1863 to Establish the Practicability of a Trade-route Between the Irawaddi and the Yang-tse-kiang*, 1868.
Wills, Arthur Winkler, *Sunny Days in Burma*, 1905.
Younghusband, G.J., *Eighteen Hundred Miles on a Burmese Tat: Through Burmah, Siam, and the Eastern Shan States*, 1888.
Yule, Henry, *A Narrative of the Mission Sent by the Governor-General of India to the Court of Ava in 1855*, 1858.

## BURNES, ALEXANDER (1805–1841)

***British Colonial Officer and Traveler***

Alexander Burnes, the grandnephew of the poet Robert Burns, was born in Montrose in Scotland. Obtaining a cadetship in the East India Company through his father, Burnes embarked on 31 December 1821 for Bombay together with his elder brother James. The youth quickly learnt Urdu and other languages, and was employed from 25 December 1822 as Urdu interpreter in Surat, then as Persian interpreter. He rose quickly in the army in western India. In 1826, he prepared the statistics for Vagar (Kutch), and in 1827 was sent to explore the mouth of the Indus (then not a part of British India) and in 1830 the Thar desert. In 1831, he escorted a government gift of horses to Lahore, then the capital of the independent Sikh kingdom ruled by Ranjit Singh. According to his commission he traveled through the lower Indus country, then ruled by the independent emirs of Sind. En route he observed the course of the Indus and tried to establish relations with the emirs. Proceeding to the Punjab he spent some time in Lahore and returned through Simla to Delhi. Burnes never published a journal of this first expedition, but wrote of his observations in a few learned articles. The sharp observations made during the journey earned the favor of his superiors, and, supported by the governor-general, Lord Bentinck, he was soon sent on new travels.

Together with the military physician and Himalayan explorer James Gerard (1795–1835) and four Indian companions, he left Delhi on 2 January 1832. The route went via Delhi, Lahore, and Attock to Kabul and further northwest via Bamiyan, Khulum, and Balkh to Bokhara, then the capital of an independent central Asian emirate. From Bokhara they turned southwest, to Meshed on the Iranian border. Here Gerard turned back to India, while Burnes continued to Iran, traveling via Mazandaran, Astrabad, Ashraf, Isfahan, and Shiraz to Abushir, arriving on 18 December, and from there by ship to Bombay, where he arrived on 18 January 1833. In October 1833, Burnes came to London as a celebrated hero, published his journal (*Travels into Bokhara*), and was accepted into the Royal Society. In December 1834, he visited Paris, and on 3 April 1835 left again for Egypt and India.

Burnes was now sent on an official mission to study the commercial possibilities of the Indus and Afghanistan (and, less openly, to observe the political situation). Soon he was also charged with the task of warning Dost Muhammad, the emir of Afghanistan, against continuing hostilities with the Sikhs. His companions on this mission were lieutenants Robert Leech and John Wood (the discoverer of the sources of the Oxus) and Dr. Percival Lord. They arrived in Sind on 18 January 1836 and continued northward, conferring with local emirs. On 5 June, they left Dera Ghazi Khan, and arrived in Attock on 5 August, and Kabul on 20 September. After largely unsuccessful negotiations Burnes returned in spring 1838 together with Charles Masson (a.k.a. James Lewis, 1800–1853) to Peshawar, where they met Allard and Court, the French generals in Sikh service, and also Lord and Wood, who had come from Kunduz. The return journey continued via Lahore and Simla. In addition to doing his political work Burnes collected much ethnographic information, especially on the Kafirs (non-Muslims) of the Hindu Kush. His journal (*Cabool*) appeared posthumously in 1842.

Burnes supported an alliance with Afghanistan, but his superiors were against it. When Dost Muhammad started negotiations with Russia, the British answer was a military expedition, though all the specialists on the area criticized this. Burnes was sent to Sind and Baluchistan to prepare the way for the army. Then he accompanied the military expedition to Kabul, where Dost Muhammad was deposed and the exiled prince Shah Shuja was crowned. When the main force returned to India in September 1839, a British garrison was left in Kabul with Burnes as the British political agent. However, the new government was not accepted by the population, who began a mutiny in autumn 1841. During its course the majority of the British residing outside the cantonment in Kabul, including Burnes and his younger brother Charles, were killed. Dost Muhammad was reinstated as emir and the long period of isolation, suspicion, and occasional wars between Afghanistan and British India began.

The three journeys of Burnes, though mainly serving the political and military interests of the Indian government, also increased considerably the sum of European knowledge about northwestern and central Asian geography and ethnography. Like many nineteenth-century travelers he was as keen a political and economic observer as a geographer and ethnographer, and also had some antiquarian interests, attempting to reconstruct the route followed by Alexander the Great in his central Asian and northwest Indian campaigns. He understood the political situation well, though he perhaps had an exaggerated idea of Russian ambition in central Asia, which only really started much later; however, his outspoken ambition often made him leave out of his reports whatever he thought would not please his superiors. Among his peers this ambitious and rash man was rather unpopular, but his books brought him great fame.

KLAUS KARTTUNEN

### Biography

Born in Montrose, Scotland, 16 May 1805. Brother of James Burnes (1801–1862, physician and author of travel books on Sind and Kutch) and grandnephew of the poet Robert Burns. Educated at Montrose College. Went to Bombay, India, in the East India Company's military service, in India, 1821. Urdu and Persian interpreter in Surat, 1822–1825. Transferred to the Quartermaster-General's Department, 1825, and to the Political Department as Assistant to the Resident in Kutch, 1829. Explored the Thar desert, 1830; traveled to Lahore on a mission to Ranjit Singh, 1830–1831. Explored Sindh, 1831; Afghanistan, the Hindu Kush, and Persia, 1832. Returned to England, 1833. Elected a member of the Royal Society, 1834. Awarded gold medal of the Geographical Society of England and the silver medal of the Geographical Society of Paris, 1834. Private audience with King William IV, 1834. Returned to India, 1835; resumed position in Kutch. Traveled on a political mission to Kabul, 1836. Returned to India, 1838. Promoted to rank of lieutenant-colonel and knighted, 1839. Second political officer in the British army, 1839. Died a victim of the mutiny in Kabul, 2 November 1841.

### References and Further Reading

Burnes, Alexander, *Travels into Bokhara: Being the Account of a Journey from India to Cabool, Tartary and Persia in the Years 1831, 1832 and 1833*; also as *Narrative of a Voyage on the Indus*, 3 vols., 1834; with an introduction by James Lunt, 1973.

Burnes, Alexander, *Cabool: A Personal Narrative of a Journey to, and Residence in That City: In the Years 1836, 1837, 1838*, 1842.

Burnes, Alexander, "Memoir on the Eastern Branch of the River Indus, Giving an Account of the Alterations Produced on It by an Earthquake, Also a Theory of the Formation of the Runn, and Some Conjectures on the Route of Alexander the Great; Drawn up in the years 1827–1828," *Transactions of the Royal Asiatic Society of Great Britain and Ireland*, 3 (1835): 550–588.

Burnes, Alexander, "On the Siah Posh Kafirs, with Specimens of Their Language and Costume," *Journal of the Asiatic Society of Bengal*, 7 (1838): 325–333; and other articles in this journal.

*See also* **Great Game**

## BURTON, RICHARD FRANCIS (1821–1890) *British Explorer, Diplomat, and Translator*

One of the most controversial figures of the Victorian era, Burton was a swordsman, brawler, traveler, linguist, soldier, war correspondent, diplomat, translator, archaeologist, anthropologist, and lover. But perhaps more than anything else, Burton was a perpetual outsider—not quite at home even at home, always looking over the next horizon, he had no regard for traditional English values and seemed happiest when disguised as someone else.

Richard Francis Burton was born in England in 1821, but grew up on the European continent. By his teenage years he had displayed considerable precocity in donning disguises, brawling, and investigating his sexuality, and his father thought to rescue him by returning him to the chillier climes of England and enrolling him in college. But Burton didn't fit in at Oxford, despite his brilliance. He insisted, for example, on speaking Greek as he had actually heard it spoken instead of the antique Greek favored by his teachers. When at last Burton was "rusticated"—expelled—both Oxford and Burton were relieved.

Burton's father purchased a commission in the East Indian army for him in 1842, and in India Burton soon found his way into an occupation perfectly suited to his gifts. He became an intelligence agent, learning the native languages and then passing himself off as an Indian by staining his skin with walnut juice. His first great feat of exploration made use of this experience: in 1852, Burton became one of the first Westerners to make the pilgrimage to Mecca. He did so by disguising himself as an Afghan Muslim, one "Mirza Abdullah." As Burton recounted in *Personal Narrative of a Pilgrimage to El-Medinah and Mecca* (1855–1856), he visited the holy city of Medina and then the holiest shrine of the Islamic faith, the Ka'ba in Mecca, all the while believing that if his disguise were pierced he would be killed by indignant pilgrims.

His next travel exploit was to enter the forbidden Islamic city of Harar on the Horn of Africa. The citizens of Harar had an ancient legend that if a Frank (European) were ever to set foot in their city it would signal the end of their culture. Burton made a daring desert crossing, presented his self-forged credentials to the young emir of Harar (who to Burton's great surprise and relief received him favorably), and managed during his trip to compile detailed notes on the

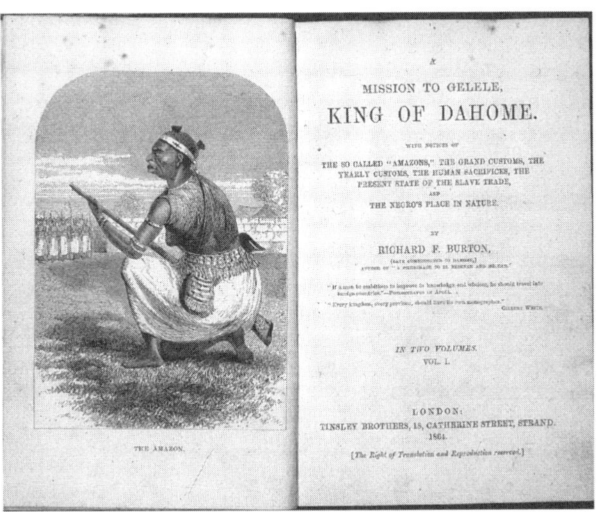

A

MISSION TO GELELE,

KING OF DAHOME.

WITH NOTICES OF

THE SO CALLED "AMAZONS," THE GRAND CUSTOMS, THE YEARLY CUSTOMS, THE HUMAN SACRIFICES, THE PRESENT STATE OF THE SLAVE TRADE,

AND

THE NEGRO'S PLACE IN NATURE.

BY

RICHARD F. BURTON,

*IN TWO VOLUMES.*

VOL. I.

LONDON:

TINSLEY BROTHERS, 18, CATHERINE STREET, STRAND.

1864.

The frontispiece to Burton's *A Mission to Gelele, King of Dahome* (1864) highlights the phenomenon of the monarch's so-called Amazon bodyguard. *Courtesy of the Stapleton Collection, London.*

people and their culture, particularly sexual practices (the branch of anthropological study that most interested him; Burton in fact claimed that the easiest way to learn a people's language was to sleep with their women). A second expedition to the land of the Somali in 1855 ended less successfully when Burton and his party were attacked by natives and Burton was badly wounded by a spear that transfixed his jaw. His experiences on these two journeys were recounted in *First Footsteps in East Africa* (1856), a work still celebrated for its detailed rendering of the Somali culture.

Burton later returned to East Africa with John Hanning Speke, a fellow officer of the East Indian army who had played a minor role in the Somali expeditions. Burton's stated objective was to explore the lake regions of central Africa; his private hope was that they might discover the source of the White Nile, the most prized geographical goal of his era. This 1857 expedition was, in many ways, more difficult than the disastrous second Somali trip. Burton suffered from a range of incapacitating diseases (including fever-induced blindness and elephantine swelling of the limbs), the desertion of bearers and subsequent loss of many supplies, attacks by hordes of insects—in fact, he and Speke were beset by virtually every calamity that could befall travelers in Africa. It also became clear that the irascible and unorthodox Burton and the traditional and plodding Speke were ill matched as companions, and long before the journey was over they had grown to dislike each other.

Five months after they set out, they attained their goal, Lake Tanganyika, the longest and one of the deepest freshwater lakes in the world, although when Burton was told that they had reached the lake, his initial reaction was disappointment:

> I gazed in dismay; the remains of my blindness, the veil of trees, and a broad ray of sunshine illuminating but one reach of the Lake, had shrunk its fair proportions. Somewhat prematurely I began to lament my folly in having risked life and lost health for so poor a prize, to curse Arab exaggeration, and to propose an immediate return. . . . Advancing, however, a few yards, the whole scene suddenly burst upon my view, filling me with admiration, wonder, and delight.

Still almost incapacitated with illness, Burton gladly agreed when Speke asked leave to search for a large lake rumored to be to the north. It was a fateful mistake, for Speke discovered Lake Victoria and immediately seized upon the notion that this huge body of water must be the fabled source of the Nile. While Burton treated Speke's intuition with skepticism because of the lack of geographical proof, he did urge the Royal Geographical Society to consider his subordinate's claim carefully, writing that he believed it highly possible that Speke's Lake Victoria might prove to be "the source or principal feeder of the White Nile."

Speke gained the greater glory from the expedition and was put in charge of the next Geographical Society expedition to East Africa, but Burton was by far the better observer of customs and cultures. His *Lake Regions of Central Africa* (1860) is a classic early work of anthropology, as are some of the books written after he was forced to abandon the field he opened and turn his attention to West Africa. Perhaps the most exciting of these journeys is related in *A Mission to Gelele, King of Dahome* (1864). Burton, who was serving as a British consul, conducted a diplomatic mission to the African kingdom of Dahomey (now Benin), where he hoped not only to convince the king to cease trafficking in slaves and put an end to frequent ritual executions, but also to observe at close hand the fabled Amazon warriors of Dahomey. Burton failed in his political aims, but perhaps his greatest disappointment was his discovery that the Amazons, instead of lovely warrior maidens, turned out to be a burly fighting force he described as being "mostly elderly and all of them hideous," an army whose officers were "chosen for the size of their bottoms."

After his journeys in West Africa, Burton left exploration in the hands of younger men and continued on in the British diplomatic service, although he never received postings appropriate to his many accomplishments. Master of 25 languages (40, counting different dialects), Burton was one of the outstanding linguists of his time. He translated a number of works into English, including his classic 16-volume rendering of the *Arabian Nights*. He authored dozens of books on his explorations of India, Africa, the Middle East, and the

Americas. He was one of the founders of the fledgling science of anthropology. And he was one of the few famous explorers of his age to travel not just to record geographical discoveries but to discover himself along the way. Burton never shrank from making people angry or uncomfortable, so he never achieved the station in society his gifts deserved. But what did he care about society? At his death, Burton was eulogized as a rarity, and indeed, he was.

GREG GARRETT

### Biography

Born Richard Francis Burton in Torquay, Devon, 19 March 1821. Lived in France and Italy in early life. Attended schools in Brighton and Richmond, Surrey. Studied at Trinity College, Oxford University, 1840–1742; was dismissed for a minor offense without a degree. Joined the Indian army, serving as an officer in the Bombay Native Infantry in Sind, 1842–1848. Caught cholera and ophthalmia; took sick leave in Goa, 1847–1849. Returned to England, 1849. Wrote about his Sind travels, 1850–1853. Visited the Muslim holy cities of Mecca and Medina and the eastern Ethiopian city of Harar, 1853–1855. Volunteer in the Crimean War, 1855. Launched Central African expedition with John Hanning Speke, 1856–1859; discovered Lakes Tanganyika and Victoria, 1857. Traveled to the United States, crossing to Salt Lake City, 1860; continued to Panama and returned to England, 1861. Married Isabel Arundell in secret, 1861. Served as British consul at Fernando Po (now Bioko), off the coast of West Africa, explored the Congo River, and journeyed to Dahomey (now Benin), 1861–1865; consul in Santos, Brazil, 1865–1869, Damascus, 1869–1871, and Trieste, 1872–1890. Died of gout and heart disease in Trieste, 20 October 1890.

### References and Further Reading

Burton, Richard Francis, *Goa and the Blue Mountains; or, Six Months of Sick Leave*, 1851.

Burton, Richard Francis, *Scinde; or, The Unhappy Valley*, 2 vols., 1851.

Burton, Richard Francis, *Sindh, and the Races That Inhabit the Valley of the Indus; and with Notices of the Topography and History of the Province*, 1851.

Burton, Richard Francis, *Falconry in the Valley of the Indus*, 1852.

Burton, Richard Francis, *Personal Narrative of a Pilgrimage to El-Medinah and Meccah*, 3 vols., 1855–1856.

Burton, Richard Francis, *First Footsteps in East Africa; or, An Exploration of Harar*, 1856.

Burton, Richard Francis, *The Lake Regions of Central Africa: A Picture of Exploration*, 2 vols., 1860.

Burton, Richard Francis, *The City of the Saints, and Across the Rocky Mountains to California*, 1861; as *The Look of the West, 1860: Across the Plains to California*, 1963.

Burton, Richard Francis, *Abeokuta and the Camaroons Mountains: An Exploration*, 2 vols., 1863.

Burton, Richard Francis, *Wanderings in West Africa, from Liverpool to Fernando Po*, 2 vols., 1863.

Burton, Richard Francis, *A Mission to Gelele, King of Dahome, with Notices of the So-Called "Amazons," the Grand Customs, the Yearly Customs, the Human Sacrifices, the Present State of the Slave Trade, and the Negro's Place in Nature*, 2 vols., 1864.

Burton, Richard Francis, *The Nile Basin*, part 1: *Showing Tanganyika to Be Ptolemy's Western Lake Reservoir: A Memoir Read before the Royal Geographical Society, November 14, 1864*; part 2: *Captain Speke's Discovery of the Source of the Nile: A Review* (part 2 by James M'Queen), 1864.

Burton, Richard Francis, *Wit and Wisdom from West Africa; or, A Book of Proverbial Philosophy, Idioms, Enigmas and Laconisms*, compiled by Burton, 1865.

Burton, Richard Francis, *The Guide-Book: A Pictorial Pilgrimage to Mecca and Medina*, 1865.

Burton, Richard Francis, *Explorations of the Highlands of Brazil; with a Full Account of the Gold and Diamond Mines; Also, Canoeing Down 1500 Miles of the Great River São Francisco, from Sabará to the Sea*, 2 vols., 1869.

Burton, Richard Francis, *Letters from the Battlefields of Paraguay*, 1870.

Burton, Richard Francis, with Charles F. Tyrwhitt-Drake, *Unexplored Syria: Visits to the Libanus, the Tulul el Safá, the Anti-Libanus, the Northern Libanus, and the 'Aláh*, 2 vols., 1872.

Burton, Richard Francis, *Zanzibar; City, Island, and Coast*, 2 vols., 1872.

Burton, Richard Francis, *Ultima Thule; or, A Summer in Iceland*, 2 vols., 1875.

Burton, Richard Francis, *Etruscan Bologna: A Study*, 1876.

Burton, Richard Francis, *Two Trips to Gorilla Land and the Cataracts of the Congo*, 2 vols., 1876.

Burton, Richard Francis, *Scind Revisited: With Notices of the Anglo-Indian Army; Railroads, Past, Present and Future, etc.*, 2 vols., 1877.

Burton, Richard Francis, *The Gold Mines of Midian and the Ruined Midianite Cities: A Fortnight's Tour in North-Western Arabia*, 1878.

Burton, Richard Francis, *The Land of Midian (Revisited)*, 2 vols., 1879.

Burton, Richard Francis, *To the Gold Coast for Gold: A Personal Narrative*, 1883.

Burton, Richard Francis, *Wanderings in Three Continents*, edited by W.H. Wilkins, 1901.

*See also* **Speke, John Hanning**

## BUSBECQ, OGIER GHISLAIN DE (c. 1520–1591) *Flemish Diplomat*

Notwithstanding the inauspicious circumstances of his birth—he was the illegitimate son of a Flemish nobleman—Ogier Ghislain de Busbecq (or Augerius Gislenius Busbequius) enjoyed an excellent upbringing. After an extensive university education he returned to Flanders to prepare himself for a career in the public service. In November 1554 he was summoned to Vienna where he accepted an assignment from Ferdinand of Austria (who in 1558 would become Ferdinand I, Holy

Roman Emperor) to undertake a diplomatic mission that was to keep him in Turkey for almost seven years. The Ottoman empire was then at the height of its power, under Sultan Suleiman I "the Magnificent" (r. 1520–1566). For decades the Turks had presented a major threat to southeast Europe, advancing as far as the gates of Vienna in 1529. Busbecq's mission was to check Turkish expansion through diplomacy. Despite his status as imperial ambassador to the Sublime Porte, the Turks, given the tense political situation and not acknowledging any diplomatic privileges, treated him initially little better than a hostage. Eventually, however, through courage and determination and thanks to his quick sympathy for and appreciation of the Turkish character, Busbecq was able to negotiate terms for a satisfactory treaty, which he presented to Ferdinand for ratification at Frankfurt am Main on 21 November 1562. Having proved himself a consummate diplomat and loyal servant, he was knighted for his efforts and remained in imperial service until his death.

Apart from his extensive official correspondence and a short treatise known as the *Exclamatio, sive de re militari contra Turcam instituenda consilium* [Appeal, or Plan to Wage War on the Turks], written in 1576, Busbecq wrote four famous letters affording vivid insights into conditions in Turkey. These "Turkish Letters" as they are generally known (a more accurate title would be "Four Letters of the Mission to Turkey") purport to have been written at Vienna on 1 September 1554, Constantinople on 14 July 1555 and 1 June 1560, and Frankfurt am Main on 16 December 1562, dates that, until recently, were taken at face value. However, Martels has shown that, though the letters are undoubtedly by Busbecq, they are not all that they seem: while the underlying information is largely authentic, they do contain elements of fiction, and were certainly not written until at least 1579. Christopher Plantin's first edition of Busbecq's writings, under the title *Itinera Constantinopolitanum et Amasianum* [Travels to Constantinople and Amasya] (Antwerp, 1581), contained only the first letter and the *Exclamatio*; Plantin reissued it in 1582, now with the second of the "Turkish Letters" appended. The third and fourth letters did not appear until the Paris edition of 1589. Not only does the publishing history of the letters itself suggest that for the most part they were not composed until the 1580s, but in addition Martels has shown that they contain factual details and stylistic features that are explicable only if we assume that they were not written until the closing years of Busbecq's life (Martels, 1989).

Despite not being as genuinely spontaneous as they have hitherto been held to be, the "Turkish Letters," written in elegant Latin, reveal Busbecq to be a man with a remarkably wide range of interests, ever eager to extend and deepen his knowledge in whatever field; nothing was beyond him, nothing beneath him. He was a frank and genial observer of human life. Unlike most sixteenth-century European commentators on the Turks, Busbecq was able to make dispassionate observations. He wrote with open admiration of the Ottoman administrative and military organization, praising in particular their system of preferment through demonstrable competence and merit rather than (as in the West) through the accident of birth; it is said that he proposed to write a book on this subject, but the plan seems not to have been carried out. The letters are important for the political information they contain, but they are also full of engaging gossip and the most delightful stories, several of which are quoted in Robert Burton's *Anatomy of Melancholy* (1621). Busbecq's interests embraced archaeological remains and epigraphy, numismatics and manuscripts, and the flora and fauna of the region. He would probably have been surprised to learn that posterity would credit him with the introduction of the tulip (the name derives from the Turkish word for turban, which it resembles in shape), the lilac, and the angora goat into western Europe, though he certainly described these. He recorded the important inscription describing the exploits of the first Roman emperor, Augustus, on the Monumentum Ancyranum at Angora (Ankara), and he collected ancient coins and acquired some 270 Greek manuscripts that still survive in the Austrian National Library (including the famous early-sixth-century Dioscorides, Cod. Med. Graec. 1).

Busbecq, an adept linguist (he is said to have spoken seven languages with native fluency), still occupies an honored place in the history of the field for his account, in the fourth of the "Turkish Letters," of Crimean Gothic, a now extinct East Germanic language. While the Gothic kingdom in northern Italy had been wiped out in the sixth century, some speakers of the language apparently still survived in the Crimea in Busbecq's day. At some point between June 1560 and late August 1562 he met two envoys from the Crimea, one of whom appears to have been a Greek-speaking Goth who claimed to have forgotten his native tongue, the other a Greek who had acquired a command of Gothic. This was a happy chance, for Busbecq tells us that he "had long hoped to meet one of these people and, if possible, obtain from him something written in their language." In his letter he records a total of 101 distinct Gothic words, mostly nouns but also a few verbs, numerals, and short phrases, and the beginning of a song. Despite the undoubted shortcomings of Busbecq's account—his interview with the men (neither of whom could be considered a reliable informant) was probably conducted through the medium of Italian and Greek—

it remains of crucial importance as the sole surviving evidence for Crimean Gothic (see Stearns, 1978).

JOHN L. FLOOD

### Biography

Born in Comines (Komen), then in Spanish Netherlands, now on the border of France and Belgium, c. 1520–1522. Studied at the University of Leuven, c. 1533–1538. Later studied at the universities of Paris, Venice, Bologna, and Padua. Entered diplomatic service, 1550s. Went to England as companion to Don Pedro Lasso, representing Ferdinand of Austria, at the marriage of Queen Mary Tudor to Philip II of Spain, July 1554. Went to Vienna to receive assignment from Ferdinand, November 1554. Ambassador to Ottoman court at Constantinople, 1555–1562. Continued in imperial service with Ferdinand (d. 1564), Maximilian II (1564–1576), and Rudolph II (1576–1612). Personal representative of Rudolph II at the French court, until 1591. Abducted by soldiers while traveling in Normandy, September 1591. Died at St. Germain, near Rouen, France, 27 or 28 October 1591.

### References and Further Reading

Busbecq, Ogier Ghislain de, *Augerii Gislenii Busbequii D. legationis Turcicae Epistolae quatuor*, 1589. There were many seventeenth- and eighteenth-century editions deriving directly or indirectly from the 1589 Paris edition. The most recent reprint is of the 1740 Basel edition: *Omnia quae extant opera*, with a preface by Rudolph Neck, 1968.

Busbecq, Ogier Ghislain de, *The Life and Letters of Ogier Ghiselin de Busbecq: Seigneur of Bousbeque, Knight, Imperial Ambassador*, edited and translated by Charles Thornton Forster and F.H. Blackburne Daniell, 2 vols., 1881.

Busbecq, Ogier Ghislain de, *The Turkish Letters of Ogier Ghiselin de Busbecq, Imperial Ambassador at Constantinople 1554–1562*, translated by Edward Seymour Forster, 1927; reprinted, 1968, 2001.

Busbecq, Ogier Ghislain de, *Ogier Ghiselin van Boesbeeck: Vier brieven over het gezantschap naar Turkije*, edited by Zweder von Martels, 1994.

Martels, Zweder von, "Augerius Gislenius Busbequius: Leven en werk van de keizerlijke gezant aan het hof van Süleyman de Grote: een biografische, literarie en historische studie met editie van onuitgegeven teksten," (dissertation), Rijksuniversiteit Groningen 1989.

Stearns, MacDonald, *Crimean Gothic: Analysis and Etymology of the Corpus*, Saratoga, California: Anma Libri, 1978.

## BUSES AND COACHES

The word *omnibus*, meaning "[transport] for all," was first applied to vehicles intended to transport members of the public more cheaply than a private coach or hackney carriage. The first primitive version of the omnibus was launched on 18 March 1662: a service of seven "*carosses a cinq sous*," each carrying a maximum of eight inside passengers. Received at first with great enthusiasm, the service was discontinued within a year, when the novelty dissipated.

In 1819, the Parisian Jacques Laffitte reintroduced the omnibus. Unwieldy and uncomfortable, it carried 16 to 18 passengers, and, in a bid to improve the design, Laffitte commissioned George Shillibeer, an English coachbuilder living in Paris, to build a better vehicle. It was Shillibeer who introduced the omnibus to London. On 4 July 1829, his first two public-service vehicles began running between Paddington and the Bank, making five round-trips daily. Their lower fares, regular service, and speediness made the new omnibus hugely popular.

> In an Omnibus there is no delay in taking up and setting down; no calling at booking offices; no twenty-minutes-waiting at "the Cellar"; no compulsive cad-cramming. In an Omnibus you may ride as far for sixpence as you can in a coach for eighteen-pence. In an Omnibus there is plenty of stretching room for the longest of legs, without knee-packing—this is a great desideratum. Lastly, an Omnibus, like most of our modern farces, is of French origin; and, therefore, must be highly appreciated by all English men and women who have any pretension to taste. (*Morning Herald*, October 1829)

Conductors were initially treated with enormous respect, hired only if they were fluent in French and English, and dressed in smart military-style uniforms to enhance their authority. However, they soon became infamous for swindling foreigners, mistreating passengers, drunkenness, and other rude behavior. The popular term for them was "cad." In *Sketches by Boz*, Dickens describes a typical London omnibus cad: "This young gentleman is a singular instance of self-devotion; his somewhat intemperate zeal on behalf of his employers, is constantly getting him into trouble, and occasionally into the house of correction."

After Shillibeer retired from the London omnibus scene, competing proprietors, in order to run profitable businesses, were all but compelled to join forces as the London Conveyance Company, which made a number of improvements. Twopenny fares (later reduced to a penny) were instituted in 1846; in the same year, advertising was introduced inside buses. Outside seats became more popular and stairways replaced ladders as a means of accessing seats on the roof of the bus, making them available to both men and women passengers. In 1855, the London General Omnibus Company was founded with 50 omnibuses, 600 horses, and a staff of more than 180 men. Although motor buses, introduced in 1899, gradually superseded horse-drawn omnibuses, these older models were still in use until 1911.

In London, 20 motor buses plied the Kensington–Victoria route in 1905; by 1908, their number had swelled to 1,000, and they were used throughout the city and its suburbs. By this time, rural areas and small towns in Britain, which maintained no other public transport, were providing regular and inexpensive bus services. Early motor buses resembled their horse-drawn counterparts: they stood high off the ground and upper-deck passengers were completely unprotected. Later improvements included a covered upper deck, upholstered seats, balloon tires that increased the comfort and speed of the vehicle, and a seating capacity of up to 70.

Motor buses remained distinct from motor coaches: the former intended for inner-city use only, the latter for touring and long-distance journeys. The development of motor coach services began after the end of World War I. Although coach journeys generally took twice as long as the same trip by rail, fares were lower and the bus could be boarded at local stops rather than a distant station. Priestley, who began writing *English Journey* in 1932, went by coach to Southampton and found coach travel "determinedly and ruthlessly comfortable."

Coach or long-distance bus travel continues to have several advantages for the modern traveler over alternative means of public transport. It is generally much less expensive than its rivals and is indeed often the only means of getting to remote areas that are not served by rail. While luxury vehicles geared for the tourist trade have a bad name among independent travelers for insulating their occupants from the countries and peoples they pass through, travel on buses used by local people offers the enterprising (and often young or impecunious) traveler an intimate personal perspective on an area. The guidebook publisher Eugene Fodor appreciated this fact when he made a three-month journey by bus through the United States in 1930, visiting 40 states and noting what his fellow passengers had to say about their region.

Like local trains, buses offer the traveler the serendipitous chance of meeting people on neutral ground. In journeys taken wholly by bus, the generating of such encounters may be a significant factor in the decision to use buses as the mode of transport. In other cases, a bus journey is merely an incident on a longer journey in which several methods of transport are used. Both sorts of bus journey have the potential to bring travelers into transitory contact with a variety of people under conditions in which they feel free to express themselves, and their opinions or personal circumstances can be poignantly juxtaposed with the traveler's observation of the passing view through the bus window. An example of this is Colin Thubron traveling by bus to Samarkand through the landscape devastated by Soviet exploitation, with an old Bukharan on one side of him and a Russian geologist on the other; in his description, this becomes a metaphor for the condition of the Central Asian republics at the end of the Soviet era (*The Lost Heart of Asia*, chapter 6).

JESSICA LANG AND JENNIFER SPEAKE

### References and Further Reading

Horne, Jon, *Lying about America*, Sittingbourne: Heartland, 1995.

Kurtz, Irma, *The Great American Bus Ride*, New York: Simon and Schuster, 1993; London: Fourth Estate, 1994.

Leather, Gertrude, *Home with the Heather: By Bus from London to John o'Groats*, London: Ian Allan, 1986.

Marnham, Patrick, *So Far from God: A Journey to Central America*, 1985.

Steinbeck, John, *The Wayward Bus*, 1947.

West, Gordon, *By Bus to the Sahara*, London: Travel Book Club, 1939; London: Black Swan, 1996.

Williams, Hugo, *No Particular Place to Go*, London: Jonathan Cape, 1981.

## BYRD, RICHARD (1888–1957) *American Polar Explorer, Aviator, and Scientist*

Richard Evelyn Byrd was born into a prominent American family in Winchester, Virginia, on 25 October 1888. His ancestors included Lord Delaware and William Byrd II, one of the founders of Richmond, Virginia. Byrd entered the U.S. Naval Academy in 1908, fought in World War I, and, when a leg injury forced him to retire from the navy in 1916, returned to the United States to train pilots in Pensacola, Florida. The first man to fly both over the North and South Poles, Byrd made five expeditions to Antarctica and is credited with naming numerous geological features and with mapping large portions of the coast of the continent. When he died on 12 March 1957, he was among the most highly decorated officers in American military history, with 22 special citations and commendations, nine of which were for bravery and two for saving the lives of others.

Byrd's career in polar exploration began in 1924, when he accompanied Donald B. MacMillan's Arctic expedition to western Greenland. The capstone of this trip occurred on 9 May 1926, when Byrd, acting as navigator, and pilot Floyd Bennett became the first men to fly over the North Pole. The round-trip flight from Spitzbergen to the North Pole in a Fokker trimotor took just over 15 hours 30 minutes.

Byrd's first and most famous expedition to Antarctica set sail from California in October 1928. Although Byrd's was a private expedition, it was exceptionally well funded, backed by corporate sponsors and donations from thousands of individuals. On 2 January

1929, the first of Byrd's three ships arrived in the Bay of Whales, and shortly thereafter the men began to set up a base camp, called Little America, some 15 miles inland on the Ross Ice Shelf. Undoubtedly, three disassembled airplanes carried in the ships' holds formed the most valuable items of Byrd's cargo on this expedition. Byrd chose a Ford trimotor monoplane capable of generating nearly 1,000 horsepower for heavy transport and longer flights. He also brought along a 425-horsepower Fokker Universal monoplane and a Fairchild folding-wing monoplane for backup, transport, and shorter reconnaissance flights.

At 3:29 PM on 28 November 1929, the heavily loaded Ford trimotor, which Byrd had named the *Floyd Bennett*, took off from Little America and headed for the South Pole, with Bernt Balchen as pilot, Harold June as copilot, Byrd as navigator, and Ashley McKinley as photographer. The plane climbed easily to 9,000 feet, but hundreds of pounds of food and empty fuel canisters had to be jettisoned to allow the plane to climb to 11,000 feet, the height necessary to clear the Liv Glacier pass in the Queen Maud Mountains. The plane cleared the pass with only a few hundred feet to spare and then continued on to the Polar Plateau. Shortly after midnight, the *Floyd Bennett* became the first plane to fly over the South Pole. The plane returned to Little America, landing at 10:10 AM, thus completing the 1,287-kilometer round-trip flight in a little less than 19 hours.

Byrd subsequently led four more expeditions to Antarctica. On his second expedition, ostensibly to map and claim land around the South Pole for the United States, Byrd spent five winter months alone at Advanced Base, a weather station hut, enduring temperatures of −60°C and colder. When Byrd was eventually rescued, he was near death, suffering from frostbite and carbon monoxide poisoning from a defective oil-burning stove. Byrd's experiences at Advanced Base provided the material for *Alone*, his most famous and popular book.

Byrd led three more expeditions to Antarctica as the director of U.S. government expeditions. On these trips, Byrd continued to map the continent from the air, but he and his fellow scientists also completed substantial work in the areas of meteorology, oceanography, glaciology, and materials testing. Byrd's ultimate goal was to make Antarctica a U.S. territory, and, to this end, he named geographic features such as Marie Byrd Land and the Rockefeller Mountains after his wife and one of his most prominent American benefactors, respectively.

One of Byrd's major contributions to polar exploration was the practical application of airplanes, radios, cameras, and other modern technologies to aid scientific research. Moreover, his numerous and lengthy expeditions provided advancements in how to cope with and survive for long periods in extremely cold weather. Unlike Amundsen, Byrd believed that modern technology should be used to supplement, not replace, traditional methods of polar exploration, so in addition to airplanes, snowmobiles, radios, and other up-to-date technological innovations, he also took along dogs, sledges, and a number of experienced dog handlers. Perhaps Byrd's most significant contribution, however, was his almost uncanny ability to navigate accurately in uncharted regions where traditional navigational aids such as the compass were all but useless.

TERRY REILLY

### Biography

Born in Winchester, Virginia, 25 October 1888. Attended the Shenandoah Valley Military Academy, Virginia Military Institute (1904–1907), University of Virginia (1907–1908), and the U.S. Naval Academy; graduated and commissioned ensign, 1912. Married Marie Donaldson Ames, 1915: four children. Served on a number of battleships before and during World War I; retired because of injury, 1916; received flight training at the U.S. Naval Air Station, Pensacola, Florida, 1917–1918. Commander of air stations in Nova Scotia; developed navigational equipment and methods for Navy/Curtiss (NC) flying boats. Conducted tests and preparations for first successful NC flight over the Atlantic, 1919. Assistant director of naval aviation and liaison officer to Congress, 1919–1921. Accompanied the Donald B. MacMillan expedition to Greenland, 1924–1925. Awarded the U.S. Congressional Medal of Honor, the Distinguished Service Medal, and the National Geographic Society's Hubbard Medal for claim of the first flight over the North Pole, 1926 (subsequently disputed). Promoted to rank of commander, U.S. Navy, 1926. Assisted Charles Lindbergh with solo transatlantic flight, May 1927. Made transatlantic flight with three others, landing at Ver-sur-Mer, Brittany, June 1927. Appointed commandant of the French Légion d'honneur, 1927. Made first Antarctic expedition, 1928–1930. Completed the first flight over the South Pole, November 1929. Awarded the Navy Cross; promoted to rank of rear admiral, 1929. Second Antarctic expedition, 1933–1935. Honorary chairman of the No-Foreign-War-Crusade, 1930s. Commanding officer of the U.S. Antarctic Service, 1939. Third expedition to Antarctic at request of President Franklin D. Roosevelt, 1939–1941. Visited the Pacific during World War II. Received Legion of Merit, January 1945. Founded Iron Curtain Refugee Campaign of the International Rescue Committee after World War II. Commander of U.S. Navy's Operation Highjump mapping and photographic expedition to

Antarctica, 1946. Final polar flight, January 1956. Supervised preparations for Operation Deep Freeze I for further exploration of the Antarctic during International Geophysical Year, 1957–1958. Received the Department of Defense Medal of Freedom, 1957. Died in Boston, Massachusetts, 12 March 1957.

### References and Further Reading

Byrd, Richard, *Skyward: Man's Mastery of the Air as Shown by the Brilliant Flights of America's Leading Air Explorer*, 1928.

Byrd, Richard, *Little America: Aerial Exploration in the Antarctic; the Flight to the South Pole*, 1930.

Byrd, Richard, *My Flight to the North Pole*, edited by Alfred Hoschke, 1933.

Byrd, Richard, *Discovery: The Story of the Second Byrd Antarctic Expedition*, introduction by Claude A. Swanson, 1935; as *Antarctic Discovery*, 1936.

Byrd, Richard, *Alone*, 1938.

Byrd, Richard, *To the Pole: The Diary and Notebook of Richard E. Byrd, 1925–1927*, edited by Raimund E. Goerler, 1998.

## BYRD, WILLIAM (1674–1744) *Virginia Planter-Legislator and Travel Writer*

Although William Byrd II was born into one of the first families of Virginia, or within the elite society that constituted the American South's aristocracy, he spent over a third of his life in England. Educated in the classics, business, and law, Byrd returned to Virginia only twice, for brief visits with his family, between the ages of 7 and 30. After claiming his father's estate in 1705, Byrd returned to England in 1715 for business reasons and to represent Virginia before the Board of Trade, and he remained there for the better part of the following decade. Byrd was a habitual journal keeper throughout his life and, from 1717 to 1721, kept a diary about his observations and experiences in London. In addition, the two other journals that sandwich his London diary have served as valuable instruments in determining the fabric of life among the colonial elite in Virginia. Byrd also wrote a treatise on English government and was one of the better-known letter writers among his contemporaries. His correspondence with friends he made in London's elite literary, political, and social circles includes letters from Sir Hans Sloane, Robert Boyle, Mark Catesby, and Sir Robert Walpole.

Byrd first traveled to Britain at the age of seven, thought to be the age of reason according to the prevailing doctrines of the day. At the age of 16, he received firsthand knowledge of the merchant trade under Dutch tradesmen in Holland and, after a brief stint there, returned to England in 1690 to learn more about the world of business from the firm Perry and Lane, Byrd-family agents in London. Then came three years at the Middle Temple, where he was trained in law and was called to the bar in 1695. Byrd returned to Virginia later that year and was elected to the House of Burgesses, but he quickly reintroduced himself to London society as legal representative of the Virginia Assembly.

In 1704, Byrd's father died, and in 1705, he returned home to claim the 26,000 acres of prime Virginia soil and two houses on the James River, Belvidere and Westover, that awaited him. In 1706, Byrd married Lucy Parke, and, five years after taking over his father's estate, he was appointed to the 12-member Council, or the upper body of the Virginia Assembly.

By 1715, Byrd was back in England for personal commercial purposes as well as on official business for the colony as representative of the Board of Trade. This time he returned not as an unattached bachelor initially, but as a family man. However, shortly upon her arrival in London, Lucy died of smallpox, leaving Byrd to care for the two surviving daughters, whom he later sent for, produced during their often volatile ten-year union. Byrd spent much of the next decade, during which time he primarily resided in England, looking for a new wife, and he finally married Maria Taylor of Kensington, who bore him four children, including his only surviving son, William III, who was born in 1726.

What is most remarkable about this interval of Byrd's life spent in England is his London diary, kept from 13 December 1717 to 19 May 1721. In it, as he did in his Virginia diaries, he described in detail the activities of his days, a typical one usually starting anywhere between the hours of five and nine o'clock and beginning with a reading in one of the classical languages he knew. Meant for private use during Byrd's lifetime, this journal and travel narrative reveals the intimate details of his life, including his dalliances with several women prior to his second marriage, and his obsessions with fashionable English ladies, including the heiress Mary Smith, a widow Pierson, and Lady Elizabeth Lee, the granddaughter of King Charles II.

Byrd also had much to say about his male friends and contemporaries, including Admiral Sir Charles Wager, who became first lord of the Admiralty in 1733; John Percival, who was created the first earl of Egmont in the same year; and Sir Hans Sloane, physician and president of the Royal Society, of which Byrd was a member.

In 1726, Byrd returned to his primary residence at Westover, and he was able to travel and explore areas closer to home. Two years later, he was appointed to a commission that surveyed the boundary between Virginia and North Carolina. Byrd told the misadventures of this experience in *The History of the Dividing Line betwixt Virginia and North Carolina* and *The Secret History of the Line*. In *The History of the Dividing Line*, he describes in vivid detail the local Indian and white backcountry cultures that he encountered, as well as the topography itself on the North Carolina frontier. Typical of his observations was this: "The high land in North Carolina was barren, and covered with deep sand; and the low grounds were wet and boggy, insomuch that several of our horses were mired, and gave us frequent opportunities to show our horsemanship." As this passage demonstrates, Byrd often combined the scientific and the personal. In *The Secret History of the Line*, he satirized the men of the North Carolina delegation to the commission by giving them fictionalized names such as Jumble, Shoebrush, and Puzzlecause.

In 1732, Byrd visited and wrote about one of the operating mines in Virginia at the time. *A Progress to the Mines* was a report for Alexander Spotswood, a former governor of Virginia who encouraged westward expansion along both sides of the Blue Ridge Mountains and ran the mines that Byrd inspected. Byrd had aspirations to start his own mining works, and, in the following year, he visited a 26,000-acre tract of land that he had purchased in North Carolina with the salary he received as a boundary commissioner. He recorded this sojourn in *A Journey to the Land of Eden*, which was quite similar to *History of the Dividing Line*. It is important to note that none of Byrd's travel narratives were published during his lifetime. Although he traveled extensively, Byrd remained active in politics, and, a year before his death in 1744, he served as president of the Virginia Council.

KOLBY W. BILAL

### Biography

Born in Charles City County, Virginia Colony, 28 March 1674. Son of William Byrd, a plantation owner, trader, and slave importer. Sent to live in England with an uncle, 1681. Attended Felsted Grammar School, Essex, England, 1681–1690. Sent to Rotterdam to study commerce, 1690. Apprenticed to merchants Perry and Lane in London, 1690. Studied law at the Middle Temple, 1692–1695. Returned to Virginia briefly, 1695. Elected fellow of the Royal Society, 1696; elected to council of the Royal Society, 1697. Appointed agent for Virginia in London, 1698. Returned to Virginia to manage father's estate after his death, 1705. Inherited posts of receiver general and auditor, 1705. Married Lucy Parke (died 1716), 4 May 1706: four children, two of whom survived infancy. Member of the Virginia Council, 1709. Chief military commander for counties of Henrico and Charles City, 1710. Returned to England as Board of Trade representative for the colony of Virginia, 1715. Married Maria Taylor, 1724: four children, including William Byrd III. Returned to primary residence in Virginia, 1726. Member of a commission to survey the boundary between Virginia and North Carolina, 1728. Built a mansion, Westover, on the James River, 1730–1734. Visited Governor Alexander Spotswood's plantation and iron foundry at Germanna, Virginia, to study iron mining, 1732. Prospected for coal, iron, and copper, traveling to land he had purchased in North Carolina, 1733. Founded the cities of Richmond and Petersburg; farmed tobacco and cultivated vineyards. President of the Virginia Council, 1743. Died at Westover, Charles City County, Virginia, 26 August 1744.

### References and Further Reading


Byrd, William, *The History of the Dividing Line betwixt Virginia and North Carolina*, 1728; in *The Westover Manuscripts*, 1841.

Byrd, William, *The Secret History of the Line*, 1728; in *William Byrd's Histories of the Dividing Line betwixt Virginia and North Carolina*, edited by William K. Boyd, 1929; as *Histories of the Dividing Line betwixt Virginia and North Carolina*, with a new introduction by Percy G. Adams, 1967.

Byrd, William, *A Progress to the Mines*, 1732; in *The Westover Manuscripts*, 1841.

Byrd, William, *A Journey to the Land of Eden*, 1733; in *The Westover Manuscripts*, 1841.

Byrd, William, *A Journey to the Land of Eden and Other Papers by William Byrd*, edited by Mark Van Doren, 1928.

Byrd, William, *The Secret Diary of William Byrd of Westover, 1709–1712*, edited by Louis B. Wright and Marion Tinling, 1941.

Byrd, William, *Another Secret Diary of William Byrd of Westover, 1739–1741*, edited by Maude H. Woodfin and Marion Tinling, 1942.


## BYRON, GEORGE GORDON, LORD (1788–1824) *British Poet and Dramatist*

Byron was born into an aristocratic family noted for its restlessness and eccentricity. Yet he himself appeared destined at birth to occupy only an obscure position within it. He was born in London, to a spendthrift father and an impoverished mother, and brought up in Aberdeen. Only through the chance death of a young relative did he become heir presumptive to the peerage, assuming the title on the death of his great-uncle in 1798. Thereafter, though habitually short of money, he increasingly led the lifestyle that his new social position implied. He entered Harrow School in 1801 and Cambridge University in 1805.

Byron's wish to travel abroad emerges in his correspondence from 1806 on. At first, his interest extended no further than the idea of a conventional Grand Tour. Later, however, a different tone intrudes into the letters, one of urgency, even desperation, and, in April 1809, he wrote to his lawyer, "I have no alternative . . . quit the country I must immediately." This apparently abrupt shift in attitude has been plausibly linked to Byron's homoerotic desires and his developing perception of travel as an escape from the potential consequences of those desires in contemporary England.

Byron finally left for his European tour in July 1809. He was accompanied by his friend John Cam Hobhouse, who in 1813 published an account of their journey. From England they went to Portugal and on into Andalucia, which was then under threat of French invasion. For the first time, and at first hand, Byron learned about the sufferings of a people at war. Afterward they went to Gibraltar, then sailed for Malta and Greece, landing at Patras in the Peloponnese on 26 September. They subsequently traveled through northern Greece and Albania, where they met the already legendary Ali Pasha. Returning south, they passed through Mesolóngion, crossed and recrossed the Gulf of Corinth, visiting Patras, Delphi, and Thebes, and arrived in Athens on Christmas Day. From there, they made a journey to western Turkey, between March and July 1810. Hobhouse then returned to England, while Byron remained in Greece, with Athens as his base, until April 1811. By his own account, this was one of the happiest times of his life, a period of small-scale travel in the Greek countryside, quixotic social engagements, and extensive homosexual encounters.

Byron's next journey to Europe was undertaken in very different circumstances. His marriage failed at the beginning of 1816, and, in April of that year, he left England, never to return. He traveled south from Ostend, visiting Bruges, Ghent, Antwerp, and Brussels, then journeyed up the Rhine. Byron settled for a time near Geneva, where he first met the poet Shelley. In September, he toured the Bernese Oberland with Hobhouse, then left for Italy at the beginning of October. The next seven years of his life were spent there, first in Venice, then Ravenna, Pisa, and Genoa.

In July 1823, having been persuaded to offer his services in the cause of Greek independence, Byron left Italy, arriving on the Ionian island of Kefallinia on 3 August. The Ionian Islands were, at that time, under British control and so outside the Greek war zone. Byron discovered that the domestic situation on mainland Greece was confused in the extreme and that the country was descending into civil war. In search of a role, he remained in Kefallinia until the end of December. Then, on the invitation of the Greek legislative senate, he left for Mesolóngion to work with Alexandros Mavrokordatos, the Greek political leader. On 19 April 1824, he died in Mesolóngion of fever.

Byron's travels thus fall into three distinct groups: the youthful visit to southern Europe in 1809–1811; the journey through northern Europe to Italy in 1816; and the final adventure in Greece in 1823–1824.

The epitome of the Romantic poet: Byron in Albanian costume, an image that has been reproduced in numerous editions of his works (steel engraving by William Finden from the portrait by Thomas Phillips). *Courtesy of the National Portrait Gallery, London.*

*Childe Harold's Pilgrimage* was the most obvious outcome of Byron's early travels. He began the poem at the end of October 1809, while in northern Greece, and cantos 1 and 2 were a loose transposition of his journey through Portugal, Spain, and the eastern Mediterranean. They were published on 12 March 1812 and made Byron instantly famous. Transparently autobiographical, with a mysterious, brooding hero ("The wandering outlaw of his own dark mind"), *Childe Harold* helped to create a new fashion for travel as romance rather than antiquarian pursuit. It also stimulated interest in the unfamiliar landscapes and cultures of the East, which Byron himself fed in a succession of Eastern tales (*The Giaour*, *The Corsair*, *Lara*, *The Siege of Corinth*).

Canto 3 of *Childe Harold's Pilgrimage*, written and published in 1816, took up the story of Byron's life in the aftermath of his definitive departure from England. His hero, now "grown aged in this world of woe," retraces Byron's path from the English Channel as far south as Switzerland. Canto 4, published in 1818, is a meditation on Byron's Italian experience. He saw himself as "A ruin amidst ruins; there to track / Fall'n states and buried greatness."

From 1818 to 1823, Byron was engaged in the writing of his parody epic poem *Don Juan*, a reflection on the upheavals in European history between the French Revolution and the Restoration. The poem is less immediately dependent on Byron's personal experience of travel than is *Childe Harold*, but it inevitably draws widely on such experience, not least in the famous passage from canto 3 ("The Isles of Greece, the Isles of Greece!").

Byron's travels were vital to his evolution as a writer, as he confirmed in a remark to his friend Trelawny: "If I am a poet . . . the air of Greece made me one." His poetry relies more heavily than Shelley's or Wordsworth's on the sensory impressions of a tangible world. His travels also served to stimulate the critical attitude toward his native land that found its fullest expression in *Don Juan*, and they played a vital role too in awakening his social and political conscience. From the time of the early travels, Byron's direct observation of poverty and suffering led him progressively, if unsystematically, toward an ideal of action. If Byron's time in Greece began as hedonistic escape, it ended with an affirmation of the values of commitment. The last months in Greece, almost completely barren in literary terms, testify to the enduring vitality of a reflective process.

STEPHEN MINTA

### Biography

Born George Noel Gordon Byron in London, 22 January 1788. Lived in Aberdeen as a child; attended Aberdeen Grammar School, 1794–1798. Inherited uncle's title and estate, Newstead Abbey, 1798 (sold Abbey, 1817). Attended Harrow School, Middlesex, 1801–1805; Trinity College, Cambridge, 1805–1808. Traveled in southern Europe, July–December 1809. Took seat in House of Lords, 1809. Based in Athens, 25 December 1809–5 March 1810 and 18 July 1810–22 April 1811. Visited western Turkey, 8 March 1810–14 July 1810. Married Annabella Milbanke, 1815 (separated, 1816): one daughter; ostracized for supposed incestuous affair with his half sister, Augusta Leigh: left England, 1816. Traveled in northern Europe, April–May 1816. Based near Geneva, May–September 1816. Lived and traveled in Italy, 1816–1823. Had affair with Claire Clairmont (stepsister of Mary Shelley), 1816–1817: one daughter. Published *Childe Harold's Pilgrimage* (1812–1818); *Don Juan* (1819–1824). Settled with Teresa, Countess Guiccioli, 1819. Lived in Venice and Ravenna, 1819–1820. Actively supported Italian patriots from 1820. Lived in Leghorn (Livorno), 1822; Genoa, 1823. Editor, with Leigh Hunt, of the *Liberal*, 1822–1823. Traveled to Argostólion, Kefallinía, August 1823; arrived in Mesolóngion, Greece, January 1824. Died of fever in Mesolóngion, 19 April 1824.

### Poetry

Byron, Lord, *Childe Harold's Pilgrimage*, 1812–1818; complete edition, 1819.
Byron, Lord, *The Bride of Abydos: A Turkish Tale*, 1813.
Byron, Lord, *The Giaour: A Fragment of a Turkish Tale*, 1813.
Byron, Lord, *The Corsair: A Tale*, 1814.
Byron, Lord, *Lara: A Tale*, 1814.
Byron, Lord, *The Prisoner of Chillon and Other Poems*, 1816.
Byron, Lord, *The Siege of Corinth*; *Parisina*, 1816.
Byron, Lord, *Beppo: A Venetian Story*, 1818; revised edition, 1818.
Byron, Lord, *Don Juan*, 1819–1824; complete edition, 1826.

*See also* **Greece, 1600–1821**

## BYRON, ROBERT (1905–1941) *British Writer and Art and Architectural Critic*

Robert Byron was born in London on 26 February 1905. His father, Eric Byron, was a civil engineer who was distantly related to Lord Byron. His mother, Margaret (Robinson), came from a gentry background. However, the family, though comfortably off, was not wealthy. Robert was educated at Eton and then at Merton College, Oxford, where he read modern history, graduating with a third-class degree in 1925. Byron's travel writing is remembered for two main qualities: its capacity to entertain, and its interest in art and architecture as expressions of cultures. He was particularly interested in the cultures of the later Hellenistic period and the Islamic culture of (what was then) Persia and Afghanistan. Many, including Paul Fussell and Bruce Chatwin, regard Robert Byron as the supreme English travel writer of his generation (though others favor his Etonian contemporary Peter Fleming for this distinction).

Byron was far from fully engaged in his academic studies, taking advantage of several opportunities for travel: he visited Italy in 1923 and Hungary in 1924 before traveling to Greece immediately after finishing his degree. His name and the assumption of a family connection tended to ensure a warm reception, and he deeply enjoyed his experience of the Greek culture of which, of course, he already knew much. His first publication was a book called *Europe in the Looking-Glass: Reflections of a Motor Drive from Grimsby to Athens* (1926), based on his travels by car across Europe to Greece. The book showed the capacity of Byron's travel writing to discover, or create, comic potential from his experiences. In later works, he adopted a subtler style, reporting events and conversations mainly in an understated and apparently straight-faced manner. Equally, this first book suggested the serious interest in culture in the widest sense that is also part of Byron's approach to travel writing. Byron asserted in the book's first chapter that he wished to counteract the fragmented nationalism of Europe and restore English readers to a sense of their membership of a European whole.

Despite Byron's lackluster performance at Oxford, soon after graduating he discovered a more personally satisfying form of scholarship—one of an "amateur" in the word's older and fuller sense. In 1932, he published *The Appreciation of Architecture*, the first sign of his commitment to the public understanding of architecture—which he developed through not only his travel writings, but also several more specialized book-length projects and extensive publication of articles in architectural journals. In 1928, his second travel book appeared: *The Station: Athos, Treasures and Men*. This was based on his journey to the Orthodox holy site of Mount Athos on the shore of the Aegean in 1927. He and three friends were welcomed as guests at the ancient monastery of Docheiariou. It was during this journey and the writing of his account of it that Byron formulated his passionate ideas about Byzantine culture—what he called "my chosen past." He thenceforth became the champion of the Christian culture of Byzantium against what he regarded as its neglect in favor of the classical culture of pagan and rational Greece. A more specialized exploration of Byzantine culture came in his next book, *The Byzantine Achievement: An Historical Perspective, AD 330–1453* (1929).

Martin Coyle (1998) argues that the trademark characteristics of Byron's travel writing first appear in a recognizable form in *The Station*. In particular, he suggests that the influence of Ruskin can be seen in the book's combination of travel writing and wide-ranging artistic and cultural critique. Less Ruskinian is the comic element in the book, often based on what appears to be verbatim quotation of curious conversations. Paul Fussell identifies this comic vein as reaching maturity in *The Station*, quoting the dialogue between Byron and the monk who would like some English medals:

> "When you return to England will you send me some?"
> . . .
> "But why? You have done nothing."
> "No, but I will. I will do great things. I love England."
> "You must do them first." (Fussell, *Abroad*)

Byron's next work was art criticism rather than travel writing; he and David Talbot Rice (who had been one of his traveling companions at Mount Athos) co-wrote *The Birth of Western Painting* during 1929. In the same year, Byron was able to travel to India as special correspondent for the *Daily Express*. He also managed a brief expedition into Tibet while in India. From this, and from six weeks of travel in the Soviet Union with Christopher Sykes in 1931, came his third travel book, *First Russia, Then Tibet*, which appeared two years after the Tibetan journey (in 1933), and also *An Essay on India* (1931). The Indian essay had a typically Byronesque project—to give an account of what Indian art and culture might tell us about the difficulties, and indeed failures, of British imperial culture in its understanding of India.

*First Russia, Then Tibet* was markedly skeptical of the achievements of Soviet culture, and it was more sympathetic to Tibetan culture. However, as Martin Coyle points out, the book was interested not merely in denouncing Russia, but in conducting a quite complex cultural comparison between the cultures of Western Europe, Soviet Russia, and Tibet: "The ideas of Russia are preached, and act, as a challenge to those of the West . . . the ideas of Tibet offer no challenge; they maintain, simply, a passive resistance towards those of the West" (Coyle, 1998).

In 1933, Byron set off, again accompanied by Christopher Sykes, for Iraq, Persia, and Afghanistan. This journey, funded by a £100 advance from Macmillan for the travel book expected to result, produced his outstanding achievement—*The Road to Oxiana* (1937). Byron and Sykes traveled, amid considerable difficulties in obtaining permissions to travel, to the area in the north of Afghanistan bordering the Oxus River. His traveling companion, writing the *Dictionary of National Biography* entry after Byron's premature death, describes "the best of his books" as "an inquiry into the origins of Islamic art presented in the form of one of the most entertaining travel books of modern times." This high valuation of the book is widely shared. Paul Fussell writes that "it may not be going too far to say that what *Ulysses* is to the novel between the wars and what *The Wasteland* is to poetry, *The Road to Oxiana* is to the travel book" (1982). The book is notably different in form from any of the earlier books, using a daily journal format rather than a continuous narrative. This gives the book an apparently fragmentary but intensely immediate flavor. Martin Coyle acutely suggests that the effect of "Byron's form and style [is] virtually anti-narrative, emphasising not so much the connections among successive experiences as the singularity of each" (1998). Nevertheless, the book also contains in the highest state of development the pleasures and insights offered by the earlier travel writing. There is still the comedy generated by the assumptions of different cultures, the cultural analysis based on specific and detailed description of particular examples, especially of art and architecture, and the serious comparison between modern European culture and alternative historical and regional views of the world.

Though Byron did a good deal of traveling between 1934 and 1937, *The Road to Oxiana* was to be his last travel book. Byron expressed his hatred of Nazi Germany at a number of points in his writing, and from 1938 on, he was committed to rousing Britain from what he regarded as culpable complacency. When war broke out in 1939, he joined the overseas news department of the BBC. In February 1941, he boarded a Royal Navy destroyer, bound for the Middle East. The ship was torpedoed off the coast of Scotland on 24 February 1941, with the loss of the entire crew. Byron was apparently going to the Middle East as a special correspondent for a group of newspapers. However, there was speculation at the time that he had in fact been engaged in intelligence work. This is borne out by work by Paul Fussell that suggests Byron was, indeed, going to report to British intelligence on Soviet activities in the area.

CHRIS HOPKINS

### Biography

Born in Wembley, London, 26 February 1905. Son of a civil engineer, a distant relative of the poet Lord Byron. Attended Eton College and Merton College, Oxford, graduating in 1925. Traveled in Italy, 1923; Hungary, 1924; Greece, 1925 and 1927; journeyed to India and Tibet, 1929; to Soviet Russia, 1931; and to Persia and Afghanistan, 1933. Worked as foreign news subeditor for the BBC from 1939. Departed by sea for Iran on a journalistic commission, February 1941. Killed by enemy action off the coast of Scotland, 24 February 1941.

### References and Further Reading

Byron, Robert, *Europe in the Looking-Glass: Reflections of a Motor Drive from Grimsby to Athens*, 1926.
Byron, Robert, *The Station: Athos, Treasures and Men*, 1928.
Byron, Robert, *The Byzantine Achievement: An Historical Perspective, AD 330–1453*, 1929; reprinted, 1987.
Byron, Robert, and David Talbot Rice, *The Birth of Western Painting: A History of Colour, Form and Iconography*, 1930.
Byron, Robert, *An Essay on India*, 1931.
Byron, Robert, *The Appreciation of Architecture*, 1932.
Byron, Robert, *First Russia, Then Tibet*, 1933; reprinted, 1985.
Byron, Robert, and Christopher Sykes (as Richard Waughburton), *Innocence and Design* (a parodic novel based on their travels in Oxiana), 1935.
Byron, Robert, *Shell Guide to Wiltshire*, 1935.
Byron, Robert, *Imperial Pilgrimage*, 1937.
Byron, Robert, *The Road to Oxiana*, 1937.
Coyle, Martin, entry on Robert Byron in *British Travel Writers, 1910–1939*, edited by Barbara Brothers and Julia M. Gergits, Detroit: Gale, 1998.
Fussell, Paul, "Sancte Roberte, Ore Pro Nobis" in his *Abroad: British Literary Traveling between the Wars*, New York and Oxford: Oxford University Press, 1980.
Fussell, Paul, Introduction to *The Road to Oxiana*, Oxford: Oxford University Press, 1982.

## BYZANTIUM

The term *Byzantium* is not an easy one to define. Byzantion was the name of a town on the Bosphorus that was founded, according to myth, by one Byzas, son of the god Poseidon, and grandson of Zeus and the nymph Io. In 330, the Roman emperor Constantine formally made the town his capital, calling it Nova Roma Constantinopolitana (Constantine's New Rome). After this date, the town became known as New Rome, or Constantinople, although occasionally, both Byzantium and Byzantion were used by classicizing authors. Often, however, it was simply called "the city"—a term that lived on after the sack of 1453 by the Ottoman Turks: indeed, the name of Istanbul is merely an adulterated variant of the Greek *stin polis*, that is to say, "in (or to) the city."

Of course, the name Byzantium is now more commonly used to describe the eastern part of the Roman empire, or more precisely that part of the empire that did not capitulate with the sack of Rome in the fifth century. But even this can be misleading. In the first place, the inhabitants of this part of the empire never referred to themselves as Byzantines, rather as Romans, and the emperor always as emperor of the Romans. It was only much later that the territory dominated and controlled by the emperor came to be known as Byzantium, and it is not insignificant that this term came to be employed by those outside the empire rather than by those within.

Nonetheless, even if we do talk of Byzantium as referring to the territory of the empire, rather than the town known in various guises as Byzantion, New Rome, Constantinople, and Istanbul, it does not solve all our problems. Over the course of the ten centuries that followed the sack of Rome, the territory of the Byzantine empire was subject to considerable geographical changes. In the mid-sixth century, for example, the empire included much of the Mediterranean basin—from Spain and North Africa to the Balkans and Palestine. At the end of the eleventh century, however, little remained apart from the capital city itself. Indeed, after 1204, not even Constantinople itself remained in Byzantine hands after the establishment of a Latin empire based on that city, and the political and administrative capital of Byzantium was effectively removed to Nicaea until 1261. It makes it all the more difficult that such changes often proved to be temporary: understandably, over the course of the 1,100 years between Constantine's dedication and the sack of Constantinople in 1453, the empire saw periods of considerable expansion and of tremendous contraction—often in quick succession. Nonetheless, it should be stressed that, while the precise geographical boundaries were subject to great change, it is those territories subject to the emperor of the eastern part of the Roman empire, who was based, apart from a brief interlude, in Constantinople, that is meant by the term *Byzantium*.

The centrality of Constantinople to Byzantium was not only political and symbolic. The physical location of the city goes a long way toward explaining the growth, development, and importance of the Byzantine empire as a whole. Located at the crossroads between Europe and Asia, the city came to be, at least over time, the meeting point of the Greek and Roman worlds, of Christianity and Islam, of Orthodoxy and Catholicism, of civilization and barbarism. It was not for nothing that in the late antique and medieval worlds, Constantinople was by far the largest city in the Christian, Western world, and, throughout its history, it was to attract many visitors.

While travelers were not drawn to the city by its sheer size, primary sources written by those who had journeyed to, or passed through, Constantinople between the fourth and fifteenth centuries make it plain that the city was a remarkable and wondrous place. The town was dominated by the imposing and supposedly impregnable walls that had been built by Emperor Theodosius II (c. 408–450) and later rebuilt and reinforced by Manuel I Comnenus (c. 1143–1180).

If the land walls did not impress the visitor, then the many monuments inside the city were bound to: the scale of the buildings such as the Golden Gate (the principal entry point to the capital, which lay at the eastern extremity of the road—known as the Via Egnatia—that linked Constantinople with Rome), the Great Palace, the Hippodrome, the various triumphal arches, the many churches in the city, and particularly, of course, the extraordinary church of St. Sophia (or Agia Sophia) made a profound impact on those who visited the city for the first time. The description provided in the *Povest' vremennykh let* (*The Russian Primary Chronicle*) of the reactions of travelers to Constantinople is typical of many of the sources: "We did not know whether we were in heaven or on earth. For on earth there is no such splendour or such beauty, and we are at a loss to describe it. We only know that God dwells there among men, and that their service is fairer than the ceremonies of other nations. We cannot forget that beauty."

The Byzantines were only too well aware of the impact that the physical splendor of the city had on visitors. Accordingly, elaborate rituals, ceremonies, and routines were devised in order to impress official visitors and to drive home the point that Byzantium was God's kingdom on earth. Two primary sources are particularly useful here, both dating from the ninth or tenth century, which elucidate how the emperor and his court sought to deal with foreigners who visited the city. The texts, known as the *De cerimoniis aulae byzantinae* [About the Ceremonies of the Byzantine Court] and the *De administrando imperio* [About the Governing of the Empire], provide an invaluable insight into the reception and treatment of foreigners in Byzantium.

There were several reasons why an individual might visit Constantinople or pass through Byzantine territory. Even before the emperor's rededication in 330, the town had been an important location for trade. Indeed, as early as the fourth century BCE, the merchants of Byzantion had acquired a reputation (as well as a certain notoriety) for their sharp practices. Over the centuries that followed, increasing numbers of traders established themselves in the capital, seeking to take advantage of the large local market and the large range of commodities available in Constantinople—which ranged, as *Biblion Eparkhion* (*The Book of the Eparch*) reveals, from agricultural produce to fine silks. Although there is evidence to show that there had always been a sizable contingent of foreign merchants living in Constantinople, it appears that the numbers of those who came to settle in the capital grew steadily and substantially from around the middle of the eleventh century on. Visitors such as Benjamin of Tudela remarked on the fact that Constantinople was populated by merchants from "Babylon and Mesopotamia, from Media and Persia, from Egypt and Palestine, and from Russia, Hungary, Patzinakia, Budia, Lombardy and Spain." There are many other sources—written both by locals, such as John Tzeztes, and by visitors, such as Hugh Eteriano—that attest to the wide ethnic diversity in Byzantium, particularly in the later centuries.

Increasing numbers of merchants led to the formalization of at least some of the communities in Byzantium—in Constantinople, as well as in other important trading posts in the empire, such as Dyrrachium (modern Dürres in Albania). By the early 1100s, Venetian, Pisan, Genoese, and Amalfitan quarters could be found in some of the towns of Byzantium.

However, not all visitors to Constantinople and Byzantium had trade in mind. For many of those who journeyed from western Europe, Byzantium only served as a stopping point on a more ambitious and longer journey to Jerusalem and the Holy Land. As early as the fourth century, pilgrims were already beginning to make their way to the holy places. This necessitated passing through Constantinople and through Byzantine territory in Asia Minor if not in Europe as well. For the most part, a pilgrim would journey along the Via Egnatia, which led from Rome to Brindisi and then on to Constantinople after crossing the Adriatic Sea. The impressive and famous relics held in the capital—as well as the magnificent churches themselves—made it a religious destination in its own right. The pilgrim would then proceed overland across Asia Minor or, alternatively, go by boat via Rhodes to Cyprus and then on to Palestine.

Political upheaval in the Middle East made this journey both arduous and dangerous and had a direct impact on the routes that pilgrims could use, as well as on the volume of traffic. The rise and sudden growth of Islam in the seventh century, for example, severely limited numbers traveling on pilgrimage until the situation stabilized. Similarly, the Seljuk conquest of Anatolia in the late eleventh and twelfth centuries had a crucial effect on the route followed by pilgrims, meaning that, unless accompanied by a large host of armed men (as was the case with the First and Third Crusades), access to Palestine across Asia Minor was essentially impossible.

The Crusades themselves—as well as the establishment of the crusader states, based initially on Jerusalem, Antioch, Edessa, and Tripoli—played an important role in increasing the frequency of contact between Byzantium and western Europe. They also facilitated travel to Constantinople and beyond, since not only were new lines of communication opened (through the Balkans, for example), but availability also increased dramatically. The collapse of the crusader position in Palestine and the sack of Acre in 1291 had a devastating effect on pilgrim traffic and on travel to Constantinople and to Byzantium in general. The subsequent Ottoman expansion into Europe and, finally, the fall of Constantinople to the Turks in 1453 did not only affect the numbers of travelers from the West; it also sharply curtailed trade in the Aegean and in the eastern Mediterranean.

There was one other reason why an individual would journey to Byzantium, besides trade and as part of a pilgrimage. There is a large body of primary evidence relating to diplomatic missions dispatched to Constantinople over the centuries. Among the best examples are the accounts of Liudprand of Cremona, a cleric who was twice sent to Byzantium, to negotiate in turn with the emperors Constantine VII Porphyrogenitus ("born in the purple") and Nikephoros II Phocas in the middle of the tenth century. The evidence, however, often raises as many questions as it provides answers, since such missions invariably go unrecorded in the Byzantine sources. Nonetheless, such travel constitutes an important part of the picture of who would visit Constantinople, as well as providing an invaluable insight into the motivations of at least some of those who journeyed to the capital.

Delegations were regularly sent to the court at Constantinople for various reasons, whether to win Byzantine support for local disputes in the Caucasus, to arrange alliances against common enemies in Italy, to demand tribute, or, after a major displacement of peoples in the ninth and tenth centuries, to seek holy baptism from the emperor. A common theme, however, as we learn from the *De administrando imperio* (as well as from other sources) was to secure a marriage alliance and obtain an imperial bride. Before the twelfth century, there were a few, isolated cases of this happening. During the reign of the Comneni emperors (and particularly that of Manuel I Comnenus), however, such marriage ties became much more common, and alliances came to be formed with many of the leading royal and aristocratic houses of western Europe.

The change of attitude to marriage alliances is an important indicator of the fact that, by the twelfth century, Byzantium had become aware of the need to cement and strengthen the levels of contact with the outside world. In the centuries that followed the sack of Rome, the Byzantine empire had survived and existed as a single, superpower state in Europe. The Goths, Avars, and Slavs, and, later, the realm of Charlemagne had presented certain rivalries, albeit temporary. With the rise of Islam, the empire was faced with a more permanent rival that offered its own political, religious, and economic rewards. So too, with consolidation and development of the West in the medieval period, even Byzantium's position as the true successor of Rome came to be challenged and disputed. The irony, of course, was that it was precisely Constantinople's location and the magnificence of its buildings, the elaborate rituals, and the spiritual supremacy articulated so powerfully and regularly by the emperor and his court that attracted more and more visitors. This served to fan and stimulate rivalries not only with Byzantium's immediate neighbors, but also farther afield. It was these rivalries that lay behind not only the sack of Constantinople by the Fourth Crusaders in 1204 and by the Turks in 1453, but also the failure of the West to come to Byzantium's help as it moved toward its final collapse.

PETER FRANKOPAN

## References and Further Reading

Blöndal, Sigfus, *The Varangians of Byzantium: An Aspect of Byzantine Military History*, Cambridge: Cambridge University Press, 1978.

Ciggaar, Krijnie, "Une description de Constantinople du XIIe siècle," *Revue des Études Byzantines*, 31 (1973): 335–354.

Ciggaar, Krijnie, "Une description de Constantinople traduite par un pèlerin anglais du XIIe siècle," *Revue des Études Byzantines*, 34 (1976): 211–267.

Comnena, Anna, *The Alexiad*, translated by E.R.A. Sewter, 1969.

Constantine Porphyrogenitus (Emperor), *De cerimoniis aulae byzantinae libri duo* [About the Ceremonies of the Byzantine Court], edited by Johann Jacob Reiske, 2 vols., 1829–1830; as *Le Livre des cérémonies*, edited and translated by Albert Vogt, 4 vols., 1935–1940.

Constantine Porphyrogenitus (Emperor), *De administrando imperio* [About the Governing of the Empire], edited by Gyula Moravcski and translated by R.J.H. Jenkins, 1967.

Liudprand of Cremona, *The Works of Liudprand of Cremona*, translated by F.A. Wright, 1930; as *The Embassy to Constantinople and Other Writings*, 1993.

Odo of Deuil, *De profectione Ludovici VII in orientem / The Journey of Louis VII to the East*, edited and translated by Virginia Gingerick Berry, 1948.

*See also* **Constantinople**

## CÀ DA MOSTO, ALVISE DA (c. 1430–1483) *Venetian Nobleman, Merchant, and Travel Diarist*

Alvise da Cà da Mosto's father, Giovanni da Cà da Mosto, had served as administrator of the Venetian mercantile marine, and at least two of his four sons, Alvise and Antonio, followed him in that service. However, the importance of Alvise da Cà da Mosto in the history of travel and exploration rests not on his voyages undertaken in the service of the Venetian republic, but on his narrative of the two voyages he made from Portugal to the west coast of Africa in 1455 and 1456. His is the first account of Portuguese voyages in the Atlantic to have been composed after Zurara's *Chronicle of the Discovery and Conquest of Guinea*, which only takes the story up to 1448. Although his claim that he was the first European to set eyes on the Cape Verde Islands has been contested by some scholars, his description of them probably led directly to their colonization by Antonio da Noli three years later.

When Cà da Mosto returned to Venice from a trading voyage to Flanders in 1453, he found that his father had been involved in a lawsuit and banished, and this may have played a part in his decision to embark almost immediately on the voyage that was to lead by chance to his settling in Portugal. In August 1454, he and his brother Antonio boarded one of a fleet of three Venetian galleys bound for England. Contrary winds obliged them to stop over at Cape St. Vincent near the villa at Sagres from where Prince Henrique, son of João I of Portugal and known to posterity as Henry the Navigator, directed his voyages of trade and exploration. One of Henrique's principal objectives was to gain access by sea to the valuable caravan trade in gold, slaves, ivory, and other products that were taken from the vaguely defined region known as Guinea across the Sahara to the ports of the Barbary Coast. So when one of Henrique's secretaries and the Venetian consul came to the galleys, Cà da Mosto gained permission to join one of his expeditions, and accordingly, on 22 March 1455, sailed in a Portuguese caravel from Lagos, Portugal, "southwards to the land of the blacks of Lower Ethiopia, where Henrique's men had been the first to navigate." He soon became a fervent admirer of Portuguese caravels, which he declared were "the best ships afloat."

The fleet sailed to Porto Santo, to Madeira, which Cà da Mosto calls "one large garden," and to the Canaries, where he notes that the Spanish settlers would carry off the inhabitants to Spain to be sold as slaves, and thence to the trading post established by Henrique at Arguin, where he says the Portuguese took a thousand slaves a year, formerly by "descending on the land at night," but now peaceably, because Henrique "would not permit any further injury." Cà da Mosto describes the silent barter trade in salt from Taghaza, first noted by Herodotus in the fifth century BCE, and relates how the salt was taken by Arab and Azanaghi or Sanhaja Tuaregs to Mali, where it was exchanged for gold. He refers to Wadan, about 350 miles east of Cape Blanco, from where Arab merchants sent caravans with brass and silver to Timbuktu, and describes the region beyond the Senegal River, which like most of his contemporaries he thought was a tributary of the

Nile. He observes that the ruler of Senegal derived his chief revenue from horses and other presents given him by the lords of the country and from slaves captured in raids on his neighbors. Cà da Mosto he was struck by the beauty of the people, whom he describes as "black, tall and with large well-formed bodies," and by the fertile and densely forested country, unlike the north, where the country was arid and the people "brownish, lean, ill-nourished and short." Beyond the Senegal River, he reached Cayor, land of the Wolof people. Continuing south, he came upon two ships, one of which belonged to a Genoese merchant named Antoniotto Usodimare, and accompanied them to Cape Verde and thence probably as far as the Gambia River.

Cà da Mosto gives revealing accounts of his encounters with different West African peoples, noting how they marveled at Portuguese firearms, which they declared must be the work of the devil; at their musical instruments, which they thought were singing animals; at their ships, which they believed were fish or birds with portholes for eyes; at the beeswax candles he made for them, from which they deduced that Christians were omniscient; and at his white skin, which they rubbed with their spittle to see if the white color was paint.

In May 1456, Cà da Mosto set sail again from Lagos, Portugal, for Africa, this time accompanied by Usodimare. On this, his second voyage, he discovered some uninhabited islands that appear from his description to be the Cape Verde Islands, although he states incorrectly that he reached them by sailing west northwest from Cape Blanco. Cà da Mosto he reached the Gambia River again, sailed up it some 60 miles, traded with the local ruler, and sampled a dish of stewed elephant, which he found somewhat unpalatable, though he had some of the meat salted and on his return to Portugal sent it, together with the elephant's trunk and one foot, to Prince Henrique. He then sailed on beyond Cape Roxo, perhaps as far as the Geba River.

The original manuscript of Cà da Mosto's account of his travels is lost and there are many inaccuracies and inconsistencies in the surviving copies, so it is not possible to establish exactly when he wrote it, but it was probably some time after he left Portugal and returned to Venice in 1464. Contemporary cartographers, notably Grazioso Benincasa and Andrea Bianco, used information provided by Cà da Mosto, Andrea Bianco. Benincasa's charts are the first on which the Cape Verde Islands appear, and they use Cà da Mosto's place names, which are given in Portuguese, not Italian. Bianco's chart of 1448 shows the West African coast as far as Cape Verde and Cape Roxo. The great map made in Venice in 1559 for Afonso V of Portugal by Fra Mauro, whom Bianco assisted, also appears to owe much to Cà da Mosto, although it does not show the Cape Verde Islands.

The two surviving manuscripts of Cà da Mosto's voyages are in the Marciana Library in Venice. The later one contains an introduction describing the work of Prince Henrique and seems to have been used for the first printed edition, which was published in Vicenza in 1507 in Fracanzano da Montalboddo's compilation of travel accounts entitled *Paesi nouamente retrovati*, together with narratives of Pedro da Sintra's voyages to Sierra Leone in 1460–1461, the voyages of Columbus and Cabral, and the *Mundus Novus* of Amerigo Vespucci. The *Paesi retrovati* proved very popular and was soon translated into many languages. It was published in Latin in Milan in 1508, in German in Nuremberg in the same year, and in French in Paris in 1515. Another printed version of Cà da Mosto's original account was that included by Giovanni Battista Ramusio in the first volume of his *Navigationi et viaggi* [Navigations and Travels], published in Venice in 1550. However, it was not included either in Hakluyt or in Purchas and the first edition in English was an abridged translation of Ramusio's version in the first of the four volumes of *A New General Collection of Voyages and Travels*, published by Thomas Astley in London between 1745 and 1757.

John Villiers

## Biography

Born in Venice, c. 1430 or 1432. Sailed to Crete with Andrea Barbarigo, 1445–1446. Elected a *nobile balestriere* (noble bowman) on the Alexandria galleys, 1451. Sailed as a *nobile balestriere* with the Flanders galleys, 1452–1453. Embarked with his younger brother Antonio on a Flanders galley under the command of Marco Zeno; forced to stop at Cape St. Vincent, Portugal, 1454. Sailed with a fleet licensed by Prince Henrique of Portugal (Henry the Navigator) to the West African coast, 1456. Made second voyage to West Africa with a fleet licensed by Prince Henrique, accompanied by Antoniotto Usodimare; possibly discovered Cape Verde Islands, 1456. Left Portugal and returned to Venice to administer his family estates, conduct trade, and enter public service, 1456. Married Elisabetta Venier, 1466. Ambassador to the ruler of Herzegovina; assisted in organizing the defense of Cattaro, 1474. Governor of the Venetian fortress of Corone in the Morea, 1476–1479. Commanded trading galleys sent to Alexandria, 1481. Died in Venice, while on an official mission to Rovigo, 18 July 1483.

## References and Further Reading

Machado, João Franco, and Damião Peres (editors), *Viagens de Luis de Cadamosto e Pedro de Sintra* [Voyages of Luís de

Cadamosto and Pedro de Sintra], Lisbon: Academia Portuguesa de História, 1948; reprinted, 1988.

Montalboddo, Francanzano da, *Paesi nouamente retrovati, et Nouo Mundo da Alberico Vesputio Florentino intitulato*, 1507.

Ramusio, Giovanni Battista, *Navigationi et viaggi* [Navigations and Travels], 1550–1559; facsimile, edited and with an introduction by R.A. Skelton, 3 vols., 1967–1970; edited by Marica Milanesi, 4 vols., 1978–1983.

## CAIRO

Cairo is many cities. It forces breathless sentences and mixed metaphors out of the best of writers. It is itself used as a highly ambiguous metaphor in much of the literature of the Arab world.

In the travel literature of Africa and the Near East, Cairo is unavoidable. Ibn Battuta (1304–1377) traveled the world for 30 years. He had a self-imposed rule: never to go the same way twice. And he kept it, with one exception: he passed through Cairo five times. Cairo exerts an immense cultural and spiritual gravitational pull for thousands of miles. It has pulled writers in ever since it started. When that was is very difficult to say. The ancient Egyptians said that life began in On, now in the northeastern suburbs of the city. Everyone who followed maintained that there was something fundamentally important about the place that is roughly Cairo, although they shuffled their capitals around. The city has shed names as a snake sheds skins.

The Greek architects of modern travel writing—Herodotus (c. 484–430 BCE), Demetrius of Phaleron (c. 350–280 BCE), Posidonius (c. 135–51 BCE), Artemidorus (fl. 100 BCE), Diodorus Siculus (fl. first century BCE), and Strabo (c. 64 BCE–23 CE)—Strabo (c. 64 BCE–23 CE)—were all here, and, until the eighteenth century, all Western travelers following them saw Egypt with Herodotus's eyes.

Cairo was one of the first and brightest feathers in the Prophet's cap. His soldiers took it in 641, and since then, Islamic poets, scholars, and pilgrims have rhapsodized, loved, lamented, and deprecated the place, wrapping it in fantasies so thick that its stones are now invisible. The Baghdadi doctor Abd al-Latif (fl. late twelfth–early thirteenth century), Ibn Battuta, who was arguably the greatest traveler ever, and the great Leo Africanus (al-Hasan al-Wazzan al-Zayyati) (1494(?)–1552) all wrote humble, puzzled, wondering accounts of the city.

The Cairenes bought off the crusaders very cheaply in 1167, and so the first medieval European writers about Cairo were prosaic merchants, merchants' scouts, or diplomats like the Venetian Emmanuele Piloti (fl. early fourteenth century) and the Florentine Leonardo Frescobaldi (fl. 1380–1390), both of whom were more interested in profit margins than minarets.

Economic decline under the Mamelukes stemmed the flow of travelers to the city, and apart from Muslim pilgrims' travelogues and the diaries of some wild Englishmen (more interesting as chronicles of their wildness than of the city), there is little real travel writing until the eighteenth century, when the number of Western visitors increased hugely. These early Europeans were hardy and enterprising, but generally inarticulate. They put little on paper that has weathered well. Napoleon's invasion in 1798 was a crucial literary catalyst. He brought with him 167 researchers and told them to write down everything about Egypt. They produced the colossal 21-volume *La Description de l'Égypte* (Jomard, 1809–1828), which is the cornerstone on which all subsequent scholarly writing on Egypt has built. The chief artist to the expedition was Dominique Vivant Denon (1747–1825), who had already made his name with the light, feisty, ironic, and extremely un-French *Voyage dans la basse et la haute Egypte (Travels in Upper and Lower Egypt*, 1802) by the time *La Description* was published.

Napoleon (although not his influence) was ousted by the British, and, from the early nineteenth century, Egypt became a popular stop for the educated rich on extended Grand Tours. These people produced some of the most lasting writing on Cairo. Cairo generated the ornate essay "The Court of Egypt" (1832) by the young Benjamin Disraeli (1804–1881), some of the finest parts of *Itinéraire de Paris à Jérusalem* (1811) by Chateaubriand (1768–1848), the quirky, immortal *Eothen* (1844) by Alexander Kinglake (1809–1891), the fast, real-life Rider Haggard *The Crescent and the Cross* (1845) by Eliot Warburton (fl. mid-nineteenth century), *Eastern Life, Present and Past* (1848) by Harriet Martineau (1802–1874), the retrospective *Visits to Monasteries in the Levant* (1849) by Robert Curzon (1810–1873)—which contains some whimsical musings on Cairo and whose admirers talk of it in the same breath as *Eothen—Letters from Egypt* (1854) by Florence Nightingale (1820–1910), and the notes and letters of Gustave Flaubert (1821–1880). An improbable place to find a magnificent account of 1850s Cairo is in *Pre-Raphaelitism and the Pre-Raphaelite Brotherhood* (1905) by William Holman Hunt (1827–1910). These are his reminiscences: in writing, he had a painter's eye for color and a pre-Raphaelite's eye for parable.

Egypt went down-market toward the end of the nineteenth century with the advent of Thomas Cook's package tours and the huge sales of *A Thousand Miles up the Nile* (1877) by Amelia Edwards (1831–1892), both of which made Egypt seem less exotic and more accessible than before. But although the number of

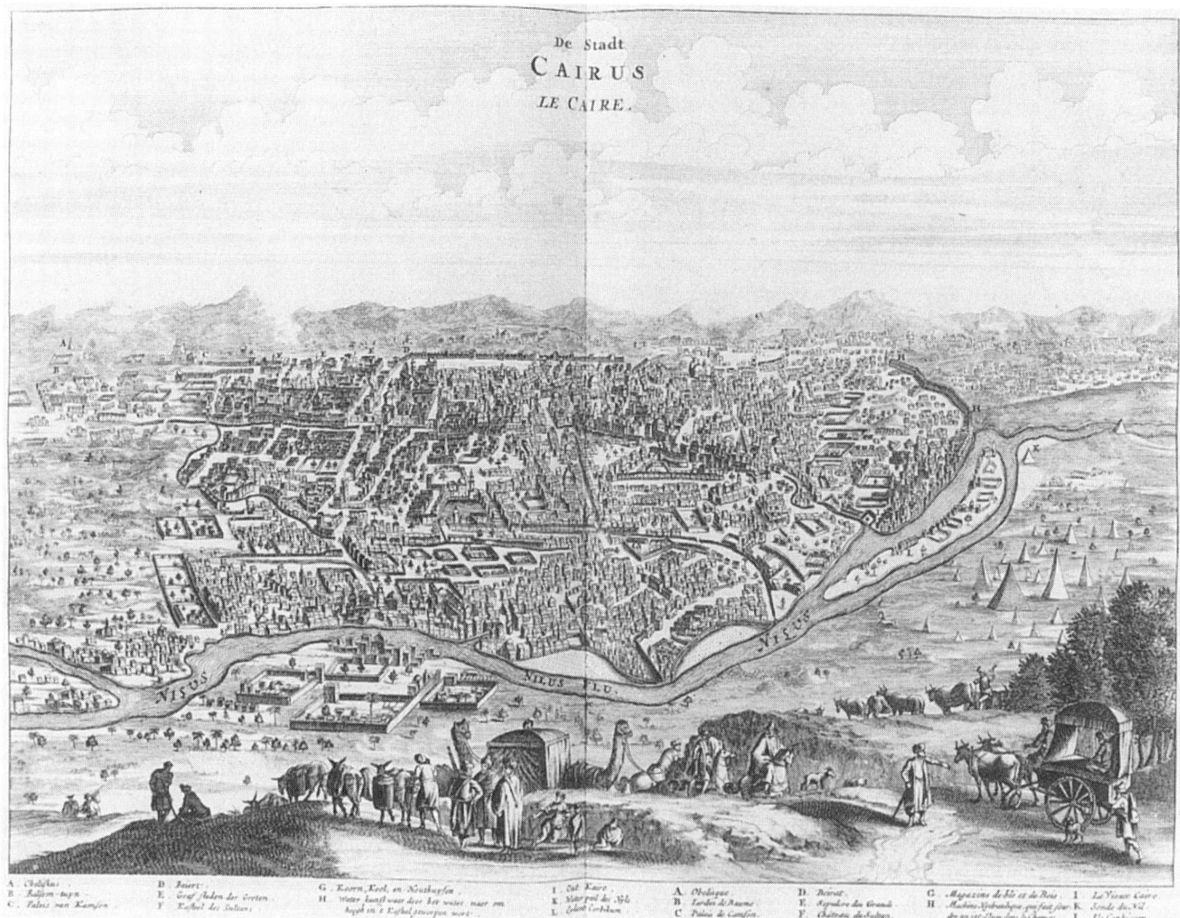


Bird's-eye view of Cairo from the west bank of the Nile (from O. Dapper's *Description de l'Afrique* . . . translated from the Flemish, 1686). *Courtesy of the Travellers Club, London; Bridgeman Art Library, agent.*

travel books went up, and the average standard went down, the last few decades of the nineteenth century and the first few of the twentieth produced some of the finest books about Cairo ever written. Perhaps the best of the Victorian offerings is the intimate and learned *Cairo: Sketches of Its History, Monuments and Social Life* (1892) by Stanley Lane-Poole (1854–1931), an Arabist and archaeologist who knew Cairo with the knowledge that only passion can generate, and loved it with the passion that only real knowledge can sustain. *Orientations* (1937), a thoughtful, wistful retrospective by Sir Ronald Storrs (1881–1955), is also outstanding: Storrs's long tenure in the city in the Egyptian Civil Service and his startling lack of cynicism or tiredness make this a quietly penetrating book.

During World War II (even more than during World War I), Cairo was the home of hard-drinking, hard-intriguing soldiers and spies planning decisive desert victories, and the khaki café culture generated some lasting writing. Freya Stark (1893–1993) painted a detailed picture of wartime Cairo in her autobiography *Dust in the Lion's Paw* (1961). Noel Coward (1899–1973) visited Cairo in 1943, and his *Middle East Diary* (1944) contains a depressingly predictable account of his mincings around the city. Coward was more interested in cocktails than scarabs, but he redeemed himself by evoking poignantly the sense that Cairo had somehow escaped the war and was living in an unreal haze of pink-champagned denial.

Post-war Cairo was an uneasy no-man's land: its ambiguities and tensions were grist for several literary mills. Notable from this period are *Egypt in Transition* (1958) by Jean and Simonne Lacouture and *At the Jazz Band Ball* (1983) by Philip Oakes. Of recent books, the towering text is *Cairo: The City Victorious* (1998) by Max Rodenbeck, a beautifully woven piece of work in which personal impression, historical perspective, and analysis combine to form the nearest approach to a definitive biography of the city yet written.

CHARLES FOSTER

### References and Further Reading

Butler, Alfred J., *Court Life in Egypt*, 1887.
Caillard, Mabel, *A Lifetime in Egypt 1876–1935*, 1935.
Chateaubriand, Francois René de, Viscount, *Itinéraire de Paris à Jérusalem*, 1811.
Chennells, Ellen, *Recollections of an Egyptian Princess, Being a Record of Five Years' Residence at the Court of Ismael Pasha, Khédive*, 1893.
Coward, Noel, *Middle East Diary*, 1944.
Curzon, Robert, Baron Zouche, *Visits to Monasteries in the Levant*, 1849.
Denon, Dominique Vivant, *Voyage dans la basse et la haute Egypte pendant les campagnes du général Bonaparte*, 2 vols., 1802, edited by Hélène Guichard, Adrien Goetz, and Martine Reid, 1998; as *Travels in Upper and Lower Egypt*, translated by Francis Blagdon, 2 vols., 1802; translated by Arthur Aikin, 3 vols., 1803.
Diodorus Siculus, *On Egypt*, translated by Edwin Murphy, 1985.
Diodorus Siculus, *The Antiquities of Asia*, translated by Edwin Murphy, 1989.
Disraeli, Benjamin, "The Court of Egypt," *New Monthly Magazine* (June 1832).
Edwards, Amelia, *A Thousand Miles up the Nile*, 1877.
Flaubert, Gustave, *Flaubert in Egypt: A Sensibility on Tour*, edited and translated from the French by Francis Steegmuller, 1972; reprinted, 1996.
Fraser, G.S., *A Stranger and Afraid: The Autobiography of an Intellectual*, 1983.
Frescobaldi, Leonardo, *Viaggio di Lionardo di Niccolò Frescobaldi in Egitto e in Terra Santa*, 1818.
Herodotus, *The Histories*, translated by Aubrey de Sélincourt, revised by John Marincola, 1996.
Holman Hunt, William, *Pre-Raphaelitism and the Pre-Raphaelite Brotherhood*, 1905.
Ibn Battuta, *Travels of Ibn Battuta AD 1325–1354*, translated by H.A.R. Gibb, 5 vols., 1958–2000 (vol. 4 with C.F. Beckingham).
Joly, Cyril, *Take These Men*, 1955.
Jomard, Edme François (editor), *La Description de l'Égypte*, 21 vols., 1809–1828.
Kinglake, Alexander, *Eothen; or, Traces of Travel Brought Home from the East*, 1844.
Lacouture, Jean, and Simonne Lacouture, *Egypt in Transition*, translated by Francis Scarfe, 1958.
Lane-Poole, Stanley, *Cairo: Sketches of Its History, Monuments and Social Life*, 1892.
al-Latif, Abd, *Abdollatiphi historiae Aegypti compendium* (Arabic, with a Latin version by Edward Pocock the younger), 1680.
Leo Africanus, *A Geographical History of Africa*, translated by John Pory, 1600; reprinted, 1846; as *The History and Description of Africa*, edited by Robert Brown, 3 vols., 1896.
Martineau, Harriet, *Eastern Life, Present and Past*, 3 vols., 1848.
Muller, William, "An Artist's Tour in Egypt," *Art Union*, (September 1839).
Nightingale, Florence, *Letters from Egypt*, 1854; edited by Anthony Sattin, 1987.
Oakes, Philip, *At the Jazz Band Ball: A Memory of the 1950s*, 1983.
Olin, Stephen, *Travels in Egypt, Arabia, Petraea and the Holy Land*, 1843.
Piloti, Emmanuele, *De modo, progressu, ordine ac diligenti providentia habendis in passagio Christianorum pro conquesta Terra Sanctae*, 1420.
Piloti, Emmanuele, *L'Égypte au commencement du quinzième siècle, d'après le Traité d'Emmauel Piloti de Crète—incepit 1420*, with an introduction by Herman Dopp, 1950.
Poole, Sophia, *The Englishwoman in Egypt: Letters from Cairo during a Residence There in 1842–44*, 3 vols., 1844–1846.
Rodenbeck, Max, *Cairo: The City Victorious*, 1998.
Rowlatt, Mary, *A Family in Egypt*, 1956.
Russell, Thomas Wentworth, *Egyptian Service, 1902–1946*, 1949.
Stark, Freya, *Dust in the Lion's Paw: Autobiography, 1939–1946*, 1961.
Storrs, Sir Ronald, *Orientations*, 1937.
Strabo, Megasthenes, *The Geography of Strabo*, translated by Horace Leonard Jones, 8 vols., 1917–1933.
Warburton, Eliot, *The Crescent and the Cross; or, Romance and Realities of Eastern Travel*, 2 vols., 1845.

*See also* **Egypt, Islamic Travelers**

## CALDERÓN DE LA BARCA, FRANCES (1804–1882) *Scottish Traveler and Wife of Spanish Ambassador to Mexico*

Frances Erskine Inglis, the fifth of ten children, was born to a distinguished family whose ancestral connections included the royal house of Stuart. By the time of her travels to Mexico in 1838, she had traveled to Italy, lived in Normandy, and emigrated to the United States. Frances's cosmopolitan life prepared her well for the journey to Mexico as the wife of the Spanish ambassador to the newly recognized nation, and her travel narrative of her two years in the country, *Life in Mexico, during a Residence of Two Years in That Country*, provides vivid detail and astute observations of the social, political, and cultural customs. Her careful observations also provide important information about the volatile political situation in Mexico following its independence and the many important political figures that emerged during this period of Mexican history.

Having married Angel Calderón de la Barca in New York on 24 September 1838, Frances accompanied him on his diplomatic mission to Mexico in October 1839. For the next two years of her life, she lived in, traveled through, and explored the Mexican social, cultural, political, and ecological environments. First stopping in Havana, Cuba, de la Barca describes her initial impressions of the bay by stating, "everything struck us as strange and picturesque." She and her husband remained in Havana from 12 to 24 November before continuing on their journey to Vera Cruz. The journey from Havana to Vera Cruz took 25 days at sea, and the de la Barca couple arrived on 18 December 1839.

De la Barca traveled from Vera Cruz into the interior of Mexico through Jalapa, Perote, and Puebla, but not before stopping to visit the infamous General Antonio Lopez Santa Anna at Manga de Clavo, his country estate. Describing him as "a gentlemanly, good-looking, quietly-dressed, rather melancholy person," de la Barca found that "knowing nothing of his past history, one would have said [he was] a philosopher, living in dignified retirement." After a month's journey inland, the de la Barcas arrived at the gates of Mexico City on Christmas Day.

Once in Mexico City, de la Barca explored the city with great zeal. Balls, parties, processions, and singing all welcomed the ambassador and his wife to the city. De la Barca describes in detail the "display of diamonds and pearls, silks, satins. . . in which the ladies have paid their first etiquette visits." Visits to Chapultepec and the Shrine of Our Lady of Guadalupe engaged her vivid attention. Much of her time in Mexico City included participating in the many religious festivities celebrated including Holy Week, where, on Holy Thursday, "nothing can be more picturesque than the whole appearance of Mexico." The religious rites of Mexico preoccupied much of de la Barca's descriptive powers. She visited many convents and observed several novices take the veil. De la Barca exclaimed that "unlike pulque (the national drink of choice) and bullfights," the novice inaugurations she "dislike[d] more and more upon trial."

During her stay in Mexico, de la Barca visited many different regions. The silver mines to the north of the city, the gambling town of San Agustin, the surrounding haciendas (traditional country houses) of the sugar country including the beautiful caves of *cacahuamilps*, the many volcanoes, and the state of Michoacan all engaged her time and attention throughout her two-year residence. Her careful descriptions detail all aspects of her journey from the "stupendous natural scenery" surrounding the silver mine of Real del Monte to the baths of Michoacan in Patzuaro, where "the place is quite wild, the scenery very striking."

Although de la Barca's travels and family kept her very busy (her niece and nephew visited her in the latter half of her stay), she also witnessed and described with astute observations the two *pronunciamientos*, or revolutions, that occurred while she and it her husband were in Mexico. Her journal provides invaluable accuracy and detail for this significant period in Mexican history, and it includes many of the public declarations written by the various *pronunciados* and the government responses.

The de la Barcas returned to the United States by way of Havana on 29 April 1842 after a two-and-a-half-year absence. *Life in Mexico* was published simultaneously in London and New York in 1843 and was well received in both places. This was not the case in Mexico, where the narrative was roundly criticized and de la Barca was denounced as a new Mrs. Trollope, the British author whose travel narrative *Domestic Manners of the Americans*, published in 1832, disparaged the United States. However, de la Barca's narrative was fundamental for William Hickling Prescott's history of Mexico, *History of the Conquest of Mexico*, and is now a respected text everywhere, including Mexico.

Angel Calderón de la Barca remained minister of Spain to the United States until he was recalled in 1854. The couple then returned to Spain, and Angel was named minister of state in the cabinet of the Conde de San Luis. The troubled rule of Isabel II forced them into exile in France in 1854. Frances Calderón de la Barca's second book, *The Attaché in Madrid*, published in New York in 1856, describes those events.

Soledad M. Caballero

## Biography

Born Frances Erskine Inglis in Edinburgh, 23 December 1804. Lived in Normandy, 1828–1830. Emigrated to Boston after her father's death, 1830, with her mother, three sisters, and three nieces. Helped her mother to establish schools in Mount Vernon Street, Boston (1831–1835); Staten Island, New York (1835); and possibly Baltimore (c. 1836). Married the Spanish diplomat Angel Calderón de la Barca, 24 September 1838. Lived in Mexico during Calderón de la Barca's appointment as Spanish minister to Mexico, 1839–1842. Published *Life in Mexico*, 1843. Returned to the United States on her husband's transfer to Washington, April 1842. Lived in Madrid, 1843–1844. Converted to Catholicism, 10 May 1847. Moved to Madrid when her husband was recalled to Spain, 1853. Exiled to France with her husband during political upheaval in Spain, 1854. Returned to Spain, 1856. Retired briefly to a convent in the Spanish Pyrenees after her husband's death in San Sebastian, 1861. Requested by Queen Isabel to act as the Infanta Isabel's governess, 1861–1868. Traveled to the United States after the infanta's marriage to the count of Girgenti, 1868; returned to Spain after the count of Girganti committed suicide, c. 1870. Created marquesa de Calderón de la Barca, in recognition of services to Spain, by King Alfonso II, 1876. Died in Madrid, 6 February 1882.

## References and Further Reading

Calderón de la Barca, Frances, *Life in Mexico, during a Residence of Two Years in That Country*, 1843; reprinted, with an introduction by Manuel Romero de Terreros, 1954.

Calderón de la Barca, Frances, *The Attaché in Madrid; or, Sketches of the Court of Isabella II*, 1856.

Calderón de la Barca, Frances, *Life in Mexico: The Letters of Fanny Calderón de la Barca*, edited by Howard T. Fisher and Marion Hall Fisher, 1966.

## CAMELS

As the "ship of the desert," the camel has enabled large tracts of the most arid areas of the earth's surface to be explored. The special structural modifications of its stomach allow it to travel for three days and more without drinking. A Bactrian camel can cover a steady 25 miles over a ten-hour day; an Arabian camel, in a kind of gentle, easy ramble, twice this distance. The camel was one of the earliest animals to be domesticated, and it is referred to in the Bible as the gift Pharaoh gave to Abraham and in other contexts, yet the Egyptologist John Gardner Wilkinson found no reference to it in ancient Egyptian portrayals, as it did not flourish at first in Egypt. The camel is now only known as a domestic, and mainly pack, animal, apart from a few wild camels in the deserts of central Asia and a few thousand feral camels descended from those released since the nineteenth century into the Australian desert.

There are two species of camel: the single-humped Arabian *Camelus dromedarius* and the stockier Asian two-humped *Camel bactriarius*. These two species have been interbred, and the Swiss traveler John Lewis Burckhardt, who journeyed widely in Egypt and Arabia in the period 1813–1817, described some of the results: for example, the unsatisfactory beast produced by the Arab she-camel cross with the double-humped male-camel of the Crimea, and the dromedary and she-Turkman cross that produces a handsome small camel with two small humps. Male dromedaries, he noted, are never used as beasts of burden, but kept for breeding and riding (1829). In Arabia, those from Oman are regarded most and are celebrated in Arab songs. Burckhardt spoke highly too of the white Nubian camels, whose pace is "so swift and pleasant an amble that they supply the want of horses better than any other." He reports the Arab saying about a good riding camel: "His back is so soft that you may drink a cup of coffee while you ride upon him." The camel was also used in war (as described by Herodotus, by central Asian travelers, during Napoleon's expedition to Egypt, and by various camel corps in the Middle East), mainly as a pack animal but also in battle.

Since the Middle Ages, vast caravans, sometimes of thousands of camels, have crossed North Africa carrying pilgrims to Mecca and traded goods from one side of Africa to another. Huge caravans of Bactrians crossed Asia along the Silk Route from China to the Mediterranean, the camels following nose to tail, roped together in groups. Ibn Battuta traveled with such caravans from Tangier to Cairo and beyond, from 1325 on. Christian pilgrims, like Friar Felix Fabri in 1483, visiting the Holy Land and including Sinai and Egypt in their itinerary, went by camel. In 1876, C.M. Doughty joined the pilgrim caravan from Damascus, which stretched out two miles in length with three to five camels traveling abreast. During the journey, he gleaned much about the animal and its work, recorded in his *Arabia Deserta* (1888).

Camels are loaded according to the length of the journey and the number of wells on the route. The common load for an Arabian camel is up to 500 pounds for short journeys, and more for local work, but a hundredweight less for longer journeys. Burckhardt observed that a camel in Egypt could endure four days' thirst in summer, but no traveler should expect to go more than five without being watered; yet the camels of Darfur (Sudan) had to travel up to ten days to reach Egypt, though many died on the way. Egypt-bred camels, accustomed to verdure, often expired on the Mecca pilgrimage across the desert. The Bedouin boasted to Burckhardt of amazing journeys, but he deemed them fanciful. The best record known to him was 130 miles (with two crossings of the Nile) in 11 hours, after which the animal collapsed. Doughty found that in a caravan the pace is little more than two miles an hour. Once set, the pace can be so regular that travelers used to measure distance by the hours ridden.

Francis Galton in his *Art of Travel* (1872) wrote camels off as "only fit for a few countries." Arabian camels from Egypt were introduced into America in 1857 for a camel corps survey of the unexplored territory around the Colorado River, but they were little used and sold off in 1865. The camels on which Burke and Wills set off on their ill-fated expedition across central Australia in 1860 were Arabian, brought in from India with "Afghan" camel drivers, and there were further imports of camels into Australia throughout the nineteenth century.

The camel is a strange-looking creature with awkward ways that often make it the butt of travelers' descriptions. Nor is it always easy to ride. Those mounting a camel for the first time give amusement whether in China, Arabia, Mongolia, or the Sahara, as James Gilmour, Dominique Vivant Denon (1747–1825), and many others attested. Once up, some people settle into the pace easily; others, like Harriet Martineau, crossing the desert to Sinai in 1846, prefer walking to the pain the camel gives them. Isabella Bird, also on her way to Sinai in 1873, after a bad start thought the experience no worse than elephant riding and spent her days reading. James St. John in Egypt in 1832–1833 wrote with exhilaration of camel riding in the desert, but to many travelers the camel was a "beast of burthen" only: while they rode asses or horses, the camel carried the equipment, the water, the biscuit, the wine, and other provisions, including in some areas its own fodder. Among the best detailed European accounts of the Arabian camel are those of Burckhardt in 1813–1817, and the naval surveyor James Wellsted (1805–1842), who traveled with the Bedouin while surveying the Arabian peninsula in the early 1830s.

In 1844, two Frenchmen, Huc and Gabet, were sent to support the Chinese Christians in Mongolia and traveled in a great circle around China, Mongolia, and Tibet. They describe the use of camels for transport in some detail. James Gilmour (1843–1870) traveled widely in Mongolia dispensing medicines and the Gospel, at first on camelback or by camelcart, but later, finding that in the summer the camels were put to pasture to gather fat and strength, abandoning them for oxcarts. On a journey from northern China to southern Russia (some 840 miles), his caravan traveled from sunrise to noon, and then again from before sunset to almost dawn, as caravans had done along the Silk Route for at least 2,000 years. Huc reported that caravans passing at resting places exchanged news up and down the "road." North of Urga, Gilmour hired oxen to haul the carts over mountain passes "too lofty to be accomplished by camels," though in the event the pack camels climbed without difficulty.

DEBORAH MANLEY

### References and Further Reading


Bartlett, W.H., *Forty Days in the Desert on the Track of the Israelites*, 5th edition, 1862.

Blunt, Lady Anne, *Bedouin Tribes of the Euphrates*, 2 vols., 1879.

Blunt, Lady Anne, *A Pilgrimage to Nejd, the Cradle of the Arab Race*, 2 vols., 1881.

Bovill, E.W. (editor), *Missions to the Niger*, 4 vols, 1964–1966.

Burckhardt, John Lewis, *Travels in Arabia, Comprehending an Account of Those Territories in Hedjaz Which the Mohammedans Regard as Sacred*, 2 vols., 1829.

Burckhardt, John Lewis, *Notes on the Bedouins and the Wahabys, Collected during His Travels in the East*, 2 vols., 1830; reprinted, 1993.

Burton, Richard F., *Personal Narrative of a Pilgrimage to El-Medinah and Meccah*, 3 vols., 1855–1856.

Cable, Mildred, and Francesca French, *Dispatches from North-West Kanzu*, 1925.

Cable, Mildred, and Francesca French, *The Gobi Desert*, 1943.

Cailliaud, Frédéric, *Voyage à Meroë, au fleuve blanc, au-delà de Fâzoql dans le midi du royaume de Sennâr, à Syouah et dans cinq autres oasis*, 2 vols., 1826–1827.

Carruthers, Douglas, *Unknown Mongolia: A Record of Travel and Exploration in North-West Mongolia and Dzongaria*, 1913.

Church, Percy W., *Chinese Turkestan, with Caravan and Rifle*, 1901.

Clapperton, Hugh, *Difficult and Dangerous Roads: Hugh Clapperton's Travels in Sahara and Fezzan (1822–1825)*, edited by Jamie Bruce-Lockhart and John Wright, 2000.

Denon, Dominique Vivant, *Voyage dans la basse et la haute Egypte pendant les campagnes du général Bonaparte*, 2 vols., 1802; edited by Hélène Guichard, Adrien Goetz, and Martine Reid, 1998; as *Travels in Upper and Lower Egypt*, translated by Francis Blagdon, 2 vols., 1802; translated by Arthur Aikin, 3 vols., 1803.

Doughty, Charles M., *Travels in Arabia Deserta*, 2 vols., 1888.

Ellis, Tristram James, *On a Raft, and through the Desert: The Narrative of an Artist's Journey through Northern Syria and Kurdistan, by the Tigris to Baghdad, and of a Return Journey across the Desert by the Euphrates and Palmyra to Damascus*, 2 vols., 1881.

Elwood, Anne Katherine, *Narrative of a Journey Overland from England, by the Continent of Europe, Egypt, and the Red Sea to India, Including a Residence There and Voyage Home in the Years 1825–1828*, 2 vols., 1830.

Fabri, Felix, *Felix Fabri (circa 1480–1483 AD)* [Wanderings in the Holy Land], translated by Aubrey Stewart, 2 vols., 1892–1893.

Faulk, Odie B., *The U.S. Camel Corps: An Army Experiment*, 1976.

Ferrier, J.P., *Caravan Journeys and Wanderings in Persia, Afghanistan, Turkistan and Beloochistan, Translated from the Original Unpublished Manuscript by Captain William Jesse*, edited by H.D. Seymour, 1856.

Galton, Francis, *The Art of Travel; or, Shifts and Contrivances Available in Wild Countries*, 1885; 5th edition, 1872.

Gielchen, Count, *With the Camel Corps up the Nile*, 1884.

Giles, Ernest, *Australia Twice Traversed: The Romance of Exploration, Being a Narrative Compiled from the Journals of Five Exploring Expeditions into and through Central South Australia, and Western Australia, from 1872 to 1876*, 2 vols., 1889.

Gilmour, James, *Among the Mongols*, 1916.

Gladstone, Penelope, *Travels of Alexine: Alexine Tinne, 1835–1869*, 1970.

Guarmani, Carlo, *Northern Najd: A Journey from Jerusalem to Anaiza in Qasim*, translated by Lady Capel-Cure, 1938.

Hedin, Sven, *My Life as an Explorer*, translated by Alfhild Heubsch, 1925; reprinted, 1996.

Hill, Gray, *With the Beduins: A Narrative of Journeys and Adventures in Unfrequented Parts of Syria*, 1891.

Huc, Évariste Régis, *Souvenirs d'un voyage dans la Tartarie, le Thibet et la Chine*, 2 vols., 1850; as *Travels in Tartary, Thibet and China, during the Years 1844–46*, translated by William Hazlitt Jr., 2 vols., 1852.

Ibn Battuta, *The Travels of Ibn Battuta*, translated by Samuel Lee, 1829.

Ibn Battuta, *Travels in Asia and Africa 1325–1354*, translated and edited by H.A.R. Gibb, 1929.

Ibn Jubayr, *Travels*, translated by R.J.C. Broadhurst, 1952.

Irwin, Eyles, *A Series of Adventures in the Course of a Voyage up the Red-Sea, on the Coasts of Arabia and Egypt: And of a Route through the Deserts of Thebais*, 1780.

Kinglake, Alexander, *Eothen; or, Traces of Travel Brought Home from the East*, 1844.

Laborde, Leon, *Journey through Arabia Petraea to Mount Sinai and the Excavated City of Petra*, 1836.

Lamartine, Alphonse de, *A Pilgrimage in the Holy Land*, 3 vols., 1835.

Lane, Edward William, *An Account of the Manners and Customs of the Modern Egyptians*, 2 vols., 1837–1838.

Lawrence, T.E., *The Seven Pillars of Wisdom*, 1922.

Lawrence, T.E., *The Diary of T.E. Lawrence, 1911, during a Visit to Northern Syria*, 1937; as *The Diary Kept by T.E.*

*Lawrence While Travelling in Arabia During 1911*, with an introduction by Robin Bidwell, 1993.
Lesley, Lewis Burt (editor), *Uncle Sam's Camels: The Journal of May Humphreys Stacey, Supplemented by the Report of Edward Fitzgerald Beal (1857–1858)*, 1929.
Linant de Bellefonds, L.M.A., *Journey of Navigation of the Bahr-el-Abiad or the White Nile*, 1828.
Ludwig Salvator, Archduke of Austria, *The Caravan Route between Egypt and Syria*, translated by Ernst von Hesse-Wartegg, 1881.
Lushington, Sarah, *Narrative of a Journey from Calcutta to Europe by Way of Egypt in 1827–1828*, 1829.
Madox, John, *Excursions in the Holy Land etc.*, 2 vols., 1834.
Martineau, Harriet, *Eastern Life, Present and Past*, 3 vols., 1848.
Mattingley, K.V., *Dentist on a Camel*, 1986.
Melly, George, *Khartoum and the Blue and White Niles*, 1851.
Montulé, Edouard de, *Travels in Egypt during 1818 and 1819*, 1821.
Morier, J.P., *Memoir of a Campaign with the Ottoman Army in Egypt, from February to July, 1800*, 1801.
Niebuhr, Carsten, *Travels through Arabia and Other Countries in the East*, translated by Robert Heron, 1792.
Palgrave, William Gifford, *Narrative of a Year's Journey through Central and Eastern Arabia, 1862–1863*, 2 vols., 1863.
Petherick, John, *Egypt, the Soudan and Central Africa*, 1861.
Petherick, John, and Katherine Harriet Petherick, *Travels in Central Africa and Explorations of the Western Nile Tributaries*, 1869.
Prescott, H.F.M., *Once to Sinai: The Further Pilgrimage of Friar Felix Fabri*, 1957.
Raunkiar, Barclay, *Through Wahhabiland on Camel-Back: An Account of a Journey of Exploration in Eastern and Central Arabia, Undertaken at the Instance and the Cost of the Royal Danish Geographical Society in 1912*, 1916.
St. John, James Augustus, *Egypt and Mohammed Ali; or, Travels in the Valley of the Nile*, 2 vols., 1834.
St. John, James Augustus, *Egypt and Nubia*, 1841.
Shafer, Edward H., *The Golden Peaches of Samarkand: A Study of T'ang Exotics*, 1963.
Shaw, Thomas, *Travels or Observations Relating to Several Parts of Barbary and the Levant*, 1721.
Steevens, G.W., *Egypt in 1898*, 1898.
Steevens, G.W., *With Kitchener to Khartum*, 1898.
Stein, Marc Aurel, *Sand-Buried Ruins of Khotan, Personal Narrative of a Journey of Archaeological and Geographical Exploration in Chinese Turkestan*, 1903.
Waddington, George, and Barnard Hanbury, *Journal of a Visit to Some Parts of Ethiopia*, 1822.
Warburton, Eliot, *The Crescent and the Cross; or, Romance and Realities of Eastern Travel*, 2 vols., 1845.
Wellsted, James R., *Travels in Arabia*, 2 vols., 1838.
Wellsted, James R., *Travels to the City of the Caliphs, along the Shores of the Persian Gulf and the Mediterranean*, 2 vols., 1840.
Whitfield, Susan, *Life along the Silk Road*, 1999.
Wriggins, Sally Hovey, *Xuanzang: A Buddhist Pilgrim on the Silk Road*, 1996.

## CAMERON, VERNEY LOVETT (1844–1894) *British Explorer and Children's Writer*

In 1876, a shy, diffident naval officer returned home to a hero's welcome. Three years before, Verney Lovett Cameron had set out from Zanzibar, off Africa's east coast, and had traveled clear across the continent to Benguela on the west coast of present-day Angola. His epic journey made him the first European to cross Africa from east to west, and his personal tale of the adventure was published in a two-volume expedition account. But Cameron did not limit himself to writing for adults: he also published a number of books for boys, using his own experiences to produce exciting adventure stories.

Cameron was born on 1 July 1844 in Radipole, Weymouth, Dorset. He had seven siblings and grew up in the comfortable, privileged atmosphere of a country vicarage. Just after his 13th birthday, he joined the Royal Navy, and he had a successful, if unremarkable, early career, spending four years in the Mediterranean and joining the West Indian Squadron in 1861. In October 1865, he was promoted to lieutenant and later saw eight months' service in the Red Sea on HMS *Star* during the British punitive campaign against Emperor Theodore of Abyssinia, for which he earned a service medal.

It was during this period that Cameron began to learn Swahili, and his appetite was whetted for the exploration of the hinterland of central Africa. At the time, the great Scottish missionary David Livingstone was "missing" in central Africa, and Cameron applied for a place on an expedition sent to find him. His first application was unsuccessful (and Henry Morton Stanley had "found" Livingstone anyway), but he was appointed to a second expedition that aimed to "find" Livingstone again and to assist the explorer in completing his discoveries.

Cameron and fellow expedition members Dr. W.E. Dillon and Lieutenant Cecil Murphy arrived in Zanzibar in 1873; shortly afterward, they were joined by Robert Moffatt, Livingstone's nephew. The expedition left Zanzibar on 2 February 1873. Despite setbacks, including Moffatt's death in May, the party had traveled 550 miles by early August. However, all three Europeans then went down with severe fever, and Cameron was stricken blind for six weeks. In October 1873, the party met a small retinue of men who were carrying Livingstone's body to the coast. With Livingstone dead, the expedition was without purpose, and Dillon and Murphy decided to accompany Livingstone's body home. Cameron, however, determined to travel to Ujiji to collect Livingstone's journals—and perhaps do a little exploring of his own.

Three months later, Cameron reached Ujiji and started to explore the unknown southern extremity of Lake Tanganyika. Now fully fired with enthusiasm for exploring, Cameron sent Livingstone's papers and his own journals back to the east coast, and he proceeded westward, reaching the Lualaba River in August 1874.

In the company of a famous Arab trader named Hamed ibn Hamed (or Tippu Tib), Cameron turned south, spending much of this time plotting elevations and recording the flow of rivers. On 28 December 1874, he declared a British protectorate over the Congo basin. However, when he later forwarded the relevant documents to the British Foreign Office, it declined to approve them.

Cameron traveled along the watershed between the Congo and the Zambezi, then pushed on toward the Atlantic Ocean, but weather, disease, and weariness proved too much for his men. When still 126 miles from the coast, he decided to make a forced march to fetch help. This was successfully completed, but on the night of his arrival, blood began to flow from his mouth and clots in his throat began to choke him. He was hurried to nearby Benguela for treatment, and advanced scurvy was diagnosed.

Cameron's journey showed him to be a humanitarian traveler in a time when other explorers, such as Stanley, frequently used firepower to overcome obstacles. Indeed, Cameron, unlike most of his contemporaries, had no taste even for hunting, except to feed his men. He also proved an enlightened and detailed observer of both natural and local customs and interactions, and, although not as good a writer as Richard Burton, he showed solid ethnographic abilities. His diaries were published in 1877 as a book, *Across Africa*, which became a popular and acclaimed work.

Cameron's self-effacing manner endeared him to the British public. He was created a Companion of the Bath, promoted to commander in the Royal Navy, and awarded a gold medal by the Royal Geographical Society. He returned to regular naval duty, but the routine soon bored him, and in 1878–1879, he journeyed from Turkey to India. His subsequent book, *Our Future Highway to India* (1880), gave an account of his travels and argued for the building of a railway from the Mediterranean to India, which did not have to follow the course of the Euphrates River. The book made little impact, however, and Cameron turned his attentions back to Africa.

In 1881–1882, Cameron joined Burton on a mission to West Africa. The two explorers examined the interior of the Gold Coast, searching for evidence of its gold-producing potential. Cameron also plotted the course of the Ankobrah River, and together they sent 151 native plants to Kew Gardens. Their book about the journey, *To the Gold Coast for Gold*, was published the next year.

Following Cameron's retirement from the active list of the Royal Navy at age 39, he married Amy Morris; they did not have children. For a number of years, both the Camerons concentrated on writing, and his first of numerous adventure books for boys, *Jack Hooper*, appeared in 1885. Cameron spent a number of years involved with the companies seeking to develop and manage Africa. He also spent a great deal of time at his country house in Soulbury near Leighton Buzzard, Bedfordshire. He was returning to his home from hunting on Easter in 1894 when he was thrown from his horse. He subsequently died from brain damage and was buried at the parish church at Shoreham, Kent, where his father had been vicar.

BEAU RIFFENBURGH

### Biography

Born in Radipole, Dorset, 1 July 1844. Son of a clergyman. Joined the Royal Navy, August 1857. Saw active service in the Mediterranean, the West Indies, and the Red Sea. Went to the United States, 1862. Took part in two major African expeditions: crossing the continent from Zanzibar, Lake Tanganyika, to Benguela on the west coast, 1873–1875; to the Gold Coast with fellow explorer Burton, 1881–1882. Achieved rank of commander, 1876. Traveled from Turkey to India, 1878–1879. Published children's books. Retired from active list of Royal Navy, 1883. Married Amy Mona Reid Morris, 1885. Companion of the Bath, 1876; awarded gold medal by the Royal Geographical Society, 1876. Honorary DCL, Oxford University, 1876. Awarded Order of the Crown of Italy. Died from brain damage following a riding accident at Soulsbury, near Leighton Buzzard, Bedfordshire, 27 March 1894.

### References and Further Reading

Cameron, Verney Lovett, *Journal*, April to September 1875, during the Livingstone Relief Expedition of 1873–1875, Royal Geographical Society, London.

Cameron, Verney Lovett, *Across Africa*, 1877.

Cameron, Verney Lovett, *Our Future Highway to India*, 1880.

Cameron, Verney Lovett, and Richard Francis Burton, *To the Gold Coast for Gold: A Personal Narrative*, 1883.

## CAMINHA, PERO VAZ DE (c. 1449–1500) *Portuguese Traveler and Writer*

Pero Vaz de Caminha was living quietly in Oporto when he was assigned the unrefusable position of writer to the trading station that was to be established at Calicut, on India's Malabar Coast. Caminha was no longer a young man when he embarked for what was to be not only his first but also his last major journey, as he was killed at the end of 1500. Travel enlarged his geographical horizons, until then confined to the narrow streets of Oporto and the fresh and green fields of the province of Entre Douro e Minho, which would be the object of analogy with the Brazilian terrain in the letter that he wrote to the Portuguese king. The letter is an important document for comparative ethnography. However, from a cultural point of view, far beyond the information value of what was reported, its importance was determined by its views about Amerindians, interesting both in their own right and when compared with those given by Columbus.

On 23 April 1500, the fleet commanded by Pedro Álvares Cabral anchored in front of a territory that had never before been seen by Europeans. For eight days, the Portuguese stayed at the place later called Cabrália Bay, Brazil, making contact with the local natives, the Pataxó (Tupinamba). The amazing wonder, counterbalanced by the strictness demanded by Caminha's belief in knowledge being attainable through observation, inspired him to write one of the most important Portuguese texts regarding the discoveries overseas. Although first written as a letter, it was classified, following its discovery in the eighteenth century in Torre do Tombo, the Portuguese national archive, and following the first of several editions in the last two centuries, as a travel narrative, and so included in the annals of travel literature. It was also used as a political instrument and, following official historiography, publicized as the "birth certificate" of Brazil in textbooks and courses. The concept is controversial, and it was called into question during the celebrations of the 500th anniversary of Cabral's voyage. Such use of this particular letter, written to announce news so special that it justified the order for a ship to sail back to Portugal with it, thus diminishing the naval force that was to sail to India, is a reminder of the multiple significances of any text at the points of both production and reception.

Caminha revealed remarkable literary skills, unexpected from a man who was formerly the master of the mint. The manuscript of the letter to King Manuel makes evident that he was used to the pen, for it was written in a good hand. If Caminha wrote some other account of the voyage, as his position on board leads us to guess he may have done, it has since been lost. The letter is not exactly a true account, but "the news of the finding" of Brazil. The writer had a double role to perform: as an actor in the living reality that he proposed to *relate and tell*, and as a creator, through the act of writing, of the same reality. Although the letter carried the date of 1 May, it had been composed over several days and, thus, enables us to analyze the evolution of knowledge about the Pataxó people and their way of life, starting from the point of complete ignorance. In the letter, daily events and issues of knowledge are very closely related: what happens may ascertain or rectify what was already known, and what was known frames the analysis of what happens. *To see* was the main requisite to achieve true knowledge, and the sense of vision was clearly favored. However, the observer only saw what he was able to understand, while looking at the natural and human landscape in front of him.

Caminha stressed the fruitful beauty and the healthy air of the new-found land. But the people were the most impressive novelty. With their naked, hairless bodies, sometimes colored with a black dye, good-looking faces with pierced lips, wearing caps of feathers, and carrying bows and arrows that were soon left aside, the local natives received the newcomers (who had, as soon as they arrived, as was usual, given new names to the land and the mountain nearby), danced with them to the sound of a bagpipe played by a sailor, and even imitated their pious reverence toward the holy cross. At the moment of the first contact, Caminha inferred from earlier Portuguese experiences in Africa that it would be possible to speak with the natives. He stated that the captain chosen by Cabral to go on shore "could not have any speech with them there [on the beach], nor understanding which might be profitable, because of the breaking of the sea on the shore." But he soon understood that the only possible means of communication was to use signs, and stressed their ambiguous nature:

> A native brought on board made a sign towards the land and then to the beads and to the collar of the captain, as if to say that they would give gold for that. We interpreted this so, because we wished to, but if he meant that he would take the beads and also the collar, we did not wish to understand because we did not intend to give it to him.

Caminha looked at women's bodies in terms of a beautiful landscape. The descriptions of the land and the people appeal to the *myth of Eldorado* (an image at Caminha's disposal that could enable him to grasp the sense of that new reality). This myth framed the image of the *good Amerindian*. But such a mythical approach straitened the understanding of everything observed by him. The benevolent intellectual disposition of the writer toward those men and women gave rise to the theme of the innocence and the amorality of the nude Amerindians, who, from Caminha's point of view, were unable to distinguish between good and evil, as Adam had been in the earthly paradise, and so were available for evangelization. However, innocence suggests also an infantile condition, an idea that was strengthened in particular by the lack of pubic hair. So the concept of the good Amerindian concealed two deprecating features, for it reduced the Amerindians to some kind of "infra-manhood" and to a "precivilized" level, making the assumption that they lived within nature and without policy. Caminha compared them to sparrows and wild animals, having in mind their sidestepping behavior, though he stressed too their trustful and fearless attitudes after the initial contact. He also thought (reporting this as a fact) that they had no political or social organization or religious belief. However, Caminha knew they built houses, and he depicted these from the account given by some Portuguese who went to an indigenous village. Caminha felt Europeans to be superior, except for a few physical details, notwithstanding being amazed by the "new mankind" he had found. But the pure simplicity of the people and the land had moved approximately five Portuguese to run away and settle there.

ISABEL BOAVIDA

### Biography

Born in Oporto, c. 1449, son of a cavalier of the household of the duke of Guimarães. Inherited from his father the position of *mestre da balança da moeda* (master of the balance of mint) at Oporto, 1476. Wrote the Request of Oporto Council to be presented to the royal court, 1498. Assigned the position of writer in the fleet under the command of Pedro Álvares Cabral, and to the trading station to be established at Calicut, India, 1500. Wrote a letter to King Manuel from the Land of Vera Cruz (Brazil), describing the new discovery, 1 May 1500. Died in Calicut, India, 16 December 1500.

### References and Further Reading

Caminha, Pedro Vaz de, Carta [Letter] in *Corografia Brazilica; ou, Relação histórico-geográfica do Reino do Brazil* [Description of Brazil; or, Historical and Geographical Account of the Kingdom of Brazil], vol. 1, edited by Manuel Ayres de Casal, 1817; numerous subsequent editions, including *A Carta de Pêro Vaz de Caminha*, edited by Jaime Cortesão, 1943; as "Letter of Pedro Vaz de Caminha to King Manuel, Written from Porto Seguro of Vera Cruz the 1st of May 1500," in *The Voyage of Pedro Álvares Cabral to Brazil and India*, edited and translated by William Brooks Greenlee, 1938.

## CAMÕES, LUÍS VAZ DE (c. 1524–1580)

***Portuguese Soldier and Writer***

Portugal's greatest poet and national symbol, Luís Vaz de Camões, was probably born in Lisbon. Although there is little verifiable biographical information, it is believed that he was born into an impoverished aristocratic family headed by Simão Vaz de Camões and Ana Sá e Macedo of Santarém. His universal reputation as one of the great poets of the European Renaissance rests mainly on his *Os Lusíadas* (*The Lusiads*, 1572), the epic whose title—literally, the sons of Lusus—reflects the founding of Portugal by Lusus, a mythical settler of the Roman region of Lusitania. In this account of the Portuguese travels of exploration to the East, Camões traces the nation's history within the context of his own experience abroad, where he was employed in the Portuguese overseas maritime administration. In this capacity, he traveled to India and as far as Macao.

Although Camões is mainly remembered for this epic work, he is also purported to be one of a handful of truly great writers of the sonnet form, along with Shakespeare and Petrarch. In his lyric sequence, in keeping with Petrarchan and earlier traditions of courtly love, Camões often expresses the unfolding saga of his own experience abroad. He accomplishes this not only in his formal compositions of classic style (sonnets, eclogues, and so forth), but also in those that echo the popular Iberian folk songs (in the *redondilhas* or verse quatrains of five- or seven-syllable lines based on a *mote* or refrain). Such is the case with the celebrated poem dedicated by the author "To a captive, called Barbara, that he fell in love with in India." In this well-known composition, Camões also explores, not without a strong dose of irony, the transformative impact of the overseas encounter on the European traveler. The poet's Barbara, "prisoner" and "captive" at once, becomes the vehicle for the paradoxical and alluring confrontation of the European traveler in the "Barbarian Gulf." Her very name echoes the primitive and orientalist expectations of the Western voyager, who is instead seduced and ultimately won over by the beauty of her dark complexion: "This ebony Love, / of such sweet sort, / that brightest snow / would trade its hue."

Many of the orientalist themes pertaining to the first European contacts in the Eastern realms—racist condescension, arrogance, and a strong sense of European superiority—are traced, and sometimes overturned, by the amorous Camões, whose verses invariably mirror his fortuitous life overseas. It is believed that Camões's first experience away from home may have resulted from a prohibited, and perhaps unrequited, liaison that sent him into exile in Ceuta, Morocco (1547), where he lost an eye in battle. In his letters, especially from Ceuta and India (published in 1598), Camões is disheartened by the tribulations of banishment and glosses his sadness with extended literary allusions. In the letter from India, unlike the platonic response to Barbara's exotic appeal, Camões denigrates these "ladies of the land," reporting their lack of nobility and courtesy (*Obras completas*, 1985: 246–247); the gentlewomen of Lisbon, however, do not fare better. Camões's duplicitous rhetoric of love (often courtly and sometimes antifeminist) recalls the words of David Quint, who has observed that in these matters of colonial discourse "the otherness of the Easterner, becomes the otherness of the second sex" (*Epic and Empire*).

Similarly, after imprisonment for a brawl in Lisbon (1552), Camões was freed from the ominous Tronco dungeon on the condition that he serve in India as a common soldier. It was in the East, then, that Camões found not only personal freedom but also justification for his epic masterpiece, *The Lusiads*. This story of Portuguese nationhood poetically transforms Vasco da Gama's commercial enterprise of expansion (he first departed from Lisbon on 8 July 1497) into a moral tale framed by European conventions of imperial discourse in the age of exploration. Much of the poem was completed by the time of Camões's shipwreck (1559), an incident that has become emblematic of national pride: the author is often represented as saving his manuscript from the waters off Cambodia.

The structure of *The Lusiads* follows that of classic models as suggested especially by Virgil's *Aeneid*. The story is launched *in medias res* with da Gama's passage up the east coast of Africa (through Mozambique, Mombasa, and finally Melinde) in search of a new empire, a voyage that ends only after the weary Portuguese soldiers, upon their return home, become symbolic masters of the Eastern lands. In the final analysis, Camões presents an apocalyptic vision of the physical and metaphysical love that rewards the "honorable" task of discovery and conquest. In canto 9, the protective Venus pays homage to the fatigued Western soldiers with the notorious "Isle of Love" ("Ilha dos Amores") that she gently floats before them. The cradled island has become one of the most acclaimed encounters in the history of travel literature, for the willing nymphs—schooled by the Eastern goddess and incited by her son—playfully evade their lustful hunters, only to submit in the end. In the ensuing orgy, even the star-crossed lover, Lionardo Ribeiro, claims a "prize," as his nymph falls "in rapture at her victor's feet / who melted utterly in passion's heat." This sensuous paradise—where the Portuguese mariners mate with the Eastern sea nymphs—illustrates not only the conquest and conversion of the new peoples, but also the Portuguese mastery of the oceans leading to the coveted Eastern realms.

371 372

ESTANCIA I.

IA Neste tempo o lucido Planeta,
que as horas vay do dia destinguindo,
chegava à desejada, e lenta meta,
a luz celeste às gentes encobrindo:
E da casa maritima secreta,
lhe estava o Deos Nocturno a porta abrindo,
quando as fingidas gentes se chegàram
a as naos que pouco avia que ancoràram.

YA En este tiempo el lucido Planeta, que vá destinguiendo las horas del dia, llegava a la deseada, i templada meta, encubriendo la celeste luz a las gentes: i el Dios Nocturno le estava abriendo la puerta de la secreta, i maritima casa, quando las infidas gentes llegaron a las naves, que de poco avian ancorado.

¶ *Ia neste tempo, &c.* Todas las entradas de los Cantos deste Poema son a imitacion de las de los de Virgilio; prosiguiendo la materia del antecedente; pero rompiendola con destreza en ocasiones sazonadas, encendiendo con el fin de un libro, o Canto, el deseo para entrar en el otro, siendo menester entrar en él con la memoria de lo passado, i por otra parte abriendo lugar a que descansen los Letores en la corriente de aquel deseo de leer. Vease sobre esto lo que contiene el num. 22. del Iuizio deste Poema.

A

¶ *Lucido Planeta, que as horas vay do dia destinguindo.* Perifrasis del Sol sacado de Petrarca, Soneto 9. *Quando il Pianeta che destingue l'hore.* Panfilo Sasso, Soneto 163. *Piu bel Pianeta che destingue l'hore.* Del Martirano en su Aretusa, *Veggonsi mesi che distingon l'anno.* Porque el Sol es el dueño, i Presidẽte destas distinciones, Ovid. Met. 1.

*.........In solio Phœbus, &c.*
*A dextra, lævaque dies, & mensis, & annus,*
*Seculaque, & positæ spatijs æqualibus horæ.*

Llamanse horas aquellas porciones de tiempo, de *horin*, que en Griego vale termino, i dél se llamó orilla la margen de los rios, o la punta de los vestidos. Son en diferentes maneras las horas: pe-

By Renaissance epic convention, the pagan gods take a hand in the action: Venus appeals to Jupiter to protect Vasco da Gama and his men in their encounter with the treacherous inhabitants of the East African coast (*Lusíadas*, canto 2, in the 1639 Madrid edition). *Courtesy of British Library, London.*

Camões made good use of the many genres of travel literature before him: *Relação da viagem de Vasco da Gama* (attributed to Álvaro Velho), *História do descobrimento e conquista da Índia pelos Portugueses* (Fernão Lopes de Castanheda, 1551), *Décadas da Ásia* (João de Barros), and many more. In *The Lusiads*, however, for all of its eclectic blending of pagan and Christian elements, there is much that Camões himself experienced in his journeys. In 1570, Camões returned to Lisbon, where he published his Christian epic. It is believed that he died in poverty in 1580, defeated also by the impending national disaster that King Sebastian's death (in Alcácer-Kebir, Morocco) symbolized to the vast Portuguese empire.

René P. Garay

## Biography

Born probably in Lisbon (in the Mouraria district), Portugal, 1524 or 1525. Probably studied at the University of Coimbra. Later moved back to Lisbon; became involved, according to legend, with Donna Caterina de Ataide, c. 1544. Exiled from Lisbon, either for personal reasons or by royal decree as the result of a love affair, 1546. Joined the royal garrison in Ceuta, Morocco, 1547; lost his left eye in action. Pardoned by King John III and returned to Lisbon, 1550. Arrested for brawling during the Corpus Christi procession, 1552. Imprisoned and released subject to payment of fine and enlistment for military duty in India. Sailed for India on board *São Bento*, 1553. Lived in Goa, 1552–1556. Took up post in Macao, 1556. Shipwrecked in the Mekong Delta in Cambodia while returning to Goa, 1559; managed to save some writings (probably *The Lusiads*). Reportedly had his passage back to Lisbon from Mozambique paid for in part by the historian Diego do Couto. Taken to Lisbon on *Santa Clara*, 1569–1570. Published *Os Lusíadas* (*The Lusiads*), 1572. Died in Lisbon, 10 June 1580.

### References and Further Reading

Camões, Luíz Vaz de, *Os Lusíadas*, 1572; as *The Lusiad; or, Portugals Historicall Poem*, translated by Richard Fanshawe, 1655; as *The Lusiads*, translated with an introduction by Leonard Bacon, 1950; translated with an introduction by Landeg White, 1997.

Camões, Luíz Vaz de, *Rhythmas*, 1595; as *The Lyricks*, translated by Richard F. Burton, 2 vols., 1884.

Camões, Luíz Vaz de, *Letter I* (from Ceuta), 1598.

Camões, Luíz Vaz de, *Letter II* (from India), 1598.

## CAMPBELL, JOHN (1766–1840) *Scottish Minister and Missionary*

Deeply religious from an early age, John Campbell had decided to join the ministry by 1789, after meeting in London the Methodist hymn writer John Newton. He was active in both religious and social causes, working to improve living conditions for fallen women by serving as a founder of the Magdalene Society of Edinburgh and a similar society in Glasgow. Campbell was keenly interested in the condition of slaves, and he arranged for the education of 30 or 40 Bantu children, who returned home after five years of schooling in London. Traveling within Scotland and England, Campbell helped found and promote Sunday schools and participated in lay preaching in isolated villages. In addition, he was continually active in promoting religious literature. Campbell was one of the founders of the Religious Tract Society of Scotland in 1793 (six years before the London society was formed). While at Kingsland, he founded the Bible and Foreign Bible Society, and he was for 18 years the editor of *The Youth's Magazine*, a religious publication.

Campbell made two trips to southern Africa. Both were funded by the London Missionary Society, for whom he agreed to inspect mission outposts. However, Campbell also used the opportunity to gather artifacts for the London Missionary Society museum. Campbell was the first missionary to travel far into the continent's interior, where he performed both missionary and medical work for the native peoples. He later published a record of his journeys (*Travels in South Africa . . . Second Journey . . .* , 1822) that was considered important for its geographic value, as these regions were little known to Europeans. For instance, one writer for the *London Quarterly Review* noted, "Mr. Campbell, by his Travels, has considerably enlarged the sphere of our knowledge of Southern Africa" (quoted in Allibone). Importantly, the second volume of *Travels* contained a map of the continent. During the first journey, which lasted from June 1812 to May 1814, Campbell traveled more than 2,000 miles, and he was the first missionary to travel beyond Lattakoo, the capital of the Bechuana tribe of the Bachapins. Campbell's second journey, 1819–1821, took him farther north, to Griquatown and Lattakoo by way of the Orange River. From there, he traveled as far north as Mashow and Kurreechane. The village of Campbell (also called Campbelldorp), which lies between Kimberley and Griquatown, was originally a station of the London Missionary Society and was named for him.

*Travels in South Africa* is Campbell's best-known work. Unlike his other books, it is primarily anecdotal and observational, not religious. It includes information on southern Africa's people, landscape, terrain, foliage, weather, and other similar topics. Examples of chapter headings include "Departure from Mashow—Description of the Scenery on the Journey— Passed a Village of Bushmen—Slaughter of a Rhinoceros" (vol. 1), and "Bootchuana Manners and Customs" (vol. 2). Campbell also wrote a book called *African Light Thrown on a Selection of Scripture Texts* (1835), in which he "intended to elucidate passages of scripture from what he had seen in travelling."

Several of Campbell's other works use the theme of travel as a way of directing the reader's attention to religious matters. Even domestic travel, such as that in *Walks of Usefulness in London and Its Environs* (1808), "might remind us of important matters. For example, the river might remind us of the river of life that enriches and enlivens the city or church of God." *Walks of Usefulness* reads the people and events in everyday London metaphorically, so that the physical world might be of spiritual use:

> The streets being wet and dirty in the morning, the people were all walking with caution, lest their clothes should be splashed with the dirt. This reminded me of the apostle's admonition, to walk circumspectly, not as fools . . . we live in a polluted and polluting world. Many things that meet the eye and the ear will pollute the mind, if we are not guarded against them.

A work intended "For the Use of Young People" is *Alfred and Galba* (1805), which incorporates the themes of travel, geography, and religious conversion. This story consists of the narrator's dream, after he falls asleep while studying geography. He "frequently seemed to traverse the globe in a night while asleep" after such studies. This narrative, in the tradition of Robinson Crusoe, has its main characters stranded on an isolated island. Highly anti-Catholic, its theme of travel creates "many opportunities of conveying useful hints about eternal things" to the narrator's acquaintances—and to Campbell's readers.

Ginny Crosthwait

### Biography

Born in Edinburgh, 1766. Attended the Royal High School in Edinburgh. Engaged in successful business enterprises; associated with many religious and philanthropic activities. Cofounder of the Religious Tract Society of Scotland, 1793. Founded and promoted, with J.A. Haldane, the movement to establish Sunday schools in Scotland; also served as a lay preacher in Scotland. Helped to establish the Magdalene Society in Edinburgh and Glasgow. Appointed minister of Kingsland independent chapel, London, 1802; assisted in the founding of the Bible Society. Traveled to southern Africa on behalf of the London Missionary Society to inspect their missions, journeying extensively in the interior, 1812–1814, Settled in Cape Town, 1814. Traveled in the southern African interior again, 1819–1821. Returned to London, 1821. Worked on behalf of missionary activity in Africa until his death. Died 4 April 1840.

### References and Further Reading

Campbell, John, *A Journey to the Moon, and Interesting Conversations with the Inhabitants, Respecting the Condition of Man*, n.d.

Campbell, John, *Worlds Displayed, for the Benefit of Young People, by a Familiar History of Some of Their Inhabitants*, 1800.

Campbell, John, *Alfred and Galba, or the History of Two Brothers, Supposed to be Written by Themselves*, 1805.

Campbell, John, *Voyages and Travels of a Bible*, 1808; 7th edition, 1821.

Campbell, John, *Walks of Usefulness in London and Its Environs*, 1808.

Campbell, John, *Travels in South Africa, Undertaken at the Request of the Missionary Society*, 1815; abridged as *Journal of Travels in South Africa, among the Hottentot and Other Tribes, in 1812, 1813 and 1814*, 1834.

Campbell, John, *Voyages to and from the Cape of Good Hope, in the Years 1812 and 1814: For the Entertainment of Young People*, 1816.

Campbell, John, *The African Traveller; or, Select Lives, Voyages, and Travels, Carefully Abridged from the Original Publications of Bruce, Barrow, Campbell, and Park*, 1817.

Campbell, John, *Travels in South Africa . . . Being a Narrative of a Second Journey in the Interior of That Country*, 2 vols., 1822; abridged as *A Journey to Lattakoo, in South Africa*, 1835.

Campbell, John, *The Juvenile Cabinet of Travels and Narratives for the Amusement and Instruction of Young Persons*, 1825.

Campbell, John, *Pacaltsdorp, ou le village hottentot*, 1825.

Campbell, John, *Hottentot Children, with a Particular Account of Paul Dikkop, the Son of a Hottentot Chief, Who Died in England, September 14, 1824*, 1830.

Campbell, John, *The Life of Africaner, a Namacqua Chief of South Africa*, 1830.

Campbell, John, *Life of Kaboo, a Wild Bushman*, 1830.

Campbell, John, *African Light Thrown on a Selection of Scripture Texts*, 1835; 3rd edition, 1852.

Campbell, John, *Africaner, Part I; or, Missionary Trials*, 1843.

Campbell, John, *Africaner, Part II; or, Missionary Pleasures*, 1843.

## CANADA

Records by European explorers searching for dominions, resources, and a shortcut to Cathay in the northern waters and regions of the "New World" assume a foundational position in the history of Canadian literature aside from the indigenous oral tradition. Richard Hakluyt's two encyclopedic compilations of exploration literature, *Divers Voyages Touching the Discovery of America* (1582) and *The Principal Navigations of the English Nation* (1589; 2nd edition, 1598–1600), include writings by and about fifteenth- and sixteenth-century explorers and their journeys along Canadian shorelines: among those mentioned are Giovanni da Verrazzano, John and Sebastian Cabot, Jacques Cartier, Humphrey Gilbert, Martin Frobisher, and John Davis. Hakluyt left a mass of manuscript that was subsequently published by Samuel Purchas in several editions, penultimately in *Hakluytus Posthumus; or, Purchas His Pilgrimes* (1625); this collection incorporates works by and about the sixteenth- and early-seventeenth-century explorers Charles Leigh, Samuel de Champlain, Henry Hudson, and William Baffin.

Inland explorers, fur traders, and surveyors from the seventeenth to nineteenth centuries produced a wealth of engaging literature documenting their encounters with the land and its people. Nature is often represented as a wilderness promising adventure or death, while natives are variously portrayed as noble or brutal savages, although some reports rise above the ethnocentrism of their time. Widely read classics of the Canadian exploration genre that thrilled audiences back home include Alexander Henry's memoir, *Travels and Adventures in Canada and the Indian Territories between the Years 1760–1776* (1809), a self-dramatizing depiction of Pontiac's 1763 attack on the English fort at Michilimackinac; Samuel Hearne's *A Journey from Prince of Wales's Fort in Hudson's Bay, to the Northern Ocean* (1795), featuring a graphic eyewitness account of the Chipewyan massacre of the Inuit near the mouth of the Coppermine River; and John Franklin's harrowing story of frostbite, murder, and death by starvation, *Narrative of a Journey to the Shores of the Polar Sea* (1823). Of particular literary interest are the journal and 90-line poem by Henry Kelsey, an unassuming servant of the Hudson's Bay Company who voyaged as far west as the prairies with the Cree from

1690 to 1692, and David Thompson's reflective journals relating his extensive peregrinations and portages in the northwest in the period 1784–1812. Frances Simpson, Letitia Hargrave, and Isobel Finlayson, who were affiliated with the fur trade through marriage, composed letters and diaries during the first half of the nineteenth century that are among the earliest documents by women of European origin in the west and northwest.

While explorers were still mapping routes westward and northward in the nineteenth century, tourists from Europe and the United States began visiting the colonies and backwoods settlements of pre-Confederate British North America. The itinerary of the popular Canadian "northern tour"—often an addendum to travels in the northeastern United States—might have included the cities of Quebec and Montreal and the scenic Saguenay region in Lower Canada, the cities of Bytown (Ottawa), Kingston, and Little York (Toronto) in Upper Canada, capped by the obligatory pilgrimage to Niagara Falls for seekers of the sublime. So successful was one of the earliest accounts of the northern tour, Isaac Weld's *Travels through the State of North America and the Provinces of Upper and Lower Canada* (1799), that it was published in successive editions and translated into several European languages. Many travel books by northern tourists or temporary residents written with an audience of potential emigrants in mind report on the politics, economy, and agriculture of the provinces and the customs, manners, and culture of the colonials. The number of travel reports on emigration increased in the years following the Napoleonic wars. After a sojourn from 1818 to 1820, John Howison wrote *Sketches of Upper Canada, Local, Domestic, and Characteristic* (1829), which recommends emigration to Upper Canada for the penurious of Great Britain as well as for the educated and titled gentlemen of meager independent incomes. Similar counsel is made in William Tiger Dunlop's *Statistical Sketches of Upper Canada, for the Use of Emigrants* (1832) and Isaac Fidler's *Observations on Professions, Literature, Manners, and Emigration in the United States and America* (1833).

Glimpses of native life on the margins of settlement continued to titillate nineteenth-century European readers, while English-speaking travelers also constructed French-Canadian culture as an exotic "other." Montreal and Quebec were frequently celebrated for their quaint, romantic, Old-Worldly qualities—veritable gardens in the perceived cultural barrens of Canada. Alternatively, and often in the same text, French Canada was condemned as unprogressive, old-fashioned, and stultified by Catholicism. John Lambert's *Travels through Lower Canada and the United States of North America* (1810) and Francis Hall's *Travels in Canada and in the United States* (1818) are two early exemplary texts on Lower Canada. The Maritimes became a destination of choice as the century progressed, particularly after the enthusiastic worldwide reception of Henry Wadsworth Longfellow's poem "Evangeline: A Tale of Acadie" in 1847. Longfellow, an American who never visited Nova Scotia, was nonetheless stirred by a tale of young lovers torn asunder by the mid-eighteenth-century deportation of the rural Acadians, and his idyllic representation of Acadia inspired others to make the voyage. In *Acadia; or, A Month with the Bluenoses* (1859), Frederick Cozzens seeks relief from his gastric disorder among the pastoral relics of Acadia, but the real often intrudes on the romance as the distinct ethnic and racial communities of the province disturb his American sensibilities of national unity and assimilation.

Anna Brownell Jameson's *Winter Studies and Summer Rambles in Canada* (1838) has justifiably attracted much critical attention and praise. Following a dreary, solitary, yet studious winter in Toronto in 1837 as the unloved and unloving wife of the provincial attorney general of Upper Canada, the author summers in the relative wilderness of the upper Great Lakes, where she becomes a participant-observer of native life and gender relations. Jameson's foray off the beaten tourist path with native companions was personally liberating and quite remarkable, given the gender restrictions of her own culture. During the century, the Canadian wilds were increasingly represented as an irresistibly dangerous playground for sportsmen, and hunting and camping narratives like Viscount Milton and Dr. Cheadle's *The North West Passage by Land* (1865) were immensely popular. Toronto-born artist Paul Kane took part in a native buffalo chase on the Canadian prairies in *Wanderings of an Artist among the Indians of North America* (1859), an illustrated account of his journey of 1845–1849 across the northwest, through the Rocky Mountains, to the Pacific coast. Hunting aside, Kane's principal mission was to sketch portraits of traditionally garbed Indian chiefs in an effort to immortalize a race and culture he believed faced extinction. His text is also an elegy to regions of Canada's wilderness soon to be transformed by a transcontinental railroad that would open the west for settlement and tourism.

Framing the construction of the Canadian Pacific Railway (CPR) are George Grant's *Ocean to Ocean: Sanford Fleming's Expedition through Canada in 1872* (1873)—Sanford Fleming being the engineer in chief of the historic project—and *England and Canada: A Summer Tour between the Old and New Westminster* (1884) by Fleming himself. The former book recounts the coordination of survey parties, and the latter depicts a project nearing completion; both ac-

The immensity of the northern Canadian wilderness is conveyed in Back's 1825 drawing of the view from a portage on the Clearwater River (from Franklin's *Narrative of a Second Expedition to the Shores of the Polar Sea . . .* , 1828). *Courtesy of the Travellers Club, London; Bridgeman Art Library, agent.*

counts exude the expansionist, nationalist, and imperialist zeitgeist that surrounded the Canadian Confederation in 1867. Following the completion of the CPR in 1886, travel books reflected the trend of the cross-Canada train trip. Mrs. Arthur Spragge catches the first through-train in Winnipeg in *From Ontario to the Pacific by the C.P.R.* (1887); Sara Jeannette Duncan rides the cowcatcher through the Rockies in *A Social Departure* (1890); Douglas Sladen entertains with the intrigues of railway travel and insightful observations of the nation in *On the Cars and Off* (1895); and Australian James Francis Hogan promotes the line's potential to fortify the unity of the British empire and its antipodal colonies in *The Sister Dominions: Through Canada to Australia by the New Imperial Highway* (1896).

Since the nation-building events of the later nineteenth century stimulated foreign appetites for information, early-twentieth-century travel writers bloated the marketplace with investigative reports on all facets of Canadian life. While some propagandistic observers touted Canada as an incipient world power, others of a more skeptical mindset tempered visions of glory with reports of a lingering backward colonialism and unbearably cold weather. As the title of *Canada As It Is* (1905) implies, author John Foster Fraser attempts to give a fair appraisal of the Dominion that debunks sensational, extremist representations of Canada. Many of these travel-based reports focus on employment possibilities, functioning as admonishment or encouragement to readers wanting to sift fact from fiction before joining the tidal wave of European immigration flooding western Canada. James Lumsden's *Through Canada at Harvest Time: A Study of Life and Labour in the Golden West* (1903) directs men unafraid of a hard day's work to western Canada, even though all the "pretty girls" reportedly reside in Montreal. In *A Woman in Canada* (1911), Marian Cran inspects the west from a woman's perspective, identifying opportunities in homesteading, domestic work, and independent farming for women who are hearty and hale.

As European civilization spread across Canada, robust adventurers of both sexes lured by the untamed Canadian wilds inevitably headed northward. We find Agnes Deans Cameron traveling by steamship, tugboat, and scow to northern forts and native settlements in *The New North: An Account of a Woman's 1908 Journey through Canada to the Arctic* (1909) and Prentice Gilbert Downes questing for Lake Nu-thel-tin-tu-eh in *Sleeping Island: The Story of One Man's Travels in the Great Barren Lands of the Canadian North* (1943). Adventurers of another ilk sought excitement and made headlines crossing Canada using alternative routes and modes of transportation other than the CPR. Thomas Wilby's *A Motor Tour through Canada* (1914) and Percy Gomery's *A Motor-Scamper cross Canada* (1922), which predate the construction of the Trans-Continental Highway, are tragicomedies of corduroy roads, dead ends, broken bridges, portentous potholes, and disintegrating cars. Katherine Trevelyan's *Unharboured Heaths* (1934) is a spirited narrative by a daring young British woman who hitchhikes across Canada in 1930, and her countrywoman Mary Bosanquet, in *Saddlebags for Suitcases* (1942), provides a moving, coming-of-age account of her liberating, solo journey across Canada on horseback.

The bulk of post-war Canadian travel books are by Canadians fumbling for self-definition, reflecting the vicissitudes of a proliferating nationalism and national identity crisis. Bristling at unflattering national stereotypes, archpatriotic traveler Bruce Hutchison strives to make his country known to fellow Canadians in *The Unknown Country* (1942). The popularity of Hutchison's book was as unprecedented in Canadian publishing history as the notoriety of Norman Levine's *Canada Made Me* (1958). Levine, temporarily returning from exile in England to travel across his natal land, displays little more than contempt for a nation he represents as a repository for the physically grotesque and the intellectually, culturally mediocre. In *Le Canada sans passeport* (1967), translated by Joyce Marshall as *No Passport: A Discovery of Canada* (1968), French Canadian writer Eugène Cloutier opens with some wickedly funny jabs at English Canada, but he warms up to his subject and comes to see the country as an original tapestry of eccentric personalities. As the urgent need for national definition subsided in the 1980s, so did the polemical, blanket-statement travel book. We find quirky texts like David McFadden's *A Trip around Lake Huron* (1980) and *A Trip around Lake Erie* (1980), where mom, dad, kids, and the family dog, Bruce, jump into the yellow Volkswagen van for a brief road trip.

Postmodernism precipitated a more experimental, intertextual form of travel writing in the 1990s. In *Places Far from Ellesmere* (1990), Canadian feminist writer Aritha van Herk travels with Leo Tolstoy's *Anna Karenina* to the High Arctic—geography she reads as a tabula rasa, a space where she may free Anna from the nineteenth-century gender and literary conventions that doomed her. *Enduring Dreams* (1994), by Canadian literary critic John Moss, is a literal and metatextual exploration of the Arctic in that the author's treks are interspersed with philosophical reflections on the process of transforming landscape into geography and history through writing. So intertextual is Moss's fragmented book that it functions on one level as an annotated bibliography on Arctic exploration and travel writing.

Denise Adele Heaps

### References and Further Reading

Aberdeen, the Countess of, *Through Canada with a Kodak*, 1893.
Bird, Isabella L., *An Englishwoman in America*, 1856.
Brooke, Rupert, *Letters from America*, 1916.
Carr, Emily, *Klee Wyck*, 1941.
Coke, E.T., *A Subaltern's Furlough*, 1833.
Cumberland, Stuart C., *The Queen's Highway from Ocean to Ocean*, 1887.
Dickens, Charles, *American Notes for General Circulation*, 1842.
Duncan, Dorothy, *Here's to Canada*, 1941.
Fitzgibbon, Mary, *A Trip to Manitoba; or, Roughing It on the Line*, 1880.
Fitzroy, Yvonne, *A Canadian Panorama*, 1929.
Garland, Hamlin, *The Trail of the Goldseekers*, 1899.
Haldane, J.W.C., *3,800 Miles across Canada*, 1900.
Hasell, F.H. Eva, *Across the Prairie in a Motor Caravan*, 1922.
Hasell, F.H. Eva, *Through Western Canada in a Caravan*, 1925.
Hubbard, Mina, *A Woman's Way through Unknown Labrador*, 1908.
Jason, Victoria, *Kabloona in the Yellow Kayak: One Woman's Journey through the Northwest Passage*, 1996.
Kalm, Pehr, *En resa till Norra America*, 3 vols., 1753; as *Travels into North America*, translated by John Reinhold Forster, 3 vols., 1770–1771.
Kipling, Rudyard, *Letters to the Family: Notes on a Recent Trip to Canada*, 1908.
Kipling, Rudyard, "Tideway to Tideway" in his *Letters of Travel*, 1920.
Kohl, J.G., *Reisen in Canada, und durch die Staaten von New York und Pennsylvanien*, 1856; as *Travels in Canada, and through the States of New York and Pennsylvania*, translated by Mrs. Percy Sinnett, 1861.
Mackenzie, Alexander, *Voyages from Montreal, on the River St. Laurence, through the Continent of North America, to the Frozen and Pacific Oceans*, 1801.
Manning, Ella Wallace, *Igloo for the Night*, 1946.
Manning, Ella Wallace, *A Summer on Hudson's Bay*, 1949.
Morris, Elizabeth Keith, *An Englishwoman in the Canadian West*, 1913.
Ogden, John Cosens, *A Tour through Upper and Lower Canada*, 1799.
Raban, Jonathan, *Passage to Juneau: A Sea and Its Meanings*, 1999.
Thoreau, Henry David, *A Yankee in Canada*, 1866.
Trollope, Anthony, *North America*, 2 vols., 1862.
Vyvyan, Clara, *Arctic Adventure*, 1961.
Warburton, George Drought, *Hochelaga; or, England in the New World*, 1846.
Westbury, G.H., *Misadventures of a Working Hobo in Canada*, 1930.
Whitman, Walt, *Specimen Days in America*, 1887.
Whitman, Walt, *Walt Whitman's Diary in Canada*, edited by William Sloane Kennedy, 1904.
Woodcock, George, *Ravens and Prophets: An Account of Journeys in British Columbia, Alberta, and Southern Alaska*, 1952.

*See also* **Great Lakes and Saint Lawrence River; Hudson's Bay Company; Niagara Falls; Northwest Passage; Rocky Mountains**

## CANOES

A slim, sleek boat with upturned ends and typically propelled by single-bladed paddle, the canoe was first widely used for exploration and trade by both Polynesians and Native Americans. Beginning at least 2,000 years ago, explorers originally from the islands of Samoa, Fiji, and Tonga fanned out over 10 million square miles of ocean in dugout or plank canoes, often with twin hulls, outriggers, and full sails, to explore the countless islands between New Zealand and Hawaii. Fashioned by burning, chipping, and scraping out the center of huge logs, dugouts had hulls as long as 100 feet. The navigational skills of the island explorers were remarkable: after voyages of 2,000 miles, they were able to find islands that were sometimes less than a mile in diameter on which the highest landmark was a coconut tree. Though the double-hulled canoes had less carrying capacity than the broad-beamed ships of the European explorers, the Polynesian canoes were faster: one of Captain Cook's crew estimated a Tongan canoe could sail "three miles to our two." After a visit to the Society Islands in 1774, Andia y Varela described canoes that were "as fine forward as the edge of a knife, so that they travel faster than the swiftest of our vessels; and they are marvellous, not only in this respect, but for their smartness in shifting from one tack to the other."

Although early North American exploration narratives lack detailed descriptions of canoe travel, canoes were certainly already long in use by natives before the arrival of Europeans in the sixteenth century. Jacques Cartier was the first European to record a sighting, in 1535, of a bark canoe; he reported seeing two boats carrying 17 Algonquin men. Seventy years later, Champlain first described canoe dimensions: the boats he saw were eight to nine paces (about 23 feet) long and one-and-a-half paces (about 50 inches) wide. It was the birchbark canoe that carried explorers like Jacques Marquette, Sir Alexander Mackenzie, and David Thompson on their journeys across Canada, and served fur traders on their westward journeys as well. One of La Salle's officers reported seeing a canoe carrying 30 men, probably 14 paddlers on each side alone with a steersman and an officer.

Early French and English explorers were particularly impressed by the speed of bark canoes, typically made from the bark of birch trees; in 1603, near the coast of Maine, Captain George Weymouth reported seeing bark canoes paddled by three men zip past his own boats powered by four oarsmen. Baron de Lahontan, one of La Salle's officers, wrote that lightweight and shallow-draft canoes were convenient for wilderness travel but easily damaged. Their thin skins required that heavy cargo be loaded and unloaded while the boats were still in the water, and at the end of each day, abraded hulls often had to be repaired. Unlike traditional wooden longboats, bark canoes had to be staked down at night to keep from blowing away. These drawbacks were offset, however, by the bark canoes' extremely light weight. Champlain was among the first to recommend the use of bark canoes for trade, since the central and eastern sections of North America were laced by powerful rivers that required many portages—sections of impassably turbulent water that forced travelers to carry their boat and gear from one body of water to another. During portages, this canoe, typically about 16 feet in length and weighing just 50 pounds, could be lifted on one's shoulders and easily carried from lake to lake or around a dangerous set of river rapids. Traditional European sailing vessels, though efficient for travel across large lakes, were useless on most rivers, and the canoe remained a critical means of traversing large regions well into the twentieth century—and well after the advent of the railroad.

McKay B. Jenkins

### References and Further Reading


Bliss, William, *Rapid Rivers*, 1935.

Boggis, R.J.E., *Down the Jordan in a Canoe*, 1939.

Cartier, Jacques, *The Voyages of Jacques Cartier*, edited and translated by H.P. Biggar, 1924.

Cartwright, George, *Captain Cartwright and His Labrador Journal*, edited by Charles Wendell Townsend, with an introduction by Wilfred T. Grenfell, 1911.

Chater, Melville, *Two Canoe Gypsies: Their Eight-Hundred-Mile Canal Voyage through Belgium, Brittany, Touraine, Gascony and Languedoc, Being an Account of Backdoors Life on Bargeman's Highway*, 1932.

Crook, Sally, *Distant Shores: By Traditional Canoe from Asia to Madagascar*, 1990.

Downie, Robert Angus, *The Heart of Scotland by Waterway: Canoe Adventure by River and Loch*, 1934.

Jenkins, Mark, *To Timbuktu*, 1997.

McGuise, Thomas, *99 Days on the Yukon: An Account of What Was Seen and Heard in the Company of Charles A. Wolf, Gentleman Canoeist*, Anchorage: Alaska Northwest, 1977.

Neidé, Charles A., *The Canoe Aurora: A Cruise from the Adirondacks to the Gulf*, 1885.

Nisbet, Jack, *Sources of the River: Tracking David Thompson across Western North America*, 1994.

Raven-Hart, Rowland, *Canoe Errant*, 1935.

Raven-Hart, Rowland, *Canoe Errant on the Nile*, 1936.

Raven-Hart, Rowland, *Canoe Errant on the Mississippi*, 1938.

Raven-Hart, Rowland, *Canoe to Mandalay*, 1939.

Rising, Thomas, and Tean Rising, *"Kingfisher" Abroad*, 1938.


## CAPE OF GOOD HOPE, PRE-1806

The earliest European records of the Cape of Good Hope were observations made by sailors passing to and from the East. First came the Portuguese: Bartholomeu Dias sailed around the Cape in 1488, but his storm-tossed ships were so far out at sea that only on his return voyage did he sail close enough to the peninsula to give it a name—Cabo Tormentoso (Cape of Storms). Later Portuguese fleets called in along the Cape coast to replenish water supplies and perhaps obtain fresh food from the Khoi inhabitants. An anonymous writer who sailed with Vasco da Gama described one such encounter at Mossel Bay in December 1497. The practice of stopping at the Cape was subsequently followed by English and Dutch mariners. Francis Drake, sighting it in June 1580, famously called it "the fairest cape in the whole circumference of the earth." The Cape also offered a rudimentary poste restante service: inscribed stones under which sailors left letters to be picked up and forwarded by the next ship heading in the right direction.

For well over 100 years, the Cape of Good Hope featured in journals and letters merely as an incident on the long voyage between Europe and the East. These accounts generally amount to no more than a journal note or a few paragraphs in a longer work; remarks focus on the hazards of the anchorage, other shipping (if any), and the primitive character of the native inhabitants. Tavernier, who stopped for 28 days at the Cape in 1649, gives a slightly more extended description in his *Six Voyages* (1676), with the usual disobliging remarks about the indigenous peoples.

In 1652, the Dutch East India Company (VOC) dispatched Jan van Riebeeck to establish a fort and gardens on the site of present-day Cape Town, with the aim of providing reliable supplies of fresh food for the company's ships. Reports and correspondence between officials at the Cape and the board in Holland now augment the impressions of transient visitors to give a picture of the developing settlement. By the

1680s, the European population, no longer comprising just VOC employees, was expanding beyond the immediate area of Table Mountain, as farmers and hunters opened up the hinterland, and a few visitors too began venturing beyond the shores of Table Bay. Several later seventeenth-century voyagers included quite substantial descriptions of the Cape in longer works, some referring to the 1685 expedition by Governor van der Stel into the hinterland. Among such visitors were in 1685, Father Guy Tachard, a Jesuit mathematician en route to Siam (*Voyage de Siam*, 1691); in 1687, Simon de le Loubère, the French ambassador to Siam, who wrote more sympathetically than most about the Hottentots (*Du Royaume de Siam*, 1691); John Ovington, homeward bound in 1690 (*Voyage to Suratt . . .*, 1696); William Dampier in 1691 (*New Voyage around the World*, 1697); and Martin Wintergerst in 1699 (*Schwabe oder Reissbeschreibung*, 1712). Abraham Bogaert wrote a lively account of climbing Table Mountain in 1702 (*Historische Reizen door d'oostersche deelen van Asia*, 1711). A description of the Cape in its VOC context is provided by François Valentijn (1656–1727) as part of his survey of the Dutch East Indies enterprise in *Oud en nieuw Oost-Indiën* (1724–1726).

An early and recurrent theme in writings about the Cape of Good Hope was ethnographic observations on the indigenous Khoi population, usually referred to as Hottentots. Such observations form an important part of the influential book by the Prussian traveler Peter Kolb (1675–1726), who was at the Cape in the first decade of the eighteenth century. Another work with valuable ethnographic content is the later *Resa till Goda Hopps-udden* (vol. 1, 1783)—quickly translated into English as *Voyage to the Cape of Good Hope* (1785)—by the world-circling Swede Anders Sparrman (1748–1820), who was in the Cape in the 1770s.

Under the stimulus of Linnaeus's work, scientific travelers paid increasing attention to the unique flora at the Cape, an interest exemplified in the two African volumes of *Travels in Europe, Africa and Asia* (1793–1795) by another Swede, Carl Thunberg (1743–1828), the author of *Flora Capensis* (1818–1820), who was also in the Cape in the early 1770s. William Paterson (1755–1810) made extended forays into the hinterland in 1777–1779, returning to England with a collection of natural history specimens, including a giraffe skin; he published his *Narrative of Four Journeys into the Country of the Hottentots, and Caffraria* in 1789. In the 1780s, the beauty and variety of South African birds received their due from François Le Vaillant, whose two *Voyages* were promptly translated into English.

When the British took over the Cape of Good Hope in 1795 to preserve it from the clutches of revolutionary France, major impetus was given to English-language writing about the region. An important visitor in the late 1790s was John Barrow (1764–1848). As private secretary to the governor Lord Macartney, he was sent on a dual mission to establish a modus vivendi between the Dutch Boers and the indigenous inhabitants in the newly British territory and to acquire accurate topographical information about the largely unmapped interior; Barrow's 1,000-mile journey on foot and horseback resulted in his *An Account of Travels into the Interior of Southern Africa* (1801–1804). The Cape now began to supersede the South Atlantic island of St. Helena as the stopping-off point for British vessels sailing to and from the East. Captain Robert Percival (1765–1826) compiled his *An Account of the Cape of Good Hope* (1804) on the basis of a pair of two-month visits: in 1796, en route to the East Indies with his regiment; and in 1801, when homeward bound. From the same period come the letters and journals of Lady Anne Barnard (1750–1825), wife of the colonial secretary, Andrew Barnard, who wrote lively descriptions of the people of various races that she encountered while maintaining a thoroughly British establishment in Cape Town Castle—"Scotch carpets, English linen and rush-bottom chairs, with plenty of lolling sofas," as she boasted in a letter to Henry Dundas (Lord Melville).

The expedition into the hinterland led by De Mist, Dutch governor at the Cape 1803–1806; his daughter was one of the party (from Hinrich Lichtenstein's *Travels in Southern Africa*, 1812). *Courtesy of the Travellers Club, London; Bridgeman Art Library, agent.*

During the brief period of direct rule from Holland that followed the Treaty of Amiens (1802)—the VOC being by then a spent force—the German Hinrich Lichtenstein (1780–1857) made his first journey to the hinterland as physician to the Dutch commissioner-general De Mist. Lichtenstein's observations on the Bechuana people (*Ueber der Beetjuanas*) were incorporated into his wider account of his Cape experiences (translated into English as *Travels in Southern Africa*,

1812–1815). But by 1806, the British were back, and from then on, the Cape became part of the wider British sphere of influence in southern Africa and, beyond that, the great imperialist vision of British writ running from Cape to Cairo.

JENNIFER SPEAKE

### References and Further Reading


Barnard, Anne, *The Letters of Lady Anne Barnard to Henry Dundas, from the Cape and Elsewhere, 1793–1803, Together with Her Journal of a Tour into the Interior, and Certain Other Letters*, edited by A.M. Lewin Robinson, 1973.

Barnard, Anne, *The Cape Journals of Lady Anne Barnard, 1797–1798*, edited by A.M. Lewin Robinson, Margaret Lenta, and Dorothy Driver, 1994.

Barnard, Anne, *The Cape Diaries of Lady Anne Barnard, 1799–1800*, edited by Margaret Lenta and Basil Le Cordeur, 2 vols., 1999.

Barrow, John, *An Account of Travels into the Interior of Southern Africa, in the Years 1797 and 1798*, 2 vols., 1801–1804; reprinted, 1968.

Brink, Carel Frederik, *Nieuwste en Beknopte Beschryving van de Kap der Goede-Hope*, 1778; parallel English and Dutch texts in *The Journals of Brink and Rhenius: Being the Journal of Carel Frederik Brink of the Journey into Great Namaqualand (1761–2) Made by Captain Hendrik Hop and the Journal of Ensign Johannes Tobias Rhenius (1724)*, translated and edited by E.E. Mossop, 1947.

Bütner (Buttner), Johan Daniel, *Account of the Cape; Brief Description of Natal; Journal Extracts on East Indies*, edited by G.S. Nienaber and R. Raven-Hart, 1970.

Cortemünde, Jan Pietersz, *Adventure at the Cape of Good Hope in December 1672*, edited by Henning Henningsen, translated and annotated by Douglas Varley and Vera Varley, 1962.

Grandpré, Louis de, *Voyage à la côte occidentale d'Afrique fait dans les années 1786 et 1787 . . . suivi d'un voyage fait au cap de Bonne-Espérance, contenant la description militaire de cette colonie*, 2 vols., 1801.

Kolb, Peter, *Caput Bonae Spei hodiernum; das ist, Vollständige Beschreibung des africanischen Vorgebürges der Guten Hoffnung*, 1719; as *The Present State of the Cape of Good Hope; or, A Particular Account of the Several Nations of the Hottentots . . . Together with a Short Account of the Dutch Settlement at the Cape*, translated by Mr. Medley, 2 vols., 1731; reprinted, 1968.

Le Vaillant, François, *Voyage de M. Le Vaillant dans l'intérieur de l'Afrique, par le Cap de Bonne-Espérance, dans les années 1780, 81, 82, 83, 84 et 85*, 2 vols., 1790; as *Travels from the Cape of Good Hope into the Interior Parts of Africa*, translated by Elizabeth Helme, 1790.

Le Vaillant, François, *Second voyage dans l'intérieur de l'Afrique, par le Cap de Bonne-Espérance, dans les années 1783, 84 et 85*, 3 vols., 1795; as *New Travels into the Interior Parts of Africa*, 1796.

Lichtenstein, Hinrich, *Ueber der Beetjuanas*, 1807; as *About the Bechuanas*, translated and edited by O.H. Spohr, 1973.

Lichtenstein, Hinrich, *Reisen im südlichen Africa in den Jahren 1803, 1804, 1805 und 1806*, 2 vols., 1811–1812; as *Travels in Southern Africa in the Years 1803, 1804, 1805, and 1806*, translated by Anne Plumptre, 2 vols., 1812–1815; reprinted, 1928–1930.

Mentzel, O.F., *Vollständige und zuverlässige geographische und topographische Beschreibung des berühmten und in aller Betrachtung merkwürdigen afrikanischen Vorgebirges der Guten Hoffnung*, 2 vols., 1785–1787; as *A Geographical and Topographical Description of the Cape of Good Hope*, translated by H.J. Mandelbrote, 3 vols., 1921–1944.

Paterson, William, *A Narrative of Four Journeys into the Country of the Hottentots, and Caffraria: In the Years One Thousand Seven Hundred and Seventy-Seven, Eight, and Nine*, 1789; 2nd edition 1790.

Percival, Robert, *An Account of the Cape of Good Hope*, 1804; reprinted, 1969.

Reenen, Jacob van, *A Journal of a Journey from the Cape of Good Hope, Undertaken in 1790 and 1791, by Jacob van Reenen, and Others of His Countrymen, in Search of the Wreck of the Honourable the East India Company's Ship the Grosvenor; to Discover If There Remained Alive Any of the Unfortunate Sufferers, with Additional Notes and Map by Captain Edward Riou*, 1792.

Sparrman, Anders, *Resa till Goda Hopps-udden, Södra polkretsen och omkring jordklotet, samt till Hottentott- och Caffer-landen, åren 1772–76*, 2 vols., 1783–1818; as *A Voyage to the Cape of Good Hope, towards the Antarctic Polar Circle, and round the World: But Chiefly into the Country of the Hottentots and Caffres, from the Year 1772 to 1776*, translated by George Forster, 2 vols., 1785; 2nd edition, 1786; edited by V.S. Forbes, with the translation from the Swedish revised by J. Rudner and I. Rudner, 2 vols., 1975–1977.

Thunberg, Carl, *Resa uti Europa, Africa, Asia, förrättad åren 1770–1779*, 4 vols., 1788–1793; as *Travels in Europe, Africa and Asia, Performed between 1770 and 1779*, 4 vols., 1793–1795; 2nd edition, 1795; 3rd edition, 1796; selections, as *Travels at the Cape of Good Hope, 1772–1775*, edited by V.S. Forbes, with the translation from the Swedish revised by J. Rudner and I. Rudner, 1986.

Valentijn, François, *Oud en nieuw Oost-Indiën*, 1726; selection as *Description of the Cape of Good Hope with the Matters Concerning It*, parallel English and Dutch texts, translated by Rowland Raven-Hart, edited by Petrus Serton et al., 2 vols., 1971–1973.

Velho, Alvaro (attributed), *A Journal of the First Voyage of Vasco da Gama, 1497–1499*, translated and edited by E.G. Ravenstein, 1898.

Vogel, Johann Wilhelm, *Zehen-jährige Ost-Indianische Reise-Beschreibung*, 1704; 2nd edition, 1716.


*See also* **Southern Africa**

## CARIBBEAN, PRE-1700

A map of 1502 was the first to label the known islands of the Caribbean as *Antillas del Rey de Castella*—the Antilles of the Castilian King. The designation alluded to Antilia, an island of medieval lore. As much as a statement of possession, what the map's title suggested was that, even before their unveiling of the archipelago on the fringe of the yet unfound landmass, European navigators and cartographers already had a marker in their imagination for the Caribbean islands. Columbus, who accidentally discovered them for the rest of the modern world, was in fact hoping to find Antilia on his way to the Asian continent. Such expectations colored the discovery of the islands, imposing on them yet again the name of something they stood for—Indies, albeit West Indies—rather than of what they were. Only the later name of *Caribe*, or Caribbean, derived from the natives known as Caribs, indicates a concession to non-European worldviews. But it would not be long before the basin acquired for Europe the symbolic, economic, and strategic importance thus far reserved for its own Mediterranean.

As does the conventional history of European voyages to America, that of travels to the Caribbean begins with Columbus. In the course of three of his four American voyages, Columbus and his crew effectively managed to sight, and touch upon, all but the most outlying islands of the Caribbean archipelago. The first and most celebrated landfall (1492) happened at one of the Bahamas, called San Salvador by the admiral and known today as Watling Island. Taking a southern bearing, Columbus sailed along the coast of Cuba and settled on the island of Hispaniola (modern Haiti and Dominican Republic) before returning to Spain with the news. A second voyage (1493–1494) allowed for the reconnaissance of many of the so-called Lesser Antilles—Dominica, Guadalupe (later Guadeloupe), Monserrat, San Martín (later Nevis), San Jorge (modern Saint Kitts), San Anastasia (Saint Eustatius), San Cristóbal (Saba), Santa Cruz (Saint Croix), and the Islands of the Eleven Thousand Virgins (known today simply as the Virgin Islands)—before landing at San Juan Bautista, today's Puerto Rico. It was on the same voyage that the admiral carried out further explorations of Cuba and arrived at Jamaica. A third voyage (1498–1500) completed Columbus's contribution to the area's cartography by putting Trinidad on Spanish maps and finally placing the islands in relation to the mainland.

During the early phases of the Spanish domination of America, the Caribbean served as an indispensable gateway to the New World (Enciso; Fernández de Oviedo; Hakluyt; Las Casas). Its early exploration was inevitably entwined with the exploration of the American continent. Not a single ship could enter or leave the Spanish-American main without stopping at one of the West Indies: Cortés's expedition to Mexico left from Cuba (1510); Juan Ponce de León's search for a fountain of eternal youth in Florida set off from Puerto Rico (1513); Antonio de Berrio launched his quest for El Dorado from Trinidad (1580). Meanwhile, Spanish galleons loaded with the spoils of conquest stopped at Havana and Santo Domingo on their homebound journeys. And as Amerindians were wiped out through epidemics and forced labor (see Las Casas), the first Africans were brought into the region as slaves (1510), starting a loathsome but highly profitable trade that would leave its indelible mark on the region—and on all further descriptions of it.

The most famous accounts of travel in the sixteenth century attest to the fact that Spanish domination in the Caribbean did not go uncontested for long. Anglo-Spanish rivalry had its New World expression in the tales of Elizabethan privateers such as John Hawkins and Francis Drake, whose campaigns of terror against Spanish possessions in the region—even the failed ventures—were promptly publicized in print (Bigges; Hakluyt). Tudor courtiers seemed compelled to journey to the Spanish West Indies in search of fame, riches, and royal favor (Dudley). But it was Walter Raleigh's account of *The Discoverie of the Large, Rich and Bewtiful Empyre of Guiana* (1596) that made the first English claim on the Caribbean island of Trinidad.

The possession of Bermuda, in the western Atlantic (1609), gave England a stronger foothold near the Caribbean. Although the island's common name is attributed to its first discoverer, Juan Bermúdez—a Spaniard who was shipwrecked on the homeward leg of a provisioning trip to Hispaniola in 1505—it became known to English cartographers as Sommer Island, in honor of one of the English colonists who had been on their way to Virginia when a hurricane forced their ship onto the island's treacherous coral shoals (Jourdain; Hughes, 1615, 1621).

Thereafter, under a policy of "no peace beyond the line" (that is, beyond the meridian established by the Treaty of Tordesillas), the Caribbean became a stage for the settling of European disputes. Piracy—notably by Dutch and English seamen or buccaneers (Exquemelin)—and forceful conquest were the usual alternative means by which governments pursued their continental politics and acquired their Caribbean possessions (I. S.). France took over Martinique, Guadeloupe, Antigua, Monserrat, and Saint Kitts (Du Puis; Labat). The English occupation and colonization of Barbados, Bermuda, Jamaica, and Tobago generated vast amounts of published correspondence, descriptions, and chronicles of travel (Anonymous, *An Account of the Late Earthquake* . . . ; Anonymous, *The Present State of Jamaica* . . . ; Blome; Golding; Hardy; Hickeringill; Ligon; Littleton; Lynch; Poyntz) and as many more that remain in manuscript. What emerges through these personal narratives is a vivid and often harrowing portrait of life in West Indian plantation societies.

A particular type of account flourished during England's civil war, when conflict on the islands between royalist rebels and Parliament's navy echoed the troubles at home (Aisene; Anonymous, "From aboard the *Rainbow* . . ."; Anonymous, *Newes from the Sea* . . . ; Foster). Especially riveting are the accounts by those who survived Cromwell's policy of transportation of political prisoners to Barbados (Rivers and Foyle; Uchteritz). Thus, by the end of the seventeenth century, reports by travelers to the Caribbean spoke of a conquered region that reflected both domestic and inter-European strife—even if tempered by the kinder climate and made more brutal by the aberrations of slavery.

ÁNGEL GURRÍA QUINTANA

### References and Further Reading


Aisene, George, "Journal de ce qui s'est passé en la navigation de la flote du Parlament d'Angleterre vers l'isle de Barbades . . . envoyé a Londres par le Chevalier Georges Aisene, et traduit de l'original Anglois" ["Diary of Events Regarding the Sailing of Parliament's Fleet toward the Isle of Barbados . . . Sent to London by George Aisene, and Translated from the Original English"], *Gazette de France, Supplement* (7 June 1652)

Anonymous, *Newes from the Sea, concerning Prince Rupert, Capt. Pluncket, Capt. Munckel, and Others, with Some Transactions betwixt the King of Portingal and Them, Together with the Taking of Certain Ships, and a Relation Touching the Strange Newes of Barbadoes*, 1650.

Anonymous, "From aboard the *Rainbow* in Carlisle Bay, before the Island of Barbados, 19 October 1651," *Mercurius Politicus*, London, no. 90 (1652).

Anonymous, *A Book of the Continuation of Foreign Passages: That is, of the Peace Made between This Commonwealth and That of the United Provinces of the Netherlands . . .*, 1657.

Anonymous, *Recueil de divers voyages faits en Afrique et en l'Amerique, qui n'ont point esté encore publiez*, 1674.

Anonymous, *The Present State of Jamaica: With the Life of the Great Columbus the First Discoverer: To Which Is Added an Exact Account of Sir Hen. Morgan's Voyage to, and Famous Siege and Taking of Panama from the Spaniards*, 1683.

Anonymous, *An Account of the Late Earthquake in Jamaica, June 7th, 1692: Written by a Reverend Divine There to His Friend in London. With Some Improvement Thereof by Another Hand*, 1693.

Biet, Antoine, *Voyage de la France Equinoxiale en l'isle de Cayenne, entrepris par les François en l'Annee M.DC.LII . . .*, 1664.

Bigges, Walter, *A Summarie and True Discourse of Sir Francis Drake's West Indian Voyage, Wherein Were Taken the Townes of Saint Jago, Sancto Domingo, Cartagena & Saint Augustine*, edited by Thomas Cates, 1589.

Blome, Richard, *A Description of the Island of Jamaica; with Other Isles and Territories in America, to Which the English Are Related, viz. Barbadoes, St. Christopher, Nievis, or Mevis, Antego, St. Vincent, Taken from the Notes of Sir Thomas Linch . . . Governour of Jamaica, and Other Experienced Persons*, 1672; 2nd edition, 1678; as *The Present State of His Majesty's Isles and Territories in America*, 1686.

Bry, Theodor de, et al. (editors), *Collectiones peregrinationum in Indiam orientalem et Indiam occidentalem*, 25 vols., 1590–1634; as *Americae*, 1590–1634; edited by Gereon Sievernich, 1990.

Burton, Robert, *The English Empire in America; or, A Prospect of His Majesties Dominions in the West-Indies . . . with an Account of the Discovery, Scituation, Product, and Other Excellencies of These Countries . . .*, 1685.

Champlain, Samuel de, *Narrative of a Voyage to the West Indies and Mexico, in the Years 1599–1602*, translated from the original and unpublished manuscript, edited by Norton Shaw, with a biographical note by Alice Wilmere, 1859.

Clarke, Samuel, *A True, and Faithful Account of the Four Chiefest Plantations of the English in America: To Wit, Virginia, New England, Bermudas, Barbados . . .*, 1670.

Columbus, Christopher, *Journal and Other Documents on the Life and Voyages of Christopher Columbus*, edited and translated by Samuel Eliot Morison, 1963.

Columbus, Christopher, *The Journal of Christopher Columbus*, edited by L.A. Vigneras, translated by Cecil Jane, 1968.

Crafford, John, *A New and Most Exact Account of the Fertile and Famous Colony of Carolina*, 1683.

Dampier, William, *A New Voyage round the World*, 1697.

Dampier, William, *A Voyage to New Holland &c. in the Year 1699*, part 1, 1703; part 2, 1709; edited by James Spencer, 1981.

Doyley, Edward, *A Narrative of the Great Success God Hath Been Pleased to Give His Highness Forces in Jamaica, against the King of Spain Forces*, 1658.

Dudley, Robert, *The Voyage of Robert Dudley, afterwards Styled Earl of Warwick and Leicester, and Duke of Northumberland, to the West Indies, 1594–95, Narrated by Captain Wyatt Himself, and Abraham Kendall, Master*, edited by George F. Warner, 1899; reprinted, 1967.

Du Puis, Mathias, *Relation de l'establissement d'une colonie françoise dans la Gardeloupe, isle de l'Amérique, et des moeurs des sauvages*, 1652.

Enciso, Martín Fernández de, *Suma de geographia que trata de todas las partidas y provincias del mundo; en especial de las Indias . . .*, 1519; as *A Briefe Summe of Geographie*, translated by Roger Barlow, edited with an introduction by E.G.R. Taylor, 1932; reprinted, 1967.

Exquemelin, A.O., *De Americaensche Zee-Rovers*, 4 vols., 1678; as *The Bucaniers of America; or, A True Account of the Most Remarkable Assaults Committed of Late Years upon the Coasts of the West-Indies, By the Bucaniers of Jamaica and Tortuga, Both English and French. Wherein Are Contained More Especially, the Unparallel'd Exploits of Sir Henry Morgan, Our English Jamaican Hero . . .*, 2 vols., 1684–1685; reprinted, 1923; as *The Buccaneers of America*, translated by Alexis Brown, 1969.

Eyndhoven, Jan vans, *Journael, ofte Dagh-register, over de reyse, gedagen door de Heer Luytenant Admirael M.A. de Ruyter. In de West Indies. Door A.F.* [Journal or Diary about the Trip Done by Lt. Admiral M.A. de Ruyter in the West Indies. By A.F.], 1665.

Fernández de Oviedo y Valdés, Gonzalo, *De la natural hystoria de las Indias*, 1526; as *Natural History of the West Indies*, translated and edited by Sterling A. Stoudemire, 1959.

Fernández de Oviedo y Valdés, Gonzalo, *Historia general y natural de las Indias*, 2 vols., 1547; in part as *The Conquest and Settlement of the Island of Boriquen or Puerto Rico*, edited and translated by Daymond Turner, 1975.

Foster, Nicholas, *A Briefe Relation of the Late Horrid Rebellion Acted in the Island Barbadas, in the West Indies. Wherein Is Contained Their Inhumane Acts and Actions, in Fining and Banishing the Well-Affected to the Parliament of England . . . Anno 1650*, 1650; reprinted, 1927.

Gardyner, George, *A Description of the New World; or, America Islands and Continent*, 1651.

Golding, William, *Servants on Horse-Back: or, A Free-People Bestrided in Their Persons, and Liberties, by Worthlesse Men; Being a Representation of the Dejected State of the Inhabitants of Summer Islands*, 1648.

Hakluyt, Richard, *Divers Voyages Touching the Discovery of America and the Islands Adjacent*, 1582; facsimile, 1966.

Hakluyt, Richard, *De Orbe Novo Petri Martyris Anglerii Mediolanensis . . . decades octo, diligenti temporum observati-*

*one, & utilissimis annotationibus illustratae, suoque nitori restitutae, labore & industria Richardi Hakluyti Oxoniensis Angli. Additus est in usum lectoris accuratus totius operis index*, 1587; as *De Nouo Orbe; or, The Historie of the West Indies, Contayning the Actes and Adventures of the Spanyardes, Which Have Conquered and Peopled Those Countries . . . Comprised in Eight Decades. Written by Peter Martyr a Millanoise of Angleria, Chiefe Secretary to the Emperour Charles the Fift . . . Whereof Three, Have Beene Formerly Translated into English, by R. Eden, Whereunto the Other Five, Are Newly Added*, translated by Michael Lok, 1612.

Hakluyt, Richard, *The Principal Navigations, Voiages, and Discoveries of the English Nation, Made by Sea or over Land, to the Most Remote and Farthest Corners of the Earth*, 1589; revised edition as *The Principal Navigations, Voyages, Traffiques, and Discoveries of the English Nation*, 3 vols., 1598–1600.

Hardy, John, *A Description of the Last Voyage to Bermudas, in the Ship Marygold . . . Begun in November the Twelfth, 1670. And Ending May the Third, 1671, with Allowance*, 1671.

Hartgers, Joost, *Beschrijvinghe . . . Bermudes*, 1651.

Hickeringill, Edmund, *Jamaica Viewed; with All the Ports, Harbours, and Their Several Soundings, Towns, and Settlements thereunto Belonging. Together with the Nature of Its Climate, Fruitfulnesses of the Soile, and Its Suitablenesse to English Complexions . . .*, 1661.

Hughes, Lewes, *A Letter Sent into England from the Summer Islands (Containing an Account of Them)*, 1615; reprinted, 1971.

Hughes, Lewes, *A Plaine and True Relation of the Goodness of God toward the Sommer Islands, Written by Way of Exhortation, to Stirre Up the People There to Praise God*, 1621.

Hughes, William, *The American Physitian; or, A Treatise of the Roots, Plants, Trees, Shrubs, Fruit, Herbs, etc. Growing in the English Plantation in America*, 1672.

I. S. *A Brief and Perfect Journal of the Late Proceedings and Success of the English Army in the West-Indies, Continued until June the 24th 1655 . . . by I.S. an Eyewitness*, 1655.

Jourdain, Silvester, *A Discovery of the Barmudas, Otherwise Called the Ile of Divels, by Sir Thomas Gates, Sir George Sommers and Captayne Newport, with Divers Others . . .*, 1610; reprinted, 1940; as *A Plaine Description of the Barmudas, Now Called Sommer Ilands. With the Manner of Their Discoverie Anno 1609, by the Shipwrack and Admirable Deliverance of Sir Thomas Gates and Sir George Sommers . . .*, 1613; reprinted, 1971.

Labat, Jean Baptiste, *Nouveau Voyage aux isles de l'Amérique*, 2 vols., 1724; as *The Memoirs of Père Labat, 1693–1705*, translated by John Eaden, with an introduction by Philip Gose, 1931.

Laet, Joannes de, *Nieuw Wereldt, Ofte Beschrijvinghe van West-Indien*, 1625.

Laet, Joannes de, *Historie ofte iaerlijck verhael van de verrichtinghen der Geoctroyeerde West-Indische Compagnie*, 1644; as *Iaerlyck van de verrichtinghen der Geoctroyeerde West-Indische Compagnie*, edited by S.P. L'Honoré Naber, 4 vols., 1931–1937.

Las Casas, Bartolomé de, *Brevissima relación de la destruyción de las Indias*, 1552; in part as *The Spanish Colonie; or, Briefe Chronicle of the Acts and Gestes of the Spaniards in the West Indies*, 1583; as *The Devastation of the Indies: A Brief Account*, translated by Herma Briffault, 1974.

Ligon, Richard, *A True and Exact History of the Island of Barbadoes, Illustrated with a Mapp of the Island as Also the Principall Trees and Plants There Set Forth in Their Due Proportions and Shapes . . . Together with the Ingenio That Makes Sugar . . .*, 1657.

Linschoten, John Huyghen van, *Itinerario: Voyage ofte Schipvaert, naer Oost ofte Portugaels Indien*, 1596; as *Discours of Voyages into ye East and West Indies*, translated by W.P., 1598; reprinted, 1974.

Littleton, Edward, *The Groans of the Plantations; or, A True Account of Their Grievous and Extreme Sufferings by the Heavy Impositions upon Sugar, and Other Hardships: Relating More Particularly to the Island of Barbadoes*, 1689.

Lynch, Thomas, *A Description of the Island of Jamaica; with the Other Isles and Territories in America, to Which the English Are Related . . . Taken from the Papers of Sr. Thomas Linch Knight, Governour of Jamaica; and Other Experienced Persons in the Said Place*, 1672.

Marvell, Andrew, "Bermudas" in *Miscellaneous Poems*, 1681.

Mocquet, Jean, *Voyages en Afrique, Asie, Indes Orientales & Occidentales*, 1617; translated as *Travels and Voyages into Asia, Africa, and America . . .*, 1696.

Monardes, Nicolás, *Primera y segunda y tercera partes de la historia medicinal de las que se traen de nuestras Indias Occidentales, que siruen en medicina*, 1574; as *Joyfull Newes out of the New-Found Worde: Wherein Are Declared the Rare and Singuler Vertues of Divers Herbs, Trees, Plants, Oyles, and Stones, with Their Applications, as Well to the Use of Phisicke, as of Surgery*, translated by John Frampton, 1577.

Montanus, Arnoldus, *Die Nieuwe en Onbekende Weereld . . .*, 1671; as *America: Being the Latest and Most Accurate Description of the New World; Containing the Original Account of the Inhabitants, and the Remarkable Voyages Thither*, translated by John Ogilby, 1655.

Naipaul, V.S., *The Loss of El Dorado: A History*, 1970.

Peake, Thomas, *America: or, An Exact Description of the West Indies: More Especially of Those Provinces Which Are under the Dominion of the King of Spain*, 1655.

Pelleprat, Pierre, *Relation des missions des pp. de la Compagnie de Jésus dans les îles et dans la terre ferme de l'Amérique méridionale*, 1655.

Peter Martyr (Pietro Martire d'Angleria), *De Orbe Novo decades*, 1516; as *The Decades of the Newe Worlde or West India: Conteyning the Nauigation and Conquestes of the Spanyeards, with the Particular Description of the Most Ryche and Large Llandes Founde in the West Ocean*, translated by Richard Eden, 1555; reprinted as *The History of Travayle in the West and East Indies . . .*, 1577.

Phillips, Thomas, *A Journal of a Voyage Made in the Hannibal of London, from England to Cape Monseradoe in Africa . . . and So Forward to Barbadoes . . . 1693*, 1694; in *A Collection of Voyages and Travels*, published by Awnsham Churchill, vol. 6, 1732.

Poyntz, John, *The Present Prospect of the Famous and Fertile Island of Tobago: With a Description of the Scituation, Growth, Fertility, and Manufacture, of the Said Island*, 1683.

Purchas, Samuel, *Hakluytus Posthumus; or, Purchas His Pilgrimes: Contayning a History of the World in Sea Voyages and Lande-Travells, by Englishmen and Others . . .*, 4 vols., 1625.

Raleigh, Walter, *The Discoverie of the Large, Rich and Bewtiful Empyre of Guiana . . .*, 1596.

Rivers, Marcellus, and Oxenbridge Foyle, *England's Slavery; or, Barbados Merchandize: Represented in a Petition to the High and Honourable Court of Parliament, by Marcellus Rivers and Oxenbridge Foyle, Gentlemen, on Behalf of*

*Themselves and Three-Score and Ten More of Freeborn Englishmen, Sold (Uncondemned) into Slavery*, 1659.

Rochefort, Charles de, *Histoire naturelle et morale des îles Antilles de l'Amerique*, 1658.

Sloane, Hans, *A Voyage to the Islands of Madera, Barbados, Nieves, St. Christophers, and Jamaica; with the Natural History of the Herbs and Trees, Fourfooted Beasts, Fishes, Birds, Insects, Reptiles, . . . of the Last of Those Islands . . .*, 2 vols., 1707–1725.

Spörri, Felix Christian, *Americanische Reiss-Beschreibung nach den Caribes Insslen, und Neu Engelland*, 1677.

Stubbes, Dr. [Henry], "Observations Made by a Curious and Learned Person, Sailing from England to the Caribe-Islands," *Philosophical Transactions of the Royal Society*, 2/27 (1668); 3/36 (1669).

Uchteritz, Heinrich von, *Kurtze Reise-Beschreibung Hrrn. Heinrich von Uchteritz, Lieutenants, erbassen auf Modelwitz in Meissen, und Worinnen vermeldet was er auf Derselben für Unglück und Glück gehabt sonderlich wie er Gefangen nach West-Indien Geführet zur Sclaverey verkaufft und auf der insul Barbados*, 1666.

Van Berkel, Adriaan, *Amerikaansche voyaigen*, 1695; as *Adrian van Berkel's Travels in South America between the Berbice and Essequibo Rivers and in Surinam, 1670–1689*, translated and edited by Walker Edmund Roth, 1942.

Ward, Ned, *A Trip to Jamaica: With a True Character of the People and Island*, 1698; reprinted in *Five Travel Scripts Commonly Attributed to Edward Ward*, 1933.

*See also* **Cuba; Haiti**

## CARIBBEAN, POST-1700

To consider the Caribbean in terms of travel writing is to open up a rich and diverse field. Broadly speaking, there are two main types of representation of the region: those written by European commentators, who historically have represented a colonial perspective; and Caribbean writers, for whom travel has always held a specific and culturally central significance.

Travel is not a distant or abstract metaphor in Caribbean literature, but part of the region's heterogeneous sense of culture, roots, and identity. Central concerns in Caribbean literature are an exploration of the problematic nature of defining identity and an awareness of the decenteredness of any single tradition. This is tied to a recognition of a cultural history of travel and its implications for conceptualizing what constitutes roots and self-image. Historically, the ethnically mixed base of Caribbean experience derives from centuries of emigration into the region (either forced, as in slavery, or voluntary). With the introduction of sugar planting at the close of the sixteenth century, travel as an experience in African slave narratives takes on specific qualities of the diaspora and rootlessness. Olaudah Equiano's *The Interesting Narrative of the Life of Olaudah Equiano* (1789) offers an early written expression of this oral tradition. Equiano's text provides a prescient model for African American writers and an unacknowledged source for the development of the American protest novel in works such as Harriet Beecher Stowe's *Uncle Tom's Cabin* (1851–1852).

Until the end of the Napoleonic wars, the region was a contested zone among European powers, who all claimed the islands for their own interests and who all left marks on Caribbean culture. This legacy is recognized by the Dominican novelist Jean Rhys, who gives expression to the Creole experience of liminality with regard to inclusion and exclusion. Travel, in Rhys's novels, becomes a metaphor for spiritual homelessness. The particular quality of twentieth-century Caribbean migration (predominantly to the urban centers of North America and Britain) has produced its own form of travel literature. Claude McKay's novels *Home to Harlem* (1928) and *Banjo* (1929) provide an early-twentieth-century expression of what the experience of migration and metropolitan exile means for the Caribbean writer. V.S. Naipaul's *Guerrillas* (1975), George Lamming's novels *Of Age and Innocence* (1958) and *Water with Berries* (1971), and Andrew Salkey's *Come Home, Malcolm Heartland* (1976) are, as Rhonda Cobham draws attention to, texts that reveal the disjuncture that the experience of travel produces:

Black and mixed-race revelers, from the near-naked black drummer to the tall-hatted mulatto couple in European finery, take part in genteel jollity amid Edenic tropical abundance on St. Vincent—note the prominently displayed fruits (from Bryan Edwards's *The History, Civil and Commercial, of the British Colonies in the West Indies*, revised edition, 1794). *Courtesy of the Travellers Club, London; Bridgeman Art Library, agent.*

these are novels that speak of the difficulties of reconnecting the experience of metropolitan exile with "back home." The strength of Derek Walcott's work derives from his deep consciousness, as a St. Lucian educated in an Anglophile tradition, of the diverse qualities of Caribbean experience: both in its heritage of European literary models and in its indigenous oral traditions. A specifically Jamaican expression of the meanings of exile is voiced by Rastafarian poets, for whom the West represents the state of bondage, and whose poetry celebrates the utopian future of return to Africa.

Historically, representations of the Caribbean in European travel writing serve as a trope for "otherness," the exotic, the strange, or serve as a metaphor for appropriation where apparent differences allow a writer to contrast and comment on his or her society. Père Labat's *Nouveau Voyage aux isles de Amérique* (1722), while ostensibly an island-hopping travel autobiography, reveals a vein of fantasy expectation in its representation of the region as a zone of potential idyllic fulfillment; Labat is particularly taken with the beauty and promise of West Indian women. Sir Walter Raleigh's *Discoverie of Guiana* (1596) offers an earlier indication of how fiction can mask itself as a factual travel document. Supposedly based on Raleigh's own expedition to Guyana, his mythical El Dorado (a place of untold riches) provides a powerful signifier for later writers such as Daniel Defoe. Even though Defoe is deliberately vague about the location of Crusoe's island in *Robinson Crusoe* (1719), references suggest that it is off the coast of Guyana. Crusoe's island experiences serve as a setting for a metaphoric exploration of mercantile ideology and as a critique of English society, while facilitating the hero's inclusion in that society through his acquisition of wealth. Tobias Smollett (1721–1771), who did, in contrast to Defoe, have personal experience of Caribbean life, uses the region in a similar eurocentric manner in *The Adventures of Roderick Random* (1748), where the hero's Caribbean experiences serve as a satiric indictment of the ills in English society. As novelists, neither Defoe nor Smollett is particularly interested in the actual geography or economy of the region, and when either describe fauna or terrain, their descriptions are vague and impressionistic. James Granger's long poem *The Sugar-Cane* (1764) provides a counterbalance to this tendency in its detailed scientific observation, but Granger reveals an equally distanced perspective on his own imbrication in a system of slavery.

Often in European literature of the eighteenth century, the Caribbean functions as a literary device to explain characters' rise in fortune or bring about closure of plotlines. It functions in this way in Richard Cumberland's *The West Indian* (first produced 1771), a play in which the Enlightenment discourse of primitivism is yoked to this economic metaphor, and in Jane Austen's *Mansfield Park* (1814), where resolution is brought about by the success of Uncle Bertram's West Indian sugar plantation.

By the nineteenth century, as Michael Cotsell (1990) points out, the West Indies had deeply permeated British culture as a result of the extent of its contribution to the British economy, the moral insistence of antislavery agitation, and the fate of the white "owners" after emancipation (1838). All these factors had by midcentury created a complex nexus of guilt and hostility, which was intensified by British associations of dark peoples with repressed, feared aspects of themselves. In Charlotte Brontë's *Jane Eyre* (1847), the heroine's inclusion in societal kinship patterns is premised on a polarization of racial stereotyping whereby Bertha Mason (the mad Creole first wife of Mr. Rochester) functions as the dark other, thus allowing Jane to assume the position of her opposite. Jean Rhys's *Wide Sargasso Sea* (1968) revises Brontë's reading by offering a fictional account from Bertha's perspective. But as Gayatri Chakravorty Spivak's postcolonial critique of both novels (1985) reveals, neither novelist has managed to free herself of the colonial metaphor. This is also true of supposedly factual accounts of travel in the Caribbean. Froude's *The English in the West Indies* (1888) reflects the deep-seated unease of the colonial consciousness in its attempt to justify a racialized reading on the terms of Darwinism. Charles Kingsley's *At Last: A Christmas in the West Indies* (1871), while offering a more sympathetic version of cultural exchange, persists in placing its value system on an English model of social relations.

June Jordan's "Report from the Bahamas" (1989) embraces the interrelated nature of gender, race, and imperialistic structures from her personal experience as an Afro-American woman of Caribbean extraction. What Jordan's travel to the Bahamas reveals is the complex relations between power, powerlessness, and identity—experiences that form a bedrock for the Caribbean understanding of the meaning of travel.

GAIL BAYLIS

## References and Further Reading

Austen, Jane, *Mansfield Park*, 1814.
Bayley, Fredrick William Naylor, *Four Years' Residence in the West Indies*, 1830; 3rd edition, 1833.
Behn, Aphra, *Oroonoko; or, The Royal Slave*, 1688.
Brathwaite, Edward, *The Arrivants: A New World Trilogy*, 1973.
Brontë, Charlotte, *Jane Eyre*, 1847.
Cotsell, Michael, "Trollope: The International Theme" in *Cred-*

*itable Warriors, 1830–1876*, edited by Cotsell, London: Ashfield Press, 1990.
Cumberland, Richard, *The West Indian*, 1771.
Defoe, Daniel, *Robinson Crusoe*, 1719.
Equiano, Olaudah, *The Interesting Narrative of the Life of Olaudah Equiano, or Gustavus Vassa, the African*, 2 vols., 1789; edited by Werner Sollors, 2001.
Fox, George, *A Journal*, 2 vols., 1694–1698.
Froude, James Anthony, *The English in the West Indies*, 1888.
Grainger, James, *The Sugar-Cane*, 1764.
Hemingway, Ernest, *The Old Man and the Sea*, 1952.
Hughes, Richard, *A High Wind in Jamaica*, 1929.
Jordan, June, "Report from the Bahamas" in her *Moving towards Home: Political Essays*, 1989.
Kingsley, Charles, *At Last: A Christmas in the West Indies*, 2 vols., 1871.
Labat, Jean Baptiste, *Nouveau Voyage aux isles de l'Amérique*, 6 vols., 1722; as *The Memoirs of Père Labat*, translated and abridged by John Eaden, 1931.
Levo, J.E., *The West Indian Adventure*, 1929.
Lewis, Matthew Gregory, *Journal of a West Indian Proprietor*, 1834.
Luffman, John, *A Brief Account of the Island of Antigua . . . Written in the Years 1786, 1787, 1788*, 1789; reprinted in *The History of the Island of Antigua*, by Vere Langford Oliver, 3 vols., 1894–1899.
McKay, Claude, *A Long Way from Home*, 1937.
Naipaul, V.S., *Guerrillas*, 1975.
Nugent, Maria, *A Journal of a Voyage to, and Residence in, the Island of Jamaica, from 1801 to 1805*, 2 vols., 1839; as *Lady Nugent's Journal*, edited by Philip Wright, 1966.
Prince, Mary, *The History of Mary Prince, a West Indian Slave, Related by Herself*, 1831.
Raleigh, Walter, *The Discoverie of the Large, Rich, and Bewtiful Empyre of Guiana*, 1596.
Rhys, Jean, *Wide Sargasso Sea*, 1968.
Salkey, Andrew, *Come Home, Malcolm Heartland*, 1976.
Smollett, Tobias, *The Adventures of Roderick Random*, 2 vols., 1748.
Spivak, Gayatri Chakravorty, "Three Women's Texts and a Critique of Imperialism," *Critical Inquiry* 12 (1985): 243–246.
Trollope, Anthony, *The West Indies and the Spanish Main*, 1859.
Walcott, Derek, "The Fortunate Traveller" in his *Collected Poems, 1948–1984*, 1986.
Walcott, Derek, *Omeros*, 1990.

*See also* **Cuba; Haiti**

## CARPINI, GIOVANNI DI PIANO (c. 1182–c. 1252) *Ambassador of Pope Innocent IV to the Mongol Khan*

Very little is known about Giovanni di Piano Carpini. Probably born in the 1180s, he was among the first to join the order of St. Francis. From 1221 to 1245, he had several important functions in the Franciscan hierarchy in Saxony as well as in the Iberian Peninsula. In 1245, Piano Carpini attended the Council of Lyons, where Innocent IV ordered him to go to the Mongol khan in order to persuade the latter to put an end to the invasions of his armies, which, in the early 1240s, had set Poland and Hungary on fire and which nobody seemed able to stop. The ecclesiastical authorities also thought that the Mongols could be persuaded to embrace Christianity; if they did so, they would be marvelous allies in the struggle against Islam. The ambassador of the pope was also instructed to gather as much information as possible about the organization and capacities of the Mongol armies.

Piano Carpini left Lyons on 16 April 1245, in the company of Benedict of Poland. The two friars went to Kiev. In February 1246, they left that town in order to join Batu, at that time the commander in chief in Mongol Russia, whose camp was situated on the banks of the Volga. Since the Mongol general did not have the authority to deal with the European travelers, he sent them to the court of the Great Khan at Caracarum. In August, the two friars reached the Mongol capital, where they were allowed to attend the installation of Kuyuk. On 13 November, they set out on the journey back to Lyons, where they arrived in November 1247.

Friar Giovanni was not the only ambassador sent by Pope Innocent. In 1247, Lawrence of Portugal, another Franciscan, went to the Mongol military commander in Armenia. Two years later, a Dominican by the name of Ascelin was ordered into Asia Minor. Nothing is known about Lawrence's trip. Ascelin's journey was mentioned by Vincent of Beauvais, who inserted Piano Carpini's *Ystoria Mongalorum* into his *Speculum historiale*.

The *Ystoria* is a remarkable document because of its coherent and from time to time even rigid organization, strongly influenced by the rhetorical traditions of medieval teaching. It ranges from the description of the exterior aspects of Mongol society to what might be called the interior or even ethnographic characteristics of the traditions and customs of that people. However, notwithstanding the respect of contemporary rhetorical formalism, the *Ystoria* is a curious combination of information obtained from the spokesmen the two friars had met during their long journey and from personal observations. Piano Carpini carefully distinguishes between the information provided by eyewitnesses on the one hand and the details produced by himself on the other. It is difficult to say whether the information obtained from the spokesmen, among whom were Christian Russians and Hungarians and other Christians living at the court of the Great Khan, was rendered correctly. Since Piano Carpini did not master the local languages and was compelled to use interpreters who were more-or-less familiar with Turkish, the lingua franca in Asia, many details must have been interpreted with a distinct lack of precision.

From time to time, the author falls back on legendary material, but he does so sparingly. The main part of

Piano Carpini's account is based on things he actually witnessed, and this is what makes the *Ystoria* so important a document. Friar Giovanni knew that his information was valuable as well as unusual and would need some official confirmation. In Giovanni's prologue, he explicitly states that the things he has recorded, either from personal observation or from the accounts of trustworthy people, are strange but nonetheless true. Even if such a caveat on reliable witnesses was strictly rhetorical, it was unavoidable because the information was new and did not correspond with the general European ideas about the Mongols. It is therefore hardly surprising to see Piano Carpini introduce witnesses at the end of his history of the "Mongols whom we call Tartars." In doing so, he gave his account the formal status of an official authoritative document.

The *Ystoria* contains a prologue and nine chapters, each of which is centered on one specific aspect of Mongol society. The first one, for instance, gives general information on the country the enemies live in. The second chapter focuses on the Mongols themselves. The third discusses their religion and customs. As far as Mongol religious life is concerned, Piano Carpini only sees the exterior part, which is obvious since he lacks the necessary linguistic knowledge to appreciate Mongol customs correctly. Thus, in chapter 3, he states that the Mongols believe in "one God whom they think is the creator of all things visible and invisible . . . Even so, they do not worship him with praises or ritual. Nevertheless they do have idols of felt made in the image of men and they place these on both sides of the doorway of a tent." Giovanni's discussion of Mongol religious practices is characterized by total incomprehension. Since he does not understand their language, he can only register the exterior, ritual side of Mongol religion. However, Friar Giovanni is not to be blamed. All Christian travelers in those days committed the same "sin."

The sections that must have been of great interest to the people at the papal court are chapters 6–8, in which the author discusses the organization of the Mongol military machine. Piano Carpini explains the ferocious discipline and cruelty of the Asiatic warriors, which Christian Europe had already experienced. Mongol units never retreat, since desertion is always punished by death. This explains their ruthless behavior toward their enemies, whom they either kill or enslave. It is hardly surprising that the Mongols who lived in the northern parts of Asia were identified with the apocalyptic people of Gog and Magog, whose natural habitat was supposed to be in those hostile regions. Carpini advises the Christian rulers to put an end to the terror of the Mongols. That mission is all the more urgent, since the Great Khan himself had announced his decision to attack all the countries in the West. Since such an enterprise has to be avoided at all costs, Piano Carpini dedicates a whole chapter to the military countermeasures to be taken by Christian Europe.

Giovanni di Piano Carpini's *Ystoria* is a rather technical account of a difficult journey under dangerous and hostile circumstances. Although Giovanni frequently notes that his Mongol hosts steal, lie, and try to extort money or gifts from any stranger they meet, he limits himself to mere moral comments. He fails to see that life on the Asiatic steppes is so harsh that the Mongols themselves have difficulties surviving. Although Piano Carpini presents himself as an eyewitness, he does not really speak about himself. His successor, Guillaume de Rubruck, will produce a far more personal account. It is only in the last chapter that Giovanni shows some gratitude to those who have helped him and Benedict during their exacting journey and their long and unpleasant stay at the court of the Great Khan: "Unless God had not sent us a certain Ruthenian called Cosmas . . . who supported us somewhat, or if God had not helped us in some other way, we would have died."

Friar Giovanni di Piano Carpini's account did not receive much attention. Since the Mongols were not interested in embracing the true faith, they would never help the Christians fighting Islam. Moreover, the Asian warriors were so arrogant that the ecclesiastical authorities abandoned all hope of coming to terms with them. Since, toward the end of the 1240s, the direct danger of a Mongol invasion was over and other enemies were manifesting themselves at the frontiers of Christian Europe, Piano Carpini's information had no more news value. If it had not been for Vincent of Beauvais, Giovanni's *Ystoria* might even have been lost.

MARTIN GOSMAN

## Biography

Born in Perugia, c. 1182. Disciple of St. Francis of Assisi; was one of the first members of the order of St. Francis. Held several important positions in the Franciscan hierarchy in Saxony and the Iberian Peninsula, 1221–1245. Sent by Pope Innocent IV on embassy to the Mongol khan, 1245–1247. Papal ambassador at the court of Louis IX of France, c. 1250–1251. Archbishop of Antivari, Dalmatia, 1252. Died c. 1252.

## References and Further Reading

Carpini, Giovanni di Piano, in *Contemporaries of Marco Polo: Consisting of the Travel Records to the Eastern Parts of the World of William of Rubruck (1253–1255); the Journey of John of Pian de Carpini (1245–1247); the Journal of Friar Odoric (1318–1330) and the Oriental Travels of Rabbi Benjamin of Tudela (1160–1173)*, edited by Manuel Komroff, 1928.

Carpini, Giovanni di Piano, *The Mongol Mission: Narratives and Letters of the Franciscan Missionaries in Mongolia and China in the Thirteenth and Fourteenth Centuries*, translated by a nun of Stanbrook Abbey, edited by Christopher Dawson, 1955; reprinted, 1980.
Carpini, Giovanni di Piano, *Histoire des Mongols*, translated by Jean Becquet and Louis Hambis, 1965.
Carpini, Giovanni di Piano, *The Story of the Mongols, Whom We Call the Tartars*, translated by Erik Hildinger, 1996.
Simon de Saint-Quentin [fl. 1245–1248], *Histoire des Tartares*, edited by Jean Richard, 1965.

## CARTIER, JACQUES (1491–1557) *French Explorer*

It is considered that Jacques Cartier discovered "Canada," although the toponym, which means "house" in Iroquois, referred at the time to the area surrounding the present-day city of Quebec. He made three official voyages in the name of Francis I, searching for the passage to Asia and "grande quantité d'or" (a great quantity of gold).

Cartier's first voyage lasted from 20 April to 5 September 1534. With two ships and 61 men, he sailed around the Gulf of St. Lawrence. While other navigators had undoubtedly ventured into the area before him, Jacques Cartier was the first to have explored it in a systematic manner. He was harsh in his description of the north coast, which he judged to be "la terre que Dieu donna à Cayn" (the land God gave to Cain). Everywhere Cartier stopped, he established contact with the natives. Domagaya and Taignoagny, sons of the Iroquois chief Donnacona, accompanied him back to France and would serve as interpreters on his next trip. During Cartier's lifetime, an Italian account of his first journey, written by Giovanni Battista Ramusio, was published (1556), which was later translated into English (1580) and French (1598). A manuscript has also been preserved.

The second voyage was made a year later. With three ships and some 110 men, guided by the two Iroquois whom Cartier brought back to America, he set out on 19 May 1535 to discover the true importance of the Hochelaga (St. Lawrence) River. Cartier was convinced he had found the passage to the Orient. Upon hearing of the wonders of the Saguenay to the north, he sailed up the St. Lawrence, the "route towards Canada," and settled near Stadacona (Quebec City) where the estuary narrows. Cartier soon realized he could no longer trust his interpreters, who had attempted to deceive him although their motives were unclear. In spite of opposition from Donnacona, Cartier continued upstream to Hochelaga (present-day Montreal), an enclosed and fortified community in the Iroquois style. After a brief stay, he returned to Stadacona for the winter, which was extremely difficult due to the intense cold and scurvy: the disease killed 25 men; the others owed their lives to *annedda* (probably white cedar) tea, the secret of which was revealed to them by Domagaya. The voyage ended on 16 July 1536.

Of Cartier's own three travel narrations, only that of the second voyage was published, in French (1545), during the traveler's lifetime. It is this voyage that appears to have contributed the most to Cartier's fame. As with the first narration, it was also published in Italian (1556) and English (1580). Three different manuscripts of this second narration have been preserved, which are distinct from the French edition and in all likelihood copies of a lost original.

The third voyage (23 May 1541–1542) was under the authority of Jean-François de La Rocque de Roberval, a Protestant, Cartier setting sail with five ships and approximately 1,500 men. Because of the mutual distrust between the French and the Iroquois, Cartier established a settlement some distance from Stadacona, which he named Charlesbourg-Royal. He went back to Hochelaga. Shortly after Cartier's return to Stadacona, the account of his voyage ends abruptly. However, it is common knowledge that Cartier brought gold and diamonds back to France, which in fact turned out to be iron pyrites and quartz. Disillusionment set in. The only known version of this narration is an English translation by Richard Hakluyt in his collection *Principall Navigations*.

Cartier's travels did not have the repercussions one might have expected. A narration of the second voyage, *Brief Recit* [A Brief Account], was published in Rouen in 1545. But it was not until a year before Cartier's death, when the accounts of his first two voyages were published in Ramusio's famous Venetian collection, that the navigator received the recognition he deserved in Europe. It is this version that was later used by François de Belleforest in his *Cosmographie universelle* (1575) and André Thevet in his *Singularitez de la France Antarctique* (1558), notwithstanding the credence one may give to a possible encounter between Thevet and Cartier, and to the confidences the cosmographer claimed he received from the traveler. Insofar as any connections with Rabelais are concerned, they remain purely hypothetical, more a seductive idea than a real probability. While it has been thought that the two men might have met (Ch.-A. Julien, *Les voyages de découverte* . . . [Travels of Discovery], 351[-]360), indeed that it was Rabelais who wrote Cartier's narrations, this appears to be unfounded. It is nevertheless quite possible that Rabelais's works were influenced by Cartier's travels.

NORMAND DOIRON AND GILLIAN LANE-MERCIER

### Biography

Born in Saint-Malo, France, between June and December 1491. Nothing known of his navigations before 1532. Married Catherine des Granches, 1520: probably had no children. Was perhaps part of Giovanni da Verrazzano's expeditions, 1524 and 1528. Commissioned by King Francis I of France to sail to North America, traveling to the Gulf of St. Lawrence, 1534; made two further voyages, traveling to Stadacona (present-day Quebec) and Hochelaga (present-day Montreal), 1535 and 1541–1542. Probably traveled to Brazil and to Newfoundland, as alluded to in his writings. Retired to his estate of Limoilou, near Saint-Malo, after completing his final voyage, 1542. Died at Limoilou, Saint-Malo, 1 September 1557.

### References and Further Reading


Cartier, Jacques, *Brief Recit, & succincte narration, de la navigation faicte es ysles de Canada*, 1545.

Cartier, Jacques, "Relationi della Nova Francia" in *Delle navigationi et viaggi*, compiled by Giovanni Battista Ramusio, vol. 3, 1556; in *A Shorte and Briefe Narration of the Two Navigations and Discoveries to the Northweast Partes Called Newe Fraunce*, translated by John Florio, 1580; as *Discours du voyage fait par le capitaine Jaques Cartier*, 1598.

Cartier Jacques, *The Voyages of Jacques Cartier* (published from the originals), edited and translated by H.P. Biggar, 1924.

Cartier, Jacques, *Voyages au Canada, avec les relations des voyages en Amérique de Gonneville, Verrazzano et Roberval*, edited by Charles-André Julien, René Herval, and Théodore Beauchesne, 1981; reprinted, 1992.

Cartier, Jacques, *Relations*, edited by Michel Bideaux, 1986.

Hakluyt, Richard, *The Principal Navigations, Voyages, Traffiques, and Discoveries of the English Nation*, 3 vols., 1598–1600.


## CASOLA, PIETRO (1427–1507) *Milanese Clergyman and Pilgrim*

Besides Rome and Santiago de Compostela, Jerusalem and the Holy Land are among the most important destinations of Christian pilgrims. In the late Middle Ages, pilgrims from western Europe could reach Jerusalem only by ship. Pilgrims nevertheless undertook the dangerous and expensive voyages, which were organized by Venetian patricians, and some of the pilgrims wrote down their experiences after their return. From the period between 1450 and 1500 in particular, numerous accounts have come down to us that sharply differ as to volume, content, and the reason they were written.

The account of Pietro Casola, written as a diary, is one of the most remarkable and most detailed in the late medieval period, together with the accounts of the German pilgrims such as Felix Fabri, Bernhard of Breydenbach, and Arnold von Harff and the Milanese Santo Brasca. In 1494, in spite of his advanced age of 67, Casola was finally "freed of every impediment" and possessed the necessary financial means to fulfill the vow he had made. Devotion and also curiosity were Casola's motives.

Casola started his pilgrimage on 15 May 1494, and it was to last until he returned to Milan half a year later on 14 November. After a few days, he reached Venice and used the time until the sea departure to visit the town. Well informed, Casola described the city's topography, buildings, and inhabitants. He noted down the rebuilding and renovation at the palace of the doge as well as the behavior and fashion of the Venetians. The climax of Casola's stay was his participation in a procession during the festival of Corpus Christi.

Casola paid the "Patrono" Agostino Contarini, the captain of the pilgrim galley and also the pilgrims' guide in the Holy Land, 60 gold ducats for the whole journey, for food and for accommodation in Palestine. Casola's detailed description of the special type of galley used for pilgrimages confirms the drawings of pilgrim galleys made by Erhard Reuwich and Konrad of Grünemberg on their pilgrimage some years before. Casola counted 170 pilgrims. One of these, a German pilgrim called Reinhard of Bemmelberg or Konrad of Parsberg (according to Stolz, the name of Ludwig of Württemberg as the author is a mistake), also wrote an account of the pilgrimage. The galley followed the usual route along the Dalmatian coast, with stops at Venetian bases, and then continued on to Crete, Rhodes, and Cyprus, then to Jaffa, where the pilgrims arrived after a six-week trip.

The pilgrims were in Palestine for about a month, where they faced hardship and harassment by the Muslim authorities, who, as Casola described, tried to enrich themselves at the pilgrims' expense. Only after two weeks were the pilgrims allowed to continue their voyage from Jaffa to Jerusalem, where some pilgrims were arrested under the pretext of espionage and had to be ransomed by the "Patrono." Because of these incidents, Casola had a negative attitude toward Muslims and always called them "dogs." The guided tour in and around Jerusalem, which was done by the friars of St. Francis, was similar to the programs described in other accounts: it included the Mount of Olives, Mount Zion, three overnight stays in the Church of the Holy Sepulchre, and excursions to Bethlehem and to the Jordan River.

When contrasted to the parallel account, it becomes obvious that Casola did not intend to give a complete report of all the holy places he had seen. He confines himself to describing only the most important spots in full detail. Casola was not at all impressed by the holy city: the only building he thought to be beautiful was the Dome of the Rock. Several times, he criticizes the behavior of the "Ultramontani," pilgrims from north of the Alps, who always tried to be the first at the holy places. In contrast to the accounts of the German pilgrim and many others, Casola never mentioned the indulgences that could be gained at any holy place. Before their return, the pilgrim group was asked by the Franciscan prior of Mount Zion, Francesco Suriano (himself the author of one pilgrim account), to warn other prospective pilgrims about coming to Palestine because of the conflicts with the Muslim authorities. Because of this, Casola even had to cancel his planned voyage to Mount Sinai. On the two-month journey back, Casola heard for the first time, through meeting Venetian galleys, of the French king Charles VIII's campaign to Italy. Back in Venice, Casola met the French ambassador and famous historian Philippe de Comines (1447–1511).

The account Casola gave of his pilgrimage is very different from other reports. It is not simply a list of the towns and places he visited combined with historical and biblical notes. Every object was commented on, and Casola often shared his personal feelings with his readers. In Casola's account, he mentioned that he knew many Italian and even non-Italian reports, but the stylistic devices and the composition are determined by his individual impressions. In addition to that, Casola is not only a keen observer in his narration, he even introduces himself as an active participant in the events described in his account. Aware of his status as both pilgrim and narrator, Casola occasionally lets us know this difference by making ironic comments. His writing style is one of simple elegance. With great knowledge and the experience of a long life, Casola was able to describe both intimate and strange things in a complex but comprehensible way.

Because of Casola's social status as a high Milanese clergyman, as a respected expert on the Ambrosian ritual (he was author and editor of manuscripts on this theme), and with his links to the ducal court of Milan, he enjoyed special attention from, for example, Agostino Contarini. This also helped Casola to be well informed about every event on the journey.

Only one manuscript of Casola's account, written in Italian, has survived (Milan, Biblioteca Trivulzina, Cod. 141). According to Casola, he was asked to write down his experiences in full detail. The first page of the manuscript stating the year of the journey is missing, but the date can nevertheless be definitely reconstructed by, inter alia, Casola's description of political events in Italy. Another page is missing with parts of the description of Crete. In 1855, the account was published for the first time by Giulio Porro, in an edition of 100 copies. Mary Margaret Newett edited an English translation with a comprehensive introduction and notes in 1907.

Stefan Schröder

### Biography

Born in Milan, 1427. Appointed rector of the church of St. Vittore al Pozzo in Milan and curate of a chapel of the church of San Tommaso in Terramara, 1452. Member of the Milanese legation at the papal court in Rome, from 1460. Confirmation of the benefice over the provosty of the church of St. Vittore in Corbetta by the duchess of Milan, Bianca Maria Visconti, 1467. Appointed canon of the collegiate church of St. Stefano in Brolo in Milan, 1476; canon of the basilica of San Ambrogio in Milan, 1486. Made a pilgrimage to the Holy Land, 1494. Appointed dean of the theological college in Milan, 1502. Died in Milan, 6 November 1507.

### References and Further Reading

Casola, Pietro, *Viaggio di Pietro Casola di Gerusalemme, tratto dall'autografo esistente nella Biblioteka Trivulzio*, edited by Giulio Porro, 1855.

Casola, Pietro, *Canon Pietro Casola's Pilgrimage to Jerusalem in the Year 1494*, edited by M. Margaret Newett, 1907.

## CATLIN, GEORGE (1796–1872) *United States Painter, Writer, and Explorer*

George Catlin was born on 26 July 1796 in Wilkes-Barre, Pennsylvania. He was the fifth of 14 children born to Putnam (a lawyer) and Polly Catlin. Two important events shaped his life and his respect for Native Americans: the kidnapping of his mother (18 years before he was born, when she was seven) and his meeting with the Iroquois On-O-Gong-Way. Catlin's mother was abducted by Native Americans during the Wyoming Massacre in July 1778, which occurred in Wyoming Valley, Pennsylvania. She was returned unharmed, and young George Catlin was impressed when his mother told him, years later, that her captors had treated her well. When Catlin was nine, he was about to shoot his first buck when On-O-Gong-Way shot it just before he did; the Iroquois later returned and shared the venison with George, and the two became friends.

Catlin attended the Gould and Reeve Law School in Litchfield, Connecticut, and then, on passing the bar in 1819, moved to Lucerne, Pennsylvania, to practice law. However, he soon became bored with law and longed to change to a different profession. Although a lawyer, Catlin preferred to travel and to paint; because he lacked formal training as a painter, he taught himself the art. Subsequently, Catlin relinquished law in order to travel across the country—and later to other continents—in order to meet Native Americans and paint their portraits. Catlin's goal was partly to explore other regions and partly to preserve Native American heritage and culture, which he realized were being obliterated by the aggressive expansion of white men in the United States.

Peter Matthiessen (1989) remarks:

> If Meriwether Lewis and William Clark were the first white Americans to explore the west half of the continent, from the Mississippi at St. Louis to the northwest Pacific coast, George Catlin traveled at least as many miles on his journeys by canoe and horse from Minnesota and the Montana border south to eastern Texas, as well as forays to the Gulf states and South Carolina, seeking to record the Indians in paintings and journals. Taken together, Catlin's works constitute the first, last, and only "complete" record of the Plains Indians ever made at the height of their splendid culture, so soon destroyed by traders' liquor and disease, rapine, and bayonets.

Catlin initiated his travels with short journeys to local reservations, where he painted portraits of Native Americans. Shortly thereafter (1830), Catlin traveled to St. Louis to meet with General William Clark, who took an instant liking to the painter and encouraged him to travel west, where he could paint Native Americans in areas where they still maintained their autonomy, freedom, and dignity. In 1831, Catlin went to the plains, where he encountered different tribes, who permitted him to paint portraits. In the autumn of 1831, Catlin traveled west of Missouri, where he made portraits of Native Americans in Leavenworth (now located in the northeastern section of Kansas) and Kansa (on the Kansas River). The painter also claimed that in 1831 he went to what is now Wyoming and past the Rocky Mountains to the Great Salt Lake, but some scholars dispute his claim, because on this alleged trip, unlike on all his others, he made no paintings and no diaries or notes. Matthiessen (1989) notes that Catlin was aboard for the maiden voyage of the American Fur Company steamboat *Yellow Stone*, which sailed 2,000 miles up the wide Missouri; Catlin painted portraits of Native Americans in Fort Pierre (now Pierre, South Dakota) and eventually ended up at the mouth of the Yellowstone, which is currently the North Dakota–Montana border; here, Catlin painted the Blackfoot, Assiniboin, Ojibwa, Crow, and Plains Cree. In 1832, Catlin made his famous voyage to the Mandan Sioux in the upper Missouri; during his three-week stay, he became the first to paint the Mandans. He made at least 20 portraits and wrote a book entitled *O-kee-pa*, which is the name of the religious festival in which the tribesmen inflict cruel punishments on themselves. Concerned that his observations about this bizarre ritual would not be believed, Catlin enlisted three white men to corroborate his story (see Kipp, 1873, the journal of a retired fur trader). Five years after his visit, smallpox wiped out the Mandans.

In 1835, Catlin, along with his wife, Clara, and his children, sailed up the Mississippi River to Fort Snelling, near the Falls of Saint Anthony, where they encountered and befriended Ojibwas. The Catlins made frequent visits to the Ojibwas here. Catlin also visited the Chinooks (Flatheads) on the lower section of the Columbia River. (They are known as the Flatheads because of their custom of squeezing and flattening the heads of their infants.) When Catlin was not traveling, he was showing his paintings at public exhibitions. In July and August 1836, for instance, his paintings were shown in Buffalo, New York, before moving to Philadelphia, Washington, DC, and Baltimore; in 1839, Catlin's gallery, consisting of 310 paintings of Native Americans and 200 other paintings, appeared in England. In 1843, Catlin showed paintings of Ojibways at an exhibition in England. Catlin attempted to show Iowas in Paris in 1845 and Ojibways in Belgium, but the results proved financially disastrous. King Louis Philippe of France commissioned Catlin to paint copies of 15 of his paintings, but before the painter could complete the works, the monarch was overthrown in the February Revolution of 1848. In July 1845, Catlin's wife, Clara, died of pneumonia (the painter blamed himself for her death because he refused her request to return to the United States), and the painter's son George died of typhus in 1848.

In 1852, enticed by the legend of the Crystal (also known as Tumucumache) mountains in northern Brazil and inspired by his cupidity, Catlin traveled there in search of gold. According to the legend, Spanish miners discovered great wealth but were massacred by natives before they could take the gold with them. Catlin's route to the Crystal mountains was first via Havana in Cuba, then to Caracas, Venezuela, and thence to the Orinoco and Demerara. He intended to ascend the Essequibo River to the base of the Crystal mountains, but political conflict between British Guiana and Brazil forced him to take a land route. In *Last Rambles* (1867), Catlin mentions that he found an Arowak village, where he obtained a guide who took him "across the mountains into the valley of the Amazon, which we accomplished, but with great fatigue and some distress, to the forks of the Trombutas, from which we descended in an Indian pirogue to the Amazon, to Santarem, and to Para." After many miles of wading through thick brush and vegetation, Catlin came to the Crystal mountains—only to find that they were actually many mountains that were too hazardous to climb. A mule stepped on Catlin's only gold-washer, preventing him from finding gold; he returned to the

Catlin at his easel (frontispiece to Catlin's *Letters and Notes on . . . North American Indians*, vol. 1, 1841). *Courtesy of British Library, London.*

Amazon valley and subsequently to the United States starving and with only two ounces of gold—but much wiser.

George Catlin was the greatest and most significant painter of Native Americans. A visionary, Catlin foresaw the destruction of the Native American people and culture by expansionist white Americans and decided to help preserve their culture. He painted portraits of Native Americans and wrote valuable and insightful books about his experiences with them. Catlin's portraits manifest the pride and dignity of a people that he admired and respected, a people that would soon lose their land, power, and autonomy—and ultimately be pushed onto reservations.

ERIC STERLING

### Biography

Born in Wilkes-Barre, Pennsylvania, 26 July 1796. Attended the Gould and Reeve Law School in Litchfield, Connecticut; passed the bar, 1819, and moved to Lucerne, Pennsylvania, to practice law. Abandoned law practice to become a portrait painter, 1823. Member of the Pennsylvania Academy of Fine Arts, 1824. Member of the National Academy of Design, 1826. Moved to New York, 1827. Married Clara Bartlett Gregory, 1828 (died 1845): four children. Decided to travel and paint Native American life, 1829. Moved to St. Louis, Missouri, 1830. Traveled to Fort Union, 1832; the southern plains, 1834; the Mississippi River and the Great Lakes, 1835. Established a Native American gallery in New York, 1838. Moved to England, 1839, and Paris, 1845; exhibited his work in both places. Moved back to England, 1848; became bankrupt, 1852. Traveled to Brazil in search of gold, 1852–1857. Returned to Europe, 1858, and to the United States, 1871. Tried unsuccessfully to gain financial help from the U.S. government for his collection of Native American paintings. Died in Jersey City, New Jersey, 22 or 23 December 1872.

### References and Further Reading

Catlin, George, *Letters and Notes on the Manners, Customs, and Conditions of the North American Indians: Written during Eight Years' Travel (1832–1839) amongst the Wildest Tribes of Indians in North America*, 2 vols., 1841; reprinted, 1973.

Catlin, George, *Adventures of the Ojibbewa and Joway Indians in England, France, and Belgium: Being Notes of Eight Years' Travels and Residence in Europe with His North American Indian Collection*, 2 vols., 1848.

Catlin, George, *An Account of an Annual Religious Ceremony Practised by the Mandan Tribe of the North American Indians*, 1865.

Catlin, George, *Last Rambles amongst the Indians of the Rocky Mountains and the Andes*, 1867.

Catlin, George, *O-kee-pa: A Religious Ceremony and Other Customs of the Mandans*, 1867; reprinted, 1967.

Catlin, George, *The Boy's Catlin: My Life among the Indians*, edited by Mary Gay Humphries, 1909.

Kipp, James, "On the Accuracy of Catlin's Account of the Mandan Ceremonies" in *Annual Report of the Smithsonian Institution*, Washington, DC: Smithsonian Institution Press, 1873.

Matthiessen, Peter (editor), *iIntroduction to North American Indians*, New York: Viking Penguin, 1989.

## CAUCASUS, RUSSIAN EXPLORATION

Russian scientific exploration of the Caucasus began during the reign of Catherine II under the auspices of the Academy of Sciences, which sponsored five major expeditions during the years 1768–1774, two of which crossed into the Caucasus. Their purpose was a comprehensive study of the nature and population of Russia, and they did just that, offering a wealth of data of all kinds, from the flora and fauna of a region to its economy and ethnography. Johann Güldenstädt, a Riga-born doctor of medicine trained in Germany, made the most extensive foray into the Caucasus, traveling all the way to Tbilisi and from there in various directions. His two-volume diaries, written in German, were published in St. Petersburg in 1787 and 1791. The second expedition that explored a small part of the northern Caucasus was headed by Samuil Gmelin, a doctor of medicine from Tübingen.

Peter Pallas, a prominent naturalist from Germany who spent about 40 years in Russia, much of it as an academician, described the northern Caucasus in his *Travels through the Southern Provinces of the Russian Empire in the Years 1793 and 1794*. A travelogue replete with precise observations on nature and people but omitting "every trivial circumstance" of journey, *Travels* includes an extended essay on the ethnic and social profile of the northern Caucasus, which aims to establish a taxonomy of its numerous tribes and peoples. Thankfully, Pallas eschews blanket generalizations about the moral character of the Caucasians. Instead, he attributes their notorious contentiousness to customary laws, which make of revenge a major duty shared by relatives and offspring. Yet Pallas characterizes individual ethnicities in moral terms—the Chechens, for example, are deemed "the most turbulent, hostile, and predatory inhabitants of the mountains."

The exploration of the Caucasus became a popular topic in the 1820s, during the rise of romanticism in Russia and increased interest in orientalism. The year 1823 saw the publication of two works written in starkly different genres: Semen Bronevskii's *New Geographical and Historical Information on the Caucasus* and Aleksandr Pushkin's *The Prisoner of the Caucasus*.

Bronevskii's unfinished study, written in 1810, is a reasoned compilation from available sources, augmented by his personal observations while crossing the Caucasus during the Persian campaign of 1796 and, subsequently, while stationed in Georgia as a civil servant. In his introduction, the author states that the Caucasus is as little known as the interior of Africa. His moral description of the Caucasian tribes—which he presents as staunchly independent, willing to endure poverty for the sake of freedom, generally greedy, cruel, perfidious, and vindictive, yet meek, faithful, and chaste in family life—shows already many of the ingredients of the Caucasian peoples' stereotypical image. Yet it lacks the Rousseauesque admiration for the noble savage, as well as a sense of awe at the sublimity of the mountains (Bronevskii compares the Elbrus to "two heads of sugar, one lower than the other").

Pushkin's *The Prisoner of the Caucasus* is a long narrative poem in the Byronic style, featuring the adventures of a jaded Russian nobleman taken captive by the Circassians (*Circassian* was used as a generic term for peoples of the northern Caucasus) and protected by a young native woman, who falls in love with him and sets him free. The poem raises interesting gender issues, as well as the question of Pushkin's relationship to Russian imperialism. Indeed, the admiration for the Circassians implicit in the story is thoroughly undercut by an epilogue written in odic style, in which Pushkin celebrates the Russian occupation.

*The Prisoner of the Caucasus* includes a variety of poetic set pieces, including descriptive poems about the sublime mountains and the proud lifestyle of the Chechens, and it is equipped with footnotes that convey factual information. In fact, Pushkin called his poem a "geographical article" in the draft of a private letter, and a prominent critic hailed the poem as a travel account. Pushkin had not in fact traveled deep enough into the Caucasus to gain firsthand knowledge of the poem's setting, and it has been impossible to ascertain what written sources he might have used. Whatever these were, Pushkin's hugely influential poem fulfilled the readership's desire for romantic adventure and for descriptive information about the Caucasus. It firmly established the romantic credentials of the Caucasus and unleashed a flood of descriptions and poetic evocations of the area, which, as Susan Layton (1994) points out, paradoxically celebrated both blissful communion with nature and exhilarating confrontation with hostile tribes and mountains.

This heady mix was recycled through a number of travelogues, fiction pieces, and poems by authors such as Mikhail Lermontov, Aleksandr Bestuzhev-Marlinskii, Aleksandr Polezhaev, and others. Taken together, this corpus of texts proclaimed the notion that the Caucasus was Russia's Orient, in imitation of the way in which Western empires had constructed their own discursive Orient. Pushkin was the first to puncture the ambivalent exotic seductiveness of this orientalized Caucasus. In his *Journey to Arzrum*, based on his 1829 trip to join the Russian war against Turkey, Pushkin documented painstakingly the annoying incidents, missed encounters, and nonevents he experienced on his way to Tbilisi and then Arzrum. His depiction of thc mountains is in turn parodic and starkly matter-of-fact, and his contacts with indigenous people consist of nothing but misunderstandings. Lermontov's *Hero of Our Times*, a novel encapsulating a fictionalized travelogue, rests on a kind of irony of origins whereby the orientalist clichés about the Caucasus arise from the pen of naive or unsavory characters. This exercise in defamiliarization was completed by Leo Tolstoy. In *The Cossacks*, in several short stories, and finally in *Hadzhi-Murat*, Tolstoy returned epic objectiveness to the depiction of the Caucasus and foregrounded the cultural gap between well-meaning Russian noblemen and indigenous people.

Until the 1860s, the scientific discovery of the Caucasus was concentrated on the northern Caucasus and Georgia. After the complete subjugation of mountain tribes in 1864, explorations intensified and extended into the high mountains. A history of specialized expeditions, such as the geological studies of G.V. Abikh or the well-written botanical studies of G.I. Radle, can be found in Gvozdetskii's book.

Writers continued to be interested in the Caucasus after the Soviet revolution. Suffice it to mention Osip Mandel'shtam's highly elliptical *Journey to Armenia* (1931–1932). For writers loyal to Soviet power, journeys to the Caucasus became an occasion for surveying the construction of a new Armenia undertaken by the Soviets (see Andrei Belyi's *Armeniia* and Marietta Shaginian's *Journey through Soviet Armenia*).

ANDREAS SCHÖNLE

### References and Further Reading


Belyi, Andrei, *Armeniia*, 1985; reprinted, 1997.

Berezin, I., *Puteshestvie po Dagestanu i Zakavkaz'iu*, 1850.

Gmelin, Samuil, *Puteshestvie po Rossii dlia issledovaniia trekh tsarstv estestva*, 1771–1785.

Güldenstädt, Johann Anton, *Reisen durch Russland und im Caucasische Geburge*, 2 vols., 1787–1791.

Gvozdetskii, N.A. et al, *Russkic geografich eskic issledavaniia kavkaza sredei Azii v XIX-nachale* xxv., Moscow: Nauka, 1964.

Khersonets, "Gori, drevniaia stolitsa Kartalinii," *Moskovskii Telegraf*, 4/16 (1833): 493–512.

[Lakubovich, A.L.,] "Otryvki o Kavkaze (iz pokhodnykh zapisok)," *Severnaia Pchela* (1825), 138 (17 November).

Layton, Susan, *Russian Literature and Empire: Conquest of the Caucasus from Pushkin to Tolstoy*, Cambridge and New York: Cambridge University Press, 1994.

Mandel'shtam, Osip, *Journey to Armenia*. translated by Sidney Monas, 1979; translated by Clarence Brown, with an introduction by Bruce Chatwin, 1989.

Marlinskii, A.A. Bestuzhev, *Sochineniia*, vol. 2, 1958.

Mukhanov, P.A., "Vziatie Ganzhi," *Moskovskii Telegraf*, 19 (1825): 242–250; "Krasnyi most," *Ibid.* 21 (1825): 57–68; "Elizavetpol'skaia dolina (Pis'mo iz Gruzii)," *Ibid.* 8 (1826): 28–32.

Nefed'ev, N.A., *Vzgliad na armianskuiu oblast' (iz putevykh zapisok)*, 1839.

Pallas, P.S., *Bemerkungen auf Einer Reise in die Sudlichen Statthaltershaften des Russischen Reichs in den Jahren 1793 und 1794*, 2 vols., 1799–1801; as *Travels through the Southern Provinces of the Russian Empire in the Years 1793 and 1794*, 2 vols., translated from the German, 1802–1803.

"Poezdka v Gruziiu," *Moskovskii Telegraf*, 4/15 (1833): 327–367.

Pushkin, A.S., "Kavkazskii plennik," *Polnoe Sobranie Sochinenii*, vol. 4, Moscow: Akademiia nauk SSSR, 1937.

Pushkin, A.S., "Puteshetvie v Arzrum," *Polnoe Sobranie Sochinenii*, vol. 8, Moscow: Akademiia nauk SSSR, 1937.

Radozhitskii, I.T., "Doroga ot reki Dona do Georgievska na prostranstve 500 verst," *Otechestvennye zapiski*, 40 (August 1823): 343–375.

Rovinskii, I.V., *Khoziaistvennoe opisanie Astrakhanskoi i Kavkazskoi gubernii po grazhdanskomu i estestvennomu ikhsostoianiiu, v otnoshenii k zemledeliiu, promyshlennosti i domovodstvu . . .* , 1809.

Shaginian, Marietta, *Puteshestvie po Sovetskoi Armenii*, 1950; as *Journey through Soviet Armenia*, 1954.

Shishkov, A.A., *Vostochnaia liutnia*, 1824.

Sumarokov, Petr, "Pis'ma iz Kavkaza," *Moskovskii Telegraf*, 10 (1830): 167–196; 11: 313–339.

Vedeniktov, M., "Vzgliad na kavkazskikh gortsev," *Syn Otechestva*, 88 (1837): 21–59.

Zubov, Platon, *Kartina kavkazskogo kraia prinadlezhashchego Rossii i sopredel'nykh odnomu zemel'*, 4 vols., 1834–1835.


*See also* **Black Sea**

## CAUCASUS, WESTERN VISITORS

The Mongols held suzerainty and Genoese trading posts were established on the Black Sea when the Dominican Johannes de Galonifontibus, bishop of Nakhichevan from 1377 (archbishop of Sultanieh from 1398), completed in 1404 an account of his oriental experiences. Enumerating the Caucasian peoples and languages, he perspicaciously demarcated Circassia ("Zyquia sive Tarquasia"), Abkhazia, Mingrelia, and Georgia ("J/Ioriania"—the form *Georgiania* is known from the mid-thirteenth century) as countries with separate languages. Constantinople's fall in 1453 subsequently hampered communication with the West.

Travel restarted with seventeenth-century missionaries, whose medical and pedagogical expertise helped counterbalance Orthodox (or pagan) reservations. In the 1630s, the Dominican prefects Dortelli D'Ascoli and Giovanni da Lucca extended Giorgio Interiano's description of Circassia (and Abkhazia). Theatine proselytizers targeted Mingrelia/western Georgia, Capuchins the eastern provinces—the Vatican's Fide Press further contributed by printing the first Georgian books (see Chikobava and Vateishvili). Many, including mission head Don Pietro Avitabile (1624–1638), recounted their experiences. Prefect to Mingrelia, Arcangelo Lamberti (resident 1633–1649) penned valuable observations on every aspect of Mingrelian life. During the same period, Don Christoforo de Castelli, who lived locally from 1627/28 to 1654, composed not only *De Iberia orientalis regni eiusque recentulis bellis* but two albums of sketches (more than 500 survive) vividly depicting, inter alia, architecture and the dress of different Abkhazian, Mingrelian, Imeretian, and east Georgian social classes. Another prefect to Mingrelia, Giuseppe Maria Zampi, who lived there for 23 years from approximately 1645, contributed a third significant source in his description of Mingrelian religious practice. This he handed to Jean Chardin (1643–1713) in 1672. A French traveler who became English ambassador to Holland, Chardin translated and incorporated this text as a substantial part of his own description of a sometimes perilous journey through Transcaucasia (1672–1673), which reflects Ottoman and Persian influence in western and eastern parts, respectively—a Turkish-organized slave trade flourished from various Mingrelian ports, for example. Linguistically, Zampi revealingly observed that the ecclesiastical language, Georgian, was as difficult for even the

Mingrelian priesthood to understand as Latin was for Italian peasants.

The first to provide concrete examples of the local languages was the illustrious (half-Abkhazian, half-Turkish) traveler Evliya Çelebi (1611–1682/83), who in the 1640s transcribed precious words and phrases from Circassian, Abkhaz, their now-extinct sister tongue Ubykh, Mingrelian, and Georgian (Gippert). The Latvian-born German Johann Anton Güldenstädt (1745–1781) included more extensive materials from most of the Caucasian languages as part of his comprehensive survey of the entire Caucasus, undertaken between 1770 and 1773 at the behest of the Russian Academy. Another German, Jacob Reineggs (1744–1793), while serving east Georgian monarch Erek'le II from 1779, attracted Potemkin's attention and became Russian Resident in Tiflis (Tbilisi), leaving historico-geographical and ethnographic writings for posthumous publication. Captain de Grailly de Foix, a French officer in the Russian military, wrote an eyewitness account of Count Todtleben's expedition to Georgia (1769–1771), which allows glimpses of Russian attitudes shortly before Russo–(east) Georgian relations were formalized in the Treaty of Georgievsk (1783). Marie Félicité Brosset (1802–1880), a midcentury French traveler to Transcaucasia, again on behalf of the Russian Academy, published vast quantities of mainly philological work on Georgian (and Armenian).

Chardin had drawn the first panorama of Tbilisi; the second appeared in the work of Joseph Pitton de Tournefort (1656–1708), French traveler and botanist, who stayed with missionaries in the city in 1701 on his scholarly tour of the Near East. The Swiss antiquarian and geologist Frédéric Dubois de Montpéreux (1798–1850) and the Polish-born German naturalist and ethnographer Gustav Radde (1831–1903), who helped Tbilisi's Caucasian Museum reopen in 1867, also published volumes of scientific and general interest after de Montpéreux's travels in 1831–1834 and Radde's residence in 1863–1903.

Commercial potential was investigated by the Frenchmen Jacques François Gamba (1763–1833), consul to Tbilisi 1821–1824, who was well acquainted with Georgian-speaking regions and traveled to Circassia, Abkhazia, and Mingrelia, and the aristocrat Jacques Victor Edouard Taitbout de Marigny (1793–1853), who, at first in Russian service, familiarized himself with coastal Circassia in particular in 1813–1818, becoming Holland's (vice-) consul for the Black Sea from 1821.

The focus shifted to political/humanitarian issues with the first Briton to set foot in Circassia, Scotsman David Urquhart (1805–1877), a social activist and sometime diplomat who designed Circassia's national flag. His brief sojourn in 1834 had profound, if atypical, consequences. Vehemently pro-Turkish, he championed Circassian opposition to Russia's dubious claims to their country and was indirectly responsible for two of the most important travel books to emerge from nineteenth-century peregrinations in the Caucasus. James Stanislaus Bell, having arranged in 1836 for *Vixen* to run Russia's blockade of Circassia with a cargo of salt, saw the vessel illegally impounded. Lord Palmerston declined to demand restitution, setting a precedent for the insouciance toward unwarranted aggression against north Caucasians that the West has manifested ever since. With strengthened determination, Bell took up residence in Circassia (1837–1839), accompanied for a year by *Times* correspondent J.A. Longworth. Both published poignant journals relating the Circassian, Ubykh, and Abkhazian mountaineers' heroic struggle to defend their independence against often wanton brutality, while giving sympathetic insights into a lifestyle that within 25 years was to vanish forever. The moral of Bell's and Longworth's intimate memoirs is summed up in Urquhart's stinging rebuke: "When she [England] proclaims herself the friend of the powerful and the ally of the aggressor, she ceases to have a situation among mankind, not because her fleets are disarmed, but because her character has sunk." Captain Edmund Spencer authored parallel accounts, and all these British travelers were branded "spies" by Russian/Soviet tradition. By contrast, the Caucasus's first American guest, George Leighton Ditson, severely disappoints, questioning Spencer's (indeed all Englishmen's) veracity and dedicating his book to Russia's Caucasian viceroy, Prince Vorontsov.

The French governess Anna Drancy (see Merlieux, 1857) became an unwilling visitor of the Daghestan of Shamil, guerrilla leader in the northeast Caucasus, where she observed village life. After her release, she described her captivity of 1854–1855, which followed a raid that seized aristocratic Georgian hostages to be bargained in exchange for Shamil's eldest son. After Russia's final conquest in 1864 and the flight to Ottoman lands of most of the autochthons from the northwest together with some from the northeast, more conventional travel to these remote parts was undertaken by the Hon. John Abercromby, Sir Arthur Augustus Thurlow Cunynghame, and John Frederick Baddeley (1854–1940), whose trek encountered Ingush-Chechens.

Sport is represented by Douglas William Freshfield, conqueror of Elbrus, Europe's highest peak, and other Caucasian challenges in the period from 1860 through the 1880s, who produced wonderful evocations of the mountains and a peregrination from Europe's highest inhabited village (Ushguli in Svanetia) through Abkhazia. Freshfield, Mrs. Harvey, and Britain's (thus far) sole consular representative to Abkhazia, William

Gifford Palgrave, all allude to Abkhazia's desolation after the mass exodus of its indigenous population. Sir Clive Phillips-Wolley's journal of usually unsuccessful attempts to slaughter Svanetia's wildlife pales in comparison.

Sir John Oliver Wardrop's (1864–1948) postuniversity jaunt through Georgia in 1887 led to not only a charmingly illustrated travel book, but a lifelong love affair with the country and its language, shared subsequently by his sister, Marjory Scott (1869–1909). Both translated important literary works, laying the foundation for Georgian studies in the United Kingdom. Sir John became the British government's representative (1918–1921) to independent Georgia (Roberts, 1921), establishing the Wardrop Collection at the Bodleian Library and the Wardrop Scholarship in Marjory's memory.

In 1929, the U.S. war correspondent Negley Farson was perhaps the last to enjoy the freedom to travel across the range before Stalin sealed his native region to foreign eyes. His sensitive account cautions: "[The mountains] 'possess' you. Once you have felt the spell of the Caucasus you will never get over it."

George Hewitt

### References and Further Reading


Abercromby, John, *A Trip through the Eastern Caucasus, with a Chapter on the Languages of the Country*, 1889.

Abich, Hermann, *Aus kaukasischen Ländern*, 2 vols., 1896.

Avitabile, Don Pietro, *Relazione di Georgia, anni 1624–1638*, 1650.

Baddeley, John F., *The Rugged Flanks of Caucasus*, 2 vols., 1940.

Barbaro, Giosafat, and Ambrogio Contarini, *Travels to Tana and Persia by Josafa Barbaro and Ambrogio Contarini*, translated by William Thomas and S. [i.e., E.] A. Roy, edited by Lord Stanley of Alderley, 1873; reprinted, 1963.

Bell, James Stanislaus, *Journal of a Residence in Circassia during the Years 1837, 1838 and 1839*, 2 vols., 1840.

Bernoville, Raphaël, *La Souanétie libre*, 1875.

Bodenstedt, Friedrich Martin von, *Die Völker des Kaukasus und ihre Freiheitskämpfe gegen die Russen*, 1848; 2nd edition, 1849; revised edition, 2 vols., 1855.

Borromeo, Andrea, *Relazione di Georgia* [Letter of 8 June 1658].

Borromeo, Andrea, *Relazione della Georgia, Mingrelia, e Missione de Padri Teatini in quelle parti*, 1704.

Bryce, Viscount James, *Transcaucasia and Ararat, Being Notes of a Vacation Tour in the Autumn of 1876*, 1877; reprinted, 1970.

Cameron, George Poulett, *Personal Adventures and Excursions in Georgia, Circassia and Russia*, 2 vols., 1845.

Chardin, Chevalier Jean, *Journal de voyage de Chevalier Jean Chardin en Perse*, 1686.

Chardin, Chevalier Jean, *Voyages de Monsieur le Chevalier Chardin en Perse, et autres lieux de l'Orient*, 3 vols., 1711; as *A New and Accurate Description of Persia and Other Eastern Nations*, translated by Edmond Lloyd, 1724; abridged as *The Travels of Sir John Chardin through Mingrelia and Georgia into Persia*, 1777; as *Travels in Persia, 1673–1677*, 1927.

Chikobava, A.S. and J.L. Vateishvili (editors) *First Printed Books in Georgian*, Tbilisi: Khelovneba, 1983.

Cunynghame, Arthur Augustus Thurlow, *Travels in the Eastern Caucasus, on the Caspian and Black Seas, Especially in Daghestan, and on the Frontiers of Persia and Turkey during the Summer of 1871*, 1872.

da Lucca, Giovanni, "17th Century Description of Circassia and Western Caucasia (continuing D'Ascoli)," in *Recueil des voyages au nord, contenant divers mémoires trés utiles au commerce et à la navigation*, 10 vols., 1715.

Dapper, Olfert, *Asia, of Naukeurige beschryving van het rijk des grooten Mogols . . . Beneffens een volkome beschryving van geheel Persie, Schirwan, Adirbeitzan, Karabach, Sagistan, Dagestan, Georgie, Mengrelie, Imereti, Kacheti, Karduel, Guriel, Avagasie, Circassie, Kurdistan en andere gebuur-gewesten*, 1672.

D'Ascoli, Dortelli, *Descritione del Mar Negro e della Tartaria*, 1634.

de Castelli, Don Christoforo, *Relazione e album dei schizzi sulla Georgia del secolo XVII*, text and drawings prepared for publication with Georgian translation and commentary by Bezhan Giorgadze, 1976.

de Galonifontibus, Johannes, *Libellus de notitialorbis*, 1404.

Ditson, George Leighton, *Circassia; or, A Tour to the Caucasus*, 1850.

Dubois de Montpéreux, Frédéric, *Voyage autour du Caucase, chez les Tcherkesses et les Abkhases, en Colchide, en Géorgie, en Arménie et en Crimée*, 6 vols., 1839–1843.

Dumas, Alexandre, père, *Impressions de voyage: Le Caucase*, 3 vols., 1865; as *Adventures in Caucasia*, translated by A.E. Murch, 1 vol., 1962.

Dunsheath, Joyce, *Guest of the Soviets: Moscow and the Caucasus, 1957*, 1959.

Eichwald, Ed., *Reise auf dem Kaspischen Meer und in den Caucasus unternomen in den Jahren 1825–1826*, 1837.

Ellis, George, *Memoir of a Map of the Countries Comprehended between the Black Sea and the Caspian; with an Account of the Caucasian Nations, and Vocabularies of the Languages*, 1788.

Evliya Çelebi, *Narrative of Travels in Europe, Asia and Africa in the Seventeenth Century*, translated from the Turkish by R. Joseph von Hammer, 2 vols., 1834–1850.

Farson, Negley, *Caucasian Journey*, 1951; as *The Lost World of the Caucasus*, 1958.

Ferrand, N., *Voyage de Crimée en Circassie: Lettres édifiantes et curieuses des missions étrangères*, 1820.

Freshfield, Douglas W., *Travels in the Central Caucasus and Bashan, Including Visits to Ararat and Tabreez and Ascents of Kazbek and Elbruz*, 1869.

Freshfield, Douglas W., *The Exploration of the Caucasus*, 2 vols., 1896; 2nd edition, 1902.

Gamba, Jacques François, *Voyage dans la Russie méridionale, et particulièrement dans les provinces situées au-delà du Caucase, fait depuis 1820 jusqu'en 1824*, 3 vols., 1826.

Graham, Stephen, *A Vagabond in the Caucasus*, 1911.

Graham, Stephen, *Changing Russia*, 1913.

Grove, Florence Craufurd, *The Frosty Caucasus: An Account of a Walk through Part of the Range and of an Ascent of Elbruz in the Summer of 1874*, 1875.

Güldenstädt, J.A., *Reisen durch Russland und im Caucasischen gebürge*, 2 vols., 1787.

Güldenstädt, J.A., *Reisen nach Georgien und Imerethi*, 1815.

Güldenstädt, J.A., *Beschreibung der kaukasischen Länder*, 1834.

Harvey, Annie Jane, *Turkish Harems and Circassian Homes*, 1871.
Herbert, Agnes, *Casuals in the Caucasus: The Diary of a Sporting Holiday*, 1912.
Hommaire de Hell, Adèle, and Xavier Hommaire de Hell, *Travels in the Steppes of the Caspian Sea, the Crimea, the Caucasus, etc.*, 1847.
Interiano, Giorgio, *La Vita et Sito de Zychi, chiamati Ciarcassi*, 1502.
Keun, Odette, *In the Land of the Golden Fleece: Through Independent Menchevist Georgia*, translated by Helen Jessiman, 1924.
Koch, Karl Heinrich E., *Reise durch Russland nach dem Kau Kasischen Isthmus in den Jahren 1836, 1837 und 1838*, 2 vols., 1842–1843.
Koch, Karl Heinrich E., *Die kaukasischen Länder und Armenien, in Reiseschilderungen von Curzon, K. Koch, Macintosh, Spencer und Wilbraham*, 1855.
Lamberti, Arcangelo, *Relatione della Colchide, hoggi detta Mengrellia, nella quale si tratta dell' origine, costumi e cose naturali di quei paesi*, 1654.
Lamberti, Arcangelo, *Colchide Sacra*, 1657.
Longworth, J.A., *A Year among the Circassians*, 2 vols., 1840.
Lyall, Robert, *Travels in Russia, the Krimea, the Caucasus and Georgia*, 2 vols., 1825; reprinted, 1970.
Maclean, Fitzroy, *To Caucasus, the End of All the Earth: An Illustrated Companion to the Caucasus and Transcaucasia*, 1976.
Marlinsky, Alexander, *Esquisses Circassiennes: Esquisses sur le Caucase*, 1854.
Marnier, Xavier, *Du Danube au Caucase: Voyages et littérature*, 1854.
Merlieux, Edouard, *Souvenirs d'une Française captive de Shamyl*, 1857.
Milaneli, Don Dzhuzep'e Dzhudiche [Don Giuseppe Giudice Milanese], *C'erilebi sakartveloze. XVII sauk'une* [Letters about Georgia. Seventeenth Century], 1964.
Mounsey, Augustus H., *A Journey through the Caucasus and the Interior of Persia*, 1872.
Mourier, Jules, *La Mingrélie, ancienne Colchide*, 1883.
Mummery, A.F., *My Climbs in the Alps and Caucasus*, 1936.
Oliphant, Laurence, *The Russian Shores of the Black Sea in the Autumn of 1852, with a Voyage Down the Volga, and a Tour through the Country of the Don Cossacks*, 2nd revised and enlarged edition, 1853.
Palgrave, William Gifford, *Essays on Eastern Questions*, 1872.
Phillips-Wolley, Clive, *Savage Svânetia*, 2 vols., 1883.
Radde, Gustav, *Reisen und Forschungen im Kaukasus in 1865*, 1867.
Radde, Gustav, *Die Chews 'uren und ihr Land*, 1878.
Radde, Gustav, *Ornis caucasica*, 1884.
Reineggs, Jacob [Christian-Rudolf Elich], *Allgemeinehistorisch-topographische Beschreibung des Kaukasus*, 2 vols., 1796; as *A General, Historical, and Topographical Description of Mount Caucasus*, translated by C. Taylor, 2 vols., 1807.
Roberts, C.E. Beckhofer, *In Denikin's Russia and the Caucasus, 1919–1920*, 1921.
Serena, Carla, *Excursion au Samourzakan et en Abkhasie, 1881*, 1885.
Spencer, Edmund, *Travels in Circassia, Krim-Tartary etc.*, 2 vols., 1837.
Spencer, Edmund, *Travels in the Western Caucasus*, 2 vols., 1838.
Taitbout de Marigny, Edouard, *Three Voyages in the Black Sea to the Coast of Circassia*, 1837.
Telfer, J. Buchan, *The Crimea and Transcaucasia, Being the Narrative of a Journey*, 2 vols., 1876.
Tournefort, Joseph Pitton de, *Relation d'un voyage du Levant, contenant l'histoire ancienne et moderne de . . . l'Arménie, de la Géorgie*, 2 vols., 1717.
Urquhart, David, *Progress and Present Position of Russia in the East*, 1836.
Ussher, John, *A Journey from London to Persepolis*, 1865.
Thielman, Max von, *Streifzüge im Kaukasus, in Persien, und in der asiatischen Türkei*, 2 vols., 1875; as *Journey in the Caucasus, Persia, and Turkey in Asia*, translated by Charles Heneage, 1875.
Wagner, Moritz, *Reise nach Kolchis und nach den deutschen Colonien jenseits des Kaukasus*, 1850.
Wagner, Moritz, *Travels in Persia, Georgia and Koordistan with Sketches of the Cossacks and the Caucasus*, 3 vols., 1856.
Wanderer [Elim Henry d'Avigdor], *Notes on the Caucasus*, 1883.
Wardrop, John Oliver, *The Kingdom of Georgia: Notes of Travel in a Land of Women, Wine and Song*, 1888; reprinted, 1977.
Wilbraham, Capt. Richard, *Travels in the Trans-Caucasian Provinces of Russia*, 1839.
Wilford, Francis, *On Mount Caucasus*, 1799.
Zampi, Giuseppe Maria, *Relatione della Colchida*, seventeenth century [vide Chardin].

*See also* **Black Sea**

## CAVENDISH, THOMAS (1560–1592)

### *English Sailor and Circumnavigator*

Thomas Cavendish led the third expedition to circumnavigate the world and was the first to set out with the expressed and planned purpose of circling the globe. He followed Sir Francis Drake by about six years, and, like Drake, he captured a major Spanish shipment of rich treasure off the western coast of America, returning to England with great wealth just after the Spanish Armada had been repulsed. A relatively young man of strong intelligence and great energy, Cavendish set forth again in 1591 to build on his success with a more ambitious expedition. This voyage, of which Cavendish himself wrote an extensive account, ended disastrously with Cavendish dying in mid-Atlantic on the return to England from Brazil after a protracted but unsuccessful effort to sail through the Strait of Magellan.

Cavendish was born in 1560 at Trimley in Suffolk. His father, William, died when Thomas was 12, leaving him a wealthy young man. At the age of 15, Thomas went to Corpus Christi College, Cambridge, departing two years later without taking a degree. In 1585, he took part in Raleigh's first expedition to Virginia, sailing with Sir Richard Grenville and commanding a small ship, *Elizabeth*.

By 1586, Cavendish had had a larger ship built, *Desire*, to follow the path of Drake. Setting out from

Harwich on 27 June 1586, his small fleet reached the Strait of Magellan by 6 January 1587, where they encountered "most vile and filthie fowle weather" (Hakluyt, 1600, 11: 301). Nevertheless, Cavendish emerged from the strait on 24 February into the Pacific and headed up the western coast of South America.

By October 1587, Cavendish had reached the southern tip of Lower California, where he awaited a Spanish treasure ship rumored to be in the area. In early November, Cavendish and his small band captured the 600-ton Spanish galleon, *Santa Ana*, after stiff resistance, despite the fact that all her cannon were stored in the hold. His small ships were unable to carry all the treasure, and he had not the men to sail the great Spanish galleon across the Pacific. Although it was one of the richest treasures to fall into English hands, much of it was burned along with the galleon and sent to the bottom of the harbor.

Cavendish also captured a Spanish pilot, Alonso de Valladolid, who knew the route across the Pacific. Sailing through the Philippine Islands, Cavendish picked up a great deal of information on Japan and the Chinese coast, which he hoped to use on a second expedition to the area. A large map of China also came into his possession. Cavendish did not follow Drake's passage through the Spice Islands, nor apparently did he make efforts to continue the trade relations that Drake had inaugurated, but he did spend nearly three months exploring and mapping the Philippines, the Moluccas, and the southern coast of Java, providing a much more detailed picture of the Far East. Cavendish could envisage English trade in the Far East by the circuitous route, not depending on plunder to make such long voyages profitable. By 14 May 1588, he had reached the coast of Africa, east of the Cape of Good Hope. Finally, on 9 September, after enduring Atlantic storms, the bedraggled but richly laden *Desire* sailed into Plymouth. Cavendish had accomplished the circumnavigation some nine months faster than his predecessor, Drake.

The voyage was hugely successful, and Elizabeth was pleased with her young courtier's accomplishment; Cavendish was still only 28. To make a round-the-world trading route a viable option for English ships was certainly a great achievement. But Cavendish's voyage fell in the long shadow cast by the defeat of the Spanish Armada. Although Elizabeth received Cavendish and his ship, she did not knight him; and some believed his ostentatious display of captured riches did not endear him to his monarch or her subjects.

In 1590, Cavendish prepared a fleet of five ships to repeat his round-the-world voyage. Although Cavendish planned to capture Spanish shipping in the eastern Pacific, he also hoped to establish trade with the Chinese and Japanese. In addition, John Davis, who was sailing with Cavendish, planned to leave the fleet when it reached California and continue to sail north in search of the Pacific outlet of the elusive Northwest Passage.

From the beginning, the voyage was conducted at an extraordinarily casual pace. They were late leaving Plymouth, languished for nearly a month in the doldrums, and dawdled down the coast of Brazil, so that they did not reach the Strait of Magellan until 8 April 1592, where autumn storms slowed their progress even more. In May, they were stuck in small harbors in the strait while the crew was gradually dying of disease, starvation, and the cold. Cavendish became increasingly violent and paranoid, in part owing to his frustration. Finally, the ships turned around and headed with the wind east out of the strait and back into the Atlantic, where they became separated. Davis in *Desire* and with *Black Pinnace* lost sight of Cavendish in the galleon *Leicester* and with *Roebuck*. No rendezvous had been arranged, and the two parties were never reunited.

Cavendish's retreat to England continued as a sailing disaster. Natives and the Portuguese attacked shore parties looking for food and water. Crew members who had not starved or been killed were mutinous. Cavendish himself became increasingly despondent, and he began writing an account of the voyage largely to vindicate his own actions. At some point in the Atlantic, he died, possibly by his own hand. Eventually, *Leicester* and *Roebuck* returned to Portsmouth, though the exact date of their arrival is not recorded. *Desire* reached Ireland with 16 survivors on 11 June 1593.

Cavendish's last voyage was as tragic as his first had been triumphant. At least 80 percent of the men he sailed with perished on the fruitless journey, and those who survived endured unspeakable privation. Ironically, Cavendish's last voyage demonstrated the terrible difficulties of circumnavigation, particularly with a large and fully manned fleet.

DAVID JUDKINS

## Biography

Born at Trimley St. Martin, Suffolk, 1560. Attended Corpus Christi College, Cambridge University, 1575–1577. Served at the court of Elizabeth I; member of Parliament for Shaftesbury, Dorset, 1584. Sailed with Sir Richard Grenville to Virginia, 1585. Member of Parliament for Wilton, 1586. Circumnavigated the world, 1586–1588, in *Desire*, seizing the treasure galleon *Santa Ana* off the coast of California, 1587. Embarked on a second, unsuccessful circumnavigation in *Leicester*, 1591. Died of unknown causes in the North Atlantic, 1592.

### References and Further Reading

Cavendish, Thomas, in *The Principal Navigations, Voyages, Traffiques, and Discoveries of the English Nation*, edited by Richard Hakluyt, 12 vols., 1903–1905 (modern reprint of the 1598–1600 edition; for Cavendish, see vol. 11, pp. 290–348).

Cavendish, Thomas, *The Last Voyage of Thomas Cavendish, 1591–1592: The Autograph Manuscript of His Own Account of the Voyage, Written Shortly before His Death*, edited by David B. Quinn, Chicago: University of Chicago Press, 1975.

Cavendish, Thomas, *Last Voyages: Cavendish, Hudson, Ralegh: The Original Narratives*, edited by Philip Edwards, 1988.

## CELA, CAMILO JOSÉ (1916–2002)

### *Spanish Novelist, Travel Writer, Poet, and Literary Critic*

Camilo José Cela was the best known of the Spanish novelists who emerged in the years immediately after the Spanish civil war of 1936–1939. His first novel, *La familia de Pascual Duarte* (1942) (*Pascual Duarte's Family*, translated by John Marks, 1946), has become a modern classic of Spanish literature, and for more than 50 years, the author maintained a steady output of full-length fiction.

In June 1946, Cela spent ten days traveling, mainly on foot, around the Alcarria district, a hilly area some 120 kilometers from Madrid. His account of the trip, subtitled *Viaje a la Alcarria*, was published in 1948. In the brief prefatory material to this work, Cela insists that travel narratives should simply record what is seen and should shun invention. Fiction, Cela notes, belongs in novels, and he also suggests that geography is the discipline that travel writers should seek to emulate.

The account of the Alcarria journey is narrated in the third person, with Cela referring to himself throughout as "the traveler." At a leisurely pace, he visits towns and villages, describes the physical features of the district, and records his encounters with various inhabitants. However, the most striking feature of the work is the description of the contrasting fortunes of those living in the Alcarria. In the lowland regions, where the soil is good, there is prosperity. In the hillier parts, on the other hand, the traveler encounters a good deal of poverty and hardship. In this respect, *Viaje a la Alcarria* can be viewed as a microcosm of 1940s Spain: while many were struggling to survive, others were reasonably well fed and leading comfortable existences. A fascinating silence in the work is to be found in the lack of comment (from the locals and the traveler) on what is happening elsewhere in the country during the difficult post-war period. Nor is there reference to the fact that Franco's Spain was being shunned, economically and diplomatically, by virtually the whole of the international community.

Cela's second travel book, *Del Miño al Bidasoa*, appeared in 1952. It describes a journey from the area of the Miño River (which forms Portugal's northern border with Spain), through the Atlantic region of Galicia, and thence across the north of Spain to the Bidassoa and the French border. In fact, the narrative draws heavily on a series of newspaper articles that Cela published in 1948 as he made his way around Spain by car, and which described his travels to government-sponsored holiday hostels for workers. In the 1952 narrative, the author introduces a French companion and man of the road, Dupont, and the work soon evolves into a breezy and lighthearted account of the travel experiences of the two men.

*Judíos, moros y cristianos* (1956) is presented as a seven-week journey around Old Castile. The focus here is essentially historical. The traveler shows particular interest in the towns and cities that were fought over by Christians and Moors during the Middle Ages and also in the sites of the dynastic struggles that culminated, toward the close of the fifteenth century, in the foundation of modern Spain. However, at the end of the work, the author acknowledges that his narrative is not a single journey, but a conflation of trips made during the period 1946–1952.

The concern with Spain's past is maintained in *Primer viaje andaluz* (1959), a narrative in which the author features some of the great southern towns and cities, especially Seville. Indeed, the journey gradually develops into a kind of cultural pilgrimage to and then through the region that produced many of Spain's greatest writers and painters, and where many of the country's most enduring works of literature were set. However, a good deal of the itinerary follows sections of the route of the car journey of 1948, and, from time to time in the early parts of the text, passages from the 1948 newspaper articles are reworked and interpolated. It seems certain that the Andalusian book is, once more, a conflation of several trips.

Cela's last two travel narratives do, however, recount single journeys. In August 1956, he traveled, mainly on foot, around the heart of the Spanish Pyrenees. The account of this trip was serialized in the newspaper *ABC* between October 1963 and June 1964, and the definitive version was published in book form as *Viaje al Pirineo de Lérida* in 1965. While Cela pays a good deal of attention to the majestic beauty as well as to the smaller-scale charms of the area, he also becomes increasingly aware of the intrusions of tourism and of how the landscape is being scarred by the large-scale development of hydroelectric schemes.

In the 1960s, Cela stated that he was getting too old for tramping around Spain and suggested that the

Pyrenean book would be his last travel work. However, many years later, he was persuaded by the weekly magazine *Cambio 16* to make a return trip to the Alcarria district. Consequently, in June 1985, Cela undertook a much-publicized tour, in a chauffeur-driven Rolls-Royce, of many of the places he had visited 39 years earlier. Now a famous literary figure, Cela was feted in towns and villages in the area, saw some familiar faces, reported on those people he had met in 1946 who had since moved away or died, and also shed light on some intriguing omissions from the account of the first visit. But above all, *Nuevo viaje a la Alcarria* (1986), with its descriptions of a much changed, modernized, and prosperous Alcarria, is a recognition that a new Spain had emerged, and it reveals the author musing on the benefits as well as the disadvantages of Westernization and consumerism.

All of Cela's travel books employ third-person narration and are marked by the author's wry sense of humor, his depth of knowledge of Spanish culture, and his frequent interest in the pleasures of food and drink. The works also increasingly betray Cela's inability to remain the detached observer and recorder that, in his essays on travel writing, he proclaims as being central to his approach to the genre.

David Henn

### Biography

Born Camilo José Cela y Trulock in Iria Flavia, Galicia, Spain, 11 May 1916. Attended school in Vigo, Galicia; moved to Madrid and studied at high school there, 1925–1933. Studied medicine at the University of Madrid, 1934–1937. Enlisted in General Franco's Nationalist Army, 1937; wounded in action and granted an honorable discharge, 1938. Studied law at the University of Madrid, 1939–1941. Started working solely as a writer, publishing novels, short stories, poetry, plays, and other work, beginning with the novel *La familia de Pascual Duarte*, 1942. Married María del Rosario Conde Picavea, 1944 (marriage disolved): one son. Traveled widely in Spain, France, and North and South America, 1948–1986. Lived in Palma, Mallorca, 1954-Mid-1980s. Founded the literary and cultural magazine *Papeles de son Armadans*, 1956; remained editor until it ceased publication, 1979. Elected to the Royal Spanish Academy, 1957. Honorary doctorates, University of Santiago de Compostela, 1980; Univesity of Sarajevo, 1993; the Universidad Ciencias Empresariales y Sociales, Buenos Aires, 1998; and others. Nobel Prize for Literature, 1989; Cervantes Prize, 1995. Married Marina Castaño, 1991. Received the title marqués de Iria Flavia, 1996. Honorary rector for life, Camilo José Cela University, Madrid, from 1999. Died in Madrid, 17 January 2002.

### References and Further Reading

Cela, Camilo José, *Las botas de siete leguas: Viaje a la Alcarria*, 1948; as *Journey to the Alcarria*, translated by Frances M. López-Morillas, 1964; reprinted, 1990.

Cela, Camilo José, *Del Miño al Bidasoa: Notas de un vagabundaje* [From the Miño to the Bidassoa], 1952.

Cela, Camilo José, *Judíos, moros y cristianos: Notas de un vagabundaje por Ávila, Segovia y sus tierras* [Jews, Moors, and Christians], 1956.

Cela, Camilo José, *Primer viaje andaluz: Notas de un vagabundaje por Jaén, Córdoba, Sevilla, Huelva y sus tierras* [First Andalusian Journey], 1959.

Cela, Camilo José, *Viaje al Pirineo de Lérida: Notas de un paseo a pie por el Pallars Sobirà, el Valle de Arán, y el Condado de Ribagorza* [Journey to the Lérida Pyrenees], 1965.

Cela, Camilo José, *Nuevo viaje a la Alcarria* [New Journey to the Alcarria], 1986.

## CENDRARS, BLAISE (1887–1961) *French Poet and Novelist*

This writer's life and work are inextricable: each is prolix and extravagant, full of dazzling marvels and glaring inconsistencies. Blaise Cendrars was an inveterate mythomaniac who, proclaiming that "truth is imaginary," used literature to embroider preposterously and without qualm upon his ubiquitous adventures. Even when Cendrars gave a series of radio interviews, in his sixties, he still contrived to serve up an impromptu novelty for every tall tale he disavowed. He would surely have reveled in the tags "the Homer of the Trans-Siberian" and "the Marco Polo of the twentieth century," accorded to him by, respectively, his friend John Dos Passos and his first biographer, Jean Buhler.

Born Frédéric Sauser in La Chaux-de-Fonds, Switzerland, the man who went on to construct himself as "Blaise Cendrars" typically loved to hint that he had come into the world in more exotic circumstances: in a decrepit Paris hotel, for instance, or on board an Italian railway train during his Scottish mother's journey back from Egypt. (His mother was in fact Swiss, like his father.) Cendrars's lifelong wanderlust—or, to put it more skeptically, his lifelong compulsion to project the image of globetrotter supreme—colors nearly all his writings, whether of a fictional or a documentary cast. His first escapade was a teenage joyride on an express train out of his hometown of Neuchâtel. This led to a three-year stay in St. Petersburg, where he worked for a Swiss watchmaker. By 1904, at the age of 17, he was traveling through prerevolutionary Russia on the newly built Trans-Siberian Railway. This and other unverified trips of his adolescence—to China, Armenia, Bombay, and elsewhere—were made in the company of Rovogine, a maverick friend whom many suspect was a pure invention. Two decades later,

Rovogine reappears as the eponymous hero of Cendrars's adventure yarn *Moravagine:* its first-person narrator is starstruck by this charismatic psychotic and anarchist revolutionary, and follows him across four continents. *Moravagine* was the first in a cycle of loosely configured travel books that vacillate between being thinly disguised memoirs and semiautobiographical novels.

Cendrars was also a pioneering poet. A long and penniless stay in New York prompted his 1912 elegy "Les Pâques à New York" [Easter in New York], which, back in France, asserted itself as the paradigmatic city-poem of modernism, a free-verse stream of emotional impressions that crystallize moments of urban ecstasy and despair. A second landmark work appeared in 1913 as *La Prose du Transsibérien* (*The Trans-Siberian Express*). Relayed in staccato style, its episodes reenact the Moscow–Peking rail journey of nine years earlier. Announced as "the first simultaneous book," the text was printed on a single scroll measuring two meters and designed to unfold vertically, and it was illuminated by a railway map and a parallel band of colored patterns devised by the simultaneist artist Sonia Delaunay. It is both a unique instance of avant-garde artistic collaboration and a forceful instance of a text seeking to mimic the rhythm and momentum of traveling.

Striving for more immediacy, Cendrars later amassed dozens of short poems under the title *Feuilles de route* (*Ocean Letters*), using brief, rapid phrases to produce diary-like notations of a journey aboard a liner bound for Brazil. The poems range from banal observations about the traveler's fellow passengers or the "snoring" of the air-conditioning in his cabin to more lyrical evocations of strolling on deck beneath the equatorial constellations or sniffing at the fragrant islands just over the horizon.

Despite being wounded on the Marne front during World War I, Cendrars assiduously maintained the legend of the restless writer-vagabond who keeps embarking with several trunkfuls of books and a suitcase of manuscripts forever on the verge of completion. Among many other activities, Cendrars found time to run a publishing house, and to work as actor and scriptwriter with the director Abel Gance on films like *J'Accuse* [I Accuse] (1919), an antiwar documentary, and *La Roue* [The Wheel] (1921–1924), the acclaimed railway sequences and rapid cutting of which owe much to the poet's impetus. *Bourlinguer*—which roughly translates as "knocking about the world"—is the title of one of four long autobiographical novels produced in the 1940s: its chapter headings advertise the names of a dozen European cities, including Antwerp, Genoa, Hamburg, and Paris. An earlier novel, *L'Or* (*Sutter's Gold*), had exploited the true-life story of a Swiss wanderer caught up in the California gold rush, whereas another, *Les Confessions de Dan Yack* [The Confessions of Dan Yack], had ventured more obviously toward the pole of the imaginary, given that its plot deals with an adventurer who establishes a whaling town on the Antarctic continent, albeit Cendrars took care to incorporate strict cartographical references within this phantasmagoria.

As if directly voiced by some latter-day Sinbad the Sailor, Cendrars's prose idiom is typically boisterous and freewheeling. In the Paris of the mid–1930s, it earned him the admiration of Henry Miller, who saluted him as the man "exploding in all directions at once." Yet while Cendrars loved to confound the distinction between "knocking about" and putting pen to paper, boasting that he did all his writing on trains, on board ship, or in obscure hotels, his career embraces several periods of sedentariness: for instance, after a few hectic months as a war correspondent in 1940, Cendrars retreated to the country for several years, closed off from the world and mobile only in his imagination. By his death in 1961, his writings had spilled across a dozen separate genres, nearly always with some reference to travel: novels, poems, memoirs, various pieces of reportage, and radio interviews, not to mention art criticism, opera libretti, and an anthology of African folktales. One project nourished in the 1930s was a world trip to document on film such phenomena as levitation and ritual trances. In 1939, a more realistic plan to sail around the globe had to be canceled because of the impending war. Typical of Cendrars's truculent self-image was his late boast that he had secured a reservation for the first rocket flight to the moon.

ROGER CARDINAL

## Biography

Born Frédéric Louis Sauser in La Chaux-de-Fonds, Switzerland, 1 September 1887. Attended schools in Naples and Basel, 1895–1897. Studied at School of Commerce in Neuchâtel, 1901–1902. Ran away from home, taking trains through Germany to Russia, 1903. Employed by a Swiss jeweler in St. Petersburg, 1904–1907. Journeyed from Moscow to Peking by rail, 1904. Returned to Europe, 1907. Kept bees and maintained a pear orchard in Meaux, 1908. Studied medicine and philosophy in Bern, 1909. Lived in Paris, St. Petersburg, and New York, 1910–1912. Settled in Paris, frequenting avant-garde literary and artistic circles and adopting the pen name Blaise Cendrars, 1912. Published the poetry collections *Les Pâques à New York* [Easter in New York]; 1912, and *La Prose du Transsibérien et de la petite Jehanne de France* (*The Prose of the Trans-Siberian and of Little Jehanne of France*,

1913). Married Féla Poznanska (died 1942), September 1914: two sons, one daughter. Joined French Foreign Legion; posted to the front line, wounded, leading to amputation of his right arm, 1915. Returned to Paris; took French citizenship, 1916. Made films with Abel Gance and ran the Éditions de La Sirène publishing house, 1917–1923. Made five ocean voyages to Brazil, 1924–1929. Met Henry Miller, 1934. Traveled on *Normandie* on its maiden crossing to New York, 1935. Active as a war correspondent, 1940. After the fall of France, settled in Aix-en-Provence, 1940. Wrote four autobiographical novels, 1943–1949. Moved to Villefranche, 1948. Married the actress Raymone Duchâteau, 1949. Settled in Paris; recorded several radio interviews, 1950. Suffered increasingly from hemiplegia from 1956. Commandeur, Légion d'honneur, 1958. Awarded Grand Prix Littéraire de la Ville de Paris, 1961. Died in Paris, 21 January 1961.

### References and Further Reading

Cendrars, Blaise, *La Prose du Transsibérien et de la petite Jehanne de France*, 1913; as *The Trans-Siberian Express*, translated by Anselm Hollo, 1964.
Cendrars, Blaise, *Du Monde entier* [From the World at Large], 1919.
Cendrars, Blaise, *Feuilles de route I: Le Formose*, 1924; with parts 1 and 2 in *Poésies complètes*, 1944; in *Complete Postcards from the Americas*, translated by Monique Chefdor, 1976.
Cendrars, Blaise, *Kodak (Documentaires)*, 1924; in *Complete Postcards from the Americas*, translated by Monique Chefdor, 1976.
Cendrars, Blaise, *L'Or*, 1925; as *Sutter's Gold*, translated by Henry Longan Stuart, 1926.
Cendrars, Blaise, *Moravagine*, 1926; translated by Alan Brown, 1968.
Cendrars, Blaise, *Les Confessions de Dan Yack* [The Confessions of Dan Yack], 2 vols., 1929.
Cendrars, Blaise, *Rhum: L'aventure de Jean Galmott*, 1930.
Cendrars, Blaise, *L'Homme foudroyé*, 1945; as *The Astonished Man*, translated by Nina Rootes, 1970.
Cendrars, Blaise, *Du Monde entier au coeur du monde* [From the World at Large to the Heart of the World], 1947.
Cendrars, Blaise, *Bourlinguer*, 1948; as *Planus*, translated by Nina Rootes, 1972.
Cendrars, Blaise, *Le Lotissement du ciel* [Dividing Heaven into Plots], 1949.
Cendrars, Blaise, *Emmène-moi au bout du monde!* 1956; as *To the End of the World*, translated by Alan Brown, 1967.

## CENSORSHIP AND TRAVEL WRITING

Travel writing gained in readership between 1600 and 1900, evolving from often romanticized and idealized accounts to the political and social commentaries of today. However, out of concern for audience sensibilities, the need for privacy, or fear of reprisals, many writers practiced self-censorship. Editors too censored material, often acting as gatekeepers, withholding or adapting accounts to meet the audience expectations.

Some information was withheld to protect commercial interests. With the race to establish colonies in the New World, some governments, such as Portugal, censored maps and travel chronicles to protect the secrecy of trade routes. The fall of Constantinople in 1453 brought the Ottoman empire closer to Christian Europe. Travel accounts perpetuated the vision of Moorish countries as barbarous, treacherous, and a threat to Christianity. One late-sixteenth-century writer, Frauncis Billerbege, could not bring himself to describe a conversion to the Islamic faith for fear of distressing his readers (Matar, 1998). Some Christians who converted worried about a hostile reception of their works in Europe. Such was the case of Thomas Arcos (1568–(?)), former secretary to Cardinal Joyeuse, who converted and remained in Tunisia following his release from captivity. When he proposed to publish his *Relations d'Afrique* in France, his French correspondent, the magistrate Nicolas-Claude Fabri de Peiresc, hesitated, fearful that news of the conversion would not be well received in a Catholic country. Peiresc recommended publishing under a pseudonym.

Some travel writers attempted to justify European policies of imperialism, omitting accounts of the mistreatment of natives or justifying this action, as in the case of Henry Savage Landor's beating of a native Tibetan, recounted in his *In the Forbidden Land* (1898) (Procida, 1996). Other accounts were modified by editors in order to reconcile travelers' experiences with accepted European values. In John Gabriel Stedman's (1744–1797) *Narrative of a Five Years' Expedition against the Revolted Negroes of Surinam* (1790), his editor made changes to the original manuscript to "insulate his readers from shock" at accounts of interracial relationships, torture, and mistreatment of slaves.

Other travel accounts were censored by host countries because of commentaries on existing social conditions. Garcilaso de la Vega's book *Royal Commentaries of the Incas* (1723) was banned by the Spanish colony where it was published because the authorities anticipated a revolt among the upper class (Pratt, 1992). Social worker Flora Tristan (1803–1844), born in France to a French mother and Peruvian father, presented an unflattering portrayal of the problems in Peru in her book, *Pérégrinations d'une pariah* (*Peregrinations of a Pariah*, 1838). Although the work was not actually censored, Peruvian aristocrats took issue with her account and burned her in effigy (Pratt, 1992).

The possibility of circumnavigation, the search for the origin of the Nile, and a growing interest in science contributed to an increasing number of expeditions to Africa. Although some writers went for the purpose of investigating commercial opportunities, their accounts stressed instead other interests to protect potential investments, as in the case of Sir John Barrow in his *An Account of Travels into the Interior of Southern Africa, in the Years 1797 and 1798* (1801–1804).

Some travelers omitted information that might detract from the dramatization of their narrative. According to Barrow's *Travels*, the French naturalist François Le Vaillant (1753–1824) did not describe regions of the interior of southern Africa as inhabited by colonialists, which Barrow said "would have diminished the interest he intended to excite."

Travel provided a means of escaping social restrictions. The German geographer Alexander von Humboldt (1769–1859) traveled in South America for five years (*Personal Narrative of the Travels to the Equinoctial Regions of the New Continent*, 1814) and wrote on indigenous cultures and archaeology, avoiding mention of his own homosexual relationships. Writing in the late seventeenth and early eighteenth-centuries as the wife of the ambassador to the sultan's court in Constantinople, Lady Mary Wortley Montagu (1689–b1762) did not reveal her infatuation with the Italian writer Count Francesco Algarotti or her family problems (for example, her marital life and her sister's deteriorating mental health) in her published letters to friends and family. Instead, she focused on her impressions of customs and scenery.

An increasing number of archaeological expeditions introduced readers to exotic landscapes of the Levant, or the eastern Mediterranean, and China. Sir Aurel Stein (1862–1943), born in Hungary and naturalized a British citizen, gained renown for his travels along the Silk Route in Chinese Turkestan to the Caves of the Thousand Buddhas near Dunhuang. Here, he located a cache of ancient manuscripts and numerous wall paintings. In personal letters, Stein criticized the destructive methods of other anthropologists: "Big temples, monasteries, etc., were dug into with the method of a scholarly treasure-seeker, barely approached to archaeological thoroughness" (quoted in Hopkirk, 1980). But this criticism was missing in his published accounts.

Some travel writers have had an important role in transmitting a cultural identity, as in the case of the Russian poet Osip Mandel'shtam (1891–1938), who died in the Gulag. Mandel'shtam, who already faced persecution prior to his eight-month visit to Armenia, used his trip (*Journey to Armenia*) as a metaphor for an idealized vision contrasted with the stark reality of Soviet Russia under Stalin. Numerous passages were expurgated by Soviet censors, including the parable used by Mandel'shtam to criticize Stalin and the Communist regime.

Many of today's travel writers journey to former Eastern bloc countries and provide an analysis of political and social conditions. Some of these writers are viewed with suspicion by foreign governments. Although accounts may not be censored, access to information and to interview sources may be restricted. The Briton Colin Thubron (b. 1939) risked having his notes confiscated when visiting Russia. Fellow British citizen Geoffrey Moorhouse (b. 1931) recounted his travels across Pakistan in his book *To the Frontier* (1984) and raised the ire of President Zia because of his narrative of the oppression and torture in prisons.

In *Open Lands* (1997), the American Mark Taplin (b. 1957) visited a Russian zone recently open to foreign visitors. However, he pointed out, "Soviet maps had been purposefully made incomplete or inaccurate in order to throw off snooping foreigners like ourselves." Hence travel writers continue to contend with various forms of censorship, not only self-censorship but problems with restricted access to information and censorship of published works.

JANE T. TOLBERT

### References and Further Reading

Barrow, John, *An Account of Travels into the Interior of Southern Africa, in the Years 1797 and 1798*, 2 vols., 1801–1804; reprinted, 1968.

Billerbege, Frauncis, *Strange News from Constantinople*, 1585.

Hopkirk, Peter, *Foreign Devils on the Silk Road: The Search for the Lost Cities and Treasures of Chinese Central Asia*, London: John Murray, 1980.

Landor, A. Henry Savage, *In the Forbidden Land*, 2 vols., 1898.

Mandel'shtam, Osir, *The Complete Critical Prose and Letters*, edited by Jane Gary Harris, translated by Harris and Constance Link, Ann Arbor, Michigan: Ardis, 1979.

Matar, Nabil, *Islam in Britain, 1558–1684*, Cambridge and New York: Cambridge University Press, 1998.

Moorhouse, Geoffrey, *To the Frontier*, 1984.

Procida, Mary A. "A Tale Begun in Other Days: British Travelers in Tibet in the Late Nineteenth Century," *Journal of Social History*, 30 (1996): 185–208.

Speke, John Hanning, *Journal of the Discovery of the Source of the Nile*, 1863.

Stedman, John Gabriel, *Narrative of a Five Years' Expedition against the Revolted Negroes of Surinam*, edited by Richard Price and Sally Price, 1988.

*See also* **Publishing**

## CENTRAL AFRICA

In the Western imagination, the quintessence of the continent that has stood for "darkness" has been—as Joseph Conrad's (1857–1924) *Heart of Darkness* (1902) attests—Central Africa. Europe has seen Central Africa as the most primitive, most savage, and thus most "other" location within the landmass that German philosopher G.W.F. Hegel, in his 1837 *Vorlesungen über die Philosophie der Geschichte* (*The Philosophy of History*), describes as "compressed within itself . . . enveloped in the dark mantle of night . . . [where lives] man in his completely wild and untamed state." Such presumptions have made Central Africa the explorer's and travel writer's equivalent of the Arthurian holy grail. Central Africa has been the antipode against which European difference—and supposed superiorities physical, intellectual, and spiritual—could best be proved; it is no wonder that perhaps the three most famous explorers of Africa—David Livingstone (1813–1873), Sir Richard Francis Burton (1821–1890), and Henry Morton Stanley (1841–1904)—distinguished themselves there.

This "othering" of Africa is already evident in the description of the fifth-century BCE historian Herodotus, in *The Histories*, of some Africans as "dog-headed," some as "headless . . . with eyes in their breasts," and others who "squeak like bats" (334, 332). Herodotus also introduces what would become the most alluring and long-standing of quest(ion)s for explorers in Africa: "the Nile and the riddle of its source" (141). Six centuries later, Ptolemy, in his *Geography*, both reinforces the allure of this riddle and more clearly situates its solution in a savage Central Africa when he writes that in "Aethiopia Interior" (that is, sub-Saharan Africa) are both *Anthropophagi* (cannibals) and "the Mountains of the Moon [*Lunae Montes*] from which the lakes of the Nile receive snow water" (109 and "Africa: Fourth Map").

The earliest travel narratives, such as mid-fourteenth-century Sir John Mandeville's (composite) *Voyages* (1357) and Leo Africanus's (c. 1485–c. 1554) *Descrittione dell' Africa* (1550; *A Geographical Historie of Africa*, 1600), refer to northern approaches toward this mysterious "Interior," and Richard Hakluyt's (c. 1552–1616) three-volume *The Principal Navigations, Voyages, Traffiques, and Discoveries of the English Nation . . .* (1598–1600) touches on Central Africa's west coast. But it was not until some 23 centuries after Herodotus that European exploration of Central Africa began in earnest, approaching this cartographically blank region sometimes from the north—for instance, Heinrich Barth (1821–1865), who traveled in Africa during 1850–1855, and Georg Schweinfurth (1836–1925), who traveled 1868–1871—but more typically from the southeast by, for instance, David Livingstone, who traveled 1850–1856, 1858–1864, and 1866–1873, and from the east, usually setting out from Zanzibar as did John Hanning Speke (1827–1864) and Richard Burton for their 1856–1858 expedition and later James Augustus Grant (1827–1892) and Speke for their 1860–1863 travels.

Scottish missionary David Livingstone set much of the tone and goals of nineteenth-century travel in Central Africa when he abandoned the proselytizing of missionary work to focus on the "Commerce and Civilization" that he declared would "open" the continent to both Christianity and the abolition of slavery—the proclaimed raisons d'être of European involvement in sub-Saharan Africa. The importance of rivers to "commerce" catalyzed not only the quest for the source of the Nile, but also the quest to map the major rivers of the region.

More importantly, the twin "halos" of Christianity and abolitionism "sanctified" exploration, and travel literature worked to strengthen this sanctification by associating Europeans with an empirical metaperspective based on "the truth" of science. The analysis of African languages, physiognomies, political structures, and the industriousness of "tribes" relative to each other situated the traveler in a godlike position from which both the writer and the reader (home in Europe) were able to see how things "really are." Repeated emphasis on, for instance, place, time, geology, and the collection and classification of fauna and flora proclaimed the European traveler as rational and grounded in empirically verifiable details that exemplified the "truth" of Europe's Enlightenment enterprise in the darkest region of the "dark continent."

The nineteenth-century traveler in Central Africa typically exhibited a noblesse oblige air of paternalism, typified by Burton's description of indigenous people, in *The Lake Regions of Central Africa* (1860), as "of those childish races." Even in moments of greatest appreciation, such as Stanley's tearful encomium to "these gallant fellows" who had made up his caravan during his nearly three-year (and first European) east–west crossing of Central Africa, Stanley declares: "For me, too, they are heroes, these poor ignorant children of Africa, for . . . they had never failed me" (*Through the Dark Continent*, 1878).

The importance of leading—whether leading Africans into "the future" already attained by Europe or merely over the next hill—diminished acknowledgment of the roles Africans, and especially African women, played in the success of expeditions. Texts and accompanying illustrations magnified the crisply dressed European whose upright stature and faraway gaze signified an inherent ability to lead, and these scenes typically included a national flag, as Central Africa quickly became an arena in which not only men but, metonymically, nations competed to prove themselves and their "natural" superiorities. Livingstone may have declared himself a "pioneer of Christianity," but "grop[ing] in the interminable forests" for the source of the Nile, he "stuck to it like a Briton" (*Livingstone's Africa*, 1872).

Although twentieth-century writers have continued to use Central Africa's magnificent landscape as a place to test and inspire, the atrocities committed under the rule of Leopold II of Belgium (1835–1909)—sovereign of the État Indépendant du Congo from 1885 to 1908—helped move most Central African travel literature toward a more critical political stance.

Although not strictly travel literature and despite its frequent ambivalence, Conrad's *Heart of Darkness* marks a turn away from "Euro"-celebration toward a more honest engagement with the violences of Western involvement in Central Africa. André Gide's (1869–1951) *Voyage au Congo* (1927; *Travels in the Congo*, 1929), for instance, denounces colonialism, but the critique is mild compared with such recent works as Helen Winternitz's *East along the Equator: A Journey up the Congo and into Zaire* (1987) and Paul Hyland's *The Black Heart: A Voyage into Central Africa* (1988).

The National Geographic tradition of essentializing and exoticizing Central Africa as "the most remote place I've ever seen" (to quote National Geographic photographer Jim Sugar's description of the Ituri forest in *Secret Corners of the World*, 1982) continues. Travel writers like Ryszard Kapśucinski ("A Tour of Angola," *Granta*, 20; "Christmas Eve in Uganda," *Granta*, 26, selections from *The Soccer War*), Mark Doyle ("Captain Mbaye Diagne," *Granta*, 48), and Sousa Jamba ("Brothers," *Granta*, 48), however, work against the nineteenth-century tradition of using Central Africa merely as a foil—what Christopher L. Miller (1985) calls "blank darkness"—by giving voice to the individual humanity of a "darkness" whose existence has been in the ignorance of foreigners and in the violences those foreigners have perpetrated on those who live in the place so much of Europe's making: Central Africa.

KEVIN M. HICKEY

### References and Further Reading

Barth, Heinrich, *Travels and Discoveries in North and Central Africa: Being a Journal of an Expedition Undertaken under the Auspices of H.B.M.'s Government, in the Years 1849–1855*, 5 vols., 1857–1858.

Becker, Jérôme, *La Vie en Afrique; ou, Trois ans dans l'Afrique centrale*, 2 vols., 1887.

Burton, Richard F., *The Lake Regions of Central Africa: A Picture of Exploration*, 2 vols., 1860.

Büttner, Richard, *Reisen im Kongolande*, 1890.

Coquilhat, Camille, *Sur le Haut-Congo*, 1888.

Frobenius, Leo, *Im Schatten des Kongostaates: Bericht über den Verlauf der ersten Reisen der D.I.A.F.E. von 1904–1906, über deren Forschungen und Beobachtungen auf geographischem und kolonialwirtschaftlichem gebiet*, 1907.

Gide, André, *Voyage au Congo*, 1927; as *Travels in the Congo*, translated by Dorothy Bussy, 1929.

Hakluyt, Richard, *The Principal Navigations, Voyages, Traffiques, and Discoveries of the English Nation*, 2nd edition, 3 vols., 1598–1600; reprinted, 12 vols., 1903–1905.

Hallet, Jean-Pierre, and Alex Pelle (editors), *Congo Kitabu*, 1965.

Hilton-Simpson, M.W., *Land and Peoples of the Kasai: Being a Narrative of a Two Years' Journey among the Cannibals of the Equatorial Forest and Other Savage Tribes of the South-Western Congo*, 1911.

Horn, Alfred Aloysius, and Ethelreda Lewis, *Trader Horn: Being the Life and Works of Alfred Aloysius Horn*, with a foreword by John Galsworthy, 1927.

Hyland, Paul, *The Black Heart: A Voyage into Central Africa*, 1988.

Lindqvist, Sven, *Utrota varenda jävel*, 1992; as "*Exterminate All the Brutes*," translated by Joan Tate, 1996.

Livingstone, David, and Charles Livingstone, *Narrative of an Expedition to the Zambesi and Its Tributaries, and of the Discovery of the Lakes Shirwa and Nyassa, 1858–1864*, 1865.

Livingstone, David, *Livingstone's Africa: Perilous Adventures and Extensive Discoveries in the Interior of Africa*, 1872.

Livingstone, David, *The Last Journals of David Livingstone, in Central Africa*, 2 vols., 1874.

Miller, Christopher L., *Blank Darkness: Africanist Discourse in French*, Chicago: University of Chicago Press, 1985.

Petherick, John, and Katherine Petherick, *Travels in Central Africa, and Explorations of the Western Nile Tributaries, by Mr. and Mrs. Petherick*, 2 vols., 1869.

Schweinfurth, Georg, *Im Herzen von Afrika: Reisen und Entdeckungen im Centralen Aequatorial-Afrika während der Jahre 1868 bis 1871*, 2 vols., 1874; as *The Heart of Africa*, translated by E.E. Frewer, 2 vols., 1873.

Speke, John Hanning, *Journal of the Discovery of the Source of the Nile*, 1863.

Speke, John Hanning, *What Led to the Discovery of the Source of the Nile*, 1864.

Stanley, Henry M., *How I Found Livingstone*, 1872.

Stanley, Henry M., *Through the Dark Continent; or, The Sources of the Nile around the Great Lakes of Equatorial Africa, and down the Livingstone River to the Atlantic Ocean*, 2 vols., 1878.

Stanley, Henry M., *The Congo and the Founding of Its Free State*, 2 vols., 1885.

Stanley, Henry M., *In Darkest Africa; or, The Quest, Rescue and Retreat of Emin, Governor of Equatoria*, 2 vols., 1890.

Tayler, Jeffrey, *Facing the Congo: A Modern-Day Journey into the Heart of Darkness*, St. Paul, Minnesota: Ruminator Books, 2000.

Thomson, Joseph, *To the Central African Lakes and Back: The Narrative of the Royal Geographical Society's East Central African Expedition, 1878–80*, 2 vols., 1881.

Thomson, Joseph, *Through Masai Land: A Journey of Exploration among the Snowclad Volcanic Mountains and Strange Tribes of Eastern Equatorial Africa*, 1885.

Ward, Herbert, *Five Years with the Congo Cannibals*, 1890.

Winternitz, Helen, *East along the Equator: A Journey up the Congo and into Zaire*, 1987.

Wissmann, Hermann, *Unter deutscher Flagge quer durch Afrika von West nach Ost: Von 1880 bis 1883 ausgeführt von Paul Pogge und Hermann Wissmann*, 1889.

*See also* **White Nile**

## CENTRAL AMERICA, POST-1524

As a geographical region, Central America includes the seven nations of Belize (known as British Honduras until 1973), Guatemala, Honduras, El Salvador, Nicaragua, Costa Rica, and Panama, which together make up the isthmus separating North and South

America. As a political region, Central America is generally regarded as including only five countries: Guatemala, Honduras, El Salvador, Nicaragua, and Costa Rica. A former British colony and a predominantly English-speaking country, Belize has long been on the political margins of the region. Panama, on the other hand, has shared a political identity with Colombia, beginning with its voluntary annexation to Colombia in 1821, rather than with the five countries that briefly constituted the Provincias Unidas del Centro de América (The United Provinces of Central America) (1823–1838).

The earliest travel writings on the region were written by explorers intent on subjugating local inhabitants, such as Pedro de Alvarado (1485(?)–1541), who brutally conquered the Mayas of Guatemala in 1524, and Hernán Cortés (1485–1587), who traveled from Mexico to Honduras in 1525. There were few travelers in the first two centuries following the Conquest. For the sixteenth century, there is *Relación breve y verdadera de algunas cosas de las muchas que sucedieron al padre fray Alonso Ponce en las provinicias de la Nueva España . . . escrita por dos religiosos, sus compañeros* [Brief and True Relation of Some of the Many Things That Happened to Father Alonso Ponce (1551–1617) in the Provinces of New Spain, . . . Written by Two Religious, His Companions] (1873). Another priest provided one of three narratives for the seventeenth century: Thomas Gage (1603(?)–1656), the Irish Dominican who converted to the Anglican Church after his travels in Central America (1625–1637), published his informative and anti-Spanish *A New Survey of the West Indies* in London in 1648. The other seventeenth-century narratives are seamen's tales: William Dampier's (1652–1715) *A New Voyage round the World* (1697) was wildly popular, and it preceded by two years the account by his sometime traveling companion, the physician Lionel Wafer (1660(?)–1705(?)), *A New Voyage and Description of the Isthmus of America* (1699). Another Englishman, John Cockburn, reported his adventures in *The Unfortunate Englishmen* (1735). Captain George Henderson wrote an account of early British activity on the eastern coast in *An Account of the British Settlement of Honduras* (1809).

Spain had jealously guarded her American colonies against foreign influences for nearly three centuries when they rose up and won their independence, stimulating a veritable flood of foreign visitors with a range of interests from the economic to the scientific. Orlando W. Roberts points to the advantages of commerce with the natives of the Nicaraguan coast in *Narratives of Voyages and Excursions on the East Coast and in the Interior of Central America* (1827). James Wilson (1799–1827) and Henry Dunn (1800–1878) depict life in Guatemala in *A Brief Memoir of the Life of James Wilson* (1829) and *Guatimala; or, The Republic of Central America, in 1827–8* (1828), respectively. L.H.C. Obert, like many subsequent travelers, explains the economic conditions of the region in *Mémoire contenant un aperçu statistique de l'état de Guatemala* (1840). George Washington Montgomery (1804–1841) authored the first major North American travel account, *Narrative of a Journey to Guatemala in Central America, in 1838* (1839). Sent on a commission by the U.S. government, he visited Belize and Cuba as well. Another commissioned traveler published what may still be the most famous travel narrative on the region. U.S. envoy John Lloyd Stephens (1805–1852) met with the major political figures of the time, including the "Indian" president Rafael Carrera and, more importantly, "discovered" many Mayan ruins. In fact, Stephens purchased the ruins at Copán, Honduras, for $50, and he considered shipping the huge stone monuments back to the museums of the United States. Frederick Catherwood (1799–1854) accompanied Stephens, providing exquisitely detailed illustrations of Mayan artifacts for the text; Stephens's descriptions together with Catherwood's illustrations is the work (*Incidents of Travel in Central America, Chiapas, and Yucatan*, 1841) that essentially founded Mesoamerican archaeology. Stephens apparently died of a tropical disease contracted in Panama. Désiré Charnay (1828–1915) traveled in Mexico and Central America from 1857 to 1882 in search of native ruins. John Boddam-Whetham (1843–(?)) and Frederick Boyle (1841–(?)) searched for indigenous antiquities in Guatemala and Nicaragua, respectively.

The second half of the nineteenth century saw the advent of geographers, geologists, and engineers from the United States, France, and Germany, many eager to find an interoceanic route to shorten the lengthy trip from the west to the east of the United States, particularly after the gold rush in California increased travel and commerce between the two coasts. According to Captain Robert Fitzroy (1805–1865), four routes were under investigation: the Mexican line, between the Gulf of Mexico and Tehuantepec; the Nicaragua line, through the two lakes of Nicaragua; the Panama line, site of the current Panama Canal; and the Atrato and Cupica line, in the Darien region of Panama. Scientific studies quickly short-listed only the Nicaraguan and Panama lines. Other travelers commenting on possible canal routes include the American diplomat E.G. Squier (1821–1888), Félix Belly (1816–1886), Commander Bedford Pim (1826–1886), and Armand Reclus (1843–1927). Scientists, in turn, found the tropical flora and fauna of Central America unique and fascinating. Auguste Dollfus (1840–1869) observed the many and sometimes active volcanoes with fascination in his *Voyage géologique* (1868); George Byam discussed animal life and the hunting of it in *Wild Life in the Interior of Central America* (1849); Thomas Belt (1832–1878) blended social commentary with botanical and zoological data in *The Naturalist in Nicaragua* (1874); and the Swedish scientist Carl Bovallius (1844–1907) included an index to the species of animals and plants referred to in his text, *Resa i Central-Amerika, 1881–1883* [Travels in Central America, 1881–1883] (1887). The first Russian to visit Nicaragua, Jegórs von Sivers (1823–1879), published his travels in German as *Ueber Madeira und die Antillen nach Mittelamerika* (1861).

Germans colonized the Alta Verapaz province of Guatemala along with areas of Costa Rica, becoming the primary coffee producers of the region, which may account for the many German travelers who visited Central America. Moritz Wagner (1813–1887), Karl Scherzer (1821–1903), Julius Fröbel (1805–1893), Wilhelm Marr (1818–1904), and Karl Sapper (1866–1945) all authored major works.

Though women travelers were few in the nineteenth century, they produced important texts with astute observations on domestic life and customs— aspects of life often overlooked by male travelers. Lady Emmeline Stuart-Wortley (1806–1855) describes her travels in Central America, particularly Panama, in volume 2 of her *Travels* (1851), while Mrs. Foote, widow of Henry Grant Foote, gives a very personal view of her eight years' residence in Nicaragua and El Salvador in *Recollections of Central America and the West Coast of Africa* (1869). Dora Hort wrote an account of her journey to California via Nicaragua, returning by the Isthmus of Panama. Helen Sanborn (1857–1917), daughter of Charles Sanborn of the American coffee firm Chase and Sanborn, accompanied her father on a coffee-buying trip to Guatemala, serving as his interpreter after three months' study of Spanish. Perhaps the most famous traveler of the late nineteenth century was Richard Harding Davis (1864–1916), who describes his tour of most of Central America on his way to Venezuela in *Three Gringos in Venezuela and Central America* (1896), with many fine illustrations.

In the twentieth century, Central America continued to be the travel destination for those seeking adventures off the beaten path. Francis Nicholas (1862–1938) explored "the gold regions, the timber lands, the rubber forests, and other resources of the tropics" (1903) for the South American Land and Exploration Co., and he found the indigenous population better company than many of the other Americans with whom he was forced to work. William Richard Dean Harris (1847–1923) formed the opposite opinion, claiming that "a savage is a savage" and that "a high material civilization can only be developed in temperate regions" so "we must not judge the people of these lands by our standards" (1905).

Mario Barone (1893–(?)) drove through Central America in a Studebaker, during a 26-month trip (1927–1929) from Rio de Janeiro to the Bronx, New York, losing three companions on the way—one from tropical disease and two as the result of car accidents in the days before seat belts—and wrote a fascinating account of his journey with its many dangers and inconveniences (*Heart and Will Power*, 1930). The years between World War I and World War II are illuminated in lively travel accounts by Eugene Cunningham (1896–1957) and Morley Roberts (1857–1942). Aldous Huxley (1894–1963), J.H. Jackson (1894–1955), and Erna Fergusson (1888–1964) focus particularly on Guatemala in the 1930s.

Accounts written by journalists include the *Time* magazine reporter William Krehm's (1913–) day-by-day account of events in the 1940s, the Swedish journalist Tord Wallström's perceptive observations of the 1950s, and Paul P. Kennedy's comments on the Guatemala and El Salvador of the late 1960s. When their citizenries tired of many decades of repressive totalitarian governments, civil wars broke out in the region, attracting a number of reporter-travelers. Fernando da Cunha (1957–) covered the war in El Salvador (1980–1992) in *El Salvador: Reportajes de guerra* [El Salvador: War Reports] (1987), and Tom Buckley wrote an account of his travels in the war zone of Central America in *Violent Neighbors* (1984), focusing on El Salvador. Guatemala's civil war (1966–1996) is the backdrop for the observations of the naturalist Jonathan Maslow (1948–). The apparent success of socialist revolution as a result of the civil war in Nicaragua (1979–1990) attracted the Italian writer Aldo De Jaco (1923–) and the American poet Lawrence Ferlinghetti (1919–), both of whom wrote about "Free Nicaragua."

The Maya and their ancient ruins continued to attract both professional and amateur attention. Thomas Wright (1927–), Mario Zeledón Cambronero, Carol Miller (1933–), Luis de la Sierra, and David Hatcher Childress are among the travelers whose accounts focus on Mayan antiquities. Nigel Pride's (1940–) narrative, *A Butterfly Sings to Pacaya* (1978), is illustrated with fine line drawings by the author. The finest account of the indigenous people themselves is to be found in the British-turned-Canadian Ronald Wright's (1948–) *Time among the Maya* (1989), whose title reflects Wright's sensitivity to the notion of time as he passes it and time as a concept understood differently by the Maya and Lacandón natives.

Several important travel accounts were published in the last decade of the twentieth century. Stephen Connely Benz (1958–) published a sensitive exploration of Guatemala and its people after his 1988–1990 stint as a Fulbright scholar, years when the guerrillas still blew up electrical towers and physicians were kidnapped by paramilitaries for providing medical treatment to alleged guerrillas. Gordon Chaplin, whose relative Frederick Catherwood had preceded him to the region, set sail along the "fever coast" of Central America, "looking for stories that would be good enough to help [him] remember who [he] was" (1992). Peter Ford sailed a similar terrain in his lengthy journey *Around the Edge* (1991). Anthony Daniels (1949– ) traveled throughout Guatemala, reflecting on social customs; Peter Canby traveled among the Maya and Lacandón of Chiapas, Mexico, and the Petén jungle and northern highlands of Guatemala.

The sheer quantity of travel accounts on Central America as a whole, the isthmus in part, and individual countries is astonishing. Many early authors begin by asserting the need to write and publish an account of their travels in order to enlighten the general public about a little-known region with a grand future. The lure of gold brought the conquistadores to the Americas, but the lure of commercial profits, whether from cochinelle or coffee production, bananas or hardwoods, or the construction of trains, roads, and bridges, kept the travelers coming throughout the nineteenth and early twentieth centuries. Volcanoes, rain forests, and tropical flora and fauna brought many scientific travelers to the area. In the later twentieth century, as travelers more frequently went in search of themselves in the face of the Other, Central America continued to provide that alien Other to the domestic Self abroad, through the political crises of civil wars and especially through the ongoing presence of the ever-fascinating Maya, who have survived despite the Conquest through what they call "500 years of resistance."

LINDA LEDFORD-MILLER

## References and Further Reading


Alvarado, Pedro de, *An Account of the Conquest of Guatemala in 1524 by Pedro de Alvarado*, edited by Sedley J. Mackie, 1924; reprinted, 1969.

Arlach, H. de T. d', *Souvenirs de l'Amérique Centrale*, 1850.

Babson, Roger W., *A Central American Journey*, 1920.

Baily, John, *Central America: Describing Each of the States of Guatemala, Honduras, Salvador, Nicaragua, and Costa Rica; Their Natural Features, Products, Population, and Remarkable Capacity for Colonization*, 1850.

Barone, Mario, *Heart and Will Power: Twenty Thousand Miles through the Three Americas*, 1930.

Bell, Charles Napier, *Tangweera; Life and Adventures Among Gentle Savages*, 1899; reprinted with an introduction by Philip A. Dennis, 1989.

Belly, Félix, "La Question de l'Isthme Américain. Episode de l'histoire de notre temps," *Revue des Deux Mondes*, 30/2 (1860): 328–368.

Belt, Thomas, *The Naturalist in Nicaragua: A Narrative of a Residence at the Gold Mines of Chontales; Journeys in the Savannahs and Forests. With Observations on Animals and Plants in Reference to the Theory of Evolution of Living Forms*, 1874; with a foreword by Daniel H. Janzen, 1985.

Benz, Stephen Connely, *Guatemalan Journey*, 1996.

Boddam-Whetham, J.W., *Across Central America*, 1877.

Bovallius, Carl, *Resa i Central-Amerika, 1881–1883* [Travels in Central America, 1881–1883], 2 vols., 1887.

Boyle, Frederick, *A Ride Across a Continent: A Personal Narrative of Wanderings Through Nicaragua and Costa Rica*, 1868.

Brasseur de Bourbourg, Charles Étienne, *Aperçus d'un voyage dans les états de San-Salvador et de Guatemala*, 1857.

Buckley, Tom, *Violent Neighbors: El Salvador, Central America, and the United States*, 1984.

Byam, George, *Wild Life in the Interior of Central America*, 1849.

Byam, George, *Wanderings in Some of the Western Republics of America: With Remarks upon the Cutting of the Great Ship Canal through Central America*, 1850.

Canby, Peter, *The Heart of the Sky: Travels among the Maya*, 1992.

Chaplin, Gordon, *The Fever Coast Log*, with an introduction by Jan Morris, 1992.

Charnay, Désiré, *Les anciennes villes de Nouveau Monde*, 1885; as *The Ancient Cities of the New World, Being Travels Explorations in Mexico and Central America from 1857–1882*, translated by J. Gonino and Helen S. Conant, 1887.

Childress, David Hatcher, *Lost Cities of North and Central America*, 1992.

Ciudad Real, Antonio de, *Relación breve y verdadera de algunas cosas de las muchas que sucedieron al padre fray Alonso Ponce en las provincias de la Nueva España: Siendo comisario general de aquellas partes . . . escrita por dos religiosos, sus compañeros* [Brief and True Relation of Some of the Many Things That Happened to Father Alonso Ponce (1551–1617) in the Provinces of New Spain . . . Written by Two Religious, His Companions] 2 vols., 1873.

Cockburn, John, *The Unfortunate Englishmen; or, A Faithful Narrative of the Distresses and Adventures of John Cockburn, and Five Other English Mariners . . . Who Were Taken by a Spanish Guarda Costa [in the John and Ann, Edward Burt, Master,] and set Set on Shore at [a Place Call'd] Porto-Cavallo . . . Containing a Journey over Land from the Gulf of Honduras to the Great South Sea . . . as Also an Account of the Manners, Customs, and Behaviour of the several Indians Inhabiting a Tract of Land of 2400 miles . . .* , 1735.

Cortés, Hernán, *Cartas y relaciones de Hernan Cortés al emperador Carlos v*, 1866; as *The Letters of Cortés: The Five Letters of Relation from Fernando Cortés to Emperor Charles V*, edited and translated by Francis Augustus MacNutt, 1908.

Cunningham, Eugene, *Gypsying through Central America*, with photographs by Norman Hartman, 1922.

da Cunha, Fernando, *El Salvador: Reportajes de guerra* [El Salvador: War Reports], 1987.

Dampier, William, *A New Voyage round the World*, 1697.

Daniels, Anthony, *Sweet Waist of America: Journeys around Guatemala*, 1990.

Davis, Richard Harding, *Three Gringos in Venezuela and Central America*, 1896.

De Jaco, Aldo, *Nica libre, ouvero, visita a una giovane rivoluzione* [Free Nica, or, Visit to a Young Revolution], 1984.

Dollfus, Auguste, *Voyage géologique dans les républiques de Guatemala et de Salvador par MM. A. Dollfus et E. de Mont-Serrat*, 1868.

Dunn, Henry, *Guatimala; or, The Republic of Central America, in 1827–8; Being Sketches and Memorandums Made during a Twelve Month's Residence in That Republic*, 1828; with a foreword by James C. Andrews, 1981.
Fergusson, Erna, *Guatemala*, 1937.
Ferlinghetti, Lawrence, *Seven Days in Nicaragua Libre*, 1984.
Fisk, Erma J., *Parrots's Wood*, 1985.
Fitzroy, Robert, *Considerations on the Great Isthmus of Central America*, 1851.
Foote, Mrs. Henry, *Recollections of Central America and the West Coast of Africa*, 1869.
Ford, Peter, *Around the Edge: A Journey among Pirates, Guerrillas, Former Cannibals, and Turtle Fisherman along the Miskito Coast*, 1991.
Fröbel, Julius, *Aus Amerika*, 1857–1858; as *Seven Years' Travel in Central America, Northern Mexico, and the Far West of the United States*, 1859.
Gage, Thomas, *A New Survey of the West Indies*, 1648; edited and with an introduction by A.P. Newton, 1929.
Harris, Dean, *Days and Nights in the Tropics*, 1905.
Henderson, George, *An Account of the British Settlement of Honduras . . . to Which Are Added, Sketches of the Manners and Customs of the Mosquito Indians . . .* , 1809.
Hort, Dora, *Via Nicaragua: A Sketch of Travel*, 1887.
Huxley, Aldous, *Beyond the Mexique Bay*, 1934.
Jackson, Joseph Henry, *Notes on a Drum: Travel Sketches in Guatemala*, 1937.
Kennedy, Paul P., *The Middle Beat: A Correspondent's View of Mexico, Guatemala, and El Salvador*, edited by Stanley K. Koss, 1971.
Krehm, William, *Democracies and Tyrannies of the Caribbean*, with an introduction and notes by Gregorio Selser, 1984.
Marr, Wilhelm, *Reise nach Centrall-Amerika* [Journey to Central America], 1863.
Maslow, Jonathan Evan, *Bird of Life, Bird of Death: A Naturalist's Journey through a Land of Political Turmoil*, 1986.
Mayle, Simon, *The Burial Brothers*, 1996.
Miller, Carol, *Mundo maya: Viajes* [Mayan World: Travels], 1993.
Montgomery, G.W., *Narrative of a Journey to Guatemala in Central America, in 1838*, 1839.
Nicholas, Francis Child, *Around the Caribbean and across Panama*, 1903.
Obert, Henri, *Memoire contenant un aperçu statistique de l'etat de Guatemala*, 1840.
Pim, Commander Bedford, *The Gate of the Pacific*, 1863.
Pride, Nigel, *A Butterfly Sings to Pacaya: Travels in Mexico, Guatemala, and Belize*, 1978.
Reclus, Armand, *Panama et Darien: Voyages d'exploration par Armand Reclus, 1876–1878*, 1881.
Roberts, Morley, *On the Earthquake Line: Minor Adventures in Central America*, 1924.
Roberts, Orlando W., *Narratives of Voyages and Excursions on the East Coast and in the Interior of Central America*, 1827.
Sanborn, Helen, *A Winter in Central America and Mexico*, 1886.
Sapper, Karl, *In den vulcangebieten Mittelamerikas und Westindiens* [In the Volcanic Region of Central America and the West Indies], 1905.
Scherzer, Karl, and Moritz Wagner, *Wanderungen durch die mittel-amerikanischen Freistaaten: Nicaragua, Honduras and San Salvador*, 1854; as *Travels in the Free States of Central America: Nicaragua, Honduras, and San Salvador*, 1857; reprinted, 1970.
Sierra, Luis de la, *Viaje a Mesoamérica: Por tierras de México, Guatemala y Honduras* [Travel to Mesoamerica through the Lands of Mexico, Guatemala, and Honduras], 1991.
Sivers, Jegórs von, *Ueber Madeira und die Antillen nach Mittelamerika*, 1861.
Squier, E.G., *Nicaragua: Its People, Scenery, Monument, and the Proposed Interoceanic Canal*, 2 vols., 1852.
Squier, E.G., *Notes on Central America, Particularly the States of Honduras and San Salvador: Their Geography, Topography, Climate, Population, Resources, Productions, etc., etc., and the Proposed Honduras Inter-Oceanic Railway*, 1855.
Stephens, John L., *Incidents of Travel in Central America, Chiapas, and Yucatan*, 2 vols., 1841; edited by Richard L. Predmore, 1949.
Stuart-Wortley, Lady Emmeline, *Travels in the United States, etc., during 1849 and 1850*, 3 vols., 1851.
Trollope, Anthony, *The West Indies and the Spanish Main*, 1859.
Wafer, Lionel, *A New Voyage and Description of the Isthmus of America*, 1699.
Wagner, Moritz, and Carl Scherzer, *Die republik Costa Rica in Central-Amerika, mit besonderer Berücksichtigung der Naturverhältnisse und der Frage der deutschen Auswanderung und Colonisation: Reisestudien und skizzen aus den Jahren 1853 und 1854* [The Republic of Costa Rica in Central America, with Special Consideration of the Natural Circumstances and the Question of German Immigration and Colonization: Travel Study and Sketches in the Years 1853 and 1854], 1856.
Wallström, Tord, *A Wayfarer in Central America*, translated from the Swedish by M.A. Michael, 1955.
Wilson, James, *A Brief Memoir of the Life of James Wilson*, 1829.
Wright, Ronald, *Time among the Maya: Travels in Belize, Guatemala, and Mexico*, 1989.
Wright, Thomas E., *Into the Maya World*, 1969.
Zeledón Cambronero, Mario, *En busca de los mayas* [In Search of the Maya], 1976.

*See also* **Mexico**

## CENTRAL ASIA, RUSSIAN EXPLORATION

The German geographers Carl Ritter and Alexander von Humboldt were the first to use the term *Central Asia* to describe the main continental part of the Asian mainland, as opposed to the outlying plains and peninsulas surrounding the massif. According to the wide application of the term, it covered the whole area limited by the Caucasus range and Caspian Sea in the west, by Siberia in the north, by inland China in the east, and by India and Iran in the south. In prerevolutionary Russia, the same notion of Central Asia was current, the "Russian part" of the region being named "Sredniya Asia" (Middle Asia).

The Tatar Baybiriy Tayshev was one of the earliest Russian travelers to Bokhara, traveling there in 1589 as an envoy of Czar Boris Godunov. Russian knowledge of Central Asia around this time is summed up in the 1598 *Bol'shoy Chertezh* [Great Drawing] of the whole Muscovite state and its borders with its neighbors, and its 1627 successor. Neither map has survived, but a description—*Kniga Bolshomu Chertezhu* [Book [attached] to the Great Drawing]—is extant and includes references to around 50 geographical names in Central Asia.

During the seventeenth century, Russians traveled intermittently in Central Asia, pursuing trade or diplomatic aims: Tikhanov and Bukharov visited Khiva and Bokhara in 1614; the nobleman I.D. Khokhlov was in Bokhara 1618–1620; the Astrakhan merchants Savin Gorokhov and Onisim (Anisa) Gribov went to Bokhara and Khiva in 1642 and Gribov to Persia and Bukharia in 1646; B.A. Pazukhin and N. Medvedev journeyed to Bokhara, Khiva, and Balkh in 1669–1673; V.A. Daurov, M.I. Kasimov, N. Venyukov, and I. Shishkin went to Bokhara and Khiva; and Kasimov and Shishkin went to Balkh and Kabul in 1675–1677. Baykov's mission from Tobolsk to Beijing (1654–1658) took in Dzhungaria, Zaysan Lake, and the upper reaches of the Irtysh River.

Throughout the eighteenth and early nineteenth centuries, Russia continued to strengthen its ties with the Central Asian lands. Russian colonists had reached the Irtysh River by the start of the eighteenth century, which led to more regular contact with Dzhungaria and attempts to penetrate into eastern Turkestan. Official expeditions under Colonel Bukhgol'ts (1715) and Major M.I. Likharev (1719) explored eastern Turkestan, and, around the same time, Dzhungaria was visited by several other Russians. The Tobolsk nobleman F. Grushnikov was sent east to prospect for gold in 1713–1716. Prince Alexander Bekovich-Cherkasskii led two expeditions (1714–1715 and 1716–1717). The Italian Florio Beneveni went as Russian envoy to Khiva and Bokhara (1718–1725), and among other visitors to Khiva were Lieutenant Gladyshev and the geodesist Muravin between 1740 and 1741 (see Khanykov, 1843), the merchant Rukavkin in the period 1753–1765, and the physician N. Blankenagel in 1793–1794. Ensign F. Efremov, who was captured on his travels and sold as a slave in Bukharia, succeeded in escaping and, between 1774 and 1782, made a perilous journey through Ferghana and eastern Turkestan to India, of which exploit he wrote a popular account (1852). Information obtained during these travels, as well as discussions with Siberian *bukhartsy* (Central Asian natives who came to Siberia as traders), provided Georg F. Müller (1705–1783) with the data for his *Izvestie o pesochnom zolote v Bukharii* [Information about Alluvial Gold in Bukharia] (1760), in which he described in detail Small and Great Bukharia (western and eastern Turkestan).

In 1759–1760, Chinese forces invaded Dzhungaria, and between the 1770s and 1810s, the Russians dispatched a number of expeditions there, the majority being unofficial and undercover. Manuscript materials of the following expeditions have survived in the Russian archives: Quartermaster Neznaev (1771), Cossack *ataman* Voloshanin (1771), Second Major Zelenov (1784), Second Major Bogdanov (1784), Captain Grening (1791), and First Lieutenant Telyatnikov (1797). In 1803–1804, Lieutenant Gaverdovskii covered a route from Orsk fortress to the Syr-Darya River. A Cossack party under Mamed'yarov in 1811 came to Kokand, visiting Turkestan and Tashkent, and in the same year, the Siberian interpreter Putimtsov reached Kuldja. Filipp Nazarov in 1813–1814 crossed the Ferghana Valley. Few materials of these journeys were published, but an account of Nazarov's travels was printed in 1821.

Explorers of Central Asia of the next three decades, such as N.N. Murav'ev (1819), A. Negri and Freiherr G. von Meyendorff (1820), E.A. Eversman (1820 and 1825), Nikivorov (1841), G.I. Danilevskii and Th. F.L. Basiner (1842), and A.I. Butakov (1848–1849), studied regions adjacent to the Caspian Sea. As the most thorough general Russian publication on Central Asia of this period, N.V. Khanykov's *Opisanie Bukharskogo khanstva* [Description of Bokhara Khanate] deserves mention.

Russian and Chinese possessions in Central Asia came into close contact at that time. In 1865–1866, the Russian army occupied Tashkent, Khodzhent, and Dzhizak. The Uzbek khanate of Kokand was annexed in 1876; those of Khiva and Bokhara became Russian protectorates in 1873 and 1868, respectively. The conquest of the Turkmens in the last quarter of the nineteenth century defined Russia's (now Turkmenistan's) southern frontier with Iran and Afghanistan. On 12 February 1867, Russia and China signed the St. Petersburg Treaty, which marked out a boundary between the Central Asian possessions of the two empires. The foundation of Russian colonies in Turkestan led to active exploration in eastern Central Asia.

Nikolai M. Przhevalskii (1839–1888), during his four journeys to Central Asia (1870–1873, 1876–1877, 1879–1880, and 1883–1885), traveled to Urga (now Ulan Bator), Mongolia, crossed the Gobi desert, the drifting sands of the Taklamakan, and the peaks of the Tien Shan, reaching Lop Nor Lake, the northern regions of Tibet, the Tarim basin, and the upper reaches of the Yellow River. After Przhevalskii's death, Mikhail V. Pevtsov (1842–1902) continued explorations of Central Asia with the Imperial Russian Geographical Society's support. Another Russian Geographical Society expedition was led by Grigorii E. Grumm-Grzhimaylo. In 1884–1887, he traveled in Altaii, the Pamirs, the Tien Shan, Kashgaria, and the Karakoram, explorations described in works such as *Le Pamir et sa faune lepidopterologique*. In 1889–1890, Grumm-Grzhimaylo led an expedition to Central Asia, written up in his three-volume *Zapadnaya Mongoliya i Uryankhayskiy kray* [Western Mongolia and Uryankhay Province] (1896–1906).

Grigorii N. Potanin (1835–1920) also undertook major explorations in Mongolia and China, between 1876 and 1899. His wife, Alexandra V. Potanina (1843–1893), accompanied and assisted him. The first Russian female explorer of Central Asia, Alexandra Potanina died while on an expedition on the bank of the Yangtse River. In 1899–1902, the Russian Geographical Society's Buriyat scientist G. Ts. Tsybikov (1873–1930) visited Tibet in the disguise of a Buddhist lamaist and was accepted in Potala as a worshipper of "the Living God," the Dalai Lama. He was the first Russian subject to cross Central Asia from Kyakhta to Lhasa.

The famous Russian geologist and geographer Vladimir A. Obruchev (1863–1956) began his field studies in Central Asia. In 1892–1893, as a member of G.N. Potanin's expedition, he crossed Mongolia, explored the Nan Shan mountain chain, and finished his journey in Kuldja. In 1905–1906 and 1909, Obruchev investigated the Dzhungarian depression and the mountains on its borders, where he discovered oil fields and gold and other metal deposits.

In 1893–1895, a participant in the third and fourth of Przhevalskii's expeditions, Vsevolod I. Roborovsky (1856–1910), carried out explorations of the Tien Shan, the Nan Shan, northern Tibet, and the Khami desert; Roborovsty's explorations ended in tragedy for him when apoplexy left him paralyzed. Another participant in the last of Przhevalskii's expeditions, Petr K. Kozlov (1863–1935), continued Roborovsky's explorations, leading the Mongolian–Tibetan Expedition of 1899–1901, which traversed the Mongolian Altai, the central Gobi, the huge Tsaidam depression, and northeastern and southeastern Tibet (Kam). Kozlov wrote up the expedition's results in *Mongoliia i Kam*. In the course of Kozlov's next journey (1907–1909), he sensationally discovered in the Gobi desert the remains of the thirteenth-century Tangut town Khara-Khoto. The expedition and its outstanding scientific findings were described in Kozlov's main Monograph, *Mongoliia i Amdo: Mertvyi gorod Khara-Khoto* (1923).

In 1870–1890, Russian travelers and military topographers were performing many geographical explorations and surveys in the Pamirs region, which in that period had become of great geopolitical interest to Russia. Alexei P. Fedchenko (1844–1873) carried out three expeditions to the Zeravshan valley, Iskandrkul Lake, and Kokand khanate, reaching the northern outskirts of the Pamirs. In the summer of 1876, a military-scientific expedition under Mikhail D. Skobelev (1843–1882) explored the Alai valley and the northern part of the Pamirs, including the region of Rang Kul Lake. In 1877–1878, Nikolay A. Severtsov (1827–1885) led the so-called Ferghana–Pamirs Expedition, studying Great Kara Kul Lake and the southwestern part of its basin, the region around Rang Kul Lake, and the whole area of Alichur-Pamir as far as Yashil Kul Lake. In 1879, a scientific expedition under the anthropologist Vasilii F. Oshanin studied the mountain chains of Petr I, Darvaz, and Karategin, visiting Sarydzhut, Regat, Karatag, Gissar, Kafirnigan, Feyzabad, and Karategin. In 1874–1880, the well-known Russian geologist Ivan V. Mushketov (1850–1902) explored the Tien Shan spurs near Tashkent, the Pamir-Alai mountains, the Ferghana depression, and a region where the Alai and Ferghana chains join. His fundamental work, *Turkestan*, outlines the exploration of the region and analyzes the geological structure of the western parts of the Tien Shan, the Pamir-Alai, and the Turan basin. In 1883, the members of the so-called Great Pamirs Expedition, Dmitrii V. Putyata, Dmitri L. Ivanov, and Nikolai A. Benderskii, virtually crisscrossed the whole Pamirs area and made topographic surveys of their routes. On the basis of these surveys, the best Pamirs map of the time was compiled in the same year. In 1891 and 1892, a regiment under Colonel Mikhail Ionov carried out a detailed study and mapping of the Pamirs region, and it also took the necessary military measures to secure the country for the Russian empire.

Extensive expeditions in Central Asia were carried out by a Russian officer of Polish origin, Bronisłav L. Grąbczewski (1855–1926). In 1885–1886, he visited Kashgar, the Tien Shan, and Ferghana province. In 1888–90, Grąbczewski's travels took in the regions of Raskem and western Tibet, as well as the nexus of the Kunlun, Hindu Kush, and Karakoram mountain ranges. Grąbczewski was the first Russian explorer to survey the Nagar River valley, which is a part of the Indus River basin. Grąbczewski's rich entomology collection was studied and published by A. Semenov (1889–1890), and Grąbczewski himself compiled a description of his travels and published it in four volumes in Polish (1924–1926). In 1958, the Polish Academy of Sciences brought out a scientific edition of these memoirs.

ALEXEI V. POSTNIKOV

## References and Further Reading

Curzon, George Nathaniel, *Russia in Central Asia in 1889 and the Anglo-Russian Question*, 1889; reprinted, 1967.

Efremov, Filipp, *Devyatiletnee stranstvovanie* [Nine Years' Long Travel], 1852.

Grąbczewski, Bronisław, *Kaszgaria: Kraj i ludzie*, 1924.

Grąbczewski, Bronisław, *Przez Pamiry i Hindukusz do 'zródel rzeki Indus*, 1925.

Grąbczewski, Bronisław, *W pustyniach Raskemu i Tibetu*, 1925.

Grąbczewski, Bronisław, *Na słuzbie rosyjskiej*, 1926.

Grąbczewski, Bronisław, *Podróże po Azji Środkowej*, 1958.
Grumm-Grzhimaylo, Grigorii E., *Le Pamir et sa faune lepidopterologique*, 1890.
Grumm-Grzhimaylo, Grigorii E., *Zapadnaya Mongoliya i Uryankhayskiy kray* [Western Mongolia and Uryankhay Province], 3 vols., 1896–1906.
Grumm-Grzhimaylo, Grigorii E., *Istoricheskoe proshloe Beyshanya v svyazi s istoriey Sredney Azii* [Historical Past of Beyshan' in Connection with the History of Central Asia], 1898.
Kemp, P.M (editor and translator), *Russian Travellers to India and Persia [1624–1798], Kotov, Yefromov, Danibegov*, Delhi: Jiwan Prakashan, 1959.
Khanykov, N.V., *Opisanie Bukharskogo khanstva* [Description of Bokhara Khanate], 1843.
Khanykov, Nikolai, *Bokhara: Its Amir and Its People*, translated by Clement de Bode, 1845.
Kozlov, Petr K., *Mongoliia i Amdo: Mertvyi gorod Khara-Khoto*, 1923.
Kozlov, Petr K., *Mongoliia i Kam*, 2nd edition, 1947.
Kuropatkin, A.N., *Kashgaria, Eastern or Chinese Turkistan: Historical and Geographical Sketch of the Country* [Anglo-Russian Borders in Central Asia], translated by Walter E. Gowan, 1882.
Kuropatkin, A.N., *Les Confins Anglo-Russes dans l'Asie Centrale*, translated into French by G. Le Marchand, 1885.
Levshin, A., *Opisanie kirgiz-kazach'ikh ili kirgis-kaysatskikh ord i stepei* [A Description of Kirgiz-Koysak Hordes and Steppes], part 1, 1832.
Lobanov-Rostovsky, André, *Russia and Asia*, 1933; revised edition, 1951.
Meyendorff, Freiherr G. von, *Voyage d'Orenboug à Boukhara, fait en 1820*, 1826.
Morgan, E. Delmar, "Notes on the Recent Geography of Central Asia from Russian Sources," *Supplementary Papers of the Royal Geographical Society*, 1/2 (1884): 203–263.
Morgan, E. Delmar, "The Russian Pamir Expedition of 1883," *Proceedings of the Royal Geographical Society*, new series, 6 (1884): 135–142.
Murav'ev, Nikolai, *Puteshestvie v Turkmeniyu i Khivvu v 1819 i 1820 gg. Gvardii General'nogo Shtaba kapitana Nikolaya Murav'eva, poslannogo v sii strany dlya peregovorov* [General Staff Guard Captain Nikolai Murav'ev's Travel to Turkmenia and Khiva in 1819 and 1820 for Discussion], parts 1–2, 1822.
Murav'ev, Nikolai, *Journey to Khiva through the Turkoman Country, 1819–20*, 1871.
Nazarov, Filipp, *Zapiski o nekotorykh narodakh i zemlyakh Sredney Azii* [Commentaries about Peoples and Countries of Central Asia], 1821.
Nazarov, Filipp, *Russian Missions into the Interior of Asia: Nazaroff's Expedition to Kokand; Eversmann and Jakovlew's Account of Buchara; Captain Muraviev's Embassy to Turkomania and Chiva* in *New Voyages and Travels*, edited by Richard Phillips, vol. 9, 1823.
Pevtsov, M.V., *Trudy tibetskoy ekspeditsii* [Proceedings of Tibet Expeditions], 1895.
Potanin, Grigorii N., *Ocherki severo-zapadnoy Mongolii* [Essay on Northwestern Mongolia], 1883.
Potanin, Grigorii N., *Tangutsko-tibetskaya okraina Kitaya i tsentral'naya Mongoliya* [Tangut-Tibetan Outskirts of China and Central Mongolia], 1895.
RGVIA, Fund VUA, # 24668: *Sobraniye zagranichnykh opisaniy puteshestvuyushchikh v raznye vremena chrez Sibirskuyu step'... polkovogo kvartirmeystera Neznaeva i kazatskogo atamana Voloshanina 1771-go goda, kapitana Greninga 1791-go goda, podporuchika Telyatnikova 1797 g. [o Tashkente], Mamed'yrova 1811-go goda, pyatidesyatnika Vyatkina, pogranichnogo tolmacha Nazarova i gubernskogo sekretarya Bubenkova 1813 goda; v Omske 1816 goda* [Collection of Travel Descriptions of Those Who from the Siberian Steppe Visited Foreign Countries at Different Times, Namely: Regimental Quartermaster Neznaev and Cossack *ataman* Voloshanin 1771, Captain Grening 1791, First Lieutenant Telyatnikov 1797 [around Tashkent], Mamed'yarov 1811, Cossack Captain Vyatkin, Translator Serving on Boundary Nazarov and Secretary of Gubernia Bubenkov 1813; Compiled in Omsk, 1816].
Semenov, Petr Petrovich, *Travels in the Tian'-Shan' 1856–1857*, edited by Colin Thomas, translated by Liudmila Gilmour et al., 1998.
Valikhanov, Chokhan Ch., *The Russians in Central Asia, Their Occupation of the Kirghiz Steppe and the Lives of the Syr-Daria; Their Political Relations with Khiva, Bokhara, and Kokan; Also Descriptions of Chinese Turkestan and Dzungaria. By Captain Valikhanoff, M. Veniukof and Other Russian Travellers*, translated by J. Michell and R. Michell, 1865.

*See also* **Turkestan**

## CENTRAL ASIA, WESTERN TRAVELERS

Defining Central Asia is difficult. The term has a distinctive smell about it: it is easy enough to say how Central Asian a place is by the strength of the smell, but using that smell to draw clear boundaries is impossible. Broadly, though, it means the land east of the Caspian but south of European Russia, the wild steppe lands around the Oxus River, Afghanistan, the Pamirs, the Karakoram, western China, and Tibet. It is the place where continents, mountains, and ideologies collide. It is a no-man's land that has attracted travelers who hate labels, and imperial sculptors who have tried to force it to fit their own dreams of empire.

Since very ancient times, there was some east–west traffic along the Silk Route, but few accounts survive. The literature begins, as serious travel there began, with Alexander the Great (356–323 BCE). Everyone who followed him was relatively anemic. Alexander crossed the Hellespont in 334 BCE, conquered the entire Persian empire, marched on through Afghanistan into the Punjab, and then, having failed to persuade his men to press further east, went south by river to the Indus delta before cutting west through Baluchistan, and back to Babylon. His exploits were recorded hagiographically by Arrian (died c. 180 CE) in *The Life of Alexander the Great*.

Central Asia does not like being owned: most of it resisted the Hellenization that so transformed the Near East. But Alexander's travel-conquest opened doors through which all later Western travelers to the region passed. Writers, though, were slow in coming, although merchants were not. With the exception of a few peripatetic Greeks such as Megasthenes

(c. 350–290 BCE), Western travelers kept silent or expressed themselves only in ledgers throughout the Hellenic and Roman periods and the European Dark Ages.

In the twelfth and thirteenth centuries, the Western missionary conscience and its historical bedfellow, Italian entrepreneurism, drove literate men out of the cloisters and the markets of Venice and across the steppes. The greatest of the writer-merchants was Marco Polo (c. 1254–1324), who, in 1271, traveled from Venice to Kublai Khan's court at Beijing via Hormuz, the Hindu Kush, the Pamirs, Kashgar, and the Gobi. Later, locked up for two years by the Genoans, he wrote the fast-moving, crystalline classic *Travels*, still the best guidebook to most places between Caspian and the Pacific.

Of the clerics, the (deservedly) best remembered are Friar Ascelin (fl. 1247), who traveled throughout Central Asia, seeking better treatment for Christians from the rulers there, and the Italian friar Odoric of Pordenone (1274(?)–1331), who traveled for 14 years in Central Asia, China, and India, baptized 10,000 people, and recorded it all in colorful, whimsical prose. Throughout the later Middle Ages, merchants and diplomats crossed the region, but left little of literary note behind. An exception is the Spanish nobleman Gonzalez de Clavijo (d. 1412), whose account of his diplomatic journey to Tamerlane's court at Samerkand is a great read.

From the early seventeenth century on, Central Asia groaned under the weight of all the European words spent on it. The trailblazer was the English merchant Anthony Jenkinson (d. 1611). He was followed by Thomas Coryate (c. 1577–1617), whose amiably written, opinionated meanderings make the labyrinthine court intrigues of Central Asia seem as cosy and parochial as the market tittle-tattle in his native Somerset; John Frampton (fl. 1577–1596); and the Italian traveler Pietro della Valle (1586–1652), a canny, close observer of colorful minutiae.

Tricky moment at Herat: the author's dervish disguise threatened with exposure (from Arminius Vambéry's *Travels in Central Asia . . . in . . . 1863*, 1864). *Courtesy of the Travellers Club, London; Bridgeman Art Library, agent.*

The travelers of the eighteenth and early nineteenth centuries were often on serious scientific or missionary journeys, or were hardy extended Grand Tourists, going more than the extra mile in search of watercolors, dinner-party stories, or relief from the tedium of stuffy parlors. They notably included George Forster (d. 1792), the German naturalist Alexander von Humboldt (1769–1859), the English pioneer of Chinese studies Thomas Manning (1772–1840), the German missionary Joseph Wolff (1795–1862), the English geographer and naval officer John Wood (1811–1871), the French missionary Évariste Régis Huc (1813–1860), and the English governess and semiprofessional gossip Lucy Atkinson (fl. 1849–1853), whose travels with her husband through Siberia and the Kirghiz Steppe amounted to nearly 40,000 miles.

From the mid-nineteenth century, the area had a new interest for Westerners. It became the playground of the Great Game. Russia looked lasciviously at British India, and Great Britain looked with a new interest at the buffer states that stood between Russia and India. English and Russian officers saw Bokhara, Samarkand, the Hindu Kush, and the Pamirs no longer as mere fairy-tale lands, but as gladiatorial arenas. Hide and seek, disguised as a fakir, became intelligent careerism. The spies were all soldiers holidaying, and all holidaying soldiers were spies.

Perhaps the greatest Great-Gamer of them all was Sir Francis Younghusband (1863–1942), whose exploits included traverses of the Gobi and the Karakoram and the assault on Lhasa. His *The Heart of a Continent* (1896) is the best distillation of the spirit of the times. Others include Sir Alexander Burnes (1805–1841), eventually killed in the Kabul massacre, Arthur Conolly (1807–1842), famously murdered with Colonel Stoddart in Bokhara, Sir James Abbott (1807–1896), Sir Charles MacGregor (1840–1887), and Sir George Scott Robertson (1852–1916). Increasingly recognized are the "Pundits," Indians recruited by the British to do covert surveying work beyond India's frontiers. Their reports contain accounts of epic journeys, but most are known only by their initials.

The Great Game both resulted from and resulted in supreme individual initiative. The most colorful of the travelers who ran along the sidelines of the Great Game was the colossal Fred Burnaby (1841–1885), speaker of many languages and said to be the strongest man in the British Army. He traveled through Central Asia in 1876, eventually arriving in Khiva frostbitten and nauseated by Russian bureaucracy and insolence. The story is in the classic *A Ride to Khiva* (1876).

The suspicion engendered by the Cold War between Russia and Britain made travel difficult and dangerous, but Central Asia continued to attract enterprising individuals such as George Curzon (1859–1925), Sven Hedin (1869–1952), Alexandra David-Néel (1869–1968), Frederick Bailey (1882–1967), Ella Maillart (1903–1997), and Peter Fleming (1907–1971).

In the early Soviet era, the Soviet Central Asian republics were more-or-less out of bounds to Westerners. Only a few penetrated them, notably Fitzroy Maclean (1911–1996). Central Asia was the reluctant host of the dreamy Western wanderers to Kathmandu in the 1960s and 1970s, but by and large their eyes were on their navels rather than on publication. Since the 1980s, travel to, and travel writing on, the region has expanded hugely, and writers like Colin Thubron (1939–), William Dalrymple (1962–), and Nick Danziger (1958–) have written best-selling accounts of journeys there.

Charles Foster

### References and Further Reading


Abbott, James, *Narrative of a Journey from Heraut to Khiva, Moscow and St. Petersburg during the Late Russian Invasion of Khiva*, 1843.

Ambolt, Nils Peter, *Karavan*, 1935; as *Karavan*, translated by Joan Bulmar, 1939.

Atkinson, Lucy, *Recollections of Tartar Steppes and Their Inhabitants*, 1863.

Ascelin, Friar, *The Travels of Friar Ascelin and His Companions, towards the Tartars in 1247* [from the memoirs of Friar Simon de St. Quentin, in Book 32 of *Speculum historiale* by Vincent of Beauvais, 1473; abstracted in Astley IV], 1745.

Ascelin, Friar, *A General Description of Western Tartary, A Generalized Description of Turkestan, Taken from Various Sources*, and *A Generalized Description of the Kingdom of Karazm from Various Sources*, 1745.

Bailey, F.M., *Mission to Tashkent*, 1946.

Bailey, F.M., *No Passport to Tibet*, 1957.

Bellew, H.W., *Journal of a Political Mission to Afghanistan in 1857 under Major (Now Colonel) Lumsden, with an Account of the Country and People*, 1862.

Bellew, H.W., *From the Indus to the Tigris: A Narrative of a Journey through the Countries of Balochistan, Afghanistan, Khorassan and Iran in 1872*, 1874.

Bellew, H.W., *Kashmir and Kashghar: A Narrative of the Journey of the Embassy to Kashgar in 1873–74*, 1875.

Bruijn, Cornelis de, *Travels into Muscovy, Persia and Part of the East Indies*, 1720.

Burnaby, Fred, *A Ride to Khiva: Travels and Adventures in Central Asia*, 1876.

Burnes, Alexander, *Travels into Bokhara, Being the Account of a Journey from India to Cabool, Tartary, and Persia*, 1834.

Burnes, Alexander, *Cabool, Being a Personal Narrative of a Journey to, and Residence in That City in the Years 1836, 7 and 8*, 1842.

Cable, Mildred, and Francesca French, *Through Jade Gate and Central Asia*, 1927.

Cable, Mildred, and Francesca French, *The Gobi Desert*, 1942.

Church, Percy William Palmer, *Chinese Turkestan with Caravan and Rifle*, 1901.

Coryate, Thomas, *Coryat's Crudities*, 1611.

Coryate, Thomas, *Greeting from the Court of the Great Mogul*, 1616.

Cumberland, C.S., *Sport on the Pamirs and Turkistan Steppes*, 1895.

Curzon, George Nathaniel, *Tales of Travel*, 1923.

Dalrymple, William, *In Xanadu: A Quest*, 1989.

Danziger, Nick, *Danziger's Travels: Beyond Forbidden Frontiers*, 1987.

David-Néel, Alexandra, *My Journey to Lhasa*, 1927.

David-Néel, Alexandra, *With Mystics and Magicians in Tibet*, 1931.

Deasy, H.H.P., *In Tibet and Chinese Turkestan*, 1901.

Fleming, Peter, *News from Tartary: A Journey from Peking to Kashmir*, 1936.

Forster, George, *A Journey from Bengal to England, through the Northern Part of India, Kashmire, Afghanistan, and Persia and into Russia, by the Caspian Sea*, 1798.

Frampton, John, *A Discourse of Tartaria, Scithia, etc: The Region of Tartaria and of the Lawes and Power of the Tartares, of the Cuntrey of Scithia and the Manner of the Scithians, of the Cuntrey Called the Other Side of Gange, of Cataia and the Region of Sina, a Cuntrey of the Great Cham and of the Mervelous Wonders That Haue Ben Seene in Those Cuntreyes*, 1500.

Franklin, William, *Observations Made on a Tour from Bengal to Persia in the Years 1786–87, with a Short Account of the Remains of the Celebrated Palace of Persepolis*, 1790.

French, Evangeline, Mildred Cable, and Francesca French, *A Desert Journal: Letters from Central Asia*, 1934.

Glazebrook, Philip, *Journey to Khiva*, 1992.

González de Clavijo, Ruy, *Narrative of the Embassy of Ruy Gonzalez de Clavijo to the Court of Timour, at Samarkand, AD 1403–06*, translated by Clements R. Markham, 1859.

Hedin, Sven, *My Life as an Explorer*, 1925.

Huc, Évariste Régis, *Travels in Tartary, Thibet and China, during the Years 1844–5–6*, translated by William Hazlitt, 1852.

Jamie, Kathleen, *The Golden Peak: Travels in Northern Pakistan*, 1992.

Jenkinson, Anthony, et al., *Early Voyages and Travels to Russia and Persia*, edited by E.D. Morgan and C.H. Coote, 2 vols., 1886.

Kemp, Emily Georgiana, *Wanderings in Chinese Turkestan*, 1914.

Le Coq, Albert von, *Buried Treasures of Chinese Turkestan*, 1928.

Macartney, Lady, *An English Lady in Chinese Turkestan*, 1931.

MacGregor, C.M., *Narrative of a Journey through the Province of Kharassan and on the N.W. Frontier of Afghanistan in 1875*, 1879.

MacGregor, C.M., *Wanderings in Baluchistan*, 1882.

Maclean, Fitzroy, *Eastern Approaches*, 1949.

Maclean, Fitzroy, *Back to Bokhara*, 1959.

Maclean, Fitzroy, *To the Back of Beyond*, 1974.

Maillart, Ella, *Des Monts Célestes aux Sables Rouges*, 1934; as *Turkestan Solo: One Woman's Expedition from the Tien Shan to the Kizil Kum*, translated by John Rodker, 1934.

Maillart, Ella, *Oasis interdité: De Pekin au Cachemire*, 1937; as *Forbidden Journey*, translated by Thomas McGreevy, 1937.

Maillart, Ella, *The Cruel Way*, 1947.

Malcomson, Scott L., *Empire's Edge: Travels in South-Eastern Europe, Turkey and Central Asia*, 1994.

Masson, Charles, *Narrative of Various Journeys in Balochistan, Afghanistan and the Panjab, Including a Residence in Those Countries from 1826 to 1838*, 1842.

Moorhouse, Geoffrey, *Apples in the Snow: A Journey to Samarkand*, 1990.

Newby, Eric, *A Short Walk in the Hindu Kush*, 1958.

Olearius, Adam, *The Voyages and Travels of the Ambassadors Sent by Frederick, Duke of Holstein, to the Great Duke of Muscovy and the King of Persia*, translated by John Davies, 1662.

Polo, Marco, *The Travels of Marco Polo*, translated by Ronald Latham, 1958.

Robertson, George Scott, *The Kafirs of the Hindu Kush*, 1896.

Seth, Vikram, *From Heaven Lake: Travels through Sinkiang and Tibet*, 1983.

Stein, Aurel, *On Alexander's Track to the Indus: Personal Narrative of Explorations on the North-West Frontier of India*, 1929.

Strabo, *The Geography*, translated by Horace Leonard Jones, 8 vols., 1917–1933.

Struys, Jean, *Les Voyages de Jean Struys: En Moscovie, en Tartarie, en Perse, aux Indes et plusieurs autres pais étrángers*, 1681; as *Voyages and Travels through Italy, Greece, Muscovy, Tartary, Media, Persia, East India, Japan, and Other Countries in Europe, Africa and Asia*, 1684.

Tavernier, Jean Baptiste, *Les Six Voyages de Jean-Baptiste Tavernier, qu'il a faits en Turquie, en Perses et aux Indes, pendant l'espace de quarante ans et par toutes les routes que l'on peut tenir*, 2 vols., 1676–1677; as *Through Turkey into Persia and the East Indies, for the Space of Forty Years*, translated by J.P., 1677.

Teichman, Eric, *Journey to Turkistan*, 1937.

Terzani, Tiziano, *Goodnight Mister Lenin: A Journey through the End of the Soviet Empire*, 1993.

Theroux, Paul, *Riding the Iron Rooster*, 1988.

Thesiger, Wilfrid, *Among the Mountains: Travels through Asia*, 1998.

Thubron, Colin, *The Lost Heart of Asia*, 1994.

Vambéry, Arminius, *Travels in Central Asia, Being the Account of a Journey from Teheran across the Turkoman Desert on the Eastern Shore of the Caspian to Khiva, Bokhara and Samarcand, Performed in the Year 1863*, 1864.

Vambéry, Arminius, *Sketches of Central Asia: Additional Chapters on My Travels, Adventures and on the Ethnology of Central Asia*, 1868.

Whittell, Giles, *Extreme Continental: Blowing Hot and Cold through Central Asia*, 1995.

Wolff, Joseph, *Narrative of a Mission to Bokhara in the Years 1843–1845, to Ascertain the Fate of Colonel Stoddart and Captain Conolly*, 1845.

Wolff, Joseph, *Travels and Adventures of the Rev. Joseph Wolff*, 1860.

Wood, John, *A Personal Narrative of a Journey to the Source of the River Oxus, by the Route of the Indus, Kabul and Badakhshan*, 1841.

Wood, John Nicholas Price, *Travel and Sport in Turkestan*, 1910.

Younghusband, Francis, *The Heart of a Continent*, 1896.

*See also* **Great Game; Turkestan**

## CENTRAL EUROPE

The lands of Central Europe extend, from west to east, from the eastern Alps to the Carpathian Mountains encircling the eastern regions of the former Habsburg empire, and from north to south, from Germany, Bohemia, and Moravia to Italy, the Adriatic, and the Balkans. The extension northward of the Roman empire combined with the advent of Christianity to generate a concept of a "civilized" Europe of the "true faith," geographically coextensive with the empires of the Romans and of Charlemagne. Beyond lay the barbarian culture of the infidel. Renaissance writers also accepted this distinction.

By the end of the Middle Ages, the most direct and important route through the western region led from Augsburg in Germany, across the Brenner Pass, and on to Verona and Venice. Another route led from Dresden, through Bohemia to Vienna, and on to Venice. Travelers to the east and southeast usually traveled through Moravia to Poland, turning south along the old trade routes from the Baltic, leading down the Dnieper to the Balkans and the Bosporus. Alternatively, they could travel along the Danube valley from Linz to Vienna and on into Hungary and Transylvania to Temesvar and the Balkans.

During the sixteenth and seventeenth centuries, most accounts of the regions were written by Habsburg officials, traveling through the region on business, who often provided detailed accounts of the local populations. Foreign travelers were deterred by the Turks who reached the gates of Vienna in 1539 and 1683, and by the Thirty Years' War (1618–1648). However, Dr. Edward Browne (1604–1708) made two tours of Hungary in 1668, visiting the gold mines of northern Hungary and making detailed observations of the local bathing practices. Browne was reminded of the cultural complexities and ambiguities of the region by the juxtaposition of the visible signs of the Turkish occupation with Dacian and Roman relics linking the region to Mediterranean civilization. It appeared to Browne that on entering the country "a man seems to take leave of our World . . . and before he cometh to Buda, seems to enter upon a new stage of world, quite different from that of the western countrys" (1685).

Lady Mary Wortley Montagu (1689–1762) entertained similar feelings as she contemplated her forthcoming trip to the Ottoman empire, for, even though the Turks had retreated from Hungary, her Viennese acquaintances still regarded the inhabitants of the eastern region with deep apprehension. Departing by the Temesvar route, Lady Mary declared, "I think I ought to bid Adeiu to my freinds with the same Solemnity as if I was going to mount a breach, at least if I am to beleive the Information of the peple here, who denounce all sorts of Terrors to me . . . I am threaten'd at the same time with being froze to death, bur'd in the Snow, and taken by the Tartars who ravage that part of Hungary I am to passe" (Letter, 16 January 1717). Lady Mary's observations of the ruinous effects of the conflict between the Habsburgs and the Turks in the lack of cultivation, sparseness of the population, and extreme backwardness of the region were to be echoed by foreign travelers for the next two centuries as the disparities between northwestern and southeastern Europe increased.

Foreign travelers were again discouraged by the outbreak of the Wars of the Austrian Succession (1740–1748) and the Seven Years' War (1756–1763), but, as peace returned, the number of Grand Tourists passing through the region began to increase. Vienna, established as the principal social and cultural focus of Central Europe, was particularly popular with German travelers, many of whom also visited Prague. A few, like Johann Georg Keyssler (1693–1743), extended their tour to northern Hungary or Budapest.

Few foreigners ventured further, although there was a fairly steady stream of travelers passing through Poland to Russia and to Turkey via Bukovina and the Balkans, as diplomats traveling east were joined by adventurers, antiquarians, scholars, and merchants. In the second half of the eighteenth century, western travelers, observing the dirt, poverty, and decay of the eastern provinces, compared them unfavorably that the cleanliness and order that they now began to associate with "civilized" Europe and "enlightened" values. Traveling through Poland in 1778, William Coxe (1747–1828) noted the bad state of the Galician roads, the villages "few and wretched beyond description," and wooden hovels full of filth and misery that gave everything "the appearance of extreme poverty" (1784). Cracow's "grandeur" was that of a "city in ruins." William Hunter, Lady Elizabeth Craven (1750–1828), Edward Daniel Clarke (1769–1822), and Adam Neale (d. 1832) contrasted the misery of the peasants with the lifestyle of the nobility and the gentry. The images of sheepskin-clad peasants and unwashed Jews with their matted tresses continued to figure in travelogues into the twentieth century.

Foreign travelers were invariably fascinated by the ethnic, linguistic, and religious diversity of the peoples of Central Europe, although their sense of the differences was less acute than that of domestic travelers. The mixture of costumes and languages they encountered on city streets provided an endless source of anecdotal material. The habits and dress of the eastern Jews were regarded with horrified fascination, while the term *Orientals* was frequently used, not just of the Balkan Muslims, but also of the extensive Jewish populations found throughout the empire. German-speaking travelers passing through Bohemia were increasingly conscious of the linguistic and cultural differences of the Slavic races. The composer Mozart (1756–1791), a German-speaking resident of Vienna, regarded his visits to Prague as excursions into a culturally different world. The influence of Johann Herder (1744–1803) and Alberto Fortis (1741–1803) led some Germans to take an interest in the folklore and customs of the south. Fortis had participated in a scientific expedition in 1770 from Venice to Dalmatia, and his account helped to prepare the way for nineteenth-century perceptions of the southern Slavic lands as a kind of ethnic folk museum. The sense of a lack of clear-cut cultural boundaries was evident in the persistence of terms like *Tatars* to refer to the non-Germanic peoples. Friedrich Stolberg (1750–1819) noted that Carniola was inhabited by "Vandals." In some areas, northern Protestants sometimes found the intense and superstitious Catholicism disturbing.

After the end of the Napoleonic wars in 1814, the growth in traffic to Italy brought more visitors to Vienna's palaces, art collections, and gardens. While the city's cultural life appealed to middle-class German tourists, the British were usually more interested in the city's reputation for its thriving social life. Visitors continued to view the city and its multiethnic population as a gateway to the East. The poet Gérard de Nerval (1808–1855) associated it with the imaginary world of literary Bohemia in which conventional standards of behavior were weakened or inverted: in Munich, he visited museums, but in Vienna, he chased women.

Although the spas of the "real" Bohemia and the eastern Alps attracted visitors like Peter Turnbull (1786–1852) and Augustus Granville, M.D. (1783–1872), Frances Trollope (1780–1863) was still able to observe in 1838 that "there was no country in Europe so little known, and so little understood" as Austria. One of the first British travelers to make the eastward journey to the Balkans using the new Danubian steamboats was Michael Quin (1796–1843). Others, like Adolphus Slade (c. 1802–1877), soon followed. Taking a train through Germany, once in Prague this naval officer's familiarity with the East enabled him to detect the "influence of Turkishness on tastes," which "becomes more evident, the further one advances eastwards, until in Transylvania and Croatia, distinctions cease." Johann Georg Köhl (1808–1878) felt Bohemia to be separate from the rest of the world and, anticipating the future, noted that Prague "has become a city full of ruins and palaces, that will secure to the city an enduring interest for centuries to come" (1843).

Unlike Julia Pardoe (1806–1862), Slade escaped quarantine in the lazaretto on the Balkan border. Instituted by the Habsburgs in 1770, quarantine was compulsory for all travelers from the Balkans and was enforced by the army stationed along the military frontier. British travelers saw the real function of the restrictions as the prevention of intercourse between the peoples of the Balkans and those of the empire. In the 1840s, John Paget (1808–1892) made several tours of Hungary, including one down the Danube to Orsova, then overland to Temesvar, and on into Transylvania. His influential *Hungary and Transylvania*

(1839) stimulated the interest of other travelers. Like Julia Pardoe, Archibald Paton (1811–1874), and Charles Boner (1815–1870), Paget also took a relatively positive view of the Magyars, who were generally seen as the victims of Austrian repression. These ethnographic observations, together with those of Emily Gerard (1849–1905), served as useful background for the fictional travelogue of Bram Stoker's *Dracula* (1897).

By the 1870s, the clientele of the west Bohemian spas was international. The hinterland was still primarily of interest only to writers and artists, like Walter Crane (1845–1915), who, under the influence of the Arts and Crafts movement, were becoming interested in folk art. The frontier town of Cracow and the port of Trieste were now easily accessible from Vienna and Budapest, now the Hungarian capital, while the Orient Express linked Central Europe to Paris and Constantinople. The new carriage road over the Brenner Pass was overtaken by the railway. The increased accessibility of the resorts of the eastern Alps, the Dolomites, and the Carpathians made them more popular with climbers, pedestrians, and those taking cures. The mythical status of the Carpathians, described by Charles Boner in 1865 as "a barricade against northern barbarism, and Turkish hate and tyranny," was indicated by their representation in maps and atlases as a continuous physical boundary around Hungary. Standing on a ridge in the Tatra Mountains, James Bryce (1838–1922) was taken aback to see before him an "undulating land of forest covered hills" no more real than the "Mountains of the Moon" over which one "could see out over the plains into Russia."

The persistent anti-Austrian feelings that had generated sympathy for the Magyar rebels of 1848, whom the British and French associated with romantic notions of liberty and independence, had not yet extended that sympathy to the Slavic peoples, although Georgina Mackenzie (Sebright) and her niece Adeline Irby adopted the cause of the southern Slavs. In the last quarter of the nineteenth century, the gradual political decay of the Habsburg empire and the backward state of its eastern territories led some western travelers to describe their inhabitants in the language of Western colonialism. Andrew Crosse, a firm believer in "self-help" and technological progress, toured the Banat and Transylvania in the 1880s. Crosse compared the Wallachians (Romanians) to "children" who needed guidance and a "firm hand," and he viewed the "contentment" of the Saxons as possibly the first sign of "rottenness" and "the deterioration of a race which does not progress." He described the empire as an anachronistic "hotch-potch of races, so to speak, all in one boat, but ready to do anything rather than pull together." By the end of the century, the unresolved nature of the Eastern question and a growing awareness of the nationalities question led some travelers to regard the heedless gaiety of imperial Vienna as a symptom of the empire's political decay. The robber bands on the Balkan frontiers appeared as a sign of the permeable, fragile nature of the political and cultural boundaries separating internal order from external anarchy.

At the same time, tourists were attracted to Poland and Hungary by the mountains and the Hungarian romances of Mór Jókai (1825–1904), while the lack of amenities testified to the "authenticity" of the traveler's journey. Ellen Browning, Margaret Fletcher, and Nina Elizabeth Mazuchelli (1832–1914), a "Fellow of the Carpathian Society," painted lively, if romanticized, pictures of the Hungarian countryside and its colorful inhabitants. Lion Phillimore, camping in the Carpathians, associated gypsy music with a romantic independence of spirit that transcended territorial borders. Actual encounters with real gypsies and peasants newly returned from America dissolved the magic.

The historian Robert Seton-Watson (1879–1951), traveling in Hungary from 1906 to 1908, found that Hungary's political system was not as liberal as he had thought. His subsequent writings did much to promote interest in the Slavic lands, especially sympathy for the Czechs. After World War I, when the Habsburg empire collapsed into separate states, through the interwar period and the subsequent rise and fall of Communist Eastern Europe, the ghost of the old Habsburg empire continued to haunt travelogues of *Mittel Europa* (Central Europe). Recent travelers have included Patrick Leigh Fermor, Stephen Brook, Dervla Murphy, and Jan Morris, while Claudio Magris's *Danube* retraces the old route to the Bosporus.

JILL STEWARD

## References and Further Reading

Bahr, Hermann, *Dalmatinische Reise*, 1909.

Boner, Charles, *Transylvania: Its Products and Its People*, 1865.

Bovill, W.B. Foster, *Hungary and the Hungarians*, 1908.

Bright, Richard, *Travels from Vienna through Lower Hungary; with Some Remarks on the State of Vienna during the Congress in the Year 1814*, 1818.

Brook, Stephen, *The Double Eagle*, 1988.

Browne, Edward, *Travels in Europe: A Brief Account of Some Travels in Divers Parts of Europe, viz Hungaria, Servia, Bulgaria, Macedonia, Thessaly, Austrian Styria, Carinthia, Carniola and Friuli. As Also Some Observations on the Gold, Silver, Copper and Quick-silver Mines . . . in Those Parts*, 1673; reissued with additions as *An Account of Several Travels through a Great Part of Germany: In Four Journeys*, 1677; with more additions in 1685.

Browning, H. Ellen, *A Girl's Wandering in Hungary*, 1896.

Bryce, James, *Memories of Travel*, 1923.

Clarke, Edward Daniel, *Travels in Various Countries of Europe, Asia and Africa*, vol. 1, 1810.

Coxe, William, *Travels into Poland, Russia, Sweden and Denmark: Interpersed with Historical Relations and Political Inquiries*, 1784.

Crane, Nicholas, *Clear Waters Rising: A Mountain Walk across Europe*, 1996.

Crosse, Andrew F., *Round about the Carpathians*, 1878.

Esmark, Jens, *Kurze Beschreibung einer mineralogischen Reise durch Ungarn, Siebenbürgen und das Banat* [Short Description of a Mineralogical Journey through Hungary, Transylvania, and the Banat], 1798.

Fermor, Patrick Leigh, *A Time of Gifts: On Foot to Constantinople from the Hook of Holland to the Middle Danube*, 1977.

Fermor, Patrick Leigh, *Between the Woods and the Water: On Foot to Constantinople from the Hook of Holland: The Middle Danube to the Iron Gates*, 1986.

Fletcher, Margaret, *Sketches of Life and Character in Hungary*, 1892.

Gerard, Emily, *The Land beyond the Forest: Facts, Figures and Fancies from Transylvania*, 2 vols., 1888.

Granville, A.B., *The Spas of Germany*, 2 vols., 1837.

Hervé, Francis, *A Residence in Greece and Turkey: With Notes of the Journey through Bulgaria, Servia, Hungary and the Balkans*, 1837.

Holman, James, *Travels through Russia, Siberia, Poland, Austria, Saxony, Prussia, Hanover, &c. Undertaken during the Years 1822, 1823, and 1824, while Suffering from Total Blindness, and Comprising an Account of the Author Being Conducted a State Prisoner from the Eastern Parts of Siberia*, 2 vols., 1825.

Hunter, William, *Travels in the Year 1792 through France, Turkey and Hungary to Vienna*, 1796; with additions as *Travels . . . to Which Are Added Several Tours in Hungary in 1799 and 1800 in a Series of Letters to His Sister in England*, 2 vols., 3rd edition, 1803.

Keyssler, Johann Georg, *Neueste Reisen durch Deutschland, Böhmen, Ungarn, die Schweiz, Italien und Löthringen*, 1740; as *Travels through Germany, Bohemia, Hungary, Switzerland, Italy and Lorrain*, 1756.

Köhl, Johann Georg, *Austria: Vienna, Prague, Hungary, Bohemia, and the Danube*, 1843; as *Austria . . . : With Additional Galicia, Styria, Moravia, Bukovina, and the Military Frontiers*, 1843 (condensed from the original five volumes of *Reisen . . .* , 1842).

Mackenzie, Georgina Mary Muir, and Adeline Irby, *Across the Carpathians*, 1862.

Mazuchelli, Nina Elizabeth, *"Magyarland": Being the Narrative of Our Travels through the Highlands and Lowlands of Hungary*, 2 vols., 1881.

M., B.v. *Reise durch Oesterreich nach Konstantinopel und Triest* [Journey through Austria to Constantinople and Trieste], 1839.

Monroe, Will S., *Bohemia and the Czechs: The History, People, Institutions, and the Geography of the Kingdom, Together with Accounts of Moravia and Silesia*, 1910.

Montagu, Lady Mary Wortley, *Letters of the Right Honourable Lady Mary Wortley Montagu: Written during her Travels in Europe, Asia and Africa to Persons of Distinction, Men of Letters etc. in Different Parts of Europe*, 1763, with many revisions.

Morris, Jan, *Trieste and the Meaning of Nowhere*, 2001.

Morritt, John B.S., *The Letters of John. S.B. Morrit of Rokeby, Descriptive of Journeys in Europe and Asia Minor in the Years 1794–1796*, edited by G.E. Marindin, 1914; as *A Grand Tour: Letters and Journeys 1794–96*, with an introduction by Peter J. Hogarth, 1985.

Moryson, Fynes, *An Itinerary Written by Fynes Moryson, Gent, First in the Latin Tongue and Then Translated by Him into English: Containing His Ten Years Travel through the Twelve Dominions of Germany, Behmerland, Switzerland, Netherland, Denmarke, Poland, Italy, Turkey, France, England, Scotland and Ireland*, 1617.

Neale, Adam, *Travels through Some Parts of Germany, Poland, Moldavia and Turkey*, 1818.

Nerval, Gérard de, *Voyage en Orient*, 1851; as *Journey to the Orient*, translated by Norman Glass, 1972.

Novello, Vincent, and Mary Novello, *A Mozart Pilgrimage, Being the Travel Diaries of Vincent and Mary Novello in the Year 1829*, edited by Rosemary Hughes, transcribed and compiled by Nerina Medici di Marignano, 1955.

Paget, John, *Hungary and Transylvania: With Remarks on Their Condition, Social, Political and Economical*, 2 vols., 1839.

Pardoe, Julia, *The City of the Magyar, or Hungary and Her Institutions in 1839–40*, 3 vols., 1840.

Paton, Archibald Andrew, *Travels in Hungary; or, Sketches of the Goth and the Hun: In Transylvania, Debreczin, Pesth, and Vienna, in 1850*, 1851.

Paton, Archibald Andrew, *Researches on the Danube and the Adriatic, or Contributions to the Modern History of Hungary and Transylvania, Dalmatia and Croatia, Servia and Bulgaria*, 1861.

Phillimore, Lion, *In the Carpathians*, 1912.

Quin, Michael J., *A Steam Voyage down the Danube: With Sketches of Hungary, Wallachia, Servia and Turkey etc.*, 2 vols., 1835.

Riesbeck, Johann Kaspar, *Briefe eines reisenden Franzosen über Deutschland an seinen Bruder zu Paris*, 1784; as *Travels through Germany, in a Series of Letters*, translated by the Rev. Maty, 1787.

Salaberry, d'Irumberry, Charles Marie, Marquis de, *Voyage à Constantinople, en Italie, et aux Îles de l'Archipel, par l'Allemagne et la Hongrie*, 1799.

Sartori, Franz, *Neuste Reise durch Oesterreich, ob und unter der Ens, Salzburg, Berchtesgaden, Kärnthen, und Steyermark*, 1811.

Schwigger, Salomon, *Eine neue Reysbeschreibung auss Teutchsland nach Konstaninopel und Jerusalem: Darinn die Gelegenheit derselben Laender/Staedt/Flecken/geben etc. der inwohnenten Voelker Art/Sitten/Gebraech/Trachten/Religion und Gottesdienst etc.*, 1608.

Slade, Adolphus, *Travels in Germany and Russia: Including a Steam Voyage by the Danube and the Euxine from Vienna to Constantinople, in 1838–39*, 1840.

Starke, Mariana, *Travels on the Continent: Written for the Use and Particular Information of Travellers*, 1820; reissued as *Information and Directions for Travellers on the Continent of Europe*, 1824.

Stolberg, Friedrich Leopold, Graf zu, *Reise in Deutschland, der Schweiz, Italien und Sicilien*, 1795; as *Travels through Germany, Switzerland, Italy, and Sicily*, translated by Thomas Holcroft, 2 vols., 1796–1797.

Strand, John, *Germany in 1731*, 2 vols., 1731.

Street, C.J.C., *East of Prague*, 1924.

Suleiman, Susan Rubin, *Budapest Diary: In Search of the Motherbook*, 1996.

Sulzer, Francis Joseph, *Altes und Neues, oder dessen litterarischen Reise durch Siebenbürgen, den Temeswarer Banat, Ungarn, Oesterreich, Bayern, Schwaben, Schweiz und Elsass* [Old and New, or His Literary Journey through Transylvania, Temeswar, the Banat, Hungary, Austria, Bavaria, Swabia, Switzerland and Alsace], 1782.

Tissot, Victor, *Vienne et la vie Viennoise:*, 1878; as *Un Hiver à Vienne: Vienne et la vie Viennoise*, 1878; as *Vienna and the Viennese, Based upon the work of Victor Tissot*, translated with revisions and additions by Maria Horner Landsdale, 1902.

Tissot, Victor, *Voyage au pays des Tziganes, la Hongrie inconnue*, 1880; as *Unknown Hungary*, translated by Mrs. A. Oswald Brodie, 1881.

Tissot, Victor, *La Hongrie de l'Adriatique au Danube: Impressions de voyage* [Hungary from the Adriatic to the Danube], 1883.

Trollope, Frances, *Vienna and the Austrians; with Some Account of a Journey through Swabia, Bavaria, the Tyrol, and the Salzburg*, 1838.

Turnbull, Peter Evan, *Austria: Narrative of Travels*, 2 vols., 1840.

White, Walter, *A July Holiday in Saxony, Bohemia and Silesia*, 1857.

Wilmot, Martha, *More Letters from Martha Wilmot: Impressions of Vienna 1819–1829*, edited by the Marchioness of Londonderry and H.M. Hyde, 1935.

Wraxall, Nathaniel William, *Memoirs of the Courts of Berlin, Dresden, Warsaw and Vienna, in the Years 1777, 1778 and 1779*, 1779.

*See also* **Danube River**

## CHAMPLAIN, SAMUEL DE (1567–1635)

***French Explorer, Geographer, and Administrator***

A man of action with an inordinate amount of energy, Champlain is the true founder of New France. Very little is known about him before his first voyage to Canada in 1603. He himself claimed to have traveled to the West Indies before that date, although it is uncertain whether *Bref Discours des choses plus remarquables que Samuel Champlain de Brouage a reconneues aux Indes occidentales* (*Brief Narrative of the Most Remarkable Things That Samuel de Champlain of Brouage Observed in the West Indies, 1599–1601*) may be attributed to him. Whatever the case may be, the explorer never saw fit to publish the text under his own name. One should therefore be extremely careful when judging its authenticity.

On 15 March 1603, with no official title, Champlain embarked on his first trip to Canada. From Tadoussac to Quebec City, and then on to Hochelaga (Montreal), Champlain followed in Jacques Cartier's steps, displaying remarkable intuition when he guessed the existence of Hudson Bay to the north and was able to get an accurate idea of the Great Lake system to the west. He nonetheless remained convinced that the Asian Sea was not far off and that direct access was from Acadia, rather than from Canada. Moreover, the Sieur de Prévert had expressed the hope that mines could be found in Acadia. For these two reasons, both of which proved groundless, Acadia would be the destination of Champlain's next voyage.

Upon returning to France, Champlain published a narration entitled *Des Sauvages* (*Of Savages*) (1603). In it, he enters into a theological dispute with Tessouat, an Amerindian chief, thus providing a unique source of information on Amerindian mythology. This first narration is clearly a response to the humanist aesthetics of foreign "wonders," which required that readers marvel at the eloquent harangue in praise of the king delivered by a Sagamore grand chief; at the depiction of women and girls who, as they danced, "commencerent à quitter leurs robbes de peaux, & se meirent toutes nuës, monstrans leur nature" (proceeded to cast off their mantles of skins, and stripped themselves stark naked, showing their privities); and at men "qui parlent au diable visiblement" (who speak to the Devil face to face) or who are "du tout monstrueux pour la forme qu'ils ont" (of a perfectly monstrous shape). Such an influence is confirmed at the end of the narration when the traveller describes

> un monstre espouvantable que les sauvages appellent Gougou . . . [de] la forme d'une femme, mais fort effroyable, & d'une telle grandeur, qu'ils me disoient que le bout des mats de nostre vaisseau ne luy fust pas venu jusques à la ceinture.
> (a dreadful monster, which the natives call Gougou . . . it had the form of a woman, but most hideous, and of such a size that according to them the tops of the masts of our vessels would not reach his waist.)
> (*Des Sauvages*, 1603, xiii)

In March 1604, Champlain set sail on the Acadian expedition, commanded by the Protestant Pierre du Gua de Monts. Searching for a site to establish a permanent colony, he explored the Baie Française (Bay of Fundy), discovering within it another bay he named Port-Royal (Annapolis, Nova Scotia), which a year later would become, and would remain, the capital of Acadia. The small island of Sainte-Croix, however, was chosen as the site for the first winter (1604–1605), a choice that proved disastrous because of the cold and scurvy. The next summer, Champlain explored and charted the coastline of what would become New England, sailing as far as Mallebarre (Nauset Harbor). Jean de Biencourt de Poutrincourt, accompanied by, among others, the lawyer and poet Marc Lescarbot, arrived in the course of the summer of 1606. That winter, Champlain created the Ordre de Bon Temps (Order of Good Cheer), a gargantuan corporation of joyful eaters. In the early spring, the revocation of the trade monopoly forced the entire colony to return to France.

Invested for the first time with an official function, Champlain embarked as lieutenant to the Sieur de Monts in April 1608, heading once again for the St. Lawrence, on the banks of which he established, on 3 July, a habitation. According to tradition, this is his first claim to fame: the founding of Quebec City. Over the next two years, he helped the Algonquin, Huron, and Montagnais allies in their wars against the Iroquois. From this point on, his prestige was enormous in the eyes of the Amerindians. He arbitrated their disputes, played the role of peacemaker, and persuaded them to settle near Quebec so they might clear and cultivate the land. They even accepted his idea that no chief might be elected without French approval.

The year 1612 was a turning point: Champlain became lieutenant to New France's viceroy, Charles de Bourbon, who was succeeded by Henry de Bourbon, prince of Condé. The publication of *Les Voyages* (*The Voyages*) (1613) enhanced the explorer's notoriety. At the end of the same year, he published *Quatriesme Voyage* (*The Fourth Voyage*), in which he relates his disappointing expedition to Huron country and how he was deceived by the lies of a certain Nicolas de Vignau, who claimed to have seen Hudson Bay. In 1615, Champlain set out along the Ottawa River to follow the same route, this time going as far as Lake Huron. He took part in an important offensive against the Iroquois, spent the winter in Huron country against his will, and wrote a fascinating description of the land and its inhabitants.

De Monts lost his monopoly at the end of 1608, partially as a result of unsuccessful colonization, and trade was opened up to everyone. In 1614, Champlain created the Company of the Merchants of Rouen, which pledged to support the colony. The agreement, however, was shaky and the competition fierce. In 1618, Champlain convinced the Chamber of Commerce and the king to adopt a vast program of colonization designed to better exploit the riches of New France. The passage to Asia was once again given top priority. Granted a pension of 600 livres, he became the de facto administrator of the colony. In 1619, Champlain published a sequel to *Voyages*, wherein he recounts what were to be his last great exploratory travels between 1615 and 1618. In 1627, at the peak of Champlain's career, he was appointed governor of New France in the absence of Cardinal Richelieu (Louis François Armand de Vignerot du Plessis), who, taking the colony under his personal supervision, created the Compagnie des Cent-Associés (Company of the 100 Associates). Henceforth, trade and commerce no longer depended on two or three towns, but rather on a financial institution in which each of the 100 members had invested 300 livres. It was hoped that this capital would allow for extraordinary development and profits. Such hopes proved to be short-lived, primarily as a result of the war against the English, which, from the outset, pushed the company to the brink of bankruptcy.

One event was to cast a shadow over Champlain's final years. In 1629, he was forced to hand Quebec over to the Kirke brothers (Sir David, the eldest; Sir

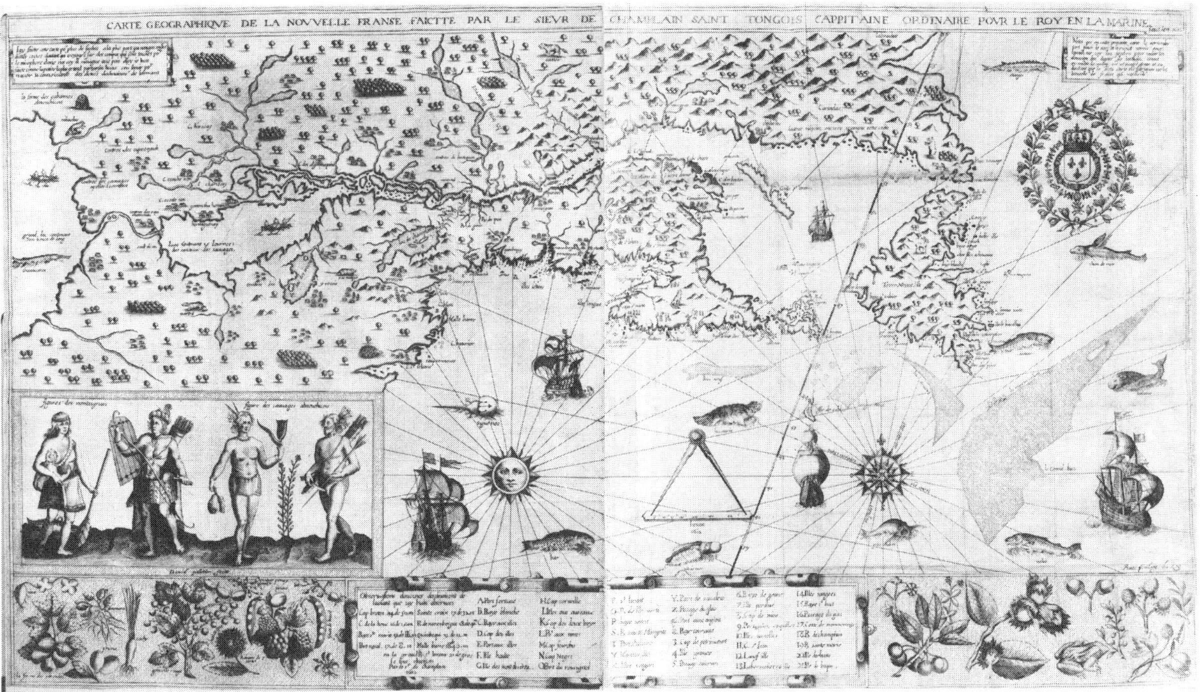

Champlain's 1612 map of eastern Canada ("Nouvelle Franse") records the earliest European knowledge of the Great Lakes region (from *Les Voyages du Sieur de Champlain*, 1613). *Courtesy of British Library, London.*

Lewis; Thomas; John; and James; they were five privateers), to whom he had no choice but to capitulate. Three years later, in 1632, the Treaty of Saint-Germain-en-Laye restored the colony to France. The same year, the complete edition of *Les Voyages de la Nouvelle France* (*The Voyages*, 1632), containing Champlain's travels since 1603, an account of the year 1631, and a "Traitté de la marine" (Treatise on Seamanship), was published.

Returning to Quebec City in 1633, Champlain had a chapel constructed on the point: Notre-Dame-de-la-Recouvrance. He was certainly by no means the devout man portrayed by the Jesuits in their *Relations* (*Narrations*). Indeed, the 1632 edition attributes to the traveler, after the fact, a religious zeal he did not always show. Nonetheless, Champlain's religious convictions were profound. It is noteworthy that the Recollet Order came to New France at his request in 1615. The Jesuits were to follow ten years later. Father Charles Lalemant was at the great explorer's bedside when he died on Christmas Day 1635.

NORMAND DOIRON AND GILLIAN LANE-MERCIER

### Biography

Born in Brouage, in Saintonge (Charente-Maritime), France, c. 1567, to Antoine de Champlain, a captain in the navy, and Marguerite Le Roy. Possibly of noble birth. Appears to have been from a Protestant family. Fought against the League (an ultra-Catholic confederation, also known as the Saint League, which, during the wars of religion, refused to recognize Henry IV as king of France, even after he had abjured the Protestant faith) in the army of Henry IV until 1598. Received honorary title at court of Henry IV. Claimed to have journeyed from Spain to the West Indies. Sailed for Canada, 1603. Crossed the Atlantic 21 times, 1603–1633. Lieutenant to Pierre du Gua de Monts, 1608–1612; to Lieutenant General Charles de Bourbon, count of Soissons, 1612; to Viceroy Henry de Bourbon, prince of Condé, 1612–1620; to Viceroy Henry II, duke of Montmorency, 1620–1625; to Viceroy Henry de Lévis, duke of Ventadour, 1625–1627. Married 12-year-old Hélène Boullé, December 1610. Accompanied to New France once by his wife, 1620. Governor of New France, under the direct authority of Richelieu, 1629–1635. Died of a stroke in Quebec, New France, 25 December 1635.

### References and Further Reading

Champlain, Samuel de, *Des Sauvages*, 1603; edited by Alain Beaulieu and Réal Ouellet, 1993; as *Of Savages*, translated by H.H. Langton, 1922.

Champlain, Samuel de, *Les Voyages du Sieur de Champlain*, 1613; separate parts as *The Voyages, 1613. Book 1, 1604–07*, translated by W.F. Ganong, 1922; *The Voyages, 1613. Book 2, 1608–12*, translated by J. Squair, 1925.

Champlain, Samuel de, *Quatriesme Voyage du Sr de Champlain*, 1613; as *The Fourth Voyage*, translated by J. Squair, 1925.

Champlain, Samuel de, *Voyages et descouvertures faites en la Nouvelle France . . . par le Sieur de Champlain*, 1619; as *The Voyages, 1619*, translated and edited by H.H. Langton and W.F. Ganong, 1929.

Champlain, Samuel de, *Les Voyages de la Nouvelle France occidentale, dicte Canada, faits par le Sr de Champlain . . . avec un Traitté de la Marine*, 1632; separate parts as *The Voyages, 1632. Part 1*, translated by H.H. Langton, 1929–1932; *The Voyages, 1632. Part 2, books 1 and 2*, translated by W.D. LeSueur, 1933; *The Voyages, 1632. Part 2, book 3*, translated by W.D. LeSueur, H.H. Langton, and W.F. Ganong, 1936; *An Account of What Took Place in 1631*, translated by W.D. Le Sueur and H.H. Langton, 1936; *Treatise on Seamanship*, translated by H.H. Langton, 1936.

Champlain, Samuel de [authorship questionable], *Brief Discours des choses plus remarquables que Samuel Champlain de Brouage a reconneues aux Indes Occidentales (1598–1601)*, 1859; as *Brief Narrative of the Most Remarkable Things That Samuel de Champlain of Brouage Observed in the West Indies, 1599–1601*, translated by H.H. Langton, 1922.

Champlain, Samuel de, *Œuvres de Champlain* [Champlain's Works], edited by C.-H. Laverdière, 6 vols., 1870; reedited by Georges-Émile Giguère, 3 vols., 1973.

Champlain, Samuel de, *The Works of Samuel de Champlain*, edited by H.P. Biggar, 6 vols., 1922–1936.

## CHANCELLOR, RICHARD (d. 1556)

***English Navigator, Mathematician, and Astronomer***

Richard Chancellor is one of the more elusive figures of the early Tudor age. There is no modern biography of him, and little is known of his life other than what relates to his voyages. However, Chancellor enjoyed a very high reputation among his contemporaries and made significant contributions to the theory and practice of Tudor navigation. His first western European sighting of Russia had lasting implications for English trade and navigation.

Probably born in Bristol, an important Tudor port, Chancellor spent his early years in the household of Sir Henry Sidney. His tutor was the extraordinary mathematician, astronomer, scholar, imperialist, and adviser to Elizabeth I, Dr. John Dee. Chancellor and Dee became close friends, and the latter regarded his pupil as his intellectual equal—an indication of Chancellor's exceptional abilities. Together, they worked on a new version of the ephemerides for 1553. This was a calendar used for navigation, and it required accurate astronomical data, which were obtained using instruments made by Chancellor. Accurate solar observations were also an essential part of Tudor navigation, and, in 1572, Thomas Digges, who probably worked with Dee and Chancellor on the ephemerides, credited Chancellor with the invention of the diagonal scale on the sailor's quadrant. This innovation made solar observations much easier (see Waters, 1958).

Chancellor's first known voyage was made to Chios, under Roger Bodenham in 1550, although he may have made other voyages before then. Chancellor claimed, for example, to have visited the French court, but there is no record of the visit. Bodenham's voyage was promoted by Sebastian Cabot, and it is first recorded in Richard Hakluyt's *Principal Navigations, Voyages, Traffiques, and Discoveries of the English Nation* (1598–1600). Probably intended as a training mission, it was an eventful voyage. The Levant was under Turkish rule, and a dangerous place for English ships. There were skirmishes with Turkish ships, a flight from Chios, and a militant crew—an eye-opening trip that provided Chancellor with real insights into life at sea. No wonder, then, that Bodenham claimed "all those mariners that were in my sayd shippe . . . for the most part were within five or sixe yeeres after, able to take charge, and did. Richard Chanceller, who first discovered Russia, was with me in that voyage" (Hakluyt, 1598–1600). That Chancellor was in charge of a fleet within two years of his return suggests his remarkable abilities, although he may already have been of a more senior rank than mariner.

The trip on which Chancellor sighted Russia, or Muscovy, took place in 1553–1554. He was pilot to the fleet of three ships and captain of one of them. Investors hoped that he would find a northeast passage to the Moluccas and China, but the search for gold and spices went alongside a desire to find new markets for the export of woolen cloth after the slump in exports in 1550–1552. The voyage itself revealed much about the conditions of Tudor navigation. It took three weeks to sail from Deptford to Yarmouth, from where the fleet was blown back to the Orwell River. They spent a further three weeks on the Suffolk coast waiting for a southerly wind. During that time, much of the food putrefied and the barrels leaked. On their way northward, the three ships were separated by a storm. Under Sir Hugh Willoughby, two ships sailed to "Arzina in Lapland" (Hakluyt, 1598–1600), where they wintered. Unprepared for the hard winter, the crews froze to death. Chancellor's ship made it to Archangel, in Russia, from where Czar Ivan IV invited him to Moscow. Not the least of Chancellor's achievements was the completion of this lengthy journey by sled in winter. At Moscow, Chancellor was received by the czar, to whom he presented letters from Edward VI, and a mutually beneficial trade began.

Chancellor's description of Russia was first published by Richard Hakluyt some 40 years after it was written. It describes the Russian court, the armed forces, the legal system, and Russian religion, but it gives little account of the voyage. It also details the commodities available for trade, such as hemp, flax, wax, furs, and hides. In 1554, Clement Adams also wrote an account of the journey in *Noua Anglorum ad Moscouitas nauigatio* [The New Navigation of the English to Muscovia]. The earliest surviving copy of the text is in Hakluyt's 1589 work, *The Principall Navigations, Voiages, and Discoveries of the English Nation,* but a version also appeared in 1600 in Marius's *Rerum Moscoviticarum auctores varii* [Various Writers on Moscovite Matters]. Reputed to have come from an interview with Chancellor, this account gives more detailed descriptions of the whole voyage, including details of northern Russia.

Chancellor's voyage failed to reach China, but it did open a trade that had far-reaching consequences. It ended the monopoly of the Hanse merchants on English naval materials and in the long term challenged the English Hanse Leaguers' position. The Tudor navy had great demand for Russian cordage, which it regarded as the best available, and a steady trade continued in this and other commodities until the 1590s.

The immediate impact of Chancellor's voyage was the creation of the Muscovy Company, which obtained its charter in 1555. The Muscovy Company organized another voyage to Russia, and this time Chancellor returned from the czar with privileges guaranteeing a monopoly to the company. In 1556, Chancellor returned to Russia again and tried to recover Willoughby's two ships. The combined fleet left Russia in July with a rich cargo and a Russian ambassador on board, but some of the fleet took four months to reach the coast of Scotland, while others were lost on the voyage. On 10 November 1556, Chancellor's ship was driven on to rocks, and he drowned while saving the Russian ambassador. Hakluyt compared his achievements to those of Vasco da Gama, but perhaps Dee provided the most appropriate epitaph when he described him simply as the "incomparable" Richard Chancellor.

MATTHEW DAY

## Biography

Probably born in Bristol, date unknown. Tutored by Dr. John Dee in the household of Sir Henry Sidney, father of Sir Philip Sidney. Visited France. Voyaged to Chios, 1550. Made voyages to Russia, going overland to Moscow from Archangel, 1553–1554, 1555, and 1556. Negotiated trade terms with the Czar, facilitating the establishment of the Muscovy Company, 1555; wrote a brief account of his experience of Russia. Married: two sons. Died in a shipwreck in in Pitsligo Bay, Scotland, 10 November 1556.

### References and Further Reading

Chancellor, Richard, "The Booke of the Great and Mighty Emperor of Russia, and Duke of Moscovia, and of the Dominions Orders and Commodities thereunto Belonging: Drawen by Richard Chanceler," in *The Principal Navigations, Voyages, Traffiques, and Discoveries of the English Nation*, edited by Richard Hakluyt, 3 vols., 1598–1600; 12 vols., 1903–1905.

Waters, David W., *The Art of Navigation in England in Elizabethan and Early Stuart Times*, London: Hollis and Carter, 1958; second edition, Greenwich: National Maritime Museum, 1978.

*See also* **Muscovy Company**

## CHARCOT, JEAN-BAPTISTE (1867–1936) *French Polar Explorer and Oceanographer*

In the history of man's conquest of Antarctica, Jean-Baptiste Charcot's name should be numbered with those of Scott, Amundsen, and Shackleton. "No one has surpassed him and few have equaled him as a leader and as a scientific observer," wrote Edwin Balch, the historian of polar expeditions (1913). With the support of the Académie des Sciences, the Musée d'Histoire Naturelle, and the Société de Géographie (and the national subscription organized by the Parisian newspaper *Le Matin*), Charcot sailed to Antarctica in August 1903 to chart the area between Graham Land and Alexander Island and to collect the scientific data required by his sponsors. Although Charcot and his crew were unable to sail back to France on their ship *Français* (battered by two Antarctic winters) in 1905, the expedition was considered a success because of all the hydrographic, botanical, zoological, and meteorological data they had gathered. Five volumes of scientific research would be published at the state's expense. The imagination of the general public was stirred by the fact that Charcot, reaching the limits of the known territories, had mapped over 1,000 kilometers of the frozen continent. The results of his second Antarctic expedition on *Pourquoi pas?* (1908–1910) were equally impressive. Charcot claimed discovery of an unknown land within the Antarctic Circle (which he named Charcot Land, after his father), mapping in the process some 2,000 kilometers of territory, so accurately that his maps were to be in use for the next 25 years. The data collected during this expedition (with an emphasis on terrestrial magnetism, optics, and the polar ecosystem) would eventually fill 28 volumes.

Charcot's journals of his South Polar expeditions—(*Journal de l'expédition antarctique française, 1903–1905* (1906) and *Le "Pourquoi pas?" dans l'Antarctique . . . 1908–1910*, (1911)—reached a wide public in France and (in the case of the latter) in Britain and northern Europe, where polar expeditions were events of great importance. In these extensive and, at times, didactic journals, very few private or egotistical considerations are to be found. Whether written in the style of a captain's logbook or as an adventure narrative, these journals reveal a man of knowledge and sensibility, gifted with a wonderful command of language.

Charcot's descriptions concern themselves with the coastline of the White Continent, as his two expeditions, despite some occasional travels into the hinterland, were not intended to reach the South Pole itself. Descriptions are more numerous than might be expected (considering the monotonous nature of the polar landscape), because Charcot came to experience a profound attraction exerted on him by Antarctica: "I have felt for a long time now that in the midst of this desolation and death, I had a more vivid sense of delight in my own life. But now I feel that these regions make a kind of religious impression on one" (*Journal de l'expédition antarctique français*).

Years later, Charcot was to publish a book on Christopher Columbus (*Christophe Colomb vu par un marin*, 1928). The ostensible purpose was to make the Italian explorer "better known as a navigator," but one can also sense that Charcot wanted to recapture the exhilaration of exploration, the sense of wonder produced by new lands, in whatever part of the earth: "It was here [just beyond the Antarctic Circle] that the *Herta, Belgica*, and *Français* met the pack-ice, and, driven back by it, had to turn away from land. We are the first to penetrate into this region. The Unknown, the Unforeseen are in front of us. How far can we advance?" (*Le "Pourquoi pas?" dans l'Antarctique*).

There is a human dimension in these journals that reflects most favorably on the captain of the expedition. Charcot was indeed, as Scott called him, "the gentleman of the Pole." Charcot was always prepared to acknowledge the explorations of his predecessors, to give a full account of the scientific work conducted by his subordinates, and to offer generous praise to any member of the crew (cook, carpenter, or stoker) whenever circumstances made them play a crucial part in the success of the expedition. It seems as if Charcot, who had to spend so much time in the crow's nest of his ship looking for navigable channels, adopted a similar perspective in the writing of his journal: "I wish to encourage the utmost initiative in everyone, to direct operations, as it were, from the rear, and, above all, to show that I do not try to monopolize things" (*Le "Pourquoi pas?" dans l'Antarctique*).

Charcot, himself a talented doctor, was keen to study what he termed the "cafard polaire," the polar homesickness that had plagued so many expeditions during the long period of wintering over "when the months pass quickly but the hours are long" (*Le "Pourquoi pas?" dans l'Antarctique*). Charcot's second journal shows how he perfected the strategies adopted during the first expedition. Some aspects of the French national culture here come to the fore. Charcot made sure that, whatever the initial storage difficulties, there would be sufficient wine on board for the sailors to have their "regular rations" with every meal, and that these meals (taken communally) would be of good and palatable food (including fresh seal and penguin meat) so as to prevent tempers having free play and scurvy becoming prevalent.

A well-furnished library was also taken on board (about 1,500 volumes of scientific works, travel books, novels, and plays), and, true to Charcot's republican belief in popular education, he recommended the assiduous reading of the *Dictionnaire Larousse* for the wardroom. The complete files of *Le Matin* and *Le Figaro* for the two years before the departure of the expedition were also available, distributed on the anniversary of their publication. The detailed record of the necessities of ordinary life at the end of the world is not the least interesting or original part in Charcot's journals, particularly when their description is associated with the dangers always facing the expedition.

Charcot would never return to Antarctica, but he frequently sailed to Greenland and Iceland on *Pourquoi pas?* (see *La Mer du Groenland*, 1929). During a storm off the coast of Iceland, in 1936, Charcot and his crew went down with the old ship.

PIERRE DAPRINI

### Biography

Born Jean-Baptiste-Étienne-Auguste Charcot in Neuilly-sur-Seine, near Paris, 15 July 1867. Son of Jean-Martin Charcot, a well-known neurologist. Attended the École Alsacienne, Paris, 1876–1885. Studied medicine and worked at the Salpêtrière Hospital, Paris, 1892–1894. Served as chief of the clinic of the faculty of medicine at the University of Paris, 1896–1898; worked also at the Pasteur Institute from 1897. Married Jeanne Hugo, 1896 (divorced 1905). Developed an interest in sailing during vacations: bought his first boat, a sloop (*Courlis*), 1892; built a three-masted schooner (*Français*) with the considerable inheritance received at the death of his father, 1893). Cruised in the Mediterranean and the Greenland Sea before embarking on Antarctic exploration in *Pourquois pas?*, 1903–1905 and 1908–1910. Published reports of the expeditions as *Journal de l'expédition antarctique française*, 1906, and *Le "Pourquois pas?" dans l'Antarctique*, 1911. Married Marguerite Cléry, 1907. Published *Autour du Pôle sud*, 1912. During World War I, mobilized as a marine doctor in a Cherbourg hospital, 1914–1915, and later as a commander on a whaler with the British Navy, patroling the Hebrides, 1915–1918: awarded the Distinguished Service Cross. Joined the reserve corps of the French Navy after World War I. Led scientific missions for the French Navy in the North Atlantic, 1918–1925; promoted to commander, 1924. Retired from the navy, 1925; acted as *chef de mission* to all the oceanographic studies of the *Pourquoi pas?* in or near the Arctic Circle, 1918–1925. Published a number of oceanographic and geological maps and charts, and also *Christophe Colomb vu par un marin*, 1928. Sailed frequently to Greenland and Iceland on *Pourquois pas?* 1929–1936. Died at sea after *Pourquoi pas?* was wrecked off the Iceland coast, 16 September 1936.

### References and Further Reading


Charcot, Jean-Baptiste, *Expédition antarctique française (1903–1905), commandée par le dr. Jean Charcot. Sciences naturelles: Documents scientifiques*, 5 vols., 1906–1911.

Charcot, Jean-Baptiste, *Journal de l'expédition antarctique française, 1903–1905: Le "Français" au Pôle sud*, 1906.

Charcot, Jean-Baptiste, *Deuxième expédition antarctique française (1908–1910), commandée par le dr. Jean Charcot. Sciences naturelles: Documents scientifiques*, 28 vols., 1911–1921.

Charcot, Jean-Baptiste, *Le "Pourquoi pas?" dans l'Antarctique: Journal de la deuxième expédition au Pôle sud, 1908–1910*, 1911; as *The Voyage of the "Why Not?" in the Antarctic: The Journal of the Second French South Polar Expedition, 1908–1910*, translated by Philip Walsh, 1911.

Charcot, Jean-Baptiste, *De la participation de la marine nationale aux recherches maritimes scientifiques*, 1924.

Charcot, Jean-Baptiste, *Christophe Colomb vu par un marin*, 1928.

Charcot, Jean-Baptiste, *La Mer du Groenland: Croisières du "Pourquoi pas?"* 1929.

Charcot, Jean-Baptiste, *Voyages aux îles Feroë*, 1934.

Balch, Edwin Swift, *The North Pole and Bradley Land*, Philadelphia: Campion, 1913.


## CHARDIN, JEAN (1643–1713) *French Traveler*

Throughout the seventeenth century, many different forms of harassment and encouragement were employed against the Protestants, in an attempt to convert them to Catholicism. These attacks eventually culminated in the Edict of Fontainebleau, or revocation of the Edict of Nantes, in October 1685, which effectively abolished all their rights and precipitated the clandestine flight of about a quarter of the million Protestants then remaining in France.

Chardin was born into a family of Protestant jewelers just at the beginning of the reign of Louis XIV (r. 1643–1715), architect of so many of the problems encountered by the Huguenot minority. It was hardly surprising that Chardin began at a very early age to seek his fortune elsewhere, traveling to Persia for the first time in 1664 with the merchant Raisin in order to sell jewels to the Persian court. They traveled in Persia until 1666, then moved on to Surat in 1667 and elsewhere in India in 1668 before returning to France in the spring of 1670. Barely 15 months after Chardin's return from this successful trip, he determined to set out again, having as he said discovered "que la Religion dans laquelle j'ai été élevé, m'éloignoit de toute sorte d'Emplois; et qu'il falloit, ou en changer, ou renoncer à tout ce qu'on appelle honneurs et avancement" (that the religion in which I was brought up excluded me from many professions, and I either had to change my religion or give up all hope of honors and social success). For indeed, restrictions on the careers that could be pursued by Huguenots had begun to be introduced in 1664, and in the 1670s, the profession of jeweler, like so many others, was barred to them. The contrast with Persia was striking, since there, as Chardin remarked, "sans être pressé de changer de Religion, ni sans sortir aussi de la condition de Marchand, je ne pouvois manquer de remplir une ambition modérée" (without having to rush to change my religion and without having to give up business, I could not fail to achieve some modest ambitions).

Chardin's second journey took him through the Ottoman empire and Georgia to Persia, from Paris (August 1671) to Smyrna (February 1672), Constantinople (March 1672), and on to Qom and Isfahan (June 1672), from where he pursued his travels returning to Europe in 1677. The account that Chardin published in both French and English soon after having returned and settled in England (because of the ongoing religious persecution in France) was immediately considered to be extremely authoritative. Entitled *Journal du voyage du Chevalier Chardin en Perse et aux Indes Orientales par la Mer Noire et par la Colchide*, it was translated into English as *The Travels of Sir John Chardin into Persia and the East Indies*. Thanks to Chardin's previous journey in the 1660s, he spoke Persian, Turkish, and Arabic, which gave him the added advantage of being able to converse with people in their own language and consult local written sources. Indeed, unlike some other travelers (for example, Tavernier or Thévenot), Chardin paid careful attention to the checking of facts. In the preface to the English translation, which appeared in 1686, Chardin remarks that he always tried "to inform my self in all things that were Curious and New to us in Europe, concerning a Country that may well be called, Another World, both in respect of the Distance of place it has from us; and the different Manners and Maximes of it." Chardin goes on to explain that he does not really feel qualified to write about India, since he spent merely five years there and only spoke the "vulgar languages" of Persian and Hindi and, hence, could not converse with the Brahmins!

No believer in Western superiority, Chardin saw Persia as a tolerant society that provided him with opportunities no longer offered by France. A curious, enterprising man, his account is rigorous, moderate, objective, and serious, at once scholarly and full of useful practical information for potential travelers and merchants. Chardin ranges widely over history, economics, politics, and sociology, seeks to avoid value judgments, and emphasizes accuracy and truth, informing potential readers that he is an authority on Persia and can therefore be consulted in all confidence. The account was quickly translated into English (1686), Dutch (1687), and German (1687), and the 1735 edition stretched to four volumes and included numerous high-quality illustrations (maps, portraits, and so on) executed by Joseph Grelot, who traveled with Chardin from Constantinople to Isfahan (although he is never mentioned by Chardin and they are said to have quarreled).

Thought to have been read by writers such as Montesquieu and Rousseau (one is reminded, for example, of the former's *Lettres persanes* (*Persian Letters*) of 1721), Chardin's account stands apart from those of other travelers to the region at this time through its awareness of cultural difference and relativity and in its desire to place accuracy above romanticism.

JOY CHARNLEY

The royal guard setting out from Ispahan (from *Voyages du Chevalier Chardin en Perse . . .*, 1811). *Courtesy of the Stapleton Collection, London.*

## Biography

Born in Paris, 16 November 1643. Son of a Protestant jeweler. Traveled to Persia and India, 1664–1670; stayed at Isfahan at the court of Shah Abbas II. Returned to France, 1670; made a second journey to Persia, traveling through Turkey, the Crimea, and the Caucasus, 1671–1677. Returned to France via India and the Cape of Good Hope, 1677. Forced to flee from religious persecution in France, 1681. Settled in London; ennobled by Charles II, 1681. Married Esther Peigné, a Huguenot refugee (died 1691), 1681: two sons and two daughters. Elected a member of the Royal Society, 1682. Representative of the English East India Company in the Netherlands, 1683–1712. Died near London, 26 January 1713.

### References and Further Reading

Chardin, Jean, *Journal du voyage du Chevalier Chardin en Perse et aux Indes Orientales par la Mer Noire et par la Colchide*, 1686; as *The Travels of Sir John Chardin into Persia and the East Indies*, 1686; as *Voyages de M. le Chevalier Chardin en Perse et autres lieux de l'Orient*, 3 vols., 1711; as *Voyages du Chevalier Chardin en Perse et autres lieux de l'Orient*, 4 vols., 1735, and 10 vols., 1811; as *Voyage de Paris à Ispahan*, edited by Stéphane Yerasimos (based on the 1811 edition), 2 vols., 1983.

## CHATEAUBRIAND, VICOMTE DE, FRANÇOIS-RENÉ (1768–1848) *French Author and Politician*

François-René, the tenth child of the count of Chateaubriand, was born into the French aristocracy just in time to see the Revolution deprive the nobles of their hereditary privileges. Faced with a need to make his fortune, Chateaubriand embarked for America in 1791, persuaded that he would be the one to discover the fabled Northwest Passage.

This trip to America illustrates the hazards of travel in the late eighteenth century. The ship that departed from Saint-Malo for the island of Saint Pierre in Canada was blown so far off course by an Atlantic storm that their first stop was the Azores, where they waited for the ship to be repaired. Finally reaching Canada and descending the east coast to Baltimore, Chateaubriand disembarked after three months of travel. He spent five months in America, going up the Hudson and across what was then the wilderness of New York State to Niagara Falls. Hurt in a fall and nursed back to health by local natives, Chateaubriand abandoned his quest for the Northwest Passage. After descending the Ohio River, he encountered a settler who had a New York newspaper, already weeks old, that announced the flight of Louis XVI and his recapture.

Realizing how dangerous things had become for his family, Chateaubriand hastened home, the return voyage taking less than a month, where he fought against the Revolution and eventually went into exile in England. Meanwhile, he composed his short novel, *Atala* (1801), the story of a Native American princess in America doomed to an early death by the conflict between a Christian religious vow and her love for Chactas. *Atala* contains many descriptions of America, but Chateaubriand drew these less from his own experiences, though the final scene does take place near Niagara Falls, than from other published travel narratives of the time. Chateaubriand would revisit these travels, however, in *Les Natchez* (*The Natchez*, 1826), *Voyage en Amérique* (*Travels in America*, 1827), and his autobiographical *Mémoires d'outre-tombe* [Memoirs from Beyond the Grave] (1849–1850).

In 1806, Chateaubriand set out on his second major trip, this time to the Mediterranean. Visiting Greece, Constantinople, the Holy Land, Egypt, Tunisia, and Spain, Chateaubriand followed a route that would become increasingly popular with French travelers, many of them guided by his published narrative, *Itinéraire de Paris à Jérusalem ...* (1811; *Travels in Greece, Palestine, Egypt and Barbary*, 1812).

The two trips exhibit major contrasts. Chateaubriand went to America as a young man with meager funds; more affluent by the time he reached Greece, Chateaubriand bought, or simply stole, fragments of antiquities to take home, and in Jerusalem, he and his servants rode about heavily armed and in French dress. This show of force may have been necessary, as he points out that while the beginnings of a tourist trade could be found in Greece, in the Holy Land travelers were in constant danger of being robbed. In Chateaubriand's *Itinéraire*, he repeatedly asserts the superiority of Europeans over the natives. He sees the latter as having fallen off from the greatness of classical times and presenting an impediment to his quest for the relics of antiquity. Chateaubriand also felt that his decisions should prevail. En route to Constantinople, Chateaubriand wanted to visit the site of Troy and threatened legal action against his guide, who refused to take him into the area merely because war had broken out.

European influence could not open all doors. Similarly, in Egypt, Chateaubriand was unable to visit the pyramids, because he had arrived at the season of the Nile floods. As Chateaubriand left Egypt, however, he commissioned a friend to carve his name on the monuments as soon as the water had receded. A major purpose of the pyramids seemed to be, in his mind, recording the visits of European travelers.

Another contrast between the two trips lay in the differences between visiting a land that was thinly settled and little known to Europeans and countries that were long settled and documented in classical texts. Chateaubriand went to America with few preconceptions beyond the vague hope of finding the Northwest Passage. In Greece, he experienced a different disappointment. He had set out for the East in part to collect imagery that might illustrate his epic, *Les Martyrs* (*The Martyrs*). By the time Chateaubriand reached Jerusalem, he took satisfaction from documenting camels and palm trees, features of the region that would not have changed with the centuries. But in Greece, he found in the poor shepherds no adequate echo of his vision of the heroes of antiquity.

Paradoxes dominate Chateaubriand's narrative. While he eagerly collected souvenirs, he decried the Europeans' wholesale removal of artifacts and the Turkish occupation of Greece that wiped out monuments during the fighting. The principal contrasts come from the failure of the peoples of the lands visited to correspond to their literary models. Chateaubriand describes the filthy lodgings and bad food he encountered in Greece, noting that this was at the same place where the *Odyssey* described sumptuous hospitality.

On the one hand, Chateaubriand resolved to publish his travel journal so that those fatigued by Europe's revolutions and industrial pollution could find ease in the brilliant Mediterranean sunlight. But on the other, he concludes that the gods no longer live on Olympus. Approaching Constantinople, Chateaubriand records scenes worthy of the *Thousand and One Nights* but characterizes the people of the city as a herd of persecuted beasts. In Egypt, when literary associations did not come so readily to mind, Chateaubriand described a row of palm trees as resembling the regular plantings around a French chateau, but he noted that there nature must provide this element of civilization in a country that had returned to barbarism.

Chateaubriand raises the question of how well the traveler should get to know the lands he visits. Conditions of travel were changing rapidly, and Chateaubriand was helping the French to learn of exotic countries, both through his writings and through the numerous messages he was to bring back to France. The extensive hospitality Chateaubriand received, from the monastery where he lodged in Jerusalem to the family with whom he stayed for six weeks in Tunis, obliged him to help with communications but also gave him ideal opportunities to observe. Chateaubriand would later write, however, that he pitied travelers who would come after him, because for them these countries would no longer have secrets. He recalled with nostalgia his experience in the wilds of America but concluded that this was an appropriate adventure for a man of 20. With age and with time, mystery fades and with it a compellingly attractive ideal.

DOROTHY M. BETZ

## Biography

Born in Saint-Malo, Brittany, 4 September 1768. Studied at the Collège de Dol, and in Rennes, 1781–1782; attended the naval school in Brest, 1783. Lieutenant in the regiment of Navarre, 1786. Lived in Paris during the early days of the Revolution; sailed to America, April 1791. Returned to France, January 1792; married Céleste Buisson de la Vigne, February 1792. Went into exile in England; lived in London and Suffolk, 1793–1800. Published *Essai historique, politique, et moral sur les révolutions anciennes et modernes*, 1797. Returned to France, 1800; worked as a freelance journalist; published *Atala*, 1801. Met Juliette (Madame) Récamier in 1801 and developed long-standing relationship with her. Appointed secretary to the French embassy in Rome by Napoleon Bonaparte, 1803; resigned, 1804. Traveled to the Middle East, Greece, Constantinople, Jerusalem, and Egypt, 1806. Elected to the Académie Française, 1811; created viscount and member of the House of Peers, 1815. Ambassador to Berlin, 1821, and to London, 1822. Represented France at the Congress of Verona, 1822; minister for foreign affairs, 1822–1824. Ambassador to Rome, 1828–1829. After the July Revolution of 1830, he retired to his house in Paris and edited his memoirs (*Mémoires d'outre-tombe*) for posthumous publication (1849–1850). Died in Paris, 4 July 1848.

## References and Further Reading

Chateaubriand, Vicomte de, François-René, *Atala*, 1801.

Chateaubriand, Vicomte de, François-René, *René*, 1802.

Chateaubriand, Vicomte de, François-René, *Itinéraire de Paris à Jérusalem et de Jérusalem à Paris*, 3 vols., 1811; as *Travels in Greece, Palestine, Egypt and Barbary*, 2 vols., 1812.

Chateaubriand, Vicomte de, François-René, *Les Aventures du dernier Abencérage*, 1826; as *The Adventures of the Last Abencerrage*, translated by H.W. Carter, 1870.

Chateaubriand, Vicomte de, François-René, *Les Natchez*, 1826; as *The Natchez*, 1827.

Chateaubriand, Vicomte de, François-René, *Voyage en Amérique, Voyage en Italie*, 2 vols., 1827; as *Travels in America and Italy*, 2 vols., 1828.

Chateaubriand, Vicomte de, François-René, *Mémoires d'outre-tombe* [Memoirs from Beyond the Grave], 1849–1850; as *The Memoirs of Chateaubriand*, translated by Robert Baldick, 1961.

# CHATWIN, BRUCE (1940–1989) *British Travel Writer and Novelist*

Bruce Chatwin was born into a middle-class family, and his early childhood featured frequent displacement, as his mother visited other family members while his father served in the British Navy. An early career at Sotheby's earned Chatwin a reputation for having a good eye for valuable pieces, but he left, claiming to dislike the pretense and ostentation of the art world. Chatwin had already traveled widely in Europe, Africa, and the United States, including a journey to Afghanistan in the footsteps of Robert Byron, whom he admired greatly. He drew on both his childhood and his experiences at Sotheby's in several semiautobiographical pieces.

After studying at Edinburgh University and working at the *Sunday Times*, Chatwin left for South America, apparently sending his editor the telegram "Gone to Patagonia." The trip resulted in Chatwin's first book, *In Patagonia* (1977). Nearly contemporary with Paul Theroux's *The Old Patagonian Express*, it is credited with contributing to a renewed interest in the genre of travel writing. It is presented in short numbered sections, and it features a sparse prose style. As well as describing Chatwin's experiences on a journey from Buenos Aires to Punta Arenas, *In Patagonia* follows thematic concerns with little regard for a linearity of travel or narrative. Chatwin hitched and caught buses, but the passages describing travel are mostly of travel on foot; the book initiated Chatwin's reputation as a prodigious walker. Interweaving travel accounts with "literary traveling," the book is ostensibly a quest in the footsteps of Chatwin's great-uncle, and it includes writing about The Wild Bunch, indigenous Patagonians, previous explorers in Patagonia, and the texts that they produced. *In Patagonia* won the Hawthornden Prize and the E.M. Forster Award.

Chatwin continued to produce journalistic pieces, but he was now a full-time writer. His second work, *The Viceroy of Ouidah* (1980), was less well received. The narrative follows the life of a Brazilian slave-trader in Ouidah in the eighteenth and nineteenth centuries. Again difficult to classify, it was based on a mixture of travel and research. Chatwin had traveled to Benin and Brazil; a trip to the former also resulted in the short piece "A Coup," which was featured in *Granta*, a regular showcase for Chatwin's work. A third book, *On the Black Hill* (1982), received critical acclaim. The narrative draws on the experiences of Chatwin's childhood holidays in Wales and provides a contrast with the narratives of travel. *The Viceroy of Ouidah* and *On the Black Hill*, as well as *Utz*, demonstrate the capacity of Chatwin's style for encompassing an expansive time frame in carefully structured episodic scenes. A spare, elliptical prose had by now become Chatwin's trademark, clearly influenced by Flaubert, Maupassant, Babel, and Hemingway.

With *The Songlines* (1987), Chatwin achieved his greatest popular success. A "novel of ideas," the narrative is set in Australia and focuses on the Aboriginal "dreaming tracks" as a metaphor for human cultural identity. The novel proposes that walking is an essential human need, and it criticizes by implication the sedentary materialist nature of late-twentieth-century Western culture. Chatwin's own travel is to the fore, emphasizing the range of his experience, and especially of his walking, but as well as travel narrative based on his visits to urban and outback Australia, the fictional narrative features excerpts from his notebooks. These include literary and philosophical quotations as well as ethnographic and archaeological arguments to support Chatwin's thesis of nomadism. The book, despite being heavily criticized by land-rights activists in Australia and skeptical critics elsewhere, was a huge success, appealing to the taste for New Age philosophy, backpacking, and alternative lifestyles.

Despite Chatwin's marriage to Elizabeth Chanler in 1965, he pursued several homosexual relationships during the course of his travels, and he was by this time seriously ill from the effects of being HIV positive. Chatwin became unable to travel, but he continued to write, producing *Utz* (1988), a short but well-crafted novel about a collector of Meissen porcelain living in Cold War Prague. Chatwin had frequently traveled in Eastern Europe, and he drew on his knowledge of the art world as well as Communist Czechoslovakia to produce a convincing yet sympathetic portrait of the collector, who also visits France, again a favorite destination of Chatwin's. *Utz*, like his other work, is more than just travel account, combining fiction, travel, and other themes, from the history of porcelain to creation myths. Although short-listed, the novel failed to win the Booker Prize. Chatwin died having just completed the collection of short stories and journalistic pieces *What Am I Doing Here* (1989). This collection enhanced his reputation, the shorter pieces being well suited to his style. They reveal the extent of Chatwin's travel in India, China, and the United States, as well as the places described in his longer works.

Since Chatwin's death, his reputation as a stylist has grown, although biographical work on him has revealed a very different character from the one presented to the public during his lifetime. A compulsive storyteller and self-mythologizer, Chatwin appeared to typify an image of the self-sufficient modern-day nomad. To this, he added idiosyncratic preoccupations and a store of esoteric knowledge; he seemed to be as comfortable in London literary society as in a Bedouin tent. Chatwin is best known for travel in South America and Australia, but his travels ranged wider than that and, like the expression they found in his work, were invariably driven by a quest for cultural or historical knowledge. His works are read enthusiastically, including the posthumous *Anatomy of Restlessness* (1996), containing previously uncollected pieces, *Photographs and Notebooks* (1993), and *Winding Paths* (1999), another collection of photographs. The attention paid to Chatwin's reputation and public image does not detract from the fact that he wrote highly original travel novels in an unmistakable style, which helped to raise the profile of travel writing in the late 1970s and the 1980s.

Kerry Featherstone

## Biography

Born Charles Bruce Chatwin in Sheffield, Yorkshire, 13 May 1940. Son of a prominent solicitor who later became a naval officer. Traveled widely as a child. Educated at Marlborough College, 1953–1958. Worked at Sotheby's, London, 1958–1966; director, impressionist art department, from 1965. Married Elizabeth Chanler, 1965. Studied archaeology at Edinburgh University, 1966–1969. Arts consultant to the *Sunday Times*, 1972–1975. Published five full-length books, many pieces of journalism, and one collection of short pieces, 1977–1989. Traveled to Afghanistan, India, West and East Africa, the United States, Eastern and Western Europe, and South America. Awarded Hawthornden Prize, Somerset Maugham Award, and E.M. Forster Award of the American Academy of Arts and Letters, 1978, for *In Patagonia;* Whitbread First Novel Award, 1982, for *On the Black Hill.* Died of AIDS near Grasse, France, 18 January 1989.

### References and Further Reading

Chatwin, Bruce, *In Patagonia*, 1977.
Chatwin, Bruce, *The Viceroy of Ouidah*, 1980.
Chatwin, Bruce, with Paul Theroux, *Patagonia Revisited*, 1986; as *Nowhere Is a Place: Travels in Patagonia*, 1992.
Chatwin, Bruce, *The Songlines*, 1987.
Chatwin, Bruce, *Utz*, 1988.
Chatwin, Bruce, *What Am I Doing Here*, 1989.
Chatwin, Bruce, *Bruce Chatwin: Photographs and Notebooks*, 1993; as *Far Journeys: Photographs and Notebooks*, 1993.
Chatwin, Bruce, *Anatomy of Restlessness: Selected Writings, 1969–89*, edited by Jan Borm and Matthew Graves, 1996.
Chatwin, Bruce, *Winding Paths: Photographs by Bruce Chatwin*, 1999.

## CHAUCER, GEOFFREY (c. 1340–1400)

### *English Poet and Prose Writer*

Archival records prove that Geoffrey Chaucer traveled extensively in war, on the king's business, and perhaps on pilgrimage. Historical data never mention his writings, however, and those writings never mention Chaucer's own travels. To describe him as a travel writer, therefore, is to acknowledge his genius for adapting travel-related genres of traditional literature at a key moment in the linguistic and sociopolitical history of England.

Most prominently, Chaucer transformed a Latin literary convention familiar from Ovid's *Metamorphoses*, the story collection, which he found being revitalized in the vernacular during his travels around Italy. Chaucer's busy life in government service precluded completion of the innovative work that presents a story collection within a frame story of pilgrimage travel: the *Canterbury Tales*. Chaucer also broke new ground to create the general prologue, an adaptation of "estates literature" describing occupations. It introduces those Canterbury pilgrims who frequently travel, such as the Knight and Wife of Bath, alongside those who seldom do, such as the Franklin and Prioress. Some veteran voyagers in the group, such as the Shipman, tell stories with travel as a plot element; other professional travelers, such as the Merchant, tell different kinds of tales.

In other works besides *Canterbury Tales*, likewise, Chaucer was exploring and transforming the range of oral and literary genres available to him. In order to position him as travel writer, it is useful to set up distinctions regarding his sources. Chaucer's writings served as a vortex for Judeo-Christian and Greco-Roman traditions of travel narrative divisible into three overlapping categories: military expeditions, searches for something or some place on this earth, and imagined travel to another world.

Chaucer regarded himself as an adapter of Greco-Roman literature, not of the Judeo-Christian sacred text. Yet travel-related themes from the Hebrew Bible and the New Testament permeate medieval European literature. In the former text, which Christians retitled the Old Testament, various wars cause the Jewish people to wander homeless in search of the Promised Land, which has both geographical and metaphorical dimensions. The New Testament instead encourages centrifugal travel: although Jesus himself stayed quite close to his birthplace, he urged his followers to spread the word to all nations. In addition, the Christian canon came to include the Revelation, during which John of Patmos experienced dream-vision travel to a heavenly Jerusalem.

Analogous dreams of the afterlife conclude Plato's *Republic* and Cicero's derivative *De re publica*, influencing the early Christian theologians who assembled a sacred canon. Chaucer knew about the visionary travel in Cicero's work via Macrobius's fifth-century commentary on it. He also knew various intermediaries such as the thirteenth-century French *Romance of the Rose* and the *Divine Comedy* of Dante Alighieri, having encountered the latter work only while traveling in Italy. Prior to *Canterbury Tales*, with one exception, Chaucer's major poems all incorporate a first-person narrator's dream-vision travel to another world: *Book of the Duchess*, the unfinished *House of Fame, Parliament of Fowls*, and the prologue to the unfinished *Legend of Good Women.*

Among works composed before the collection of *Canterbury Tales*, that one exception, *Troilus and Criseyde*, features a first-person narrator who is not dreaming but writing. He waxes distraught at his duty to retell the sad story of a Trojan prince's love for a war widow. In the poem, Criseyde returns Troilus's affection until political negotiations force her to join her father, who has absconded to the Greek side, knowing as do we and the narrator that Troy will fall. In the *Knight's Tale* too, Chaucer depicts emotion-drenched situations caused by the dislocations of military travel. The two oldest epics in the European tradition tell of Greek armies away from home, fighting on foreign shores and thereafter trying to return. Chaucer's education included Latin reworkings of those two epics but also, most extensively, Virgil's *Aeneid*—in which books 1–6 relate Aeneas's *Odyssey*-like search for a new home for the Trojan people, and books 7–12 his *Iliad*-like battles to remove the inhabitants from the future site of Rome. Chaucer took the plots of his two major war stories quite directly from Boccaccio's vernacular versions, however, which he encountered during travel to Italy on the king's business.

Thus, the classically based *Troilus and Criseyde* and *Knight's Tale*, as is also the case for Chaucer's other works with Italian precedents, were created as a side effect of the fourteenth-century English kings' efforts to acquire allies or avoid making additional enemies in their futile attempt to conquer France. The literary traditions of France, in contrast, had long dominated England. Overall, most of Chaucer's writings have French stylistic and generic ancestry. Even stories with no extant analogues probably came to his ears from French-speaking Irish or Breton storytellers at court.

Within *Canterbury Tales*, many stories evoke two French genres that involve travel. In the fabliaux, travel may provide plot elements by sending husbands out of town (*Miller's Tale, Shipman's Tale*) or by bringing lusty young men to occupied beds (*Reeve's Tale*). Travel is more central to works classifiable within the more problematic category romance, a genre traceable to Greek descendants of the *Odyssey*. In France after 1066, the wandering protagonists were no longer warriors trying to return home but, instead, landless knights in quest of some damsel in distress who happened to be sole heir to her father's land. Like Aeneas, therefore, a romance hero would travel in search of some unknown place that might become his home. A number of the *Canterbury Tales* and their themes reflect the kaleidoscopic worlds of the romance: the unfinished *Squire's Tale*, the parodic *Tale of Sir Thopas*, the young men's search for Death in the *Pardoner's Tale*, the problems created when a husband travels in the *Franklin's Tale* and when Christian is sent to marry Muslim in the *Man of Law's Tale*, the quest in the *Wife of Bath's Tale* to discover what women most desire, and indeed that tale-teller's expansive account of her own ongoing search for someone to give her what she most desires.

Readers of English literature have perhaps most desired, these six centuries, that Chaucer's life had allowed less time for travel on the king's business and more time to finish his writings. Yet the open-endedness of his work has kept readers and writers on quests of their own ever since, exploring new and old ideas along pathways blazed by their constantly metamorphosing and fearless leader.

Betsy Bowden

### Biography

Probably born in London, c. 1340, son of John Chaucer, London vintner and deputy to the king's butler. Perhaps studied at a school in Southampton, 1347–1349, and Almonry Cathedral School, London. Served in the household of Elizabeth, countess of Ulster, 1357, and in King Edward III's army, 1359–1360 and 1366–1374; attached to the royal household, under the patronage of John of Gaunt (later his brother-in-law), from 1360. Perhaps studied law at the Inner Temple, London, early 1360s. Traveled extensively around England and France on diplomatic business, made two trips to Italy and perhaps a visit to Santiago de Compostela, Spain, 1366–1378. Married Philippa, daughter of Payne [Paon] de Roet, c. 1366 (died c. 1387): probably two sons, two daughters. Received annuity for life as yeoman of the king, 1367; king's esquire, 1368. Possible visit to Canterbury during Jubilee, 1370. Comptroller of customs, 1374–1386, traveling several times to France "on secret business of the king" and again to Italy. Clerk (steward) of the royal palaces at Eltham, Kent, and Sheen, Surrey, from 1385. Lived mainly at the royal manor in West Greenwich, 1385–1399, and also in Kent. Government service in Kent, including service as justice of the peace, 1385–1388, and knight of the shire (member of Parliament) for the county of Kent, 1386. Final journey to France authorized 5 July 1387. Clerk of the king's works, 1389–1391. Worked on *Canterbury Tales*, 1390s; unfinished at his death. Subforester of the king's park, North Petherton, Somerset, 1391–1399. Final journey around England on the king's business authorized May 1398. Leased a house in the garden of Westminster Abbey, 1399. Died sometime after 5 June 1400.

### References and Further Reading

Chaucer, Geoffrey, *The Riverside Chaucer*, 3rd edition, edited by Larry D. Benson, 1987.

*See also* **Pilgrimage, Christian**

## CHEKHOV, ANTON (1860–1904) *Russian Dramatist, Novelist, Short-Story Writer, and Traveler*

Anton Pavlovich Chekhov was born on 29 January 1860 in Taganrog, southern Russia, a city situated on the Azov Sea. It was a busy port for foreign travel, and this, together with Chekhov's avid reading of the newspapers, which were full of articles about famous travelers—Livingstone and Stanley, for example, and the Russian explorers Micklucho-Maklai and Przhevalskii—fostered in him a keen interest in travel and literature. At Moscow Medical University in 1879–1884, Chekhov studied the works of Darwin, in particular *The Voyage of the Beagle*, which influenced Chekhov's *Ostrov Sakhalin* (*The Island: A Journey to Sakhalin*): both have the same division of the text by chapters with special names, and both integrate scientific and statistical materials with descriptions of nature and the life of the natives.

Chekhov's interest in travel literature influenced his works from the beginning. Starting his literary career as a humorist, he wrote a parody of Jules Verne's novel *Le Docteur Ox* (1874). After the death of Przhevalskii, Chekhov wrote a long article about him, in which he stated that one Przhevalskii or one Stanley was worth ten institutes and 100 good books. These devoted explorers spread "the good disease of heroism." Chekhov himself traveled all over Russia in his youth. He almost never kept diaries: most of his impressions are in letters to his family and friends, and these have been published in editions of his complete works.

Chekhov traveled nearly every year. In 1887, he went from Moscow to Taganrog, where he had not been for eight years, and was to use aspects of this journey in his story "Steppe" (1888). In 1888, Chekhov went to the Ukraine, Crimea, and Caucasus, and the impressions from this journey gave him the idea for his story "Duel" (1891). In 1889, he returned to the Crimea, where he spent some time in Yalta, working on *The Dull Story*. In 1890, Chekhov undertook his longest journey—from Moscow through Siberia to Sakhalin, then via the southern seas, the Suez Canal, and the Black Sea back to Moscow. The following year, Chekhov went for the first time to western Europe—Austria, Italy, and France—traveling with his friends, the writers Gippius, Merezhkovskii, and Suvorin. The main impressions were made by Venice and Rome and by the fact that he lost 900 francs playing roulette in the casino in Monte Carlo. In 1892, Chekhov went to the central Russian districts of Voronezh and Nizhniy Novgorod to help the peasants, who were suffering from hunger. In 1894, he went from Taganrog to the Crimea and then to Italy, France, and Germany. He spent the winter of 1897–1898 in the south of France. From 1898, Chekhov lived in Yalta, in the Crimea, a healthy location for sufferers from bronchial diseases, because he had contracted tuberculosis.

In 1899, Chekhov undertook the most romantic trip of his life: he went to the northern Caucasus to meet the woman who was to become his wife—the famous Russian actress Olga Knipper, whom he married in 1901. In 1900, he traveled to the Caucasus together with the writer Maxim Gorkii and the painter V. Vasnetzov.

In 1902, Chekhov traveled twice: first to Italy, then, as a postponed honeymoon with his wife, by ship along the Volga and its tributary the Kama River. By this time, Chekhov was suffering from serious health problems. In 1902, he undertook a journey to the Urals, where the main estates and factories of S. Morozov (the sponsor of the Moscow Art Theatre, in which Olga Knipper was the principal actress) were located.

In 1904, Chekhov visited Germany and went to the health resort of Badenweiler. Chekhov died there on 15 July, and his body was taken back to Russia by his wife, who had been with him throughout. He was buried in Moscow.

In his works, Chekhov describes many characters whom he met during his trips—priests, officers, merchants, sailors, peasants, prisoners, and so forth. His play *The Three Sisters* contains traces of his journey to Siberia, in the company of young officers. His Siberian and Sakhalin impressions were written as a series of articles for the St. Petersburg newspaper *Novoe Vremya* [New Time]. *Ostrov Sakhalin* was published in Moscow in 1895. There were different reasons for this long journey; the best analysis of them is in Rayfield (1975). These include Chekhov's dissatisfaction with the absence of any serious public activity in his life, his personal disillusionment as a writer, his own religious beliefs, and his desire to be an explorer like Stanley or Przhevalskii. The human aspect was also very important; Chekhov wanted to show the real face of the czarist prisons in Siberia and Sakhalin. After *Ostrov Sakhalin* was published, a special committee was sent to Sakhalin, and the conditions of the prisoners improved slightly as a result.

Chekhov's letters and essays as collected in *From Siberia* contain much information about his travels in this vast and largely uninhabited region, where cities such as Irkutsk, with museums, theaters, orchestras, and good hotels, were extremely rare. Chekhov thought he had the same feelings about this journey as the traveler from Dante's *Divine Comedy*, who was sent to hell because of his lust for travel to the unknown. These thoughts sadly became a prophecy: after Sakhalin, Chekhov developed the tuberculosis that finally killed him. Thoughts about hell can be found in his descriptions of Sakhalin's prisons, its fires, and the suffering of women and children and in his stories about the native population of Sakhalin, the Ainu, who were rapidly disappearing. Chekhov traveled by foot, on horseback, and by boat throughout the island and, in effect, conducted a census, making record cards for more than 10,000 people. Thanks to that, and to the detailed descriptions of the ecology, fishing, agriculture, health service, and other aspects of the island's life, *Ostrov Sakhalin* has become a classic of travel literature. Chekhov spent three months on the island itself, and this, together with the time for the journey to and from Sakhalin, meant that he was away for eight months, from April to December 1890. In the course of Chekhov's return by sea, calling at Hong Kong and Singapore, he had the chance to compare Russian and British colonial policy, and, astonished to discover efficient railways, beautiful gardens, and so on, he decided that British colonial administration was superior. Vivid impressions from Chekhov's trip across the Indian Ocean appeared in the story "Gusev." The publication of *Ostrov Sakhalin* stimulated many other Russian writers to visit the Far East.

Chekhov had the desire to travel all his life. He had plans to go to Africa and America, and when the Russian war with Japan started in 1904, he even volunteered as a doctor in Manchuria. Chekhov's plans were interrupted by his early death in 1904 at the age of only 44.

GENNADY SHELUGIN
*translated by Olga Stone*

### Biography

Born in Taganrog, Russia, 29 January 1860. Attended a school for Greek boys, Taganrog, 1867–1868; Taganrog grammar school, 1868–1879; Moscow University Medical School, 1879–1884. Practiced medicine in Moscow, 1884–1892; traveled to the penal settlement on the island of Sakhalin, 1890; published a study of social and economic conditions there as *Ostrov Sakhalin* (*The Island: A Journey to Sakhalin*), 1895. Worked in Melikhov, 1892–1899, and in Yalta from 1899. Married the actress Olga Knipper, 1901. Traveled extensively across Siberia and through the Ukraine, the Caucasus, western Europe, and Asia. Published, among others, the plays *Uncle Vanya*, 1896, and *The Cherry Orchard*, 1904. Suffered from tuberculosis from 1890s; lived as a semi-invalid after a severe hemorrhage of the lungs, 1897. Awarded the Pushkin Prize, 1888. Member of the Imperial Academy of Sciences, 1900 (resigned, 1902). Died of tuberculosis in Badenweiler, Germany, 15 July 1904.

### References and Further Reading

Chekhov, Anton, "Steppe," 1888; in *The Steppe and Other Stories*, edited and translated by Ronald Hingley, 1991.

Chekhov, Anton, "Gusev," 1890; translated in *A Doctor's Visit: Short Stories*, edited by Tobias Wolff, 1988.

Chekhov, Anton, *Ostrov Sakhalin*, 1895; as *The Island: A Journey to Sakhalin*, translated by Luba Terpak and Michael Terpak, 1967; as *A Journey to Sakhalin*, translated by Brian Reeve, 1993.

Chekhov, Anton, *Letters of Anton Chekhov*, translated by Michael Henry Heim and Simon Karlinsky, 1973; as *Anton Chekhov's Life and Thought: Selected Letters and Commentary*, 1975.

Chekhov, Anton, *Letters of Anton Chekhov*, edited by Avrahm Yarmolinsky, 1973.

Chekhov, Anton, *Anton Chekhov: A Life in Letters*, translated and edited by Gordon McVay, 1994.

Rayfield, Donald, *Chekhov: The Evolution of His Art*, London: Elek, and New York: Barnes and Noble, 1975.

## CHERRY-GARRARD, APSLEY (1886–1959) *British Explorer and Writer*

Apsley Cherry-Garrard was a survivor of the fateful Scott expedition to Antarctica, which he described in *The Worst Journey in the World: Antarctic 1910–1913* (1922). Heir to two landed English families and son of a major-general in British India, Cherry-Garrard read classics and modern history at Oxford, where, despite extreme myopia, he rowed bow for the university crew. After meeting Scott's chief of scientific staff, Edward Wilson, at a hunting party, Cherry-Garrard joined their entourage at 24 as an assistant zoologist, an appointment reflecting the mission's determination to advance natural science as well as claim the South Pole for England.

In keeping with the gentlemanly amateurism of the British exploring tradition, Cherry-Garrard assumed many additional duties, including becoming the preeminent writer on the most literate of polar expeditions. Cherry-Garrard edited the *South Polar Times*, the expedition's newspaper, and in *The Worst Journey in the World*, he notes the camp's thrice-weekly lectures, his campmates filling their notebooks, and his own habit of reciting poetry to maintain consciousness on long sledge journeys. Further evidence of the expedition's belletristic atmosphere is detailed in the "good modern fiction" the party favored (Thackeray, Charlotte Brontë, Bulwer-Lytton, and Dickens); the authors who stirred discussion (Shaw, Wells); the mission's library of Arctic and Antarctic travel (Nansen and Shackleton are repeatedly cited); what books should have been carried (reference books to resolve arguments); authors whom Wilson and Scott knew as friends (Galsworthy, Barrie); and even the poetry the leaders packed for their final, fatal journey (Browning for Scott, Tennyson for Wilson).

Cherry-Garrard began writing *The Worst Journey in the World* while recovering from illness contracted during military service in Flanders in World War I. The book's title refers specifically to the 1911 winter sledge journey he made with Wilson and "Birdie" Bowers, which Scott on the party's return called "the hardest that has ever been made." More than twice as long as any previous Antarctic journey, the "Winter Journey" traversed 67 miles to Cape Crozier in five weeks with the purpose of snatching eggs from an emperor penguin rookery in order to investigate a "missing link" in the embryology of birds and reptiles.

Cherry-Garrard relates this journey partly as a minor epic, starting with Homeric catalogs of what the party carried and interlacing allusions to Dante, *The Pilgrim's Progress*, and Walt Whitman. His narrative quietly evokes the desperate self-possession with which the three men pushed into deepening darkness and temperatures 100° F below freezing. Its spare details suggest the men's "indescribable effort and hardship": on one day, eight hours of sledging gained less than three miles; the cold splits Cherry-Garrard's teeth and kills their nerves, leading him to wonder why his tongue hasn't frozen; he shivers so convulsively through the night in his damp bag that his "body chatters"; and he notes the difficulty of knowing whether one's feet are frozen or not.

At last reaching the cape and taking five eggs from the howling, eldritch rookery where rapt male penguins brooded over snowballs and rocks in addition to eggs, Cherry-Garrard exults in "doing something never done before" and being among "the first and only men to witness this marvel of the natural world." Yet the author's and reader's foreknowledge that his companions will perish on the subsequent polar journey heightens the atmosphere of peril. Grim heroics give way to grimmer comedy as Cherry-Garrard relates his efforts the following year to donate three unbroken eggs from the journey to a blasé staff member of the Museum of Natural History in South Kensington, and his chapter on the Winter Journey weirdly terminates in a microscopic addendum ostensibly written by an Edinburgh professor, who, distinguishing the embryos' papillae of feathers from the papillae of scales, insists that "the worst journey in the world was not made in vain."

*Terra Nova* sailing through pack ice, 11 December 1910; H.G. Ponting's Antarctic photographs capture the drama and the hardship of the early-twentieth-century expeditions (reproduced in Cherry-Garrard's *The Worst Journey in the World*, 1922). *Courtesy of the Royal Geographical Society, London.*

Three months after returning from Cape Crozier "with still a grace about us as we stumbled in," Cherry-Garrard accompanied the polar party across the Beardsmore Glacier but was the last man Scott left behind in his race for the Pole. *The Worst Journey in the World* reconstructs that journey from the diaries of Scott, Wilson, and Bowers, who reached their goal only to find that Roald Amundsen of Norway, forgoing science for efficiency, had preceded them by a month. On their return journey, Scott and his party perished 11 miles from a supply depot. Cherry-Garrard joined the search party for their remains and inscribed the concluding verse from Tennyson's "Ulysses" on the cross over Scott's last camp: "To strive, to seek, to find, and not to yield."

Reissued several times and regularly listed as a masterpiece of travel literature, *The Worst Journey in the World* has yet received little extended criticism. A. Alvarez has celebrated its "perfect prose: lucid, vivid, bone-simple, and full of feeling," and Francis Spufford with others has identified the Scott expedition and its posthumous glory with Britain's romantic idealization of the world's bleakest climes. The convergence of the author's measured style and the regimen of British exploration may be recognized in *The Worst Journey*'s peculiar characterization. Cherry-Garrard recognizes personality in the expedition's dogs and ponies as well as in penguins ("an almost human friend") and the killer whales who course up and down water lanes with "deliberate cunning" and "singular intelligence." The mission's human characters, however, are weighed on one Edwardian scale in which "thought for self" is given up for "cooperation and solidarity," with the result that their "clean, open life" grows as blank and beguiling as the "pure land of the south." Cherry-Garrard's account of the Scott expedition consummately depicts his nation's strenuous ethos during the heroic age of Antarctic exploration near the sunset of the British empire. For readers at a greater historical remove, the text's minutiae of late feudalism, heraldic colors, sledge flags, music-hall tunes, and old church hymns, as well as its domestic details of an all-male enterprise, may provide a unique anthropological document.

Cherry-Garrard later became friends with Mallory of Everest and Lawrence of Arabia, composing a short essay in tribute to the latter (in *T.E. Lawrence by His Friends*, edited by A.W. Lawrence, 1937), as well as introductions to biographies of Wilson and Bowers. He settled on his estate, married, and collected early travel books. In Cherry-Garrard's last years, however, he fell victim to mental breakdowns arising from survivor guilt. In *Postscript to the Worst Journey in the World* (1948), Cherry-Garrard reproached himself for not having made an impossible sacrifice to reach the members of the polar party before they perished of hunger and cold.

CRAIG WHITE

### Biography

Born in Bedford, 2 January 1886. Educated at Winchester School and Christ Church, Oxford University: B.A. 1908. Inherited fortune on his father's death, 1907. Cruised round the world on cargo boats, 1909–1910. Joined Robert Falcon Scott's second expedition to the Antarctic as assistant zoologist, 1910–1913. Edited the expedition journal *South Polar Times;* was among the search party that found the bodies of Scott and his companions, 1912. Military service in Flanders in World War I, 1914–1916. During convalescence, wrote *The Worst Journey in the World*, published 1922. Settled on the family estate at Lamer Park, Hertfordshire. Married Angela Turner, 1939. Sold Lamer Park and moved to London, 1947. Associated with the writers George Bernard Shaw and H.G. Wells, and the explorers George Mallory and T.E. Lawrence. Suffered many years of physical and mental illness in later life. Died in London, 18 May 1959.

### References and Further Reading


Cherry-Garrard, Apsley (editor), *South Polar Times*, vol. 3 (April–October 1911), printed 1914.

Cherry-Garrard, Apsley, *The Worst Journey in the World: Antarctic 1910–1913*, 2 vols., 1922; corrected edition with postscript by the author, 1951; with an introduction by Paul Theroux, 1994.

Cherry-Garrard, Apsley, Introduction to *Edward Wilson of the Antarctic, Naturalist and Friend*, by George Seaver, 1933.

Cherry-Garrard, Apsley, Memoir of T.E. Lawrence, in *T.E. Lawrence, by His Friends*, edited by A.W. Lawrence, 1937.

Cherry-Garrard, Apsley, Introduction to *"Birdie" Bowers of the Antarctic*, by George Seaver, 1938.


## CHILDREN'S TRAVEL WRITING

Although a literature designed specifically for children did not exist before the eighteenth century, travel literature for children could be said to have started with Homer's *Odyssey* (c. ninth century BCE). Even though the poem was not specifically designed for children, its tales of monsters, giants, and other fantastic creatures, as well as the adventurous journeys of Odysseus, make it attractive to them. Later, this and other fictional accounts of journeys, though designed perhaps for adults, proliferated in versions for juveniles, like classics retold specifically for children: for example, Alfred J. Church's (1829–1912) two Homers (1892, 1906) prove popular even today. Padraic Colum (1881–1972) compiled his *The Children's Homer: The Adventures of Odysseus and the Tale of Troy* in 1918, and it was reissued in the 1960s, and Jane Werner Watson (1915–) also issued a children's version of Homer's poems (1956). Other poems that older children would find fascinating involve the exploits of Anglo-Saxon heroes, like *Beowulf* (c. early eighth century); Church included a children's version of this in his *Heroes of Chivalry and Romance* (1898).

Examples of travel literature in the medieval period include the works that Lady Charlotte Guest (1812–1895) translated from Welsh as *The Mabinogion* (1838–1849); another translation was published in *Book of Three Dragons* (1930) by Kenneth Morris. The tales were derived from two Welsh sources, *The White Book of Rhydderch* (1300–1325) and *The Red Book of Hergest* (1375–1425), but they were probably composed and transmitted orally as much as three centuries before. Geoffrey Chaucer's (c. 1343–1400) *Canterbury Tales* (1387–1400) also traces a journey; it, too, was reissued many times, for instance in Anne Malcolmson's (1910–) *A Taste of Chaucer* (1964) and Barbara Cooney's (1917–) *Chanticleer and the Fox* (1958). More obscure accounts of pilgrimages include the anonymous poem "The Way to Jerusalem" (c. 1425), which gives a picture of exotic peoples and places. Another anonymous poem, "The Pilgrims' Sea Voyage and Seasickness" (mid-fifteenth century), is an exciting tale of a sea voyage that would thrill any child, especially in an age lacking juvenile literature.

Children were actually participants in pilgrimages and the Crusades, and perhaps they were spurred to action or informed (in hyperbole, of course) by the mystery, the miracle, and the morality plays, biblically inspired dramas that were brought to even small towns and villages in the medieval period, from perhaps the fourteenth century. Some examples are *The York Play of the Crucifixion* (c. 1425) and *The Second Shepherd's Play* (c. 1425), which were presented in A.W. Pollard's (1859–1944) *The Towneley Plays* (1897). Children could also listen, perhaps, to the chansons de geste, rousing tales like *Orlando innamorato* [Orlando in Love] (1487) by Matteo Maria Boiardo (1441–1494) and its sequel, *Orlando furioso* [Orlando Mad] (1516) by Lodovico Ariosto (1475–1533). Some of these were again retold in the nineteenth century by Alfred J. Church in *Heroes of Chivalry and Romance* (1898). Many modern versions call the hero Roland, for instance, James Baldwin's (1841–1925) version (1930) and Eleanor Clark's (1913–) *Song of Roland* (1960).

When news of Columbus's and others' exploration of the New World got out, travel narratives proliferated. Richard Hakluyt (1553–1616) was one of many inspired by stories of the discovery of the New World. It was with the Restoration (1660–1700), however, that the New World travel story reached its apogee. John

Dryden (1631–1700) wrote the drama *The Indian Queen* (1664) and its sequel, *The Indian Emperor* (1665), with which Aphra Behn (1640–1689) was familiar. Her *Oroonoko; or, The History of the Royal Slave* (1688) gives an account of a "royal slave" and his experiences, first in his native Africa, then in the slave trade. Hannah More (1745–1833) knew of *Oroonoko: A Tragedy* (1695), Thomas Southerne's (1659–1746) stage adaptation of Behn's novel (Gallagher and Stern, 2000). More seems unaffected by these exotic tales of abducted slaves, but perhaps those of her educational efforts such as *Moses in the Bulrushes* (1782), as well as her antislavery stance, were influenced by the more picturesque tales.

Before literature for children existed as a separate genre, children focused on the fantastic journeys related in some early novels, the most prominent among them, of course, *Robinson Crusoe*—or to give it its full title, *The Life and Strange and Surprising Adventures of Robinson Crusoe of York, Mariner* (1719)—by Daniel Defoe (1659–1731) and *Gulliver's Travels into Several Remote Nations of the World* (1726) by Jonathan Swift (1667–1745). They were both inspired by actual travel narratives, but their allegorical elements allow, of course, for many interpretations. After a specifically children's literature was developed, both novels were issued in editions intended for children, but such authors as Charles Dickens and Benjamin Franklin acknowledged reading one or both, unexpurgated, as children. Voltaire's (1694–1778) *Candide* (1759), like *Gulliver's Travels*, could be viewed as a satire of travel literature.

The desire for help on the educational Grand Tour, considered essential to complete any young aristocrat's acculturation in the eighteenth and nineteenth centuries, led to a plethora of travel literature. Nonfiction works such as Johann W. von Goethe's (1749–1832) *Italienische Reise* (1816), among many others, would have been consulted by older adolescents embarking on their tour. Fictional treatments in George Eliot's (1819–1880) *Middlemarch* (1871–1872), William Makepeace Thackeray's (1811–1863) *Vanity Fair* (1848), and Charlotte Brontë's (1816–1855) *Villette* (1853) might also have shown them what to expect. In the romantic period, another genre of travel literature came to the fore: celebrations of the provincial—exemplified by Sir Walter Scott's (1771–1832) Waverley novels (1814–1824), William Wordsworth (1770–1850) and Samuel Taylor Coleridge's (1772–1834) *Lyrical Ballads* (1798), and Dorothy Wordsworth's (1771–1855) *Recollections of a Tour Made in Scotland* (1803)—brought British people back to their neglected homeland.

In the eighteenth century, a literature for children began to be developed, and with the necessity for didacticism in children's literature finally eschewed, the nineteenth century was the great age of the adventure novel. One of Coleridge's contributions to *Lyrical Ballads*, "The Rime of the Ancient Mariner," revitalized the traditional ballad form and inspired a brand of fantastic travel narratives. James Fenimore Cooper (1789–1851) popularized the romance of the American frontier all over the world, and his *The Pilot* (1823) was one of the first stories of the sea. Sir Walter Scott and Captain Frederick Marryat (1792–1848) both influenced Robert Louis Stevenson (1850–1894). Marryat wrote a series of books for children, starting with *Masterman Ready* (1841–1842) and including *Children of the New Forest* (1847) and *The Little Savage* (1848–1849). Stevenson is most famous for *Treasure Island* (1883), which was first serialized in *Young Folks* (1881–1882). The travel story also came to the fore at this time. Horace Scudder (1838–1902) wrote a series for children on a New England family called the Bodleys (1875–1880). William Taylor Adams (1822–1897) was an incredibly prolific writer, who, from the 1850s to the 1890s, under the pseudonym of Oliver

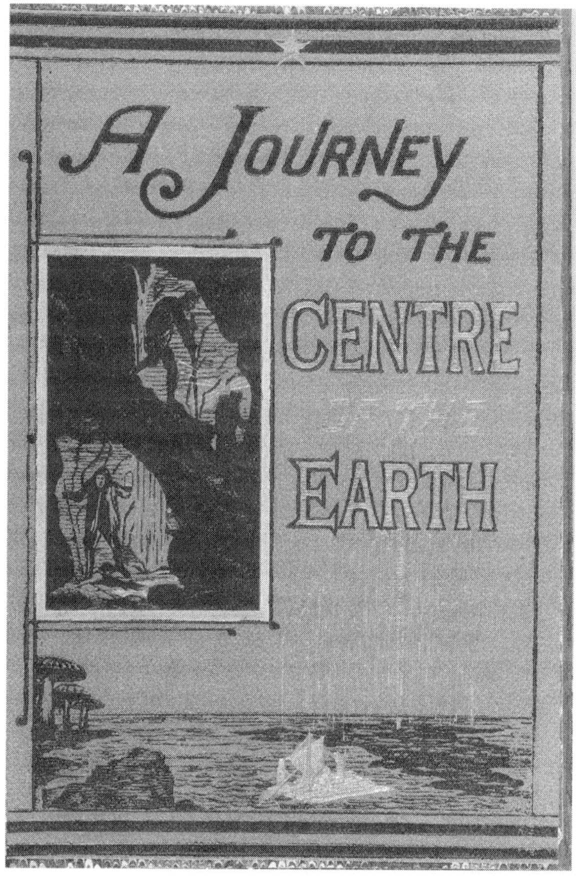


Eye-catchingly illustrated covers were a feature of late-nineteenth- and early-twentieth-century children's books. *Courtesy of British Library, London.*

Optic, wrote several series of adventure stories for boys and girls that provided lessons in geography and science. The Frenchman Jules Verne's fantasies captured the child's imagination: *Voyage au centre de la terre* (1864; *A Journey to the Centre of the Earth*, 1872) and *The Mysterious Island* (1875) are still popular.

In England, the continued rise of the British empire led to an often jingoistic literature that captured the exoticism of colonial holdings. Derring-do by brave white men in far-flung lands was the stock-in-trade of boys' adventure novels by the likes of G.A. Henty (1832–1902). Stories for children by Rudyard Kipling (1865–1936), notably the *Jungle Books* (1894, 1895), show his continued love of India. The turn of the century brought more interest to literatures other than English: Dikken Zwilgmeyer's (1859–1913) *Johnny Blossom* and *What Happened to Inger Johanne* were written in Norwegian, but translated into English in 1912 and 1919, respectively. *Donkey John of Toy Valley* (1909) by Margaret Morley (1858–1923) is set in the Tyrol. Margaret Bertha Synge's (d. 1939) *A Book of Discovery* (1912) starts with the ancients and progresses to the discovery of the South Pole; it features maps and charts.

As the western frontier of America closed, interest in the Western seemed to grow in inverse proportion. Hamlin Garland (1860–1940) wrote *Boy Life on the Prairie* (1899), George Bird Grinnell (1849–1938) authored *Wolf Hunters* (1914), and James Willard Schultz (1859–1947) penned *With the Indians in the Rockies* (1912), *Sinopah, the Indian Boy* (1913), and *Lone Bull's Mistake* (1918); all of them took knowledge gained from personal experience in the West and fictionalized it. Laura Ingalls Wilder (1867–1957) did the same in her series on the Ingalls family pioneers beginning in 1932.

World War I inevitably disrupted book publishing, but children's travel literature made a rebound in the post-war years. At this time, interest in aviation began to capture the child's imagination. Anne Morrow Lindbergh's (1906–2001) *North to the Orient* (1935) details the airplane trip to Asia she took with her husband, and Charles Lindbergh supplied maps. *Wind, Sand and Stars* (1939), a nonfiction account by Antoine de Saint-Exupéry (1900–1944), another noted aviator, gives his experiences of flight. As the world grew smaller and people could more easily voyage to other places, interest in other peoples and customs grew. Sulamith Ish-Kishor (1896–1977) wrote *A Children's History of Israel from the Creation to the Present Time* (1930–1933) as well as other histories of Judaism, though she only came to be famous in the 1960s when multiculturalism was more accepted. Nevertheless, it was in the 1930s that Arna Bontemps (1902–1973) wrote children's stories about blacks in that decade: his *Sad-Faced Boy* (1937) traces the journey of three black boys who travel to New York. Madeleine L'Engle (1918–) is best known for her *A Wrinkle in Time* (1962), but her novel *And Both Were Young* (1949) is set in Switzerland and describes an American girl at a boarding school.

During and after World War II (1939–1945), there was more interest in learning about the war's participants as well as theaters of the war. *Ocean Outposts* (1943) by Helen Follett describes the Pacific Islands. Dola de Jong's (1911–) *Level Land* (1943) features Holland. Attilio Gatti (1896–) wrote *Mediterranean Spotlights* (1944), describing Greece, Gibraltar, Crete, Malta, Palestine, Sicily, and Italy; with his wife Ellen, he also composed *Here Is Africa* (1943). Scribner embarked on a whole Here Is series: Jean Kennedy (1919?–) wrote *Here Is India* (1945) for them. Grace Hogarth's (1905–) *Australia: The Island Continent* (1943) gives an account of the geography, history, and industries of that country. Books concentrating on nature also came to the fore around the time of World War II. An English translation of a Russian juvenile novel called *White Birds Island*, by Georgii Skrebitskii (1903–1964), appeared in 1948. Clifford H. Pope (1899–) wrote about his expeditions for the American Museum of Natural History (1937, 1940). Dorothy Sterling's (1913–) *The Outer Lands* (1967) gives a good introduction to coastal ecology. Jocelyn Arundel's *The Wildlife of Africa* (1965) and *Land of the Zebra* (1974) tell of her safaris in Africa and were meant to bring attention to the dangers of extinction facing the animals she describes.

Travel guides specifically for children now abound, as well. One of the more literary is E.L. Konigsburg's (1930–) *From the Mixed-Up Files of Mrs. Basil E. Frankweiler* (1967), a juvenile novel that gives a wonderful description of New York's Metropolitan Museum of Art. Similarly, Jill Krementz's (1940–) *A Visit to Washington, D.C.* (1987) is actually a novel. A new series called Sightseers, published by Kingfisher, is meant to comprise historical guides to places as they were in the past, but they are described as travel guides. And there are actual travel guides to popular destinations for children such as Disney Land and Disney World, like Kim Wright Wiley's *Walt Disney World 4 Teens by Teens* (2000). With the precocious maturity and independence of today's youth, travel literature for children may become more practical and less imaginative than in the past.

JOSEPHINE A. MCQUAIL

**References and Further Reading**

Arundel, Jocelyn, *The Wildlife of Africa*, 1965.
Arundel, Jocelyn, *Land of the Zebra*, 1974.

Baldwin, James, *The Story of Roland*, 1930.
Behn, Aphra, *The History of Oroonoko; or, the Royal Slave*, 1688.
Boiardo, Matteo Maria, *Orlando innamorato* [Orlando in Love], books 1 and 2, 1483; complete edition, 1495.
Bontemps, Arna, *Sad-Faced Boy*, 1937.
[Campen, Joachim], *Receuil de voyages interessans: Pour l'instruction et l'amusement de la jeunesse*, 7 vols., 1786–1793.
Chaucer, Geoffrey, *The Canterbury Tales*, c. 1387–1400; edited by William Caxton, 1478.
Church, Alfred J., *The Story of the Odyssey*, 1892.
Church, Alfred J., *Heroes of Chivalry and Romance*, 1898.
Church, Alfred J., *The Odyssey for Boys and Girls*, 1906.
Church, Alfred J., *The Iliad and the Odyssey of Homer*, 1964.
Clark, Eleanor, *The Song of Roland*, illustrated by Leonard Everett Fisher, 1960.
Colum, Padraic, *The Children's Homer: The Adventures of Odysseus and the Tale of Troy*, 1918; reprinted 1962.
Cooney, Barbara, *Chanticleer and the Fox*, 1958.
Defoe, Daniel, *The Life and Strange and Surprising Adventures of Robinson Crusoe of York, Mariner*, 1719.
Dryden, John, with Sir Robert Howard, *The Indian Queen*, 1665; first produced, 1664.
Dryden, John, *The Indian Emperor; or, The Conquest of Mexico by the Spaniards, Being the Sequel of The Indian Queen*, 1667; first produced, 1665.
Follett, Helen, *Ocean Outposts*, 1943.
Gallagher, Caterine, and Simon Stern (editors), *Oroonoko; or, The Royal Slave*, New York: St. Martin's Press, 2000.
Garland, Hamlin, *Boy Life on the Prairie*, 1899; revised edition, 1908.
Gatti, Attilio, and Ellen Morgan, *Here Is Africa*, 1943.
Gatti, Attilio, *Mediterranean Spotlights*, 1944.
Goethe, Johann W. von, *Italienische Reise*, 1816; as *Italian Journey*, translated by W.H. Auden and Elizabeth Mayer, 1962.
Grinnell, George Bird, *Wolf Hunters*, 1914.
Guest, Charlotte, *The Mabinogion*, 1838–1849; first complete text, 1849.
Hakluyt, Richard, *Divers Voyages Touching the Discovery of America*, 1582.
Hakluyt, Richard, *The Principall Navigations, Voiages, and Discoveries of the English Nation, Made by Sea or over Land, in the Most Remote and Farthest Distant Quarters of the Earth at Any Time within the Compasse of These 1500 Yeeres*, 1589.
Henty, G.A., *By Sheer Pluck: A Tale of the Ashanti War*, 1883.
Henty, G.A., *A Final Reckoning: A Tale of Bush Life in Australia*, 1886.
Henty, G.A., *By Right of Conquest; or, With Cortez in Mexico*, 1890.
Hogarth, Grace, *Australia: The Island Continent*, 1943.
Ish-Kishor, Sulamith, *Children's History of Israel from the Creation to the Present Time*, 1930–1933.
Jong, Dola de, *Level Land*, 1943.
Kennedy, Jean, *Here Is India*, 1945.
Kipling, Rudyard, *The Jungle Book*, 1894.
Kipling, Rudyard, *The Second Jungle Book*, 1895.
Kipling, Rudyard, *Kim*, 1901.
Konigsburg, E.L., *From the Mixed-Up Files of Mrs. Basil E. Frankweiler*, 1967.
Krementz, Jill, *A Visit to Washington, D.C.*, 1987.
L'Engle, Madeleine, *And Both Were Young*, 1949.
Lindbergh, Anne Morrow, *North to the Orient*, 1935.
Malcolmson, Anne, *A Taste of Chaucer: Selections from the Canterbury Tales*, illustrated by Enrico Arno, 1964.
Marryat, Frederick, *Masterman Ready; or, The Wreck of the Pacific, Written for Young People*, 3 vols., 1841–1842.
Marryat, Frederick, *The Children of the New Forest*, 1847.
Marryat, Frederick, *The Little Savage*, 2 vols., 1848–1849.
More, Hannah, *Moses in the Bulrushes*, 1782.
Morris, Kenneth, *Book of Three Dragons*, illustrated by Ferdinand Huszti Horvath, 1930.
Optic, Oliver [William Taylor Adams], Boat Club series, 1854–.
Optic, Oliver [William Taylor Adams], Woodville series, 1861–1867.
Optic, Oliver [William Taylor Adams], Army and Navy series, 1865–1894.
Optic, Oliver [William Taylor Adams], Starry Flag series, 1867–1869.
Picard, Barbara Leonie, *The Odyssey of Homer*, 1952.
Picard, Barbara Leonie, *Stories of King Arthur and His Knights*, illustrated by Roy Morgan, 1955.
Picard, Barbara Leonie, *Hero Tales from the British Isles*, illustrated by John G. Galsworthy, 1963.
Saint-Exupéry, Antoine de, *Wind, Sand and Stars*, 1939.
Schultz, James Willard, *With the Indians in the Rockies*, with illustrations by George Varian, 1912.
Schultz, James Willard, *Sinopah, the Indian Boy*, with illustrations by E. Boyd Smith, 1913.
Schultz, James Willard, *Lone Bull's Mistake: A Lodge Pole Chief Story*, 1918.
Scott, Walter, Waverley novels, 1814–1824; Scott's final revised version, 48 vols., 1829–1833.
Scudder, Horace E., Bodley series, 1875–1880.
Sherwood, Merriam (translator), *The Song of Roland*, illustrated by Edith Emerson, 1938.
Skrebitskii, Georgii, *White Birds Island*, 1948.
Southerne, Thomas, *Oroonoko: A Tragedy*, 1696; first produced, 1695.
Sterling, Dorothy, *The Outer Lands: A Natural History Guide to Cape Cod, Martha's Vineyard, Nantucket, Block Island, and Long Island*, 1967.
Stevenson, Robert Louis, *Treasure Island*, 1883.
Swift, Jonathan, *Travels into Several Remote Nations of the World, by Captain Lemuel Gulliver*, 1726; revised edition, 1735.
Synge, M.B., *A Book of Discovery: The History of the World's Exploration, from the Earliest Times to the Finding of the South Pole*, 1912.
Verne, Jules, *Voyage au centre de la terre*, 1864; as *A Journey to the Centre of the Earth*, 1872.
Verne, Jules, *L'Ile mysterieuse*, 3 vols., 1874–1875; as *The Mysterious Island*, 3 vols., 1875.
Voltaire, *Candide; ou, L'Optimisme*, 1759; as *Candidus; or, All for the Best*, 1759; in *Candide and Other Stories*, translated by Roger Pearson, 1990.
Watson, Jane Werner, *The Iliad and the Odyssey*, illustrated by Alice Provensen and Martin Provensen, 1956.
Wilder, Laura Ingalls, *Little House in the Big Woods*, 1932.
Wiley, Kim Wright, *Walt Disney World 4 Teens by Teens*, 2000.
Wordsworth, Dorothy, *Recollections of a Tour Made in Scotland*, 1803.
Wordsworth, William, and Samuel Taylor Coleridge, *Lyrical Ballads, with a Few Other Poems*, 1798.
Zwilgmeyer, Dikken, *Johnny Blossom*, translated from the Norwegian by Emilie Poulsson, illustrated by F. Liley Young, 1912.
Zwilgmeyer, Dikken, *What Happened to Inger Johanne*, translated from the Norwegian by Emilie Poulsson, 1919.

*See also* **Fictional Travel Writing**

## CHILE

As part of the conquest of the Inca empire by the Spaniards under Pizarro, his jealous rival Almagro spent two fruitless years in Chile (1535–1537) struggling against the elements and the native population before withdrawing, having concluded that Chile had nothing to offer but pain and grief. After the murder of Almagro by Pizarro in 1539, the victor delegated the conquest of inhospitable southern Chile to Pedro de Valdivia, before Pizarro too succumbed to assassination, by Almagro's mestizo son and the "men of Chile" in 1541. The way was now clear for Valdivia, bold soldier-son of Extremadura, who has fought his way into the history books as the conqueror of Chile. No one has captured better the adversities and triumphs of the governor than Cunninghame Graham in *Pedro de Valdivia* (1926), one of his several historical biographies of Latin American figures. With the support of his mistress Inés de Suárez, Valdivia founded the cities of Santiago (1541), Concepción (1550), and Valdivia (1552) before tragedy struck. The fierce character and achievements of the wily chief have been well portrayed in the epic poem *La Araucana* (1569–1589) of the soldier-writer Alonso de Ercilla. Published in Buenos Aires in 1945, this is one of several Latin American epic poems translated by the Scottish-Argentine writer Walter Owen (1884–1953).

That Almagro, Pizarro, and Valdivia should have found the Chilean land and climate uninviting, as well as lacking in gold and silver, is no surprise. The geography of Chile (which means "cold" in Quechua) has always been surprising, if not threatening to foreign travelers. The natives of Upper Peru are reputed to have described it to Valdivia as "the land where the earth ends." Although the country is 2,600 miles long, it averages barely 100 miles in width, hence the oft-quoted description of Benjamín Subercaseaux's *Chile o una loca geografía* (1940), a crazy geography indeed, not captured by the English translation, *Chile: A Geographic Extravaganza* (1971). The country is divided into four regions. The northern desert, though lacking gold and silver, contains the valuable minerals, especially nitrate, which in the nineteenth century were to attact the mining engineers and mineralogists, the first of the travel writers. The central valley, where it rains only in winter, houses 90 percent of the population in the main cities and contains the large agricultural estates. The dense rain forests of the south yield to Atlantic Chile of the southerly point, spanning the Strait of Magellan, touching on Tierra del Fuego and southern Patagonia, long a bone of contention with Argentina. In his *Voyage of the Beagle*, Darwin provides a memorable description of this isolated region.

Not only the geography is crazy or extravagant, however. When political independence did come to Chile, it was by circuitous and stumbling steps, in the face of royalist opposition. In fact, in 1814, Spain reconquered Chile, which was not fully liberated until Bernardo O'Higgins returned from exile to see independence proclaimed in 1818. As in the other emancipated colonies, the nineteenth century tells a story of civil war and dictatorship, constant struggles between conservatives (landowners, Catholics) and liberals (reformers, anticlericals). Dictatorship and anarchy notwithstanding, Chile made progress in spite of itself. Culturally too, it became a refuge for exiles from other countries. This was also a period of commercial progress. A whole wave of mining experts, scientists, diplomats, missionaries, and others spread out over the Pampas en route to Chile. Among the best in literary terms were Joseph Andrews, who wrote *Journey from Buenos Ayres* (1827), Alexander Caldcleugh, *Travels in South America, during the Years 1819–20–21* (1825), Samuel Haigh, *Sketches of Buenos Ayres, Chile and Peru* (1831), John Miers, *Travels in Chile and La Plata* (1826), Peter Schmidtmeyer, *Travels into Chile, over the Andes, in the Years 1820 and 1821* (1824), and others, whose reports, narratives, records, and journals were to become the stuff of British travel literature in the region. At the same time, they contributed, in translation, to the socioeconomic and cultural aspects of Chilean life, none of their work being more interesting than Maria Graham's *Journal of a Residence in Chile* (1824), which prepared the way later in the century for a whole new genre of women's writing, as captured in June E. Hahner's collection *Women through Women's Eyes* (1998).

In the twentieth century, the ground was being prepared for the *vía chilena* to socialism, which progressed steadily from the founding of the Labour Party, up through the Popular Front, to the burgeoning Communist Party, of which the poet Pablo Neruda was by far the best-known and most literate member. When Allende was elected in 1970, he was for many workers and intellectuals the long-awaited messiah. But as often happens in Latin America, the army had the last word. The 1973 coup of General Pinochet initiated a process that resulted in the death of the president, the disappearance of at least 3,000 people, and the departure of a host of artists, writers, and intellectuals, like Isabel Allende, Ariel Dorfman, and Antonio Skarmeta. The coup and its aftermath also involved foreign citizens caught in the maelstrom. One remembers the suffering of the English doctor Sheila Cassidy (*Audacity to Believe*, 1978) and the harrowing events of the 1982 film *Missing* as examples of what happens to a country that loses its civilized veneer and resorts to barbaric behavior, state-controlled torture, and terrorism. Ariel Dorfman, who now writes in English, has captured the nightmare in novels like *Hard Rain* (1973) and *Widows*

Valparaiso Bay c. 1820 (from Alexander Caldcleugh's *Travels in South America*, 1825). *Courtesy of the Travellers Club, London; Bridgeman Art Library, agent.*

(1981), the short stories of *My House Is on Fire* (1990), and his drama, for example, *Death and the Maiden* (1992).

With Pinochet gone, and democracy restored to a country that traditionally had little experience of military intervention, Chile can now enjoy *some* of the economic progress that, ironically, derived from the Pinochet years, although it never filtered down to the masses of the people, the mainstay of the Allende government. Contemporary travel writers like Tony Gould in *Death in Chile: A Memoir and a Journey* (1992) and Sara Wheeler in *Travels in a Thin Country* (1995) are the much more self-conscious modern equivalents of the nineteenth-century *viajeros ingleses* who captured, at times unwittingly, the spirit of postindependence Chile, with the civil war, anarchy, dictatorship, and material progress of that time, up through the turbulent years that ushered in the radicalism of the twentieth century, thus paving the way for Allende's socialist experiment, devoured, in Ariel Dorfman's terms (*The Last Song of Manuel Sendero*, 1982), by the legendary dragon Pinochet, now itself on its last legs and on the verge of extinction.

JOHN WALKER

### References and Further Reading

Akers, C.E., *Argentine, Patagonian and Chilian Sketches, with a Few Notes on Uruguay*, 1893.

Andrews, Joseph, *Journey from Buenos Ayres through the Provinces of Córdova, Tucumán and Salta, to Potosí, Thence by the Deserts of Caranja to Arica, and Subsequently, to Santiago de Chile and Coquimbo, Undertaken on Behalf of the Chilean-Peruvian Mining Association in the Years 1825–26*, 1827.

Caldcleugh, Alexander, *Travels in South America, during the Years 1819–20–21: Containing an Account of the Present State of Brazil, Buenos Ayres and Chile*, 1825.

Clissold, Stephen, *Chilean Scrap-book*, 1952.

Darwin, Charles, *Journal of Researches into the Geology and Natural History of Various Countries Visited by HMS Beagle, under the Command of Captain Fitzroy, R.N., from 1832 to 1836* (vol. 3 of *Narrative of the Surveying Voyages of His Majesty's Ships Adventure and Beagle*, edited by Robert Fitzroy), 1839; revised edition, 1845; as *The Voyage of the Beagle*, 1909.

Davie, John Constanse, *Letters from Buenos Ayres and Chili, with an Original History of the Latter Country*, 1819.

Gardiner, Allan F., *A Visit to the Indians on the Frontiers of Chili*, 1841.

Gould, Tony, *Death in Chile: A Memoir and a Journey*, 1992.

Graham, Maria, *Journal of a Residence in Chile during the Year 1822. And a Voyage from Chile to Brazil in 1823*, 1824.

Hahner, June E. (editor), *Women through Women's Eyes: Latin American Women in Nineteenth-Century Travel Accounts*, 1998.

Haigh, Samuel, *Sketches of Buenos Ayres, Chile and Peru*, 1831.

Hall, Basil, *Extracts from a Journal, Written on the Coast of Chile, Peru, and Mexico*, 1824.

Hibbert, Edward, *Narrative of a Journey from Santiago de Chile to Buenos Ayres in July and August, 1821*, 1824.

Keenan, Brian, and John McCarthy, *Between Extremes*, 2000.

Mathison, Gilbert Farquhar, *Narrative of a Visit to Brazil, Chile, Peru and the Sandwich Islands during the Years 1821 and 1822*, 1825.

Miers, John, *Travels in Chile and La Plata*, 1826.

Morant, George C., *Chili and the River Plate in 1891: Reminiscences of Travel in South America*, 1891.

Phelan, Nancy, *The Chilean Way: Travels in Chile*, 1973.

Sagaris, Lake, *After the First Death: A Journey through Chile, Time, Mind*, 1996.

Scarlett, Peter Campbell, *South America and the Pacific: Comprising a Journey across the Pampas and the Andes; from Buenos Ayres to Valparaíso, Lima and Panama*, 1838.

Schmidtmeyer, Peter, *Travels into Chile, over the Andes, in the Years 1820 and 1821*, 1824.

Sutcliffe, Thomas, *Sixteen Years in Chile and Peru from 1822 to 1839*, 1841.

Wheeler, Sara, *Travels in a Thin Country: A Journey through Chile*, 1995.

*See also* **Andes**

## CHINA

Traveling in China has generated a voluminous and diverse literature by Chinese writers as well as by a variety of foreigners. Although first-person narratives in Chinese did not become an established form until the eighth century, earlier texts reflect a steady growth of interest in the wider world. The legendary sage-king Yu the Great (fl. c. 2000 BCE), who was later revered as the fountainhead of knowledge about geography, was ordered while still an official to travel throughout the Chinese world to control the Deluge. He directed extensive river-control projects, divided up the land into nine provinces, and ensured the circulation of products as tribute to the capital, after which he is said to have established China's first dynasty, the Xia. Other rulers are recorded as traveling in order to conduct religious sacrifices at sacred mountains and rivers as well as for pragmatic military and political purposes.

One such royal tour was the subject of the highly fictionalized *The Travels of King Mu* (*Mutianzi zhuan*. c. fourth century BCE–fourth century), in which a tenth-century BCE ruler journeys to the ends of his empire and meets both gods and subjects who confirm his sovereignty (see Cheng Te-k'un, 1933). During the Warring States period (475–221 BCE), cosmographies were compiled to aid literate travelers in negotiating a landscape populated by innumerable gods, demons, and strange animals. The only surviving example, *Guideways through Mountains and Seas* (*Shanhaijing*, c. fourth century–first century BCE), contains a mixture of myth, legend, and other fabulous content with factual information, and it became a model for later, more verifiable geographies. The Daoist philosophers of the *Zhuangzi* (trad. c. third century BCE) extolled travel as a metaphor of the natural flow of the universal Way (Dao), while the poets of the *Songs of Chu* (*Chuci*, c. third century BCE), in such works as "The Far-Off Journey" (*Yuanyou*) and "Encountering Sorrow" (*Lisao*), represented celestial travel with gods and spirits as a refuge from the tribulations of the human political world. It was to encounter similarly transcendent beings (*xian*), said to possess the secret of longevity, that some rulers dispatched costly expeditions to the Isles of the Immortals thought to lie in the eastern sea. The most elaborate mission was the one led by Xu Shi (n.d.) with a retinue of several thousand sent by the First Emperor of Qin in 219 BCE, but it, like all the others, resulted in failure. Generally speaking, a number of factors combined to inhibit travel in the early period, including the broad extent of the Chinese cultural area surrounded by deserts, high mountains, and vast oceans, the difficulty of navigating many of the internal river systems, the unimportance of maritime trade, the settled, agricultural nature of Chinese society, and the belief in a landscape populated by demons.

With the establishment of a strong, unified empire during the Qin-Han period (221 BCE–220 CE), exploration and expansion were begun in earnest. Under Emperor Wu (r. 141–87 BCE), Zhang Qian (n.d.) was sent westward on two diplomatic missions to the states of central Asia to gather intelligence, form alliances, and secure a reliable supply of the horses necessary to defend the state against hostile nomadic tribes. He probably submitted a report on the first of his travels from 139 to 126 BCE, which is believed to have been used by the historian Sima Qian (c. 145–85 BCE) in his *Historical Records* (*Shiji*), c. 90 BCE), China's first comprehensive history. This work became a model for the 24 or so subsequent dynastic histories, which also include treatises, often based on travelers' reports, about the geography and ethnography of China and foreign regions. In subsequent centuries, during the period of disunion known as the Northern and Southern Dynasties (third–late sixth century), a number of compilations appeared that reflect in part the explorations of travelers following the tradition of the early cosmographies. The most notable of these are *Record of Lands South of Lotus Mountain* (*Huayang guozhi*, late third century) by Chang Qu and *The Guide to Waterways with Commentary* (*Shuijingzhu*, c. early sixth century) by Li Daoyuan (d. 527). Yang Xuanzhi (Hsüan-chih) (fl. c. 528–547) developed a genre of nostalgic accounts of former capitals and other urban areas with his *A Record of Buddhist Monasteries in Lo-yang* (*Luoyang gielanji*, c. 547). This work documents the personalities, places, and events in this capital during its height a few decades earlier, before it was abandoned and damaged by war. With the spread of Buddhism from India and central Asia to China that began in the first century, foreign missionary monks came to China, and Chinese monks began to travel in the reverse direction to study in the centers of Buddhist learning. A new genre of travel writing resulted, one documenting journeys to the many oasis kingdoms that dotted the Silk Route, as well as to countries along a southern sea route via Southeast Asia. These accounts include Fa-Hsien's (c. 337–418) journey to India from 399 to 413 and that of Song Yun (n.d.) and Huisheng (n.d.) from 518 to 522, later culminating in the Tang dynasty pilgrim Xuanzang's (Hsüan Tsang, c. 600–664) *Record of the Western Regions* (*Xiyuji*, 646), which describes the kingdoms he visited from 627 to 645. A revealing glimpse of China itself during the Tang can be found in the diary written by the Japanese monk Ennin (794–864), one of many who made a similar journey to China for the purpose of studying Buddhism. He can be considered among the earliest foreigners to have left a written record of his journey to China, and, like many later accounts by non-Chinese, it reveals many features of the daily life of the country not recorded elsewhere.

The earliest surviving first-person narrative by a Chinese traveler is an account by an official, Ma Dibo (n.d.), who accompanied Emperor Guangwu (r. 25–57) on a ritual tour of the sacred Mount Tai in 56. This account was preserved as a commentary to the "Treatise on the Feng and Shan Sacrifices" in the *History of the Latter Han Dynasty* (*Houhanshu*: *"Fengshan yiji,"* c. 82), and it documents not only the emperor's progress in detail, but also the writer's subjective impressions about his own journey. However, this was still subsumed within the form of an official report and did not generate an independent genre of travel writing. Although writers gradually began to record their journeys in rhyme-prose, lyric poetry, and brief letters, it was only centuries later, during the Tang, that a group of scholar-officials promoting a revival of "ancient-style prose" (*guwen*) created the classical Chinese "travel account" (*youji*), a short form combining poetic description of a landscape with documentary facts about places as well as autobiographical sentiments. Many of these accounts were the result of exile from the court to distant areas and were also covert expressions of the writer's plight. The most influential was Liu Zongyuan's (773–819) "Eight Pieces from Yongzhou" (*Yongzhou baji*, 809–812), which was later canonized as the locus classicus of the travel account.

It was not until the succeeding Song dynasty (960–1279) that the new intellectual spirit of "classifying things" (*gewu*), promoted by the ideology of neo-Confucianism, stimulated a more widespread desire to investigate the world. The rapid development of printed books also encouraged a proliferation of travel accounts, often by officials, who were frequently exiled or dispatched to distant locations. These develop earlier themes and also include more objective, quasi-scientific speculation about the natural world and the historical significance of the places visited. Classical Chinese travel accounts do not usually focus on the mundane details of the journey itself; many describe the places arrived at, celebrating scenery, outstanding buildings, social occasions, or unusual events. Among the major Song writers of travel accounts were Fan Zhongyan (989–1052), Ouyang Xiu (1007–1072), Shen Kuo (1031–1095), and Su Shi (1037–1101). Some of the places they wrote about became famous as a result and developed into popular tourist attractions. A related genre that flourished was the travel diary (*riji*), essentially strings of shorter travel accounts arranged chronologically. Two major ones, *A Journey into Shu* (*Rushuji*, c. 1170) by Lu Yu (1125–1210) and *Diary of a Boat Trip to Wu* (*Wuchuanlu*, c. 1177) by Fan Chengda (1126–1193), were written about journeys up and down the Long River (the Changjiang, or "Yangtze") and are lengthy compilations, filled with a variety of details about ethnography, historical sites, and natural formations, as well as personal reflections. Because the Song was militarily weak, it was compelled to send embassies to neighboring states, such as the Liao (907–1125) and Jin (1115–1234), that had conquered Chinese territory as well as to the ascendant Mongols. These alien forces did not regard themselves in the traditional role of barbarian tributaries. The several surviving diaries compiled by officials in the Chinese delegations, such as *Diary of a Northern Journey* (*Beixing rilu*, 1169–1170) by Lu Yu (1137–1213), *Register of Grasping the Carriage Reins* (*Lanpeilu*, 1170) by Fan Chengda, and *Embassy to the Jin* (*Shijinlu*, 1211–1212) by Cheng Zhuo (1153–1223), reveal both what these envoys observed about their enemies as well as their mixed emotions upon viewing the destruction in their former territory.

The Mongol conquest of all China by 1279 brought it within a global empire that emphasized trade while devaluing scholars and classical Chinese learning. This was the period when Marco Polo (1254–c. 1323) visited and brought back to Europe his enthralling tales about the power and wealth of China during the Mongol Yuan dynasty (1279–1368). Other travelers, such as the Franciscan monk John of Montecorvino (1247–1328) and the Muslim Ibn Battuta (1304–1377), also visited China at this time and left valuable reports. Two interesting accounts, one about a charismatic Daoist priest, Qiu Chuji (Changchun, 1148–1227), and another by his antagonist, the Confucian-Buddhist official Yelü Chucai (1189–1243), tell of their respective journeys to the Western Region at the summons of Genghis Khan (c. 1162–1227). The hagiographic account about Qiu written by a disciple in 1228–1230, after Qiu's death, describes his difficult itinerary and the magical feats he performed that led Genghis to favor him and his sect of Daoism. Yelü's 1228 account of his own journey from 1219 to 1224 offers even more concrete detail, though its realistic approach was largely designed to discredit the legend of Qiu and reduce the influence of the latter's followers back in China.

With the revival of Chinese culture under the Ming (1368–1644), travel, exploration, and travel writing entered a new, expansionary phase that produced unparalled accomplishments in both the belletristic genres of travel literature as well as in more pragmatic, documentary writing. Responding to a second wave of expansion in printed books beginning in the mid-sixteenth century, scholars wrote travel accounts in abundance and increasingly used them to express subjective, autobiographical sentiments. Among the most engaging of these are vignettes (*xiaopin*) by Yuan Hongdao (1568–1610), by Zhang Dai (c. 1597–c. 1679), and later by Yuan Mei (1716–1798), all of whom used travel writing to champion an individual sensibility in literature. The travel diary reached the peak of its development in the extensive notes of the intrepid, lifelong traveler Xu Hongzu (Xiake, 1586–1641), which first circulated in manuscript and were eventually edited and printed. Because these were not yet polished literary pieces, they reflect an immediacy of experience and an abundance of detail not found before. Moreover, these diaries hold a special interest for their record of heroic itineraries by a private individual to some of the most inaccessible parts of the Chinese empire, itineraries that were carried out in an unusually independent spirit of exploration and curiosity.

Meanwhile, the outside world was beginning to intrude again, as new kinds of foreigners knocked at the gates. Early in the Ming, the eunuch admiral Zheng He (1371–1435) had been sent on seven massively outfitted navel expeditions through Southeast and South Asia from 1403 to 1431 that reached as far as Africa

William Alexander's drawing of the Chinese emperor's reception of Macartney's embassy in 1793—at which Macartney famously avoided performing the kowtow (British Library). *Courtesy of British Library, London.*

and brought back intelligence as well as new products, exotic animals, and other curiosities for the court. Despite fictionalized celebrations of his exploits in plays and novels, Zheng's actual reports were filed away and later lost, though his journey is preserved by Ma Huan (c. 1380–1460), one of his accompanying subordinates, in *The Overall Survey of the Ocean's Shores* (*Ying-yai sheng-lan*, 1433). As these missions were intended to gauge possible threats to China from the sea and concluded that China was sufficiently strong, they did not lead to colonization abroad or the reorientation of the court away from a closed-door policy.

It remained for European traders and missionaries to make direct and forceful contacts with Ming China, and these began in the sixteenth century. The Portuguese were permitted to establish the trading post of Macao in 1557 and were later joined in the South China area by the Spanish, Dutch, French, and English, and Russian trade missions were later sent overland across Siberia to the north, especially by Peter the Great (1672–1725) and his successors. This yielded a rich literature of popular travel accounts by merchants, published back home in the tradition of Marco Polo, though with varying degrees of reliability. The Jesuit missionaries who arrived along with the traders were generally highly educated, and some were well received by Chinese scholars, Chinese officials, and the imperial court during the late Ming and early Qing (1644–1911) dynasties. Anxious to obtain more support for their missions, they wrote extensive letters, books, and reports back home describing the land and their activities. These reveal much about quotidian Chinese life while also exaggerating, to some extent, the writers' degree of success in religious conversions. Among the most successful and informative of the Jesuits was the Italian Matteo Ricci (1552–1610). As a result of these contacts, a misleading view of China as an extensive, enormously rich empire ruled benevolently by philosopher-kings emerged in Europe. This image, false though it was, appealed to the spirit of the Enlightenment, especially to such figures as Voltaire (1694–1778), and was further disseminated by bucolic scenes on porcelain and other luxury goods that stimulated the fad in Europe for chinoiserie.

During the Qing dynasty, when China was ruled by the Manchus, official embassies by European governments began to arrive in increasing number, seeking trading privileges. John Bell (1691–1780), a Scottish physician in the service of Peter the Great, described his journey to the court of the K'ang-hsi emperor (r. 1661–1722) in the company of a Russian trade mission that was personally entertained by the ruler. Further European embassies followed, led by higher-ranking figures such as the Englishman Lord Macartney (1737–1806) in 1793–1794. These were not very successful, because of lack of Chinese interest in direct diplomatic and trade relations as well as conflict over performing the court ritual of kowtowing. Still, they often produced valuable reports and illustrations, published back home in lavish editions.

By the early nineteenth century, the Enlightenment view of China had begun to change as Europe rapidly progressed both culturally and technologically. Travel writers began to depict China as, at best, a quaint land of curious customs, but, increasingly, as a backward empire burdened by a decadent, medieval culture whose stubborn rulers arrogantly refused to engage the modern world and partake of the benefits of trade and Christianity. Relations were further complicated by the growing importance of the export of opium to China and the negative effects this had on the Chinese official class, population, and economy. To protect this lucrative trade as well as sell new products to the vast Chinese market, the European imperial powers, later joined by Japan, repeatedly fought and defeated Qing forces and carved out spheres of economic influence, forcing the country to open up to a large number of foreign travelers, traders, long-term residents, missionaries, official representatives, and journalists. Modern Chinese travel literature can be said to date roughly from the Opium War of 1840–1842. This and later wars resulted in the ceding of Hong Kong as a British colony, established diplomatic relations, opened up ports such as Canton (Guangzhou), Shanghai, and Tientsin (Tianjin), and permitted travel through the interior, missionary work, and long-term residence; it also led to direct foreign bureaucratic involvement in the government. The result was that tourism also grew, as reflected in the publication of numerous guidebooks.

Classical Chinese travel writing continued during the Qing and into the modern period but generally declined in innovation and ambition. However, one noteworthy autobiographical work by the Manchu official Lin-ch'ing (Lin-ching, 1791–1846), entitled *A Wild Swan's Trail* (*Hung hsueh yin yuan*, 1849), combines vignettes of his many travels as an official with charming woodblock illustrations by artists that he took along with him. This was written not long before the widespread destruction of many of the traditional scenic places in the central and southern areas as a result of the Taiping Rebellion (1851–1864).

A new development in the second half of the nineteenth century was reports on foreign countries by Chinese travelers, who had begun to travel abroad to Japan, Europe, and America as students or diplomats; these reports present both admiring and unflattering views of the outside world. In the modern and contemporary periods, the amount of travel writing by Chinese journeying within China has further declined from the peak of the imperial era, even as writing by foreigners has greatly increased in production and popularity abroad. Among the reasons for this are the decline of the classical culture, particularly after the promotion of vernacular literature by the Literary Revolution of 1919; unsettled conditions in the country as a result of civil war, invasion, and revolution; the discouragement of personal writing for decades by the Communist Party; and, more recently, the competition with new media such as film and television.

However, travel books about China written by foreigners in the last 150 years number in the hundreds and can be seen to fall into several, overlapping categories: those written in a spirit of adventure designed to entertain readers back home or stimulate support for further expeditions; those that analyze the "problem of China" and seek to provide solutions or predict its destiny; and those written in a contrary spirit that exalt the superior values of Chinese life and culture, either traditional or revolutionary, over those of the "materialistic" West. Among the first group are a number of works by women travelers, including Mrs. Archibald Little (d. 1926), who led the campaign against foot binding, and the intrepid Victorian explorer Isabella Bird Bishop (1831–1904), whose *The Yangtze Valley and Beyond* (1899) is now considered a classic. Other explorers, like Sir Aurel Stein (1862–1943), Sven Hedin (1865–1952), and Langdon Warner (1881–1955), produced books that stimulated the competition among Westerners for obtaining antiquities, such as Stein's *Ruins of Desert Cathay* (1912).

During the first half of the twentieth century, the political, economic, and military situation in China worsened following the collapse of the Qing dynasty as the country experienced civil war, Japanese invasion, and Communist revolution. Travel writing by foreigners bifurcated: on the one hand were the more consciously literary efforts in the form of diaries, memoirs, and casual notes, written by long-term residents or insightful tourists, that paid tribute to a vanishing traditional culture, such as those by Harold Acton (1904–1994), George Kates (1895–1990), and Osbert Sitwell (1892–1969); on the other hand, there was the more journalistic reporting that focused on the realities of national survival. The Sino-Japanese War of 1937–1945 put a virtual end to tourism for pleasure and to comfortable lives for foreign residents in the occupied areas, but it produced influential accounts of the actual state of China at war such as Helen Foster Snow's (Nym Wales, 1907–1997) *Inside Red China* (1939), Agnes Smedley's (1890–1950) *Battle Hymn of China* (1943), and Edgar Snow's (1905–1972) *Red Star over China* (1937), whereas Theodore White's (1915–1986) *Thunder out of China* (1946) accurately assessed the state of the country on the eve of the civil war between the Nationalists and the Communists. Following the Communist victory in 1949, travel to China by foreigners, especially those from non-Communist countries, was severely restricted. Of those foreign writers that were admitted, most tended to produce works that admired the establishment of the revolutionary socialist order. These themes peaked during the Cultural Revolution of 1965–1976 but have virtually disappeared since China embarked on its new economic policies and reopened the country to the West. In the present, more permissive atmosphere, travel and travel writing about China are enjoying a renaissance. Among the most recent works are those concerned with observing the impact of global capitalism and market reforms on Chinese culture and society as well as those rediscovering the variety of the landscape and its peoples.

RICHARD E. STRASSBERG

## References and Further Reading


Acton, Harold, *Peonies and Ponies*, c. 1941; reprinted, 1983.

Arkush, R. David, and Leo O. Lee (translators and editors), *Land without Ghosts: Chinese Impressions of America from the Mid-Nineteenth Century to the Present*, 1989.

Arlington, L.C., and William Lewisohn, *In Search of Old Peking*, 1935; reprinted, 1987.

Auden, W.H., and Christopher Isherwood, *Journey to a War*, 1939.

Beal, Samuel (translator), *Si-yu-ki: Buddhist Records of the Western World, Translated from the Chinese of Hiuen Tsiang (629)*, 2 vols., 1884; reprinted in 1 vol., 1968.

Bell, John, *A Journey from St. Petersburg to Pekin, 1719–1722*, edited and with an introduction by J.L. Stevenson, 1966.

Bird, Isabella L., *The Yangtze Valley and Beyond: An Account of Journeys in China, Chiefly in the Province of Sze Chuan and among the Man-Tqze of the Somo Territory*, 1899.

Bland, J.O.P., *Houseboat Days in China*, 1909.

Bodde, Derk, *Peking Diary: A Year of Revolution*, 1951.

Boxer, C.R. (editor), *South China in the Sixteenth Century, Being the Narratives of Galeote Pereira, Fr. Gaspar da Cruz, O.P., Fr. Martín de Rada, O.E.S.A.*, 1953.
Bredon, Juliet, *Peking: A Historical and Intimate Description of Its Chief Places of Interest*, 1920.
Cheng Te-k'un (translator), "The Travels of Emperor Mu," *Journal of the North China Branch of the Royal Asiatic Society*, 2nd series, 64 (1933): 124–142; 65 (1934):128–149.
Ellis, Henry, *Journal of the Proceedings of the Late Embassy to China*, 1817.
Fa-Hsien, *A Record of Buddhistic Kingdoms, Being an Account by the Chinese Monk Fâ-hien of His Travels in India and Ceylon (AD 399–414) in Search of the Buddhist Books of Discipline*, translated by James Legge, 1886; reprinted, 1965.
Fracasso, Ricardo (translator), *Libri dei monti e dei mari (Shan-hai jing): Cosmographia e mitologia nella Cina Antica*, 1996.
Giles, H.A. (translator), *The Travels of Fa-hsien (399–414 AD); or, Record of the Buddhistic Kingdoms*, 1923.
Gützlaff, Charles, *Journal of Three Voyages along the Coast of China, in 1831, 1832, and 1833*, 1834; reprinted, 1968.
Hedin, Sven Anders, *The Silk Road*, translated by F.H. Lyon, 1938.
Hsu Hung-tsu, *The Travel Diaries of Hsü Hsia-K'o*, translated by Li Chi, 1974.
Ibn Batuta, *Travels in Asia and Africa, 1325–1354*, translated by H.A.R. Gibb, 1929.
Kates, George, *The Years That Were Fat: Peking, 1933–1940*, 1952.
Li Chih-ch'ang, *The Travels of an Alchemist: The Journey of the Taoist, Ch'ang-Ch'un, from China to the Hindukush at the Summons of Chingiz Khan, Recorded by His Disciple, Li Chih-Ch'ang*, translated by Arthur Waley, 1931; reprinted, 1976.
Lin-ch'ing, *Hung hsueh yin yuan*, 1849; as *A Wild Swan's Trail: The Travels of a Mandarin*, edited and translated by T.C. Lai, 1978.
Little, Mrs. Archibald, *Intimate China: The Chinese as I Have Seen Them*, 1899.
Little, Mrs. Archibald, *In the Land of the Blue Gown*, 1902.
Lu Yu, *South China in the Twelfth Century: A Translation of Lu Yu's Travel Diaries, July 3–December 6, 1170*, translated by Chun-shu Chang and Joan Smythe, 1981.
Ma Huan, *Ying-yai sheng-lan: The Overall Survey of the Ocean's Shores (1433)*, translated by J.V.G. Mills, 1970.
Macartney, George, *An Embassy to China, Being the Journal Kept by Lord Macartney During His Embassy to the Emperor Ch'ien-lung, 1793–1794*, edited by J.L. Cranmer-Byng, 1962.
Mathieu, Rémi (translator), *Le Mu tianzi zhuan*, 1978.
Mathieu, Rémi (translator), *Étude sur la mythologie et l'ethnographie de la Chine ancienne*, 2 vols., 1983
Mirsky, Jeannette (editor), *The Great Chinese Travelers: An Anthology*, 1964.
Polo, Marco, *The Description of the World*, translated and annotated by A.C. Moule and Paul Pelliot, 2 vols., 1938; reprinted, 1976.
Reischauer, Edwin O. (translator), *Ennin's Diary: The Record of a Pilgrimage to China in Search of the Law*, 1955.
Ricci, Matteo, *China in the Sixteenth Century: The Journals of Matthew Ricci, 1583–1610*, translated by Louis J. Gallagher, 1953.
Ripa, Matteo, *Memoirs of Father Ripa*, translated by Fortunato Prandi, 1846.
Russell, Bertrand, *The Problem of China*, 1922.
Salzman, Mark, *Iron and Silk*, 1986.
Sitwell, Osbert, *Escape With Me! An Oriental Sketch Book*, 1939.
Smedley, Agnes, *Battle Hymn of China*, 1943.
Snow, Edgar, *Red Star over China*, 1937.
Stein, Aurel, *Ruins of Desert Cathay; Personal Narrative of Explorations in Central Asia and Westernmost China*, 1912; reprinted, 1985.
Strassberg, Richard E. (translator), *Inscribed Landscapes: Travel Writing from Imperial China*, 1994.
Trigault, Nicolas, *The China That Was: China as Discovered by the Jesuits at the Close of the Sixteenth Century*, translated by Louis J. Gallagher, 1942.
Verbiest, Ferdinand, *Correspondance de Ferdinand Verbiest de la Compagnie de Jésus (1623–1688)*, edited by H. Josson and L. Willaert, 1938.
Wales, Nym [Helen Foster Snow], *Inside Red China*, 1939.
Warner, Langdon, *The Long Old Road in China*, 1926.
Watters, Thomas, *On Yuan Chwang's Travels in India, 629–645* AD, 1904–1905.
White, Theodore H., and Annalee Jacoby, *Thunder out of China*, 1946.
Yang Hsüan-chih, *A Record of Buddhist Monasteries in Loyang*, translated by Yi-t'ung Wang, 1984.
Yule, Henry (translator and editor), *Cathay and the Way Thither, Being a Collection of Medieval Notices of China*, revised by Henri Cordier, 3 vols., 1913–1916.
Zhang Dai, *Souvenirs rêvés de Tao'an*, translated by Brigitte Teboue-Wang, 1995.

*See also* **Beijing (Peking)**

## CIEZA DE LEÓN, PEDRO (c. 1520–1554)

***Spanish Conquistador and Chronicler***

Pedro Cieza, the son of a merchant from the town of Llerena in Extremadura, was only a teenager when in 1534 the sensational news of the conquest of Peru by Francisco Pizarro reached Seville, together with the treasure ruthlessly extracted from the Incas. The following year, Cieza crossed the ocean to spend the next 15 years of his life in South America, as conqueror, settler, and, more exceptionally, self-appointed chronicler of the discovery and conquest of Peru. By the time Cieza returned to Seville in 1550, he had traveled through many of the regions of modern Panama, Colombia, Ecuador, Peru, and Bolivia. Largely on the basis of this personal experience, he had also written *The Chronicle of Peru*, surely one of the most ambitious, coherent, and balanced historical accounts of the dramatic encounter between the Spanish and the Incas.

Pedro Cieza began collecting notes and writing while he participated (between 1536 and 1546) in the exploration, plunder, conquest, and settlement of the northern Andes, in the western parts of modern Colombia. He thus combined arms and letters, fulfilling one of the aristocratic ideals of his age. In Cieza's description of these regions were recorded many aspects of native life at a time when the dramatic impact of the Spanish arrival was just beginning to be felt. He also described in detail the enormous physical obstacles that the Spanish had to overcome in order to accomplish their conquests. According to Cieza, what gave the Spanish their ultimate advantage over the more numerous natives was their military superiority. While in his chronicle Cieza often deplored with genuine concern the destruction that the Spanish brought upon the native world, condemning their cruelty, he never hid that he personally shared their aim of finding gold or other sources of wealth and satisfaction (including indigenous labor and women). However, Cieza took the moral side of the conquest equally seriously. He was in no doubt that the whole conquest obeyed a divine plan against the devil's hold over the native population and was concerned with their Christianization. Cieza was also worried about with the neglected task of leaving a proper written record of a historical process that he understood to be of obvious significance.

Although Cieza was already writing before traveling to Peru, from at least as early as 1541, it was in the former Inca empire that he would both find a more decisive patronage and define his true subject, by obtaining the support of royal commander Pedro de la Gasca (a talented bureaucrat sent from Spain) for his ambition to write comprehensively about the conquest of Peru. It was in Peru that the Spanish found the greatest wealth and also the most sophisticated native civilization of South America. It was also in Peru, between 1547 and 1550, that Cieza's research became more wide-ranging and systematic. He relied on interviews with both Spaniards and natives in order to reconstruct events, thus contrasting opinions and correcting rumor with fact when possible. La Gasca also allowed Cieza to consult the correspondence of the leaders of the civil war and facilitated his travels throughout the kingdom, where local royal officials assisted him in gathering information. In Cuzco, Cieza interviewed the *quipucamayos*, the keepers of the Inca mythological and dynastic memory. Thus, Cieza's personal travels allowed him to complete his historical research, by making the geographical and ethnographic setting of the conquest and subsequent civil wars both more vivid and more realistic. It seems that the bulk of the four-part chronicle was written during these years in Peru, although it is clear that further revisions were introduced well into 1553.

The *Chronicle of Peru* is distinguished by its ambition. It is divided into four parts, of which only the first was published, with illustrations, during the author's lifetime (Seville, 1553; twice in Antwerp, 1554). This first part described the geographical setting of the Andes province by province, and it is especially important for its natural and ethnographic descriptions. It also recorded the extension of Spanish civilization through the foundation of their cities over the ruins of a fast-receding native world. The second part was an antiquarian investigation into the history of the Inca dynasty on the basis of native informants. This served as background for the third part, describing the discovery and conquest of Peru by a small band of Spaniards. The fourth part, more extensive and perhaps never fully completed, narrated in five sections the various civil wars between the Spanish for the spoils of conquest, up until President la Gasca's establishment of royal authority.

This dramatic structure allowed Cieza to emphasize two themes: the fact that the conquest as a whole could only be rationalized as providential, and the stark contrast between the civilizing Incas and the cruel and wasteful Spaniards. The Incas were depicted as a civilizing force within the context of a native world dominated by the devil, in which, for example, cannibalism and sodomy were rife (Cieza was especially keen to contrast the well-organized imperial Incas with the wilder, less rational Peruvian natives whom they had conquered, or those whom Cieza had himself encountered in Colombia). The Spanish, on the other hand, while heroic in their willingness to withstand extreme hardship, and despite their allegiance to Christianity, were often dominated by greed and ambition. In many ways, observed Cieza, the Inca's excellent political order had degenerated, for lack of good government, after the coming of the Christians. The continuous civil wars among the conquerors left a particularly strong impression on Cieza. It was God's desire to offer salvation to the indigenous population that gave meaning to the conquest, not the moral virtues of the Spanish themselves.

Cieza did not idealize the Incas for purely rhetorical aims: their rationality and civilization were only relative, comparable to the ancients but also marked by barbarism and cruelty. His analysis implied the existence of a complex ranking of levels of civilization. Equally revealing was Cieza's portrayal of Atahualpa as a tragic figure, intelligent but fatally flawed by the circumstances of the civil war that his own ambition had brought upon Peru. Cieza was, however, not totally faithful to native self-understanding: he also rationalized their myths in order to clear the way for a Christian monopoly of divine power. His intention was humanistic: the more he could rationalize Inca myths as historical events, the less would the real specter of devilish influences that pervaded indigenous idolatry and customs stand in the way of a synthesis between Inca civilization and Christian values. Cieza was firm in his Christian conviction in the unity of destiny in the whole of mankind.

The greatest mystery about Pedro Cieza is his education, or lack thereof. Cieza was very young when he traveled to the New World, and it is difficult to imagine that he would have had any opportunity to pursue higher education. As the son of a merchant, Cieza must of course have learned to read and write in Spain. It is nevertheless probable that his reading of classical historians such as Diodorus Siculus or Livy was in the vernacular. It was from these classical models, together with some of the already existing historians of the New World, especially his older contemporary Gonzalo Fernández de Oviedo, that Cieza derived his inspiration as historian. What is nevertheless remarkable is that Cieza worked largely on his own initiative, with little formal training, intellectually isolated in the most difficult of circumstances, reading voraciously, one imagines, when opportunity offered, but otherwise left to his own devices. In stark contrast with Oviedo, who had spent a number of formative years in Italy and at the court before settling in Santo Domingo, Pedro Cieza transformed what must have been the romantic dream of a teenager into an original work that in some ways superseded what he could have learned from his models. He wished to represent his undertaking of writing history as heroic given the circumstances. Modern commentators have agreed that while Cieza styled himself as chronicler, his methods and vision were those of a historian.

Although not without ideological contradictions, what makes Cieza's book so extraordinary is the writer's ability to take an informed and balanced view of the historical viewpoint and human qualities of both natives and Europeans. Cieza dramatized perhaps better than most other early chroniclers and travelers, in America or Asia, the fact that, in their conquests overseas, the Europeans failed to live up to the crucial assumption that the Christians were always the more civilized.

Despite the success of the first part, which Cieza himself presented to Philip II in 1552, his early death in 1554 prevented him from publishing the second and third parts (he was aware that the fourth part, depicting the civil wars, dealt with too sensitive a theme and should not be published for a number of years). In Cieza's last will, he expressed his desire that his unpublished manuscripts should be sent to the Dominican missionary Bartolomé de Las Casas, notorious for his defense of the rights of the natives at court. This probably reveals an ideological sympathy. But the unpublished parts remained instead in the possession of the Council of the Indies and the Inquisition, and they were eventually used by successive royal cosmographers. Eventually, the official court historian of the Indies, Antonio de Herrera, plagiarized Cieza extensively in his *General History of the Deeds of the Castilians in the Islands and Mainland of the Ocean Sea* (Madrid, 1601–1615).

JOAN-PAU RUBIÉS

## Biography

Born in Spain, c. 1520 or 1522. Son of a merchant from the town of Llerena in the region of Extremadura. Left Spain for the New World, 1535. Settled initially in present-day Colombia; participated in the *entradas*, the Spanish expeditions of exploration and plunder. Served under the conquerors Alonso de Cáceres, 1536; Juan de Vadillo, 1537–1538; and Jorge Robledo, 1539–1546. Lost his grant of natives and his mines in the province of Arma after Robledo's fall, 1546. Traveled to Peru, as participant in the royalist camp in the war that followed the rebellion of Gonzalo Pizarro. Attracted the patronage of royal commander Pedro de la Gasca for his literary project, *The Chronicle of Peru;* traveled to the southern parts of Peru as far as the silver mines of Potosí. Completed first draft of the *Chronicle* by 1550. Left Peru and returned to Seville, 1550; married Isabel, the daughter of a Seville merchant, as previously arranged in Peru with the bride's brother, Pedro López de Abreu. Settled in Seville and undertook the publication of his work; went to Toledo to present a copy of the first part to Philip II, 1552. Died in 1554.

## References and Further Reading

Cieza de León, Pedro, *Parte primera de la crónica del Perú: Que tracta la demarcación de sus provincias; la descripción dellas; las fundaciones de las nuevas ciudades; los ritos y costumbres de los Indios; y otras cosas estrañas dignas de ser sabidas*, 1553; 2nd edition, 1554; as *The Travels of Pedro Cieza de León*, translated by Clements R. Markham, 1864.

Cieza de León, Pedro, *Segunda parte de la crónica del Perú: Que trata del Señorío de los Incas*, edited by Marcos Jiménez de la Espada, 1880; as *Crónica del Perú: Segunda parte*, edited by Francesca Cantù, 1985; as *The Second Part of the Chronicle of Peru*, translated by Clements R. Markham, 1883.

Cieza de León, Pedro, *Crónica del Perú: Tercera parte*, edited by Francesca Cantù, 1987; as *The Discovery and Conquest of Peru: Chronicles of the New World Encounter*, edited and translated by Alexandra Parma Cook and Noble David Cook, 1998.

Cieza de León, Pedro, *Guerras civiles del Perú*, edited by José Sancho Rayón, 3 vols., 1877–1881; as *Crónica del Perú: Cuarta parte*, edited by Pedro Guibovich Pérez, Gabriela Benavides de Rivero, and Laura Gutiérrez Arbulú, 3 vols., 1991–1994:

1. *Guerra de las Salinas*, 1877; as *The War of Las Salinas*, translated by Clements R. Markham, 1923.
2. *Guerra de Chupas*, 1881; *as The War of Chupas*, translated by Clements R. Markham, 1918.
3. *La Guerra de Quito*, edited by Manuel Serrano y Sanz, 1909; the first 53 chapters as *The War of Quito*, translated by Clements R. Markham, 1913.

Cieza de León, Pedro, *Obras completas* [The Complete Works], 3 vols., edited by Carmelo Sáenz de Santa María, 1984–1985.

## CIRCUMNAVIGATION NARRATIVES

Nearly every literate person who has circumnavigated the world has written about the experience, which is often seen as pivotal or life altering. It took Charles Darwin five years to sail around the world in *Beagle*, but he spent the rest of his life sifting through the materials he collected and writing about his experience and findings. More recently, Robin Lee Graham, an American teenager, sailed around the world alone in a small sailboat. His memoir *Dove* (1972), has become an inspiration to countless adolescents the world over, many of whom have never been near the ocean.

Ferdinand Magellan was the first to lead a successful expedition to circle the globe (1519–1522). Magellan himself was killed in the Philippines, but Antonio Pigafetta, one of 17 survivors who straggled back to Spain, wrote a short book, *The First Voyage around the World*, an abbreviated English version of which was included by Richard Eden in his *Decades of the Newe World* (1555). The first full English translation did not appear until 1625, in Samuel Purchas's *Hakluytus Posthumus; or, Purchas His Pilgrimes*. Purchas included accounts of the first six circumnavigations in his massive three-folio-volume compilation of travel stories and documents. All the early circumnavigators traveled west from Europe, sailing southwest to Brazil and following the coast to Patagonia. At first, navigators believed that South America was attached to a great southern continent, and the Strait of Magellan was seen as the only route to the Pacific. The Dutch captain Willem Cornelisz Schouten van Hoorn went further south to avoid the Spanish claim on the Strait of Magellan (the Portuguese had a similar claim on the Cape of Good Hope), and he was the first to round Cape Horn in 1616. His discovery was important, because doubling the Horn was found to be faster and less hazardous than sailing through the Strait of Magellan.

Nevertheless, circumnavigation was a very dangerous activity. Magellan began with five ships and 270 men. Three years later, one ship and 17 men returned to a Spanish harbor near the one they had left. Sir Francis Drake, the first captain to lead an expedition around the world and live to tell the tale, lost well over half of his men and two of the three ships he began with. Drake did not actually write an account of his voyage, but an anonymous sailor did leave a short account, which Richard Hakluyt published in his great compendium, *Principal Navigations* (1598–1600). It was not just storms, poor maps, and uncertain navigational equipment that made these voyages dangerous; disease, notably scurvy, was the chief cause of death. In some cases, the danger and loss of life were considered worth the reward, largely plunder. The Spanish stole from the indigenous populations, the English stole from the Spanish, and the Dutch would take what they could where they could.

This was not just a sixteenth-century pattern. Open privateering, plundering, and stealing went on well into the eighteenth century. Henry Morgan, William Dampier, and George Shelvocke, to mention just three prominent pirates, found the risks worth the rewards. Morgan never circumnavigated the world but was content to confine his raids to the West Indies. Dampier wrote a lengthy account of his travels around the world: *A New Voyage round the World* (1697) gave a patriotic spin to his story of robbery and plunder. Dampier wrote two other books on his travels. In part because of these books, he was given command of a warship, *Roebuck*, to explore Australia. Dampier planned to sail around the Cape of Good Hope and, remaining in the southern latitudes, look for the southern continent before returning to England via Cape Horn. Had Dampier completed the mission, he would have been the first to sail from west to east around the world. Unfortunately, he failed so famously that he was court-martialed and declared unfit for further command. The judgment did not prevent Dampier from publishing an account of his expedition, *Voyage to New Holland* (1703–1709).

A west-to-east circumnavigation was first completed by Captain James Cook in his second great expedition, 1772–1775. Cook is perhaps the greatest circumnavigator and explorer of all time, and he marks a welcome change from piracy to genuine exploration. On his first circumnavigation, he sailed to Tahiti with the noted astronomer Joseph Banks to observe the transit of Venus over the sun. Cook then went on to discover the southeastern corner of Australia and to circumnavigate both islands of New Zealand and chart their coastlines. On Cook's second expedition, he sailed from Plymouth in 1772 for the Cape of Good Hope, where he rested for several weeks before heading southwest into uncharted seas. Cook confronted the great ice floes surrounding the seventh continent as he reached 71°10′ south latitude, and he concluded that either there was no southern continent or it was so far south as to be bound by impenetrable snow and ice and of no use to mankind. Cook's account, *A Voyage towards the South Pole*, was published in 1777. It is a detailed story with invaluable information for future sailors. Among other things, he noted that seawater does not freeze at 0° C and that icebergs are formed of freshwater not salt water. In this long journey with great periods of time spent at sea, Cook lost only four men and only one of those to scurvy. He not only proved that scurvy could be prevented by a good diet, but his proof finally convinced other captains to protect their crews in a like manner.

On Cook's third voyage, the great explorer was killed during a skirmish with the local inhabitants on

Mid-ocean incident during the 1615–1616 Dutch circumnavigation by Le Maire and Schouten (from Burney's *Chronological History of the Voyages and Discoveries in the South Sea or Pacific Ocean*, vol. 2, 1806). *Courtesy of the Travellers Club, London; Bridgeman Art Library, agent.*

Hawaii. His account up to that point was edited and augmented by James King and published in 1784. Not only are these books valuable sources of geographical and navigational information, but they also contain useful ethnographic observations on the people of the North and South Pacific along with data on the flora and fauna of the regions.

Following Cook's circumnavigation, narratives move in three different directions. Exploration continues, but now largely confined to the polar regions. The most notable of these narratives was James Ross's *A Voyage of Discovery and Research 1839–43* (1847), in which the author/explorer describes his charting of the coast of Antarctica. The second direction is narratives of expeditions to make more detailed charts of previously discovered areas. On a French charting expedition led by Louis Claude de Freycinet, his young wife, Rose, dressed as a man, stowed away with her husband's knowledge. She was one of the first women to sail around the world and leave a written account. Her journal was not published until 1927, in a very limited and expensive edition. An English translation by M.S. Rivière, *A Woman of Courage*, appeared in 1996. Rose was just 22 when she accompanied her husband on the long and arduous voyage.

Perhaps the most famous charting and scientific expedition was the voyage of *Beagle*. Charles Darwin had just graduated from Cambridge when he was selected as the ship's naturalist. Although the great product of this voyage, Darwin's *Origin of the Species*, was not published until much later, his personal account of the voyage in the form of a diary was printed in 1839 as the third volume of the *Narrative of the Surveying Voyages of the Adventure and Beagle between the Years 1826 and 1836*. Owing to its popularity, the third volume soon became available by itself; and in 1845, prior to yet another edition, Darwin made extensive and final revisions and retitled his book, as *Journal of Researches*.

The third direction these narratives take is the travelogue, that is, a journey undertaken to gather material for a book. Mark Twain's *Following the Equator* (1897) is a satirical meander around the world. Twain makes wry comments on the people and places visited while on a lecture tour. Near the end of the nineteenth century, newspapers in the United States found that round-the-world trips by clever journalists were an easy way to stimulate circulation. In 1889, Nellie Bly and Elizabeth Bisland raced each other around the world, sending back lively accounts of their adventures to their respective newspapers.

By this time, sailing around the world had become so commonplace that, to gain any notice, one had to do something different or dangerous. The first known individual to circumnavigate the world single-handedly was the Canadian Joshua Slocum, in a 36-foot sloop, *Spray*, which he had built himself. Leaving Gloucester, Massachusetts, in May 1895, he returned to the same port in July 1898 to great acclaim. Slocum's book, *Sailing Alone around the World*, was published in 1899. A particularly poignant circumnavigation was undertaken by 16-year-old Robin Lee Graham in 1965. He took seven years to complete his journey in a 24-foot sloop, *Dove*. Although young Graham began alone, he picked up a wife and daughter along the way plus countless adventures that keep his book, *Dove* (1972), still in print.

The most famous solo circumnavigation was by Sir Francis Chichester, who was 65 and a survivor of lung cancer by the time he set out to sail around the world faster than any previous solo mariner. He made only one stop, in Sydney, Australia, where *Gypsy Moth* was extensively repaired and refitted before the second and final leg of his journey eastward around Cape Horn and then back to Plymouth, where he arrived on 28 May 1967, nine months and one day after departing. Chichester's achievement caught the imagination of the British and indeed the entire world. He was knighted by Elizabeth II, and, perhaps more importantly, his book, *Gypsy Moth Circles the World*, was rushed to press later that year and became an instant best-seller. There remained only the final triumph of sailing around the world single-handedly with no stops. That was accomplished the following year by Robin Knox-Johnston, winner and only finisher of the first nonstop round-the-world race. His book *A World of My Own* (1969) recounts the adventure.

This, of course, did not put an end to the interest in circumnavigation. Round-the-world nonstop yacht races are organized periodically. Other sailors looking for adventure and solitude find themselves sailing around the world and, more often than not, writing about their experiences. And for good reason: the worry of scurvy and pirates has largely passed, and the Panama and Suez Canals eliminate the need for doubling the Capes Horn and Good Hope, but there is still plenty of adventure for anyone undertaking a surface circumnavigation of the world.

DAVID JUDKINS

### References and Further Reading

Chichester, Francis, *Gypsy Moth Circles the World*, 1967.

Cook, James, *A Voyage towards the South Pole, and round the World. Performed in His Majesty's Ships the Resolution and Adventure, in the Years 1772, 1773, 1774, and 1775 . . .*, 1777.

Cook, James, and James King *A Voyage to the Pacific Ocean Undertaken by the Command of His Majesty, for Making Discoveries in the Northern Hemisphere in the Years 1776, 1777, 1778, 1779 and 1780*, 3 vols. and atlas, 1784.

Cook, James, *The Journals of Captain James Cook on His Voyages of Discovery*, edited by J.C. Beaglehole, 4 vols., 1955–1974.

Dampier, William, *A New Voyage round the World*, 1697.

Dampier, William, *A Voyage to New Holland &c. in the Year 1699*, part 1, 1703; part 2, 1709; edited by James Spencer, 1981.

Dampier, William, *Voyages and Discoveries*, edited by Clennell Wilkinson, 1931.

Darwin, Charles, *Journal of Researches into the Geology and Natural History of Various Countries Visited by HMS Beagle, under the Command of Captain Fitzroy, R.N., from 1832 to 1836* (vol. 3 of *Narrative of the Surveying Voyages of His Majesty's Ships Adventure and Beagle*, edited by Robert Fitzroy), 1839; revised edition, 1845; as *The Voyage of the Beagle*, 1909.

Darwin, Charles, *Charles Darwin's Beagle Diary*, edited by Richard Darwin Keynes, 1988.

Eden, Richard (translator), *The Decades of the Newe World; or, West India . . . by Peter Martyr of Angeleria*, 1555.

Freycinet, Rose Marie Pinon de, *A Woman of Courage: The Journal of Rose de Freycinet on Her Voyage around the World 1817–1820*, translated and edited by Marc Serge Rivière, 1996.

Graham, Robin Lee, *Dove*, 1972.

Hakluyt, Richard, *The Principall Navigations, Voiages, and Discoveries of the English Nation, Made by Sea or over Land, to the Most Remote and Farthest Corners of the Earth*, 1589; revised edition as *The Principal Navigations, Voyages, Traffiques, and Discoveries of the English Nation*, 3 vols., 1598–1600; 12 vols., 1903–1905.

Knox-Johnston, Robin, *A World of My Own: The Single-Handed, Non-Stop Circumnavigation of the World in Suhaili*, 1969.

Pigafetta, Antonio, *The First Voyage around the World (1519–1522): An Account of Magellan's Expedition*, edited by Theodore J. Cachey Jr., 1995.

Ross, James Clerk, *A Voyage of Discovery and Research in the Southern and Antarctic Regions, during the Years 1839–43*, 1847.

Slocum, Joshua, *Sailing Alone around the World*, 1899.

Twain, Mark, *Following the Equator: A Journey around the World*, 1897.

## CLAPPERTON, HUGH (1788–1827) *British Explorer*

Hugh Clapperton led an extremely adventurous life, which culminated in two expeditions to the Sudanic region of West Africa. It is on these that his fame chiefly rests. Yet that fame is not as great as such an effective as well as genial, entertaining, and informative a traveler deserves. Unsympathetic editing of his journals in the 1820s, combined with the fact that the second journey was something of an anticlimax both geographically and politically, has meant that Clapperton's name does not always spring readily to mind as that of a major explorer.

One of 21 children of a Scottish surgeon, Clapperton was apprenticed to the sea as a cabin boy. Press-ganged into the navy, Clapperton deserted but was forgiven and made a midshipman, and he began to serve with distinction in the Mediterranean, in the East Indies, on the Canadian Great Lakes, and, most importantly, at the capture of Mauritius from the French in 1810. The end of the Napoleonic wars and half-pay did not appeal, so Clapperton leaped at the chance opened up for him by Walter Oudney, his fellow Scottish ex-sailor, to join an official expedition that was to penetrate to the West African interior across the desert from Tripoli. The Colonial Office added Major Dixon Denham to the party. It was, unfortunately, not clear who was in overall charge, and Denham was a difficult man whose poor relations with Clapperton undermined the enterprise. Yet the achievements were considerable, not least on Clapperton's part. On this expedition of 1822–1825 and its follow-up in 1825–1827, he came near to solving the problem of the course and termination of the Niger that was so exercising European geographers, found out what had happened to Mungo Park, provided the first reliable report of the results among the Hausa kingdoms of the great jihad of Uthman dan Fodio, and more generally gathered a wealth of information on the basic nature of the Sahara, Bornu, and Hausaland, to which was added data on Yoruba societies on the second venture. Clapperton was also the means by which the British government began to implement a policy of curtailing both the Saharan and maritime slave trades and introducing "legitimate" trade.

The available writings consist essentially of daily journals, which have been published in edited form, and some correspondence, a small part of which has also been published. In the cases of both expeditions, the journals were edited by John Barrow, the formidable second secretary at the Admiralty. Barrow perhaps found the ex-cabin boy déclassé and certainly had theories about the Niger that the explorer seemed to be disproving. His editing of Clapperton, as he confessed,

The camp at Woodie (Ouidi) on the northwest shore of Lake Chad in 1823 (from a drawing by Dixon Denham in his *Narrative of Travels and Discoveries in Northern and Central Africa*, 1826). *Courtesy of British Library, London.*

involved "dishing him and trimming him as much as I dare." No doubt much was lost in the process, but comparison of edited and unedited Clapperton prose suggests that Barrow did not prevent Clapperton's essential nature and approach from emerging.

Although making conscious efforts to relieve suffering, as when Clapperton upbraided some guards with "how unworthy it was of brave men to behave with cruelty to their prisoners" or when he condemned the effects of the slave trade, it is the story he less consciously tells of his capacity for commanding respect and fellowship across racial, cultural, and religious divides—in the latter respect, no mean feat in the aftermath of a jihad—that impresses. Claperton never denied his Christianity despite the initial hostility of many of those Muslims he encountered. His relationship with the son and successor of Uthman, Mohammed Bello, is particularly important as well as constituting a fascinating feature of the record of the two journeys. More intellectual than Clapperton, Bello asked questions about Nestorianism and Socinianism, which the explorer evaded by saying that he was a Protestant and trying to explain Protestantism instead. Clapperton says that he told everyone at Sokoto that he had found "not naked savages," but people "civilized, learned, humane and pious." While this was said as diplomatic flattery, it was also a truth that Clapperton was sensible enough to comprehend. This made him all the more anxious to negotiate a means of developing Anglo-Sokoto relations. It was hardly Clapperton's fault that realpolitik meant that Bello was less helpful in 1827 than he had been in 1824. The disappointment may not only have made Clapperton uncharacteristically irritable and untactful but also helped on the explorer's death, which left his servant Lander to return home with the story. Another result of the difficulties with Bello and Clapperton's demise was that it was not possible to establish conclusively that the Niger flowed to the Bight of Benin.

Personally, Clapperton became racially tolerant. He wondered what the Prophet would have made of the black men who so vigorously promoted the faith but concluded that racial differences soon faded away. Denham maliciously retailed a story that Clapperton was homosexual, but, in fact, he seems to have been very much taken with women and they with him—not least the widow Zuma, who tried to marry him for a mixture of political as well as presumably sexual reasons. Clapperton's sense of humor was more often directed against himself than others, as when he tells of dressing up in his best naval uniform to enter Kano only to find that no one took any notice of him at all. Those best qualified to judge have found Clapperton an impressive figure. Curtin praises his sympathy for and interest in the people he met. Even though rancor entered their final relationship, Mohammed Bello had been able to tell George IV that Clapperton was "an intelligent and wise man."

The story of the first expedition is probably best followed in the Hakluyt Society volumes edited by Bovill, and the second in the original albeit unsatisfactory volume of 1829. Bruce-Lockhart has recently produced two volumes reprinting some of this material from the first expedition. There are careful annotations, but it is a pity that introductory material anachronistically puts Clapperton in the context of explorations of the "dark continent." Some original letters, journals, and papers survive, many in official collections.

Roy Bridges

## Biography

Born in Annan, Dumfriesshire, May 1788. Apparently received little schooling, but learned some navigation. Apprenticed as a cabin boy on a Liverpool trading ship, 1801. Charged with smuggling offenses at Liverpool. Press-ganged into the Royal Navy as a cook; deserted his frigate at Gibraltar, 1806. Joined a privateer ship but was caught, forgiven, and made a midshipman. Volunteered on *Clorinde* frigate, 1808. Served on the Spanish coast, in the East Indies, at the storming of Port Louis, Mauritius, 1810, and in Canada, where he was promoted to lieutenant. Reportedly nearly married a Huron princess. Returned to Scotland on half-pay, 1817; lived in Lochmaben. Recruited by Walter Oudney to join the Admiralty and Colonial Office mission to the interior of Africa, 1821. With Dixon Denham and Oudney, traveled from Tripoli to Lake Chad and Bornu. Oudney died; Clapperton traveled on to Kano and Sokoto, 1824. Promoted to rank of commander, 1825; returned to Sokoto via Guinea coast, 1825–1827.

Died of dysentery at Chungary, near Sokoto, Fulani empire, 13 April 1827.

### References and Further Reading

Clapperton, Hugh, et al., *Narrative of Travels and Discoveries in Northern and Central Africa in the Years 1822, 1823 and 1824 . . . by Major Denham, Captain Clapperton, and the late Doctor Oudney*, 1826.

Clapperton, Hugh, *Journal of a Second Expedition into the Interior of Africa, from the Bight of Benin to Soccatoo, to Which Is Added the Journal of Richard Lander*, 1829; facsimile, 1966.

Clapperton, Hugh, and Richard Lander, *Records of Captain Clapperton's Last Expedition to Africa by His Faithful Attendant . . .*, 2 vols., 1830.

Clapperton, Hugh, *Travels and Discoveries in Northern and Central Africa in 1822, 1823 and 1824 . . . with a Short Account of Clapperton and Lander's Second Journey in 1825, 1826 and 1827*, 4 vols., 1831.

Clapperton, Hugh, *Missions to the Niger*, edited by E.W. Bovill, 4 vols., 1964–1966.

Clapperton, Hugh, *Clapperton in Borno: Journals of the Travels in Borno of Lieutenant Hugh Clapperton, R.N., from January 1823 to September 1824*, edited by Jamie Bruce-Lockhart, 1996.

Clapperton, Hugh, *Difficult and Dangerous Roads: Hugh Clapperton's Travels in Sahara and Fezzan (1822–25)*, edited by Jamie Bruce-Lockhart and John Wright, 2000.

*See also* **Denham, Dixon; Lander, Richard Lemon and John**

## CLARKE, EDWARD DANIEL (1769–1822) *British Mineralogist, Antiquarian, and Travel Writer*

Edward Daniel Clarke was a scientist and antiquarian whose travels ranged from as far north as Lapland to as far south as Egypt. The six volumes of Clarke's *Travels* united his extensive knowledge with his flair for dramatic narrative, so that he became internationally famous as "a literary and scientific traveller" (Gunning, 1854).

Clarke was able to travel thanks to the institution of educational tours. He came from a family of clerics and was not well off, although his father, Edward Clarke, had written *Letters concerning the Spanish Nation: Written at Madrid during . . . 1760 and 1761* (1763) while chaplain to the British embassy there. On graduating Cambridge, the son took a post as tutor to the Hon. Henry Tufton and accompanied him on a tour of Britain. This resulted in his first published work, *A Tour through the South of England, Wales and Part of Ireland* (1793). As his biographer wrote, the *Tour* "abounds with trifling incidents of life, and florid descriptions of scenery" (Otter, 1824). Clarke came to consider the work unworthy of him. Although lively and entertaining, it was not marked by the vast tracts of factual information that characterized his later work.

In 1792–1794, Clarke made the Grand Tour as companion to Thomas Hill, second Lord Berwick, his near-contemporary at Cambridge. While at Naples, he met Sir William Hamilton and formed collections of pictures, books, prints, and minerals. The experience, however, left Clarke cynical about the value of the traditional Grand Tour, and he wrote *Letters on Travel* (unfinished), which urged the young traveler to go instead to Greece, Asia Minor, Syria, and Egypt to help "rescue the inestimable monuments of antiquity from the jaws of everlasting oblivion" (Otter, 1824).

On Clarke's return from Italy, another tutoring post allowed him to travel to Scotland and the Western Isles in 1797. His journal from this tour was never published, but extracts survive in *The Life and Remains* (Otter, 1824).

Back in Cambridge, Clarke, now elected a Fellow of Jesus College, took on another student, John Marten Cripps, with whom he was to make his most extensive tour. Together with two other Fellows—his biographer-to-be, William Otter, and Thomas Robert Malthus, who was looking for data for his work on population—Clarke and Cripps set off for Scandinavia in May 1799. They intended to be back in Cambridge in time for the autumn term. However, while Otter and Malthus came home as planned, Clarke and Cripps decided to press on. After visiting St. Petersburg and Moscow, they traveled down through the Crimea and crossed the Black Sea to Constantinople.

Although nominally traveling for the benefit of his young student, "the cause and companion of my travels," and financed by Cripps's inheritance, Clarke

Clarke visits the ruins of a temple in the Troad, a popular destination for travelers keen to establish the topography of Homer's Troy (from *Travels in Various Countries of Europe, Asia and Africa*, part 2, *Greece, Egypt and the Holyland*, 1812). *Courtesy of the Travellers Club, London; Bridgeman Art Library, agent.*

clearly was pursuing his own interests as much as his pupil's. The amenable Cripps, he remarked, "would go to the mountains of the moon, if I would consent to accompany him" (Otter, 1824). Their route was also dictated by the course of the Napoleonic wars, as British victories gradually opened up the Levant to them.

After exploring the Plain of Troy, Clarke and Cripps made their way to Rhodes and sailed for Egypt, where Clarke's brother was stationed with Nelson's fleet in Aboukir Bay, then to Cyprus and next the Holy Land. After the capitulation of Alexandria, they were able to enter the city with the British army. In autumn 1801, they sailed north to Greece, the highlight of the tour for the Hellenist Clarke. There, they made substantial acquisitions of manuscripts, sculpture, and inscriptions and witnessed the removal of friezes from the Parthenon by Lord Elgin's agents, which Clarke later described in typically dramatic language. They returned to Constantinople and, finally, set off home via Hungary, Vienna, and Paris.

Throughout their travels, Clarke and Cripps had made copious notes and collections. In Constantinople, Clarke wrote of sending home 76 cases. Cripps's acquisitions were even more extensive. The *Monthly Magazine* was to report (1 April 1803) that Clarke and Cripps had "brought home a greater variety of natural and literary curiosities, minerals, plants, pictures, busts, manuscripts, &c. than was ever, as is supposed, brought by any individual into England before."

Returning to Cambridge, Clarke presented the university with a collection of ancient sculpture, notably the so-called Ceres of Eleusis, a colossal bust removed from its site despite the protests of local inhabitants. In return, he was awarded the degree of LL D. In the next few years, Clarke published several antiquarian works relating to objects acquired while traveling, including *The Tomb of Alexander* (1805) and *Greek Marbles* (1809). In 1807, he began to lecture on mineralogy, using materials gathered on his tour, and, in 1808, was appointed professor.

The first volume of Clarke's *Travels in Various Countries* was published in 1810. It met with immediate success, although his critical comments on Russia proved controversial. Further volumes followed in 1812, 1814, 1816, and 1819. Clarke earned £6,595 from the work and attained some measure of celebrity: his visitors and correspondents included Byron, Maria Edgeworth, and the Near Eastern traveler John Lewis Burckhardt. However, dogged by ill health and busy with lectures and chemical experiments, he was often hard-pressed to find time to write. Clarke died in 1822, and the final volume appeared posthumously, completed by Robert Walpole.

Clarke's *Travels* are characteristic of their period in that they combine strong national sentiment with copious scientific data. They also manifest developments in the science of archaeology: Clarke was among the first to apply rigor to the study of the antiquities of the Holy Land. However, it should be remembered that, in spite of the scientific tone, he was not above altering details to improve the narrative. His writing fulfilled the contemporary criteria by being as entertaining as it was useful. Clarke's talent as a communicator is well conveyed by Gunning's story of receiving a packet of his letters while dining:

> The first letter began with these words:—"Here I am, eating strawberries within the Arctic Circle." We were so intent on his dessert that we quite forgot our own.

KATHERINE EDGAR

### Biography

Born in Willingdon, Sussex, 5 June 1769. Attended Tonbridge Grammar School, 1779–1786, and Jesus College, Cambridge University, 1786–1790. Traveled as tutor in England, Wales, and Ireland, 1791; traveled as companion to Lord Berwick on Grand Tour of Germany, Switzerland, and Italy, 1792–1794; toured Scotland and Western Isles, 1797. Fellow and bursar of Jesus College, 1798. Made extensive tour with his pupil, John Marten Cripps, through Scandinavia, Russia, the Crimea, Turkey, Egypt, the Holy Land, and Greece, returning through Transylvania, Hungary, Vienna, and Paris, 1799–1802. Honorary LLD from Cambridge University, 1803. Ordained; appointed vicar of Harlton, near Cambridge, 1805. Senior tutor at Jesus College, 1805–1806. Married Angelica Rush, 1806: five sons, two daughters. Appointed professor of mineralogy, 1808. Published on antiquarian and mineralogical subjects. Rector of Yeldham, Essex, from 1809. Published *Travels* from 1810 on. Appointed librarian of Cambridge University, 1817. Member of the Geological Society of England and the Royal Academy of Sciences at Berlin. Died of fever in London, 9 March 1822.

### References and Further Reading

Clarke, Edward, *A Tour through the South of England, Wales and Part of Ireland, Made during the Summer of 1791*, 1793.

Clarke, Edward, *Travels in Various Countries of Europe, Asia and Africa*, 6 vols., 1810–1823.

Clarke, Edward, *Critique on the Character and Writings of Sir George Wheler, Knt., as a Traveller*, 1820.

Gunning, Henry, *Reminiscences of the University, Town and Country of Cambridge from the Year 1780*, 2 vols., London: Bell, 1854.

Otter, William, *The Life and Remains of the Rev. Edward Daniel Clarke, L.L. D.*, London: Dove, 1824.

## COLERIDGE, SAMUEL TAYLOR (1772–1834) *British Poet and Essayist*

Samuel Taylor Coleridge was born on 21 October, 1772 in Ottery St. Mary, a small town in Devon where his father was vicar and headmaster. After his father's death in 1781, the young Coleridge was sent to Christ's Hospital School in London, where Charles Lamb and Leigh Hunt were also pupils. Coleridge was not happy there, suffering badly from homesickness, lack of privacy, and the sadism of the headmaster, but his constant reading of classical texts attracted attention, and he joined the "Grecians," senior students being prepared for Oxford and Cambridge. Coleridge also read *Arabian Nights* and the fictional travel narrative *The Hermit* by Philip Quarll.

In 1791, Coleridge went up with two scholarships to Jesus College, Cambridge, where he began by working hard as well as drinking and socializing, and won the Brown Gold Medal for a Greek "Ode on the Slave Trade." In Coleridge's second year, he became increasingly involved in radical politics. He did not get the scholarships he applied for and was deeply in debt by the beginning of his final year. Coleridge began to drink heavily and disappeared at the end of November 1793. He was found by his brother George three months later, having enlisted while drunk in the 15th Light Dragoons as Silas Tomkyn Comberbach. Eventually, Coleridge's family bought his discharge, and he returned to Cambridge. That summer, on a walking tour, he met Robert Southey in Oxford, and the two men began to plan "Pantisocracy," an egalitarian colony of young couples on the banks of the Susquehanna River in Pennsylvania. In Bristol, Southey introduced Coleridge to his own fiancée, Edith Fricker, and played a significant role in Coleridge's marriage to her sister Sara. Coleridge also met Tom Poole, a radical thinker and the owner of a tannery in Nether Stowey, and when the Pantisocratic scheme fell apart the following year, Coleridge married Sara Fricker and settled in Dorset, where he visited Poole regularly and lectured, sometimes against the slave trade, in Bristol. In 1795, Coleridge met Wordsworth, who moved to the southwest to be near him in 1797, beginning the annus mirabilis of artistic partnership and friendship between the two men. Traditionally, it was on one of many seaside walks that Wordsworth suggested that the account of an albatross in Shelvocke's *Voyage round the World* would figure well in the "Ancient Mariner." It was also at this time that Coleridge wrote *Kubla Khan*, for which travel sources including Purchas's *Pilgrimage*, Maurice's *History of Hindostan*, and Bartram's *Travels in North and South Carolina* have been suggested. In 1798, Coleridge, Wordsworth, and Dorothy Wordsworth went to Germany to study the new philosophy and Higher Criticism. Coleridge was delighted by this first overseas journey, and he wrote enthusiastic letters home about the winter landscape and German Christmas traditions. After Coleridge's eventual return, both households settled in the Lake District, where it first became clear that Coleridge's long-standing opium addiction was becoming debilitating. (The consumption of opium, which formed an important part of British trade with Asia, was legal and widespread at this time.) Coleridge's marriage, which had never been comfortable, became increasingly tense as Coleridge saw more of Sara Hutchinson, the sister of Wordsworth's future wife Mary, and Sara Coleridge was absorbed in rearing their two sons. In the summer of 1803, Wordsworth, Dorothy, and Coleridge went on a walking tour of Scotland, partly in an attempt to alleviate Coleridge's addiction, but by the spring of 1804, he was seriously ill and decided that time alone in a hot climate was his last hope. This was Coleridge's first long sea voyage, and he nearly died of the side effects of opium combined with seasickness. The memory of this voyage has been seen to color the annotations to the 1807 version of "Rime of the Ancient Mariner." Little of Coleridge's writing from this period survives, because his papers were lost at sea on the way home, but he enjoyed exploring Malta and also worked for the British embassy, although his addiction did not abate.

Coleridge returned to England in 1804 and for several years lived alternately with his family and the Wordsworths in the north of England and alone in London or Dorset, where he worked as a journalist and lecturer. In 1807, de Quincey, author of *Confessions of an Opium Addict*, sought out Coleridge, who became a major influence on the younger writer. By the autumn of that year, Coleridge was seriously ill again and took refuge at the house of his London friends, the Morgans. Coleridge lived with them for the next four years, lecturing and publishing his periodical, *The Friend*, and it was they who found Coleridge when he disappeared after a bitter and hurtful argument with Wordsworth in 1809. In 1813, Coleridge's play *Remorse*, set in Moorish Spain, was performed at Drury Lane and met with great success, but he seems to have spent all the profits in an unsuccessful attempt to stave off the Morgans' bankruptcy. John Morgan left the country, and Coleridge escorted Mary and Charlotte to Dorset, where there was an argument that resulted in Coleridge leaving them and appearing destitute and "suffering from the most acute opium overdose of his life" in Bath. (Holmes, 1999) The landlady of Coleridge's inn called the local doctor, who was Caleb Parry, father of the polar explorer and a friend of Coleridge, and Coleridge was again, rescued and taken to friends in Bristol. By the summer of 1814, he was writing again and in 1815, *Biographia Literaria* was finished and a volume of poems, *Sibylline Leaves*, was under way. He returned to London in 1816 and began to take large quantities of opium again. Morgan found Coleridge a doctor, who asked his friend James Gillman, a member of the RCS, to take Coleridge into his house and cure his addiction. Coleridge and the Gillmans found each other very congenial, and Coleridge stayed with them for the rest of his life, keeping his addiction more or less under control. He continued to write, publishing *Aids to Reflection* and *On the Constitution of the Church and State*, and met Byron and Keats. On 15 July 1834, Coleridge died of heart disease at the Gillmans' house in Highgate.

SARAH MOSS

### Biography

Born Ottery St. Mary, Devon, 21 October 1772. Educated Christ's Hospital School and Jesus College, Cambridge. Poet, journalist, essayist; published in *Morning Post*, *Watchman*, *Friend*; friend of Wordsworth and Charles Lamb. Married Sara Fricker: three sons (Derwent, Berkeley, Hartley) and one daughter (Sara); died of heart disease and opium addiction in Highgate, London, 15 July 1834.

### References and Further Reading

Bartram, W., *Travels through North and South Carolina*, 1792.
Coleridge, Samuel Taylor, *Collected Letters of Samuel Taylor Coleridge*, edited by Earl Leslie Griggs, Oxford: Clarendon Press, 1956.
Coleridge, Samuel Taylor, *The Notebooks of Samuel Taylor Coleridge*, edited by Kathleen Coburn, London: Routledge and Kegan Paul, 1957.
Coleridge, Samuel Taylor, *Lectures 1795 on Politics and Religion*, edited by Lewis Patton and Peter Mann, Princeton, New Jersey: Princeton University Press, 1971.
Coleridge, Samuel Taylor, *Lectures 1808–1819 on Literature*, edited by R.A. Foakes, Princeton, New Jersey: Princeton University Press, 1987.
Coleridge, Samuel Taylor, *Poems*, edited by John Beer, London: Everyman, 1993.
Cooper, T., *Some Information Respecting America*, 1794.
Empson, William, "The Ancient Mariner," *Critical Quarterly*, 6 (1964): 298–319.
Holmes, Richard, *Coleridge: Early Visions*, London: HarperCollins, 1989.
Holmes, Richard, *Coleridge: Darker Reflections*, London: HarperCollins, 1998.
Keane, P.J, *Coleridge's Submerged Politics*, 1994.
Leask, Nigel, *British Romantic Writers and the East: Anxieties of Empire*, Cambridge and New York: Cambridge University Press, 1992.
Lowes, John Livingston, *The Road to Xanadu: A Study in the Ways of the Imagination*, Boston: Houghton Mifflin, and London: Constable, 1927; revised edition, Houghton Mifflin, 1930.
McGann, Jerome J, "The Meaning of the Ancient Mariner," *Critical Inquiry*, 8/1 (1981): 35–69.
Maurice, Thomas, *The History of Hindostan*, London, 1795.
Purchas, Samuel, *Purchas His Pilgrimage*, 1617.
Quarll, Philip, *The Hermit, or The Unparalleled Sufferings and Surprising Adventures of Philip Quarll*, London, 1794.
Roe, Nicholas, *Wordsworth and Coleridge: The Radical Years*, Oxford: Clarendon Press, 1988.
Southey, Robert, *Madoc: A Poem in Two Parts*, London: Longman, Hurst, Rees and Orme, 1805.
Shelvocke, George, *A Voyage round the World by Way of the Great South Sea*, London, 1726.
Wilkinson, C.S., *The Wake of the Bounty*, London: Cassell, 1953.

## COLLECTIONS OF LITERATURE OF TRAVEL AND EXPLORATION

The activities of travelers and explorers have had a major impact on literary endeavor with the travelogues of exploits and discoveries in strange and distant lands that have appealed to a wide readership. Whether it is the splendid series of volumes published by the Hakluyt Society or a single-volume account written by the explorer himself or one of his contemporaries that was later included as part of a multivolume series, collections in the literature of exploration are a readily recognized genre, a well-tilled field of scholarly study.

Early peoples, such as the ancient Egyptians and Mesopotamians, produced literature related to travel and exploration. The libraries in Brucheion, at Pergamum, and in Alexandria, among the better known, undoubtedly contained small collections in these areas. A surviving papyrus from the period of the Middle Kingdom describes the wanderings of a mythical hero who was shipwrecked, endured much suffering and hardship, and then miraculously obtained another ship upon which to return home. Similarly, Gilgamesh, the hero of the well-known Mesopotamian epic, was a wayfarer who crossed seas and trackless deserts. These tales and other ancient works are prototypes of the *Odyssey*, based on a collection of oral traditions commonly ascribed to the blind poet Homer, which contains elements that reappear throughout such literature.

The Loeb Classical Library, a series named for its founder, James Loeb (1867–1933), and published by Heinemann (London) and Harvard University Press (Cambridge, Massachusetts), was the most comprehensive collection of ancient Greek and Latin literature ever assembled; in each green (Greek) or red (Latin) pocket-size volume, the original text is displayed opposite an English translation. The first volume of each work contains an introduction summarizing the author's life and writings with an explanation of how the work has survived. Among the authors represented who are connected with travel writing are Apollonius of Rhodes, Herodotus, Homer, Polybius, Strabo, Xenophon, and Pliny.

Medieval literature drew on folk legends, which carried echoes of events from classical antiquity. It encompassed the daring Atlantic voyages of the Vikings and other Scandinavian peoples and sagas, eddas, and epic poems associated with them with examples of exploratory endeavor in literature, delightful tales of reconnaissance that remain at the heart of the Scandinavian and Icelandic cultural heritage. The Icelandic sagas remain one of the great marvels of exploration literature, a great human achievement, which has not really been surpassed. Examples of the manuscripts that make up Icelandic sagas can be studied in the Fiske Icelandic Collection, Cornell University Libraries, Ithaca, New York, and at the Icelandic Collection, Elizabeth Dafoe Library, University of Manitoba, Canada. These repositories, in conjunction with the National and University Library of Iceland, held a conference at the Library of Congress in May 2000, "Saga Literature and the Shaping of Icelandic Culture," accompanied by a traveling exhibition, "Living and Reliving the Icelandic Sagas."

Also important were the literary works of the Crusades. Out of these religiously inspired undertakings came numerous chronicles and related writings, such as the account of the monumental travels of Marco Polo. Both India and China had highly advanced civilizations with traditions that included tales of noble discoveries, but it was in Elizabethan England that exploration in literature really achieved heights of grandeur with the overseas achievements of daring adventurers such as Francis Drake, Humphrey Gilbert, and John Hawkins. Writers, most notably William Shakespeare, Ben Jonson, Christopher Marlowe, Edmund Spenser, and Sir Walter Raleigh, glorified newfound worlds and their conquerors in an ecstasy of patriotic fervor, with distant lands and noble travelers highlighted in media ranging from sonnets to plays. In this, Richard Hakluyt was a master. He gave his name to one of the most important collections of travel and exploration literature.

The Hakluyt Society was formed at a small meeting of distinguished men of letters and science, held at the London Library in December 1846. Most of the members were already members of the Royal Geographical Society, and there continued to be an association between the two organizations. The Hakluyt Society's purpose was "to print for distribution among the members the most rare and valuable voyages, travels, and geographical records, from an early period of exploratory enterprise to the circumnavigation of Dampier." A high proportion of the Hakluyt Society's publications are reprints of original English texts or English translations, covering the writings of medieval travelers and cosmographers, the classical narratives of the age of the great discoveries, and reports by modern explorers. Publication of the volumes is arranged by series; to date, there are three, covering the periods 1847–1899 (First), 1899–1995 (Second), and 1995– (Third); there is also a catchall Extra Series of occasional booklets and talks in annual reports. Over 300 titles have been released.

Leading writers of the seventeenth and eighteenth centuries utilized exploration and travel information to shape their works, focusing on commercial expansion, which had less literary attraction than journeys motivated by a simple desire to probe the unknown. The Royal Society, created in England early in the reign of Charles II, had a marked impact on scientific travel, and both the society and its French counterpart (created a few years later) included many literary figures in their membership. Awnsham and John Churchill booksellers, published their *Collection of Voyages and Travels, Some Now First Printed from Original Manuscripts; Others Translated Out of Foreign Languages and Now First Published in English . . . With a General Preface, Giving an Account of the Progress of Navigation* in four folio volumes in 1704. The collection consisted of extracts compiled in no particular order, but it was a popular success; it was reissued in six volumes (1732), then reprinted (1744–1746). Two further volumes (The Harleian Collection) were added by Thomas Osbourne in 1747.

By the mid-nineteenth century, new areas of discovery were opened to the world and to its writers. Between 1850 and 1900, the rage was tropical Africa and the scramble for colonial possessions on the continent. Starting with James Bruce's five-volume *Travels to Discover the Source of the Nile* (1790), there was an undisguised attempt, even among the most noted explorers of Africa, to embellish their travelogues with the sensational or the lurid, often to call attention to the supposed inferiority of the peoples among whom they traveled.

The Royal Geographical Society, with the Institute of British Geographers, was founded in 1830, for the advancement of geographical science. It is the largest geographical society in Europe and one of the largest in the world, supporting research, education, and training; it has a membership of approximately 13,000. Along with an Expedition Advisory Centre to train field scientists, it has a library, archives, and map and photographic collections to support its research, and it publishes three journals, two newsletters, and a popular magazine. The society's archives consist of its administrative papers along with journal manuscripts from 1830; diaries, logbooks, and letters, not all connected to the society; the papers of David Livingstone, H.M. Stanley, and other noted explorers; and observation files of astronomical, meteorological, and topographical notes.

The major feats of African discovery had been completed by the turn of the twentieth century, and there was a rapid decline soon thereafter in works based on its grand geographical mysteries. The last unexplored area on earth was the polar regions, which provided their own icy imagery. The polar regions have not generated as many works as has travel in warmer climates, but it is a comparatively new field. The Scott Polar Research Institute (SPRI) was founded in 1920 and formally inaugurated in 1926 to finance polar expeditions and the publication of their findings as scientific reports. The SPRI is the oldest international research center in the world covering both the Arctic and Antarctic regions. Its library and the Thomas H. Manning Polar Archives are considered two of the most comprehensive in the world. The SPRI library holds a unique collection of books, documents, and maps. The archives hold one of the largest collections of manuscript and other unpublished material relating to the Arctic and Antarctic regions, including documents on the exploration of northern Canada, Greenland, and Svalbard. The picture library contains many original works of art and a photographic collection from both the Arctic and Antarctic, mostly on the history of exploration in the polar regions, including much material from the expeditions of Scott and Shackleton. Today, the SPRI is part of the Faculty of Earth Sciences and Geography, School of Physical Sciences, University of Cambridge.

The Van Riebeeck Society was founded in Cape Town, South Africa, in 1928 after the publication by the South African Library Board of the diary (1705–1706) of Adam Tas and Baron van Pallandt's observations on the Cape (1803) highlighted the considerable interest in South African historical documents. On the initiative of the South African Library's chief librarian, the society was formed to print, or reprint, rare and valuable books, manuscripts, and documents relating to the history of South Africa, in volumes similar in format to those of the Hakluyt Society and the Linschoten-Vereeniging in The Hague. Several of the volumes are related to the history of exploration and travel, such as *The Diary of the Reverend F. Owen, Missionary with Dingaan* (1926), *The Diary of Dr. Andrew Smith, Director of the "Expedition for Exploring Central Africa," 1834–6* (1939–1940), and *A Voyage to the Cape of Good Hope towards the Antarctic Polar Circle round the World and to the Colony of the Hottentots and the Caffres from the Years 1772–1776* by Anders Sparrman (1975). The society is named after Jan van Riebeeck (1619–1677), the Dutch East India Company official who founded the Dutch settlement at Cape Town in 1652.

The Broadway Travellers was a series of travel and exploration literature classics, published by George Routledge and Sons in the 1920s and 1930s, that enjoyed a long life, with one or two of the titles still being reprinted in the 1950s. The series was not confined to well-known books; some had never appeared in English, had become scarce, or needed annotations in the light of research not previously reprinted or translated. Most of the travelers selected for inclusion were men who ventured into strange climates, while others were tourists whose personality and literary merits lent them a special interest. Each volume was introduced by an acknowledged authority and included an appendix containing notes necessary to clarify difficulties in the text. E. Denison Ross and Eileen Power were the general editors. Sample titles in the series included *Akbar and the Jesuits: An Account of the Jesuit Missions to the Court of Akbar* by Father Pierre du Jarric (C.H. Payne), *Don Juan of Persa: A Shi'ah Catholic, 1560–1604* (Guy Le Strange), *Thomas Gage: The English American, a New Survey of the West Indies, 1648* (A.P. Newton), *Diaz del Castillo: Discovery and Conquest of Mexico, 1517–1521* (A.P. Maudsley), *Jewish Travellers* (Elkan N. Adler), and *An Account of Tibet: The Travels of Ippolito Desideri of Pistoia, 1712–1727* (C. Wessels).

Also published in the same time period, Classics of Travel and Exploration was a collection of heavily annotated scholarly editions of original accounts and translations published by the Argonaut Press but later available from Nico Israel in Amsterdam. Titles included *The World Encompassed* and *Analogous Contemporary Documents concerning Sir Francis Drake's Circumnavigation of the World*, Sir Walter Raleigh's *The Discoverie of the Large and Bewtiful Empyre of Guiana, The Most Noble and Famous Travels of Marco Polo Together with the Travels of Nicolo de Conti*, and *The Voyages of Christopher Columbus, Being the Journals of His First and Third, and the Letters concerning His First and Last Voyages, to Which Is Added the Account of His Second Voyage Written by Andres Bernaldez.*

The *Cambridge History of the British Empire* was intended to "exhibit the present state of knowledge of the subject and lay a foundation on which future generations of students may build." There were eight volumes. The first, *The Old Empire from the Beginnings to 1783* (1929), had a special bibliography on exploration and seapower; volume 2, *The Growth of the New Empire, 1783–1870* (1940), had a chapter by E.A. Heawood on "The Exploration of Africa" with an accompanying bibliography. The last volume in the series, *South Africa, Rhodesia and the High Commission Territories* (1963), contained "Africa in Ancient and Medieval Times" (E.H. Warmington), "The Portuguese in South Africa" (Edgar Prestage), and "Foundations of Cape Colony" (Leo Fouche). Another collection, the *Cambridge Modern History*, in 12 volumes (1902–1910), was considered one of the world's great multivolume, cooperative works of scholarship, in which a particular historical event of outstanding importance was chosen as the theme for each volume.

Each one included a number of chapters, and an extensive bibliography, relating to discovery and exploration; for example, the first volume, *The Renaissance* (1902), opened with the chapters "The Age of Discovery" and "The New World" by E.J. Payne; the last volume, *The Latest Age* (1910), ends with "Modern Exploration" (J.D. Rogers), which considers exploration in Asia, Africa, Australasia, and the polar regions. In the 1960s, the *Cambridge Modern History* was replaced by the *New Cambridge Modern History*. Also appearing at the same time was the Colonial History series, which included such titles as *The Proceedings of the Association for Promoting the Discovery of the Interior Parts of Africa* (2 vols., 1810).

The Golden Hind series was edited by Milton Waldman and published by John Lane in the 1920s and 1930s; the volumes were presented as "in a form suitable for the general reader new lives of great explorers written by well-known men of letters which are at the same time reliable history and attractive biographies." Each author was allowed to present his subject in the manner he wanted, so long as he examined all available material, especially the documents left by the explorer and his contemporaries. Each volume contained illustrations from contemporary prints and maps and a working bibliography. Titles in the series included *Sir Francis Drake* (E.F. Benson), *Captain John Smith* (E. Keble Chatterton), *Henry Hudson* (Llewelyn Powys), *Captain Scott* (Stephen Gwynn), *Sir John Hawkins* (Philip Gosse), and *Mungo Park and the Quest of the Niger* (Stephen Gwynn). Another series, Great Explorer, was conceived by Vilhjalmur Stefansson, who had previously edited *Great Adventures and Explorations*, an anthology of carefully selected quotations from original source material. The series was published by Delacorte Press, and it reflected Stefansson's belief that "the true discoverers of every land were those who stepped upon shores where human foot had never trod." The first volume was *Beyond the Pillars of Hercules: The Classical World Seen through the Eyes of Its Discoverers* (Rhys Carpenter, 1966); others were *Silk, Spices and Empire* (Owen and Eleanor Lattimore), *South by the Spanish Main* (Earl P. Hanson), and *West and by North* and *The Moving Frontier* (both by Louis B. Wright and Elaine W. Fowler).

A new area of research, previously unexplored by scholars, has been collections of books, journals, diaries, and personal papers by women explorers. One of the most comprehensive collections is in the Arthur and Elizabeth Schlesinger Library on the History of Women in America, part of the Radcliffe Institute, at Harvard University, Cambridge, Massachusetts, and is a collection on women and their travels for fun, for exploration, for adventure, and for missionary work. Along with first-person accounts, such as *"She Was a Sister Sailor": The Whaling Journals of Mary Brewster, 1845–1851* (1992) and *A White Nurse in Africa* by Maria Haseneder (1951), there are selected manuscript collections for world traveler Mabel Hall Colgate (1895–1985), Maud Wood Park (1871–1955), with her Around the World reports for the Far East and the Orient, and the Women's Travel Club, Boston, Massachusetts.

The National Geographic Society, founded by Alexander Graham Bell in 1888 in Washington, DC, has done much, like its British equivalent, the Royal Geographical Society, to popularize man's exploits. With its widely circulated magazines, *National Geographic* and *National Geographic Traveler*, along with its educational programs, exhibitions, and other special publications, the world of travel and exploration has been brought to a wider audience than ever before. Its library has over 63,000 books, manuscripts, pictures, and maps concerning land, sea, and space exploration.

The National Maritime Museum (NMM) was formally established by act of Parliament in 1934 and was opened in the Queen's House, Greenwich, London, on 27 April 1937. It preserves British maritime history, and its rich collections cover the voyages of discovery undertaken by the Royal Navy, the history of navigation, and nautical astronomy. In collaboration with the Society for Nautical Research and other bodies, the museum conducts conferences, symposia, and other educational activities. Its Caird Library is considered one of the largest and most significant research collections of its kind in the world, with over 100,000 books, many pre-1850; more than 20,000 pamphlets; and 20,000 bound periodicals, charts and atlases, and press clippings. There is a series of volumes, extensively annotated, on voyages and travel, biography, atlas and cartography, piracy and privateering, and naval history. NMM, with its Centre for Maritime Research, has the most important holdings in the world on the history of British maritime activities, including art, cartography, manuscripts of official public records, ship models and plans, scientific and navigational instruments, timekeeping, and astronomy. Its website is http://www.nmm.ac.uk.

Many libraries and archives have books and periodicals on travel and exploration, but, along with those collections mentioned already, several are noteworthy for the valuable substance of their holdings on travel and exploration. Not all of them are easily recognizable. In the United States, the Library of Congress, Washington, DC is one of the best known in the world, and the breadth of its resources is overwhelming. Especially important is its Geography and Map Reading Room. Another well-known repository in the same city is the Smithsonian Institution, with its extensive holdings on travel and exploration, including many rare books in its Dibner Library, that are spread throughout the institution's wide array of branch libraries. Also of interest are the Pacific Grove Public Library, Pacific Grove, California, which has the Alvin Seale South Seas Collection, including rare and unusual items, accounts of early voyages, ships' logs, and artifacts; the Mandeville Department of Special Collections, Central University Library, University of California, San Diego, with its Hill Collection of Pacific Voyages, with reports and commentaries on important voyages by explorers such as Magellan and Sir Francis Drake; the Otto G. Richter Library, University of Miami, Florida, which has a rare Floridiana collection on Spanish exploration and colonization in that area; the John Carter Brown Library, Brown University, Providence, Rhode Island, with its manuscript collections on the exploration of the Americas; and the Sandor Testler Library, Wofford College, Spartanburg, South Carolina, a miscellaneous collection relating to voyages, travel, and descriptions of various parts of the world.

In Canada, the Special Collections and University Archives Division, University of British Columbia Library, Vancouver, British Columbia, has several important resources on exploration and travel, including the A.J.T. Taylor Arctic Collection, manuscripts, maps, and photographs on Pacific Northwest exploration; the History Department, Metropolitan Toronto Library, Ontario, includes among its holdings reports, diaries, and personal narratives of travels and voyages of exploration and discovery from the Renaissance to the present day, with emphasis on the North American interior, early oceanic voyages of discovery, and accounts of travelers to Russia; the Thomas Fisher Rare Book Library, University of Toronto, Ontario, contains a great variety of material on the early exploration and settlement of Canada, including the search for the Northwest Passage, the Barren Lands, and the subsequent exploration of the Arctic; Victoria University Library, Toronto, Ontario, has a unique collection of books, pamphlets, and government reports detailing missionary enterprises among the Native American tribes in Canada; and the National Archives of Canada, Ottawa, and the National Library of Canada both have extensive book and manuscript collections on discovery and exploration in Canada.

For a more complete list, see the latest edition of *Subject Collections* (New Providence, New Jersey: Bowker). Note that many of these libraries have home pages with links to their collections' catalogues.

MARTIN J. MANNING

### References and Further Reading

*Aldus Encyclopedia of Discovery and Exploration*, 18 vols., London: Aldus, 1971.

Bettex, Albert W., *The Discovery of the World: The Great Explorers and the Worlds They Found*, translated by Daphne Woodward, New York: Simon and Schuster, and London: Thames and Hudson, 1960.

Day, Alan Edwin, *Discovery and Exploration: A Reference Handbook*, vol. 1: *The Old World*, New York: Saur, and London: Bingley, 1980 (no more volumes published).

Delpar, Helen (editor), *The Discoverers: An Encyclopedia of Explorers and Exploration*, New York: McGraw Hill, 1980.

McCarry, Charles (editor), *From the Field: A Collection of Writings from National Geographic*, Washington, DC: National Geographic Society, 1997.

Parker, John (editor), *Merchants and Scholars: Essays in the History of Exploration and Trade, Collected in Memory of James Ford Bell*, Minneapolis: University of Minnesota Press, 1965.

Stefansson, Vilhjalmur (editor), *Great Adventures and Explorations from the Earliest Times to the Present, as Told by the Explorers Themselves*, New York: Dial Press, and London: Hale, 1947.

## COLLECTIONS OF LITERATURE OF TRAVEL AND EXPLORATION, ANTHOLOGIES

Collections of travel narratives by different authors were an early product of the printing press. Although effort was sometimes made to hush up sensitive commercial information, the widespread interest fueled by the New World discoveries and other exploits of European seafarers from the end of the fifteenth century meant that their narratives were sought out by publishers and often promptly translated into several languages. Latin remained the learned lingua franca until much later, but the rapidity with which exploration narratives were also made available in languages other than that of their original writing shows a readership extending well beyond scientific geographers or officers of state. Patriotic pride and national self-aggrandizement competed with dissemination of information as the motivating force behind the early collections.

Venice saw the publication of the first major collection: Ramusio's three-volume *Navigationi et viaggi* (1550–1559). This is unsurprising for two reasons: first, the acquisition of accurate geographical information was important to Venice's mercantile ventures overseas; second, the city was a major center of the book trade. Although not the first Venetian travel compilation (Antonio Manuzio, of the scholar-printer family that ran the great Aldine publishing house, had put together *Viaggi fatti da Vinetia* in 1543), Ramusio's was exceptional in its scope and authority. As a librarian and an accomplished linguist, Ramusio would have been aware of the importance of obtaining and publishing accurate texts of significant works, both past and present, and through this role and as an official in the Venetian state, he was extremely well placed to obtain material from a Europe-wide network of contacts.

As England grew into a major player in exploration and overseas trade, Ramusio's example was followed by Richard Hakluyt, whose first collection, *The Principall Navigations, Voiages, and Discoveries of the English Nation*, appeared in 1589. The core of this book was greatly expanded in the three-volume *Principal Navigations, Voyages, Traffiques, and Discoveries of the English Nation* (1598–1600) to bring the story of English exploration up to date with narratives by Hakluyt's contemporaries. Like Ramusio, Hakluyt was in contact with many leading explorers and geographers of his day, playing an active role in information exchange among them, and although his principal subject was the exploits of English explorers and travelers, he also published foreign accounts, often making his own translations. The naming of the Hakluyt Society, founded in 1846 to publish scholarly editions of travel narratives, was a recognition of his pioneering achievement. The clergyman Samuel Purchas, originally interested in travel narratives as sources for a universal survey of religion (*Purchas His Pilgrimage*, 1613), took up where Hakluyt left off when, around 1620, he acquired Hakluyt's unpublished manuscripts. His four-volume *Hakluytus Posthumus; or, Purchas His Pilgrimes* (1625) was a major publishing feat.

The potential for enhancing travel texts with high-quality engravings (as opposed to the often crude woodcuts that adorned early works) was pioneered by the de Bry family at Frankfurt, whose magnificently illustrated volumes set a standard for subsequent illustrators. Publication of *Collectiones peregrinationum in Indiam orientalem et Indiam occidentalem* was begun by Theodor in 1590, continued by his sons, and only completed in 1634. Other long-running de Bry projects were the 10-volume *Grands Voyages*, on the New World, and the 15-volume *Petits Voyages*, on Africa and Asia. The illustrations in these and many later large-format collections are often a major aspect of their value and interest.

As the material available expanded, editors often chose to focus on particular themes, such as Commelin's Dutch East India Company voyages (1645) or Anderson's circumnavigation narratives (1784(?)). In Portugal, pamphlets containing heart-rending accounts of shipwrecks, usually en route to the East, and the often tragic fates of the survivors had been published since the mid-sixteenth century; Bernardo Gomes de Brito gathered together 12 such texts under the title *História trágico-marítima* (1735–1736), which gave its name to a specifically Portuguese subgenre of travel writing. Other more modest compilations, such as John Ray's (1693), were not so much compendia as texts on a particular topic with supporting material by several hands.

The de Bry/Merian compilations, and those of their contemporary Hulsius, set a trend for long-running projects in travel publishing. The eighteenth century saw a burgeoning of collections of travel and exploration narratives as the pace of European exploration worldwide continued to quicken under pressure from imperial and commercial rivalries, especially between the English and French. New narratives continued to be written and translated, and booksellers saw golden opportunities in the gathering of texts old and new into ever-enlarging numbers of volumes, whether handsomely illustrated folios or easily portable duodecimos, their title pages emblazoned with hyperbolic claims of completeness, novelty, or authenticity. A typical publication history is that of *A Collection of Voyages and Travels*, first published in four folio volumes by the Churchill brothers, booksellers in London, in 1704 and sold by subscription. Two further volumes appeared in 1732 "printed by assignment from Messrs. Churchill," while sheets of the first four volumes were reissued with new title pages in the same year. A so-called third edition of all six volumes appeared in 1744–1746, and in 1752 another bookseller, Thomas Osborne, brought out a further edition.

Titles that were variations on the theme of "Collection of Travels and Voyages" by no means were, or aimed to be, all accurate editions of original manuscripts. Compilers often substantially rewrote their material, the better to accommodate it to the educational or imperial program that they had in mind—to provide a "regular series of information," as Burney wrote in the dedication of his Pacific volume to Banks. Thus, although the compiler (the geographer John Green?) of the *New General Collection of Voyages and Travels* states in his lengthy preface that the three uses of collections are (1) "to preserve valuable Books from being lost," (2) "to render scarce Books common," and (3) "to bring the best Authors relating to all Parts of the World into one Body," his actual treatment of the texts he collected shows scant regard for their integrity. In the interests of a better read, the longueurs (for the general reader) of navigational observations were excised from journals, and contradictions between various accounts smoothed over. The merits and demerits of arrangement by chronology, by originating nation, or by region visited were debated, the virtues and shortcomings of abridgments weighed up, and the texts altered accordingly. Under such editorial regimes, with compilers copying or translating material from other collections without reference to an authoritative text, the textual authority of the narratives quickly degraded, and the line between a "Collection" and a "History" or "Universal Geography" increasingly blurred.

The abundance of these titles, of which a small, mainly English-language selection is listed following this entry, indicates their considerable popularity, and the book trade was certainly alert to the publication opportunities provided by such major events as Cook's voyages and the departure of Ross's 1818 Northwest Passage expedition. The appetite for all these works is illustrated by the enterprise of the London printer Hogg, who brought out a folio edition of Anderson's *Collection* in 80 instalments at 6d. each, to be bound by the purchaser into one or two volumes, thus bringing the price of a large-format illustrated work within range of a readership that could not afford 20 guineas for a luxury production. Across the Channel, Laporte's *Le Voyageur françois* in 26 volumes, praised more for its elegance than its accuracy, continued to be expanded by other hands long after its author's death.

Since the mid-nineteenth century, the Hakluyt Society has published, in addition to single-author volumes, scholarly collections of accurate texts on particular places or themes. Examples from the society's early years include Markham's edition of texts on Amazonia, Major's on India and Australia, and Rundall's on the Northwest Passage and Japan. More recent examples are Wilkinson's *Jerusalem Pilgrimage 1099–1185* (1988), which combines new and previously published translations from various languages, and Lorimer's *English and Irish Settlement on the River Amazon 1550–1646* (1989), which brings together material from manuscript sources in several countries.

With the advent of recreational travel, entertainment has come to the fore as a raison d'être of travel collections. Eric Newby, for instance, writes in the introduction to his anthology, *A Book of Travellers' Tales* (1985), that his aim in assembling it was "to produce a feast" and that its purpose is "to entertain rather than to instruct." In an even more informal vein, a collection of Indian reminiscences recorded for BBC Radio 4 became the basis for Charles Allen's *Plain Tales from the Raj* (1975); the formula was repeated in the African context with *Tales from the Dark Continent* (1979). Another kind of anthology is the San Francisco-based country-by-country *Travelers' Tales* series, which supplies easily assimilable background reading for both would-be visitors and armchair travelers in the form of other travelers' accounts of their experiences: in the series editors' words, "a kind of experiential primer that guidebooks don't offer."

JENNIFER SPEAKE

### References and Further Reading


Allen, Charles (editor), *Plain Tales from the Raj: Images of British India in the Twentieth Century*, London: Deutsch and BBC, 1975.

Allen, Charles (editor), *Tales from the Dark Continent: Images of British Colonial Africa in the Twentieth Century*, London: Deutsch, and New York: St. Martin's Press, 1979.

Anderson, George William, *A New, Authentic, and Complete Collection of Voyages round the World, Containing a Complete Historical Account of Captain Cook's First, Second, Third and Last Voyages, Newly Written from the Authentic Journals and Published under the Direction of G.W. Anderson Assisted by Many Other Gentlemen*, London: Hogg [1784?]; illustrated folio edition published in installments, c. 1786; octavo edition in 6 vols., revised by James Hogg, London: Miller, Law and Cater, 1790.

Barrow, John, *A Chronological History of Voyages into the Arctic Regions . . .*, London: John Murray, 1818.

Bradshaw, George (editor), *A Collection of Travel in America by Various Hands*, New York: Farrar Strauss, 1948.

Brito, Bernardo Gomes de, *História trágico-marítima, em que se escrevem chronologicamente os naufrágios que tiveram as naus de Portugal, depois que se poz em exercício a navegação da Índia*, 2 vols., Lisbon: Congregação do Oratorio, 1735–1736; edited by António Sérgio, 3 vols., Lisbon: Sul, 1956–1957.

Bry, Theodor de, et al. (editors), *Collectiones peregrinationum in Indiam orientalem et Indiam occidentalem*, 25 vols., 1590–1634.

Burney, James, *A Chronological History of the Discoveries in the South Sea or Pacific Ocean*, 5 vols., London: Luke Hansard, 1803–1817.

Burney, James, *A Chronological History of North-Eastern Voyages of Discovery; and of the Early Eastern Navigations of the Russians*, London: Payne and Foss, 1819.

Churchill, Awnsham (editor), *A Collection of Voyages and Travels, Some Now First Printed from Original Manuscripts; Others Translated Out of Foreign Languages and Now First Published in English . . .*, 4 vols., London: A. and J. Churchill, 1704; further editions, 1732, 1744–1746, and 1752.

Commelin, Isaac, *Begin ende voortgangh van de Vereenighde Nederlandtsche Geoctroyeerde Oost-Indische Compagnie. Vervatende de voornaemste Reysen, by de inwoonderen der selver Provintien derwaerts gedaen*, 2 vols., Amsterdam, 1645; as *Recueil des voyages qui ont servi à l'établissement et aux progrès de la Compagnie des Indes Orientales*, translated and adapted by Constantin de Renneville, 2 vols., Amsterdam, 1702; 2nd edition, 7 vols., Amsterdam, 1754; vol. 1 as *A Collection of Voyages Undertaken by the Dutch East-India Company, for the Improvement of Trade and Navigation*, London: Freeman et al., 1703.

Dalrymple, Alexander (editor), *An Account of the Discoveries Made in the South Pacifick Ocean, Previous to 1764*, 1767.

Dalrymple, Alexander (editor), *An Historical Collection of the Several Voyages and Discoveries in the South Pacific Ocean*, 1769.

Dalrymple, Alexander (editor), *An Historical Collection of the Several Voyages and Discoveries in the South Pacific Ocean*, 2 vols., 1770–1771.

Dalrymple, Alexander (editor), *A Collection of Voyages Chiefly in the Southern Atlantick Ocean*, 1775.

Davidson, Robyn (editor), *The Picador Book of Journeys*, London: Picador, 2001.

Deleury, Guy, *Les Indes florissantes: Anthologie des voyageurs français (1750–1820)*, Paris: Laffont, 1991.

Deperthe, J.L.H.S., *Relations d'infortunes sur mer*, 1781; as *Histoire des naufrages; ou, Recueil des relations les plus interessantes des naufrages, hivernements, de laissemens, incendies, famines at autres évenmens funestes sur mer; qui ont été publiés depuis le quinzième siècle jusqu'à présent*, Paris: Cuchet, 1789.

Forster, R.P. (editor), *A Collection of the Most Celebrated Voyages and Travels from the Discovery of America to the Present Times: Arranged in Systematic Order, Geographical and Chronological . . .* , 4 vols., Newcastle upon Tyne: Mackenzie and Dent, 1817–1818.

Fulford, Tim, and Peter J. Kitson (editors), *Travels, Explorations and Empires 1770–1835*, 4 vols., London: Pickering and Chatto, 2001.

Green, John (editor), *A New General Collection of Voyages and Travels: Consisting of the Most Esteemed Relations Which Have Been Hitherto Published in Any Language*, 4 vols., London: Thomas Astley, 1745 [1743–1747].

Hakluyt, Richard (editor), *The Principall Navigations, Voiages, and Discoveries of the English Nation, Made by Sea or Overland, to the Most Remote and Farthest Distant Quarters of the Earth at Any Time with the Compasse of These 1500 Yeeres*, London, 1589; edited with an introduction by D.B. Quinn and R.A. Skelton, Cambridge: Hakluyt Society, 1965.

Hakluyt, Richard (editor), *The Principal Navigations, Voyages, Traffiques, and Discoveries of the English Nation, Made by Sea or Over-land, to the Remote and Farthest Distant Quarters of the Earth at Any Time within the Compasse of These 1500 Yeeres: Divided into Three Severall Volumes, According to the Positions of the Regions, Whereunto They Were Directed*, 3 vols., London: Bishop Newberie and Barker, 1598–1600; 12 vols., Glasgow: MacLehose, 1903–1905.

Harris, John (editor), *Navigantium atque Itinerantium Bibliotheca; or, A Compleat Collection of Voyages and Travels: Consisting of above Four Hundred of the Most Authentick Writers . . .* , 2 vols., London: Thomas Bennet, John Nicholson and Daniel Midwinter, 1705; revised and augmented editions, 1744–1748 and 1764.

Herrmann, Frank, and Michael Allen (editors), *Travellers' Tales*, London: Castlereagh Press, 1999.

Hulsius, Levinus, *[Sammlung von] 26 Schiffahrten*, Nuremberg, Frankfurt, and Hannover: Hulsius and successors, 1598–1660.

Kerr, Robert (editor), *A General History and Collection of Voyages and Travels Arranged in Systematic Order*, 18 vols., 1811–1824; Edinburgh: Blackwood, 1824.

Laporte, Joseph de, *Le Voyageur françois; ou, La Connoissance de l'Ancien et du Nouveau Monde*, 26 vols., Paris: Cellot, 1769.

Lorimer, Joyce (editor), *English and Irish Settlement on the River Amazon, 1550–1646*, London: Hakluyt Society, 1989.

Major, R.H. (editor), *India in the Fifteenth Century*, London: Hakluyt Society, 1857; reprinted, New York: Franklin, 1963.

Major, R.H. (editor), *Early Voyages to Terra Australis, Now Called Australia: A Collection of Documents, and Extracts from Early Manuscript Maps, Illustrative of the History of Discovery on the Coasts of That Vast Island, from the Beginning of the Sixteenth Century to the Time of Captain Cook*, London: Hakluyt Society, 1859.

Manuzio, Antonio (editor), *Viaggi fatti da Vinetia, alla Tana, in Persia, in India, et in Constantinopoli . . .* , Venice: Aldus, 1543; 2nd edition, 1545.

Markham, Clements R. (editor and translator), *Expeditions into the Valley of the Amazons, 1539, 1540, 1639*, London: Hakluyt Society, 1859.

Mavor, William, *Historical Account of the Most Celebrated Voyages, Travels, and Discoveries from the Time of Columbus to the Present Period*, 25 vols., London: E. Newbery, 1796–1801; New York: T. and J. Swords, 1796–1803.

Moore, John Hamilton (editor), *A New and Complete Collection of Voyages and Travels, Containing All That Have Been Remarkable from the Earliest Period to the Present Time*, 2 vols., London: Hogg, 1778(?).

Newby, Eric (editor), *A Book of Travellers' Tales*, London: Collins, 1985.

Osborne, Thomas (editor), *A Collection of Voyages and Travels, Consisting of Authentic Writers in Our Own Tongue . . . and Continued with Others of Note . . .* , 2 vols., London: Osborne, 1745.

Pelham, Cavendish (editor), *The World; or, The Present State of the Universe: Being a General and Complete Collection of Modern Voyages and Travels: Selected, Arranged, and Digested, from the Narratives of the Latest and Most Authentic Travellers and Navigators . . . Embellished with Upwards of One Hundred and Thirty Beautiful Engravings*, 2 vols., London: J. Stratford, 1806–1808.

Peres, Damião (editor), *Viagens e naufrágios célebres dos séculos XVI, XVII e VIII*, 4 vols., Porto: Oliveira, 1937–1938.

Pinkerton, John (editor), *A General Collection of the Best and Most Interesting Voyages and Travels in All Parts of the World: Many of Which Are Now First Translated into English. Digested on a New Plan*, 17 vols., London: Longman Hurst Rees and Orme, 1808–1814; Philadelphia: Kimber and Conrad, 1810–1812.

Prévost, Abbé François, *Histoire générale des voyages; ou, Nouvelle Collection de toutes les relations de voyages par mer et par terre, qui ont été publiées jusqu'à présent dans les differentes langues de toutes les nations connues . . .* 19 vols., Paris: Didot, 1746–1789.

Purchas, Samuel, *Hakluytus Posthumus; or, Purchas His Pilgrimes: Contayning a History of the World, in Sea Voyages and Lande-Travells, by Englishmen and Others*, 4 vols., London: Fetherstone, 1625; reprinted New York: AMS Press, 1965.

Ramusio, Giovanni Battista, *Navigationi et viaggi* [Navigations and Travels], 3 vols., Venice: Giunti, 1550–1559; facsimile, edited and with an introduction by R.A. Skelton, Amsterdam: Theatrum Orbis Terrarum, 1967–1970.

Ray, John (editor), *A Collection of Curious Travels and Voyages*, 2 vols., London: Smith and Walford, 1693; 2nd edition, 1705.

Roberts, David (editor), *Points Unknown: A Century of Great Exploration*, London: Norton, 2001.

Rundall, Thomas (editor), *Narratives of Voyages towards the North-West, in Search of a Passage to Cathay and India, 1496 to 1631: With Selections from the Early Records of the Honourable the East India Company and from MSS. in the British Museum*, London: Hakluyt Society, 1849.

Rundall, Thomas (editor), *Memorials of the Empire of Japon in the XVI and XVII Centuries*, London: Hakluyt Society, 1850.

Stevens, John (editor), *A New Collection of Voyages and Travels: With Historical Accounts of Discoveries and Conquests in All Parts of the World. None of Them Ever Before Printed in English; Being Now First Translated from the Spanish, Italian, French, Dutch, Portuguese and Other Languages. Adorn'd with Cuts*, London: Knapton, 1708–1710; reissued, 2 vols., 1711.

Wilkinson, John, Joyce Hill, and W.F. Ryan (editors), *Jerusalem Pilgrimage 1099–1185*, London: Hakluyt Society, 1988.

*See also* **História Trágico-Marítima; Publishing**

## COLONIST AND SETTLER NARRATIVES

At least since Tacitus recorded his observations of the Roman empire's expansion into Europe and Asia

Minor, western European colonists and settlers have written about their frontier experiences. Whether used for official purposes, for popular distribution in published form, or as records of private attempts to comprehend unfamiliar environments, settler and colonist narratives have much in common. The focus and scope of each narrative differs with the writer's background and nationality, the location and nature of the colony or frontier, and the writer's assumptions about the audience and the colonial authority itself. In general, however, colonist and settler narratives are varieties of comment, from the perspective of the colonizer, on the clash of ideologies inevitable in the process of colonization, a liminal space Pratt (1992) describes as a "contact zone."

Surviving colonist and settler narratives include texts written for both public and private purposes. Colonist narratives include writing about the wide range of social, political, economic, and religious contexts that arise in the aftermath of colonial activity. Many early colonist narratives were official, public reports to colonial governments and investors; these narratives often reflect the values and goals of the colonizer while promoting the career and reputation of the writer. Some writers of colonist narratives became sympathetic to the plight of the colonized and attempted to use their reports to alleviate the suffering they witnessed in the colonial setting (for example, Nuñez; Las Casas).

Settler narratives describe the hardships experienced by individuals actually settling or expanding a frontier. Often private reflections, such narratives mediate the gap between an author's cultural assumptions and frontier experiences. Most narratives recast colonial experiences in European terms while responding with ambivalence to encounters with native peoples. Settler narratives by women, in particular, recount the loneliness and isolation of frontier life. Whereas earlier settler narratives focus on the problems of day-to-day survival, later narratives recount travel episodes and inventory natural resources.

Because they mediate conceptual divides, many colonist and settler narratives use conflicting rhetorical strategies that attempt to reinscribe the new landscape within preconceived ideas about the intrinsic nature of social and political order, property, and land use. One common rhetorical strategy in colonist narratives is to exaggerate the benefits of relocation while underestimating the likely hardships: the land is described as unused but fertile, the climate as temperate, and resources as plentiful, whereas subsequent settlers report the land filled with indigenous peoples, the weather harsh, and food scarce.

Similarly, colonial and settler narratives often describe the same indigenous people in contradictory terms: native people are described both as "noble savages" (naturally good, physically beautiful, and living in a golden age state of Edenic innocence) and as treacherous, lawless, savage, and even demonic. Paradoxically, both views are used at times to justify imposing legal, military, and civil authority as a civilizing influence that "improves" the native culture while establishing and protecting European property rights.

Captivity narrative, a subgenre of the colonist or settler narrative, reenacts a version of property seizure (namely, kidnapping) in countless variations and locales. Varieties of captivity narrative have enjoyed popularity for centuries. A permutation of captivity narrative, promulgated by abolitionists, is the slave narrative. Yet another variety is the Barbary Coast captivity narrative, in which European merchants are seized and held to ransom by Turkish or Algerine captors. Some scholars have seen accounts of recent hostage standoffs in the Near East as the latest version.

For colonists and settlers, who tended to see their colonial activities and the act of writing itself as justified within their own established ethnocentric or nationalistic traditions and frameworks, writing became a way of mediating between past and present and between subject and other. The unfamiliar colonial landscapes and peoples are consequently described and viewed through preconceived belief systems that fit poorly with indigenous landscapes and peoples. Although first contact with native peoples in the Americas, Africa, and Asia occurred centuries earlier, some recent scholars have commented that similar rhetorical strategies are used in anthropological writing of the earlier twentieth century.

Narratives of the Spanish conquest of the Americas include both supportive and critical accounts. Narratives that support the Spanish position include accounts of Columbus's voyages, López de Gómara on the expeditions of Cortés, and Diaz del Castillo on those of Pizarro. For narratives that criticize Spanish cruelty, see Nuñez's account of six years afoot among indigenous people from Florida to Mexico. See also Cieza de León for a comparison of Incan and Roman systems of justice and ethics. Highly critical of the Spanish was Las Casas, whose writing was co-opted to justify English and French colonial activities.

Important French narratives include that of Lescarbot, who criticizes French culture by praising native people in Nova Scotia, then part of New France. Samuel de Champlain praises French over Spanish colonial behavior. Captivity narratives include those of the martyred French Jesuits Jogues and Brébeuf (recounted by Regnaut in Sayre, 2000).

English colonists and settlers from all classes emigrated or were exiled to the Americas, Australia, India, and other far-off places, some to govern, trade, or claim land, and others to flee religious persecution or serve prison terms. Consequently, colonist and settler narratives written in English are diverse in form and focus. Richard Hakluyt's early translations of continental exploration narratives encouraged further English colonization. Hariot's descriptions of the land in Virginia encouraged emigration, as did images of native life by engravers like de Bry and such pamphlets as *Virginia Richly Valued* (1609) and *Nova Britannia* (1609). Captain John Smith wrote self-promotional reports of his activities in Virginia that may draw upon his earlier experiences as a captive in the Mediterranean (Sayre). William Penn's 1735 pamphlet praises the civilizing nature of colonization and predicts the American colonies will fuel prosperity.

In 1682, Mary Rowlandson initiated the Puritan captivity narrative; in contrast with French narratives, it describes indigenous peoples as demonic tests sent by God. This genre developed into a highly stylized form that increasingly turned upon issues of property and law. The racial conventions of captivity narrative were later inverted by slavery abolitionists, who created a new genre.

Benezet's later work influenced abolitionists in France and England by portraying Africans as noble savages living in an Arcadian pastoral setting. This strategy was instrumental in fashioning the "noble Negro" abolitionist myth. Opposing views, such as that of Edward Long's *History of Jamaica* (1774), argue that Africans need the civilizing structure of the colonist, even suggesting that Africans are a separate species. Clarkson (1788) argues more forcefully that the races are equal (Fulford and Kitson, 1998).

Another form of English-language settler narrative comprises published journals and diaries that chronicle settlement of the western United States, western Canada, the Australian continent, Africa, South America, and the West Indies. Australia's role as a penal colony also produced a distinct form of settler narrative, the convict narrative.

Earlier narratives about Africa follow conventions similar to those already described: narratives diverge as Arcadian pastorals, exploration reports, and accounts of settlement. In pastoral narratives, a mode favored by abolitionists, Africa is populated by noble savages. Later exploration reports inventory the undeveloped land and commodities, including gold, potential slaves, and (later) diamonds. Other narratives describe impassable land and wild beasts, often accompanied by instructions for killing them. Similarly, accounts of taking slaves are sometimes told alongside accounts of African slavery practices; later captivity narratives about whites in Barbary Coast or Algerine captivity are perhaps an extension of this practice. Later narratives of Africa depict European efforts to survey and establish domestic economies (such as Dinesen's account of life on a Kenyan coffee plantation) and industrial operations, such as gold and diamond mines.

ROXANNE KENT DURY

## References and Further Reading


Adams, Cecilia, and Parthenia Blank, *The Oregon Trail Diary of Twin Sisters Cecilia Adams and Parthenia Blank in 1852: The Unabridged Diary*, 1990.

Allison, Susan, *A Pioneer Gentlewoman in British Columbia: The Recollections of Susan Allison*, edited by Margaret A. Ormsby, 1976.

Anderson, Andrew A., *Twenty-Five Years in a Waggon in the Gold Regions of Africa*, 2 vols., 1887.

Baker, Samuel White, *The Nile Tributaries of Abyssinia*, 1867.

Beeson, Welborn, *The Oregon and Applegate Trail Diary of Welborn Beeson in 1853: The Unabridged Diary*, 1987.

Benemann, William (editor), *A Year of Mud and Gold: San Francisco in Letters and Diaries, 1849–1850*, 1999.

Benezet, Anthony, *Some Historical Account of Guinea: Its Situation, Produce, and the General Disposition of Its Inhabitants, with an Inquiry into the Rise and Progress of the Slave-Trade, Its Nature and Lamentable Effects*, 1771; new edition, 1788; reprinted, 1968.

Bennett, James, *Overland Journey to California: Journal of James Bennett, Whose Party Left New Harmony in 1850 and Crossed the Plains and Mountains until the Golden West Was Reached*, 1987.

Bickham, William Dennison, *A Buckeye in the Land of Gold: The Letters and Journal of William Dennison Bickham*, edited by Randall E. Ham, 1996.

Black, Mary Louisa, *The Oregon and Overland Trail Diary of Mary Louisa Black in 1865*, introduction by Marguerite Black, contemporary comments and maps by Bert Webber, 1989.

Blome, Richard, *A Description of the Island of Jamaica; with the Other Isles and Territories in America, to Which the English Are Related . . . Taken from the Notes of Sir Thomas Linch, Knight, Governour of Jamaica, and Other Experienced Persons*, 1672.

Blome, Richard, *The Present State of His Majesties Isles and Territories in America . . . with New Maps of Every Place, Together with Astronomical Tables, Which Will Serve as a Constant Diary or Calendar, for the Use of the English Inhabitants in Those Islands, from the Year 1686 to 1700*, 1687.

Bourneuf, François Lambert, *Diary of a Frenchman: Frangçois Lambert Bourneuf's Adventures from France to Acadia, 1787–1871*, translated and edited by J. Alphonse Deveau, 1990.

Bradford, William, *History of Plymouth Plantation, 1620–1646*, edited by William T. Davis, 1952.

Brewer, Henry Bridgman, *The Journal of Henry Bridgman Brewer, September 3, 1839, to February 13, 1843: To Which Is Appended Some Information on Chloe Aurelia Clarke Willson, Both of Whom Came Out on the French Ship Lausanne*, 1986.

Burton, Richard F., *Explorations of the Highlands of the Brazil, with a Full Account of the Gold and Diamond Mines*, 2 vols., 1869.

Champlain, Samuel de, *Les Voyages du Sieur de Champlain*, 2 vols., 1613; and *Voyages et découvertes faites en la Nou-*

*velle-France*, 1619; as *Voyages of Samuel de Champlain, 1604–1618*, translated by Charles Pomeroy Otis, 1907.
Champlain, Samuel de, *The Works of Samuel de Champlain*, translated and edited by H.P. Biggar et al., 7 vols., 1922–1936.
Churchill, Randolph Henry Spencer, *Men, Mines, and Animals in South Africa*, 1892.
Cieza de León, Pedro de, *Crónica del Perú*, written 1536–1553; selection, as *The Incas*, translated by Harriet de Onis, 1959.
Clarkson, Thomas, *An Essay on the Slavery and Commerce of the Human Species, Particularly the African, Translated from a Latin Dissertation*, 2nd edition, 1788.
Clayton, William, *William Clayton's Journal: A Daily Record of the Journey of the Original Company of "Mormon" Pioneers from Nauvoo, Illinois, to the Valley of the Great Salt Lake*, 1921; reprinted, 1973.
Clyman, James, *Journal of a Mountain Man*, edited by Linda M. Hasselstrom, 1984.
Coccola, Nicolas, *They Call Me Father: Memoirs of Father Nicolas Coccola*, edited by Margaret Whitehead, 1988.
Coleman, Ann Raney, *Victorian Lady on the Texas Frontier: The Journal of Anne Raney Coleman*, edited by C. Richard King, 1972.
Colmer, John, and Dorothy Colmer (editors), *The Penguin Book of Australian Autobiography*, 1987.
Columbus, Christopher, *Colección de los viages y descubrimientos*, edited by Martin Fernandez de Navarrete, 5 vols., 1825–1837; as *Four Voyages to the New World: Letters and Selected Documents*, translated by R.H. Major, 1961.
Cortés, Hernán, *Letters from Mexico*, translated and edited by Anthony Pagden, with an introduction by J.H. Elliott, 1986.
Daniels, Sylvester, *Frontier Times: The 1874–1875 Journals of Sylvester Daniels*, edited by Tim Purdy, 1985.
Dawbin, Annie Baxter, *A Face in the Glass: The Journal and Life of Annie Baxter Dawbin*, edited by Lucy Frost, 1992.
Dawson, George Mercer, *The Journals of George M. Dawson*, edited by Douglas Cole and Bradley Lockner, 1989.
Dean, Harry, *Umbala: The Adventures of a Negro Sea-Captain in Africa and on the Seven Seas in His Attempts to Found an Ethiopian Empire: An Autobiographical Narrative*, 1929; reprinted, 1989.
Densley, Lillian Cummings, *Saints, Sinners, and Snake River Secrets, from Memories Recorded in Jessie's Journals*, 1987.
Derounian-Stodola, Kathryn Zabelle (editor), *Women's Indian Captivity Narratives*, 1998.
Díaz del Castillo, Bernal, *Historia verdadera de la conquista de la Nueva España*, 1632; as *The Conquest of New Spain*, translated by J.M. Cohen, 1963.
Dickson, Albert Jerome, *Covered Wagon Days: A Journey across the Plains in the Sixties and Pioneer Days in the Northwest*, 1929.
Dinesen, Isak, *Out of Africa*, 1937.
Drury, Clifford Merrill, *First White Women over the Rockies: Diaries, Letters, and Biographical Sketches of the Six Women of the Oregon Mission Who Made the Overland Journey in 1836 and 1838*, 3 vols., 1963–1966.
Dunderdale, George, *The Book of the Bush: Containing Many Truthful Sketches of the Early Colonial Life of Squatters, Whalers, Convicts, Diggers, and Others Who Left Their Native Land and Never Returned*, 1870; facsimile, 1973.
Durieux, Marcel, *Ordinary Heroes: The Journal of a French Pioneer in Alberta*, translated and edited by Roger Motut and Maurice Legris, with an introduction by L.G. Thomas, 1980.
Ebey, Winfield Scott, *The 1854 Oregon Trail Diary of Winfield Scott Ebey*, edited by Susan Badger Doyle and Fred W. Dykes, 1997.
Ewbank, Thomas, *Life in Brazil; or, The Land of the Cocoa and the Palm*, 1856; reprinted, 1971.
Farnham, Thomas J., *Travels in the Great Western Prairies, the Anahuac and Rocky Mountains, and in the Oregon Territory: An 1839 Wagon Train Journal*, 1977.
Farnsworth, Martha, *Plains Woman: The Diary of Martha Farnsworth, 1882–1922*, edited by Marlene Springer and Haskell Springer, 1986.
Fowler-Lunn, Katharine, *The Gold Missus: A Woman Prospector in Sierra Leone*, 1938.
Fraser, Maryna, *Johannesburg Pioneer Journals, 1888–1909*, 1985.
French, Emily, *Emily: The Diary of a Hard-Worked Woman*, edited by Janet Lecompte, 1987.
Froude, James Anthony, *The English in the West Indies; or, The Bow of Ulysses*, 1888; reprinted, 1969.
Fulford, Tim, and Peter J. Kitson (editors), *Romanticism and Colonialism: Writing and Empire, 1780–1830*, Cambridge and New York: Cambridge University Press, 1998.
Gage, Thomas, *A New Survey of the West-Indies: Being a Journal of Three Thousand and Three Hundred Miles within the Main Land of America . . . with His Abode XII Years about Guatemala . . . an Account of the Spanish Navigation Thither, Their Government, Castles, Ports, Commodities, Religion, Priests and Friers, Negro's, Mulatto's, Mestiso's, Indians, and of Their Feasts and Solemnities; with a Grammar, or Some Few Rudiments of the Indian Tongue, called Poconchi or Pocoman*, 4th edition, 1699.
Garrettson, Freeborn, *American Methodist Pioneer: The Life and Journals of the Rev. Freeborn Garrettson, 1752–1827: Social and Religious Life in the U.S. during the Revolutionary and Federal Periods*, 1984.
Glass, Anthony, *Journal of an Indian Trader: Anthony Glass and the Texas Trading Frontier, 1790–1810*, edited by Dan L. Flores, 1985.
Gould, Jane, *The Oregon and California Trail Diary of Jane Gould in 1862: The Unabridged Diary*, 1987.
Gray, Charles Glass, *Off at Sunrise: The Overland Journal of Charles Glass Gray*, edited by Thomas D. Clark, 1976.
Green, Ephraim, *A Road from El Dorado: The 1848 Trail Journal of Ephraim Green*, edited by Will Bagley, 1991.
Hafen, Le Roy R., and Ann W. Hafen, *Handcarts to Zion: The Story of a Unique Western Migration, 1856–1860, with Contemporary Journals, Accounts, Reports; and Rosters of Members of the Ten Handcart Companies*, 1960.
Hafen, Le Roy R., and Ann W. Hafen (editors), *Journals of Forty-niners: Salt Lake to Los Angeles, with Diaries and Contemporary Records of Sheldon Young, James S. Brown, Jacob Y. Stover, Charles C. Rich, Addison Pratt, Howard Egan, and Henry W. Bigler*, 1998.
Hakluyt, Richard, *The Principal Navigations, Voyages, Traffiques, and Discoveries of the English Nation*, 2nd edition, 3 vols., 1598–1600; reprinted, 12 vols., 1903–1905.
Hall, Sarah Harkey, *Surviving on the Texas Frontier: The Journal of an Orphan Girl in San Saba County*, 1996.
Hammer, Jacob, *This Emigrating Company: The 1844 Oregon Trail Journal of Jacob Hammer*, with commentary by Thomas A. Rumer and a preface by Aubrey L. Haines, 1990.
Hance, Gertrude R., *The Zulu Yesterday and To-day: Twenty-nine Years in South Africa*, 1916; reprinted, 1969.
Hariot, Thomas, *A Briefe and True Report of the New Found Land of Virginia*, 1588; facsimile, 1903.
Hayes, Benjamin Ignatius, *Pioneer Notes from the Diaries of Judge Benjamin Hayes*, edited by Marjorie Tisdale Wolcott, 1929; reprinted, 1976.

Hays, Lorena Lenity, *To the Land of Gold and Wickedness: The 1848–1859 Diary of Lorena L. Hays*, edited by Jeanne Hamilton Watson, 1985.

Heiskell, Hugh Brown, *A Forty-niner from Tennessee: The Diary of Hugh Brown Heiskell*, edited by Edward M. Steel, 1998.

Helmcken, John Sebastian, *The Reminiscences of Doctor John Sebastian Helmcken*, edited by Dorothy Blakey Smith, with an introduction by W. Kaye Lamb, 1975.

Howell, Elijah Preston, *The 1849 California Trail Diaries of Elijah Preston Howell*, edited by Susan Badger Doyle and Donald E. Buck, 1995.

Hudson, John, *A Forty-niner in Utah: With the Stansbury Exploration of Great Salt Lake: Letters and Journal of John Hudson, 1848–50*, edited by Brigham D. Madsen, 1981.

Hunter, William W., Missouri '49er: *The Journal of William W. Hunter on the Southern Gold Trail*, edited by David P. Robrock, 1992.

Jogues, Isaac, "Novum Belgium," written 1665; in *American Captivity Narratives*, edited by Gordon Sayre, 2000.

Johnson, Robert, *Nova Britannia: Offring Most Excellent Fruites by Planting in Virginia: Exciting All Such as Be Well Affected to Further the Same*, 1609; facsimile, 1969.

Johnson, Rolf, *Happy as a Big Sunflower: Adventures in the West, 1876–1880*, edited by Richard E. Jensen, 2000.

Knox, Alexander A., *The New Playground; or, Wanderings in Algeria*, 1881.

Korns, J. Roderic, and Dale L. Morgan (editors), *West from Fort Bridger: The Pioneering of the Immigrant Trails across Utah, 1846–1850*, revised and updated by Will Bagley and Harold Schindler, 1994.

Larkin, James Ross, *Reluctant Frontiersman: James Ross Larkin on the Santa Fe Trail, 1856–57*, edited by Barton H. Barbour, 1990.

Las Casas, Bartholomé de, *Brevissima Relación de la destruyción de las Indias*, 1552; as *The Devastation of the Indies*, translated by Herma Briffault, with an introduction by Bill M. Donovan, 1992.

Laudonnière, René Goulaine de, *L'Histoire notable de la Floride situé es Indes Occidentales*, 1586.

Lescarbot, Marc, *Histoire de la Nouvelle France*, 3rd edition, 1618; as *The History of New France*, translated by W.L. Grant, 3 vols., 1907–1914.

Livingstone, David, *Livingstone's Africa: Perilous Adventures and Extensive Discoveries in the Interior of Africa . . . Together with the . . . Results of the Herald-Stanley Expedition . . . to Which Is Added a Sketch of Other Important Discoveries in Africa, Including the Celebrated Diamond Diggings at Colesberg Kopje*, 1872.

Long, Edward, *The History of Jamaica*, 3 vols., 1774; facsimile, 1970.

López de Gómara, Francisco, *Historia de la conquista de Mexico*, edited by Pedro Robredo, 1943.

López de Gómara, Francisco, *Historia general de las Indias y vida de Hernán Cortés*, edited by Jorge Gurria Lacroix, 1979.

Luark, Patterson Fletcher, and Michael Fleenen Luark, *From the Old Northwest to the Pacific Northwest: The 1853 Oregon Trail Diaries of Patterson Fletcher Luark and Michael Fleenen Luark*, edited by Howard Jablon and Kenneth R. Elkins, 1998.

Martin, Maria, *An Historical Account of the Kingdom of Algiers: Including a Description of the Country, the Manners and Customs of the Natives, Their Treatment to Their Slaves, Their Laws, Religion, &c.: To Which Is Annexed, a History of the Captivity and Sufferings of Mrs. Maria Martin, Who Was Six Years a Slave in Algiers*, 1815.

Matthews, J.W., *Incwadi Yami; or, Twenty Years' Personal Experience in South Africa*, 1887.

Matthews, John, *A Voyage to the River Sierra-Leone, on the Coast of Africa, Containing an Account of the Trade and Productions of the Country, and of the Civil and Religious Customs and Manners of the People; with an Additional Letter on the Subject of the African Slave Trade*, 1788; reprinted, 1966.

Mayer, Frank Blackwell, *With Pen and Pencil on the Frontier in 1851: The Diary and Sketches of Frank Blackwell Mayer*, edited by Bertha L. Heilbron, 1932; enlarged edition, 1986.

McCrae, Georgiana Huntly Gordon, *Georgiana's Journal*, edited by Hugh McCrae, 1992.

McMicking, Thomas, *Overland from Canada to British Columbia*, edited by Joanne Leduc, illustrations by William G.R. Hind, 1981.

Merrill, Julius, *Bound for Idaho: The 1864 Trail Journal of Julius Merrill*, edited by Irving R. Merrill, 1988.

Moore, George Fletcher, *Diary of Ten Years Eventful Life of an Early Settler in Western Australia, and also a Descriptive Vocabulary of the Language of the Aborigines*, 1884; facsimile, 1978.

Morgan, Dale (editor), *Overland in 1846: Diaries and Letters of the California–Oregon Trail*, 1993.

Mumey, Nolie, *Amos Steck (1822–1908), Forty-niner: His Overland Diary to California: A Pioneer Coloradan, Prominent Citizen, Jurist, Educator, Builder, and Philanthropist*, 1981.

Nicholson, Thomas, *An Affecting Narrative of the Captivity and Sufferings of Thomas Nicholson . . . Who Has Been Six Years a Prisoner among the Algerines*, 1816.

Nuñez Cabeza de Vaca, Alvar, *La relacion y comentarios . . . del governador Alvar Nuñez Cabeça de Vaca*, 1555; as *Castaways*, translated by Frances M. López-Morillas, 1993.

Nunis, Doyce B. Jr., *The Bidwell-Bartleson Party: 1841 California Emigrant Adventure: The Documents and Memoirs of the Overland Pioneers*, 1991.

Okeley, William, *Eben-ezer; or, A Small Monument of Great Mercy Appearing in the Miraculous Deliverance of William Okeley, William Adams, John Anthony, John Jephs, John Carpenter, from the Miserable Slavery of Algiers, with the Wonderful Means of Their Escape in a Boat of Canvas*, 1675.

Paddock, Judah, *A Narrative of the Shipwreck of the Ship Oswego, on the Coast of South Barbary, and of the Sufferings of the Master and the Crew While in Bondage among the Arabs*, 1818.

Parke, Charles Ross, *Dreams to Dust: A Diary of the California Gold Rush, 1849–1850*, edited by James E. Davis, 1989.

Parrish, Edward Evans, *The Oregon Trail Diary of Reverend Edward Evans Parrish in 1844: The Unabridged Diary*, 1988.

Pattie, James Ohio, *Personal Narrative of James O. Pattie of Kentucky*, edited by Richard Batman, 1988.

Peck, John Mason, *Forty Years of Pioneer Life: Memoir of John Mason Peck, DD*, edited by Rufus Babcock, introduction by Paul M. Harrison, foreword by Herman R. Lantz, 1965.

Penn, William, *The Benefit of Plantations or Colonies*, 1732.

Phillips, Daisy, *Letters from Windermere, 1912–1914*, edited by R. Cole Harris and Elizabeth Phillips, 1984.

Pratt, Mary Louise, *Imperial Eyes: Travel Writing and Transculturation*, London and New York: Routledge, 1992.

*The Present State of the West Indies: Containing an Accurate Description of What Parts Are Possessed by the Several*

*Powers in Europe; Together with an Authentick Account of the First Discoverers of Those Islands*, 1778.
Reid, Bernard Joseph, *Overland to California with the Pioneer Line: The Gold Rush Diary of Bernard J. Reid*, edited by Mary McDougall Gordon, 1983.
Rowlandson, Mary, *A True History of the Captivity and Restoration of Mrs. Mary Rowlandson*, 1682; in *Classic American Autobiographies*, edited by William L. Andrews, 1992.
Royce, Sarah, *Sarah Royce and the American West*, edited by Jane Shuter, 1994.
Salaices, Jose, *The Journal of Jose Salaices, 1789–1818*, translated by Diana Ortega DeSantis, 1998.
Sayre, Gordon M. (editor), *American Captivity Narratives*, 2000.
Scamehorn, H. Lee, Edwin P. Banks, and Jamie Lytle-Webb (editors), *The Buckeye Rovers in the Gold Rush: An Edition of Two Diaries*, revised edition, 1989.
Seaver, James E., *A Narrative of the Life of Mrs. Mary Jemison Who Was Taken by the Indians in the Year 1755 . . . and Has Continued to Reside amongst Them to the Present Time*, 1824; reprinted, 1992.
Sessions, Patty Bartlett, *Mormon Midwife: The 1846–1888 Diaries of Patty Bartlett Sessions*, edited by Donna T. Smart, 1997.
Shape, William, *Faith of Fools: A Journal of the Klondike Gold Rush*, 1998.
Smedley, William, *Across the Plains: An 1862 Journey from Omaha to Oregon*, with a foreword by Merrill J. Mattes, 1994.
Smith, Azariah, *The Gold Discovery Journal of Azariah Smith*, edited by David L. Bigler, 1990.
Smith, John, *The Generall Historie of Virginia, New-England, and the Summer Isles*, 1624; facsimile, with an introduction and notes by A.L. Rowse and Robert O. Dougan, 1966.
Smith, John, *The Complete Works of Captain John Smith (1580–1631)*, edited by Philip L. Barbour, 3 vols., 1986.
Staden, Hans, *Hans Staden: The True Story of His Captivity, 1557*, translated by Malcolm Letts, 1928.
Staples, James M., *A Journal Kept by James M. Staples of Brunswick, Mo., during His Stay in California, 1850–1851*, 1988.
Storrs, Monica, *God's Galloping Girl: The Peace River Diaries of Monica Storrs, 1929–1931*, edited by W.L. Morton, 1979.
T.S., *The Adventures of Mr. T.S., an English Merchant, Taken Prisoner by the Turks of Argiers, and Carried into the Inland Countries of Africa; with a Description of the Kingdom of Argiers*, 1670.
Tacitus, Cornelius, *Agricola*, translated by M. Hutton, revised by R.M. Ogilvie, 1992.
Tacitus, Cornelius, *Germania*, translated with an introduction and commentary by J.B. Rives, 1999.
Thwaites, Reuben Gold (editor), *The Jesuit Relations and Allied Documents: Travels and Explorations of the Jesuit Missionaries in New France, 1610–1791*, 73 vols., 1896–1901.
Trent, William, *Journal of Captain William Trent from Logstown to Pickawillany, AD 1752*, 1871; reprinted, 1971.
Tyler, Royall, *The Algerine Captive; or, The Life and Adventures of Doctor Updike Underhill, Six Years a Prisoner among the Algerines*, 2 vols., 1797.
VanDerBeets, Richard (editor), *Held Captive by Indians: Selected Narratives 1642–1836*, 1973; revised edition, 1994.
Vaughan, Alden T., and Edward W. Clark (editors), *Puritans among the Indians: Accounts of Captivity and Redemption, 1676–1724*, 1981.
*Voyages and Discoveries in South-America*, 1698.
Ward, Herbert, *Five Years with the Congo Cannibals*, 1890.
Washburn, Wilcomb E. (editor), *Garland Library of Narratives of North American Indian Captivities*, 111 vols., 1975–1979.
Weeks, John H., *Among Congo Cannibals: Experiences, Impressions, and Adventures during a Thirty Years' Sojourn amongst the Boloki and Other Congo Tribes*, 1913.
Wells, Zaccheus William, *Diary of Zaccheus William Wells, 1 January 1861 to 31 December 1864*, transcribed by Herbert D. Mullon, 2nd edition, 1971.
Wilson-Haffenden, James Rhodes, *The Red Men of Nigeria: An Account of a Lengthy Residence among the Fulani or "Red Men," and Other Pagan Tribes of Central Nigeria, with a Description of Their Head-hunting, Pastoral and Other Customs, Habits, and Religion*, 1930.
Wingfield, Lewis Strange, *Under the Palms in Algeria and Tunis*, 2 vols., 1868.

*See also* **Imperialist Narratives**

## COLUMBUS, CHRISTOPHER (1451–1506) *Italo-Hispanic navigator*

Christopher Columbus, an Italo-Hispanic navigator and mercantile entrepreneur, is among the most famous travelers in world history, and has often been called "the discoverer of America." Despite Columbus's celebrity in his own time and the huge volume of scholarship devoted to him since, he remains in important respects a shadowy figure or, perhaps, a Rorschach's inkblot in whom the aspirations or anxieties of the historical moment have been confidently discovered. From the Columbian celebrations of 1892, he emerged as a proto-American heroic individualist, a visionary giant among the pygmies of his age. In the mood of the Quincentenary of 1992, he became a grasping imperialist and the brutal agent of genocide. For many, the "discoverer" and the "explorer" have yielded to the "invader" and the "conqueror."

Columbus was in fact a fifteenth-century merchant-mariner with certain remarkable abilities and certain lamentable limitations. He was born in Genoa into a mercantile family. We know little of his youth. He took to the sea early, but not without attaining a respectable level of Latin humanistic education. Columbus's life's work must be understood within the social and economic worlds of the potentially lucrative, intensely competitive, and often literally buccaneering Mediterranean merchant marine of the fifteenth century as well as within the political and spiritual climate attendant upon an apparently invincible Ottoman expansion. Yet Columbus clearly had distinctive features of personality that should not be underestimated: the genius of a great sailor, unflagging energy, visionary persuasiveness, persistence in the face of adversity, and a religious sensibility tending to the mystical that led him, eventually, to a nearly megalomaniacal view of his own role in the providential history.

The precise origins of Columbus's plan to establish a westward route to the Orient—he called it his "enterprise of the Indies"—are unclear. But he became seized of an idea—fundamentally sound, though grossly ignorant or errant in its geographical details—destined to alter world history. By the mid-1470s, however, when Columbus took up protracted residence in Portugal, the navigation of that country was already in effect committed to the program of incremental exploration of the West African coastline aimed at rounding the southern tip of the continent and finding an eastern sea-road to India—finally achieved only in 1498 by Vasco da Gama. Unable to sell his idea to the preoccupied Portuguese, Columbus turned to the court of the Catholic monarchs, Ferdinand and Isabella of Spain, where, after considerable lobbying and some good luck, he gained the financial backing to launch the small exploratory fleet that sailed from Palos (Seville) on 3 August 1492 and, ten weeks later, famously sighted an uncertain Caribbean landfall in the Bahamas by the bright early-morning moon of 12 October. His belief that he had reached the fabled East is yet preserved in the appellation of "Indians" given to the American aborigines.

Columbus made four successive trips between Spain and America, which can be thus summarized:

1. August 1492–March 1493. The Bahamas and the larger islands of Cuba and Hispaniola, where Columbus left a small garrison.
2. September 1493–June 1496. Returned to the Lesser Antilles, landed on Puerto Rico—the only piece of current U.S. territory Columbus ever touched—sailed under Cuba, found Jamaica, and set up a long-term base on Hispaniola, where he discovered that the pioneer garrison had been exterminated by natives.
3. May 1498–October 1500. This confused trip included the first European sighting of Trinidad and the beginnings of exploration of the South American coast from central Venezuela to the delta of the Orinoco, but it ended in utter ignominy when Bobadilla, the newly arrived Spanish viceroy in Santo Domingo (Hispaniola), arrested Columbus for gross administrative incompetence and sent him back to Spain a prisoner.
4. May 1502–September 1504. Sailed between Cuba and Hispaniola to Jamaica, through the Caymans to make significant exploration of the Central American coastline from modern Honduras to Panama. The return journey was delayed by an involuntary yearlong sojourn on Jamaica.

Each of Columbus's voyages, especially the second and third, was attended by great difficulty and material catastrophe in which the admiral variously exhibited remarkable courage, culpable obduracy, great maritime abilities, and administrative incompetence. At the high point of Columbus's success, after the first voyage, he enjoyed the prestige of an international European hero, but he was already a has-been at the time of his death in Valladolid on 20 May 1506.

Columbus has left us a miscellaneous body of more-or-less incidental writings that, when gathered together, fill two octavo volumes. Columbus could read and write Latin, and he is probably the author of at least one Latin poem. Most of his documents, of an epistolary or legal cast, are written in the undistinguished Castilian of a non-native speaker of that language. Several of Columbus's letters relate directly or indirectly to his travels, as does his most distinctive work, a so-called *Libro de las profecías* (*Book of Prophecies*), in which Columbus sought to record—from the Bible, the ancient geographical traditions, and elsewhere—all the testimonies and "predictions" he could make to relate to his enterprise of the Indies. As an actual travel writer, Columbus's fame depends on a single work perhaps typical of the problematic nature

Letter from Columbus dated December 1504 and addressed to "the most learned Doctor Oderigo" (reproduced in *Memorials of Columbus; or, A Collection of Authentic Documents of That Celebrated Navigator*, 1823). *Courtesy of the Travellers Club, London; Bridgeman Art Library, agent.*

of everything he touched: the journal of the first voyage of 1492–1493, a book that has been published, republished, translated, annotated, and analyzed more frequently than nearly any other work of travel literature—and this despite the fact that it does not, strictly speaking, exist. Columbus certainly did keep some kind of logbook of the first journey though, surprisingly, perhaps not of the others. But the original of it has been lost. What we have instead—and what is repeatedly published as "Columbus's log"—is an edited and quite probably editorialized summary of the log by Barthomé de Las Casas, OP, the famous "Apostle to the Indians," a believer in the greatness of Columbus and in the providential guidance of his project, but also a critic of his unjust dealings with Indians. Las Casas recasts the log as a third-person narrative recounting the words of "the admiral."

Though of the greatest importance as evidence of the European mentality in its first encounters with America, Columbus's travelogue, written in the language of cliché in an undistinguished style, is largely lacking in sharp observation, suggestive reflection, or even much of a sense of extraordinary novelty. The admiral strongly though inconsistently resisted the fact, obvious to so many others, that he had found not Asia but some very large archipelago or landmass entirely unknown to European geography, indeed a veritable "New World." He intensely desired that Cuba should be Japan, and Hispaniola China or India. Furthermore, with Columbus as with so many other European pioneers in America, believing was seeing. Thus, the journal, ostensibly an eyewitness report, includes items from his readings in the fabulous zoology, botany, and anthropology of the ancient geographers and Jean de Mandeville. Certain aspects of the log strongly suggest that Columbus regarded it as the raw material for a report to his royal patrons and others whose strongest interest in the newly sighted lands would lie in the economic sphere. His understanding of early contacts with indigenous Americans was, of course, vitiated by linguistic incomprehension. Yet insofar as Columbus initiated the "western policy" first of Spain and then of other European countries, he must continue to be regarded as one of the most influential travelers in the history of the world.

JOHN V. FLEMING

### Biography

Born Cristoforo Colombo in Genoa, Italy, between August and October 1451, son of Domenico Colombo, a Genoese merchant and wool weaver. Little is known of his early life; possibly apprenticed as a weaver as a youth. Probably began sailing in the Mediterranean on mercantile missions for his father, 1474. Settled in Lisbon as a map dealer with his brother Bartholomew after surviving a shipwreck off Cape St. Vincent, Portugal, 1476. Probably sailed to Iceland and Ireland on a Portuguese ship, 1477. Traveled to Madeira on a commercial mission for a Genoese company, 1478. Married Felipa Perestrello e Moniz, 1479 (d. 1485): one son. Returned to Madeira and settled there; making commercial voyages to Guinea and equatorial West Africa, 1482–1485. Began relationship with Beatriz Enriquez de Harana of Córdoba after the death of his wife, 1485–1486: one son. Obtained patronage from King Ferdinand and Queen Isabella of Spain for a crossing of the Atlantic; awarded by the Spanish crown the title Admiral of the Ocean Sea, 1492. First voyage, August 1492–March 1493: established a base in Hispaniola and sighted and explored Cuba and islands in the Bahamas. Second voyage, September 1493–June 1496: made first European sighting of Jamaica and Puerto Rico and explored the Lesser Antilles and Cuba. Third voyage, May 1498–October 1500: explored Trinidad and Venezuela. Fourth voyage, May 1502–September 1504: sailed from Cape Honduras to Nicaragua, Costa Rica, and Panama. Returned to Seville, September 1504; lived in Seville, traveling to Salamanca and Valladolid with the Spanish royal court in attempts to receive more substantial financial reward from the Spanish Crown for his explorations. Died in Valladolid, Spain, 20 May 1506.

### References and Further Reading

Columbus, Christopher, *The Four Voyages of Christopher Columbus*, edited and translated by J.H. Cohen, 1969.

Columbus, Christopher, *Cartas de particulares a Colón y Relaciones coetáneas*, edited by Juan Gil and Consuelo Varela, 2 vols., 1984.

Columbus, Christopher, *The Diario of Christopher Columbus's First Voyage to America, 1491–1492, Abstracted by Fray Bartolomé de las Casas* (bilingual edition), edited and translated by Oliver Dunn and James E. Kelley, Jr., 1989.

*See also* **Atlantic Ocean, Explorations Across**

## CONRAD, JOSEPH (1857–1924) *Polish-Born English Novelist and Travel Writer*

Joseph Conrad was born in Berdyczów in the Russian-dominated Ukraine. In 1861, his father was arrested for anti-Russian conspiracy, and in 1862, the family was exiled to Vologda in Russia. After the deaths of Conrad's parents (Eva in 1865, Apollo in 1869), he was looked after by his uncle, Tadeusz Bobrowski. Conrad left Poland for Marseilles in 1874 to become a seaman in the French merchant navy (and thus evade military service in the Russian army). As Conard had been taught French since he was a small child, this first move from one culture to another was not as difficult as his second in 1878, when he joined his first British ship and had to learn English from scratch. After a number of voyages (to Australia and the Far East) as an ordinary seaman, he was made third and, later, second mate. He passed the first mate's examination in 1884, then became a naturalized British subject and passed the master's examination in 1886; he was released from the status of Russian subject in 1889. Conard made voyages (as first mate and, once, from January 1888 to March 1889, as master) between Britain and Singapore, Bangkok, the Dutch East Indies, Borneo, Celebes, Mauritius, and Australia. In 1890, Conard secured a three-year appointment with the Société Anonyme Belge pour le Commerce du Haut-Congo as officer on its steamboats on the Congo, but he returned prematurely after six months because of severe illness. After further voyages (from Britain to Australia), his sea career ended on 17 January 1894.

Strictly speaking, Conrad did not publish any literature of travel or exploration as such. Instead of writing reports of his travels, on the whole he used his experiences and the books he read as raw material that he artistically transformed according to his imaginative intentions and capability. The following are debatable exceptions: *The Mirror of the Sea: Memories and Impressions* (1906), which combines descriptive, analytic, and reflective passages on the nature of the sea, different kinds of wind and weather, the role of the land (its rivers and ports), and the culture of seamanship (with particular emphasis on processes of initiation as well as the craft of seamanship as a fine art and its heroes); *A Personal Record: Some Reminiscences* (1912), which, among other things, covers the genesis of Conrad's first novel, *Almayer's Folly*, which he began in 1889, continued over the next five years (in England, the Ukraine, the Congo, on board ships), and finally published in 1895; and "Geography and Some Explorers" (1924), which crucially links Conrad's avid reading of books of travel and exploration (works on or by, for example, Tasman, Cook, Franklin, McClintock, Mungo Park, Heinrich Barth, Burton, Speke, Livingstone, and Hugh Clifford) with his personal experiences.

The Malay Archipelago plays a vital part in Conrad's early work: *Almayer's Folly* (1895), *An Outcast of the Islands* (1896), *Lord Jim* (1900), and a number of tales, such as "The Lagoon" (1896), "Karain" (1897), "Falk" (1901), and "Typhoon" (1902), are set there. A four-month period of work (1887–1888) as first mate of the small steamer *Vidar*, trading between Singapore and the Dutch East Indies, Borneo, and Celebes, had provided Conrad with a concrete body of experience and a particular setting that later enabled him to write about this part of the world—its complex social and cultural conflicts, its brutalized and disillusioned colonizers and colonized—successfully and with unusual accuracy, so that early reviews of Conrad's texts stressed their "pioneering quality" (Najder, 1983). Moreover, Conrad benefited from the fact that the archipelago was not part of the British empire and had hardly been used as a fictional subject before: he was not faced by an "embarrassing division of loyalty" and "could allow his knowledge and imagination relative freedom" (Najder, 1983). These advantages induced Conrad to return to this setting again and again, as in his tales "The Secret Sharer" (1910), "A Smile of Fortune" (1911), and "Freya of the Seven Isles" (1912), his late novels *Victory* (1915) and *The Rescue* (1920), and his novella *The Shadow-Line* (1916).

In Conard's European novels and tales, his quality as a writer is to be found not so much in the settings—London in *The Secret Agent* (1906) and Geneva in *Under Western Eyes* (1910)—as in the subjects and their narrative realization. For the context of *Nostromo* (1904), Conard's great South American novel, he had to rely on his reading (and, perhaps, his early experiences in the Caribbean, where he had sailed on French ships between 1874 and 1876). His output deriving from his experiences in Africa consists of his tale "An Outpost of Progress" (1897) and his novel *Heart of Darkness* (1899). The so-called Congo Diary, kept by Conrad during his trek from Matadi to Kinshasa between 28 June and 1 August 1890, was not published in his lifetime (and quite clearly was not intended for publication), as it is no more than a record of "immediate impressions" (Najder, 1983) for the purpose of future remembering and imaginative transformation.

Conrad's work marks a particular conjuncture. He witnessed, chronicled, and, both critically and creatively, responded to the apex and decline of two historical developments: the age of sail and the British empire. Both of these had found their preeminent literary expressions in the travel writing (of Brooke, Speke, McClintock, Livingstone, Wallace, and others) and adventure fiction (of, for example, Marryat, Kingsley, Ballantyne, Henty, and Haggard) of the Victorian age and, thereby, had succeeded in securing a popular forum for espousing the ideals of the British empire and the imperial subject. But while Conrad was profoundly influenced by these two different, if complementary, genres (see White, 1993), he also challenged many assumptions of their conventions, affording and demanding new ways of viewing and dealing with their objects. Steeped deeply in the nineteenth-century realist tradition, Conrad confronted political, cultural, and moral issues in increasingly complex narrative constructions whose disrupted chronology, polyphonic voices, and powerful irony precluded any conclusive message. Moreover, the fact that Conrad wrote in his third language made him acutely aware both of the challenge of exploiting the linguistic possibilities of English and of the limits of any language as a means of creating even an approximate representation of the world. His work persuasively documents the transition from nineteenth-century realism to literary modernism.

JÜRGEN KRAMER

### Biography

Born Józef Teodor Konrad Natęcz Korzeniowski in Berdyczów (now Berdichev), Ukrainian Province of Poland (now the Ukraine), 3 December 1857. Educated by tutors in Lwów and Cracow, 1868–1873. Moved to Marseilles, 1874. Worked as a seaman on French ships, traveling to the West Indies, 1874–1876, then as an able seaman in England, 1878; sailed on British ships in the Orient trade, 1879–1894, passing the first mate's and master's examinations, 1884 and 1886. Became British subject, 1886. Received first and only command, 1888. First mate on *Torrens*, 1891–1893. Retired from the Merchant Service; moved to England, 1894. Married Jessie George, 1896: two sons. Lived in the south of England from 1896. Published 13 novels (and two more in collaboration with Ford Madox Ford), including *Lord Jim* (1900) and *Heart of Darkness* (1899), 28 novellas and tales, and two volumes of memoirs and reminiscences, 1895–1924. Declined the offer of a knighthood, May 1924. Died in Bishopsbourne, near Canterbury, 3 August 1924.

### References and Further Reading

Conrad, Joseph, *The Mirror of the Sea: Memories and Impressions*, 1906.

Conrad, Joseph, *A Personal Record: Some Reminiscences*, 1912.

Conrad, Joseph, *The Works of Joseph Conrad*, uniform edition, 22 vols., 1923–1928.

Najder, Zdzisław, *Joseph Conrad: A Chronicle*, Cambridge: Cambridge University Press, New Brunswick, New Jersey: Rutgers University Press, 1993.

White, Andrea, *Joseph Conrad and the Adventure Tradition: Constructing and Deconstructing the Imperial Subject*, Cambridge and New York: Cambridge University Press, 1993.

## CONSTANTINOPLE

As the repository for a staggering supply of miracle-working relics, Constantinople was a major center for (mainly eastern) Christian pilgrims throughout the medieval period. The pilgrim's itinerary invariably began with the church of St. Sophia, before encompassing a host of smaller, but hardly less magnificent shrines. Associated with the pilgrim traffic was a brisk trade in souvenirs. "Getting hold of . . . miracle-working objects was the dream of many travellers, especially those with a clerical background," writes Ciggaar (1996). "The common visitor, however, had to make do with small mementos of a religious character. Pilgrim tokens could be bought in gold, silver, copper, bronze, lead, and even in glass, bearing the portraits of Christ, the Virgin, a saint or some other religious symbol."

Despite its lively pilgrim trade, there is a remarkable dearth of commentary about Constantinople prior to the eleventh century, when non-Greeks began visiting it in significant numbers. Considering that the early visitors were privileged to witness one of the world's great cities in its heyday, the brevity of their accounts makes for disappointing reading. The only description longer than a few lines was penned by a Syrian, probably a Jew, Harûn-ibn-Yahya, who visited Constantinople shortly after 910. Unlike most other visitors, who were Christians doing the rounds of the city's holy sanctuaries, Harûn was primarily interested in its secular monuments. More typical of medieval accounts are the effusions of Foucher of Chartres's *Historia hierosolmitana*, written around 1100:

> Oh, how great is that noble and beautiful city! How many monasteries, how many palaces are there, fashioned in a wonderful way! How many wonders there are to be seen in the squares and in the different parts of the city! I cannot bring myself to tell in detail what great masses there are of every commodity: of gold, for example, of silver, of many-shaped garments and relics of saints. All the time merchants, with busy shipping traffic, were bringing in everything that people needed. (translated by J.P.A. van der Vin)

Virtually identical impressions of Constantinople's sumptuous monuments and flourishing commerce were conveyed by other twelfth-century visitors, including Odo of Deuil, chaplain to the French king Louis VII, who passed through the city in 1147 en route to the Holy Land, and Benjamin of Tudela, a Spanish Jew who visited it in about 1160. But indicative of growing anti-Greek sentiment, which rose sharply in the last half of the century, was a passage in which Odo pointed out that the much-vaunted magnificence of the city's churches and palaces coexisted with widespread urban squalor:

> The city itself is squalid and fetid and in many places harmed by permanent darkness, for the wealthy overshadow the streets with buildings and leave these dirty, dark places to the poor and to travelers; there murders and robberies and other crimes which love the darkness are committed. (translated by J.P.A. van der Vin)

In 1204, in one of the most infamous episodes of medieval history, Constantinople was extensively plundered by the crusaders. Although the two richest palaces, the Blachernae and the Bucoleon, and some other larger buildings narrowly escaped the same fate, the city never fully recovered. As we lack accounts for a period of more than a century afterward, the decline is first registered in an account written by a Dominican monk who visited the city around 1330. According to Brocardus, "Although the city is large only a modest number of people live there, in relation to its size. For barely a third of the city is inhabited. The rest consists of gardens or fields or vineyards, or waste land." With the exception of a few palaces, its buildings were all made of wood and destined, he thought, to "go up in a sea of flame" in the event of a fire (quoted in van der Vin, 1980).

From the 1330s on, visitors from the Latin West were as likely to comment on Constantinople's degraded condition as its splendid edifices. The Spanish nobleman Ruy González de Clavijo, who was in Constantinople in the winter of 1403–1404, noted not only that the city was thinly populated, but also that most churches and monasteries were in ruins. Although St. Sophia itself remained largely intact, "Near the church there are many fallen edifices, and doors leading to the church, closed and ruined" (van der Vin, 1980). That parts of the Great Church remained in superb condition is testified to by another Spanish visitor, Pero Tafur, who saw it in about 1437: "the church itself is in such a fine state that it seems to-day to have only just been finished" (van der Vin, 1980). Johannes Schiltberger, a German soldier who passed through in 1427, observed that one could "see one's self on the walls inside the church as if in a mirror, because the marble and lapis-lazuli on the wall is clear and clean." By this date, however, its fine state of repair was exceptional. The imperial palace "is in such a state that both it and the city show well the evils which the people have suffered and still endure," Tafur wrote (van der Vin, 1980). As for the people, they were "but sad and poor, showing the hardship of their lot" (van der Vin, 1980). Written shortly after his return to Spain in about 1452, Tafur's would have been the last major account written before the eastern capital fell to the Turks the following year.

Curiously, the pace of Constantinople's decline can only be followed in texts written by visitors from the Catholic West. The Arab traveler Ibn Battuta, who was there in 1332, wrote a lengthy, vivid account but noted few signs of decay. His description consists rather of detailed impressions of the buildings retaining their ancient splendor intact, notably St. Sophia (which, as a Muslim, he was only allowed to view from the outside) and the Blachernae palace. Finally, the five Russian accounts that survive from the postcrusader period are so preoccupied with sacred relics that scant attention is paid to the city's material condition or even its secular monuments. But, as they were written by visitors who fully participated in the devotional world that was Byzantium, anyone interested in recovering Constantinople's significance to the pilgrims who made up the bulk of its tourists throughout its long history needs to start with these fascinating texts, recently collected and translated by Majeska.

The tombstone of British ambassador Edward Barton (died 1597) recycled over a monastery gate in the Princes Islands (from Robert Walsh's *Residence at Constantinople*, 1836). *Courtesy of the Travellers Club, London; Bridgeman Art Library, agent.*

James Paterson

## References and Further Reading


Brock, Sebastian, "A Medieval Armenian Pilgrim's Description of Constantinople," *Revue des Études Arméniennes*, new series, 4 (1967): 81–102.

Ciggaar, Krijnie N., *Western Travellers to Constantinople: The West and Byzantium, 962–1204: Cultural and Political Relations*, Leiden and New York: Brill, 1996.

Clavijo, Ruy González de, *Embassy to Tamerlane, 1403–1406*, translated by Guy le Strange, 1928.

Ibn Battuta, *The Travels of Ibn Battuta, AD 1325–1354*, translated by H.A.R. Gibb, 3 vols., 1958–1971.

Majeska, George P. (editor), *Russian Travelers to Constantinople in the Fourteenth and Fifteenth Centuries*, 1984.

Odo of Deuil, *De profectione Ludovico VII in orientem / The Journey of Louis VII to the East*, edited and translated by Virginia Gingerick Berry, 1948.

Schiltberger, Johannes, *The Bondage and Travels of Johann Schiltberger, a Native of Bavaria, in Europe, Asia, and Africa, 1396–1427*, translated by J. Buchan Telfer, 1879.

Tafur, Pero, *Travels and Adventures, 1435–1439*, translated and edited by Malcolm Letts, 1926.

Vin, J.P.A. van der, *Travellers to Greece and Constantinople: Anicient Monuments and Old Traditions in Medieval Travellers' Tales*, 2 vols., Leiden: Netherlands Historisch-Archeologisch Institut te Istanbul, 1980.

Wright, Thomas (editor), *Early Travels in Palestine: Comprising the Narratives of . . . Benjamin of Tudela, etc.*, 1848.

*See also* **Byzantium; Istanbul**

## CONTI, NICCOLÒ DEI (c. 1395–1469)

***Italian Merchant and Traveler***

After the collapse of the prosperous trade system in the distant parts of Asia around the middle of the fourteenth century, very few Europeans traveled to India. This was a result of the plague, the breakup of the Mongolian empire following the assumption of power in China by the xenophobic Ming dynasty in 1368, and the disintegration of the kingdom of the Mongol Timur, an Islamic convert, after his death in 1405. One who did travel in this period, however, was Niccolò dei Conti, a merchant from Chioggia, who spent some 25 years between c. 1415 and 1439/42 traveling around the Near East and Southeast Asia. Conti's travels were a risky undertaking, but he was fortunate enough to return home, where an eager scholar, Poggio Bracciolini, took an interest and wrote down Conti's impressions and experiences.

As an adolescent, Conti studied Arabic in Damascus, one of the main crossroads for trade in the Levant. Since Europeans were forbidden to trade with Persia and India as a result of a trade monopoly, he joined an Arabian caravan en route to Baghdad, then sailed via Basra, the Persian Gulf, and Hormuz as far as Kalhat in present-day Oman, where he learned Persian. While Conti was returning via Arabia, his disguise as a Persian merchant was uncovered. At the Egyptian border, with his life and those of his wife and his four children under threat, he was forced to convert to Islam. On Conti's return to Italy, he begged absolution for his conversion from Pope Eugene IV at the Council of Florence and thus came to know the eminent humanist and private secretary to the pope, Gian Francesco Poggio Bracciolini (1380–1459).

In 1448, the scholarly Poggio, who had been in the service of the pope since 1404, published the authenticated details of his thorough interview of Conti in *Historia de varietate fortunae*, a work designed to demonstrate the fickleness of fortune, which he dedicated to Pope Nicholas V. Cooperative works of this kind (for example, Odoric of Pordenone with William of Solagna, Marco Polo with Rustichello) traditionally acquired greater credibility. Poggio divided the story of Conti's travels into two parts—itinerary and detailed summary—which he added to the first of three volumes of his work, written between 1432 and 1435 and covering the history of Rome, of Europe in the fourteenth and fifteenth centuries, and of the pontificate of Eugene IV. Poggio's purpose was to provide reliable knowledge on Asian cosmography, supported and complemented by two short reports from envoys in Cathay and Ethiopia.

Conti traveled via the usual trade routes; personal details, such as his motivations, have not been passed down. Traveling as a tradesman in a Persian vessel, Conti set off for Cambay via the west coast of India, and from there, via the Malabar coast, he went south toward Delhi via Barkur, crossing India by land via the capitals of Vijayanagar as far as "Pudifetania" (probably what we now know as Madras Chennai) on the Indian east coast. In Mailapur, he visited the grave of St. Thomas the Apostle and a community of Nestorians, before heading south along the Coromandel Coast toward Cayal and to the island of Ceylon (Sri Lanka), rich in precious stones and cinnamon. From there, Conti sailed past the Andaman Islands to Sumatra, where he remained for a year and observed cruel native customs. A storm took him to Tenasserim and finally to the mouth of the Ganges, where he sailed upriver in search of a number of cities that have never been identified. The details of the route Conti took are probably an amalgamation of several different voyages. He used "Pudifetania" again as the point of departure for his crossing of the Gulf of Bengal and his journey by land from Arakan, following the Irrawaddy to Ava, the former capital of the Burmese empire. A diagram of a route to Cathay at this point in the narrative has provoked lively scholarly debate about the possibility that Conti had visited China, though this seems unlikely. After stops in Sittang and Pegu, he spent nine months in Sumatra and Java (he uses "Java minor" and "maior," which could possibly have denoted Java and Borneo). It was there that Conti heard about the remote spice islands of Sandai (Sunda) and Bandam (Banda), situated further to the east, which were reported to be sources of nutmeg Sandai (Sunda) and cloves. The furthest Bandam (Banda) mainland point to the east that he reached was Ciampa (Vietnam). His return journey to Europe took him via the Malabar Coast, the island of Socotra, Aden, the Red Sea, and Cairo. It was in Cairo that Conti lost, during an epidemic, the woman he was reputed to have married in India, two of his children, and all his servants, before finally reaching Venice accompanied by his two surviving children.

The narrative describes a total of 25 months of travel and lengthy stopovers of approximately four years; we know little about the remaining periods.

Poggio combined eyewitness accounts with professional skill and scholarship to a degree that was unique in writings about the Near East and the Ganges in the Middle Ages. Conti is often cited as an impartial source, but he rarely appears as an individual, with the result that it is difficult to distinguish between what was his actual experience and what was simply hearsay. A nonjudgmental, neutral tone (with little reference to *mirabilia* and myth) dominates Conti's travel narrative, which concentrates mainly on trade in plants (fruits, spices, timber), pearls and precious stones, and animals and on native customs, but he seldom gives detailed accounts of cities and islands. The systematic, ethnocentric textbook style of description of the Indian and Indonesian peoples is modeled on classical lines, particularly those of Pliny the Elder. Beginning with the partition of India by the Ganges and the Indus, Poggio describes everyday life (food, clothing, jewelery, prostitution), ritual (marriage, polygamy, burial, sati), gods and idols (sacrifice, ritual suicide), festivals, technical skills (navigation, shipbuilding, calendars, currency, weapons), Asian views of Europeans, writing, justice, diseases, and idiosyncracies. The result is a wealth of new and precise writing that takes its inspiration from classical historiography and contemporary Asian studies (such as those of the male and female islands in Socotra or the tale of hunting for diamonds using birds of prey borrowed from Marco Polo).

The Castilian nobleman and global wanderer Pero Tafur (1410–c. 1479), who from 1435 to 1439 traveled throughout the Holy Land and nearly all over Europe, covered the same journey as Conti, but his writings reveal completely different observations. He is supposed to have met up with Conti in 1436 or 1437 at the monastery of St. Catherine on the Sinai peninsula as Conti arrived with a caravan from India. It is said that Conti so energetically advised him not to continue to India that Tafur joined the caravan heading for Egypt. Conti, who was supposedly in the service of the sultan in Cairo, reportedly sent Tafur on ahead to Venice with letters and notes. This encounter has been the subject of intense scholarly debate, because Tafur claims that Conti had spent 40 years in India, giving an entirely different route for his travels (Alexandria, Babylon, the court of Tamerlane and the kingdom of Prester, conversion in Mecca), and that he had given Tafur his notes does not quite ring true. The stereotypical description and the numerous *mirabilia* give one reason to doubt their encounter, especially as Tafur was, like Bracciolini and perhaps Conti, also in Florence in 1439 and only committed his account to paper in 1450. Other elements, however, support the view that the encounter did occur: the urgent warning against traveling to India (which corresponds with Conti's own opinion in his last will), the denial of the existence of mammoths in India, and the accounts of necromancy on windless days, which are found only in Poggio's writings.

Poggio's report survives in 52 of the 59 known manuscripts of *Historia de varietate fortunae* (of these, 28 contain all four books and one has books 1 and 4). Twenty-three manuscripts contain only book 4, which was circulated widely and keenly read as a separate volume. All the manuscripts, with the exception of three originated in central Italy, are exclusively from the fifteenth century. The early printed versions (the first being that of Ulrich Scinzenzeler in Milan in 1492) reproduce only the fourth book, and then often in the context of other eyewitness accounts. The Latin edition was followed in 1502 by a Portuguese edition and in 1503 by the first Spanish translation. An Italian version was published in 1550 in the famous collection of travel writings by Giovanni Battista Ramusio, gaining wide circulation, but it was riddled with errors. The foreword for this work claims that Conti was forced to dictate his experiences as a penance. Proof that interest was concentrated in Italy (for instance, it was not published in Germany) can be found in the clear evidence contained in the Genoese Portulan map of 1457, in Fra Mauro's 1459 map of the world, in Enea Silvio Piccolomini's (Pope Pius II) geographical compendium *De Asia* (1461), in an annex to the foreword of Ansel Adorno's journey to the Holy Land (1470–1471), and in other treatises of the sixteenth century.

INGRID BAUMGÄRTNER

## Biography

Little known about his life. The only certain dates are those concerning the period following his 25 years traveling in India. Born c. 1395 in Chioggia, a port in the republic of Venice; supposed to have headed for Damascus in 1415, to have married an Indian woman, and to have returned to Italy between 1439 and 1442 accompanied by his surviving children, Maria and Daniele. We know that he was a member of the *Maggior consiglio* in 1451, that he was elected procurator of the churches of San Francesco in 1453 and Santa Croce in 1460, *giudice di proprio* in 1456, and that he was subsequently a member of various trade missions tasked with buying cereals and oil in Faenza and Apulia. His will was read on 10 August 1469, apparently soon after his death.

## References and Further Reading

Conti, Niccolò dei, "The Travels of Nicolò Conti in the East in the Early Part of the Fifteenth Century," translated by J.

Winter Jones, in *India in the Fifteenth Century: Being a Collection of Narratives of Voyages to India*, edited by R.H. Major, 1857; reprint, 1994: 1–39.
Conti, Niccolò dei, in *Viaggi in Persia, India e Giava di Nicolò de' Conti, Girolamo Adorno e Girolamo da Santo Stefano*, compiled by Poggio Bracciolini, edited by Mario Longhena, 1929; 2nd edition, 1960: 117–196.
Conti, Niccolò dei, in *Navigazioni e viaggi* [Navigations and Travels], compiled by Giovanni Battista Ramusio, edited by Marcia Milanesi, vol. 2, 1979: 781–820.
Conti, Niccolò dei, in *De varietate fortunae*, compiled by Poggio Bracciolini, edited by Outi Merisalo, 1993.
Conti, Niccolò dei, *L'India di Nicolò de' Conti: Un manoscritto del Libro IV del De varietate fortunae di Francesco Poggio Braccioloni da Terranova (Marc. 2560)*, edited by Alessandro Grossato, 1994.
Conti, Niccolò dei, in *Indien und Europa im Mittelalter*, edited by Wilhelm Baum and Raimund Senoner, 2000: 154–204.

## COOK'S TOURS

Thomas Cook's tours made leisure travel easy and affordable for the middle classes. By providing escorted and lower-cost journeys, and taking care of all the mundane and intimidating details of travel (choosing an itinerary, buying the proper tickets, finding a decent hotel, exchanging currency), Cook made large strides toward the democratization of travel.

A one-time itinerant Baptist preacher and devoted temperance advocate, Thomas Cook (1808–1892) understood his work as having a moral purpose. Travel, he believed, broadened the mind. It provided cultural enrichment for ordinary people, broke down barriers of class and nationality, and promoted tolerance. His first excursion was intended to further promote the antidrink cause by transporting 570 people from Leicester to a temperance rally at Loughborough and back on a specially chartered train. The success of this and other temperance outings led Cook to try his hand at holiday travel for the general public.

Rail travel in Britain in this period could be confusing and complicated because of the numerous different lines and the gaps between them. Cook's organized tours made leisure travel simple. In 1845, he conducted a trip from Leicester, Nottingham, and Derby to Liverpool and back. A more complex outing than his previous efforts, this trip required connections between four different railway lines and offered in addition a steamer trip to Caernarvon and an opportunity, for those who wished it, to climb Mount Snowdon. As Cook would for all his trips, he scouted out the route in advance and prepared a handbook detailing the sights to be seen. As many as 350 people took part, and the jaunt was repeated two weeks later by popular demand. Cook next looked to Scotland, which had recently become a fashionable destination. Although his first excursion there—which attracted 350 people in 1846—was something of a fiasco, his Tartan Tours soon became the heart of a thriving business. Between 1848 and 1863 (with the exception of 1851, when Cook reinforced his reputation by organizing excursions to the Great Exhibition in London, bringing 165,000 people there), Cook spent two months every summer conducting four tours to Scotland, with a total of 5,000 visitors per season. The tours lasted two weeks and enabled participants to visit all Scotland's major attractions, including destinations in the western Highlands. Cook estimated that, by 1861, he had taken 40,000 people to Scotland.

In 1863, the Scottish railway companies, eager to capture a bigger share of the tourist business and to save the cost of Cook's agency, refused to allow Cook's Tours the use of their lines for his Scottish tours. This action effectively banned his business from Scotland. In response, Cook turned to the Continent, where he had already made a few forays, chiefly short tours to Paris. In 1863, he escorted 500 people on a three-week tour of Switzerland. His first tours to Italy took place in 1864. Destinations offered by the firm soon included Holland, Belgium, France, Germany, Austria, Spain, the United States, India, Australia, and New Zealand. By 1868, Cook claimed to have organized the travels of 2 million people.

Tours to the Middle East began in 1869, soon becoming a central part of the company's business. By the 1880s, Thomas Cook and Son dominated tourist traffic on the Nile, having been granted exclusive control of all steamers on that river. Sometimes called the "Booking Clerk to the Empire," the company became a central element of British military and administrative authority in Egypt and Palestine, arranging transportation of casualties during the Arabi Pasha revolt of 1882 and providing transport and supplies for the 1884–1885 effort to evacuate Khartoum and relieve General Gordon. In 1872, Cook took a small group on a round-the-world tour, and the circumnavigation of the globe became a regular feature of his program.

Thomas Cook was not the first to organize group tours, and he had several competitors throughout his career. However, he took an unusual degree of care with his tours and his tourists. Those who lacked the confidence to travel by themselves (or those, like single women, for whom traveling alone was not socially acceptable) could feel completely comfortable under Cook's care. Women were often in the majority among his customers, for the protection offered by Cook's Tours provided new opportunities for single women to travel. The tours cost less than individual travel, as Cook's tourists could take advantage of group rates everywhere from trains to restaurants. Clients on his English and Scottish tours were largely tradesmen,

Steamship cruises, mountain scenery, and classical antiquities—all the delights of Cook's Tours promised in the publicity for the 1902 season. *Courtesy of Thomas Cook Archives.*

clerks, artisans, and other skilled workers. In expanding to the Continent and beyond, the firm successfully appealed to the upper middle classes, a move in which Cook's son, John Mason Cook (1834–1899), who joined the firm full-time in 1865, played a central role. As Thomas Cook and Son offered longer, more distant, and more elaborate tours, the firm also worked to combine the benefits of structured tourism with the freedom to choose among options. Cook's could sell customers all the tickets needed for a given itinerary (drawn up by the firm), allowing them to decide how and when to use the tickets. Clients could also buy hotel coupons covering room, board, and some amenities; these were accepted in establishments recommended by Cook in most countries in which the firm did business. In 1873, the firm began issuing "circular notes," precursors of modern travelers' cheques. By the 1870s, most of Cook's customers made use of the various tickets to travel independently rather than on escorted tours. For much of the century, however, Cook's was identified with large escorted tours, and it was frequently criticized for bringing crowds of "Cockneys" to locales that they allegedly could not truly appreciate.

In the late nineteenth century and in the Edwardian period, the company worked to appeal to a higher class of clientele, offering "select, first-class" tours to expensive locations, thus moving ever further from their founder's more democratic goals. In the twentieth century, Cook's continued to offer personally conducted tours, usually to exotic locations. Most of their business, however, was directed toward other aspects of the tourist industry.

KATHERINE HALDANE GRENIER

### References and Further Reading

Thomas Cook and Son published a newspaper, *Cook's Excursionist*, from 1851 to 1939, which was the company's primary means of reaching the public. (From 1903 to 1939, it was known as *Cook's Traveler's Gazette.*) The company also published numerous guidebooks to its destinations. The Thomas Cook Company Archives in Peterborough, United Kingdom, has an extensive collection of these materials.

*See also* **Tourism**

## COOPER, JAMES FENIMORE (1789–1851) *American Novelist and Travel Writer*

James Fenimore Cooper was the twelfth of 13 children born to William and Mary Cooper in Burlington, New Jersey, on 15 September 1789. Though his father, a judge and landowner, arranged for the boy's earliest education under the guidance of an episcopal clergyman in Albany, New York, Cooper was by February 1803, after the death of his tutor, enrolled at Yale College. An underage student, Cooper was expelled in the spring of 1805 for pulling a prank on an unpopular teacher. The young man stayed at home for more than 18 months, but in October 1806, William Cooper decided to send his son to sea. He spent the next year as a common sailor on *Sterling*, a merchant vessel bound for England and the Mediterranean. The son saw a great deal of London, and he visited Spain, but his memories of this period were colored by the perils of pirates and impressment gangs encountered on the journey. By the summer of 1807, Cooper found himself back in America, and on 1 January 1808, he was commissioned a midshipman in the U.S. Navy. Over the next three years, the death of Cooper's father and his marriage to Susan DeLancey helped persuade him to resign from the service and assume the responsibility of his inheritance.

Cooper farmed in New York State, and after the death of the last of his brothers in 1819, he took responsibility for the family estate. He published his first novel, *Precaution* (1820), anonymously, but over the following five years, he established a commercial and critical reputation for himself as a writer of fiction with works like *The Pilot* (1823), drawing upon his experiences at sea. In June 1826, Cooper left with his family for an extended tour of Europe. While biographers point out that Cooper was interested both in securing a European education for his children and in bettering his health in milder climates, he also desired an opportunity to improve arrangements for the publication of his books abroad. *The Last of the Mohicans* (1826), his best-known and most enduring work, appeared just before his departure.

With the help of De Witt Clinton, governor of New York, Cooper was appointed as U.S. consul for Lyons. He originally planned a five-year tour to include Scandinavia and North Africa, but though he stayed abroad for more than seven years, he realized much less of his ambitious itinerary. The family established a residence in Paris, a city in which Cooper would spend more than half the trip. The author was celebrated in France, and he found life there agreeable, in notable contrast to the time he spent in England. He had returned to London briefly upon arriving in Europe, but he did not spend significant time in England until the spring of 1828. By that summer, he found himself in Switzerland, where the family took a small house in Bern. Cooper spent the winter of 1828–1829 in Italy, where he fell in love with the city of Florence. He visited Rome and Naples, setting up residence in Sorrento. His enduring affection for the Italian coast was captured in novels like *The Bravo* (1831) and *Wing-and-Wing* (1842), though readers might also recognize echoes of Europe in Cooper's rendering of Long Island Sound in *The Water-Witch* (1830). In the spring of 1830, he traveled again through northern Italy on his way to Germany, finally reestablishing the family in Paris by the end of the year. Illness kept Cooper close to the French capital for most of the rest of his stay, and his correspondence with America in 1831 began a period of preparation for a return to the United States. The summer and early autumn of 1832 saw Cooper undertake a trip up the Rhine that reacquainted him with Belgium, Germany, and Switzerland. His experience in these countries helped inform *The Heidenmauer* (1832) and *The Headsman* (1833). After spending the summer in England, Cooper returned to New York in November 1833.

Cooper's life after his return to America effected the further diversification of his work. He experienced the scrutiny afforded a famous writer, and his conflicts with townspeople over land rights in Cooperstown, New York, eventually led him to sue certain newspapers for libel. Many of Cooper's novels reflected his new concerns, and his works of nonfiction addressed issues from the development of democracy in America to the history of the U.S. Navy. His travels in Europe sharpened his opinions on a range of political and moral issues; some later works of fiction had foreign settings, and he drew upon European examples to help illustrate his polemical texts. Cooper's experiences abroad were captured most directly, however, in a series of five travel books assembled from notebooks and published between 1836 and 1838. *Sketches of Switzerland* (1836) recorded his journeys after leaving England for the Continent in 1828; *Sketches of Switzerland, Part Second* (1836) looked at Cooper's later stay in France, as well as his Rhine journey and return to Switzerland itself. In these works, the author's enthusiasm for tourism is quite clear. None of these books is carefully constructed, yet all are lively. *Gleanings in Europe: France* (1837) dealt in great detail with Cooper's early years in France, and it is here that he proves his eye for recording manners and customs observed at the heart of French society. *Gleanings in Europe: England* (1837) drew upon his three months in London at the beginning of his travels abroad. Cooper's skepticism about the English way of life contrasts with the Anglophilia that defined many of his countrymen's view of English society and institutions. *Gleanings in Europe: Italy* (1838) recorded the happiest two years in his European travels. While Cooper himself dismissed this last work as less important than, for example, his studies of France and England, the enthusiasm it betrays made it, during his lifetime, his most popular travel book. Cooper died at Otsego Hall, his family home in Cooperstown, on 14 September 1851.

CRAIG MONK

**Biography**

Born in Burlington, New Jersey, 15 September 1789. Moved to Cooperstown, New York, 1790. Attended Yale College, New Haven, Connecticut, 1803–1805; dismissed for misconduct. Visited England and Spain as a common sailor on the merchant ship *Sterling*, 1806–1807. Midshipman in the U.S. Navy, 1808–1811. Married Susan Augusta DeLancey, 1811: five daughters, two sons. Lived in Mamaroneck, New York, 1811–1814; Cooperstown, 1814–1817; Scarsdale, New York, 1817–1821. Took his family on an extended tour of Europe, 1826–1833. Published *The Last of the Mohicans*, 1826. Lived mostly in Paris, 1826–1828, 1830–1832, 1832–1833. Lived in Italy, 1828–1830 and also visited Belgium, England, Germany, and Switzerland. Returned to the United States, 1833. Lived in Cooperstown from 1834. Published a series of five travel books, 1836–1838. Died in Cooperstown, New York, 14 September 1851.

### References and Further Reading

Cooper, James Fenimore, *Sketches of Switzerland, by an American*, 2 vols., 1836; as *Excursions in Switzerland*, 2 vols., 1836; as *Gleanings in Europe: Switzerland*, 1980.

Cooper, James Fenimore, *Sketches of Switzerland, Part Second: A Residence in France; with an Excursion up the Rhine, and a Second Visit to Switzerland*, 2 vols., 1836; as *Gleanings in Europe: The Rhine*, edited by Thomas Philbrick and Maurice Geracht, with an introduction by Ernest Redekop and Maurice Geracht, 1986.

Cooper, James Fenimore, *Recollections of Europe*, 2 vols., 1837; as *Gleanings in Europe*, 1837.

Cooper, James Fenimore, *Gleanings in Europe*, vol. 1: *France*, edited by Robert E. Spiller, 1928; edited by Thomas Philbrick and Constance Ayers Denne, with an introduction by Thomas Philbrick, 1983.

Cooper, James Fenimore, *England: With Sketches of Society in the Metropolis*, 1837; as *Gleanings in Europe*, vol. 2: *England*, edited by Robert Spiller, 1930; revised edition, 1982.

Cooper, James Fenimore, *Gleanings in Europe: Italy*, 1838; as *Excursions in Italy*, 1838; revised edition, 1981.

## CORONADO, FRANCISCO VÁSQUEZ DE (1510–1554) *Spanish Explorer and Soldier*

Few adventures in the history of man can surpass, or even equal, the journey of Francisco Vásquez de Coronado from Mexico City to the plains of Cíbola (now Kansas). The name of the great explorer still evokes the picture of a handful of men riding boldly in search of gold into the unknown natural furnace of the southwestern dry country.

Coronado came to Mexico with Viceroy Antonio de Mendoza in 1535. In 1538, Coronado was appointed governor of the province of New Galicia, and in that same year, Friar Marcos de Niza returned from the north with the news that he had, with his own eyes, actually seen one of the fabled Seven Golden Cities of Cíbola. Viceroy Mendoza, dazzled at the thought of the legendary wealth of the Seven Cities, organized an elaborate expedition to go and take the land in the name of the king of Spain. Mendoza appointed Coronado to lead the expedition and named him captain general of the Spanish army overseas.

Coronado's army consisted of 300 soldiers and a large body of friendly Native American allies. The Spanish outpost farthest north in New Spain was the village of Culiacán (in Sinaloa), and from there, Coronado set forth in the spring of 1540. Mendoza ordered Coronado to show the Native American allies the greatest consideration, something that had not been done by all the conquistadores. They had to be dealt with as freemen, and permitted to turn back "rich and contented," supplied with provisions for the return march, with, if necessary, an escort of horsemen for their protection. Natives encountered on the way were likewise to be treated considerately. They were expected to render obedience to his Majesty, "as their sovereign and ours," but they were not to be molested, nor their food or other belongings taken from them without compensation. To this end, many bales of petty merchandise (*rescates*) were carried on the backs of mules as presents for the natives encountered on the way and to barter for provisions. Some of the Native Americans took their wives and children with them on the long march. Families left behind, Mendoza decreed, were to be provided with what was necessary for their sustenance until the husband should return. This order was "well known and public," and there is good evidence that it was carefully observed.

Coronado's trail led across modern Sonora and southwest Arizona to the Zuñi country in New Mexico, and from there into the plains now called Kansas. None of the Spaniards found splendor or wealth in Cíbola; they found only primitive natives and wild buffalo. Instead of a great city sparkling with jewels, the weary treasure seekers saw before them little pueblos "all crumpled together." And when the soldiers beheld it, and realized what it was, "such were the curses which some of them hurled at Fray Marcos," wrote Pedro de Castañeda, expedition chronicler, "that I pray God to protect him from them." Coronado sent the friar back to Mexico City, telling the viceroy, "He has not told the truth in a single thing that he said, but everything is the opposite of what he related, except the name of the cities and the large stone houses."

For Coronado, there was no turning back. After taking Cíbola by force, Coronado made it his headquarters, then sent scouting parties out in several directions. Pedro de Tovar led a group that headed to the northwest, climbed the Colorado Plateau, and crossed the Painted Desert to investigate the people called Hopi, a Shoshonean-speaking group rumored to dwell in seven cities. Tovar found the Hopi, living in isolated towns, nestled at the bases of windswept mesas. He returned to Cíbola bearing reports of a great river still farther west, so Coronado dispatched another scouting party, this time led by his lieutenant García López de Cárdenas. On 25 August 1540, the expedition encountered the Grand Canyon, which they named Nuestra Señora (Our Lady). Along the way, the Spaniards had their first encounters, some peaceful, others violent, with many native groups, including the massacres of the Tiguex and Cicuye. The same month that López de Cárdenas saw the Colorado from the rim of the Grand Canyon, another Spanish party entered the river through its mouth on the Gulf of California. Later,

García López de Cárdenas was tried in Spain for various crimes against the natives; he died in prison.

Coronado pushed deeper into the continent, now seeking a kingdom called Quivira, described by a native as fabulously wealthy. This search took him onto the high plains of today's west Texas, then northeast across the panhandles of Texas and Oklahoma, before ending in frustration at a Wichita village on the Arkansas River near the present-day town of Lyons, in central Kansas. He planned to explore beyond this place, but a riding injury, from which he never fully recovered, thwarted him. Coronado therefore decided to go home. In the spring of 1542, his expedition returned the way it had come, taking with it nothing more than hard-won knowledge of the new land.

Coronado never located the supposed cities of gold. He notified the king that the lands were poor in metal but rich in livestock and very suitable for farming. In his journey, Coronado covered more territory in a shorter period of time than any other Spanish explorer to date, and in so doing, he prepared the way for future settlement of what would become the Southwest of the United States. It was the legend of the gilded man that brought the Spaniards into what is now Central and South America; it was the legend of the Seven Golden Cities of Cíbola that led them into New Spain and northward into the dry country of the American Southwest. That legend died forever when Coronado returned empty-handed to Mexico City. For a Spanish conquistador, failure meant oblivion, and although Coronado resumed his duties as governor of New Galicia, he fell from favor and was no longer as welcome at the royal court in Mexico City. By 1544, he had been dismissed from his post and stripped of his property. Coronado died in poverty in Mexico City and only a few marked the passing of this historic adventurer and soldier. Only the passage of time has elevated his name to the recognition he deserved, long ago, as the explorer of the great Southwest.

Because Coronado found no precious metals in the regions he explored, it has been the fashion to regard his expedition as a pointless jaunt. Nothing could be further from the truth. Exploration was a necessary antecedent to the colonization, exploitation, and social development of any part of the New World. Whether negatively or positively, each reconnaissance helped to prepare the way for the next step in the historical process by which the New World became what it is today.

Coronado performed in North America a service analogous to what was done in South America by Pizarro, Almagro, Benalcázar, and Quesada; and in Central America by Balboa, Alvarado, and Cortés. He converted the old trail up the west coast corridor into a well-known road that is still in use. To the map of the interior of North America, he added Cíbola, Tusayán, Tiguex, the Llanos del Cíbola, and Quivira, regions later combined under the name of the Southwest, or the Spanish Borderland, by Anglo-Americans. Historical tradition in this vast area, all the way from California to Nebraska, runs back to the reconnaissance made by Coronado. Another of his notable contributions to the larger features of North American geography was the discovery of the Continental Divide, the watershed between the Pacific and Atlantic Oceans from which two river systems run in opposite directions.

In all, Coronado's was one of the significant expeditions of that remarkable era during which Europeans opened up the Western Hemisphere.

JUAN CARLOS MERCADO

### Biography

Born in Salamanca, Spain, 1510. Studied humanities at the University of Salamanca for a short time; left for the West Indies, 1534. Arrived in Mexico; attached to the court of the Spanish viceroy Antonio de Mendoza, 1535. Appointed governor of Nueva Galicia (New Galicia), 1538. Organized expedition of several hundred Spaniards and Native American allies and two ships on an expedition to seek Cíbola or Quivira, rumored to be the location of the Seven Cities of Gold, reaching present-day New Mexico and Arizona, 1540. Made further exploration of present-day Texas, 1541–1542. Returned to New Galicia, 1542. Dismissed from post of governor, by 1544. Unsuccessfully indicted for conduct on the expedition, 1546. Retained seat on Council of Mexico City until his death. Died in Mexico City, 22 September 1554.

### References and Further Reading

Castañeda, Pedro de, "Relación de la jornada de Cíbola compuesta por Pedro de Castañeda de Nájera donde se trata de todos aquellos poblados y ritos y costumbres, la cual fue el año de 1540," manuscript at Lennox Library in the New York Public Library.

*See also* **New World Chronicles**

## CORTÉS, HERNÁN (1485–1547) *Spanish Soldier and Conquistador*

Hernán Cortés was just seven years old in 1492, when Spain triumphed over the last Moorish stronghold of Granada and rejoiced in Columbus's discovery of America. As the child of a noble but impoverished family, the adult Cortés could choose between the law and the army. Though his parents hoped he would take the robe of law, he chose the adventure and possibilities of the sword. In 1504, Cortés made his first voyage to the exotic, opportunity-filled Americas; he sailed to Hispaniola (today's Haiti and Dominican Republic), where he lived the life of a landowner of modest means for seven years. He then traveled to Cuba and spent another seven years there. Cortés's real entry into history began with his trip to mainland Mexico in 1519, a voyage at first sanctioned and then forbidden by Diego Velásquez, the governor of Cuba. The five *Cartas de relación* (*Letters of Relation*), written between 1519 and 1526 from Mexico chronicling his travels and conquests in Mexico, Guatemala, and Honduras, constitute one of the central documents in the historiography of the Americas.

Cortés's first letter, also known as the *Letter from Veracruz*, may be a substitute for a true "lost" first letter of relation to which he and his secretary Gómara refer. Dated 20 July 1519, the *Letter from Veracruz* describes the difficulties of previous expeditions by other Spaniards, who were attacked and killed by natives. Cortés takes great pains to criticize his former supporter, Diego Velásquez, the governor of Cuba, and pleads for Queen Joanna and her son Charles's support. Until Cortés and his men founded the "Villa Rica of Vera Cruz" [Rich Village of the True Cross] and appointed municipal officials, the expedition was under the command of Velásquez in Cuba. But Cortés made the journey to Mexico against Velásquez's wishes, and his enemies were conspiring all around him. Cortés knows he must present himself in a favorable light to the queen and her son: he includes a long list of all the indigenous objects being sent as gifts, in addition to the gift of a new town (Veracruz) in a new country (Mexico) from which the group would launch the conquest of that country. Among the gifts of most interest to the Crown were some colorful featherwork and precious gold objects. Thus, the first *Letter* is as much a political document as a relation, and it may properly be read as "a brilliant piece of special pleading, designed to justify an act of rebellion" and advance Cortés's claims over those of Velásquez (Pagden in Cortés's, 1971).

Cortés wrote the second *Letter* in April 1522, after the Spanish position at the Aztec capital of Tenochtitlán (now the site of Mexico City) had been considerably weakened by the brutal behavior of his lieutenant, Pedro de Alvarado. The letter is divided into three sections. The first section narrates the long march from Veracruz to the expedition's entry into Tenochtitlán. The second gives a detailed description of the city built in the middle of a lake, including its people and customs and everything related to Montezuma, the Aztec emperor. The third section begins with the arrival of Pánfilo de Narváez at Veracruz, sent by Velásquez against Cortés, relates Narváez's defeat and Cortés's return to Tenochtitlán, where the Indians had surrounded the Spanish, and describes the valiant battle in which the Aztecs expelled the Spanish from the city. Cortés's second *Letter* ends with his preparations and plans to reconquer Tenochtitlán. Cortés has lost the Mexican empire he had won for Charles V, yet his letter manages to place blame on his enemies in the Americas and, by implication, at court. His descriptions of Montezuma ring with Christian overtones, and his narrative often mentions gold in great quantities. Indeed, it is no accident that he relates the battle with Narváez and the Spanish loss of Tenochtitlán only after his detailed descriptions of the enormous wealth of Montezuma and the Aztecs.

The third *Letter* contains two sections. The first relates the successful conquest of Tenochtitlán and the capture of the Aztec leader, Cuauhtémoc; the second attempts to demonstrate that the conquest, and Cortés's leadership in it, are just beginning.

Spanish miniature, probably from a near-contemporary account, apparently showing the landing of Cortés in Mexico in 1519, with authentic detailing of the natives and vegetation; underneath is a medallion portrait of Cortés. *Courtesy of British Library, London.*

In the fourth *Letter*, Cortés again demonstrates his abilities to govern New Spain, and he again decries the efforts of his enemies against him, which he portrays as dangerous to the interests of Spain. And by now, a great deal of Mexican gold had made its way into the king's coffers.

The fifth *Letter* is the relation of Cortés's arduous trip from central Mexico, through the jungles of Guatemala, to Honduras to punish Cristóbal de Olid for rebelling against his authority in much the same way Cortés had rebelled against Velásquez. The second section of the letter sets forth Cortés's responses to all the charges brought against him by his enemies at the king's court, yet he closes by reaffirming his loyalty to the Crown.

The second, third, and fourth *Letters* were published in Spain soon after arriving, in 1522, 1523, and 1524, respectively, and were widely disseminated. In 1527, the *Letters* were banned, however, and no further printings allowed in Spanish, perhaps because even so early in its history the press revealed its power. The first *Letter* was not discovered until 1777 in the National Library of Vienna, where the fifth *Letter* was also found. They were published in 1842 and 1844, respectively.

Cortés's *Letters* are unique among letters of the period by virtue of their much greater length and their structure as letters, or true narratives, rather than as itemized accounts. The *Letters* are much more than a mere narrative of political and military events during the conquest of Mexico. Cortés describes and interprets the reality in which he finds himself, fusing data with ideas, facts with proposals. His detailed descriptions provided the first image of a New World—a New Spain—for many Spaniards. Though Cortés's *Letters* were written with a single reader in mind—Charles V—and were not intended as histories of the era and its events, they remain even today central documents of the conquest of Mexico.

LINDA LEDFORD-MILLER

### Biography

Born in Medellín, Extremadura, Spain, 1485. Studied law at the University of Salamanca, 1499–1501. Planned to sail to Hispaniola (Haiti and the Dominican Republic), 1502; an accident prevented his departure. Left for Hispaniola, 1504. Participated in conquest of Cuba under Diego Velásquez, 1511. Married Catalina Suárez Marcaida, probably 1515 (died in mysterious circumstances, 1522). Twice elected alcalde (mayor) of Santiago. Sent by Velásquez to the mainland of Mexico, 1518; arrived in Tenochtitlán, the Aztec capital, 1519. Fought the Aztecs and completed their conquest after a four-month siege of Tenochtitlán, 1521. Mounted expeditions to the territories of Honduras and Guatemala, 1524–1527. Accused of having poisoned a colleague, was dispossessed of his titles and his American lands and forced to return to Spain, 1528. Married Juana de Zúñiga, 1528: at least two daughters and a son. Created marqués del Valle by King Charles of Spain, 1529. Returned to New Spain, 1530. Traveled to the Pacific coast. Discovered the coast of Baja California, 1536. Lived on his estates at Cuernavaca, near Mexico City. Returned to Spain to contest his appointment as viceroy of New Spain, 1540. Had several illegitimate children with several different women, including a son with the Indian noblewoman la Malinche (this child, Martín, was thus the first mestizo). Spent the rest of his life in Spain in poverty. Died of illness in Castilleja de la Cuesta, near Seville, 2 December 1547.

### References and Further Reading

Cortés, Hernán, *Cartas de relación: Primera carta* [Letters of Relation; First Letter], July 1519, published 1842; *Segunda carta* [Second Letter], April 1522, published November 1522; *Tercera carta* [Third Letter], May 1522, published March 1523; *Cuarta carta* [Fourth Letter], October 1524, published 1525; *Quinta carta* [Fifth Letter], 1526, published 1844.

Cortés, Hernán, *Cartas y relaciones de Hernan Cortés al emperador Carlos v*, 1866; as *The Letters of Cortés: The Five Letters of Relation from Fernando Cortés to Emperor Charles V*, edited and translated by Francis Augustus MacNutt, 1908.

Cortés, Hernán, *Letters from Mexico*, edited and translated by A.R. Pagden, 1971; with an introduction by J.H. Elliott, 1986.

*See also* **New World Chronicles**

## CORYATE, THOMAS (c. 1577–1617)

***English Traveler and Writer***

At about 10 AM on Saturday 14 May 1608, Thomas Coryate embarked at Dover to travel to Venice, and at about 5 PM he arrived, very seasick, in Calais. Thenceforth until 3 October, when he returned to London, he kept a daily account of his observations and adventures that would be published in *Coryats Crudities* (1611). Coryate proclaimed himself the "Peregrine of Odcombe" (his Somerset birthplace) and the "Odcombian Legstretcher," but it is wrongly stated that most of this European journey was on foot. A map in Strachan's *The Life and Adventures of Thomas Coryate* (1962) details his itinerary and various modes of transport. He did walk long distances, one day in May covering 36 miles, but also used horse, coach, and cart, was carried over the Mont Cenis pass in a "chaise-à-porteurs," and made much of his homeward journey by boat. Coryate intended that his *Crudities* should encourage the courtiers and gallants surrounding Henry, Prince of Wales, who accepted the dedication, to enrich their minds by Continental travel. It is the first guidebook in English to the countries Coryate traversed, and it includes practical information about prices, exchange rates, food and drink, and local customs and much historical data. The guidebook is illustrated and contains many architectural descriptions, but it is far too diffuse and bulky—655 numbered pages plus many unnumbered in the 1611 edition, and 864 in that of 1905—to become a handy companion, even if the traveler wished to follow Coryate's itinerary.

From Calais, Coryate made his way to Paris, where he spent five days and found it even dirtier and smellier than London. At Fontainebleau, he made friends with members of Henry IV's Garde Ecossaise and was thus able to get a closer look at the royal household. He paused for two days in Lyons, then proceeded through Savoy to Turin, Milan, and Mantua. Table forks, almost unknown in England, were already in general use in Italy; Coryate adopted the Italian fashion of eating. "Furcifer" (fork-bearer) became one of his nicknames. His description of how Italians shielded themselves from the sun resulted in the word *umbrella* being introduced into English. Coryate enjoyed concocting new words from Greek and Latin roots—one at least, *refocillate*, has survived. Ben Jonson, a bantering friend, called him a "bold carpenter of words," most evident in his euphuistic orations, of which he was very proud; but his narrative style is straightforward and vigorous, reminiscent of the Authorized Version of the Bible (1611).

Coryate arrived in Venice on 24 June, carrying two letters of introduction to the English ambassador, Sir Henry Wotton, who did him many kindnesses. For six weeks, Coryate spent the day exploring, observing, measuring, and copying inscriptions, then writing up his notes and reading far into the night. Few subsequent descriptions of Venice ignore Coryate's wide-ranging account. He left Venice by boat for Padua, then walked to Vicenza, Verona, and Bergamo, arrived in Zurich by boat, and walked on to Basel. While in Switzerland, Coryate recorded the story of William Tell; his account appears to be the earliest in English. Arriving in Strasbourg by boat, he then got lost in the Black Forest alone and on foot, unarmed save for a staff and a knife. However, the only threat of armed violence Coryate experienced in Europe was from a German peasant who resented his picking grapes from a vineyard. He was hospitably received in Heidelberg and walked to Mainz. After a detour to visit Frankfurt's fair, he sailed down the Rhine, with a brief stop at Cologne, continuing by river down what was then the temporary truceline between the armies of Spain and the United Provinces. After calling on the English merchants established at Middelburg, Coryate was entertained by the English garrison at Flushing. Thence he embarked on 1 October and landed in London two days later. With the rector's permission, he hung his shoes in Odcombe church.

For the next four years, Coryate seems to have divided his time mainly between Odcombe and London, where he officiated as beadle at the monthly meetings of the Mermaid Tavern Club, whose members presented him with a mock passport before he sailed for Constantinople on 20 October 1612. During the voyage, he visited Zante, Chios, and Alexandria Troas, then thought to be the site of Troy. Here, a companion dubbed Coryate "the first English Knight of Troy," and he responded with an oration. Toward the end of March 1613, Coryate arrived in Constantinople and presented a letter of introduction to the English ambassador, Paul Pindar, who treated him kindly and frequently included him in his suite on state occasions. Here, he learned Turkish and Italian, the lingua franca of the Levant; few but his countrymen knew English. In January 1614, he sailed from Constantinople, landed at Iskenderun, and walked via Aleppo and Damascus to Jerusalem, arriving on 12 April in time for Easter. Coryate had the crusaders' and pilgrims' fitchy crosses tattooed on his wrists, and he visited Nazareth, Bethlehem, Jericho, and the Jordan River before walking back to Aleppo, where he spent six months writing up his notes. These, covering his travels since leaving England but drastically abbreviated, were published in *Purchas His Pilgrimes* (1625). In September 1614, Coryate joined an enormous caravan and walked via Diarbekr, where he was robbed of much of his money, Tabriz, and Kazvin to Isfahan, spending two months there writing up his notes, which disappeared. Joining another caravan in February 1615, he walked via Kandahar, Multan, Lahore, Delhi, and Agra to Emperor Jahangir's court at Ajmer, arriving in mid-July 1615. Coryate measured his walk from Jerusalem as being 2,700 miles in ten months, but he actually must have walked 3,300 miles, during which he spent only £3, often living reasonably for one penny sterling per day. At Ajmer, he lived at the expense of the East India Company's servants and that of Sir Thomas Roe (whom Coryate had known in England), when Roe arrived as England's first ambassador in December. Coryate earned his keep by entertaining them with his tales, meanwhile learning Persian, the language of the Moghul court, Arabic, that of the learned, and Hindustani. In about August 1616, he made an oration in Persian before Jahangir, asking him to facilitate a contemplated journey to Samarkand and the tomb of Tamerlane. Jahangir declined but rewarded him with 100 rupees. In September, Coryate resumed his explora-

"I have rid upon an Elephant since I came to this Court, determining one day (by Gods leave) to have my picture expressed in my next Booke, sitting upon an Elephant" (from *Letters from India*, in *Coryats Crudities*, vol. 3, 1776 (reprinted from the 1611 edition)). *Courtesy of the Travellers Club, London; Bridgeman Art Library, agent.*

tions northward, reaching Kangra and Hardwar, where the Ganges issues from the Himalayan foothills. In September 1617, he rejoined Roe and Jahangir's court at Mandu in Malwa. Soon after Jahangir resumed his progress toward Ahmadabad, Coryate decided to make for Surat in Gujarat, the East India Company's main base, where he died of dysentery in December 1617. Of his intended second great travel book, only scraps survive.

MICHAEL STRACHAN

### Biography

Born in Odcombe, Somerset, c. 1577. Only son of the rector of Odcombe. Attended Winchester College, 1591–1596, and Gloucester Hall (now Exeter College), Oxford, 1596–c. 1599. Played the role of unofficial jester at the court of James I; met many eminent people of the day; later attached to household of Princess Elizabeth and Prince Henry, who granted him a pension. Inherited property on the death of his father, c. 1607. Traveled through France and Italy to Venice; returned via Switzerland, Germany, and the Netherlands, May–October 1608. Published *Coryats Crudities* and *Coryats Crambe*, 1611. Traveled to Constantinople and the Holy Land, 1612–1614. Walked through Turkey, Persia, and Moghul India to Emperor Jahangir's court at Ajmer, Gujarat, 1615–1616. Continued to travel northward, September 1616. At invitation of Sir Thomas Roe, visited imperial court at Mandu, Malwa, September 1617; left for Surat in Gujarat, November 1617. Died of dysentery in Surat, December 1617.

### References and Further Reading

Coryate, Thomas, *Coryats Crudities, Hastily Gobled Up in Five Moneths Travells in France, Savoy, Italy, Rhetia, Commonly Called the Grisons Country . . . Helvetia Alias Switzerland, Some Parts of High Germany, and the Netherlands* 1611; 3 vols., 1776 [volume 3 includes most of the contents of *Coryats Crambe*, 1611; most of John Taylor the Water Poet's works lampooning Coryate; one of Coryate's published letters from India; all the material published by Samuel Purchas; and extracts from Edward Terry's *A Voyage to East India*, 1655. Terry, Sir Thomas Roe's chaplain, gives a convincing character sketch, but is unreliable about Coryate's itinerary]; 2 vols., 1905 [1611 pagination in margin]; facsimile, with an introduction by William M. Schutte, 1978.

Coryate, Thomas, "Master Thomas Coryates Travels to, and Observations in Constantinople and Other Places in the Way Thither," in *Purchas His Pilgrimes*, edited by Samuel Purchas, 4 vols., 1625; reprinted as *Hakluytus Posthumus*, 20 vols., 1905–1907.

Coryate, Thomas, in *Early Travels in India, 1585–1618*, edited by William Foster, 1921; reprinted, 1975.

## COXE, WILLIAM (1747–1828) *British Traveler, Historian, and Political Biographer*

As a respected "bear-leader," or traveling tutor, William Coxe embarked on a series of European travels in the 1770s and 1780s that spurred interest in areas previously less known or appreciated by British Grand Tourists, particularly Switzerland and Russia. From the fame of his travel writings, Coxe's later admirers referred to him as the "traveling Archdeacon" or simply "the Russian traveler." Even critics of his prolixity paid tribute to his accomplishments: "Or from the Alps extend to Norway's rocks/With Switzer-Russico-Kamtschatcan Coxe" begins T.J. Mathias's satirical vignette in *The Pursuits of Literature* (1794). Coxe earned a more lasting reputation as a historian and political biographer. His memoirs of eminent eighteenth-century figures—Robert Walpole (1798), Horace Walpole (1802), and the duke of Marlborough (1818–1819)—are examples of Coxe's historical writings that introduced new methods and standards of archival research to biographical scholarship.

Coxe first traveled to the Continent in November 1775 as tutor to Lord Herbert, eldest son of Henry, tenth Earl of Pembroke. With Herbert, who stayed abroad until 1780, Coxe resided in Strasbourg before touring Switzerland in summer 1776. Coxe found the region amenable to his aesthetic enjoyment of the pleasures of horror, an attitude to the sublime that was to become commonplace in Swiss travelogues only after

Coxe's. A staunch Whig, he also tracked "the general spirit of liberty" throughout the cantons, with notices of important landmarks (such as the chapel of William Tell in Uri) and with numerous inquiries into social and political structures at the local level. Before he returned from the Continent, Coxe published his account of the tour as *Sketches of the Natural, Civil, and Political State of Swisserland* (1779).

After parting company with Herbert in Italy, Coxe revisited Switzerland (particularly the Grison Alps) in summer 1779, too late to incorporate the tour into *Sketches*. Before this, Coxe and Herbert had extended their travels to the northern kingdoms of Europe, entering Poland in July 1778 and Russia in August. Four months in and around St. Petersburg between October 1778 and January 1779 gave Coxe ample time to research the discoveries of Russian travelers farther east, while ingratiating himself at the court of Catherine the Great. His return journey included the Scandinavian kingdoms, particularly Sweden and Denmark. With the two Swiss tours, these experiences furnished the basis of Coxe's most important travel writings in the following decade: a new edition of *Sketches*, refashioned as *Travels in Switzerland* (1789), and *Travels into Poland, Russia, Sweden, and Denmark* (1784). In St. Petersburg, Coxe also translated and adapted an anonymous German account of Russian voyages between 1745 and 1770, and he edited three subsequent journals by Russian travelers. Supplemented by Coxe's own research, these materials were published by him in 1780 as *Account of the Russian Discoveries*.

In *Sketches*, Coxe describes travel itself as a research methodology. The traveler bears "eye-witness" to what he describes, while social, political, and historical conclusions are ascertained by comparing first-hand interviews with "different persons of all ranks" with "written accounts, if there be any." Coxe's subsequent travels and editions of his travel writings extend these principles by conceiving the account of a given region as an unfinished project pending the collation of repeated investigations. In 1784–1785, Coxe retraced much of his previous itinerary (Denmark, Sweden, Norway, Russia, Poland, Switzerland) this time as tutor to Samuel Whitbread Jr. Coxe then conducted a further tour of Switzerland in order to explore the Grisons in more depth, probably in the summer of 1786, as tutor to Henry William Portman. The results of all of these tours (and subsequent political events) were incorporated into further editions of *Travels in Switzerland* and *Travels into Poland*. In the latter instance, for example, Coxe added a supplementary volume in 1790 detailing places not mentioned in 1784; the fourth edition (1792) dispensed with such divisions and collated all the visits, providing a historical continuum by which further comparisons and conclusions might be arrived at; the fifth edition (1802) incorporated new material regarding the final partition of Poland in 1795.

Coxe visited the Continent once more in summer 1794 with Lord Brome, eldest son of Lord Cornwallis. They toured Germany and Hungary but were hampered by war—the exclusion of British travelers from the Continent during the counterrevolutionary and Napoleonic years had begun. In the early 1790s, Coxe entered the controversy over the Revolution with a response to Richard Price, the dissenting minister whose sermon provoked Edmund Burke's more famous reply, *Reflections on the Revolution in France* (1790). Coxe's opposition to French republicanism also found voice in additions to *Travels in Switzerland*, published separately in 1802. Coxe approved of the 1789 Genevan "revolution" as a restoration of balance between popular and aristocratic factions, yet the weakening of the Helvetian confederacy before the 1798 French invasion struck him as the work of a systematic Jacobin conspiracy. For once, Coxe elected not to update the text of his travels (4th edition, 1801): "I have. . . made no alteration in the original work, but left it as a memorial of Switzerland in a state of independence, freedom, and prosperity, and a contrast to its present state of subjugation and misery."

From the 1790s, Coxe occupied himself increasingly with literary and historical projects. In the company of Sir Richard Colt Hoare, as friend rather than mentor, Coxe conducted a tour of south Wales in autumn 1798. With Hoare's encouragement and artistic collaboration, Coxe supplemented his initial itinerary with two subsequent tours in spring and autumn 1799, a total of five months and 1,500 miles according to his own estimate. The three tours were collated in Coxe's last new travel book, *An Historical Tour in Monmouthshire* (1801), two handsome quarto volumes illustrated with engravings of Hoare's sketches. The volumes were quintessential Coxe, blending enthusiastic appreciation of picturesque landscape with weighty historical inquiries, antiquarian researches, and biographical anecdotes.

In 1802, Coxe's sister published a pocket abridgment of the *Historical Tour*, in an attempt to broaden his readership among those who could not afford expensive quartos or who wished to consult Coxe on the spot. Despite this attempt at popularization, Coxe was not a popular writer, nor did he court the status. As a traveling tutor, he mixed with privileged nobility, received church preferment from them, and gained entrance to the courts of Europe. His reputation as a scholar of discretion gave him access to privy matters of state; the fifth edition of *Travels into Poland* (1802) reveals sources concealed in earlier editions, including the king of Poland himself. Coxe's works appeared in expensive editions, and his readership both at home and abroad included many leading statesmen, men of letters, and titled families, as witnessed by the subscribers' list to *Travels into Poland* (1784).

BENJAMIN COLBERT

### Biography

Born in London, 7 March 1747. Attended Eton College, 1753–1765, and King's College, Cambridge University, 1765; Fellow, 1768. Ordained deacon, 1771; curate of Denham, middlesex, briefly. Tutor to marquis of Blandford, later duke of Marlborough, c. 1772–1773. Traveled to Switzerland and later to Russia as tutor to Lord Herbert, later 11th earl of Pembroke, 1775–1780. Traveling tutor in Europe to Samuel Whitbread, 1784–1785, and to Henry William Portman, probably 1786. Traveled to Hungary with Lord Brome, eldest son of Lord Cornwallis, 1794. Traveled in Wales, 1798 and 1799. Member of Society of Antiquarians, April 1788. Took college living of Kingston-on-Thames, Surrey, 1786, and presented as rector of Bemerton, Wiltshire, by Lord Pembroke, 1788. Presented to rectory of Stourton, Wiltshire, by Richard Colt Hoare, 1800. Married Eleanor (née Shairp), widow of Thomas Yeldham of the British factory in St. Petersburg, 1803. Appointed archdeacon of Wiltshire, May 1804. Resigned rectorship of Stourton; presented with rectory of Fovant, Wiltshire, by Lord Pembroke, 1811. Died in Bemerton, Wiltshire, 8 June 1828.

### References and Further Reading


Coxe, William, *Sketches of the Natural, Civil, and Political State of Swisserland; in a Series of Letters to William Melmoth, Esq.*, 1779.

Coxe, William, *Account of the Russian Discoveries between Asia and America: To Which Are Added, the Conquest of Siberia, and the History of the Transactions and Commerce between Russia and China*, 1780; 4th edition, 1803.

Coxe, William, *Account of the Prisons and Hospitals in Russia, Sweden and Denmark*, 1781.

Coxe, William, *Travels into Poland, Russia, Sweden, and Denmark*, 2 vols., 1784; 2nd edition, 4 vols., 1787; 5th edition, 5 vols., 1802.

Coxe, William, *Supplement to the Russian Discoveries*, 1787.

Coxe, William, *Travels in Switzerland: In a Series of Letters to William Melmoth, Esq.*, 3 vols., 1789; 3rd edition, 2 vols., 1794; 4th edition, 1801; *Additions to "Travels in Switzerland": Containing an Historical Sketch and Notes on the Late Revolution*, 2 vols., 1802.

Coxe, William, *An Historical Tour in Monmouthshire: Illustrated with Views by Sir R.C. Hoare, Bart.*, 1801.

Coxe, William, *A Picture of Monmouthshire, or An Abridgement of Mr. Coxe's Historical Tour in Monmouthshire: By a Lady*, 1802.


## CRETE

At the dawn of Western literature, in the eighth century BCE, Crete is already remembered as a place endowed with legendary power. In Homer's *Iliad* (2: 649), the island is called "Crete of a hundred cities," and in the *Odyssey* (19: 172f.), Odysseus famously sings its praises: "There is a land called Crete, in the midst of the winedark sea, lovely and fertile, sea-girt. Many men live there, past counting." Behind such passages lie memories of Crete's first major civilization, the Bronze Age "Minoan" culture of c. 3500–1100 BCE, and an enduring fascination with that culture has been the inspiration for many travelers' accounts.

The position of Crete on the sea routes between western Europe, Cyprus, the Levant, and Egypt has made it one of the most frequently visited places in the Mediterranean. It lies, as *Mandeville's Travels* (chapter 5) suggests, "right in the myd weye."

Following the Minoans, the island's history was one of occupation by a succession of invaders: Dorian Greeks, Romans, Byzantines, Arabs, Venetians, and Ottoman Turks. In all that time, Crete remained Greek speaking, but its development was often sharply different from that of the Greek mainland. Crete played a marginal role, for example, during the Greek classical period, and, in modern times, the island remained subject to Turkish control until 1898, almost 70 years after Greece had achieved its independence. Crete was formally united with Greece only in 1913.

The island is meticulously described by Strabo (c. 64 BCE—after 21 CE) in his *Geography*. In the Middle Ages, the Italian Cristoforo Buondelmonti (c. 1385–c. 1430) gives one of the most detailed accounts in his *Liber insularum*, the *Descriptio insule Candie*, and *Descriptio Cretae*. He is particularly impressed by the remains of the city of Gortyn in central Crete. The ruins were those of Roman Gortyn, but Buondelmonti knows that the city had once belonged to "King Minos." In its grandeur, the place reminds him of his native city of Florence.

The period of the island's subjection to Venice (1204–1669) was one of gradually renewed interest in Crete's past. It was also a time when Cretan trade and commerce made it one of the most coveted centers in the Levant. The Cambridge scholar Fynes Moryson visited in 1596. Though too ill to explore the locally celebrated site of the Labyrinth, where Theseus had supposedly slain the Minotaur, he gives a precise account of Crete's agricultural munificence: "It hath great plentie of all kinds of Corne, of all manner of Pulse, of Oyle, of all kinds of flesh, of Canes of sugar, of Hony, of Cedar trees, of all coloured Dyings, of Cypres trees . . . and of all the necessaries for human life" (1617).

William Lithgow was on the island in about 1610 and records being robbed almost as soon as he landed. He, too, marvels at the flourishing state of agriculture, and he gets as far as the entrance to the Labyrinth ("It

The late-sixteenth-century Venetian facade of the church of Arkhadi monastery near Rethymnon; the monastery became a potent symbol of Crete's struggle for liberty in 1866 when its Greek defenders blew it up rather than surrender to Turkish besiegers (from Pashley's *Travels in Crete*, 1837). *Courtesy of the Travellers Club, London.*

is cut forth with many intricating wayes, on the face of a little hill," 1614). George Sandys, who was in Crete at about the same time, gives a vivid account of both people and places (1615). He observes a ritual bow dance ("The Country people do dance with their Bows ready bent on their arms . . . imitating therein their Ancestors"); he notes that the Cretan women wear loose veils on their heads, "the breasts and shoulders perpetually naked, and dyed by the Sun into a loathsom tawny." He goes into the Labyrinth, near Gortyn, but finds, as Pierre Belon had already noted 60 years before, that the site is nothing more than a quarry. The true Labyrinth had been at the Minoan palace of Knossos, and all trace of it has long since vanished.

One of the most important books of the seventeenth century was Bernard Randolph's *The Present State of the Islands in the Archipelago* of 1687. His work is especially valuable for the light it throws on the effects of the Turkish occupation of the island, which had begun with the capture of Chania in 1645 and Candia (now Herakleion), the capital, in 1669.

Richard Pococke wrote an interesting account of a month's visit to Crete in 1739. He is a shrewd observer of the prevailing economic and social conditions and the founder of modern topographical research in Crete. In the nineteenth century, that research reached a peak with Robert Pashley's *Travels in Crete* (1837). Pashley, in the words of the archaeologist John Pendlebury (1939), "identified most of the important sites with an accuracy which had never before been attained and has in few cases since been challenged." Another nineteenth-century traveler with scholarly interests was Thomas Spratt, who wrote an account of the island's natural history, geology, and archaeology (*Travels and Researches in Crete*, 1865). Edward Lear was on the island in 1864, and J.E. Hilary Skinner joined in the abortive insurrection against the Turks of 1866 and left a record entitled *Roughing It in Crete*.

The twentieth century saw the final reemergence of the Minoans from legend into archaeology, with the excavations at Knossos under Arthur Evans, from 1900 on. Evans built the Villa Ariadne to serve as his base at Knossos, and the atmosphere of the early years of excavation is well caught in Dilys Powell's book of the same name. Evans eventually handed over control of the site to John Pendlebury, who later fought against the Germans and died in an attack on Herakleion in 1941. The battle of Crete generated a large number of publications, notably by George Psychoundakis, a Cretan participant, and by Evelyn Waugh, in his novel *Officers and Gentlemen*.

Thereafter, the story of Crete is of the gradual erosion of traditional patterns of life under the impact of mass tourism. Several writers describe this period of transition: David Doren, in *Winds of Crete* (1974), Christopher Thorne, in *Between the Seas* (1992), and, perhaps most memorably, Jackson Webb, in *The Last Lemon Grove* (1977).

STEPHEN MINTA

### References and Further Reading

In earlier travel literature, Crete is often called by its Venetian name of Candia. This name was also that of the island's capital city, renamed Herakleion at the beginning of the twentieth century.

Albin, Célestin, *L'Île de Crète: Histoire et souvenirs*, 1898.

Baud-Bovy, Daniel, and Frédéric Boissonnas, *Des Cyclades en Crète au gré du vent*, 1919.

Belon, Pierre, *Les Observations de plusieurs singularitez et choses memorables, trouveés en Grèce etc.*, 1553.

Bickford-Smith, Roandeu A.H. [R.A.H.], *Cretan Sketches*, 1898.

Brewster, Ralph, *The Island of Zeus: Wanderings in Crete*, 1939.

Buondelmonti, Cristoforo, *Description des îles de l'Archipel*, edited and translated by Émile Legrand, 1897; reprinted, 1974.

Buondelmonti, Cristoforo, *Descriptio insule Crete et liber insularum, cap.XI: Creta*, edited by Marie-Anne van Spitael, 1981 [Latin text and French translation].

Burch, Oliver, *Under Mount Ida: A Journey into Crete*, 1989.

Dandini, Girolamo, *Missione apostolica al Patriarca, e Maroniti del Monte Libano*, 1656; as *A Voyage to Mount Libanus*, 1698.

Dapper, Olfert, *Naukeurige beschryving der eilanden, in de Archipel der Middelantsche Zee*, 1688; as *Description exacte des isles de l'Archipel*, 1703.

Doren, David MacNeil, *Winds of Crete*, 1974.

Edwardes, Charles, *Letters from Crete*, 1887.

Fielding, Xan, *The Stronghold: An Account of the Four Seasons in the White Mountains of Crete*, with photos by Daphne Bath, 1953.

Hakluyt, Richard, *The Principall Navigations, Voiages, and Discoveries of the English Nation*, 1589; as *The Principal Navigations, Voyages, Traffiques, and Discoveries of the English Nation*, 2nd edition, 3 vols., 1598–1600; 12 vols., 1903–1905.

Lear, Edward, *The Cretan Journal*, edited by Rowena Fowler, 1984; 2nd edition, 1985.

Lithgow, William, *A Most Delectable, and True Discourse of an Admired and Painefull Peregrination . . . to . . . Europe, Asia and Affricke*, 1614; as *Discourse of a Peregrination in Europe, Asia and Affricke*, 1971.

Miller, Henry, *The Colossus of Maroussi*, c. 1941.

Moryson, Fynes, *An Itinerary Written by Fynes Moryson . . . Containing His Ten Yeeres Travell etc.*, 1617; facsimile, 1971.

Pashley, Robert, *Travels in Crete*, 2 vols., 1837; reprinted, 1970.

Pendlebury, J.D.S., *The Archaelogy of Crete: An Introduction*, London: Methuen, 1939.

Pococke, Richard, *A Description of the East and Some Other Countries*, 2 vols., 1743–1745.

Postlethwaite, Edward, *A Tour in Crete*, 1868.

Powell, Dilys, *The Villa Ariadna*, London: Hodder and Stoughton, 1973.

Pschhoundakis, George, *The Cretan Runner: His Story of the German Occupation*, translated with an introduction by Fermor, edited by Fermor and Van Fielding, London: John Murray, 1955.

Randolph, Bernard, *The Present State of the Islands in the Archipelago, or Arches, Sea of Constantinople, and Gulph of Smyrna; with the Islands of Candia and Rhodes*, 1687; reprinted, 1983.

Sandys, George, *A Relation of a Journey Begun An. Dom. 1610*, 1615.

Savary, Claude Étienne, *Lettres sur la Grèce*, 1788; as *Letters on Greece*, 1788.

Scott, C. Rochfort, *Rambles in Egypt and Candia*, 2 vols., 1837

Sieber, F.W., *Reise nach der Insel Kreta . . . im Jahre 1817*, 1823; as *Travels in the Island of Crete, in the Year 1817*, in *New Voyages and Travels*, vol. 8, 1823; reprinted, 1975.

Skinner, J.E. Hilary, *Roughing It in Crete in 1867*, 1868.

Spratt, T.A.B., *Travels and Researches in Crete*, 2 vols., 1865; reprinted, 1984.

Strabo, *The Geography*, translated by Horace Leonard Jones, 8 vols., 1917–1933.

Thevet, André, *Cosmographie de Levant*, 1554; edited by Frank Lestringant, 1985.

Thorne, Christopher G., *Between the Seas: A Quiet Walk through Crete*, 1992.

Tournefort, Joseph Pitton de, *Relation d'un voyage du Levant*, 2 vols., 1717; as *A Voyage into the Levant*, 2 vols., 1718.

Webb, Jackson, *The Last Lemon Grove*, illustrated by Delia Delderfield, 1977.

*See also* **Greece, Ancient Hellenic World**

## CRIMEA

The Crimean peninsula (in ancient times known as Tavrida) is situated in the Ukraine. It is bordered by the Black and Azov Seas and is connected with the mainland by a narrow isthmus about seven to eight kilometers wide. The northern part of the Crimea is steppe, while the southern coast is separated from the rest by three ranges of mountains, the highest point of which is Roman-Kosh (1,545 meters). In the southeast, there is a volcanic mountain, Kara-Dag. There are very few rivers in the peninsula. In the north, there are several salt lakes, the clay from which is used for medical purposes. The mountains cut off the cold air from the north, giving much warmer winters on the south coast. This led to the development of tourist and health resorts.

The history of the Crimea covers several thousand years, and the first traces of human beings can be dated to the Paleolithic era. The most ancient peoples were Scythians. One of the first mentions of the Crimea was made by Herodotus (fifth century BCE), the ancient Greek historian. The Greeks inhabited it from c. 700 BCE and built the powerful city-states Chersonesus (later Khersones), now on the outskirts of Sebastopol, and Panticapaeum, on the site of the city of Kerch. Mithridates, the emperor of Pontus, was, according to Cicero, one of the most dangerous enemies of the Roman empire. After a war in 63 BCE, Mithridates was defeated and stabbed himself to death in Panticapaeum. After that, his state never recovered, and it eventually disappeared. The next main state, after c. 500, was Scythian, with the capital Neapol (now within Simferopol). From the third century, tribes of Hazars, Goths, Pechenegs, and Huns frequently invaded the Crimea and destroyed its cities. Christianity came to the Crimea in the fourth century, under the influence of Byzantium. The first Christian principality with its capital, Feodoro, was built on the high plateau of Mangup. In the tenth century, Prince Vladimir of Kievan Rus conquered Khersones, becoming Christian himself in 988. During the medieval period, many Genoese colonies were founded—Sugdea (now Sudak), Kaffa (now Feodosiia), and Balaklava, among others.

From the thirteenth century, the Crimea was occupied by Mongols, Tatar tribes of the Golden Horde. In 1427, an independent Muslim state developed and became more prominent under the khan Hadji-Girey, with his capital at Bakchisaray (the palace of which still exists). In 1475, the Ottoman empire conquered the Crimea, ruling it for three centuries. Having trained cavalry, the Crimean khans often attacked southern Ukraine and Russia, taking many people into slavery. Russia obviously needed to defend its borders and started serious action, as a result of which the Crimea became part of the Russian empire in 1783. In the same year, Sebastopol was founded as a navy base on the Black Sea, and in 1784, Simferopol was founded as the capital.

European countries did not welcome the Russian presence on the Black Sea, because of the threat posed to the Bosporus and the Dardanelles. In 1853–1856, during the Crimean War, the British and, French allies

Horse, ox, and camel power in Perekop on the Crimean isthmus (from Pallas's *Travels through the Southern Provinces of the Russian Empire in the Years 1793 and 1794*, 2nd edition, 1812). *Courtesy of the Travellers Club, London; Bridgeman Art Library, agent.*

besieged Sebastopol and, after 365 days, finally occupied it. One of the defenders of Sebastopol was the great writer Leo Tolstoy, and the scene in his military expedition attracted the attention of Western writers such as Koch and Scott.

At the start of the twentieth century, the period of rapid development of the Crimean economy started, centered on tourism and wine-making. The Black Sea coast became a popular health resort. The czarist palace in Yalta and other palaces of the Russian upper classes were built. Famous artists liked to spend holidays in the Crimea—Shaliapin, Tolstoy, Gorkii, Rachmaninov, and Chekhov, for example. World War I and the revolution put an end to this period. In November 1920, the Crimea became part of the Soviet Union. The Crimea was handed over to the Ukraine by Khrushchev in 1955, and since 1991, it has been an autonomous republic of the Ukraine.

The Crimea has attracted travelers since ancient times. It is mentioned in Herodotus, Ptolemy, and Strabo. The Arabian historian of the twelfth century, Idrisi, and the Italian Visconti in 1318 both described the peninsula. In the sixteenth century, Dortini d'Ascoli, a Jesuit, visited the Crimea, and in 1578, the ambassador of the Polish king Stephen Batory, Martin Bronevski (Broniowski), traveled for eight months in the Crimea and recorded detailed information about it. One of the best documents about the medieval Crimea was that of the Turkish traveler Evliya Çelebi, who stayed there between 1641 and 1667. His *Narrative of Travels* gives a full description of the life of the local population.

Many travelers visited the Crimea after it became Russian. In 1786, Catherine the Great herself undertook a long visit there. There were more than 138 carriages in her retinue, and the emperor of Austria, Joseph II, the French ambassador, Prince de Ségur, and Prince de Linne accompanied her. Her memoirs of the Crimea were published in 1865 in St. Petersburg.

An example of a visit for a special purpose was that made by Lady Elizabeth Craven, who in 1786 came to the Crimea, fulfilling a secret mission for the British prime minister William Pitt to examine the system of defense. Britain was anxious about the plans of General Potemkin to liberate the Balkans from the Turks. Lady Craven visited northern Crimea (where she noticed weak points in the defense), Bakchisaray, and Sebastopol. She made a map of the peninsula and departed to Istanbul, where she reported her conclusions. Her diary, *Letters to a Friend*, was published in London immediately, and the next year, Turkish groups invaded northern Tavrida.

There were two major scientific expeditions at this time. The first was in 1782 by V. Zuev, a member of the Russian Academy of Science, who wrote a book, *Extracts from a Travel Diary*, concerning the botany, geography, agriculture, and ethnography of the Crimea (published in 1783 in St. Petersburg). The second was in 1793–1794 by the academician Pallas, who gave a detailed description of the Crimean flora and fauna, mineralogy, mountains, and salt lakes and the ancient cave towns.

The historical heritage of the Crimea was the subject of the president of the Foreign Department of Russia, I.M. Muraviev-Apostol, who in 1823 published *Travels along the Tavrida*, in which he described ancient monuments and explained some myths by detailing the historical evidence for them. It was he who first connected the old name of the peninsula, Tavrida, with the tribe of Tavres, who lived on the Crimean mountains in ancient times (in Assyrian, *taura* means "mountain"). At the same time, a law was issued by Alexander I concerning the protection of the Crimean heritage.

Interesting impressions about Crimea can be found in the letters of Aleksander Pushkin, who visited the Crimea in 1820s and wrote a poem called "The Fountain of the Palace of Bakchisaray." The fountain can still be seen. Other relevant writers are Tolstoy (*Sebastopol Sketches*), Chekhov, and Ivan Bunin.

GENNADY SHELUGIN
*translated by Olga Stone*

### References and Further Reading

Alexander, James Edward, *Travels to the Seat of War in the East, through Russia and the Crimea, in 1829*, 2 vols., 1830.
Craven, Elizabeth, *A Journey through the Crimea to Constantinople*, 1789.
Evliya Çelebi, *Narrative of Travels in Europe, Asia and Africa in the Seventeenth Century*, translated from the Turkish by Joseph von Hammer, 2 vols., 1834–1850.
Gerakov, G.V., *Travel Notices in 1820*, 1828.
Markov, Evgenii, *Ocherki Kavkaza* [Caucasian Essays], 1902.
Muraviev-Apostol, I.M., *Travels along the Tavrida in 1820*, 1823.
Pallas, P.S., *Travels through the Southern Provinces of the Russian Empire in the Years 1793 and 1794*, 2nd edition, 1812.
Ségur, Louis-Philippe, *Mémoires; ou, Souvenirs et anecdotes*, Paris: Eymery, 1824–1826; as *The Memoirs and Anecdotes of Count de Ségur*, translated by Gerard Shelley, 1928.
Tolstoy, Leo, *Sebastopol Sketches*, 1856.
Zuev, V., *Extracts from a Travel Diary*, 1782.

*See also* **Black Sea; Russia**

## CRUSADES

History has made of the Crusades a far more orderly and better-defined undertaking than existed in the Middle Ages. All the major expeditions by Westerners to wrest control of the Levant from Muslims have been neatly numbered, while the myriad smaller efforts made in the name of the church or Western culture have received but little attention. Much recent historical scholarship has helped to resurrect those nearly forgotten crusades, to question the sharp distinctions between various campaigns, and generally to present a more realistically complex picture of crusading. An important part of this has been unearthing and publishing more documentary evidence both from the crusaders and from those whose lands were invaded by them. Nevertheless, it is to the chronicles of the Christians who traveled east to participate in the Crusades that we naturally turn for travel writing.

Motivation and purpose aside, the actual experience of crusading was travel: the movement of thousands of people from western Europe through difficult territory to the lands around the Mediterranean and back again. A pilgrim route between West and East was well established, but this new undertaking of mass militarized pilgrimage brought with it overwhelming new challenges. In addition to underestimating their adversaries, the crusaders, in their pious belief that they were under God's protection, also tended to underestimate the difficulties of travel to and life in what would be a very foreign land. Thus, even the most enthusiastic chroniclers were forced to catalog campaigns filled with mishaps, tragedies, and countless avoidable deaths.

French priest and future chronicler Foucher (or Fulcher) of Chartres (c. 1059–c. 1127) was in Clermont in 1095 when Pope Urban II (c. 1042–1099) exhorted the faithful to embark on the First Crusade (1096–1102). From then on attached to the households of various crusade leaders, Fulcher observed the entire expedition from a vantage point near the top. He lived in Jerusalem from 1099 till his death in 1127, and it was there that he wrote his reliable *Gesta Francorum Iherusalem peregrinantium*. In it, Fulcher notes generally what appears to have applied to him personally: namely, that Westerners had little trouble assimilating to Eastern culture once disabused of their misconceptions about Muslims.

Controversy has long surrounded three important accounts of the First Crusade, namely, the anonymous *Gesta Francorum et aliorum Hierosolimitanorum*, the *Historia Francorum qui ceperunt Iherusalem* by Raymond of Aguilers (fl. 1100), and the *Historia de Hierosolymitano itinere* by Peter Tudebode (fl. 1100). They are so similar as to invite accusations of plagiarism, but they contain enough significant differences to suggest that they are truly individual accounts based on a common written source. Raymond and Peter were genuine eyewitnesses; the former served as chaplain to Count Raymond IV of Toulouse, and the latter was a priest of Civray. Taken together, these three sources offer too much information about the journey and the subsequent events of the First Crusade for them to be discounted because of questions about their provenance.

Writing between the Second (1147–1149) and Third (1189–1192) Crusades was William, archbishop of Tyre (c. 1130–1190). Born of European stock in the Kingdom of Jerusalem, he was commissioned by Amalric I (d. 1174) to produce various histories of the region, for which William found himself drawing on the works of his predecessors and recording current events from his privileged positions in the church and at court. William transformed his early works into what has become known as the *Historia rerum in partibus transmarinis gestarum*, covering the period from the Christian loss of Jerusalem in 614 to just before its capture by Saladin in 1187.

The return of Jerusalem to Muslim hands prompted the Third Crusade, personally led by the great rulers of Europe. Frederick Barbarossa, king of Germany and Holy Roman emperor (c. 1123–1190), struck out via the land route. While that arm of the crusade was meeting with disaster outside Acre, Richard I of England (1157–1199) and King Philip II of France (1165–1223) were successfully moving their armies and provisions into the Levant by sea; no major crusade would again take the land route. The latter excursion was sympathetically recorded by Richard's own jongleur, Ambroise, who captured the spirit of the average crusader in his verse narrative, *L'Estoire de la guerre sainte*, written around 1196.

What are perhaps the best-known chronicles of the Fourth Crusade (1199–1207) provide two very different perspectives on that campaign. Robert of Clary, a knight of no particular distinction, imbued his *La Conquête de Constantinople* with his own obvious enthusiasm for exploration, aided by his keen powers of observation. It is almost as much a record of the wonders of Constantinople as a narrative history of the crusade. A far more significant figure within the Fourth Crusade itself was Geoffrey of Villehardouin, the marshal of Champagne (c. 1150–c. 1213). He was a leader of the crusade from the outset and distinguished himself during the expedition. Geoffrey's unfinished *Histoire de l'empire de Constantinople* ultimately spawned his enduring version of the events of the Fourth Crusade, *La Conquête de Constantinople*.

Though the Fifth Crusade included the journey of St. Francis from Assisi to Egypt, neither it nor its successor produced chronicles as significant as those of the other major crusades. The Seventh Crusade (1248–1254) was led by Louis IX of France (1215–1270), later St. Louis, and documented in *Histoire de Saint-Louis* by John of Joinville (c. 1224–1317). Commissioned by French royalty, it is an unusual hagiography in that it reveals almost as much about the writer as it does the subject and unflinchingly chronicles the many travel, subsistence, and military problems encountered throughout the crusade. John wisely refused to join Louis on the Eighth Crusade (1269–1272), which he thought foolish and advised against—and during which Louis indeed met his death.

While eyewitness accounts of the Crusades provide invaluable insights into the unique experiences of some of the men who took the cross, they inevitably vary widely in scope, perspective, and accuracy. Recent compilations such as Peter Edbury's *The Conquest of Jerusalem and the Third Crusade* and Elizabeth Hallam's *Chronicles of the Crusades* facilitate comparisons of original source materials and thus allow individual chronicles to be put into perspective. The vast body of secondary literature must also be consulted to establish a proper understanding and appreciation of the travel writings of the crusaders.

VERONICA MELNYK

## References and Further Reading

Ambroise, *L'Estoire de la guerre saint*, edited by Gaston Paris, 1897; as "The History of the Holy War" in *Three Old French Chronicles of the Crusades*, translated by Edward Noble Stone, 1939; as *The Crusade of Richard Lion-Heart*, translated by Merton Jerome Hubert, edited by John L. La Monte, 1941.

*Crusade Texts in Translation*, 8 vols., 1996–2001.

De Sandoli, Sabino (editor), *Itinera Hierosolymitana Crucesignatorum*, 4 vols., 1978–1983.

*Documents relatifs à l'histoire des Croisades*, 17 vols., 1946–1995.

Edbury, Peter W. (editor and translator), *The Conquest of Jerusalem and the Third Crusade: Sources in Translation*, 1996.

Foucher of Chartres, *Historia hierosolymitana (1095–1127)*, edited by Heinrich Hagenmeyer, 1913; as *Chronicle of the First Crusade*, translated by Martha E. McGinty, 1941; as *A History of the Expedition to Jerusalem 1095–1127*, translated by Frances Rita Ryan, edited and with an introduction by Harold S. Fink, 1969.

Geoffrey of Villehardouin, *La Conquête de Constantinople*, edited by Natalis de Wailly, 1872; as "The Conquest of Constantinople" in *Chronicles of the Crusades*, by Villehardouin and De Joinville, translated by Frank Marzials, 1908; in *Chronicles of the Crusades*, translated by Margaret R.B. Shaw, 1963.

*Gesta Francorum et aliorum Hierosolimitanorum* in *Gesta Dei per Francos*, 1611; as *The First Crusade: The Deeds of the Franks and Other Jerusalemites*, translated by Somerset de Chair, 1945; as *The Deeds of the Franks and the Other Pilgrims to Jerusalem*, translated by Rosalind Hill, 1962.

Hallam, Elizabeth (editor), *Chronicles of the Crusades: Nine Crusades and Two Hundred Years of Bitter Conflict for the Holy Land Brought to Life through the Words of Those Who Were Actually There*, 1989; as *Chronicles of the Crusades: Eye-Witness Accounts of the Wars between Christianity and Islam*, 2000.

Housley, Norman (editor and translator), *Documents on the Later Crusades, 1274–1580*, 1996.

John of Joinville, *Histoire de Saint-Louis*, 1761; as *Mémoires du Sire de Joinville*, 1824, many later editions; as "Memoirs of Louis IX, King of France" in *Chronicles of the Crusades*, translated by J.A. Giles and Thomas Johnes, 1848; as "The Life of St. Louis" in *Chronicles of the Crusades*, translated

by Frank Marzials, 1908; as *The History of St. Louis*, translated by Joan Evans, 1937; as *The Life of St. Louis*, translated by Rene Hague, 1955; in *Chronicles of the Crusades*, translated by Margaret R.B. Shaw, 1963.
Krey, August C., *The First Crusade: The Accounts of Eye Witnesses and Participants,* 1921.
Peters, Edward (editor), *The First Crusade: The Chronicle of Fulcher of Chartres and Other Source Materials*, 1971; 2nd edition, 1998.
Raymond of Aguilers, *Historia Francorum qui ceperunt Iherusalem* in *Recueil des historiens des croisades: Historiens Occidentaux*, 5 vols., 1844–1895; reprinted 1967; translated under its original title by John Hugh Hill and Laurita L. Hill, 1968.
*Recueil des historiens des croisades*, 5 series, 1841–1906: *Lois: Assises de Jérusalem*, 2 vols., 1841–1843; all reprinted, 1967; *Historiens Occidentaux*, 5 vols., 1844–1895; *Documents Armeniens*, 2 vols., 1869–1906; *Historiens Orientaux*, 5 vols., 1872–1906; *Historiens Grecs*, 2 vols., 1875–1881.
Robert of Clary, *La Conquête de Constantinople*, edited by Philippe Lauer, 1924; as *The Conquest of Constantinople*, translated by Edgar Holmes McNeal, 1936; as "The History of Them That Took Constantinople" in *Three Old French Chronicles of the Crusades*, translated by Edward Noble Stone, 1939.
Tudebode, Peter, *Historia de Hierosolymitano itinere* in *Recueil des historiens des croisades: Historiens Occidentaux*, 5 vols., 1844–1895; reprinted, 1967; translated under its original title by John Hugh Hill and Laurita L. Hill, 1974.
William, Archbishop of Tyre, *Historia rerum in partibus transmarinis gestarum* in *Recueil des historiens des croisades: Historiens Occidentaux*, 5 vols., 1844–1895, reprinted, 1967; as *The History of Godefrey of Boloyne and of the Conquest of Iherusalem*, translated by William Caxton, 1481, reprinted, 1893; as *A History of Deeds Done beyond the Sea*, translated by Emily Atwater Babcock and A.C. Krey, 1943.

*See also* **Constantinople; Jerusalem**

## CUBA

Columbus claimed Cuba as a Spanish colony in 1492, and the influence of Spain, especially upon the architecture, is a recurring theme in travel writing about the country. However, in the first half of the nineteenth century, the most noteworthy aspect of life on the island was how dependent it was upon slavery, as the economy was based upon sugar and tobacco. This reliance drew in critical observers such as David Turnbull, a leading British antislavery figure, who visited Cuba in the 1830s, and Richard Robert Madden (1798–1886), who arrived during the following decade. Madden was later implicated in the 1844 Ladder Conspiracy, an alleged abolitionist plot that led to a Spanish massacre of thousands of blacks, both enslaved and free.

Naturally, both Madden and Turnbull expounded at length about the evils of slavery, but Turnbull's account is perhaps more enlightening as he had a wider focus. Along with sugar and tobacco production, he also addressed smaller industries like coffee and mining as well as the lives of free blacks and life in Havana. Two Spanish-backed travelers, Cirilo Villaverde (1812–1894) and Alexander von Humboldt (1769–1859), also addressed these themes, with perhaps less overt political sentiment. Villaverde was especially interested in cigar production, and his account captures the atmosphere of this industry in the 1830s and 1840s. Von Humboldt journeyed round the island as part of a much wider tour of South America and the Caribbean. At this time, Cuba was a near-obligatory stop on such tours because of its size, its closeness to the United States, and the fact that the Spanish influence meant that it was much more developed than most other islands in the Caribbean.

Traveling around the island in the 1820s meant that von Humboldt witnessed some of the instability within Cuba that was beginning to undermine Spanish rule. His book is a classic record of a society going through profound changes, and these eventually led to a war of independence in the eastern half of the island (1868–1878). *New York Herald* journalist James O'Kelly's reports on this conflict were subsequently published as a book, which despite being mainly war reportage—at one point, O'Kelly escaped from a Spanish jail—does show something of a rarely traveled part of Cuba. Other travelers during this period included the illustrator Samuel Hazard (1834–1876), who showed the diverse Spanish, Caribbean, and African influences in Havana before visiting the rest of the country, and Maturin M. Ballou (1820–1895), who was a perceptive writer, especially upon social conditions.

The United States took Cuba from the Spanish in 1898, and even after the island became independent three years later, repeated interventions meant that Americans greatly influenced Cuban life. This was especially true once Prohibition was enacted, as Cuba soon became a playground for the rich and crooked, being one of the more agreeable and convenient places in which to drink legally. Basil Woon (1890–?) evocatively captured the atmosphere of this period as he portrayed Americans at play upon the island. By contrast, another American, Sydney Clark (1890–1975), focused much more upon the life of Cubans and how they were affected by the social and economic upheavals of the 1920s and the subsequent depression.

Cuba's reputation as an American playground was ended by the Socialist revolution of 1959. Fidel Castro's government soon became a pariah in the West, but some left-wing intellectuals began to see it as a possible model for future political developments, as the Soviet Union had been after its revolution in 1917. Elizabeth Sutherland (b. 1925), for instance, published a sympathetic account of the revolution, complimenting social programs such as health and education reforms. Susan Sontag (b. 1933) similarly returned with praise for the new regime's treatment of artists and intellectuals—not one was imprisoned or denied publication, she erroneously claimed—while Angela Davis (b. 1944) felt that the newly empowered sugar cutters—whose lives had barely changed—had been given a palpable "sense of human dignity" by the new regime. Another visitor was Ernesto Cardenal, a Nicaraguan poet and priest who later became the minister for culture in the Sandinista government. He interviewed a number of Cubans, including Castro, who readily made himself available for sympathetic authors.

However, as in the Soviet Union, left-wingers came to write critical accounts of the new regime once Castro's gleam began to fade. The Argentinean socialist Jacobo Timerman (b. 1923), for instance, condemned the revolution for distorting the lives of the peoples through cultural and intellectual repression. Maurice Halperin (b. 1906), an American who had known prerevolutionary Cuba and had visited the island as a guest of Ché Guevara in the 1960s, argued after a monthlong trip in 1989 that Cuba had regressed under Castro.

Less ideological authors to have written about trips to Cuba include journalist Joe Nicholson (b. 1943), who penned a somewhat upbeat account of life there in the 1970s when U.S.-Cuban relations looked to be thawing; Nicholson disliked the imposed uniformity but found support for Fidel. Another nonideological visitor was Tom Miller (b. 1947), who wrote an idiosyncratic account of Cuban life, speaking to, among others, graffiti artists and Cuba's most famous chef. Carlo Gébler (b. 1954), a Briton, wrote a similarly personal account of a three-month trip he took with his wife and children. His anecdotal book sidelines politics in favor of breakdowns and nonfunctioning hotel equipment. Another Briton, Stephen Smith (b. 1961), has written the best account of life in Cuba since the collapse of the USSR, which had underpinned the Cuban economy. He showed how this had greatly affected the country and also asked what will happen once Castro dies. Furthermore, like many other authors, he was enraptured by the fact that an American embargo has forced Cubans to continue to drive American motorcars from the 1950s.

NEIL DENSLOW

### References and Further Reading


Ballou, Maturin M., *Due South; or, Cuba, Past and Present*, 1885; reprinted, 1969.

Cardenal, Ernesto, *En Cuba*, 1972; as *In Cuba*, translated by Donald D. Walsh, 1974.

Clark, Sydney, *Cuban Tapestry*, 1936.

Gébler, Carlo, *Driving through Cuba: An East–West Journey*, 1988; as *Driving through Cuba: Rare Encounters in the Land of Sugar Cane and Revolution*, 1988.

Halperin, Maurice, *Return to Havana: The Decline of Cuban Society under Castro*, 1994.

Hazard, Samuel, *Cuba with Pen and Pencil*, 1871.

Humboldt, Alexander von, *Essai politique sur l'île de Cuba*, 2 vols., 1826; as *The Island of Cuba*, edited and translated by J.S. Thrasher, 1856; reprinted, 1969.

Madden, R.R., *The Island of Cuba: Its Resources, Progress, and Prospects*, 1849.

Miller, Tom, *Trading with the Enemy: A Yankee Travels through Castro's Cuba*, 1992.

Nicholson, Joe, Jr., *Inside Cuba*, 1974.

O'Kelly, James J., *The Mambí-Land; or, Adventures of a Herald Correspondent in Cuba*, 1874.

Pérez, Louis A., Jr. (editor), *Slaves, Sugar and Colonial Society: Travel Accounts of Cuba, 1801–1899*, 1992.

Smith, Stephen, *The Land of Miracles*, 1998.

Sontag, Susan, "Some Thoughts on the Right Way (for Us) to Love the Cuban Revolution," *Ramparts* (April 1969).

Sutherland, Elizabeth, *The Youngest Revolution: A Personal Report on Cuba*, 1969.

Timerman, Jacobo, *Cuba hoy, y después*, 1990; as *Cuba: A Journey*, translated by Toby Talbot, 1990; with a new foreword by the author, 1992.

Turnbull, David, *Travels in the West: Cuba; with Notices of Puerto Rico and the Slave Trade*, 1840; reprinted, 1969.

Villaverde, Cirilo, *Excursión a vuelta abajo*, 1981.

Woon, Basil, *When It's Cocktail Time in Cuba*, 1928.


*See also* **Caribbean, Pre-1700; Caribbean, Post-1700**

## CURZON, GEORGE (1859–1925) *British Statesman and Viceroy of India*

George Nathaniel Curzon came from a long line of Curzons who, in his own words, went "straight back to a Norman who came over with the Conqueror." Unlike most of his ancestors, who were "content to remain in possession of the same estate since the twelfth century," George Curzon was marked out for great things, amply fulfilling the prophecy of his preparatory school headmaster that he would "certainly be a distinguished man in the best sense of the term." An outstanding career at Eton was followed by five years at Balliol College, Oxford, the "kindergarten for aspiring politicians and diplomats" (Gilmour, 1995) attended by future prime minister H.H. Asquith, future foreign secretary Edward Grey, and Alfred Milner, who, alongside Curzon and Lord Cromer, would later be spoken of as forming the triumvirate of Britain's imperial proconsuls.

The future viceroy of India began his travels in the East as a young graduate, smarting from the humiliation of gaining only a second-class degree. In 1883, he set out for the eastern Mediterranean with the aim of researching the Byzantine emperor Justinian, the subject of one of Oxford's hardest essay prizes. En route from Naples to Athens, he sat on his bunk writing his essay, in between paroxysms of seasickness. Curzon left his party of Oxford friends in Greece, going

Books are brought out from their satchels for Curzon's inspection at a monastery in Wadi Natron, in Egypt's western desert (from *Visits to Monasteries in the Levant*, 1849). *Courtesy of the Travellers Club, London; Bridgeman Art Library, agent.*

on to Egypt, where he cruised the Nile and had an affair with an exotic Englishwoman but resolutely refused to enjoy the seductiveness of Cairo. From there, he proceeded to Palestine and Syria, where he "spent most of the time comparing the sites . . . with the events associated with them in the Bible" (Gilmour, 1994)—much to the detriment of the former.

This was to set a pattern for Curzon's subsequent travels in Persia and central Asia (though not in India), where he continually came across ruins on or near sites celebrated for their former glories. Despite such disappointments, Curzon's travels for a purpose had yielded a result: on his way home via Turkey and the Balkans, he read a copy of the *Times* announcing that his essay on Justinian, dispatched some weeks earlier, had won the Oxford prize. This vindication of the journey through and by the text (for Curzon always read everything written on the target area by other authors ancient and modern, then endeavored to supersede them himself) was to set a precedent for his later books on central Asia and Persia.

Between 1887 and 1894, Curzon made five journeys to the East, including two that took him around the world. His political aspirations were the main motive, the aim being to establish himself as the foremost expert on Asian affairs as they impinged upon the British empire. But he was also captivated by the East in a manner that served to accentuate his orientalism. In 1886, Curzon crossed the Atlantic, traversed eastern Canada and the Midwest, and sailed from San Francisco to Japan, returning via Hong Kong, Singapore, and Ceylon. Calcutta, seat of an empire "not far short of the entire size of Europe," furnished the climacteric for his pride in British governance over the East, while his aesthetic pleasure was no less fulfilled by the Taj Mahal. In 1888, Curzon journeyed across central Asia on the newly completed Trans-Caspian Railway, from Uzun Ada on the Caspian, to Merv, Ashkabad, Bokhara, and Samarkand, and then on horseback to Tashkent. The following year found him on the same railway, this time crossing the Persian frontier into Khorassan, traveling from Meshed to Tehran by post-horse (the only means of transport through a terrain devoid of roads), south to Bushire, and down the Persian Gulf. Curzon's second round-the-world trip, in 1892, gave him the opportunity to observe China, Japan, and Korea. In 1894, Curzon made his last journey east—to the Pamirs and Afghanistan—prior to his appointment as viceroy of India (1898). His later career on the Conservative front bench and in government (his last years spent as foreign secretary) precluded extensive travel outside Europe.

Curzon's journeys are recorded in three volumes, each of which contains not only travel writing, but copious historical research and political analysis on the East. *Russia in Central Asia* (1889) and *Persia and the Persian Question* (1892) are both framed by a concern with Russia's spreading power in the region and the putative threat this posed to British India, while *Problems of the Far East* (1894) concentrates on Britain's providential role in that area of the globe. These writings are in several key respects characteristic of orientalism as delineated by Edward Said. The primary purpose of their publication was to establish for their author an acknowledged expertise on his subject—Asia and the Orient—so furthering a political career that would in turn be founded on a bedrock belief in British imperial dominance over large areas of the East. Curzon's mastery of his oriental subjects was intended to facilitate his imminent participation in Britain's political sway over the regions studied. The peoples of the East, with the exception of the Japanese, toward whom he is at best ambivalent, are presented as unchanging, picturesque, often corrupt, and generally incapable of reforming themselves. This backwardness is both the object of the traveler's censure and, on occasion, the source of his satisfaction. "Do we ever escape from the fascination of a turban, or the mystery of the shrouded apparitions that pass for women in the dusty alleys?" (*Persia and the Persian Question*). The Orientals having long forgotten their past, this is left to the Western traveler and scholar to reconstruct. European encroachment on and conquest of their lands is inevitable. The Turkomans of central Asia, recently so brutally conquered by the Russians, make willing imperial subjects, while the effete and cowardly Persians, steeped in the mire of centuries of oriental decay, represent a conundrum to British imperial interests given the vital strategic importance of Persia within the Great Game:

> An enemy could march into Nishapur as easily as he could march down Brompton Road, and would find about as much to reward him as if he occupied in force Brompton Cemetery. (*Persia and the Persian Question*, 1892)

GEOFFREY NASH

## Biography

Born at Kedleston Hall, Derbyshire, 11 January 1859. Attended Eton College, 1872–1878, and Balliol College, Oxford University, 1878–1882. Traveled in the Near East, 1883. Elected Fellow of All Souls College, Oxford, 1883. Elected member of Parliament for Southport, Lancashire, 1886. Journeyed round the world for the first time, 1886–1888. Traveled in central Asia, 1888, and Persia, 1889–1890. Entered government of Lord Salisbury as parliamentary undersecretary at the India Office, 1891. After defeat of the Salisbury government, made second round-the-world trip, 1892. Traveled to the Pamirs and Afghanistan, 1894. Married Mary Leiter (d. 1909) in Washington, DC, 1895: three daughters. Parliamentary undersecretary for foreign affairs, 1895–1896. Viceroy of India, 1898–1904. Created Baron Curzon of Kedleston, 1898. Resigned as viceroy, 1905. Retired temporarily from political life during Liberal government, 1906–1916. Elected chancellor of Oxford University, 1907. Lord rector of Glasgow University, 1907. Entered House of Lords as an Irish representative peer, 1908. President of the Royal Geographical Society, 1911. Created Earl Curzon of Kedleston, 1911. Appointed lord privy seal, 1915. Joined Lloyd George coalition government as member of war cabinet, 1916. Married Grace Duggan, née Hinds, 1917. Foreign secretary, 1919–1924. Failed to secure Conservative leadership, 1923. Died in London, 20 March 1925.

### References and Further Reading


Curzon, George, *Russia in Central Asia in 1889 and the Anglo-Russian Question*, 1889; reprinted, 1967.
Curzon, George, *Persia and the Persian Question*, 2 vols, 1892.
Curzon, George, *Problems of the Far East*, 1894.
Curzon, George, *The Pamirs and the Source of the Oxus*, 1896; revised edition, 1898.
Curzon, George, *Tales of Travel*, 1923.
Gilmour, David, *Curzon*, London: John Murray, 1994.


## CURZON, ROBERT (1810–1873) *British Traveler and Book Collector*

Robert Curzon, the fourteenth Baron Zouche (or de la Zouche), was born at the family's country seat at Parham near Pulborough in Sussex. He had two passions in life: rare books and his country house. Having studied paleography, Curzon left Christ Church in Oxford without a degree in 1831 to become member of Parliament for Clitheroe. His family borough was, however, disenfranchised by the Reform Bill of 1832. Unemployed, he assuaged his distress by embarking on three Grand Tours to the Near East.

Curzon's first journey (1833–1834) took him to Egypt and Palestine, St. Catherine's on Mount Sinai, Corfu, and the Meteora monasteries in Albania (now Greece). He rescued valuable manuscripts from the neglected monastic libraries and showed the way to other explorers, notably Dr. Tattam. On Curzon's second Levantine voyage in 1837, he first visited the monasteries of the Natron Lakes in the Libyan desert and then traveled via Constantinople to Mount Athos, where he followed in the footsteps of Pierre Belon, John Covel, Joseph Dacre Carlyle, and others, knowing that the Paris and Vatican libraries had been enriched from Mount Athos.

Curzon's account of the library conditions in Pantokratoros on Mount Athos is revealing:

> By the dim light which streamed through the opening of an iron door in the wall of the ruined tower, I saw above a hundred ancient manuscripts lying among the rubbish which had fallen from the upper floor, which was ruinous . . . I advanced cautiously along the boards, keeping close to the wall, whilst every now and then a dull cracking noise warned me of my danger . . . At last, when I dared go no farther, I made them bring me a long stick, with which I fished up two or three fine manuscripts . . . When I had safely landed them, I examined them more at my ease, but found that . . . the pages were stuck tight together into a solid mass, and when I attempted to open them, they broke short off in square bits like a biscuit. Neglect and damp and exposure had destroyed them completely. (*Visits to Monasteries in the Levant*, 1849)

Western travelers have often been accused of rifling the libraries of the Near East. However, by purchasing manuscripts, they saved quite a few of them, as Curzon did from the monastery of Karakallou, where the abbot valued the reparation of the buildings more than its literary treasures:

> I picked up a single loose leaf of very ancient uncial Greek characters, part of the Gospel of St. Matthew, written in small square letters and of small quarto size. I searched in vain for the volume to which this leaf belonged . . . I made bold to ask for this single leaf as a thing of small value.
> "Certainly!" said the Hegoumenos. "What do you want it for?"
> My servant suggested that, perhaps, it might be useful to cover some jam pots or vases of preserves which I had at home.
> "Oh!" said the Hegoumenos, "take some more"; and, without more ado, he seized upon an unfortunate thick

> quarto manuscript of the Acts and Epistles, and drawing out a knife cut out an inch thickness of leaves at the end before I could stop him.
> It proved to be the Apocalypse, which concluded the volume, but which is rarely found in early Greek manuscripts of the Acts: it was of the eleventh century . . . I pocketed the Apocalypse, and asked him if he would sell me any of the other books . . .
> "Malista, certainly," he replied. "How many will you have? They are of no use to me, and as I am in want of money to complete my buildings, I shall be very glad to turn them to some account." (*Visits*)

In 1841, Curzon made his third journey to the Levant as an attaché at the British embassy in Constantinople and private secretary to the ambassador, Sir Stratford Canning. During his leisure hours, he roamed around in the bazaars or the old city ruins. Using his acquired manuscripts as notebooks, he jotted down amusing pieces of information concerning their acquisition or oddments he associated with the pleasures of the trip. This information, along with letters posted back to England, helped Curzon in writing his *Visits to Monasteries in the Levant* more than ten years after his first journey:

> I was staying by myself in an old country-house [Parham] belonging to my family . . . having nothing to do in the evening, I looked about for some occupation to amuse the passing hours. In the room where I was sitting there was a large book-case full of ancient manuscripts, many of which had been collected by myself in various out-of-the-way places, in different parts of the world. Taking some of these ponderous volumes from their shelves, I turned over their wide vellum leaves, and admired the antiquity of one, and the gold and azure which gleamed upon the pages of another. The sight of these books brought before my mind many scenes and recollections of the countries from which they came, and I said to myself, I know what I will do; I will write down some account of the most curious of these manuscripts, and the places in which they were found, as well as some of the adventures which I encountered in the pursuit of my venerable game. (*Visits*)

Five years later, Curzon wrote a book on his one-year mission as an attaché in Constantinople, entitled *Armenia: A Year at Erzeroom, and on the Frontiers of Russia, Turkey, and Persia* (1854). He also made a trip to Italy with the specific purpose of discovering manuscripts. In 1854, the Philobiblon Society published his "Account of the Most Celebrated Libraries of Italy."

Curzon's *Visits to Monasteries* provides the first systematic record of the conditions of the libraries and the attitudes of the monks toward their literary treasures. In 1983, Meridel Holland evaluated Curzon's books as "a perfect combination of travel-book (complete with recipes for yoghourt and shish-kebab) and bibliomaniac history."

René Gothóni

### Biography

Born in London, 16 March 1810, son of Viscount Curzon and Baroness de la Zouche. Educated at Charterhouse School. Entered Christ Church, Oxford University, as a gentleman commoner, 1829; left without a degree, 1831. Member of Parliament for Clitheroe, a family borough, 1831–1832. Traveled in Egypt and Palestine in search of manuscripts, especially in monastery libraries, 1833–1834. Continued his travels in the Meteora monasteries of Albania; visited Mount Athos, 1837. Appointed attaché at the British embassy in Constantinople and private secretary to Sir Stratford Canning (later Viscount Stratford de Redcliffe), 1841. Traveled to Erzurum, Armenia (now Turkey), as joint commissioner, with Lieutenant Colonel (afterward, Sir W. Fenwick) Williams, for defining the boundary between Turkey and Persia, 1843–1844. Decorated with the Lion and Sun of Persia and the Nishan (or "Pour le mérite") of Turkey by the shah and the sultan, respectively. Returned to England, 1844. Published two accounts of his explorations and a description of the major libraries of Italy. Married Emily Wilmot-Horton (died 1866), 1850: one son, one daughter. Succeeded his mother in the barony of de la Zouche, 1870. Died at the family estate at Parham, Sussex, 2 August 1873.

### References and Further Reading

Curzon, Robert, *Visits to Monasteries in the Levant*, 1849; 5th revised edition, 1865.

Curzon, Robert, *Armenia: A Year at Erzeroom, and on the Frontiers of Russia, Turkey, and Persia*, 1854.

*See also* **Manuscript Collecting**

## CYPRUS

> *The island is in the power of whichever nation is overlord in these seas.*
>
> —al-Muqaddesi in 985

The location of Cyprus at the crossroads of Europe, Asia, and Egypt has given it an importance disproportionate to its size, and many nations have left their mark upon it; but the island was settled originally from Syria. Fifty years ago, the streets of old Nicosia were still closer to those of Damascus than of Athens. During the Arab raids (mid-seventh to mid-tenth century) this beautiful island changed hands 11 times according to the historian Étienne de Lusignan. "Inter Graecos et Saracenos," an English traveler who journeyed through in 723 observed.

Throughout the Middle Ages, Cyprus remained Christian, first as a Byzantine province, then, from the time of the Third Crusade and for 300 years after, as a Frankish kingdom. After the fall of Acre in 1291, Cyprus became the only Christian country left in the eastern Mediterranean, the only road to the Holy Land, and a honey pot for European merchants trading with the Orient. The wealth poured in. "And the tongues of every nation under heaven are heard and read and talked," wrote Ludolf von Suchen, a German priest visiting c. 1340. "The princes, nobles, barons and knights are the richest in the world . . . but they spend all on the chase." It was only a matter of time before predators from without and corruption within broke up this bonanza; in 1489, the kingdom fell into Venetian hands. Travelers during the fifteenth and sixteenth centuries remarked upon the now-rundown countryside and the oppression of the people, and they warned of the unhealthy air that constantly struck visitors down.

The Turkish conquest in 1570 brought no rescue from the West. Although it was the talk of Europe, with numerous eyewitness reports of both the horror and the heroism, Western interests were already turning toward the Atlantic. Cyprus was absorbed once again into the East—and there it remained, an obscure backwater, until the middle of the nineteenth century. Only the reports of a few stray visitors brought news of its plight. The Russian monk Vasilii Barskii came twice, in 1726 and 1735. He trudged through the mountains from monastery to monastery, sketching and making notes on their precarious survival (see Barsukov, 1885–1889).

It was in the eighteenth century that travel broadened. A new kind of traveler came to face the hardships of a land that had one rough road only and made no provision for strangers: the explorer and scholar. Men such as Richard Pococke, there in 1738, were the first of a long line that included Edward Daniel Clarke in 1801 and William Turner shortly after. General interest in antiquities was growing. From the mid-nineteenth century, some tourists included Cyprus in their Levant itinerary. Usually, they stayed in Larnaca with their consuls, who arranged expeditions, including a spot of digging for souvenirs. Archaeology was a young science, but 1871 saw the foundation in London of the Cyprus Exploration Fund, and properly organized digs were started. The American consul, Luigi di Cesnola, excavated for his own benefit, and in the 11 years he was on the island, tens of thousands of objects were unearthed and exported. His book, *Cyprus: Its Ancient Cities, Tombs and Temples* (1877), is still highly readable.

At this time, in view of Turkish weakness against Russia, the West once more looked at Cyprus. The arrival in 1878 of British troops and officials was fully covered by journalists and official artists, and it was followed by a rush of Victorian ladies and gentlemen curious to see for themselves the forgotten island. Shortly afterward, travel books began to appear with titles such as *In an Enchanted Island* (Mallock, 1889), *A Lady's Impressions of Cyprus in 1893* (Lewis, 1894), and *Through Cyprus with a Camera* (Thomson, 1879); all good of their kind, they found a ready market. Later travelers were greatly assisted by two things: the reliable map drawn up by Lord Kitchener—then a lieutenant—and a proper highway between the towns. In 1896, Camille Enlart, an eminent French archaeologist specializing in medieval Gothic, made an appraisal of those Lusignan monuments that had survived. His work, *Gothic Art and the Renaissance in Cyprus* (French edition: 1899), is still unsurpassed. In the preface, he remarks upon the continuing lack of facilities for visitors. Four years later, Rider Haggard observed that a hotel now existed in Larnaca, but elsewhere, "he who would journey here must either rely upon tents . . . or upon the freely offered hospitality of the Government officials." One of these officials was C.D. Cobham, commissioner for Larnaca, whose *Excerpta Cypria*, first published in 1908, has been a valuable sourcebook ever since.

By World War I, the tide of travel books had ebbed. Instead, by the middle of the century, a number of well-researched works on the topography, archaeology, and history of Cyprus had appeared, as well as personal memoirs written by diplomats such as Sir Ronald Storrs, governor from 1926 to 1932. From World War II through the Turkish invasion and beyond, unrestricted travel was not always possible. Nevertheless,

The ruined walls and Gothic churches of Famagusta evoke Cyprus's historic links with the medieval West (frontispiece to W. H. Mallock's *In an Enchanted Island*, 1889). *Courtesy of the Travellers Club, London; Bridgeman Art Library, agent.*

Lawrence Durrell's enduring classic, *Bitter Lemons* (1957), is an evocative account of his three-year residence during the EOKA campaign. In 1972, amid increasing intercommunal tension, Colin Thubron walked the length and breadth of the island, a modern Barskii, and was warmly received in both Greek villages and Turkish enclaves. Sir David Hunt summarized the effect of the final catastrophe in his epilogue to *Footprints in Cyprus* in 1982: "A piece of the old Levant has been brought violently into the divided Near East." More recently, Marc Dubin has traveled widely and, in his book *Cyprus: The Rough Guide* (1999), writes of the gradually widening gap between the two communities. The south, he says, has wrought an economic miracle, but at a price; while in the less-developed north, "the grass grows between the cracks."

GWYNNETH DER PARTHOG

### References and Further Reading


Baker, Sir Samuel, *Cyprus as I Saw It in 1879*, 1879.

Balfour, Patrick (Lord Kinross), *The Orphaned Realm: Journeys in Cyprus*, 1951.

Barsukov, Nicolai (editor), *Stranstvovaniia V.G. Barskogo po sviatym mestam Vostoka s 1723 po 1747 g. Izdany pravoslavnym palestinskim obšcestvom po podlinnoi rukopisi, pof redakcieiu Nikolaia Barsukova* [The Travels of Vasilii Grigorovich Barskii to Holy Places in the East from 1723 to 1747. Publication of the Orthodox Palestine Society according to the Original Manuscript, edited by Nikolai Barsukov], 1885–1889.

Cesnola, Luigi Palma di, *Cyprus: Its Ancient Cities, Tombs and Temples*, 1877; reprinted with a foreword by Stuart Swiny, 1991.

Cotovicus, Dr. Iannes, *Itinerarium Hierosolymitanum et Syriacum*, 1619; translated by Claude Delaval Cobham in *Excerpta Cypria*, 1908.

Dixon, W. Hepworth, *British Cyprus*, 1879.

Dubin, Marc S., *Cyprus: The Rough Guide*, 1999.

Durrell, Lawrence, *Bitter Lemons*, 1957.

Enlart, Camille, *Gothic Art and the Renaissance in Cyprus; 1899*, edited and translated by David Hunt, Coldstream: Trigraph Press, 1987, French edition, 1899.

Faber, Felix, *Evagatorium in Terra Sancta, Arabie et Egypti Peregrinationem*, 1484, translated from his autobiography by Claude Delaval Cobham in *Excerpta Cypria*, 1908.

Fellman, Arno, *Voyage en Orient du Roi Erik Ejegod et sa mort à Paphos* [in 1103], 1938.

Gjerstad, Einer, *Ages and Days in Cyprus*, 1980.

Haggard, Rider, *A Winter Pilgrimage . . . Travels through Palestine, Italy and the Island of Cyprus*, 1901.

Hogarth, D.G., *Devia Cypria: Notes of an Archaeological Journey in Cyprus in 1888*, 1989.

Hunt, David (editor), *Footprints in Cyprus: An Illustrated History*, London: Trigraph, 1982; revised edition, 1990.

Lazarides, Stavros G., *Cyprus, 1878–1900*, 1984.

Lewis, E.A.M., *A Lady's Impressions of Cyprus in 1893*, 1894.

Lithgow, William, *The Total Discourse of the Rare Adventures and Painefull Peregrinations of Long Nineteen Years Travailles from Scotland to the Most Famous Kingdomes in Europe*, 1632.

Mallock, W.H., *In an Enchanted Island; or, A Winter's Retreat in Cyprus*, 1889.

Mariti, Giovanni, *Viaggi per l'isola di Cipro*, 1769; as *Travels in the Island of Cyprus*, translated by Claude Delaval Cobham, 1909; reprinted, 1971.

Ross, Ludwig, *A Journey to Cyprus (February and March 1895)*, translated from the German by Claude Delaval Cobham, 1910.

Smith, Agnes, *Through Cyprus*, 1887.

Storrs, Ronald, *Orientations*, London: Nicholson and Watson, and New York: Putnam, 1937.

Strabo, *The Geography* (first century CE), translated by Horace Leonard Jones, 1917–1933.

Thomson, John, *Through Cyprus with a Camera in the Autumn of 1878*, 2 vols., 1879; reprinted, 1985.

Thubron, Colin, *Journey into Cyprus*, 1975.


*See also* **Levant**

# D

## D'ANCONA, CYRIACO (c. 1391–c. 1450)

***Italian Merchant, Antiquarian, and Archaeologist***

Cyriaco d'Ancona (Cyriaco di Filippo de' Pizzicolli by family name, Cyriac of Ancona in English) was born in Ancona on the Italian Adriatic toward the end of the fourteenth century, probably in 1391, and died shortly after 1450 in Cremona. He was a merchant with extensive commercial connections on the eastern shores of the Adriatic (Dalmatia and Greece), in the Aegean Islands, and in the countries of the Levant. In all these places, he traveled extensively. Cyriac's reputation for learning gained him access to the rich and the powerful, including the Giustinianis, Pope Eugenius IV, and the Ottoman conqueror of Constantinople, Mehmet II. His unique position in the history of travel literature resides in his pioneering archaeological interests, for he was among the very first of the European antiquarians. Cyriac developed a well-informed interest in the Greco-Roman antiquities he encountered in his travels, of which he made extensive descriptive notes, often with drawings, in notebooks. He was particularly interested in ancient monuments and, especially, ancient inscriptions. As a competent amateur draughtsman who frequently made sketches of what he saw, Cyriac anticipates many of the great travelers of the Grand Tour and the philhellenes of the Romantic and Victorian periods. In his love for the ruins of Turkey, he anticipates Rose Macaulay in the twentieth century. He himself was a modest collector of small antiquities. Chiarlo calls him "the undisputed father of modern archaeology and epigraphy." We may also find in his union of an active mercantile life with literary and antiquarian attainments a truer model of the genuine Renaissance man than those more conventionally advanced.

Among the historical circumstances of Cyriac's career, two related factors are of particular importance. He was active in the final age of Byzantium as the Byzantines retreated rapidly in the face of expanding—eventually conquering—Ottoman power. The Roman Catholic West found a quickened if largely ineffectual interest, born of fear and desperation, in the embattled Greek Orthodox East. Cyriac appears in his last years to have played a minor role in papal diplomacy in Greece. The political and military situation further stimulated a burgeoning humanistic interest in the Greco-Roman past and, especially, in the Greek language. Cyriac, apparently without formal tuition, became proficient in the classical form of that tongue as well as in Latin. As with many of the other Italian humanists from the time of Dante on, Cyriac's classicism was connected with a more-or-less vague and impractical sense of the renovation of political imperium. We find him at one point, for example, advancing the idea of a European crusade against the Turks.

Cyriac's lifelong passion for ruins evidently began in his native Ancona, where there still stood a richly decorated triumphal arch from the time of the emperor Trajan. We have several of his sketches of that monument. Indeed, Cyriac seems to have kept systematic notebooks—or to use his term, *commentaria*—on the sites he visited. They were widely circulated and sometimes copied by the growing band of Italian humanists who shared his classical interests. Although all the originals seem to have perished—with the possible exception of MS Trotti 373 in the Ambrosiana Library, Milan—numerous copies or extracts exist in many of the libraries of Europe, above all in Italy. There are also surviving letters and minor poetic works in Latin and Italian.

Cyriac recorded important information about the ancient monuments of Egypt and the Greco-Roman remains in Italy, Greece, and Turkish Asia Minor. In many instances, he is the earliest modern witness to important remains, and he is the only surviving witness to several important monuments destroyed since his time. Among Cyriac's most interesting and important work are accounts of his visits to Egypt in 1435 and to Athens, the islands of the northern Aegean (especially Samothrace), and the Sea of Marmara (especially the temple of Hadrian at Cyzicus, now in northwestern Turkey) in 1444 and 1445. Among his more remarkable drawings are those of the Parthenon in Athens and of the great church of Hagia Sophia in Constantinople.

Cyriac, at heart an archaeologist, rarely betrays an interest in the current inhabitants of the places he visits. We do have preserved in a manuscript in the Bodleian Library in Oxford (Canon. Misc. 280) his charming sketches, or copies thereof, of an elephant and a giraffe he encountered in Egypt. The influence of one of Cyriac's archaeological sketches has plausibly been detected in the woodcut iconography of one of the greatest of early Renaissance books, the *Hypnerotomachia Polifili* (1497). Certainly in a general sense, his reverent and studious approach to the visual monuments of antiquity is widely evidenced in the classicizing humanism of northern Italy in the second half of the fifteenth century. His surviving work still lies scattered among the great libraries of Europe or partially published in journals not always easy of access. A just evaluation of his cultural importance must await the much-desired comprehensive collection and edition of his manuscripts and a complete catalog of all of his surviving drawings and their derivatives.

John V. Fleming

### Biography

Born Cyriaco di Filippo de' Pizzicolli in Ancona, Papal States (now Italy), probably 1391. Traveled widely as a merchant in the Middle East, Greece, Egypt, and southern Italy, also documenting ancient monuments and writing accounts of his journeys. Produced six volumes of *commentaria* on his travels, most of which were destroyed by fire, 1514. Died in Cremona, Duchy of Milan (now Italy), c. 1450.

### References and Further Reading

d'Ancona, Cyriaco, *Cyriacus of Ancona's Journeys in the Propontis and the Northern Aegean, 1444–1445*, edited by Edward W. Bodnar and Charles Mitchell, 1976.

Chiarlo, Carlo Roberto, "Cyriac of Ancona" in *The Dictionary of Art*, edited by Jane Turner, London: Macmillan, and New York: Grove, 1996.

## DA GAMA, VASCO (c. 1460–1524)

***Portuguese Admiral and European Discoverer of India***

Vasco da Gama was born into the class of the military aristocracy at Sines in the Algarve, where his father was the municipal governor. Little is known of his career before he undertook command of the first European commercial fleet to sail around Africa to reach India (1497–1499), but the very fact that he was entrusted with such a vital mission argues a formidable reputation for competence in navigation and military command. Da Gama's great achievement must be viewed within a complex historical context. The Iberian experience of the fifteenth century, both in Spain and Portugal very different from that elsewhere in Europe, was one of Christian triumphalism and consolidation of a gradual and hard-won victory over Muslim power in the peninsula. In their outward expansion, the Iberian nations almost instinctively assumed a crusading mentality. As the spice trade, the principal economic object of the search for a sea route to India, was monopolized by Muslim traders in Moghul India, Persia, Arabia, and East Africa, the Portuguese tended to view their quest as an extension of their warfare against Islam. Furthermore, Portugal was itself in often explicit competition with its much larger and more populous neighbor, Spain. By the Treaty of Tordesillas (1494), it was formally agreed that the Spaniards would be allowed supremacy in the western sphere of "discoveries" (the Americas) and Portugal would enjoy sovereignty in the East (Africa and what lay beyond, India). Throughout the fifteenth century, and especially under the influence of the celebrated Prince Henry the Navigator (1394–1460), Portuguese navies systematically and incrementally explored the west coast of Africa and its offshore islands—"cape-hopping" ever southward from one promontory to the next, in an attempt to get around Africa. Unlike the wildly speculative route of Columbus, sea routes between East Africa and India were long known to Indian, Arabian, and African merchants; but it was no mean trick to circumnavigate Africa. Around midcentury, Cà da Mosto found the Cape Verde Islands, roughly a third of the way along the African flank; by 1488, Bartolomeu Dias was at the southern tip of Africa, the Cape of Good Hope (which he called the Cape of Storms—*Cabo Tormentoso*).

Da Gama had been groomed as early as 1490 to command the fleet that would attempt the final push to India, but only in July 1497, after meticulous and protracted preparations, did his fleet (*São Gabriel, São Rafael, Bérrio*, and a supply ship) depart. He took a route through the Cape Verde Islands, then more or less due south at 17° W to about 23° S, when he pointed toward the Cape, which he rounded on 22 November. The supply ship was emptied and demolished. All was now terra incognita. Ever hopeful of finding Prester John and his eastern Christian kingdom, da Gama's three ships moved up the east coast of the continent from Mossel Bay to the Copper, thence to Kilimane, Mozambique, Mombasa, and Malindi. By now, many of his crew had scurvy. The frequently treacherous, hostile, or simply uncomprehending reception of the native Africans, and even more so the Muslim Arab traders who controlled the coast as far south as Mozambique, was answered with artillery and brutality. The headman of Malindi, hoping to gain new allies in his own hostilities against the Mombasans, welcomed the Portuguese and secured for da Gama the services of an experienced Indian Ocean pilot, Ahmad Ibn Majid.

With remarkable speed, the Portuguese crossed the Indian Ocean in less than a month, arriving off the great commercial hub of Calicut on the Malabar Coast on 20 May 1498, thus completing a journey unprecedented in distance, difficulty, and danger. Da Gama's actual commercial dealings with the local potentate, the samorim of Calicut, were at best an anticlimax, at worst a tragicomedy of errors. The Indians were insulted by the gimcracks with which da Gama proposed to dazzle them. Facing the genuine hostility of Muslim traders who hated him both as infidel and competitor, he reacted with ruthless brutality. Just as his personal demeanor was marked by arrogance, irascibility, and violence, his little fleet left in its path on the Malabar Coast of India, as it had along the African coast, longlasting feelings of hostility, outrage, and fear. Though he would arrive home with only some modest specimens of the alimentary and lapidary riches of the East, da Gama nonetheless did open up India for European trade and laid the foundation for tiny Portugal's astonishing if short-lived Eastern empire. His journey, like the first journey of Columbus—in comparison with which it was, from the nautical point of view, far more impressive—is one that truly changed history. It was quite literally an epic journey that became the subject of what is probably the greatest of Renaissance heroic poems, *The Lusiads* of Luís de Camões.

The trip home, which took more than a year, was horrendous. Da Gama attempted to retrace his outward path, but the ships drifted aimlessly in the doldrums of the Indian Ocean for weeks on end. Many sailors died, mostly of the horrible death of scurvy. By the time they reached Malindi, their numbers were insufficient to man three ships, and *São Rafael* was scuttled. Its captain, da Gama's beloved brother Paulo, became increasingly ill with tuberculosis. Da Gama, whose own ship had become separated from *Bérrio*, stopped in the Azores long enough to allow his brother to die and be buried in dry ground. The king of Portugal heaped social, political, and monetary rewards upon Vasco da Gama; but it is doubtful that his egomania was ever sated.

Following da Gama's success, Pedro Álvares Cabral took a second fleet to India in 1500, and da Gama himself sailed again, with a very powerful force, in 1502. By now, there was no distinction between trading mission and crusade against Islam, and da Gama proceeded with atrocious brutality to secure an exclusive market with the zamorin of Calicut. King John III named him viceroy of India in 1524, but he had hardly arrived again on the Malabar Coast when he died, at Cochin, on 24 December.

JOHN V. FLEMING

### Biography

Born c. 1460 in Sines, Portugal, son of Estevão da Gama, a nobleman, municipal governor, and commander of the fortress of Sines. Little is known of his early life; may have studied mathematics and navigation at Évora. Sent by King John II of Portugal to attack French ships, at Setúbal and on the Algarve, 1492. After his father's death in 1497, took his place as leader of expedition to Africa and India, via the Cape of Good Hope, commissioned by King Manuel I, 1497–1499. Granted title of *Dom* (Sir) and royal pension and estates by Manuel I. Married Catarina de Ataíde, c. 1500: six sons. Promoted to rank of admiral, 1502. Second voyage to India, 1502–1503. Possibly retired to Évora. Named first count of Vidigueira, 1519. Appointed Portuguese viceroy of India by King John III; third voyage to India, 1524. Arrived in Goa but fell ill shortly afterward. Died in Cochin, India, 24 December 1524.

### References and Further Reading

No significant writings of Vasco da Gama survive, and there probably were none. There is a partial *roteiro* (log) of the first journey kept by one Alvaro Velho, published as *Roteiro da primeira viagem de Vasco da Gama (1497–1499)*, edited by A. Fontoura da Costa, 3rd edition, 1969. A splendid English translation by E.G. Ravenstein appeared as *A Journal of the First Voyage of Vasco da Gama, 1497–1499*, 1898.

## DALRYMPLE, ALEXANDER (1737–1808)

***British Hydrographer***

Alexander Dalrymple, a younger son in a large family of Scottish gentry, entered the service of the East India Company in 1752. While in India he became obsessed with the potential for British trade in East and Southeast Asia, an area from which the British had been driven by the Dutch in the seventeenth century. Dalrymple's travel writings were produced for the purpose of encouraging and guiding this expanding trade, for which it was absolutely vital to obtain navigational and geographical information. Obtaining this information was a particular challenge due to the Dutch dominance of Indonesia and the Spanish rule of the Philippines.

Dalrymple's first-person travel writing recounted his voyages in Southeast Asia and the China coast in search of navigational information and trading opportunities. Most were devoted to the first of these, the voyage of the East India Company schooner *Cuddalore* between 1759 and 1762. Although Dalrymple was not a seaman, he was in overall command of the *Cuddalore* expedition with the mission to explore the possibility of a southern route to China bypassing the Strait of Malacca and to establish trade relations with the indigenous rulers of the Southeast Asian archipelagos. The first two *Cuddalore* journals, published in *General Introduction to the Charts and Memoirs Published by Alexander Dalrymple, Esq.*, recount Dalrymple's observations and experiences on the China coast and the island of Hainan. In addition to navigational and geographical information, these journals, based on the notes Dalrymple took during the voyage, include accounts of his encounters with the Chinese and Hainanese peoples. Dalrymple praises ordinary Chinese people, particularly on the coast away from Canton, although he had far less respect for the Chinese upper classes. China, he claimed, was the only country where one could expect the fishermen to be polite. His description of Hainan is one of the few by a European in the period. Dalrymple observed that the indigenous people of Hainan disliked the Chinese, at one point urging the British to kill some Chinese who had their backs turned. In an unpublished letter to the British prime minister, William Pitt the Elder, he suggested that Hainan would be a possible acquisition for Britain in the case of a war with China. Dalrymple planned to publish more of the *Cuddalore* journals, but only one more volume came out many years later (1793), published separately and recounting some of his experiences on the islands. This volume is very rare.

Dalrymple's book on the cruise of *London* in the Philippines between 1762 and 1763 is less colorful than his writings on the China coast. It concentrates even more than the *Cuddalore* volumes on navigational information, and does not describe the peoples of the area at all. It does have some interesting descriptions of geography and of remarkable atmospheric and oceanic phenomena.

Dalrymple's collections and editions of the travels of others were far more voluminous than the writings recounting his own experiences. His major collections of voyage accounts were not produced for literary or entertainment reasons, but for utilitarian purposes. The most important were a series of publications connected with the South Pacific, and culminating in the two-volume *An Historical Collection of the Several Voyages and Discoveries in the South Pacific Ocean*. The South Pacific writings were the result of a shift, in the 1770s, of Dalrymple's interests away from the China trade to the hypothetical southern continent, after the failure of the British to establish a base for trade at Balambagan. *An Historical Collection* was intended to stir up enthusiasm for the project of discovering and exploring the great southern continent (*Terra Australis Incognita*). Dalrymple's introduction set forth a heroic vision of exploration invoking Columbus and Magellan as heroes suitable for emulation. He claimed that the southern continent was equal in size to Asia from Turkey to China and inhabited by more than 50 million people. He also suggested that this continent was the original home of the highly civilized Inca empire. Although most of the first volume is composed of narratives of Spanish explorers of the South Pacific, Dalrymple also included navigational information on the South Seas and the Solomon Islands, and some of his own observations of the natural curiosities of Sulu, including pearl fisheries, edible birds' nests, and corals. The narratives included, among others, the voyages of Magellan, Ferdinand Grijalva. Juan Fernandes (whom Dalrymple identified as the discoverer of the great southern continent), Adelanto Alvarado Mendana de Neyras, and Pedro Fernandez de Quiroz. Dalrymple did not wish for or anticipate a British conquest of the new continent. His vision of British oceanic expansion was based on trade rather than conquest and colonization. He argued that the Spanish would have gained more by trading with Mexico and Peru than by conquering them.

The second volume of *An Historical Collection* was devoted to Dutch voyagers. It includes accounts of the voyages of Le Mair and Schouten in 1616, Abel Janszoon Tasman in 1642, and Jacob Roggewein in 1722. Dalrymple also included a history and chronology of previous explorations and a program for further exploration. *An Historical Collection* attracted interest outside Britain, and was translated into French and German. Both volumes accompanied James Cook on his *Endeavour* voyage to observe the transit of Venus and explore the southern seas in 1769, a command that Dalrymple wanted for himself hoping to be the one to find the continent. The Admiralty refused to allow a non-sailor to captain one of its vessels. Ironically, it was this voyage and Cook's second that disproved the existence of the great southern continent.

*A Collection of Voyages Chiefly in the Southern Atlantick Ocean* collects the voyages of Edmond Halley in *Paramore* in 1698, 1699, and 1700; Des Loziers Bouvet's voyage in 1738 and 1739; S. Ducloz Guyot's voyage; and a journal of the weather at the Falklands Islands. Dalrymple also edited dozens of maritime logs, charts, and journals of Asian waters and the south seas for the East India Company. These concentrated on navigational and hydrographical information.

WILLIAM BURNS

### Biography

Born at New Hailes, Scotland, 24 July 1737. Appointed Writer to the East India Company 1 November 1752; arrived at Madras 11 May 1753; deputy secretary, Fort St. George, 1757; passenger on *Winchilsea* from Madras to Malacca, 1759; commander of *Cuddalore* from Malacca, 1759–1762; negotiated commercial treaty with the sultan of Sulu, 28 January 1761; commander of *London* from Madras, 1762–1763; passenger on *Neptune* to Sulu and the Philippines, 1763–1764; deputy governor of Manila, 1764. Returned to England 10 July 1765; departed England on *Grenville*, 1775; member of the Council at Madras, 1776; returned to England, 1776; appointed hydrographer to the East India Company, 1779; hydrographer to the British Admiralty, 1795; forced to resign his position as Admiralty hydrographer, 1808. Fellow of the Royal Society, 1771. Died in Marylebone, London, 9 June 1808.

### References and Further Reading

Dalrymple, Alexander, *An Account of the Discoveries Made in the South Pacifick Ocean, Previous to 1764*, 1767; reprinted, 1996.

Dalrymple, Alexander, *An Historical Collection of the Several Voyages and Discoveries in the South Pacific Ocean*, 2 vols., 1769–1971; reprinted, 1967.

Dalrymple, Alexander, *A Collection of Charts and Memoirs*, 1772; 2nd edition, 1786.

Dalrymple, Alexander, *A Collection of Voyages Chiefly in the Southern Atlantick Ocean*, 1775.

Dalrymple, Alexander, *Journal of the Ship London, Captain Walter Hues, along the North Coast of Magindanao, October, 1764*, 1781.

Dalrymple, Alexander, *Journal of the Schooner Cuddalore through the Strait of Sapy, and on the South Coast of Man–e–rye, in February, March, and April 1761*, 1793.

## DALRYMPLE, WILLIAM (1965–) *British Travel Writer and Journalist*

In 1986 William Dalrymple set out to retrace Marco Polo's route from Jerusalem to the legendary palace of Kubla Khan in China. Equipped with a copy of Sir Henry Yule's edition of Polo and a £700 travel grant from Trinity College, Cambridge, he carried a vial of oil from the holy sepulchre 12 thousand miles through a region made hazardous by war and politics. With the publication of *In Xanadu: A Quest* (1989), he achieved immediate acclaim as a travel writer. This expedition was a sequel to his walk from Rouen to Jerusalem, following the route of crusader Robert Curthose (c. 1054–1134), which was the first summer holiday he took as an undergraduate.

Dalrymple's passion for the East had been kindled when, after a Scottish childhood and a decade at a Catholic school in Yorkshire, he spent a year in India's capital, where he worked in a home for the destitute. He found the experience transforming, and says it led him to return to India repeatedly. Having embarked on a career as a writer, Dalrymple went to Delhi in 1989 as an "India correspondent," and began describing South Asia and its people in a stream of articles for both British and American journals. He revised 20 of these essays for publication as his fourth book, *The Age of Kali* (1998). His second book, *City of Djinns* (1993), quickly garnered praise as well as prizes. Dalrymple revealed aspects of Delhi's multilayered history and culture to the surprise of some who thought they knew the city well. He led his readers from the present back through the time of the Raj, the Moghuls, and beyond, in a series of affectionately drawn character sketches and discursive accounts of monuments and architecture.

Dalrymple's special gift as a travel writer lies in his artful ability to blend incisive descriptions of place, conversations, historical erudition, and his sense of humor in a prose that is neither pedantic nor patronizing. His ability to guide readers through time as well as space was fully developed in his third and most ambitious book, *From the Holy Mountain* (1997). Inspired by the 30-year journey of Byzantine monk John Moschos (d. 619), Dalrymple resolved

> to spend six months circling the Levant, following roughly in John Moschos' footsteps. Starting at Athos and working my way through the Coptic monasteries of Upper Egypt, I wanted to do what no future generations of travellers would be able to do: to see wherever possible what Moschos . . . had seen, to sleep in the same monasteries, to pray under the same frescoes and mosaics, to discover what was left, and to witness what was in effect the last ebbing twilight of Byzantium.

Dalrymple used Moschos's *The Spiritual Meadow* as both itinerary and point of reference for his own investigation of the Eastern Christian communities from Turkey to Egypt, which are so little known in the West. Everywhere, except in Syria, he found them in serious decline, and ruefully predicted that within the foreseeable future Christianity would all but disap-

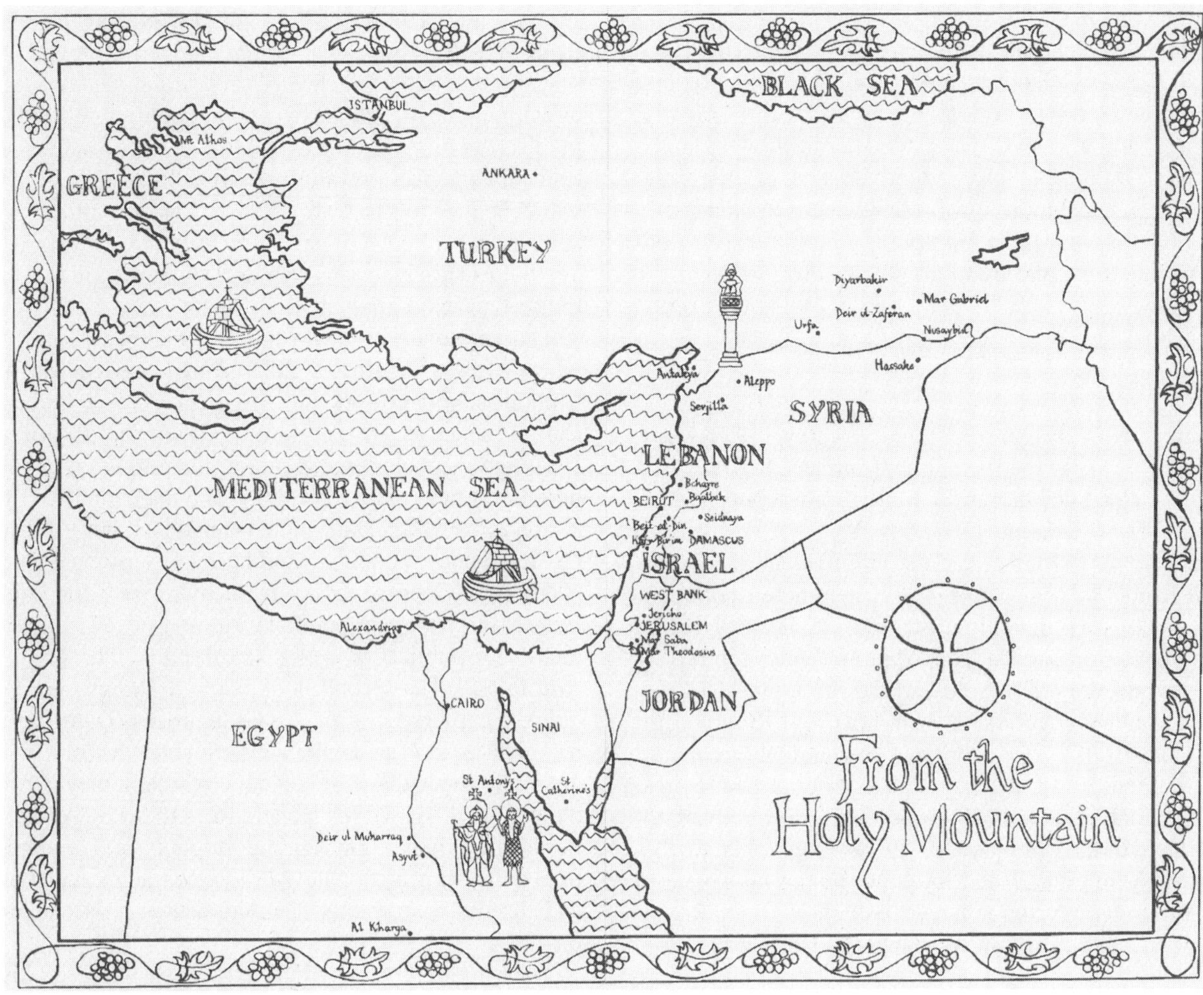


Sketch map by Olivia Fraser showing Dalrymple's route around early Christian sites in the Near East in the footsteps of the sixth-century monk John Moschos (endpapers of Dalrymple's *From the Holy Mountain*, 1997). *Courtesy of HarperCollins, London.*

pear from its original heartland. The churches, monasteries, and shrines visited by Moschos that had not already succumbed to destruction were in danger of being reduced to empty museums. Only in Egypt did Dalrymple find Islamic fundamentalism to be a significant factor in this decline. Indeed, his delineation of the intimate historical relationship between Christianity and Islam is one of the book's great achievements, and his implied criticism of government policy in Turkey, Israel, and Egypt reflects the depth of his own indignation.

The accolades with which *From the Holy Mountain* was received included inevitable comparisons with other travel writers such as Bruce Chatwin and Robert Byron. Although Dalrymple acknowledges Chatwin's stature as a great travel writer, he categorically denies being influenced by his work. On the other hand, he has called *In Xanadu* a homage to Byron's *The Road to Oxiana*, which he describes as his favorite travel book. Like Byron, Dalrymple's technique is to compile a mosaic of anecdote and incident, present and past, with a mordant eye for the ironic. He has a keen ear as well as eye, and steadily records sights, sounds, and dialogue in his ever-present stock of notebooks—35 of them on his journey for *From the Holy Mountain*.

Similarly, the essays that make up *The Age of Kali* form a mosaic of images described by the author himself as somewhat grim. Composed over a decade of residence and travel, they focus on many of the unattractive aspects of India and its neighbors, Pakistan and Sri Lanka, such as violence, crime, and political corruption. Many of those whom Dalrymple interviewed fatalistically attributed these woes to living in the "Kali Yug," the fourth epoch of Hindu cosmology, a time of advancing "strife, corruption, darkness, and disintegration," which provided the book's title. Despite attracting some criticism for its strong focus on the anarchic and, in the case of suttee (the ritual burning of widows), on the infrequent, *The Age of Kali* succeeds in depicting a region struggling to reconcile tradition with modernity, and it became another critical and commercial success.

Living in England with a young family, Dalrymple turned his hand to the writing of documentaries for television; six episodes of *Stones of the Raj* (1997) and three of *Indian Journeys* (2000) drew upon his favorite themes. Whether following the Hindu pilgrimage to the source of the Ganges in the Himalayas, retracing St. Thomas's legendary mission to bring Christianity to Southern India, or simply exploring Delhi, Dalrymple deftly blended history and travel. After abandoning a similar project based on *From the Holy Mountain*, perhaps because of obstacles to filming in countries whose governments the book portrayed in a bad light, Dalrymple announced that his fifth book, *White Mughals*, would deal with eccentric Englishmen who, sharing his passion for India, adopted native ways to a degree deemed unseemly. Although this may herald a change of direction, Dalrymple's first four books have already secured his reputation as a travel writer.

MERRILL DISTAD

### Biography

Born in Edinburgh, 20 March 1965. Brought up in Scotland. Attended Ampleforth College, Yorkshire, until 1983; Senior History Scholar, Trinity College, Cambridge University, 1984–1987; MA, 1992. Traveled from Jerusalem to China in Marco Polo's footsteps, 1986. Lived in Delhi, 1989–1994. Began journey in Moschos's footsteps, June 1994. Feature writer for the *Independent Magazine*, 1988–1989, and India correspondent for the *Sunday Correspondent*, 1990–1991. Contributor to *Condé Nast Traveler, Granta, Islands Magazine, New Statesman, Observer, Spectator, Sunday Telegraph Magazine, Sunday Times Magazine, Tatler*, and *Times Literary Supplement*. Wrote and presented *Stones of the Raj* for television, 1997, and *Indian Journeys* for the BBC, 2000. Married the artist and illustrator of his books, Olivia Fraser, 1991: two sons and one daughter. *Yorkshire Post* Best First Book Award, 1990; Thomas Cook Travel Book Award, 1994. Elected youngest Fellow of the Royal Society of Literature, 1993; Fellow of the Royal Geographical Society, 1993, and of the Royal Asiatic Society, 1998.

### References and Further Reading


Dalrymple, William, *In Xanadu: A Quest*, 1989.
Dalrymple, William, *City of Djinns: A Year in Delhi*, 1993.
Dalrymple, William, "Beyond Turkman Gate," "Breaking the Fast," "The Other Raj," and "A Sufi Spring," in *Travelers' Tales: India*, edited by James O'Reilly and Larry Habegger, 1995.
Dalrymple, William, *Stones of the Raj*, television scripts, 1997.
Dalrymple, William, *From the Holy Mountain: A Journey in the Shadow of Byzantium*, 1997; as *From the Holy Mountain: A Journey among the Christians of the Middle East*, 1998.
Dalrymple, William, *The Age of Kali: Indian Travels and Encounters*, 1998; as *At the Court of the Fish-Eyed Goddess: Travels in the Indian Subcontinent*, 1998.
Dalrymple, William, foreword to *Sacred India*, by Masood Hayat et al., 1999.
Dalrymple, William, "Shiva's Matted Locks," "City of Djinns," and "Doubting Thomas," for *Indian Journeys*, television scripts, 2000.
Dalrymple, William, *White Mughals*, 2002.


## DAMASCUS

Damascus is too significant a place for any reasonably sensitive writer ever to feel at home. All the good writing about the city has in it a groping reverence—an acknowledgement that the essence of the city cannot be distilled. "Whether you ride to Damascus by a short cut or by a high road," wrote Gertrude Bell, "it is always further away than any known place."

For all writers it is first of all a desert city, but a desert city with gardens and clear water, and therefore holy. To the Prophet, Damascus was an earthly paradise. To Alexander Kinglake (1844), Damascus was "a city of hidden palaces, of copses, and gardens, and fountains, and bubbling streams. The juice of her life is the gushing and ice-cold torrent that tumbles from the snowy sides of Anti-Lebanon." Sand, water, greenery, palaces within palaces, and silent eyes behind every door: these are the recurring alchemical elements in the literature of Damascus.

Damascus is very, very old; no one knows how old. Certainly there were people there in the third millennium BCE. It flits mistily in and out of the Old Testament, always with a sense of immense remoteness. Colin Thubron (1967) notes that "Damascus arrived at the gates of classical history so hoary with centuries that her foundation was already traced to giants among men." Paul's conversion on the road to Damascus made the city a metaphor and gave it a significance for Westerners that it has never shaken off. It was a holy city for the crusaders, as well as a logistically important one, but despite attacks in 1113 and 1129, they never took it. This added to the established legend of Damascus's inaccessibility.

Traveling there was a lot easier for Arabs than for Westerners: Mukaddasi (fl. tenth century) thought that the fountains did not make up for the squalor. Ibn Jubayr (1145–1217) rhapsodized over the city, but found Damascenes pretentious. Ibn Battuta (1304–1368(?)), who had seen more of the world than anyone else, was enraptured. He had a son by a Damascene woman, and however bad Damascus was, it was bound to be better than most of the places he had visited.

There has long been a substantial Jewish community in Damascus, and throughout the Middle Ages Jewish travelers visited the city. They were a quiet lot, scared of going public, apart from Benjamin of Tudela (fl. twelfth century) who arrived from Naverre in 1160 and left a beautifully observed, whimsical account of the medieval city. The fourteenth and fifteenth centuries saw few Western travelers. The ubiquitous and colorful Sir John Mandeville (fl. fourteenth century) apparently got there; so did Frescobaldi (fl. c. 1384), Johannes Schiltberger (c. 1380–(?), and Bertrandon de la Brocquière (fl. fifteenth century). The German knight Arnold von Harff (fl. late fifteenth–early sixteenth century) arrived in 1499 and wrote a splendidly illustrated and wildly exaggerated guidebook to Christian Damascus.

From the early sixteenth century onward merchant adventurers, particularly Italians, began to exploit the Levant, and contacts in Damascus were of course crucial. The merchants themselves had things other than books on their minds, but they opened up the country to romantics, thrill-seekers, and articulate gypsies like William Biddulph (fl. c. 1600), Ludovico di Varthema (before 1470–1517), and Thomas Coryate (1577(?)–1617). Contemporaries in Damascus, but coincident in nothing else, were the rough and smelly Scotsman, William Lithgow (1582–1645) and the exhaustingly refined, overeducated, and probably overscented Italian, Pietro della Valle (1586–1652). They both reached the city in 1614. Lithgow, whose ears had been cut off by the enraged brothers of a wench with whom he had been caught *in flagrante*, was a refugee from convention, but had enough European sensibility to be appalled by the Turks and wooed into poetry by Damascus, "the most beautiful place in all Asia." Della Valle was wooed into poetry by almost everything, and that included Damascus. He did some serious academic sightseeing there, bought some Hebrew manuscripts, and wrote some lovely romantic prose. Thomas Coryate took the cosiness and integrity of a Somerset alehouse with him wherever he went. He was contented enough in Damascus, which says nothing other than that he would have been a tremendous traveling companion anywhere.

The Portuguese priest, Frei Sebastião Manrique (fl. seventeenth century), arrived in Damascus in 1630 and was lucky to leave alive. His ability to describe the place was hampered by two things: his abysmal Spanish and the fact that most of his time there was spent in a cellar in hiding from brigands who believed that he was loaded with priceless gems from Constantinople. Diligent, thorough, and dull were the two main seventeenth-century travelers from the West, the Frenchman Jean de Thévenot (1633–1667), who wrote a dowdy travel guide bristling with footnotes, and the English clergyman Henry Maundrell (fl. c. 1697), whose was briefer but just as gray. These two accounts were conflated and spiced up by "The late Charles Thompson Esq.," who could write but not travel. His account of his stay in Damascus is the best of the seventeenth-century accounts. It is also complete fraud: he never went there.

Damascus had been overdescribed by the end of the seventeenth century. In the eighteenth century it was measured, weighed, and its history systematized, usually wrongly, by a host of solid, lantern-jawed worthies like Count Volney (1757–1820), Richard Pococke (1704–1765), and Carsten Niebuhr (1733–1815). Thus, when the curtain rose on nineteenth-century Damascus, the set had been painted well. Damascus had been drenched with superlatives, but it was still difficult to get there. The desert still started in the suburbs and blew into the windows if they weren't sealed properly. Some of the people who followed used Damascus as the backdrop to their own personal dramas. Their descriptions of the city were intended to throw romantic, shocking, or heroic light on their own magnificent souls. Lady Hester Stanhope (1776–1839) is the classic example. In her dubious image, and very much in her shadow, were Lamartine (1790–1869) and James Silk Buckingham (1786–1855).

"After the apotheosis of Lady Hester," writes Colin Thubron, "there was little left for a romantic to do." She certainly took the wind out of all aspirant Byronics' sails, but people with personalities of their own found plenty to do. Kinglake was the best of them. He found Damascus to be "safer than Oxford." "There is nothing in all Damascus," said a friar to Kinglake, "half so well worth seeing as our cellars." And Kinglake seems to have agreed. He went

> to see and admire the long range of liquid treasure that [the friar] and his brethren had laid up for themselves on earth. And these, I soon found, were not as the treasures of the miser that lie in unprofitable disuse' for day by day, and hour by hour, the golden juice ascended from the dark recesses of the cellar to the uppermost brains of the friars. Dear old fellows! In the midst of that solemn land, their Christian laughter rang loudly and merrily.

Published in the same year as *Eothen* was *The Modern Syrians* (1844) by Andrew Paton. Paton was an intelligent romantic, intoxicated by the Near East, who wrote beautifully and penetrated deeply into ordinary Damascene life.

Probably the best guidebook to Damascus yet written was *Five Years in Damascus* (1855) by Josias Porter. Porter was a master of many moods, handling ideas as deftly as landscapes. His book combines serious historical and geographical scholarship with highly readable accounts of his wanderings, and is illustrated with whimsical drawings of locals and landmarks. The orientalist veil, which hung over most previous and subsequent accounts of the city, was penetrated by Mrs Mackintosh, who lived for seven years there and produced *Damascus and its People* (1883), a sympathetic set of sketches of ordinary Damascene life.

Smaller writers then bridge the gap to the twentieth century, and to the three great prose-poets of Damascus: Gertrude Bell (1868–1926), Freya Stark (1893–1993), and Colin Thubron (1939–). Damascus features prominently in Bell's *The Desert and the Sown* (1907) and in her *Letters* (1927). She was of course supremely well connected, but she used her connections not only to get to every diplomatic cocktail party, but to procure support for her intimate and magnificently self-confident journeys. She was passionate, poetic, and magnetic. The passion and the magnetism come through best in her books; the poetry best in her letters. Freya Stark's *Letters from Syria* (1942) are among the best things she ever wrote. Lawrence Durrell said that what lent Freya Stark's books their poetic density was that "as she covers the ground outwardly, so she advances towards fresh interpretations of herself inwardly." When this is not tedious onanism, it is definitively good travel writing. What makes Freya Stark great is the unusual intimacy of the correlation between geographical movement and personal discovery, the fact that she never waves her soul intrusively in her readers' faces, and the fact that she writes like an aphoristic angel, drilled in Wordsworth, but slightly embarrassed by her own fluency. Colin Thubron's *Mirror to Damascus* (1967) is a tremendous, evocative biography of the city through its ages. Conversational, learned, and anecdotal, it is the gate through which most thoughtful modern travelers enter Damascus.

CHARLES FOSTER

## References and Further Reading

Anonymous, *Familiar Letters from a Gentleman at Damascus, to His Sister in London . . . Also an Account of the Lives, Travels, Miracles, Sufferings and Deaths of Our Blessed Saviour, and His Apostles*, 1750.

Anonymous [C.G.], *A Fortnight's Tour amongst the Arabs on Mount Lebanon, Including a Visit to Damascus, Ba'albek, etc.*, 1876.

Bell, Gertrude, *The Desert and the Sown*, 1907.

Bell, Gertrude, *Letters of Gertrude Bell*, edited by Lady Bell, 1927.

Biddulph, William, *The Trauels of Certaine Englishmen into Africa, Asia, Troy, Bythinia, Thracia and to the Blacke Sea; and into Syria, Cilicia, Pisidia, Mesopotamia, Damascus, Canaan, Galile, Samaria, Iudea, Palestina, Ierusalem, Iericho, and to the Red Sea, and to Sundry Other Places: Begunne in the Yeere of Iubile 1600, and by Some of Them Finished in This Yeere 1608—the Others Not Yet Returned*, 1609; facsimile, 1968.

Buckingham, James Silk, *Travels among the Arab Tribes Inhabiting the Countries East of Syria and Palestine; Including a Journey from Nazareth to the Mountains beyond the Dead Sea, and from Thence through the Plains of the Hauran to Bozra, Damascus and Aleppo; with an Appendix, Containing a Refutation of Certain Unfounded Calumnies Industriously Circulated against the Author*, 1825.

Byron, Robert, *The Road to Oxiana*, 1937.

Coryate, Thomas, "Master Thomas Coryates Travels to, and Observations in Constantinople and Other Places in the Way Thither," in *Purchas His Pilgrimes*, edited by Samuel Purchas, 4 vols., 1625; reprinted as *Hakluytus Posthumus*, 20 vols., 1905–1907.

Farman, Samuel, *Damascus, and Some of Its Recollections*, 1857.

Frescobaldi, Leonardo, Giorgio Gucci, and Simone Sigoli, *Visit to the Holy Places of Egypt, Sinai, Palestine, and Syria, in 1384*, translated by Theophilus Bellorini and Eugene Hoade, 1948.

Green, John, *A Journey from Aleppo to Damascus, with a Description of Those Two Cities and the Neighbouring Parts of Syria: To Which Is Added, an Account of the Maronites Inhabiting Mount Libanus . . . also the Surprising Adventures and Tragical End of Mostafa, a Turk*, 1736.

Harff, Arnold von, *The Pilgrimage of Arnold von Harff . . . Which He Accomplished in the Years 1496 to 1499*, translated by Malcolm Letts, 1946.

Harvey, Annie Jane, *Our Cruise in the Claymore, with a Visit to Damascus and the Lebanon*, 1861.

Hogg, Edward, *Visit to Alexandria, Damascus, and Jerusalem, during the Successful Campaign of Ibrahim Pasha*, 2 vols., 1835.

Ibn Battuta, *Travels in Asia and Africa 1325–1354*, translated by H.A.R. Gibb, 1929.

Ibn Jubayr, *The Travels of Ibn Jubayr*, translated by R.J.C. Broadhurst, 1952.

Jones, George, *Excursion to Cairo, Jerusalem, Damascus and Balbec, from the United States Ship, Delaware, during Her Recent Cruise*, 1836.

Kelman, John, *From Damascus to Palmyra*, 1908.

Kinglake, Alexander William, *Eothen; or, Traces of Travel Brought Home from the East*, 1844.

Kinnear, John G., *Cairo, Petra and Damascus, in 1839; with Remarks on the Government of Mehemet Ali, and on the Present Prospects of Syria*, 1841.

La Brocquière, Bertrandon de, *The Travels of Bertrandon de La Brocquière to Palestine, and His Return from Jerusalem Overland to France during the Years 1432 and 1433*, translated by Thomas Jones, 1807.

Lear, Edward, *Journals of a Landscape Painter in Albania, Illyria &c*, 2nd edition, 1852.

Lithgow, William, *Discourse of a Peregrination in Europe, Asia, and Affricke*, 1614; facsimile, 1971.

Mackintosh, Mrs., *Damascus and Its People: Sketches of Modern Life in Syria*, 1883.

Mandeville, John, *The Voiage and Travaile of Sir John Maundevile, Which Treateth of the Way to Hierusalem, and of Marvayles of Inde, with other Ilands and Countryes*, 1725.

Manrique, Sebastião, *Itinerario de las missiones que hizo el Padre F. Sebastião Manrique Religioso Eremita de S. Agustin Missionario Apostolico treze años en varias Missiones del India Oriental*, 1649; as *Travels of Fray Sebastien Manrique 1629–1643*, edited by C. Eckford Luard, 2 vols., 1927.

Margoliouth, D.S., *Cairo, Jerusalem and Damascus: Three Chief Cities of the Egyptian Sultans*, 1907.

Martineau, Harriet, *Eastern Life, Present and Past*, 3 vols., 1848.
Maundrell, Henry, *A Journey from Aleppo to Jerusalem at Easter, AD 1697*, 1703; facsimile of the 1810 edition, with an introduction by David Howell, 1963.
Mukkadasi, *Description of Syria, Including Palastine*, translated by Guy Le Strange, 1886.
Niebuhr, Carsten, *Beschreibung von Arabien*, 1772; abridged edition as *Travels through Arabia*, vol. 2, translated by Robert Heron, 1792.
Paton, Andrew Archibald, *The Modern Syrians; or, Native Society in Damascus, Aleppo, and the Mountains of the Druses, from Notes Made in Those Parts during the Years 1841, 2, 3, by an Oriental Student*, 1844.
Pococke, Richard, *A Description of the East, and Some Other Countries*, 1743–1745.
Porter, Josias Leslie, *Five Years in Damascus . . . with Travels and Researches in Palmyra, Lebanon and the Hauran*, 2 vols., 1855.
Richardson, Robert, *Travels along the Mediterranean and Parts Adjacent . . . Extending as far as the Second Cataract of the Nile, Jerusalem, Damascus, Balbec &c*, 2 vols., 1822.
Schiltberger, Johannes, *The Bondage and Travels of Johann Schiltberger, a Native of Bavaria, in Europe, Asia and Africa, 1396–1427*, translated by J. Buchanan Telfer, 1879; reprinted, 1970.
Sinclair, Olivia, *Impressions of Cairo, Jerusalem, and Damascus*, 1876.
Stanhope, Hester, *Memoirs of the Lady Hester Stanhope, as Related by Herself in Conversations with Her Physician*, 3 vols., 1845.
Stanhope, Hester, *Travels of Lady Hester Stanhope, Forming the Completion of Her Memoirs, Narrated by Her Physician*, 3 vols., 1846.
Stark, Freya, *Letters from Syria*, 1942.
Stewart, Frederick William Robert, Viscount Castlereagh, *A Journey to Damascus: Through Egypt, Nubia, Arabia Petraea, Palestine and Syria*, 2 vols., 1847.
Thévenot, Jean de, *Relation d'un voyage fait au Levant*, 3 vols.: 1664–1684; as *The Travels of Monsieur de Thevenot into the Levant*, 1687.
Thompson, Charles, *The Travels of the Late Charles Thompson, Esq; Containing His Observations on France, Italy, Turkey in Europe, the Holy Land, Arabia, Egypt, and Many Other Parts of the World*, 1744.
Thubron, Colin, *Mirror to Damascus*, 1967.
Valle, Pietro della, *Viaggi di Pietro della Valle il Pellegrino*, 4 vols., 1650–1663.
Volney, Constantin François, Comte de, *Voyage en Syrie et en Égypte*, 2 vols., 1787; as *Travels through Syria and Egypt*, 1787.

*See also* **Levant**

## DAMPIER, WILLIAM (1651–1715) *English Buccaneer, Explorer, and Travel Writer*

It is hard to overestimate William Dampier's contribution to British travel writing. In the eighteenth century, voyages and travels were the second most popular form of writing among the reading public, after theology: it was Dampier, more than any other individual, who brought the genre so hugely into vogue. His writings signal a new spirit among British travelers, marked by a new emphasis on accurate observation and detailed description. Seen in this light, Dampier inaugurates a tradition of scientific exploration that leads to James Cook in the late eighteenth century. Dampier also stimulated the literary as much as the scientific imagination of the period: the novel, in English especially, owes a huge debt to this seminal traveler.

The work that made Dampier's name was *A New Voyage round the World* (1697). The *New Voyage* was an instant success, going through three editions in its first year, and two further editions by 1705. Thereafter it features prominently in many of the collections of travel literature published in the eighteenth and early nineteenth centuries. It describes a 12-year period during which Dampier lived what he termed a "loose, roving way of life." This life began in 1679, when Dampier joined a group of privateers at Negril Bay, Jamaica. These privateers, or buccaneers, were in practice little more than pirates. Dampier and his comrades lived precariously by harrying Spanish shipping in the Caribbean and South Seas, and by raiding Spanish settlements in the New World. Periodically switching ships and captains, Dampier crossed and recrossed the Isthmus of America (present-day Panama) on foot, rounded Cape Horn, sailed up and down the Pacific coast of South America, and lived for a short period in Virginia. Eventually, he crossed the Pacific to Southeast Asia via the Philippines and Australia. At the Nicobar Islands, northwest of Sumatra, he broke with the privateers, embarked in an open boat for Sumatra, and sailed to England, where he arrived in 1691.

These events provide the framework for Dampier's *New Voyage*, and were an important part of its appeal. Dampier's narrative has its origins in the buccaneer literature that was so popular in the late seventeenth and early eighteenth centuries. Into this material, moreover, Dampier has transposed some of the conventions of spiritual autobiography often found in seventeenth-century shipwreck narrative: thus the voyage from the Nicobar Islands is fashioned into a scene of crisis and repentance. These elements, however, were not the most novel feature of the book. Dedicated to the president of the recently founded Royal Society, the *New Voyage* bears witness throughout to that society's Baconian outlook, which stressed the accumulation of empirical data. Inserted into the main action of the narrative are many passages of a more static and descriptive nature. These relay an abundance of ethnographical, zoological, and botanical data, in a prose that is precise yet homespun. Although writing before Linnaean classification, Dampier displays a remarkable observational rigor. "I speak it experimentally," he declares (*New Voyage*); he means that he is recording what he has proven with his own senses. Often this

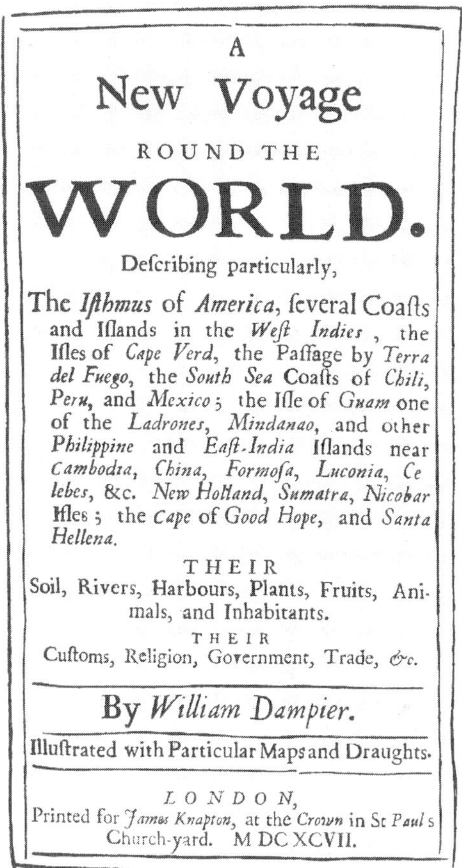

A

New Voyage

ROUND THE

WORLD.

Deſcribing particularly,

The *Iſthmus* of *America*, ſeveral Coaſts and Iſlands in the *Weſt Indies*, the Iſles of *Cape Verd*, the Paſſage by *Terra del Fuego*, the *South Sea* Coaſts of *Chili*, *Peru*, and *Mexico*; the Iſle of *Guam* one of the *Ladrones*, *Mindanao*, and other *Philippine* and *Eaſt-India* Iſlands near *Cambodia*, *China*, *Formoſa*, *Luconia*, *Celebes*, &c. *New Holland*, *Sumatra*, *Nicobar* Iſles; the *Cape* of *Good Hope*, and *Santa Hellena*.

THEIR

Soil, Rivers, Harbours, Plants, Fruits, Animals, and Inhabitants.

THEIR

Cuſtoms, Religion, Government, Trade, *&c.*

By *William Dampier*.

Illuſtrated with Particular Maps and Draughts.

*LONDON*,

Printed for *James Knapton*, at the *Crown* in St *Paul's* Church-yard. M DC XCVII.

*Title-page of the first edition of "A New Voyage Round the World"*

Title page of the first edition of William Dampier's *A New Voyage round the World*, 1697. *Courtesy of Senate House, University of London Library.*

involved no small degree of risk or discomfort, and consequently a rather touching vulnerability runs through Dampier's writing. We learn that eating guava fruit affects the bowels, while prickly pears color the urine red. To cure a fever, Dampier is buried up to the neck in sand; to cure the dropsy, he considers a local remedy, pulverized alligator testicles. Luckily for the alligators—and perhaps for Dampier himself—there were none to be found nearby. These accounts of flora and fauna, and of the practices of other cultures, provided a wealth of data for scientists and for subsequent travelers: William Bligh, for example, begins the narrative of his ill-fated voyage with Dampier's description of the breadfruit.

More such information came in a second volume entitled *Voyages and Descriptions, Part II*, published in 1699. This work falls into three parts. The first describes in more detail the Southeast Asian leg of the earlier voyage around the world, while the second recounts Dampier's first years in the Caribbean, from 1674 to 1676. The third, a "Discourse on Winds," is an outstanding piece of meteorological observation, quoted in textbooks as recently as 1942.

However engaging his authorial persona, in life Dampier was clearly a troublesome character. In 1699 he captained a naval expedition to Australia. In exploratory terms the voyage was successful: Dampier visited Australia, New Guinea, New Britain, and New Ireland, and subsequently published *A Voyage to New Holland* (which appeared in two parts, in 1703 and 1709). This work contains much useful information, but lacks the zest of the *New Voyage*. In other ways, however, the voyage was less happy: Dampier was later court-martialed for his treatment of his lieutenant. Similar tensions marred Dampier's subsequent command, a privateering venture that embarked for the South Seas in 1703. William Funnell, who served on the voyage (as mate according to himself, as steward according to Dampier), subsequently wrote a hostile account of Dampier, who responded with an angry, self-vindicating pamphlet: such acrimony is not uncommon in the publications of privateers in this period.

It was on this latter voyage that Alexander Selkirk asked to be marooned on one of the islands of Juan Fernández, off the coast of present-day Chile. Dampier duly obliged, and Selkirk survived alone until 1709 (when he was rescued by a vessel in which, ironically, Dampier was serving as pilot). It was Selkirk's story, together with an account in Dampier's *New Voyage* of a Mosquito Indian who was similarly abandoned on Juan Fernández, that provided the raw material for Daniel Defoe's *Robinson Crusoe* (1719). The travel-writing vogue Dampier inspired also stimulated another fictionalized travel account, Jonathan Swift's *Gulliver's Travels* (1726), which opens with Gulliver referring to "my cousin *Dampier*." Later in the century, Romantic writers such as Wordsworth and Coleridge similarly drew upon Dampier for incidents and imagery. Such borrowings remind us that while Dampier's fame rests primarily on his status as an early scientific explorer, we must not underestimate the extent to which his *New Voyage* fascinated his age more generally. It reflects—and helped to bring about—a new outlook in Britain, and in time a new relationship with the wider world.

CARL THOMPSON

### Biography

Born in East Coker, Somerset, September 1651 or 8 June 1652 (sources vary). Orphaned, 1667. Began career as seaman, 1668. Fought in Dutch War, 1673. Sailed to Jamaica to take up post as assistant manager of a plantation, 1674. Lived and worked in the logging business in Honduras, c. 1675–1678. Returned to England briefly and married Judith (about whom nothing is known other than her name), 1678. Engaged in buccaneering in the Caribbean and South Seas, 1679–1691. Crossed the Pacific to Southeast Asia, reaching Australia, 1688. Returned to England via South Africa, 1688–1691. Captained *Roebuck* on exploratory voyage to Australia, 1699–1701. Court-martialed for treatment of lieutenant on that voyage, 1702. Captained controversial privateering voyage to South Seas, 1703–1704; several crew members, including Alexander Selkirk, marooned on the Juan Fernández Islands off the coast of Chile. Unable to find a command of his own, served as pilot on Woodes Rogers's privateering voyage to the south seas, 1708–1711. Died in London, March 1715.

### References and Further Reading

Dampier, William, *A New Voyage round the World*, 1697.
Dampier, William, *Voyages and Descriptions, Part II*, 1699; edited by N.M. Penzer, Clennell Wilkinson, and A.C. Bell, 1931.
Dampier, William, *A Voyage to New Holland &c. in the Year 1699*, Part 1, 1703; Part 2, 1709; edited by James Spencer, 1981.
Dampier, William, *Captain's Dampier's Vindication of his Voyage to the South Seas*, 1707.
Dampier, William, *Dampier's Voyages*, edited by John Masefield (contains all of Dampier), 2 vols., 1906.
Dampier, William, *William Dampier: Buccaneer Explorer*, edited and with an introduction by Gerald Norris, 1994.

*See also* **Circumnavigation Narratives; Pirates and Bandits**

## DANTE ALIGHIERI (1265–1321) *Italian Poet and Prose Writer*

With his poetic masterpiece *The Divine Comedy*, one of the founding texts of the Western literary tradition, Dante Alighieri expressed a powerful synthesis of the Middle Age theological beliefs and visions that informed the motif of the spiritual journey and put it firmly at the center of the Christian conception of life. Dante's travel writing therefore documents an *itinerarium mentis in Deum* (the journey of the mind into God) where man is a pilgrim (*homo viator*) who is simply passing through earth in his divine quest for God.

Originally entitled simply *La Commedia* (the adjective "divina" was added to the 1555 Venetian edition), Dante's masterpiece was probably begun around 1304, when he had already been exiled from Florence for his unyielding desire for the city's independence from the papacy, and was finished just before his death in 1321. Its title is explained by Dante in his 1316 letter to Cangrande della Scala with respect to content and style. The poem develops from harsh and terrible events to a peaceful ending (and this positive development is what distinguishes, in Dante's view, comedy from tragedy), and its style is intermediate between the high tragic style and the low elegiac one. *The Divine Comedy* was written in *lingua volgare* (gross language), which had its base in Dante's native Tuscan. Dante opposed the assumptions that prescribed Latin as the only appropriate literary language and advocated, instead, the use of a courtly Italian enriched with the best of every spoken dialect.

The allegorical poem is divided into three parts, according to a symbolic use of numbers that is one of the recurring patterns of *La Commedia: Inferno* (Hell), *Purgatorio* (Purgatory), and *Paradiso* (Paradise). It chronicles Dante's journey in the Beyond. To redeem himself from a condition of sin and spiritual danger, the protagonist begins his journey toward spiritual salvation by descending into Hell, a funnel-shaped pit made of nine circles situated just under Jerusalem. Led by the Latin poet Virgil, Dante arrives in Hell at the center of the earth, where Lucifer is nailed. Following a subterranean path he reemerges in the Southern Hemisphere, and finds himself on the beach of an island at the antipodes of Jerusalem. The high mountain of Purgatory (composed of seven circles) springs up from the beach. The mountain was originally created by the fall of Lucifer. Dante climbs it and arrives at Eden, from which he begins his ascension through Paradise toward the Empyrean and the final contemplation of God, accompanied first by Beatrice and then by St. Bernard of Clairvaux. The characters Dante meets on his spiritual quest are taken mainly from classical history or mythology and from recent and contemporary Italian history, including Dante's personal friends and political enemies.

The cosmology of the work is firmly based on the Aristotelian-Ptolemaic system as conceptualized by the scholastic philosophy (and by Dante himself in his work *Convivio*), even though he regarded the church of his time as a "harlot" no longer serving God and was therefore frequently considered a heretic. The earth is at the center of the universe and nine other spheres turn around it. These are all included in the tenth sphere, the Empyrean, which does not move as it is the seat of God. Only the Northern Hemisphere of the earth is populated; its borders are the Pillars of Hercules (the Straits of Gibraltar) on the west side and the river Ganges on the eastern side and its center is Jerusalem. Dante's journey highlights man's crucial and intermediate position on the earth: he is both material (body) and spiritual (soul), and being on the earth he is close to the degraded center as well as surrounded by the skies leading to the Empyrean. Such a position displays the main tension of the Christian world: will man follow his own material nature in a downfall leading him to the corrupt center or will he follow his soul toward God? Dante's journey becomes a source of knowledge: Dante, the living historical character, is able to grasp the absolute or religious dimension of reality that is always the ultimate meaning of the reality he experiences as a man.

Man's desire to pursue "virtue and knowledge high" can, however, lead him astray when he is prompted to transgress the world's established frontiers and boundaries. This is very clearly the case of Ulysses (*Inferno*, Canto XXVI). At the end of his adventurous life, Ulysses decides to launch himself into the extreme quest for knowledge, which will bring him "to the strait pass, where Hercules ordain'd/The boundaries not to be o'erstepp'd by man" (lines 106–107). In his journey through "the unpeopled world," Ulysses breaches the natural and divine boundaries and therefore must be punished: "Joy seized us straight; But soon to mourning changed. From the new land A whirlwind sprung, and at her foremost side Did strike the vessel. Thrice it whirl'd her round With all the waves; the fourth time lifted up The poop, and sank the prow: so fate decreed: And over us the booming billow closed" (lines 129–135).

Overstepping the frontier is a "witless flight," a concept that is reiterated throughout the poem and closely associates the notion of "frontier" with "prohibition," stressing the importance of staying within the known and shared beliefs. On this point, *La Commedia* is connected to several other medieval literary texts such as the Arthurian romances of Chrétien de Troyes, the *Alexandreis* by Gautier de Châtillon, and the *Libro de Alexandre*, as D'Arco Silvio Avalle has demonstrated (*Modelli semiologici nella Commedia di Dante*, Milano: Bompiani, 1975).

Luca Prono

### Biography

Born in Florence into a family of minor Florentine aristocracy, 1265. Little known of his early life; grew up in Florence. Studied philosophy and literature. Probably attended the University of Bologna. Met Beatrice Portinari, subject of his first poetical work, *La Vita Nuova* (1283–1295), 1274. Married Gemma di Maretto Donati, c. 1285: at least four children. Occupied several official positions in Florence, 1295–1302. Exiled from Florence for political reasons, 1302. Traveled around a number of aristocratic courts in northern Italy, including those at Verona (1303; 1317); Bologna (c. 1304–1305); Lucca (1306–1308); Ravenna (1317–1321). Wrote *De Vulgari Eloquentia* (1303–1305), *Il Convivio* (1304–1307), *De Monarchia* (1312–1313 and 1317), and *La Commedia* (1307–1321). Died of malaria in Ravenna, 14 September 1321.

### References and Further Reading

Dante Alighieri, *La Commedia*, written c. 1307–1321; as *The Divine Comedy*, translated by John Ciardi, 1977; many other translations.

## DANUBE RIVER

Arrian, the second-century Greek historian and philosopher, provides one of the earliest literary references to the Danube in his *Anabasis* (describing the campaigns of Alexander the Great) when he tells us that Alexander made an expedition through what is now Bulgaria to subjugate the tribes that might otherwise have posed a threat to his rear when he set off to conquer Asia. He reached the Ister (Danube) and decided to cross it to demonstrate his power to the Getae and force their submission but, as Arrian says, Alexander had a longing to cross to the other side. Although it is no more than a passing reference to this great river, it serves to emphasize how, even then, the Danube was seen as both barrier and highway.

The Danube has always been regarded as a military river, and literary references to it occur frequently in books describing the endless wars and campaigns along its banks or the exploits of great military commanders such as Marlborough or Napoleon. Because the Danube divided the Romans from the barbarians and the Ottomans from the Hapsburgs, it has long been regarded as an imperial boundary.

The river rises in the Black Forest of southern Germany and to trace its course is to sense half the history of Europe. The river runs over 2,840 kilometers through Germany and Austria, cutting Hungary in half; another 500 kilometers runs through Croatia and Serbia before reaching the Iron Gates, the gorge now submerged by a great reservoir. In its final broad stretch, the river is more than a mile wide, as it marks the boundary between Bulgaria and Romania. Strabo, another Greek whose life (c. 64 BCE–c. 19 CE) spanned the formal emergence of the Roman empire, describes the Danube Basin and Black Sea in his *Geography* (book 7). The Danube delta is Europe's greatest bird sanctuary, where it is possible to meander in a small boat through 4,403 square kilometers of wetland, willows, and lagoons whose egrets and other birds and unique wildlife make up one of Europe's last remaining sanctuaries (Arnold, 1989).

Rome's influence on the Danube and the river's influence on Rome were equally profound. During the reign of Augustus (27 BCE–14 CE) the territories bounding the Danube from Switzerland to the Black Sea were annexed to the empire, and under his successors a system of roadways was created to cover these Danube lands. The river then became the frontier of Rome for four centuries. Emperor Trajan built a great bridge

Typical seventeenth-century Danube craft negotiate a river hazard (from Edward Browne's "Journey from Colen to Vienna" in his second travel book *An Account of Several Travels*, 1677). *Courtesy of the Travellers Club, London; Bridgeman Art Library, agent.*

across the Danube at the Iron Gates so that his army could invade Dacia (Romania) and annex it to Rome, and his name is still celebrated in Romanian street names. The philosopher-emperor Marcus Aurelius spent half his reign (161–180) on the Danube with his army facing the barbarians who threatened Rome; he is said to have composed his *Meditations* while on watch with his troops. A Roman fleet patrolled the river, and Roman strongholds later became great European capitals: Vindobona (Vienna), Aquincum (Budapest), Singidunum (Belgrade). The *Notitia Dignitatum*, a fourth-century Roman register of officials, describes the lower and middle Danube as guarded by armies and providing a shield for Italy. By the end of the fourth century, however, the Danube was no longer able to hold the barbarians at bay, and their coming signaled the breakup of the Roman empire.

The legend of the Nibelungs relates equally to the Rhine and the Danube: the Nibelungs followed the Danube to the court of King Etzel (Attila) and their destruction; the epic poem of *Das Nibelungenlied* (encompassing the story of Siegfried), which would later inspire Wagner to compose the Ring Cycle, was written in Austria in the thirteenth century. Charlemagne saw the Danube as the farthest extent of his empire and built fortresses such as Wurfenstein along the river. Richard I, the "Lionheart," returning from the Third Crusade, was obliged to pass through Austria in disguise because he had offended Leopold V, Duke of Austria, but he was recognized in Vienna and imprisoned by his enemy in Durnstein Castle on the Danube. This event gave rise to one of the best medieval legends, that of the troubadour Blondel searching for Richard; the story is told in the thirteenth-century *Narrative of the Minstrel of Reims*.

Then came the Ottoman Turks: when in 1396 they captured Nikopolis, the Bulgarian city due north of Plevna, which commands the lower Danube, their victory heralded 500 years of Turkish rule. It was at Nikopolis that Wulfila translated the Greek Bible into Gothic, a beginning of German literature. The river became the frontier between the Ottoman empire and the Hapsburgs, the divide between Islam and Christianity. Under the Hapsburg empress Maria Theresa (r. 1740–1780) the river ceased to be a barrier between two empires and reverted to being a highway. In 1830 a riverboat made the first known trip from Vienna to Budapest. Gradually the river came to be recognized as an international waterway, and in the 1920s an International Danube Commission was created to control navigation along the river from Ulm in southern Germany to the Black Sea.

War was never long absent from the river's banks. Marlborough's greatest victory was at Blenheim (Blindheim) on the Danube, and Napoleon's campaigns brought him to the Danube, about which he had a good deal to say. Napoleon wrote of his defeat at Aspern-Essling: "It was not my fault that the Danube rose sixteen feet in one night. But for that, I should have finished off the Hapsburgs once for all." Referring to the river as a symbol of imagination, Napoleon also said: "It is like the Danube: at the source of the river one can cross it in a bound." The Danube was again a major theater of fighting during World War II when the Russians advanced into Europe.

The twentieth century saw the Danube become popular with travel writers. Patrick Leigh Fermor, in his two books *A Time of Gifts* (1977) and *Between the Woods and the Water* (1986), describes his walk across Europe as a young man in 1933 and 1934, much of it along the Danube. Although he wrote his books later in life, well after he took his original notes, he describes encounters in Germany and Austria just after Hitler came to power and provides a wonderful feel for that era. The Italian Claudio Magris traveled the length of the river in what he describes as a sentimental journey during the 1980s, and his *Danube* (1989) is a mixture of travel, politics, and history. Trost's *Die Donau* (1968) is a detailed examination of the river from end to end: scenery and music, history and politics. Arnold's *Down the Danube: From the Black Forest to the Black Sea* (1989) is a tale of walking from the Black Forest to Regensburg, travel by barges (by special arrangement with the First Danube Steamship Company) as far as Vienna, hovercraft to Bratislava, and then bus or train or walking again to the delta.

Acting as a boundary and highway for thousands of years, the Danube has also acted as a conduit for the spread of cultures: from western Europe to the east, and in the reverse direction. Three capital cities, monasteries, and castles adorn its banks, and every major European war has seen the river defended and attacked because of its strategic significance. John Buchan's World War I novel *Greenmantle* features the Danube, as its hero, Richard Hannay, makes his way behind enemy lines across Europe to Constantinople. In the Furstenberg Park in Donaueschingen a plaque reads: "Hier Entspringen die Donau." As the historian Norman Davies says: "Rivers to the geographer are the bearers of sediment and trade. To the historian they are the bearers of culture and sometimes conflict. They are like life itself." Few rivers, anywhere, have been so fought over, so traveled, and so romanticized; it may not be the Blue Danube that Johann Strauss immortalized, but it has contributed unceasingly to the growth of European history and culture.

Guy Arnold

### References and Further Reading


Arnold, Guy, *Down the Danube: From the Black Forest to the Black Sea*, 1989.

Arrian, *The Life of Alexander the Great*, translated by Aubrey de Sélincourt, 1958; also as *History of Alexander and Indica*, translated by P.A. Brunt, 2 vols., 1976–1983 (Loeb edition).

Browne, Edward, "Journey from Colen to Vienna" in *An Account of Several Travels*, 1677.

Davies, Norman, *Europe: A History*, Oxford and New York: Oxford University Press, 1996.

Fermor, Patrick Leigh, *A Time of Gifts: On Foot to Constantinople, from the Hook of Holland to the Middle Danube*, 1977.

Fermor, Patrick Leigh, *Between the Woods and the Water: On Foot to Constantinople, from the Hook of Holland: The Middle Danube to the Iron Gates*, 1986.

Klaudy, Klinga, *The Danube Bend, A Landscape Set in Time*, photographs by Andre Balla, et al., 1994.

Magris, Claudio, *Danube: A Sentimental Journey from the Source to the Black Sea*, translated from the Italian by Patrick Creagh, 1989.

Pierre, Bernard, *Le Roman du Danube*, 1987.

Strabo, *The Geography*, translated by H.L. Jones, 8 vols., 1917–1933 (Loeb edition; several reprints).

Trost, Ernst, *Die Donau: Lebenslauf eines Stromes*, 1968.


*See also* **Central Europe; Eastern Europe**

## DARWIN, CHARLES (1809–1882) *British Scientist*

Charles Robert Darwin was born into a wealthy and well-connected gentry family in the English Midlands. He began a medical education in Edinburgh before switching to divinity at Cambridge. Here Darwin cultivated his interest in natural history, and it was on the strength of this, a growing interest in geology, and his gentlemanly standing, that the Rever end J.S. Henslow, professor of botany, recommended Darwin to the Admiralty in connection with the planned voyage of HMS *Beagle* to South America. Although Darwin was to spend most of his important scientific career in rural Kentish solitude, that career was built upon *Beagle*'s voyage around the world between 1831 and 1836, which he described as "the most important event in my life."

*Beagle* was a survey vessel charged with charting and sounding the coastal waters of South America, with an eye to Britain's strategic advantage in the region; so science was inextricably linked to colonial commerce. Darwin's appointment to *Beagle* was linked closely to his social position: he was knowledgeable about natural history, but not the official ship's naturalist (a role occupied by the surgeon), and his main role was as gentleman companion to the captain, the aristocratic Robert FitzRoy.

The voyage was scheduled to be completed in two years, but in fact it lasted for five: of the 57 months *Beagle* was at sea, 42 were spent in the waters of South America. The east coast and Falkland Islands were surveyed between February 1832 and March 1834, the west coast from June 1834 to September 1835. Then, in order to take accurate longitudinal measurements with state-of-the-art chronometers, FitzRoy steered his ship to the Galapagos Islands in the South Pacific, afterward visiting in turn Tahiti, New Zealand, Australia, the Keeling Islands in the Indian Ocean, Mauritius, St. Helena, and Ascension Island, before anchoring at Falmouth in October 1836. Thus, in circumnavigating the globe, Darwin observed diverse forms of tropical island life, but also the grandeur of the South American, mainland, which he explored extensively while *Beagle* was surveying: out of the five years he traveled, three years and one month were spent on land.

Darwin's experience of the voyage and his explorations were meticulously recorded in a variety of written forms. As he explained to his father in a letter of 1832, "whenever I enjoy anything I always look forward to writing it down in my Log Book (which increases in bulk) or in a letter—so you must excuse raptures" (*Correspondence*, vol. 1). Darwin compiled a massive logbook or diary; in addition, he made extensive scientific notebook entries to record his fieldwork observations. The letters to family and scientific mentors in England were also extensive and in all, Darwin's rapturous enjoyment of what he encountered ensured that *Beagle*'s voyage was one of the best-recorded nineteenth-century expeditions. Although the diary and correspondence have subsequently been published in their own right, Darwin integrated his diverse writings into what became the classic account of the voyage, the *Journal of Researches* (1839, 1845), now popularly known as *The Voyage of the Beagle*. He also produced more specialized scientific works on the geology along the route of the voyage.

The *Journal* brings together a rich variety of impressions and observations. Darwin is overwhelmed by "noble forests . . . which completely surpass in magnificence all that the European has ever beheld in his own country"; and registers an aesthetic appreciation of tropical atmospheres in which "lucid" light and bright color shade at greater distance "into a most beautiful haze, of a pale French grey, mingled with a little blue." His narrative also records something of the texture of overseas and colonial life, from the pastoral charms of a New Zealand settler farm, to the rough hospitality of Brazilian *vendas* (inns), and the gilded domesticities of Brazilian *fazendas* (estates). The latter's use of slaves revealed a darker side of the society, which Darwin abhorred. Indeed, his narrative does not flinch from reporting the horrific genocidal onslaught that Argentine General Rosas inflicted on the indigenous populations of the Pampas. The destructive human consequences of colonization and overseas scientific exploration add an important dimension to Darwin's *Journal*: *Beagle* carried as passengers three Fuegian natives from Tierra del Fuego, who had been captured on a previous voyage and were being returned to their homeland in order to disseminate further the "civilization" that had been bestowed on them. Darwin narrates the collapse of this mission with some poignancy, speculating on the absence of central authority and property in Fuegian "savage" society as the cause of its failure.

Otherwise, Darwin's *Journal* is best known for its speculations on the structure of the earth and the origins and distribution of organic life in space and time—the important preliminary work to his theory of evolution by natural selection as set out in *The Origin of Species*. Darwin was reading Charles Lyell's newly published and revolutionary *Principles of Geology* (1830–1833) as the voyage progressed. Orthodoxy held that the earth's surface was a consequence of massive catastrophes during a relatively brief history, whereas Lyell contended that constant, gradual, and unimaginably slow movement and change over aeons of time were the key to the earth's formation. Darwin looked to confirm Lyell's theory during his geological observations conducted in St. Jago, the Andes, and his work on coral reefs in the South Seas. A slowly changing earth's surface was also, potentially, the key to the question of the origin of new species, in the sense that new land, such as a volcanic island, could be colonized by species from nearby land masses, which would then begin to vary in structure as nature selected the most beneficial adaptations for the new environment. Similar thinking underpins Darwin's account of the differences between finches on the Galapagos that are unique to those islands. Thus, by the second edition (1845) of the *Journal of Researches*, a subtextual polemic concerned with the origin of species, controversial in both theological and natural historical terms, is woven subtly into Darwin's rapturous celebration of traveling amidst tropical nature.

David Amigoni

## Biography

Born in Shrewsbury, Shropshire, 12 February 1809. Son of an eminent physician. Attended school in Shrewsbury. Studied medicine at Edinburgh University, 1825–1827. Studied divinity at Cambridge University, 1827–1831. Independent naturalist on HMS *Beagle*, 1831–1836. Resided in London, elected to the governing council of the Geological Society, 1837; began secretive work on so-called "transmutational speculations." Elected to the Athenaeum, 1838; elected to the Royal Society, 1839. Married his first cousin, Emma Wedgwood, granddaughter of Josiah Wedgwood, 1839: ten children, of whom seven survived to adulthood. Moved to Down House, Downe, Kent, September 1842; lived there until his death. Worked continuously on the differences between species and varieties. Reading of joint papers on natural selection (Darwin and A.R. Wallace), Linnean Society, July 1858. *Origin of Species* published, 1859. *Descent of Man* published, 1871. Died at Down House, Downe, Kent, 19 April 1882.

## References and Further Reading


Darwin, Charles, *Journal of Researches into the Geology and Natural History of Various Countries visited by HMS Beagle, under the Command of Captain Fitzroy, R.N., from 1832 to 1836* (vol. 3 of *Narrative of the Surveying Voyages of His Majesty's Ships Adventure and Beagle*, edited by Robert Fitzroy), 1839; revised edition, 1845; as *The Voyage of the Beagle*, 1909.

Darwin, Charles, *The Structure and Distribution of Coral Reefs: Being the First Part of the Geology of the Voyage of the Beagle*, 1842.

Darwin, Charles, *Geological Observations on the Volcanic Islands Visited during the Voyage of HMS Beagle, Together with Some Brief Notices on the Geology of Australia and the Cape of Good Hope: Being the Second Part of the Geology of the Voyage of the Beagle, under the Command of Capt. Fitzroy . . . during the Years 1832 to 1836*, 1844.

Darwin, Charles, *Geological Observations on South America: Being the Third Part of the Geology of the Voyage of the Beagle*, 1846.

Darwin, Charles, *Charles Darwin's Diary of the Voyage of HMS Beagle*, edited by Nora Barlow, 1933.

Darwin, Charles, *The Correspondence*, edited by Frederick Burkhardt and Sydney Smith, vol. 1: *1821–1836*, Cambridge and New York: Cambridge University Press, 1985).

*See also* **Scientific Traveling**

## DAVID, ARMAND (1826–1900) *French Missionary and Natural Historian*

Jean-Pierre Armand David, the son of the local doctor at Espelette in the Basses-Pyrénées, was intended by his family for the study of medicine. As a boy his scientific interests focused on natural history, and he became an enthusiastic collector of plants, insects, and birds' eggs from the surrounding countryside. His religious feelings, however, led him toward the priesthood rather than his father's profession. Even as a young man it was apparent that the two defining forces in David's life—his Catholic spirituality and a passion for natural history—were interdependent. He later wrote, "All science is dedicated to the study of God's works and glorifies the Author; science is praiseworthy and even holy in its objective" (*Diary*, 1949).

At the age of 22, David became a novice in the order of St. Vincent de Paul and, after ordination in 1851 as a Lazarist priest, he was sent to Savona on the Italian Riviera, where he was employed as a science teacher until 1861. But as early as 1852 he was writing to his superior-general, Bishop Mouly, wishing to be sent as a missionary "to the Celestial Empire, Mongolia, and other similar places as soon as possible in order to learn new languages, customs, and climates" (*Diary*). At Savona he collected an impressive cabinet of specimens from the area for the benefit of his pupils. The collection was later bequeathed to the town—the first instance of David's public acclaim as a natural historian. Of his pupils at Savona, d'Albertis later gained recognition as an explorer in Melanesia, and the Marquis of Doria, a lifelong friend, founded Genoa's natural history museum.

In 1862 his order finally recalled David to Paris for ordination as a missionary in China. Before his departure he was introduced to Henri Milne-Edwards, the director of the Muséum National d'Histoire Naturelle, who requested that David collect specimens of the flora, fauna, animals, and insects found during his missionary work. David went as a science teacher, with two other priests, to establish a Lazarist mission school at Beijing. He assembled a natural history cabinet for the instruction of his pupils and traveled widely in the regions around his school seeking out suitable specimens. Those sent back to France impressed Milne-Edwards, who persuaded Bishop Mouly that David should be allowed to undertake further natural history researches for the government, under the offical title of "Missions Scientifiques."

Père David made three major collecting expeditions while in China: the first from 12 March to 26 October 1866 in the regions of Inner Mongolia; the second from 26 May 1868 to 25 July 1870 from Kiukiang, up the Yangtze River to Chungking, then overland through Sichuan's Red Basin into Muping in Sikang, before returning down the Yangtze; the third from 2 August 1872 to 1 April 1874 in the Chin Ling mountains in the Shensi and Shansi provinces (*Diary*). By 1874, however, fever had seriously affected David's health and he was obliged to return permanently to France. This was a great disappointment because he was planning to extend his explorations into Japan and the Philippines. Nevertheless, he maintained an active interest in natural history until his death in 1900.

Of the plants discovered by David in China, the most famous are *prunus davidiana* (spring-flowering peach with pink blossoms), *lilium davidii* (lily with orange-red flowers), *buddleia davidii* (butterfly bush with purple flowers), *clematis davidiana* (climbing shrub with blue flowers), and *davidia involucrata* (dove tree). He also identified some 58 new species of birds (including the pheasant, *crossoptilon auritum*; the passerines, *pyrgilanda davidi* and *propasser davidianus*; and an owl, *syrnium davidi*); about 100 new insects; various butterflies (*armandia thaitina, lycaena atroguttata, lycaxna coeligena*, and *pieris davidis*); and numerous fish, although many of his samples dissolved because Chinese alcohol was too weak to act as a preservative.

David is now best remembered for his interest in Chinese mammals. The *elaphurus davidiensis* (Père David's deer) had already been long extinct in the wild when he arrived in China, but a captive herd had been maintained in the Imperial Hunting Park south of Beijing. David managed to obtain two skins in 1865 and later some live specimens, from which breeding pairs were introduced into France and England (Woburn Abbey, Bedfordshire), and then, remarkably, in 1985 back into Beijing. Other important mammal specimens were also collected on his 1866 expedition: the red-brown squirrel, *sciurus davidianus*; the jerboa, *dipus annulatus*; and a golden-furred rodent, *siphneus armandii*. On his expedition between 1868 and 1870 he discovered the takin, *budorcas taxicolor*, a goat-shaped antelope with lyre-shaped horns; and the *rhinopithecus roxellanae*, a golden monkey, so named after Roxellana, the mistress of the Turkish sultan Suleiman II.

David's most memorable discovery was undoubtedly the so-called giant panda (*ailuropoda melanoleuca*; known to the Chinese as *bai xiong/bei-shung*, white bear, or *zhu xiong*, bamboo bear). On 11 March 1869 Père David first saw a panda skin ("of the famous white and black bear") at "the home of a certain Li, the principal landowner in the valley" (*Diary*). On 21 March David compared the animal to a bear, naming it as *ursus melanoleucus*. (See Catton, 1990; Schaller, 1994; and Laidler, 1992, for the ongoing debate over the giant panda's genetic relationship to either the bear genus or the red panda/firefox, which had been known to Europeans since the early 1820s.) On 23 March the hunters brought him a freshly killed young giant panda, followed by the carcass of an adult female on 1 April. It has even been claimed, but without corroboration, that David was ultimately successful in sending home a live giant panda. (See *Diary* and Morris, 1981.) Through its enduring popularity and its adoption as the symbol of the World Wildlife Fund, the giant panda remains Père David's most lasting memorial.

MICHAEL G. BRENNAN

## Biography

Born in Espelette, Basses-Pyrénées, France, 7 September 1826. Son of the local doctor, who was also justice of the peace and mayor. Attended the Petit Seminaire de Larsorre for six years, and then the Grand Seminaire de Bayonne. Entered as a novice into the order of St. Vincent de Paul, Paris, 4 November 1848; took vows, 1850; ordained as a Lazarist priest, 1851. Employed by the order of St. Vincent de Paul as a science teacher in Savona, Italy, 1851–1861. Member of the Lazarist mission school at Beijing, 1862–1874. Traveled extensively in China, including Mongolia, 1866, and Tibet, 1868–1870. Collected specimens, sending them to the Muséum National d'Histoire Naturelle, Paris. Made an extended visit to France and Italy, 1871–1872; elected a member of the French Academy of Sciences and a correspondent of the French Institute. Returned to France, 1874, settling at the order's main house in the rue de Sèvres, Paris. From 1874 worked as a priest and as an instructor to missionaries; cataloged his collections; prepared exhibitions and publications. Visited Tunisia and Constantinople for natural history purposes, 1881. Delivered address to the International Scientific Congress of Catholics, Paris, 1888. Awarded the Cross of the Légion d'honneur, 1896. Died in Paris, 10 November 1900.

## References and Further Reading

David, Armand, "Journal d'un voyage en Mongolie fait en 1866," bulletin appended to the *Nouvelles Archives du Muséum National d'Histoire Naturelle*, 3 (1867): 3–83.

David, Armand, *Recherches pour servir à l'histoire naturelle des mammifères: comprenant des considérations sur la classification de ces animaux*, with A. Milne-Edwards, 1868–1874.

David, Armand, "Journal d'un voyage dans le centre de la Chine et dans le Thibet Oriental," three bulletins appended to the *Nouvelles Archives du Muséum National d'Histoire Naturelle*, 8 (1872): 3–128; 9 (1873): 15–48; 10 (1874): 3–82.

David, Armand, *Journal de mon troisième voyage d'exploration dans l'empire Chinois*, 2 vols., 1875.

David, Armand, *Les Oiseaux de la Chine*, with M.E. Oustalet, 1877.

David, Armand, *Plantae Davidianae ex sinarum imperio* (catalog of his botanical collections), 2 vols., 1884–1888.

David, Armand, *Abbé David's Diary: Being an Aaccount of the French Naturalist's Journeys and Observations in China in the Years 1866 to 1869*, edited and translated by Helen M. Fox, 1949.

Laidler, Keith, and Liz Laidler, *Pandas: Giants of the Great Bamboo Forest*, London: BBC Books, 1992.

Morris, Ramona, and Desmond Morris, *Men and Pandas,* London: Hutchinson, 1966; New York: McGraw-Hill, 1967; as *The Giant Panda,* revised by Jonathan Barzdo, London: Kogan Page, 1981; New York: Penguin, 1982.

Schaller, George B., *The Last Panda: With a New Afterword,* Chicago: University of Chicago Press, 1994.

# DAVID-NÉEL, ALEXANDRA (1868–1969)

### *French Travel Writer and Tibetan and Sanskrit Scholar*

Alexandra David-Néel, travel writer, Tibetan and Sanskrit scholar, anarchist, and humanist, was born in Saint-Mandé, France, on 24 October 1868. She was the daughter of Louis David, of French Huguenot descent, a prominent journalist and friend of Victor Hugo. Her mother had a Catholic background and was of Scandinavian descent. According to her letters, Alexandra first wandered from home at the age of four in order to escape the cold, bourgeois environment of her parents' home, having an instinctive urge to find out what lay beyond the garden gate. As a serious reader from an early age, she read the Bible and important philosophical works during her childhood, and was also an avid reader of the science fiction author Jules Verne.

In the 1880s David-Néel undertook studies of Eastern religion and philosophy at the Sorbonne, in the lecture halls of prominent specialists of the era, and spent hours studying at the Musée Guimet, where she discovered her vocation as a scholar of Asian studies. In 1892 David-Néel traveled to London to improve, through immersion, her English skills and to study in preparation for travel to India. While in London she met members of esoteric groups, the Theosophists and the gnostics. In 1898 her anarchist treatise *Pour la vie* was published in Brussels. In the late-nineteenth century and well into the twentieth century she published articles on women's issues and Asian religion and philosophy (some signed "Alexandra Myrial" or "Alexandra David") for magazines such as *Mercure de France* and *Le Lotus bleu*.

David-Néel's mission in writing popular accounts of her travel experiences was first and foremost to ren-

Alexandra David-Néel in China in October 1937; photograph taken with her 6X6 Rolleiflex by her adoptive son, the lama Yongden. *Courtesy of Fondation Alexandra David Neel, Digne-les-Bains.*

der more accessible basic notions about Eastern philosophy and religion, an area of scholarship that she considered to be overly esoteric and erudite. She strongly believed that the best way to learn about Asian cultures was through complete cultural and linguistic assimilation, which she actively sought by leaving the library behind and taking to a nomadic life on the trail.

In her travel narrative *Le Sortilège du mystère* (published posthumously in 1972), David-Néel describes in detail her experiences within the worlds of the gnostics and the theosophists of Paris, London, and northern India at the turn of the century, a time of prophecy and great interest in the occult and spirit travel. It is noteworthy that while describing the beliefs of some of the members of these esoteric circles in *Le Sortilège du mystère*, she maintains a tone of sceptical rationalism throughout the narrative.

David-Néel achieved international renown for her forbidden entry into Lhasa, the capital of Tibet and seat of the Dalai Lama's palace, in 1924. Disguised as a poor Tibetan pilgrim, with face and hands covered in dark clay to disguise her fair skin, she and her Sikkimese traveling companion Aphur Yongden made the crossing by night to avoid being caught by border-control authorities. She claimed to have been the first Western woman to have crossed the border successfully. Her published account of this adventure appeared in 1927 in Paris and London, as *Voyage d'une parisienne à Lhassa* (*My Journey to Lhasa*). It was published during an era when it was rare for women's contributions to world travel and discovery to be published in newspapers and books. There are moments in *My Journey to Lhasa* when David-Néel's narration blurs the lines of the real and the fantastic. This is one of David-Néel's relatively adventurous narrative styles, which she also employs in some of her later works, such as *Magie d'amour et magie noire* (1938).

*Magic and Mystery in Tibet* (1929) is a travel narrative which, like *Le Sortilège du mystère*, is an exploration of travel into the realm of heightened mystical and psychological states. Within this narrative, David-Néel traces both her literal and metaphysical path into the worlds of Tibetan lamas and their practice.

David-Néel's nomadic life in Asia covered more than 20 years of her life. Although she married Philippe Néel in 1904, she shared an address with him only until 1911, when she embarked upon the first of two lengthy stays in Asia. These two periods (1911–1925 and 1937–1946) kept her away from Europe during both world wars.

The *Journal de voyage: Lettres à son mari* (1975–1976) is a remarkable collection of letters that David-Néel wrote almost daily to her husband while traveling through India, Nepal, Sikkim, Tibet, China, and Japan. Volume one of the *Journal* begins with letters from the earliest days of her marriage to Philippe in 1904. It includes detailed descriptions of her life in the high Himalayas, where she went into a two-year retreat with a lama, the *Gomchen* of Lachen, in order to practice the Tibetan language and study essential aspects of Tantric Buddhism. Volume two of her letters includes a personal description of her entry into Lhasa.

The *Journal de voyage* provides us with a rich autobiographical glimpse of Alexandra David-Néel's life in Asia. In it she writes about everything from the rudimentary details of bath and kettle to her ruminations about her marriage to Philippe, as well as making important philosophical reflections on Eastern and Western ways of life. Her vantage point from her Himalayan home, Dechen Ashram (the hermitage of peace), provides us with a fascinating glimpse of Europe from the eyes of a European woman who has adopted the Tibetan language and a hermetic, contemplative lifestyle. Likewise, her daily descriptions of travel to remote regions of the Himalayas give us a clear understanding of the physical efforts she made in travel.

In the years after her two lengthy stays in Asia, David-Néel moved to the home in Digne in southern France that she purchased in 1928, Samten Dzong (the fortress of meditation). There she wrote both prolifically and with diversity, experimenting with genres ranging from the epic (*La Vie Surhumaine de Guésar de Ling*) to the suspense thriller (*Magie d'amour et magie noire*, 1938).

MARGARET E. MCCOLLEY

### Biography

Born Louise Eugénie Alexandrine David in Saint Mandé, Paris, France, 24 October 1868. Daughter of Louis David, a prominent journalist and political activist and a Belgian mother. Studied music in Paris, 1880s; became interested in Eastern philosophy and Theosophy. Studied Asian religion, literature, and philosophy at the Sorbonne University and the Musée Guimet, late 1880s. Attended lectures and studied in the library of the Theosophical Society in London and Paris, early 1890s. Traveled to India and Ceylon (Sri Lanka) with money from an inheritance, 1891. Toured French Indo-China as "première chanteuse," under the name Mademoiselle Alexandra Myrial, with the Opéra-Comique of Paris, 1894–1900. Became director of the casino at Tunis, 1902. Married a distant cousin, Philippe Néel, a railroad executive, in Tunisia, 1904; separated shortly afterward, communicating by letter and receiving financial and emotional support for her travels from him. Commissioned by the French Ministry of Education to travel to Asia and meet the Dalai Lama, 1910. Started first major Asian journey, August 1911, traveling to India and becoming the first Western woman to have an audience with the 13th Dalai Lama, at Kalimpong, near Darjeeling, 1912. Met and became close to the crown prince of Sikkim, Sidkeong Tulka. Went into spiritual retreat north of Sikkim, 1914. Successfully crossed the forbidden border of Lhasa, disguised as a Tibetan pilgrim, with her Sikkimese traveling companion, Yongden, 1924. Returned to France, 1925. Adopted Yongden as her son and heir, 1925. Purchased home, Samten Dzong, in Digne, near Nice, 1928. Returned to China with Yongden, traveling by Trans-Siberian Railway from Moscow, 1936; met both Mao Tse-Tung and Chiang Kai-Shek. Lived in southern China, near the border with Tibet, during World War II. Repatriated to France, 1944. Wrote prolifically, including scholarly works on Buddhism, travel narratives, epics, and suspense thrillers. Named Chevalier de la Légion d'Honneur, 1927; promoted to Premier Commandeur, 1964. Awarded the Grande Médaille d'Or by the Société de Géographie de Paris, 1928; Grand Prix de l'Athlétisme Féminin, Société des Sports, 1929. Died in Digne, 8 September 1969.

### References and Further Reading

David-Néel, Alexandra, *Pour la vie*, 1898; reedited in her *En Chine*, 1969.

David-Néel, Alexandra, *Souvenirs d'une parisienne au Thibet*, 1925, as *Voyage d'une parisienne à Lhassa*, 1927; as *My Journey to Lhasa*, 1927, with an introduction by Peter Hopkirk, 1983, with foreword by His Holiness the Dalai Lama and introduction by Diana Rowan, 1993.

David-Néel, Alexandra, *Mystiques et magiciens du Thibet*, 1929; as *Magic and Mystery in Tibet*, 1932; many reprints.

David-Néel, Alexandra, *Initiations lamaïques*, 1930, revised edition, 1957; as *Initiations and Initiates in Tibet*, translated by Fred Rothwell, 1931, reprinted, 1970.

David-Néel, Alexandra, *Au Pays des brigands gentilshommes: grand Tibet*, 1933; as *Tibetan Journey*, 1936.

David-Néel, Alexandra, *Le Bouddhisme: ses doctrines, ses méthodes*, 1936, revised as *Le Bouddhisme du Bouddha*, 1960; as *Buddhism: Its Doctrines and Methods*, translated by H.N.M. Hardy and Bernard Miall, 1939, reprinted, 1977.

David-Néel, Alexandra, *Magie d'amour et magie noire: scènes du Tibet inconnu*, 1938; as *Tibetan Tale of Love and Magic*, translated by Vidar l'Estrange, 1983.

David-Néel, Alexandra, *Sous des nuées d'orage*, 1940.

David-Néel, Alexandra, *A l'Ouest barbare de la vaste Chine*, 1947.

David-Néel, Alexandra, *Au coeur des Himalayas: le Népal*, 1949.

David-Néel, Alexandra, *L'Inde Hier, aujourd'hui, demain*, 1951, as *L'Inde où j'ai vécu, avant et après l'indépendance*, 1969.

David-Néel, Alexandra, *Les Enseignements secrets dans les sectes Bouddhistes tibétaines*, 1951, 2nd edition, 1961; as *The Secret Oral Teachings in Tibetan Buddhist Sects*, translated by H.N.M. Hardy, 1967.

David-Néel, Alexandra, *Textes Tibétains inédits*, translated by David-Néel, 1952.

David-Néel, Alexandra, *Le Vieux Tibet face à la Chine nouvelle*, 1953.

David-Néel, Alexandra, *Le Sortilège du mystère*, 1972.

David-Néel, Alexandra, *Journal de voyage: lettres à son mari (11 août 1904–27 décembre 1917)* and *(14 janvier 1918–31 décembre 1940)*, edited by Marie-Madeleine Peyronnet, 2 vols., 1975–76.

David-Néel, Alexandra, *Vivre au Tibet: Cuisine, traditions, et images*, 1975; as *Gargantua aux pays des neiges*, 1993.

David-Néel, Alexandra, *Le Tibet d'Alexandra David-Néel*, edited by Françoise Borin, 1979.

David-Néel, Alexandra, *Grand Tibet et vaste Chine: récits et aventures*, with a preface by Marie-Madeleine Peyronnet, 1994.

## DAVIS, JOHN (c. 1550–1605) *British Sailor and Explorer*

John Davis, "that excellent pilot and skilful navigator, and fortunate discoverer of unknown countries," was the son of a gentleman of Devonshire. His family appears to have been intimate with the Gilberts and the Raleighs, who lived in the neighborhood, and who were prominent families in maritime Elizabethan England. Of his youth, little is known, but it is obvious that he must have gone to sea at an early age.

In the early 1580s Davis was among those who were convinced of the possibility of the existence of a Northwest Passage and who believed that the passage was a practicable means of reaching the Orient. Letters patent were granted conferring a right of search for such passage to China, to a company presided over by Adrian Gilbert. The result of this was the dispatch of *Sunneshine* and *Mooneshine*, under Davis's command in 1585. This was the first voyage, after those of Frobisher in the 1570s, to search for a Northwest Passage. Davis himself left a short note of this voyage, and there is a full account of it by John Jane (or Janes), who was the supercargo on Davis's own ship, *Sunneshine*. Davis sighted the eastern coast of Greenland on 20 July 1585, "the most deformed, rocky, and mountainous land that ever wee sawe," and after passing Cape Farewell, which he named, he proceeded along the west coast and, on landing, established friendly relations with the Inuit. He then headed across the strait that now bears his name toward Cumberland Sound on Baffin Island. Although he hoped he had found the passage, the season was far advanced and he returned to Dartmouth in Devon, arriving on 30 September. This voyage convinced Davis that the Northwest Passage was "a matter nothing doubtfull, but at any tyme almost to be passed, the sea navigable, voyd of yce, the ayre tollerable, and the waters very depe."

A second attempt was speedily arranged. In 1586 Davis had four ships: *Mermayde*, of 120 "tunnes," *Sunneshine*, *Mooneshine*, and a "pynace" of ten "tunnes," *Northstarre*. Davis left a full account of this voyage. On arrival at Greenland, Davis divided his fleet, sending two ships under Captain Pope to survey the east coast, while he, with the rest, proceeded north along the west coast. There he met more Inuit and kidnapped one as a hostage, but the man soon died. Because of sickness, Davis decided to send *Mermayde* home and in *Mooneshine* he sailed west and surveyed much of the coast originally seen on his first voyage. He did not prosecute his discoveries up Cumberland Sound, but passed southward along the Labrador coast, where he observed large numbers of cod, some of which he caught. Davis arrived home in early October to find that all of his ships save *Northstarre*, which had been lost in a storm, had preceded him.

Davis was determined to continue the following year and in order to guarantee some income from the venture for his sponsors it was decided that, of the three ships to go forth, two were to be used entirely for fishing. Jane wrote an account of this voyage, and Davis's *Traverse Booke*, or log, has survived. On arrival in the area, Davis left the two fishing vessels and proceeded north in the other vessel, probably a small pinnace called *Ellen*. Sailing along the west Greenland coast, he eventually reached the prominent point he named "Sanderson, his hope" (72° 40' N) after one of the sponsors of his voyages, the name reflecting the hope of the passage. This was Davis's northern most destination, reached on 30 June 1587. He then headed west, passed the middle pack of the Baffin Bay ("a mighty banke of yce"), and arrived at Mount Raleigh, where he wrote that "there was no yce towards the north, but a great sea, free, large, very salt, and blue, and of an unsearchable depth." Davis then moved southward—noting a "mighty" tidal race at the mouth of what is now called Hudson Strait, although he did not investigate it—toward the rendezvous with the fishing vessels, but finding them absent, he sailed to England.

Davis realized that his work in the north was open to "this objection, why hath not Davis discovered this passage being thrice that wayes imploied?" It is notable that although Davis was criticized by some, they were not practical navigators; all those with real experience of the craft, from Baffin to the present day, have been full of admiration for what he was able to achieve.

Davis's next voyage of discovery was as the captain of *Desire*, one of the vessels which, in 1591, accompanied Thomas Cavendish on his second voyage. Davis reveals his two motives by commenting that he was "onely induced to goe with M. Candish . . . vpon his constant promise vnto me, that . . . I should haue his Pinnce with my owne Barck . . . to search that Northwest discouery vpon the backe parts of America." In the Straits of Magellan, *Desire* became separated from the rest of Cavendish's ships. Davis tried three times to enter the South Pacific, but was driven back by contrary winds. It was during this period that he sighted the Falkland Islands on 14 August 1592.

Towards the end of his life, Davis undertook several voyages as pilot, pilot major, or master, including three to the East Indies. It was on the third of these, as master of *Tiger*, that he left England for the last time on 5 December 1604. In December the following year, *Tiger* fell in with a vessel manned by Japanese pirates, with whom the English established, they thought, friendly relations. On 29 or 30 December 1605, however, the Japanese attacked the English on board *Tiger*. Davis was one of the first victims and received "sixe or seven mortall wounds." A severe battle took place, during which the Japanese were forced into the cabin, where they were destroyed by the desperate expedient of firing guns directly into it through the door. The loss of Davis caused *Tiger* to return to England.

Davis was one of the most skilled navigators who ever sailed the sea. He appears never to have lost a ship in which he sailed, and for the period, relatively few men. He was in the forefront in adopting innovations and invented the back staff, an improvement on the old cross staff. He was also an author and has two major works to his credit. Davis's language is clear and straightforward, as one would expect from such a practical man, yet it is also elegant, indicating that he had some formal education. His first work, *The Seamans Secrets*, published in 1594 and covering some

100 pages, is nothing less than a practical guide for the sailor. It is arranged in the form of a dialogue, the first question of which is "What is Navigation?", to which the response, surely never improved upon since, is "Navigation is that exellent art which demonstrateth by infallable conclusion how a sufficient Ship may bee conducted the shortest good way from place to place by Corse and Trauers." Many of the questions are highly technical, for example, "The Moone Being 21 Days olde at what time is the full sea at Dartmouth?" The answer, after much complicated instruction, is "10 of the clock and 48 minutes past." His book was very popular and went through eight editions between 1594 and 1657.

Davis's second publication, *The Worldes Hydrographical Description*, published in 1595, concentrates on his enthusiasm for the Northwest Passage. He rejects all the arguments used against it and seeks to prove that America is an island. He includes information from his own voyages and touches on the floatation of ice and the formation of icebergs, and concludes with a firm enunciation of the advantages to be gained from the passage.

Ian R. Stone

### Biography

Born in Sandridge, near Dartmouth, Devon, c. 1550. Went to sea as a boy; made voyages with Adrian Gilbert. Undertook three voyages to seek the Northwest Passage, 1585, 1586, and 1587. Probably commanded *Black Dog*, active in operations against the Spanish Armada, 1588. Joined the Earl of Cumberland's fleet in the Azores, 1590. Commanded one of the vessels of Thomas Cavendish's fleet, 1591. Separated from Cavendish in the Straits of Magellan and sighted the Falkland Islands. Probably master of Sir Walter Raleigh's ship at Cadiz and the Azores, 1596–1597. Pilot of the Dutch vessel *Leeuw* on a voyage to the East Indies, 1598; helped defend the vessel in two actions. Participated in James Lancaster's voyage to the East Indies, 1600–1603. Master of *Tiger*, commanded by Sir Edward Michelborne, on another voyage to the East Indies, 1604. Died in attack on *Tiger* off Bintan Island, near Singapore, by Japanese pirates, 29 or 30 December 1605.

### References and Further Reading

Davis, John, *The Seamans Secrets*, 1594; facsimile with an introduction by A.N. Ryan, 1992.
Davis, John, *The Worldes Hydrographical Description*, 1595.
Davis, John, *The Voyages and Works of John Davis the Navigator*, edited and with an introduction by Albert Hastings Markham, 1880.

*See also* **Northwest Passage**

## DEFOE, DANIEL (1660–1731) *English Merchant, Secret Agent, Journalist, and Novelist*

The son of a butcher and candle merchant in London, Daniel Defoe (born Foe) had an unlikely upbringing for the "father of the English novel." Although well educated, he was barred from Oxford and Cambridge because of his Presbyterian upbringing. He did, however, attend Charles Morton's Newington Green Academy for Dissenters where he studied science, mathematics, philosophy, and use of English. This was perhaps a better training, and certainly a more modern one, for a new breed of writer addressing a new but rapidly growing audience, the middle classes. Defoe's first hero, Robinson Crusoe, personified this audience's bourgeois values of self-reliance, driven in equal measure by the sometimes conflicting ideologies of Christian doctrine and trade capitalism.

Defoe came to writing fiction late in life, producing most of his major works in his sixties. He enjoyed a remarkably prolific period between 1719 and 1725, when he wrote *Robinson Crusoe* (1719), *Moll Flanders* (1722), *A Journal of the Plague Year, Captain Singleton* (1720), *Roxana* (1724), *A New Voyage round the World* (1724), and *A Tour thro' the Whole Island of Great Britain* (1724–26). Always hardworking, Defoe amassed over 500 titles to his name, varying from pamphlets of a few pages to the 5,000-plus pages of journalism he produced for *The Review* (his total output is difficult to ascertain because most of what he wrote appeared anonymously). This prolific output may be partly due to the fact that writers in Defoe's time were paid by the page, and Defoe, it seems, for all his political connections, education, and industry, was no stranger to the bankruptcy courts—he needed the cash. In 1709 he leased a large house in Stoke Newington, London, by which time he had the reputation of being very well paid, but he never quite banished the ghosts of his dubious financial past (he was the defendant in eight lawsuits between 1688 and 1694, and was bankrupt twice, in 1692 and 1703).

In his younger days, Defoe was active in various trade ventures, dealing in hosiery, tobacco, wine, and other goods. He acted as political agent for William III in England and Scotland between 1697 and 1701, and subsequently as a secret agent for Robert Harley, speaker of the House of Commons and later earl of Oxford. It was Harley who secured Defoe's release from Newgate prison in 1703, recognizing that such a talented writer could serve his political ambitions. Indeed, Defoe served Harley well, traveling extensively through England and Scotland surreptitiously acquiring political intelligence and defending Harley's policies through pamphlets and articles in *The Review*.

Defoe's experience as merchant, political agent, and spy furnished him with much of the background for

Bernard Picart's portrait of Robinson Crusoe, which closely followed the text in its details, in particular the large goatskin umbrella, has become the enduring image of Defoe's castaway (frontispiece to the first French translation, *La Vie et les aventures surprenantes de Robinson Crusoe*, 1720). *Courtesy of London Library.*

his fiction, while his experience as a journalist furnished him with the skill to put observations and impressions into narrative. His extensive journeys through England and Scotland on horseback in his early years supplied him with much of the information he was to present in *A Tour thro' the Whole Island of Great Britain* (1724–1726), written long after the actual journeys. The *Tour* is written in the form of letters, each describing a journey supposedly carried out between 1722 and 1724, but it is a literary re-creation of earlier impressions and observations. Hardly travel writing in the modern sense, the *Tour* is a wonderfully realistic piece of social history at a fascinating juncture between the seventeenth and eighteenth centuries, when economic and demographic changes were giving a foretaste of the great upheavals of the Industrial Revolution.

Although Defoe traveled extensively, there is no evidence that he ventured beyond western Europe. When he describes the wider world of *Robinson Crusoe, Captain Singleton*, and *Robert Drury* (1729), it is secondhand, derived mainly from his wide reading in contemporary history and travel. Not having been born into the aristocracy, Defoe did not take the Grand Tour. The wider world, for Defoe and his fellow middle-class armchair travelers, was to be mastered through books, as he advises in *The Compleat English Gentleman*: "If he has not travell'd in his youth, has not made the grand tour of Italy and France, he may make the tour of the world in books . . . He may go round the globe with Dampier and Rogers, and kno' a thousand times more in doing it than all those illiterate sailors."

Defoe had an enormous number of travel books to choose from, including the accounts of William Dampier, Woodes Rogers, and Jean-Baptiste Tavernier. A lesser-known work of Defoe's, *Atlas Maritimus et Commercialis* (1728), gives a very full account of the commercial possibilities of the coasts of the world, but it is his fiction, and in particular his travel romances (loosely based on real travels), that have proved most popular and enduring. *Robinson Crusoe* is a fictional account of a young Englishman shipwrecked on a small island off the coast of South America. The novel was suggested by the experiences of Alexander Selkirk, who spent four years on the islands of Juan Fernández, barely surviving the ordeal. *Robinson Crusoe* has been translated into many languages, testifying to its universal appeal. It has become something of a modern myth, an *Odyssey* for the emerging bourgeois class and proto-colonialists of Europe.

Most of Defoe's novels, including *Roxana* and *Moll Flanders*, owe something to the genre of travel literature, but *Captain Singleton, The Farther Adventures of Robinson Crusoe, Robert Drury's Journal*, and *A New Voyage round the World* are properly travel fictions. *Captain Singleton* is the story of a young man's journey across Africa and his exploits as a pirate on the high seas. *The Farther Adventures of Robinson Crusoe* brings China and Central Asia within the compass of Defoe's eurocentric vision of the world, and is notable for the envy expressed through Crusoe for superior Chinese wealth and trade. *Madagascar; or, Robert Drury's Journal* is a fictional autobiography of an early eighteenth-century adventurer. But of all these travel fictions, *A New Voyage round the World* perhaps best articulates Defoe's vision of European colonial enterprise through a realistic narrative of exploration. The unnamed narrator describes an eastward circumnavigation via the Cape of Good Hope, the Philippines, and across the South Pacific to Peru, before returning home, his ship loaded with silver. Half a century before Captain Cook, Defoe's narrator discovers many islands in the South Pacific rich with provisions and pearls, and indulges in one of the author's recurring fantasies of an English colony in Patagonia.

PAUL SMETHURST

### Biography

Born Daniel Foe in London, 1660 (known as Daniel Defoe from c. 1703). Attended school in Dorking and then Charles Morton's Academy, Newington Green, 1671–1679. Established as hosiery merchant, 1683; later expanding into tobacco, wine, and other goods, 1685–1692. Married Mary Tuffley, 1684: eight children, of whom six survived to adulthood. Fought with the Duke of Monmouth's rebellion, 1685; joined William of Orange's march on London, 1688. Political agent for William III, 1697–1701. Arrested, pilloried, and imprisoned for seditious libel, 1703, after publishing a pamphlet, *The Shortest Way with Dissenters* (1702). Secret agent for Robert Harley, earl of Oxford, 1703–1714, traveling extensively in England and Scotland. Established and wrote for *The Review*, 1704–1713. Published *Robinson Crusoe*, 1719, and other works of fiction, social history, and economics, 1719–1729. Died in London, 24 April 1731.

### References and Further Reading

Defoe, Daniel, *The Life and Strange Surprising Adventures of Robinson Crusoe of York, Mariner*, 1719.
Defoe, Daniel, *The Farther Adventures of Robinson Crusoe*, 1719.
Defoe, Daniel, *The Life, Adventures, and Piracies of the Famous Captain Singleton*, 1720.
Defoe, Daniel, *A New Voyage round the World, by a Course Never Sailed Before*, 1724.
Defoe, Daniel, *A Tour thro' the Whole Island of Great Britain*, 3 vols., 1724–1726.
Defoe, Daniel, *The Four Years Voyages of Capt. George Roberts*, 1726.
Defoe, Daniel, *Madagascar; or, Robert Drury's Journal, during Fifteen Years Captivity on That Island*, 1729.

*See also* **Fictional Travel Writing**

## DELLA VALLE, PIETRO (1586–1652)

***Italian Traveler and Antiquarian***

Pietro della Valle was one of the most influential travelers of the seventeenth century. His long and detailed letters describing his extensive travels in Turkey, Persia, and India, written in Italian and published between 1650 and 1663, were highly personal in tone and conception. They created a new standard of independent, philosophical scrutiny in the growing genre of travel literature. Della Valle styled himself as "the pilgrim" and his pilgrimage was, decisively, a pilgrimage of curiosity. Unlike many earlier travelers in America or Asia, della Valle was not primarily concerned with trade, conquest, or missionary work. Neither was he an adventurer seeking fortune, but rather a truly educated gentleman, with connections at the Roman court, fully aware that he was creating his own myth as traveler. His journey to the East was a luxury, a form of aristocratic ostentation that certainly went beyond the conventions of the northern European Grand Tour, challenging the limits of a classical education by seeking to embrace the civilizations of the East. In effect della Valle's pilgrimage represents an original form of baroque self-fashioning, based on the social and religious values of the chivalric Renaissance and the Catholic Counter-Reformation. While in some ways della Valle was very much the product of his specific early-seventeenth-century Roman context, on the other hand his wide-ranging and dilettantish curiosity, secular and independent, set a standard for travelers from a variety of European backgrounds in the following two centuries.

Della Valle's immediate motivation for his travels was his desire to forget a frustrated love. He departed Venice for Constantinople with ceremony and pomp in 1614. He was accompanied by servants and painters, carried with him a small library on oriental matters, and once in Ottoman lands devoted himself to learning Turkish and acquiring old manuscripts and curios. However, after visiting Constantinople, Egypt, and Jerusalem (where he performed a conventional religious pilgrimage), in 1616 he decided to continue his travels toward Baghdad. There he fell in love with an 18-year-old Syrian Christian woman, Sitti Maani Joerida, whom he duly married (despite the fact that her family were Nestorian—and therefore considered heretics by the Catholic church). Della Valle went on to Isfahan, followed by Sitti Maani's family, and spent the next six years (1617–1622) in Persia, immersing himself in the local languages and cultures and devising schemes for an anti-Ottoman alliance with the Safavid ruler Shah Abbas. The attempt to settle a Syrian-Catholic Christian community near Isfahan, under Rome's ecclesiastical authority, eventually failed. He decided to leave Persia, but, on the way to Hormuz, Sitti Maani fell sick, miscarried, and died. Della Valle continued his travels toward India in an English ship, with the embalmed body of his wife hidden in his luggage. He reached the commercial city of Surat, visited a few Jain and Hindu temples, and then traveled south to Portuguese Goa. He used Goa as a base from which to visit the nearby gentile lands under the authority of petty Hindu rulers—Ikkeri, Olala, and Calicut. In 1624 he began his return journey, reaching Rome in 1626 after a long detour in Sicily.

Della Valle's letters were in reality whole sections of a carefully kept journal, which he sent regularly to his erudite friend Mario Schipano in Naples. This accounts for their immediacy and precision. Rather than hiding his personality behind his observations, della Valle combined the most intimate matters with learned disquisitions. He dressed according to the custom of each place and engaged in religious and political conversation with a variety of hosts—Christians, Muslims, and Gentiles of various persuasions. He researched Arabic science, translated Persian literature, copied ancient inscriptions, dug up mummies in Egypt, and wrote poetry in Italian, Turkish, and Persian. His collection of manuscripts included Samaritan, Coptic, Turkish, Persian, and Sanskrit texts. He not only observed, but also discussed all the subjects of scientific curiosity of the age: politics, religion, manners, morality, music and architecture, food and dress, landscape, antiquities, and history were all open to the traveler's scrutiny. Della Valle was thus both a recorder and interpreter of the East.

There is a sense in which della Valle was, for all his openness to exoticism, still a conventional man. His Catholicism was unwavering, and his social ideals were chivalric and aristocratic. His political schemes were ultimately those of a sophisticated crusader capable of seeking allies in the East, and his attitude to oriental religions was sympathetic but not syncretic. For example, he interpreted the Nestorian creed of his wife's family as an ethnic identity rather than as a firm belief, and ultimately no more than a result of ignorance—he assumed that their destiny was the Roman Church. Similarly, while he was a pioneer in establishing the seventeenth-century hypothesis of a primitive philosophical truth behind the universal system of idolatry uncovered by antiquarian research (one that identified the philosophical core of Hinduism as a form of Pythagoreanism), he had no doubt that Indian gentiles worshipped the devil. One can also consider that della Valle's linguistic skills were often limited. All this being said, what is most striking in his letters is the power of his romanticism, which led him to seek common human qualities outside Europe and outside the Roman Church. More than a thinker, della Valle was someone willing to explore the limits of humanity through the direct experience of cultural diversity. On the basis of his Neoplatonic and neo-Stoic Christian philosophy, he saw virtuous behavior in all cultures, beyond the diversity of ethnic or religious backgrounds.

A good example of this attitude is of course his marriage to Sitti Maani. His interest in other women is also significant. For example, what is remarkable of his account of a *sati* in Ikkeri, the Telinga widow Giaccamà, is the way he individualized her experience of sacrifice, even writing three sonnets in her honor. This represented a break with centuries of European tradition of simply expressing horror at the ritual.

On his return home, della Valle reentered the life of Rome, then under the liberal-minded Barberini pope Urban VIII. Following the funeral rites for Sitti Maani, whose body he finally buried, della Valle married (not without scandal in the Roman court) Mariuccia, a Georgian orphan girl adopted by his former wife, who had accompanied Pietro in India and Europe. He offered Urban VIII (who for this reason made him chamberlain of honor) an optimistic account of the prospects for a Catholic mission in Georgia, based on his observations in Persia, and afterward, under the umbrella of the Propaganda Fide (a congregation set up by the papacy in 1622 to promote missions outside Europe), he continued to provide regular diplomatic advice for a group of Theatine missionaries who had been dispatched accordingly. However, della Valle was disappointed as he met with censorship for his encomiastic portrait of Shah Abbas, published in 1628 and in fact dedicated to the pope's nephew Cardinal Francesco Barberini. The Roman censorship refused to allow the distribution of the book because it portrayed an infidel ruler as a heroic and prudent king, justifying his harsh policies toward Christians as no worse than Christian policies toward Jews and infidels. It was probably in the light of this experience that della Valle delayed the publication of his letters, and the first volume, dealing with Turkey, only appeared (censored) in 1650. The remaining two parts, dealing with Persia and India, were published by his sons in 1658 and 1663.

In the same Roman court that condemned Galileo, della Valle learned that his universalistic cultural ideals needed to be kept within the limits imposed by a fresh ideological retreat. In contrast, the intense flowering of orientalist projects in Rome, Paris, and Vienna in the decades following his return to Rome effectively ensured that della Valle's Samaritan and Coptic manuscripts, through contacts with men like the French antiquarian Peiresc and the Jesuit polymath Athanasius Kircher, were published, and their significance (ultimately theological) discussed by Catholic and Protestant scholars alike. If we can judge from the circulation of his letters in Italian, French, Dutch, English, and German in quick succession over less than 15 years, his own correspondence with the international network of antiquarians of the seventeenth century, his participation in the life of learned academies like the Umoristi of Rome, and finally, the existence of no fewer than two biographies of his life, which prefaced the Italian edition of his letters, it is clear that della Valle's self-fashioning as a curious and cosmopolitan pilgrim found a strong echo in baroque Europe.

JOAN-PAU RUBIÉS

### Biography

Born in Rome 11 April 1586. Son of aristocratic parents, received a good education. Lived in Naples in 1609–1614, where he participated in expeditions against North African corsairs and joined a local academy. Fathered some illegitimate children. Began pilgrimage to the Holy Land, 1614, traveling from Venice to Constantinople (Istanbul); stayed in Constantinople, 1614–1615, learned Arabic and Turkish. Continued to Egypt and the Holy Land. Traveled from Jerusalem to Damascus and Baghdad (1616); met and married a Syrian Christian, Sitti Maani Joerida (d. 1621). Lived near the court of Shah Abbas at Isfahan, 1617–1621. Traveled to India, 1621. Reached Surat, Gujerat, 1623; traveled on to Goa, visiting a number of petty courts in southern India. Began his return via the Middle East and Sicily, 1624, reaching Rome, 1626. Married his adopted Georgian daughter Mariuccia in Rome: 14 children. Appointed to the papal court of Urban VIII as gentleman of the bedchamber; acted as advisor on missionary work in Georgia; corresponded with foreign orientalists and hosted scholars in his palace. As a member of the *Accademia degli Umoristi*, delivered an oration concerning his travels. Banished from Rome after killing a servant of Cardinal Barberini in a brawl, 1636. Published a treatise in praise of modern music, 1640. Died in Rome, 21 April 1652.

### References and Further Reading


Della Valle, Pietro, Biblioteca Apostolica Vaticana, MS Ottob. 3,382 (the original journal of della Valle, covering the years 1616–1626).

Della Valle, Pietro, *Nel funerale de Sitti Maani Gioerida sua consorte*, 1627.

Della Valle, Pietro, *Delle conditioni di Abbàs rè di Persia*, 1628.

Della Valle, Pietro, *Viaggi de Pietro della Valle il pellegrino*, 1650 (part 1 only, *La Turchia*).

Della Valle, Pietro, *Viaggi di Pietro della Valle il pellegrino descritti da lui medesimo in lettere familiari all'erudito suo amico Mario Schipano*, 3 parts in 4 books, including *La Turchia* (2nd edition), 1662; *La Persia*, 1658; and *L'India*, 1663; critical edition, for the first half of the second part only: *I viaggi di Pietro della Valle: Lettere dalla Persia*, edited by Franco Gaeta and Laurence Lockhart, 1972; for the third part only, in English: *The Travels of Sig. Pietro della Valle into East India and Arabia deserta*, translated by George Havers, 1665; edited by Edward Gray, 2 vols., 1892, reprinted 1991; as *The Pilgrim: The Travels of Pietro Della Valle*, translated and edited by George Bull (abridged version of the whole journey), 1990.

Della Valle, Pietro, "Informatione della Giorgia," in *Relations de divers voyages curieux, qui n'ont point esté publiées*, by Melchisédec Thévenot, 1663.

Della Valle, Pietro, "Letters," in *Antiquitates Ecclesiae Orientalis*, by Jean Morin et al., edited by Richard Simon, 1682.


## DENHAM, DIXON (1786–1828) *British Traveler in the Sahara and Sudan*

Dixon Denham was greeted as a considerable hero on his return to Britain from West Africa in June 1825. He had crossed the Sahara from Tripoli to Lake Chad and Bornu, experienced many adventures, and amassed much information that he then turned into a well-received book. His fame did not last, however, and he has generally a rather bad reputation among commentators on African travel and exploration. Dr. Robert Brown said in 1892 that Denham "was not regarded by his contemporaries as burdened by many scruples," and that his association with a slave raid was "a discreditable episode in the history of British exploration." It has been implied that his purchase of a slave girl was for sexual purposes. The modern editor (1964–1966) of the materials relating to the expedition, Bovill, judges that "it is difficult to recall in the checkered history of geographical discovery . . . a more odious man." These negative verdicts are in part a response to the fact that Denham was unfair to his fellow explorers, Walter Oudney and Hugh Clapperton, underplaying their work and suppressing information about it as well as giving credence to allegations of sexual misconduct by Clapperton, which he knew to be untrue. In fact, many commentators feel that Denham's own geographical work was relatively unimportant, for example, Curtin says that his understanding of Africa was that of a temporary tourist.

Although it may seem difficult to rescue Denham's reputation in the face of this barrage of condemnation, there is much to be said for him. Some of the blame for his bad relations with Oudney and Clapperton attaches to the Colonial Office and Admiralty, who organized the expedition, because they did not make clear who was in charge. Denham was capable of good feeling toward other subordinate Europeans on the trip, and even toward Clapperton at times. Moreover, and more importantly, as Boahen (1964) points out, he was, like Clapperton, a "model of patience, tact and prudence" in dealing with African rulers. Although it is true that his reaction to reaching "the great Lake Tchad, glowing with the golden rays of the sun in its strength" is a ridiculous parody of Park's words on reaching the Niger—to reach and describe Lake Chad was an achievement. That he appears a champion of the erroneous idea that the Niger flowed eastward through this lake toward the Nile was John Barrow's fault. In fact, Denham's desire to reach the eastern side of the lake to see if there was an outlet (there is not) was the reason for his taking part in a slave raid in April 1823; there seemed no other way of getting away from the Bornu capital, Kukawa. Unwise as he certainly was in this episode, Denham was also personally brave, surviving being speared, having his clothes stripped from him, and near death by drowning. The geographical problem of the Niger partly explains the disputes with Oudney and Clapperton, who favored the theory that the Niger flowed into the Gulf of Benin (as it does).

Perhaps the best reason for forgiving Denham his failings lies in his writings. The major part of his 1826 volume is the production of someone who had considerable sensitivity, culture, and was able to write well and interestingly. His narrative is based on three folio volumes that contained his original manuscript records of his experiences. The published work was undoubtedly an enhanced and improved version in which Barrow probably also had a hand. Its faults, however, appear to lie in its passing over the work of Oudney and Clapperton rather than in major distortion of Denham's own activities or of the information he gathered about Africa.

Denham reports that the expedition members "had determined to travel in our real characters as Britons and Christians, and to wear, on all occasions, our English dresses." While this demonstrates a growing British self-confidence—or arrogance—about their place in the world, the decision was wise: to have appeared in disguise among the reforming Muslims of the western Sudan, where El-Kanemi of Bornu vied with Sultan Bello of Sokoto to demonstrate orthodoxy, would have been to court disaster. On the whole, Denham seems to have gained more respect for his attitude than otherwise. For his own part, he was understanding of Muslims and realized that African Islam was not simply the religion of the Arabs of North Africa. He was inclined to believe that it was the North African slave-trading Arabs who were responsible for the thousands of slave skeletons they saw in the desert, and that figures like El-Kanemi might be persuaded to work with Britain to end slaving. For Denham, El-Kanemi was someone of "fearless bravery, virtue and simplicity." Despite this, the traveler condemned El-Kanemi's severe treatment of erring women. This is all the more understandable in view of Denham's very obvious admiration for the women he encountered, especially those who had the agreeable habit of "shampooing" weary travelers.

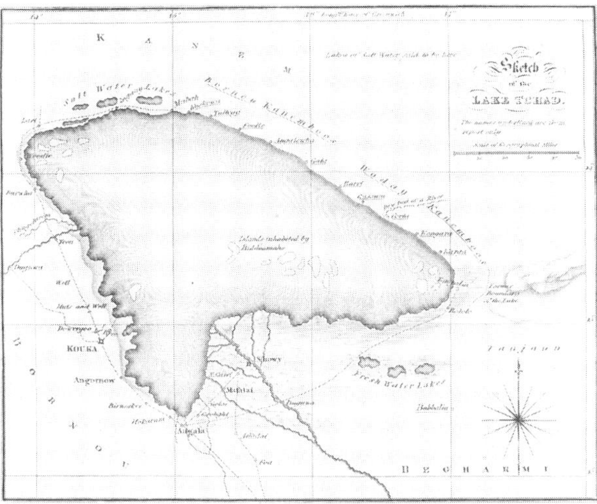


Denham's map of Lake Chad; his expedition with Clapperton established that the lake was not the source of the River Niger (from *Narrative of Travels and Discoveries in Northern and Central Africa*, 1826). *Courtesy of British Library, London.*

Modern readers may well be surprised to discover that Denham, interested as he was in seeing elephants and other African fauna, lacked the normal upper-class Englishman's passion for the hunt, "not being a very keen or inhuman sportsman, for the terms appear to me to be synonymous," he said. As for people, none are so savage "but that gentle kind treatment, with a frank and liberal manner will gain their confidence and regard." Denham warmly praised his own African servants and those in the interior who, albeit "untutored children of nature," possessed "feelings and principles which would do honour to the most civilized Christian." A cynical interpretation would be that Denham included such sentiments to gain favor with the great humanitarian Colonial Secretary Earl Bathurst, so that he would be offered another job. If so, he succeeded—only to bring about his own death in Sierra Leone. However, a reading of his work suggests that Denham was a traveler deserving of some personal reassessment as well as one who produced an important and highly readable narrative. The best and fullest text is the second edition of the narrative of 1826. The 1828 version is the same as that of 1831, but the latter is a four-volume, pocket-sized edition. Bovill's edition (1964–1966) uses the 1826 text and may be the most useful version for modern readers. In addition to the published material, there are relevant official reports by Denham and others in CO2 and FO76 files at the Public Record Office (some printed by Bovill) and many of his manuscripts are in the archives of the Royal Geographical Society.

ROY BRIDGES

## Biography

Born in London, 1 January 1786. Attended Merchant Taylors' School, 1793; later articled to a solicitor. Joined the army as a volunteer with the Royal Welsh Fusiliers, 1811; fought in Spain, Portugal, and France; in reserve at Waterloo. Received Waterloo medal, 1815. After traveling in Europe, including Belgium, France, and Italy, obtained a post at Sandhurst, 1819. Volunteered to travel in Africa; appointed by the Colonial Office to join Walter Oudney and Hugh Clapperton in their expedition across the Sahara from Tripoli, 1821. Reached Lake Chad and then Kukawa in Bornu, February 1823. Narrowly escaped death during a slave raid, May 1823. Made four other exploratory trips near Lake Chad, 1824; unable to complete a circuit. Returned across the Sahara desert, September 1824–January 1825. Returned to Britain to prepare his writings for publication, 1825. Promoted to lieutenant colonel, 1826; elected Fellow of the Royal Society. Went to Sierra Leone, 1827, as Superintendent of Liberated Africans; appointed lieutenant-governor of Sierra Leone, 1828. Died from malaria in Freetown, Sierra Leone, 8 May 1828.

### References and Further Reading

Denham, Dixon, *Narrative of Travels and Discoveries in Northern and Central Africa in the Years 1822, 1823 and 1824*, 1826; 2nd edition, in 2 vols., 1826 [with fewer appendices and illustrations]; 3rd edition, in 2 vols., 1828. New edition, 1985.

Denham, Dixon, *Travels and Discoveries in Northern and Central Africa in 1822, 1823 and 1824: With a Short Account of Clapperton and Lander's Second Journey in 1825, 1826 and 1827*, 4 vols., 1831.

Denham, Dixon, *Missions to the Niger*, edited by E.W. Bovill, 4 vols., 1964–1966.

*See also* **Clapperton, Hugh**

## DEZHNEV, SEMYON (c. 1608–c. 1672)

***Russian Explorer***

Semyon Ivanovich Dezhnev is the first European known to have sailed through the strait dividing Asia from North America.

Russians reached the Pacific coasts in the first half of the seventeenth century. In 1639 a party under I. Yu. Moskvitinov traveled by the Ulya River to the Sea of Okhotsk. The following year Cossacks from the party sailed the Pacific to the north as far as the mouth of the Okhota River, and to the south as far as the Shantarskie Islands. Okhotskiy *ostrog* (stronghold) was founded in 1647. During the same period there was already substantial regular use of the Lena-Kolyma section of the Northeast Passage. The first Cossacks descended the Lena to its delta in 1633, and within a decade the entire coast from the mouth of the Olenek River to the mouth of the Kolyma had been explored. By 1645 the first trading vessels were plying between the Kolyma and the Lena along the Arctic coast. In 1646 Isay Ignat'ev was the first to voyage in the Polar Ocean to the east of the mouth of the Kolyma River, reaching Chaun's *guba* (inlet). He returned to Nizhnekolymsk with a rich supply of *rybiy zub* ("fish tooth," as Russians called walrus tusks at that time). Under the influence of Ignat'ev's reports about those regions' abundance in game for furs and precious walrus bone, a small trading and hunting company was organized to look for a sea passage from the Kolyma to the Anadyr. Fedot Alekseev (Popov) was made leader of the enterprise and Semen Dezhnev joined the company; he was also officially appointed as government representative to the expedition party, with the sole purpose of ensuring that the state made a profit.

In June 1647 the expedition sailed in four *koches* (a *koch* is a one-deck vessel, approximately 25 meters long, which can run under sail and be rowed) from the mouth of the Kolyma to the east, but shortly afterward had to return because impassable ice fields barred their way.

The following year Fedot Alekseev (Popov) and Gerasim Ankudinov set up a new expedition; Dezhnev, with a party of Cossacks, again joined them to collect the tsar's *yasak* (levy) and to search for new peoples who had not yet been forced to pay. The expedition was very imposing for that time: no fewer than 90 men sailed in six (some sources say seven) vessels. The travelers left the mouth of the Kolyma in late June. The ocean near the coasts was nearly free of ice, which allowed them to sail without difficulty. In August the vessels began to turn south, and at the beginning of September they sailed into the strait between Asia and America. Just three of the expedition's vessels reached Bolshoy Kamennyi Nos (Great Nose [promontory] of Stone, now Cape Dezhnev), three months after setting out. It was a high (800 meters), rocky massif with a steep slope to the sea. Writing from Anadyr in April 1655 to the *voevoda* (military governor) of Yakutsk, Semyon Dezhnev's description of the Bering Strait is in such detail that his course can be traced on the modern landscape. The travelers could not see an American shoreline, but they did point out two islands in the strait (now called the Diomid Islands) inhabited by *Chukochi* (in fact by Eskimos).

Not far from Bol'shoy Kamennyi Nos, the Russians landed and fought the Chukchi. They then visited one of the islands in the strait and got acquainted with its natives, describing them as *zubatye chukochi* or "Chukchi with teeth," which fits the Eskimos of these islands, who pierced their lips with seals' teeth. Ankudinov's *koch* was shipwrecked near the island, and his men boarded Alekseev's (Popov's) vessel. At the beginning of October violent storms separated the expedition's ships. Dezhnev's *koch*, with its 25-man crew, was beached at Cape Olyutorsky some ten days' walking distance to the south of the mouth of the Anadyr. Later Semyon Dezhnev discovered that Alekseev's (Popov's) and Ankudinov's *koch* had landed on the coast near the Kamchatka River, where all the men had perished from scurvy and fights with natives. Dezhnev's party, in very difficult winter conditions, traveled on foot to the mouth of the Anadyr: only 12 men survived this trip. In the summer of 1649 Dezhnev constructed a boat and sailed up the Anadyr, reaching Chukchi settlements. In the middle course of the Anadyr the Russians built a winter village, which was later called Anadyr *ostrog* (stronghold).

Dezhnev proved that Asia was separated from North America, but did not fully comprehend the geographical importance of his discovery. His expedition did not pass unnoticed by representatives of the Siberian administration. The two earliest surviving manuscript maps of Siberia, dating from 1667 and 1673, prove this fact as both show uninterrupted water space between the Kolyma and Anadyr rivers. The legend of the 1673 map even contains confirmation that expeditions like Dezhnev's were attempted by other Russians: they "move from the River Kolyma and farther round the land . . . by sail to reach the Stone [i.e., the Chukotskii Peninsula], and on crossing the Stone reach the River Anadyr and there buy fish bone [walrus tusks] from natives; and the Stone is difficult to cross." Dezhnev's journey was not known at the time by the world at large because his report lay buried in the archives at Yakutsk until the German historian Gerhard Friedrich Müller (1705–1783), serving in the St. Petersburg Academy of Sciences, found it in 1736. Therefore the discovery was not known until nearly a century had passed and after Vitus Bering and others had explored the area.

G.F. Müller was the first to publish information about Deshnev's expedition, in Russian and German, in 1758. In 1761 an English translation was published. In 1890 N. Oglobin discovered and published some new material on Deshnev's journey. Genuine documents on the journey were issued by T.D. Lavrentsova in 1964, and the most thorough English rendering of these sources is to be found in the Hakluyt Society edition of 1981.

In 1898, to commemorate the 250th anniversary of Semyon Dezhnev's voyage from the Polar into the Pacific Ocean, the Imperial Russian Geographical Society proposed that the eastern cape of Chukotskii Peninsula be named the Cape of Dezhnev or Dezhnev Cape. This proposition was accepted by the international scientific community, and since that time the promontory with the coordinates 66°3′ N and 169°44′ E has borne the name of the traveler who was the first to discover and describe it for Europeans.

Alexei V. Postnikov

### Biography

Born in Velikiy Ustyug, Russia, c. 1605 or 1608. Left Ustyug in early youth; visited the Russian frontier towns of Siberia; worked as a state's (czar's) officer responsible for collecting taxes in furs (*yasak*) from the natives in Tobolsk and Eniseysk. During 20 years of service was seriously injured nine times. Moved to Yakutsk, 1638; in the party of 15 Cossacks led by Mikhaylov, traveled to collect the *yasak* (levy) on the Yana River, 1641. Lived on the Kolyma River, 1642–1645, gathering furs and other booty. With 13 Cossacks, withstood the assault of 500 Yukagirs in the Kolyma encampment (*ostrozhek*). Served as official representative on Fedor Alekseev's (Popov's) expedition to look for a sea passage from the Kolyma to the Anadyr rivers, 1648; proved the geographical separation of Asia and North America. Settled on the Anadyr River, 1648–1662, hunting and traveling. Returned to Yakutsk, 1662. Lived in Moscow, 1664–1665, compiling reports on his travels and attempting to obtain retrospective payment for his work. Served as Yakutsk's *ataman* (military commander) 1665–1672; returned to Moscow. Died in Moscow, 1673.

### References and Further Reading

Dezhnev, Semyon, "Nachrichten von Seereisen und zur Seegemachten Entdeckungen," *Sammlung Russischer Geschichte*, 9/1 (1758).

Dezhnev, Semyon, *Voyages from Asia to America for Completing the Discoveries of the North West Coast of America: To Which is Prefixed a Summary of the Voyages Made by the Russians on the Frozen Sea, in Search of a North East Passage*, 1761.

Dezhnev, Semyon, "Semen Dezhnev (1638–1671 gg): Novye dannye i peresmotr starukh" [Semyon Dezhnev (1638–1671): New Materials and a Revision of Old Ones], *Zhurnal Ministerstva narodnogo prosvyashcheniya*, 272/11 (1890).

Dezhnev, Semyon, *The Voyage of Semen Dezhnev in 1648: Bering's Precursor, with Selected Documents*, edited by Raymond H. Fisher, 1981.

## DIARIES

The diary could be considered the stealth genre of travel literature. Some travel books announce their status as diary right up front, like James Boswell's *Journal of a Tour to the Hebrides* (1785) or Stephen Spender and David Hockney's *China Diary* (1982). Some use a subtitle to mark the presence of a diary as in Robert Walpole's *Memoirs Relating to European and Asiatic Turkey: Edited from Manuscript Journals* (1817). But others, such as *A Pilgrimage to Nejd* (1881) by Lady Anne Blunt or *Ultimate High: My Everest Odyssey* (1999) by Goran Kropp, contain many passages from their authors' diaries without any indication thereof, while the specific dates, times, and descriptions in works like Mary Kingsley's *Travels in West Africa* (1897) clearly reveal their origins in a diary or diarylike notes, despite the lack of any reference to the genre. To make things more complicated, *The Journal of Friar Odoric* (1318–1330), an account of the Asian journeys of an Italian monk, is nothing of the sort. As these few examples begin to suggest, diaries show up in travel literature in numerous guises: as books, as parts of books, as sources of books, not to mention as unpublished, though frequently shared, manuscripts.

What accounts for the near omnipresence of the diary in travel literature? Stuart Sherman offers a persuasive set of answers to this question in *Telling Time: Clocks, Diaries, and English Diurnal Form, 1660–1785*. Looking at how "the numbers of time structure the narrative of motion through space," he suggests that the travel diary allows for "the greatest comprehensiveness of coverage." That is, organized by time, rather than topic, event, or place, the diary offers the traveler a framework that can encompass everything that happens, everything seen, every possible kind of information gathered. At the same time, the familiarity of its daily structure "mediates a growing sense of 'simultaneity' between the sedentary reader and the outwandering narrative": even as the diary functions as an organizing structure for the writing traveler, it provides a source of pleasurable identification for the traveler's reader. Of course not everything worth writing is worth reading; one danger of any diary, but especially the travel diary, as Sherman points out, is that it can become what Daniel Defoe criticized as "a Journal of Trifles" (quoted in Sherman, 1996): a list of distances, sights, prices, and meals that reveals little or nothing of the traveler or the travels. The boring monotony of many travel diaries, both published and manuscript, testifies loudly to this danger. Revising a diary into a narrative, even partially, can be seen as an effort to distill and develop a more compelling account out of the diary's "comprehensiveness." Such revisions also allow a writer to enhance the diary's immediate observations with the benefits of hindsight and reflection.

A PAGE OF DAMPIER'S JOURNAL (SLOANE MSS. 3236)

[*Note.* A comparison of this page with page 155 of the present edition shows that the text and marginal notes were subjected to considerable revision before publication of the book.]

A page from Dampier's journal (British Library MS Sloane 3236) recording the seizure and firing of the Central American Spanish settlement of Leon in August 1685; comparison with the published version of the same episode (in *A New Voyage round the World* (1697), pp. 218–221) shows how extensively the journal was reworked for publication. *Courtesy of Senate House, University of London Library.*

The efficacy of the diary format for travel writing can be seen in its persistence across cultures and time. Some of the oldest extant travel diaries are Japanese and Chinese. These range from the Japanese Buddhist monk Ennin's record of his nine-year trip to China on legal business, begun in 838, to medieval Japanese literary travel diaries full of poems and symbolism, to seventeenth-century Chinese geographer Hsü Hsia-k'o's diaries of his exploratory travels throughout China. Maritime logs and journals were a significant prototype for the travel diary in the West, particularly during the sixteenth and seventeenth centuries, as European ships set out to create new trade routes and colonies in Africa, Asia, and the Americas. Following this precedent, the daily format of the journal became the conventional textual model for producing accounts of new places and peoples, and nineteenth-century Western land-based explorers in the Americas, Africa, and the Arctic kept meticulous daily records of their travels. American emigrants in the nineteenth century may not have seen themselves as national or imperial explorers, but they too relied on diaries to mark their individual paths through new ground.

While the diaries of explorers and emigrants suggest that one important role of the travel diary has been to compile information about uncharted regions, by the seventeenth century the diary was also becoming a conventional means of documenting leisure travel. Indeed, mid-eighteenth-century diarists on the Grand Tour seem to practically repeat each other's words as they follow in each other's tracks. Travel diaries were particularly popular throughout the eighteenth and nineteenth centuries among continental visitors to

Great Britain, tourists in England's Lake District and in Scotland, European visitors to America, and American visitors to Europe. Travel diarists of the twentieth century, like so many other twentieth-century writers, wrote self-consciously in their generic tradition, even as they maintained its conventions. Some still set out to explore new ground, but this ground was as likely to be social as geographical, as in the case of Western travelers to Communist countries. Many travel diaries of this time also reflected the diary's general turn toward introspection and self-reflectiveness. At the beginning of the twenty-first century, the daily entries of the diary remain a significant form for travelers, but the medium of those entries has been expanded by technology; while many diarists still rely on pen and paper, others create daily records of their travels through video cameras, laptop computers, and Internet websites.

In all its variations, the travel diary is distinguished from other travel writing by its temporal framework and its immediacy: through its daily entries the text generally maintains the impression of having been written in the thick of things, as the journey unfolds, though in published travel diaries that impression can be as artful as it is actual. The travel diary is distinguished from other diaries by its specific focus and, significantly, by its public nature. More often than other kinds of diaries, indeed, more often than not, the travel diary is written for or shared with friends and family members, kept by one diarist on behalf of a group or by more than one diarist, and/or published, frequently soon after its composition. Queen Isabella and King Ferdinand of Spain commissioned Christopher Columbus to keep his *Diarios* (1492–1504), American explorers Meriwether Lewis and William Clark kept journals of their expedition to the Pacific (1804–1806) at the behest of President Thomas Jefferson, and 19th-century emigrants, particularly women, frequently sent their diaries back to friends and family at home. Percy and Mary Shelley kept and published a joint diary of their travels on the Continent (*History of a Six Weeks' Tour*, 1817). Nineteenth-century British explorers Mungo Park, David Livingstone, Henry Stanley, and John Speke, among others, kept journals of their travels in Africa which, published soon after their composition, were widely read and reprinted. Mountain-climber Sandy Hill Pittman posted daily dispatches on the Internet from her 1996 climb up Everest. One result of the travel diary's public nature is that the psychological dimension so frequently emphasized in other kinds of diaries is less central, sometimes even absent, as the diarist focuses on outward circumstances and surroundings more easily shared with others.

It is important to note that the travel diary's public nature does not always equate with publication. Indeed, the travel diary also stands out from other kinds of travel writing as a genre highly accessible to the amateur. A significant percentage of the entries in John Stuart Batts's bibliography, *British Manuscript Diaries of the Nineteenth Century* (1976) are travel diaries. Some of these come from the pens of habitual diarists who kept up their habit on journeys, but the number of freestanding travel diaries suggests that the genre had a broader appeal to travelers who wanted a tangible and personal reminder of their experiences. That these diaries remain in manuscript form testifies to their limited readership, although some expressly indicate an interest in readers, like Henry Bishop's "A Journal from London to Paris &c" (1814), a carefully formatted manuscript volume, complete with cover page, footnotes, and annotations, and helpful comments like "This is the first Village from *Abbeville* where it is possible to get any thing in the shape of Food, which may be a useful information to Travellers, as it is some distance from Abbeville!" Often, especially in the eighteenth and nineteenth centuries, published travel diaries had their origin in manuscripts circulated among family and friends, though the claim that the readers of the manuscript insisted on its publication is so common in published diaries as to become a convention. This was especially true for women writers who were prolific travel diarists but, for propriety's sake, often needed a practical or pedagogical excuse for publication.

Today, the popularity of the travel diary shows no sign of fading. Even with the omnipresence of snapshots and videos, the written diary maintains its appeal for the ordinary traveler, as seen in the number of blank books with titles like *Travel Journal, Kid's Trip Diary*, and *RVer's Travel Diary* stocked by popular bookshops. Readers also continue to respond to the genre, as demonstrated by the large numbers of travel diaries, old and new, published each year. Indeed, reading published travel diaries often inspires travelers to write their own, whether they be medieval Japanese poets, eighteenth-century tourists like James Boswell, nineteenth-century American emigrants, or twenty-first-century teenagers and grandmothers. Its ability to traverse the boundary between reader and writer is thus one more instance of the travel diary's powerful presence in the world of travel literature.

REBECCA STEINITZ

### References and Further Reading

Bartlett, John Russell, *Personal Narrative of Explorations and Incidents in Texas, New Mexico, California, Sonora, and Chihuahua, Connected with the United States and Mexican Boundary Commission during the Years 1850, '51, '52 and '53*, 2 vols., 1854.

Batts, John Stuart, *British Manuscript Diaries of the Nineteenth Century: An Annotated Listing*, Fontwell: Centaur Press, Totawa, New Jersey: Rowman and Littlefield, 1976.
Beauvoir, Simone de, *L'Amérique au jour le jour*, 1948; as *America Day by Day*, translated by Patrick Dudley, 1952.
Bishop, Henry, "A Journal from London to Paris &c," 1814.
Bligh, William, *A Narrative of the Mutiny, on Board His Britannic Majesty's Ship Bounty: and the Subsequent Voyage of Part of the Crew, in the Ship's Boat, from Tofoa, One of the Friendly Islands, to Timor, a Dutch Settlement in the East Indies*, 1790.
Blunt, Anne, *A Pilgrimage to Nejd: The Cradle of the Arab Race*, 1881.
Boswell, James, *The Journal of a Tour to the Hebrides*, 1785.
Columbus, Christopher, *Diarios des viajes*, 1492–1504; as *The Voyage of Christopher Columbus: Columbus's Own Journal of Discovery Newly Restored and Translated*, translated by John Cummins, 1992.
Cook, James, *A Voyage to the Pacific Ocean: Undertaken by the Command of His Majesty, for Making Discoveries in the Northern Hemisphere*, 3 vols., edited by John Douglas, 1784; as *The Journals of Captain James Cook on His Voyages of Discovery*, 4 vols., edited by J.C. Beaglehole, 1955–1974.
Dana, Richard Henry, *Two Years before the Mast: A Personal Narrative of Life at Sea*, 1840.
Darwin, Charles, *Journal of Researches into the Geology and Natural History of the Various Countries Visited by H.M.S. Beagle*, 1839.
Ennin, *Ennin's Diary: The Record of a Pilgrimage to China in Search of the Law*, translated by Edwin O. Reischauer, 1955.
Fowler, John, *Journal of a Tour in the State of New York in the Year 1830*, 1831.
Gammelgaard, Lene, *Climbing High: A Woman's Account of Surviving the Everest Tragedy*, 1999.
Kemble, Frances Anne, *Journal of a Residence on a Georgian Plantation in 1838–1839*, 1863.
Kingsley, Mary, *Travels in West Africa: Congo Français, Corisco and Cameroons*, 1897.
Kropp, Goran, *Ultimate High: My Solo Ascent of Everest*, 1999.
Leake, William Martin, *Travels in the Morea*, 3 vols., 1830.
Leake, William Martin, *Travels in Northern Greece*, 4 vols., 1835.
Lewis, Meriwether, and William Clark, *Original Journals of the Lewis and Clark Expedition, 1804–1806*, 8 vols., edited by Rueben Gold Thwaites, 1904–1905; as *The Journals of the Lewis and Clark Expedition*, 12 vols, edited by Gary E. Moulton, 1983–1999.
Livingstone, David, *The Last Journals of David Livingstone, in Central Africa, from 1865 to his Death*, 1874.
Livingstone, David, *Livingstone's Private Journals, 1815–53*, edited by I. Schapera, 1960.
Malinowski, Bronislaw, *A Diary in the Strict Sense of the Term*, translated by Norbert Guterman, 1967.
McElwee, Ross, *Sherman's March*, 1986.
Melville, Herman, *Journal of a Visit to Europe and the Levant*, edited by Howard C. Horsford, 1955.
Morrell, Abby Jane, *Narrative of a Voyage to the Ethiopic and South Atlantic Ocean, Indian Ocean, Chinese Sea, North and South Pacific Ocean, in the Years 1829, 1830, 1831*, 1833.
Parry, William, *Journal of a Voyage for the Discovery of a North-West Passage from the Atlantic to the Pacific*, 1821; *Journal of a Second Voyage for the Discovery of a North-West Passage from the Atlantic to the Pacific*, 1824; *Journal of a Third Voyage for the Discovery of a North-West Passage from the Atlantic to the Pacific*, 1826.
Plutschow, Herbert (translator), *Four Japanese Travel Diaries of the Middle Ages*, 1981.
Scott, Robert Falcon, *Scott's Last Expedition: The Personal Journal of Captain R.F. Scott, on His Journey to the South Pole*, 1923.
Shelley, Mary, and P.B. Shelley, *History of a Six Weeks' Tour*, 1817.
Sherman, Stuart, *Telling Time: Clocks, Diaries, and English Diurnal Form, 1660–1785*, Chicago: University of Chicago Press, 1996.
Spender, Stephen, and David Hockney, *China Diary*, 1982.
Stanley, Henry M., *How I Found Livingstone: Travels, Adventures and Discoveries in Central Africa*, 1872.
Victoria, Queen, *Leaves from the Journal of Our Life in the Highlands, from 1848 to 1861*, 1868.
von Ehingen, Jörg, *Itinerarium*, 1600; as *The Diary of Jörg von Ehingen*, translated and edited by Malcolm Letts, 1929.
Walpole, Robert (editor), *Memoirs Relating to European and Asiatic Turkey: Edited from Manuscript Journals*, 1817.
Willard, Emma, *Journal and Letters from France and Great-Britain*, 1833.
Wilson, Edmund, *Red, Black, Blond, and Olive: Studies in Four Civilizations*, 1956.

*See also* **Letters; Logbooks**

## DÍAZ DEL CASTILLO, BERNAL

**(c. 1496–1584)** ***Spanish Soldier and Chronicler***

When Columbus landed in the Caribbean, those islands were to be the stepping-stones not only to a new continent, but to a whole new world—a new concept of civilization, for which Spain was ill prepared. Having waged a long war of reconquest against the Moors, Spanish warriors carried their crusade into new territories, proud of their newly won title of God's chosen race—the sword in one hand and the cross in the other. These two images were to symbolize the objectives of the Spanish mission in the New World—territorial expansion and religious conversion. The important factor for the literature was the novelty—all was new for these discoverers and conquerors, who had the extraordinary distinction of creating history and literature simultaneously. In the early literature, which was necessarily in the chronicle genre, in letters, reports, and commentaries, they marveled at the new lands, the flora and fauna, and the new people, the indigenous inhabitants. In Columbus's *Cuatro viajes del almirante* [Four Voyages of the Admiral] one finds the seeds of the potential lyric poet, while in the *Cartas de relación*, (1519–1526) [Letters of Relation] of Cortés, one is struck by the epic grandeur of mighty civilizations. In both one also finds awareness of the precious metals that were soon to overthrow the economy of Europe.

Side by side with Cortés in the epic battle to capture the vast Aztec empire was a Castilian soldier named Bernal Díaz del Castillo. Born in Medina del Campo

(c. 1496) of a modestly noble family, Bernal Díaz went to the Indies at the age of 18 to seek fortune and glory. After brief and fruitless stays in Darien and Cuba, he served on various expeditions to the Yucatán under Francisco Hernández de Córdoba and Juan de Grijalva, again without success. In February 1519 he set out anew from Cuba on an expedition to the Yucatán, this time under the command of Hernán Cortés, to seek fame, land, gold, and other compensations for spreading the word of God and extending the Spanish empire at the expense of the native Indians. This story has been told elsewhere by Cortés himself in his letters, and by his secretary-chaplain Francisco López de Gómara in his *Historia de las Indias y conquista de México*, 1552 [History of the Indies and Conquest of Mexico], a work that inspired Bernal Díaz to write his own *Historia verdadera de la conquista de la Nueva España* [True History of the Conquest of New Spain], which was not published until 1632, almost 50 years after his death. Although this chronicle of the Spanish conquest of the Aztec empire eventually gained Bernal Díaz the posthumous fame that he had sought in life, his military career extended beyond the fall of Tenochtitlán. He served Cortés in other forays to different regions, including Honduras. Disillusioned and disappointed with his lack of reward, the old soldier went to Spain in 1540 to demand recompense and recognition. Still dissatisfied, he returned to the New World and settled in Santiago de los Caballeros de Guatemala, where he became a member of the local town council and married Teresa Becerra, the comparatively wealthy daughter of a conquistador. Now in his sixties, Bernal Díaz had the financial security and the peace of mind not only to reflect on his days of military action, but to record his own memories of the conquest of Mexico, as opposed to the egotistical and self-centered letters of his chief, Cortés, and even worse the eulogistic history by Cortés's chaplain, López de Gómara, who had never even been in the New World.

To counterbalance this work of eulogy, Bernal Díaz's aim was to write a work of distributive justice that would give credit not only to the leader Cortés, but to the other captains and ordinary soldiers who had fought courageously but had received no reward or recognition (financial or otherwise). Not least among these unappreciated warriors was Bernal Díaz himself. As the oldest of the five survivors who left Cuba in 1519 with Cortés, he displays his prodigious memory more than half a century later in recollecting the men and events. If the letters of Cortés constitute a document of self-justification, and López de Gómara's pure adulation, Bernal Díaz's history is more democratic, even proletarian, and certainly fairer to the soldiers (and the Indians). Although Bernal Díaz recognizes Cortés's soldierly qualities, he is not afraid to criticize him and point out the self-promotion at the heart of his master's narrative. Bernal Díaz's attitude (and his literary style) is more that of the man in the street and around the campfire. As such, he is the chronicler of the ordinary soldiers and their desires for wealth, land, and *encomienda*—control over the native Indians. Although not a butcher or a fanatic like some of the other conquistadores, Bernal Díaz was a typical Castilian soldier of his time, with much of the ambivalent medieval attitude (cross/sword) toward the indigenous people, as his narrative reveals. Reading his chronicle, one never doubts his courage, his spirit, his sense of justice and fairness, or his common sense. If not completely a true history, as he claims, Bernal Díaz's version is certainly more balanced than those of his fellow conquistadores. If not a defender and apologist of the Indians like the "Apostle" Las Casas, whose exaggerated statistics and hyperbolic descriptions helped propagate the black legend of Spanish cruelty and barbarity in the New World, Bernal Díaz shows himself to be just and fair. In fact, his moving description of the deaths of Montezuma and Cuauhtémoc, which reduced the author to tears, is one of the highlights of the narrative. His recording of these events and other examples of the mistreatment of the Indians implies a criticism of Cortés's methods and decisions. Bernal Díaz, who appears to have treated his own Indians in a more humane fashion, openly condemns the practices of postbattle enslavement and branding.

Although Bernal Díaz's *Historia verdadera* was not highly regarded in the seventeenth and eighteenth centuries, it was beginning to be more appreciated in the nineteenth century, not only as a counterbalance to the narrow focus of his compatriots, but as literary work of Mexican *costumbrismo* and even autobiography, in its detailed self-portrait of the old soldier. Bernal Díaz may have decried his own literary powers, but the *Historia verdadera*, with its unique style of oral expression, is a fine collection of memoirs by a man who, as he always claimed, was there, and saw and experienced what he wrote. It may be the prose of the campfire, but it is a true record of lived events, as in his portrayal of the battles for Tenochtitlán, with all their color and drama. This Castilian eyewitness, however, in his description of *la grandeza mexicana*, writes under the influence of the old novels of chivalry in vogue at that time. His constant references, for example, to the *Amadis de Gaula*, in his description of the plants and animals, the bridges and palaces, the gardens and markets, and his general sense of wonder and enchantment in the face of the marvels and the novelties of the fantastic New World, prepare the way for the imaginative, creative literature of the coming centuries. This is no mean achievement for a self-confessed simple old soldier, devoid of artistic pretensions, who only wanted to tell the truth, in the name of justice, before he died in Guatemala on 3 February 1584.

JOHN WALKER

### Biography

Born in Medino del Campo, Castile, c. 1496. Went to Cuba on the voyage of Pedrarias Davila to Tierra Firme, 1514. Stayed in Cuba until 1517. Served in expeditions to Yucatán peninsula under Francisco Hernández de Córdoba (1517) and possibly with Juan de Grijalva (1518). Took part in the conquest of the Aztec capital of Tenochtitlán with Hernán Cortés, 1519 and 1521. Made expedition to the Mexican interior with Gonzalo de Sandoval, c. 1520s. Settled in Espiritú Santo, Coatzacoalcos, Mexico. Later served on ill-fated expedition with Cortés to explore Honduras, 1524–1526. Returned to Mexico, 1526. Two daughters by a native Mexican woman, before 1540. Returned to Spain to demand recognition and reward for his conquests, 1539–1540. Returned to Mexico briefly and moved to Santiago de los Caballeros de Guatemala, 1541. One son by common-law wife, Angelina, c. 1542. Married Teresa Becerra, 1543 or 1544: five sons and three daughters. Traveled to Spain again to seek financial reward, 1549–1550. Elected as *regidore* to the Guatemala *cabildo*, 1551. Died in Santiago de los Caballeros de Guatemala, January or February 1584.

### References and Further Reading

Díaz del Castillo, Bernal, *Historia verdadera de la conquista de la Nueva España* [True History of the Conquest of New Spain], written 1568, published 1632; edited by Miguel Leon-Portilla, 2 vols., 1984; as *The Discovery and Conquest of Mexico, 1517–1521*, edited by Genaro García, translated by A.P. Maudslay, 1928; with an introduction by Irving A. Leonard, 1956; as *The Bernal Díaz Chronicles: The True Story of the Conquest of Mexico*, translated and edited by Albert E. Idell Gardenlith, 1956; as *The Conquest of New Spain*, translated and with an introduction by J.M. Cohen, 1963.

## DICKENS, CHARLES (1812–1870) *English Novelist*

Charles John Huffam Dickens, acknowledged to be England's greatest writer of fiction, was an inveterate traveler, who exercised his acute powers of observation to assess characters and situations, as well as social and political conditions, in a series of comparative meditations on the locations he visited, including France, Belgium, Switzerland, Italy, Ireland, the United States, and Canada.

The nineteenth century saw an expansion of the available modes of transportation—particularly the railway and steamship, but also roads and canals, thus facilitating the democratization of foreign and domestic travel, and placing it within reach of the young Dickens. His first journey abroad to France (particularly Calais) and Belgium in 1837, conceived as a result of a childhood spent partly in Kent, established a convenient route for retreat and escape that he followed for the rest of his life. Early on he recognized the insight that could be gained from comparing French and English values, character, and modes of behavior; this comparison emerged in various forms in his writing—including "A Monument of French Folly" (*Household Words*), 2 (8 March 1851): 553–558) and, most spectacularly, *A Tale of Two Cities* (1859).

Dickens was struck by French republican egalitarianism, and as he consolidated his social vision and his reputation as a writer he turned his attention to that other great republic, the United States, which for him appeared to be a utopian dream. Prompted partly by the urgings of the writer Washington Irving, Dickens sailed for Boston in January 1842, hoping to use his visit (for which he had borrowed money from his English publishers) as an opportunity to confirm his complimentary opinion. He traveled through Massachusetts, Connecticut, Pennsylvania, New York, Virginia, Ohio, Kentucky, and as far west as St. Louis; in Washington he was received by President John Tyler. At first he and his wife enjoyed the attention lavished on them at private and public functions (including the "Boz Ball" in New York, attended by 3,000 people); however, his American hosts were troubled and offended by Dickens's public remarks concerning the highly debated issue of international copyright—the absence of which allowed for the publication of countless pirated American editions of his work. He keenly felt that this "unmanly and ungenerous treatment has been to me an amount of agony such as I have never experienced since my birth"; he also disliked what he considered vulgar American habits, including spitting, inadequate personal hygiene, and crude table manners, as well as their informality, which made for uninvited advances by complete strangers. His observations led him to conclude that "This is not the Republic I came to see. This is not the Republic of my imagination" (*Letters*). Dickens was also repelled, in Virginia, by the sight of slaves, though he never spoke about this issue in public.

Dickens reserved his most sustained critique for the travelogue published on his return, *American Notes for General Circulation*—a work for which he prepared by reading the accounts of such writers as Harriet Martineau. He used the many journal-letters he wrote to his friend John Forster as *aides mémoires*, and introduced into his manuscript (preserved at the Victoria and Albert Museum) cuttings from printed material he had gathered on his tour. The book is divided in two: the first part provides details of Dickens's voyage, covering his travels as far as Washington D.C., and his analysis of various American institutions, including prisons, schools, and government; the second deals with the novelist's journey to the West, and concentrates on the rigors of travel, undertaken by train, canal, riverboat, and stagecoach. He also includes details of his brief sojourn in Canada, where he visited Niagara Falls, Toronto, Kingston, and Montreal, before returning to the United States for the voyage home.

Despite Dickens's disappointment with the country, he did not approach his subject with invective in mind; rather he wished to catalog his impressions, and to report on various foibles and abuses as honestly as he would have done at home. These intentions were made clear in Dickens's introduction, written in July 1842 but suppressed (it was first reprinted in Forster's *Life of Charles Dickens*). The absence of these prefatory remarks from the published volume may have added to the distress felt by American readers of *American Notes*, which nevertheless sold well in the United States—especially in pirated editions. Though the book went comparatively unnoticed in England, American reviewers generally saw it as a vituperative misrepresentation of republican virtues. They had a second opportunity to vent their anger at Dickens's impressions when in 1843–1844 he issued his sixth novel, *Martin Chuzzlewit*, which, in its acerbic account of Martin's American adventures, highlights selfishness in its various aspects.

When Dickens embarked for Italy in July 1844, he longed for an extended period of rest, and hoped to defray the expenses of his Continental sojourn by compiling a second travel book, *Pictures from Italy*. On his way to Genoa (which he made his base) he passed through Boulogne, Paris, Lyons, Avignon, Marseilles, and Nice. During his 11 months in Italy he traveled as far north as Milan, and ventured south to Capri. His stated interest was in developing a "new picturesque" with which to describe the country's social and political difficulties (*Letters*). He adopted the persona of a strongly independent *flâneur*, strolling through Italian society in order to compile a critique of what he observed. The first half of *Pictures from Italy* describes Dickens's journey through France, his life in Genoa, and his brief return to London in December 1844. In the second half he describes his two visits to Rome and his journey to Pompeii, including a fascinating account of a nighttime ascent of Vesuvius; he concludes with a "Rapid Diorama" of Florence, and the return journey through Switzerland. The volume was not particularly successful: critics believed that Dickens was not well versed in Italian affairs, and lacked the education necessary to write convincingly about the country. The volume also drew strong disapproval from readers who objected to his negative presentation of Roman Catholicism.

Dickens did not document his later travels in such a structured or expansive manner. He had an extended stay in Switzerland in 1846, during which he wrote the opening portions of *Dombey and Son* (1846–1848), and his professional reading tours, begun in 1858, took him to many parts of Britain and Ireland, as well as to America in 1867–1868. After England, the country that attracted him most was France—particularly Paris, which he described in "Travelling Abroad" and "Some Recollections of Mortality" (in *The Uncommercial Traveller*, 1860 and 1865), and Boulogne, where he found that he could work fruitfully, and which in later years he used as a refuge from both personal and professional pressures.

LEON LITVACK

## Biography

Born in Portsmouth, 7 February 1812. Formal education sporadic: attended the small preparatory school run by the Reverend William Giles, 1821–1822; after his father's release from Marshalsea debtors' prison, attended Wellington House Academy, London, 1824–1827, and Mr. Dawson's school, Brunswick Square, London, 1827. Employed as a legal clerk, then a freelance shorthand reporter at Doctors' Commons, 1827–1829. Parliamentary reporter for the *True Sun*, 1830–1832; *Mirror of Parliament*, 1832–1834; *Morning Chronicle*, 1834–1836. Married Catherine Thompson Hogarth, 1836 (separated, 1858): seven sons, three daughters. Editor, *Bentley's Miscellany*, 1837–1839. Visited the United States, 1842; lived in Italy, 1844–1845; lived in Switzerland and Paris, 1846. Editor, London *Daily News*, 1846. Managed an amateur theatrical tour of England, 1847. Founding editor, *Household Words*, London, 1850–1859; *All the Year Round*, 1859–1870. Conducted reading tour of the United States, 1867–1868. Developed an intimate friendship with Ellen Lawless Ternan, who may have been his lover, from 1858. Lived at Gad's Hill Place, near Rochester, Kent, from 1860. Published sketches and tales in newspapers and journals, eventually collected as *Sketches by Boz*, 1836. Produced 14 complete novels and *The Mystery of Edwin Drood*, 1870, unfinished at the time of his death. Also published two travelogues, *American Notes*, 1842, and *Pictures from Italy*, 1846; and five Christmas books, including *A Christmas Carol*, 1843. Died of a stroke at Gad's Hill, Kent, 9 June 1870.

## References and Further Reading

Dickens, Charles, *American Notes for General Circulation*, 2 vols., 1842.
Dickens, Charles, *Pictures from Italy*, 1846.

## DIGBY, JANE (1807–1881) *British Traveler and Artist*

In the coterie of nineteenth-century travelers and travel writers, perhaps in particular the women, Jane Elizabeth Digby stands out because of her unwillingness to publish accounts of her adventures and travel. Because of her much-publicized love life as wife to aristocrats and lover to royalty, including King Ludwig of Bavaria, Digby's steamy reputation became the subject of eight novels during her lifetime and more after her death. In spite of her notoriety as an adult, Digby ironically began, at a young age, to guard her privacy, writing to her family in a secret code that she continued to use throughout her lifetime in diaries and letters.

This zealous desire to protect her privacy is revealed in a letter to her sister-in-law written in response to a false report of her own death and Isabel Burton's public announcement of being Digby's officially sanctioned biographer. Digby wrote: "I certainly *always* deprecated every idea of publishing anything relating to myself or my former existence, as you can easily believe . . . she [Isabel Burton] knew the horror and aversion I have to this kind of thing" (21 May 1873 [Lovell, 1995]). In her later years, when a visitor to Damascus suggested that she ought to write her memoirs, she replied with a chuckle that she was afraid they would be a rather naughty edition of the *Almanach de Gotha*, and then added rather primly that a prayer book was more suitable to her declining years.

One example of her unconventional life is illustrated by her affair with Christodoulos Hadji-Petros, a chieftain of a band of Albanian *palikares*. They lived in the open air in camps, in deserted, ruined castles, in caves. They cooked on an open fire and rode horseback on dangerous mountain roads. Digby, in the colorful dress of the *palikares*, rode beside her lover at the head of the band. Her friend Edmond About said: "Ianthe [Greek for Jane], imagined that she was born Palikar . . . this delicate woman lived with drunkards, galloped on horseback in the mountains, ate literally on the move, drank retsina, slept in the open beside a great fire" (Lovell, 1995). The delicate woman herself said, "This was freedom, this was life!"

The knowledge and experiences Digby gained through her freedom informed the works of other travel writers who wandered through Damascus, including Amy Fullerton-Fullerton's *A Lady's Ride through Palestine and Syria* (1872), Emily Beaufort's *Egyptian Sepulchres and Syrian Shrines* (1861), and works by Wilfrid and Anne Blunt, most notably *Bedouin Tribes of the Euphrates* (1878) by Lady Anne Blunt.

Digby's other significant literary contribution occurred through her collaboration with Sir Richard Burton on his translation of *The Arabian Nights* and in particular the controversial "Terminal Essay." Digby's intimate insider knowledge of harem life and her fluency in languages made her an invaluable resource for Burton's. Burton's biographer, Sefton Dearden, acknowledged her contribution, explaining that "her knowledge of Arab life almost equalled his own [Burton's], her acquaintance with the female side far exceeded it and many were the evenings they spent on the leafy logia at Salhiyeh, talking under the stars." Dearden adds: "How much of the knowledge of Moslem female sexual psychology which was later embodied in the famous "Terminal Essay" to *The Arabian Nights* came from the lips of Jane Digby one can only guess, but knowing the vigorous secrecy surrounding the harem . . . and remembering the minuteness of Burton's descriptions, we must conclude that it was much" (Lovell, 1995).

Digby's knowledge of desert and harem life came from her travels in Syria. In June 1853, dressed as a native and astride a camel in a small caravan headed by Medjuel el Mezrab, her hired guide, she began the journey to Palmyra to view the ancient ruins of Tadmor, the fabled city founded by King Solomon. Calling this the "greatest adventure, probably of all my journeys," she followed in the footsteps of the well-known British eccentric, Lady Hester Stanhope, who had made the arduous journey 30 years before.

Digby loved the city, the desert, and the ruins, and eventually grew to love Medjuel. At the age of 47 she married Medjuel in a Muslim ceremony and took a honeymoon journey back to Palmyra in the spring of 1855, a trip she said was the happiest time of her life. For the next 30 years she divided her time between her villa in Damascus and the low black tents of her husband's tribe. On 3 April 1857, she wrote in her diary, "My Birthday! Fifty! . . . all the romance and poetry of life ought to be long past and over and here I am still with a beating and burning heart."

While Digby's passionate search for love and adventure remains unscripted, her insistence on defining life on her own terms becomes her lasting legacy and greatest contribution to the annals of nineteenth-century travel. Her desire for privacy and the freedom to live as she wished, against Western ideas of decorum, sets her in stark contrast to many of her literary sisters such as Mary Kingsley, Isabella Bird, and other Victorian women travel writers who felt compelled to define their unconventional lives in conventional literary texts. By her literary silence, which to a great extent continues today, she removed herself from the need for public approval and the court of public judgment.

By refusing to masquerade as a writer of history, geography, or anthropology, or as a doer of good deeds, she represents for her fellow travelers and for us a symbol of romance, intrigue, and passion. Through her passionate pursuit of travel, Jane Digby expands not only geographical borders but also the borders of acceptable feminine behavior for her time.

LORRAINE GALLICCHIO MERCER

### Biography

Born at Forston House, Dorset, 3 April 1807, to Admiral Sir Henry Digby, GCB and Jane Elizabeth Coke, Lady Andover, widow of Viscount Andover. Educated at her grandfather's estate, Holkham Hall, Norfolk, by private tutor, Miss Margaret Steele, and at the Seminary for Young Ladies, Tunbridge Wells, Kent. Traveled extensively in Europe, the Mediterranean, and the Middle East including Turkey, Egypt, Greece, Albania, Jerusalem, and Syria. Married Edward Law, Lord Ellenborough, 15 September 1824 (divorced, 1830): one son. Liaison with Prince Felix Schwarzenberg and lived with him in Paris, 1829–1831: one son and one daughter. Married Baron Carl-Theodore von Vennigen, 1832 (divorced, 1840): one son and one daughter. Lived in Palermo, Italy, 1832–1834, and in Munich, 1835–1840. Entered affair with Count Spiridion Theotoky; went to Paris with him, 1839: one son. Married Theotoky, 1840 (marriage annulled, early 1850s), lived in Corfu, Athens, and Tuscany, 1840–1848. Returned to Athens; entered relationship with Christodoulos Hadji-Petros, 1850–1853. Traveled to Syria, 1853. Married Sheikh Medjuel el Mezrab, 1854; lived in Homs, later settling in Damascus. Died of fever and dysentery in Damascus, 11 August 1881.

### References and Further Reading

The Minterne House Collection contains primary sources including: a summary of Digby's life from 1807–1856 (compiled by a member of the family from documents since destroyed); diaries kept by Digby from December 1853–1881; poetry written 1824–1834; letters by Digby; collected paintings and sketches of Digby.

## DIPLOMATIC AND TRADE MISSIONS

Diplomacy and commercial interests have been intertwined from ancient times, and embassies between rulers to discuss matters of politics and trade have generated informal travelogues, diaries, or letters outside the official reports sent back to the ambassadors' masters. The earliest recorded diplomatic missions took place when the kings of Babylonia, Assyria, and Egypt sent envoys to negotiate with other rulers. Although little is known about the earliest trade missions, one of the first was by Eudoxus of Cyzicus (b. c. 135 BCE), who made two trading journeys to India on behalf of the Ptolemaic kings of Egypt, and embassies, such as that of the Rhodians under Poseidonius of Apamea to Rome in 87 BCE, were a frequent feature of the Hellenistic and Roman worlds.

In the Christian era papal missions to convert the "enemies of Christ" often used members of religious orders—Dominicans and Franciscans and later the Jesuits—as ambassadors to make contact with rulers whose subjects were viewed, usually on the basis of total ignorance, as likely candidates for conversion. Medieval friars who undertook major embassies include Giovanni di Piano Carpini, William of Rubruck (Guillaume de Rubruck), John of Montecorvino, Odoric of Pordenone, Andrew of Longjumeau, and John of Marignolli. Carpini's report, *Historia Mongalorum quos nos Tartaros Appellamus*, or *Liber Tartarorum*, is considered one of the most detailed, comprehensive, and accurate of all the medieval Christian accounts. John of Montecorvino, leader of a mission sent by Pope Nicholas IV to convert the Mongols in 1289, spent 13 months in India en route, writing a long report describing southern India, the first ever by a European. (His reports are included in *The Mongol Mission*, edited by Christopher Dawson, 1955.) On the secular, commercial front, the most famous medieval Westerner to visit the courts of the Far East was Marco Polo, who accompanied his father and his uncle on their second journey to the court of Kublai Khan at Cambulac (Khan-balik), the present-day Beijing.

Outward embassy traffic was not confined to Christian Europe. One of the greatest medieval travelers, the

Intimidating reception at the Chinese imperial palace in Beijing for Czar Peter the Great's embassy led by Dutchman Evert Isbrandz. Ides (from Ides's *Three Years Travels from Moscow Overland to China*, 1706). *Courtesy of the Travellers Club, London; Bridgeman Art Library, agent.*

fourteenth-century scholar Ibn Battuta, who journeyed throughout the Islamic world, led a mission from the sultan of Delhi to the Mongol emperor of China. In the 1360s the Nasrid sultan Mohammed V of Granada in Spain employed another great Islamic traveler, Ibn Khaldun, as ambassador to Pedro the Cruel of Castile. Cheng Ho, a eunuch at the imperial Chinese court at the beginning of the fifteenth century, was placed in command of a series of seven commercial and diplomatic voyages to the Malay peninsula, the East Indies, the islands of the Indian Ocean, and the Malabar coast ports of Calicut, Cochin, and Quilon (1405–1431), although he did not actually travel with the fleet on every occasion. The official records of Cheng Ho's voyages have not survived; it is thought that they were deliberately destroyed by his enemies at court but a pillar discovered in the city of Ch'ang-ho, the port from which the expeditions sailed, lists the dates and destinations of each of the voyages. Other records include the books of four senior officers: Kung Ch'en, *Record of the Barbarian Countries in the Western Ocean* (1434); Hsin Fei, *Triumphant Visions of the Starry Raft* (1436); Huan Ma, *Ying-Yai Sheng-Lan: "The Overall Survey of the Ocean's Shores"* (1433); and *Record of the Tribute Paying Western Countries* (1520). The actual routes followed were charted on a map included in Wu Pei Chili, *Notes on Military Preparation* (1621).

One of the first official embassies to the African continent was that of Pero da Covilhã, who was entrusted by John II of Portugal to seek, among other things, the source of the spices reaching Europe via Arab and Venetian merchants and to establish whether it was possible to bypass these routes by circumnavigating Africa. He carried with him letters for "Prester John," the legendary Christian ruler who had haunted the imagination of medieval European potentates with the illusory promise of a Christian ally in the pagan East. Covilhao died some time after 1525 in Ethiopia, where he had been detained for three decades at the court of the Negus, Prester John's real-life equivalent. Vasco da Gama, captain-general of the Portuguese expedition that departed from the Tagus on 8 July 1497 "to make discoveries and go in search of spices," was empowered to negotiate a commercial treaty, which he attempted to do with the samorim, the local ruler at Calicut (Kozhikode) on India's Malabar Coast. As a diplomatic mission this was not an unqualified success, but it opened the way to Portuguese enterprise in India.

Some of the most important written reports to reach Europe, characterized by their coverage of all aspects of the countries to which they related, are those of the Jesuits who were attached, often for long periods, to the courts of foreign powers. The Moghul emperor Akbar sent a two-man embassy to the Jesuits in Goa in 1579 requesting the presence of some of their number at his court. Another Jesuit, Matteo Ricci, fulfilled the role of ambassador for Christendom at the imperial Chinese court for many years.

The princes of the emergent nation-states of Renaissance Europe engaged in a busy round of diplomacy that involved frequent exchanges of ambassadors. These embassies were as much prestige-boosting exercises—such as that involving the principals themselves, Francis I of France and Henry VIII of England, at the Field of the Cloth of Gold in 1520—as negotiations over matters of substance: royal marriages, political alliances, trade agreements, or religious questions. Diplomatic activity intensified in periods of crisis such as that leading up to the fall of Constantinople in 1453 when the beleaguered Palaeologan emperors sent envoys to Catholic Europe in an attempt to reach an accommodation that would bring the Catholic powers into an effective alliance with Byzantium against the Ottoman Turks. Around the same time the Sienese humanist Enea Silvio Piccolomini (later Pope Pius II) traveled on church business as far as the court of James I of Scotland, and his autobiographical *Commentarii rerum memorabilium* describes places he visited on his travels. A more systematic account of a then little-known host country was provided by the *Rerum Muscoviticarum commentarii* [Notes upon Russia] of the German Sigmund von Herberstein, based on his embassies in 1517 and 1526. Sir Jerome Horsey, who acted as go-between for Elizabeth I of England and the czars Ivan the Terrible and Feodor I in the 1580s, and Giles Fletcher, who was English ambassador to Moscow in 1588, also left accounts of Russia.

Embassies continued to operate on an ad hoc basis to deal with matters of immediate concern, but from the mid-fifteenth century onward the Venetians, building on their long-standing tradition of trade consuls, began keeping a representative permanently stationed in the capital cities of the countries with which they had dealings. These men filed regular reports (*relazioni*), which were read out formally in the Venetian senate. Other powers copied the practice of maintaining a permanent presence in foreign capitals, which led to the beginnings of the diplomatic service as understood today. Men with a talent for languages and negotiation became career diplomats; an English protodiplomat was Sir Henry Wotton (1568–1639), whose remark "An ambassador is an honest man sent to lie abroad for the good of his country," all but wrecked his career.

The sultan's court in Istanbul, power base of the Muslim threat to the heart of Europe but also the center of a vast trading empire, was the focus of intensive diplomatic activity from the sixteenth century onward. The centralized nature of Ottoman decision making encouraged the dispatch of a stream of ambassadors to the Sublime Porte, and the Pera district north of the Golden Horn, long the residence of foreign traders, became the established diplomatic quarter. Records in various forms other than bare official reports survive from a number of these Western missions: those of the envoys of the Holy Roman Emperor Ogier Ghislain de Busbecq in 1554–1562, Hans Ludwig von Kuefstein (1628), and the nineteenth-century J. von Hammer-Purgstall, author of the massive *Histoire de l'Empire Ottoman* (1835–1846); the Britons Sir Thomas Roe (1620s), Sir John Finch (1670s), Edward Wortley Montagu (1716–1718), and Lord Elgin (1799–1803); the French Marquis de Nointel (1670s), Vicomte d'Andrezel (1724–1727), and Comte de Choiseul-Gouffier (1780s); the Dutchman Cornelis Calkoen (1727). Montagu's embassy is now chiefly memorable for the *Letters* of his wife, Lady Mary Wortley Montagu, and the gossipy letters of Lady Elgin; the memoirs of the doctor, William Wittman, who accompanied the military mission associated with the Elgin embassy, also described the life of foreigners in the Ottoman capital. The rarefied and obsessive ceremonial at the Ottoman court was noted by virtually all visitors, and *l'affaire du sofa*, a disagreement over the seating arrangements at an audience involving the Marquis de Nointel, nearly resulted in a diplomatic rupture between France and the Porte.

Ambassadors to the Porte and elsewhere often took along an artist in their entourage to make a visual record of the embassy, in particular the splendor of their reception: von Kuefstein, envoy of Holy Roman Emperor Ferdinand II to Sultan Murad II in 1628, not only kept a diary of his embassy but also commissioned paintings to commemorate it; the Vicomte d'Andrezel and the Comte de Choseul-Gouffier likewise patronized artists. A notable pictorial record of the journey of Thomas Howard, 2nd earl of Arundel, on his abortive embassy from Charles I of England to the holy Roman emperor in 1636 was made by Wenceslaus Hollar.

The Ottoman sultan was not the only potentate who required elaborate obeisances from ambassadors presented to him: the court of the Chinese emperor was notorious for its protocol for receiving envoys from what the Chinese regarded as inferior nations. Tsar Peter the Great of Russia sent the Dutchman Evert Ysbrants Ides at the head of an embassy to Beijing in 1692, and Ides wrote a full account of his experiences (originally in Dutch). The question of how to avoid kowtowing to the emperor greatly exercised Lord Macartney in his embassy of 1792 and 1793. Macartney was an experienced diplomat, having made his reputation by successfully negotiating a commercial treaty with Russia on an embassy to St. Petersburg in the mid-1760s (of which an account was printed for private circulation in 1768). His mission to China failed in its purpose of obtaining permission for the posting of a permanent British representative, but it brought back much valuable information.

While intra-Europe embassies continued to concern themselves with the negotiation of political, religious, commercial, and matrimonial alliances, the expansion of European interests around the globe from the 1600s onward meant that a great deal of well-informed travel literature, much of it from Dutch, French, and English sources and based heavily on the diplomatic and trade reports, was published in Europe. Tales of "the wealth of the Indies" remained seductive and also rather misleading, as the English found out when they sent Roe as ambassador to the Moghul emperor Jahangir in 1615 with expectations of a generous handout of gold and other treasures; instead he received only a female slave, a male criminal, and a wild boar. Embassies were dispatched to faraway courts in the expectation of opening up whole new spheres of influence—and of excluding the influence of rival European powers. Books published by Jesuit mathematician Guy Tachard (*Voyage de Siam*, 1686) and ambassador Simon de La Loubère (*Du Royaume de Siam*, 1691) were spin-offs from Louis XIV's scheme to establish a French sphere of influence in Indochina.

By the nineteenth century the increasing professionalization of diplomacy was militating against the production of travelogues as a by-product of formal embassies. In dealings with rulers outside Europe and North America, embassies between putative equals were frequently replaced with missions by agents of the imperial powers who were in a position to enforce compliance upon indigenous rulers by "gunboat diplomacy," or the threat of it. Furthermore, the mores of foreign courts and capitals were no longer novelties to European readers, and as opportunities to travel spread throughout society, the experiences of returned ambassadors no longer had an automatic claim upon public attention except insofar as they offered privileged insights into momentous events in countries to which they were posted—which makes their diaries and memoirs more the stuff of history than of travel writing. Diplomats' wives' memoirs, a subgenre that continues to thrive with such titles as *Pay, Pack and Follow* (Ewart-Biggs) or *A Military Memsahib* (Watts), may offer a more personal view of the countries in which they find themselves and of the vagaries of diplomatic life.

MARTIN J. MANNING

### References and Further Reading

Alvares, Francisco, *Verdadeira Informação das terras do Preste João das Indias*, 1540; as *Narrative of the Portuguese Embassy to Abyssinia during the Years 1520–1527*, translated and edited by Lord Stanley of Alderley, 1881.

Busbecq, Ogier Ghislain de, *The Turkish Letters of Ogier Ghiselin de Busbecq, Imperial Ambassador at Constantinople, 1554–1562*, translated from the 1633 Elzevir edition by Edward Seymour Forster, 1927.
*A Complete View of the Chinese Empire . . . and a Genuine and Copious Account of Earl Macartney's Embassy from the King of Great Britain to the Emperor of China*, 1798.
Crowne, William, *A True Relation of all the Remarkable Places and Passages Observed in the Travels of the Right Honourable Thomas Lord Howard*, 1637.
Dawson, Christopher (editor), *The Mongol Mission: Narratives and Letters of the Franciscan Missionaries in Mongolia and China in the Thirteenth and Fourteenth Centuries*, translated by a nun of Stanbrook Abbey, 1955.
Ewart-Biggs, Jane, *Pay, Pack and Follow: Memoirs*, 1984.
Ferguson, Mary Nisbet, *The Letters of Mary Nisbet of Dirleton, Countess of Elgin*, edited by John Patrick Nisbet Hamilton Grant, 1926.
Fletcher, Giles, *Of the Russe Common Wealth*, 1591; as *Of the Rus Commonwealth*, edited and with an introduction by Albert J. Schmidt, 1966; as *Of the Russe Commonwealth*, with an introduction by Richard Pipes, 1966.
Gonzalez de Clavijo, Ruy, *Narrative of the Embassy of Ruy Gonzalez de Clavijo to the Court of Timour, at Samarcand, AD 1403–6*, translated by Clements R. Markham, 1859.
Herberstein, Sigismund von, *Notes upon Russia: Being a Translation of the Earliest Account of That Country, Entitled Rerum Moscoviticarum commentarii, by the Baron Sigismund von Herberstein, Ambassador from the Court of Germany to the Grand Prince Vasiley Ivanovich, in the Years 1517 and 1526*, translated and edited by R.H. Major, 2 vols., 1851–1852.
Horsey, Jerome, *The Travels of Sir Jerome Horsey* in *Russia at the Close of the Sixteenth Century*, edited by Edward A. Bond, 1856.
Huan Ma, *Ying-Yai Sheng-Lan: "The Overall Survey of the Ocean's Shores,"* edited by Feng Cheng-Chun, 1433, with an introduction by J.V.G. Mills, 1970.
Ides, Evert Ysbrants, *Driejaarige reize naar China*, 1704; as *Three Years Travels from Moscow Over-land to China*, 1706.
La Loubère, Simon de, *Du Royaume de Siam*, 2 vols., 1691; as *A New Historical Relation of the Kingdom of Siam*, translated by A.P., 2 vols., 1693; facsimile, with an introduction by David K. Wyatt, 1969.
Macartney, George, Earl, *An Account of Russia, 1767*, 1768.
Marignolli, John of, "Recollections of Travel in the East" in *Cathay and the Way Thither, Being a Collection of Medieval Notices of China*, translated and edited by Henry Yule, vol. 2, 1866; in vol. 3 of revised edition, 1913–1916.
Montagu, Mary Wortley *Embassy to Constantinople: The Travels of Lady Mary Wortley Montagu*, edited by Christopher Pick, 1988.
Montagu, Mary Wortley, *The Turkish Embassy Letters*, edited by Malcolm Jack, 1993.
Odoric of Pordenone, *Itinerarium fratris Odorici . . . de Mirabilibus Orientalium Tartarorum* in *Cathay and the Way Thither, Being a Collection of Medieval Notices of China*, translated and edited by Henry Yule, vol. 1, 1866, in vol. 2 of revised edition, 1913–1916.
Roe, Thomas, *The Negotiations of Sir Thomas Roe, in His Embassy to the Ottoman Porte, from the Year 1621 to 1628 Inclusive*, 1740.
Roe, Thomas, *The Embassy of Sir Thomas Roe to the Court of the Great Mogul, 1615–1619, as Narrated in His Journal and Correspondence*, edited by William Foster, 2 vols., 1899; revised edition, as *The Embassy of Sir Thomas Roe to India, 1615–19*, 1926.
Rubruck, William of, and Giovanni di Piani Carpini, *The Journey of William of Rubruck to the Eastern Parts of the World, 1253–55, as Narrated by Himself, with Two Accounts of the Earlier Journey of John of Pian de Carpine*, translated and edited by William Woodville Rockhill, 1900; reprinted, 1967.
Staunton, George, *An Authentic Account of an Embassy from the King of Great Britain to the Emperor of China . . . Taken Chiefly from the Papers of His Excellency the Earl of Macartney . . . and of Other Gentlemen*, 2 vols., 1797.
Tachard, Guy, *Voyage de Siam*, 1686; as *A Relation of the Voyage to Siam, Performed by Six Jesuits*, 1688.
Velho, Alvaro, *Roteiro da Viagem de Vasco da Gama em MCCCCXCVII*, 1861; as *A Journal of the First Voyage of Vasco da Gama, 1497–1499*, translated and edited by E.G. Ravenstein, 1898.
Watts, Rosemary, *A Military Memsahib: The Lighthearted Impressions of a Defence Attaché's Wife, Islamabad, Pakistan, 1982–1985*, 1994.
Wittman, William, *Travels in Turkey, Asia-Minor, Syria, and across the Desert into Egypt during the Years 1799, 1800, and 1801, in Company with the Turkish Army, and the British Military Mission*, 1803; reprinted, 1972.
Yule, Henry (translator and editor), *Cathay and the Way Thither, Being a Collection of Medieval Notices of China . . . with a Preliminary Essay on the Intercourse between China and the Western Nations Previous to the Discovery of the Cape Route*, 2 vols., 1866; revised edition, 4 vols., 1913–1916.

*See also* **East India Company, British; East India Company, Dutch; East India Company, French; Muscovy Company**

## DOGSLEDS

Dogsledding was once a principal method of transportation among the Inuit people of the circumpolar North. Used then for travel, hauling, and daily chores, dogsleds have recently been replaced in their utilitarian purpose by airplanes and snowmobiles.

Dogsleds became extremely important during the period of Arctic and Antarctic exploration in the nineteenth and early twentieth centuries. Although many explorers felt that the North Pole could be reached by ship, they often brought along dogs and sleds in case they were needed to make a final dash across the ice to the pole. In the 1893 *Fram* expedition, for example, Fridtjof Nansen and a companion set out from the icebound ship by dogsled for a run to the North Pole, but were stopped by rough terrain at 86°14′ N. By the first decade of the twentieth century, travel by both ship and dogsled had become the norm in Arctic exploration and on 6 September 1909 Robert E. Peary, along with Matthew Henson and four Inuit guides, arrived at the North Pole on dogsleds.

In the race to the South Pole, dogsleds became, perhaps, even more important. Prior to his 1901 through

1904 expedition in the *Discovery*, for example, Robert Falcon Scott met with Nansen who advised him to buy a large number of Greenland dogs. The number of Arctic expeditions over the previous 40 years had depleted the supply of Greenland dogs, however, and Scott was eventually able to buy only 23 smaller and wilder Russian dogs in Archangel. Scott's experience with dogs on the *Discovery* expedition can only be described as disastrous: only two of his men had dog-mushing experience; the stockfish brought as dog food became tainted during the sea voyage; and finally, the dogs were extremely quarrelsome and cannibalistic. "The dogs take away all idea of enjoying the marches," Scott lamented, "certainly dog driving is the most terrible work one has to face in this sort of business." Within the first year of the *Discovery* expedition, all of Scott's dogs had died.

Scott's adverse experiences with dogs and dogsledding on the *Discovery* expedition caused him to all but abandon the use of dogs in favor of ineffective Siberian ponies and motorized sleds on his ill-fated and ultimately fatal *Terra Nova* expedition of 1910 through 1913. On the other hand, Roald Amundsen's success in reaching the South Pole in December 1911 was due, in large part, to experienced mushers and 97 well-trained Greenland dogs who pulled the Norwegians' sleds from the Bay of Whales to the pole and back. While the extreme hardships and eventual death of Scott's party can be attributed to the breakdown of the motorized sleds and the deaths of the ponies, Roland Huntford (1979), comparing the two expeditions, asserts that "Scott would have had an easy time of it with an adequate number of well-trained dogs."

Within a decade of the Amundsen and Scott expeditions and within a few years of World War I, airplanes and dirigibles had all but replaced dogsleds in polar exploration. The exploits of Richard E. Byrd, the first man to fly over both poles, perhaps best epitomizes this transition in the 1920s and 1930s, as does Amundsen's death in an airplane crash in 1928 while searching for a downed dirigible. One exception to this trend, however, was a six-man international expedition that took 221 days to cross 3,700 miles of Antarctica by dogsled in 1990.

Dog team kicks over the traces on the approach to the Yukon River (from Frederick Whymper's *Travel and Adventure in the Territory of Alaska*, 1868). *Courtesy of British Library, London.*

Today, dogsledding is both a formal and a recreational sport in parts of Scandinavia, Canada, Alaska, and areas of the northern United States. Organized dogsled races include, among others, three annual races in Alaska and Canada: the Fur Rendezvous in Anchorage; the Iditarod, a 1,049-mile race each March that commemorates the delivery of diphtheria antitoxin serum by dogsled from Nenana to Nome in 1925; and the Yukon Quest, a 1,000-mile winter race from Fairbanks to Whitehorse, which dogsled enthusiasts regard as the toughest race in the world. Other mushers prefer not to race; instead, they often hook up their dogs and head out into the northern wilderness for weeks at a time, touring, vacationing, and visiting people and sites in remote locations.

Although touring sleds, working sleds, and racing sleds differ in size and weight, a typical generic sled weighs around 33 pounds and is constructed of steam-bent ash. Early sleds were lashed together with leather or strips of sinew, and while modern sleds often include these materials, they frequently use metal hardware as well. Runners originally made solely of wood were later made more durable by encasing the wood in steel or aluminium.

Dogs used to haul the sleds are often specially bred, although many trace their ancestry to Alaskan malemutes, Siberian huskies, samoyeds, Greenlanders, or Eskimo dogs. Because of their large size, malemutes and Greenlanders were bred to haul heavy freight—including wood and food such as moose, bear, and sea mammals—long distances from remote areas to villages. Smaller, faster dogs such as huskies and samoyeds were used to herd reindeer, haul loads, and race. All of these types of dogs eventually came together in Alaska during the Gold Rush of the late 1890s, and various types of breeding produced the mixed-breed sled dogs of today. In fact, with the emphasis on either speed or endurance in dogsled racing today, it is not unusual to see dogs whose parentage might include some greyhound, Labrador, collie, and/or golden retriever.

While a small, lightly loaded sled may be pulled by a single dog, working or racing sleds are usually drawn by teams of between 5 and 15 dogs. Most mushers prefer an odd number of dogs because the team is connected and driven in a gang hitch—a single lead dog followed by the rest in pairs. A well-bred and well-trained team of 5 to 7 dogs can comfortably pull a loaded sled and musher at speeds of more than 20 miles per hour over flat ground, while a larger team of 10 to 15 dogs can easily cover 100 miles per day under racing conditions.

TERRY REILLY

### References and Further Reading

Allan, Alan Alexander, *Gold, Men and Dogs*, 1931.

Armitage, Albert, *Two Years in the Antarctic: Being a Narrative of the British National Antarctic Expedition*, 1905; reprinted, 1984.

Bernacchi, L.C., *To the South Polar Regions: Expedition of 1898–1900*, 1901; reprinted, 1991.

Bernacchi, L.C., *Saga of the "Discovery,"* 1938.

Huntford, Roland, *Scott and Amundsen*, London: Hudder and Stoughton, 1979, New York: Putnam, as *The Last Place on Earth: Scott and Amundsen's Race to the South Pole*, London: Hudder and Stoughton, 1985, New York: Modern Library, 1999.

Klerekoper, Fred G., *Dogsled Trip from Barrow to Demarcation Point, April 1937*, 1977.

Murphy, Joseph E., *To the Poles: By Ski and Dogsled*, 1996.

Paulsen, Gary, *Winterdance: The Fine Madness of Alaskan Dog-Racing*, 1995.

Scott, Robert Falcon, *The Voyage of the "Discovery,"* 2 vols., 1905.

Stuck, Hudson, *Ten Thousand Miles with a Dog Sled: A Narrative of Winter Travel in Interior Alaska*, 1914.

Turk, Jon, *Cold Oceans: Adventures in Kayak, Rowboat, and Dogsled*, 1999.

## DOUGHTY, CHARLES (1843–1926) *British Poet and Explorer*

Charles Montagu Doughty was born into a county gentry that in the previous two centuries had produced six admirals, three generals, a bishop, a judge, and a colonial governor. Orphaned by the age of six, he developed a desire to join the navy and a precocious sense of patriotism. He endured a lonely childhood immersing himself in solitary pursuits, in particular digging for fossils and flint artifacts in the Suffolk chalk, a subject about which he presented a paper to the British Association for the Advancement of Science while still a schoolboy. The skills of scientific methodology and the powers of observation that were the basis for *Travels in Arabia Deserta* (1888) were thus formed early in life. Not considered robust enough for the navy, he went to Cambridge to study natural history. Gaining a poor degree he abandoned his scientific ambitions for the study of medieval literature and poetry, a passion that would inform all his future writings. His patriotic zeal had at last found an outlet and his life's work would be devoted to a fight against the decay of the English language and an attempt to restore it to what he considered its "Golden Age," a period bounded by the writings of Chaucer and Spenser.

Most of Doughty's life was dogged by financial worries, which he addressed by adopting the life of a peripatetic scholar on the Continent, living cheaply and pursuing his literary studies. In 1870 he left for Holland and then Belgium, France, Italy, and Sicily to begin a circumnavigation of the Mediterranean before traveling the Levant to the Holy Land. In 1875 he reached Petra, one of the few Europeans since Burkhardt to do so, and there heard tales of another carved city unvisited by Europeans and abandoned in the Arabian desert. His determination to visit Medain Salih was the genesis of *Travels in Arabia Deserta*, described by T.E. Lawrence in his introduction to the second edition as a "book not like other books, but something particular, a bible of its kind." The surviving notebooks and letters from the preceding years of travel show the disparate elements of Doughty's character to be fully formed—the self-contained traveler, the geologist, the archaeologist, the patriotic scholar, and poet—but they give no indication of the fusion these elements would undergo in the crucible of the desert.

The Arabia that Doughty entered was a remote part of the Ottoman empire riven by feuds and vendetta, and ruled by local emirs perpetuating ancient traditions of warfare and raiding. The impoverished and ignorant populace, although adhering to strict codes of hospitality, were capable of instant hostility and a brutality commensurate with the harshness of their lives. They were deeply antagonistic to foreigners and their religious fanaticism was inflamed by the advocates of Wahhabism. The interior was unmapped and unknown to the West; the few Europeans who traveled there had done so like Burton and Palgrave, disguised as Muslim pilgrims. Doughty traveled alone and lived with the bedouin openly declaring himself to be an "Engleys" (Englishman) and a "Nasrany" (Christian).

Having failed to get official or financial backing from England and without a travel firman from the Sublime Porte, Doughty determined to join the Hajj caravan and reach Medain Salih unaided. In 1876 he left Damascus with the Hajj and *Travels in Arabia Deserta* records in minute detail his two years wandering in northwest Arabia. His observations, scientific measurements, and sketches were recorded in small notebooks often written in secret and concealed under his cloak. Being almost penniless, he carried in his saddlebags a barometer, a thermometer, a sextant, and a set of scales to measure out the medicines he hoped to dispense for payment. He also carried a seventeenth-century edition of Chaucer. After copying the Nabatean inscriptions at Medain Salih, he set off with Fukara nomads crisscrossing the Nefud, dependent on the hospitality of the "booths of hair" and existing on camel's milk and dates. Arriving in Hayil, court of the murderous emir Ibn Rashid, he was met with hostility and expelled to the legendary town of Kheybar, where he suffered months of virtual imprisonment. Eventually freed, he traveled through the Nejd to Boreyda where, after being beaten and robbed, he fled to the town of Aneyza. Although he was befriended by educated merchants, they were unable to defend him from the hostility of local fanatics. Eventually joining a caravan taking butter to Mecca, he endured arduous travel through the western Nejd to be robbed, beaten, and nearly murdered before being kindly received by the Sherif of Mecca under whose protection he reached Jeddah and the end of his Arabian journey.

*Travels in Arabia Deserta* took nine years to write and was published in 1888. The two volumes of 600,000 words are as epic as the journey itself, the style full of archaisms and constructions drawn from medieval English, the Old Testament, and Latin, the text littered with Arabic words and phrases. The descriptive passages are often of great poetic beauty and Doughty himself called the book only "nominally prose." The geological and geographical descriptions are of such accuracy and detail that it became a military textbook for the British army in the final phase of the Arab Revolt. The sensitive observation of bedouin life is unsurpassed, whether describing how scarlet dye is made from toadstools and camels' urine or the construction of tent ropes. In his introduction to the second edition, T.E. Lawrence describes Doughty as coming away with "the soul of the desert." With its poetic vision and the extraordinary personality of its author, the book with its description of "Old Arabia" now vanquished by the car and airplane holds a singular place in the travel literature of Arabia. It inspired a generation of travelers that included Freya Stark, Gertrude Bell, Wilfred Thesiger, Harry St. John Philby, Bertram Thomas, and of course T.E. Lawrence.

Doughty spent the rest of his life in genteel poverty on the south coast of England writing immensely long poems of a patriotic or prophetic nature. He never visited or wrote about Arabia again.

ANTHONY HAZLEDINE

## Biography

Born at Theberton Hall, Leiston, Suffolk, 19 August 1843. Educated at Beach House, a naval school in Portsmouth. Attended Caius College, Cambridge, 1861–1863; Downing College, Cambridge, 1863–1865. Undertook field trip to Norway to study glaciers, 1863–1864; became life member of British Association, 1864. Engaged in private study in London and Oxford, 1865–1870. Adopted the life of a scholar gypsy, visiting Holland, Belgium, France, Italy, Sicily, Malta, Tunisia, Algeria, Spain, Portugal, Greece, Turkey, Lebanon, Palestine, Sinai, and Egypt, 1871–1875. Joined Hajj caravan and traveled in Arabia, 1876–1878. Visited India; returned to England, 1878. Lived in Italy and wrote *Travels in Arabia Deserta*, 1879–1884. Lectured to Royal Geographical Society, 1883. Married Caroline Amelia McMurdo, 1886: two daughters. Lived in Europe, settling in Tunbridge Wells, England, 1898. Later lived in Eastbourne; moved to Sissinghurst, Kent, 1923. Awarded honorary doctorate from Oxford, 1908. Awarded Founder's Gold Medal by the Royal Geographical Society, 1912. Honorary doctorate from Cambridge, 1920. Honorary Fellow of the British Academy, 1922. Died in Sissinghurst, Kent, 20 January 1926.

## References and Further Reading

Doughty, Charles, "Travels in N.W. Arabia and Nejd," 1883.
Doughty, Charles, *Travels in Arabia Deserta*, 2 vols., 1888, 2nd edition with an introduction by T.E. Lawrence, 1921; abridged as *Wanderings in Arabia*, 2 vols., with an introduction by Edward Garnett, 1908, and as *Passages from Arabia Deserta*, 1931.

## DOUGLAS, DAVID (1799–1834) *British Botanist and Journalist*

Reading David Douglas's expedition journal and letters today, there is little doubt as to why his story still fascinates. This unassuming Scotsman of humble background not only collected and sent back to England more plants and seeds than any botanist in history, he described in detail the circumstances under which he worked. Douglas described the primeval forests and thunderous rainstorms of Oregon and Washington states, how undammed rivers controlled human fate, and the extent to which he was dependent on the people of Native American nations as deep-forest guides and fellow plant collectors. While much has been made of Douglas's unrelenting heroism as a botanist, little has been said of his journal and letters as a comprehensive documentation of the Hudson's Bay Company traders among their native nations' employees. With his base at Fort George (Astoria, Oregon), Douglas found his guides and canoe-men among the "Chenooks, Cladsaps, Clikitats, and Killimucks." In October 1826, along the Willamette River (Oregon), Douglas met one of the Umpqua nation who led him to discover the largest sugar pine (*Pinus lambertiana*), with 14- to 16-inch pine cones, called *Natelé* by the Umpqua. Not only did Douglas send many Native Americans on plant- and seed-hunting forays—no doubt to their amusement—he also observed their salmon-fishing methods, and hat- and basket-making efforts with the native wild grass *Quip-Quip*, or *xerophyllum tenax*. Douglas also observed that in long-distance travel, native people of the Columbia River region exchanged the tobacco *Nicotiana pulverulenta* with the Snake people living much further east near the Missouri River. With self-conscious amusement, Douglas noted that among native men he stood high "as a marksman and passable as a hunter" (Davies, 1980), and was known to be the best marksman "from King George." The Chinook named him Olla-piska for his ability to light his tobacco pipe using a lens and the sun, and he was also called "the Grass Man." Douglas had little time for romantic feelings toward the native Chinook, particularly when he felt personally threatened during times that may have been characterized by tribal warfare or poor trading relations with whites.

For three years, Douglas collected, dried, and shipped his specimens to England; on his return, his work was celebrated to such an extent that his self-consciousness and sensitivity to publicity became too much to bear and he wished himself traveling again. What may have contributed to the popularity with which Douglas was so uncomfortable were his journal entries recounting the adventurous circumstances under which he gathered specimens: rough conditions in the company of pioneer trappers and *voyageurs*, scenes of bear shooting and solitary rides through dense, silent forests, and the display of cool nerves while encountering unpredictable indigenous peoples who were in a strong position as the majority population. We may never know if these adventures unwittingly played upon the romantic sensibilities of his readers, but Douglas turned down offers of assistance in preparing his journal for publication; and unable to concentrate sufficiently to complete it alone, he planned a second voyage to the Columbia River. Again traveling with the Hudson's Bay Company, with the financial assistance of the Horticultural Society and the Colonial Office, Douglas left England in October 1829, and arrived six months later at the base camp, Fort Vancouver (Oregon). All that we know of Douglas's second voyage from 1830–34 to the Columbia River (Oregon), to British Columbia, the Sandwich Islands (Hawaiian Islands), and the California coast as far south as Santa Barbara, is through letters to England: the journal and botany notes of this second voyage were destroyed in a canoe accident on the Fraser River in British Columbia on 13 June 1833. In a letter to William J. Hooker, professor of botany at Glasgow University, Douglas explained that all personal belongings and scientific research were lost, and "I cannot detail to you the labor and anxiety this occasioned me, both in body and mind, to say nothing of the hardships and sufferings I endured" (Hooker, 1836).

Aside from his tireless work, which astounded the botanical world, one can see how Douglas's friends were charmed by simple expressions of enjoyment such as the view from the summit of Mauna Kea, the live volcano near Hilo on the island of Hawaii. In a letter to Hooker, January 1834, Douglas writes:

> Man feels himself as nothing—as if standing on the verge of another world. The death-like stillness of the place, not an animal nor an insect to be seen—far removed from the din and bustle of the world, impresses on his mind with double force the extreme helplessness of his condition, an object of pity and compassion, utterly unworthy to stand in the presence of a great and good, and wise and holy God, and to contemplate the diversified works of His hands! (Hooker, 1836)

Six months later, on 12 July 1834, Douglas died under mysterious circumstances. While walking alone at the northeastern base of Mauna Kea, Douglas may have paused to observe a bull standing in a pit dug for the purpose of capturing wild cattle, fell in, and was trampled. Though no one witnessed Douglas's death, two missionaries, the Reverends Goodrich and Diell, reported the particulars in a long letter to the British consul reprinted in Hooker (1836) and Douglas (1914). Further evidence suggests Douglas may have been moody that day, his eyesight having much deteriorated, and the ground around the bull pit may have been loose or muddy. Douglas was buried in Honolulu, and a monument stands at the northeast base of Mauna Kea. Perhaps the greatest monument to Douglas is the American Christmas tree of choice, a conifer named for him, the Douglas fir (*Pseudotsuga menziesii, P. taxifolia* or *P. douglasii*), and also the *Douglasia nivalis*, the mountain pink. He introduced into England more than 200 North American trees, shrubs, and herbaceous plants (listed in Hooker and Douglas).

TAMARA M. TEALE

**Biography**

Born in Scone, Perthshire, Scotland, 25 July 1799. Educated at schools in Scone and Kinnoul. Apprenticed as gardener to the earl of Mansfield at Scone, 1810–1817. Assistant gardener at Sir Robert Preston's Valleyfield gardens, Culross, Fife, 1818. Appointed to Glasgow Botanical Garden; met William Jackson Hooker, new Chair of Botany at Glasgow University, 1820; accompanied him on botanical expeditions in the Highlands. Introduced to Joseph Sabine at the Royal Horticultural Society and sent by him on a six-month botanical expedition to the east coast of Canada and the United States, 1823–1824. Sponsored by the Royal Horticultural Society, traveled on a three-year expedition with the Hudson's Bay Company from Gravesend (England) to a base on the Columbia River, "Northwest America" (Oregon-Washington state border), 1824–1827. Sailed via Rio de Janeiro, Juan Fernandez, and Galapagos Islands. Returned to Portsmouth, England, via annual overland Hudson's Bay Company express from Oregon to York Factory, Hudson Bay, via Rocky Mountain House (Alberta) and Norway House and Fort Garry, near Winnipeg (Manitoba). Made second expedition to the Columbia River region and British Columbia, including ascents of the live volcanoes Mauna Kea and Mauna Roa, 1829–1834. Died after being attacked by a wild bull near Hilo, Sandwich Islands (now Hawaii), 12 July 1834.

### References and Further Reading

Davies, John (editor), *Douglas of the Forests: The North American Journals of David Douglas*, Seattle: University of Washington Press and Edinburgh Harris: 1980.

Douglas, David, *Journal Kept by David Douglas during His Travels in North America 1823–1827*, edited by W. Wilks, 1914.

Hooker, W. J. (editor), *A Brief Memoir of the Life of Mr. David Douglas, with Extracts from His Letters*, reprinted from the *Companion to the Botanical Magazine*, vol. 2, London, 1836.

## DRAKE, FRANCIS (c. 1540–1596) *English Admiral and Circumnavigator*

Francis Drake was born a commoner near Tavistock, just north of Plymouth in southern Devon. His naval career involved more fighting than exploring; nevertheless, he was an extraordinarily good navigator and contributed to the further development of accurate maps and charts of newly discovered areas of the globe. His greatest exploratory achievement was the circumnavigation of the world between 1577 and 1580, but the voyage was secondary to his main purpose: attacking Spanish settlements and shipping on the west coast of South America. He gave further impetus to British initiatives of exploration and colonization, and continued to attack the concept of national monopolistic control of trading ports and trading routes.

Drake was a small man with incredible energy, quick intelligence, and undeniable courage. He went to sea early, apprenticed to the master of a coastal cruiser hauling small cargoes in the English Channel. By the mid-1560s Drake found employment with the Hawkins brothers sailing out of Plymouth for Spain or West Africa, and in 1567 he was given command of *Judith* by John Hawkins on a voyage from Plymouth to Africa for slaves, and on to the West Indies, selling the slaves before returning to England. On this voyage Drake acquired his lifelong animosity for the Spanish when the British fleet, which had been promised safe harbor at San Juan de Ulúa on the Mexican coast, was surprised and attacked, and Drake, in *Judith*, narrowly escaped. In all the British lost nearly three-quarters of their men and all the profit they had accumulated from the voyage. Drake appealed to the Spanish authorities for restitution, but later, when it was not granted, he took matters into his own hands.

In 1572 he sailed to the West Indies and Panama with *Pasha* and *Swan*, two small ships carrying 73 men including his two brothers, John and Joseph, both of whom died on the voyage. In 1577 Drake prepared for a more ambitious project: attacking Spanish shipping on the west coast of South America. The fleet's destination was kept a secret from everyone, including the crew, and there is no evidence that Drake planned or even considered a circumnavigation of the world. Three ships wintered at San Julian in southern Patagonia, and on 17 August 1578 they headed for the Strait of Magellan. Though they made it through the straits in 14 days, they were soon hit by a huge storm out of the northwest that broke up the fleet. The smallest ship, *Marigold*, foundered and all her crew were lost. A second ship, *Elizabeth*, took refuge at the western opening of the Straits of Magellan, but after three weeks waiting for Drake she returned to England. Only Drake's ship, *Pelican*, now rechristened *Golden Hind*, continued up the western coast of South America after the storm, attacking undefended ports and unsuspecting trading ships. Finally, in December, north of Valparaiso, Drake paused for a full month to clean, repair, and caulk his ship. It may have been at this point that he made the decision to proceed northward and then head homeward west across the Pacific. Before leaving South America Drake captured his greatest prize—*Nuestra Señora de la Concepción*, known as the *Cacafuego*. He continued north capturing other ships, but finally left the area of Spanish occupation, moving up the coast to California.

How far north *Golden Hind* traveled is a matter widely disputed by historians, but it is important in defining the journey as at least in part a voyage of exploration. Specifically, Drake is reported to have searched for the western outlet of the elusive Northwest Passage. John Drake, his cousin, said that he went as far north as 48°, which would put him near Vancouver Island, but four years later the same commentator put him at 44° N. Traditionally he is associated with the San Francisco Bay area at about 38° where he stopped, met the Indians, and claimed the land, which he named New Albion, for the queen. However, Drake's most recent biographer, Harry Kelsey, claims all of this is a fiction allied to the original official secrecy of the voyage; the story was subsequently concocted to confuse the Spanish and give a slightly more positive spin to Drake's privateering. Kelsey believes that Drake went no further than Catalina Island at 33° before turning west in his heavily laden ship, anxious to get his rich, stolen cargo safely home.

The voyage across the Pacific required about two months before landing in the Palau Islands. They lingered in the Moluccas until early April 1579 trading for spices and taking on six tons of cloves along with ginger and pimiento. Although Drake still had a great journey before him, it all passed without notable incident. On about 26 September 1580 he arrived back in Plymouth with a ship full to overflowing with gold, silver, fine fabrics, and spices.

After consultation and a reasonable lapse of time, Queen Elizabeth ordered Drake to sail *Golden Hind* up the Thames to Deptford, where on the deck of his ship she knighted him for his heroic achievement. Drake presented Elizabeth with a map of the route he had taken around the world, but because the voyage was controversial, to say the least, Drake's route was kept something of a secret, and the map disappeared. However, maps that claimed to be copied from Drake's work were drawn by the Dutch cartographers and engravers Nicola van Sype in the early 1580s and Jodocus Hondius around 1596. The great English compiler, translator, and editor of early voyages, Richard Hakluyt, did not include an account of Drake's voyage in the first edition of his *Principall Navigations*, published in 1589. At some point, probably in the mid-1590s, the story came out as a ten-page insert to the 1589 edition and is included in the following edition (1598–1600), though the authorship of the story is never made clear and scholars today still debate its origins.

Drake went on to serve as vice-admiral during the attempted invasion of England by the Spanish Armada in 1588, and is credited with being instrumental in its defeat. His last voyage departed for the West Indies in 1595. Drake shared command with John Hawkins, and though well armed and well equipped, the expedition was a disaster. Hawkins died of an illness on 11 November. Drake continued to look for spoil and booty, but became ill himself in mid-January with fever and dysentery, and died on 27 January 1596 off the coast of Panama.

David Judkins

### Biography

Born at Tavistock, Devon, c. 1540. Son of a tenant farmer. Grew up in Devon and Kent. Apprenticed to a pilot and coastal mariner, mid-1550s. Sailed with John Hawkins on a slave-trade mission to the West Indies in 1567 and commanded *Judith* when the British fleet was attacked by the Spanish at San Juan de Ulúa, on the coast of Mexico. Married Mary Newman (d. 1583). Engaged in raids on Spanish ports and shipping in the New World, 1570s. Completed the second circumnavigation of the world, largely to plunder Spanish ports on the Pacific coast of South America; in the process mapped areas hitherto little known to English sailors, 1577–1580. Elected mayor of Plymouth, Devon, and knighted, 1581. Purchased Buckland Abbey estate in Devon, 1580s. Married Elizabeth Sydenham, 1585. Appointed vice-admiral of the British fleet defending against the Spanish Armada, 1588. Died of a fever and dysentery at sea, off Portobello, Panama, during another expedition in the West Indies, 27 January 1596.

### References and Further Reading

Cumming, Alex A., *Sir Francis Drake and the Golden Hinde*, Norwich: Jarrold, 1975.

Drake, Francis, *The World Encompassed by Sir Francis Drake*, London: Nicholas Bourne, 1628; edited by G.E. Hollingworth, London: University Tutorial Press, 1933.

Hakluyt, Richard, *The Principall Navigations, Voyages, Traffiques and Discoveries of the English Nation*, 2nd edition, 3 vols., London: Bishop Newberie and Banker, 1598–1600; reprinted, 12 vols., Glasgow: James MacLehose, 1903–1905 (for Drake see vol. 11, pp. 101–162).

Hanna, Warren L., *Lost Harbor: The Controversy over Drake's California Anchorage*, Berkeley: University of California Press, 1979.

Kelsey, Harry, *Sir Francis Drake: The Queen's Pirate*, New Haven, Connecticut, and London: Yale University Press, 1998.

Nichols, Philip, *Sir Francis Drake Revived*, London: Nicholas Bourne, 1626.

Purchas, Samuel, *Purchas His Pilgrimes*, 4 vols., London: Fetherstone, 1625; reprinted, 20 vols., Glasgow: James MacLehose, 1905–1907 (for Drake see pp. 119–148).

Quinn, David B., *Drake's Circumnavigation of the Globe: A Review*, Exeter: University of Exeter, 1981.

Quinn, David B., "Early Accounts of the Famous Voyage," in *Sir Francis Drake and the Famous Voyage, 1577–1580*, edited by Norman J.W. Thrower, Berkeley: University of California Press, 1984.

Thrower, Norman J.W. (editor), *Sir Francis Drake and the Famous Voyage, 1577–1580: Essays Commemorating the Quadricentennial of Drake's Circumnavigation of the Earth*, Berkeley: University of California Press, 1984.

Wallis, Helen, *Sir Francis Drake: An Exhibition to Commemorate Francis Drake's Voyage around the World, 1577–1580*, London: British Museum, 1977.

*See also* **Circumnavigation Narratives**

## DUFFERIN AND AVA, MARQUIS OF (FREDERICK TEMPLE-BLACKWOOD) (1826–1902) *British Diplomat, Sailor, and Writer*

*The Marquess of Dufferin and Ava . . . Diplomatist, Viceroy, Statesman*, the title chosen by Charles E. Drummond Black for one of the two voluminous biographies published after Dufferin's death, rings like a herald's proclamation. The image that it creates is, however, only partially accurate. Educated at Eton and

Christ Church, Oxford, Dufferin did become an eminent figure in Victorian public life, adding "and Ava" to his title on advancement to a marquisate in 1888. The other side to service in government at home, as viceroy in India and as ambassador in the major capitals, was a love of the sea. In an age when decorous yachting in sight of Cowes satisfied many of his class, Dufferin liked nothing more than the adventure of a cruise, and the longer the better, especially if there would be something unusual to see at the end. Perhaps it was his ancestry coming out. His father, before coming into his title and entering politics, had reached the rank of captain in the Royal Navy, while his uncle, Henry Blackwood, had earned the high regard of Nelson himself as a skillful and intrepid frigate commander.

In an article published in 1898 Dufferin recalls an early adventure. In 1854—in his late twenties but already an Irish representative peer in the House of Lords and after serving as a lord-in-waiting to Queen Victoria under Lord John Russell and Lord Aberdeen—Dufferin, being the "happy possessor of a small schooner yacht of eighty tons called the *Foam*," decided to head "for the Baltic, in the hope of seeing something of the naval warfare between ourselves and Russians." Only a rich man in a bygone age could call *Foam* "small," and few today would contemplate a jaunt for the pleasure of witnessing a fleet in action. Setting out from Portsmouth, Dufferin and his companion, Lord Arthur Russell, arrived just in time for the bombardment of the Russian fortress of Bomarsund on the island of Åland at the entrance to the Gulf of Bothnia. Cordially welcomed by Sir Charles Napier aboard his flagship, *Duke of Wellington*, Dufferin jumped at the chance of a closer view and embarked on *Penelope*, a paddle frigate armed with two 10-inch guns. He was lucky to escape unscathed when she ran aground and came under fire, suffering heavy casualties. Undaunted, he gladly ran further risks when he landed a few days later and spent some time with the besieging French soldiers.

A bout of typhoid obliged Dufferin to abandon a proposed visit to the Black Sea to round out his experience of the Crimean War. Two years later, however, he set off on his great adventure. He recorded it in epistolary form with many a literary, mythological, and historical allusion and plenty of rather ponderous humor, in his *Letters from High Latitudes* (1857). It was promptly published with the explanatory subtitle *Being Some Account of a Voyage in the Schooner Yacht "Foam" to Iceland, Jan Mayen and Spitzbergen*. A detail conveys the style of the enterprise. The early pages dwell on the fitting of a new figurehead in the form of a portrait bust of the duchess of Argyle. The bronze was the work of Carlo Marochetti, who, since the Great Exhibition of 1851, Queen Victoria and her subjects had ranked among the greatest living sculptors; his *Richard Coeur de Lion* was placed in a prime position outside the Palace of Westminster. Commissioning the figurehead was aristocratic patronage; screwing this work of art to the bows of a yacht about to brave rough seas was lordly insouciance.

Though Dufferin enjoyed small boat sailing with a minimal crew into old age, he was accompanied to the north by a friend with medical skills and scientific knowledge, an Icelandic law student who was to help with language problems, a valet (William Wilson by name, and a Dickensian melancholic), a steward, two cooks, five seamen, and a ship's boy under a master and a mate. Not surprisingly, Dufferin enjoyed the first long leg of the journey, from Oban to Reykjavik, and a lyric passage on his snug cabin is the counterpart of accounts of mountainous waves and other people's prostrating seasickness. Arriving in Reykjavik, Dufferin devoted his time to enjoying hospitality from the more respectable local people and to exploring the island's remarkable volcanic landscape. He responded to everything with enthusiasm. For want of other means of communication, he had on occasion, as he records, no choice but to thank his generous hosts in Latin, while sightseeing, which in the Victorian tradition also involved wild-fowling as well as geologizing, required a "cavalcade" of no fewer than 26 ponies. On returning to what Dufferin plainly regarded as only the relative civilization of Reykjavik, he found the steam corvette *Reine Hortense* in port; her officers, including Prince Napoleon, made him very welcome. Accepting a tow from the French warship part of the way, Dufferin next headed northeast beyond the Arctic Circle to remote Jan Mayen Island. Landfall was a thrill, and mountains and glaciers made an astonishing panorama in the mist, though navigation was difficult amid the ice. In fact Dufferin thoroughly enjoyed "one of the prettiest and most exciting pieces of nautical manoeuvring that can be imagined." He allowed himself only a short time on shore, however, before heading for Hammerfest, 800 miles away on the Norwegian coast. The town held little appeal for him, but he found more to admire in the nearby country and then sailed north again, steering for Bear Island and Spitzbergen. Arrival there was everything Dufferin had expected: a pristine world with no sound, not even the lapping of waves, under the midnight sun. Leaving before the ice closed in for the winter, *Foam* sailed back to England via Copenhagen.

Eleven English editions of *Letters from High Latitudes* in half a century, reprints in three popular series, as well as translations into French, German, and Dutch, show that Dufferin had touched a chord. With a light touch he told of a daring voyage to places that were still largely unfamiliar; narrative and characterization were combined with quite a lot of factual information; and as the years passed, interest grew in this portrayal of a great proconsul at leisure, not just enjoying his very superior holiday but describing it so well that readers could share all his pleasures.

CHRISTOPHER SMITH

### Biography

Born in Florence, Italy, 21 June 1826. Son of Fourth Baron Dufferin. Educated at Eton and at Christ Church, Oxford University, 1844–1846. Entered the House of Lords as Irish peer Baron Clandeboye, 1850. Lord-in-waiting to Queen Victoria, 1849–1852; 1854–1858. Sailed to the Baltic in his yacht *Foam*, 1854. Attaché to Vienna conference to resolve Crimean war, 1855. Sailed in *Foam* to Iceland, Jan Mayen, and Spitzbergen, 1856. Traveled to Egypt, Constantinople, and Syria; as British commissioner, assisted the British Ambassador in Syria, Sir Henry Lytton Bulwer, 1860. Appointed civil K.C.B., 1861. Married Harriet Hamilton, 1862: three sons and three daughters. Lord-lieutenant of County Down, Ireland, 1864. Under-secretary for India, 1864–1866; under-secretary, war office, 1866–1868. Chancellor of the Duchy of Lancaster, 1868–1872. Created Earl of Dufferin, 1871. Governor-general of Canada, 1872–1878. British ambassador, St. Petersburg, 1879–1881. British ambassador to Ottoman Turkey, 1881. Viceroy of India, 1884–1888. Created Marquess of Dufferin and Ava, 1888. British ambassador to Italy, 1889–1891; ambassador to France, 1892–1896. Warden of the Cinque Ports, 1891–1895. Retired to his estate at Clandeboye, 1896. Chairman of the London and Globe Finance Corporation, 1897–1901. Died at Clandeboye, Ireland, 12 February 1902.

### References and Further Reading

Dufferin, Marquis of, *Letters from High Latitudes: Being Some Account of a Voyage in the Schooner Yacht "Foam," 85 O.M., to Iceland, Jan Mayen and Spitzbergen, in 1856*, 1857; 11th edition, 1903; reprinted with an introduction by Vigdís Finnbogadóttir, 1990.

Dufferin, Marquis of, "At the Siege of Bomarsund as Seen from the Deck of the 'Foam,' " *Cornhill Magazine*, new [3rd] series, 5 (November 1898): 595–605.

## DUFF-GORDON, LUCIE (1821–1869)

### *British Translator and Travel Writer*

Born into a family of reform-minded radicals, Lucie Duff Gordon became a shrewd critic of imperialist policies in Egypt, where she lived as an expatriate from 1862 to 1869. Suffering from tuberculosis, she sought relief in South Africa, then Egypt, traveling up the Nile from Alexandria to Cairo, later settling in Luxor, site of ancient Egyptian temples, tombs, and excavations. Gordon witnessed firsthand the effects on rural Egyptians of the construction of the Suez Canal and the gradual European infiltration of Egyptian commerce and politics, a process that culminated after her death in a European takeover of the canal, a British invasion of Egypt in 1882, and more than 40 years of British occupation. Already established as a translator in England, Gordon discovered new scope for her literary talents in Egypt. *Letters from Egypt, 1863–65* (1865), distinguished by its wit, erudition, ironic humor, and cross-cultural sensitivity, gained immediate popularity and became a classic of travel literature about the Middle East.

Egyptians emerge as subjects in *Letters from Egypt* to a degree not found in the texts of many other Western visitors of the period. Unlike Edward William Lane, whose distanced, scientific style precluded any personal tone in *Manners and Customs of the Modern Egyptians* (1836), Gordon represents Egyptian people as individuals with distinct voices. Although at first Gordon displays an orientalist tendency to represent Egypt as an unchanging landscape, the longer she remains in Egypt, the more her discourse diverges from the rhetoric of the picturesque and exotic. At the beginning of her stay in Egypt, Cairo is a city "out of the real Arabian Nights . . . It is a golden existence, all sunshine and poetry and, I must add, kindness and civility." However, appealing characters quickly occupy the landscape, especially when Gordon settles into community life in Luxor. The reader meets Mustapha Agha Ayat, the richest man in Luxor and the local British consular representative, who lends Gordon his horse before she purchases a donkey. There is Seleem Effendi, the magistrate and Shaikh Ibrahim, the judge. In addition to notables, Gordon befriends old Sidi Omar, a modest farmer who loses all his water buffalo to disease. Most developed as characters are the members of Gordon's household. Omar Abu Halaweh, translator and personal assistant, becomes Gordon's most devoted and dependable servant, nursing her as her tuberculosis worsens. Her Arabic teacher, Shaikh Yussef, is characterized by integrity and intelligence. Other household members include Mohammed, the guard; Suleyman, the Christian gardener; and Ahmed, the small houseboy. As these people become part of Gordon's life, they speak often in her text. Although Gordon's tone is sometimes paternalistic, people in her text emerge as individuals, not mere Arabs.

Gordon's religious and cultural tolerance contrast sharply with the racist attitudes of other British visitors to Egypt. Florence Nightingale, for example, described Egyptians as "an intermediate race, they appeared to me, between the monkey and the man, [with] the ugliest most slavish countenances." Gordon's desire to "sit among the people" allowed her to identify with Egyptians and critique the imperialist attitudes of her countrymen abroad. She sympathized with indigent Egyptian peasants, just as she had opposed injustices against laboring men in England. Critical of aristocratic privilege and pretension in Britain, she despised the bullying attitudes of middle-class Englishmen in Egypt on their way to India, who "try their hands here on the Arabs in order to be in good training for insulting Hindus . . . I hate the sight of a hat here now." Gordon exposed the collusion of Westerners with the Khedive Ismail in exploiting peasants to build modernization projects such as the Suez Canal. She pleaded for better treatment for her Luxor neighbors, who, subject to forced labor, were "marched off in gangs like convicts and their families starve and (who'd have thought it) the population keeps decreasing."

Although life in Egypt was inexpensive by English standards, Gordon's funds were limited. However, she also deliberately cultivated an aesthetic of the spare and simple, repelled by the crassness of bourgeois European consumerism. In the words of her houseboy Ahmed:

> Our Lady is almost like the children of the Arabs. One dish or two, a piece of bread, a few dates, and Peace (as we say, there is an end of it). But thou shouldst see the merchants of Alexandria, three tablecloths, forty dishes, to each soul seven plates of all sorts, seven knives and seven forks and seven spoons, large and small and several different glasses for wine and beer and water.

Gordon also developed a deep respect for Islamic culture and opposed European efforts to convert Muslims. She learned spoken Arabic and the conventions of Arabic poetry, and ordered books in Arabic sent from England to share with her Luxor friends: "I can't read the *Arabian Nights*, but it is a favorite amusement to make one of the party read aloud. A stray copy of *Kamar-es Zaman* and *Sitt Boodoora* went all round Luxor, and was much coveted for the village soirees. But its owner departed and left us to mourn over the loss of his MSS."

Ironically, after Gordon's death, her letters were used as propaganda to legitimize British rule after 1882. Because Gordon portrayed Ismail and his Turko-Circassian officials as corrupt and cruel, reporting that her neighbors sometimes expressed a desire to have the British deliver them from the Turks, British administrators made her letters required reading in Egyptian schools to counter the rising tide of Arab nationalist sentiment. By emphasizing that Gordon had been hailed by Egyptians with such epithets as "Noor ala-Noor" (light of the light of God), "Sitt el Kebir" (the great lady), and "el Beshoosheeh" (the one with the kindly face), propagandists promoted the idea that British rule was popular and benevolent.

Despite or perhaps because of Gordon's orientalist tendency to romanticize Arabs and highlight herself as their benefactor, *Letters from Egypt* has survived numerous revisions and reprints to be read by travelers to Egypt even today. Its enduring popularity may be linked to Gordon's masterful handling of what Mary Louise Pratt has called the sentimental as opposed to scientific mode of travel writing. As Caroline Norton recognized in a memorial essay on her friend, it is Gordon's engaging persona to which readers respond: "That feeling of sympathy with humanity,—above all, suffering humanity—which is here evidenced, was a distinctive feature in Lady Gordon's mind."

Anne Lockwood

## Biography

Born Lucy or Lucie Austin in Westminster, London, 24 June 1821, the only child of John Austin, a legal scholar and utilitarian who helped reform the British legal system, and Sarah Taylor Austin, who edited her husband's work on jurisprudence and translated works from German. Educated in Latin and Greek; learned German and French while traveling with her parents to Bonn, Boulogne, and Malta. Attended boarding school in Bromley, 1836. Married Sir Alexander Cornewall Duff Gordon, 1840: one son, two daughters. Lived in Queen Square (now Queen Anne's Gate), London, establishing a literary circle at their home. Published English translations of works by Berthold Niebuhr, W. Meinhold, Clemons Lamping, Anselm Ritter von Feuerbach, Leopold von Ranke, Leon De Wailly, Sophie d'Arbouville, and Helmuth von Moltke, 1840s and 1850s. Lived in Weybridge, Surrey, 1850; established a working men's library and reading room. Suffering acutely from tuberculosis, traveled to South Africa, 1861–1862. Moved to Egypt for health reasons, 1862; lived in Cairo until her death. Died of complications from tuberculosis in Cairo, 14 July 1869.

## References and Further Reading

Duff-Gordon, Lucie, "Letters from the Cape," in *Vacation Tourists and Notes of Travel in 1862–3*, edited by Francis Galton, 1864.

Duff-Gordon, Lucie, "Extracts from Lady Duff-Gordon's Letters from Egypt," *Macmillan's Magazine* (January 1865): 362–370.

Duff-Gordon, Lucie, *Letters from Egypt, 1863–65*, edited by Sarah Austin, 1865; revised edition, with a memoir by Janet Ross, 1902; revised, with an introduction by Gordon Waterfield, 1969; reprint of 1902 edition, with an introduction by Sarah Searight, 1983.

Duff-Gordon, Lucie, "Longshore Life at Boulak," *Macmillan's Magazine* (March 1867): 365–370.
Duff-Gordon, Lucie, "Life at Thebes," *Macmillan's Magazine* (August 1867): 299–305.
Duff-Gordon, Lucie, *Last Letters from Egypt, to Which Are Added Letters from the Cape*, with a memoir by Janet Ross, 1875.

## DURRELL, LAWRENCE (1912–1990)

***British Novelist, Poet, and Travel Writer***

For more than 40 years Lawrence Durrell made the Mediterranean region, primarily Greece and Provence, his home. A British subject not born in Britain, Durrell was never intrinsically English, but felt spiritually connected to the landscape and peoples of the Mediterranean. His travel works, which Richard Aldington described more aptly as books of foreign residence, recreate the ambience of Greece and Provence, the characters of people he knew, and the history and mythology unique to each region.

Durrell was seduced by the siren song of the Mediterranean in 1935, when he and his first wife moved to Corfu on the encouragement of expatriate friends. The product of that four-year experience is *Prospero's Cell* (1945). In his subtitle, Durrell labels the work "a guide to the landscape and manners of the island of Corcyra," but it is more a prose-poem than a guidebook to the island. A lyrical rather than literal rendering of Corfu and his life there, *Prospero's Cell* takes the form of a diary, with entries dated from late 1937 to 1941. The diary form gives the work a sense of immediacy and spontaneity that is deceptive because Durrell did not write the work until several years later while living in Alexandria. Durrell describes how he immersed himself in Corfiot life by buying a house and boat, becoming friendly with the locals, and cultivating bonds with unconventional fellow foreign travelers and residents. He frequently digresses from autobiography to explore the island's history, festivals, and social customs. For Durrell, Greece was a spiritual revelation: "Other countries may offer you discoveries in manners or lore or landscape; Greece offers you something harder—the discovery of yourself."

*Prospero's Cell* begins with Durrell's poetic evocation of his island paradise and ends with his forced exile from that idyllic land as a result of the onset of World War II. After six years in Greece, Durrell fled the country in 1941, just ahead of the advancing Nazi army, settling first in Cairo and then in Alexandria. He returned to Greece in 1945. Posted to Rhodes as British public information officer, he traveled extensively around the Dodecanese, gathering material for his second travel book, *Reflections on a Marine Venus* (1953). While detailing Durrell's impressions of postwar Rhodes and the surrounding islands, the work more fully explores the relationship between the individual and the landscape, a recurring theme in Durrell's travel books. The landscape here, as in most of his travel books, is that of the Mediterranean islands. Durrell describes the intention of the book as "a sort of anatomy of islomania," "a rare but by no means unknown affliction of spirit." "Islomanes" like himself "find islands somehow irresistible." Durrell was not simply obsessed with the natural beauty of the Mediterranean islands; he was drawn to them because they formed the ideal landscape for the spiritual exploration and contemplation needed to achieve self-knowledge, the ultimate goal of travel.

After leaving Rhodes in 1947, Durrell resided first in Argentina and then in Yugoslavia. In 1952 he returned to the Mediterranean region he so loved. Moving to Cyprus, where he hoped to find the tranquillity to write, Durrell bought and restored an old stone house in the village of Bellapaix and began earning a living teaching English, but peace in Cyprus proved to be elusive. During that period, war broke out between the Cypriot Greeks, who desired independence from Britain and union or enosis with Greece, the British who were trying to hold on to the island as a colony, and the Turkish Cypriots who favored partition. Durrell eventually accepted a position as British public relations officer in Nicosia, a government post that put him in conflict with the warring factions and even made him a target for terrorist attacks. He captured these troubled times in his finest work, *Bitter Lemons* (1957), which along with *Prospero's Cell* and *Reflections on a Marine Venus*, completes his island trilogy.

*Bitter Lemons* is at once a highly personal and a political book. Durrell writes of his divided loyalties: on the one hand, given his years of residence among the Greeks and his fluency in the language, he was a philhellene, yet his philhellenism was at odds with his support of the British position. Durrell is not overtly political; he attempts to "evaluate [the Cyprus tragedy] in terms of individuals rather than policies," focusing particularly on how violence destroys human bonds. His own friendship with the Greek Cypriot Panos comes to an abrupt end when the latter is shot dead, apparently for fraternizing with Durrell.

Scholars tend to agree that the travel books Durrell produced later in his career are inferior to his island trilogy. *Spirit of Place* (1969), a collection of letters, short works, and excerpts from early novels, contains Durrell's essay "Landscape and Character," significant for the light it sheds on his view of environmental determinism (i.e., that place shapes character). Durrell followed this work with *Sicilian Carousel* in 1977. Unlike his island trilogy, which captures Durrell on his journeys of self-discovery, *Sicilian Carousel* follows him on a package vacation, a tourist's bus holiday. Durrell examines the nature of tourism as well as highlights the similarities and connections he saw between Sicily and Greece. His next travel book, *The Greek Islands* (1978), is a beautifully illustrated, very personal guide to 56 islands, in which Durrell gives his opinions on the places and experiences that no traveler (or islomane) should miss. In his final travel book, *Caesar's Vast Ghost* (1990), he distills the affection and understanding derived from 30 years' residence in Provence, describing its rich culture and giving breath to the history of the land.

In part, the value of Durrell's travel books is that they capture the landscape and spirit of a now vanished Greece as well as the writer's almost mystical sympathy with the Mediterranean region in general. Of greater value, however, is the way in which his works show the reader that travel is ultimately about the search for self-knowledge: "Journeys, like artists, are born and not made . . . and the best of them lead us not outwards in space, but inwards as well" (*Bitter Lemons*).

HARICLEA ZENGOS

### Biography

Born Lawrence George Durrell in Jullundur, Punjab, India, 27 February 1912. Older brother of the naturalist and writer Gerald Durrell. Attended St. Joseph's College, Darjeeling, India; St. Olaf's and St. Saviour's Grammar School, Southwark, London, 1925–1926; St. Edmund's School, Canterbury, 1927. Married Nancy Isobel Myers, 1935 (divorced, 1947): one daughter. Lived in Corfu, 1935–1939. Moved to Athens to work for the British Information Services and British Council, 1939. Teacher at British Institute, Kalamata, Greece, 1940–1941. Columnist for *Egyptian Gazette*, Cairo, 1941. Foreign press service officer, British Information Office, Cairo, 1941–1942. Posted to Alexandria, Egypt, as press attaché, 1942–1945. Posted to Rhodes as director of public relations for the Dodecanese, 1945–1947. Married Eve Cohen, 1947 (divorced, 1957): one daughter. Director of the British Council Institute, Cordoba, Argentina, 1947–1948. Press attaché, British legation, Belgrade, 1949–1952. Moved to Cyprus, 1952. Director of public relations for the British Embassy, Cyprus, 1954–1957. Moved to Sommières, Provence, France, 1957; lived there until his death. Married Claude-Marie Forde, née Vincendon, 1961 (d. 1967). Married Ghislaine de Boysson, 1973 (divorced 1979). Andrew Mellon Visiting Professor of Humanities, California Institute of Technology, Pasadena, 1974. Duff Cooper Memorial Prize, 1957, for *Bitter Lemons*. Prix du Meilleur Livre Etranger, 1959, for *Justine* and *Balthazar*. James Tait Black Memorial Prize, 1975, for *Monsieur; or, The Prince of Darkness*. First prize in international competition, Union of Hellenic Authors and Journalists of Tourism, 1979, for *The Greek Islands*. Cholmondeley Award for Poetry, British Society of Authors, 1986. Fellow, Royal Society of Literature, 1954. Died of emphysema in Sommières, France, 7 November 1990.

### References and Further Reading


Durrell, Lawrence, *Prospero's Cell: A Guide to the Landscape and Manners of the Island of Corcyra*, 1945; republished with *Reflections on a Marine Venus*, 1960; with an introduction by Carol Pierce, 1996.

Durrell, Lawrence, *Reflections on a Marine Venus: A Companion to the Landscape of Rhodes*, 1953; republished with *Prospero's Cell*, 1960; with an introduction by David Roessel, 1996.

Durrell, Lawrence, *Bitter Lemons*, 1957; with an introduction by Ian S. MacNiven, 1996.

Durrell, Lawrence, *Spirit of Place: Letters and Essays on Travel*, edited by Alan G. Thomas, 1969.

Durrell, Lawrence, *Sicilian Carousel*, 1977; with an introduction by Madeline Merlini, 1997.

Durrell, Lawrence, *The Greek Islands*, 1978.

Durrell, Lawrence, *Caesar's Vast Ghost: Aspects of Provence*, 1990; republished as *Provence*, 1994.

# E

## EAST AFRICA

John Milton knew of the "less maritime kings, Mombaza and Quiloa and Melind" (*Paradise Lost*, Book XI), possibly from acquaintance with Camões's *Lusiads*. There was little enough in English on East Africa with Hakluyt having been able to include only secondhand Portuguese information in 1589. The first recorded English visit to Zanzibar of 1591 by James Lancaster did figure in the 1600 edition, but since Lancaster and his men were forced to stay aboard their ship in the harbor, they were "cut off from all knowledge of the state and traffique of the countrey." There was no information on the fifteenth-century Chinese visits to East Africa nor even any translation available of the testimony of the greatest of all Arab travelers, Ibn Battuta, who had been at Kilwa in 1332.

This state of ignorance continued up to about 1800. The Portuguese remained secretive and in any case had lost effective power north of Mozambique while India-bound English ships normally sailed east of Madagascar. If knowledge of the coast was hazy, any information on the interior in geographical compendia was based on garbled if not mythical data from Ptolemy's second-century *Geography* or Portuguese sources. As Enlightenment principles took hold, competent geographers and mapmakers left the region blank south of the "Mountains of the Moon," which even savants still assumed to lie east to west across the continent just north of the equator. Many assumed that blank region would in any case turn out to be desert.

By 1800, changes were in process that would profoundly affect East Africa and open the way for visitors who would produce some of the most striking and popular travel literature ever. The Indian Ocean system of trade, which the Portuguese had vainly tried to capture, began to revive, principally because of the stimulus of British, French, and Dutch trading activities. Arabs from Oman who had done much to break Portuguese power established a loose control of Zanzibar and the coastal cities. Seyyid Said, ruler of Oman from 1806 to 1856, actually made Zanzibar his headquarters from about 1840. Said encouraged Indian traders to come to the coast. French from Mauritius sought slaves from Kilwa. American merchants from Salem began regular visits to Zanzibar from the 1830s. Responding to these new economic opportunities, Africans from the interior brought increasing numbers of slaves or tusks of ivory to sell on the coast; for the first time, there were regular and significant contacts between the coast and deep interior. Soon the Arabs would follow the Africans back inland in order to dominate the slave and ivory business, "Tippu Tip" becoming the best known and a considerable traveler. Britain's position was ambiguous. There were few direct contacts with East Africa but as British power in India extended, more of the Indian traders became British subjects. More significantly, the British Indian authorities, especially at Bombay, for strategic reasons, felt the need to dominate the Persian Gulf and the Omani peoples at its entrance and so were pulled toward East Africa with Seyyid Said. Said was happy enough to accept British protection from some of his enemies even if one of the prices was having to agree to limitations on the slave trade in treaties of 1822 and 1847.

Despite the changes, comparatively little travel literature was produced in the first half of the nineteenth

A *Punch* cartoon of 1863 expresses British gratification at the successful solution of a centuries-old puzzle. *Courtesy of British Library, London.*

century. A naval visit of 1812 did yield James Prior's account. William Owen's hydrographic survey of Africa's coasts in the 1820s led to the temporary British takeover of Mombasa, but only two rather dull and unsatisfying books by Thomas Boteler and Owen himself. Visits by Indian Navy ships to the coast were followed by useful accounts, but these were not published in Britain or in popular form. Henry Salt provided some information on the coast and even a Swahili vocabulary, but his real focus was on Ethiopia and Egypt. The American trading connection produced sparse literature: John Osgood's short book was little known in America, much less Britain. The French admiral Guillain's scholarly compilation on the coast peoples seems to have made little impact even in France itself. Some speculative geographical work was published, but any travel literature on East Africa remained hard to find until about 1850, when the situation changed very quickly and dramatically.

East Africa became the focus of great popular interest for the next 50 years as a result of a series of publications recording the exploits of famous explorers and missionaries. Rebmann saw Mount Kenya in 1848, Lewis Krapf saw Kilimanjaro in 1849; both reported stories of lakes farther in the interior. Richard Burton and John Hanning Speke reached Lake Tanganyika in 1857 and Speke alone Lake Victoria in the following year, while David Livingstone saw Lake Malawi in 1859. Speke and James Grant explored the Nile source region in 1862 and Samuel Baker reached Lake Albert in 1864. Livingstone was subsequently lost in the interior looking for the ultimate Nile source, which many believed Speke had not actually located. Henry Morton Stanley famously "found" Livingstone in 1871 and later led the expedition of 1874 through 1877, which solved most of the remaining geographical problems. Verney Cameron, also originally in search of Livingstone, crossed the continent between 1873 and 1876. Joseph Thomson explored the area between Lake Malawi and Lake Tanganyika, and later penetrated what is now Kenya between 1883 and 1884. Samuel Teleki and Ludwig von Höhnel reached Lake Turkana (Rudolf) in 1888. By this date, European control was being established, and later expeditions by Stanley, Frederick Lugard, and others were more imperialist than exploratory.

All this activity meant that East Africa had become the archetypal setting for the equally archetypal intrepid European traveler able to overcome natural and human obstacles. Why was this the case? Most important is the fact that East Africa was the last major inhabited region of the world to be opened to Western attention. Steamships, railways, telegraphs, printing, and many other technological developments made it possible for Europeans to reach East Africa easily and to disseminate information about it. Paradoxically, though, technology was of no use in East Africa itself, except to a limited extent with firearms; everything still depended on the traveler walking and fending for himself—which was part of the appeal of reading about the explorers. In fact, the adventure element is present in all the great travel narratives with dangers including supposedly backward and warlike peoples as well as wild animals. The popular concept is reflected in boys' stories like R.M. Ballantyne's *Gorilla Hunters* (1861). Interestingly, explorers themselves, notably Cameron, Stanley, and Thomson, felt it necessary to write fiction based on their experience of East Africa.

Emerging knowledge of the region's physical geographical characteristics was as important as the adventure element in directing attention to East Africa. Not everyone believed Krapf and Rebmann had seen snow on the summits of Kenya and Kilimanjaro, while there was controversy and debate about their further reports of lakes and, of course, about the source of the White Nile. The first great scientific expedition led by Burton in 1856 appropriately produced a long article for his sponsors, the Royal Geographical Society (RGS), but this was followed by the two-volume *Lake Regions* (1860) for the public; a pattern had been set. Burton made some claim to provide ethnographic information on the people encountered. Natural history was given a tremendous boost as tropical flora and fauna were revealed. The self-taught Livingstone was supreme here, but Marischal College-educated Grant made a very significant contribution.

It was, in fact, a scientific society, the RGS, which dominated British relations with East Africa for about 20 years beginning in 1856. Although naturally wanting its travelers to fill the geographical blanks on the map and produce scientific data, the society, dominated as it was by Roderick Murchison, was also keen to make its travelers great popular figures and to persuade the government that scientific exploration was an important matter of public policy.

Adventure and science certainly did become entwined with questions concerning East Africa's future. The prospects for the propagation of the Christian gospel and the related matter of ending the slave trade and slavery were the most immediately important. The greatest influence on East African concerns was not the book Krapf produced after ten years of East African experience, but Livingstone's South-African-based *Missionary Travels* of 1856, which pointed the way for commerce and Christianity to conquer this new field. Livingstone was seen as a great Christian—eventually, perhaps, a martyr—a scientific explorer and something of a public official. Essentially, his appeal lay in his belief that it was necessary and possible to use European expertise and technology to end the slave trade and prepare the way for new Christian societies to develop. His own efforts on the Zambezi with steamboats were disappointing, although he did discover another lake. His tragic last journey generated immense public interest and further important exploratory journeys by Cameron and Stanley, as well as several major missionary initiatives that yielded popular travel literature by figures like Annie and Edward Hore, Henry Drummond, and Alexander Mackay.

With the notable exception of Thomson, all the explorers suggested that "legitimate commerce" was possible and would be profitable. Apart from Livingstone himself, Cameron was the most important prophet of east and central Africa's economic potential because of the impact he had on King Leopold II. Baker's encouragement of Egyptian initiatives in the upper Nile region was hardly less important in its consequences, followed as it was by expeditions part exploratory and part imperialistic by Charles Gordon, Emin Pasha, and others. Although most British merchants and manufacturers remained wary of involvement in East Africa, several, notably William Mackinnon, a few explorers and missionary figures, and some public men connected with either the Indian or metropolitan administrations, were by the late 1870s trying to create a new East Africa. This "unofficial empire," as it has been called, created more opportunities for travel literature to be produced. On the whole, however, high-minded attempts to redeem East Africa failed, discredited by association with King Leopold's increasingly questionable activities and overtaken by developing rivalries between Europeans, which led to political partitioning of the region. French and especially German travelers had made some, albeit mostly minor, contributions to exploration. Hermann von Wissmann was a distinguished explorer, but Carl Peters was more a political traveler. His direct British counterpart was Lugard, whose book is a classic of imperialist exploration. Most famous was Stanley whose controversial expedition to rescue Emin Pasha for imperialist purposes spawned his own bestseller and many other books, the most distinguished by Arthur Mounteney Jephson.

By the 1880s, many writers had become racist, their descriptions of the region downgrading its African inhabitants on a presumed scale of civilization. This implicitly or explicitly justified calls for European control of some kind, although it is important to remember that until the 1890s, general sentiment was opposed to creating new political dependencies in Africa. Whatever was advocated, older ideals were overtaken by the idea of the "dark continent," a phrase coined and popularized by Stanley in the 1870s. If in reality some of the people proved not to be entirely lacking in sophistication, they were presumed to be non-negro elites. Some of these might have elements of the exotic about them, perhaps the heirs of a lost civilization. Speke's discovery of the Baganda in 1861 and his inauguration of the "Hamitic hypothesis"—that more advanced people from the north had come to rule—was just as important as his discovery of the Nile source. Clearly, it inspired Rider Haggard's *King Solomon's Mines* (1885), but more importantly suggested to whom the Europeans should look for local allies.

The scramble in East Africa produced miseries for Africans associated with punitive expeditions and exacerbated the environmental and disease afflictions of the ecological catastrophe of the 1890s. Elephant hunters like Arthur Neumann and W.D.M. Bell contributed to the difficulties, and books like theirs perhaps mark the end of the classic period of East African travel literature. By the 1890s, a few lady travelers had entered the picture; Mrs. Hore was the first but May French-Sheldon's narrative was the more readable. Essentially, however, the exploration of East Africa had been very much a male affair.

It is unfortunate that, until recently, most of the available secondary literature on East Africa's famous nineteenth-century travelers has been unimpressive in terms of either historical or literary analysis. Travel discourses have been accepted at face value and used as the basis of narratives about the exploration pure and simple and the relationships between the travelers involved. There are numerous biographies of the travelers, of greatly varying merit. Burton is a favorite subject, although not principally for his East African work. Speke has surprisingly attracted only one book-length biography, but there are innumerable studies of Livingstone. No one has successfully covered all facets of this remarkable man's life and work. Stanley is also much written about, Hall's (1974) being the best of recent biographies. Disputes about the Nile source or the snow mountains certainly developed into malarial fever-fueled personal antagonisms, and there is something to be said for accounts that explore the psychological characteristics of the travelers, but to concentrate on these matters alone ignores historical realities about Europe and its outreach, about Africa and Africans and, equally important, considerations concerning the nature of the literary discourses in the explorers' publications. Within these limitations, Moorehead's book (1960) is the best popular account of the exploration of the nineteenth century. McLynn's works are ambitious but in the end more concerned with psychology than history or literature. Hall's *Empires of the Monsoon* (1996) is impressive in its scope: it deals with two thousand years of writing about East Africa in its Indian Ocean setting.

The first serious large-scale academic study of East Africa's history by Coupland (1938 and 1939) and the old *Cambridge History of the British Empire* (1929–1940) tended to see the explorers as providing the prelude to (inevitable) British rule, but later works on imperialism generally do not regard the travelers as significant. For different reasons, the *Oxford History of East Africa* (vol. 1, 1963) ignored explorers as a historical phenomenon and the same has largely been true of other works concerned with the history of Africa and Africans. However, some new historical appraisals have emerged in recent years and there has been a tendency to examine travelers' writings in a more critical sense. Among historians, Simpson (1975), while having no theory to propound, added an important perspective by showing how much travelers depended on their African porters. Rotberg's biography of Thomson (1971) was something of a departure and his edited volume on travelers was designed to show the explorers in relation to the African societies they encountered; the results were mixed. Bridges (2000) regards the explorers, missionaries, and their allies as having tried to create an "unofficial empire."

The development of interest in East African travelers' discourses by literary experts has begun to yield important insights—not least for historians. It becomes apparent that much more is involved than descriptions of adventures in unknown lands among exotic peoples; many questions arise on the extent to which the discourses themselves were a product of European desires to justify their own culture and to justify the domination of other peoples. In 1965 Cairns examined travelers' and missionaries' texts to find strong evidence of racist and imperialist assumptions. Some chapters of Brantlinger's work (1988) examine similar themes in more subtle ways. The most penetrating analysis of East African travelers' texts as texts has been made by Youngs (1994). Like other scholars, he has been affected by Said's concept of orientalism and also believes that "what travellers describe in Africa is mainly Britain." Bridges (1987 and 1998), however, points out that behind the published discourses there are notebooks and journals which, carefully used, allow the historian to approach the reality of what the travelers and those Africans they encountered actually experienced. In other words, East African travel literature, whatever it tells us about the writer's own psychological state and about the cultural milieu from which he emerged, can also tell us about East Africa.

In the twentieth century, some travelers attempted to follow in the footsteps of the first explorers and nineteenth-century traditions were in a sense perpetuated by the dozens of accounts of hunting expeditions. Nothing can relieve their tedious and often distasteful nature, even if the hunter happened to be a president of the United States or the heir to the British throne. An exception should perhaps be made for Winston Churchill, who made shrewd comments on politics and economics as well as describing his shooting exploits in 1907. Julian Huxley also made shrewd comments in 1929, but he was hunting information about education, not animals. At about the same time, the young Margery Perham was traveling to record information about politics and administration, although the full account of her tour was not published until 1976. Evelyn Waugh passed through East Africa and was present long enough to record something of the decadent lifestyle the Kenya white settlers had so rapidly developed. John Gunther saw East Africa, at the end of the colonial period. Regardless, twentieth-century travel literature on East Africa is inevitably something of an anticlimax: no longer could the traveler be the "first to see" and no longer would travel works be the key repositories of information about the region. Hence East Africa is to be regarded as important in the story of travel literature chiefly because of the combination of circumstances that produced the works by the explorers and missionaries of the later nineteenth century.

ROY BRIDGES

### References and Further Reading

Arkell-Hardwick, A., *An Ivory Trader in North Kenia*, 1903.
Ashe, Robert P., *Two Kings of Uganda*, 1889; reprinted, 1970.
Baker, Samuel White, *The Albert N'yanza: Great Basin of the Nile, and Explorations of the Nile Sources*, 2 vols., 1866.
Baker, Samuel White, *Ismailïa: A Narrative of the Expedition to Central Africa for the Suppression of the Slave Trade*, 2 vols., 1874.
Baumann, Oscar, *Durch Massailand zur Nilquelle*, 1894.
Beardall, William, "Exploration of the Rufiji River," *Proceedings of the Royal Geographical Society*, new series, 3 (1881): 641–656.

Becker, Jérôme, *La Vie en Afrique*, 2 vols., 1887.
Bell, W.D.M., *The Wanderings of an Elephant Hunter*, 1923.
Bellville, Alfred, "Journey to Magila, Borders of Usambara Country," *Proceedings of the Royal Geographical Society*, 20 (1876): 74–78.
Boteler, Thomas, *Narrative of a Voyage of Discovery to Africa and Arabia*, 2 vols., 1835.
Brantlinger, Patrick, *Rule of Darkness: British Literature and Imperialism 1830–1914*, Ithaca, New York: Cornell University Press, 1988.
Bridges, R.C., "Nineteenth-Century East African Travel Records with an Appendix on 'Armchair Geographers' and Cartography," *Paideuma*, 33 (1987): 179–196.
Bridges, R.C., "Explorers' Texts and the Problem of Reactions by Non-Literate Peoples", *Studies in Travel Writing*, 2 (1998): 65–84.
Bridges, R.C., "Towards the Prelude to the Partition of East Africa" in *Imperialism, Decolonization and Africa: Studies Presented to John Hargreaves*, edited by R.C. Bridges, 2000.
Broyon-Mirambo, P., "Description of Unyamwesi," *Proceedings of the Royal Geographical Society*, 22 (1878): 28–37.
Burton, Richard F., *First Footsteps in East Africa; or, An Exploration of Harar*, 1856.
Burton, Richard F., *The Lake Regions of Central Africa: A Picture of Exploration*, 2 vols., 1860; reprint 1961.
Burton, Richard F., *Zanzibar: City, Island and Coast*, 2 vols., 1872.
Cameron, Verney Lovett, *Across Africa*, 2 vols., 1877.
Casati, Gaetano, *Dieci anni in Equatoria, e ritorno con Emin Pascia*, 2 vols., 1891; as *Ten Years in Equatoria, and the Return with Emin Pasha*, translated by Mrs. J. Randolph Clay, 2 vols., 1891.
Chaillé Long, Charles, *Central Africa: Naked Truths of Naked People*, 1876; reprinted, 1968.
Chippindall, W.W., "Journey beyond the Cataracts of the Upper Nile towards the Albert Nyanza," *Proceedings of the Royal Geographical Society*, 20 (1876): 67–69.
Churchill, Winston, *My African Journey*, 1908.
Cooley, William Desborough, "The Geography of Nyassi," *Journal of the Royal Geographical Society*, 15 (1845): 185–235.
Cotterill, H.B., "On the Nyassa and Journey to Zanzibar," *Proceedings of the Royal Geographical Society*, 22 (1878): 233–251.
Coupland, Reginald, *The Exploitation of East Africa, 1856–1890: The Slave Trade and the Scramble*, London: Faber, 1939.
Decken, Carl Claus von der, *Reisen in Ost-Afrika in den Jahren 1859 bis 1865*, 4 vols., 1869–1879.
Dodgshun, Arthur W., *From Zanzibar to Ujiji: The Journal of Arthur W. Dodgshun, 1877–1879*, edited by Norman Robert Bennett, 1969.
Drummond, Henry, *Tropical Africa*, 1888.
Elton, J. Frederic, *Travels and Researches among the Lakes and Mountains of Eastern and Central Africa*, edited and completed by H.B. Cotterill, 1879; reprinted, 1968.
Emery, James B., "A Short Account of Mombas and the Neighbouring Coast of Africa," *Journal of the Royal Geographical Society*, 3 (1833): 280–283.
Emin Pasha, *Die Tagebücher von Dr Emin Pascha*, edited by Franz Stuhlmann, 6 vols., 1916–1927.
Emin's journeys from 1876 to 1890. Translations by Sir John Gray on sections bearing on Uganda appeared in the *Uganda Journal* in 13 parts from vol. 25 (1961) to vol. 32 (1968).
Farler, J.P., "Usambara Country," *Proceedings of the Royal Geographical Society*, new series, 1 (1879): 81–94.
Faulkner, Henry, *Elephant Haunts, Being a Sportsman's Narrative of the Search for Doctor Livingstone, with Scenes of Elephant, Buffalo and Hippopotamus Hunting*, 1868; reprinted, 1984.
Fischer, G.A., *Das Massai-Land*, 1885.
Fitzgerald, William Walter Augustine, *Travels in the Coastlands of British East Africa and the Islands of Zanzibar and Pemba*, 1898; reprinted, 1984.
Frere, H. Bartle, "Zanzibar and the East Coast of Africa," *Proceedings of the Royal Geographical Society*, 17 (1873): 343–354.
Gamitto, A.C.P., *O Muata Cazembe*, 1854; as *King Kazembe*, translated by Ian Cunnison, 2 vols., 1960.
Gordon, Charles G., *Colonel Gordon in Central Africa, 1874–1879*, edited by George Birkbeck Hill, 1881; reprinted, 1969.
Gordon, Charles G., and Romolo Gessi, "The Khedive's Expedition up the White Nile," *Proceedings of the Royal Geographical Society*, 20 (1876): 50–54; 21 (1877): 48–630.
Grant, James Augustus, *A Walk across Africa; or, Domestic Scenes from My Nile Journal*, 1864.
Grant, James Augustus, "Summary of Observations . . . Made by the Speke and Grant Expedition," *Journal of the Royal Geographical Society*, 42 (1872): 243–342.
Grogan, Ewart S., and Arthur H. Sharp, *From the Cape to Cairo*, 1900.
Guillain, Charles (editor), *Documents sur l'histoire, la géographie et le commerce de l'Afrique orientale*, 3 vols., 1856.
Gunther, John, *Inside Africa*, 1955.
Hall, Richard, *Stanley: An Adventurer Explored*, London: Collins, 1974; Boston: Houghton Mifflin, 1975.
Hall, Richard, *Empires of the Monsoon: A History of the Indian Ocean and Its Invaders*, London: HarperCollins, 1996.
Hannington, James, *The Last Journals of Bishop Hannington*, edited by E.C. Dawson, 1888.
Höhnel, Ludwig, Ritter von, *Discovery of Lakes Rudolf and Stefanie*, translated by Nancy Bell, 2 vols., 1894.
Holmwood, Frederic, "Kingani River, East Africa," *Journal of the Royal Geographical Society*, 47 (1877): 253–267.
Hore, Annie B., *To Lake Tanganyika in a Bath Chair*, 1886.
Hore, Edward Coode, *Tanganyika: Eleven Years in Central Africa*, 1892.
Huntingford, G.W.B. (translator and editor), *The Periplus of the Erythraean Sea*, 1980.
Huxley, Julian, *Africa View*, 1931.
Ibn Battuta, *Travels of Ibn Batutta* AD *1325–1354*, translated by H.A.R. Gibb, vol. 2, 1962.
Jephson, A.J. Mounteney, *Emin Pasha and the Rebellion at the Equator*, 1890.
Jephson, A.J. Mounteney, *The Diary of A.J. Mounteney Jephson: Emin Pasha Relief Expedition, 1887–1889*, edited by Dorothy Middleton, 1969.
Johnson, William P., "Seven Years' Travels East of Nyassa," *Proceedings of the Royal Geographical Society*, new series, 6 (1884): 512–533.
Johnston, Harry Hamilton, *The Kilima-Njaro Expedition: A Record of Scientific Exploration in Eastern Equatorial Africa*, 1886; reprinted, 1968.
Kirk, John, "Notes on Two Expeditions up the Rovuma," *Journal of the Royal Geographical Society*, 35 (1865): 154–169.
Kirk, John, "Visit to the Coast of Somali Land," *Proceedings of the Royal Geographical Society*, 17 (1873): 340–343.
Kirk, John, "Examination of the Lufiji River Delta," *Proceedings of the Royal Geographical Society*, 18 (1874): 74–76.
Krapf, J. Lewis, *Travels, Researches and Missionary Labours during an Eighteen Years' Residence in Eastern Africa*, 1860.

Lancaster, James, "A Voyage with Three Tall Ships . . . to the Iles of Comoro and Zanzibar on the Backeside of Africa," in *The Principal Navigations, Voiages, Traffiques and Discoveries of the English Nation*, by Richard Hakluyt, 3 vols., 1598–1600; reprinted in 12 vols., 1903–05: vol. 6, 392–395.

Lacerda, Francisco José Maria de. *The Lands of Cazembe: Lacerda's Journey to Cazembe in 1798*, translated by R.F. Burton, 1873.

Last, J.T., "Journey into the Nguru Country," *Proceedings of the Royal Geographical Society*, new series, 4 (1882): 148–157.

Laws, Robert, "Journey along Part of the Western Side of Nyassa," *Proceedings of the Royal Geographical Society*, new series, 1 (1879): 305–320.

Livingstone, David, *Missionary Travels and Researches in South Africa*, 1857.

Livingstone, David, *The Last Journals of David Livingstone*, edited by Horace Waller, 2 vols., 1874; reprinted, 1970.

Livingstone, David, *David Livingstone and the Rovuma*, edited by George Shepperson, 1965.

Livingstone, David, and Charles Livingstone, *Narrative of an Expedition to the Zambesi and Its Tributaries*, 1865; reprinted, 1971.

Lugard, Frederick Dealtry, *The Rise of Our East African Empire*, 2 vols., 1893; reprinted, 1968.

Macdonald, J.R.L., *Soldiering and Surveying in British East Africa, 1891–1894*, 1897; reprinted, 1973.

Mackay, Alexander M., "Boat Voyage along the Western Shores of Victoria Nyanza," *Proceedings of the Royal Geographical Society*, new series, 6 (1884): 273–283.

Maples, Chauncy, "Masasi and Rovuma District, East Africa," *Proceedings of the Royal Geographical Society*, new series, 2 (1880): 337–352.

Maples, Chauncy, "Makua Land," *Proceedings of the Royal Geographical Society*, new series, 4 (1882): 79–86.

M'Queen, James, "The Visit of Lief bin Said to the Great African Lake," *Journal of the Royal Geographical Society*, 15 (1845): 371–374.

Mullens, J., "A New Route to Central Africa," *Proceedings of the Royal Geographical Society*, 21 (1877): 233–247.

Neumann, Arthur H., *Elephant-Hunting in East Equatorial Africa*, 1898.

New, Charles, *Life, Wanderings and Labours in Eastern Africa*, 1873; reprinted, 1971.

New, Charles and R. Bushell, "Ascent of Kilima Njaro," *Proceedings of the Royal Geographical Society*, 16 (1872): 167–168.

Osgood, John Felt, *Notes of Travel; or, Recollections of Majunga, Zanzibar, Muscat, Aden, Mocha, and Other Eastern Ports*, 1854.

Owen, W.F.W., *Narrative of Voyages to Explore the Shores of Africa, Arabia and Madagascar*, 2 vols., 1833; reprinted, 1968.

Patterson, J.H., *The Man-Eaters of Tsavo and Other East African Adventures*, 1907.

Perham, Margery, *East African Journey: Kenya and Tanganyika, 1929–30*, 1976.

Peters, Carl, *New Light on Dark Africa*, translated by H.W. Dulcken, 1891.

Pringle, Mrs M.A., *Towards the Mountains of the Moon: A Journey in East Africa*, 1884.

Prior, James, *Voyage along the Eastern Coast of Africa*, 1819.

Roosevelt, Theodore, *African Game Trails*, 1910.

Rotberg, Robert I., *Joseph Thomson and the Exploration of Africa*, London: Chatto and Windus, and New York: Oxford University Press, 1971.

Salt, Henry, *A Voyage to Abyssinia and Travels to the Interior of That Country*, 1814; reprinted, 1967.

Sheldon, May French, *Sultan to Sultan: Adventures among the Masai and Other Tribes of East Africa*, 1892.

Simpson, Donald, *Dark Companions: The African Contribution to the European Exploration of East Africa*, London: Elek, 1975; New York: Barnes and Noble, 1976.

Smee, Thomas, and L. Hardy, "Observations during a Voyage of Research on the East Coast of Africa," *Transactions of the Bombay Geographical Society*, 6 (1841–1844): 23–61.

Southon, Ebenezer J., "Notes on a Journey through Northern Ugogo," *Proceedings of the Royal Geographical Society*, new series, 3 (1881): 547–553.

Speke, John Hanning, *Journal of the Discovery of the Source of the Nile*, 1863.

Speke, John Hanning, *What Led to the Discovery of the Source of the Nile*, 1864; reprinted, 1967.

Stanley, Henry M., *How I Found Livingstone*, 1872.

Stanley, Henry M., *Through the Dark Continent*, 2 vols., 1878; reprinted, 1969.

Stanley, Henry M., *In Darkest Africa; or, The Quest, Rescue and Retreat of Emin*, 2 vols., 1890.

Stanley, Henry M., *The Exploration Diaries of H.M. Stanley*, edited by Richard Stanley and Alan Neame, 1961.

Stanley, Henry M., *Stanley's Despatches to the New York Herald, 1871–1872, 1874–1877*, edited by Norman R. Bennett, 1970.

Stewart, James, "Observations on the Western Side of Lake Nyassa and the Country . . . between Nyassa and Tanganyika," *Proceedings of the Royal Geographical Society*, new series, 2 (1880): 428–431.

Stewart, James, "Survey of Eastern Coast of Nyassa," *Proceedings of the Royal Geographical Society*, new series, 5 (1883): 689–692.

Swann, Alfred J., *Fighting the Slave Hunters in Central Africa*, 1910.

Thomson, Joseph, *To the Central African Lakes and Back*, 2 vols., 1881.

Thomson, Joseph, "Basin of the River Rovuma," *Proceedings of the Royal Geographical Society*, new series, 4 (1882): 65–79.

Thomson, Joseph, *Through Masai Land*, 1885; revised edition, 1887; reprinted, 1968.

Thornton, Richard, "Expedition to Kilimanjaro," *Proceedings of the Royal Geographical Society*, 6 (1862): 47–51.

Tippu Tip, *Maisha ya Hamed bin Muhammed el Murjebi*, translated by W.H. Whiteley, 1959.

Waugh, Evelyn, *Remote People*, 1931.

Waugh, Evelyn, *The Diaries of Evelyn Waugh*, edited by Michael Davie, 1976.

Wilson, C.T., and R.W. Felkin, *Uganda and the Egyptian Soudan*, 2 vols., 1882.

Windsor, Edward, (later Duke of), *Sport and Travel in East Africa . . . Compiled from the Private Diaries of H.R.H. the Prince of Wales*, edited by Patrick R. Chalmers, 1934.

Wissmann, Hermann von, *My Second Journey through Equatorial Africa, from the Congo to the Zambesi, in the Years 1886 and 1887*, translated by Minna J.A. Bergmann, 1891.

Young, Edward Daniel, and Horace Waller, *The Search after Livingstone*, 1868.

Young, Edward Daniel, and Horace Waller, *Nyassa: A Journal of Adventures*, 1877.

Youngs, Tim, *Travellers in Africa: British Travelogues, 1850–1900*, Manchester: Manchester University Press, 1994.


*See also* **Ethiopia/Abyssinia; Blue Nile**

## EAST INDIA COMPANY (BRITISH)

The history of the East India Company is a history of commerce and politics that began with Henry VIII and Sir Francis Drake, who were concerned with advancing British power and fascinated with discovering and exploring new territory. Following their lead, Elizabeth I granted a royal charter establishing the East India Company on 31 December 1600, formalizing what had previously been loosely structured and unregulated maritime interactions between Britain and other nations. Initially, its goal was to give British merchants the power to establish binding commercial exchanges with foreign countries, to engage in exploratory voyages, and to establish national outposts in countries of the East. Later its ventures would extend into the American colonies under the jurisdiction of the Virginia Company and it would be influential in the search for the Northwest Passage.

Historians note that the Company's primary intent was to compete with the Dutch spice trade in India, but suggest that it would soon have other, wider goals, including attempting to establish national superiority over other commercial nations, such as Portugal and Spain, and the wish to spread Christianity. Whatever its stated charter, however, from its very inception, the Company was both institution and metaphor for British national interest. It was always much more than a mere commercial enterprise. Indeed, it advanced the British empire from the reign of Elizabeth through to the mid-nineteenth century and its commercial goals were intertwined with Britain's political and, later, military objectives.

The original charter was unique in many ways, and included several features that ensured the Company's early financial success. According to Philip Lawson, in *The East India Company: A History* (1993), four aspects of the charter were distinct. The Company was granted a "monopoly of all trade" in the East; it was authorized to carry bullion out of England to be used in purchasing foreign goods; it was subsidized by shareholders whose assets pooled risk and limited individual liability; and it was internally organized in a way that allowed for efficient decision making. In addition to its radical charter, the business practices of the Company altered the typical way of trading. Most importantly, it began the practice of erecting factories or warehouses to store commodities in foreign lands. Thus, ships could be easily loaded and sent back to sea without the burden of time-consuming interactions with local merchants.

Technically the Company was directed from London by an administrative board, but the great distance between England and India actually meant that regional field directors and overseas agents had enormous power. They began diplomatic relations with Moghul India without much direction from the mother country, as letters often took a year to be delivered to England from remote stations. Overseas directors established independent trade agreements with local authorities, many of which resulted in enormous political power for the company. These regional directors also insisted on the right to establish their own armies and garrisons, initially to protect their interests against piracy, smuggling, and rival companies, but later as protection against the local populations. The forts eventually served as outposts from which military initiatives could be undertaken. For these and many other reasons, the Company quickly produced considerable profits, despite the recurring economic problems in England throughout the seventeenth century.

During the seventeenth century, complicated relationships existed between the Company and the rulers in England, and during this period many parliamentary challenges to the company's monopoly were made both by commercial rivals and by politicians. However, the revenues that the company returned to England essentially silenced public opposition so that the era saw the frequent renewal of the initial charter granting a monopoly on trade, resulting in the dramatic expansion of the Company and an increase in its power.

In addition to the significant revenue it sent to England, the Company also changed British dietary habits and culture. It distributed tea and sugar, saltpeter and molasses, and other spices that were used to enhance flavor and as preservatives. It also brought cotton and other textiles from new sources. One of the company's earliest successes was establishing a trade agreement with China and importing silk and porcelain, which ultimately gave rise to new industries in England. Early in the seventeenth century it was also one of the first trading companies to import coffee, which found a

Bombay (Mumbai) in the mid-eighteenth century under Company control: the "Green" overlooked by the "extremely neat, commodious, and airy" church (from John Henry Grose's *Voyage to the East Indies*, second edition, 1766). *Courtesy of Travellers Club, London; Bridgeman Art Library, agent.*

ready market in European countries as the habit of drinking coffee on a daily basis quickly spread.

In the eighteenth century, the Company established three centers of power in India: Bombay, Madras, and Calcutta. Favored by good management, it stabilized operations and was granted generous concessions from Moghul rulers. According to John Keay in *The Honourable Company* (1991), the concessions took many forms, including "preferential trade agreements," "custom-free movement," and titles conferring rank and authority on agents of the Company. All of these concessions allowed it to maintain a huge competitive advantage over its rivals.

In addition, the Company began to exercise considerable authority within India, handling the collection of taxes and other revenue, as well as supervising and enforcing legal regulations. By 1750 its power was enormous. Under the leadership of Robert Clive, the Company became the de facto ruler of Bengal, collecting taxes and enforcing laws through military intervention. Eventually it controlled a very considerable part of the world, estimated at one-fifth of the world's population. In addition to trading, the Company engaged in many other operations, such as the engineering of transport systems across India.

Despite the Company's public authority, historians agree that internal corruption was widespread. Many of its employees sought personal gain and established private trade agreements that cheated the parent company of profits. Smuggling was commonplace, but tolerated as spoils. Many Englishmen who were drawn to service in the company came with the express intent of making independent fortunes, and records suggest that many succeeded admirably. Many of the higher-ranking officers were virtually equivalent in power and prestige to local rulers. Although the authorities in England were aware of these practices, at first many went largely unchallenged because the Company still showed reliable profits to its shareholders. Supervising the firm from England proved difficult because of distance, and as a result, many decisions were made in India and elsewhere that had never been authorized in London.

Eventually the Company's growth in power and autonomy worried members of parliament and the general public at home. Parliament sought to curtail its power, and during the latter third of the eighteenth century legal actions restricted its authority. An outside agent, a governor-general of India, was appointed to supervise British interests, and the Company was essentially directed to resume its emphasis on trade, not imperial expansion. Other political developments, however, including the American Revolution and the Napoleonic wars, interfered with Britain's ability to maintain control, and by the start of the nineteenth century, British efforts to promote territorial expansion in India clearly involved using the resources of the company. Its militia initiated wars with local authorities, and its officers promoted the British domination of Indian culture. Where previous administrators largely respected the various Indian religions, new regulations fostered evangelical missionary conversions to Christianity.

In addition, changing British attitudes toward local populations led to policy changes. According to Matthew Edney's *Mapping an Empire* (1997), public figures such as Thomas Babington Macaulay advocated the anglicization of India and insisted on the supremacy of British authority and way of life. In 1835 for example, administrators insisted on the mandatory use of the English language in all educational programs in India, in stark contrast to earlier systems that promoted the use and preservation of local languages, especially Persian, which had been used extensively.

Although the Company held enormous political, military, and cultural power during the early nineteenth century, many factors contributed to its economic decline. Profits dwindled and were replaced by enormous debt, which parliament refused to underwrite. Its trading privileges were curtailed, and the military actions it undertook were costly financially and politically. Local Indian rulers began to stage insurrections against British authority, arguing for their right of self-government, while the military leaders of the Company refused to concern themselves with trade, preferring to enforce expansionist goals instead.

Eventually, following the so-called Indian Mutiny of 1857, British control of India was transferred officially back to England, eliminating the Company's last vestiges of jurisdiction. In 1858 Queen Victoria announced that the Crown would take over the jurisdiction of India, which had "heretofore [been] administered for us by the Honourable East India Company." In praising the Company for its efforts, she also spoke of the need to begin a new era, "draw[ing] a veil over the sad and bloody past." Speaking directly to the abuses by the Company, she emphasized that the Crown would not insist on religious conversion and that it would honor all treaties with local authorities (Anderson and Subedar, 1918).

Thus, through Victoria's official proclamation, the Company ceased to be a world power, although its influence continued. During its height, the Company had established railway and irrigation systems in India, significantly changed the country's political, legal, and educational systems, and in England and elsewhere it had forever altered public taste by the provisions it had brought to market.

Many book-length studies of the East India Company exist, as do extensive discussions within the works of Anglo-Indian and trade (such as those on tea and spices) history. Historical accounts make use of extensive archival materials, from newspaper articles to cartographic surveys to statistical trade records to first-person narratives and correspondence. According to many scholars, the Company's archives are so meticulous that there are case studies of individual decades, virtually tracing the Company's productivity and importance year by year. In addition, given the Company's frequent appearance in fictional and even cinematic accounts, the corpus of legend and myth associated with it extends its reputation even further. As a result, recent studies contain extensive bibliographies of both primary and secondary materials.

Most archival records associated with the Company are housed in the India Office, Waterloo, London, under the supervision of the British Library. Several bibliographic tools exist to assist scholars in locating and identifying cataloged materials. An annotated description of archival materials can be found in Edney's *Mapping an Empire*, page 409.

Electronic sources are also available that provide links, citations, and archival materials; the website maintained by the reestablished East India Company, www.theeastindiacompany.com, includes materials related to Company history, notices about forthcoming exhibitions and publications, as well as a glossary of Anglo-Indian words. It also includes lists of fictional works that mention the original Company.

NANCY V. WORKMAN

## References and Further Reading


Anderson, G. and M. Subedar, *The Expansion of British India (1818–1858)*, vol. 1: *The Last Days of the Company*, London: Bell, and New York: Macmillan, 1918; reprinted, New Delhi: Uppal, 1987.

Beeckman, Daniel, *A Voyage to and from the Island of Borneo, in the East Indies*, 1718; with an introduction by Chin Yoon Fong, 1973.

Best, Thomas et al., *The Voyage of Thomas Best to the East Indies, 1612–14*, edited by William Foster, 1934.

Blakiston, John, *Twelve Years' Military Adventure in Three Quarters of the Globe; or, Memoirs of an Officer Who Served in the Armies of His Majesty and of the East India Company, between the Years 1802 and 1814, in Which Are Contained the Campaigns of the Duke of Wellington in India, and His Last in Spain and the South of France*, 2 vols., 1829.

Cocks, Richard, *Diary of Richard Cocks, Cape-Merchant in the English Factory in Japan 1615–22, with Correspondence*, edited by Edward Maunde Thompson, 2 vols., 1883.

Conolly, Arthur, *Journey to the North of India, Overland through Russia, Persia, and Affghaunistan*, 2 vols., 1834.

Dalrymple, Alexander, *Journal of the Ship London, Captain Walter Hues, along the North Coast of Magindanao, October, 1764*, 1781.

Dalrymple, Alexander, *Journal of the Schooner "Cuddalore" through the Strait of Sapy, and on the South Coast of Man–e–rye, in February, March, and April 1761*, 1793.

Daniell, Thomas, and William Daniell, *A Picturesque Voyage to India, by Way of China*, 1810.

D'Oyly, Charles, *Sketches on the New Road in a Journey from Calcutta to Eyah*, 1830.

Edney, Matthew H., *Mapping an Empire: The Geographical Construction of British India, 1765–1843*, Chicago: University of Chicago Press, 1997.

Forster, George, *A Journey from Bengal to England, through the Northern Part of India, Kashmire, Afghanistan, and Persia and into Russia, by the Caspian Sea*, 1798; reprinted, 2 vols., 1987.

Foster, William (editor), *Early Travels in India, 1583–1619*, 1921; reprinted, 1975.

Grose, John Henry, *A Voyage to the East Indies*, 1757; 2nd edition, 2 vols., 1766; 3rd edition, 1772.

Hedges, William, *The Diary of William Hedges Esq. . . . during His Agency in Bengal; as well as on His Voyage out and Return Overland (1681–1687)*, 3 vols., 1887–1889.

Hodges, William, *Select Views in India, Drawn on the Spot in the Years 1780, 1781, 1782 and 1783*, 1786–1788.

Hunter, William, *A Concise Account of the Kingdom of Pegu, Its Climate, Produce, Trade and Government: The Manners and Customs of Its Inhabitants, Interspersed with Remarks Moral and Political*, 1785.

Keay, John, *The Honourable Company: A History of the English East India Company*, London: HarperCollins, 1991; New York: Macmillan, 1994.

Lal, Mohan, *Journal of a Tour through the Panjab, Afghanistan, Turkistan and Khorasan and Part of Persia in Company with Lieut. Barnes and Dr. Gerard*, 1834.

Lal, Mohan, *Travels in the Panjab, Afghanistan and Turkistan*, 1846.

Lawson, Philip, *The East India Company: A History*, London and New York: Longman, 1993.

Malcolm, John, *Sketches of Persia, from the Journals of a Traveller in the East*, 2 vols. (published anonymously), 1827; new edition (published as John Malcolm), 1 vol., 1845.

Markham, Clements R. (editor), *Narratives of the Mission of George Bogle to Tibet, and of the Journey of Thomas Manning to Lhasa*, 1876.

Markham, Clements R. (editor), *The Voyages of Sir James Lancaster, Kt, to the East Indies . . .*, 1877; as *The Voyages of Sir James Lancaster to Brazil and the East Indies, 1591–1603*, edited by William Foster, 1940.

Masson, Charles, *Narrative of Various Journeys in Balochistan, Afghanistan and the Panjab, Including a Residence in Those Countries from 1826 to 1838*, 3 vols., 1842; reprinted, with an introduction by Gavin Hambly, 1974.

Methwold, William, "Relations of the Kingdome of Golchonda and Other Neighbouring Nations within the Gulfe of Bengala" in *Purchas His Pilgrimes*, by Samuel Purchas, fourth edition, 1626; in *Relations of Golconda in the Early Seventeenth Century*, edited by W.H. Moreland, 1931.

Middleton, Henry, *The Voyage of Sir Henry Middleton to Bantam and the Maluco Islands, Being the Second Voyage Set Forth by the Governor and Company of Merchants of London Trading into the East-Indies*, edited by Bolton Corney, 1855; new edition as *The Voyage of Sir Henry Middleton to the Moluccas 1604–1606*, edited by William Foster, 1943.

Moorcroft, William, and George Trebeck, *Travels in the Himalayan Provinces of Hindustan and the Panjab; in Ladakh, and Kashmir; in Peshawar, Kabul, Kunduz and Bokhara . . . from 1819 to 1825*, edited by Horace Hayman Wilson, 2 vols., 1841; reprinted, with an introduction by G.J. Adler, 1979.

Purchas, Samuel, *Purchas His Pilgrimes*, 4 vols., 1625.

Roe Thomas, *The Embassy of Sir Thomas Roe to the Court of the Great Mogul, 1615–1619, as Narrated in His Journal and Correspondence*, edited by William Foster, 2 vols., 1899; revised edition, as *The Embassy of Sir Thomas Roe to India, 1615–19*, 1926.
Strachan, Michael, and Boies Penrose (editors), *The East India Company Journals of Captain William Keeling and Master Thomas Bonner, 1615–1617*, 1971.
Thomson, John Turnbull, *Some Glimpses into Life in the Far East*, 1864; as *Glimpses into Life in Malayan Lands*, edited and with an introduction by John Hall-Jones, 1984.
Turner, Samuel, *An Account of an Embassy to the Court of the Teshoo Lama in Tibet*, 1800; reprinted, 1971.
Williamson, Thomas, *The European in India . . .*, 1813.

## EAST INDIA COMPANY (DUTCH)

The Dutch East India Company (Vereenigde Oostindische Compagnie; VOC) is often described as the largest shipping and trade company in the world during the seventeenth and eighteenth centuries. After the first Dutch voyages to Asia, starting around 1595, the Dutch trading companies soon gained a firm position in Asia. In 1602 the VOC was formed as a merger of several smaller companies. The first 50 years were a period of great expansion. The VOC settled at the Cape of Good Hope, in Sri Lanka and many South Indian harbor towns, in Taiwan, and in the Indonesian archipelago, especially Java and the Moluccas. From 1641 the Dutch were the only Europeans granted the right to trade with Japan. Between 1595 and 1800 the ships of the VOC made 4,721 voyages, carrying nearly a million people to Asia. After 1700 the Dutch–Asian trade slowly declined. During the French revolutionary wars, the VOC was dissolved and taken over by the Dutch state government.

In the first 50 years of the seventeenth century, not only did Dutch overseas trade boom, but so too did the book trade. Dutch printers and publishers produced books for the national and international market. Many readers in the Netherlands and elsewhere in Europe were interested in books on Dutch voyages overseas. The most important handbook for the first Dutch voyages to the Far East was the magnum opus by Jan Huygen van Linschoten, the *Itinerario* (1595–1596; in English as *Jan Huighen van Linschoten His Discours of Voyages into ye Easte West Indies*, 1598). Van Linschoten lived in India in the 1580s as a secretary of the Portuguese archbishop of Goa. During his stay, van Linschoten collected information on Asian trade and shipping. His book was translated into English, French, German, and Latin. Accounts of several other early Dutch voyages undertaken around that time were printed within weeks or months after the return of a fleet, and were translated into the leading European languages almost as soon as they appeared in Dutch. This includes for example, the voyage of Willem Barents and Jacob van Heemskerck, who tried their luck on a northeastern passage to China. Gerrit de Veer, one of the men on board, used Barents's journals, as well as his own, to write the *Waerachtige Beschryvinghe* (as *True and Perfect Description of Three Voyages*, 1609), published in 1598. At the same time, Willem Lodewycksz, who went with Cornelis de Houtman on the first successful Dutch voyage to Asia, published *D'Eerste boeck: Historie van Indien, waer inne verhaelt is de avontueren die de hollandtche schepen* [The First Book: History of the Indies, Relating the Adventures of the Dutch Ships] in 1598. A few years later the safe return of Olivier van Noort, the first Dutchman to circumnavigate the globe (fourth after Magellan, Drake, and Cavendish), resulted in the *Beschryvinghe vande voyagie om den gehelen werelt cloot* [Description of the Voyage around the Entire Globe, 1602].

The Amsterdam-based printer-publisher Cornelis Claesz was the leading publisher in this genre in those early years. He worked with some of the best engravers of his time, producing high-quality work. Thanks to Claesz, around 1600 the Dutch travel account could already be described as a literary genre, with distinct formal characteristics. For Claesz and other Dutch publishers, it was common practice to print editions in French and Latin shortly after completing the Dutch edition. Translations were usually printed and published in England and Germany.

During the first 30 years of the seventeenth century, the printed travel account hardly changed. The most important subject of most travel accounts was the voyage itself. Not the adventurous events during the voyage itself, but the fact that any important voyage was undertaken at all, was reason enough for an account to be published. By the time people grew accustomed

A Dutch landing party ambushed (from Valentijn's *Oud en Nieuw Oost-Indiën*, 1724[-]1726). *Courtesy of Travellers Club, London; Bridgeman Art Library, agent.*

to the idea of voyages overseas, the subject of the travel accounts had changed. Simultaneously around 1630, two subgenres appeared: the disastrous travel account and the personal travel account. In the disastrous accounts, sensational events during a voyage were the most important subject of the story: shipwreck, mutiny, and general misery sell, as both writers and publishers soon found out. The most popular Dutch travel account was the one about the disastrous voyage of the skipper Willem Ysbrantsz Bontekoe of Hoorn, first published in 1646. Another famous voyage is that of the ship *Batavia*, shipwrecked in 1629 on the Abrolhos Islands off the west coast of Australia. The survivors of the shipwreck were subsequently terrorized by a demonic merchant who killed many men, women, and children before he and his accomplices were captured, tried, and hanged. The *Ongeluckige Voyagie van't Schip Batavia*, 1647 [Disastrous Voyage of the Ship Batavia] (a summary appears in John Harris's *Collection of Voyages*, 1705) was published many years after the disaster, but was still thought worthy of eight reprints. Disastrous travel accounts remained very popular throughout the seventeenth and eighteenth centuries.

In the personal travel account, the author himself is the subject of the story. Such an autobiographical account follows his adventures from the day he leaves home until his safe return, often many years later. Starting in the 1630s, the personal travel account slowly developed into the most important genre of travel writing during the eighteenth century, with some elaborate, expensive, and beautifully illustrated publications. Examples are Wouter Schouten's *Oost-Indische Voyagie* [East Indian Voyage], first published in 1676, and *Reisen van Nicolaus de Graaff* [Travels of Nicolaus de Graaff], first published in 1701. The *Reize van Zeeland over de Kaap de Goede Hoop, naar Batavia, Bantam, Bengalen enz. . . . door den heer J.S. Stavorinus*, 4 vols., 1793 (as *Voyages to the East Indies: By the Late John Splinter Stavorinus*, 1798) was translated into English, German, French, and Swedish.

A significant number of personal travel accounts (approximately 30) were written by German VOC employees. The VOC had quite a large number of foreign employees, mostly poor Germans and Scandinavians who were hired as soldiers or craftsmen and joined the company as a last resort. Some, however, were well educated and clearly longed for adventure before settling down. When they returned home, they published their stories. To explain them to their readers—stay-at-homes who had never seen a ship—these writers gave many details of the daily routines on board ship and of life in Asia, facts often ignored by Dutch sources. In the seventeenth and eighteenth centuries, some of these German accounts were translated into Dutch.

Between 1640 and 1665, Dutch travel accounts reached a widespread audience when three Amsterdam-based publishers—Johannes Janssonius, Joost Hartgers, and Gillis Joosten Saeghman—each published a large collection of travel accounts. Janssonius's collection, *Begin ende Voortgangh van de Vereenigde Neederlandtsche Geoctroyeerde Oost-Indische Compagnie* (1644; as *A Collection of Voyages Undertaken by the Dutch East India Company*, 1703) was the most expensive, with several new texts supplementing the older pioneering voyages, many of them beautifully illustrated with fine copper engravings, while the collection published by Saeghman, *Verscheyde Oost-Indische Voyagien*, 1663 [Several East Indian Voyages], balances on the threshold of popular publishing, consisting of reprints only, sometimes shortened with some rough editorial cuts, and illustrated with smaller and cheaper woodcut pictures. Janssonius's *Begin ende Voortgangh* was translated into French and English. The collections of Hartgers and Saeghman reached Dutch readers only.

During the VOC period, some important works on Asia were published by the Dutch. A true encyclopedia of the history and nature of the VOC territory appeared: *Oud en Nieuw Oost-Indiën* (1724–1726) by François Valentijn is a monumental work that is still of great value, especially with respect to his descriptions of the Moluccas, Ceylon, and the Cape of Good Hope. The chapters on Ceylon were translated into English as *François Valentijn's Description of Ceylon* and published by the Hakluyt Society in 1978.

During the time that the VOC resided in Deshima, Japan, the VOC officials had to visit the emperor in Edo (present-day Tokyo) once a year. Arnoldus Montanus wrote the *Gedenkwaerdige Gesantschappen der Oost-Indische Maetschappy . . . aen de Kaisaren van Japan* [*Atlas Japanensis, being Remarkable Addresses by Way of Embassy from the East India Company to the Emperor of Japan*, 1670], using the logs of the Dutch embassy from 1649 through 1661.

Around the same time, the Dutch tried to establish better relations with China. In 1655 the first Dutch embassy to the Chinese court in Beijing was undertaken. Johan Nieuhof was assigned to join the party as the official writer and artist, and in 1665 his *Het Gezantschap der Neêrlandsche Oost-Indische Compagnie aan den Grooten Tatarischen Cham, den tegenwoordigen Keizer van China* [An Embassy from the East India Company of the United Provinces to the Grand Tartar Cham, Emperor of China] was published.

The large number of VOC travel accounts (over 150 first editions) published up to 1800 poses the question of copyright and ownership. By contract, all those in service of the VOC were sworn to secrecy on any subject regarding the company and its Asian trade, so in theory no travel account could have been published without the consent of the VOC. In reality, the governors of the company appear to have been rather indifferent on this subject. Much information on VOC territory was not exclusively Dutch—English, French, Portuguese, Danish, and Swedish ships also crossed the Indian Ocean to find fortune in the Far East. But more than any other nation, the Dutch travelers and publishers provided the whole of western Europe with detailed information and exciting stories. The engravings and woodcuts illustrating these books still dominate our image of seventeenth- and early eighteenth-century Asia.

VIBEKE ROEPER and DIEDERICK WILDEMAN

### References and Further Reading

Anonymous, *Ongeluckige Voyagie van't Schip Batavia* [Disastrous Voyage of the Ship Batavia], 1647; a summary appears in John Harris's *Collection of Voyages*, 1705.

Bontekoe, Willem Ysbrantsz, *Iovrnael ofte gedenckwaerdige beschrijvinghe vande Oost-Indische reyse van Willem Ysbrantsz Bontekoe van Hoorn*, 1646.

Graaff, Nicolaus de, *Reisen van Nicolaus de Graaff, na de vier gedeeltens des Werelds, als Asia, Africa, America en Europa* . . . [Journey of Nicolaus de Graaff, around the Four Parts of the World, Asia, Africa, America and Europe . . ., 1701; 2nd edition, enlarged, as *Reysen*, 1704; translated as *Voyages de Nicolas de Graaf aux Indes Orientales et en d'autres lieux de l'Asie; avec une relation curieuse de la ville de Batavia, et des moeurs & du commerce des Hollandois établis dans les Indes*, 1719.

Hartgers, Joost, *Oost-Indische Voyagien door dien begin en voortgangh van de Vereenighde Nederlandtsche geoctroyeerde Oost-Indische compagnie*, 1648.

Janssonius, Johannes, *Begin ende Voortgangh van de Vereenigde Neederlandtsche Geoctroyeerde Oost-Indische Compagnie*, 1644; as *A Collection of Voyages Undertaken by the Dutch East India Company*, 1703.

Linschoten, Jan Huygen van, *Itinerario*, 1595–1596; as *Jan Hughen van Linschoten His Discours of Voyages into ye Easte West Indies*, 1598.

Lodewycksz, Willem, *D' Erste boeck: Historie van Indien, waer inne verhaelt is de avontueren die de hollandtche schepen* [The First Book: History of the Indies, Relating the Adventures of the Dutch Ships], 1598.

Montanus, Arnoldus, *Gedenkwaerdige Gesantschappen der Oost-Indische Maetschappy . . . aen de Kaisaren van Japan*, 1669 [*Atlas Japannensis, Being Remarkable Addresses by Way of Embassy from the East India Company to the Emperor of Japan*], 1669.

Nieuhof, Johan, *Het Gezantschap der Neêrlandsche Oost-Indische Compagnie aan den Grooten Tatarischen Cham, den tegenwoordigen Keizer van China* [An Embassy from the East India Company of the United Provinces to the Grand Tartar Cham, Emperor of China], 1665.

Noort, Olivier van, *Beschryvinghe vande voyagie om den gehelen werelt cloot* [Description of the Voyage around the Entire Globe], 1602.

Saeghman, Gillis Joosten, *Verscheyde Oost-Indische Voyagien* [Several East Indian Voyages], 1663.

Schouten, Wouter, *Oost-Indische Voyagie* [East Indian Voyage], 1676.

Stavorinus, J.S., *Reize van Zeeland over de Kaap de Goede Hoop, naar Batavia, Bantam, Bengalen enz. . . . door den heer J.S. Stavorinus*, 4 vols., 1793; as *Voyages to the East Indies; By the Late John Splinter Stavorinus*, 1798.

Valentijn, François, *Oud en Nieuw Oost-Indiën*, 1724–1726; the chapters on Ceylon (Sri Lanka) as *François Valentijn's Description of Ceylon*, edited by Sinnappah Arasaratnam, 1978; the section on the Cape of Good Hope as *Description of the Cape of Good Hope with the Matters Concerning It*, translated by Rowland Raven-Hart, edited by P. Serton et al., 1971–1973.

Veer, Gerrit de, *Waerachtige Beschryvinghe*, 1598; as *True and Perfect Description of Three Voyages*, 1609.

## EAST INDIA COMPANY (FRENCH)

France was the fourth of the five great maritime powers of the sixteenth and seventeenth centuries to enter the race for commercial success in the East and the Far East. Initial attempts to establish trading companies made in 1604 (La Compagnie des Mers Orientales), in 1615 (La Compagnie des Moluques), and in 1642 (La Compagnie d'Orient) proved to be unproductive. French trading ventures truly began only when Colbert came to power during the reign of Louis XIV. He created new ports like Rochefort and reconstituted old ones like Brest and Toulon in order to support his ambitious economic policies and to facilitate maritime commerce. In 1664 he founded La Compagnie des Indes Orientales, and granted it the exclusive right of commerce in India for 50 years. Under the leadership of Francis Caron, director general of French commerce in India, the company's second expedition reached Surat where the first French settlement was founded in 1668. Later settlements were established in the south at Masulipatam in 1669 and Pondicherry in 1673. Chandernagore in Bengal was established in 1690. Mahé on the Malabar Coast was acquired in 1721 and Yanaon (present-day Yanam) in 1723. Karaikal came under French rule in 1738 and 1739.

Even though the company enjoyed state protection and patronage it was an autonomous body depending primarily on its directors, who never seriously strengthened the financial resources of the company and took the easy way out by allowing outsiders to make use of its trading privileges. In the first 50 years of its existence, the Compagnie des Indes Orientales, could not implement regular trade despite considerable maritime movement between France and India. The decline of the Moghul empire in India could have favored commercial activities especially in Surat, but lack of capital and inefficient administration hampered the progress of commercial activities in all the settlements. Apart from the lack of capital and business enterprise in France, another factor that crippled the company was the protectionist doctrine that triumphed after the death of Colbert in 1683.

Although Louis XIV's wars at the end of the seventeenth century prevented France from having a long-term, sustainable policy on its settlements overseas, the company was fortunate to have competent agents like François Martin handling its affairs in the Indian settlements. Using native resources, Martin transformed the town of Pondicherry into a viable commercial and colonial stronghold for the French. Captured by the Dutch in 1693, Pondicherry was restored to the French in 1697 by the Treaty of Ryswick. By 1706 this settlement, with its 40,000 inhabitants, had a solid foundation upon which to build a French India.

In 1714, when the 50-year monopoly granted to the company founded by Colbert came to an end, a continuance for 10 years was issued but with a condition that ten percent of its profit had to revert to France. In 1719 the regent entered fully into the financial schemes of the Scottish banker, Law, and decreed that the newly formed Company of the West (Compagnie d'Occident) would be merged with the Compagnie des Indes Orientales, under a new name, Compagnie des Indes. New shares were issued to the tune of 25 million francs to raise capital for this huge new company. Law's financial scheme failed in 1720 and the company was reorganized in 1723, but Law's failure was not the end of the company. In fact his scheme had given it a new lease on life. The port of Lorient in northwest France, acquired by Law for the company, remained in its possession until 1764. He strongly encouraged the construction and acquisition of ships. Between 1725 and 1759 an average of 15 ships plied between France and India, and at the peak of its prosperity the company made 200 percent profit on its Indian trade. During this period, the French commercial settlements prospered tremendously under the leadership of Lenoir (1721–1723, 1726–1735), Benoit Dumas (1735–1741), and Dupleix (1741–1754).

From the very beginning the company paid its shareholders a fixed dividend regardless of the results of trade. Secure sources of income (e.g., monopoly of tobacco sales) that could have been floating capital for the company were diverted for the benefit of shareholders. Consequently, the company was forced to depend on financial expedients and could not make long-term plans. In 1745 it faced yet another financial crisis after the War of the Austrian Succession. Governor general Dupleix wished to transform the mercantile nature of the company into a political one, but the company was unable to meet additional expenses arising from Dupleix's political and military enterprises. At the same time, the growing dominance of the English in south India and the appearance on the scene of Robert Clive rendered a military conflict between the two European powers inevitable. France, under Louis XV, did not see India with an imperial eye. Neither Dupleix's policy of constructing military and political alliances with local rulers nor his vision of a French India was supported by his compatriots in France. Although the governor and his councillors administered laws in the name of the French government in the settlements, they remained servants of the company and hence liable to removal without any reference to the sovereign. The directors, led to believe by the English as well as the French that the personal ambitions of Dupleix had caused insecurity in the settlements, recalled the governor general in 1754.

After the fall of Pondicherry in 1761 the company faced yet another financial crisis in 1765. A few years of peace and commercial revival could have helped the company recover, but the Seven Years' War dealt it a mortal blow. A colossal amount of money was spent to reconstruct the settlements that had been destroyed by the English. (Chandernagore had also been captured by the English in 1757.) Despite efforts to salvage the situation, the company was liquidated in 1769 and its capital returned to the Crown. A new company was formed in 1785 on the initiative of Calonne, but it was abolished by the Convention Nationale, in 1794.

SRILATA RAVI

## References and Further Reading

Bernier, François, *Histoire de la dernière révolution des États du Grand Mogol*, 4 vols., 1670–1671; as *Voyage dans les États du Grand Mogol*, edited by France Bhattacharya, 1981; as *Travels in the Mogul Empire, A.D. 1656–1668*, translated by Irving Brock, revised and annotated by Archibald Constable, 1891; 3rd edition, 1934.

Deleury, Guy (editor), *Les Indes florissantes: anthologie des voyageurs français (1750–1820)*, 1991.

La Haye, Jacob de, and François Caron, *Journal du voyage des Grandes Indes, contenant tout ce qui s'y est fait et passé par l'escadre de Sa Majesté envoyée sous le commandement de Mr de la Haye, depuis son départ de La Rochelle au mois de mars 1670*, 1698.

Modave, Louis Laurent de Féderbe, Comte de, *Voyage en Inde du Comte de Modave, 1773–1776: nouveaux mémoires sur l'état actuel du Bengale et de l'Indoustan*, edited by Jean Deloche, 1971; selection, as *Comte de Modave's Account of Bengal, 1773–1774*, translated by Pranabendra Nath Ghosh, 1992.

Pyrard de Laval, François, *The Voyage of François Pyrard of Laval to the East Indies, the Maldives, the Moluccas and Brazil*, translated from the 3rd French edition of 1619, and edited by Albert Gray, 2 vols., 1887–1890.

Sonnerat, Pierre, *Voyage aux Indes Orientales et à la Chine, fait par ordre du Roi, depuis 1774 jusqu'en 1781*, 2 vols., 1782; revised and corrected edition, 4 vols., 1806.

Tavernier, Jean Baptiste, *Les Six Voyages de Jean Baptiste Tavernier . . . qu'il a fait en Turquie, en Perse et aux Indes, pendant l'espace de quarante ans*, 2 vols., 1676; as *The Six Voyages of John Baptista Tavernier*, 1678.

Thévenot, Jean de, *Voyages de M. Thevenot, contenant la relation de l'Indostan, des nouveaux Mogols et des autres peuples et pays des Indes*, 1684.

## EASTERN EUROPE, PRE-WORLD WAR II

Eastern Europe, depending on the period of history, is either a geographical or a political term. In some periods of the past the two overlap. There is also a considerable overlap, in terms of territories, between central or middle Europe and eastern Europe, and indeed, between certain parts of the Balkans and eastern Europe—mainly for political reasons. This became fairly obvious during the period of Soviet domination (1945–1989/1990): one sympathetic, and typical, commentator, Hewlett Johnson (1874–1966), visited most of the Danubian countries for his *Eastern Europe in the Socialist World* (1955). If we look at the map today the reemerging countries such as Estonia, Ukraine, and Latvia might be grouped, with eastern Europe geographically, but could be grouped with equal justification, with northern eastern Europe. Territories such as Galicia, which included North Bukowina, were once part of the Austrian (later the Austro-Hungarian) empire, but are now submerged and form part of other units. The break-up of Yugoslavia—which can be considered part of southern eastern Europe, or simply the Balkans—has resulted in the reemergence of Croatia and Slovenia.

The specialist book catalog of the Cambridge bookseller de Visser is entitled *Central and Eastern Europe*; it carries an inclusive map on its cover, the western limits being Cologne and Bern, the northern limits Berlin and Gdansk, the eastern limits Lvov and Brasov, and the southern limits the southern borders of present-day Hungary.

It is, therefore, partially justifiable to concentrate on Hungary and Romania in this article, but which Hungary? The present-day country is one-third of its historic self. Travelers through the ages visited many parts of historic Hungary, from Hainburg (Dévény), the "Danube gate" in the west, to Verecke hágó in the east; from the Lomniczi peak (2,663 meters) in the northern Carpathians to Orsova in the south, just beyond the "Iron Gates," as the Danube flows toward its delta.

And of which Romania shall we speak? The country as we know it at present was internationally recognized in 1919 by the Versailles Treaty, having achieved unity in 1918. Later, after some loss of Transylvanian territory between 1941 and 1944, it was re-created in 1945. The Romanians as a people go back a long way; Dacians, Sarmatians, Scythians, and Sclavonians being some of their ancestors, but the territories—Transylvania, Wallachia, Moldavia—remained disunited and lacked full independence.

According to the Romanian view, Transylvania was, certainly in ancient times, the Romanian heartland. Graphic testimony of this is found on Trajan's Column in Rome, which shows the Roman emperor's two triumphant campaigns in Dacia (101–102 and 105–106) in stone bas-relief. It is described in words by Wilhelm Froehner (1834–1925) in *La Colonne Trajane* (1872–1874). Sources are lacking for much of the Middle Ages in Transylvania, and in the sixteenth century all territories inhabited by Romanians fell to the Turks.

Travelers from the sixteenth century to the mid-nineteenth would have visited certain parts of the Turkish empire when they sojourned in Jassy or Bucharest. The provinces of Wallachia and Moldavia were united in 1859, but the eastern part of Moldavia was earlier referred to as "Little Tartary," and remained under Russian rule. J.R. McCulloch (1789–1864) in his *Dictionary* (1841–1842) refers to "Eastern Moldovia" as the most westerly province of Russia. In the *Historical Dictionary of Romania* (1996) by Kurt W. Treptow and Marcel Popa the historical provinces of Romania include Maramures (now Ukraine), Crisana and Banat (formerly Hungary, or Partium, then part of Turkey, later administered by Austria), Transylvania (formerly Hungary, or semi-independent), Oltenia, Wallachia, Dobrodgea (the Black Sea and the Danube delta territories), and Bessarabia, which on one of the maps in this book takes a slice of Bukovina and Little Tartary.

When going to Transylvania, with its mixed Hungarian-Romanian-Saxon population, travelers would have visited the eastern part of Hungary, between the eleventh and the early sixteenth centuries; a semi-independent princedom between the middle of the sixteenth century and the beginning of the eighteenth; a Hapsburg province between 1711 and 1848; a part of Hungary for one further year, 1849; an Austrian province between 1850 and 1866; a part of Hungary between 1867 and 1918; and then Romania, except for the years 1941 through 1944, mentioned above.

Travel and exploration in these territories, a historical Hungary and a present-day Romania, began long ago. *The Danube in Prehistory* (1929) by V. Gordon Childe (1892–1957) dates the appearance of "Danube men," moving slowly upstream on the river in boats, to 3000 BCE; their remains have been found by archaeologists. The Danube has seen many modes of travel since then: paddle boats, sailing boats, boats pulled by horses, barges, canoes, kayaks, steamships, diesel-powered boats; walking, riding a bicycle, wearing skis (in the Carpathians); riding on horseback, traveling in horse carts, coaches, then by buses, motorcars, trains, and airplanes. Both Hungary and Romania are hospitable territories for all modes of travel. Discounting those who came to build empires and to conquer, such as the Yazyges, Scythians, the Avars, Attila's Huns, and the Magyars, the first known medieval travelers were pilgrims and crusaders. The army of the Second Crusade was let through Hungary in 1147 without any consequences. The Fifth Crusade in 1218 had a Hungarian contingent led partly by the Magyar king, András II (1176–1235), who had transferred the possession of the port of Zara (then in Hungary) in exchange for the Venetians' agreement to transport his troops. This had dire consequences: in the king's absence a rebellion broke out and the queen was murdered.

The best and truest narrator of the Turkish times in Hungary was the papal legate Antonio Burgio (1490–1538), who lived and traveled in Hungary between 1523 and 1526 and was a married man with two children. We learn more from his letters to Sadoleto (published in *Mohács emlékezete*, 1979: 181–244) about the country, its politics, leaders, and military strengths and weaknesses than from anyone else in the sixteenth century.

The country fell in 1526 to the force of Suleiman II who reinforced his conquest in 1541, dividing Hungary into three parts. The middle became part of the Ottoman empire, Transylvania became a semi-independent state under Turkish suzerainty, and northern and northwestern Hungary were managed by the Austrian Hapsburgs as the Kingdom of Hungary. The curious thing is that travelers to any of these territories for the next 150 years did not call it "Turkey" but "Occupied Hungary." One such traveler was a doctor who visited Hungary in 1667: Edward Browne (1644–1708). His *A Brief Account of Some Travels in Hungaria . . .* (1673) describes some of the mineral resources of the country, the military situation as he found it, and the customs, language, and various political, historical, and geographical details derived in part from observation and in part from hearsay. Those who got as far as Transylvania were equally aware of its recent ties with Hungary, although they also pointed out its distant link with Dacia.

Among the celebrated travelers in the eighteenth century was Mary Wortley Montagu (1689–1762), who traversed Hungary on her journey from Vienna to Belgrade, en route to Istanbul. Her book, written in the form of letters to friends between 1716 and 1718, gives an account of the kinds of people she met, the atrocious roads, the scenery, and the accommodation, and includes Temesvár in the Banat.

Many people's favorite travel book on eighteenth-century Hungary is *Travels through Germany, Bohemia, Hungary, Switzerland, Italy and Lorrain . . .* (1756) by Johann Georg Keyssler (1693–1743). Written in the form of letters from a tutor to a pupil between 1729 and 1731, Keyssler's book is an admixture of early quasi-encyclopedic reporting on several countries: their natural, literary, and political history, geography, manners, laws, commerce, manufactures, painting, sculpture, architecture, coins, and antiquities. Although all these things could be found in Hungary, Keyssler's reporting from Pest and Buda pointedly blames Turkey for the devastation he found.

One of the last reports on the state of Hungary in the eighteenth century was *Travels in Hungary* (1797) by Robert Townson (1763–1827). He traveled in coaches overland and by boat down the Danube, and describes Hungarian life in its diversity: the castle in Buda, trips to the theater, hospitals, libraries, prisons, agriculture, mineralogy, and military taxes.

The nineteenth century was the golden age of travel to eastern Europe. The initial interest seems to have been mineralogical. *Travels in Hungary in 1818* (1823) by F.S. Beudant (1787–1850) is an abridged English version of his original four-volume work. Beudant appears to have had very good initial information from Baron E. Podmaniczky (1760–1830), the ambassador to Paris, who furnished him with addresses before his departure and must be at least partly responsible for the excellent introduction to the book.

Because of her extensive historical and geographical coverage, Julia Pardoe (1806–1862) is regarded as a pioneer. Her book, *The City of the Magyar* (1840), is an account of Hungary as a country of reform and renewal; she was the first to describe many of its institutions, some unique, some Westernized. A well-informed freelance writer and journalist, Pardoe gained admittance to the drawing rooms and offices of the powerful: politicians, lawyers, writers. To a large extent, therefore, her book was based on interviews with the well-informed, though she had no spokesperson for the lowest classes. Her first volume presents the typical traveler making her way from west to east, recording notable events, buildings, characters, institutions, and topography on the way. The second inquires into the national character, the third into history, folklore, and social customs. The style is straightforward; the few engravings in the volumes are romantic.

Contemporary with Pardoe, John Paget (1808–1892), a doctor from Edinburgh and a seasoned traveler, spent two years in exploration (1837–1838); then settled down as a landowner in Transylvania. Paget married the niece of Baron Miklós Wesselényi (1796–1850), the famous radical Hungarian politician whose activities merit two chapters in his book, *Hungary and Transylvania* (1839). Paget wrote with the precision of an examining doctor, and the book became one of the main sources for Hungarian and Transylvanian exploration in the nineteenth century. Paget measured, weighed, and counted everything: countries, towns, villages, habits, natural phenomena, literature, economy. The book was illustrated by George Hering (1805–1879), a notable artist in his own right, who traveled with Paget in Hungary and Transylvania, then again on his own in Switzerland. Hering published an album of 26 lithographs, entitled *Sketches on the Danube in Hungary and Transylvania* (1838). He traveled, partly on the Danube, with Paget to Orsova; from there they took an overland round journey to Mehadia, the Banat, staying at Temesvár, the valley of the Maros River, Kolozsvár, Hunyad, Zsibó, Torda, Enyed, Marosvásárhely, the Székely land, the Saxon land, and Brassó, and returned to Kolozsvár. Hering briefly described Wallachia and Moldavia without actually having visited them.

The third traveler of note remained incognito a long time. Joseph Blackwell (1798–1886) was first a secret, then a recognized, diplomatic agent of Britain in Hungary. He sent diplomatic dispatches to his ambassador in Vienna and to the foreign secretary in London. Out of the diplomatic bag the whole political spool of Hungary is unwound from the 1830s to the 1850s. Blackwell initially traveled from London to Pest, at 18 years of age. Still carefree, he went on the Grand Tour of the well-to-do young in the 1820s crossing France, Germany, and Switzerland and stopping in Austria. There, in 1827, he married in Graz and went honeymooning with his wife to Vienna. In the Austrian capital he was informed of a bad turn of his family's fortune back in England, so he returned to London and looked for employment. Blackwell translated archaeological works, and eventually compiled *A Handbook for Travelers in Southern Germany . . . and Austria* (1852) for John Murray in London: at that time Hungary was part of Austria. Blackwell's guide is a mine of information for travelers in Hungary, giving favorite sites, coach routes, and ship and train timetables. His own travels include a sojourn in Hungary between 1832 and 1836 for the purpose of reporting on the Hungarian parliament at Pozsony. Four further diplomatic missions between 1843 and 1849 followed, which took him far and wide across Transdanubia: trips to Pest, Szeged, and to various great houses of Hungarian nobles; a secret mission to Zagreb in Croatia across southern Hungary and several journeys to Graz and back (where his wife and, after a while, his small son stayed); and numerous trips to Pozsony, with journeys to London and back. There is a vivid description of his hurried travel from London to Pozsony, written in a letter to a friend in England, and worth quoting, as it encapsulates the modes and possibilities of transport and the maximum speed to be achieved by a traveler in 1847. Writing from Pozsony (the seat of the Hungarian parliament) to his friend Francis Emery in Staffordshire on 7 January 1848, Blackwell recalled his journey the previous November:

> when I got to Ghent I was so hungry and fatigued that I sat down to a very good dinner and put a whole bottle of excellent claret in me and then fell fast asleep and by the time I awoke—I was, no doubt in Antwerp. I left Ghent the next morning November 20—but was obliged to stop a night (sadly against my inclination) at Cologne—the night Steamers having (2 days before) ceased to go. On the 21st however it steamed up the Rhine but we were not able to go further than Coblenz on account of the lowness of the water. From Coblenz I went night and day in the Diligence without stopping and arrived at Gratz at 8am on the twenty-seventh just as they were getting up and had the pleasure of finding all well . . . It took a further 15 hours railway travel to Pressburg (Pozsony) next day. (Kabdebó, 1984)

Some of the sources of Blackwell's travels and missions are more available than others: basically an anthology, *Magyarországi Küldetései* (1989) is about his missions in Hungary. Kabdebó's Ph.D. thesis (1984) presents Blackwell's life and activities with reference to his known journeys. The two main sources of his writings—all his surviving diplomatic dispatches and many of his letters—are in the Foreign Office Archives in London (F.O.7). Copies of much of this material are in the Blackwell Archives in the Hungarian Academy, together with original pieces of diary fragments and personalia.

The wife of the prominent diplomat Francis Pulszky (1817–1890), Theresa Pulszky (1819–1866) was forced to escape from Hungary at the end of the Hungarian-Austrian war of 1848 and 1849. Apart from giving an account of the main events of the war in her book, *Memoirs of a Hungarian Lady* (1850), Theresa Pulszky vividly described three of her journeys, from Vienna to Pest in 1848, from Pest to Debrecen, and from Debrecen to Prussia via Pest and the north of Hungary.

Many travelers to Hungary and other parts of eastern and central Europe, included Transylvania on their itineraries, and land journeys to the Turkish empire often crossed Wallachia and Moldavia, now part of Romania. The *Novum Lexicum Geographicum* (published 1738) of Philippus Ferrarius (d. 1626) treats Temesvar and Daciae Ripensis as part of European Turkey, and the *Compleat Geographer* (1723) lists three Turkish provinces: Wallachia, with details on Tergowisch Bucharest and Brasow; Moldavia, with details on Jassy, Suchow, Chotzyn, and Braila; and Bessarabia, or "Little Tartary."

The land of the Carpathian basin in Roman and early medieval times was described as "Pannonia, Moesia, Dacia" (see *Geographia Antiquae* [1701–1706] by Christoph Cellarius [1638–1707]) while the Dacian presence, at least in terms of names, is attested by Balthasar Hacquet (1740–1815) in *Neueste Physikalisch-politische Reisen* . . . (1790–1796). But the most interesting of these early Danubian land travels is a set of letters by Ignaz Born (1742–1791), *Travels through the Bannat of Temeswar, Transylvania and Hungary* . . . (1777). Born, a German nobleman and counselor of the Royal Mint in Bohemia, traveled in 1770 and wrote his letters to a certain professor Herber describing the mines and mountains of Transylvania and Hungary together with learned notes on the origins of the Dacians, Scythians, and Wallachs, describing their language, religion, and habits and noting that according to the Wallachs "fornication is not a sin."

The routes were, generally, Vienna to Pozsony to Esztergom to Pest to Buda (the new name Budapest was used only after 1868), then either directly east via Debrecen to Kolozsvár (Cluj since 1919), Gyulafehérvár (Alba Julia since 1919), Nagyszeben (Sibine since 1919), Brassó (Brasow), Bucharest, Jassy, then Constanta on the Black Sea, or alternatively via Russe (Turkish Bulgaria) to Silistra (Turkish Wallachia) and proceeding to the port of Varna and Burgas (Turkish Bulgaria), finally ending at Constantinople (Istanbul).

These routes were variously taken by three notable travelers of the nineteenth century: Patrick O'Brien (1823–1895), author of *Journal of a Residence in the Danubian Principalities* (1854); Emily Gerard (1849–1905), author of *The Land beyond the Forest* (1888), with facts, figures, and fancies from Transylvania; and, best of all, Charles Boner (1815–1870), author of *Transylvania* (1865). Boner's book describes the products, the people, and their ethnographical characteristics, in the form of a travelogue. Boner had been a foreign correspondent of the *Times* and his work was used as a source by Arthur Griffith (1872–1922) in writing his *The Resurrection of Hungary* (1904).

Very few would have crossed the Balkan mountains as a direct approach. Those wishing to explore Transylvania in a round trip would have traveled first from Debrecen to Nagyvárad (Oradea), then to Kolozsvár (Cluj) and Marosvásárhely (Tirgu Mures), back along the line of the Maros (Mures) River via Vajdahunyad (Hunadeora), Arad, then diverting to Temesvár (Timisoara) and crossing back to Hungary, reaching Szeged. Those who sojourned in the Wallachian heartland would have made excursions from Bucharest to Ploiesti northward, to Craiova, Slatina, and Turneu Severin eastward, and to Pitesti in the northwest. Until the railroads were built to link these towns (1848 onward) travel was by road: these generally ran along the banks of the rivers, such as the Arges, the Jiu, and the Danube. After unification in 1918 and 1919 Romania, no longer just a landscape on either side of the Carpathians, became a state to visit. The accounts of three travelers stand out in the first third of the twentieth century. Maude Parkinson's *Twenty Years in Roumania* (1921) is a good autobiography with a woman's observation of dresses, dances, and customs. Henry Baerlein (1875–1960) wrote an anthology of Romania and her people, *Romanian Oasis* (1948), from material mainly collected in the 1930s. Baerlein's "field book" was the highly amusing and quasi-sociological *And Then to Transylvania* (1931); the writer is particularly informative about the tension between Romanians and Hungarians, the new and former possessors of this land. The third traveler was Walter Starkie (1901–1979), whose *Raggle-Taggle* (1933) is an adventure story of a violinist who, in 1929, traveled with gypsies, crossing Lake Balaton, then on to Mezökövesd, Hortobágy, Debrecen and across to Huedin, Cluj, Saliste, Fagaras, and Bucharest. Starkie was professor of Spanish at Trinity College Dublin and is the only twentieth-century visitor to Romania who does not refer to animosities between the Magyars and the Romanians.

The Danube delta had its own attraction for travelers, who usually pass through Rasova, Hirsova, Braila, Galati, Tulcea, and end up at Sulina and S. Gheorghe. This presents us with the most typical of east European explorations: travel on the Danube. The earliest recorded Rhine and Danube travelers might have been the Nibelungs, of the early medieval German saga, the *Nibelungenlied* (eighth century, but referring back to earlier times). Among the late medieval representations of the Danube, in terms of a description of Buda, is the *Schedel Chronicle* (1493); later is the etching with a view of Visegrad (1595), the artist of which has not been positively identified.

Before the dramatic improvements to roads and the introduction of railways, the Danube was the main thoroughfare for commercial, diplomatic, or military travel. The oldest "Danube books" report on the Turkish wars and so describe the kingdoms, provinces, and towns on the river banks, from the river's source to its mouth in the Black Sea. A "novel", *Der Donau-Strand* (1664) by Sigmund von Birken (1626–1681), was, according to Zoran Konstantinovič (*Deutsche Reisebeschreibungen über Serbien und Montenegro*, 1960), used and is retrospectively usable as a guidebook.

This was followed by *Der ungarische Kriegs-Roman* (1685–1689) by Eberhard Werner Happel (1647–1690). The six volumes of this book cover wars, towns, culture, and hearsay heavily borrowed from Birken's work, which incidentally seems also to have been the inspiration for an anonymous work from Venice: *L'origine del Danubio* (1689). After these voluminous but amateurish books, a master came along in the person of the chief engineer of the Christian siege of Turkish Buda, who decided to explore the river from its source in Bavaria to Orsova—at that time recently regained from the Turks. Count Luigi Ferdinando Marsili (1658–1730), with his engineers and oarsmen, traveled up and down the Pannonian and Moesian course of the river, traversing and measuring it countless times between 1687 and 1702. The result is two books; one is a set of short descriptions and maps, *Danubialis operis* (1700); the other is the record of the most thorough exploration of the river, *Danubius Pannonico-Mysicus* (1726). The later describes the river's hydrology, currents, navigability, flora, fauna, mineralogy, geography, history, and palaeontology in faultless Latin; with copious illustrations it will never be surpassed. With this work Marsili's last exploration led him to Donaueschingen and above to the sources of the Danube. The result of this was a book of 24 exquisite maps with scant text, *Hongrie et le Danube* (1741). The king of the Danube's illustrators, and a keen traveler on the whole course of the river, was the graphic artist Jacob Alt (1789–1872), whose *Donau Ansichten* (1820–1828) consists of 246 drawings, published successively, then in two volumes. These lithographs depict all the notable towns and beautiful spots on the entire length of the river. Less ambitious in his itinerary was Richard Bright (1789–1858), author of *Travels from Vienna through Lower Hungary* (1818), who did some of his travels in a boat on the Danube. His most interesting observations are on the state of Vienna during the Congress in 1814 and 1815.

A notable traveler, indeed the captain of a steamship on the Hungarian and Romanian stretch of the river, was Michael J. Quin (1796–1843), who wrote *A Steam Voyage down the Danube* (1835). Apart from reaching Wallachia, Serbia, and finally Turkey, Quin sojourned at Orsova, there visiting Count István Széchenyi (1791–1860), the most active reformer in nineteenth-century Hungary, who at that time was trying to cut a road above the Iron Gates on the northern side of the river. (The Iron Gates disappeared between 1968 and 1978 because of the building of the dam at Ada Kaleh. Széchenyi's diary, containing short entries in German, English, Hungarian, and French covers the period of 1814 through 1860, including his travels (Széchenyi, 1978). Judging by the stunning illustrations in *Picturesque Europe* (6 vols., 1844), the Danube section of which was written by George Adam Smith (1810–1870), the author covered the full length of the river.

In the nineteenth century Danube travel by small craft became fashionable. Robert Blanchford Mansfield (1846–1889), author of *The Water Lily on the Danube* (1852), rowed down the Danube, covering the upper and middle part; F.D. Millet (1846–1912), in *The Danube from the Black Forest to the Black Sea* (1892), covers the whole length, touching on the notable parts of the Romanian Danube, Tulcea, Braila, Galati, and Sulina. Julia Clara Byrne (1819–1894), in her *Pictures of Hungarian Life* (1869), traveled more comfortably by steamboat from Vienna to Pest, where she was shocked to see that men and women swam together in a mixed pool.

Perhaps somewhat dry, but extremely accurate, is *Die Donau* (1881) by Alexander Heksch (d. 1883); this describes the length of the river, its historic past, each town and notable village, and many natural phenomena and constructions. He is very good on the Danubian ports: Serbian, Bulgarian, and Romanian. The historical data and the Danube guide are still usable today. *The Danube with Pen and Pencil* (1911), by Captain B. Granville Baker (1870–1957), is a pre–World War I artist's book. Lively and informative on those cities Baker liked, such as Vienna, Pozsony, and Budapest, it reflects the picture of a peaceful Danubian Carpathian Austro-Hungarian monarchy.

In the final years before World War II, the most poetic description of the Danube is given by Patrick Leigh Fermor (1915–) in *Between the Woods and the Water* (1986). In 1933 Fermor set out to walk across Europe living on a pound a week. This book describes the second part of his voyage in the forest of Transylvania and on the waters of the Danube.

THOMAS KABDEBÓ

### References and Further Reading


Alt, Jacob, *Donau Ansichten*, 1820–1828.
Anonymous, *L'Origine del Danubio*, 1689.
Baerlein, Henry, *And Then to Transylvania*, 1931.
Baerlein, Henry (editor), *Romanian Oasis*, 1948.
Baker, B. Granville, *The Danube with Pen and Pencil*, 1911.
Beudant, F.S., *Voyage minéralogique et géologique en Hongrie*, 4 vols., 1822; abridged and translated as *Travels in Hungary in 1818*, 1823.
Birken, Sigmund von, *Der Donau-Strand*, 1664.
Birmingham, George A., *A Wayfarer in Hungary*, 1925.
Blackwell, Joseph Andrew, *Magyarországi Küldetései, 1843–1851*, edited by Eva Haraszti, 1989.
Blackwell, Joseph Andrew, *A Handbook for Travellers in Southern Germany . . . and Austria*, 1852.
Boner, Charles, *Transylvania*, 1865.
Born, Ignaz, *Travels through the Bannat of Temeswar, Transylvania and Hungary in the Year 1770*, translated by R.E. Raspe, 1777.
Bright, Richard, *Travels from Vienna through Lower Hungary*, 1818.
Browne, Edward, *A Brief Account of Some Travels in Hungaria, Servia, Bulgaria, Macedonia, Thessaly, Austria, Styria, Carinthia, Carniola, and Friuli*, 1673; 2nd edition, 1677.
Byrne, Julia Clara, *Pictures of Hungarian Life*, 1869.
Çelebi, Evliya, *Seyahatnamesi* [Book of Travels], 10 vols., 1896–1938; in part as *Narrative of Travels in Europe, Asia and Africa*, translated from the Turkish by Joseph von Hammer, 1834–1850.
Cellarius, Christoph, *Geographia Antiquae*, 2 vols., 1701–1706.
Childe, V. Gordon, *The Danube in Prehistory*, 1929.
*The Compleat Geographer*, fourth edition, 1723.
Crosse, Andrew, *Round about the Carpathians*, 1878.

Fermor, Patrick Leigh, *Between the Woods and the Water: On Foot to Constantinople from the Hook of Holland, the Middle Danube to the Iron Gates*, 1986.
Ferrarius, Philippus, *Novum Lexicum Geographicum*, 2 vols., 1738.
Froehner, Wilhelm, *La Colonne Trajane*, 2 vols., 1872–1874.
Gerard, Emily, *The Land beyond the Forest: Facts, Figures and Fancies from Transylvania*, 2 vols., 1888.
Griffith, Arthur, *The Resurrection of Hungary: A Parallel for Ireland*, 1904; 3rd edition, 1918.
Hacquet, Balthasar, *Neueste Physikalisch-politische Reisen in den Jahren 1788 und 1789 durch die Dacischen und Sarmatisehan* . . . 4 vols., 1790–1796.
Happel, Eberhard Werner, *Der ungarische Kriegs-Roman*, 5 vols., 1685–1689.
Heksch, Alexander, *Die Donau*, 1881.
Hering, George, *Sketches on the Danube in Hungary and Transylvania*, 1838.
Johnson, Hewlett, *Eastern Europe in the Socialist World*, 1955.
Josten, Jacob, *Reise Beschreibung durch die Türkey, Ungarn* . . ., 1652.
Kabdebó, Thomas, "Joseph Andrew Blackwell", (Ph.D. thesis, University of Manchester), 1984; translated into Hungarian as *Blackwell küldetése*, 1990.
Keyssler, Johann Georg, *Neueste Reisen durch Deutschland, Böhman, Ungarn, die Schweiz, Italian und Lothrigon* . . ., 4 vols., 1740; as *Travels through Germany, Bohemia, Hungary, Switzerland, Italy and Lorrain* . . . 4 vols., 1756.
Konstantinovič, Zoran, *Deutsche Reisebeschreibungen über Serbien und Montenegro*, 1960.
Magris, Claudio, *Danube: A Sentimental Journey from the Source to the Black Sea*, translated from the Italian by Patrick Creagh, 1989.
Mansfield, Robert Blanchford, *The Water Lily on the Danube, Being a Brief Account of the Perils of a Pair-Oar during a Voyage from Lambeth to Pesth*, 1852.
Marsili, Luigi Ferdinando, *Danubialis operis*, 1700.
McCulloch, J.R., *A Dictionary, Geographical, Statistical, and Historical*, 2 vols., 1841–1842.
Marsili, Luigi Ferdinando, *Danubius Pannonico-Mysicus*, 6 vols, 1726.
Marsili, Luigi Ferdinando, *Hongrie et le Danube*, 1741.
Millet, F.D., *The Danube from the Black Forest to the Black Sea*, 1892.
*Mohács emlékezete* [The Memory of Mohács], 1979.
Montagu, Lady Mary Wortley, *Letters of the Right Honourable Lady M[ar]y W[ortle]y M[ontagu]e, Written during her Travels in Europe, Asia, and Africa to Persons of Distinction*, 1763; as *The Turkish Embassy Letters*, edited by Malcolm Jack, with an introduction by Anita Desai, 1993.
O'Brien, Patrick, *Journal of a Residence in the Danubian Principalities, in the Autumn and Winter of 1853*, 1854.
Paget, John, *Hungary and Transylvania*, 1839; new edition, 1850.
Pardoe, Julia, *The City of the Magyar; or, Hungary and Her Institutions in 1839–40*, 3 vols., 1840.
Parkinson, Maude, *Twenty Years in Roumania*, 1921.
Planché, James Robinson, *Descent of the Danube from Ratisbon to Vienna during the Autumn of 1827*, 1828; as *The Danube from Ulm to Vienna*, 1836.
Pulszky, Theresa, *Memoirs of a Hungarian Lady*, 2 vols., 1850.
Quin, Michael J., *A Steam Voyage down the Danube*, 2 vols., 1835.
Smith, George Adam, Danube section in *Picturesque Europe*, vol. 6, 1844: 271–288.
Starkie, Walter, *Raggle-Taggle: Adventures with a Fiddle in Hungary and Roumania*, 1933.
Széchenyi, István, *Napló*, 1978.
Tekeli, Dominic, *Reisen durch Ungarn*, 1805.
Townson, Robert, *Travels in Hungary, with a Short Account of Vienna in the Year 1793*, 1797.
Treptow, Kurt W. and Marcel Popa, *Historical Dictionary of Romania*, Lanham, Maryland: Scarecrow Press, 1996.
Wilden, J., *Nouveau Voyage d'un chrétien esclave, de 1604–1611 de la Hongrie à Constantinople* . . ., 1623.

*See also* **Danube River**

## EBERHARDT, ISABELLE (1877–1904)

***Russian Writer and Journalist***

A European woman who traveled in North Africa masquerading as an Arab man, Isabelle Eberhardt was heralded as a "champion of decolonization," romanticized as "la bonne nomade," and excoriated as a decadent parasitical pretender.

In 1897 Eberhardt and her mother moved from Geneva to Bône, a port city in Algeria. Algeria had been under French colonial rule for over 60 years, but Isabelle and her mother had no interest in *colon* society. They embraced Islam and Isabelle began wandering the city dressed as a young Arab man. She had essentially been brought up as a boy, spoke fluent Arabic, and was well versed in the tenets of Islam. Eberhardt considered Africa her fatherland and saw herself as a "nomad who has no country beside Islam" (*The Passionate Nomad*, 1923, 1987). Accounts of her travels appear in her essays, reports, stories, and journals, most of which remained unpublished until after her death.

In the summer of 1899 Eberhardt moved to Tunis, then traveled the Algerian Sahara visiting the towns of Timgad, Batna, Biskra, Sidi Okba, Touggourt, and El Oued. Identifying herself as Si Mahmoud Saadi, a Tunisian student, she received instruction at *zawiyas* (centers of religious learning) and also immersed herself in the local nightlife, often to excess. She repeated this pattern of searching for religious enlightenment and overindulging in more secular pleasures throughout her short life.

Eberhardt returned to Tunis in September 1899, but for her, "vagrancy [was] emancipation" (*Prisoner of Dunes*, 1995), so she set off for the Tunisian Sahel without plan or itinerary. She met and accompanied a native man who was collecting a French poll tax from Tunisians, gathering material for her writing along with taxes. Her description of this trip is included in *Notes de route* (1904).

After a series of trips around Europe visiting family, consulting with editors, and attempting to settle her inheritance, Eberhardt returned to Algeria in July 1900 with plans to devote herself to writing. In the oasis town of El Oued, she maintained her identity as Si

Mahmoud Saadi, but also began a relationship with Slimène Ehnni, a member of the *spahis*, a native cavalry within the French army. She traveled the region on horseback and was initiated into the Qadrya brotherhood of the mystical sufi order of Islam. Accounts of her travels in Tunisia and Algeria and her experiences in El Oued are collected in *Prisoner of Dunes*.

In this militarized area, Eberhardt was suspected of being an anti-French activist, or at least a disrupting influence. Hoping to remove her from the region, the military command posted Slimène to Batna. In January 1901 an attempt was made on her life by a member of a rival non-sufi sect; she was expelled from Algeria five months later. Although the French considered Eberhardt provocative and repellent, Africans' attitudes are less clear. There was some hostility and resentment, as evidenced by the attack, and while the Arab custom of tact and courtesy may explain why her masquerade was not challenged, it is also possible that she was simply tolerated by a colonized people who had no real choice. There is evidence, that her devotion to Islam and proficiency in Arabic gained her respect, but both sides in this colonial locale also seem to have hoped to use her as a source of information about the other. All of these factors contributed in various degrees to her relative freedom of movement.

After her expulsion, Eberhardt stayed with her brother in Marseilles. In October 1901 she married Slimène, who had become a naturalized French citizen, and was able to return to Algeria as such. Isabelle traveled alone to Bou-Saâda and from there visited the *zawiya* of a woman *maraboute*, or holy teacher. With Slimène, she relocated to Ténès, where the couple found themselves embroiled in political intrigue. Isabelle decamped to Algiers to work with Victor Barrucand; she had been making contributions to his newspapers and he recognized her unique position among the Muslim population as a potential advantage for the gathering of news. In the autumn of 1903 she embarked on a tour of the Algerian southwest, covering French attempts to subdue nomadic tribes and push into Morocco. She spent most of the remainder of her life traveling this region, sleeping in the open, relishing the "life of the desert" (*In the Shadow of Islam* 1906, 1993).

Eberhardt also undertook reconnaissance work for General Hubert Lyautey, gauging the moods and positions of the tribes. She wrote articles on the military situation and sketches about Algerian people, locales, and customs. These pieces appeared in Barrucand's newspaper *El Akhbar* and were later included in *Dans l'ombre chaude de l'Islam* (*In the Shadow of Islam*) and *Notes de route* [Notes along the Way]. In the summer of 1904, at Lyautey's request, she went to stay at a Moroccan *zawiya* considered important to French control of the border area, but the hardships and excesses of her traveling life had taken their toll. In September 1904 a recurring fever sent her to a military hospital at Aïn Sefra; Eberhardt died in a flash flood shortly after her release at 27 years of age.

Barrucand recovered her notebooks and in 1906 published *Dans l'ombre chaude de l'Islam*, which consisted of sketches about her travels in the south and her stay in the Moroccan *zawiya*. He inserted his own (often purple) prose and listed himself as coauthor, causing an uproar in French and Algerian literary circles. In 1908 he released *Notes de route*, a collection of Eberhardt's stories and sketches to which he made fewer changes. *Pages d'Islam* [Pages on Islam], also compiled of material from her notebooks, appeared in 1920. Eberhardt's diaries were recovered in 1923 and published without alteration by René-Louis Doyon, who also published collections of her short stories, *Contes et paysages* and *Au Pays des sables*. A collection of her complete works was issued in 1988, and new translations and collections continue to appear.

Eberhardt's writing blurs the boundaries commonly erected between fiction and autobiography, pulling together elements of travel, religious, literary, and ethnographic writing. Her journals reveal a woman of profound inner conflicts, crossing, recrossing, and double-crossing colonial lines of race and gender. Dressing as an Arab man, taking lovers, and marrying an Algerian, she flouted the norms of white womanhood so central to the preservation of European culture in Africa. After her marriage she did as she pleased, traveling alone and attempting to mold and educate her Arab husband. In this sense she assumed the position of power and dominance traditionally reserved to men and to colonizers. On the other hand, her life among Arabs threatened European complacency and unsettled the appearance of colonial superiority. Eberhardt both decried the effects of colonial dominance and at certain times supported French hegemony in North Africa. She claimed freedom for herself, but remained unsympathetic to other women. Her religious devotion was tempered by her promiscuity and addictions to alcohol and drugs, and although she immersed herself in everyday Algerian life, she often wrote about her experiences in the orientalizing discourses of exoticism, eroticism, and escapism.

These contradictions suggest a woman in search of a comfortable sense of identity in a place and at a time when uncomfortably rigid lines separated European and Arab, man and woman, colonizer and colonized. Isabelle Eberhardt defined herself through travel, yet also acknowledged that "what keeps thrusting me on to life's roads, is not the wisest voice in my soul; it is a side of me that finds the earth too limited, and is unable to find in myself a sufficient universe" (*In the Shadow of Islam*).

MARY PANICCIA CARDEN

### Biography

Born Isabelle Wilhelmine Marie Eberhardt in Geneva, 17 February 1877. Illegitimate daughter of Nathalie de Moerder, née Eberhardt, a Jewish Russian aristocrat, and Alexander Trophimowsky, a former Russian Orthodox priest. Received no formal education; tutored at home by her father. Left Geneva and traveled to Algeria with her mother, May 1897. Lived in Bône from 1897, often identifying herself as Si Mahmoud Saadi. Returned to Geneva, December 1897. Traveled in Tunisia and Algeria, June–September 1899. Returned to Europe and attempted to organize her inheritance, traveling to Paris, Geneva, and Sardinia, 1899–1900. Returned to Algeria, July 1900; settled in El Oued. Attempt on her life in Béhima, January 1901. Expelled from Algeria, June 1901. Married Slimène Ehnni, an Arab military officer, in Marseilles, October 1901. Returned to Algeria, January 1902. Traveled to Bou-Saâda and El Hamel *zawiya* and met Lella Zeyneb, June 1902. Traveled between Ténès and Algiers; contributed to Victor Barrucand's newspaper *Les Nouvelles*, 1902–1903. Left for southwest Algeria to report on conflicts between French troops and nomadic tribes for Barrucand's new newspaper, *El Akhbar*, September 1903. Met General Hubert Lyautey; made reporting and reconnaissance trips along the border with Morocco. Made second trip to the southwest region, early 1904; spent the summer at Moroccan *zawiya*. Became ill and was taken to the military hospital in Aïn Sefra, September 1904. Died by drowning in a flash flood in Aïn Sefra, Morocco, 21 October 1904.

### References and Further Reading


Eberhardt, Isabelle, *Dans l'ombre chaude de l'Islam*, edited by Victor Barrucand, 1906; as *In the Shadow of Islam*, translated by Sharon Bangert, 1993.

Eberhardt, Isabelle, *Notes de route: Maroc–Algérie–Tunisie*, with a preface by Victor Barrucand, 1904; reprinted, 1998.

Eberhardt, Isabelle, *Pages d'Islam* [Pages on Islam], edited by Victor Barrucand, 1920.

Eberhardt, Isabelle, *Mes journaliers*, 1923; as *The Passionate Nomad: The Diary of Isabelle Eberhardt*, translated by Nina de Voogd, edited and with an introduction by Rana Kabbani, 1987.

Eberhardt, Isabelle, *The Oblivion Seekers and Other Writings*, translated by Paul Bowles, 1975.

Eberhardt, Isabelle, *Ecrits sur le sable*, edited by Marie Odile Delacour and Jean René Huleu, 1988.

Eberhardt, Isabelle, *Lettres et journaliers: Sept années dans la vie d'une femme*, edited by Eglal Errera, 1989.

Eberhardt, Isabelle, *Ecrits intimes: Lettres aux trois hommes les plus aimés*, edited by Marie Odile Delacour and Jean René Huleu, 1991.

Eberhardt, Isabelle, *Prisoner of Dunes: Selected Writings*, edited and translated by Sharon Bangert, 1995.


## ECUADOR

Ecuador has mainly attracted a particularly hardy breed of traveler, more interested in danger and exploration than in the local Ecuadorian people. Lately there have been some accounts redressing the balance, but writers usually visit in order to see the Andes and Ecuador's incredibly diverse range of flora and fauna on both the mainland and the Galapagos Islands, and for the challenge of exploring the unknown, and the indigenous population in the heart of the country.

The most notable visitor to the area was Charles Darwin (1809–1882) who explored Ecuador and the Galapagos Islands as part of the voyage of HMS *Beagle* (1831–1836). The great variety of flora and fauna he found, especially on the Galapagos Islands, was to greatly influence his subsequent theory of evolution. He was not, however, the first scientist to publish an account of explorations in Ecuador. Among his predecessors were Charles-Marie de la Condamine (1701–1774) and Pierre Bouguer (1698–1758), two Frenchmen who traveled in the region between 1735 and 1744. The main purpose of their expedition was to investigate whether the world was a perfect sphere or not, but they were also fascinated by Ecuador's varied wildlife. Upon their return to Europe, both men published a wide range of scientific data and gained fame from their adventurous stories of battling nature and exploring the unknown, which they published and recounted in numerous lectures.

This fight against nature is a recurring theme in travel writing about Ecuador. It can, for instance, be seen in the works of Alexander von Humboldt (1769–1859), whose explorations at the beginning of the nineteenth century greatly inspired Darwin. Other explorers to have been drawn to the country include Englishmen Alfred Simson and Edward Whymper (1840–1911), who made separate journeys to the region in the 1880s. Both wrote about nature (Whymper is especially noteworthy on botany) but they were also interested in writing exciting yarns about facing death and overcoming the elements.

Indeed, well into the twentieth century much of Ecuador remained unexplored and so a possible site of adventure. Men like Joseph H. Sinclair (1879–(?)) disappeared into the Amazonian jungle and came back with stories "filled with great hardships and dangers of death" (Sinclair, 1932). Others who explored the region include Scotsman Alexander Mann, whose long

Mule carrying boxes of archaeological trophies falls en route to Quito—the mule survived, the pots did not (from Edward Whymper's *Travels amongst the Great Andes of the Equator*, 1892). *Courtesy of Travellers Club, London; Bridgeman Art Library, agent.*

connection with Ecuador gave him particularly good knowledge of the country, G.M. Dyott (1883–1972), and American Blair Niles. All emphasized the dangers of travel in Ecuador, from epidemic yellow fever and leprosy to the savage indigenous population.

A refreshing change came from Janet MacKay, who wrote much more about Guayaquil and Quito, Ecuador's two main cities, which normally just featured as starting points for trips into the jungle. MacKay, a Canadian barrister, still considered her trip to be a mad adventure, but focused much more on the people, whom she describes as very honest and generous. The Belgian poet Henri Michaux (1899–1984) similarly noted that the "Ecuadorian is not simply hospitable in an unheard-of-style. He actually enjoys giving." Alexander Mann agreed and also had much respect for the indigenous people, about whom Simson was more divided; he applauded the noble Jívaros, or headhunters but dismissed the trivial, drunken Canelos. Michaux shared the latter view and described whole indigenous population settlements as being drunk for weeks on end.

The indigenous Ecuadorian peoples have generally been badly treated ever since the first Spanish conquistadores arrived. The conquistadores' letters, records, and later testimony recount numerous examples of rape or torture as the Spanish looked for gold. The Northern Inca capital, Quito, was thought to be full of untold wealth, but when Sebastián de Benalcázar arrived in June 1534 he was disappointed. Others soon struck out into the Andes looking for the fabled El Dorado, but without success. They did, however, start a long tradition of exploring the mountains of the Andes, which continues to the present day. These mountaineers have faced as much danger as their counterparts in the jungle and have written similarly adventurous stories. One of the more modern, by Richard Snailham, records a doomed attempt to climb the world's most active volcano, Mount Sangay, which resulted in two deaths and serious injuries to the author himself.

Like the Andes, the Galapagos Islands, volcanic islands pushing up through the Pacific 600 miles west of the mainland, have constantly drawn travelers and adventurers. Some, like Victor Wolfgang von Hagen (1908–), and later, Toby Green (1974–) arrived while re-creating or marking Darwin's *Beagle* voyage, but for some the islands are an end in themselves. Tui De Roy has produced some stunning images of the islands' volcanoes and wildlife; the title of her book of photo essays, *Islands Born of Fire* (1998), aptly sums up the Galapagos's mysterious charm. Others, however, have made an effort to ignore these natural wonders and to instead focus on the people living on what is a remarkably isolated outpost. Von Hagen's account contains a great deal on this theme, as does a much later book by the British diplomat John Hickman.

Hickman is part of a growing band of travel writers to have paid much more attention to the Ecuadorians themselves, rather than the nature that surrounds them. The Americans Moritz Thomsen, Paul Theroux, and Tom Miller have written very different accounts of time in Ecuador, but all share this basic similarity. Thomsen's account records the two years he spent in the country during the 1960s as a Peace Corps volunteer. He felt numerous frustrations while dealing with Third World problems, but also hope for the future and a sympathetic attitude toward the local population. Theroux, who passed through the country as part of a longer journey in the 1970s, was troubled by the Ecuadorians' poor treatment of the indigenous population, but considered Quito to be a happy place in contrast to the repression found in the rest of South America. Miller visited the country 20 years later and sought out examples of the misnamed Panama hat (they originated in Ecuador). His highly personalized account includes interviews with a diverse range of people and shows that there is more to the country than just the jungle.

NEIL DENSLOW

## References and Further Reading

Bouguer, Pierre, "An Abridged Relation of a Voyage to Peru" [1749], in *A General Collection of the Best and Most Interesting Voyages and Travels in All Parts of the World*, edited by John Pinkerton, vol. 14, 1813: 270–312.

Darwin, Charles, *Journal and Remarks, 1832–1836* in *Narrative of the Surveying Voyages of His Majesty's Ships Adventure and Beagle*, edited by Robert Fitzroy, vol. 3, 1839; as *Voyage of the Beagle: Charles Darwin's Journal of Researches*, edited and with introduction by Janet Browne and Michael Neve, 1989.

De Roy, Tui, *Galapagos: Islands Born of Fire*, 1998.

Dyott, George Miller, *On the Trail of the Unknown in the Wilds of Ecuador and the Amazon*, 1926.

Green, Toby, *Saddled with Darwin: A Journey through South America*, 1999.

Hagen, Victor Wolfgang von, *Ecuador the Unknown: Two and Half Years' Travels in the Republic of Ecuador and Galápagos Islands*, 1939.

Hickman, John, *The Enchanted Islands: The Galapagos Discovered*, 1985.

Humboldt, Alexander von, *Ansichten der Natur*, 1808, revised edition, 1826 and 1849; as *Views of Nature*, translated by E.C. Otte and Henry G. Bohn, 1850, reprinted, 1975.

Humboldt, Alexander von, *Vues des Cordillères, et monumens des peuples indigènes de l'Amérique*, 2 vols., 1810; as *Researches Concerning the Institutions and Monuments of the Ancient Inhabitants of America*, translated by Helen Maria Williams, 2 vols., 1814.

Humboldt, Alexander von, *Relation historique du voyage aux régions équinoxiales du Nouveau Continent*, 3 vols. (vol. 3 unfinished), 1814–1825, reprinted, 1970; as *Personal Narrative of Travels to the Equinoctial Regions of the New Continent*, translated by Helen Maria Williams, 7 vols., 1814–1829, reprinted, 1971.

La Condamine, Charles-Marie de, *Relation abrégée d'un voyage fait dans l'interieur de l'Amérique meridionale*, 1745; as *A Succinct Abridgment of a Voyage Made within the Inland Parts of South-America*, 1747.

Mann, Alexander, *Yachting on the Pacific: Together with Notes on Travel in Peru, and an Account of the Peoples and Products of Ecuador*, 1909.

Melville, Herman, "The Encantados," in *The Piazza Tales*, 1856.

Michaux, Henri, *Ecuador: journal de voyage*, 1929, revised editions, 1968, 1980, 1990; as *Ecuador: A Travel Journal*, translated by Robin Magowan, 1968.

Niles, Blair, *Casual Wanderings in Ecuador*, photographs by Roberts L. Niles Jr., 1923.

Simson, Alfred, *Travels in the Wilds of Ecuador, and the Exploration of the Putumayo River*, 1886.

Sinclair, Joseph H., "Some Reminiscences of Travel in Ecuador," *Proceedings of the American Antiquarian Society* (October 1931); reprinted as pamphlet, 1932.

Snailham, Richard, *Sangay Survived: The Story of the Ecuador Volcano Disaster*, 1978.

Theroux, Paul, *The Old Patagonian Express: By Train through the Americas*, 1979.

Thomsen, Moritz, *Living Poor: A Peace Corps Chronicle*, 1969; as *Living Poor: An American's Encounter with Ecuador*, 1989.

Whymper, Edward, *Travels amongst the Great Andes of the Equator*, 1892; edited and with an introduction by Eric Shipton, 1972; introduction by Loren McIntyre, 1987.

*See also* **South America, The North**

## EDEN, EMILY (1797–1869) *British Traveler*

The vivacious personality of its author has ensured the continuing popularity of *Up the Country*, although its hauteur makes it disconcerting to find Eden's work still being introduced as "indispensable to the book-bag of a 'griffin' [newcomer to India]" in 1983. Indira Ghose has refuted claims that Eden represents "The Ugly Victorian," that she was her brother's adoring apologist, that she was bearing the white woman's burden or her civilizing banner. She was a homesick traveler who used humor (a rare quality in colonial writings) to "transgress the ideological values of the society she represents" (1998). But she pretended (at least) to be uninterested in the values and culture of the society her brother governed: "I never ask questions, I hate information" (28 December 1837).

The colossal camp that assembled at Benares when the governor-general and his sisters set out in October 1837 to tour the upper provinces required an entourage of 12,000 persons and their animals. Mrs. Fanny Parks recorded its awesome dimensions in her *Wanderings of a Pilgrim in Search of the Picturesque* (1850). It was to be on the move for the next two and a half years, apart from hot-weather respite at Simla. Eden's account of the hill station's romances, fancy-work bazaars, and amateur theatricals is very like Kipling's, 50 years later, but without Kipling's Victorian certainties:

> Twenty years ago no European had ever been here [Simla], and here we were, with the band playing the "Puritani" . . . and eating salmon from Scotland, and sardines from the Mediterranean . . . and all this in the face of those high hills, some of which have remained untrodden since the creation, and we, 105 Europeans, being surrounded by at least 3,000 mountaineers, who, wrapped up in their hill blankets, looked on at what we call our polite amusements, and bowed to the ground if a European came near them. I sometimes wonder they do not cut all our heads off, and say nothing more about it. (25 May 1839)

No wonder, perhaps, that Simla was also a "cradle of . . . political insanity" (as Sir John Kaye put it), where Auckland was persuaded in 1838 to embark on the policy that led to the rout of the "Army of the Indus" in the First Afghan War.

Eden's letters afford only occasional glimpses of the political maneuvers behind either the "polite amusements" or the extravagant durbars, partly no doubt for security reasons and partly because she could rely on readers at home being well informed from other sources. To expect a historical record, however, is to mistake Eden's primary purpose. Her mission was the traditional function of women's letter writing: the preservation of family bonds. "I am interested in Indian politics just now," she wrote as more news of Russian "meddling" reached the hills (14 June 1838) "but could not make them interesting on paper." Her intimate, idiosyncratic style was ideal for "bringing her home" to her readers, but not for analysis.

Eden's prose has the informality, self-deprecation, and humor of Jane Austen's letters, and like the novelist her apparent preference for the domestic and the trivial over the momentous and political is in the end revelatory. What she *inadvertently* records is the fragility of the enterprise: "Two Russian letters were intercepted . . . only unluckily nobody in India can read them" (14 June 1838). Her emphasis on trappings reflects the common infantilizing of Indian princes, but alongside the feminine/imperial consumerism evident in the operations of the *Tosha Khanna* (the official system for exchange of diplomatic gifts) is the anxiety that accompanies these transactions: "very pretty pickings if they had been private presents, but I saw C. twisting his moustaches in agonies, because they were not intrinsically worth the diamond rings he gave in exchange" (14 December 1839). In the long wake of the Warren Hastings impeachment, the company was acutely sensitive to charges of profiteering.

Although her aristocratic demeanor is frequently chilling, her Whig tolerance alerted her to the pettiness of her compatriots, and despite her sometimes relentless flippancy she could disconcertingly register both the spoliation and the transience of the regime her family headed: "Delhi is a very suggestive and moralising place—such stupendous remains of power and wealth passed and passing away—and somehow I feel that we horrid English have just 'gone and done it', merchandised it, revenued it, and spoiled it all" (20 February 1838).

CICELY PALSER HAVELY

### Biography

Born in Westminster, London, 3 March 1797, seventh daughter of William Eden, first baron Auckland. Family were supporters of the Whigs in opposition after Waterloo. Went to Calcutta with her sister Frances as shared consort to their brother, George Eden, second baron Auckland, after his appointment as governor-general of India, 1835–1842. Kept house for George Eden at Eden Lodge, Kensington, 1842–1849. Lived in later life in Richmond, Surrey, as a political and artistic hostess and novelist. Published the novels *The Semi-Detached House* (edited by Lady Theresa Lewis) 1859; *The Semi-Attached Couple* (by E.E.), 1860. Died in Richmond, 5 August 1869.

### References and Further Reading

Eden, Emily, *Portraits of the Princes and People of India*, 1844.
Eden, Emily, *Up the Country: Letters Written to Her Sister from the Upper Provinces of India*, 2 vols., 1866; reprinted with notes by Edward Thompson, 1983.
Eden, Emily, *Letters from India*, edited by Eleanor Eden, 1872.
Eden, Emily, *Miss Eden's Letters*, edited by Violet Dickinson, 1919.
Ghose, Indira, *Women Travellers in Colonial India: The Power of the Female Gaze,* New Delhi and New York: Oxford University Press, 1998.

## EDWARDS, AMELIA (1831–1892) *British Novelist and Travel Writer*

Amelia Blandford Edwards was a woman of multiple talents and wide-ranging interests who, in the earlier part of her life, found both release and stimulus in the opportunities provided by travel. Abroad she was free of the social restrictions of home and able to indulge her desire for independence and claim the liberty to go as and where she chose. Her first travel book, published in 1862, was meant for a juvenile audience and belongs to a period when she was still trying to establish a financially viable career as a writer. Although is of little intrinsic interest now, the story of a holiday tour provided the basis of her far more sophisticated and accomplished major travel books, *Untrodden Peaks and Unfrequented Valleys* (1873) and *A Thousand Miles up the Nile* (1877).

*Untrodden Peaks and Unfrequented Valleys*, originally entitled *A Midsummer Ramble in the Dolomites*, was the result of a holiday in which Amelia Edwards, together with a woman friend (identified only as L.), undertook what was virtually a pioneering exploration of an area almost totally unknown to any but mountaineers. Roads were often nonexistent and even mule tracks were sometimes lacking. Accommodation was scarce, amenities at best minimal and sometimes primitive, but Amelia Edwards was determined, whatever the obstacles, to see all that was to be seen whether it was a mountain, a particular view, or an alleged Titian in a local church. She intended her book to be a practical guide, scrupulously noting both good and bad, but the emphasis lies decisively on the unspoilted attractions of a region available to all with the enterprise and fortitude to depart from usual tourist routes. She was a mountain enthusiast, avidly studying maps and all available material, but all aspects of local life and scenery engaged her attention and she made a point of talking in their own language to as many people as she could. She had nurtured ambitions to be an artist and her artist's eye helps her to paint vivid scenes. Earlier experience as a novelist and short-story writer is also evident in the skillful handling of narrative and the lively treatment of individual episodes. Her personal observations are supported and amplified by further research. Amelia Edwards fully shared the Victorian enthusiasm for gathering and diffusion of knowledge, but she also had the rarer gift of conveying information gracefully and without taint of pedantry. The book is seasoned and enlivened throughout by her own zest for exploration and the wide range of responses she brings to the culture and history of the region.

The characteristics that make *Untrodden Peaks and Unfrequented Valleys* both attractive and instructive are even more evident in *A Thousand Miles up the Nile*. By 1873 Egypt was already much visited and the book could not have *Untrodden Peaks'* quality of quasi-exploration, but the historical and cultural background is much richer and Amelia Edwards's mind and imagination are stimulated to maximum effect. As in the Dolomite book there is the propelling urge to open readers' eyes to experiences beyond their usual ken, whether of the physical, the artistic, or the intellectual world, and Amelia Edwards deploys all her writer's skills to stimulate understanding and appreciation of the extraordinary achievements of ancient Egypt. With practiced assurance in the handling of pace, tone, and image she absorbs the latest results of archaeological research into a whole composed of lively narrative and descriptions in which cameralike precision is infused with an artist's sensitivity. The success of this amalgam is largely a result of the character of the author herself as it is projected in the pages of both her major travel books. This persona, to whatever extent it may or may not be biographically accurate, functions as a brilliant literary device, holding together all the varied elements of narrative, description, and instruction in the person of an ideal companion, wonderfully well informed, alert to every feature of a site or a landscape but wearing her knowledge lightly, quick to recognize the humor of a situation or a quirk of personality and with a capacity for subtle irony from which she herself is not exempt.

*Untrodden Peaks and Unfrequented Valleys* and *A Thousand Miles up the Nile* are still read by today's travelers. Amelia Edwards's account of her Egyptian journey, in particular, has stirred the minds and imaginations of many. Her dedicated study and her gifts as a writer still sharpen awareness and understanding of the powerfully evocative and resonant civilization of ancient Egypt.

JOAN REES

### Biography

Born in Islington, London, 7 June 1831. Educated at home under the supervision of her mother. Showed early talent in music, art, and writing. After an unsuccessful engagement, built an independent career: worked as a journalist and writer, from 1850s. Published eight novels, 1855–1880. Her parents died, 1860; settled with an elderly woman friend in Westbury-on-Trym, near Bristol, 1864. Traveled to the Dolomites, 1872; Egypt, 1873–1874. Initiated the founding of the Egypt Exploration Fund (currently the Egypt Exploration Society), with Reginald Poole in London, 1882 to raise funds to conduct excavations in the Delta. Corresponded on the society's behalf; wrote reports for *The Times* on the progress of Flinders Petrie's excavations. Conducted lecture tour in the United States, 1889. Received honorary degrees from three U.S. universities; awarded a civil pension in recognition of her services to literature and archaeology. Suffered from severe ill health from 1890. Died in Westbury-on-Trym after contracting influenza, 15 April 1892.

### References and Further Reading

Edwards, Amelia, *Sights and Stories: Being Some Account of a Holiday Tour through the North of Belgium*, 1862.

Edwards, Amelia, *Untrodden Peaks and Unfrequented Valleys: A Midsummer Ramble in the Dolomites*, 1873; reprinted, with a new introduction by Philippa Levine, 1986.

Edwards, Amelia, *A Thousand Miles Up the Nile*, 1877; 2nd edition, 1989.

## EGERIA (FOURTH CENTURY) *Spanish Nun and Pilgrim*

Egeria was a wealthy nun from Galicia in northwestern Spain, who wrote an account of her pilgrimage to the Holy Land between 381 and 384 for her religious community (*dominae sorores*). A seventh-century letter from the monk Valerius (d. 691) to his brethren at El Vierzo refers three times to a courageous pilgrim called "the blessed nun Egeria." Although her name appears in the eight surviving copies of the letter in different spellings, including Echeria, Etheria, Eutheria, Aetheria, Heteria, Eitheria, Eucheria, and Silvia, Egeria has been identified as the writer of the account and, like Valerius, a native of Galicia.

Although we know little about Egeria, we do know that she was by nature curious, eager to visit biblical places, and always planning new excursions. Travel conditions being what they were, she cannot have been an ordinary woman. An almost four-year journey required ample means, good connections, and knowledge of the countries and their languages. The fact that she referred to discussions with archbishops and bishops, and inserted some Greek words, suggests that she knew Greek. Thus it can be said that Egeria was financially well off, with a good education, benevolent relations, and the mind of an adventurer determined to see the visible proofs of the truth of the biblical narratives. She used an Old Latin Bible as a guidebook during her journey, reading on the spot the appropriate narratives about the holy places. This is reflected in the style of her *Itinerarium*, which is written in the Vulgar, or Late, Latin of her time interspersed with indirect citations from the Old Latin Bible.

When the Italian scholar Gian Francesco Gamurrini (1835–1923) discovered Egeria's *Itinerarium* in the library of the Lay Fraternity of Santa Flora at Arezzo in 1884, only the middle portion of the manuscript had survived. However, the extant text and other sources of travels at that time reveal that Egeria used the common pilgrimage route. From Galicia, her assumed place of birth, she traveled first to Constantinople, then on foot to Bithynia, Galatia, and Cappadocia, reaching Tarsus through Cilicia. On her way down to Jerusalem she followed the coastal road (*via maris*) to Caesarea. The southern road continued through Lod/Diospolis and Emmaus/Nicopolis to Jerusalem but, eager to reach the holy city, she took the northern way straight through Samaria and reached Jerusalem in autumn 381.

Egeria made numerous excursions from Jerusalem. At the end of the year, or early in 382, she made her first journey to Egypt along the coastline through Ascalon and Pelusium to Alexandria. She then sailed up the Nile, visiting Tanis, Memphis, Babylon/Cairo, and Heliopolis. She visited the monks and clergy in Nitria and the Thebaïd, and then returned through Goshen, arriving in Jerusalem probably at the end of the year, but certainly before 18 May 383.

In the summer of 383 Egeria explored Galilee. She visited the almond tree at Bethel; the temple and the tomb of Eli the priest at Shiloh; the well of Jacob and the tomb of Joseph at Shechem; the tombs of John the Baptist, Elisha, and Obadiah at Sebastia (Samaria); the mountains of Gilboa; the well at Jezreel; the little Hermon; the house of Shunamite at Shunem; and Nain, Tabor, and Nazareth. She even climbed Mount Carmel. After a short stay in Tiberias she toured the places by the Sea of Tiberias where Jesus had ministered: Capernaum, the springs and the temple at Tabgha, Mount Eremos, and the synagogue at Chorazin. She also went to Hebron and Mamre, and to Jericho where she climbed the Mount of Temptations. From Jerusalem she visited Bethlehem; the tower at Anathoth, where the prophet Jeremiah once uttered his Lamentations; Gibeon, where the Lord had supper with his disciples after the Resurrection; the tomb of Joshua the son of Nun at Timnat-serah; and the church at Kiriath-jearim.

At the end of 383 her second journey to Egypt took her through Ascalon, Pelusium, and Clysma/Suez to Sinai. From Clysma, having localized the miracle at the Red Sea, she continued along the west coast of the Gulf of Suez and then turned inland, entering the Valley of Rest (Wadi er Raha), where she saw the Graves of Craving. Egeria's travel account begins with this part of the journey describing her approach to Sinai. She climbed Mount Sinai and Horeb, visiting the cells of the Forty Martyrs on the way up to the church on the summit of Gebel Musa, and on the way down passing the Burning Bush before returning the way she came and then making a detour to Goshen. She then saw the sites of the Exodus to Egypt in reverse order:

> So we were shown everything which the Books of Moses tell us took place in the valley beneath holy Sinai, the Mount of God. I know it has been rather a long business writing down all these places one after the other, and it makes far too much to remember. But it may help you, loving sisters, the better to picture what happened in these places when you read the holy Books of Moses.

Back in Jerusalem in early January 383, Egeria took part in the Epiphany services, and later that spring in the feast of Easter celebrated in the "Great Church built by Constantine on Golgotha behind the Cross." Early the following year she climbed Mount Nebo, where Moses viewed the Promised Land, and visited the tomb of Job four miles outside Jerusalem.

At the end of March 384 her return journey took her to Antioch, where she made a detour to Edessa, the martyrium of the apostle Thomas, and the palace of King Abgar. She also visited Charra (Haran), the site of Abraham's house, on 22 April. Having seen the well where Jacob watered Rachel's animals, Egeria returned to Antioch. In May and June, by way of Tarsus, she reached Seleucia, where she visited the martyrium of Thecla, and met her dear friend the deaconess Marthana, before returning to Constantinople.

Egeria's meticulous *Itinerarium* is invaluable regarding the topography, the early church architecture, and the piety of the Holy Land, as well as the liturgy in Jerusalem during the fourth century.

René Gothóni

## Biography

Born fourth century AD. Traveled to the Holy Land in 381–384. No further biographical details are known.

## References and Further Reading

Egeria, *Egeria's Travels*, translated by John Wilkinson, 1971; revised edition, 1981.

Egeria, *Journal de Voyage*, edited by Pierre Maraval, 1982.

Egeria, *Itinerarium/ Reisebericht*, Latin text and German translation by Georg Röwekamp and Dietmar Thönes, 1995.

*See also* **Pilgrimage, Christian**

## EGYPT, ANCIENT TO 680 CE

Ancient Egypt, roughly defined from the fourth millennium BCE to the Islamic explosion of the seventh century CE, exuded a natural magnetism for travel writers. By 1500 BCE it acted as a hub for prodigious international trade routes that stretched in all directions: north across the Mediterranean into the Hittite and Hurrian kingdoms and up to the Black Sea; west through Crete and Greece, touching southern Italy through Minoan and Mycenaean continuation; east through Babylonia and Afghanistan to the Indus and China; and south down the Nile and Red Sea into the southern African kingdoms of Nubia and Ethiopia. Yet for all this prodigious contact with the outside world, contemporary travel literature is fairly scarce. There are many engraved records of trade, and some accounts of Egypt's conflicts, yet there are relatively few personal accounts from travelers to Egypt itself. Those that can be classified as travel writing tend to mix fabulous expectations of Egypt's promissory opulence with a style of factual accounting that suggests an emerging consciousness of, if not reportage, then at least the obligation to reliable witness.

One historical force dominates the earliest writings of exploration to Egypt: Hellenization. As Minoan and Mycenean trading propelled Greek influence throughout the ancient Mediterranean, Egypt became a region about which speculation and fantasy accrued, usually because of presumptions about its wealth and agricultural opulence. Homer's *Iliad* has but a single mention of Egypt, but the *Odyssey* reveals more of a preoccupation with over 20 references. These go beyond generalized reflections of Egypt's cultural, agricultural, and metallurgical fecundity, and include historical details such as pirate raids against Egypt's northern coastline, and eyewitness details like accurate references to the islet of Pharos and the workings of the Nile.

The interest in Egypt continued as Hellenization expanded with conquest and commercialism. Enter Herodotus, probably the high-water mark of travel writing concerning ancient Egypt. Herodotus was born between 490 and 480 BCE at Halicarnassus on the southern coastline of Asia Minor. We know little concerning him as a person, but his *Histories* have left us a contentious account (focused mainly in Books II and III) of the geography, mythology, theology, and social customs of contemporary Egypt, and an account of Egypt's conquest by Cambyses II, the Achaemenid king of Persia, in 525 BCE. Though it has been contested, there seems little doubt that Herodotus actually visited Egypt; his text clearly differentiates between first- and secondhand reporting. For example, when discussing the southerly course of the Nile, Herodotus admits that "as far as Elephantine I speak as an eyewitness, but further south from hearsay." This type of self-reflective narratizing does not solve all problems, however. His theological and geological explanations often ring of subservience to other's deferential accounts, and the "father of history"/"father of lies" debate continues with alacrity.

Around the time of Herodotus, philosophical tourism started to mingle with trade visitations: Solon, Thales, and Hecataeus are all said to have traveled to Egypt in the sixth century BCE with only exploratory purpose. Yet Hellenization really exploded after Alexander the Great's conquest of Egypt in 332 BCE and the subsequent stewardship of Egypt under the Macedonian Ptolemies. Though not strictly first-person travel writing, literature exploring Alexander's foreign adventures was prolific. Alexander himself was accompanied by his official historian, Callisthenes of Olynthus (Aristotle's nephew), whose works plotted Alexander's Asiatic expedition; these works no longer exist except through references by other writers. By the third century, however, Alexander's travels in Egypt were given life through anonymous works such as *The Alexander Romance*, a mix of historical aggrandizement and Herodotean description (*The Alexander Romance* appears to have borrowed detail directly from Herodotus).

By the first century BCE Egypt was a magnet for much of the Greek world, and many Greek citizens took up residence in fashionable new cities, such as the transparently Hellenized Alexandria. The travelers came from an amazing breadth of locations: Sinope (a city on the Black Sea), Illyria, Thrace, Syracuse, and Marseilles. The Ptolemaic period yielded an amazing diversity of literary styles, but particularly sketches of everyday Egyptian life from the new settlers. We have the *Mimes* of Herondas, written about 270 BCE, which reflects on the bright-lights lure of Egypt to the young, while Theocritus in his *Idylls* builds vignettes around his experience of settlement in Alexandria. More famous are the works of Diodorus Siculus, writer of the substantial *Biblioteca Historia* [Library of History]. Though born in Agyrium, Sicily, in the first century, Diodorus visited Egypt around between 60 and 56 BCE, and gives an ethnography of Egypt that is mostly derived from Hecataeus. Indeed, the value of Diodorus is not so much his writing as the sources of his writing, though he does show an intimacy with some aspects of Egyptian life, such as mummification. A more intimate account of Egypt in the same period was given in an anonymous text known as the *Periplus*, from a Greek resident of Alexandria. The *Periplus* is a detailed account of journeying along Africa's east coast and is excellent for filling in many gaps in our knowledge about pre-Christian African geography and travel.

The island of Philae encapsulated the picturesque qualities of ancient Egypt for traveling artists (from Edouard du Montulé's *Recueil des cartes et des vues du voyage en Amerique en Italie en Sicile et en Egypt fait pendant les Années 1816, 1817, 1818, 1819*, 1821). *Courtesy of Travellers Club, London; Bridgeman Art Library, agent.*

As we enter the Christian era, Hellenization is replaced by Romanization. Egypt was annexed by Rome in 30 BCE, and there began an alternative influx of tourism and exploratory writings. Strabo heads this cast. Born in Pontus he spent several years in Alexandria, and gives an account of this in the eighth book of his *Geography*. Strabo also reflected somewhat on the nature of Egyptian tourism itself. Many Romans made the journey from Italy in some measure inspired by the cult of Isis, which was flooding into the Roman world and elicited works such as Plutarch's *De Iside et Osiride*. One of the tourists' favorite destinations was the Colossi of Memnon, and the inscriptions scrawled by Roman tourists on the stonework there make fascinating travel reading in their own right.

By the end of Constantine's reign, Christianity was taking over as the hegemonic worldview in the west. As this Christian world became more entrenched, we can add a final strand to the pattern of ancient travel writing in Egypt: pilgrimage. Early pilgrimage writing tended to dwell on descriptive accounts of Holy Land places of scriptural significance or prominent churches. Yet looking prior to 680, one of the most representative and individuated names in this context is Egeria. Egeria was a nun of the fourth century who, around 385 wrote an account of her travels through the Holy Land, including Egypt. Her *Itinerarium* or *Peregrinatio ad terram sanctam* [Travels to the Holy Land] was written mainly as an illustrative rendition of the state of the church in the Holy Land for her sisters back in Europe. An inquisitive, fresh, and enthusiastic voice, Egeria provides a striking illustration of the language of faith-tourism. This type of voice became dominant after 680, when both Islam from the east and Christianity from the west all attempted to gain descriptive purchase over Egypt and all the nations of the Holy Land.

CHRISTOPHER MCNAB

## References and Further Reading

Diodorus Siculus, *The Antiquities of Asia: A Translation with Notes of Book II of the Library of History*, edited by Edwin Murphy, 1989.

Egeria, *Egeria's Travels*, translated and edited by John Wilkinson, 1971.

*The Greek Alexander Romance*, translated and with an introduction by Richard Stoneman, 1991.

Herodotus, *Herodotus, Book II*, edited by W.G. Waddell, 1939.

Herodotus, *The Histories*, translated by Aubrey de Sélincourt, with an introduction and notes by A.R. Burn, 1972.
Herodotus, *The Histories*, translated by Walter Blanco, edited by Blanco and Jennifer Tolbert Roberts, 1992.
Homer, *The Odyssey*, translated by Richmond Lattimore, 1967.
Plutarch, *Plutarch's De Iside et Osiride*, edited and translated by J. Gwyn Griffiths, 1970.
Strabo, *The Geography of Strabo*, 8 vols., translated by Horace Leonard Jones, 1917–1932; reprinted, 1983.

## EGYPT, ISLAMIC TRAVELERS

The geographic centrality of Egypt to the Islamic world has ensured it a rather steady influx of travelers throughout the centuries. After the Islamic conquest of Egypt the country became an important station for many travelers en route, particularly North Africans heading for the Muslim religious center of Mecca or the political and cultural centers of the successive Muslim states in Damascus, Baghdad, Cairo, and Istanbul. Stopping off in Egypt in the Middle Ages, however, meant long sojourns in the country, and although few travelogues take Egypt as their exclusive topic, almost all include at least a chapter on it. Islamic travel literature of Egypt is, therefore, interspersed in accounts that cover other parts of the Islamic world as well, depending on the traveler's itinerary and the political scene.

Muslims are attracted to travel by their beliefs and culture. Many travelers start off as pilgrims, some as traders, but the majority of the travelogues are by scholars. Scholarly travelogues stand prominently in Islamic literature, partly as a result of the conceptual link between travel and learning and partly because the academics were the most prolific writers of all travelers. Learning basically meant an exchange of cultural and religious ideas, observing natural phenomena, and reporting on the cultural and social scenes. The academic tendency is particularly remarkable in sufi travelogues such as that of Al-Harawi (d. 1215). Another example is Al-Tugaibi Al-Sabti (1271–?). The earliest Islamic academic trip to Egypt on record is that of the imam Al-Shaf'i (787–820). Whether in the role of students or teachers, many travelers visited Egypt in pursuit of religious learning, in particular at its college-mosque Al-Azhar. While the preoccupation with religious learning persists, the Middle Ages mark the emergence of interest in other sciences. Muslim's contribution to geography, history, botany, and medicine, along with a wide range of sciences, dates back to early oriental travelers.

As early as the pre-Islamic period, trade was the basic economic activity of the Arabs. With the Arab conquest of the neighboring lands, this mode of economic activity widened to encompass the newly annexed regions, taking traveling tradesmen as far as Morocco in the west and China in the east. Al-Zaheri (d. 1468) is one such traveler. Travelogues by such travelers mainly supply economic studies of the diverse markets, products, modes of exchange, prices, and standard of living.

The fact that the vast lands of the Islamic world were predominantly ruled by centralized governments at once created a political need for travel—to convey news and information and to maintain control—and allowed freedom of movement among the different provinces. The extension of the Muslim empire in the Middle Ages resulted in the construction of roads and waystations, hotels, and an efficient mail service, which facilitated travel. This political need was partly responsible for the emergence of a specific genre of travel writing that is predominantly interested in describing the road, the predecessor of the modern travel guide. *Masalik* and *mamalik* (roads and kingdoms) books such as Al-Istakhri those by (d. 951) and Al-'Omari (1301–1347) came to the fore between the tenth and thirteenth centuries, and were meant to supply information to civil servants, tradesmen, and other travelers. Many of the more popular travelers, like Ibn Battuta, took the trip for the mere love of travel and adventure.

Although many women travelers visited Egypt on their way to Mecca, often residing there at length while working as catechists and writers—for example, Um-al-Yemen Bint-Mohalla (traveled 1226), Fatima Bint-'Aiash al-Baghdadiah [d. 1314], and Sit-al-Wozaraa Bint-'Omar Al-Damashqiah (1226–1316)—their literature is lost.

However, the long history of travel in Egypt is far from monolithic. As the travelers' motives for travel, their individual preferences, and the political and cultural scenes in the Islamic world changed, so too did the points of interest and perceptions in the successive texts. The earliest extant travelogue that includes a section on Egypt is that of Al-Mas'udi (d. 957). A renowned historian, geographer, and literary figure, Al-Mas'udi was also a prolific traveler and a professional writer. His travelogue partly derives its importance from the fact that it is the earliest account written by the traveler himself and is therefore a record of firsthand impressions and genuine information as well as deep perception. His main focus is Egypt's economic activities, its agriculture, industries, and trade, which he relates to its environment, hence confirming his climatological theory relating geography and history, and evaluating the effect of the place and climate on the mode of life and economic production.

The eleventh and twelveth centuries witnessed a remarkable fluidity of movement in Islamic lands and a proliferation of cultural production. Many travelers still stopped off in Egypt while heading for other destinations, but more chose it as their desired destination. Fustat (now part of Cairo) was the capital of the prosperous Fatimid state. Travelers flocked into Egypt from both east and west parts of the Islamic state. In 1046 the Persian Nasir-i Khusro [or Khosrau] (1003–1088) began with the aim of going on a pilgrimage to Mecca and arrived in Egypt the following year. During his journey Khusro kept a journal and produced sketches of the road which were later turned into an account of his travels. Although *Sefar Nameh* (1881), is a complete account of his journey, based on his itinerary, the major part of it is devoted to Egypt. Khusro reveals a remarkable interest in architecture, craftsmanship, economic and social aspects, and the organization of government. He reports on the general plan of Cairo, its hotels, baths, palaces, mosques, shops, marketplaces, and houses. *Sefar Nameh* is also an account of Egyptian industries and trade that relates these activities to the daily life of the people, revealing how the transactions were carried out rather than simply listing what was on exchange, just as it covers life in the royal palaces to which Khusro had access. Also heading for Mecca, but starting from west of the Islamic state, from Valencia, Ibn Jubayr (c. 1145–1217) arrived in Egypt in 1182. His text is the first Islamic travelogue written in diary form and one of the best pieces of Islamic travel writing. It is remarkable for its literary style, spontaneity, and sincerity of sentiment. It records social and economic life in Egypt at the time and is particularly interesting in its description of the monuments, both Islamic and ancient. The different mosques, the Nilometer and the Maristan (hospital), which represent different epochs in Egyptian history, stand side by side in the text, and Ibn Jubayr gives details of the interior of the pyramid as well as its use. The text reveals a remarkable sensitivity to history. The land is not a mere site that lends itself to description but is steeped in historic narratives: the Nile recalls Moses and Joseph. The text has a further historical value as it relates a wanderer's perception of the crusades and an evaluative representation of Saladin's social rather than military achievements.

After the crusades the trip to Palestine gained popularity and travelers to Jerusalem, the Muslims' second holy city, often landed in Egypt. In addition, Saladin's interest in the promotion of scientific studies instigated scientists to travel, particularly between Baghdad, Damascus, and Cairo. 'Abd-al-Latif Al-Baghdadi (1162–1231), a linguist and biologist who was particularly interested in botany and anatomy and who established a reputation as a medical practitioner, visited Egypt twice in pursuit of its scientists. His *Al-ifadah wa'l-i'tibar* stands out in the history of Islamic travel writing for many reasons. It is a text dedicated exclusively to the representation of Egypt, an outstanding scientific research on the plants and animals of that country, and a record of his work on anatomy in which he challenged and corrected some of the then current theories. The text also has a historic importance as it gives a vivid account of the famine that arose in Egypt in betwee 1200 and 1202 because of a low Nile. It describes the topography and climate of the country, its plants and animals, its monuments and architecture, its food, the Nile, and the famine. Classic though these topics may seem, in 'Abd-al-Latif's hand they are turned into topics for scientific observation and investigation: rather than merely describing the buildings, he gives an account of the process of their construction while the Nile's water invites chemical analyses.

The fourteenth century witnessed the travels of the most renowned of all oriental travelers, Ibn Battuta (1304–1377). Initially heading for Mecca, Ibn Battuta traveled extensively for 28 years and recorded his travels after his return to his home in Tangier. He reached Egypt by sea, first landing in Alexandria, then sailed up the Nile, stopping at Cairo and many other places en route. His account of Egypt comprises references to buildings, mosques, the pyramids, gardens, the Maristan, and the Nile. However, these places are not merely picturesque scenes or natural phenomena, but cultural signs that are pretexts for speculations on the mode of life, ideas, and beliefs as well as the economy of the country. He traces their history and their effect on the life of the people through individualized anecdotes he learned during his tour of the country. He reveals an interest in the sheikhs, revealing their way of life and ideas, and his text shows an understanding of and an interest in the manners and customs of the Egyptians. His extensive travels and comparative approach place Egypt in relation to other Islamic countries and cultures, hence revealing Islamic cultural diversity as well as its shared background. Almost at the same time as Ibn Battuta was traveling, Ibn Khaldun fled to Egypt where he wrote his notorious *Moqademah* and his travelogue, *Al-ta'rif b'Ibn Khaldun*.

Egypt remained a popular destination for travelers, particularly scholars, until the sixteenth century. Travelers from eastern and western Islamic regions visited Egypt, revealing a wide range of interests and a rich diversity of perceptions in texts on exploration, catechism, history, geography, and literature. After the Ottoman occupation, however, Egypt gradually lost its academic supremacy. This period is remarkable for the proliferation of ambassadorial travels, but most Islamic travelers headed first for Europe and next for Asia. Egypt's share of official and academic travelers went into decline, although it remained a popular stopping-off point for many pilgrims. However, during this period an interesting and remarkable traveler visited Egypt, one who adds to the diversity of travelers to visit the country. Ibn al-Wazzan (Leo Africanus) (1495/1500 ? – ?) was born in Granada, raised in Morocco, traveled in Africa, went on the Hajj, and was captured by Italian pirates, as a result of which he spent ten years in captivity. Although his travelogue opens on a soberly geographic note, it is one of the most vivid and animated accounts of Egypt. Cairo springs to life with its festivities: its streets are filled with chatting women in colorful dress and jesters performing their tricks and sketches. The book represents a mature form of manners' and customs' travel writing.

The nineteenth century witnessed a further decline of interest in Egypt among Islamic travelers. After the French incursion of 1798 and 1799, more Islamic travelers headed for Europe and the United States, and in their place Westerners flocked into Egypt. However, since the nineteenth century, a new trend in Egyptian travel has emerged: exploration journeys undertaken by Egyptians who, as much following their traditions as the newly emerging desire for scientific exploration, produced narratives of distant parts of their own country. Between 1839 and 1841 Selim Effandi headed south with the aim of discovering the sources of the Nile, and in 1922 Ahmad Hassanein explored the Libyan desert and rediscovered long-lost wells, roads, and oases. In addition, references to certain sites in Egypt, usually coastal cities, are interspersed in Egyptians' travelogues of their journeys elsewhere. Rereading the homeland after long absence has become something of a tradition. In her *Rihlat al-sharq wa al-gharb* (1986), for example, Ne'mat Fouad includes a descriptive, informative, poetic account of Hurghada, where she landed on her return. The focus of interest in Islamic travelogues has shifted among religious learning, geography, history, botany, and medicine, but the basic preoccupation with recording what the traveler has heard and learned from his fellow travelers, rather than what he has only seen, persists throughout. Modern travelogues are mainly exploration narratives that tend to be more subjective, centralizing the traveler's own perception and decoding of the visited place.

SAHAR SOBHI ABDEL-HAKIM

### References and Further Reading


Ahmad, Mahmoud, *Bayan tarikhi 'an masjed 'Amr Ibn-Al-'As: Rihalat Farouk wa Faiza wa Fauziah lizyarat al-masajed al-athariah*, Cairo, n.d.

Ahmad, Mahmoud, *Bayan tarikhi 'an masjed al-sultan Hassan wa sharh mumaizatahu al-faniah: Rihalat Farouk wa Faiza wa Fawziah lizyarat al-masajed al-athariah*, Cairo, n.d.

Al-'Abdari, Mohammad Ibn Abu-'Abd-Allah Al-Himi, *Rihlat Al-'Abdari al-mosammah al-rihla al-maghribiah*, 1968.

Al-Baghdadi, 'Abd-al-Latif, *Kitab al-ifadah wa'l-i'tibar*, edited by Ayman Fu'ad Sayyid, 1983; as *The Eastern Key*, translated by Kamal Hafuth Zand, John A. Videan and Ivy E. Videan, 1965.

Al-Bakri, Abu 'Ubayd, *Kitab al-masalik wa'l-mamalik*, 2 vols, 1992; as *Description de l'Afrique septentrionale*, translated by MacGuckin de Slane, 1859; revised edition, 1965.

Al-Balawi, Khalid Ibn 'Isa, *Taj al-mafriq fi tahliyat 'ulama' al-mashriq*, 2 vols., 1980.

Al-Gizi, Rabi' Ibn Suliman, *Rihlat Al-Imam Al-Shaf'i min Macca ila Yanbu'*, 1950.

Al-Harawi, 'Ali Ibn Abi-Bakr, *Kitab al-isharat ila ma'rifat al-ziyarat*, 1953; as *Guide des lieux de pèlerinage*, translated by Janine Sourdel-Thomine, 1957.

Al-Idrisi, (Mohammed Ibn Mohammed), *Kitab Nuzhat al-mushtaq fi ikhtiraq al-afaq*, edited by Mohammed Hajj Sadiq, 1983; as *Géographie d'Édrisi*, translated by P. Amédée Jaubert, 2 vols., 1836–1840; as *Opus Geographicum*, translated by A. Bombaci et al., 9 parts, 1970–1984.

Al-Istakhri, Abu-Ishaq Ibrahim Al-Faresi, *Kitab al-masalik wa-al-mamalik*, edited by M.J. de Goeje, 1870; as *The Oriental Geography of Ebn Haukal*, translated by William Ouseley, 1800.

Al-Mas'udi, 'Ali Ibn al-Hussain, *Muruj al-dhahab wa ma'adin al-jawhar / Les Prairies d'or*, edited and translated by C. Barbier de Meynard and Pavet de Courteille, 9 vols., 1861–1877; selection, as *The Meadows of Gold: The Abbasids*, translated by Paul Lunde and Caroline Stone, 1989.

Al-Mas'udi, 'Ali Ibn al-Hussain, *Kitab Al-tanbih wa'l ishraf*, edited by M.J. de Goeje, 1894; as *Le Livre de l'avertissement et de la révision*, translated by B. Carra de Vaux, 1896.

Al-Muqaddasi, Shams Al-Din Mohammad Ibn Ahmad, *Kitab Ahsan al-taqasim fi ma'rifat al-aqalim*, edited by M.J. de Goeje, 1877, 2nd edition, 1906; as *The Best Divisions for Knowledge of the Regions*, translated by Basil Anthony Collins, 1994.

Al-'Omari (Shihab Al-Din Abu'l-Abbas), Ahmad Ibn Yahya Ibn Fadl-Allah, *Masalik al-absar fi mamalik al-amsar*, 1924; facsimile, 1988.

Al-Rihani, Amin (Fares), *Muluk al-Arab, aw Rihlah fi al-bilad al-Arabiah*, 2 vols., 1924–1925; 2nd edition, 1929.

Al-Ya'qubi, Ahmad Ibn Abi Ya'qub Ibn Jafar, *Kitab al-buldan*, edited by M.J. de Goeje, 1892.

Al-Zaheri, Ghars al-Din Khalil Ibn Shahin, *Zubdat kashf al-mamalik: Tableau politique et administratif de l'Égypte, de la Syrie et du Hidjaz*, edited by, Paul Ravaisse, 1894.

Azm, Nazih Mu'ayyad, *Rihlah fi -bilad al-Arabiah al-sa'idah: min Misr ila Sana'a*, 1937.

Fouad, Ne'mat, *Rihlat al-sharq wa al-gharb*, 1986.

Ibn al-Faqih al-Hamadhani, Ahmad Ibn Mohammad, *Kitab al-buldan*, edited by Yusuf al-Hadi, 1996; as *Abrégé de livre des pays*, translated by Henri Massé, edited by Charles Pellat, 1973.

Ibn al-Ma'mun, *Passages de la chronique d'Égypte*, edited by Ayman Fu'ad Sayyid, 1983.

Ibn Battuta, *Tuhfat al-nuzzar fi ghara'ib al-amsar wa 'aja'ib al-asfar*, 2 vols., 1905; as *Voyages d'Ibn Batoutah*, translated by C. Defrémery and B.R. Sanguinetti, 1853–1859; as *The Travels of Ibn Battuta A.D. 1325–1354*, translated by H.A.R. Gibb, 3 vols., 1958–1971; as *The Adventures of Ibn Battuta: A Muslim Traveller of the Fourteenth Century*, translated by Ross E. Dunn, 1986.

Ibn-Hawqal, Abu al-Qasim Mohammad Ibn Ali al-Nasibi, *Kitab Surat al-ard*, 2 vols., edited by J.H. Kramers, 1938–1939; as *Configuration de la terre*, translated by J.H. Kramers and G. Wiet, 2 vols., 1964.

Ibn Jubayr, *The Travels of Ibn Jubayr*, translated by R.J.C. Broadhurst, 1952.

Ibn Khaldun, 'Abd-al-Rahman Ibn Mohammad, *Al-ta'rif b' Ibn Khaldun wa rihlatuhu gharban wa sharqan*, edited by Mo-

hammed Ibn Tawit al-Tanji, 1951; as *Le Voyage d'occident et d'orient*, translated by Abdessalam Cheddadi, 1980.
Ibn Khurradadhbib, Abu al-Qasim Ibn 'Ubayd Allah, *Al-masalik wa al-mamalik*, edited by Mohammed Makhzum, 1988.
Khosro, Nasir-i, *Sefer Nameh: relation du voyage de Nassiri Khosrau en Syrie, en Palestine, en Égypte, en Arabie et en Perse*, edited and translated by Charles Schefer, 1881; reprinted, 1970; as *Sefarnamah*, Arabic translator Yehia Al-Khashab, 1993.
*Kitab al-istibsar fi 'ajab'i al-amsar: wasf Makkah wa al-Madinah wa Misr wa bilad al-Maghrib / Description de la Mekke et de Médine, de l'Égypte et de l'Afrique septentrionale, par un écrivain marocain du VIe siècle de l'Hégire (XIIe s. J.C.)*, text in Arabic and French, edited and partially translated by Saad Zaghlul 'Abd al-Hamid, 1958.
Leo Africanus, *Della descrittione dell' Africa*, 1526; as *Wasf Ifriqi*, 1980; as *The History and Description of Africa*, translated by John Pory, edited by Robert Brown, 3 vols., 1896; reprinted, 1965.
Musa, Sabri, *Fi al-sahara*, 1964.
Thabit, Karim, *Rihlat galalat al-malik Fouad al-awal bin Misr wa Europa fi saif 1929*, 1931.
Yaqut Ibn 'Abd-Allah (al-Rumi) al-Hamawi, *Kitab Mu'jam al-buldan*, 8 vols, 1906; as *Jacut's geographisches Wörterbuch*, edited by Ferdinand Wüstenfeld, 6 vols., 1866–1873.

*See also* **Cairo**

## EGYPT, WESTERN TRAVELERS

Western travelers to Egypt fall into three broad groups. Among the earliest were pilgrims who completed their itinerary by visiting Matariya on the edge of Cairo, where Mary and Joseph reputedly rested in their flight, or by journeying through the land of the Exodus, to St. Catherine's Monastery in the Sinai peninsula, and entering Egypt across the desert from Palestine to Suez. Pilgrims (like Egeria, fl. 385) came from the early centuries after Christ, and on through the crusading centuries and after. In the nineteenth century, clergymen traveled with a growing interest in the geography and natural history of the holy places. Alongside them came merchants seeking spices, scents, and silks, and all the luxuries of the East to trade for Suffolk wool, Spanish cork, and much else. For them Cairo was the mart of the world where everything could be bought and sold, and where mummies' hands and ancient jewelry could be purchased and taken home for show. The merchants were seldom writers, but there were exceptions: John Sanderson (1560–1627) took a cursory look at the pyramids; Abraham Parsons (d. 1785) watched and recorded the seven-hour procession of the Mecca caravan leaving Cairo in 1780. In the eighteenth century came adventurers, explorers, collectors, scholars and artists, and travelers who were, in reality, tourists. Among them were military men and government officials as the pivotal position of Egypt became of increasing interest to Europe. These groups of travelers came mainly from Europe, including European Russia, but from the 1830s, Americans were becoming more familiar.

Knowledge of Egypt in Europe became widespread, fed by travelers' books that were often translated into many languages. Bernhard von Breydenbach's *Pilgrimage to Jerusalem in 1483* (1486) appeared in Dutch, German, Italian, and French before the English edition in 1594. Editions of the *Narrative* (1821) of Giovanni Belzoni (1778–1823) in German, Italian, and French appeared almost simultaneously with the English edition in 1822. Many travel accounts had several editions. The topographical artist W.H. Bartlett (1809–1854) did not live to see his *Nile Boat* (1850) go into five editions within ten years. The monthly journals gave considerable space to the accounts of the discoveries of travelers like John Lewis Burckhardt (1784–1817), Belzoni, and Captain Caviglia (1770–1845) and to observations about the people, the country, and the monuments by such people as Comte de Forbin (1777–1841) and Dr. Robert Richardson (1779–1847), both in Egypt in 1817. Travelers read widely before they set out and often took a library with them. James Bruce (1730–1794) cut down his luggage in Cairo in 1768 by reducing the numbers of pages in the books he carried. Dr. R.R. Madden (1798–1886) complained in 1826 that in visiting Troy, Memphis, Thebes, and Jerusalem, "It is difficult to carry Herodotus and Hamilton, Strabo and Sir William Gell, Pococke and Pausanius in one small head, albeit enveloped in a large turban." The travelers' own large output (for which we mainly have the publishers Henry Colbourn and John Murray to thank) provided a record of great value not only for other travelers but also for historians, geographers, scientists, and others. In Europe people who had never been there could talk knowledgeably about Egypt, and in 1741 the short-lived Egypt Society was formed in London so that travelers, including Richard Pococke (1704–1765), Frederick Norden (1708–1742), and the Earl of Sandwich (1718–1792) could share their experiences and their souvenirs, just as members of the

Dominique Vivant Denon, head of the team of artists who accompanied Napoleon to Egypt in 1798, at work in Upper Egypt (from *Voyage dans la Basse et la Haute Égypte . . .*, 1802, after Denon's own pen-and-wash drawing). *Courtesy of Travellers Club, London; Bridgeman Art Library, agent.*

Society of Dilettanti, formed in 1734, could for the classical world.

Western travelers came into Egypt by three main routes: to Alexandria, up the Red Sea from India and across the desert to the Nile from either Cosseir or Suez. From Alexandria or the south, they hired boats or took a place on a passenger boat to Cairo. In 1858 the railway joined Alexandria and Cairo; in 1869 the Suez Canal linked the Red Sea and the Mediterranean; in the same year Thomas Cook himself accompanied the first Cook's tour of Egypt. Soon there were tourist steamers on the Nile and many more visitors, and the patterns of travel greatly changed, as S.S. Hill commented in 1866: everything has been "brought within such easy reach, that they have lost the charm of strangeness."

Before the early nineteenth century travel was erratic, uncomfortable, and sometimes perilous. The Danish naval captain Frederick Norden, sent by his king to investigate possibilities in Egypt, was often advised not to go ashore lest the people molest him. Eyles Irwin (1751–1817), returning from India in 1768, was abducted and had to be ransomed by his consul. Eliza Fay (1756–1816) journeying from Cairo to Suez was delayed by battles between warring tribes in the desert in 1779. In 1806 Lord Valentia's (1770–1844) outing at the pyramids was guarded by a large contingent of infantry for fear of attack.

The impact and consequences of Napoleon's invasion of Egypt in 1798 brought both change within and interest from beyond Egypt. He brought with him 165 savants to observe and record. Vivant Denon (1747–1825) published his *Voyage dans la basse et la haute in Égypte* in 1802 and the elephant-folio volumes of the savants' researches, *La Description d'Egypt*, was published from 1809, arousing further interest. Meanwhile the Albanian Ottoman general Mehemet Ali (1769–1848) seized power and was forcing peace upon the country. Egypt became a peaceful and attractive destination. Travelers' accounts of the ancient monuments and the present beauties and discoveries encouraged others to follow.

From earliest times travelers brought back souvenirs of Egypt's past: obelisks, statuary, and mummies, papyrus, and stones covered with the unknown language of the hieroglyphs. In 1801 the British expeditionary force, having ousted Napoleon's army, conveyed the savants' collections to the British Museum, including the supposed sarcophagus of Alexander, and the trilingual Rosetta Stone, the key to the hieroglyphs. In 1823 Belzoni's exhibition on his finds in Piccadilly's Egyptian Hall brought in thousands of amazed visitors. His *Narrative* was a bestseller. At the same time, outstanding objects were purchased from Consul-General Henry Salt (1780–1827) and others and displayed in the Louvre, the Royal Museum in Turin, the Hermitage, and the British Museum. And there was so much left to collect. Amelia Edwards (1831–1892) discovered an unknown temple at Abu Simbel in 1873, and in her massively popular *A Thousand Miles up the Nile* (1877) wrote of Sakkarah: "the plateau is thickly strewn with scraps of broken pottery, limestone, marble and alabaster . . . presently someone picks up a little noseless head of the common blue-ware funereal statuettes, and immediately we all fall to work, grubbing for treasure." In the mid-1820s journeys by scholar-artist-travelers increased. Architects extended their study tours into the Islamic and ancient Egyptian worlds. Charles Barry (1795–1860) was up the Nile in 1819; John Gardner Wilkinson (1797–1875) in 1824; Joseph Bonomi (1796–1878) arrived with Robert Hay (1799–1863) in 1826. Francis Frith (fl. seventeenth century) in 1858 added photographs with text to the Nile record. In 1823 J.F. Champollion (1790–1832) turned the key that unlocked the secrets of the hieroglyphs and, although it was five years before he went to Egypt himself, others began to be able to decipher the inscriptions on the monuments and the papyrii. At about the time that Edward William Lane (1801–1876) published *Manners and Customs of the Modern Egyptians* in 1836, travelers in creasingly turned their attention to Egypt's present and their accounts took in everyday life and political and economic concerns. James Augustus St. John (1801–1875), for example, entitled his first book *Egypt and Mohammed Ali* (1834).

In the ordinary life of the people, women travelers always took an interest. The Prussian Baroness Wolfradine Menu von Minutoli (fl. eighteenth–nineteenth centuries) and English woman Anne Katharine Elwood (fl. eighteenth–nineteenth centuries) give insights both into the lives of the foreign communities in Egypt and those of the ordinary people. Lady Lucie Duff Gordon (1821–1865) who came for her health but died in Egypt, introduced readers through her *Letters from Egypt* (1865), to ordinary life around her. On the whole travelers took a tolerant and understanding view of local people, both the "Arabs" and their "Turkish" overlords, though not all travelers were as involved with them as Burckhardt, Wilkinson, and Lady Duff Gordon, for the "Franks" or Christian foreigners were separated from the local community by laws that kept them in foreigners' enclaves. The India-bound passengers on the overland route, hurrying through, the British troops going to Khartoum, and the Cook-type tourists from Europe or America, had more arrogant attitudes toward the people they met, who were, of course, mainly the donkey-boys or people trying to sell them something.

At this time too there was growing interest in the geography of the Bible lands, with travelers like E.H. Palmer (1840–1882), who walked 600 miles with a companion from Sinai to Jerusalem, Harriet Martineau (1802–1876), who traveled through Sinai after the Nile, and the American scholar Edward Robinson (fl. seventeenth century) who debated the route of the Exodus through the Sinai peninsula. The main journey through Egypt was ordained by the Nile, but a few travelers, like Sir Archibald Edmonstone (1795–1871), the Frenchman Linant de Bellefonds (1799–1883), and the mineralogist Frédéric Cailliaud (1787–1869) branched off to explore the oases of the surrounding deserts.

Most travelers followed a customary pattern. They arrived at Alexandria, spent a few days looking at the sites, complained about the disrepair, and wondered at the strangeness of the East. They took a boat up the Nile, reaching it on the Mahmoudieh Canal after 1819, stayed for a week or more in Cairo visiting "the lions," making a trip to the pyramids and Sphinx (where some stayed overnight), and preparing for their journey southward. Several wrote about the special experiences of Cairo: a wedding party, the bazaar, the celebration of the inundation, the departure of the Mecca caravan, the *psylli* or snake charmers, the dervishes, the dancing girls, the slave market, and the horrors of the insane asylum. Male travelers of quality were presented by their consul to the pasha of Egypt.

The arrangements for the Nile journey included making contract with a dragoman, who would act as interpreter, guide, and general factotum, and hiring a *dahabeeyah* (a refitted Nile boat) and the crew to man it. Women, particularly, gave very detailed pictures of the interior of these boats, while the men listed the provisions and equipment, including materials for measuring and recording, and guns for the shoot.

The Nile journey south was usually swift, taking advantage of the prevailing wind, as the Italian janissary, Giovanni Finati (1787–c. 1829) put it: stopping "only at those objects that were of paramount interest, or when the wind failed us" (1830), except at night. Travelers went as far as Aswan and the first cataract; a few turned back there. Most went on into Nubia to Abu Simbel and Wady Halfa, and a very few, like George Waddington (1793–1869) and Barnard Hanbury (1793–1833) in 1820, went farther south. Some hardy souls (like Harriet Martineau), stayed onboard while their boat went through the terrors of the cataract, and gained a very healthy respect for the skills of the sailors. In Nubia they visited temple after temple along the river, all of which are now situated above the waters of Lake Nasser or merged into other lands; important records of history no longer in place. Even after Belzoni, Irby and Mangles, and others entered the great temple at Abu Simbel in 1817, it constantly filled with sand, and travelers paid local men to clear it while they continued up to the second cataract at Abu Sir, where convention led even such people as Harriet Martineau to carve her name. The sailors then shipped the sails, took the oars and, with the stream, went north again, stopping at Abu Simbel and at the dream island of Philae, of which Richard Madden wrote in 1826: "There are four recollections of a traveller, which might tempt him to live forever: the sea view of Constantinople, the sight of the Coliseum by moonlight, the prospect from the summit of Vesuvius at dawn, and the first glimpse of Philae at sunset."

Leaving Nubia they sailed north, stopping at major sites and often spending a much longer period at Luxor on both banks of the river, studying the two great temples on the east bank and the complexity of tombs and temples on the west. Several of the men lived here for months and even years, drawing and collecting.

Up to the mid-nineteenth century the temples were often filled with sand, but more or less intact, and still retained a great deal of their original colors, as the paintings of David Roberts (1796–1864) show. To satisfy Mehemet Ali's desire to build factories, barracks for his large army, and palaces for his governors, many monuments were used as quarries; in a few, European collectors took away not only the parts already separated but also sawed off sections to carry home. The local people, eager to satisfy the demand for antiquities, removed more and sold them to the travelers. Thus the travelers' descriptions of the buildings as they saw them provide an irreplaceable record. Their pictures carried the excitement of Egypt to Europe, so Amelia Edwards could look at the painted tombs at Gournu near the Valley of the Kings in 1873 and remember how, when she was a child, Gardner Wilkinson's *The Manners and Customs of the Ancient Egyptians* had shared her affections with *The Arabian Nights*: "I had read every line of the old six-volume edition over and over again. I knew every one of the six hundred illustrations by heart. Now I suddenly found myself in the midst of old and half-forgotten friends. Every subject on those wonderful walls was already familiar to me."

DEBORAH MANLEY

## References and Further Reading

Abu Talib Khan, *Travels of Mirza Abu Taleb Khan in Asia, Africa, and Europe, during the Years 1799, 1800, 1801, 1802 and 1803*, translated and edited by Charles Stewart, 1810.

Ampère, J.J.A., *Voyage en Egypte et en Nubie*, 1868.

Annesley, George, *Voyages and Travels to India, Ceylon, the Red Sea, Abyssinia, and Egypt in the Years 1802, 1803, 1804, 1805 and to 1806*, 3 vols., 1809.

Arundale, Francis, *Illustrations of Jerusalem and Mount Sinai: Including the Most Interesting Sites between Grand Cairo and Beirout*, 1837.

Athanasi, Giovanni d', *A Brief Account of the Researches and Discoveries in Upper Egypt Made under the Direction of Henry Salt Esq.*, 1836.

Aveling, T.W., *Voices of Many Waters; or, Travels in the Lands of the Tiber, Jordan and the Nile*, 1855.

Baltimore, Frederick, *A Tour to the East, in the Years 1763 and 1764*, 1787.

Barsky, Vasily Grigorovich, *Pilgrimage to the Holy Places in the East from 1727 to 1747*, 1778.

Barth, Heinrich, *Wanderungen durch die Kustenlander, des Mittelmeers, Ausgefahrtin der Jahre 1845, 1846 und 1847*, 1849.

Barth, Heinrich, *Travels and Discoveries in North and Central Africa*, 5 vols., 1857–1858.

Bartlett, S.C., *From Egypt to Palestine, through Sinai, the Wilderness, and the South Country, Observations of a Journey Made with Special Reference to the History of the Israelites*, 1879.

Bartlett, W.H., *Forty Days in the Desert, on the track of the Israelites; or, a Journey from Cairo, by Wady Feiran, to Mount Sinai and to Petra*, 1848.

Bartlett, W.H., *Scripture Sites and Scenes: From Actual Survey, in Egypt, Arabia and Palestine*, 1849.

Bartlett, W.H., *The Nile Boat; or, Glimpses of the Land of Egypt*, 1850.

Beamont, William, *A Diary of a Journey to the East, In the Autumn of 1854*, 1856.

Beamont, William, *Cairo to Sinai and Sinai to Cairo: Being an Account of a Journey in the Desert of Arabia, November and December 1860*, 1861.

Beaton, Cecil, *Near East*, 1943.

Beaufort, Emily A., *Egyptian Sepulchres and Syrian Shrines*, 2 vols., 1861.

Belzoni, Giovanni Battista, *Narrative of the Operations and Recent Discoveries within the Pyramids, Temples, Tombs, and Excavations, in Egypt and Nubia*, 1821.

Belzoni, Giovanni Battista, *Plates Illustrative of the Researches and Operations of Belzoni in Egypt*, 1820.

Belzoni, Sarah, "Short Account of the Women of Egypt, Nubia, and Syria," in Belzoni's *Narrative*, 1821.

Bevan, Samuel, *Sand and Canvas: A Narrative of Adventures in Egypt*, 1849.

Bibescu, Martha, *Egyptian Day*, translated by Helen Everitt and Raymond Everitt, 1930.

Biddulph, William, *The Travels of Certaine Englishmen . . . into Africa, Asia, Troy, Bythinia, Thracia, and to the Blacke Sea*, edited by Theophilus Lavender, 1609; facsimile, 1968.

Blount, Henry, *A Voyage into the Levant*, 1636.

Bramsen, John, *Travels in Egypt, Syria, Cyprus, the Morea, Greece, Italy, etc.*, 1820.

Breasted, James Henry, *Egypt through the Stereoscope: A Journey through the Land of the Pharoahs*, 1905.

Bremer, Fredrika, *Travels in the Holy Land*, 2 vols., translated by Mary Howitt, 1862.

Breydenbach, Bernhard von, *Peregrinatio in terram sanctum* [Pilgrimage to Jerusalem], 1486; German edition, 1486.

Briggs, Martin, *Through Egypt in Wartime*, 1918.

Bromfield, William Arnold, *Letters from Egypt and Syria*, 1856.

Browne, W.G., *Travels in Africa, Egypt and Syria from the year 1792 to 1798*, 1799.

Bruce, James, *Travels to Discover the Source of the Nile, in the years 1768–1773, Containing a Journey through Egypt*, vol. 1 of 5 vols., 1790.

Buckingham, James Silk, *Autobiography of James Silk Buckingham: Including his Voyages, Travels, Adventures, Speculations, Successes and Failures*, 2 vols., 1855.

Burckhardt, John Lewis, *Travels in Nubia and the Interior of North-eastern African performed in 1813 to Which Arte Prefixed Life and Memoir of the Author*, 1819.

Burton, Nathanael, *A Narrative of a Voyage from Liverpool to Alexandria*, 1838.

Burton, Richard, *Personal Narrative of a Pilgrimage to Al-Madinah and Meccah*, vol. 1 of 3, 1856.

Cailliaud, Frédéric, *Travels in the Oasis of Thebes, and in the Deserts situated East and West of the Thebaid*, 1822–1824.

Cailliaud, Frédéric, *Voyage à Méroé, au fleuve blanc, au delà de Făzoql dans le midi di sennâr á Syouah et dans cinq autres oases*, 1826–1827

Camp, Maxime du, *Le Nil, ou Lettres de l'Égypte et la Nubie*, 1852.

Capper, James, *Observations on the Passage to India, through Egypt*, 1783.

Carey, M.L.M., *Four Months in a Dahabeéh, or, Narrative of a Winter's Cruise on the Nile*, 1863.

Carne, John, *Letters from the East; Written during a Recent Tour through Turkey, Egypt, Arabia, the Holy Land, Syria and Greece*, 1826.

Carne, John, *Recollections of Travels in the East Forming a Continuation of Letters from the East*, 1830.

Champollion, J.F., *Lettres écrits d'Égypte et de Nubie, en 1828 et 1829* [Letters from Egypt and Nubia 1828–1829], 1833.

Charmes, Gabriel, *Five Months at Cairo and in Lower Egypt*, translated by William Conn, 1883.

Chateaubriand, François René de, vicomte de, *Travels in Greece, Palestine, Egypt and Barbary, during the Years 1806 and 1807*, translated by Frederic Shoberl, 1811.

Chubb, Mary, *Nefertiti Lived Here*, 1954.

Churchill, Awnsham, *A Collection of Voyages and Travels*, 4 vols., 1703–1704.

Clarke, Edward Daniel, *Travels in Various Countries of Europe, Asia and Africa*, 6 vols., 1810–1823.

Clayton, Robert, *A Journal from Grand Cairo to Mount Sinai and Back Again*, 1753.

Cocteau, Jean, *Maalesh: A Theatrical Tour of the Middle East*, translated by Mary C. Hoeck, 1956.

Conder, Josiah, *The Modern Traveller: Egypt*, 1824.

Cooper, Edward J., *Views in Egypt and Nubia: From a Collection of Drawings Taken on the Banks of the Nile by S. Bossi*, 1824–27.

Coward, Noel, *Middle East Diary*, 1944.

Cumming, C.F. Gordon, *Via Cornwall to Egypt*, 1885.

Curtis, George William, *Nile Notes of a Howadji, or the American in Egypt*, 1851.

Curzon, Robert, *Visits to Monasteries in the Levant*, 1849; 3rd edition, 1850.

Dalton, Richard, *Views and Engravings in Greece and Egypt 1790–91.*

Damer, G.L. Dawson, *Diary of a Tour in Greece, Turkey, Egypt and the Holy Land*, 2 vols., 1841.

Denon, Vivant, *Voyage dans la Basse et la Haute Egypte pendant les campagnes du général Bonaparte*, 2 vols., 1802, edited by Hélène Guichard, Adrien Goetz and Martine Reid, 1998; as *Travels in Upper and Lower Egypt*, translated by Francis Blagdon, 2 vols., 1802; translated by Arthur Aikin, 3 vols., 1803.

Disraeli, Benjamin, *Home Letters*, 1885.

Dorr, Benjamin, *Notes of Travel in Egypt, the Holy Land, Turkey and Greece*, 1856.

Duff Gordon, Lucie, *Letters from Egypt, 1863–65*, 1865; and *Last Letters from Egypt*, 1875.

Dumas, Alexandre, *Impressions of Travel, in Egypt and Arabia Petraea*, 1839.

Du Mont, Baron John, *Voyages en France, en Italie, en Allemagne, á Malthe et en Turquie*, 1699.
Durrell, Lawrence, *Spirit of Place: Letters and Essays Essays on Travel*, edited by Alan G. Thomas, 1969.
Eden, Frederic, *The Nile without a Dragoman*, 1871.
Edmonstone, Archibald, *A Journey to Two of the Oases of Upper Egypt*, 1822.
Edwards, Amelia, *A Thousand Miles up the Nile*, 1877.
Edwards, Matilda Bethune, *Holiday Letters from Athens, Egypt and Weimar*, 1873.
Egeria (or Etheria), *The Pilgrimage of St. Silvia of Aquitania to the Holy Places* (c. 385 AD), translated by J.H. Barnard, 1896.
Egeria, *Egeria's Travels*, translated by John Wilkinson, 1971.
Elwood, Anne Katharine Curteis, *Narrative of a Journey Overland from England, by the Continent of Europe, Egypt, and the Red Sea, Including a Residence There, and Voyage Home, in the Years 1825–28*, 1830.
Enemannius, Michael, *Resa i Orienten, 1711–12*, 1889.
English, George Bethune, *A Narrative of the Expedition to Dongola and Sennaar under the Command of His Excellency Ismael Pasha*, 1822.
Fabri, Felix, *Felix Fabri (c. 1480–1483 AD)* [Wanderings in the Holy Land], translated by Aubrey Stewart, 2 vols., 1892–1893.
Fairholt, Frederick, *Up the Nile and Home Again: A Handbook for Travellers and a Travel-book for the Library*, 1862.
Falkland, Amelia Cary, Viscountess, *Chow-Chow: Being Selections from a Journal Kept in India, Egypt and Syria*, 1857.
Fay, Eliza, *Original Letters from India (1779–1815)*, edited by E.M. Forster, 1925; with an introduction by M.M. Kaye, 1986.
Field, Henry M., *From Egypt to Japan*, 1877.
Field, Henry M., *On the Desert: With a Brief History of Recent Events in Egypt*, 1883.
Finati, Giovanni, *Narrative of the Life and Adventures of Giovanni Finati*, edited by William J. Bankes, 1830.
Fitzclarence, G.A., [George Augustus Munster], *Journal of a Route across India, through Egypt, to England, in the Latter End of the Year 1817, and the Beginning of 1818*, 1819.
Fitzmaurice, William Edward, *A Cruise to Egypt, Palestine and Greece*, 1834.
Flaubert, Gustave, *Flaubert in Egypt: A Sensibility on Tour*, edited and translated from the French by Francis Steegmuller, 1972; reprinted, 1996.
Forbin, Louis N.P.A., Comte de, *Travels in Egypt in 1817–18, Being a Continuation of the Travels in the Holy Land*, 1819.
Frith, Francis, *Egypt and Palestine Photographed and Described*, 1858–1860.
Frith, Francis, *Egypt, Sinai and Palestine, Photographed and Described*, c. 1862.
Frith, Francis, and Joseph Bonomi, *Egypt, Nubia and Ethiopia Illustrated by One Hundred Stereoscopic Photographs*, 1862.
Fuller, John, *Narrative of a Tour through Some Parts of the Turkish Empire*, 1830.
Gadsby, John, *My Wanderings: Being Travels in the East*, 2 vols., 1855.
Gleichen, Edward, *With the Camel Corps up the Nile*, 1888.
Gleichen, Edward, *Report on the Nile and Country between Dongola, Suakin, Kassala and Omdurman*, 2nd edition, 1898.
Golding, William, *An Egyptian Journal*, 1985.
Grey, Catharine Thérèse, *Journal of a Visit to Egypt, Constantinople, the Crimea, Greece etc. in the Suite of the Prince and Princess of Wales*, 1869.
Hahn-Hahn, Ida, *Letters of a German Countess: Written during Her Tour in Turkey, Egypt, the Holy Land, Syria, Nubia, etc. in 1843–44*, 3 vols., 1849.
Haight, Sarah, *Letters from the Old World, by a Lady of New-York*, 1840.
Hakluyt, Richard, "Voyage to the Cities of Alexandria and Cairo, 1585," in *The Principal Navigations, Voyages, Traffiques and Discoveries of the English Nation*, vol. 2, 1598.
Hakluyt, Richard, *Hakluyt's Collections of the Early Voyages, Travels and Discoveries of the English Nation*, 1809–1812.
Halls, J.J., *Life and Correspondence of Henry Salt*, 1834.
Hamilton, William Richard, *Remarks on Several Parts of Turkey*, Part 1: *Aegyptica or Some Account of the Ancient and Modern State of Egypt Obtained in the Years 1801–02*, 1809.
Hasselquist, Frederick, *Voyages and Travels in the Levant in the years 1749–52*, 1766.
Hay, Helen Selina, Countess of Gifford, *Lispings from Low Latitudes, or Extracts from the Journal of the Hon. Impulsia Gushington*, 1863.
Head, C.F., *Eastern and Egyptian Scenery, Ruins, etc.*, 1833.
Henniker, Frederick, *Notes during a Visit to Egypt, Nubia, the Oasis, Mount Sinai and Jerusalem*, 1823.
Heuglin, Theodor von, *Reise in das Gebiet des weissen Nil und seiner westlichen Zuflusse in den Jahren 1862–64*, 1869.
Hill, S.S., *Travels in Egypt and Syria*, 1866.
Hogg, Edward, *Visit to Alexandria, Damascus and Jerusalem, during the Successful Campaign of Ibrahim Pasha*, 1835.
Holthaus, P.D., *Wanderings of a Journeyman Tailor, during the Years 1824 to 1840*, translated by William Howitt, 1842.
Hopley, Howard, *Under Egyptian Palms, or, Three Bachelors, Journeyings on the Nile*, 1869.
Hornby, Emily, *A Nile Journal*, 1906.
Hornby, Emily, *Sinai and Petra: The Journals of Emily Hornby in 1899 and 1901*, 1907.
Hornemann, Friedrich, *The Journal of Frederick Hornemannis Travels, from Cairo to Mourzouk, the Capital of the Kingdom of Fezzan, in Africa*, 1802.
Hoskins, G.A., *Travels in Ethiopia, above the Second Cataract of the Nile*, 1835.
Hoskins, G.A., *Visit to the Great Oasis of the Libyan Desert*, 1837.
Hoskins, G.A., *Winter in Upper and Lower Egypt*, 1863.
Huxley, Julian, *From an Antique Land*, 1954.
Irby, Charles Leonard, and James Mangles, *Travels in Egypt and Nubia, Syria and Asia Minor*, 1823.
Irwin, Eyles, *A Series of Adventures in the Course of a Voyage up the Red-Sea, on the Coasts of Arabia and Egypt*, 1780.
Jarvie, William, *Letters Home from Egypt and Palestine, 1903–04*, 1904.
Joliffe, T.R., *Letters from Palestine, Descriptive of a Tour through Galilee and Judaea to Which Are Added Letters from Egypt*, 2nd edition, 1820.
Kelly, R. Talbot, *Egypt: Painted and Described*, 1902.
Kennedy, Douglas, *Beyond the Pyramids: Travels in Egypt*, 1996.
King, Annie, *Dr. Liddon's Tour in Egypt and Palestine in 1886*, 1891.
Kinglake, Alexander, *Eothen; or, Traces of Travel brought Home from the East*, 1844.
Kingsford, W.E., *Assouan as a Health Resort*, 1899.
Koning, Hans, *A New Yorker in Egypt*, 1976.
Kusel, Baron Samuel Selig de, *An Englishman's Recollections of Egypt, 1863 to 1887*, 1915.
Laborde, Léon de, *Journey through Arabia Petrea to Mount Sinai, and the Excavated City of Petra, with Linant de Bellefonds*, 1836.

Lamartine, Alphonse de, *Souvenirs, impressions, pensées et paysages pendant un voyage en Orient, 1832–1833*, 1935; as *Travels in the East*, 1839.
Lane, Edward, *An Account of the Manners and Customs of the Modern Egyptians*, 1836.
Lane, Edward, *Description of Egypt*, edited by Jason Thompson, 2000.
Lear, Edward, *Selected Letters*, edited by Vivien Noakes, 1988.
Legh, Thomas, *Narrative of a Journey in Egypt and the Country behind the Cataracts*, 1816.
Leland, Charles G., *The Egyptian Sketch Book*, 1874.
Leo, John, *Geographical Historie of Africa Written in Arabic and Italian*, translated by John Pory, 1600.
Lepsius, Richard, *Discoveries in Egypt, Ethiopia, and the Peninsula of Sinai*, edited by Kenneth R.H. Mackenzie, 1852.
Lepsius, Richard, *Letters from Egypt, Ethiopia and the Peninsula of Sinai*, translated by Leonora and Joanna B. Horner, 1853.
L'Hôte, Nestor, *Lettres écrites d'Égypte en 1838 et 1839*, and *Lettres d'Égypte 1840–41*, 1840 and 1841.
Light, Henry, *Travels in Egypt, Nubia, Holy Land, Mount Lebanon and Cyprus, in the Year 1814*, 1818.
Linant de Bellefonds, L.M.A., *Journey of Navigation of the Bahr-el-Ablad or the White Nile*, 1828.
Linant de Bellefonds, *Account of a Journey into the Oases of Upper Egypt, 1822*, 1829.
Lindsay, Lord Alexander, later Earl of Crawford, *Letters from on Egypt, Edom, and the Holy Land*, 2 vols., 1838.
Lithgow, William, *The Totall Discourse of the Rare Adventures and Painfull Peregrinations of Long Nineteen Years Travayles from Scotland to the Most Famous Kingdomes in Europe, Asia and Affrica*, 1614 (part), 1632 (fully).
Lobo, Jerónimo, *A Short Relation of the River Nile, of its Source and Current, of its Overflowing the Campagnia of Egypt till it Runs into the Mediterranean: and on other Curiosities, Written by an Eye Witness*, 1669.
Loftie, W.J., *A Ride in Egypt from Sioot to Luxor, with Notes on the Present State and Ancient History of the Nile Valley, and Some Account of the Various Ways of Making the Voyage out and Home*, 1879.
Lorimer, Norma, *By the Waters of Egypt*, 1909.
Loti, Pierre, *Egypt*, 1909.
Lott, Emmeline, *The Grand Pacha's Cruise on the Nile in the Viceroy of Egypt's Yacht*, 1869.
Lucas, Paul, *Troisièene Voyage du siure Paul Lucas: Dans le Turquie, l'Asie, la Sourie la Palestine, la Haute et a Basse Égypte*, 3 vols., 1719.
Lushington, Mrs. Charles (Sarah), *Narrative of a Journey from Calcutta to Europe, by Way of Egypt, in the Years 1827–28*, 1829.
Lynch, Jeremiah, *Egyptian Sketches*, 1890.
Macgregor, John, *The Rob Roy on the Jordan, Nile, Red Sea, and Gennesareth*, 1870.
Madden, R.R., *Travels in Turkey, Egypt, Nubia and Palestine in 1824, 1825, 1826 and 1827*, 1830.
Madden, R.R., *Egypt and Mohammed Ali: Illustrative of the Condition of His Slaves and Subjects*, 1841.
Madox, John, *Excursions in the Holy Land, Egypt, Nubia, Syria, etc.*, 2 vols., 1834.
Mannin, Ethel, *Aspects of Egypt: Some Travels in the United Arab Republic*, 1964.
Manning, Samuel, *The Land of the Pharoahs: Egypt and Sinai: Illustrated by Pen and Pencil*, 1875.
Marcellus, Comte de, *Souvenirs de l'Orient*, 1839.
Marmont, A.F.L., Duc de Raguse, *Voyage du maréchal duc de Raguses en Hungrie: . . . eter Égypte*, 3 vols., 1837.
Martineau, Harriet, *Eastern Life: Past and Present*, 1848.
Maspero, Gaston, *Egypt: Ancient Sites and Modern Scenes*, 1910.
Melly, George, *Khartoum and the Blue and White Niles*, 1851.
Menu von Minutoli, Wolfradine, *Recollections of Egypt 1820–21*, 1827.
Merrick, E.M., *With a Palette in Eastern Palaces*, 1899.
Meyer, Luigi, *Views in Egypt . . . with Historical Observations . . . of the Customs of the People*, 1804.
Millard, David, *A Journal of Travels in Egypt, Arabia Petraea, and the Holy Land during 1841–42*, 1843.
Monconys, Balthasar de, *Voyage en Égypte de Balthasar de Monconys 1646–47*, edited by Henry Amer, 1973.
Montagu, John, 4th Earl of Sandwich, *A Voyage Performed by the Late Earl of Sandwich Round the Mediterranean in the Years 1738–39*, edited by J. Cooke, 1799.
Montefiore, Judith, *Private Journal of a Visit to Egypt and Palestine by Way of Italy and the Mediterranean*, 1838.
Montefiore, Moses, *Diaries of Sir Moses and Lady Judith Montefiore*, edited by L. Loewe, 1890.
Montulé, Édouard, *Travels in Egypt during 1818 and 1819*, 1821.
Morier, J.P., *Memoir of a Campaign with the Ottoman Army in Egypt*, 1801.
Nightingale, Florence, *Letters from Egypt: A Journey on the Nile*, edited Anthony Sattin, 1987, from *Letters from Egypt*, 1834, privately circulated.
Norden, Frederick, *A Compendium of the Most Approved Modern Travels*, vol. 4, *The Travels of F.L. Norden through Egypt and Nubia*, 1757.
North, Marianne, *Recollections of a Happy Life*, 1892.
Olin, Stephen, *Travels in Egypt, Arabia Petrea and the Holy Land*, 1843.
Palmer, E.H., *The Desert of the Exodus*, 1871.
Parsons, Abraham, *Travels in Asia and Africa*, 1808.
Petherick, John, *Egypt, the Soudan and Central Africa*, 1861.
Petrie, W.F., *Ten Years Digging in Egypt (1881–91)*, 1892.
Petrie, W.F., *Seventy Years in Archaeology*, 1931.
Petrie, W.M., *A Season in Egypt*, 1887.
Pfeiffer, Ida, *Visit to the Holy Land, Egypt, and Italy*, 1852.
Pinkerton, John, *A General Collection of the Best and Most Interesting Voyages and Travels in All Parts of the World*, 17 vols., 1808–1814.
Pococke, Richard, *A Description of the East, and Some Other Countries*, 1743–1745.
Prime, William C., *Boat Life in Egypt and Nubia*, 1868.
Pryce-Jones, Alan, *The Spring Journey*, 1931.
Pückler-Muskau, Prince Hermann von, *Egypt under Mehemet Ali*, translated by H. Evans Lloyd, 2 vols., 1845.
Pye-Smith, Charlie, *The Other Nile: Journeys in Egypt, the Sudan and Ethiopia*, 1986.
Queiroz, José Eça de, *O Egipto: A notas de viágem* [A Portuguese Naturalist in Egypt], 1926.
Quibell, Annie, *A Wayfarer in Egypt*, 1925.
Rawnsley, Hardwick D., *Notes for the Nile*, 1892.
Rhind, A. Henry, *Egypt: Its Climate, Character, and Resources as a Winter Resort*, 1856.
Rhind, A. Henry, *Thebes, its Tombs and their Tenants, Ancient and Present, including a Record of Excavations in the Necropolis*, 1862.
Richardson, R.R., *Travels along the Mediterranean and Parts Adjacent, in Company with the Earl of Belmore during the Years, 1816–18, Extending as Far as the Second Cataract of the Nile, Jerusalem, Damascus, Balbec, etc.*, 2 vols., 1822.

Rifaud, J.J., *Voyage en Égypte, en Nubie et lieux circonvoisins, depuis 1805 jusqu'en 1927*, 1829.

Rifaud, J.J., *Notice analytique des voyages de M. Rifaud en diverse contrees et particuliarement Égypte*, n.d.

Roberts, David, *The Holy Land: Syria, Idumea, Arabia, Egypt and Nubia*, with text by George Croly, 1842–1849.

Roberts, David, *Egypt and Nubia, from Drawings Made on the Spot, by David Roberts, with Historical Descriptions by William Brockedon*, vol. 3, 1846–1849.

Roberts, Emma, *Notes of an Overland Journey through France and Egypt to Bombay*, 1841.

Robinson, Edward, and Eli Smith, *Biblical Researches in Palestine, Mount Sinai, Arabia Petrea, and Egypt: A Journal of Travels in the Year 1838*, 3 vols., 1841.

Robinson, George, *Three Years in the East, Being the Substance of a Journal Written during a Tour and Residence in Greece, Egypt, Palestine, Syria, and Turkey in 1829–1830*, 2 vols., 1831–1832.

Romer, Isabella, *A Pilgrimage to the Temples and Tombs of Egypt, Nubia and Palestine*, 2 vols., 1846.

Rose, George (writing as Arthur Sketchley), *Mrs. Brown up the Nile*, 1869.

Ruppell, Eduard, *Reisen in Nubia, Kordofan, unddem Peträischei Arabien*, 1829.

Russell, Michael, *View of Ancient and Modern Egypt, with an Outline of its Natural History*, 1831.

Russell, William Howard, *A Diary in the East during the Tour of the Prince and Princess of Wales*, 1869.

St. John, Bayle, *Adventures in the Libyan Desert and the Oasis of Jupiter Ammon*, 1849.

St. John, Bayle, *Village Life in Egypt; with Sketches of the Saïd*, 1852.

St. John, James Augustus, *Lives of Celebrated Travellers*, 1831.

St. John, James Augustus, *Egypt and Mohammed Ali; or, Travels in the Valley of the Nile*, 1834.

St. John, James Augustus, *Egypt and Nubia: Their Scenery and Their People*, 1845.

Salt, Henry, *Egypt: A Descriptive Poem*, 1824.

Sandys, George, *A Relation of a Journey Begun* A.D. *1610: Foure Bookes containing a Prescription of The Turkish Empire, of Aegypt Egypt, of the Holy Land, etc.*, 4 vols., 1615.

Saulnier, M., *A Journey in Egypt by M. Lelorrain, and Observations on the Circular Zodiac of Denderah*, 1819–1823.

Savary, Claude (called Nicolas), *Letters on Egypt, with a Parallel between the Manners of Its Ancient and Modern Inhabitants*, 2 vols., 1786.

Savigny de Moncorps, Vicomte, *Journal d'un Voyage en Orient, 1869–70, Égypte, Syria et Constantinople*, 1873.

Seetzen, Ulrich Jasper, *Ulrich Jasper Seezen's Reisen durch Syrien, Palästina, Phlönicien, die Transjordan-länder, Arabia Petraea und Unter-Aegypten*, 4 vols., 1854–1859.

Senior, Nassau William, *Conversations and Journals in Egypt and Malta*, 2 vols., 1882.

Shaw, Thomas, *Travels; or, Observations Relating to Several Parts of Barbary and the Levant*, 1738.

Sherer, Moyle, *Scenes and Impressions in Egypt and in Italy*, 1824.

Sitwell, Constance, *Lotus and Pyramid*, 1928.

Sitwell, Constance, *Bright Morning*, 1942.

Skinner, Thomas, *Adventures during a Journey Overland to India, by Way of Egypt, Syria, and the Holy Land*, 2 vols., 1837.

Sladen, Douglas, *Egypt and the English*, 1908.

Sladen, Douglas, *Queer Things about Egypt*, 1910.

Smith, Agnes (Mrs. Lewis), *Eastern Pilgrims: The Travels of Three Ladies*, 1870.

Smith, Alfred Charles, *Attractions of the Nile and its Banks: A Journal of Travels in Egypt and Nubia Showing Their Attractions to the Archaeologist, the Naturalist and the General Tourist*, 2 vols., 1868.

Smith, Jeromean Crowninshield, *A Pilgrimage to Egypt, Embracing a Diary of Explorations on the Nile; with Observations Illustrative of the Manners, Customs and Institutions of the People, and of the Present Condition of the Antiquities and Ruins*, 1852.

Smyth, C. Piazzi, *Life and Work at the Great Pyramid during the Months of January, February, March and April,* A.D. *1865*, 3 vols., 1867.

Sonnini, C.S., *Travels in Upper and Lower Egypt*, translated by Henry Hunter, 1799.

Sopwith, Thomas, *Notes of a Visit to Egypt, by Paris, Lyons, Nismes, Marseilles and Toulon*, 1857.

Sowden, William, *Another Australian Abroad: Travel Notes in Egypt and Palestine, 1924–25*, 1925.

Stanhope, Hester Lucy, *Memoirs of the Lady Hester Stanhope as Related by Herself in Conversations with Her Physician*, 3 vols., 1845.

Stanley, Arthur Penrhyn, *Sinai and Palestine, in Connection with Their History*, 1856.

Stark, Freya, *East is West*, 1945.

Stark, Freya, *Dust in the Lion's Paw: Autobiography, 1939–1946*, 1961.

Steevens, G.W., *With Kitchener to Khartum*, 1898.

Steevens, G.W., *Egypt in 1898*, 1898.

Stephens, J.L., *Incidents of Travel in Egypt, Arabia Petrea, and the Holy Land, by an American*, 1837.

Stephens, J.L., *Incidents of Travel in Egypt, Arabia, Patrae, and the Holy Land*, 1837; chapters 1–12 revised as *Notes of Travel in Egypt and Nubia, Revised and Enlarged, with an Account of the Suez Canal*, 1876.

Stuart, Villiers, *Nile Gleanings: Concerning the Ethnology, History and Art of Ancient Egypt as revealed by Egyptian Paintings and Bas-Reliefs*, 1879.

Sumner, Mrs. George (Mary Elizabeth), *Our Holiday in the East*, 1881.

Tafur, Pero, *Travels and Adventures 1435–39*, translated by Malcolm Letts, 1926.

Taylor, Bayard, *Life and Landscapes from Egypt to the Negro Kingdoms of the White Nile*, 1854.

Taylor, Bayard, *Egypt and Iceland in the Year 1874*, 1874.

Thackeray, William Makepeace (writing as Mr. M.A. Titmarsh), *Notes of a Journey from Cornhill to Grand Cairo*, 1846.

Thévenot, M., *Recueil de Voyages de M. Thevenot*, 5 vols., 1681.

Thompson, Charles, *Travels through Turkey in Europe Asia, the Holy Land, Arabia, Egypt, and Other Parts of the World, Giving an Account of Manners, Religion, Polity, Antiquities and Natural History*, 1767.

Tilt, Charles, *The Boat and the Caravan: A Family Tour through Egypt and Syria*, 1847.

Tinne, Alexine, *Travels in the Region of the White Nile*, 1869.

Traill, H.D., *From Cairo to the Soudan Frontier*, 1896.

Trevisan, Domenico, *Le Voyage d'Outre-Mer de Jean Thenaud, suivi de la Relation de l'Ambassade de Domenico Trevisan amprès du Soudan d'Égypte 1512*, 1884.

Turner, William, *Journals of a Tour of the Levant*, 3 vols., 1820.

Twain, Mark (Samuel Clemens), *The Innocents Abroad; or, the New Pilgrims' Progress*, 1870.

Tyndale, Walter, *Below the Cataracts*, 1907.

Tyndale, Walter, *An Artist in Egypt*, 1912.

Varthema, Ludovico de, *Itinerario de Ludovico de Varthema Bolognese nello Egypto, nella Suria, nella Arabia deserta & felice, nella Persia, nella India & nella Ethiopia. La fede, el vivere & costumi de tutte le prefate provincie*, 1510; as *The Travels of Ludovico di Varthema*, translated by J. Winter Jones, edited by G.P. Badger, 1863.
Volney, Constantin-François, *Travels through Egypt and Syria in the Years 1783–85*, 2 vols., 1787.
Vyse, Howard, *Operations Carried out at the Pyramids of Gizeh in 1837; with an Account of a Voyage in Upper Egypt*, 3 vols., 1840.
Waddington, George and Barnard Hanbury, *Journal of a Visit to Some Parts of Ethiopia*, 1822.
Waghorn, Thomas, *Particulars of an Overland Journey from London to Bombay by Way of the Continent, Egypt, and the Red Sea*, 1831.
Waghorn, Thomas, *Egypt as It Is in 1837*, 1837.
Walpole, Robert, *Memoirs Relating to European and Aisiatic Turkey*, 1817.
Walsh, Thomas, *Journal of the Late Campaign in Egypt: Including Descriptions of That Country*, 1803.
Warburton, Eliot, *The Crescent and the Cross, or Romance and Realities of Eastern Travel*, 1845.
Webbe, Edward, *The Rare and Most Wonderful Things Which Edward Webbe an Englishman Hath Seen and Passed in his Troublesome Travails: In the Cities of Jerusalem, Damasco, Bethlehem and Galely and in the Landes of Iewrie, Egypt, Gracia, Russia, and Prester John*, 1590.
Webster, James, *Travels through the Crimea, Turkey and Egypt, Performed during the Years 1825–28*, 2 vols., 1830.
Wellsted, James Raymond, *Travels in Arabia*, 2 vols., 1838.
Wellsted, James Raymond, *Travels to the City of the Caliphs, along the Shores of the Persian Gulf and the Mediterranean*, 1840.
Whately, Mary L., *Ragged Life in Egypt, and More about Ragged Life in Egypt*, 1870.
Whately, Mary L., *Letters from Egypt to Plain Folks at Home*, 1879.
Whately, Richard, *On The Present State of Egypt, Compiled from the Unpublished Journals of Recent Travellers*, 1858.
Wild, Johann, *Neue Reysbeschreibung eines Gefangenen Christen Anno 1604*, 1613; edited by Georg A. Narciss, 1964.
Wilde, W.R., *Narrative of a Voyage to Madeira, Teneriffe and along the Shores of the Mediterranean, Including a Visit to Algiers, Egypt, Palestine, Tyre, Rhodes, Telmessus, Cyprus and, Greece*, 1840.
Wilkinson, John Gardner, *Modern Egypt and Thebes: Being a Description of Egypt, Including the Information Required for Travellers in That Country*, 1843.
Williams, Josiah, *Life in the Soudan: Adventures amongst the Tribes, and Travels in Egypt in 1881 and 1882*, 1884.
Wilson, John, *The Lands of the Bible Visited and Described*, 1847.
Wilson, William Rae, *Travels in Europe, Egypt and the Holy Land*, 2 vols., 1823.
Wolff, Joseph, *Sketch of the Life and Journal*, 1827.
Wolff, Joseph, *Journal . . . Containing an Account of His Missionary Labours*, 1839.
Wolff, Joseph, *Travels and Adventures of the Rev. Joseph Wolff*, 2 vols., 1860–1861.
Yates, William Holt, *The Modern History and Condition of Egypt, Its Climate, Diseases, and Capabilities; Exhibited in a Personal Narrative of Travels in That Country*, 1843.
Young, Cuthbert G., *A Wayfarer's Notes on the Shores of the Levant and the Valley of the Nile*, 1848.

*See also* **Cairo**

## ENGLAND, PRE-1603

The travel literature of England before 1603 was primarily focused on travel outside the country. Beginning as epic, it moves to devotion as the major image of the journey becomes that of pilgrimage. This pilgrimage gradually becomes interior and individually allegorical, allowing for more characterization and analysis by the authors. By the end of the sixteenth century, England's travel writers were caught up in the tremendous movement of exploration and colonization that has shaped the modern world. The last narratives of this period reflect the new spirit of enquiry, commerce, and conquest characteristic of the early modern era as a whole.

English travel writing during this period must be discussed from a number of perspectives: it is fictional and nonfictional, and sometimes the lines between fiction and nonfiction are blurred; it is writing about England by those visiting or traveling within the country; and, finally, it is writing by English people venturing outside their nation's borders. Though the final category is by far the largest, most formal, and best preserved, English travel writing starts with epic fiction.

Travel narratives begin in England before the advent of writing, with the retelling of the great Germanic epics by bards connected to the courts of regional kings. In fact, the greatest extant Germanic epic, *Beowulf*, could be categorized as the first travel writing in English (Anglo-Saxon), with its account of the hero's journey to the hall of Hrothgar in search of lasting fame. The developing tales of King Arthur of England and his knights of the Round Table, given their theme of quest, influence the structure of the narratives that follow them. In both epics and romances, the landscape through which the characters travel, though sometimes identified as England, is not realistic, but an idealized presentation of magic and wonder.

The medieval movements of crusade and pilgrimage generated the largest number of nonfictional narratives, including both writings about England and writings about the Middle East. Such accounts as that of the Anglo-Saxon pilgrim Saewulf epitomize both the structure and the content of medieval travel writing. Though travel for purposes of trade and exploration did occur, records preserve remarkably few written accounts of this kind of journey. Instead, pilgrimage is seen as the characteristic form of travel throughout the Middle Ages in England, with crusade thought of as armed pilgrimage. The crusades brought about a system of indulgences that promised remission of the temporal punishment for sin upon the completion of specific acts of devotion. The practice of indulgences transformed pilgrimage into one of the premier religious and social movements of the medieval period. Traveling to shrines and venerating relics were the main acts of devotion for which indulgence was granted.

Travel as pictured in pilgrimage narratives is both purposeful and allegorical. Travelers describe the landscape in terms of its allegorical significance to their religious lives as Christian pilgrims. Crusade narratives, though ostensibly of armed pilgrimage, describe activities and landscape less idealistically. Crusade narratives tell of the often underhanded political and martial maneuverings as Islamic and Christian armies struggle to hold the sacred city of Jerusalem and the holy lands around it. Pilgrimage writings vary from formal narratives, which both informed and inspired their readers, to relatively sketchy guides and itineraries designed merely to give information. Many examples of all these kinds of writing exist in manuscript.

Ultimately, medieval pilgrimage developed into an industry comparable to modern tourism, with many hospitality services along the main pilgrimage routes and at major destinations. Although the most important destinations for Christian pilgrimage were Rome and Jerusalem, many shrines attracted pilgrims, notably Santiago de Compostela in Spain and Canterbury in England. In general, only pilgrimages to the two major destinations merited narratives, however.

By the 1300s, writers of fiction and nonfiction began to use the content and structure of pilgrimage innovatively. Margery Kempe, an illiterate middle-class woman of the fourteenth century, dictated a book, which in the opinion of literary historians, stands as the first autobiography in English; because of Margery's long and consistent journeying, both in England and abroad, one can also consider it an important travel narrative. Margery, a visionary in the female mystical tradition, chronicled in detail her life's journeys to Rome, Jerusalem, shrines in the Low Countries, and around England. Though most of these journeys are religious in nature, they ultimately concentrate on Margery Kempe as a character, one whose personal story contains much ironic humor. In the same way, Geoffrey Chaucer's masterpiece, *Canterbury Tales*, uses the device of the journey to tie together disparate tales and characterize the tellers of those tales, individuals from many walks of medieval life.

One of the most intriguing and unusual travel narratives to come out of the late medieval period is *The Travels of Sir John Mandeville*. Purportedly written by a fourteenth-century English knight who first made a pilgrimage to Jerusalem and then continued east, the book melds the structure and information of the pilgrimage narrative with the geographical wonders of the medieval encyclopedias (compendia of the exotic wonders—plant, animal, climatic, and human—of the unexplored Eastern world). Until well into the 1600s, the book was thought to be essentially nonfictional, or at least as nonfictional as *The Travels of Marco Polo*. A number of fifteenth- and sixteenth-century explorers, including Christopher Columbus, used Mandeville's *Travels* as a source of reference during their voyages. Modern scholars, however, question the identity of the author, his English origins, and most of all, the extent of his travels. Twentieth-century critics have shown that the author of Mandeville's *Travels* cribbed extensively from a number of other travel sources, but even editors as early as Richard Hakluyt (1552(?)–1616) and Samuel Purchas (1575–1626) treated the account with either caution or cynicism.

If pilgrimage characterizes the journey in English medieval travel writing, exploration characterizes the Renaissance. Beginning in 1498, with Henry VII's support for the exploratory voyage by John Cabot to Newfoundland, England took an interest in world exploration, especially that of the New World. A number of economic, social, and intellectual factors kept England from following up on its early exploratory venture, but by the 1550s private trading companies were sponsoring voyages of trade and exploration to Russia and the Middle East, and by the 1570s and 1580s to America. The expeditions of the Muscovy Company, the Levant Company, and the Virginia Company produced a wealth of travel writing. Some of this writing is as prosaic as expedition supply lists or lists of rules for mariners, but elsewhere it lays the groundwork for both scientific description and modern personal travel narratives. In addition, these writings have an important social function, aiming to persuade future backers of expeditions as well as to inform future travelers to the same areas. They are also intimately tied to the movement of colonization by the European powers of the time.

The last two decades of the sixteenth century in England witnessed not only an abundance of travel writing, but also the first great English collection of travel and exploration narratives, Richard Hakluyt's *Principall Navigations, Voyages and Discoveries of the English Nation* (1589). Richard Hakluyt the younger, a clergyman, worked to collect, translate, and publish as much information about exploration up to that time as possible. His motives for publishing were manifold: to disseminate eyewitness accounts, to show the grandeur of the English exploratory and trading enterprise, and to stimulate further endeavors in exploration and colonization. The two editions of the *Principal Navigations* (1589 and 1598–1600) function as geographical compendia comprising not only narratives, but maps and other documents as well. These characteristics, along with their monumental size (more than three million words in the second edition), prompted Victorian critic A.J. Froude to call them "the prose epic of the English nation." The collections contain most English travel writing up to that point in history, among the longest and most important of which is Sir Walter Raleigh's *The Discovery of the Large, Rich, and Beautiful Empire of Guiana* (1596). This masterpiece of narrative prose and political maneuvring epitomizes the positive and negative attitudes and characteristics of the English Renaissance gentleman explorer: sycophancy, gullibility, optimism, greed, and determination. As English exploratory activity increased, so did the practical need for information; many foreign accounts of exploration were translated into English during this period.

During the second half of Elizabeth's reign, a new kind of English traveler emerged: the youth on what came to be called the Grand Tour. Sons of the English nobility, after completing their collegiate education, toured continental Europe with a view to schooling themselves in the culture of other countries. Then (as now) travel of this type was castigated by some authorities as an incentive to idleness and vice. Such a view of the Grand Tour can be seen in Thomas Nashe's short work of prose fiction *The Unfortunate Traveller* (1594).

Though some of the writings of chroniclers and historians during the early period contain descriptions of the English countryside, travel within the country does not seem to have merited significant narration and description by its natives. The few informal letters and descriptions penned by visitors to England concentrate mostly on matters of court and diplomacy, and seldom venture beyond descriptions of play-going and other upper-class social activities.

JAMES P. HELFERS

### References and Further Reading


Hakluyt, Richard, *The Principall Navigations, Voyages, and Discoveries of the English Nation, Made by Sea or Over Land, to the Most Remote and Farthest Corners of the Earth*, 1589; revised edition as *The Principal Navigations, Voyages, Traffiques and Discoveries of the English Nation*, 3 vols., 1598–1600; reprinted, 12 vols., 1903–1905.

Hakluyt, Richard, *Hakluyt's Voyages to the New World: A Selection*, edited by David F. Hawke, 1972.

Kemp, Margery, *The Book of Margery Kempe*, edited and with an introduction by Sanford Brown Meech, 1940.

Malory, Thomas, *The Works of Sir Thomas Malory*, edited by Eugène Vinaver, 1967.

Mandeville, John, *The Bodley Version of Mandeville's Travels*, edited by M.C. Seymour, 1967.

Nashe, Thomas, *The Unfortunate Traveller*, 1594; edited by J.B. Steane, 1972.

Raleigh, Walter, *The Discoverie of the Large, Rich, and Bewtiful Empyre of Guiana*, 1596; as *The Discoverie of the Large and Bewtiful Empyre of Guiana*, with an introduction, notes, and appendices by V.T. Harlow, 1928.

Saewulf, *Saewulf*, translated by the Lord Bishop of Clipton, 1892.

Speight, E.E. (editor), *Hakluyt's English Voyages*, 1905.

Stewart, Aubrey (translator), *Anonymous Pilgrims I–VIII*, 1894.

Taylor, E.G.R. (editor), *The Original Writings and Correspondence of the Two Richard Hakluyts*, 2 vols., 1935; reprinted, 1967.

Taylor, E.G.R. (editor), *The Troublesome Voyage of Captain Edward Fenton 1582–1583: Narratives and Documents*, 1959.

Wilkinson, John (editor and translator), *Jerusalem Pilgrims before the Crusades*, 1977.


*See also* **Scotland; Wales**

## ENGLAND, SEVENTEENTH AND EIGHTEENTH CENTURIES

*I do not think there is a people more prejudiced in its own favour than the British people . . . they look on foreigners in general with contempt, and think nothing is as well done elsewhere as in their own country.*

So spoke the Swiss visitor César de Saussure of his experiences of traveling in England at the beginning of the eighteenth century. During the seventeenth and eighteenth centuries travel in England underwent radical changes in its practical accessibility, cultural meanings, and imaginative range.

In the sixteenth and seventeenth centuries, travel was seen primarily through a biblical metaphor as a journey of life or in its more secularized form as a means to improvement, economic, or moral, or both. For example, William Camden (1551–1623) made tours of England for antiquarian research; while his *Britannia* (1586) reveals an awareness of nature, this is framed within the improving impetus of acquiring greater knowledge. At the close of the sixteenth century Thomas Nashe named his picaresque tale *The Unfortunate Traveller; or, The Life of Jacke Wilton* (1594), a title that tells us a lot about how travel in England was conceptualized at the time. During the seventeenth century travel remained an arduous ordeal, undertaken only out of necessity or for improvement. Travel by road from Newcastle to London at the beginning of the seventeenth century took nine days; communications were slow, involving numerous inconveniences and potential dangers. By the 1780s the same journey by post coach took under two days.

Travel as an ordeal, as something to be undertaken only out of necessity, underscores the journey metaphor in Bunyan's *The Pilgrim's Progress* (1678; revised edition, 1679; part 2, 1684): "As I walked through the wilderness of this world, I lighted on a certain place, where was a den [gaol]; and I dreamed a dream. I dreamed, and behold I saw a man clothed with rags, standing in a certain place, with his face from his own house, a book in his hand, and a great burden upon his back."

John Bunyan (1628–1688) is clearly seeing travel within an allegorical frame of Christian iconography, but he also introduces realistic details to describe the journey, as in the hardships of travel and the features of the Bedford landscape with which the author was familiar. The overriding impression of the journey that Christian and his fellow travelers undertake, both in its religious and secularized meanings, is that travel is a struggle and a hardship. At the close of the century even a seasoned and enthusiastic traveler such as Celia Fiennes, who traveled on horseback into every county in England between 1685 and 1703, could lose her way and have to endure difficulties as the road just disappeared back into the natural landscape (*The Journeys of Celia Fiennes*, 1947). This is a very different conception from the imaginative appeal of traveling in England voiced by Dr. Johnson in the latter half of the eighteenth century as he journeyed along the Stratford road and proclaimed, "Life has not many things better than this" except "driving briskly in a post-chaise with a pretty woman" (quoted in Porter, 1982). What changed during these two centuries was not only that the means of travel became easier, but also that the idea of travel became something signifying pleasure, fun, and leisure as well as functionality.

These changes derive from a number of obvious causes and from some that reflect wide-ranging shifts in cultural perception. Improvements in methods of transportation undoubtedly made traveling a more enjoyable experience. The building of canals alleviated the damage caused by heavy commercial vehicles churning up the roads. Turnpike roads made travel by certain routes far easier and allowed for improvements in communications generally. Improvements in coach design and the introduction of sprung upholstery also made the experience of traveling more comfortable, while the use of stronger horses to pull coaches made journeys smoother and quicker. Without these changes it would have been inconceivable for domestic tourism to have taken off in the manner that it did from the mid-eighteenth century. The term *tourist* in the domestic context first came into use in the 1780s and 1790s (Brewer, 1997), a period that also witnessed the birth of the seaside town as a tourist resort (for example, Brighton, Margate, and Scarborough).

View of Rochester in 1669, drawn by an artist in the entourage of Cosmo III and published in the English translation of the Italian manuscript (from the *Travels of Cosmo the Third, Grand Duke of Tuscany, through England, During the Reign of King Charles II*, 1821). *Courtesy of Travellers Club, London; Bridgeman Art Library, agent.*

Along with these changes came the development of a new conception of identity, place, and nation. During the Tudor and Stuart periods the centers of culture lay within the preserve of the aristocracy; this meant that travel for cultural enjoyment lay outside the bounds of all but the very few. What developed in the eighteenth century, as J.H. Plumb points out, is that travel for cultural reasons becomes more democratic, creating a new climate: "Never before had so many people seen so much of Britain" (Plumb, 1980). Country houses, ruins, and natural phenomena (especially in the late eighteenth century when the picturesque comes into vogue) quickly become tourist attractions.

An offshoot of this process was that knowledge of England through travel (which increased during the Seven Years' War and the French Revolution when travel on the Continent became more difficult for the British) fostered a new sense of national identity. At the beginning of the seventeenth century Elizabeth I called herself "mere English"; by the latter half of the eighteenth century George III, expressing similar sentiments, claimed to "glory in the name of Briton." This process of forging a national identity was undoubtedly influenced by political considerations (the Act of Union between Scotland and England dates from 1707), but it was also propelled by travel literature and a newfound sense of knowing England. Writing at the close of the century William Mavor claimed in *The British Tourists* (6 vols., 1798–1800) that tourism had made Britain British. Murray G.H. Pittock (1997) has shown how the eighteenth century was the period when British identity emerged: this process was provisional, uncertain, and forged by "alienizing" differences of regionality by a process of "othering" that fostered a new sense of definition by differences, in which London, the English southeast, and the East Midlands became the "core" of English culture and dominant national identity, a movement whose legacy under which we are still living, Pittock points out.

The rise of regionalism, travel to remote areas classed as picturesque, would appear to contradict Pittock's arguments, but as John Brewer (1997) points out, "regional and national cults of the late eighteenth and early nineteenth centuries" were rarely an attempt at cultural separatism but aimed "to imagine the British nation." Similarly, foreign travel, rather than solely denigrating home culture, feeds into a process of defining nationhood, especially from the late 1760s when Continental travel became more accessible for those other than the aristocracy. Continental commentators like Cesar de Saussure noted the xenophobic character of the British abroad: for most British travelers, experience of being abroad was an inverse opportunity to define what was British. This trend is illustrated by the titles of domestic travel literature such as Leopold Berchtold's *An Essay to Direct and Extend the Inquiries of Patriotic Travellers* (1789). Of course such valuations were riddled with political, social, religious, and xenophobic biases, but they fostered a culture of domestic tourism, aided by the experience of being a tourist abroad.

The dominance of London from the Restoration onward as a center of Englishness created a distinctive type of domestic travel literature. Exploring England, touring its length and breadth, was unconsciously or consciously underscored by an imaginative compass point: the "great wen," as Cobbett described London in *Rural Rides* (1830). Daniel Defoe's *A Tour thro' the Whole Island of Great Britain* (1724–1726) exemplifies this tendency in that however far the author travels from the metropolis, it still remains his benchmark of worth. The romantic reaction against metropolitan sophistication in the flight from the city to the country is itself an acknowledgement of the dominance of London in the cultural imagination.

London was the preeminent seat of conspicuous consumption, a center where what J.H. Plumb has termed the "commercialization of leisure" was revealed in its fullest dimensions. Indeed the concept of leisure and its concurrent notion of travel for pleasure hardly existed before the eighteenth century. Older conceptions of travel still held currency but, as the century progressed, such ideas were increasingly incorporated into or usurped by newer notions of travel for pure pleasure. William Gilpin (1724–1804), the foremost popularizer of the picturesque, claimed by the close of the eighteenth century, that "we dare not promise . . . more from picturesque travel, than a rational and agreeable amusement" (quoted in Brewer, 1997). Indeed by the late eighteenth century, tourist travel took on many of the trappings we now think of as distinctively modern, such as souvenir shops with the sale of travel memorabilia, and the rifling of monuments for mementos of the trip. Brewer draws attention to the fact that "by the 1790s tourists in the Lake District were complaining of the commercialism for which they themselves were largely responsible." The Lake poets had to travel to Scotland to experience the "authentic nature" that other tourists were flocking to the Lakes to experience, following the example of their works.

Gail Baylis

## References and Further Reading


Archenholz, Johann Wilhem von, *A Picture of England*, 1789.

Berchtold, Leopold, *An Essay to Direct and Extend the Inquiries of Patriotic Travellers*, 1789.

Brewer, John, *The Pleasures of the Imagination: English Culture in the Eighteenth Century*, London: Harper Collins, and New York: Farrar Straus, 1997

Brome, James, *Travels over England, Scotland and Wales*, 1700.

Camden, William, *Britannia*, 1586.

Cobbett, William, *Rural Rides*, 1830.

Defoe, Daniel, *A Tour thro' the Whole Island of Great Britain*, 4 vols., 1724–1726.

Fielding, Henry, *The History of the Adventures of Joseph Andrews*, 1742.

Fielding, Henry, *The History of Tom Jones, a Foundling*, 1749.

Fiennes, Celia, *The Journeys of Celia Fiennes 1685–1712*, edited by Christopher Morris, 1947.

Gilpin, William, *Observations on the River Wye and Several Parts of South Wales*, 1782.

Gilpin, William, *Observations Relative Chiefly to Picturesque Beauty. . . Particularly the Mountains and Lakes of Cumberland and Westmoreland*, 1786.

Gray, Thomas, *A Supplement to the Tour of Great Britain*, 1787.

Macky, John, *A Journey through England*, 1714.

Mavor, William Fordyce, *The British Tourists; or, Traveller's Pocket Companion*, 6 vols., 1798–1800.

Morden, Robert, *The New Description and State of England*, 1701.

Moritz, C.P., *Journeys of a German in England in 1782*, edited by Reginald Nettel, 1965.

Nashe, Thomas, *The Unfortunate Traveller*, 1594; edited by J.B. Steane, 1972.

Ogilby, John, *Britannia; or, An Illustration of the Kingdom of England*, 1675.

Pittock, Murray G.H., *Inventing and Resisting Britain: Cultural Identities in Britain and Ireland. 1685–1789*, Basingstoke: Macmillan, and New York: St. Martins Press, 1997.

Plumb, J.H. *The Commercialisation of Leisure in Eighteenth-Century England*, Reading: University of Reading, 1973.

Plumb, J.H., *Georgian Delights*, Boston: Little Brown, and London: Weidenfeld and Nicolson, 1980.

Porter, Roy, *English Society in the Eighteenth Century*, London: Allen Lane, 1982; revised edition, Harmondsworth and New York: Penguin, 1990.

Saussure, Cesar de, *A Foreign View of England in the Reigns of George I and George II*, translated and edited by Madame von Muyden, 1902.

Simond, Louis, *An American in Regency England: The Journal of a Tour in 1810–1811*, edited by Christopher Hibbert, 1968.

Smollett, Tobias, *The Adventures of Roderick Random*, 1748.

Smollett, Tobias, *The Expedition of Humphry Clinker*, 1771.

Torrington, John Byng, *The Torrington Diaries: Containing the Tours through England and Wales of the Hon. John Byng*,

edited and with an introduction by C. Bruyn Andrews, 4 vols., 1934–1938.
Voltaire, *Letters on England*, 1733; translated by Leonard Tancock, 1980.
West, Thomas, *A Guide to the Lakes*, 1778.
Young, Arthur, *A Six Month Tour through the North of England*, 1770.
Young, Arthur, *Annals of Agriculture and Other Useful Arts*, 46 vols., 1784–1815.

*See also* **Scotland; Wales**

## ENGLAND, NINETEENTH CENTURY

Travel in the nineteenth century becomes a major preoccupation in literature. Its thematic importance derives from the recognition of the significance of developments in modes of transportation (and concurrent communications) during the century, and the connotative meanings attributed to these changes as indices of the cultural health of England.

The improvements in road construction and coach design of the previous century were capitalized on by the "macadamizing" of road surfaces, which made travel more comfortable for passengers. Because roads could carry heavier goods, road systems could be linked by bridges (Thomas Telford (1757–1834) being a notable innovator in bridge building) with canal systems, which developed rapidly under the impetus of industrialization. Birmingham rivaled Venice in its mileage of canal waterways during the nineteenth century. Developments in transportation were in large measure the result of the dictates of industrial change, which they also made, through improved access, more visible to the traveler.

Early in the century William Cobbett traveled the byways of southern England on horseback. His assessment of the changes he saw in the rural economy is heavily colored by a radical political agenda. In the 1850s Anthony Trollope, another enthusiastic horseman, traveled widely in the southeast of England in his capacity as surveyor clerk for the post office with the commission of modernizing the rural postal system. He recorded these experiences in his *Autobiography* (1883, lamenting the fact that transfer to Northern Ireland disallowed him the opportunity to ride all over England) and they feed into the texture of his fiction, specifically *The Warden* (1855) and the later Barsetshire novels (1857–1867).

However, popular notions of Victorian travel derive in large measure from Charles Dickens's *Pickwick Papers* (1836–1837), a work in which the texture of "Old England" is represented by coach travel and camaraderie. Even when Dickens was writing *Pickwick Papers*, this vision of travel was largely anachronistic. The great age of coach occurred during the first three decades of the century; by the 1840s travel by train was

"Doctor Syntax Sketching the Lake": the Romantic thrill of the picturesque that motivated many early nineteenth-century travelers to search out England's most dramatic scenery was caricatured in Rowlandson's *The Tour of Doctor Syntax in Search of the Picturesque* (1812). *Courtesy of Senate House, University of London Library.*

quicker, cheaper, and more comfortable. Dickens's portrait of travel is imaginative and nostalgic; it is a recognition of the knowledge that one model of England (an imaginative sense of nation as family) was being displaced by newer, more amorphous forms of connectedness.

For the Victorians, domestic travel becames a metaphor for conceptualizing nation, serving as an experience both of assimilation and difference. The form of transportation that most significantly marked a sense of visible cultural transition is the railway. The rapid development of railway construction between 1840 and 1860 (popularly known as the age of "Railway Mania") produced great cultural as well as economic changes. In *Dombey and Son* (1848) Dickens offers a pessimistic vision of the imaginative possibilities of travel in the railway age: the train becomes the symbol of the devouring, accelerated pace of life that is eating England up; it is indicative of a homogenizing culture that denies differences. However, with the coming of the railway it became, for the first time, possible for those other than the well-to-do to live away from their place of employment; this development had significant effects on demographic shifts and urban planning (Mitchell, 1996). The introduction of the Bank Holidays Act (1871) made travel and the notion of leisure far more democratic. Thomas Cook, whose name has become synonymous with foreign travel, began his tourist business by responding to a new market for cheap excursions in England.

The coming of the railway created new conceptions of time and space: distances appeared shorter, instilling not only a sense of the smallness of England but also aggravating anxieties about speed and the pace of modern life. The railway became a symbol for both progress and degeneration, engendering responses of excitement and fear: Robert Browning was an enthusiastic rail traveler (though he wrote no poems about trains) while Matthew Arnold saw the train as a symbol of the philistine nature of the age. Significantly, George Eliot in *Middlemarch* (1871–1872) situates her rendition of middle England (based on Warwickshire and Coventry) chronologically at the juncture where its own distinctiveness is at the point of dissolution because of the coming of the railway and the Reform Bill. In doing so Eliot expresses a commonly held nineteenth-century belief that the coming of the railway marked a point of divide between past and present. At the close of the century Thomas Hardy registers a similar consciousness in his Wessex novels. In *Jude the Obscure* (1896) the railway has already deeply permeated the traditions of rural life: access to travel does not offer any alternative to the insufficiency of modern life for Jude. Nineteenth-century fiction is deeply permeated by an awareness of changes in forms of travel: the novel both reflects these changes and attempts to consolidate a sense of values in their wake.

England was a destination on the tourist map for many foreign travelers. The author of *London of To-day* (1888) was indignant about how the capital had become "a pleasure lounge for the idlers of the globe" where "Americans, Frenchmen, Germans, Indians, Colonials and persons of leisure and wealth from all parts of the world flock" (quoted in Porter, 1994). Not all tourists were impressed by the opportunities for conspicuous consumption that London afforded. Hippolyte Taine considered the experience of walking in a London fog melancholic enough to induce thoughts of suicide. Dostoevsky was appalled by the contrasts of luxury and poverty in the metropolis; he considered a nation that could allow such a capital city as being doomed to entropy. However, he argues that the social oppression and waste of human lives so visible in the London streets is preferable to the French system which, he claims, masks the same inequalities with a veneer of moral concern. Henry James (a confirmed anglophile) epitomizes the shock that the contrasts of London provoked when he describes, in a single day in 1869, the metropolis as being a place where "all history appears to live again" yet where he experienced "a sudden horror of the whole place." He registers the extreme responses and often the puzzlement that London provoked in many visitors.

Apart from James, other major nineteenth-century American writers who visited England and recorded their experiences include Mark Twain, Nathaniel Hawthorne, who was American consul at Liverpool from 1853 to 1857, and Herman Melville. Of course the gaze of the foreign traveler was no more neutral than that of English commentators: Twain, for example, came to England with an agenda of assessing what he saw there in terms of its contrast to his notion of democratic American values, overwhelmingly to the detriment of the former. However, the cultural distance of travelers to England did allow them to register the shock of its inherent contradictions. This was also a preoccupation of indigenous writers, but their immersion in a culture of change meant that their focus was different in important ways.

The central question at the heart of much nineteenth-century travel writing on England is the question of how England could be defined. Technological changes in methods of transportation compressed notions of geography, space, and time differentials. The time that it took to reach people and correspond with them became far shorter, creating the possibility of understanding England as a whole and a breakdown of regional differences, but the rapidity of change and the perception of accelerated pace (prompted by responses to industrialism, the mechanism of clock time, and the railway as a symbol of increased speed) created a sense of displacement. Travel in this climate became the experience of making visible the alien and different. Emily Brontë's *Wuthering Heights* (1847) satirizes the romantic expectations of the traveler-narrator Lockwood, whose notion of northernness is shattered by the alienness of the world he encounters.

The articulation of a sense of "other" finds its most common expression in the fascination that the industrial town (and the working class) holds for the traveler. As Alun Howkins points out (1986), until the 1860s, and possibly later, England is seen primarily as an industrial nation whose individuality is symbolized by the industrial town. For foreign visitors especially it is these centers of manufacture that represent the sights of England. However, not all tourists were impressed with what they saw: Taine describes Manchester as a "Babel built of brick"; Tocqueville and Dickens both see Birmingham as satanic (quoted in Newsome, 1997). In the nineteenth-century imaginative landscape of England it becomes a cliché to see the industrial city as foreign, demonic, and dangerous while endlessly fascinating and potentially exotic, representing all that is and is not England. Disraeli's notion of "Two Nations" (the subtitle to his novel *Sybil*, 1845) gives expression to the sense that gulfs between classes produce foreignness and different types of England.

The use of travel as a means of depicting changes in the cultural, social, and demographic constancy of England was not an isolated procedure: it often reflected conscious or unconscious familiarity with dominant discourses of the time, most notably the discourses of imperialism, gender, class, and race. Nineteenth-century travel literature (like these other discourses) is deeply embedded in systems of "othering": the result is a tendency to displace a fixed sense of home and elsewhere, Englishness and abroad. The paradox at the heart of much of the travel writing of the period is that it registers these two senses of England: its potential knowability and its foreignness.

GAIL BAYLIS

### References and Further Reading


Allen, Walter, *Transatlantic Crossings: American Visitors to Britain and British Visitors to America in the Nineteenth Century*, 1971.

Cobbett, William, *Rural Rides*, 1830 (originally appeared in the *Political Register* from 1821).

Dickens, Charles, *The Posthumous Papers of the Pickwick Club*, 1836–1837 (published serially).

Dickens, Charles, *The Uncommercial Traveler*, 1860.

Dostoevskii, Fedor, *Summer Impressions*, translated and with an introduction by Kyril Fitzlyon, 1955.

Engels, Friedrich, *The Condition of the Working Class in England in 1844*, translated by Florence Kelley Wischnewetsky, 1887.

Faucher, Léon, *Manchester in 1844*, translated by J.P. Culverwell, 1844.

Hawthorne, Nathaniel, *Our Old Home: A Series of English Sketches*, 1863.

Hawthorne, Nathaniel, *Passages from the English Note-Books*, edited by Sophia Peabody Hawthorne, 2 vols., 1870; also published in full as *The English Notebooks*, edited by Randall Stewart, 1941.

Howkins, Alun, "The Discovery of Rural England" in *Englishness: Politics and Culture 1880–1920*, edited by Robert Colls and Philip Dodd, London and Dover, New Hampshire: Croom Helm, 1986.

James, Henry, *Transatlantic Sketches*, 1875; revised edition as *Foreign Parts*, 1883.

James, Henry, *The Art of Travel: Scenes and Journeys in America, England, France, and Italy, from the Travel Writings of Henry James*, edited by Morton Dauwen Zabel, 1958.

Mayhew, Henry, *London Labour and the London Poor*, 3 vols., 1851; 2nd edition, 4 vols., 1861–1862.

Melville, Herman, *Journal of a Visit to London and the Continent 1849–1850*, edited by Eleanor Melville Metcalf, 1948.

Mitchell, Sally, *Daily Life in Victorian England*, Westport, Connecticut, and London: Greenwood Press, 1996.

Munby, Arthur, *The Diaries and Letters of Arthur J. Munby (1829–1910) and Hannah Cullwick (1833–1909)*, microfilm holding, Trinity College, Cambridge.

Newsome, David, *The Victorian World Picture: Perceptions and Introspections in an Age of Change*, London: John Murray, 1997.

Olmsted, Frederick Law, *Walks and Talks of an American Farmer in England*, 1852; new edition, 1859; reprinted, 1967.

Porter, Roy, *London: A Social History*, London: Hamish Hamilton, 1994; Cambridge, Massachusetts: Harvard University Press, 1995.

Reach, Angus B., *The Railway Note-Book*, 1852.

Taine, Hippolyte, *Notes sur l'Angleterre*, 1872; as *Taine's Notes on England*, translated by Edward Hyams, 1957.

Tocqueville, Alexis de, *Journeys to England and Ireland*, translated by George Lawrence and K.P. Mayer, 1958.

Trollope, Anthony, *An Autobiography*, 2 vols., 1883; reissued with an introduction by Bradford Allen Booth, 1947.

Trollope, T.A., *What I Remember*, 3 vols., 1887–1889.

Twain, Mark, *The Travels of Mark Twain*, edited by Charles Neider, 1961.

Twain, Mark, *The Complete Travel Books*, edited by Charles Neider, 2 vols., 1966–1967.


*See also* **Scotland; Wales**

## ENGLAND, TWENTIETH CENTURY

Still riding high on the U.K. bestseller lists at the end of the twentieth century was *Notes from a Small Island* (1995). An account of a tour by Bill Bryson shortly before his return to the United States after nearly 20 years in England, this hugely successful book offered humorous—and self-consciously American—observations on the British character and way of life. As such, it harks back to a tradition popular in the nineteenth century, but subsequently in decline—a trend confirmed by the fact that the twentieth-century antecedents its author does refer to are mostly English, writing about their own country.

Three authors he mentions—H.V. Morton, J.B. Priestley, and George Orwell—may serve to highlight a flourishing of the documentary impulse between World War I and World War II. There are striking differences between their accounts. Morton's *In Search of England* (1927) shows a predilection for the countryside and historic towns, while in *English Journey* (1934) Priestley homes in on scenes of urban work and public leisure. In contrast to both, Orwell's *The Road to Wigan Pier* (1937) pays particular attention to the domestic life of the unemployed working class. Yet they all exhibit a modernist fascination with everyday details (speech, diet, manners) that cuts across these preferences, evident also (and perhaps above all) in the vast amount of material produced by the field workers for the Mass Observation project, selectively showcased in books such as its *Britain* (1939).

A different approach is adopted by two other writers mentioned by Bryson: John Hillaby and Paul Theroux. Here the route itself, mapped out in advance and pursued single-mindedly, takes center stage. Hillaby's *Journey through Britain* (1968) is the best known of the Land's End to John o' Groats narratives. Theroux, in *The Kingdom by the Sea* (1983), made another popular choice: to follow the coastline—in his case, by land, while others have taken to the seas, most notably in *Coasting* (1986) by Jonathan Raban, who pays homage to a number of predecessors including Hilaire Belloc. A more recent innovation is to trace a line of longitude—the method adopted by Stephen Sankey and Nicholas Crane—or some other artificial route as in Janet Street-Porter's *As the Crow Flies* (1999). Such itineraries may appear to be stunts, but their very arbitrariness is often partly contrived to ensure the author encounters a true cross-section of national life.

Many of these accounts are preoccupied with the nature of Englishness and are haunted by the kind of lists offered by T.S. Eliot ("Derby Day . . . a cup final . . . Wensleydale cheese . . . nineteenth-century Gothic churches") in *Notes* (1948), later critically revised and updated by Raymond Williams ("steelmaking, touring in motor cars, mixed farming") in *Culture and Society* (1958) and Hanif Kureishi ("hamburgers, visits to gay bars, the dole office and the taking of drugs") in "Bradford" (1986). The travel writer is constantly measuring his or her experiences against a changing set of conventional images, silently captioning particular scenes as "typical"—or, conversely, pointedly avoiding them. This is particularly evident in those books that, rather than attempting to cover the entire country, focus on particular towns or communities.

The choice of location is often quite explicitly determined by its ability to represent the nation as a whole. The subject of *Oxford* (1965) by Jan Morris is, for her, at the heart of England—touched by key events in its history, the training ground of many of its leaders, and displaying its social structure "as in geological layers." The 1997 general election in the Calder Valley in West Yorkshire, a marginal parliamentary constituency equidistant from London, Cardiff, and Edinburgh, provides the setting of *This England* (1997) by Pete Davies. The subtitles of *Townscape with Figures* (1994) by Richard Hoggart ("Portrait of an English town") and of *Akenfield* (1969) by Ronald Blythe ("Portrait of an English village") suggest likewise. And the initial metropolitan sneer at suburbia in *Park and Ride* (1999) loses its force as Miranda Sawyer comes to realize that its features are inescapable.

Other writers adopt a contrasting rhetoric of invisibility and marginality. Following in the tradition of the social explorers of the nineteenth century, *Danziger's Britain* (1996) is a record of visits to depressed rural and urban areas, "places that only their residents, the postman and the occasional traveling salesman are likely to visit." What interests Nigel Richardson in *Breakfast in Brighton* (1998) is precisely its un-English hedonism. Both works use the word "edge" in their subtitles, suggesting they explore aspects of the nation and national character that rarely figure in popular images of the country.

The same might be said of Dervla Murphy's study of "Brown" and "Black" districts of Bradford and Birmingham in *Tales from Two Cities* (1987), and of *Behind the Frontlines: Journey into Afro-Britain* (1988) by Ferdinand Dennis, outsider and insider perspectives, respectively. In *Robinson in Space* (1999), Patrick Keiller is fascinated by the depopulated, ugly landscapes on the edge of towns, the locations of some of the more profitable sectors of the U.K. economy: manufacturing plants, distribution centers, ports.

England tends to take a back seat in books written about particular regions which, more often than not, seek out specifically local history and culture, without making it representative (or otherwise) of the country at large. As examples one could cite Daphne Du Maurier's *Vanishing Cornwall* (1967), less elegiac than its title might suggest, or the many portraits of Cumbria, such as Hunter Davies's *A Walk Around the Lakes* (1979). Similarly, a keen eye and ear for the vernacular unites the otherwise very different *Up North* (1995) by Charles Jennings (a Londoner who exaggerates the differences) and *All Points North* (1998) by Simon Armitage (a resident who almost takes them for granted).

Apart from a handful of accounts by North American authors, one of the few travel books by overseas visitors is *England: A Travel Journal* (Greek original, 1940) by Nikos Kazantzakis, who offers rather old-fashioned Emersonian reflections on national character on the eve of World War II. As an imperial center, England has received countless official visits from representatives of many colonies, though the few published records of their impressions tend to focus, predictably enough, on London. A notable exception, however, is Ham Mukasa's *Uganda's Katikiro in England* (1904), an account of a tour of Britain by a Ugandan dignitary invited to Edward VII's coronation. By no means uncritical in its admiration, the book offers a fascinating counterpart to the works of Victorian explorers who wrote about his homeland a few decades before.

Alasdair Pettinger

## References and Further Reading

Armitage, Simon, *All Points North*, 1998.
Belloc, Hilaire, *The Cruise of the "Nona,"* 1925.
Blythe, Ronald, *Akenfield: Portrait of an English Village*, 1969.
Bryson, Bill, *Notes from a Small Island*, 1995.
Collis, John Stewart, *An Irishman's England*, 1937.
Crane, Nicholas, *Two Degrees West*, 1999.
Danziger, Nick, *Danziger's Britain: A Journey to the Edge*, 1996.
Davies, Hunter, *A Walk around the Lakes*, 1979.
Davies, Pete, *This England*, 1997.
Dennis, Ferdinand, *Behind the Frontlines: Journeys into Afro-Britain*, 1988.
Du Maurier, Daphne, *Vanishing Cornwall*, with photographs by Christian Browning, 1967.
Eliot, T.S., Notes towards the Definition of Culture, London: Faber, 1948; New York: Harcourt Brace, 1949.
Hillaby, John, *Journey through Britain*, 1968.
Hoggart, Richard, *Townscape with Figures: Farnham—Portrait of an English Town*, 1994.
Jennings, Charles, *Up North: Travels beyond the Watford Gap*, 1995.
Kazantzakis, Nikos, *Taxideuontas: Anglia*, 1940; translated as *England: A Travel Journal*, 1965.
Keiller, Patrick, *Robinson in Space*, 1999.

Kureishi, Hanif, "Bradford," *Granta*, 20 (1986).
Mass Observation, *Britain*, 1939.
Morris, Jan (as James Morris), *Oxford*, 1965.
Morton, H.V., *In Search of England*, 1927.
Mukasa, Ham, *Uganda's Katikiro in England*, 1904.
Murphy, Dervla, *Tales from Two Cities: Travel of Another Sort*, 1987.
Orwell, George, *The Road to Wigan Pier*, 1937.
Priestley, J.B., *English Journey*, 1934.
Purves, Libby, *One Summer's Grace: A Family Voyage round Britain*, 1989.
Raban, Jonathan, *Coasting*, 1986.
Richardson, Nigel, *Breakfast in Brighton: Adventures on the Edge of Britain*, 1998.
Sankey, Stephen, *Three Degrees West: A Walk through Britain's Local and Natural History*, 1990.
Sawyer, Miranda, *Park and Ride: Adventures in Suburbia*, 1999.
Somerville, Christopher, *The Other British Isles: A Journey through the Islands Off England, Wales and Scotland*, 1990.
Street-Porter, Janet, *As the Crow Flies: A Walk from Edinburgh to London in a Straight Line*, 1999.
Theroux, Paul, *The Kingdom by the Sea: A Journey round the Coast of Great Britain*, 1983.
Wharton, Margaret, *Back to Britain: The Holiday Journals of a G.I. Bride*, 1995.
Williams, Raymond, *Culture and Society*, London: Chatto and Windus, 1958.

*See also* **Scotland; Wales**

## EPISTOLARY TRAVEL FICTION

It has been commonplace in literary criticism to observe that the epistolary form—a narrative composed of letters flowing either one way or back and forth to and from a single correspondent or many—performed a vital role in the development of modern fiction from heroic and comic romances to the more realistic and psychologically satisfying fictions that began to appear in the eighteenth century. However improbable the compulsion to document every emotional nuance may seem to a later generation, novels like Richardson's *Clarissa* (1747–1748) and Goethe's *Sorrows of Werther* (1774) both owe their intensity to the absence of an all-seeing and manipulating narrator through whom the protagonists' passion would otherwise be filtered. The epistolary form, therefore, may be seen as a means both for establishing verisimilitude and stimulating self-examination.

Because an ongoing correspondence can have no sense of its ending, epistolary fiction is characterized by a looser conception of story, and in this amorphousness of plot, epistolary fiction has much in common with travel narratives and journals. Like such classic fictional travel narratives as Defoe's *Robinson Crusoe* (1719) and Swift's *Gulliver's Travels* (1726), the objectives of the spurious letters may be less to delineate imaginary worlds than to illuminate real ones.

This, at any rate, appears to have been the purpose of what is frequently cited as the first modern epistolary novel, *Letters of a Turkish Spy*, by the Italian Giovanni Paolo Marana (1684; English translation 1694). Based on a tradition of hostile letter exchanges between representatives of the Ottoman empire and Christian princes, Marana's spy insinuated himself into France as an observer and commentator on current events and Western ways to friends and confidants in Constantinople. By assuming the identity of an outlandish character, the author was thus at liberty to criticize and question freely the institutions of Christendom. The formula was widely imitated during the eighteenth century yielding, among others, the purported correspondence of German, Jewish, and Chinese secret agents.

Subtler and more refined social and political commentary appears in the *Persian Letters* of Montesquieu (1721), in which the satire is somewhat double-edged, for while the travelers Usbek and Rica remark on the failings and inconsistencies of the foreign lands they visit, despite the graciousness of their deportment, they reveal as well the despotism inherent in their own society. By removing the sinister element from his correspondents, Montesquieu was able to introduce a more reflective character in their observations. Like *The Turkish Spy*, the *Persian Letters* inspired a host of English imitations, from the feebly derivative *Letters from a Persian in England to his Friend at Ispahan* of George, Lord Lyttelton (1735) to William Lloyd's *Letters from a Moore at London to His Friend at Tunis* (1740) to Viscount Pery's *Letters from an Armenian in Ireland to his Friend in Trebizond* (1757). The most widely known of these traveler-critics was Oliver Goldsmith's Chinese visitor to England, Lien Chi Altangi, whose letters home, which appeared serially in the *Public Ledger*, comprise a *Citizen of the World* (1762). However shrewd the observations, the veneer of fiction is quite thin, and the work is actually more a series of discrete essays than an account of adventures or a revelation of character.

In France the spin-offs from the *Persian Letters* were on the whole more philosophical, filled with fewer details of local color and more of the imagined responses of citizens of an alien culture to a nominally more civilized one. The prolific Marquis d'Argens composed novels of Kabbalistic, Jewish, and Chinese letters. Less learned perhaps in its references to the civilization of the Incas but more incisive for its examination of relations between the sexes is Mme de Graffigny's *Letters from a Peruvian Woman* (1747), which begins as an epistolary captive narrative, develops into a commentary on the frivolousness of French society, and ends as an allegory of the poisonous consequences of artificial manners on natural affections.

By far the most enduring survivor of the vogue of epistolary travel fiction is the semipicaresque *Expedition of Humphry Clinker* (1771) by Tobias Smollett, unique for having multiple correspondents, each with a distinctive outlook and idiom, describing the same adventures, and for allowing the eponymous hero to make his appearance only halfway through the novel. The principal letter writer is the irascible Matthew Bramble, a wealthy Welsh landowner, who, with an entourage consisting of his old-maid sister, a nephew and niece, and servants, has undertaken a circular tour of the island of Britain in search of his health. Borrowed from the successful verse letters of Christopher Anstey's *New Bath Guide* (1766), the scheme of multiple correspondents in Smollett's novel breaks down, like the conveyance in which they are traveling, as a conventional narrative plot line begins to impose itself on the journey. The most distinctive contribution of Smollett's novel to the genre is Bramble's deflation of popular guidebook descriptions of such touristic magnets as Bath and London and his championing of the natural beauty of Scotland, still largely unknown to the English.

It is obvious from the foregoing that the intent of epistolary travel fiction is hardly to impart geographical or historical information, but to convey a response to a contemporary cultural scene. Whether the fictional characters traversing the landscape are total inventions, like Montesquieu's Persians, or plausible self-projections, like Smollett's Bramble and Graffigny's Zilia, the effects are similar: because all travel, whatever its purpose, is discommoding, it stimulates reflection and comparison between the accustomed and the unfamiliar. For a moment in the history of European literature the popular interest in the exotic voyage or voyager and the epistolary mode of narration coalesced to produce works of considerable social analysis, a function performed comparably in our own time by the genre of science fiction.

IRA GRUSHOW

### References and Further Reading


Altman, Janet Gurkin, *Epistolarity: Approaches to a Form*, Columbus: Ohio State University Press, 1982.

Beebee, Thomas O., *Epistolary Fiction in Europe, 1500–1850*, Cambridge and New York: Cambridge University Press, 1999.

Black, Frank Gees, *The Epistolary Novel in the Late Eighteenth Century: A Descriptive and Bibliographical Study*, Eugene: University of Oregon, 1940.

Day, Robert Adams, *Told in Letters: Epistolary Fiction before Richardson*, Ann Arbor: University of Michigan Press, 1966.

Dunlop, John Colin, *History of Prose Fiction*, edited by Henry Wilson, London: Bell, 1888; New York: Franklin, 1970.

Giraud, Yves, *Bibliographie du roman épistolaire en France: des origines à 1842*, Fribourg: Editions Universitaires, 1977.

Gove, Philip Babcock, *The Imaginary Voyage in Prose Fiction: A History of Its Criticism and a Guide for Its Study, with an Annotated Checklist of 215 Imaginary Voyages from 1700 to 1800*, New York: Columbia University Press, 1941; London: Holland Press, 1961.

Kany, Charles E., *The Beginnings of the Epistolary Novel in France, Italy, and Spain*, Berkeley: University of California Press, 1937.

Perry, Ruth, *Women, Letters, and the Novel*, New York: AMS Press, 1980.

Singer, Godfrey Frank, *The Epistolary Novel: Its Origin, Development, Decline, and Residuary Influence*, Philadelphia: University of Pennsylvania Press, 1933; New York: Russell and Russell, 1963.


*See also* **Fictional Travel Writing**

## ETHICS, ISSUES OF

The issue of ethical questions in travel writing can be dealt with from a number of perspectives. Here, I suggest that the primary ethical questions in travel writing stem from the ideological bases, and material consequences of the representational practices and prescriptive qualities of much travel writing. These concerns of the material consequence of travel writing raise two central ethical questions that much travel writing has, since its formative stages, overlooked: questions of reflectiveness and reflexivity. While travel writing tends to pass judgment on the morality of people and places visited, it rarely engages in moral reflection on the author's own position. This includes the author's personal history and experience and the role he or she plays in the production of knowledge of people and place and subsequent representations. The absence of reflectiveness delimits the possibility of reflexivity in travel writing, including a consideration of the material effects of its own production and circulation. Rarely does it deal with the implicit values and beliefs that underlie the presentation of the world it represents. This is perhaps more true of colonial-era travel writing than it is today, but even as it references colonial predecessors, rarely does contemporary travel writing stop to seek out, confront, or question the colonial ideologies and value hierarchies grounded in racial and gender difference that give rise to the differential and quite arbitrary treatment of people and places as they exist within the social relations that constitute travel and tourism.

In writing of the ethics of travel and exploration, it is impossible to escape the historical legacies of capitalist development and accumulation, of imperialist expansion, and of numerous forms of inequity that persist today. It is also difficult to avoid a discussion of historical and contemporary attempts to delineate the kinds of activities that constitute travel and exploration, primarily those that produce a literature of travel. Rarely included in this are forms of travel that do not leave as direct a literary trace as "travel for leisure"—travels that result from or result in forced migration, immigration, employment as bearers, homelessness. Accordingly, travel and questions of representation raised by dominant practices of travel writing must consider how descriptions of people and place are bounded by the differential ability of people to travel. Certainly, financial ability provides the capacity for some to engage in travel in ways or to places that are out of reach of others simply because of the willingness to pay for exclusivity. But the difference in the ability to travel is most marked in those places where mobility is disproportionately skewed, both legally and economically, toward those from so-called developed nations. Ironically the capacity of many people to travel to destinations in so-called poor countries exists precisely because a significant portion of the population in those countries is poor. It is the difference in purchasing power—the value of currency—that permits the extension of a localized leisure activity into the sphere of global travel. This is nothing new. Any perusal of early travel narratives reveals that the emergence of professional travelers in the eighteenth and nineteenth century was facilitated by the ability to take advantage of wealth differentials grounded in the exploitation of difference typically on the basis of race. Indeed, travel itself is historically grounded in, and reproduced, racial typifications that served its own interest. The identification, description, and categorization of particular populations from within the ideological frames of colonialism, and common in much early travel writing, not only denigrated native people but also detailed their usefulness in the service of travel. Despite the inequitable social relations of production engaged in travel, and their unethical reliance on arbitrary discrimination, much travel writing has historically adopted a liberal rhetoric concerning the moralizing effect of the encounter; an assertion that travel, particularly under the guise of colonialism, was not simply a mechanism of discovery—of unearthing and codifying facts of people and place—but a mode of capturing difference within a common language of morality. This was typically produced through a discourse of liberal humanism as it emerged from the Enlightenment to emphasize values of freedom and self-realization. These values, when socially contextualized, however, were not free from the chains of a religious morality that saw the route to their realization as lying within a religious and educational conversion of native populations to European beliefs and values. Hence the association of travel with education and missionary activity. Both of these activities, and the travel writing associated with them, can be read as disciplining activities or vehicles through which to reorient worldviews and the bodily practices associated with them. Like many other forms of writing, travel literature has disciplinary qualities in the way that it explicitly or implicitly prescribes certain modes of behavior that have material consequences.

An example of this lies in the ethical problems related to the production of the object of much travel—cultural authenticities. This is, in part, related to the arrogance of the tourist/traveler divide. In the popular lexicon of much travel and exploration writing, it is the true traveler who seeks to find the real and the tourist who corrupts it, seeking only to satisfy base desire. Ironically, "the real" is itself produced through the ideological norms of early travel writing, which assumed as a primary function the production of objective descriptions of the world—descriptions of people and place that Mary Louise Pratt and Edward Said, among others, have described as the "customs and manners" trope of travel writing. This "knowledge" is subsequently reproduced through the social norms and practices that govern travel writing: the reference of authority—itself produced within a delimited economy of meaning that relies on the act of travel as the basis for the production of legitimate meaning—and the adherence to institutional sanction. Travel and the accounts of travellers then, are sanctioned within and through power relations that arbitrarily promote the accounts of those who serve the ideological interests of dominant institutions. In the past, these were frequently colonial institutions or institutions of the state. Increasingly, as the ideology of adventure has become more pervasive in Western society, these have become the institutions of capital. Through the process of the arbitrary institutional sanction of legitimate travel, another ethical thorn emerges; enquiries into the points of view of those who have been visited are rarely offered in travel accounts, nor are the accounts of those who have accompanied sanctioned travelers in the role of employees or servants. Even in the case of exceptions, accounts of native people are commonly heavily edited by institutional hands and emerge at political moments when they can be of use to the institutions of travel. A notable exception is Jamaica Kincaid's "A Small Place."

A concern with authenticity and the historical textual reproduction of manners and customs representations exposes ethical concerns regarding the encounter between traveler and the "travelled." Among these is the manufacture of a performative authenticity through which the textual production of "the real" generates a material expectation on the part of the tourist/traveler. It also provides guidelines for action, as the textual representation of authenticity in travel writing assumes a prescriptive dimension and encourages the reproduction of oppressive conditions of interaction through particularized forms of cultural exploitation. The construction of authenticity, for example, implies pressure for the reproduction of cultural practice as performance and raises ethical concerns related to the devaluation of meaning in such geographically and socially contextualized practices. Of course, there is the response that those performing the cultural practice, often rituals, recognize the manufactured context and engage in a particular form of performance for the travel market while reserving separate spaces for their own meaningful performances. This, however, can be counterproductive as these new sites become the authentic spaces of cultural performance and, as such, are sought out by travelers seeking to differentiate themselves from the mainstream. Even in cases where a community sanctions cultural performance for a travel market, that community is rarely inclusive or homogeneous and decisions can be made by a selective group that is not necessarily representative of the interests of all community members. A differential in power relations within communities often facilitates exploitation on the basis of gender and social status, and can generate new sources of tension within communities as some members try to capture the benefits flowing from a travel market. These concerns are directly related to the discursive authority assumed by travel literature, which relies on an appeal to wisdom and social superiority to discern the "real" or the essence in any cultural encounter and to represent it to potential travelers.

The role of travel writing in the production of desire, the demarcation of possibility, and as a signifier of class and social status carries with it some specific ethical concerns. Perhaps most obvious of late are environmental concerns associated with the representation of particular locales as attractive destinations. The onslaught of tourists in Niagara Falls during the late nineteenth century makes it clear that the material environmental effects of travel writing's seductive power are not new, but the stakes have become higher. An expanding global leisure class combined with a vastly expanded spatial reach made feasible through jet travel (and the environmental hazards associated with airports and fuel consumption) has not been accompanied by an associated shift in practice to minimize the environmental impacts of tourism. Even the advent of so-called ecotourism, now the subject of a new genre of travel writing, simply relies upon a continued process whereby a discursively produced environment is commodified, consumed as spectacle, all the while remaining subject to the whims of a fairly fickle free market.

Ultimately, travel writing cannot be held apart from the material consequences of the act of travel. It is one element in an economy of meaning that underpins travel and exploration. Travel writing brings the objects of tourism into being. It creates desire through the social status accorded to travel and the markers of class distinction inserted into a hierarchy of travel, manifest in the distinction between traveler and tourist, provides people with the conceptual apparatus through which to interpret their experiences, and quite often structures their experience by creating iconic objects associated with particular places. Travel writing, in other words, provides a textual map to navigate the material experience of place. It brings people and place into being through its own discursive mechanisms that cannot be dissociated from the prior ideological representations grounded in the value hierarchies of colonialism, value hierarchies that continue to maintain inequitable social and environmental relations.

KENNETH IAIN MACDONALD

### References and Further Reading


Adler, J., "Travel as Performed Art," *American Journal of Sociology*, 94 (1989): 1366–1391.

Bartowski, Frances, *Travelers, Immigrants, Inmates: Essays in Estrangement*, Minneapolis: University of Minnesota Press, 1995.

Bassnett, Susan, "Constructing Cultures: The Politics of Travelers' Tales," in *Comparative Literature: A Critical Introduction*, Oxford and Cambridge, Mass.: Blackwell, 1993.

Behdad, Ali, *Belated Travelers: Orientalism in the Age of Colonial Dissolution*, Durham, N.C.: Duke University Press, 1994.

Butz, David, and Kenneth I. MacDonald, "Serving Sahibs with Pony and Pen: The Discursive Uses of 'Native Authenticity,' " *Environment and Planning D: Society and Space*, 19 (2001): 179–201.

Clifford, James, *Routes: Travel and Translation in the Late Twentieth Century*, Cambridge, Mass.: Harvard University Press, 1997.

Cocker, Mark, *Loneliness and Time: British Travel Writing in the Twentieth Century*, London: Secker and Warburg, and New York: Pantheon, 1992.

Duncan, James, and Derek Gregory, *Writes of Passage: Reading Travel Writing*, London and New York: Routledge, 1999.

Greenblatt, Stephen J., *Marvelous Possessions: The Wonder of the New World*, Chicago: University of Chicago Press, and Oxford: Clarendon Press, 1991.

Griffiths, G., "The Myth of Authenticity: Representation, Discourse and Social Practice," in *De-Scribing Empire: Post-Colonialism and Textuality*, edited by Chris Tiffin and Alan Lawson, London and New York: Routledge, 1994.

Kaplan, Caren, *Questions of Travel: Postmodern Discourses of Displacement*, Durham, N.C.: Duke University Press, 1996.

Kowalewski, Michael (editor), *Temperamental Journeys: Essays on the Modern Literature of Travel*, Athens: University of Georgia Press, 1992.

Krishnaswamy, Revathi, "Mythologies of Migrancy: Postcolonialism, Postmodernism and the Politics of (Dis)location," *Ariel*, 26/1 (1995): 125–146.

Leed, Eric J., *The Mind of the Traveler: From Gilgamesh to Global Tourism*, New York: Basic Books, 1991.

Lippard, Lucy R., *On the Beaten Track: Tourism, Art and Place*, New York: New Press, and London: Tauris, 1999.

MacCannell, Dean, *Empty Meeting Grounds: The Tourist Papers*, London and New York: Routledge, 1992.

MacCannell, Dean, *The Tourist: A New Theory of the Leisure Class*, New York: Schocken, and London: Macmillan, 1976; revised edition, Schocken, 1989; new edition, Berkeley: University of California Press, 1999.

Maggi, Wynne, *Our Women Are Free: Gender and Ethnicity in the Hindukush*, Ann Arbor: University of Michigan Press, 2001.

Martels, Zweder von (editor), *Travel Fact and Travel Fiction: Studies on Fiction, Literary Tradition, Scholarly Discovery, and Observation in Travel Writing*, Leiden and New York: E.J. Brill, 1994.

Mezciems, J., "'Tis Not to Divert the Reader': Moral and Literary Determinants in Some Early Travel Narratives," in *The Art of Travel: Essays on Travel Writing*, edited by Philip Dodd, London: Cass, 1982.

Mills, Sara, *Discourses of Difference: An Analysis of Women's Travel Writing and Colonialism*, London and New York: Routledge, 1991.

Mitchell, T., "Orientalism and the Exhibitionary Order," in *Colonialism and Culture*, edited by Nicholas B. Dirks, Ann Arbor: University of Michigan Press, 1992.

Nerlich, Michael, *Ideology of Adventure: Studies in Modern Consciousness, 1100–1750*, translated by Ruth Crowley, foreword by Wlad Godzich, Minneapolis: University of Minnesota Press, 1987.

Porter, Dennis, *Haunted Journeys: Desire and Transgression in European Travel Writing*, Princeton, N.J.: Princeton University Press, 1991.

Pratt, Mary Louise, *Imperial Eyes: Travel Writing and Transculturation*, London and New York: Routledge, 1992.

Robertson, George, et al. (editors), *Travellers' Tales: Narratives of Home and Displacement*, London and New York: Routledge, 1994.

Rojek, Chris, and John Urry (editors), *Touring Cultures: Transformations of Travel and Theory*, London and New York: Routledge, 1997.

Said, Edward W., *Orientalism*, New York: Pantheon, and London: Routledge and Kegan Paul, 1978; with new afterword, New York: Vintage, 1994, London: Penguin, 1995.

Said, Edward W., *Culture and Imperialism*, New York: Knopf, and London: Chatto and Windus, 1993.

Spurr, David, *The Rhetoric of Empire: Colonial Discourse in Journalism, Travel Writing, and Imperial Administration*, Durham, N.C.: Duke University Press, 1993.

Thomas, Nicholas, *Colonialism's Culture: Anthropology, Travel and Government*, Princeton, N.J.: Princeton University Press, and Cambridge: Polity Press, 1994.

Tiffin, Chris, and Alan Lawson, *De-Scribing Empire: Post-Colonialism and Textuality*, London and New York: Routledge, 1994.

Todorov, Tzvetan, *La Conquête de l'Amérique: La Question de l'autre*, Paris: Seuil, 1982; as *The Conquest of America: The Question of the Other*, New York: Harper and Row, 1984.

Urry, John, *Consuming Places*, London and New York: Routledge, 1994.

*See also* **Ethnography; Tourism**

## ETHIOPIA / ABYSSINIA

When Father Francisco Álvares published his famed account of the first visit by a Portuguese, indeed a European, embassy to the Christian kingdom of Abyssinia (between 1520 and 1526), he gave it the curious title of *True Information of the Kingdom of Prester John of the Indies* (1540, 1881). Only once or twice in the account does he refer to the lands he visits as Ethiopia, and "Abyssinia" is never used. He, like many European writers of that period, speaks of that regional and political entity as the "kingdoms of Prester John." By Ethiopia, travel writers and cosmographers generally meant the African continent, whereas Africa (in Arabic, *Ifryqia*) was used to identify the coastal areas of North Africa, in antiquity and in the Middle Ages. Since ancient Greek times, Aethiops has generally designated the "land of the [people with] burned faces." So, when used in a more strict sense, the word required some specification: the eastern African region was called High Ethiopia, also known as Third India.

*Abyssinia* is generally acknowledged to be derived from the Arab *habesh* ("people of mixed breed"), a word that is of common use in modern Ethiopia to designate the semiticized populations of the northern high plateaus. The term appears in medieval maps and texts: for instance, Marco Polo says that "Abash" is a "very large province in Middle India," but its use in European travel literature became more widely adopted after publication of the writings of the Jesuits (Fathers Manuel Almeida and Jerónimo Lobo, among others) who, in the early seventeenth century, gained some influence at the Christian Orthodox emperors' court. They would distinguish between *Abassia* (Abyssinia)—the Christian areas of the country they referred to as the High Ethiopia of Prester John—and the southern and western surroundings populated by pagans and Muslims.

To better understand the ambiguities and confusions arising from the superimposition of these different geographical qualifiers, one must bear in mind the ideological weight of the medieval crusading myth of the eastern Christian potentate Prester John. According to the twelveth-century *Letter of Prester John of the Indies*, this "king of kings," who proposed an alliance to Western rulers for a joint conquest of the Holy Land, lived in the neighborhood of the Earthly Paradise. In medieval European visions of the world, the Earthly Paradise lay in the Far East, and was therefore represented at the top of the T in O maps (thus called because the three known continents were depicted within an O divided by a T representing the Danube, the Nile and the Mediterranean). The eastern regions of the inhabited world bore the mark of the proximity of God. So if India, or rather the "three Indies," were this legendary emperor's original home, the later identification of the Ethiopian Christian kingdom with the Indian Prester John, in the fourteenth century, was facilitated by the fact that medieval maps accentuated the eastern location of the Red Sea and the Horn of Africa—the Nile River acting as a separator between Hesperian (or

VOYAGE
HISTORIQUE
D'ABISSINIE,
DU R. P. JEROME LOBO
DE LA COMPAGNIE DE JESUS.
Traduite du Portugais, continuée & augmentée de plusieurs Dissertations, Lettres & Memoires.
Par M. LE GRAND, Prieur de Neuville-les-Dames & de Prevessin.

A PARIS. & A LA HAYE.
Chez P. GOSSE & J. NEAULME.
MDCCXXVIII.

The 1728 French translation and abridgement of Father Jerónimo Lobo's *Itinerario* introduced his *Voyage to Abyssinia* to the European public, but his complete manuscript remained undiscovered for a further 200 years. *Courtesy of Travellers Club, London; Bridgeman Art Library, agent.*

western) Ethiopia, a land of monsters and evil, and High (or eastern) Ethiopia—a rich and beneficial land. Also the Horn of Africa was frequently drawn to the southeast of the Indian subcontinent, thus stressing the conception of High Ethiopia as the "third India."

The oriental characteristics that European travel writers and cosmographers attributed to Ethiopia, and more specifically to the Abyssinian plateaus, became an important framework for the descriptions and images produced by travelers to that country, well into the twentieth century. The stereotypical distinction between Christian Ethiopia and the rest of Africa was so strong throughout the centuries that it was even reflected in the more or less benign attitude of European imperial powers toward Emperor Menelik II in the late nineteenth century, and in the general acceptance of Ethiopia's exceptional independent status; Menelik aptly manipulated mutual rivalry between the Western powers and expanded southward, thus effectively carving an African empire.

In a region that compounded Western prejudices about oriental sophistication and African barbarism, Ethiopians were described accordingly by travelers from a large number of European countries in a spiral of clichéd visions that were only partially abandoned with the fall of Emperor Haile Selassie in 1974. The source of the Nile, the Red Sea, the mountainous landscape, the ancient presence of Christianity, and the physical characteristics of the Abyssinians have been the usual background for a relatively large number of travel accounts about Ethiopia. From very early on these accounts have swayed between the traveler's mythical and fantastical expectations, dependent on the images of Prester John, and the confrontation with a frustratingly different reality. Some elements are thus recurrent in European travel literature about Ethiopia since the sixteenth century, which enunciates a sometimes very negative stanza: the treachery of the people, the tyrannical character of the imperial rulers, the heretical character of Ethiopian Christianity, the harshness of natural disasters.

Tales of the inaccessibility of Ethiopia have proliferated from the earliest times in European travel literature, and yet visitors to the country have not failed to notice the continuous cultural interpenetration of that region with Egypt, Sudan, the Arabian peninsula, and to the East with India. In his *Christian Topography*, Cosmas Indicopleustes (sixth century) refers to how Aksum showed evidence of Egyptian and Middle Eastern influence. The first-century itinerary *Periplus of the Erythraean Sea* is further proof of how the Ethiopian highlands were part of an international merchant circuit. Later, the expansion of Islam effectively created the conditions for developing the European vision of an inaccessible Christian kingdom perched near the mountainous sources of the Nile, far behind enemy lines. The fourteenth-century travelers Pietro Rombulo and Pero Tafur (whose travels are mentioned in Nicolò de Conti's account of his own travels in the Orient) reflect this perspective. Marco Polo; Jordanus Catalani of Severac, self-styled bishop of India; and friar Simon Simeonis stressed the idea of the interchangeability between India and Ethiopia. It was at this period that Catalan and Genoan cartography began placing Prester John in eastern Africa, on the right bank of the Nile River.

Meanwhile, a rich travel literature in Arabic also developed in the wake of Ibn Hisham's accounts of Arab migrations to Abyssinia. Ibn Hawqal (943–977), Ibn Khaldun (1332–1406), al-Idrisi (c. 1099–1154) and Ibn Battuta (1304–1368(?)) are some of the writers who recorded Islam's vision of that country—the ideas of inaccessibility being much mitigated.

Although most travelers reporting on Ethiopia in the fifteenth century were Italian, the sixteenth and early seventeenth centuries were the golden age of Portuguese literature on the country. A string of Jesuit writers produced report after report, not only on their missionary labors, but also on their extensive travels. Their expulsion by Emperor Fasiladas in 1634 resulted in a partial closing of the country to Western travelers. Even so, the Italian traveler Giacomo Baratti, the Czech Franciscan Remedius Prutky, and the French doctor Charles-Jacques Poncet forwarded precious information on the rising Gondarine civilization in the seventeenth century. Sparse Turkish and Yemenite reports, as well as indigenous literature in Ge'ez and in Amharic languages, gave further details of northern Ethiopia. While in Germany, Hiob Ludolf (1624–1704) developed a long collaboration with the Ethiopian monk Abba Gregorius and became the father of modern Ethiopian studies. In Great Britain, Samuel Johnson (1709–1784) translated Father Jerónimo Lobo's *Itinerary* (from the French version of Joachin Legrand), and wrote his influential novel *Rasselas, Prince of Ethiopia*, which stressed the vision of a country almost totally cut off from the rest of the world. Around the same time, the Scottish traveler James Bruce published his *Travels to Discover the Source of the Nile* (1790). Dr. Johnson scorned Bruce's claims to be the discoverer of the mythical river's source, reminding the public that the Jesuits had been there more than one century before. Even so, his book still became a model for later European travelers in Ethiopia, the descriptions of the Nile and its source pervading most accounts.

During the nineteenth century, a growing number of foreigners began visiting the region, the Abyssinian plateaus and Eritrea featuring high in most travelogues. Travelers, merchants, and missionaries romanticized the country. The British explorer Richard Burton (1821–1890) and the French poet Arthur Rimbaud (1854–1891) greatly contributed to the mystique of Harar. Samuel Gobat (1799–1879), Henry Salt (1780–1835), Antonio Cecchi (1849–1896), and Jules Borelli (1853–1941) wandered through Gondar, Gojjam, and Shewa. The German missionaries C.W. Isenberg (1806–1864), J.L. Krapf (1810–1887), and Henry Stern (1820–1885), the Italian priest Guglielmo Massaia (1809–1889), the explorers Samuel Baker (1821–1893) and F.J. Bieber (1873–1924), and journalists C. François Mondon-Vidhailet (1847–1910) and Achile Bizzoni (1841–1904), among others, further pictured Ethiopia as a lost, feudal, and oriental empire.

Diplomatic missions were sent from diverse countries: from Great Britain (Cornwallis Harris in 1841–1843, Walter Plowden in 1843–1847, Hormuzd Rassam in 1864–66, and James Rennell in 1896), from France (Ferret and Galinier in 1840, Rochet d'Héricourt in 1839–1848, and Anton Klobokowski in 1908), from Italy (Marchese Antinori in 1876, and Pietro Antonelli in 1887–1889), from Germany (Gerhard Rohlfs in 1881, and Friedrich Rosen in 1905–1906), from Austria (T. von Heuglin with the Swiss Werner Munzinger, in 1857, Ludwig von Höhnel in 1905), from Russia (Nicholas Ashinov and Vladimir Mashkov in 1888–1889, and Nicholas Leontev in 1895), from the United States (Skinner, in 1903–1904), and from Greece (Demosthenes Mitzakis' in 1879).

There was also a fair amount of scientific exploration in the region. Geographical knowledge of the country progressed in the wake of Antoine and Arnauld d'Abbadie's intensive explorations, soon followed by surveys in such areas as archaeology, ethnography, zoology, etc. Scientific expeditions were led by Eduard Rüppell (1831–1833), Théophile Lefebvre (1839–1843), W.T. Blandford and C.R. Markham (1867–1868), Philipp Paulitschke (1885), Enno Littmann (1905–1910), and a profusion of others. Lalibela, Gondar, and Aksum formed the favorite triangle for foreign visitors who could thus blend evocations of late antiquity, orientalist traits, and rude native interpretations of Christianity, while in the southeast Harar's status as a Muslim closed city further fed the orientalist curiosity of European readers. Attention paid to the southeastern flatlands (particularly by anthropologists) became more evident from the early twentieth century onward.

Emperors Menelik and Haile Selassie strongly stimulated European and American presence in the country because it favored the assertion of their own imperial authority in a multinational and fractured state. For more than a century now, scientific expeditions, Protestant missions (in the southern marches), adventurers, and explorers have been criss-crossing the country, and producing an extensive international bibliography that, until very recently, still echoed the old vision of Ethiopia as an oriental, non-African country.

MANUEL JOÃO RAMOS

## References and Further Reading


Abbadie, Arnauld d', *Douze ans dans la Haute-Éthiopie*, 1868.

'Abd al-Qadir, Shihab al-Din Ahmad ibn (Arab-Faqih), *Histoire de la conquête de l'Abyssinie*, edited and translated by René Basset, 2 vols., 1897–1909.

Abu al-Fida, *Kitab Taqwim al-buldan*, edited by J.T. Reinaud and William MacGuckin de Slane, 1840.

Almeida, Manuel de, *Historia geral de Ethiopia a Alta ou Abassia* in *Rerum aethiopicarum scriptores occidentales inediti a saeculo XVI ad XIX*, edited by Camillo Beccari, vols. 5–7, 1907–1908; parts translated as *Some Records of Ethiopia, 1593–1646*, translated and edited by C.F. Beckingham and G.W.B. Huntingford, 1954.

Álvares, Francisco, *Verdadeira informação das terras do preste João, segundo vio e escreueu ho Padre Francisco Aluarez capellã del rey nosso senhor*, 1540; as *The Prester John of the Indies: A True Relation of the Lands of the Prester John, Being the Narrative of the Portuguese Embassy to Ethiopia in 1520*, translated by Lord Stanley of Alderley (1881), revised and edited with additional material by C.F. Beckingham and G.W.B. Huntingford, 2 vols., 1961.

Antinori, Orazio, *Viaggio nel Bogos*, 1887.

Antonelli, Pietro, *Rapporti sullo Scioa . . . dal 22 maggio 1883 al 19 giugno 1888*, 1890.

Bahrey, "History of the Galla" (seventeenth century), in *Some Records of Ethiopia, 1593–1646*, edited and translated by C.F. Beckingham and G.W.B. Huntingford, 1954.

Baratti, Giacomo, *The Late Travels of S. Giacomo Baratti, an Italian Gentleman, into the Remote Countries of the Abissins, or of Ethiopia Interior*, translated by G.D., 1670.

Bieber, F.J., "Reise durch Äthiopien und den Sudan," *Mitteilungen der Kaiserlich- Königlichen Geographischen Gesellschaft*, 53 (1910).

Blandford, William Thomas, *Observations on the Geology and Zoology of Abyssinia, Made during the Progress of the British Expedition to That Country in 1867–68*, 1870.

Borelli, Jules, *Ethiopie méridionale: journal de mon voyage aux pays Amhara, Oromo et Sidama, Septembre 1885 à Novembre 1888*, 1890.

Bruce, James, *Travels to Discover the Source of the Nile, in the Years 1768, 1769, 1770, 1771, 1772 and 1773*, 5 vols., 1790.

Burton, Richard F., *First Footsteps in East Africa; or, An Exploration of Harar*, 1856.

Catalani, Jordanus (Jordan of Severac), *Mirabilia descripta: The Wonders of the East*, translated by Henry Yule, 1863.

Cecchi, Antonio, *Da Zeila alle frontiere del Caffa*, 3 vols., 1886–1887.

Combes, Edmond, and Maurice Tamisier, *Voyage en Abyssinie, dans le pays des Galla, de Choa et d'Ifat*, 4 vols., 1838.

Cosmas Indicopleustes, *Ellas topografia* in *Patrologiae Graeca*, vol. 88, 1860; as *The Christian Topography of Cosmas*, translated by J.W. McCrindle, 1897.

Crawford, O.G.S. (editor), *Ethiopian Itineraries, circa 1400–24, Including Those Collected by Alessandro Zorzi at Venice in the Years 1519–24*, 1958.

Ferret, P.V.A. and J.G. Galinier, *Voyage en Abyssinie, dans les provinces du Tigré, du Samen, et de l'Amhara*, 3 vols., 1847–1848.

Frobenius, Leo, *Unter den unsträflichen Aethiopen*, 1913.

Gobat, Samuel, *Journal of Three Years' Residence in Abyssinia*, translated by Sereno D. Clark, revised edition, 1850; reprinted, 1969.

Griaule, Marcel, *Les Flambeurs d'hommes*, 1934; as *Abyssinian Journey*, translated by E.G. Rich, 1935.

Harris, W. Cornwallis, *The Highlands of Aethiopia*, 3 vols., 1844; reprinted, 1968.

Heuglin, M.T. von, *Reise nach Abessinien, den Gala-Ländern, Ost-Sudan und Chartum in den Jahren 1861 und 1862*, 1868.

Höhnel, Ludwig, Ritter von, "In Mission bei Kaiser Menelik, 1905" in *Mein Leben zur See, auf Forschungsreisen und bei Hofe*, 1926.

Holland, Trevenen J., and Henry M. Hozier, *Record of the Expedition to Abyssinia*, 2 vols., 1870.

Huntingford, G.W.B. (translator and editor), *The Periplus of the Erythraean Sea*, 1980.

Ibn Battuta, *Travels of Ibn Battuta AD 1325–1354*, translated by H.A.R. Gibb, 5 vols., 1958–2000 (vol. 4 with C.F. Beckingham).

Ibn Hawqal, *Kitab Surat al-ard*, edited by J.H. Kramers, 2 vols., 1938–1939; as *Configuration de la terre*, translated by Kramers and G. Wiet, 1964.

Ibn Hishām, *al-Sirah al-nabawiyah*, edited by Mustafa al-Saqqa et al., 4 vols., 1936–1937; as *The Life of Muhammad*, translated by Alfred Guillaume, 1955.

Ibn Khaldun, *Kitab al-'Ibar*, 7 vols., 1867–1868; as *Tarikh al-'allamah Ibn Khaldun*, edited by Y.A. Daghir, 1956–1961.

Isenberg, C.W., and J.L. Krapf, *The Journals of the Rev. Messrs. Isenberg and Krapf, Missionaries of the Church Missionary Society, Detailing Their Proceedings in the Kingdom of Shoa, and Journeys in Other Parts of Abyssinia, in the Years 1839, 1840, 1841, and 1842*, 1843.

Krapf, J.L., *Travels, Researches and Missionary Labours during an Eighteen Years' Residence in Eastern Africa*, 1860; reprinted with an introduction by R.C. Bridges, 1968.

Lefebvre, Théophile, et al., *Voyage en Abyssinie exécuté pendant les années 1839–43*, 6 vols., 1845–1851.

Littmann, Enno, *Publications of the Princeton Expedition to Abyssinia*, 4 vols., 1910–1915.

Lobo, Jerónimo, *Itinerário, e outros escritos inéditos*, edited by Manuel Gonçalves da Costa, 1971; as *The Itinerário of Jerónimo Lobo*, translated by Donald M. Lockhart, with an introduction and notes by C.F. Beckingham, 1984.

Longhena, Mario (editor), *Viaggi in Persia, India e Giava di Nicolò de' Conti, Girolamo Adorno e Girolamo da Santo Stefano*, 1929.

Ludolf, Hiob, *Historia Aethiopica, sive brevis et succinta descriptio Regni Habessinorum quod vulgo male Presbyteri Iohannis vocatur*, 1681.

Massaia, Guglielmo, *I miei trentacinque anni di missione nell'-Alta Etiopia*, 12 vols., 1885–1895; reprinted, 1921–1930.

Mitzakis, Demosthenes, *Journey to Abyssinia* (in Greek), 1889.

Mondon-Vidhailet, François M.C., "Lettres d'Abyssinie" series, *Le Temps* (1892–1898).

Monfreid, Henri, *Vers les terres hostiles de l'Éthiopie*, 1933.

Munzinger, Werner, *Ostafrikanische Studien, von Werner Munzinger: Mit einer Karte von Nord-Abyssinien und den Ländern am Mareb, Barka und Anseba*, 1864.

Murphy, Dervla, *In Ethiopia with a Mule*, 1968.

Paez, Pero, *Historia Aethiopiae*, in *Rerum Aethiopicarum scriptores occidentales inediti a saeculo XVI ad XIX*, edited by Camillo Beccari, vols. 2–3, 1905–1906.

Paulitschke, Philipp, *Harar-Forschungsreise nach den Somâl- und Galla-Ländern Ost-Afrikas*, 1888.

Plowden, Walter Chichele, *Travels in Abyssinia and the Galla Country*, edited by Trevor Chichele Plowden, 1868.

Polo, Marco, *La Description du monde* [c. 1395] edited by Pierre-Yves Badel, 1988; as *The Book of Marco Polo*, edited and translated by Henry Yule, 3rd edition revised by Henri Cordier, 1903.

Prester, John, *The Letter and the Legend*, edited and translated by Vsevolod Slessarev, 1959.

Prutky, Remedius, *Prutky's Travels in Ethiopia and Other Countries*, translated and edited by J.H. Arrowsmith-Brown, annotated by Richard Pankhurst, 1991.

Ranzano, Pietro, *Annales omnium temporum* [c. 1450], in "Un Italiano in Etiopia," by Carmelo Trasselli, *Rassegna di Studi Etiopici*, 1/2 (1941): 173–202.

Rassam, Hormuzd, *Narrative of the British Mission to Theodore, King of Abyssinia*, 2 vols., 1869.

Rimbaud, Arthur, *Voyage en Abyssinie et au Harrar*, 1928.

Rohlfs, Gerhard, *Meine Mission nach Abessinien*, 1883; reprinted, 1983.

Rüppell, Eduard, *Reise in Abyssinien*, 2 vols., 1838–1840.

Salt, Henry, *A Voyage to Abyssinia*, 1814; reprinted, 1967.

Simeonis, Simon, *Itinerarium Symonis Semeonis an Hibernia ad Terram Sanctam*, edited by Mario Esposito, 1960.

Stern, Henry A., *The Captive Missionary, Being an Account of the Country and People of Abyssinia, Embracing a Narrative of King Theodore's Life, and His Treatment of Political and Religious Missions*, 1869.

Thesiger, Wilfred, *The Danakil Diary: Journeys through Abyssinia*, 1930–1934.
Waugh, Evelyn, *Remote People*, 1931; as *They Were Still Dancing*, 1932.

*See also* **Jesuit Narratives: Eastern Missions**

## ETHNOGRAPHY

Ethnography involves the study of sociocultural systems of meaning through participant-observation research. The first ethnographers sought to describe and record the strange and exotic customs of other cultures. A distinction has long been made between armchair ethnographers who consulted works written by others who had traveled to foreign lands and ethnographers (fieldworkers) who collected their own material. Herodotus (484–c. 425 BCE), the Greek historian and traveler, is one of the first to describe cultural and linguistic diversity with a mixture of scientific and humanistic approaches. He reported on customs, beliefs, and material culture among more than 50 peoples, with a surprising lack of ethnocentrism and a comparative approach that sought to accumulate knowledge about human lifestyles.

Ethnography began to take shape as an approach within the wider discipline of anthropology during the nineteenth century. Travel across space became associated with travel to the past (Fabian, 1983) within the framework of evolutionist thinking. It was linked to natural history, with the collection and classification of customs and beliefs recorded through field observations. Guides to such work, such as the British Association's *Notes and Queries on Anthropology* (1874), appeared. Three key figures in early ethnography are Lewis Henry Morgan (1818–1881) in the United States, and Edward Burnett Tylor (1832–1917) and J.G. Frazer (1854–1941) in Britain. Influenced by ideas of cultural evolution, they sought to categorize cultural systems according to stages of human development. Morgan, a lawyer who lived in upstate New York, lived close to the Iroquois tribe and recorded their kinship system in great detail based on visits and interviews. Tylor, while known as an armchair anthropologist, sifted through data collected by missionaries, explorers, and other observers of foreign customs, to develop a concept of culture as a complex whole. This way of thinking about culture eventually led to more systematic ethnographic studies in the next generation of field-workers. Frazer's classic, multivolume *The Golden Bough* (1890–1915) is a collection of the customs of human societies placed within an evolutionary framework in which "primitives" are seen as irrational and childlike. Like Tylor, Frazer was not a fieldworker himself. For contemporary ethnographers, fieldwork encounters are essential to breaking down abstract and racist paradigms of "primitive" and "civilized" peoples.

During the twentieth century, ethnography and fieldwork became associated with long-term participant-observation research within cultures other than that of the anthropologist. The emphasis became that of gaining the "native point of view" (Malinowski, 1922). Travels to the Pacific, Africa, and South America were common, as were those within the United States to Indian reservations in the Southwest. The so-called father of American anthropology, Franz Boas, instilled the importance of fieldwork among his students. Margaret Mead, his most famous student, went off to Samoa in the early 1920s to study female experiences of adolescence. This was the first of many field trips for Mead to various islands of the Pacific. Her collected *Letters from the Field, 1925–1975* (1977) shed light on her experiences and on her approach to recording human behavior and the influence of culture upon it. Her autobiography, *Blackberry Winter: My Earlier Years* (1972), also chronicles her fieldwork and ethnographic travel experiences. The Polish-born British social anthropologist Bronisław Malinowski (1884–1942) has long set the standard for intensive, long-term field research. He spent several years in the Trobriand Islands, resulting in several works of ethnography, including *Argonauts of the Western Pacific* (1922). His diaries of this research were posthumously published in 1967, leading to a "crisis in anthropology" (Stocking, 1992) because of the candid details on his activities and emotions during his research. Claude Lévi-Strauss (1908–) the French structuralist anthropologist, published an account of his first encounters with little-known South American tribal peoples in *Tristes Tropiques* (1955).

For several generations ethnographers wrote academic accounts of the indigenous peoples while not detailing their own experiences in the field; at the same time, many of these same writers published parallel works that gave autobiographical accounts of ethnographic encounters (Tedlock, 1991). One of these was published in novel form under a pseudonym: *Return to Laughter* (1954) by Elenore Bowen (Laura Bohannan), about ethnographic research of a West African tribe. Other early first-person accounts of ethnography include Jean Briggs's *Never in Anger: Portrait of an Eskimo Family* (1970) and Gerald Berreman's *Behind Many Masks: Ethnography and Impression Management in a Himalayan Village* (1962). Wives who accompanied their husbands in ethnographic research were also prompted to write about their experiences, most notably Elizabeth Fernea (who eventually became a professional anthropologist). Her books include *Guests of the Sheik: An Ethnography of an Iraqi Vil-*

*lage* (1969) and *A Street in Marrakech* (1975), in which she offers her view of women in Morocco.

Contemporary anthropology has been marked by what Cole calls the "reflexive tradition" (1992). Texts aiming to combine autobiographical accounts of fieldwork with theoretical and ethnographic analyses began to appear in earnest in the 1970s. Paul Rabinow chronicles his travels and adventures in *Reflections on Fieldwork in Morocco* (1977) and Jean-Paul Dumont combines personal experience and ethnography in *The Headman and I: Ambiguity and Ambivalence in the Fieldworking Experience* (1978). It is now increasingly common for all published ethnographic monographs to include some material on the experience of fieldwork. Accounts of fieldwork have been called "confessional tales" by van Maanen (1975), and "fables of rapport" by Clifford (1986). Tropes of arrival and of ways of establishing rapport with indigenous populations have been analyzed by Marcus and Cushman (1982). Numerous accounts of ethnographic experiences have recently been published in edited collections, such as DeVita's *The Naked Anthropologist: Tales from around the World* (1992) and Okely and Callaway's *Anthropology and Autobiography* (1992).

DEBORAH REED-DANAHAY

### References and Further Reading

Berreman, Gerald, *Behind Many Masks: Ethnography and Impression Management in a Himalayan Village*, 1962.

Bowen, Elenore Smith, *Return to Laughter*, 1954.

Briggs, Jean L., *Never in Anger: Portrait of an Eskimo Family*, 1970.

Clifford, James and George E. Marcus (editors), *Writing Culture: The Poetics and Politics of Ethnography*, Berkeley: University of California Press, 1986.

Cole, Sally, "Anthropological Lives: The Reflexive Tradition in Social Science" in *Essays on Life Writing: From Genre to Critical Practice*, edited by Marlene Kadar, Toronto: University of Toronto Press, 1992.

DeVita, Philip R. (editor), *The Naked Anthropologist: Tales from around the World*, 1992.

Doubleday, Veronica, *Three Women of Herat*, 1988.

Du Boulay, Juliet, *Portrait of a Greek Mountain Village*, 1974.

Dumont, Jean-Paul, *The Headman and I: Ambiguity and Ambivalence in the Fieldworking Experience*, 1978.

Fabian, Johannes, *Times and the Other: How Anthropology Makes Its Object*, New York: Columbia University Press, 1983.

Fernea, Elizabeth Warnock, *Guests of the Sheik: An Ethnography of an Iraqi Village*, 1969.

Fernea, Elizabeth Warnock, *A Street in Marrakech*, 1975.

Frazer, J.G., *The Golden Bough: A Study in Magic and Religion*, 12 vols., 1890–1915; abridged edition, 1 vol., 1922; numerous subsequent reprints.

Herodotus, *The Histories*, translated by Aubrey de Sélincourt, revised edition, with an introduction by John Marincola, 1996.

Lévi-Strauss, Claude, *Tristes Tropiques*, 1955; as *Tristes Tropiques*, translated by John Weightman and Doreen Weightman, 1997.

Malinowski, Bronisław, *Argonauts of the Western Pacific: An Account of Native Enterprise and Adventure in the Archipelagoes of Melanesian New Guinea*, with an introduction by J.G. Frazer, 1922.

Malinowski, Bronisław, *A Diary in the Strict Sense of the Term*, translated by Norbert Guterman, 1967.

Marcus, George and Dick Cushman, "Ethnographies as Texts", *Annual Review of Anthropology*, 11 (1982): 25–69.

Mead, Margaret, *Blackberry Winter: My Earlier Years*, 1972.

Mead, Margaret, *Letters from the Field, 1925–1975*, 1977.

Okely, Judith, and Helen Callaway (editors), *Anthropology and Autobiography*, 1992.

Rabinow, Paul, *Reflections on Fieldwork in Morocco*, 1977.

Stocking, George W. Jr., *The Ethnographer's Magic and Other Essays in the History of Anthropology* Madison: University of Wisconsin Press, 1992.

Tedlock, Barbara, "From Participant Observation to the Observation of Participation: The Emergence of Narrative Enthnography" *Journal of Ethnographic Research*, 47/1 (1991): 69–94.

Tylor, Edward Burnett, *Primitive Culture: Researches into the Development of Mythology, Philosophy, Religion, Art, and Custom*, 1871.

van Maanen, John, *Tales of the Field: On Writing Ethnography*, Chicago: University of Chicago Press, 1988.

*See also* **Ethics, Issues of**

## EUSTACE, JOHN (c. 1762–1815) *Irish Traveler*

John Chetwode Eustace was a latitudinarian Roman Catholic priest and a close friend of Edmund Burke, whose deathbed he attended and on whom he composed an elegy (1798). He wrote his celebrated and popular work on Italy as a result of his experiences as the traveling personal tutor of young relatives of Lord Petre between 18 February and 7 October 1802. Initially titled *A Tour through Italy, Exhibiting a View of its Scenery, Its Antiquities and Its Monuments, Particularly as They Are Objects of Classical Interest and Elucidation, with an Account of the Present State of Its Cities and Towns, and Occasional Observations on the Recent Spoliations of the French* (1813), it became known by its later title as Eustace's *A Classical Tour through Italy* (2nd edition, 1814) and reached eight editions by 1841.

Its pedagogical origins (Eustace addressed the work "solely to persons of a liberal education") are evident in its structure, beginning with the preliminary discourse on the necessary preparation for travel to Italy, which included a grounding in the classics and in modern Latin and Italy-loving poets; knowledge of the Italian language and of the history of Italy, and familiarity with its fine arts, although music was more safely avoided as it "too often leads to low and dishonourable connexions". In the next 44 chapters, he describes many cities he visited on his journey, pursuing a route from Salzburg through the Brenner Pass to Venice, then Bologna, across the Apennines to Rome, Naples, Vesuvius, Herculaneum, Paestum, Capua, back to Rome, Florence, Pistoia, Lucca, Pisa, Livorno, Genoa, Milan, the lakes, Turin, and returning via Mont Cenis. Rome is most fully treated, with nine chapters on the way out and three on the way back. Following this, Eustace gives a dissertation on the geography and history of Italy and on the language, literature, and character of Italians. Next there is an appendix on the institution of the papacy as spiritual and civic authority and a postscript containing a report "from a friend" of the French excavations under Napoleonic rule.

The book was well reviewed by Whig and high church publications. The *Edinburgh Review* (July 1813), and the *British Critic* (three successive articles, March, April, May 1814) were both attracted by its easy manner and the pleasure of the copiously quoted classical illustrations. However, the author's francophobia and uncritical partisanship for the government of ancient Rome, "habitually mild, and only teazed into resentment," particularly in the discursive chapters when returning to Rome, were severely criticized by both reviews and seen as approaching the "turgid declamation of a fifth-form school boy" by the *British Critic*. Many inaccuracies of geographical location, ancient history, and classical and Italian language were challenged. So were some of Eustace's political sentiments, ranging from his praise for the moderation of Augustus to his declaration of the superiority of having a mediocrity ("without either defect or excellency") as king of Naples. Even the high Tory *Quarterly Review* (October 1813) jibbed at Eustace's notion "that nothing hostile to the French can possibly be wrong," and chided him for recommending a "form of government which furnished the most abundant cause for complaint." Another criticism was that Eustace was verbose and repetitious.

When John Cam Hobhouse also attacked Eustace (deceased at the time) in his notes to Byron's *Childe Harold's Pilgrimage*, canto 4 (1816), he was not breaking new ground, except by the force of his dismissal of *A Classical Tour*, which he unfavorably compared to Forsyth's *Italy*. He accused Eustace of being so inaccurate "as to induce a suspicion that he had either never visited the spots described, or had trusted to the fidelity of former writers" and his commentary of being "swelled out by those decorations which are so easily supplied by a systematic adoption of all the common places of praise . . . The unction of a divine and the exhortations of the moralist, may have made the work more and better than a book of travels, but they have not made it a book of travels." These charges were sufficient to polarize opinion. The *British Critic*, which had recommended Forsyth as having "a large proportion of the best qualifications for a traveler, full possession of the language, and of the attainments of a scholar, with a mind of prompt and active powers, a judgment on works of art already informed and exercised" (January 1817) transformed him into "grumbling" Forsyth (July 1819) and declared, "Mr. Eustace will be our closet companion, and one in whom we shall most and longest delight" (September 1819).

The second edition of 1814 added a map of Italy (copied from Zannoni, whom Eustace had recommended in his Preliminary Discourse), two more plans of churches (making a total of ten), and the index that the *British Critic* asked for. Purchasers of the first edition could buy these additions for five shillings. In 1821 Joseph Mawman's editor added a preface to the sixth edition, defending Eustace against the various attacks, and counterattacking Forsyth's *Italy*. At the same time, the work was made more accessible by the addition of translations of all quotations. The book had become more like a guidebook for the general public than an instructive companion for those who could afford a "liberal education" and it continued to please with what the *Edinburgh Review* called "its principal object [of] classical illustration."

In 1814 Eustace wrote *A Letter from Paris*, which recounted his experience of a visit in June of that year. It runs to 100 pages and laments the destruction of churches, the prevalence of "dry science and atheism," and the retention of artworks despoiled from Italy, which would, he claimed, retard the progress of art in the country to which they belonged. The restored monarchy was precarious and the French had not gained from the recent wars: their literature was in decline and their military tactics were exploded. The war had "corrupted their morals, and perverted their principles; had it lasted one generation more, France would have been inhabited by monsters." The *British Critic* favorably reviewed this jeremiad in September 1814, contrasting Eustace's considered approach with the unthinking "childish, impotent, and vapid curiosity" of "cockney tourists" who rushed to Paris at that time.

KEITH CROOK

## Biography

Born in Ireland, c. 1762. Probably educated at Sedgley Park School, Staffordshire, 1767–1774. Attended the Benedictine convent of St. Gregory, Douai, France, from 1774, but did not become a full member of the order. Taught rhetoric at Maynooth College, Ireland; ordained as a Roman Catholic priest there. Returned to England; became confidential adviser to Edmund Burke. Taught in schools at Southall Park and Cossey

Park, near Norwich. Tutor at Oxford and Cambridge Universities. Traveled to Italy through France and Switzerland with three pupils, 1802. Lived at Jesus College, Cambridge, 1805, as tutor to George Petre. Traveled with Petre to Greece, Sicily, and Malta, c. 1808. Wrote an account of his Italian travels in *A Classical Tour* (1813). Visited France with Lords Carrington and Essex, June 1814. Returned to Italy, 1815, to collect materials for a new edition of *A Classical Tour*. Died of malaria in Naples, 1 August 1815.

### References and Further Reading

Eustace, John, *A Tour through Italy, Exhibiting a View of its Scenery, Its Antiquities and Its Monuments, Particularly as They Are Objects of Classical Interest and Elucidation, with an Account of the Present State of Its Cities and Towns, and Occasional Observations on the Recent Spoliations of the French*, 2 vols., 1813; 2nd–8th editions, as *A Classical Tour through Italy*, 1814–1841.

Eustace, John, *A Letter from Paris, to George Petre, Esq., with Critical Remarks on the State of Society, and the Moral Character of the French People*, 1814.

## EVELYN, JOHN (1620–1706) *English Diarist*

John Evelyn was born of a wealthy family at Wotton House in a wooded parish of Surrey. As a child he developed a love of the countryside and a lifelong loyalty to the Church of England. A royalist sympathizer, he did not fight in the civil war, but spent a large part of the 1640s traveling on the Continent. After 1660 he became known as a horticulturalist and held positions of trust to improve London streets, repair St. Paul's Cathedral, and care for wounded soldiers. He was also involved in the Royal Society's beginnings.

Evelyn's life spanned the end of the English Renaissance and the beginning of the scientific age, and these are viewpoints combined in his *Diary*, but his early education did not provide him with intellectual discipline, and he writes little of the politics, society, or the intellectual climate of foreign lands. Although he had an artistic temperament, he was discouraged by his father from pursuing art seriously, and his visual faculties may have been channeled instead into a drive to see art, monuments, and scenery.

On his first journey to the United Provinces and the Spanish Netherlands, from July to October 1641, he visited The Hague, Gennep, Rotterdam, Amsterdam, Haarlem, Leiden, Antwerp, Brussels, and Ghent. Ostensibly at least, his aim was to gain military experience by volunteering with the Dutch forces besieging the fortress at Gennep, but he had also come into his inheritance and was financially independent. Under the influence of Thomas Howard, Earl of Arundel, connoisseur of Continental art, he may already have begun to long for a chance to visit Europe's artistic and cultural centers.

When he arrived at Gennep in August, the fortress had been surrendered. After less than two weeks' discomfort at camp, he set off for Rotterdam and found himself in the midst of a flourishing Dutch culture. He was "amaz'd" by the array of pictures in Rotterdam's marketplace—the "Landscips, and Drolleries"—bought some, and sent them back to England. Soon an indefatigable collector, he also bought maps by Joan Blaeu and exotic curiosities in Amsterdam.

He was impressed with the "state, order & accomodations" of the soldiers' hospital in Amsterdam. His horticultural and urban-planning activities seem presaged by his delight in numerous gardens and his description of Amsterdam's Emperors Street as a "Citty in a Wood" with "stately ... Lime-trees, exactly planted before each-mans doore." His later work with the Royal Society is suggested by his description of the museum of "Naturall curiosities" at the Anatomy School at Leiden, which was, he writes:

> very well furnish'd with . . . all sorts of Skeletons, from the Whale & Eliphant, to the Fly, and the Spider, which last is a very delicat piece of Art, as well as Nature, how the bones (if so I may name them) of so tender an Insect, could possibly be separated from the mucilaginous parts of that minute animal. Here is the Sceletus of a Man on Horse-back, of a Tigar, and sundry other creatures: . . . Two . . . entire Mummies, Fishes, Serpents, Shells, divers Urnes; The figure of Isis cut in wood of a greate Proportion & Antiquity; a large Crocodile.

The passage shows a tendency toward cataloging, but Evelyn's seemingly indiscriminate interests display the sense of wonder of a curious young man living just before the age of specialized knowledge.

He returned to England in October 1641, and in November 1642 tried tried to assist the king in the battle of Brentford, but arrived with "horse and Armes just at the retreate." Believing that if he joined royalist forces, the Evelyn estate would be forfeited with no benefit to his family or the king, and probably aware that he was unsuited to military life, he embarked on his most important journey, a four-year tour of France, Italy, and Switzerland, in November 1643.

He wintered in Paris, went to Tours the following summer, and arrived in Rome in November 1644, where his interests came into focus. Resolving "to spend no moment idly," he sought expert advice on what to see, hired a tour guide, and began an energetic round of monuments, artworks, libraries, natural history collections, gardens, and scenery. He was particularly impressed with the Aldobrandini and Farnese palaces and the Vatican.

That winter Evelyn went to Naples, drawing landscapes along the way. He ascended Mount Vesuvius on a mule until it became too steep, then crawled, bruised by volcanic rocks, to his reward: the view of Naples, one of "the goodliest prospects in the World." He left Rome in the spring, traveled by way of Florence and Bologna to Venice, and studied anatomy at Padua. In 1646 he crossed the Simplon Pass, contracted smallpox at Geneva, and recuperated in Switzerland before reaching Paris in July. The following year he married the 12-year-old daughter of the English ambassador to France, but left her with her mother and returned to London in October 1647.

Charles I was executed in January 1649. With no hope of employment in what he considered a regicide government, Evelyn returned to Paris that July and lived among royalist exiles associated with his father-in-law. In February 1652 he returned to England and was joined that summer by his wife. In 1654 he toured Oxford, where he saw the Bodleian Library's rarities, York, and Cambridge; a brief trip to Suffolk in 1656 included a visit to an Ipswich prison populated with Quakers, "a new phanatic sect of dangerous Principles."

Evelyn never intended to publish his *Diary*. There is no reason to doubt his intention to tell the truth in the portion detailing his travels, but de Beer's footnotes detail many factual errors, and the account is largely based on earlier travel books. The portion of the diary covering his travels was written from his notes years after the events; it is, therefore, not a true travel diary, but a memoir in diary form. Used attentively, however, de Beer's 1955 edition is indispensable to the study of seventeenth-century travel and the history of English taste.

LAURA NILGES-MATIAS

## Biography

Born at Wotton House, near Dorking, Surrey, 31 October 1620. Attended Southover School, Lewes, Sussex, 1630–1637. Studied at Balliol College, University of Oxford, 1637–1640; did not graduate. Obtained part of a chamber in the Middle Temple but did not study law, 1640. Traveled in the United Provinces and Spanish Netherlands, 1641. Served in the royalist army, 1642. Toured France, Italy, and Switzerland, 1643–1647. Lived in Paris, 1649–1652. Married Mary, daughter of Sir Richard Browne, the English ambassador to France, 1647: six sons, three of whom died as infants, and three daughters. Acquired Sayes Court, near Deptford, London, 1652. Toured England, 1654 and 1656. Published numerous original works and translations, 1649–1706, including *Sylva, or a Discourse of Forest-Trees* (1664). Named as a candidate of what would become the Royal Society, 1660; founding fellow and council member, Royal Society, 1662; secretary, 1672–1673. Appointed to the London Streets Commission, 1662, and the Mint Committee, 1663. Commissioner for seamen wounded in the Dutch Wars, 1664–1667 and 1672–1674. Appointed to a group reporting on proposals for the repair of St. Paul's Cathedral, 1666. Helped obtain the gift of the Arundel library to the Royal Society and of the Arundel marbles to the University of Oxford, 1667. Awarded DCL, University of Oxford, 1669. Member, Council for Foreign Plantations, 1671–1674; commissioner for the Privy Seal, 1685–1687. Moved to Wotton House, 1694; inherited the estate at Wotton, 1699. With Christopher Wren, laid foundation stone for Greenwich Hospital, 1696; treasurer until 1703. Died at his London house, Dover Street, 27 February 1706.

## References and Further Reading

Evelyn, John, *Memoirs, Illustrative of the Life and Writings of John Evelyn, Esq. F.R.S. Author of the "Sylva", &c. &c. Comprising his Diary, from the Year 1641 to 1705–6, and a Selection of his Familiar Letters*, 2 vols., edited by William Bray and William Upcott, 1818; revised edition, 2 vols., 1819; 5 vols., 1827; revised and enlarged, edited by William Bray and John Forster, 4 vols., 1850–1852; as *The Diary of John Evelyn*, edited by E.S. de Beer, 1955; edited by Guy de la Bédoyève, 1994; selections, as *John Evelyn's Diary*, edited by Philip Francis, 1965; and as *The Diary of John Evelyn*, edited by John Bade, 1983.

# EVLIYA ÇELEBI (1611–c. 1684) *Turkish Scholar and Official*

"The traveler of the World," as he called himself, adopted a pseudonym to disguise his true identity: "Evliya" honored a court imam, while "Çelebi" is simply a title indicating an educated person or gentleman. Evliya Çelebi was certainly well educated as an Ottoman gentleman official, but we are entirely dependent for our knowledge of his life and travels on a single work, his *Seyahatname* [Book of Travels]. He claimed to be descended from an old Ottoman family that had served the sultans as soldiers and scholars and held property in western Anatolia. The thirst for travel came, he said, in a vision and he took every opportunity to quench it. According to Joseph von Hammer, Evliya Çelebi made some 22 separate journeys, often traveling in the suite of a high Ottoman official, but sometimes on his own account.

Evliya Çelebi's travels began in the 1630s with an exploration of his native city, Istanbul, and its surrounding districts, though in 1634 he accompanied Murat IV's expedition against Persia. In 1640 he visited the cities of Bursa and Izmit (Nicomedia) before traveling to Trabzon (Trebizond) with the new governor. From there he was able to make his way through the Caucasus to Azov, then under siege, and subsequently to accompany the Tartar army through the Crimea. Shipwrecked on the voyage back to Istanbul, he was able to see Bulgaria for the first time.

In 1645 Evliya Çelebi was part of the Ottoman military expedition against Venetian-ruled Crete and witnessed the siege of Hanya (Chania). The following year he traveled through northern Anatolia in the suite of the governor of Erzerum. A special mission took him on to Tabriz and allowed him to make another foray into the Caucasus. In 1648 he was appointed chief muezzin and imam to the annual pilgrim caravan to Mecca and traveled with the governor of Damascus to Syria, where the main caravan assembled. On completing the Hajj (pilgrimage), Evliya Çelebi took part in a campaign against the Druzes and traveled in Syria and Lebanon.

Attachment to his uncle and main patron, Abaza Melik Ahmet Pasha, gave an opportunity for a second, more extensive visit to Bulgaria (1651) and subsequently to southeastern Anatolia when the pasha became governor of Van. A mission to Persia followed, allowing Evliya Çelebi to explore the western provinces of the Persian empire and to visit the Baghdad and Basra districts (1655–1656).

Between 1659 and 1665 Evliya Çelebi fought with the Ottoman army in Transylvania, and traveled in Moldavia, Serbia, Montenegro, Bosnia, Herzegovina, and Croatia. Leaving the army, in 1665 he accompanied an Ottoman diplomatic mission to Vienna, where he may have resided for some time. After that he claims to have traveled extensively in central and eastern Europe for three years before returning to Istanbul, but this seems doubtful. However, he was in Crete again between 1667 and 1670 for the Venetian surrender of Kandiye (Candia/Herakleion) and accompanied the grand vizier's punitive expedition against the Mani district in the southern Peloponnese. Further travels in the 1670s took him to western and southwestern Anatolia and Syria. He completed the Hajj again and appears to have settled in Egypt for several years. He traveled in Upper Egypt, the Sudan, and Ethiopia searching for the sources of the Nile, before he settled down to compiling his great travel book.

Evliya Çelebi's reputation rests on his 10-volume *Seyahatname*, in which his travels are arranged chronologically. It survives in several manuscript copies, but what is thought to be the archetype is clearly a rough draft, full of gaps and richly annotated with notes for inclusion and improvement, on which the author may have been working when he died. Its format largely accounts for what Pallis described as "its methodless and unliterary form," though the style of writing is both educated and conversational, sophisticated in its use of rhymed and rhythmic prose and characterized by puns and hyperbole. Its scholarly value has also been questioned: Evliya Çelebi clearly writes about places he never visited (e.g., northern Europe); the influence of professional storytellers is apparent in his delight in the fanciful and mythical, while folk tales and oral traditions are repeated uncritically; and he is guilty of carelessness and error. On the other hand, the *Seyahatname* draws upon a range of official documents, Turkish translations, and editions of prominent Western geographers, and contains the results of much firsthand observation (including measurements) recorded, although somewhat unsystematically, in notebooks. Particular interest is shown in the great cities of the Ottoman empire (one volume is devoted entirely to Istanbul), and the accounts suggest the use of a "mental questionnaire" (Faroqhi, 1999) in the collection of information. In fact, where Evliya Çelebi has been carefully checked, as in the case of Diyarbakir in southeastern Anatolia, he has been shown to be a sound and conscientious observer. "The figures he gives both regarding finance and physical measurements, were generally correct" (Bruinessen and Boeschoten, 1988), while his descriptions of buildings in the city (two-thirds of which survive) were more precise and systematic than those of all other early travelers (Kiel in Bruinessen and Boeschoten, 1988).

The doubtful reputation of the *Seyahatname* is largely the result of the poor quality of the first complete printed edition. Not only was this based on an imperfect manuscript, but the original editor bowdlerized the text in several ways, omitting difficult passages and changing others, while adding ridiculous figures for places where the archetype leaves a gap. Even if the information is incidental to Evliya Çelebi's intention of producing a piece of imaginative writing, as Faroqhi claims (1999), his *Seyahatname* does contain reliable observations about buildings seen and routes traveled, the social and economic life of his time, and Ottoman administrative arrangements. In addition, this "Ottoman Ibn Battuta" (Babinger, 1927) presents much that is of interest to students of folklore and the Turkish language, especially in his occasional use of local words and careful discussions of dialect.

MALCOLM WAGSTAFF

## Biography

Born in the Unkapani district of Istanbul (between the Golden Horn and Zeyrek Camii), 25 March 1611 (10 Muharram 1020). After elementary school, spent seven years at a *medresse* in Istanbul and trained as a reciter of the Qur'an. Later studied calligraphy, music, poetry, and Persian in the palace school. Became a cavalry soldier (*sipahi*). Explored the city of Istanbul and its neighborhood, 1630–1631. Traveled extensively within the Ottoman Empire and in neighboring territories, c. 1640–1676. Completed his travels in Egypt and worked on his *Seyahatnamesi* [Travel Book]. Died in Egypt, or possibly Adrianople or Istanbul, c. 1684.

### References and Further Reading

Evliya Çelebi, *Seyahatnamesi* [Book of Travels], 10 vols., 1896–1938; in part as *Narrative of Travels in Europe, Asia and Africa*, translated by Joseph von Hammer, 2 vols., 1834–1850.

Evliya Çelebi, *Im Reiche des Goldenen Apfels, des turkischen Weltenbummlers Evliya Celebi denkwurdige Reise in das Giaurenland und in die Stadt und Festung Wien anno 1665* [In the State of the Golden Horn. The Turkish World traveler Evliya Çelebi's Memorable Journey to the Land of the Infidel and the City and Fortress of Vienna in the Year 1665], translated and annotated by Richard F. Kreutel et al., 2nd edition, 1987.

Bruinessen, Martin van and Hendrik Boeschoten (editors), *Evliya Çelebi in Diyarbekir: The Relevant Section of the Seyahatname,* with translation, commentary and an introduction, Leiden and New York: E.J. Brill, 1988.

Faroqhi, Suraiya, *Approaching Ottoman History: An Introduction to the Sources,* Cambridge and New York: Cambridge University Press, 1999.

*See also* **Ottoman Empire**

## EXILE

Exile (from the Latin *exilium*, meaning banishment), the condition of prolonged separation from one's country or home, by force or by circumstances, has generated a large body of literary works. Adam and Eve's banishment from paradise can be viewed as mankind's first exilic experience. One can argue that ever since the Fall human beings have lived in exile, yearning for the paradise lost. Some of the fundamental themes explored by the literature of exile are to be found in the Old Testament: the Tower of Babel (Genesis 11) accounts for the geographical dispersal of humankind and for its permanent exile from a common language. Exodus, the Hebrews' return from Egypt to Canaan, is the paradigmatic narrative of an exiled people's passage from bondage to freedom.

The Exile commonly refers to the Babylonian captivity (587–538 BCE) of the Jews who, after the capture of Jerusalem, became forced laborers in the empire of Nebuchadnezzar. "By the waters of Babylon, there we sat down and wept, when we remembered Zion" (Psalm 137) has come to epitomize the exilic condition. While the dream of the self-exiled English Puritans was to build "a city upon a hill" in North America, many seventeenth-century captivity narratives (for example *The Captivity and Restoration of Mary Rowlandson*, 1682) liken the "errand into the wilderness" to the Babylonian exile.

On the whole, the literature of exile is concerned with travel and exploration in a peculiar way. Exiled writers are more inclined to introspection and nostalgia than to the exploration and description of their new surroundings. Since ancient times, banished authors have turned to the philosophical or moral essay in order to raise such existential questions as allegiance to the homeland, to religion, to political ideas and ideals. For the stoic philosopher Seneca (4 BCE–65 CE), exile is a metonymy for the human condition. Written during his exile in Corsica, "In Consolation, A Letter from Exile to his Mother, Helvia" contains the famous plea for universality, "inside the world there can be found no place of exile; for nothing that is inside the world is foreign to mankind." More often than not, the exiled writer seems frozen at the moment of arrival, unable to accept his forced removal from the homeland, from the loved ones. Banished to Tomis, a remote port on the Black Sea, the Roman poet Ovid (43 BCE–17 CE) adopts a passive stance as he complains about the miseries of solitude and pathetically appeals for clemency to the emperor Augustus (*Tristia* and *Ex Ponto*).

By and large, the literature of exiled writers and of displaced communities echoes the paradox of an impossible, yet hoped-for, return to the native country. While the separation is perceived as merely temporary, the return to the homeland would inevitably deprive the writer of the very subject matter of his work. Thus, "the exile's whole being is [necessarily] concentrated on the land he left behind" (McCarthy, 1985).

The year 1492 marked a watershed in the history of exile: the "discovery of the New World" was accompanied by the expulsion of the Arabs and the Jews from the Iberian peninsula. Contemporary Sephardic writers like Victor Perera (*The Cross and the Pear Tree: A Sephardic Journey*, 1995) consider themselves to this day as exiles from their beloved homeland. Whether through (temporary or permanent) emigration, expatriation, or (internal or external) exile, many writers were moved to leave their native country or permanent residence in the course of the twentieth century. A focus on some examples will illustrate the main trends of the literature of exile.

In the 1920s and 1930s, Paris provided a cultural shelter for many African American, Latin American, and Russian authors (for example Richard Wright, Octavio Paz, Nina Berberova); among them was Vladimir Nabokov, whose *Speak, Memory* (1966) remains the paradigmatic autobiography of a writer in exile.

The tremendous political and social upheavals that took place in this "age of the refugee" brought about the displacement of entire communities. Totalitarian regimes sent their most outspoken writers and dissidents into exile. During World War II, Thomas Mann,

Lion Feuchtwanger, Theodor Adorno, and other German and Jewish writers continued to criticize their homeland from outside its borders. Aleksandr Solzhenitzyn's *The First Circle* (a reference to Dante's Hell) is a denunciation of the Gulag based on the writer's own experience in the labor camps of the Soviet Union. Primo Levi's life and work bear witness to the ultimate form of exile—survival in the concentration camp. *If This Is a Man* (1947) retraces the everyday horror of Auschwitz, while *The Truce* (1963) follows the author's painful journey back home.

The term *diaspora*, which referred originally to the dispersal of the Jews after the second destruction of the temple in Jerusalem, is increasingly used to designate the displacement of other communities such as Cubans, Palestinians, and Native Americans. This new diasporic literature explores, mainly through autobiographical narratives and essays, the effects of deterritorialization on the writer's inner self. Cuban writers in France and especially in the United States (for example, Zoe Valdes, Reinaldo Arenas, Cristina Garcia) pursue a relentless dialogue between the present and the past, between the "here" and the "there." The separation from the homeland, and the feeling of orphanhood from the fatherland and from the mother tongue account for the shifting in narrative perspective and for the switching of languages.

Indeed, exile can be a fertile human and artistic experience as it heightens the writer's power of introspection and favors expression in the second language. As George Steiner has noted in *Extra-territorial*, "the writer as linguistic polymath, as actively at home in several languages, is something very new." *Lost in Translation: A Life in a New Language* (1989) by Eva Hoffman is an immigrant writer's attempt to translate the cultural exile from her mother tongue (Polish) into an autobiographical narrative written in English.

In his seminal essay *Imaginary Homelands*, Salman Rushdie considers that the "physical fact of discontinuity" enables exiled writers "to speak properly and concretely on a subject of universal significance and appeal." The remark is confirmed by Edward Said's *Out of Place: A Memoir* (1999), which centers around the political upheavals in the Middle East, or by Ariel Dorfman's *Heading South, Looking North: A Bilingual Journey* (1998), a Chilean expatriate's tale of multiple exiles, of switches in languages and cultures.

A significant number of exiled writers are Nobel Prize winners: Thomas Mann, Boris Pasternak, Aleksandr Solzhenitzyn, Joseph Brodsky, or Wole Soyinka. Estranged from the mother tongue, the exiled writer is driven from language to language in what may be the most radical of exiles. Some of the most outstanding contemporary literary works come from such "poets unhoused and wanderers across language" as Nabokov, Beckett, or Kafka.

Ada Savin

### References and Further Reading

Camus, Albert, *Lyrical and Critical Essays*, edited by Philip Thody, translated by Ellen Conroy Kennedy, 1968.

Conrad, Joseph, *Notes on Life and Letters*, 1921.

Dorfman, Ariel, *Heading South, Looking North: A Bilingual Journey*, 1998.

Garcia, Cristina, *Dreaming in Cuban*, 1992.

Hoffman, Eva, *Lost in Translation: A Life in a New Language*, 1989.

McCarthy, Mary, "A guide to Exile, Expatriates, and Internal Emigrés" in her *Occasional Prose*, San Diego: Harcourt Brace, and London: Weidenfeld and Nicolson, 1985.

Nabokov, Vladimir, *Speak, Memory: An Autobiography*, 1966.

Ovid, *Tristia* and *Ex Ponto*, translated by Arthur Leslie Wheeler, 1924; 2nd edition revised by G.P. Gold, 1988.

Perera, Victor, *The Cross and the Pear Tree: A Sephardic Journey*, 1995.

Rousseau, Jean Jacques, *The Reveries of a Solitary Walker*, translated by Charles Butterworth, 1979.

Rowlandson, Mary, *The Soveraignty and Goodness of God . . . Being a Narrative of the Captivity . . . of Mrs Mary Rowlandson*, 1682; as *A Narrative of the Captivity, Sufferings and Removes of Mrs Mary Rowlandson: Who Was Taken Prison by the Indians*, 1770; as *The Narrative of the Captivity and Restoration of Mrs Mary Rowlandson*, edited by Henry Stedman Nourse and John Eliot Thayer, 1903; as *The Captive: The True Story of the Captivity of Mrs Mary Rowlandson among the Indians and God's Faithfulness to Her in Her Time of Trial*, with an introduction by Mark Ludwig, 1988.

Rushdie, Salman, *Imaginary Homelands, Essays and Criticism 1981–1991*, London and New York: Granta, 1991.

Said, Edward W., *Out of Place: A Memoir*, 1999.

Seneca, *Seneca in English*, edited by Don Share, 1998.

Staël, Germaine de, *An Extraordinary Woman: Selected Writings of Germaine de Staël*, edited and translated by Vivian Folkenflick, 1987.

Steiner, George, *Extra-territorial: Papers on Literature and the Language Revolution*, New York: Atheneum, 1971; London: Faber, 1972.

## EYRE, EDWARD (1815–1901) *Australian Explorer and Colonial Governor*

The son of a British clergyman, Edward John Eyre arrived in Australia at the age of 17 and determined that he would become a successful overlander of stock. Eyre gained bush experience by droving 1,000 sheep and 600 cattle from Canberra to Adelaide, during which great hardship was experienced in what is now western Victoria. In 1839 Eyre set out on his first expedition proper, venturing north from Adelaide in search of fertile country. What he found was dry, barren land, and a crescent of salt lakes that impeded any further movement. His journals describe his deep disappointment at being unable to find land that would assist the growing colony of South Australia, and his puzzlement at finding springs to be salty at their source. These travels and his earlier experiences in the colonies are recalled in his *Autobiographical Narrative* written in 1859, but unpublished until 1984. This memoir is notable for its humane and detailed description of Aboriginal life and customs, and for its equally understanding views of the convicts whom Eyre employed.

Eyre's other travel narrative was his *Journals of Expeditions of Discovery . . . in the Year 1840–41* (1845). In 1840 Eyre and a small party departed from Port Lincoln, west of Adelaide on the southern Australian coast. His original intention was to journey north into central Australia, but initial exploratory travels proved that this would be impracticable. Two short journeys to the west, along the coast of the Great Australian Bight, had shown him that this country too was almost impassable because of its lack of water. Despite the plea of the governor of South Australia not to attempt to cross the Bight, Eyre turned west on 25 February 1841 with a small party, including his friend John Baxter and the Aboriginals Wylie, Jarry, and Joey.

Nothing of the country was known to Europeans. The coast was a long line of spectacular cliffs that prohibited any resupply from ships or any view of the land from the sea. Very little water was in evidence, and it is unlikely that Eyre and his party would have been able to travel far without the assistance of local Aborigines. Eyre was more grateful for this help than many of his fellow explorers and settlers. "In how strong a light," Eyre writes, "does such simple kindness of the inhabitants of the wilds to Europeans traveling through his country (when his fears are not excited or his prejudices violated) stand contrasted with the treatment he experiences from them when they occupy his country, and dispossess him of his all."

It must be surmised on 29 April 1841, the trust that Jarry and Joey had in Eyre's leadership had been exhausted. Awakened by a flash and the report of a gun, Eyre ran to investigate. "Upon reaching the encampment, which I did in about five minutes after the shot was fired, I was horror-struck to find my poor overseer lying on the ground, weltering in his blood, and in the last agonies of death." Joey and Jarry had murdered Baxter, taken two guns and most of the food, and decamped. Dramatically, the first volume of the journals ends at this point.

The second volume opens with Eyre in a difficult plight. He was being shadowed by the two murderers and he had grave doubts about the faithfulness of Wylie, his remaining Aboriginal companion. Eyre writes, "The frightful, the appalling truth now burst upon me, that I was alone in the desert . . . The horrors of my situation glared upon me in such startling reality, as for an instant almost to paralyse the mind." Eyre determined to shoot the elder of the two rebels, but the opportunity passed and the two disappeared into the desert and into history.

Suffering dysentery and difficulty in digesting the horse they were forced to eat, Wylie and Eyre traveled slowly west through inhospitable land. Looking south he saw the formidable cliffs that formed the border between the Australian continent and the sea. These he described as having the "romantic appearance of massy battlements of masonry" and he lamented that he was not a painter. To his north were the seemingly endless plains of the Nullarbor desert, which offered no promise of a discovery of rich pastoral country. Exiting the western end of the Bight, Eyre and Wylie came upon an inlet he later named Rossiter Bay, in which the French whaler *Mississippi* was anchored. Although his destination, King George Sound and the settlement of Albany, still lay almost 300 miles away, Eyre decided to continue with the supplies the *Mississippi*'s captain had generously given him. They arrived in Albany on 7 July 1841 after walking through several weeks of inclement weather.

Australian explorers had a wide range of attitudes toward Aborigines. Some were openly contemptuous and some were disposed toward confrontation and violence. Quite often, however, sincere if paternalistic attempts were made to understand Aboriginal culture and to offer suggestions as to how this culture might best continue in a modified form in a European settler society. The second part of volume two of Eyre's *Journals of Expeditions of Discovery*, is entitled "Manners and Customs of the Aborigines of Australia," wherein Eyre carries out a detailed and sympathetic proto-ethnography of Aboriginal culture. While bewailing the tendency of Aborigines to decorate themselves, he did admire the corroboree (a native dance), but noted that like the panorama, it was "seen to most advantage at a distance." It is in the treatment of the Aborigines by the colonial process that Eyre is at his most fierce, and his journals on these issues are timely reminders that doubts about the unequal application of laws is not solely a modern phenomenon. In attacking the law of nations Eyre notes that it "provides not for the safety, privileges, and protection of the Aborigines, and owners of the soil, but . . . merely lays down rules for the direction of the privileged robber in the distribution of the booty of any newly discovered country" (*Journals of Expeditions*). Such liberal views toward the inhabitants were generated both through his travels and his time as resident magistrate and Protector of Aborigines on the Murray River, where he brought to a halt many of the violent conflicts between Aborigines and settlers. His views toward people of other races make all the more tragic Eyre's ultimate role as the governor during the Morant Bay uprising in Jamaica in 1865, where his declaration of martial law led to the killing of 600 people. This resulted in a bitter debate in England about the criminality of his actions, obscuring his reputation as a courageous and humane explorer.

SIMON RYAN

## Biography

Born in Hornsea, Yorkshire, England, 5 August 1815. Emigrated to Australia instead of pursing a planned army career, arriving in Sydney, 1833. Became a sheep farmer on the Molonglo Plains, south of present-day Canberra. Served as a magistrate and acted as a protector of Aborigines. Drove stock from Canberra to Port Phillip and Adelaide, 1837 and 1838. Explored regions north of Adelaide but was turned back by salt lakes, 1839–1840. Turned west; with his Aboriginal companion Wylie, crossed the Great Australian Bight from east to west, 1840–1841. Returned to England, 1845. Married Fanny Ormond, 1850: four sons and one daughter. Lieutenant-governor, New Zealand, 1846–1853; St. Vincent Island, 1854–1860. Captain-general and commander-in-chief of Jamaica, 1861–1864; governor, 1865. Severely repressed the Morant Bay uprising in Jamaica, 1865. Recalled to England, 1866; persecuted by opponents of his action and threatened with indictment for murder; failed to be indicted by grand jury, 1868. Acquitted in civil murder case, 1872. Received government pension beginning in 1874. Lived in Shropshire and later near Tavistock, Devon. Awarded Founder's medal of the Royal Geographical Society, 1843. Died near Tavistock, 30 November 1901.

## References and Further Reading

Eyre, Edward, *Journals of Expeditions of Discovery into Central Australia, and Overland from Adelaide to King George's Sound, in the Year 1840–41*, 1845.

Eyre, Edward, *Autobiographical Narrative of Residence and Exploration in Australia, 1832–1839*, edited by Jill Waterhouse, 1984.

# F

## FA-HSIEN (c. 340–418) *Chinese Buddhist Monk, Pilgrim, Writer, and Translator*

Fa-hsien is one of the earliest and best-known Buddhist pilgrims from China. He was born in Wu-yang in P'ing-yang Prefecture (in Shansi Province), and was fully ordained at the age of 20. Between 399 and 414 he "practically walked from Central China across the desert of Gobi, over the Hindu Kush, and through India down to the mouth of the Hoogly, where he took ship and returned by sea, after manifold hairbreadth escapes, to China, bringing with him what he went forth to secure—books of the Buddhist Canon and images of Buddhist deities" (Giles, 1923). In 416, at the request of his colleagues, Fa-Hsien wrote an autobiographical account of his journey known as *Fo-kuo chi* [A Record of the Buddhist Countries], and died in 418 at the Hsin Monastery of Ch'ing-chou (in Hopeh province).

His name is variously spelt, as Fa-Hien, Fa-hian, Fa-Hian, Faxian, and Fa-hsien. His original name was Kung. When he assumed the religious title of Fa-Hsien, which means "Illustrious in the Law," or "Illustrious Master of the Law," he also took the appellation of Shih or Sakyaputra, the disciple of Sakya (i.e., the Buddha).

Fa-Hsien had three older brothers. When they all died young, his father entered him as *a sramanera* (novice monk), although he remained at home with the family. When he fell dangerously ill, his father sent him to the monastery, where he soon got well but refused to return to his parents. When he had finished his novitiate, Fa-Hsien undertook his journey to India.

At the commencement of his work, Fa-hsien states the aim of his travels and gives the names of some of his fellow pilgrims: "Fa-hsien had been living in Ch'ang-gan. Deploring the mutilated and imperfect state of the collection of the Books of Discipline . . . he entered into an engagement with Kwuy-king, Tao-ching, Hui-ching, and Hwuy-wei, that they should go to India and seek for the Disciplinary Rules" (trans. Legge). The account that follows describes the places they visited, the rulers, the monks and others they met, what they saw and heard, and their varied personal experiences. As Legge has observed in his introduction, "Much of what Fa-hien tells his readers of Buddhist miracles and legends is indeed unreliable and grotesque; but we have from him the truth as to what he saw and heard."

The pilgrims set out from Ch'ang-gan in 399 and passed out of China through Ch'ien-kuei, Chang-yeh, and Tun-huang (all in northwestern China). From Tun-huang they proceeded along the southern marches of the Tarim basin to the Central Asian kingdoms of Shan-shan, Agni, and Khotan. From there they traveled to Chakarka, crossed the Pamirs and Agzi, and finally, three years after leaving China, arrived at the kingdom of Udyana in northern India, via Darada and the Indus River valley.

Fa-Hsien spent a summer retreat in Udyana, then traveled south through Suvastu, Gandara, Takshasila (Taxila), and arrived at Purusapura or Peshawar. There, three members of the mission decided to return to China. Fa-Hsien and the others continued the journey, traveling to Hilo and paying homage to the Buddha's shadow at Nagarhara. They crossed over the

Lesser Snow Mountain, where Hui-ching, one of the three members of the party, died. Fa-Hsien traveled on to Lakki, where he passed the summer retreat in 403, after which he went on to Mathura via Harana and Uccha.

He passed the summer retreat in 404 at Samkasya. Turning southeastward, he then passed through Kanyakubja (Kanauj), Vaisakha, the Jetavana grove at Sravasti, and the birthplace of the Buddha at the Lumbini near Kapilavastu on the Indo-Nepal border. From there he traveled east to Ramagrama, Kusinagara, Vaisali, and finally arrived at Pataliputra (present-day Patna), the capital of the Magadha kingdom. He remained there briefly before turning southeast. In Rajagrha he performed a rite of worship at the top of Grdhra-kuta. He worshipped the Bodhi Tree at Buddh Gaya, visited other places nearby, and returned to Pataliputra. From there he moved west, made a pilgrimage to Varanasi (Benares), the Mrgadava or Deer Park at Sarnath, and concluded the trip with a visit to Kausambi. Between the years 405 and 407, Fa-Hsien stayed at the Mahayana monastery of Pataliputra, concentrating on the study of the Sanskrit language and Buddhist scriptures of various sects. After the completion of his studies at Pataliputra, Tao-ching, the other surviving member of the party, expressed his wish to stay in India permanently, leaving Fa-Hsien to complete his mission alone. In 407 he left Pataliputra for Tamralipti in northeastern India (modern Tamluk) via Champa. He remained at Tamralipti for two years (408–409), after which he traveled to Sri Lanka. He stayed on the island for two years, made pilgrimages to the holy places, and attended lectures delivered by an Indian monk.

The account of his arrival in Sri Lanka is recorded in chapter 37 of *Fo-kuo chi*; chapters 37 through 39 contain his description of the island. The last chapter (40) describes how, after remaining on the island for two years and obtaining more texts, Fa-Hsien set off for home, the disastrous voyage to Yavadvipa (Sumatra) and on to China, his arrival at Shan-tung in 412 and continuation to Nanking, where, along with the Indian Sramana (ascetic) Buddha-bhadra, he translated some of the works that he had obtained in India and Sri Lanka. However, before he could complete this work, he moved to Ch'ing-chou and died at the age of 88, to the great sorrow of all who knew him.

The value of Fa-Hsien's visit to Sri Lanka and the record he made of it has been widely acknowledged. The nineteenth-century writer James Emerson Tennent makes much use of Fa-Hsien's personal testimony as a source for his book on Ceylon. Local tradition associates his name with the Buddhist cave temple called Fahiengala or Pahiengala, situated in Yatagampitiya village near Bulathsinhala in the Kalutara District in the lowland Wet Zone. It is believed that the pilgrim stayed there on his way to Sri-Pada, the sacred footprint of the Buddha on Adam's Peak.

D.P.M. Weerakkody

### Biography

Born Sehi in Wu-yang in Shansi Province, China, c. 340. Ordained as a Buddhist monk at the age of 20. Started traveling through central Asia to India, 399, arriving there in 402. Traveled through India, returning to China via Sri Lanka, in search of Buddhist books and images, 402–414. Wrote an account of his travels, 416. Died at the Hsin Monastery of Ch'ing-chou in Hopeh province, China, 418.

### References and Further Reading


Fa-hsien, *The Pilgrimage of Fa Hian, from the French Edition of the Foe Koue Ki of MM. Remusat, Klaproth, and Landresse, with Additional Notes and Illustrations*, 1848.

Fa-hsien, *Travels of Fah-Hian and Sung-Yun, Buddhist Pilgrims, from China to India (400 AD and 518 AD)*, translated by Samuel Beal, 1869; reprinted, 1964.

Fa-hsien, *Si-yu-ki: Buddhist Records of the Western World*, vol. 1: *Travels of Fa-Hian, or Fo-kwo-ki* [and other texts], translated by Samuel Beal, 1884; reprinted in 1 vol., 1969.

Fa-hsien, *A Record of Buddhistic Kingdoms, Being an Account by the Chinese Monk Fâ-hien of His Travels in India and Ceylon (AD 399–414) in Search of the Buddhist Books of Discipline*, edited and translated by James Legge, 1886; reprinted, 1965.

Fa-hsien, *The Travels of Fa-hsien (399–414 AD); or, Record of the Buddhistic Kingdom*, translated by H.A. Giles, 1923; reprinted, 1981.

Fa-hsien, *A Record of the Buddhist Countries by Fa-hsien*, translated by Li Yung-his, 1957.


## FANTASY TRAVEL WRITING

Those who narrate their impressions of remote and exotic locations nearly always feel the urge to amaze their untraveled audience. Throughout its history, travel writing proper has never quite shaken off its own far-fetched caricature. Indeed, serious fact and fickle fabrication are often so inseparable that, rather than see fantasy travel writing as an autonomous genre, one should perhaps envisage it as a tendency or mode capable of sabotaging credibility at any given moment.

In antiquity, few travel writers resisted the temptation to embroider their text with mythological allusions. Today's reader tends to query the mindset that apparently allowed ancient audiences to give simultaneous credence to both actual and imagined topographies and exploits. In Homer's *Odyssey*, the hero's trajectory toward the real kingdom of Ithaca is hampered by unreal deviations whereby he is kept prisoner in a cave by the divine Calypso, or narrowly escapes being devoured by the one-eyed Cyclops. In another unlikely yet deeply resonant episode, Odysseus descends to Hades and meets his dead mother. Are we to swallow these tall tales without hesitation alongside the account of Odysseus' homecoming and his down-to-earth struggles with the Suitors? The question remains pertinent even to entirely serious travel narratives, such as those of Herodotus (c. 484–c. 420 BCE) and Pausanias (fl. c. 150 CE), whose firsthand documentation occasionally admits hearsay and oral invention (albeit with reluctance).

In certain instances, the unequivocal status of the imaginary is crucial to the textual impact. The Greek satirist Menippus of Gadara (third century BCE) overtly mocked the travel genre in his *A Journey to the Underworld*, now lost. In similar vein, "The True History," by his disciple Lucian of Samosata (c. 115–180), narrates a trip to the moon, where the locals use their stomachs as handbags. Lucian issues the warning: "I have no intention whatever of telling the truth . . . I am writing about things . . . that have no reality whatever and never could have." Such hand-on-heart spoofing establishes its own rule of consistency and encourages a pleasurable teetering on the verge of belief. The essential relation of garrulous teller to gullible listener is epitomized when Sindbad the Sailor spins his yarns in the folkloric Arabian compendium *Tales of the Thousand and One Nights*. A formulaic pattern of departure, shipwreck, treasure trove, and triumphant return structures each of the seven tall stories that the adventurer relays to his alter ego, the stay-at-home Sinbad the Porter.

Although if shameless mendacity may be merely entertaining, there do exist travel fictions with a serious spiritual or edifying intent, as witness the narrative of the quest for immortality that sends the eponymous hero of the ancient Sumerian *Epic of Gilgamesh* (third millennium BCE) to the ends of the earth; or Christian allegories of advancing toward grace, like *Pilgrim's Progress* (1678) by John Bunyan (1628–1688). Fabulous voyages beyond the bounds of the known world are a deeply rooted topos of oral literature, exemplified in the twelfth-century *Voyage of Saint Brendan* (which mentions a possibly authentic landfall in North America) and the medieval German tale of *Herzog Ernst* [Duke Ernest], whose hero's crusade to the Holy Land is complicated by innumerable tests and encounters with monsters, often echoing the Sindbad stories. Grotesque aberrations abound in the fifteenth-century *Travels* (1499) of the apocryphal Sir John Mandeville, whose deadpan account of Ethiopians utilizing their single large foot as a parasol is part of the folk tradition of the topsy-turvy world.

During the Renaissance, the allegorical cast of the chivalric verse epic demanded that settings be far removed from actuality. Ludovico Ariosto (1474–1533) sets his *Orlando Furioso* (1532) in a land of romance with enchanted palaces and fearful forests where knights errant do battle with monsters or cruise upon flying hippogryphs. Occasional allusions to Paris or London hardly make this imaginary domain any easier to locate. Edmund Spenser (c. 1552–1599) confined his poem *The Faerie Queene* (1589–1596)—it being, as he put it, "a continued Allegory, or darke conceit"—to an unambiguous dreamland marked by symbolic locales like the Bower of Bliss or the Cave of Despair.

During the eighteenth century, breathtaking discoveries in the actual world were matched by an upsurge of contrived supplements. French writers found in travel a pretext for philosophical and ethical reflection, as in the social critique of *Les Lettres persanes* (1721; *Persian Letters* 1961) by Montesquieu (1689–1755) or the droll travelogue *Candide* (1759) by Voltaire (1694–1778), whose innocent hero blunders through a succession of thought-provoking disasters. In *Gulliver's Travels* (1726), the great Irish satirist Jonathan Swift (1667–1745) recycles several traditional motifs dating back to Lucian and draws caustic caricatures of contemporary society. Such didactic imaginings have an affinity with the twin traditions of utopian and dysto-

An equestrian mishap overtakes Baron Munchausen in Russia (drawing by Willy Planck in *Münchhausen: Seine und Abenteuer,* Stuttgart, n.d.).

pian writing, ranging from Thomas More (1478–1535) to Aldous Huxley (1894–1963).

Hugely popular in the early nineteenth century were the outright lies of the anonymous *Travels of Baron Munchausen*, whose eponymous hero dives into the crater of Mount Etna and surfaces again in the Pacific Ocean, or reaches the moon by shimmying up a fast-growing beanstalk. First rumored to be the work of the ballad-writer Gottfried August Bürger (1747–1794), the compilation is nowadays ascribed to the geologist and conman Rudolf Erich Raspe (1737–1794), who lifted nearly all his preposterous ideas from authors such as Lucian, Rabelais, or Swift.

By the early nineteenth century, the dark fantasies of the Gothic novel had generated such hyperbolic inventions as *Melmoth the Wanderer* (1820), in which Charles Maturin (1782–1824) portrays a satanic figure condemned, like the Wandering Jew, to roam the globe forever committing horrendous crimes. In France, Romantic writers skated freely across any gaps in their practical knowledge, producing outright fictions like the orientalist extravaganza *Salammbô* by Gustave Flaubert (1821–1880), or travel narratives like *Voyage en Orient* (1851; *Journey to the Orient, 1972*) by Gérard de Nerval (1808–1855), less a guide to the Near East than to its author's mythopoeic imagination. The English romantic Samuel Taylor Coleridge (1772–1834) went, it is thought, to extraordinary lengths to incorporate hundreds of veridical sources into what are, none the less, poems of perfect fantasy, "The Rime of the Ancient Mariner" and the dream fragment "Kubla Khan." A contemporary European cult of folk literature reflected a parallel taste for blissful escapism in tales of seven-league boots and trips to fairyland.

Startling prodigies and outlandish prophecies have always caught the popular fancy, and in the twentieth century were much exploited by the entertainment industries. This gave rise to one of the most distinctive subgenres of fantasy travel, science fiction—prefigured in the hollow-earth fantasies of *The Narrative of Arthur Gordon Pym* (1838) by Edgar Allan Poe (1809–1849) and *Voyage au centre de la terre* (1864; *Journey to the Centre of the Earth*, 1872) by Jules Verne (1828–1905); developed in the pioneering story of *The Time Machine* (1895) by H.G. Wells (1866–1946), which speculates (with impeccable logic) on the implications of time travel; crystallized in stories about interplanetary expeditions in *The Martian Chronicles* (1950) of Ray Bradbury (1920–); and brilliantly reinvented in *Fantastic Voyage* (1966) by Isaac Asimov (1920–1992), which details a journey inside a human body. The serious-minded phantasmagoria of science fiction may be understood as enhanced variants of such ancient topoi as the journey to the underworld or to the moon. Typical of some science fiction is a fondness for the trappings of the documentary, as when a cryptic technological jargon mimes authenticity while in fact undermining it.

The French symbolist school held ideas to be infinitely superior to actuality, so a conjectured journey was always preferable to a material one. Charles Baudelaire (1821–1867) recognized this when, in the prose poem "Any Where Out of the World," he strove to allay his world-weariness through daydreams of Lisbon, Rotterdam, Java, or the Arctic wastes. The epitome of sedentary travel is *Voyage autour de ma chambre* [Voyage around My Room, 1794] by Xavier de Maistre (1763–1852), with its 42-day voyage of discovery between the anchorages of bed, desk, bookcase, and mirror.

For many modern writers, the glamour of the fantastic continued to win out over the sober ideal of veracity. The Belgian poet Henri Michaux (1899–1984) began his career with a highly subjective account of a true journey to Ecuador, then plunged into total invention in *Au Pays de la magie* [In the Land of Magic, 1941], presenting a coherent wonderland where water in a vase obligingly keeps its shape even if its container is smashed, and where tourists are advised to cross the province of Stomach at speed lest their feet get digested. Michaux also wrote about mescalin, contributing to a parallel tradition of drug-inspired literature, in which the trope of travel surfaces inevitably in the notion of the "trip."

It is noticeable that fantasy travel writing continues to proliferate in our own age, shifting as ever between the poles of allegorical didacticism and sheer fun, though always respecting the rule of consistency. Major exponents include the British writer J.G. Ballard (1930–), who depicts a psychic landscape in *The Drowned World* (1962); the Argentinian writer Jorge Luis Borges (1899–1984), with his polished fables of labyrinths, dreams, and time-trips; and the Italian experimentalist Italo Calvino (1923–1985). The latter's *Le Città invisibili* (1972; *Invisible Cities*, 1974) is a conscious intertextual exercise, drawing both on the veridical *Travels* of Marco Polo and Coleridge's visionary "Kubla Khan." Reviving the situation of the two Sindbads, Calvino institutes a dialogue between a sedentary emperor, the Great Khan, and his nomadic emissary, the merchant Marco Polo, who delivers reports on the cities of his far-flung empire, adumbrating dozens of descriptions at once utterly exorbitant and utterly seductive. It emerges that all Marco Polo's "invisible cities" are generated from a single matrix, his native Venice. Here, imaginary travel seems, for all its enchanting diversity, to be premised upon a fantasy of homecoming. Calvino's parable might well illuminate fantasy travel writing at large: perhaps he is saying that every pipe dream implies a longing for origins, or that the most staggering novelties usually turn out to be rooted in cultural tradition.

ROGER CARDINAL

## References and Further Reading

Ariosto, Ludovico, *Orlando Furioso*, 1532; translated by Guido Waldman, 1974.
Asimov, Isaac, *Fantastic Voyage*, 1966.
Ballard, J.G., *The Drowned World*, 1962.
*Baron Munchausen's Narrative of His Marvellous Travels and Campaigns in Russia*, 1786, enlarged edition, 1793; as *The Travels of Baron Munchausen: Gulliver Revived; or, The Vice of Lying Properly Exposed*, edited by William Rose, 1923.
Baudelaire, Charles, "Any Where out of the World," in *Petits Poëmes en prose*, 1869.
Borges, Jorge Luis, *Ficciones*, 1956; as *Fictions*, translated by Anthony Kerrigan, 1962.
Bradbury, Ray, *The Martian Chronicles*, 1950; expanded edition, 1973.
Bunyan, John, *The Pilgrim's Progress*, 1678.
Calvino, Italo, *Le Città invisibili*, 1972; as *Invisible Cities*, translated by William Weaver, 1974.
Coleridge, Samuel Taylor, "The Rime of the Ancient Mariner" (1798) and "Kubla Khan" (written 1797), in *Complete Poetical Works*, edited by W.H. Coleridge, 1912.
*The Epic of Gilgamesh*, translated by N.K. Sandars, 1960.
Flaubert, Gustave, *Salammbô*, 1862; translated by E. Powys Mathers, 1931.
*Herzog Ernst* [Duke Ernest], edited by Karl Bartsch, 1869.
Homer, *The Odyssey*, translated by E.V. Rieu, 1945.
Huxley, Aldous, *Brave New World*, 1932.
Lucian of Samosata, "The True History," in *Satirical Sketches*, translated by Paul Turner, 1961.
Maistre, Xavier de, *Voyage autour de ma chambre* [Voyage around My Room], 1794.
Mandeville, Sir John, *The Travels*, 1499; edited by A.W. Pollard, 1900.
Maturin, Charles, *Melmoth the Wanderer: A Tale*, 1820; edited by Alethea Hayter, 1977.
Michaux, Henri, *Ecuador: journal de voyage*, 1929, revised editions, 1968, 1980, 1990; as *Ecuador: A Travel Journal*, translated by Robin Magowan, 1968.
Michaux, Henri, *Au Pays de la magie* [In the Land of Magic], 1941.
Montesquieu, Charles-Louis de Secondat, *Les Lettres persanes*, 1721; as *Persian Letters*, translated by J. Robert Loy, 1961.
More, Thomas, *Utopia* (in Latin), 1516; as *Utopia*, translated by Ralph Robinson, 1551; translated by Paul Turner, 1965.
*Navigatio Sancti Brendani Abbatis* ("Voyage of St. Brendan," tenth century and later), edited by Carl Selmer, 1959.
Nerval, Gérard de, *Le Voyage en Orient*, 1851; as *Journey to the Orient*, edited by Norman Glass, 1972.
Poe, Edgar Allan, *The Narrative of Arthur Gordon Pym of Nantucket*, 1838; edited by Harold Beaver, 1975.
"Sindbad the Sailor and Sindbad the Porter," in *The Thousand and One Nights* (tenth century or earlier), translated by N.J. Dawood, 1955.
Spenser, Edmund, *The Faerie Queene*, 1589–1596.
Swift, Jonathan, *Gulliver's Travels*, 1726.
Verne, Jules, *Voyage au centre de la terre*, 1864; as *Journey to the Centre of the Earth*, 1872.
Voltaire, *Candide*, 1759; translated by Richard Aldington, 1959.
Wells, H.G., *The Time Machine*, 1895.

*See also* **Fictional Travel Writing; Mandeville's Travels; Utopias and Dystopias**

## FAWCETT, PERCY (1867–1925(?)) *British Soldier and Explorer*

Colonel Percy Harrison Fawcett made a much more lasting contribution to travel writing by disappearing in the interior of Brazil in 1925 than through any words he ever penned. He became a staple of the popular press, which eagerly reported Fawcett sightings for years; expedition after expedition set off for the Mato Grosso. If anyone had ever found him, and been able to prove it, the sensation would have rivaled that of Stanley's encounter with Livingstone. To this day there is no conclusive evidence of Fawcett's fate or that of his two companions; it is possible that there will be further additions to a bibliography that includes a number of interesting books, and one of the classics of the entire genre, Peter Fleming's *Brazilian Adventure*.

Fawcett was reluctant to divulge all the details of his extensive travels in South America before he had achieved his ultimate goal: the discovery of a lost city, which he had convinced himself was to be found somewhere in the unexplored regions of Brazil. His writings were finally collected, edited, and published by his younger son, Brian, under the title *Lost Trails, Lost Cities* (1953). The same text was republished in the Century Travellers series in 1988, with a useful new introduction by Robin Hanbury-Tenison.

As Hanbury-Tenison points out, Fawcett at his best presents valuable observations from his extraordinary journeys through some of the least accessible areas of South America. First as a surveyor engaged in establishing accurate boundaries between Brazil and Bolivia, and later as an independent adventurer following tenuous clues in search of his lost city, Fawcett amassed a remarkably extensive firsthand experience of the jungle. His technical expertise as a surveyor and his broad general knowledge equipped him to make much better sense of what he saw than most outsiders, and to write of it in prose that is usually clear and energetic.

Fawcett's narrative is characterized by a number of quirks that most modern readers will be likely to consider serious defects. For example, he depicts the jungle as a place of almost unrelenting misery, gloom, and danger. He fills his pages with often gratuitous anecdotes of unspeakably nasty insects, voracious piranhas, and homicidal snakes. He ignores no opportunity to repeat tales of atrocities, whether he witnessed them personally or merely heard of them. Lurid stories of torture, massacres, slave raids, epidemics, and cannibalism seem to occupy as much space as Fawcett's own doings. Certainly there are discomforts and dangers in the Amazon basin, and unquestionably the death rate was alarming among natives and outsiders alike, but Fawcett's insistent reiteration of these themes verges on the ridiculous. To be fair, one must acknowledge that in this respect he is not unique among adventure writers, but rather belongs to a school lampooned by Fleming in *Brazilian Adventure*. Many of Fawcett's descriptions confirm the darkest stereotypes about the jungle. Without necessarily questioning his truthfulness, one must note that his emphasis on the worst aspects of the experience seems intended to glorify his own achievement in surviving: surviving both physically and morally, as another of his recurring themes is the degeneration of most visitors to the jungle.

Fawcett's book remains eminently readable notwithstanding its flaws. He shows a warm appreciation for the generosity with which so many of the inhabitants help him in his travels, a sympathy for the indigenous peoples which was by no means universal at the time, and even a wry sense of humor. The passage on an encounter with the Guarayos shows Fawcett at his best as a writer and a person; he describes the arms, attire, ornaments, and fishing techniques of the tribe, and tells how he and his party won their friendship. One of his companions gives a lively accordion recital, and Fawcett finds just the right gesture: "I could think of only one way to show him friendship. I placed my Stetson on his head and patted him on the back. He grinned, and all the surrounding braves roared with laughter—in fact, they laughed at everything, funny or not."

No doubt Fawcett was a visionary, and the support he gives for his theories of lost civilizations seems flimsy, yet his dream seemed plausible enough at the time: Bingham reached Machu Picchu while Fawcett was involved in one of his first surveying projects. The words chosen by his son to conclude the compendium of his writings accurately represent Fawcett's idealism and courage: "Whether we get through and emerge again, or leave our bones to rot in there, one thing's certain. The answer to the enigma of Ancient South America—and perhaps of the prehistoric world—may be found when those old cities are located and opened up to scientific research. That the cities exist, I know."

Fawcett, in short, may have been the last truly romantic explorer. Conan Doyle probably got the idea for *The Lost World* from a conversation with the colonel. Hermes Leal subtitles his book "A verdadeira história do Indiana Jones," though he never discusses his conjecture that the character in the film was based on Fawcett. In the last pages of his comprehensive survey, *The Explorers of South America*, Edward Goodman observes that "After him . . . no name has appeared to capture the imagination or excite the interest of the world."

Fawcett left his book unfinished, recognizing that the only adequate conclusion, from his point of view, would be a triumphant description of how his years of self-sacrifice and investigation had culminated in the discovery of "Z," the lost city of his obsession. He acknowledges that failure would leave him open to scorn as a man who neglected his family, took advantage of friends, acquaintances, and strangers, and squandered his formidable talents in a quest of lifelong futility. His personal magnetism, and the occasional power of his writing, have been sufficient to draw a great many people on to his trail over the years, either literally into the still-remote area where he was last reliably reported, or in imagination into the legend he left behind.

PHILIP KRUMMRICH

### Biography

Born in Torquay, Devon, 31 August 1867. Attended Newton College, Devon; Westminster School, London; Royal Military Academy, Woolwich. Served with the Royal Artillery in Sri Lanka, North Africa, Malta, and Hong Kong, 1886–1906. Married Nina Paterson, 1902: two sons and one daughter. Led expeditions to survey borders in Brazil, Bolivia, and Peru, 1906–1910. Retired from the army, 1910, returning to fight in World War I in Europe, 1915–1919. Led independent expeditions in search of remains of ancient civilizations in Brazil, 1920–1922; 1925. Received Founder's medal of the Royal Geographical Society, 1917. Disappeared in the Mato Grosso, Brazil, 1925.

### References and Further Reading

Fawcett, Percy, *Lost Trails, Lost Cities*, edited by Brian Fawcett, 1953; as *Exploration Fawcett*, 1953.

Fleming, Peter, *Brazilian Adventure*, London: Jonathan Cape, 1933; New York: Scribner, 1934.

## FERMOR, PATRICK LEIGH (1915–)

***British Travel Writer***

Patrick Leigh Fermor's life and travel books have earned him comparison with Lawrence of Arabia and a reputation as one of the twentieth century's foremost travel writers. Often focusing on areas not well known to western European and American readers, he has frequently written about cultures that have since changed dramatically or disappeared.

In 1933 Leigh Fermor began a three-year walking tour from Holland to Constantinople, a journey that was to provide him with material for two important travel books and the promise of a third book yet to appear. His first publication was a translation from the Greek of C.P. Rodocanachi's *Forever Ulysses* (1937), a novel also published as *No Innocent Abroad.* After enlisting in the Irish Guards in 1939, Leigh Fermor served in Greece and Albania during World War II, and organized the resistance movement on the island of Crete, an adventure chronicled by his friend Xan Fielding in *Hide and Seek: The Story of a War-time Agent* (1954). In 1944, Leigh Fermor led a successful expedition to kidnap Major-General Heinrich Kreipe, commander of 22,000 German troops on Crete, an episode recounted by Major W. Stanley Moss in *Ill Met by Moonlight* (1950), the inspiration for a film by the same name produced in 1957. Leigh Fermors 1947 trip to the Caribbean and Central America led to his first book, *The Traveller's Tree* (1950), which won him the Heinemann Foundation Prize for Literature in 1950 and the Kemsley Prize the following year. The book contains vivid descriptions of Caribbean islands; the *Times Literary Supplement* judged the chapter on voodoo to be one of the best in the book and applauded the author's "keen eye for such vestiges of splendour and prosperity as have survived the depredations of tropical nature and the collapse of an economy based on slavery."

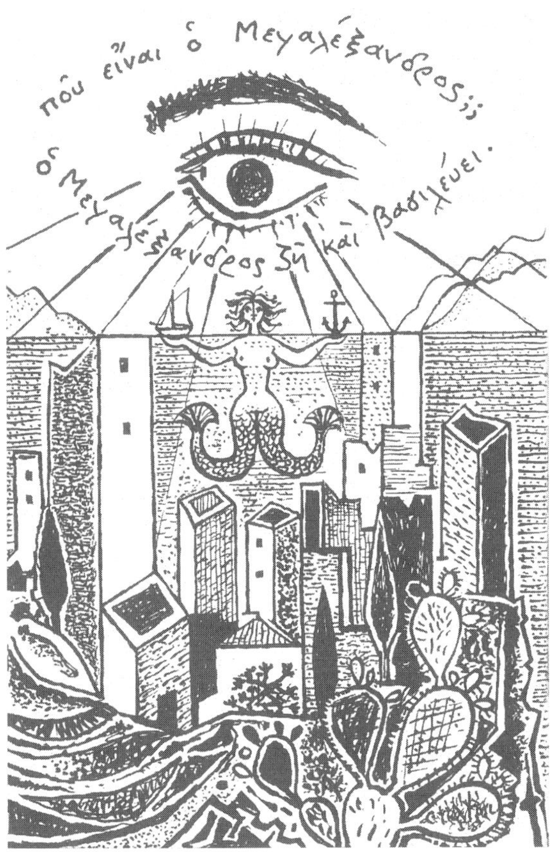


An ancient legend of the Aegean in John Craxton's frontispiece to Leigh Fermor's *Mani* (1958): the mermaid questions seafarers, "Where is Alexander the Great?", to which the proper answer is "Alexander the Great lives and reigns."

Leigh Fermor's translations of Colette's *Julie de Carneilhan* and *Chambre d'hotel* were published in 1952 as *Julie de Carneilhan and Chance Acquaintances. A Time to Keep Silence*, published in 1953, describes active monasteries in France as well as the abandoned rock monasteries of Cappadocia. In the postscript, Leigh Fermor relates that Cistercian life still seems "mysterious and perplexing"; the lost monasteries of Cappadocia he finds "as illuminating (and as irrelevant)" as ever, but Benedictine community life at Solesmes remains alive and significant to the author, himself an unbeliever.

*The Violins of Saint-Jacques*, Leigh Fermor's only novel to date, was also published in 1953. A rather short work, the story was inspired by the volcanic destruction of St. Pierre, the capital of Martinique, in 1902. The *Times Literary Supplement* termed it "excellent as a nostalgic account of a graceful, colourful, feudal way of life," but faulted it for being "a tale of travel rather than a novel." The book inspired a successful three-act opera composed by Malcolm Williamson, with libretto by William Chappell.

In 1955 Leigh Fermor's translation of *The Cretan Runner* by George Psychoundakis was published. *Mani: Travels in the Southern Peloponnese* appeared in 1958 and won the Duff Cooper Memorial Prize. Well received by critics, the book inspired reviewer John Raymond to write in the *New Statesman and Nation* that "Mr. Leigh Fermor is the best travel writer of his generation." Among the most valuable sections of *Mani* remain his analyses of the persistence of pre-Christian beliefs in modern Greek society.

Leigh Fermor's translation of Ghika's *India* was published in 1959. *Roumeli: Travels in Northern Greece* (1966) describes an area south of the Agrapha Mountains not on current maps. Freya Stark, writing in the *New York Times*, praised the author's ability to present people "as they are" as well as his "brilliance" and "exuberance of learning." *A Time of Gifts* (1977), which won the W.H. Smith Award in 1978, was written from notes made by the author during his 1930s walking tour. Beginning in Holland, Leigh Fermor traveled through Germany, a country whose towns, cathedrals, and landscapes he enjoyed, even as he worried over the changes in the mood of the people under Adolf Hitler's rule. Writing in the *New York Times Book Review*, Raymond Sokolov declared that Leigh Fermor re-creates "historically irreplaceable impressions of Central European Jews waking up to Hitler's menace, of the last days of the charming, Hapsburgian petty nobility and of the pre-Communist landscape of Hungary and Rumania."

*Between the Woods and the Water*, the long-awaited sequel to *A Time of Gifts*, appeared in 1986. The volume begins where the earlier book ended, with Leigh Fermor standing on the bridge, now ready to enter Esztergom, Hungary. Like *A Time of Gifts, Between the Woods and the Water* describes people, customs, and places in Eastern Europe as they were and no longer are. Leigh Fermor weaves accounts of history, geography, friendships, hospitality, nature, cities, and adventures using a vocabulary perhaps less esoteric than that of his previous books. The appendix to the book, titled "Thoughts at a Café Table between the Kazan and the Iron Gates," takes Leigh Fermor into the present where modernization "has now placed the whole of this landscape underwater" and destroyed historic monuments, natural beauty, and wildlife.

*Between the Woods and the Water* won the Thomas Cook Travel Book Award. In 1986, Leigh Fermor was also awarded the International PEN/Time Life Silver Pen Award. In an interview with R.W. Apple Jr. of the *New York Times*, Leigh Fermor confessed that his most difficult task lies not in remembering events and places but in refraining from making comparisons between conditions in Europe in the 1930s and the present day. He continues to work on the third volume of the account of his walking tour of Central Europe, although his goal of finishing in two years, which he stated to a *New York Times* reporter early in 1987, has long since passed. When asked by London *Times* writer Nicholas Shakespeare why his books have not appeared more frequently, Leigh Fermor replied that he feared "getting it wrong" and "forgetting the people who did marvellous things. It was awfully important to get it right, to breathe it back to life."

Leigh Fermor is a fellow of the Royal Geographical Society and of the Royal Society of Literature, a patron of the Friends of Mount Athos, and an honorary citizen of Herakleion, Crete (1947), Gytheion, Laconia (1966), and Kardamyli, Messenia (1967). What Patrick Leigh Fermor himself wrote about Sacheverell Sitwell (in his foreword to Sitwell's *Roumanian Journey*, 1992) applies equally to his own approach to life as well as to art: "Having looked at everything in the world that was worth seeing, he could spot relationships, find parallels, trace sources and identify hybrids and variants in a flash." His extraordinary contribution to twentieth-century travel literature can only be enhanced by the long-awaited publication of the final volume of his travels in the 1930s from Holland to Constantinople.

Anita G. Gorman

**Biography**

Born Patrick Michael Leigh Fermor in London, 11 February 1915. Attended Salsham Hall; King's School, Canterbury; passed London Certificate examination. Began a walking tour from Holland to Constantinople, 8 December 1933. Enlisted in the Irish Guards, 1939. Served in Greece, Albania, and Crete during World War II. Deputy director of the British Institute in Athens, 1947–1948. Married the Honourable Mrs. Joan Rayner (née Monsell), 1968. Duff Cooper Memorial Prize, 1958; W.H. Smith Award, 1978; Thomas Cook Travel Book Award, 1986; International PEN/Time Life Silver Pen Award, 1986. Fellow, Royal Geographical Society and Royal Society of Literature. Chevalier, Order des Arts et des Lettres. OBE, 1943; DSO, 1944. Honorary citizen of Herakleon, Crete, 1947; Gytheion, Laconia, 1966; Kardamyli, Messenia, 1967. Municipality of Athens gold medal of honor, 1988.

**References and Further Reading**

Fermor, Patrick Leigh, *The Traveller's Tree: A Journey through the Caribbean Islands*, 1950.
Fermor, Patrick Leigh, *A Time to Keep Silence*, 1953; republished with additions to the introduction, 1982.
Fermor, Patrick Leigh, *Mani: Travels in the Southern Peloponnese*, with photographs by Joan Eyres Monsell, 1958.
Fermor, Patrick Leigh, *Roumeli: Travels in Northern Greece*, 1966.
Fermor, Patrick Leigh, *A Time of Gifts*, 1977.
Fermor, Patrick Leigh, *Between the Woods and the Water: On Foot to Constantinople from the Hook of Holland: The Middle Danube to the Iron Gates*, 1986.
Fermor, Patrick Leigh, *Three Letters from the Andes*, 1991.

## FICTIONAL (EPIGRAPH) TRAVEL WRITING

Travel literature is often classified in libraries and bookshops as nonfiction. Fictional travel seems to be an anomaly, but there is actually a significant overlap between travel literature and fiction. The range of fictional travel is enormous. There are imaginary voyages as diverse as those of Odysseus, Baron Munchausen, and Gulliver. There are fictional journeys in realistic settings, like Jules Verne's *Le Tour du monde en quatre-vingt jours (Around the World in Eighty Days*, 1873). Sometimes there is an allegorical, religious, or philosophical subtext, as in Voltaire's *Candide* (1759), John Bunyan's *The Pilgrim's Progress* (1678–1684) and Milton's *Paradise Lost* (1667). There are embellished narratives of actual journeys, like Daniel Defoe's *The Life, Adventures and Piracies of the Famous Captain Singleton* (1720), and hoaxes of travel liars such as George Psalmanazar's *An Historical and Geographical Description of Formosa* (1704). And there are travel stories, short occasional fictions of journeys and places.

This is the safe ground of fictional travel, but there are also troublesome borderlands: novels that verge on travel literature, and travel writing that aspires to the novelistic. Of course, many novelists were also travelers and travel writers, moving between the two forms. Defoe, one of England's first novelists, had a keen interest in travel and travel narratives. *Robinson Crusoe* (1719) is partly informed by Woodes Rogers's account of the life of Alexander Selkirk on Juan Fernandez Island. In Joseph Conrad's *Lord Jim* (1900), the author's own travels in the Far East provide material for a fictional journey.

Travel literature is not very interesting when it is merely topographical and anthropological. As Samuel Johnson said, "We do not always want to be taken through wet and dry, over rough and smooth, without incidents, without reflection." This implies attention to the picturesque and the sentimental, but it can be a short step to the novelistic. Mark Twain's *A Tramp Abroad* (1880) and Bruce Chatwin's *The Songlines* (1987) are examples of travel literature on the verge of novels. *Las botas de siete leguas: Viaje a la Alcarria*, 1948 (*Journey to the Alcarria*) by Camilo José Cela is a travel narrative with the appearance of a novel because the impersonal third-person "traveler" is the subject. This breaks the conventional travel writing compact between author, traveler, and narrator presented through the first person "I."

Where to draw the line is problematic. As Johnson said, "definitions are hazardous," and new forms in literature often subvert their antecedents. *Robinson Crusoe* could be described as fictional travel because it is based on a real voyage. Charles Dickens's *The Life and Adventures of Martin Chuzzlewit* (1844) includes a journey to America based on Dickens's own travels recorded in *American Notes*, but *Martin Chuzzlewit* is clearly a novel rather than fictional travel. Many realist novels of the eighteenth and nineteenth centuries refer to real places and contain realistic journeys, but unless the narrative is dominated by a journey or by representation of a particular place, it is not really fictional travel. Based on this, Defoe's *Captain Singleton* (1720) and Herman Melville's *Omoo: A Narrative of Adventures in the South Seas* (1847) are clearly fictional travel, but although *Robinson Crusoe* and Melville's *Moby-Dick* (1851) contain journey elements, these are always secondary to the playing out of human and social drama, so these works are novels first and foremost.

The border zone between fictional travel and "real" travel writing is also hazardous. Homer's *Odyssey*, Thomas More's *Utopia* (1516), Jonathan Swift's *Gulliver's Travels* (1726), and Jules Verne's *Around the World in Eighty Days* (1873) are fictional travel. Here, places, journeys, or travelers are fictional and they are not designed to inform readers of the world as it is, but to entertain, instruct, or provoke them with alternative worlds. More difficult to define are the constructed and plagiarized *Travels* of John Mandeville (1356–1366) or the many hoaxes of the eighteenth century. Here, real places and real journeys are presented as factual, and in part they are, but the whole is an extravagant fiction. The narrator of Mandeville's *Travels* tells us that he, the author, is an English knight who traveled to the East, but there is no historical evidence of the knight or his travels. The text weaves together various contemporary and classical sources, including the *Itinerarium* (1330) of Odoric of Pordenone, the Alexander Romances, and *Wonders of the East*. Like the travel hoaxes of the eighteenth century, Mandeville's Travels seems designed to test readers' sensibility to fact versus fiction and truth versus lie dichotomies.

In the classical and medieval period, the travel romance was a common and legitimate form of literature, but between the late fourteenth century, when Mandeville's *Travels* was the most popular text of its time, and the eighteenth century, when Psalmanazar was vilified for his hoax on Formosa, attitudes to fictional travel changed. As Europe expanded its frontiers from the sixteenth century onward, a systematic approach to travel writing was introduced, dividing travel fact from travel fiction. The world beyond Europe was becoming a reality in the seventeenth and eighteenth centuries and factual information about this "other half" of the world was demanded. The Antipodes, India, Cathay, Oceania, Patagonia, and other once legendary

"Afternoon tea at Judge Wiggins"; Lady Joan Weigall Lindsay (aka Serena Livingstone-Stanley) followed the parodic tradition in fictional travel writing by poking fun at a raft of imperialist stereotypes—not least that of the intrepid, solar-topeed lady travel writer (from *Through Darkest Pondelayo. An Account of the Adventures of Two English Ladies on a Cannibal Island,* 1936).

places were no longer the exotic playgrounds for romance or for mapping the Scriptures. They became geographic realities gradually incorporated into a mundane system of knowledge. Where once monsters lurked at the fabulous margins of the eurocentric atlas, opportunity now drew a different breed of adventurer. The modern explorer and colonizer displaced the knight-errant of medieval romance. Where medieval audiences delighted in juxtapositions of the fabulous and the real, the moderns erected barriers between the world of charts and taxonomies and that of romance and fiction.

The Western history of travel and exploration, which reaches its peak in a highly organized print culture with high rates of literacy, dominates the travel literature available to us. Much of this is exotic, transforming the East into an alien but desirable elsewhere. This is pretty much a constant, from the wonders of Egypt in the *Histories* of Herodotus (fifth century BCE), to the backpackers' ideal beach in the Thailand of *The Beach* (1996) by Alex Garland.

Western travel writing, especially from the fourteenth to the nineteenth centuries, is part of a discourse that seeks to articulate and justify European expansion. Travel writing (including, and perhaps especially, fictional travel) is therefore implicated in the history of exploration, discovery, subjugation, and colonization in the East, in Africa, in the South Seas, and in the Americas. This can be traced from the Alexander Romances (myths surrounding Alexander the Great's sorties into Asia in the fourth century BCE), to Defoe's *Robinson Crusoe*. Note that Defoe himself advocated establishing a colony in Chile in *An Essay on the South-Sea Trade*. Even *The Beach* is a story of Westerners' search for, and loss of, paradise in the East. Tourism, here of the backpacker variety, is the latest episode in the West's imaginative and discursive appropriation of the exotic East, the roots of which reach back into antiquity.

Moving now from a definition of the genre to a closer look at each historical period, we might begin with the *Histories* of Herodotus, a geographer-traveler as much as a historian. Although often realistic, Herodotus strays into the fantastic when his text touches the margins of the known world centered on ancient Greece. In Egypt and the Upper Nile, he relies on hearsay and fabulation, as did Pliny, Ctesias, and Arrian. Gold-digging ants the size of dogs, unicorns, dog-faced men, men with feathers, men with one foot, one eye, or a head beneath their shoulders, all become the material of the fabulous East. Christianity did not interrupt this flow of pagan knowledge; it continued to be copied and circulated through to the Renaissance. Columbus and early modern explorers still expected to find rivers of gold, unicorns, dog-heads, pygmies, and especially cannibals. Medieval travelers such as Odoric and Marco Polo still referred to mythological and fabulous beasts for likenesses. They might have witnessed crocodiles, rhinoceroses, and monkeys, but they saw these as the fabulous toothed serpents, unicorns, and pygmies of antiquity.

Homer's *Odyssey* is the first and most enduring traveler's tale in Western literature. Odysseus' quest through a palpable yet fantastic Mediterranean is a model for the traveler's search for self-identity and a model for the travel yarn. Alcinous knows that Odysseus is lying, but his are the white lies of literature, not the "lies of an impostor who spins his lying yarns which nobody can test." They are the "lies" of a ballad-singer who uses his artistry to delight and to hint at deeper truths and realities. The *Odyssey* introduces to Western literature the journey as quest, rites of passage, and the hero against the alien Other, against the gods, and occasionally against himself. Odysseus struggles to find his true identity as the father of Telemachus, the husband of Penelope, and the king of Ithaca. Above all, the *Odyssey* celebrates telling tales, and travel is the vehicle for moving from tale to tale. There have been many attempts to rationalize the geography of the *Odyssey*, by mapping the islands of Calypso, Circe, and the Sirens to real places in the Mediterranean. The mundane is then enriched by fictional travel as myth.

Plato's (c. 428–c. 348 BCE) *Republic* is an example of utopian travel fiction. Although not really a travel story, the *Republic* describes an ideal city. In the *Timaeus*, in response to Socrates' desire to see this ideal city, Critias tells a traveler's tale. The *Critias* makes the ideal city real by making it an Athens in the Golden Age. The real Athens is then at war with the island country of Atlantis, which is destroyed and lost forever beneath the sea, establishing an enduring myth of the "lost city."

*True Story* by Lucian (c. 120–90) is a wandering sea voyage to fantastic islands and the Moon, ending up in the Antipodes. The author exploits the travel story as fiction, exploring the possibilities of plausible lies in travel. This has been read as a parody of travel romances and a use on gullible audiences. Further fantastic voyages in antiquity, including those of Jason and the Golden Fleece and Sinbad, can be found in the *Argonautica* by Apollonius Rhodius (third century BCE), and in *The Thousand and One Nights*, respectively.

After antiquity the next period of interest is the Middle Ages. Although Marco Polo's *Travels* may be based on real journeys (be they Polo's or not), the real author was a romance writer, Rustichello of Pisa. The question of authenticity in the *Travels* is debated, but the text is certainly crafted and has passing resemblance to some of Rustichello's Arthurian romances. The *Travels* of Mandeville has already been mentioned. Like Mandeville, Dante, a near contemporary, also mixed truth with fantasy and described imaginary voyages, but Dante wrote in verse, Mandeville in prose, so Dante's *La Commedia* (*Divine Comedy*) has always been read as allegorical literature rather than fictional travel.

*The Wonders of the East* is an early medieval text (fifth and sixth centuries) containing illustrated descriptions of animal and human curiosities from the East. It was something of a conduit for passing fabulous material from antiquity into medieval travel narratives. Vincent of Beauvais's *Speculum historiale* (1253) contains extracts from a number of real and literary travelers from Pliny to Giovanni di Piano Carpini. Typical of the times, it was an eclectic mix of the real and the fabulous. Medieval travel was dominated by missions and pilgrimages. Perhaps the most famous fictional pilgrimage in Western literature is Chaucer's *Canterbury Tales* (1387–1400), although the travel narrative is really only a frame for the individual tales, told at the end of each day's journey.

As new worlds began to present themselves to Europe, classical ideas of utopia and lost civilizations resurface. Thomas More's *Utopia* (1516) and Francis Bacon's *New Atlantis* (1626) revisit Plato's ideal and lost cities, but More's utopia is tied to the New World, as described in Vespucci's letters, problematically bridging the real New World with the utopia or "no-place" of antiquity.

The known world, for Europeans, expanded in the seventeenth and eighteenth centuries. For Bacon, this geographical expansion was also an epistemological expansion, to know the world fully and scientifically by understanding "the knowledge of causes, and secret motions of things; and the enlarging of the bounds of human empire." In the late seventeenth century, the Royal Society in London issued its "Directions for Sea-men, bound for far voyages." This urged travelers to "study *Nature* rather than *Books*, and from the Observations made from the Phenomena and Effects she presents, to compose such a History of Her, as may hereafter serve to build a Solid and Useful Philosophy upon."

The Royal Society may have insisted on scientific rigor in travel narratives, but the public demand for sensational stories of the exotic South Seas and the New World ensured a good market for fictional travel. The seventeenth and early eighteenth centuries produced many travel accounts that were wholly or partly fictitious, each mischievously prefaced with declarations of truthfulness from travelers, editors, and publishers. Realistic imitations of travel books include *The Isle of Pines; or, A Late Discovery of a Fourth Island in Terra Australis Incognita* (1668) by Henry Neville, and Captain William Symson's *A New Voyage to the East-Indies* (1715). Three fictional accounts of Australia may have provided material for the works of Defoe and Swift: Gabriel Foigny, *La Terre Australe connue* (1676), revised by François Raguenet as *Les Avantures de Jacques Sadeur* (1693); Denis Vairasse d'Alais, *Histoire des Sevarambes* (1677–1679); and Simon Tyssot de Patot, *Voyages et Avantures de Jaques Massé* (1710).

Two texts that press the boundaries of fictional travel in the same period are Humphrey Gilbert's *A Discourse . . . to Prove a Passage by the Northwest to Cathaia, and the East Indies* (1576) and Walter Raleigh's *The Discoverie of the Large, Rich, and Bewtiful Empyre of Guiana* (1596). Both texts are propaganda, promoting the ideas of the Northwest Passage and El Dorado, respectively. Margaret Cavendish (the marchioness of Newcastle) was one of the earliest English women writers to rewrite the adventure narrative from a female perspective; see *The Description of a New World, Called the Blazing World* (1666) and "Assaulted and Pursued Chastity" in *Natures Pictures Drawn by Fancies Pencil to the Life* (1656).

In the eighteenth century, travel accounts were often the objects of parody and satire. Captain William Dampier provides a further example of travel fact turned travel fiction. His buccaneering exploits in the South Seas, recorded in *A New Voyage round the World* (1697), furnished Defoe and Swift with rich material for their fictions. The mutiny on Captain Bligh's HMS *Bounty* and the fate of Fletcher Christian and his men among the natives of Tahiti is such a story that if it were not true, some eighteenth-century writer would surely have invented it. It has all the ingredients of an adventure novel. As with Odysseus's trials and adventures on the islands of Calypso, Circe, and the Sirens, it has exotic location, lust, deception, heroism, and conflict between duty and pleasure, action and stasis. The events gave rise to numerous conflicting accounts, novels, films, and poems, including a Miltonic poem by Byron, *The Island, or Christian and His Comrades* (1823). Christian is here cast in the role of satanic romantic hero, leading his free but guilty comrades into the lost paradise of the South Sea island.

Texts that parody and satirize travelers' tales include Daniel Defoe's *Captain Singleton* and *A New Voyage round the World* (1724), Robert Drury's *Madagascar: or, Robert Drury's Journal during Fifteen Years Captivity on That Island* (1729), Jonathan Swift's *Gulliver's Travels* (1726), Cyrano de Bergerac's *Voyage dans la lune* (1657) and *L'Histoire des états et empires du soleil* (1662), G.H. Bougeant's *Voyage merveilleux du Prince Fan-Feredin* (1735), and Voltaire's *Candide* (1759). For a feminist revision of

Defoe's *Robinson Crusoe*, in which a female Crusoe is cast adrift on the island of Britain, see Frances Burney's *The Wanderer; or Female Difficulties* (1814).

Fictional travel accounts can often be seen as the precursors of the novel. Cervantes's *Don Quijote de la Mancha* (1605), arguably the first European novel, blends the romance motifs of chivalry and quest with travels across a very real La Mancha. Travel is a major feature in many eighteenth-century English novels, adding realism to distinguish the emerging form of the novel from the romance genre that preceded it. Realistic travel was often the plot vehicle, as writers began to turn travel experience, real or of the armchair variety, into novels. Examples include Tobias Smollett's *The Adventures of Peregrine Pickle* (1751), Laurence Sterne's *A Sentimental Journey through France and Italy* (1768), and Herman Melville's *Typee* (1846) and *Omoo* (1847).

In the late nineteenth and twentieth centuries, the list of travel stories and novels in which travel dominates theme, structure, and atmosphere is extensive. Tales of the high seas and adventure, such as R.S. Ballantyne's *The Coral Island: A Tale of the Pacific Ocean* (1857) and Robert Louis Stevenson's *Treasure Island* (1883), continue the tradition of Melville and Defoe. Mark Twain's *A Tramp Abroad* (1880), with its satirical portrayal of the old country of Europe continues the tradition of Sterne and Smollett, but from an American perspective. Several of Conrad's and D.H. Lawrence's novels might be termed fictional travel; their short stories, "Youth" (Conrad, 1902) and "The Man Who Loved Islands" (Lawrence), certainly count. As Paul Fussell has noted in *Abroad* (1980), many British writers between the wars were exiles, writing both travel accounts and novels. Evelyn Waugh turned several travel narratives into novels: *Ninety-Two Days* (1934) into *A Handful of Dust* (1934), and *Waugh in Abyssinia* (1936) into *Scoop* (1938). Very different examples of modern fictional travel can be found in: Paul Bowles, *The Sheltering Sky* (1949), Bruce Chatwin, *The Songlines* (1987), Alex Garland, *The Beach* (1996), Graham Greene, *Stamboul Train* (1932), also published as *Orient Express* (1933), Jack Kerouac, *On the Road* (1957), Somerset Maugham, *The Trembling of the Leaf: Little Stories of the South Sea Islands* (1921), and Virginia Woolf, *The Voyage Out* (1915).

Anthony Trollope was a prolific writer of travel stories. See *The Complete Short Stories* (1979–1983) (vols. 3 and 5). Two recent collections of travel stories demonstrate the strength and range of the modern travel story: *The Oxford Book of Travel Stories*, edited by Patricia Craig (1996), and *The Literary Traveler: An Anthology of Contemporary Short Fiction*, edited by Larry Dark (1994).

Science fiction has provided many examples of fictional travel, continuing the tradition of imaginary voyages by Lucian, Francis Godwin, Cyrano de Bergerac, and Jules Verne. Examples range from H.G. Wells, *The First Men in the Moon* (1901), to Arthur C. Clarke's *2001: A Space Odyssey* (1968), which brings us back, rather neatly, to the first traveler's tale, Homer's Odyssey.

Finally, postmodern fictional travel invariably revisits places, journeys, and texts. *Foe* (1986) by J.M. Coetzee reinvents the process of writing *Robinson Crusoe*, but in this case a female castaway petitions the writer Mr. Foe to present the story of Friday. Italo Calvino's *Le città invisibili*, 1972 (*Invisible Cities*) reinvents Marco Polo's reports to Kublai Khan, who finds in Polo's elaborate descriptions the one thing that might prevent his empire from crumbling. As in *The Thousand and One Nights*, it is telling that postpones the end.

PAUL SMETHURST

## References and Further Reading

Alais, Denis Vairasse d', *Histoire des Sevarambes*, 1677–1679; reprinted, 1979.

Apollonius Rhodius, *The Argonautica*, translated by R.C. Seaton, 1912 (Loeb edition), many subsequent reprints; as *The Argonautika*, translated with an introduction, commentary and glossary by Peter Green, 1997.

Bacon, Francis, *The New Atlantis in Sylva Sylvarum; or, A Natural History in Ten Centuries*, 1626.

Ballantyne, R.S., *The Coral Island: A Tale of the Pacific Ocean*, 1857.

*Baron Munchausen's Narrative of His Marvellous Travels and Campaigns in Russia*, 1786; enlarged edition, 1793; as *The Travels of Baron Munchausen: Gulliver Revisited; or, The Vice of Lying Properly Exposed*, edited by William Rose, 1923.

Bougeant, G.H., *Voyage merveilleux du Prince Fan-Feredin*, 1735; edited by Jean Sgard and Geraldine Sheridan, 1992.

Bowles, Paul, *The Sheltering Sky*, 1949.

Bunyan, John, *The Pilgrim's Progress from This World to That Which is to Come*, 1678–1684.

Burney, Frances, *The Wanderer; or, Female Difficulties*, 1814.

Byron, George Gordon, Lord, *The Island; or, Christian and His Comrades*, 1823.

Callisthenes, *The Greek Alexander Romance*, translated by Richard Stoneman, 1991.

Calvino, Italo, *Le città invisibili*, 1972; as *Invisible Cities*, translated by William Weaver, 1974.

Cavendish, Margaret, "Assaulted and Pursued Chastity," in *Nature's Pictures Drawn by Fancy's Pencil*, with William Cavendish, 1656.

Cavendish, Margaret, *The Description of a New World, Called the Blazing World*, 1666; revised edition, 1668.

Cela, Camilo José, *Las botas de siete leguas: viaje a la Alcarria*, 1948; as *Journey to the Alcarria*, translated by Frances M. Lopez Morillas, 1964.

Cervantes, Miguel de, *El ingenioso hidalgo don Quijote de la Mancha*, 1605–1615; as *The History of That Ingenious*

*Gentleman, Don Quijote de la Mancha*, translated by Burton Raffel, 1995.

Chatwin, Bruce, *The Songlines*, 1987.

Chaucer, Geoffrey, *The Canterbury Tales*, edited by William Caxton, 1478; edited by N.F. Blake, 1980.

Clarke, Arthur C., *2001: A Space Odyssey*, 1968.

Coetzee, J.M., *Foe*, 1986.

Conrad, Joseph, *Lord Jim*, 1900.

Conrad, Joseph, *Youth: A Narrative, and Two Other Stories*, 1902; as *Youth, Heart of Darkness, the End of the Tether*, edited by Robert Kimbrough, 1984.

Craig, Patricia (editor), *The Oxford Book of Travel Stories*, 1996.

Cyrano de Bergerac, Savinien de, *Voyage dans la lune* (part 1), 1657; *L'Histoire des états et empires du soleil* (part 2; unfinished), 1662; complete version as *L'Autre Monde; ou, Les États et empires de la lune*, 1920; as *Other Worlds: The Comical History of the States and Empires of the Moon and the Sun*, edited by Geoffrey Strachan, 1965.

Dampier, William, *A New Voyage round the World*, 1697.

Dante, *La Commedia*, written c. 1307–1321; as *The Divine Comedy*, translated by John Ciardi, 1977.

Dark, Larry (editor), *The Literary Traveler: An Anthology of Contemporary Short Fiction*, 1994.

Defoe, Daniel, *The Life and Strange Surprising Adventures of Robinson Crusoe of York, Mariner*, 1719; *Further Adventures*, 1719.

Defoe, Daniel, *The Life, Adventures and Piracies of the Famous Captain Singleton*, 1720.

Defoe, Daniel, *A New Voyage round the World, by a Course Never Sailed Before*, 1724.

Dickens, Charles, *The Life and Adventures of Martin Chuzzlewit*, 1844.

Drury, Robert, *Madagascar; or, Robert Drury's Journal during Fifteen Years Captivity on That Island*, revised and partly written by Daniel Defoe, 1729.

Foigny, Gabriel, *La Terre Australe connue*, 1676; revised by François Raguenet as *Les Avantures de Jacques Sadeur*, 1693.

Fussell, Paul, *Abroad: British Literary Traveling between the Wars*; New York and Oxford: Oxford University Press, 1980.

Garland, Alex, *The Beach*, 1996.

Gilbert, Humphrey, *A Discourse Written by Sir Humphrey Gilbert Knight, to Prove a Passage by the Northwest to Cathaia, and the East Indies*, 1576; in *The Principal Navigations, Voyages, Traffiques and Discoveries of the English Nation*, by Richard Hakluyt, 12 vols., 1903–1905.

Goodwin, Francis, *The Man in the Moon; or, A Discourse of a Voyage Thither*, 1638.

Greene, Graham, *Stamboul Train*, 1932; as *Orient Express*, 1933.

Herodotus, *The Histories*, translated by Aubrey de Sélincourt, revised by John Marincola, 1996.

Homer, *The Odyssey*, translated by Robert Fitzgerald, 1961.

Kerouac, Jack, *On the Road*, 1957.

Lawrence, D.H., "The Man Who Loved Islands," in *The Woman Who Rode Away and Other Stories*, 1928; as *The Man Who Loved Islands*, with a foreword by Hayden Carruth, 1986.

Lucian, *Lucian*, translated by A.M. Harmon, 8 vols., 1913–1967.

Mandeville, John, *Mandeville's Travels*, edited by M.C. Seymour, 1967.

Maugham, W. Somerset, *The Trembling of the Leaf: Little Stories of the South Sea Islands*, 1921; *as Sadie Thompson and Other Stories of the South Seas*, 1928; as *Rain and Other Stories*, 1933.

Melville, Herman, *Narrative of Four Months' Residence among the Natives of a Valley in the Marquesas Islands; or, A Peep at Polynesian Life*, 1846; as *Typee*, 1846.

Melville, Herman, *Omoo: A Narrative of Adventures in the South Seas*, 1847.

Melville, Herman, *The Whale*, 1851; as *Moby-Dick; or, The Whale*, 1851.

Milton, John, *Paradise Lost*, 1667.

More, Thomas, *Utopia* (in Latin), 1516; as *Utopia*, translated by Ralph Robinson, 1551; translated by Paul Turner, 1965.

Neville, Henry, *The Isle of Pines; or, A Late Discovery of a Fourth Island in Terra Australis Incognita*, 1668.

Odoric of Pordenone, *Itinerarium*, 1330; as *Travels of Oderic of Portenau into China and the East in 1318* in *A General History and Collection of Voyages and Travels*, edited by Robert Kerr, 1824; as *The Travels of Friar Odoric*, translated by Henry Yule, 2002.

Plato, *Collected Dialogues*, edited by Edith Hamilton and Huntington Cairns, 1961.

Polo, Marco, *The Description of the World*, translated and annotated by A.C. Moule and Paul Pelliot, 2 vols., 1938; reprinted, 1976; as *The Travels*, translated and with an introduction by Ronald Latham, Harmondsworth and New York: Penguin, 1958.

Psalmanazar, George, *An Historical and Geographical Description of Formosa*, 1704.

Raleigh, Walter, *The Discoverie of the Large, Rich, and Bewtiful Empyre of Guiana*, 1596; as *The Discoverie of the Large and Bewtiful Empyre of Guiana*, with an introduction, notes, and appendices by V.T. Harlow, 1928.

Smollett, Tobias, *The Adventures of Peregrine Pickle*, 1751.

Sterne, Laurence, *A Sentimental Journey through France and Italy, by Mr Yorick*, 1768.

Stevenson, Robert Louis, *Treasure Island*, 1883.

Swift, Jonathan, *Travels into Several Remote Nations of the World, by Captain Lemuel Gulliver*, 1726.

Symson, William, *A New Voyage to the East-Indies*, 1715.

*The Thousand and One Nights* (*Arabian Nights*), translated by Sir Richard Burton, 10 vols., 1885; numerous subsequent editons.

Trollope, Anthony, *Tales of All Countries*, 2 vols., 1861–1863.

Trollope, Anthony, *Complete Short Stories*, edited and with an introduction by Betty Jane Breyer, 5 vols., 1979–1983.

Twain, Mark, *A Tramp Abroad*, 1880.

Tyssot de Patot, Simon, *Voyages et avantures de Jaques Massé*, 1710; edited by Aubrey Rosenberg, 1993.

Verne, Jules, *Le Tour du monde en quatre-vingt jours*, 1873; as *Around the World in Eighty Days*, translated by G.M. Towle, 1874.

Vincent of Beauvais, *Speculum historiale*, 1253.

Voltaire, *Candide; ou, L'Optimisme*, 1759; as *Candide*, translated by Lowell Bair, 1959.

Waugh, Evelyn, *A Handful of Dust*, 1934.

Waugh, Evelyn, *Scoop*, 1938.

Wells, H.G., *The First Men in the Moon*, 1901.

*Wonders of the East/De rebus in Oriente mirabilibus*, in *Three Old English Prose Texts in M.S. Cotton Vitellius A XV*, edited by Stanley Rypins, 1924; reprinted, 1971.

Woolf, Virginia, *The Voyage Out*, 1915; revised edition, 1920.

*See also* **Children's Travel Writing; Epistolary Travel Fiction; Fantasy Travel Writing; Picaresque Novels**

## FIENNES, CELIA (1662–1741) *British Travel Writer*

Celia Fiennes was born into a family of prominent and active parliamentarians and staunch dissenters. Her travel journal is one of only two accounts of domestic travel by a late seventeenth-century Englishwoman to survive. She began to write an account of her journeys (seemingly from notes) in 1702. Excerpts were published by Robert Southey in 1812; an incomplete and imperfect transcription was published in 1888, and a full edition in 1947.

Between approximately 1685 and 1712, Fiennes made a series of journeys through Britain, eventually visiting every English county and making brief visits to Scotland and Wales. Her earliest travels were largely social visits, combined with a moderate amount of sightseeing. In 1697 she made her first long tour, traveling by horseback as far north as Scarborough and covering over 600 miles; later the same year she made a journey through Kent. In 1698 she made her second long tour, which she described as "My Great Journey to Newcastle and to Cornwall, the account of many journeys into most parts of England." This tour was made alone, apart from one or two servants, and again traveled on horseback, staying at inns or in the homes of relations and friends. During the next 15 years she continued to travel, making additional trips throughout southern England.

In many ways, Fiennes was typical of the tourist of her day. She was financially well-off—until the advent of the railways in the nineteenth century, tourism remained the prerogative of the nobility and gentry. She followed much of the standard tourist trail and visited well-known houses and gardens, recording her reactions in a journal. The keeping of diaries and travel journals was becoming fashionable at the time, and it was common for anyone who was traveling to record their impressions, even if they did so only for their own future recollection. Instruction books for travelers emphasized the importance of keeping records of travel.

Belonging to a generation that was beginning to discover England, Fiennes traveled primarily for pleasure, taking equal interest in a stately home one day and an industrial process the next. A woman of firm opinions, she had clear ideas about what pleased or displeased her. Aware of current fashions in building and architecture, she preferred the modern to the ancient, selecting for praise those buildings that most closely conformed to contemporary tastes.

Fiennes's journal vividly describes towns, roads, country seats, paintings, gardens, and churches. She had a particular interest in mining and quarrying, and described in detail the lead mines of Derbyshire, the tin and copper mines of Cornwall, and the processes of quarrying stone and marble. Manufacturing was of equal interest and Fiennes recorded visits to over 20 different sites, including ironworks, button makers, glass blowers, shipbuilders, and paper mills. She favored the man-made landscape over the natural and complained that Derbyshire was "full of steep hills, and nothing but the peakes of hills as thick one by another is seen . . . which makes travelling tedious, and the miles long," adding, however, that the abundance of minerals in those hills showed "the wisdom and benignitye of our greate Creator to make up the deficiency of a place by an equivolent."

Conditions of travel were not easy. Roads were poor and even near London were often neglected. The increase in wheeled vehicles during the sixteenth and seventeenth centuries had caused considerable deterioration in road surfaces, and milestones and signposts were scarce and inaccurate. Fiennes's journal contains many references to the poor condition and dangers of the highway. On her way to Chester she encountered a band of highwaymen: "2 fellows all on a suddain from the wood fell into the road, they look'd truss'd up with great coates and as it were bundles about them which I believe was pistolls, but they dogg'd me one before the other behind and would . . . frequently justle my horse out of the way to get between one of my servants horses and mine." She was saved from further mishap by the presence of men haymaking in nearby fields. Characteristically, she reported the incident without any mention of fear or other emotion.

Whenever possible, Fiennes stayed with friends or relations. Frequently, however, she used local inns and lodging houses, where the accommodations were variable and unreliable. At Addison Bank, for example, the parlor was so smoky that she "could not bring myself to sit down" and in Buxton, "the Lodgings . . . sometymes are so crowded that three must lye in a bed." She was more fortunate in Brance Burton, where tenants on the estate "did entertain us kindly, made two good beds for us and also for our servants, and good bread and cheese bacon and eggs."

During the years in which Fiennes traveled, spas became centers of fashionable resort as well as places of healing. She frequently visited spas to bathe and drink the waters, and her journal records visits to over 16 different sites, including Epsom, Tunbridge, Buxton, Knaresborough, and Harrogate. She was knowledgeable about the various spas, the mineral contents of their waters, and their reputed effects, whether they were "diaretick," "a good sort of Purge if you can hold your breath so as to drinke them downe," or capable of easing "a great pain I used to have in my head."

Travel journals in the late seventeenth and early eighteenth centuries were rarely completely private documents, and it was common practice for travelers to circulate their journals among their families and friends, sometimes making multiple copies. Although Fiennes disclaimed any intention of printed publication, it is clear from her preface that she saw her journal as a book with a potential audience, even planning a supplement of errata to be added at a later date. The value of Fiennes's account for the social or economic historian is obvious, and many commentators rank it alongside that of Daniel Defoe. Beyond that, her vitality, her breathless enthusiasm, and her keen powers of observation have provided considerable reading pleasure for many modern readers.

ELIZABETH HAGGLUND

### Biography

Born Cecilia Fiennes at Newton Toney, near Salisbury, 7 June 1662. Daughter of a prominent Puritan family. Traveled in Somerset, Wiltshire, Berkshire, and Oxfordshire, c. 1685; London, Hampshire, and Surrey, 1691; Oxford and Sussex, c. 1694; Herefordshire, Gloucestershire, Hampshire, and the Isle of Wight, c. 1696. Made first grand tour through northern England and later toured Kent, 1697; completed tours to Newcastle and to Cornwall, 1698. Made several short journeys in the home counties, 1701 or later. Wrote main part of journal, 1702. Died in Hackney, London, 10 April 1741.

### References and Further Reading

Fiennes, Celia, *Omniana; or, Horae Otiosiores*, edited by Robert Southey, 1812.

Fiennes, Celia, *Through England on a Side Saddle in the Time of William and Mary: Being the Diary of Celia Fiennes*, 1888.

Fiennes, Celia, *The Journeys of Celia Fiennes*, edited by Christopher Morris, 1947.

Fiennes, Celia, *The Illustrated Journeys of Celia Fiennes, 1685–c. 1712*, edited by Christopher Morris, 1982.

## FIENNES, RANULPH (1944–) *British Explorer*

Ranulph Fiennes says, unconvincingly, that he is only a professional expedition leader because he is unqualified to do anything else, and that he would rather sit in an office than on an ice floe. If that is true, it is just as well for the prestige of British expeditions that he is unable to do anything else. Since the early 1960s he has led increasingly ambitious and dangerous expeditions, and recorded them in books that have become some of the classics of modern expedition literature.

His father, a World War II hero who commanded the Royal Scots Greys, and whom Fiennes never knew, has served as his inspiration. The demonic drive that has infuriated, intimidated, and baffled other expedition members likely comes from a desire to vindicate his father's memory. After Eton, Fiennes joined the army, served with the Royal Scots Greys and the SAS, and saw action in the Dhofar campaign in Oman.

Early trips to Norway and the Pyrenees were followed in 1969 by one of Fiennes's most colorful and engaging shoestring expeditions. On leave from his Omani secondment, and up to his eyes in debt, Fiennes thought it would be a good idea to go up the Nile from mouth to source with two mini-hovercraft. The story is told in *A Talent for Trouble* (1970). He arrived in Alexandria to find that, because of the Arab-Israeli war, permission to hover up the river had been refused. In Cairo, where he went to plead his case, the expedition was mistaken for a helicopter trade delegation and allowed to go south, although not by river. Once over the Sudanese border the hovercraft were used, and worked well, and the expedition pressed on, sometimes on the river, sometimes overland, all the way to Lake Victoria.

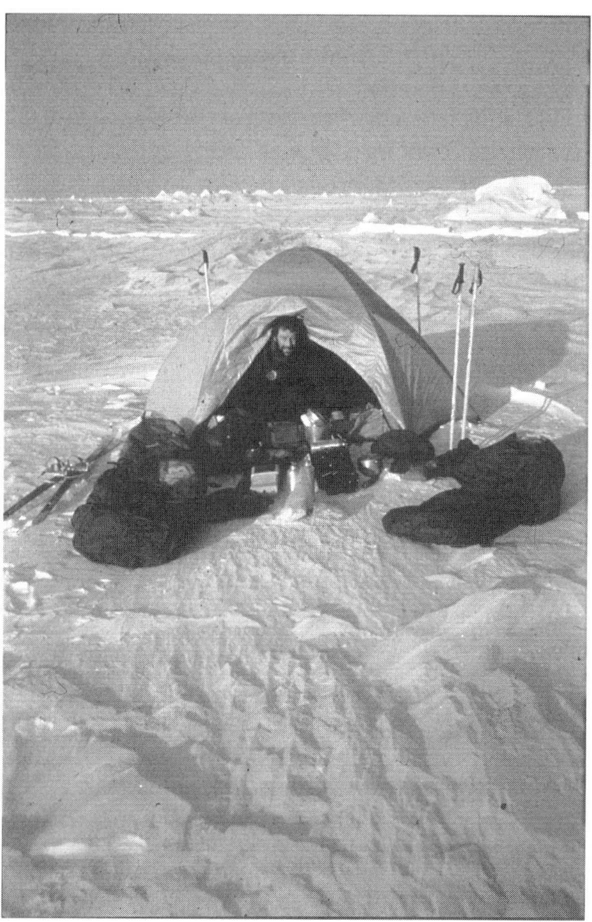

Ranulph Fiennes in his tent during his 1990 unsupported attempt on the North Pole. *Courtesy of the Royal Geographical Society, London.*

An expedition to the Jostedalsbre Glacier in Central Jotunheim, Norway (1970), led to Fiennes's second book, *Ice Fall in Norway* (1972). After being dropped by parachute on the glacier, the party planned to follow the ancient cattle trail across the glacier, and then canoe down the glacial wastewater, but things went wrong. Heavy packs, high altitude, and heavy snow proved too much for the party, and their canoes were smashed to pieces by the river. They were lucky to escape alive, and Fiennes learned a lot, very quickly, about leadership.

Another Norwegian parachute glacier trip (a survey of the Fabergstolbre Glacier) in 1970 was followed by a long river descent in Yukon and British Columbia in 1971, which resulted in *The Headless Valley* (1973), a great deal of criticism of Fiennes's leadership and organizational ability, and a portrayal of him in a BBC film as a selfish glory seeker. This did little to discourage sponsors, however, which were sorely needed for the next venture—the Transglobe and its associated expeditions.

The idea of the Transglobe expedition was to circle the globe from Greenwich to Greenwich, passing through both poles. The expedition planned to cross Europe, the Sahara, the Atlantic, and Antarctica, travel up the Pacific to the Arctic, by boat down more than 1,000 miles of the Yukon and Mackenzie rivers, through the Northwest Passage and 500 miles of Arctic archipelago, across the ice caps of Ellesmere Island, over the Arctic Ocean via the North Pole, and back to Greenwich. Fiennes recognized that Transglobe demanded more experience in cold climates than he had, and organized training expeditions in 1976 to the Greenland ice cap and in 1977 toward the North Pole. The latter expedition was forced back at just over 87° N, stopped by the transpolar drift. The terrible hardships of the 1976 and 1977 expeditions are recorded in Fiennes's usual deadpan way in *Hell on Ice* (1979).

The Transglobe expedition itself took place between 1979 and 1982. It was a complete and triumphant success—a venture so ambitious and headline-catching that it was difficult to know where Fiennes could go from there. The story of the Transglobe expedition is told in *To the Ends of the Earth* (1983), which is not only an impressive read, but an important expedition-planner's manual, full of crucial logistical information.

After Transglobe, Fiennes headed back to the North Pole in an unsupported expedition with Mike Stroud between 1986 and 1988. The pair failed to reach the pole, and Fiennes suffered gangrene in one foot. Fiennes tried again in 1990, and again failed, but set the record for the northernmost unsupported expedition.

Since his Dhofar days Fiennes had been tantalized by the notion of finding the fabled lost city of Ubar in southern Oman. He did so in 1991; the story is found in *Atlantis of the Sands* (1992).

In 1992 and 1993 Fiennes went with Mike Stroud to the Antarctic for the South Pole unsupported expedition. They became the first to cross the Antarctic continent and completed the longest polar journey ever made. The best of Fiennes's books resulted: *Mind over Matter* (1993). It is not simply a travel book, but a psychological thriller. Relations between Fiennes and Stroud were almost homicidally turbulent. The book contains excerpts from Stroud's diary, and the comparison of points of views is utterly absorbing. In February 2000, Fiennes attempted once more to reach the North Pole unsupported, but was turned back by frostbite.

Fiennes's books are written for profit, not for love, but they are fast, direct, honest, and completely unpretentious, and they have steadily improved since he started writing. There is no purple prose anywhere in them, and they are all the more evocative for it. Fiennes knows how powerful understatement can be. He has very obviously done enough to make exaggeration unnecessary, but it is unusual to find someone whose words speak almost as loudly as their actions.

CHARLES FOSTER

### Biography

Born 7 March 1944. Attended Eton College. Lieutenant, Royal Scots Greys, 1966; captain, 1968. Attached to the 22nd SAS Regiment, 1966. Served with the Sultan of Muscat's armed forces, 1968 (Dhofar Campaign Medal, 1969; Sultan's Bravery Medal, 1970). Married Virginia Pepper, 1970. Captain, RAC Expeditions: White Nile, 1969; Jostedalsbre Glacier, 1970; Headless Valley, British Columbia, 1971. Made attempt on the North Pole, 1977. Transglobe expedition (the first surface journey around the world's polar axis), 1979–1982. Reached the South Pole, 15 December 1980. Reached the North Pole, 11 April 1982. Led North Polar unsupported expeditions, 1986–1988, 1990; did not reach the pole, but achieved record for the northernmost unsupported expedition, 1990. Expedition to find the lost city of Ubar, Oman, 1991. Led South Polar unsupported expedition: first crossing of Antarctic continent and the longest polar journey to date, 1992–1993. Unsupported expedition to the North Pole, 2000. Awarded Livingstone Medal, Royal Scottish Geographical Society, 1982; Explorers' Club of New York Medal, 1983; Founder's Medal, Royal Geographical Society, 1984; Polar Medal, 1987. OBE (Order of the British Empire), 1993.

### References and Further Reading

Fiennes, Ranulph, *A Talent for Trouble*, 1970.
Fiennes, Ranulph, *Ice Fall in Norway*, 1972.

Fiennes, Ranulph, *The Headless Valley*, 1973.
Fiennes, Ranulph, *Where Soldiers Fear to Tread*, 1975.
Fiennes, Ranulph, *Hell on Ice*, 1979.
Fiennes, Ranulph, *To the Ends of the Earth*, 1983.
Fiennes, Ranulph, *Bothie the Polar Dog: The Dog Who Went to Both Poles with the Transglobe Expedition*, with Virginia Fiennes, 1984.
Fiennes, Ranulph, *Living Dangerously: The Autobiography of Ranulph Fiennes*, 1987; revised and expanded edition, 1994.
Fiennes, Ranulph, *Atlantis of the Sands: The Search for the Lost City of Ubar*, 1992.
Fiennes, Ranulph, *Mind over Matter: The Epic Crossing of the Antarctic Continent*, 1993.

## FIJI

Fijians were great travelers and explorers, making epic voyages out from Melanesia in their huge *ndrau*, or double-hulled canoes, 3,000 years ago to settle on unoccupied islands in the South Pacific. They carried with them aspects of *lapita* culture, a sedentary, agriculturist, and partially mobile maritime way of life. On a group of islands they called Viti, they adjusted to the new environment and created a new home. This became the Fiji named by European explorers who came centuries later. Reflecting the lateness of regular contact with Europeans and the inability of early observers to understand the mixture of tradition and ritual that made up the *vanua*, or way of life, Fiji was for many years known as the Cannibal Isles. The Dutchman Abel Tasman noted 12 islands in Fiji in 1643, but his report was full of references to dangerous shoals and unexpected reefs. The Englishman James Cook passed through in 1774. William Bligh headed for Batavia in 1789 after the mutiny on the *Bounty*, recorded 39 islands when he passed through the then uncharted waters, and put Fiji on English maps. Bligh published *A Narrative of the Mutiny* in 1790 and *A Voyage to the South Sea* in 1792 and then returned on HMS *Providence* to map more of the islands. The London Missionary Society supply ship *Duff* passed through in 1797 and in 1820 the Russian Fabian Bellinghausen added a few more islands to nearly complete the list. Finally, the French explorer Dumont d'Urville named Astrolobe Reef in 1834. Based on their travels and experience, as in other regions, the leaders of expeditions and naval officers mentioned Fiji in the books they published, but Fiji was never a destination imagined, known, or sought as eagerly as the fabled Tahiti and Hawaii. The books by Bligh in 1790 and 1792, Commodore John Erskine in 1853, and the pioneering missionaries Williams and Calvert in 1858, and Pritchard and Waterhouse, both in 1866, made Fiji known but to a limited audience. Rotumah Island, separate but included in the British colony declared in 1874 and later part of the modern nation of Fiji, was first visited in 1791 and then irregularly by missionary vessels after 1797. Rotumah became a major whaling and trading port of call where crews from all over the Pacific could always be found waiting to sign on, but it never attracted attention until Harry MacDonald's *Rotuma and the Rotumans* in 1917.

The first contact between Fijians and Europeans occurred during the visit of the HMS *Pandora* in 1791. By 1800, wrecks were beginning to dot the reefs as traders, naval vessels, and exploring voyages passed regularly through the Fiji group. The next phase of mapping and discovery was the result of capitalist desires to reap the rewards of Fiji's natural resources. The first traders came between 1804 and 1812. In the 1820s and 1830s, a second wave came looking for sandalwood and bêche-de-mer (sea cucumber). In 1835 the first two European missionaries arrived, and soon their colleagues were releasing books that mixed doctrine, hagiography, ethnographic observation, myth, legend, and basic geography. These missionaries, traders, and naval officers doubled as explorers by selecting harbors, mapping, listing, making charts, and recording aspects of Fijian culture. By 1840, Levuka, on the island of Ovalau, was a busy little entrepot and trading port where crew and deckhands could be signed on, routes and depots plotted, whalers reprovisioned, and ships laid over in a stormy spell. The two larger islands, Viti Levu and Vanua Levua, were not well known and Viti Levu was not crossed by Europeans until 1865. The paucity of literature was such that the travelogue in 1881 by Constance Cumming Gordan, *At Home in Fiji*, was quoted extensively when the quasi-official *Cyclopedia of Fiji* was published in 1907. In 1908 *The Fijians: A Study of the Decay of Custom* by the geographer Basil Thomson, and *The Fiji of Today* in 1910 by the Methodist missionary John Burton, therefore became the standard texts on Fiji.

The detailed surveying of Fiji by the British was closely linked to a desire to formalize, in perpetuity, the Fijian relationship with their land. The Land Claims Commission, and later the Native Lands Trust Board institutionalized Fijian ownership, boundaries, and hereditary rights. The map of Fiji began to look like a county map of rural England.

Knapman and Young have debated the role of nineteenth-century European women in creating permanent European enclaves. For Europeans, because Fiji was a scattered archipelago, there was little opportunity for the usual colonial exploration of the interior, so the urge to explore turned to material culture, crafts, linguistics, folklore, and botany. Travel within Fiji was always by cutter, whaleboat, or ketch. Fijians walked or used a variety of small and large canoes as well as bamboo rafts to negotiate river systems, deltas, and fringing lagoons. The transformation when sugarcane production began in the 1870s was therefore dramatic. Narrow-gauge train lines snaked along the coasts and river valleys, and early in the twentieth century trucks, and later passenger cars, started to motor along newly built roads.

In the 1970s the advent of the jumbo jet heralded another transformation for Fiji—it became an international travel destination. The airport at Nadi became a hub for long-distance flights from most Asian, Australian, and U.S. destinations to other Pacific airports. Lautoka, Savu Savu, and predominantly Suva became stopovers for cruise ships out of Australia and New Zealand or on longer routes out of Europe and the United States. Resorts and international hotels developed on the Coral Coast on the south of Viti Levu and the Mamanuca group off the west coast. They became snorkeling, scuba, sunbaking, honeymoon, and later backpacker havens.

Surprisingly, considering its regional prominence, Fiji has not inspired a large body of historical fiction and nonfiction and only boasts a moderate list of exploration narratives. Exploration now focuses on surfers searching for new reefs and huge barrels, and Fiji already hosts one of the world's premier surfing competitions at a reef located several kilometres off shore. Tourism remains one of the top four foreign-currency earners for Fiji, a position threatened by coups and civil unrest in 1987 and 2000. The resorts that sprouted along the coast, the mountain trails, rafting, diving, and visits to cultural villages now present a Fiji more like the imaginary South Seas paradise than the cannibal isles of 200 years ago.

MAX QUANCHI

### References and Further Reading

Allen, P.S. (editor), *Cyclopedia of Fiji*, 1907.
Bligh, William, *A Narrative of the Mutiny on Board His Majesty's Ship Bounty*, 1790; reprinted, 1952.
Bligh, William, *A Voyage to the South Sea*, 1792.
Brewster, A.B., *The Hill Tribes of Fiji*, 1922.
Brown, Stanley, *Men from under the Sky: The Arrival of Westerners in Fiji*, foreword by Raymond Burr, 1973.
Burton, J.W., *The Fiji of To-day*, 1910.
Cargill, David, *The Diaries and Correspondence of David Cargill, 1832–1843*, edited by Albert J. Schütz, 1977.
Cumming, Gordon, C.F., *At Home in Fiji*, 1881.
Diapea, William, *Cannibal Jack: The True Autobiography of a White Man in the South Seas*, 1928.
Erskine, John Elphinstone, *Journal of a Cruise among the Islands of the Western Pacific, Including the Feejees . . . in Her Majesty's Ship Havannah*, 1853.
Lockerby, William, *The Journal of William Lockerby*, edited by Everard Im Thurn and Leonard Wharton, 1925.
McDonald, Harry, *Rotuma and the Rotumans*, 1917.
Moss, Frederick J., *A Month in Fiji*, 1868.
Pritchard, W.T., *Polynesian Reminiscences; or, Life in the South Pacific Islands*, 1866; reprinted, 1968.
Smythe, Mrs W.J. [Sarah Maria], *Ten Months in the Fiji Islands*, 1864.
Tarte, Daryl, *Fiji*, 1988.
Thomson, Basil, *The Fijians: A Study of the Decay of Custom*, 1908.
Wallis, Mary Davis, *Life in Feejee; or, Five Years among the Cannibals*, 1851.
Waterhouse, Joseph, *The King and People of Fiji*, 1866.
Williams, Thomas and James Calvert, *Fiji and the Fijians*, 1858; 4th edition, 1884.

## FLAUBERT, GUSTAVE (1821–1880)

***French Novelist***

"Travelling," said Flaubert, "ought to be a serious business. Otherwise, unless you get drunk every day, it can be one of the most bitter and inane things in the world." Flaubert was undoubtedly a serious traveler. He wrote copiously about his travels in Corsica, Italy, Brittany, and Egypt, but refrained, on principle, from publishing anything that smacked of mere journalism.

Flaubert was just 18 years old when he embarked on his first real journey, to the island of Corsica, in the summer of 1840. It lasted ten weeks and was a reward for having passed his exams. Chaperoned by a friend of the family and burdened with earnest advice from his father, Flaubert set off for the south, traveling by mail coach, crossing the Pyrenees into Spain and then pausing briefly at Nîmes to visit the remains of the great Roman arena. Approaching Marseilles Flaubert had his first gloriously memorable vision of the Mediterranean. The reality of the 16-hour late-summer sea-crossing from Toulon to Ajaccio in a small paddle-steamer was less glorious: Flaubert lay in his cabin, vomiting wretchedly. When Flaubert's party arrived in Corsica the local prefect took them under his wing. Using his political influence the prefect arranged introductions and an itinerary (with military escort through bandit country). Flaubert traveled on horseback, through forests and over mountains, across the island in a diagonal line from Ajaccio to Bastia. He was fascinated by bandits, tormented by fleas, delighted by moonlit landscapes, and intrigued by distant glimpses of the Italian coast. After an unsettling return sea voyage from Bastia to Toulon, Flaubert reached Marseilles, where he savored the perfect adolescent *amour de voyage* in the person of Eulalie Foucault, the voluptuous young widow who managed the hotel.

In the spring of 1845 Flaubert set off for Italy. It was supposed to be a great romantic pilgrimage, but this journey, complicated by the company of his whole family, was miserably frustrating. No sooner had the party reached Genoa than they decided to turn back because of serious health problems. Flaubert salvaged only the memory of an encounter with Brueghel's painting of *The Temptation of Saint Antony*, an image that was to be the visual source of the author's first major work.

Flaubert now became an armchair traveler, a great connoisseur of contemporary travel writings. He read everyone, from the erudite Grand Tour aristocrats of an earlier generation, men such as Byron and Chateaubriand, to the facetiously opinionated journalists writing for the mass circulation newspapers of the day, professional journalists such as Gérard de Nerval and Théophile Gautier.

Flaubert's next journey, in the summer of 1847, was a 13-week walking tour of northwestern France. This took him through the Loire valley, visiting the chateaux of the Renaissance, and out along the wild coastline of Brittany (still one of the least French parts of France). Although he was strongly drawn to the curious, the primitive, and the grotesque: a five-legged sheep on display at the fair, a crudely voluptuous ancient granite statue of Venus, bloody scenes at the abbatoir in Quimper, the excruciating gentility of a military brothel in Brest, Flaubert was also deeply moved by more decorous literary associations. He was most eager to visit the birthplace and later the tomb of Chateaubriand, the great literary god of his adolescence. For once, the pilgrim was not disappointed. Both of these monuments met all his imaginative requirements.

In November 1849 Flaubert set off on the greatest journey of his life: to the Orient. In the company of Maxime Du Camp, he spent 20 months abroad, exploring Egypt, Palestine, Greece, and Italy. They embarked from Marseilles aboard *Le Nil*, a steam-and-sail mailboat belonging to the Messageries nationales. After an 11-day crossing, battered and almost wrecked by a storm off Malta, *Le Nil* docked in Alexandria and Flaubert was soon installed on the main square in the Hotel d'Orient. Pompey's Pillar, one of the great sights of the city, had "Thompson of Sunderland" painted around its base in black letters three feet high. Flaubert greatly relished such stupidities.

From Alexandria, Flaubert and Du Camp traveled south by steamboat up the delta to Cairo. They stayed there for the next two months in a hotel in Ezbekkiya, the modern European quarter on the edge of the old city. Although they made contact with the local circle of French expatriates, the many engineers, doctors, and soldiers who had been hired to modernize the country, Flaubert was more attracted by the colorful lowlife of the city: the transvestite dancers, the madame of a nearby brothel, the snakecharmers, and the delightfully erudite Coptic patriarch, Boutros VII, barefoot in his robes. Flaubert also seemed inexplicably depressed. His companion Maxime Du Camp wrote, "If it had been possible he would have travelled on a divan, lying down, without moving, watching the landscapes, the ruins and the cities passing in front of his eyes like the canvas unrolling in a panorama machine."

In February 1850 Flaubert and Du Camp set off up the Nile on board their hired *cange*, a 40-foot sailboat with a native crew of nine. Their Nile voyage lasted 17 weeks and took them as far south as the Second Cataract. Living on a diet of pigeons, dates, and figs, sleeping for 15 hours a night, Flaubert observed that he was becoming "ignobly plump." They visited the great temples at Karnak, Abu Simbel, and Kom Ombo. They also sampled the fabulous but unhygienic pleasures offered by Egyptian prostitutes. At their furthest point south, on the summit of the mountain above the cataract at Djebel Abousir, Flaubert supposedly gave a great cry and announced, "I'm going to call her Madame Bovary!" The travelers returned to Europe, mainly overland, visiting Jerusalem, Damascus, Beirut, Rhodes, Constantinople, Athens, Naples, Rome, and Venice (where Flaubert was reunited with his anxious mother).

Apart from a two-month solitary excursion to Algeria and Tunisia in 1858, researching his Carthaginian novel *Salammbô*, Flaubert's travels ceased when he reached the age of 30. After his return from the Orient in 1851 he lived with his widowed mother in the family home at Croisset, where he adopted an arduous and often isolated routine of writing. There he worked over his rich store of traveler's memories and imagined, with an almost equal ardor, all the great journeys that he would never attempt, to India, to China, and to California. Like many of the characters in his novels, Flaubert found that travel was best regarded as a magnificent stimulus to creative reverie.

GEOFFREY WALL

## Biography

Born in Rouen, France, 12 December 1821. Son of Achille Cléophas Flaubert, a wealthy surgeon and professor of medicine. Attended the Collège Royal, Rouen, 1831–1839; the École de Droit, Paris, 1841–1845. Gave up legal studies because of ill health, 1845. Traveled to Corsica, 1840; Italy, 1845; Brittany and the Loire valley, 1847; Egypt, Palestine, and Greece, 1849–1851; Algeria and Tunisia, 1858. Maintained a sporadic relationship with the poet Louise Colet, 1846–1855. Published six novels, including *Madame Bovary* (1856) and *L'Education Sentimentale* (1869). Died of a stroke in Croisset, near Rouen, 8 May 1880.

## References and Further Reading

Flaubert, Gustave, "Notes de voyages," in *Oeuvres Complètes*, vol. 2, 1964.

Flaubert, Gustave, *Flaubert in Egypt: A Sensibility on Tour*, edited and translated by Francis Steegmuller, 1972; reprinted, 1996.

Flaubert, Gustave, "Voyages et carnets de voyages," in *Oeuvres Complètes*, vols. 10 and 11, 1973.

Flaubert, Gustave, *Par les Champs et par les grèves*, edited by Adrianne Tooke, 1987.

Flaubert, Gustave, *Voyage en Égypte*, edited by Pierre-Marc de Biasi, 1991.

## FLEMING, PETER (1907–1971) *British Adventurer, Journalist, Soldier, and Historian*

Peter Fleming made virtually his entire contribution to travel writing while still in his twenties, with three major books in four years. Having earned an honors degree in English literature from Oxford, he traveled very extensively in Asia and the Americas. His accounts of his experiences reflect influences as diverse as Ernest Hemingway and P.G. Wodehouse; his prose is unfailingly graceful, his wit wry and exquisitely timed. In his frequent parodies of the clichés of adventure writing, Fleming seems to be reliving the dilemma of Cervantes in *Don Quixote*: clearly he believes in adventure, just as Cervantes on one level believed in chivalry, but how does one write of such things any more? Fleming's solution is to disarm his readers with word play and self-deprecation, thereby strengthening the impact of his more serious passages.

*Brazilian Adventure* (1933) opens with a droll description of how Fleming got involved in an expedition to the interior of South America in search of Colonel Percy Fawcett. He spares no one in his exposure of the absurdity of the enterprise, not even himself: it becomes obvious that no one in the group has a clear idea of where they are going or what to do when they get there. As the group gets farther from civilization and closer to the putative field of operations, however, Fleming subtly turns himself into a hero of sorts: he and those who follow him will not consider turning back without having made at least a plucky effort to solve the mystery of Fawcett's disappearance. Those of the opposing party, as Fleming depicts them, seem disposed to do nothing at all.

As if their good intentions were being rewarded, Fleming and his friends enjoy the most magical moments of the entire trip while making their ultimately futile attempt:

> For some reason, I remember that hot bright noon as being full of a curious delight. I was in that psychological state always described by the characters in Mr. Ernest Hemingway's novels as "feeling good." My perceptions were sharper than usual, my power to appreciate had suddenly expanded. All the things I saw seemed to me exactly right; I read their meanings so easily, so instinctively, that there was for once no need to try and define it. I had that uncritical exhilaration, that clear conviction that this was a good day in a good world, which one has known so seldom since childhood. (*Brazilian Adventure*)

Forced to turn back by a shortage of supplies, Fleming's party races the opposition back to civilization, both for practical reasons and as a nonviolent form of revenge. It is puerile, as Fleming freely admits, but the competition lends zest to his description of the long, slow, often frustrating river voyage.

In *Brazilian Adventure*, Fleming uses a wide range of literary techniques to transform the actual events of an ill-planned and bungled expedition into what is, in effect, a travel novel. While he emphasizes repeatedly that he is telling the truth, and prides himself on avoiding the exaggerations characteristic of much writing about exploration in the wilds, he selects and arranges his material with the skill of a literary artist.

Even before the publication of *Brazilian Adventure*, which earned him instant fame, Fleming was off to China, eager to explore Japanese-controlled Manchuria and to learn what he could of the Communist insurgents led by Mao Tse-Tung. *One's Company: A Jour-*

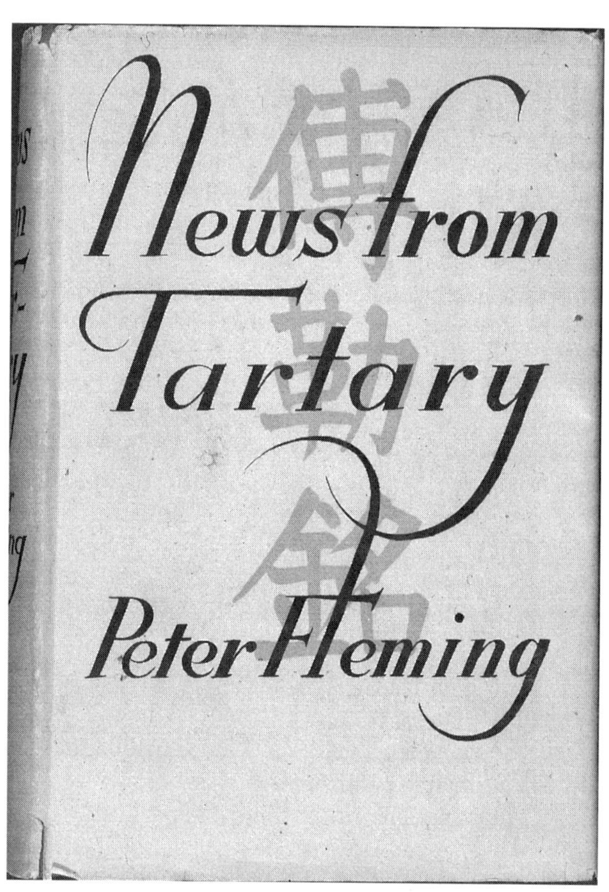


Jacket of the first edition of Fleming's *News from Tartary: A Journey from Peking to Kashir* (Jonathan Cape, 1936). *Courtesy of the Stapleton Collection, London.*

*ney to China* (1934) is written in the same urbane and witty prose as his earlier book. In this account, however, Fleming does not accentuate the farcical. He misses no chance to be funny, but he is clearly aware that he has seen many things of which even experts could have no knowledge in the rapidly changing China of the 1930s, and his narrative and descriptions convey the excitement of being involved in great events.

Whether he is riding with Japanese troops in search of Manchurian bandits, or scoring a journalistic coup by getting an interview with General Chiang Kai-Shek, Fleming thoroughly enjoys his adventures and communicates his sense of satisfaction:

> Next day, after a five-hour train journey which seemed luxury to us but might not have appealed to anyone lacking our fund of odious comparisons, we reached Canton. We were thinner, swarthier, much dirtier, but only about twenty pounds poorer than when we had started out, nearly a month ago. The route which we followed has not, I believe, been previously covered in its entirety by a foreigner, nor is there any earthly reason why it should have been. Still, it is a good journey. (*One's Company*)

Almost without a pause, Fleming then undertook his most ambitious and difficult journey, an overland trek from Beijing to India, accompanied by Ella Maillart (1903–1997), herself a famous adventurer and writer. *News from Tartary* (1936) evokes the often agonizingly slow pace of the crossing, accomplished mostly on horseback and on foot, and frequently delayed by all sorts of human and natural obstacles. As always, however, Fleming makes a point of complaining less than he might, and of celebrating the many keen and unexpected pleasures encountered along the way. As in his other books, he is writing of travel in places where his readers have almost certainly never been and will never go, and his descriptions vividly convey how it feels to contend with camels, to arrive at an oasis, to survive a sandstorm in the Gobi desert, or finally to arrive in India. His book incidentally provided the last glimpse of much of central Asia that the outside world would have for many years.

Fleming did not stop having adventures after his epic crossing of Asia, but there were no more travel books of significance. His subsequent writings were mostly light essays and serious historical studies. When he came across a diary of his travels in Soviet Russia, he merely published an unaltered transcription, with almost nothing in the way of notes or introduction: *A Forgotten Journey* (1952). Peter Fleming's work in travel writing was the first of his several brilliant careers. Although his mannerisms and his relentless wit have annoyed a small minority of readers, his humorous and elegantly written books were justifiably popular in their day, and continue to merit attention several decades later.

Philip Krummrich

### Biography

Born Robert Peter Fleming in London, 31 May 1907. Son of Valentine Fleming, later member of parliament for South Oxfordshire; older brother of the writer Ian Fleming. Suffered severe illness as a child. Attended Eton College and Christ Church, Oxford University; graduated in English literature, 1929. Visited Guatemala, 1930. Assistant literary editor, the *Spectator*, 1931. First visit to China to attend conference of the Institute of Pacific Relations, 1931. Took part in expedition to Brazil in search of missing explorer Colonel Percy Fawcett, 1932–1933. Traveled in Russia and China as special correspondent for the *Times* newspaper, 1933–1935. Traveled through China and India with Ella Maillart, 1935. Married the actress Celia Johnson, December, 1935: one son, two daughters. Journalist for the *Times*, late 1930s. Third trip to China, 1938. Joined the Grenadier Guards, 1939. Took part in covert operations and intelligence work in Norway, Egypt, England, Greece, and India, attaining rank of colonel, 1940–1945. Lived in Nettlebed, Oxfordshire, from 1945. Continued to write for the *Times* and the *Spectator*; completed several volumes of military history, including *Invasion 1940* (1957); *The Siege at Peking* (1959); *Bayonets to Lhasa* (1961). Published essays in five volumes, 1933–1961. Awarded OBE (Order of the British Empire), 1945. Died of a heart attack at Black Mount, Argyllshire, Scotland, 18 August 1971.

### References and Further Reading


Fleming, Peter, *Brazilian Adventure*, 1933.

Fleming, Peter, *One's Company: A Journey to China*, 1934.

Fleming, Peter, *News from Tartary: A Journey from Peking to Kashmir*, 1936.

Fleming, Peter, *Travels in Tartary* (contains *One's Company* and *News from Tartary*), 1948.

Fleming, Peter, *A Forgotten Journey: Diary of a Journey through Russia, Manchuria and Northern China in 1934*, 1952.


*See also* **Maillart, Ella**

## FLETCHER, GILES (c. 1549–1611) *English Diplomat and Poet*

After his first successful career as an academic at King's College, Cambridge, Giles Fletcher changed direction. He married in 1581 and then went into politics, serving as a member of Parliament for Winchelsea from 1584 to 1585. At Westminster he caught the attention of Queen Elizabeth I, who recommended him for the position of Remembrancer of the City of London before inaugurating his career as a diplomatic agent. After playing a minor role in the negotiation of the Treaty of Berwick with James VI of Scotland in 1586, Fletcher was sent on missions to the senate of Hamburg in 1587 and 1588 and to the Netherlands in 1598, but it is for his embassy to Russia in 1588 and 1589 that he is primarily remembered.

Annoyed by the behavior of certain English merchants, the Russian administration revoked the privileges of the Russia Company while demanding the repayment of what it claimed was a substantial debt. Fletcher's mission was to negotiate the restoration of the privileges and the alleviation of the debt, and more generally to smooth over the awkward diplomatic relations between the two countries. Neither well received nor well treated by the Russians, Fletcher was kept a virtual prisoner in his residence in Moscow and prevented from sending reports back to the queen. In spite of this he persisted in his diplomatic efforts, learning Russian along the way. Substantially as a result of the regent Boris Godunov's predisposition to trade with England, he returned home largely successful in the late summer of 1589. The debt remained burdensome but both diplomatic relations and trading privileges had been restored.

Fletcher's time in Russia inspired him to write. His reports, completed after his return home, are more extensive and involved than those of his other missions. Observations and studies made at the time inform the arguments from geography, etymology, and tradition that stand alongside the interpretation of scripture in his eccentric demonstration of the current whereabouts of the lost tribes of Israel, "The Tartars or, Ten Tribes," which remained in manuscript until long after his death and was finally published in 1667. Even his sequence of sonnets, *Licia*, contains passing references to Russia. Most significantly, his experiences resulted in his writing the first full-length book on the Russian state and people in English.

*Of the Russe Common Wealth* was first written between August and November 1589, and subsequently revised before its publication in 1591. Drawing liberally on the writings of earlier historians including Martin Cromer, and on Anthony Jenkinson's map of 1562, it combines this secondary research with the immediate observations of Fletcher himself and of other English travelers of the period, most notably the merchant Jerome Horsey. (Horsey himself wrote a substantial manuscript account of his experiences in Russia that was not published until 1856.) Closely structured, it is divided into three main sections, the first dealing with physical geography and commodities; the second with the political workings of the country, subdivided into the state, judicial processes, military expansion, and the church; and the third with economics or household management. As a historical source for the condition of Russia in the late sixteenth century, Fletcher's book is far from reliable. His geographical knowledge is secondhand and often inaccurate; his statistics too, while numerous, are frequently incorrect; and much of his information on Russian politics and society is clearly anecdotal. Despite their inaccuracies, these facts and figures do have considerable significance with respect to the impressions they are intended to convey.

Fletcher's book, motivated in part by his own mistreatment by the Russian regime, is a thoroughgoing portrait of a state of tyranny. In the opening dedication to the queen herself, Fletcher writes:

> In their maner of gouernment, your Highnesse may see both: A true and strange face of a *Tyrannical state,* (most vnlike your own) without true knowledge of GOD, without written Lawe, without common iustice: saue that which proceedeth from their *Speaking Lawe,* to wit, the Magistrate who hath most neede of a Lawe, to restraine his owne iniustice.

The contrast outlined here, between Russian despotism and English law, is the defining theme of the book as a whole. Whether Fletcher is describing the superstitions and theological heresies of the Orthodox Church, or the corruption and cruelty of local officials, or the absence of an elected parliament, the implied counterpoint is invariably that of Protestant, liberal, representative England. In portraying Ivan the Terrible as the archetype of an absolute tyrant, Fletcher is reminding both the reader and the queen herself of the benefits of limited and benevolent monarchy. In casting Boris Godunov as the overmighty subject turned tyrant in his own right, he is warning against the dangers of favoritism and weak rule. In alluding to rumors of political assassinations, and the sotto voce prayers for good government said at the investiture of the new emperor, Fletcher is evoking a culture of fear blessedly absent, as he presents it, from Elizabethan England. It is an irony that Fletcher was himself involved in the interrogation of Roman Catholics at Elizabeth's behest, with prescribed methods that included the use of torture.

Petitioned by the Russia Company itself, which feared that Fletcher's book would damage the trade he had restored, Lord Burghley ordered that *Of the Russe Common Wealth* be recalled. Future editions, such as that included by Hakluyt in the 1598 edition of his *Voyages*, muted the original's unfavorable portrait of the Russian state. Nevertheless, Fletcher's book continued to exert a dominant influence on how Russia was portrayed by subsequent writers, such as John Milton, Walter Raleigh, and a number of Jacobean dramatists including Ben Jonson, John Webster, and probably William Shakespeare. It also remains one of the earliest clear examples of what was to become the Whig history of England.

JOHN HOLMES

### Biography

Born in Watford, c. 1549. Attended Eton College, c. 1561–1565. Studied at and was a member of King's College, Cambridge, 1565–1581. Married Joan Sheafe, 1581: nine children, of whom two, Phineas, born 1582, and Giles, born c. 1585 or 1588, became poets themselves. Member of Parliament for Winchelsea, 1585. Remembrancer of the City of London, 1586–1605. Sent on diplomatic missions to Scotland, 1586; to Hamburg, 1587–1588; as ambassador to Russia, 1588–1589; and to the Netherlands, 1598. *Of the Russe Common Wealth* published, 1591. Poems published as *Licia*, c. 1593. Appointed Treasurer of St. Paul's, 1597. Lived in Ringwood, Hampshire, c. 1600. Died March 1611.

### References and Further Reading

Fletcher, Giles, *Of the Russe Common Wealth*, 1591; as *Of the Rus Commonwealth*, edited and with an introduction by Albert J. Schmidt, 1966; as *Of the Russe Commonwealth*, with an introduction by Richard Pipes, 1966.

Fletcher, Giles, "The Tartars; or, Ten Tribes," in *Israel Redux*, 1677; in *The English Works of Giles Fletcher the Elder*, edited by Lloyd E. Berry, 1964.

## FLINDERS, MATTHEW (1774–1814)

***British Naval Officer, Hydrographer, and Scientist***

Flinders came from a family living inland, with little previous connection with the sea, yet developed into a fine seaman and hydrographer, one of the most purposeful the world has seen. It is said that on reading *Robinson Crusoe* he determined to go to sea, and especially to explore. Indeed, his naval career was largely spent in ships of exploration, first in Bligh's second breadfruit voyage in *Providence*, which revealed his ability as a navigator, and then in *Reliance* to supply the New South Wales colony, during which he began exploratory voyages in various small craft along the Australian and Tasmanian coast, some in conjunction with George Bass. On his return to England, he approached Sir Joseph Banks, who was sufficiently impressed with him to support his proposal for a full survey of the coasts of Australia. The Admiralty consequently took up the scheme, and Flinders was appointed to command *Investigator*, with a number of scientists, which left Portsmouth in July 1801. The voyage enabled Flinders to survey much of the south and east coasts, and make a good start on the north coast, before the state of the ship compelled him to return to Sydney. No substitute being available, Flinders decided reluctantly to return home in the transport, *Porpoise*. Misfortune followed misfortune. She was wrecked on what became known as Wreck Reef, and after much diffculty, all her people were brought back to Sydney. After arranging for his crew, Flinders set off in the small schooner, *Cumberland*, for England. He reached Mauritius in December 1803, then French and therefore hostile, where the governor, General Decaen, became suspicious of his motives and interned him. Efforts to obtain his release failed until June 1810; he reached home in October, but had been able to work on the charts and journal of his voyage during his captivity. His final years were spent on completing this work, and his book was published just before his death.

Flinders's voyage on *Investigator* was certainly an expedition (with several scientists on board), when compared with later voyages, which were much more centered on surveying, relying for scientific observation much more on naval officers with appropriate interests. The results were far reaching, particularly in the botanical field, with Robert Brown and others working and collecting, and Bauer later providing engravings. The Australian continent was largely unexplored and unknown, and apart from the natural history observations, the expedition watched for great rivers or gulfs leading inland, or even forming islands of parts of the known territory. Here, it seems, Flinders did occasionally overlook important features difficult to distinguish from the sea, but his determination ensured

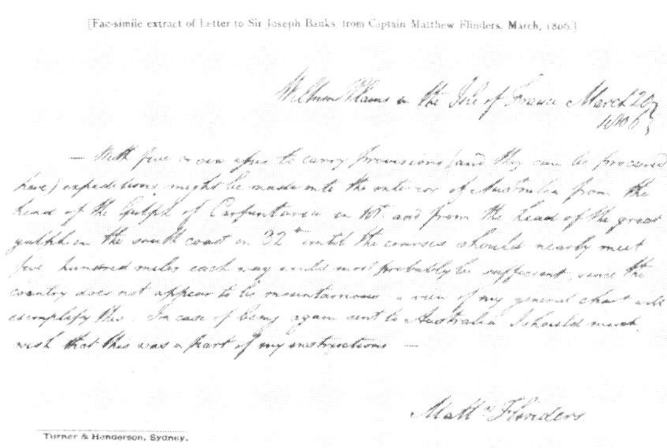

[Fac-simile extract of Letter to Sir Joseph Banks, from Captain Matthew Flinders, March, 1806.]

Wilhems Plains [?] in the Isle of France March 20 [?]
1806

— With five or six [?] asses to carry provisions (and they can be procured here) expeditions might be made into the interior of Australia from the head of the Gulph of Carpentaria in 18° [?] and from the head of the great gulph on the south coast in 32° until the courses should nearly meet; five hundred miles each way would most probably be sufficient, since the country does not appear to be mountainous: a view of my general chart will exemplify this. In case of being again sent to Australia I should much wish that this was a part of my instructions —

Matt^w Flinders

Turner & Henderson, Sydney.

Facsimile of Flinder's letter to Sir Joseph Banks, written in March 1806, with proposals for an expedition across the Australian interior; despite Flinders's optimism, the crossing was not accomplished until the 1860s (from Ernest Faven's *The History of Australian Exploration from 1788 to 1888*, 1888). *Courtesy of Travellers Club, London; Bridgeman Art Library, agent.*

that his contribution was fundamental, and when *Investigator* was found to be very decayed, he carried on with the survey for a time before returning to Sydney, and would have set out again had a suitable vessel been available. Even then, the events of the wreck and the voyage to Mauritius adequately speak for his purpose; *Cumberland* was far too small for such an oceanic voyage, and the stop at Mauritius was compelled by sheer necessity.

Flinders must also stand prominent in the world of travelers for his work on the magnetism of a ship's hull and its effect on the compass, thus making an important contribution to the improvement of navigation. He first noticed this effect during his work along the coast between 1796 and 1798, and subsequently maintained observations on the subject. After his return in 1810 he was able to make experiments in different ships, and published papers on the subject, which made him the patron saint of navigators by compass, and led to the founding of the Admiralty Compass Observatory.

*A Voyage to Terra Australis* (1814), a large and beautifully printed book, is a fine monument to Flinders's work. It contains a long historical introduction to earlier voyages, including his own previous work, followed by the account of his outward voyage in *Investigator*, during which he surveyed much of the south coast of Australia, and includes an appendix of the longitudinal observations taken during it. Volume II covers *Investigator*'s sailing from Port Jackson, the break off her survey and the return to Sydney, the account of the voyage and wreck of *Porpoise* and what followed until Flinders returned home in 1810. The last chapter is devoted to sailing directions and the weather. There are also appendices of observations on longitude, important contributions on errors of the compass, and on botany, the latter by Brown. The engravings are based on sketches by Westall, the artist on the voyage.

A.W.H. PEARSALL

### Biography

Born in Donington, near Boston, Lincolnshire, 16 March 1774. Educated locally. Entered Royal Navy, October 1789, under the patronage of Captain Sir Thomas Pasley. Midshipman in *Providence* (Captain William Bligh) to Van Diemen's Land, Tahiti, Fiji, Torres Strait to Jamaica, 1791–1793. At battle of 1 June 1794 in *Bellerophon*. Master's mate under Captain Henry Waterhouse in *Reliance* to Australia, Norfolk Island, Cape of Good Hope, returning via Australia, 1795–1800. Promoted to rank of lieutenant, January 1798; discovered Bass Strait, 1798–1799. Married Ann Chappell, 1801: one daughter. Appointed commander of *Investigator*, 16 February 1801; in command of survey of Australia, 1801–1803. Detained by the French in Île de France (now Mauritius), 1803–1810. Promoted to rank of captain, May 1810. Died of kidney disease in London, 19 July 1814.

### References and Further Reading


Flinders, Matthew, *Observations on the Coasts of Van Diemen's Land, on Bass's Strait and Its Islands, and on Part of the Coasts of New South Wales, Intended to Accompany the Charts of the Late Discoveries in Those Countries*, 1801.

Flinders, Matthew, *A Voyage to Terra Australis: Undertaken for the Purpose of Completing the Discovery of that Vast Country, and Prosecuted in the Years 1801, 1802, and 1803* . . . 2 vols. and atlas, 1814.

Flinders, Matthew, "Sur le Banc du Naufrage et sur Le Sort de M. De La Pérouse," in *Annales des Voyages, de la Géographie et de l'Histoire*, 10 (written 1807), vols. 1–25, 1808–1814.

Flinders, Matthew, *Matthew Flinders' Narrative of His Voyage in the Schooner Francis, 1798: Preceded and Followed by Notes on Flinders, Bass, the Wreck of the Sidney Cove &c by Geoffrey Rawson*, 1946.


## FLORENCE

By the eighteenth century Florence was popular among European travelers, even though the city's artistic heritage was at odds with the prevailing neoclassical fashion. Winckelmann (1717–1768) and Goethe (1749–1832) did not see anything that aroused their interest. Florentine architecture also failed to impress travelers like Boswell (1740–1795) and Horace Walpole (1717–1797). Even Madame de Staël's Corinne praised the republican spirit of Florentine art; the city's architecture is described as grim and medieval. In his *Travels through France and Italy* (1766), Smollett expresses a lack of appreciation for the celebrated Venus de Medici statue in the Uffizi Gallery. However, Goethe's friend, the philosopher Herder (1744–1803), who did not share the fashionable enthusiasm for antique Roman ruins, praised Florence as a city that embodied humanist spirit and great intellectual traditions. Florence was the ideal place for scholars and writers of the age of Enlightenment precisely because of its vivid social and intellectual life. In salons and coffee houses intellectuals could meet colleagues from all over Europe. Florentine cultural life was invigorated during the enlightened reign of Grand Duke Peter Leopold, who ruled from 1765 to 1791 and transformed Tuscany into a liberal model state where torture and the death penalty were abolished.

One of the meeting places for European men and women of letters was the salon of the Countess Albany-Stolberg (1752–1824). Before settling in Florence in 1792, Stolberg and her partner, the poet Vittorio Alfieri (1749–1803), had lived in Paris. Not only French intellectuals and writers such as Madame de Staël (1766–1817) and Stendhal (1783–1842) frequented her Florentine salon, but also English and German writers such as Byron (1788–1824), Alexander von Humboldt (1769–1859), and August Wilhelm Schlegel (1767–1845). After her death in 1824 the countess was buried next to Alfieri in the Santa Croce church, the Pantheon of Florentine genius.

In Florence, contacts between visitors and locals were much closer than in other Italian cities. Writers and scholars met their Italian colleagues in the Gabinetto Vieusseux, a mixture of library and learned debating society; Manzoni (1785–1873), Leopardi (1798–1837), Foscolo (1778–1827), Heine (1797–1856), Chateaubriand (1768–1848), Shelley (1792–1822), and Byron were among the many illustrious guests.

Florence is the city of reason, intellect, and order, says Stendhal in *Rome, Naples, and Florence, in 1817* (1818); its inhabitants behave rather passionlessly, more like people in Prussia or England than Italians. This was a frequent complaint; German writer Fanny Lewald remarked in her *Italienisches Bilderbuch* [Italian Picturebook, 1847] that Florence was extremely civilized, wealthy, and stylish, but compared with Naples, Rome, or Genoa lacked colorful Italian atmosphere. Like William Hazlitt (1778–1830), who said that Florence looked like a city planted in a garden, Lewald enjoyed the harmony between cityscape and surrounding landscape.

The orderly and rational character of Florence was probably the reason why the city was extremely popular with the British, why it was a "ville tout Anglaise" as the brothers Goncourt remarked in 1855. In 1847 Elizabeth Barrett (1806–1861) and Robert Browning (1812–1889) rented a flat in the Casa Guidi, which subsequently became a meeting place for British and American writers like William Wetmore Story (1819–1895), Harriet Beecher Stowe (1811–1896), Margaret Fuller Marchesa Ossoli (1810–1850), Anna Jameson (1794–1860), and Jessie White (1832–1906). The Brownings supported the Risorgimento, the Italian liberation movement. Elizabeth Barrett voiced her sympathy openly in her poem *Casa Guidi Windows* (1851). The political tone of this work made her popular among the liberal-minded Italians, but in Britain it damaged her reputation as a serious poet, although she only supported the moderate wing of the Risorgimento. Her friends Margaret Fuller and Jessie White were clearly on the side of the radicals. Jessie White translated the works of Mazzini and Garibaldi into English and followed Garibaldi as aide-de-camp into some of his battles. Together with her husband and fellow Garibaldian, Alberto Mario, she lived in Florence whenever the Risorgimento did not demand her presence elsewhere.

By the middle of the nineteenth century, Florence had become a focus for progressive political thinkers from all over Europe, and most of them frequented the salon of the exiled German writer Ludmilla Assing (1821–1880), where they met Italian Risorgimento activists. Among her guests were the Russian revolutionary Bakunin and the exiled Hungarian opposition leader Count Pulszky, who described Florence and its vivid cosmopolitan culture in the fourth volume of his autobiography *Meine Zeit, mein Leben* [My Times, My Life, 1883]. Assing, who translated Mazzini and portrayed the Risorgimento and its activists for German readers, was at home in both cultures. In her many essays, books, and articles, she stresses how much the Risorgimento was inspired by Florentine traditions like republicanism and renaissance.

Whether or not the Florentines invented the Renaissance and whether or not the Renaissance is an invention of the nineteenth century, Jacob Burckhardt's groundbreaking study *Die Cultur der Renaissance in Italien* (1860; *The Civilisation of the Period of the Renaissance in Italy*, 1878) changed the perception of Florence for good. For Burckhardt, Florence is indeed the place where the Renaissance, and with it modern life was invented and his view helped to form the European perception of the city. The immediate results of Burckhardt's Renaissance study included many books that developed and popularized the Renaissance theme, focusing on the men and women of the period. George Eliot's historical novel *Romola* (1863) is set in Savonarola's Florence. The rebellious monk also plays a role in Mrs. Oliphant's *The Makers of Florence: Dante, Giotto, Savonarola and Their City* (1885). German novelist Isolde Kurz evokes famous and less famous Renaissance personalities in *Die Stadt des Lebens* [1900; The City of Life] and *Florentiner Novellen* [1905; Tales of Florence].

The Renaissance fashion also produced different academic views such as John Addington Symonds's seven-volume work *The Renaissance in Italy* (1875–1886) and Walter Pater's *The Renaissance* (1873). Whereas Symonds and Pater came to Italy as visitors, the British writer Vernon Lee spent most of her life in the Florentine villa Il Palmerino. Her interest in Italian and Florentine history was not limited to the Renaissance, which she covered in *Euphorion* (1884) and *Renaissance Fancies and Studies* (1884). In 1880 she published *Tuscan Fairy Tales* and in 1884 she portrayed the Countess Albany-Stolberg, the founding figure of the cosmopolitan expatriate society in Florence. The city and its society were greatly enjoyed by Henry James, who was a frequent visitor. In *The Autumn in Florence* (1874) he expresses his love for the severe and simple beauty of Florentine Renaissance architecture, which cannot be diminished by the controversial attempts to modernize the city that were made after Italian unification. Whereas James keeps an ironic distance from this art history controversy, in *Italy Revisited* (1878) he ridicules *Mornings in Florence* (1875–1877) by John Ruskin. James regards the dry and pedantic judgments Ruskin passes on Florentine art and architecture as highly inappropriate for a city thus saturated with art, joy, and beauty.

Hermann Hesse went to Italy in 1901 and fell in love with Tuscany. In his travel essays *Anemonen, Der lustige Florentiner, Lo scoppio del carro*, and *Fiesole* (all 1901) he describes Florence as the city of flowers, beauty, wine, joy, and Renaissance. Like Hesse, D.H. Lawrence regarded Florence as a city where life was civilized yet unspoiled and authentic at the same time. In his essays "David, Looking down on the City" (1919/1920) and "Flowery Tuscany" (1927) he praises Florence for its beauty, its flowers, and its joyful atmosphere. Although Lawrence lived in Florence while writing *Lady Chatterley's Lover* in 1927 and 1928, he had no contact with Anglo-Florentine high society, which is described in Iris Origo's autobiography *Images and Shadows* (1970) as being very civilized but snobbish and aloof.

In English literature Florence often functions as the city where the English lose their reserve and overcome snobbery and Puritanism. The positive influence exercised by Florentine art and life is celebrated in E.M. Forster's *A Room with a View* (1908). This motif is still present among contemporary British writers, but the instrumental use of Florence for personal liberation is nowadays portrayed more critically. Thus, Amanda Prantera's novel *The Young Italians* (1993) contrasts Anglo-Florentine and Italian-Florentine manners between the wars and is rather critical of the British and their prejudices. Francis King's novel *The Ant Colony* (1991) describes the English community in post-World War II Florence as a decadent anachronism.

Perhaps Burckhardt was right in postulating a special affinity between modernity and the Florentine Renaissance because the city has not lost its attraction for contemporary writers. Mary McCarthy's travel essay *The Stones of Florence* (1959) is still one of the most compelling texts written about this celebrated city. Although she was in Italy during the lackluster postwar years, her work blends the history, mentality, and literary reception of Florence into one compact but complex text. McCarthy could still see the remains of the old Anglo-Florentine culture; in her day the celebrated American art historian Bernard Berenson (1865–1959) still lived in his villa I Tatti. Historian Harold Acton was the last of the Anglo-Florentines when he died in 1994; his villa La Pietra, like Berenson's I Tatti before, became a university institute. The strong presence of learned and cultural institutions from America and Europe keeps cosmopolitan Florentine traditions going; Anglo-American culture is still very much alive in Florence.

The American author R.W.B. Lewis's book *The City of Florence: Historical Vistas and Personal Sightings* (1995) shows that the appeal of Florence as a topic for travel writing is undiminished. Lewis merges historical and personal reflections on the city. He also pays homage to his predecessors, to the many English, American, and German artists and writers who came to Florence over the centuries to find inspiration for art and life.

Christina Ujma

### References and Further Reading

Acton, Harold, *Memoirs of an Aesthete*, 1948.

Acton, Harold, *More Memoirs of an Aesthete*, 1970.

Acton, Harold, *Tuscan Villas*, with photographs by Alexander Zielcke, 1973.

Alfieri, Vittorio, *The Life of Vittorio Alfieri, Written by Himself*, translated by Sir Henry McAnally, 1953.

Archenholz, Johann Wilhelm von, *England und Italien*, 3 vols., 1785; edited by Michael Maurer, 1993; Italian portion, as *A Picture of Italy*, translated by Joseph Trapp, 2 vols., 1791.

Assing, Ludmilla, foreword in *"Die nationale Presse in Italien von 1828–1860" und "Die Kunst der Rebellen." Zwei Schriften von Piero Cironi*, edited and translated by Assing, 1863.

Assing, Ludmilla, *Piero Cironi: Ein Beitrag zur Geschichte der Revolution in Italien*, 1867.

Barrett Browning, Elizabeth, *Casa Guidi Windows, a Poem*, 1851.

Bennett, Arnold, *Florentine Journal: 1st April–25th May 1910*, illustrated by the author, with an introduction by Sacheverell Sitwell, 1967.

Berenson, Bernard, *Italian Painters of the Renaissance*, 1930.

Berenson, Bernard, *Rumour and Reflection, 1941–1944*, 1952.

Boswell, James, *Boswell on the Grand Tour: Italy, Corsica and France, 1765–1766*, edited by Frank Brady and Frederick A. Pottle, 1955.

Burckhardt, Jacob, *Die Cultur der Renaissance in Italien*, 2 vols., 1860, The *Civilisation of the Period of the Renaissance in Italy*, translated by S.G.C. Middlemore, 2 vols., 1878.

Byron, George Gordon, Lord, *Childe Harold's Pilgrimage, Canto the Fourth*, 1818.

Chateaubriand, Francois-René, Vicomte de, *Voyage en Italie*, edited by J.-M. Gautier, 1968.

Dickens, Charles, *Pictures from Italy*, 1846; edited and with an introduction by Kate Flint, 1998.

Eliot, George, *Romola*, 1863.

Forster, E.M., *A Room with a View*, 1908.

Fuller Ossoli, Margaret, *At Home and Abroad, or Things and Thoughts in America and Europe*, edited by Arthur B. Fuller, 1856.

Fuller Ossoli, Margaret, *The Writings of Margaret Fuller*, selected and edited by Mason Wade, 1941; reprinted, 1973.

Goethe, Johann Wolfgang von, *Italian Journey, 1786–1788*, translated by W.H. Auden and Elizabeth Mayer, 1962.

Hawthorne, Nathaniel, *The French and Italian Notebooks*, edited by Thomas Woodson, 1980.
Herder, Johann Gottfried, *Die italienische Reise: Briefe und Tagebuchaufzeichnungen 1788–1789*, edited by Albert Meier and Heide Hollmer, 1988.
Hesse, Hermann, *Italien: Schilderungen, Tagebücher, Gedichte, Aufsätze, Buchbesprechungen und Erzählungen*, edited by Volker Michels, 1983.
James, Henry, *William Wetmore Story and His Friends: From Letters, Diaries, and Recollections*, 2 vols., 1903.
James, Henry, *Italian Hours*, 1909.
James, Henry, *Travelling in Italy with Henry James: Essays*, edited by Fred Kaplan, 1994.
Jameson, Anna Brownell, *Diary of an Ennuyée*, 1826.
Keates, Jonathan, *Italian Journeys*, 1991.
King, Francis, *The Ant Colony*, 1991.
Kurz, Isolde, *Florentiner Novellen* [Tales of Florence], 1905.
Kurz, Isolde, *Die Stadt des Lebens: Schilderungen aus der florentinischen Renaissance*, 1900.
Kurz, Isolde, *Florentinische Erinnerungen*, 1923.
Lawrence, D.H., *Sketches of Etruscan Places and other Italian Essays*, edited by Simonetta de Filippis, 1992.
Lewald, Fanny, *Italienisches Bilderbuch* [Italian Picturebook], 2 vols., 1847.
Lewis, R.W.B., *The City of Florence: Historical Vistas and Personal Sightings*, 1995.
Mario, Jessie White, *The Birth of Modern Italy: Posthumous Papers of Jessie White Mario*, edited by Duke Litta-Visconti-Arese, 1909.
McCarthy, Mary, *The Stones of Florence*, 1959.
Origo, Iris, *Images and Shadows: Part of a Life*, 1970.
Pater, Walter, *Studies in the History of the Renaissance*, 1873; as *The Renaissance: Studies in Art and Poetry*, 1877.
Prantera, Amanda, *The Young Italians*, 1993.
Pulszky, Ferencz, *Meine Zeit, mein Leben* [My Times, My Life], 4 vols., 1880–1883.
Ruskin, John, *Mornings in Florence, Being Simple Studies of Christian Art for English Travellers*, 6 vols., 1875–1877.
Seume, Johann Gottfried, *Spaziergang nach Syrakus im Jahre 1802*, edited by Albert Meier, 1985.
Sharp, Samuel, *Letters from Italy: Describing the Customs and Manners of that Country, in the Years 1765 and 1766*, 1766.
Shelley, Mary, *Rambles in Germany and Italy in 1840, 1842, and 1843*, 2 vols., 1844.
Smollett, Tobias, *Travels through France and Italy*, 2 vols., 1766; edited by Frank Felsenstein, 1979.
Staël, Germaine de, *Corinne, or Italy*, translated and edited by Sylvia Raphael, 1998.
Stendhal, *Rome, Naples, and Florence, in 1817: Sketches of the Present State of Society, Manners, Arts, Literature &c. in these Celebrated Cities*, 1818.
Symonds, John Addington, *The Renaissance in Italy*, 7 vols., 1875–1886; reprinted, 1971.
Taine, Hippolyte, *Voyage en Italie*, vol. 2, 1866; as *Italy: Florence and Venice*, translated by J. Durand, 1869.
Vidal, Gore, *The Judgement of Paris*, 1952.
Winckelmann, Johann Joachim, *Geschichte der Kunst des Alterthums*, 1764; as *The History of Ancient Art*, translated by G. Henry Lodge, 4 vols., 1849–1873.

*See also* **Italy, Post-1800**

## FODOR GUIDES

Since 1936 the name Fodor has been synonymous with travel. Founded by Eugene Fodor (1905–1991), the company has been the producer of books on travel since its first volume, which was published under the Aldor imprint in 1936. Today Fodor's publishes more than 300 titles and has branched out into a variety of media, including an interactive website.

The early years of the company are tied to its founder. Fodor was born in Leva, Hungary; he left home to study political economics at the Sorbonne and the University of Grenoble. However, it was his ability to speak five languages and his desire to travel that led to a position as an interpreter with a French shipping line in the early 1930s. In his spare time he wrote articles about life aboard ship and visits to exotic ports for the in-house magazine of the SS *France*. Subsequent travel articles appeared in newspapers in France and Hungary. Between 1930 and 1933 Fodor was travel correspondent for the *Prague Hungarian Journal*; in 1934 he moved to England and worked as foreign editor for *Query*, a magazine with an international focus, and as travel editor for Aldor, a London book publisher.

Fodor had been developing his concept of a new way to view travel. Fodor believed that travel should be a process of learning about the people and the culture of a country rather than merely an accumulation of sights to visit. This concept was a far cry from the traditional "doing" of the European continent in the style of the Grand Tour, with Baedeker in hand. Fodor sold his idea to Aldor, and the guidebook *1936—On the Continent: The Entertaining Travel Annual* was born. In the introduction Fodor stresses that forthcoming guides will be updated annually, for the most current information about hotels, exchange rates, and routes to follow. The most innovative part of the book was the shift in focus from monuments to local foods, from "must see" works of art to how much to tip in Vienna. Fodor's travel guide stresses the idea of meeting the people of a country, not just seeing their churches.

The 1936 guide, like subsequent Fodor guides, has a conversational tone. Chapters on each country are written by prominent writers and journalists. In this first volume the chapter on France is by Arthur Koestler; the 1937 guide has an introduction to the British Isles by André Maurois. The original guide not only covered all 26 countries of the Continent, but was priced modestly and promptly sold out. It was Fodor's intention to keep the price down so as to move the books quickly and facilitate the production of annual volumes.

Looking back at the 1936 travel guide, one is struck by its commonsense approach to travel. For example, in the chapter on Italy and how to see Venice, the guide advises "not dash[ing] about Venice with a guide-book in your hand," but rather taking time to stroll about and having a leisurely breakfast on the piazza at Florian or the Rosa. Observations on travel problems in London (in the 1937 guide) are still valid: "despite all the traffic reforms that have been introduced, London's traffic problem is still unresolved, and will probably always remain so." Descriptions of Germany are chilling from the perspective of subsequent history. The guide may speak of the delight of the German to "seek the friendship of every Englishman," but also notes, under a specific subheading, the proliferation of uniforms and describes the various types that, according to the guide, "have nothing to do with militarism."

The 1937 guide, *In Europe*, including the chapter on the British Isles, was adapted for the U.S. market and became a best-seller. A 1938 edition, published in England and the United States, was also a best-seller. However, World War II halted publication of the guides. Fodor was traveling in the United States in 1938 when Germany invaded Czechoslovakia and chose to stay there, working as an editor for Hyperion Press. He became a U.S. citizen in 1942 and served in the Intelligence Branch of the U.S. Army until 1947.

In 1949 Fodor set up his own guidebook company, Fodor's Modern Travel Guides, headquartered in Paris. He began producing country guides, following the same format as the 1936 guide, with emphasis on up-to-date information, local customs, shopping, and hints to facilitate getting around. The first volumes were on France, Switzerland, Italy, and Britain; all were published in 1951 by the David McKay Company in New York. By 1964, McKay was publishing 17 Fodor travel guides. Each was revised annually; in addition to the country guides, titles included *Fodor's Jet Age Guide to Europe, Fodor's Men's Guide to Europe*, and *Fodor's Women's Guide to Europe*. Part of the Fodor philosophy, then and now, is to respond to the increasingly diverse needs of travelers. Fodor himself continued to travel, often 10 months out of 12, to visit and revisit countries and the local writers who provided information for the guides.

With the escalation of the Cold War in 1950, the U.S. Central Intelligence Agency asked Fodor to take on some of their agents as guidebook writers for "cover." Fodor agreed, but requested that they send "real writers, not civil engineers." This association between Fodor and the CIA became public knowledge during hearings concerning Watergate burglar E. Howard Hunt. Fodor admitted, in an interview in the *New York Times* on 27 December 1977, that he had allowed agents to "cover" themselves as writers for his publications, but said that their work was high-quality and professional: "We never let politics be smuggled into the books."

Fodor's dream was to put out a tourist guide to the United States. In 1964 he secured agreements with McKay, as well as with publishers abroad, to publish the book simultaneously in English, French, German, Italian, Spanish, and Japanese. The genesis of the book stemmed from a three-month bus trip, covering 40 states, that Fodor took across the United States in 1930. He noted that fellow passengers were proud of their own area of the country and felt that this enthusiasm would be fascinating to the increasing number of Europeans interested in traveling to the United States. He also hoped that the book would dispel some misconceptions that Europeans had about Americans. As in all Fodor volumes, different sections of the book would be written by local authors. In an interview with Laurie O'Neill in the *New York Times* (9 March 1986), Fodor remarked, "America is still a little-known and little-understood country and we don't do much to promote ourselves abroad. But it is vastly interesting and diverse and has much to offer travelers. We may go to Europe to visit our past, but the rest of the world comes to America to see their future."

Also in 1964, Fodor shifted his seat of operations to the United States, living and working in Litchfield, Connecticut, while maintaining offices in London and Paris. By the late 1960s more than 60 travel books, in different languages, were being produced. Fodor remained editor in chief but employed a number of other editors and continued to recruit distinguished writers from many countries to write sections on history and culture. For example, James Michener wrote the introduction to *Fodor's Guide to Hawaii*, and, later, Sir Edmund Hillary wrote the introduction to Fodor's book on the Himalayas. In 1968 Fodor sold the series to the David McKay Company but continued as editor in chief.

In 1977 Robert C. Fisher was appointed editor in chief of Fodor's Modern Guides. This appointment crowned Fisher's 18-year apprenticeship to Fodor, who retired with Fisher's appointment. By 1978, Fodor's was publishing 58 titles, including city guides, country guides, regional guides, and special interest guides. Under Fisher, more than 45 titles were updated annually to provide current information on hotels and restaurants. Whereas the content of the older guides was about 70 percent interpretation and 30 percent hard facts, the guides produced under Fisher's stewardship were about 60/40. As quoted in an interview with Sarah Ferrell on 10 March 1976 in the *New York Times*, Fisher believed that a guidebook should "inspire readers, through its description of a country, to get up and go, to make the journey." Prominent among new Fodor titles are special interest guides, such as *Animal Parks of Africa* and *Fodor's Old South.*

Eugene Fodor retired from all editorial duties in 1979, yet he continued to travel and served as consultant and spokesman for the guides. To mark his half century as a writer of travel guides, his first book, *1936—On the Continent* was reissued in 1985. Fodor died in Litchfield in 1991.

In 1986 Random House bought Fodor's Travel Guides. At that time, Fodor's was publishing 121 titles. Under the direction of Michael Spring, many of the guides were revamped with a new page layout, as well as a new rating system for restaurants and hotels. The cover was redesigned in gold and black by the Italian designer Massimo Vignelli. Included in the guides were about $1 million worth of computer-generated maps. In 1993 Fodor's began publishing the Mobil Travel Guides. Under president Kristina Peterson, Fodor's Travel Publications developed a relationship with Cable News Network (CNN). In 1996 Fodor's made headlines when it became the first mainstream guidebook publisher to launch a series of travel guides for gay men and lesbians. By 1997, under current president and publisher Bonnie Ammer, Fodor's was a presence on radio with *Fodor's Travel Show*, in a partnership with New York's WOR. In 1998 Fodor's began including a full-color, fold-out, removable map from Rand McNally in the Fodor Gold Guides and introduced a new series of city guides.

Today Fodor's Travel Publications, a division of Random House, is the largest English-language travel-information publisher in the world, with more than 300 titles in print in 14 different series. In 1999 the Fodor's website (fodors.com) won the Lowell Thomas Travel in Journalism Award. The site, launched in 1996, is easy to use and provides up-to-date information. Of particular interest is the section "Create Your Own Miniguides" to 110 destinations. For example, by typing in "Cape Cod," the traveler can access not only information about hotels, restaurants, and sights to see, but warnings about when not to attempt to drive on or off the cape, as well as instructions on how to survive the infamous Cape Cod rotaries.

Fodor's original vision of a practical approach to travel still remains at the heart of the guides. Fodor once said, as quoted in *U.S. News and World Report*, 4 March 1991, "I think the American has become the world's most experienced and intelligent traveler." Thanks to his efforts and the company's continuing success, travelers from countless countries have shared the travel experience.

MARCIA B. DINNEEN

### References and Further Reading

1936—*On the Continent: The Entertaining Travel Annual*, facsimile edition, New York: Fodor's Travel Guides, and London: Hodder and Stoughton, 1985.
Baedeker's Guides.
Compass American Guides.
Fodor's Best Bed & Breakfasts.
Fodor's Citypacks.
Fodor's Escape.
Fodor's Gay Guides.
Fodor's Gold Guides.
Rivages Guides.

*See also* **Guidebooks**

## FORREST, JOHN (1847–1918) *Australian Explorer and Politician*

John Forrest was born too late to participate in the great moments of Australian exploration: too late to circumnavigate the continent with Flinders, to solve the riddle of the Blue Mountains or the inland sea, to discover "Australia Felix," or to trace the great rivers; too late even to perish in the desert and contribute through a ludicrous death to the mythology of place. But most of these accomplishments were the work of British explorers. The native-born Forrest would be able to claim he put "the finishing stroke" to their work and was proud of the fact that he was more competent than most of them.

His Scottish parents, a millwright and a shopkeeper's daughter, had migrated as servants to Western Australia in 1842, when the colony, founded with undue optimism and insufficient labor in 1829, was still struggling. Their engagement complete in 1846, they farmed and ran a mill. Mechanical ingenuity and nine sons saw them prosper, especially after 1850, when the colony began to accept convicts as a labor force. With civilization relentlessly displacing the indigenous population, it was still a masculine world that valued a practical bent, horsemanship, familiarity with the bush, and ambition to make good. At Bishop Hale's School in Perth, the young Forrest gained an education in God, Empire, and the rights of property suitable for the colony's future elite. He excelled in arithmetic, but his humble origins gave him few options. Surveying offered a promising and congenial career.

With his mix of local knowledge and book learning, he was, despite being just 21, a logical choice as second in command and navigator of an expedition to follow up new clues to the fate of the German explorer Ludwig Leichhardt, who had last been heard of in western Queensland in April 1848, attempting to cross the continent. When the prospective leader, the botanist Dr. Ferdinand von Mueller, could not take part, Forrest was given charge. Tying up such loose ends was, he said, "a proposition quite in accordance with my tastes for I had long felt a deep interest in the subject of Australian exploration, and ardently desire to take my share in the work." He covered 2,000 miles, but found no trace of Leichhardt and admitted that the land was "worthless as a pastoral or agricultural district." He was satisfied with filling in the blanks: "The additional knowledge gained of the character of the country between the settled districts of Western Australia and the 123rd meridian of east longitude, well repaid me, and those of the party, for the exertions we had undergone."

His second expedition was also tied to the older generation of explorers. In 1841 Edward John Eyre had made a precarious dash along the barren southern coast from Adelaide to Albany: no one had traveled the land route in either direction until, in 1870, Forrest, his brother, and four others made the first west–east crossing. Eyre had taken 12 months and lost all his party except one Aboriginal companion; Forrest took five months and did not lose so much as a horse. The almost waterless country again disappointed, but he demonstrated the practicality of a telegraph route that which, by 1877, would, link Perth to the would, and that would eventually be followed by a transcontinental railway, a project dear to Forrest's heart.

In 1872 the overland telegraph—the climax of inland exploration—linked north and south and provided a critical stimulus to further exploration of the central desert country: the western half of the continent had still not been crossed. Three parties set out westward in 1872–1873; only Warburton's succeeded in reaching the Indian Ocean, taking a northerly route, eating their camels along the way. In 1874 Forrest set out on the first west-east crossing and aimed to cut through the center, the "great lone land," the "Sahara of the south," the last achievement left. Cautiously moving from waterhole to waterhole, the party exploded any lingering hopes of inland waterways. They were attacked by Aborigines and endured the endless spinifex (porcupine grass) across 1,400 miles of useless country. At the last point he could have turned back, ambition drove him forward; his party was saved by a lucky shower of rain. He noted traces of earlier failed attempts to cross in the other direction. Finally the six men, with only four emaciated horses left, reached the telegraph line. Again the practical results were disappointing, but they took heart from a rapturous reception in Adelaide. On a quick visit to Melbourne, he contemplated several times the great monument to the disastrous Burke and Wills expedition: each time it sent a "thrill through my very soul."

On each journey, others had been before him, usually more flamboyantly. Forrest's his achievement was to suffer less—he was a cautious, efficient, modern professional, dubious about ineffectual heroic gestures. In 1875 he visited London and was acclaimed as "The Young Explorer." He addressed the Royal Geographical Society, who awarded him the prestigious Founder's Gold Medal in 1876. He was an effective speaker, adopting the pose of a plain man unused to his role. He arranged publication of his journals of the three expeditions as *Explorations in Australia*. He wrote as a competent, practical man, the bureaucrat politician skilled in the appropriate cliché. There was no poetry either in the names strewn in his wake: the English names of patrons, friends, and family. Careful not to give away his true feelings, he leaves us wondering whether he had any. The emptiness of the country he explored led to no existential angst, and the fact that little came of his expeditions was no particular disappointment to him. He noted temperatures and bearings and carrying capacity and then moved on. Reviewers, disappointed in the lack of derring-do, found his writing as dry and tedious as the country. Perhaps because he was born into it, he had none of the romanticism of an Ernest Giles; and because he was competent, none of the hairbreadth escapes. He was sorry when his horses died, less sympathetic when he had to shoot at Aborigines, speculating little about their lives. He was an effective leader who measured success by good management. Each party consisted of four white men and two Aborigines (Tommy Windich was on all three); he insisted that the efforts of others—including Aborigines—be recognized while accepting the privileges that went with leadership. With the complacency of the practical man, he took no unnecessary risks: when he did trust to Providence and luck he was rewarded. He observed the Sabbath and the Queen's birthday, but God and Empire were tempered by Australian nationalism.

Returning to Perth, he married into Western Australia's social elite and flourished, acquiring wealth, power, celebrity, and status. With self-government in 1890, he became the colony's first premier. He enjoyed the boom time of gold discoveries in the emptiness he had first explored, and was then one of the "founding fathers" of federation in 1901. Treasurer five times in the new federal governments, he remained committed to caution, "homely hard-headedness," and Empire, but died on his way to sit in the House of Lords.

RICHARD WHITE

## Biography

Born near Bunbury, south of Perth, Western Australia, 22 August 1847. Attended the local state school, then Bishop Hale's School, Perth, 1860–1863. Apprenticed to a surveyor, 1863; joined Surveyor-General's Office, 1865, rising to Surveyor-General, 1883. Three major expeditions eastward from Perth, 1869–1874. Married Margaret Elvire Hamersley, 1876. Appointed to Executive and Legislative Councils, 1883–1890. First premier of Western Australia, 1890–1901, federal parliament, 1901–1918, acting prime minister, 1907, treasurer five times. Became the first Australian-born peer, Lord Forrest of Bunbury. Died at sea off Sierra Leone, en route to London, 3 September 1918.

### References and Further Reading

*Explorations in Australia*, 1875; facsimile, with an introduction by Valmai Hankel, 1998.

## FORSTER, E.M. (1879–1970) *British Novelist, Essayist, and Social and Literary Critic*

Edward Morgan Forster was born to a moderately affluent family. His father, an architect, died when Forster was still very young, and the boy was brought up by his mother and paternal aunts. He studied classics and history at King's College, Cambridge University. In 1901, he was elected to the Apostles, an elite discussion group at Cambridge; there he met and became close friends with John Maynard Keynes, Lytton Strachey, Clive Bell, Leonard Woolf, and Roger Fry, who like himself were later to become members of the Bloomsbury Group. As soon as he finished his studies in 1901, Forster and his mother undertook a ten-month trip to Italy, mainly touring Milan and Florence, as well as the Arno valley. After a brief period in England in 1902, Forster went back to Italy, where he remained until 1907. During this long sojourn on the Continent, he also took the opportunity to visit Greece and other European countries.

The role of locality is seminal in Forster's writing, whether it involves his foreign travels or life in his native England. In the introduction to *The Celestial Omnibus and Other Stories* (1911), Forster claimed to have been directly moved by the genius loci—the spirit of place—three times in his life: the first, during his first trip to Italy, on a hill near Ravello, which inspired his first literary creation, "The Story of a Panic"; the second, under similar circumstances in Greece a year later, when the image of a tree near Olympia produced the remarkable "Road from Colonus"; and a third time in Cornwall at Gurnard's Head, with disappointing results.

Some of the experiences of his first Italian trip find their way into Forster's two early novels, such as the difficulties of foreign travel in *Where Angels Fear to Tread* (1905), and the disappointed desire of Mrs. Forster to have an Arno view from her *pensione* room, which is echoed by Lucy Bartlett in *A Room with a View* (1908).

Forster's classical education allowed him to experience his trips to Italy and Greece, and later to Egypt and India, with a keen appreciation of the history and culture of the places he visited, though this did not prevent him from consulting his Baedeker, the renowned travel guide. *A Room* is studded with references to this time-honored traveler's essential. In fact, in a letter to his ex-tutor Nathaniel Wedd on 1 December 1901, Forster comments that "the orthodox Baedeker-bestarred Italy—which is all that I have yet seen—delights me so much that I can well afford to leave the Italian Italy for another time." Though not the real thing, the Italy of Forster's early novels has a power all its own: ambivalent, compelling, wonderful, and at times disappointing, the land takes hold of unwitting British tourists and exposes the shallowness of their "undeveloped hearts" that lack passion, spontaneity, and imagination.

After a few years in Britain, Forster in 1912 traveled to India, where he began writing *A Passage to India* (1924), the last novel to be published during his lifetime, which he did not finish until after his second trip, in 1921, when he undertook a position as secretary to the maharajah of Dewas Senior. As with all of Forster's travel novels, *A Passage* utilizes the foreign locus as a force that propels the British visitors who come under its influence into a crisis. Time and again, Forster rehearses the encounter of the English with the genius loci of a foreign country, and each time what results is their inability to transplant well to another soil. *A Passage* captures this much better than the early novels do, presenting the incompatibility and failure to communicate of the Indian and Anglo-Indian/Raj universes. This is emblematized by the (non-)incident in the Marabar Caves, whose repercussions determine the course of the novel: a young British woman accuses an Indian doctor of attempted rape, a hallucinatory episode induced by the empty negativity of the caves.

Forster's second trip to India is documented in *The Hill of Devi* (1953), a memoir and collection of letters written during Forster's sojourn as secretary to the maharajah of Dewas, containing a wealth of cultural information as well as Forster's attempts to come to terms with this unfamiliar environment, and providing a lot of material for *A Passage to India*—most notably, the description of the Hindu festival in the last portion of the book.

Between his two Indian visits, in 1915, during World War I, Forster went to Egypt, where he worked for the Red Cross. Given his interest in travel guides, it is no surprise that his stay in Alexandria prompted him to undertake the writing of a travel guide of his own for the city. *Alexandria: A History and a Guide* (1922) is a remarkable source of information that features, as its title denotes, a history of Alexandria from its humble Egyptian origins and the splendor created by its founder, Alexander the Great, through the Ptolemaic and Christian periods and the invasions of the Arabs and Turks, to the advent of Napoleon and the various European occupations, alongside a guide describing the several historical layers and coexisting diverse civilizations that made up the international melee that characterized the city up to the 1950s. No sooner had the book been published than Forster received a letter, accompanied by considerable insurance compensation, informing him that the warehouse containing the entire stock of books had burned down. Shortly afterward, another letter followed with the information that the books had in fact escaped the fire and that the publisher had promptly burned them to avoid difficulties with the insurance claim. Forster's *Alexandria* thus met the same fate as the books of the city's legendary library. His guide was reprinted several times and served most notably as a significant source of information for the young British press attaché and novelist Lawrence Durrell during World War II, when he wrote his *Alexandria Quartet*.

While in Alexandria, Forster also produced a collection of essays entitled *Pharos and Pharillon* (1923), in reference to the two landmarks of the port of Alexandria, of which only the latter survives today. The book is divided into two parts: "Pharos" covers significant events and cultural aspects, as well as Alexandrian personalities of antiquity such as Alexander, Philo, and Clement; "Pharillon" describes the modern city since the seventeenth century and contemporary figures like the traveler Eliza Fay and the poet Cavafy, to each of whom Forster devoted an essay. Forster was among the first European intellectuals to realize the Alexandrian poet's genius and was responsible for the first published translation of a Cavafy poem—something that he claimed with great modesty might have been his most important achievement. Forster met Cavafy in person and maintained an epistolary friendship with him until the poet's death, discussing, among other things, *A Passage to India*, of which Cavafy was exceptionally fond. In *Alexandria Still* (1977), Jane Lagoudis Pinchin claims that *A Passage*, the bulk of which was written during the time Forster was preparing his two Alexandrian books, is in fact itself Alexandrian. And there may be some justification for this claim, for *A Passage* seems to focus much more closely on the relationship of the British with the Muslims than on their relationship with the Hindus, reflecting perhaps Forster's familiarity with the Muslims of Alexandria. Whatever the case, *Alexandria* and *A Passage to India*, despite the accomplishments of the early Italian novels, are in many ways the most significant fruits of Forster's encounters with foreign cultures.

BEATRICE SKORDILI

### Biography

Born in London, 1 January 1879. Educated at Kent House, Eastbourne, Sussex, 1890–1893; Tonbridge School, Kent, 1893–1897. Studied classics and history at King's College, Cambridge University, 1897–1901. Lived mostly in Greece and Italy, 1901–1907, returning to England briefly. Founded the *Independent Review* in London, 1903. Private tutor to the children of the writer Countess Elizabeth von Arnim in Nassenheide, Germany, 1905. Taught at the Working Men's College, London, 1907. Published *A Room with a View*, 1908. First trip to India with G.L. Dickinson, 1912. Cataloger, National Gallery, London, 1914–1915. Red Cross volunteer in Alexandria, 1915–1918. Private secretary to the maharajah of Dewas Senior, 1921. Published *A Passage to India*, 1924. Lived with his mother in Surrey, England, 1924–1945. Clark Lecturer at Trinity College, Cambridge, 1927. President, National Council for Civil Liberties, 1934–1935, 1942. Refused knighthood, 1946. After his mother's death, moved to Cambridge as honorary fellow of King's College, 1946. Made lecture tour of United States, 1947. Awarded James Tait Black Memorial prize, 1924; Femina Vie Heureuse Prize, 1925; Benson Medal, 1937; Companion of Literature, 1961. Honorary degrees from University of Aberdeen, 1931; University of Liverpool, 1947; Hamilton College, Clinton, New York, 1949; Cambridge University, 1950; University of Nottingham, 1951; University of Manchester, 1954; Leiden University, Holland, 1954; University of Leicester, 1958. Honorary member, American Academy and Bavarian Academy of Fine Arts. Companion of Honour, 1953. Admitted to the Order of Merit, 1969. Died in Coventry, England, 7 June 1970.

### References and Further Reading

Forster, E.M., *Where Angels Fear to Tread*, 1905.
Forster, E.M., *A Room with a View*, 1908.
Forster, E.M., *The Celestial Omnibus and Other Stories*, 1911.
Forster, E.M., *Alexandria: A History and a Guide*, 1922
Forster, E.M., *Pharos and Pharillon*, 1923
Forster, E.M., *A Passage to India*, 1924
Forster, E.M., *The Hill of Devi*, 1953

## FORSTER, GEORGE (1754–1794) *German Naturalist*

As a result of his participation in James Cook's second circumnavigation of the earth, few travelers were better known in Germany toward the end of the eighteenth century than George Forster. Prior to his departure with Cook in 1772, Forster had already played an important role in disseminating the results of recent European explorations by translating from German and French into English. He was to continue this role of translator and mediator in the cosmopolitan exchange of ideas characteristic of late Enlightenment Europe after his move to Germany in 1778, adding to his own translations a significant body of reviews. Toward the end of his short life he undertook a journey down the Rhine with Alexander von Humboldt, the romantic scientist and explorer of South America, who looked to Forster as his main inspiration. Forster's account of their journey became a classic of German prose.

The oldest of seven surviving children, George Forster received early instruction in natural history from his father, Johann Reinhold Forster, a Protestant minister and man of encyclopedic interests. Barely 11 years old, he accompanied him in 1765 on a journey of about 2,500 miles from their home near Danzig (Gdansk) to inspect the settlements of German colonists in rural Russia. The journey yielded a rich harvest of Linnean descriptions, but proved financially disappointing. His Russian employers had apparently hoped for a favorable report in order to attract more German colonists. When on his return to St. Petersburg Johann Reinhold instead reported lawlessness, enslavement, and harsh living conditions, he found himself before closed doors. Virtually penniless, he left with his son for England in 1766 to seek his fortune in the land of his ancestors. (His ancestor George Forster, a Yorkshire royalist, had emigrated to Russia/Poland sometime before 1642.)

After a brief apprenticeship with a merchant, George was soon enjoined to collaborate with his father in translations of travel accounts and works of natural history, in an effort to make ends meet. Most notable among these early works was the English version of Louis-Antoine de Bougainville's *Description d'un voyage autour du monde*, which appeared in 1772, crediting only the elder Forster as translator. The younger Forster's fortunes at this stage in his life remained firmly linked to his father's efforts at seeking patronage.

These efforts bore fruit in 1772 with the appointment of both Forsters as naturalists to accompany James Cook on his second voyage around the globe. They took the place of the gentleman-naturalist Sir Joseph Banks, who had sailed with Cook on his first voyage. Banks resigned when alterations made to Cook's ship to accommodate his entourage were removed because they had rendered the vessel unseaworthy. The Forsters were approached about joining the voyage on 26 May 1772 and departed with Cook in *Resolution*, accompanied by *Adventure*, under Tobias Furneaux, on 13 July 1772. This left them less than a fortnight—from 11 June 1772, when they received their official appointment, to 24 or 25 June 1772, when they were to leave London for Plymouth to join Cook—to prepare for a journey that was to last three years.

The primary aim of Cook's second voyage was to establish whether there existed a great southern continent, Terra Australis (Incognita or Nondum Cognita), which geographers since Greek antiquity had projected in the Southern Hemisphere as counterbalance for the land mass of the northern continents. Though the suggestion was in fact correct, Cook failed to find what is now known as Antarctica on three successive sweeps of the high southern latitudes, foiled by impenetrable pack ice. The endeavor necessitated two extended periods of rest and refreshment in more temperate zones which were rich in discovery and contact with indigenous peoples, between June and October 1773, and again between February and October 1774.

Although the Forsters were often prevented from exploring newly discovered islands at leisure, the ships' extended, repeated stays in New Zealand and Tahiti and their exploration of the Marquesas, Tonga, the New Hebrides, and New Caledonia translated into a rich description of Oceanian societies in George Forster's *A Voyage round the World* (1777). Compared with James Cook's *A Voyage towards the South Pole* (1777, with John Douglas) and his father's *Observations Made during a Voyage round the World* (1780), the narrative of the younger Forster is more engaging and excels in ethnographic detail. The training of an Enlightenment naturalist is here most fruitfully combined with the social and aesthetic sensibilities of a romantic youth.

It was therefore all the more unfortunate that until recently the book suffered from comparative neglect in anglophone countries. Although its German translation was well received and George Forster lionized when he moved to Germany in 1778, the Forsters were effectively deprived of the spoils of publishing the official account of the voyage by the English Admiralty, who subsidized Cook's narrative and awarded him the magnificent plates that were to illustrate the account.

After he settled in Germany, George Forster exercised considerable influence over how Germans in the 1780s and 1790s viewed the rest of the world. Between 1781 and 1792, he published more than 100 reviews of travel narratives, mostly in the *Göttingische Anzeigen von gelehrten Sachen*. His prodigious output as a translator of travelogues, the publication of separate essays on related topics, and, from 1788 until 1791, the publication of a yearly synopsis of literature and culture in England, strengthened his position as an authority in matters related to exploration and discovery, as well as English culture.

The strain on Forster of writing for money in a disconnected, hectic manner and of the oppressive political and social climate in the conservative Catholic electorate of Mainz, where Forster had assumed in 1788 a position as university librarian, was relieved in early 1790 by a journey to England with Alexander von Humboldt. Forster planned the journey with publication in mind. He intended to witness the effects of the French Revolution in the Low Countries and France, assemble material for a long monograph on the South Seas, and revive his flagging spirits.

Forster's account of this journey, which lasted from 25 March until 11 July 1790, was quickly acknowledged a masterpiece of German prose and an outstanding travelogue by, among others, Lichtenberg, Goethe, and Schiller—at least in private, for public appreciation of these "Views from/of the Lower Rhine" (*Ansichten vom Niederrhein*, vol. 1: 1791, vol. 2: 1792, vol. 3: posthumous fragment, 1794) was increasingly hampered by Forster's association with the French Revolution.

OLIVER BERGHOF

### Biography

Born in Nassenhuben (Mokry Dwór), near Danzig (Gdansk), 26 or 27 November 1754. Educated primarily by his father, Johann Reinhold Forster, Protestant minister and naturalist. Traveled with his father through Russia to inspect German settlements on the Volga, 1765. Left Russia with his father for England, 1766. Worked as translator of travel accounts, 1760s. Assisted his father as naturalist on James Cook's second circumnavigation, 1772–1775. Elected member of the Gesellschaft Naturforschender Freunde, Berlin, 1776; fellow of the Royal Society, 9 January 1777. Joined the Freemasons in Paris, 1777. Promoted to doctor of medicine, Halle, 1786. Professor of natural history at the Collegium Carolinum in Kassel, 1778–1784; and Vilna (Vilnius), 1784–1787. Married to Therese Heyne, daughter of Göttingen classicist Christian Gottlob Heyne, 1785: four daughters, two of whom died in infancy. Returned to Göttingen, Germany, to participate in planned Russian Pacific expedition, 1787. Became university librarian in Mainz after cancellation of the expedition due to war, 1788. Journeyed with Alexander von Humboldt through Germany, Belgium, Holland, England, and France, March–July 1790. Joined the Jacobin Club in Mainz, 1792. Sent to Paris as deputy of the Rhenish-German National Convention, March 1793. Died of natural causes in Paris, 12 January 1794.

### References and Further Reading

*A Voyage round the World in His Britannic Majesty's Sloop Resolution, Commanded by Capt. James Cook, during the Years, 1772, 3, 4, and 5*, 1777; German version in 2 vols., 1778–1780.

*Ansichten vom Niederrhein, von Brabant, Flandern, Holland, England und Frankreich im April, Mai und Junius 1790* [Views of the Lower Rhine from Brabant, Flanders, Holland, England, and France in April, May, and June 1790], 1791–1794.

Bougainville, Louis-Antoine de, *A Voyage round the World*, with Johann Reinhold Forster, 1772.

Kalm, Pehr, *Travels into North America*, with Johann Reinhold Forster, 1770–1771.

Also translated numerous works into German, including Thomas Anburey, *Reisen inm inneren Amerika* [Travels in Inner America], 1792.

## FORSYTH, JOSEPH (1763–1815) *Scottish Traveler*

Captured in Napoleon's territory in 1803, on his return from an 18-month tour of Italy, the Scotsman Joseph Forsyth was imprisoned in regimes of varying severity for 11 years, during which he wrote *Remarks on Antiquities, Arts, and Letters during an Excursion in Italy, in the Years 1802 and 1803* (1813) in a vain petition to the emperor for his release. After the fall of Paris, he was set free and returned to Britain where he prepared a greatly revised second edition, but died (in 1815) from a weakened constitution before seeing it through the press. His brother Isaac, a bookseller of Elgin, added his own memoir and also much other material from Joseph's personal notes. The work went into four editions (excluding pirated ones), with long print runs, over a period of 22 years, against the strong competition of new travel guides to Italy that appeared after the battle of Waterloo at the rate of nine a year for ten years. Its success was so great that other travel writers felt compelled to quote it and set their own works in its context. Lengthy extracts were still being incorporated in travelogues as late as 1913. *The Dictionary of National Biography* asserted in 1900, "It is still one of the best books on Italy in our language."

Forsyth gives a rare picture of Italy under Napoleon. He visited Italy during a lull in the wars between Britain and France, in 1802, after the Peace of Amiens declared a cessation of hostilities. He caught sight of an Italy on the verge of radical change. In one respect it seemed to bear out Edward Gibbon's sense of the decline and fall of the Roman empire, for its buildings were decaying and becoming buried by rubbish, and its portable artworks were being pillaged by both antiquarians and invaders. But it was also stirring with new life, which, after Forsyth's death, would swell into the rising to nationhood now referred to as the Risorgimento. Forsyth's keen eye registered elements of this in his engagement with the lively differences among Italy's many distinct peoples (whom later guidebooks often dismissed as below notice), in his appraisal of its prolific poets (including Alfieri, who first used the term *Risorgimento* in its present sense), and in his inquisitive searches of archaeological excavations, crawling through the tunnels of Herculaneum and pacing the rutted pavements of Pompeii, examining artistic treasures and evidence of ways of life that connected the ancients with contemporary Italians.

Forsyth's *Italy* is a highly readable book. It engages interest with its attractively elegant and entertaining style and its intelligent firsthand observations. Forsyth has both an eighteenth-century taste and an openness to new forms. He is enlightened, liberal, and inquiring, combining informed aesthetic judgment, practical sense, scientific curiosity, and historical reflection. He has a dry and skeptical humor, and relishes the "excellently wicked" anecdote. His praise is sparing and considered, and his adverse views are expressed with a witty compression, crediting his readers with the intelligence to catch their full implication. (In the sections containing the notes he did not intend to publish, suppressions probably dictated by his standards of decorum, he has a more expansive mode, in which contempt and enthusiasm are given freer rein, highlighting the passion that underlies his writing.)

The approach of the book is to take the reader on a journey in which Pisa, Florence, Rome, Naples, and Pompeii figure prominently. But he expressly refuses to give an exhaustive guide—a strategy that contributes much to the book's liveliness and accessibility. Nevertheless, there are descriptions that would interest the cultural historian or a modern visitor to Italy. Examples are the poetic inventiveness of the *improvvisatori* (the practitioners of extemporary verse, celebrated in Staël's *Corinne*), the beginnings of the flowering of Italian opera, the grasping immorality of Lord Acton and the faded court of the brother of the Young Pretender, the energetic bustle of the Neapolitan streets, the seemingly irresistible decay of great architectural treasures, particularly with the removal of the finest artworks to Paris by the victorious French, and the unique qualities of the wall paintings of Pompeii. The journey ends with his capture, and the following chapters (made up of the excised notes) reflect on the manners of the peoples in the different states of Italy, still so various and divided, remembering civil wars of centuries before.

The qualities that recommended Forsyth's *Italy* to his reviewers and to the younger Romantics defined, in the first decades of the nineteenth century, an ideal of travel writing and gave rise to spirited contention between admirers and detractors. In the heavyweight quarterlies and monthly reviews of the early nineteenth century, the book was the center of a detailed debate about the merits of travel writing, engaging the interest of politically opposed (and belligerent) publishers who yet found much to admire in Forsyth's text. Hobhouse's championing of Forsyth's *Italy* against Eustace's *Classical Tour* in his notes to Byron's *Childe Harold's Pilgrimage*, canto 4, briefly polarized this critical reception.

The book was read with warm approval by Byron, who saw as exceptional its "truth" and "sense" regarding Italy and its understanding of the "causes of Italian misery." The Shelleys and Clare Clairmont also endorsed it. The book it was a stimulus for Leigh Hunt's writing on Pisa (*Letters from Abroad*, 1822) and for some of Mary Shelley's *Rambles* (1844). Despite changes of taste, Forsyth's views remained accessible and worth arguing with. He clearly stated his criteria and was precise in his observations and not hidebound in his response to the new. He was also formidably learned, illustrating his points with apt literary quotations in Greek, Latin, French, and Italian, referring to a wide range of historical and contemporary figures (especially in Italy) and adroity deploying the technicalities of architecture and antiquities. This required from the reader an intellectual engagement with the reflections aroused by his observations, marking a distinction between the tradition of "remarks" and that of the guidebook. Adverse judgments among contemporaries are sparse, though his "fastidiousness" is occasionally remarked on, and regret is expressed that, with his gifts, he did not write a complete vade mecum—a process that he expressly wished to avoid but which became a more dominant purpose for later writers.

Keith Crook

## Biography

Born in Elgin, Scotland, 18 February 1763. Attended grammar school in Elgin, and King's College, University of Aberdeen; M.A., 1779. Schoolmaster, Newington Butts, London, 1788–1801. Retired because of ill health and returned to Elgin. Traveled in France and Italy, October 1801–May 1803. Captured by Napoleon's troops in Turin and imprisoned at Biche, Verdun, Paris, and Valenciennes, 1803–1814. Lived in London and set up an establishment in Elgin, 1815. Died in Elgin, 21 September 1815.

## References and Further Reading

*Remarks on Antiquities, Arts, and Letters during an Excursion in Italy, in the Years 1802 and 1803*, 1813; 2nd edition, 1816; 4th edition, 1835.

# FORTUNE, ROBERT (1812–1880) *British Plant Collector and Traveler*

Robert Fortune, the eldest son of a hedger, was born on 16 September 1812 at Blackadder in Berwickshire, Scotland. Educated at the local parish school in Edrom, near Duns, he was subsequently apprenticed to a local gardener, William Buchan of Kelloe. He joined the staff of the Royal Botanic Garden, Edinburgh, in 1839, and moved from there to Chiswick, to the garden of the Horticultural Society of London (later the Royal Horticultural Society), where he was placed in charge of the hothouse department.

The opening up of China to trade with the West led John Lindley, assistant secretary of the Horticultural Society, to choose Fortune to visit China as a botanical collector. The treaty of Nanking was concluded on 26 August 1842, granting easier access to China, which encouraged plant hunters to collect and study Chinese flora. Fortune's instructions, issued on 23 February 1843, with a salary of £100 per annum, were "to collect seeds and plants of an ornamental or useful kind, not already cultivated in Great Britain and to obtain information upon Chinese gardening and agriculture together with the nature of the climate and its apparent influence on vegetation."

Fortune, equipped with collecting kit, a heavy stick, and pistols, sailed first to Hong Kong, aboard *Emu*. The guns had been allowed in a last-minute concession from the Chinese Committee of the Horticultural Society, after Fortune's complaint that "a stick will scarcely frighten an armed Chinaman." It was Fortune's first trip abroad. He arrived on 6 July 1843, four months after his departure from England. His orders were to keep a detailed journal and to collect a number of plants, including peaches, double yellow roses, blue peonies, yellow camellias, tea and bamboo varieties, lilies, azalea, kumquats, and the true Mandarin orange. He was also instructed to write to the society at every opportunity, sending duplicate copies of each letter by separate routes, and including a complete account of his expenses. He carried with him gifts of British plants and seeds to offer to the Chinese.

Fortune took against the Chinese from the outset, pronouncing them conceited, xenophobic, and nationalistic. In China, he suffered from fevers, was caught in terrible sea storms, and was attacked by pirates and bandits on a number of occasions. Yet he never deviated from his botanical mission. He carried with him Nathaniel Bagshaw Ward's invention, known as the Wardian case—a specially constructed glass case for transporting living plants over long distances. He remained in China for three years, with headquarters in Shanghai, gradually winning the respect of local nurserymen and collecting a number of plants that were to radically change the appearance of English gardens. He collected knowledge as well as plants, most notably hints on the cultivation of tea at Ningpo, fertilizing techniques, and sophisticated irrigation principles. He left China in October 1845, arriving back in London in May 1846, when he was immediately appointed curator of the Chelsea Physic Garden. His large collection of plants arrived in perfect condition and was successfully transplanted in the Horticultural Society's garden at Chiswick. Unable to settle in Chelsea, he set out for China again two years later. This time, he was engaged by the East India Company to collect the Chinese tea plant and learn more about its cultivation in order to transplant it to the company's Indian plantations in Sikkim and Assam. With the benefit of his previous experience, he was able to successfully pass himself off as a Chinese native and managed to collect some 2,000 tea plants and 17,000 tea seedlings. He also visited Japan on this trip, returning in 1853, with his Wardian cases filled with chrysanthemums, rhododendrons, forsythia, and winter-flowering jasmine. He toured the Far East once more from 1860 to 1862, principally collecting in Japan on a self-financed expedition.

He returned to England on 2 January 1862 and spent the last years of his life comfortably in Kensington, writing occasional articles for the *Journal of the Royal Horticultural Society* and *Gardeners' Chronicle*. He died on 13 April 1880, and is buried in Brompton Cemetery. He was survived by his wife, Jane Penny, whom he married in 1838, and by four of his six children. Few of his personal papers or letters have survived, but his legacy lies in the more than 120 new species he introduced to Britain, including the Chinese shrub *Fortunearia, Fortunella* (the kumquat), *Mahonia* bealei, *Anemone japonica*, *Jasminum nudiflorum*, *Lonicera fragrantissima*, and *Forsythia viridissima*.

HELEN WARD

## Biography

Born in Blackadder, Berwickshire, 16 September 1812. Attended parish school in Edrom. Married Jane Penny, 1838: six children, two of whom died in infancy. Joined staff of Royal Botanic Garden, Edinburgh, 1839. Appointed superintendent of hothouse department at Horticultural Society's garden in Chiswick, London, 1842. Sent by Horticultural Society to collect plants in China, 1843. Returned to London, 1846. Curator of the Chelsea Physic Garden, 1846–1848. Traveled in the Far East, 1848–1853 and 1860–1862. After retirement spent some time farming in Scotland. Died in London, 13 April 1880.

## References and Further Reading

Robert Fortune's journals are housed at the Lindley Library, Royal Horticultural Society, London.

Fortune, Robert, *Three Years' Wanderings in the Northern Provinces of China, Including a Visit to the Tea, Silk, and Cotton Countries: With an Account of the Agriculture and Horticulture of the Chinese, New Plants, etc.*, 1847; facsimile, 1987.

Fortune, Robert, *A Journey to the Tea Countries of China*, 1852; facsimile, 1987.
Fortune, Robert, *A Residence among the Chinese*, 1857.
Fortune, Robert, *Yedo and Peking*, 1863.

## FOUNTAINE, MARGARET (1862–1940)

### *British Traveler and Collector*

Margaret Fountaine has been described as a traveler and collector, but these words do not do justice to the unique and unconventional nature of her life. Born in 1862, she was the eldest daughter of Reverend John Fountaine, rector of South Acre parish in East Anglia. The family lived at South Acre until shortly after John Fountaine's death in 1878, when they moved to Norwich, where Margaret spent several years leading a very conventional life full of visitations, garden parties, dances, and churchgoing. Although Margaret's father never accumulated a fortune, both her parents came from well-to-do families. It was a rich and generous uncle who provided substantial lifelong incomes for Margaret and her siblings, making it possible for them to carve out independent lifestyles. Margaret's independence began in the early 1880s when she proudly flouted convention by falling in love with and aggressively pursuing Septimus Hewson, an Irish chorister at Norwich Cathedral known for being overly fond of drink. She followed him all the way to Ireland. When, in 1890, the pursuit finally failed, Fountaine decided to spend her private income on world travel in order to collect and study butterflies. For the rest of her life, she romped through distant countryside chasing winged creatures and wild, gypsy-looking men. It was on a chase along a Trinidad road that she collapsed and died from a heart attack in 1940, butterfly net by her side.

We would know little today about Fountaine's life if it were not for a locked black box that was finally opened 38 years after her death. This box and ten mahogany display cases, containing Fountaine's butterfly collection of more than 22,000 specimens, were deposited in 1940 at the Norwich Castle Museum, as stipulated by her will. The will also made clear that the box was to remain locked until 15 April 1978. On approximately that date, several people unsealed the box to find 12 hefty volumes detailing, in a careful hand, Fountaine's life from 1878 when she was 16 until the year before she died. Thanks to W.F. Cater, these diaries have been edited and dispensed to the public in two engaging volumes that transport readers to all parts of the globe: *Love among the Butterflies* (1980) and *Butterflies and Late Loves* (1987).

Accompanying the volumes was a letter of apology in which Fountaine referred to her life as "wild and fearless" and to herself as one "who never grew up and who enjoyed greatly and suffered much" (*Butterflies and Late Loves*). One might assume that the suffering was due to her relentless pursuit of what she did not or could not have. In this sense her life was a perpetual chase, and intense wanderlust dominated her life from early on. She longed to be free both from the shackles of convention and from the constricting forces of affection. When discussing her preference for ambition over the affections, she noted how the latter "hold us back from great enterprises" and "tie us down to one spot on earth" (*Love among the Butterflies*). There was, perhaps, no Victorian woman more obsessed with traveling than Fountaine. From the time she first left her native land in 1891, she never again put down roots. She confessed proudly, "I derive the greatest pleasure from traveling, I liked the idea of knocking about the world and getting used to the ways and customs of men" (*Love among the Butterflies*).

Men functioned not only as role models for Fountaine, but also as objects to chase. She took great pride in her countless admirers, and seemed to revel in the sense of power she derived from being able both to attract and ultimately to reject the dozens of men in whose arms she rested. In only one case did she succumb to a long-lasting relationship, and that was with Khalil Neimy, a married man from Syria whom she met in 1901, who was forever torn between his responsibilities to family and his desire to accompany Fountaine on her countless journeys. Between the time they met and 1929, when he died, Neimy left home many times to meet up with Fountaine for butterfly-chasing adventures in various parts of the world. Though their relationship was never recognized, Fountaine immortalized it by christening the 22,000 cased specimens in the Norwich Museum "The Fountaine–Neimy Collection," as they are known to this day.

Fountaine first discovered the joy of capturing butterfly specimens when she traveled to Switzerland in 1891. At the time, she declared, "I was a born naturalist, though all these years . . . it had lain dormant within me" (*Love among the Butterflies*). Had she been a man, she might have been reared and trained as a naturalist, or an entomologist. But as a woman, she had to pursue her collecting interest with no training and little encouragement from others. She nevertheless became known and respected by insect enthusiasts the world over. At a meeting of entomologists in eastern Europe, she was a welcomed guest, and in Austria she met a collector who considered her a "fellow entomologist." He knew her by name and had read her articles in such publications as *The Entomologist* and the *Transactions of the Entomological Society of London*. In Budapest, where she was the only woman at a meeting of entomologists, she recounted how, after much drinking of wine, she gave a farewell address in German that "met with loud applause followed by a deal of glass-clinking" (*Love among the Butterflies*).

Fountaine's passion for butterflies sent her trekking through the wilds of every continent, net in hand. In the early 1890s, she traveled mostly by diligence and train, until a chase in the Swiss mountains made her forsake wheels and rails for foot travel. Tramping the mountains made her declaim triumphantly, "I really did feel like a traveller then" (*Love among the Butterflies*). By the time she collapsed on a Trinidad road in 1940, she had covered thousands of miles by foot, train, boat, horse, automobile, and airplane. Her first trip by plane was in South America, where she took to the air with great enthusiasm, despite being crammed into a small plane open to the elements. She opted for air travel many more times, her longest flight being from Havana to Santiago in 1931, when she coped with rough patches of turbulence by swigging brandy, an ever present part of her travel gear. Old age did nothing to dampen her traveling energies or to alter her methods of travel. Four months short of her seventieth birthday, she boasted of having sat more secure in the saddle than ever during a 45-mile collecting spree in Chile.

Fountaine was fearless, unfazed by bandits, earthquakes, lions, poisonous snakes, malaria, airplane rides, glaciers, tropical storms, or any other hair-raising perils. She experienced all of these while traveling, and let none deter her from netting yet another winged specimen. While in Rio, she was attacked by two large dogs and suffered an eight-foot fall, but neither setback put a stop to her butterfly chasing. Brazil offered more entomological excitement than she had encountered before, and she boasted of being able to pinch-catch desirable specimens off the top of fresh horse manure. But she seemed proudest of anything she did that was daring, such as sitting, drink in hand, on a Corsican mountainside with a most-wanted bandit and his gang. She also liked to remember her and her sister's crossing of the Mer de Glace on Mont Blanc, with no guide and nothing but tennis shoes and net handles to help them along. These adventures she had in her youth, but even when she was over 60, collecting in Tenerife on her way to West Africa, she was thrilled to find herself crammed, along with eight young Spaniards, into a Hudson motorcar speeding its course recklessly as if no pedestrians or mules shared the road.

W.F. Cater tells us that, though Fountaine was respected by entomologists of her time, she is summed up now "as a useful collector, perhaps a great one, but not a great scientist" (*Love among the Butterflies*). Nor can we consider her a "great" travel writer, if by travel writing we mean accounts that offer new and interesting insights into the people and places visited. Fountaine's travel diaries are more about her triumphs, trials, and tribulations, and her relationships with men. They are fascinating, nevertheless, because she was such a rare and memorable character, whose guts and determination allowed her to stretch, to the point of breaking, the boundaries imposed on women in Victorian Britain.

MARJORIE MORGAN

### Biography

Born in South Acre, Norfolk, England, 1862. Eldest of seven children of the rector of South Acre. Grew up there and in Norwich. After an unhappy love affair, traveled in Europe to collect butterflies, supported financially by an uncle's legacy. Traveled to Syria, 1901; met Khalil Neimy (d. 1929); traveled with Neimy to Turkey, Algeria, Spain, Southern Africa, the Caribbean, and India, 1901–1913. Made unsuccessful attempt to settle with Neimy in Australia, 1913; went to the USA, 1913–1919. Further travel for butterfly collecting, 1919–1940: visited Fiji, New Zealand, the Far East, West and East Africa, the Caribbean, and South America. Amassed extensive butterfly collection and contributed to a number of entomological journals. Died of a heart attack in Trinidad, 21 April 1940. At her death, left instructions for the diaries documenting her travels to remain unopened until April 1978.

### References and Further Reading

Fountaine, Margaret, *Love among the Butterflies: The Travels and Adventures of a Victorian Lady*, edited and with an introduction by W.F. Cater, 1980.

Fountaine, Margaret, *Butterflies and Late Loves: The Further Travels and Adventures of a Victorian Lady*, edited by W.F. Cater, 1987.

## FRANCE, PRE-REVOLUTIONARY

That part of Celtic Gaul approximating as a geopolitical entity to modern France was created by the Roman imperial campaigns against the Ligurians. These culminated in their crossing of the Alps in 121 BCE and the creation of the province of Gallia Narbonensis. Further military exploration of these new territories provided the Romans with ready access to the ancient trade routes between the Rhône, Saône, and Loire valleys. Julius Caesar had conquered the rest of Gaul by 50 BCE (his *Commentaries* on this campaign offer the earliest surviving account of "travels of conquest" in the region), and Augustus (27 BCE–14 CE) further subdivided the territories, and established an ordnance survey and an advanced road system. Several still popular tourist sites in France, such as the Pont du Gard, and the (amphi-)theaters in Nîmes, Arles, and Orange, date from this period.

During the next millennium, Gaul thrived as a focus for commercial, military, and Christian travelers and as a major through route for trade with Britain. It remained under Roman rule until the fifth century, with Lugdunum (Lyons), evocatively described in the *Epistulae* of Sidonius Apollinaris (fl. 450–475), as its economic and administrative metropolis. Gaul was unified under Clovis I (481–511), who became Christian and made Paris his capital in 508, rendering it a draw for European travelers. Under the Carolingians (751–987), closer links were forged with Germany and Italy, especially by Charlemagne (768–814), who was crowned Holy Roman emperor in 800, with Aix-la-Chapelle as his administrative and cultural center. However, the prevailing tradition of dividing up territories on a king's death eventually led to a large number of independent feudal states under the control of numerous minor dukes and counts. Scandinavian incursions also increased from the late ninth century, with the Vikings besieging Paris in 885 and settling at Rouen in 912, leading to the creation of the duchy of Normandy. During the rule of the Capetians (987–1328), Paris again became the administrative center. Following William of Normandy's conquest of England (1066) and the marriage (1152) of the future Henry II of England to Eleanor of Aquitaine (the divorced wife of Louis VII, whose dowry brought about one-third of France to Henry II), three centuries of dynastic power struggles between England and France generated a steady traffic of English soldiers and travelers crossing the Channel.

The international network of influence exerted by the Roman Church, along with the foundation of the great monastic abbeys, such as Cluny (910), Cîteaux (1098), and Clairvaux (1115), stimulated an ever growing amount of contact between England, France, and Rome. A remarkable surviving document from this period is the travel itinerary of Archbishop Sigeric, who journeyed from Canterbury, via France and Switzerland, to Rome in 990 to collect his pallium. Anglo-Saxon pilgrims from England habitually took one of three routes through France: down the Rhône valley to Marseilles and then by sea to Italy; from Paris to Lyons and then across the Alps; or, most commonly by the tenth century, from the Seine to Etaples, and then via various monasteries and hospices (some specifically founded for English pilgrims, such as St. Josse at Ponthieu) as far as Besançon and then on through Switzerland (Ortenberg, 1990).

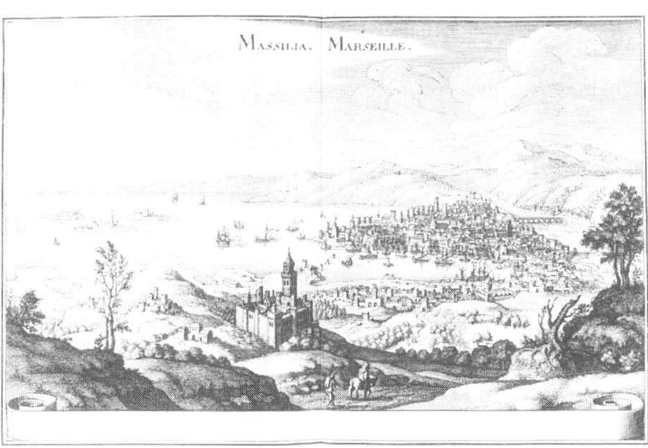


View of Marseilles from the south, shortly before Louis XIV had Fort St-Nicolas constructed to guard the southern side of the harbor entrance, facing the medieval Fort St-Jean on the north side (from Martin Zeiller's *Topographia Galliae*, 1655–1661). *Courtesy of Travellers Club, London; Bridgeman Art Library, agent.*

From the time of the First Crusade (called by Pope Urban II at Clermont in 1095) and the Second Crusade (preached at Vézelay by St. Bernard in 1146), numerous international bands of Christian volunteers crisscrossed French soil; and the building of many of the major cathedrals between 1150 and 1300 guaranteed a steady influx into France both of members of the religious orders and of skilled artisans. Following the expulsion of Pope Clement V from Rome in 1309, Avignon became a major international center of Christianity, until 1403. Complementing the centers of monastic learning, the thirteenth-century establishment of universities at Toulouse, Orléans, Montpellier, and Paris attracted many foreign students over the following centuries and nurtured the already long-established tradition of the wandering scholar, ranging from Peter Abelard (1079–1142) to Desiderius Erasmus (c. 1466–1536) and Heinrich Cornelius Agrippa (1486–1535), who moved around several countries, including France, in search of knowledge, patronage, and employment. Similarly, numerous musicians and artists of various nationalities, such as the Flemish organist and composer Heinrich Isaac (c. 1450–1517) and the German painter Albrecht Dürer (1471–1528), sought lucrative positions and commissions from the French nobility.

During the early years of the House of Valois (1328–1589), large numbers of English soldiers and foreign mercenaries were brought to France to fight in the Hundred Years' War (1337–1453), most famously at Agincourt (1415) and Orléans, where Joan of Arc defeated the English (1429). Paris was retaken by the French in 1436, and Louis XI (1461–1483) set about eradicating the great feudal lordships, gradually unifying France into a single nation. Henceforth, the geographical concept of "travels in France" became a more specifically definable one, though Picardy, Normandy, and Brittany were still regarded as outside the "true" France, which consisted of Île de France and the southern territories. From the period from 1480 to

1520, several important early travel accounts of this emerging nation survive, notably the Venetian diplomat Zaccaria Contarini's description of France in 1492; the account of Hieronymus Münzer, a German doctor fleeing the plague, who traveled through parts of France in 1494–1495; Antoine de Lalaing's description of Duke Philippe le Beau's journey through France to Spain in 1501; Francesco Guicciardini's record of his embassy from Italy via the French Mediterranean coast to Spain in 1511; accounts by Jean de Vandenesse and Laurent Vital of Emperor Charles V's progress toward Spain in 1517; the journal of Antonio de Beatis, who accompanied Cardinal Luigi of Aragon as chaplain on an extensive northern peregrination in 1517–1518; Mario Equicola's account of a pilgrimage to Marseilles made with Isabella d'Este in about 1517; and an anonymous Milanese record of a journey through Europe in 1516–1518.

Calais, the last English stronghold, was regained by France in 1558, and the Peace of Cateau-Cambrésis (1559) ended the French wars with Italy. The relatively peaceful conditions under Francis II (r. 1559–1560) and Charles IX (r. 1560–1574) saw the reopening of France to a diverse range of European travelers. Clergymen and petitioners continued to travel to and from monasteries and ecclesiastical courts, along with pilgrims heading toward shrines both within France (at Aix-la-Chapelle, Mont-Saint-Michel, and Sainte-Baume) and further afield (usually Rome, especially in jubilee years, and the Holy Land). Innumerable foreign diplomats, artisans, craftsmen, artists, scholars, and merchants continued to ply their trades, and the "art of peregrination" (the undertaking of a tour abroad for educational reasons) began to take root as training for young men of promise.

Focusing here on English travelers after 1570 (see Maçzak, 1995, for information about travelers other nationalities), the signing of the Treaty of Blois in April 1572 immediately opened up the country to English visitors. Most famously, in June of that year Philip Sidney and Lodowick Bryskett joined the diplomatic entourage of the Earl of Lincoln and resided in Paris under the protection of Sir Francis Walsingham, the resident English ambassador. But following the massacre of the Protestant Huguenots in Paris in August 1572, Sidney rapidly withdrew to Germany. The tumultuous reign of Charles IX's brother, Henry III (r. 1574–1589), who was behind the murder in Blois of the ultra-Catholic Henry, duke of Guise (which in turn led to his own assassination in Saint-Cloud in 1589), curtailed this brief flourishing of itineraries through France.

Unusually for this period, Fynes Moryson gained permission from his Cambridge college to traverse various parts of the Continent from 1591 to 1597, as recorded in his *Itinerary* (1617). In 1598 the Edict of Nantes allowed freedom of conscience to the Huguenots and ended the Wars of Religion of La Ligue (begun in 1560). From the early 1600s, France's chief minister, Maximilien de Béthune, duke of Sully (1560–1641), greatly improved the road system and instigated the Briare Canal (completed under Louis XIII), linking the Seine and the Loire. This combination of relative peace and decent transportation soon revived the idea of travel as education among the English ruling classes. James I's chief minister, Robert Cecil, earl of Salisbury (1563–1612), and the powerful Howard family were firm believers in the benefits of the Grand Tour. In 1603 Theophilus Lord Howard de Walden, later earl of Suffolk, traveled to France. Many others followed, most notably, in 1605, William Cecil, Lord Roos, the great-nephew of Robert Cecil (Stoye, 1989); and Robert Devereux, third earl of Essex, who in 1607 married Frances Howard, elder daughter of the earl of Suffolk, and then went abroad in the following year (Stoye, 1989). It became something of a custom for young nobles to disappear abroad soon after their wedding, as did Salisbury's own son, William, when he married Suffolk's younger daughter (Stoye, 1989). These inexperienced travelers were invariably accompanied by a more mature guide, such as Henry Lord Clifford's tutor, William Becher, who later became a diplomat and knight; and Thomas Lorkin, tutor in 1610 to Sir Thomas Puckering (Stoye, 1989). On a lower social level, the idiosyncratic traveler Thomas Coryate left for France on foot in the summer of 1608, recording his experiences in his *Crudities* (1611). The assassination of Henry IV in 1610 by a Catholic fanatic fuelled anti-Catholic sentiments at the English court, prompting the departure abroad of several members of the English Catholic hierarchy, including Sir Thomas and Sir Charles Somerset, the sons of the earl of Worcester. Sir Charles had also recently married; likewise, following his wedding to Salisbury's daughter, Frances, in 1610, Henry Lord Clifford was sent to study in France, as was Thomas Wentworth, later first earl of Strafford, who had married Clifford's sister, Anne (Stoye, 1989).

Tourism in France significantly diminished during the troubled reign of Louis XIII (1610–1643), although from 1623 to 1628 the planned marriage between the future Charles I of England and Henrietta Maria prompted a flurry of English travelers between London and Paris, including even a secret visit by Charles himself (1623) and, more overtly, Peter Heylin (1625). During the 1630s, Englishmen such as Sir Thomas Abdy (1633) and Richard D'Ewes (1637) once again began to cross the Channel in some numbers. The 1640s saw the departure to France of those who wished to extricate themselves from the English civil conflicts, only then to experience the outbreak of the French domestic wars (1648–1653). Such exiles included the royalist John Evelyn (in exile 1643–1651) and Sir Ralph Verney, who supported neither side (Stoye, 1989); dispossessed Oxbridge fellows like John Bargrave, who eked out a living as a traveling tutor (1645–1646); William Edgeman, who accompanied the Spanish embassy of Sir Edward Hyde and Lord Cottington through France (1649–1651); the artist Richard Symonds (1649–1652); the 15-year-old son of a parliamentarian general, Robert Montagu, Lord Mandeville (1649–1652); the Yorkshireman John Reresby (1654); William Hammond, a medical student (1656–1658), and the Londoner Francis Mortoft (1658); as well as visitors to the exiled court of Henrietta Maria.

From the Restoration until 1789, travel for pleasure, education, or health became much more common, as typified (see Lough, 1987, and Black, 1992) by Edward Browne (1664), John Locke (1675–1679), William Bromley (1692), William and John Blathwayt (1705), David Garrick (1751 and 1763), Philip Thicknesse (1777), and William Beckford (1785). By the beginning of the eighteenth century, the Grand Tour customarily included a passing visit to Paris, followed by a leisurely journey across France to Italy. Along with the merely factual recording of these itineraries, a more creative approach to travel writing developed, characterized by Tobias Smollett's *Travels* (1766) and Laurence Sterne's *A Sentimental Journey* (1768). In sharp contrast to these gentle discursive works is the vivid eyewitness account by Samuel Boddington (1766–1843) of the outbreak of the French Revolution, recorded in a series of letters to his father (Black, 307–311).

Michael G. Brennan

## References and Further Reading


Abdy, Sir Thomas, "A Journall . . . of My Travells in France [and Italy] . . . 1633–1635," Bodleian Library, Oxford, Rawlinson MS D 1285, ff. 69–138.

Andrews, John, *A Comparative View of the French and English Nations*, 1785.

Anonymous, "Account of a Journey through France in 1516–1518" [by an anonymous Milanese traveler], British Library, London, Additional MSS 24180.

A.R., *The Curiosities of Paris in Nine Letters*, 1757.

Bargrave, John, "Travels in France, 1645–46," Canterbury Cathedral Archives, U11/8.

Baudot, François-Nicolas, *Itinéraire de Normandie*, 1647; edited by Le Chanoine Porée, 1971.

Beatis, Antonio de, *Die Reise des Kardinals Luigi d'Aragona durch Deutschland, die Niederlande, Frankereich und Oberitalien, 1517–1518*, edited by Ludwig Pastor, 1905; as *Voyage du Cardinal d'Aragon en Allemagne, Hollande, Belgique, France et Italie 1517–1518*, translated by Madeleine Havard de la Montaigne, 1913; as *The Travel Journal of Antonio de Beatis: Germany, Switzerland, the Low Countries, France and Italy, 1517–1518*, translated from the Italian by J.R. Hale and J.M.A. Lindon, edited by J.R. Hale, 1979.

Beckford, William, *Letters and Observations: Written in a Short Tour through France and Italy*, 1786.

Black, Jeremy, *The British Abroad: The Grand Tour in the Eighteenth Century*, Stroud, Gloucestershire: Sutton, and New York: St. Martin's Press, 1992.

Blathwayt, William, *The Grand Tour: Letters and Accounts Relating to the Travel through Europe of the Brothers William and John Blathwayt of Dyrham Park, 1705–1708*, edited by Nora Hardwick, 1985.

Bromley, William, *Remarks in the Grande Tour of France and Italy*, 1692.

Browne, Edward, *A Journal of a Visit to Paris in the Year 1664*, edited by G. Keynes, 1923.

Contarini, Zaccaria, "Description of France in 1492," in *Relazioni degli ambasciatori veneti al senato*, edited by Eugenio Alberi, 1839–1863.

Coryate, Thomas, *Coryats Crudities: Hastily Gobled up in Five Moneths Travells in France, Savoy, Italy, Rhetia . . . Helvetia . . . Some Parts of High Germany and the Netherlands*, 1611; reprinted in 2 vols., 1905.

Dallington, Sir Robert, *A Method for Travell: Shewed by Taking the View of France as It Stoode in . . . 1598*, 1605; as *The View of France*, with an introduction by W.P. Barrett, 1936.

Downes, John, "Travels in France," British Library, London, Sloane MS 179.

Edgeman, William, "Travels in Flanders, France, Spain, 1649–51," Bodleian Library, Oxford, Clarendon MS 137.

Equicola, Mario, *De Isabella Estensis iter in Narbonensem Galliam*, *c*. 1517.

Estienne, Charles, *La Guide des Chemins de France*, 1552–1553; edited by Sir Theodore Mayerne, 1592; edited by Jean Bonneroti, 1936.

Evelyn, John, *The Diary of John Evelyn*, edited by E.S. de Beer, 6 vols., 1955.

Garrick, David, *The Journal of David Garrick, Being a Record of His Memorable Trip to Paris in 1751*, edited by Ryliss Clair Alexander, 1928.

Garrick, David, *The Journal of David Garrick, Describing His Visit to France and Italy in 1763*, edited by George Winchester Stone Jr., 1939.

Goelnitz, Abraham, *Ulysses Belgico-Gallicus*, 1631.

Guicciardini, Francesco, *Diario del viaggio in Spagna*, edited and illustrated by Paolo Guicciardini, 1932.

Hammond, William, [Travels in France and Italy], Brotherton Library, University of Leeds, MS Trv 2; another copy, British Library, London, Additional MSS 59785.

Herbert, Sir Edward, *The Life of Edward, First Lord Herbert of Cherbury*, edited by J.M. Shuttleworth, 1976.

Heylyn, Peter, *A Full Relation of Two Journeys: The One into the Mainland of France, the Other into Some of the Adjacent Islands, Performed and Digested into Six Bookes*, 1656.

Lalaing, Antoine de, "Relations du premier voyage de Philippe le Beau en Espagne, en 1501," in *Collection des Voyages des Souverains des Pays-Bas*, edited by M. Gachard, 1876.

Lister, Martin, [Travels in France, 1663–1666], Bodleian Library, Oxford, Lister MS 19.

Locke, John, *Locke's Travels in France, 1675–1679*, edited by John Lough, 1953.

Lough, John, *France Observed in the Seventeenth Century by British Travellers*, Stocksfield, Northumberland, and Boston: Oriel Press, 1984.

Lough, John, *France on the Eve of the Revolution: British Travellers' Observations 1763–1788*, London: Croom Helm, 1987.

Mączak, Antoni, *Travel in Early Modern Europe*, translated from the Polish by Ursula Phillips, Cambridge: Polity Press, and Cambridge, Massachusetts: Blackwell, 1995.

Maynard, Banister, [Travels in France, Italy, Germany, and the Low Countries, 1660–1662], Bodleian Library, Oxford, Rawlinson MS D 84.
Millard, John, *The Gentleman's Guide in His Tour through France: Wrote by an Officer in the Royal Navy, Who Lately Travelled on a Principle, Which He Most Sincerely Recommends to His Countrymen, viz, Not to Spend More Money in the Country of Our Natural Enemy Than Is Requisite to Support with Decency the Character of an Englishman*, 4th edition, 1770.
Montagu, Robert, [Travels in France, Switzerland, and Germany], Bodleian Library, Oxford, Rawlinson MS D 76.
Mortoft, Francis, *Francis Mortoft: His Books, Being his Travels through France and Italy, 1658–1659*, edited by Malcolm Letts, 1925.
Moryson, Fynes, *An Itinerary Containing His Ten Years Travel*, 1617; 4 vols., 1907–1908.
Münzer, Hieronymus, "Jérome Münzer et son voyage dans le midi de la France en 1494–1495," edited by Eugène Déprez, *Annales du Midi* (1936): 53–79.
Münzer, Hieronymus, "Le Voyage de Hieronimus Monetarius à travers la France (1494–45)," edited by E.P. Goldschmidt, *Humanisme et Renaissance* (1939): 55–75, 198–200, 324–348, 529–559.
Ortenberg, Veronica, "Archbishop Sigeric's Journey to Rome in 990 [BL Cotton Tiberius B.v.23v–24r]", *Anglo-Saxon England*, 19 (1990): 197–246.
Reresby, Sir John, *The Memoirs of the Honourable Sir John Reresby*, 1734; as *Bart*, 1813; edited by Albert Ivatt, London, 1904; as *Memoirs of Sir John Reresby: The Complete Text and a Selection from His Letters*, edited and with an introduction by Andrew Browning, 1991.
Signot, Jacques, *La Totale et Vraie Description de tous les passaiges, lieux et destroicts par lesquelz on peut passer et entrer des Gaules es ytalies*, c. 1516.
Smollett, Tobias, *Travels through France and Italy*, 1766; edited by Frank Felsenstein, 1981.
Somerset, Sir Charles, *The Travel Diary (1611–1612) of an English Catholic, Sir Charles Somerset*, edited by Michael G. Brennan, 1993.
Sterne, Laurence, *A Sentimental Journey through France and Italy*, 1768; edited by Ian Jack, 1984.
Stoye, John, *English Travellers Abroad 1604–1667: Their Influence in English Society and Politics*, revised edition, New Haven, Connecticut and London: Yale University Press, 1989.
Symonds, Richard, [Travels in France and Italy, 1649–1652], British Library, London, Harleian MSS 943, 1278; Egerton MSS 1635, 1636; Bodleian Library, Oxford, Rawlinson MS D 121.
Thicknesse, Philip, *Observations on the Customs and Manners of the French Nation*, 1766.
Thicknesse, Philip, *Useful Hints to Those Who Make the Tour of France*, 1768.
Thicknesse, Philip, *A Year's Journey through France and Part of Spain*, 1777.
Vandenesse, Jean de, "Journal des voyages de Charles-Quint, de 1514 à 1551," in *Collection des Voyages des Souverains des Pays-Bas*, vol. 7, edited by M. Gachard, 1874.
Vital, Laurent, "Premier Voyage de Charles-Quint en Espagne de 1517 à 1518," in *Collection des Voyages des Souverains des Pays-Bas*, vol. 3, edited by M. Gachard and Charles Piot, 1881.
Wentworth, Thomas, [Travels in France, 1612], Sheffield Public Library, Wentworth Woodhouse MSS.

*See also* **Paris**

## FRANCE, NINETEENTH AND TWENTIETH CENTURIES

The English agricultural theorist Arthur Young (1741–1820) traveled throughout France between 1787 and 1790. Observing the country before and during the revolution, he provides in *Travels in France* (1792) a description of the social and economic conditions of the prerevolutionary period. The events of 1789 and their aftermath triggered radical changes in attitudes toward, as well as in, the practice of travel in France. The nineteenth century witnessed, as a result, a sudden foregrounding of travel writing as a genre, with many of the period's most prominent authors—such as Chateaubriand, Hugo, Dumas, Gautier, and Flaubert—including French travel narratives in their literary output.

The revolution itself brought a number of travelers to France on unorthodox journeys. The Haitian exile Toussaint Louverture, for example, was transported to Brest in 1802 and traveled across France to his prison cell in Joux, where he would die the following year. Toussaint reversed the Middle Passage, and his traveling served as an archetypal journey for subsequent Caribbean writers and travelers, such as the Martinican Aimé Césaire (1913–), en route to France. Other visitors on more conventional journeys, such as William Wordsworth (1770–1850), came to see the postrevolutionary sociopolitical changes at firsthand, and Chateaubriand (1768–1848), evoking in *Mémoires d'outre-tombe* (1849–1850) his return from exile in 1800, was one of a number of travelers to describe journeys through a France greatly altered by Jacobin and Napoleonic "vandalism."

For domestic travelers, the development of a republican understanding of national space recast the relationship between Paris and the regions. The centralizing pull of the capital created greater opportunities for travel. To this change was added the rapid evolution of new means of transport, and, with the development of the train, car, velocipede, and balloon, the nineteenth century witnessed both technological innovation and the steady acceleration of travel. A significant turning point was the opening of the first French railway line in 1827 and the development (after 1830) of a national rail network centred on Paris, which ended travelers' reliance on horses or their own feet. Not only could greater distances be covered, but also previously marginalized or inaccessible provinces such as Brittany and the Pyrenees were opened up and made more accessible. With the development of *tourisme* (the word was borrowed from English in the 1840s), there was a simultaneous growth of the ideologies of French regionalism.

In the postrevolutionary era, however, the romantic propensity for travel outside France (and the public appetite for accounts of it) led to the creation of the neologism *exotisme* (exoticism). Greater opportunities for movement abroad and the steady mechanization of travel afforded the romantics a chance to journey beyond France and hence to come into contact with those exotic cultures that were suddenly more readily accessible. The literary geography of the period did not, however, restrict the exotic to the extra-European, and although the otherness of England was largely assimilated by the French, the Celtic fringes of France itself in Brittany were held to be one location of otherness. Yet the mix of expansionism, increased trade, improved communications, and the growth of tourism led to the opening of vast areas of Asia, the Middle East, and North Africa (known collectively as the Orient), as well as North America. The interest in journeys elsewhere (to the detriment of journeys in France) led to some chauvinistic reactions. In the preface to his *Guide du voyageur en France* [Guide for the Traveler in France] (1830–1831), for instance, the engineer and geographer Richard (1793–1851) criticizes the French for ignoring their own country:

> Alas! Ungrateful as we are, we ignore too often our own beautiful country—the France coveted by the whole of Europe; we cast a pitiful glance at the riches which surround us and spend a fortune climbing bare mountains and snow-covered peaks elsewhere . . . France seems too poor and too small; to satisfy our desire for travel, we need Switzerland, Italy, England and its three kingdoms; as if Providence, who has spoilt us as she would her own children, had not lavished its most abundant favours on the blessed climes we inhabit . . . as if we did not have our own antiquities, our own ruined castles on mountain slopes.

The extroversion implied by exoticism (and criticized here by Richard) was often a response to the perceived threats posed to France by modernization and tourism itself. The anti-tourism that characterizes much nineteenth- and twentieth-century travel literature emerged early in the period. In *En Voyage: Alpes et Pyrénées* (1890; *The Alps and Pyrenees*), for instance, Victor Hugo (1802–1885) foresees with regret the imminent transformation of the once tiny resort of Biarritz. This sense of irreparable change does not mark the travel narratives of foreign visitors to France, however, in whose eyes the country (beyond Paris) remained primarily rural. Developments in travel allowed a steady influx of foreign travelers, drawn in particular by major events such as the 1855 Universal Exposition (which attracted 130,000 foreign visitors, of whom 40,000 were British). In the first half of the century, around 70 percent of travelers from abroad were British, lured by France's climate and cuisine. Charles Dickens (1812–1870) traveled through France en route for Italy in 1844 and provides in *Pictures from Italy* (1846) a condescendingly ironic and often stereotypical account of a country he saw as picturesque if dirty and underdeveloped. An earlier traveler, Thomas Colley Grattan, offers a more sympathetic account of his journeys on foot through France in *High-Ways and By-Ways* (1823). Grattan's travels herald the slower, more modest journeys of two later British travelers, Robert Louis Stevenson (1850–1894) and Edward Barker (1849–1919), both of whom experimented with deceleration as a means of discovering the often obscured aspects of contemporary France. Stevenson's 1876 canoe trip from Anvers to Paris, described in *An Inland Voyage* (1878), is an episodic account in which river travel is used to slow down the journey and generate chance encounters; a subsequent journey on foot with his donkey Modestine, recounted in *Travels with a Donkey in the Cévennes* (1879), represents a similar reaction against mechanized transport and an exploration of the opportunities afforded to travelers who slow down. The lesser-known Barker, whose walking journeys are described in a series of accounts including *Through Auvergne on Foot* (1884), provides a realistic, detailed description of rural areas largely by-passed by the transport networks spreading across nineteenth-century France.

French travelers also observed rural France and its marginal provinces. The economist Adolphe-Jérôme Blanqui (1798–1854) visited Corsica in 1838, on the instructions of the Académie des Sciences Morales et Scientifiques. The resulting report is a travel narrative in its own right. The same is true of an account by Jules Michelet (1798–1874) of an official visit to Brittany in 1831. Alphonse Daudet (1840–1897) and Octave Mirbeau (1848–1917) also both wrote texts relating their travels in this region. However, perhaps the most

Rousseau's idyllically sited tomb attracted British visitors even during the Napoleonic era (from Colonel Thomas Thornton's *A Sporting Tour through France in a series of letters to the . . . Earl of Darlington*, 1806). *Courtesy of Travellers Club, London; Bridgeman Art Library, agent.*

important account of a Breton journey emerged from the four-month walking tour undertaken by Maxime Du Camp (1822–1894) and Gustave Flaubert (1821–1880) in 1847. *Par les Champs et par les grèves* (1886; "Over Strand and Field") describes the two travelers' flight from the literary milieux of Paris. It is a technically innovative work, consisting of a set of co-authored literary travel notes in which Du Camp and Flaubert attempt to explore the region and the people hidden behind popular myths of Brittany.

American travel narratives of the period provide a different picture of France. In the period between 1814 and 1848, 30,000 Americans undertook the difficult transatlantic journey and made the country one of the first stages (after Britain) in their newly reinaugurated Grand Tour. James Fenimore Cooper (1789–1851), Harriet Beecher Stowe (1812–1896), Mark Twain (1835–1910), Henry Longfellow (1807–1882), Henry James (1843–1916), and Edith Wharton (1862–1937) all wrote accounts of their travels in France. Many Americans were not entirely prepared for the spectacle of the country, nor for the challenges posed by its language and bureaucracy. What struck them most, however, were the architectural and cultural traditions, and their amazement is epitomized by Fenimore Cooper's astonished reaction on his arrival in Le Havre and Longfellow's surprise at the Gothic splendor of Rouen cathedral. Another aspect of the American reaction can be seen in Mark Twain, who, when traveling by train from Marseilles to Lyons, was struck by the diminutive scale of France in comparison to the American landscape.

The slow expansion and democratization of travel throughout the period led to the foundation of the Touring-Club de France in 1890. This organization regulated and promoted tourism in France, and contributed to the consolidation of this new form of popular travel. By the late nineteenth century, however, a parallel craze or *panoramania* had developed in Paris, with various shows and attractions stage-managing foreign locations in the heart of the French capital. This reached its apogee with the Universal Exposition of 1900, at which Parisians were invited on a virtual journey around the world. An exhibit with three floors of panoramas, incorporating multisensory effects, motion, and indigenous performers, would allow visitors to leave Marseilles, and tour Spain, Greece, Istanbul, Syria, Egypt, Ceylon, Cambodia, China, and Japan, enjoying a whistle-stop tour of exotic locales.

The reconstruction of elsewhere at home was an integral part of the ambivalence toward travel in fin-de-siècle French literature. While the ongoing expansion of empire continued to provide fields for journeys and exploration overseas, a growing skepticism over the future of travel began to develop in France itself. Des Esseintes, the jaded protagonist in Huysmans's *À Rebours* (1884; *Against the Grain*), epitomizes this sense of the imminent "end of travel." Tired of Paris, he plans a journey to England only to discover that he has experienced the other culture vicariously, in France itself. Des Esseintes's question, "What is the point of moving when you can travel so magnificently sitting in a chair?" reflects not only the increasing mechanization of means of transport and the separation of the traveler from outside space, but also a growing sense of crisis in travel resulting from early-twentieth-century fears of cultural homogenization. There were various responses to these fears. The French banker Albert Kahn (1860–1940) eventually ruined himself by funding an ambitious (and largely unrealized) project to photograph and film a diverse range of world cultures. His "Archives of the Planet" (founded in 1909) combine images of Asia with those of France itself, for the specific cultures of areas such as Brittany or the Auvergne were also seen to be under threat. Kahn's fear of the decline of travel, both within and beyond France, was shared by one of the most important figures in twentieth-century French travel literature, Victor Segalen (1878–1919). Segalen's *Essai sur l'exotisme* [Essay on Exoticism] and his Chinese travel narratives (such as *Equipée* [Escapade]) represent a search for new ways of traveling and of narrating travel that reject fin-de-siècle pessimism. Central to Segalen's "Aesthetics of Diversity" was a critique of the official French policy of "assimilation" of colonial territories into "Greater France." Such an expansion of France's geographical boundaries led not only to the development of colonial tourism, but also to the travel of colonial subjects to metropolitan France itself. This was particularly true in World War I, when thousands of Senegalese *tirailleurs* disembarked in France and traveled to the battlefields to discover pictures of European civilization radically different from the ones with which they had previously been supplied. The account of one such soldier's journey is the basis of the first sub-Saharan francophone African novel, *Force-Bonté* (1926), by Bakary Diallo (1892–1978).

The inter-war years witnessed radical changes in French travel. Pierre MacOrlan's *Petit Manuel du parfait aventurier* [1920; Little Manual for the Perfect Adventurer] marked an end of adventure and exploration, whereas *Le Voyage* [Travel], published by Paul Morand (1888–1976) in 1927, reflected more pragmatically on the realities of travel in an age approaching mass tourism. Authors continued to travel, however, and the emergent genre of "reportage" provided an ideal form for their narratives. During the 1930s, for example, Georges Simenon (1903–1989) undertook approximately 30 journeys in France and farther afield, which he recounted in a series of newspaper and magazine articles. Other authors persisted in their search for remoteness, with Alexandra David-Néel traveling to Tibet and Henri Michaux to Ecuador and throughout Asia. Michaux's claim in *Ecuador* that the earth is "rinsed of its exoticism" and his subsequent renunciation of geographical journeys in favor of mescaline-induced ones reflect an important shift caused by the availability of travel to an ever increasing number of people. The electoral success of the Popular Front in 1936 ensured paid holidays for all and allowed French workers leisure time to discover regions of their own country hitherto unexplored by them. This political development marks the consolidation of popular tourism in France, and Paul Morand's *Éloge du repos* [1937; In Praise of Rest], written to mark the political changes in 1936, eschews geographical exoticism to describe a rediscovery of invisible aspects of France through canoe travel along the country's rivers.

The deceleration advocated by Morand contrasts with developments in mechanized transport. In a collection of fragments entitled *Vitesse* [Speed], for instance, the poet Saint-Pol-Roux (1861–1940) recounts a car journey from Camaret to Brest on the western tip of Brittany, bemoaning the increased passivity of travel through France and the separation of travelers from their surroundings. Morand himself describes in *Flèche d'Orient* [1932; Oriental Arrow] the more radical implications of the linking of France to other countries through a rapidly expanding network of air travel. The inter-war period, and in particular the 1930s, was marked by the first regular flights between France and Africa and by a series of transcontinental car journeys—such as the Citroën "Croisière Jaune" in 1931—which catered to a public fascination with both speed and the lure of exoticism. The Colonial Exposition in 1931, the apogee of French colonial culture, depended on such increased mobility and the ability of representatives of empire to travel to France. In the exposition, France was not only presented as the center of the world, but was also transformed into a self-contained representation of the world, for once again the French were invited to travel to the limits of the empire (on a train tour of the exposition site) without even leaving Paris. In *Mirages de Paris* [1935; Parisian Mirages], Ousmane Socé describes the journey of a Senegalese character to the exposition at Vincennes, and this reverse ethnography, turning the colonial gaze onto France itself, emerged from an eclectic series of other travel accounts, such as *Cahier d'un retour au pays natal* (1939; *Notebook of a Return to My Native Land*) by the Martinican Aimé Césaire. The arrival of these francophone intellectuals from Africa and the Caribbean (and the emergence of Negritude) complemented the diversification of travel in France already triggered by the arrival of many black Americans in the 1920s, such as Claude McKay (1890–1948) and Countee Cullen (1903–1946).

After World War II, black American writers continued to travel to France, some, such as Chester Himes (1909–1984), Richard Wright (1908–1960), and James Baldwin (1924–), to escape the excesses of McCarthyism. Post-war travel was characterized, however, by a sense of exhaustion, epitomized by the obituary for travel and exploration in Claude Lévi-Strauss's *Tristes tropiques* (1955). In a period of decolonization, the potential for journeys elsewhere seemed to be in decline, paradoxically at a time when France itself was slowly becoming one of the major tourist destinations of the second half of the twentieth century. French travelers sought adventure through the choice of eccentric modes of transport, and the 1950s and 1960s witnessed a series of journeys around the world in Citroën 2CVs. Against a literary background of structuralism and the New Novel, however, new modes of travel gradually emerged as authors began to rediscover France itself. Having spent two decades traveling around the Mediterranean, for instance, Jacques Lacarrière (1925–) undertook a walking journey from Alsace to the Midi. The resulting account, *Chemin faisant* [1977; Along the Way], describes the walker's rediscovery of aspects of France hidden by modernity and steady urbanization. Far from yearning for a French rural idyll, Lacarrière describes a diverse and multilayered country, previously relegated to memory but gradually recovered by the contemporary traveler.

Lacarrière's text marked the beginning of a series of modestly disruptive journeys that honored deceleration and aspired to proximity. In 1983, Julio Cortázar and Carol Dunlop spent 30 days traveling from Paris to Marseilles, stopping at two service areas each day and never leaving the motorway. In 1990, François Maspero (1932–) traveled on one line of the RER, treating each suburban station as a stage of his journey and not returning to Paris itself for a month. The poet Jacques Réda (1929–) described in 1988 a journey to the source of the Seine. In 1997, Michel Chaillou undertook a long journey around France in a Renault Twingo, avoiding major roads and seeking what he calls in the title of his travelogue a "fleeting France." The accounts of these journeys are far removed from the anecdotal account of the Midi included in Peter Mayle's highly successful *A Year in Provence* (1989). What these domestic journeys represent instead is a recovery of the possibilities of travel and a rehabilitation of France as a place for potentially endless journeying. Later twentieth-century journeys through France reveal a shift in travel literature: the primacy of the place of travel has been replaced by considerations of speed (or its lack), of the construction of space, and of itineraries seen as specific projects in their own right.

Late-twentieth-century France witnessed the re-emergence of a complex fascination with travel. A sense of imperialist nostalgia led to the republishing of various out-of-print narratives and the return to favor of earlier travelers such as R.L. Stevenson. At the same time, however, in the journal *Gulliver* and the annual festival *Etonnants Voyageurs* (both founded in 1990), this yearning for older modes of travel and for a premodern understanding of the journey was replaced by a clear commitment to a continuation of contemporary travel. Authors such as Michel Le Bris, Jacques Lacarrière, Nicolas Bouvier, Gilles Lapouge, and Jacques Meunier—members of a hazily defined group called "Pour une Littérature Voyageuse" ("For a Traveling Literature")—continue a tradition of travel literature in French in which journeys to and within France continue to play a major role.

CHARLES FORSDICK

### References and Further Reading

Barker, Edward Harrison, *Through Auvergne on Foot*, 1884.
Blanqui, Adolphe-Jérôme, *Rapport sur l'état économique et moral de la Corse en 1838*, 1840.
Chaillou, Michel, *La France fugitive: Récit*, 1998.
Chateaubriand, François-René, Vicomte de, *Mémoires d'outre-tombe*, 6 vols., 1849–1850; as *The Memoirs of François René, Vicomte de Chateaubriand*, translated by Alexander Teixeira de Mattos, 1902; as *Memoirs*, translated by Robert Baldick, 1961.
Cooper, James Fenimore, *Recollections of Europe*, 2 vols., 1837.
Diallo, Bakary, *Force-Bonté*, 1926.
Dunlop, Carol, and Julio Cortázar, *Los Autonautas de la cosmopista o, un viaje atemporal Paris-Marsella*, 1983.
Flaubert, Gustave, *Par les Champs et par les grèves (Voyage en Bretagne)*, 1886; edited by Adrianne J. Tooke, 1987; as "Over Strand and Field: A Record of Travel in Brittany," in *The Complete Works of Gustave Flaubert*, vol. 7, 1904.
Grattan, Thomas Colley, *High-Ways and By-Ways; or, Tales of the Roadside, Picked up in the French Provinces by a Walking Gentleman*, 2nd edition, 2 vols., 1823; revised edition, 3 vols., 1840.
Hugo, Victor, *En Voyage: Alpes et Pyrenées*, 1890; as *The Alps and Pyrenees*, translated by John Manson, 1898.
Huysmans, Joris-Karl, *À Rebours*, 1884; as *Against the Grain*, translated by John Howard, 1922.
James, Henry, *A Little Tour in France*, 1884.
Lacarrière, Jacques, *Chemin faisant: Mille kilomètres à pied à travers la France*, 1977.
Longfellow, Henry Wadsworth, *Outre-mer: A Pilgrimage beyond the Sea*, 2 vols., 1833–1834.
Maspero, François, *Les Passagers du Roissy-Express*, photos by Anaïk Frantz, 1990; as *Roissy-Express: A Journey through the Paris Suburbs*, translated by Paul Jones, 1994.
Mayle, Peter, *A Year in Provence*, 1989.
Michelet, Jules, *Michelet en Bretagne: Son journal inédit d'août 1831*, edited by Auguste Dupouy, 1947.
Morand, Paul, *Éloge du repos: Apprendre à se reposer*, 1937.
Réda, Jacques, *Recommandations aux promeneurs*, 1988.
Richard, *Guide du voyageur en France*, 1823; many later editions.
Segalen, Victor, *Oeuvres complètes*, edited by Henry Bouiller, 2 vols., 1995.
Simenon, Georges, *À la découverte de la France: Textes recueillis par Francis Lacassin et Gilbert Sigaux*, 1976.
Stevenson, Robert Louis, *An Inland Voyage*, 1878.
Stevenson, Robert Louis, *Travels with a Donkey in the Cévennes*, 1879.
Twain, Mark, *The Innocents Abroad, or the New Pilgrim's Progress*, 1869.

*See also* **Paris; Pyrenees**

## FRANKLIN, JOHN (1786–1847) *British Naval Captain and Arctic Explorer*

John Franklin was born on 16 April 1786, the ninth of the 12 children of Willingham Franklin, a merchant in Spilsby, Lincolnshire. He went to Louth Grammar School, where he was the contemporary of Thomas de Quincey's brother and was followed by Alfred Tennyson. Franklin is said to have decided to be a sailor when he first saw the sea at the age of 12, and he left school at 14 to join the navy. He sailed with Matthew Flinders, a distant relation, on the official expedition to complete the survey of Australia's coast in 1801. This expedition was shipwrecked on a desert island, but Franklin survived and returned to Europe to spend the next few years climbing the naval hierarchy while fighting in the Napoleonic wars. In 1815, he was retired on half pay, and began to seek a place on one of the voyages of polar exploration that were keeping the navy busy during the peace. In April 1818, he left for the Arctic as second in command of an expedition intended to reach the North Pole while Ross and Parry sought the Northwest Passage.

This expedition reached the Arctic in May, to find that ice conditions were bad. The ships were beset off the north coast of Spitzbergen, and July storms left them so badly damaged that the expedition returned to Deptford after six months. Partly as a result of this, the Admiralty decided to concentrate on the Northwest Passage, which was at least potentially lucrative. Parry planned to lead another expedition to sail through the passage, while Franklin led a land-based party surveying the north coast of North America. This land party intended to depend on the resources of the Hudson's Bay Company, and left in May 1819, following the display in Leicester Square of a panorama based on the previous expedition. Ice made the northward voyage difficult, and by October the expedition had only reached Lake Winnipeg. They settled into an HBC trading post for the winter. As ever, the post was under-resourced and overpopulated, and they passed the winter freezing and starving. In January, Franklin left to recruit native guides from Lake Athabasca in the company of a few voyageurs. He traveled 860 miles, struggling to keep up with the voyageurs on skis. He had never skied before and left a trail of blood across the snow. The dogs got most of the food at night, while the spirits and the mercury in the thermometer froze. Unsurprisingly, Franklin had recruitment problems, and the expedition continued with too few hunters and guides, and hopelessly inadequate food supplies. By November, they were melting down pewter cups to make bullets, and by the time they reached the Coppermine River the following summer, snow blindness, fatigue, and scurvy were serious problems. After catching sight of the open Arctic Sea, they turned back with only three days' food, in rapidly worsening weather. Most of the animals had already migrated, so on the return journey the expedition lived on frozen lichen, and abandoned the books and scientific instruments in the snow. By September, they were eating shoes and bones left by wolves. The expedition split up, with the strongest few going ahead to bring back help for the weak. One of the guides produced some meat that he said was wolf, but when the rest of the group discovered that the meat came from the body of a missing companion, the guide was shot. The others ate leather and powdered bone, and two died of hunger before a Native American rescue party arrived and took them back to an HBC post, from which they left for England in May 1822.

Back in London, Franklin courted and married Eleanor Ann Porden, a well-educated young woman, who held a salon on Sunday afternoons. The marriage was not successful; Franklin held rather narrow religious views and objected to Eleanor's social life and literary activities. When their daughter was born in 1824, Eleanor's ill health worsened, but Franklin remained with his family in Spilsby while she stayed in London. Franklin began to plan another expedition with Parry to find the Northwest Passage, for which new ships were built. By January 1825, Eleanor was obviously dying, but Franklin left for the Arctic in early February. Eleanor died a few days later. Franklin's expedition was relatively successful, and when he returned in 1827 he was given a knighthood. In 1828, Franklin married Eleanor's friend Jane Griffin. He returned to naval service for a few years, and in 1836 he was appointed governor of Tasmania, which was then a penal colony. This governorship went very badly, partly because Jane's interest in the welfare of female prisoners was much resented. They were recalled in 1844. By this time, Parry and the HBC had mapped much of Arctic North America, and another expedition was planned to complete the survey. Franklin begged to go, despite his age and uncertain health, and after some hesitation he was chosen as leader. His ships, *Erebus* and *Terror*, were equipped with steam engines and supplied with food and fuel for three years.

No members of this expedition returned. Jane Franklin began an enormous publicity campaign, using her widowed status to pressure the Admiralty into sending a series of rescue expeditions over the next decade. The mortality rate on these expeditions was horrendously high, and it was not until the late 1850s that Leopold M'Clintock found a cache including a letter that said that Franklin had died in 1847. M'Clintock also found a few graves and two bodies in a boat, and heaps of equipment that had clearly come from the expedition and suggested that the explorers had been behaving in an extraordinary way, dragging curtain poles, silver cutlery, and silk shoes for miles across the snow. John Rae found evidence that the expedition had ended in cannibalism, which caused great controversy in Victorian England. The mystery was not solved until the 1980s, when the forensic archaeologists Owen Beatty and John Geiger found the remaining bodies perfectly preserved by the ice. Chemical analysis revealed serious lead poisoning from the primitive canned meats that the expedition had used; the Admiralty had employed a corrupt canner who had presented animal parts unfit for human consumption in cheaply made and badly sealed cans.

The disappearance of the Franklin expedition was hugely important to both popular and literary culture of the 1850s and 1860s. Many plays, ballads, and pictures of Lady Franklin's widowhood were produced, and Franklin was widely portrayed as a hero giving everything for the glory of England. Wilkie Collins wrote a play called *The Frozen Deep*, based on Franklin's imagined fate, for which Dickens wrote a prologue, and Tennyson wrote an epitaph for Franklin's cenotaph in Westminster Abbey.

SARAH MOSS

## Biography

Born in Spilsby, Lincolnshire, 16 April 1786. Attended Louth Grammar School. Left school and entered the Royal Navy, 1800. Sailed with Matthew Flinders as midshipman on *Investigator* to survey the Australian coast, 1801. Survived shipwreck and returned to Europe via China. Served in the battles of Trafalgar, 1805, and New Orleans, 1814. Second in command of Captain David Buchan's expedition to reach the North Pole, 1818. Led overland expedition to survey the coast of North America from Hudson Bay to the Arctic and to the east of the Coppermine River, 1819–1822. Appointed to rank of commander, 1821. Fellow of the Royal Society, 1821. Married Eleanor Ann Porden (d. 1825), 1823: one daughter. Second overland expedition mapping the coast of North America, 1825–1827.

Married Jane Griffin, 1828. Gold medal, Geographical Society of Paris, 1828. Knighted, 1829. Naval service in the Mediterranean, 1830–1833. Governor of Van Diemen's Land (Tasmania), 1837–1843. Commanded *Erebus* to the Arctic to seek Northwest Passage, 1845. Disappeared when expedition became trapped by ice in Victoria Strait, off King William Island, September 1846. Died from starvation or lead poisoning, near King William Island, British Arctic Islands (now Northwest Territories, Canada), 11 June 1847.

### References and Further Reading

Franklin, John, *Narrative of a Journey to the Shores of the Polar Sea, in the Years 1819, 20, 21 and 22*, 1823.

Franklin, John, *Narrative of a Second Expedition to the Shores of the Polar Sea, in the Years 1825, 1826 and 1827*, 1828.

*See also* **Northwest Passage**

## FRENCH INDOCHINA

There had been French missionary interest in Indochina since the seventeenth century, but it was not until economic and political imperatives took French explorers and merchants to Southeast Asia that tales of travel to the area proliferated. Throughout the 1860s and 1870s, naturalists, anthropologists, merchants, and explorers were drawn to Vietnam, Cambodia, and Laos. Henri Mouhot's travel diary of his excursion to the Cambodian temples of Angkor Wat appeared posthumously in 1863 to coincide with the formal establishment of the French protectorate over Cambodia. Mouhot's diaries and sketches of this Southeast Asian marvel aroused much attention, and stimulated the French public's appetite for information about this exotic and far-flung territory. The charting of the Red River, and the exploratory voyages to Indochina of Francis Garnier and Doudart de Lagrée (1866–1868 and 1872), were well documented in contemporary journals such as *Le Moniteur Universel, Le National*, and *Le Temps* (for collected texts see Garnier, *Voyage d'exploration en Indochine*, 1985, and Dodeman and Thibault, 1990). When news of Garnier's expedition reached the home country, most large newspapers started to send foreign correspondents to the area: columns chronicling the exploration of Tonkin appeared in *Le Figaro, Le Petit Parisien*, and *Le Globe*; Paul Bourde accompanied Garnier's *corps expéditionnaire* for *Le Temps*, Paul Bonnetain for *Le Figaro*. Both later published their collected articles, Bonnetain's *Au Tonkin* and Bourde's *De Paris au Tonkin* both appearing in 1885.

Once the Third Republic, under Jules Ferry's leadership, undertook to back these adventures with arms and men, a proliferation of travel diaries and memoirs were published by army and navy personnel. These texts documented the conquest and pacification of *Indochine française*, and were for the most part highly personal accounts of war and suffering. Of these often mediocre texts, Pierre Loti's provide perhaps the best depiction of the maritime experience of the conquest of Indochina (see extracts from *Pêcheur d'Islande*, 1893), but his *Un Pèlerin d'Angkor* (1912) was perhaps the sole example of travel writing *per se* to emerge from a period that was marked principally by war memoirs and then by colonial fiction.

The settlers and administrators newly stationed in Indochina soon began to turn their hands to fiction and produced, if not strictly travel writing as such, novels and short stories that were nonetheless viewed in France as constituting reliable sources of information about the newly acquired colonial possession. These works, like much travel writing, tended to focus upon the exotic and unusual features of Indochina; but they also emphasized the deleterious effects of the country and its climate upon the European, thus creating an abiding image of Indochina as inhospitable, untameable, and rife with disease. One example is J. Boissière's *Fumeurs d'opium*, published in 1895.

As a counterpoint to these largely exoticized accounts, Félicien Challaye's trips to Indochina in 1901, 1918, and 1919 resulted in the publication of the first critical responses to French action there. His work did not reach an equivalently large or diverse readership, appearing first in *Cahiers de la Quinzaine* and collected only later, after other critical voices had emerged in the 1930s. From the turn of the nineteenth century to World War I, travel writing thus gave way to novel writing, and French responses to Indochina were expressed principally through the medium of colonial fiction, particularly through novels depicting settlers' lives in France's "pearl" of the empire, written by such authors as Boissière, Casseville, Chivas-Baron, Daguerches, Esme, Farrère, Groslier, Leuba, Malraux, Pouvourville, Pujarniscle, Schultz, and Wild. With the exception of the Goncourt-winning Farrère (*Les Civilisés*, 1905), and Malraux's barely disguised portrayal of his own adventures in the Cambodian forest (*La Voie royale*, 1928), these writers remained comparatively obscure, their work read only by the minority of French who settled (usually briefly) in Indochina. One of the few influential writers who traveled to Indochina during this period was Paul Claudel (who visited in 1921, as part of his duties as ambassador to Japan). Claudel's positive assessment of the Franco-Indochinese relationship appeared alongside a very unflattering portrayal of Angkor in *La Revue du Pacifique* in 1922.

It was not until the mid-1920s and early 1930s, in the post-World War I climate of international scrutiny of colonial policies, that travel writing about Indochina reemerged. In response to growing humanitarian concerns over France's management of Indochina, journalists such as Roland Dorgelès, Paul Monet, and Luc Durtain traveled to Indochina in order to investigate colonial malpractice, producing a compelling indictment of French rule. Growing nationalist agitation and rebellion in Indochina culminated in the Yen Bay uprising of 1931, and provided the catalyst for the renewed output of a political and investigative form of travel writing. The most influential accounts were produced by Louis Roubaud and Andrée Viollis.

Travel writing on Indochina finally came full circle in the texts that emerged from the Franco-Indochinese War (1945–1954). As in the 1860s and 1870s, war and conflict resulted in writing that often straddled the divide between memoir and fiction. Jules Roy, Jean Lartéguy, Jean Hougron, and Pierre Schoendoerffer stand as the principal authors of France's colonial war and defeat in Indochina.

NIKKI COOPER

### References and Further Reading

Bonnetain, Paul, *Au Tonkin*, 1885.
Bourde, Paul, *De Paris au Tonkin*, 1885.
Challaye, Félicien, *Souvenirs sur la colonisation*, 1935.
Claudel, Paul, *Oeuvres complètes de Paul Claudel*, vols. 3–4: *Extrême-Orient*, 1952.
Dodeman, Jean-Louis, and Joël Thibault, *Expédition Mékong: Exploration Doudart de Lagrée–Francis Garnier, 1866–1868*, 1990.
Dorgelès, Roland, *Sur la route mandarine*, 1925.
Durtain, Luc, *Dieux blancs, hommes jaunes*, 1930.
Garnier, Francis, *Voyage d'exploration en Indochine*, edited by Jean-Pierre Gomane, 1985.
Loti, Pierre, *Pêcheur d'Islande*, 1886; as *The Iceland Fisherman*, translated by W.P. Baines, 1924.
Loti, Pierre, *Un Pèlerin d'Angkor*, 1912.
Monet, Paul, *Les Jauniers, histoire vraie*, 1930.
Mouhot, Henri, *Voyage dans les royaumes de Siam, de Cambodge, de Laos et autres parties centrales de l'Indo-Chine*, 1863; as *Travels in the Central Parts of Indo-China (Siam), Cambodia and Laos*, 2 vols., 1864; as *Travels in Siam, Cambodia and Laos, 1858–1860*, 1989.
Roubaud, Louis, *Viet Nam: La tragédie indochinoise*, 1931.
Viollis, Andrée, *Indochine S.O.S.*, 1935.

*See also* **Mekong River**

## FROBISHER, MARTIN (c. 1535–1594)

### *English Pirate, Privateer, and Explorer*

Sir Martin Frobisher is less important as a travel writer than he is as the subject of travel writing and the lore of early British exploration. Of his own writings, the most important relating to travel include the logs and observations he made on his many journeys. As a character in the literature of travel and the lore of British naval history, however, he is enshrined in various sixteenth- and seventeenth-century narratives, most notably those of his subordinates in the expeditions searching for the Northwest Passage.

Born into a Welsh family that settled near Normanton in Yorkshire, Martin himself was the fourth child and youngest son. Little schooling was available in the area, and by all existing evidence Martin's was scanty. Around 1549, he was sent to Sir John Yorke, his mother's brother, then living in London. Yorke's connections with London merchants probably involved Frobisher in his first sea journey. In 1554, Frobisher shipped on his first voyage, to West Africa, as a merchantman in a fleet headed by Thomas Wyndham. After this, Frobisher disappears from the record for a decade. We hear of him again in 1565, on a list of plunderers of Spanish merchantmen, and in 1566, observed at Newcastle-upon-Tyne arming an outgoing ship. There is evidence that he planned a slaving voyage, again to West Africa, with this vessel. These few records of Frobisher's early career, then, evidence his involvement in both piracy and the slave trade.

Frobisher's run-ins with the government had attracted another kind of attention, that of the queen's advisors, especially Lord Burghley. In 1571, Burghley was apparently concerned in the fitting-out of an expedition headed by Frobisher, this time to Ireland. It was probably in Ireland that he met Sir Humphrey Gilbert, who was attempting the pacification of the population. Frobisher's connection with Gilbert would have almost certainly introduced the geographical idea of the Northwest Passage, of which Gilbert was a popularizer. This idea impelled the expeditions that made Frobisher famous to his contemporaries and important in the history of travel and travel writing. Various Irish-related intrigues led, through Gilbert and Sir Henry Sidney, to Frobisher's presentation to the earl of Warwick (Sidney's brother-in-law) of his plan for a trading voyage to the East through the then hypothetical Northwest Passage.

Financed by Muscovy trader Michael Lok, Frobisher's fleet, numbering two small ships (*Michael* and *Gabriel*) and a pinnace, sailed for the northwest on 7 June 1576. Though the pinnace was lost off Greenland, and commander of *Michael* turned back after losing contact with *Gabriel*, Frobisher continued, braving the pack ice to reconnoiter Resolution Island and Frobisher's Strait. On the first voyage, he encountered the Inuit, and lost the expedition's only remaining boat, along with five seamen, in an attempt to trade with the natives. In return, Frobisher took one hostage, with whom he sailed to England.

An all-too-common circumstance prompted Frobisher's second and third voyages to the northwest. Though no ice-free passage to the East had been found,

Frobisher's men had picked up a black, ore-bearing rock while on Resolution Island. Assays proved inconclusive, but Michael Lok convinced himself that he had found valuable ore (gold), at a location known only to him and his crew.

In 1577, Lok formed the Cathay Company, Elizabeth I contributed a tall ship, *Aid*, and a new expedition was mounted including *Aid*, *Gabriel*, *Michael*, and two pinnaces. Abandoning his attempts to explore, Frobisher and his expedition spent the second voyage digging ore out of the Arctic islands near the strait that bears his name. They captured three further hostages in an attempt to contact their missing comrades from the first expedition.

Despite the lack of significant precious minerals in the tons of ore the second voyage had secured, a third trip was planned, this to be administered directly by the Crown. The ships assembled at Harwich on 27 May 1578 numbered 15; 12 were to make the round trip, and 3 were to winter over. One might call this effort the first attempt at the colonization of America by the English; 100 colonists shipped with the expedition, to work the supposed veins of ore over the following winter. During the course of the third expedition's explorations, Frobisher seems to have found Hudson's Strait (which he called Mistaken Strait), but did not explore it thoroughly because of his responsibility to the queen's mining project. In general, secrecy marked all three of these expeditions, especially in the matter of recording locations and in drawing charts. However, on their the return from the voyages the crew and their backers became embroiled in an ignominious round of recriminations, suits for debt, and, in some cases, imprisonment. Frobisher was saved from this last by his friends at court, but Lok was not so fortunate. The Cathay Company was disbanded.

The most important travel narratives concerning Frobisher involve these three voyages in search of the Northwest Passage. The narratives themselves are heterogeneous in style and substance; some concentrate on the specific information needed by mariners in the regions, while others are richer in narration of incidents and descriptions of American polar regions. Dionyse Settle and Thomas Ellis, two of Frobisher's fleet captains, published short descriptions of the second and third voyages. Much of the information on which they concentrate involves the specifics of navigation. Most detailed, however, is George Best's account of the three trips. Best not only narrated the action of the voyages, but also included various materials compiled and written by Frobisher himself. Best's narrative contains the most exciting account of the harrowing adventures during the expeditions. He tells how, during the course of the three voyages, Frobisher's fleet encountered the Inuit (describing both the people and aspects of their culture), braved the polar ice pack (describing Arctic animals), claimed to have sighted the (mythical) island of Frisland between Greenland and America, and attempted to plant a colony of miners on Baffin Island (the first English attempt at systematic colonization). These previously published materials (with slight alterations), along with the unpublished accounts of Christopher Hall and Thomas Wiars, are collected in the second edition of Richard Hakluyt's *Principal Navigations* (1598–1600). Much of Frobisher's career as naval officer, explorer, and privateer may be followed within the *Principal Navigations*, in mentions by other travel writers.

JAMES P. HELFERS

## Biography

Born in Normanton, Yorkshire, c. 1535. Orphaned at an early age; brought up by relatives in London. Had little education. Started work in London, c. 1549. First voyage, to Guinea coast of West Africa, 1553 and 1554. Married Isabel, widow of Thomas Rickard, of Snaith, Yorkshire, 1559. Received privateering license and worked in the English Channel; arrested several times on charges of piracy, 1560s. Captain of government-sponsored expedition to Ireland, 1571. Made voyages in search of the Northwest Passage, 1576–1578. Commanded *Foresight*, under Sir William Winter, during the pacification of Kerry, 1580. Held various naval positions under William Hawkins and Francis Drake, 1582–1588. Commander of the Fourth Squadron versus the Spanish Armada; knighted for this action, 1588. Resumed Channel patrols; commanded various naval expeditions, 1588–1594. Bought the Manor of Whitwood, Grange of Finningly, Yorkshire, 1591. Married Dame Dorothy Widmerpoole, a widow, 1591. Appointed justice of the peace for the West Riding of Yorkshire, 1593. Died in Plymouth, Devon, from a hip wound sustained during naval action during the capture of Brest, France, 22 November 1594.

## References and Further Reading

Best, George, *A True Discourse of the Late Voyages of Discouerie, for the Finding of a Passage to Cathaya, by the Northweast, under the Conduct of Martin Frobisher General*, 1578.

Ellis, Thomas, *A True Report of the Third and Last Voyage unto Meta Incognita*, 1578.

Hakluyt, Richard, *The Principal Navigations, Voyages, & Discoveries of the English Nation, Made by Sea or over Land, to the Most Remote and Farthest Corners of the Earth*, 1589; revised edition as *The Principal Navigations, Voyages, Traffiques & Discoveries of the English Nation*, 3 vols., 1598–1600; 12 vols., 1903–1905

Hakluyt, Richard, *Hakluyt's Voyages to the New World: A Selection*, edited by David F. Hawke, 1972.

Settle, Dionyse, *True Reporte of the Laste Voyage into the West and Northwest Regions . . . by Captiene Frobisher*, 1577; as *Laste Voyage into the West and Northwest Regions in the Year 1577*, 1969.

Stefansson, Vilhjalmur (editor), *The Three Voyages of Martin Frobisher in Search of a Passage to Cathay and India by the North-West, AD 1576–78*, 2 vols., 1938.

## FROMENTIN, EUGÈNE (1820–1876)

***French Painter, Writer, and Art Critic***

Eugène Fromentin was the second child of a family active in public affairs. His father, a doctor in La Rochelle, headed France's first psychiatric hospital. Clever and well behaved at school, Fromentin went on, as his family wished, to study law in Paris. This departure was also designed to get the young man away from Léocadie Chessé, a married woman with whom he had fallen in love. He became friendly with Émile Beltrémieux, Paul Bataillard, and Armand Du Mesnil.

In 1843 he joined the practice of the lawyer Denormandie, but did not like it there and began to attend painting classes, first with Jean-Charles-Joseph Rémond and then with Nicolas-Louis Cabat. He was torn constantly between pressure from his father, who would have preferred him to become an attorney, and his own ambition to be a painter. A friend, Charles Labbé, another budding artist, whose family lived in Blida in Algeria, invited Fromentin and Du Mesnil to accompany him when he went back for his sister's wedding.

That first visit to Algeria (3 March–18 April 1846), set the seal on Fromentin's liberation from family constraints and brought a revelation: he discovered for himself an Orient freed from the flashy, fanciful visions of Alexandre-Gabriel Decamps and Eugène Delacroix, and his painterly vocation grew stronger. "Everything is new to me, everything interests me, and the more I study nature here the more I believe that in spite of Marilhat and Decamps the Orient still needs to be painted" (*Lettres de jeunesse*, 12 March 1846). The same artistic impulse inspired his next two journeys. He made a second trip to Algeria, lasting from 24 September 1847 to 23 May 1848, in the company of Auguste Saltzmann and Labbé. Then from 5 November 1852 to 5 October 1853, with backing from the painter Gustave Moreau, who was a strong influence on him around this time, he made a third journey, which took him through much of Algeria. Leaving his wife in Blida, Fromentin went off with a small escort on an expedition to Laghouat, only recently (December 1852) captured by the French after much bloodshed. Another expedition, lasting five days, took the party deeper into the desert, to Ain Madhi. It was this third Algerian trip that produced *Un Été dans le Sahara*, an account, presented as an episode from a longer tour (to be described in *Une Année dans le Sahel*), of the itinerary he followed from 22 May to July 1853, starting at Médéa and ending at Ain Madhi. Ever since 1847, Fromentin had been planning a literary work based on his Algerian travels, originally conceived in the form of a book of etchings accompanied by an explanatory text. The work first appeared in its final state in the *Revue de Paris*, from 1 June to 1 December 1854. Now in the form of fictional letters addressed to Du Mesnil, it was an immediate success. "This is a unique book, a model of description that nobody, not even Théophile Gautier, has come anywhere near to. Never has the sensation of light, heat and aridity been so powerfully evoked . . . Gautier . . . said, 'It is concentrated sun' " (Maxime Du Camp, *Souvenirs littéraires*).

*Une Année dans le Sahel* appeared in the *Revue des Deux Mondes* from 15 April to 1 December 1858. With its new tendency to introspection and invention, it seems to herald the autobiographical novel *Dominique* (1863).

In 1869, thanks to his friend Charles-Edmond Chojecki, Fromentin was invited to the opening of the Suez Canal. Leaving Paris on 7 October 1869, he embarked at Marseilles on 9 October. He found himself in Egypt more or less by accident. "I wasn't expecting to come to Egypt: I came here by chance. I dash round, not grasping what I see, unable to fix it in my mind" (*Voyage en Égypte*). For three weeks he traveled up and down the Nile between Cairo and Aswan, his main stops being at El Minya, El Roda, Asyut, Qena, and Armant. He went by rail from Alexandria to attend the opening ceremonies of the canal at Ismailia on 17 November 1869. Aboard a *dahabiah*, he visited Cairo, staying until 28 November. He got back to Marseilles on 6 December. He had been keeping a log as he went along, but it remained unpublished until after his death. He had taken "instant impressions" of the trip while going about as if in a dream: "For the last 40 days we have been impelled by chance and magic . . . that is the main point about this fantastic journey, which is absolutely indistinguishable from a dream. . . . We are in the midst of the impossible and it is all real" (*Voyage en Égypte*). The only account of this journey is a set of travel notes that were put in order soon after Fromentin died, under the title *Voyage en Égypte*. Setting off, Fromentin had felt nothing but nostalgic sadness. Indeed, he embodied the paradox of the traveler who loves stasis and immobility: "I don't like things that run or flow or fly; anything that is still—stagnant water, a bird hanging in the air or perched on a bough—moves me ineffably. Perhaps one day I shall manage to convey that universal sense of repose" (*Lettres de jeunesse*, letter to Paul Bataillard, 1 November 1844). In June 1870 Fromentin went to Venice with his wife, Paul Bataillard, and Charles Busson. He made a few sketches, but the trip had to be curtailed because of the outbreak of the Franco-Prussian war.

Fromentin's destination on 5 July 1875 was Brussels, then Antwerp and Amsterdam and their art galleries. On this cultural tour he was able to admire the works of the Dutch and Flemish masters. His notes on these painters gradually built up into the last book he wrote, *Les Maîtres d'autrefois*, a combination of art criticism and traveler's guide.

Throughout his writings, Fromentin, "a painter in two languages" (Sainte-Beuve, *Nouveaux Lundis*), maintains an artist's vision, as if he saw in every landscape and oriental scene a draft for a picture. He invites the reader to attend the ballet of colors and light. In his commentary on *Un Été dans le Sahara*, Gautier talks of a "complete artistic transposition" ("Le Sahara," in *L'Orient, Voyages et voyageurs, in Oeuvres complètes*, Geneva: Slatkine, 1978: 333–372), while Fromentin envisages pen and paintbrush as two distinct and complementary means of expression.

> There are shapes for the mind as there are shapes for the eye: the language that speaks to the eye is not the same as that which speaks to the mind. And the book exists not to repeat the painter's work but to express what the painting does not say. (Preface, *Un Été dans le Sahara*)

VÉRONIQUE MAGRI-MOURGUES

## Biography

Born in La Rochelle, France, 24 October 1820. Studied for a law degree, Paris, 1839–1843. Devoted himself to painting and studied under Cabat: exhibited at the salon, 1847. Traveled to Algeria, 1846, 1848, and 1852; traveled to Egypt for the opening of the Suez Canal, 1869. A visit to Venice in 1870 was cut short by the start of the Franco-Prussian war. Visited Belgium, July 1875. Married Marie Cavallet de Beaumont, the niece of Armand Du Mesnil, 1852: one daughter, Marguerite, born 20 July 1854. Awarded second prize for five paintings on Algerian subjects at the Paris Salon of 1849: *Les Tentes de la Smala de Si-Hamed-bel-Hadj* [The Tents of the Household of Si Hamed bel Hadj], *La Smala passant l'Oued-Biraz* [The Smalah Passing through Wadi Biraz], *Les Baraques du faubourg Bab-Azoun* [Shacks in the Faubourg Bab-Azoun], *Une Rue à Constantine* [A Street in Constantine], and *La Place de la Brèche* [Place de la Brèche]. Awarded first prize and the Cross of the Legion of Honor, 1859 salon; promoted to officer of the Legion, 1869. Received another medal for two paintings at the Universal Exhibition of 1866: *Bateleurs nègres* [Black Acrobats] and *Femmes des Ouled-Nayls* [Tribeswomen of the Ouled Nail]. Died of anthrax at Saint-Maurice, France, 27 August 1876.

## References and Further Reading

Du Camp, Maxime, *Souvenirs littéraires*, 1882–1883; 2 vols., Paris: Hachette, 1892.

Fromentin, Eugène, *Un Été dans le Sahara* [A Summer in Sahara], 1857; with a preface by Fromentin, 1874; edited by Anne-Marie Christin, 1981.

Fromentin, Eugène, *Une Année dans le Sahel* [One Year in Sahel], 1859; with a preface by Denise Brahimi, 1984.

Fromentin, Eugène, *Voyage en Égypte* [Travel to Egypt], 1869; edited by Jean-Marie Carré, 1935.

Fromentin, Eugène, *Les Maîtres d'autrefois*, 1876; as *The Old Masters of Belgium and Holland*, translated by Mary C. Robbins, 1882; reprinted with an introduction by Meyer Schapiro, 1964; as *The Masters of Past Time*, translated by Andrew Boyle, 1948.

Fromentin, Eugène, *Sahara et Sahel*, 1887.

Fromentin, Eugène, *Lettres de jeunesse*, biography and notes by Pierre Blanchon, 1909.

Fromentin, Eugène, *Between Sea and Sahara: An Algerian Journal*, translated by Blake Robinson, 1999.